Government and the American Economy

Government

and the

THIRD EDITION

American Economy

Merle Fainsod
Professor of Government, Harvard University

Lincoln Gordon

Joseph C. Palamountain, Jr.
President, Skidmore College

W · W · NORTON & COMPANY · INC · New York

Library of Congress Catalog Card No. 59-6084

PRINTED IN THE UNITED STATES OF AMERICA
FOR THE PUBLISHERS BY THE VAIL-BALLOU PRESS
6 7 8 9

Contents

Preface   xi

v

Preface to the Third Edition

THIS BOOK presents an examination and analysis of one of the profoundly important developments of the last century—the assumption by government of major responsibilities for the guidance and direction of the American economy. Changing from a comparatively passive role devoted primarily to "holding the ring" for individual enterprise, government has come to exercise an active influence upon every phase of economic activity. While this trend has been vastly accelerated by the events of the last three decades, it was clearly discernible before the Great Depression of 1929. Its root causes lie deeply embedded in the technological, economic, and social transformation induced by the Industrial Revolution and by the democratic movement of the nineteenth century. The energies released by modern industrialism and democracy have given shape and content to the multiplying obligations of government in the economic realm.

The emphasis here is on the political forces which influence the formation and execution of public policy. This emphasis is based on the conviction that effective economic or other criteria of desirable public policy can be most fruitfully developed when there is a vivid realization of the potentialities and limitations of the political context in which they must be applied. Our approach does not mean that economic analysis is neglected. Every effort has been made to take account of the economic as well as the political, legal, and administrative factors which enter into the determination of public economic policies.

This edition represents a major reworking, extension, and broadening of the material contained in earlier editions of this work. New chapters have been added on transportation, antitrust policy, coal, oil, natural gas, atomic energy, monetary and fiscal policy, and the economic responsibilities of government in the international field. At the same time, the treatment of the historical evolution of public economic policies has been somewhat shortened in order to make room for more expanded discussion of contemporary themes.

The framework of analysis originally ventured in the 1941 edition has also undergone transformation over the years. The categories of promotion, regulation, and public enterprise have become so intermingled in almost every sector of the economy on which government impinges that the task today is to take account of their interrelationships rather than to use them as major classificatory tools. While the organizational scheme adopted in this edition still employs some of these categories, they are viewed by the authors as instruments of emphasis, rather than as separated realms.

The major burden of preparing this edition was assumed by Mr. Palamountain. Mr. Gordon wrote Chapter 28 and Mr. Fainsod revised the concluding chapter, now numbered 29. The remaining chapters were initially revised or drafted by Mr. Palamountain and subsequently reviewed and revised by Mr. Fainsod and Mr. Gordon.

This work has benefited at various points from the suggestions of Professors Richard Kirkendall and E. E. Schattschneider, who have kindly reviewed several chapters. Professor John V. Lintner commented helpfully on the draft of Chapter 26. We are most appreciative of the research assistance of Mrs. Kathleen Witten and Miss Grace Bacon, and of the secretarial services of Mrs. Anne Cresciamanno, Mrs. Alberta Eastwood, Mrs. Marian Haagen, Miss Willma Nash, and Mrs. Ruth Levine. We also wish to express our appreciation for the financial aid extended by the Research Fund of Wesleyan University.

MERLE FAINSOD
LINCOLN GORDON
JOSEPH C. PALAMOUNTAIN, JR.

Acknowledgments

WE ARE happy to express our appreciation to the following for permission to reproduce passages from the indicated works:

To the American Academy of Political and Social Science for material from E. E. Schattschneider, "Political Parties and the Public Interest," *Annals*, March, 1952.

To the American Economic Association for material from J. M. Clark, "Toward a Concept of Workable Competition," and from A. E. Kahn, "Fundamental Deficiencies of the American Patent Law," *American Economic Review*, Volume 30.

To the *Columbia Law Review* for material from "Collection and Survey of State Antitrust Laws," Volume 32 (1932) and from J. G. Palfrey, "Atomic Energy: A New Experiment in Government-Industry Relations," March, 1956.

To the Columbia University Press and the author for material from E. G. Campbell, *The Reorganization of the American Railroad System, 1893–1900*; and for material from H. C. Mansfield, *The Lake Cargo Coal Rate Controversy*.

To the Thomas Y. Crowell Company for material from V. O. Key, Jr., *Politics, Parties and Pressure Groups*, 3d ed.

To the Foundation Press, Inc., for material from E. C. Goddard, "The Evolution and Devolution of Public Utility Law," *Selected Essays in Constitutional Law*.

To the *George Washington Law Review* for material from C. S. Rhyne, "Work of the Interstate Commerce Commission in Railroad Reorganization Proceedings under Section 77 of the Bankruptcy Act," Volume 5.

To Harcourt, Brace and Company, Inc., for material from Thurman W. Arnold, *Bottlenecks of Business*, Felix Frankfurter, *Of Law and Men*, and Louis Hartz, *The Liberal Tradition in America*.

To Harper and Brothers for material from David E. Lilienthal, *TVA: Democracy on the March*, Charles A. Madison, *American Labor Leaders*, and Joseph A. Schumpeter, *Capitalism, Socialism, and Democracy*, 2d ed.; and to Harper and Brothers and Mrs. Woodrow Wilson for material from *The Public Papers of Woodrow Wilson*.

To the Harvard Law Review Association and the author for material from Edward S. Mason, "The Current Status of the Monopoly Problem in the United States," Volume 62 (1949).

To the President and Fellows of Harvard College and to the Harvard University Press for material from S. J. Buck, *The Granger Movement*, E. M. Dodd, "The First Half Century of Statutory Regulation of Business Corporations in Massachusetts," *Harvard Legal Essays*, Arthur N. Holcombe, *Our More Perfect Union* (1950), Edward S. Mason, *Economic Concentration and the Monopoly Problem* (1957), and John E. Sawyer, "The Entrepreneur and the Social Order," in William Miller (ed.), *Men in Business* (1952).

To Houghton Mifflin Company for material from A. J. Beveridge, *The Life of John Marshall*.

To Longmans, Green & Co., Inc., for material from W. Z. Ripley, *Railroads: Rates and Regulation*.

To the McGraw-Hill Book Company, Inc., for material from A. R. Burns, *The Decline of Competition*.

To William Morrow & Company, Inc., for material from James A. Wechsler, *Labor Baron* (1944).

To the National Industrial Conference Board for material from M. W. Watkins, *Public Regulation of Competitive Practices in Business Enterprise*.

To the National Planning Association for material from J. D. Black and J. T. Bonnen, *A Balanced United States Agriculture*.

To the *New York Times* and the author for material from Leon Keyserling, "The Economic Test: Will We Act in Time?", June 13, 1948.

To the Princeton University Press for material from Marver H. Bernstein, *Regulating Business by Independent Commission*.

To the Principia Corporation, Elsah, Illinois, for material from an address by Mr. Gordon at the Second Annual Public Affairs Conference on "The Citizen and His Government" at the Principia College, May, 1940.

To the *Public Opinion Quarterly*, Inc., for material from N. E. Long, "Public Relations of the Bell System," Volume 1.

To G. P. Putnam's Sons for material from L. A. Coolidge, *An Old Fashioned Senator: O. H. Platt*.

To Random House, Inc., for material from *The Public Papers and Addresses of Franklin D. Roosevelt.*

To Rinehart & Company, Inc., for material from E. E. Schattschneider, *Party Government.*

To Theodore W. Schultz for material from his *Production and Welfare of Agriculture.*

To Simon and Schuster, Inc., for material from L. M. Hacker, *The Triumph of American Capitalism.*

To the Twentieth Century Fund for material from the remarks of James M. Landis in George W. Stocking and M. W. Watkins, *Monopoly and Free Enterprise.*

To the University of Chicago Press for material from H. A. Millis and E. C. Brown, *From the Wagner Act to Taft-Hartley* (1950), and L. D. White, "The Origin of Utility Commissions in Massachusetts," *Journal of Political Economy*, Volume 29.

To the Viking Press, Inc., for material from T. Veblen, *Absentee Ownership and Business Enterprise.*

To the *Wisconsin Law Review* for material from R. S. Ely, "The Work of the Federal Trade Commission," Volume 7.

To the *Yale Law Journal* for material from Edward S. Mason, "Monopoly in Law and Economics," November, 1937.

To the Yale University Press for material from Thurman W. Arnold, *Folklore of Capitalism.*

PART 1

The American Setting

CHAPTER 1

The Economic Background

GOVERNMENTS function in an economic context, adopting policies which both reflect and shape this context. So important and far-reaching are these policies, and so great is the concern of the economy with them, that we can today say that ours is an *economic polity* and a *political economy*. Despite myths of a Golden Age of laissez faire, politics and economics were early intermingled in the United States. Recent research has shown that state governments played a major role in promoting economic development from the Revolution to the Civil War.[1] The economic concerns of the national government were slower to emerge, but, particularly in the last half century, they have expanded enormously.

In 1790, a year after George Washington's inauguration, the expenditures of the federal government totaled only $4 million. Its functions were narrowly limited. The conduct of foreign affairs, national defense, law enforcement, tax collection and tariff administration, the postal service, the mint, banking, patents, land grants, pensions, Indian affairs—these constituted the chief areas where the federal government touched the lives and economic activities of its people.

One hundred years later, the annual expenditures of the federal government had mounted to $318 million, but its functions were still relatively circumscribed. The burden of governmental business had increased with the growth in population, but the bulk of

[1] L. Hartz, *Economic Policy and Democratic Thought: Pennsylvania, 1776–1860* (1948); Oscar and Mary Handlin, *Commonwealth, A Study of the Role of Government in the American Economy: Massachusetts, 1774–1861* (1947).

federal activity still fell within the traditional and familiar lines marked out in the 1790's. But already harbingers of a more spacious conception of the role of government were in evidence. In 1887 the Interstate Commerce Commission was established, the first of a long line of federal regulatory commissions. Three years later came the Sherman Antitrust Act.

Since 1890 the expansion of the economic powers of the federal government has proceeded at an accelerating pace. The barest inventory of contemporary federal government activity reveals the direction of the growth. What was formerly a government limited in its assumption of responsibilities and peripheral in its effects has become intimately intertwined with the economic life of the nation. It now assumes general responsibility for maintaining high levels of employment and for piloting a rising national income between the Scylla of inflation and the Charybdis of deflation. It provides incentives to business to pursue activities contributing to national defense or other public goals. Labor has invoked the assistance of government in guaranteeing collective bargaining and in maintaining minimum labor standards. Farmers have sought and obtained large-scale federal aid for agriculture. The widening regulatory activities of government have reached far beyond the original area staked out for the Interstate Commerce Commission in 1887. Transportation, communications, electrical and gas utilities, the securities exchanges, packers and stockyards, commodity exchanges, the oil industry, and the milk business, for example, have all been subjected to special regulatory regimes. The federal government has greatly broadened its activities in the conservation of natural resources and in social welfare. It is managing and controlling the development and application of atomic energy. Responsibilities of world leadership have entailed an additional series of actions in pursuit of an affirmative foreign economic policy. One measure of government's impact on the economy is the fact that its expenditures are now almost one-fifth of the gross national product. Under the stimulus of new urgencies a heavy burden of new responsibilities has been assumed.

Major economic transformations have contributed to this tremendous growth in the economic activities of government. The expanding functions of government are in large measure a product of industrialization and its economic consequences.

1. The Rise of Modern Industry in the United States

The rise of modern industry in the United States is essentially a post-Civil War phenomenon. Pre-Civil War America was still predominantly an agrarian society. In 1860 only 16.1 per cent of the total population resided in places with eight thousand or more inhabitants. Business units were small, and were usually owned by individuals or small groups of persons. The man of business was typically a merchant or banker rather than an industrialist. Business enterprise found its outlets, for the most part, in trade, in banking, in land speculation, in mining, and in transportation ventures such as canals, bridges, turnpikes, and, later, railroads. Industrial production was small and was still predominantly of the cottage and mill type. Articles were fabricated by small independent producers and purchased by merchants or commission men who moved them into channels of commerce. Sometimes the merchant supplied the material, equipment, or credit, and thus extended his control over production. The typical workman was still the skilled artisan, craftsman, or journeyman apprentice. The modern factory system with its automatic machinery, standardized products, rationalization of operations, and wage labor was just beginning to make its appearance. It developed early in cotton textiles in New England, and by 1850 it was beginning to spread to the manufacture of iron, machinery, and leather products. But, by and large, the factory system was still relatively unimportant.

Beginning about 1850, and accelerating with the Civil War, industrialization proceeded at a rapid tempo. The following table reveals the spectacular growth of manufacturing in the years between 1850 and 1880.[2] It will be noted that the capital invested in manufacturing and the value of products turned out increased more than 400 per cent over the thirty-year period. The performance of heavy industry was particularly striking.

The explanation for this extraordinary growth was many sided. Natural resources such as coal, oil, iron, lumber, lead, copper, silver, and gold existed in great profusion. Railroad construction widened the domestic market, opened up new areas for settlement, and was itself a prime mover in stimulating demand for coal and iron. Population growth was accelerated by an influx of immigration. Labor was abundant. The tariff protected many manufactured products from foreign competition. Technological advances in transportation and industry and increasing mechanization of industrial processes opened the way to mass production, increased labor productivity, and large-scale economic organization. And, "in a society whose institutions and goals were as uniquely favorable to the individual entrepreneur as were its physical condi-

[2] This table is adapted from Louis M. Hacker, *The Triumph of American Capitalism* (1940), Appendix A, pp. 437–438.

GROWTH OF MANUFACTURES IN THE UNITED STATES
1850–1880

1. Growth of Manufactures in the United States
(in millions of dollars)

Items	1850	1860	1870	1880
Capital invested	533.2	1009.9	1694.6	2790.3
Value of products	1019.0	1885.0	3386.0	5369.6

2. Per Cent Increases

Items	1850–60	1860–70	1870–80	1850–80
Capital invested	89.4	67.8	64.7	423.5
Value of products	85.0	79.5	58.6	426.9

3. Value of Products of Selected Light Industries
(in millions of dollars)

Industries	1850	1860	1870	1880
Cotton manufactures	61.9	115.7	142.0	192.1
Woolen manufactures	48.6	73.5	159.4	238.1
Boots and shoes	54.0	91.9	145.3	196.9
Men's ready-made clothing	48.3	80.8	118.9	209.5

4. Per Cent Increases

Industries	1850–60	1860–70	1870–80	1850–80
Cotton manufactures	87.0	22.7	35.3	210.5
Woolen manufactures	51.1	117.0	49.4	389.8
Boots and shoes	70.3	58.1	35.5	264.9
Men's ready-made clothing	67.3	47.1	76.2	333.7

5. Value of Products of Selected Heavy Industries
(in millions of dollars)

Industries	1850	1860	1870	1880
Pig iron	12.7	20.9	55.7	89.3
Agricultural implements	6.8	20.8	41.7	68.6
Machinery	28.0	51.9	110.8	214.4
Lumber	60.4	97.7	168.1	233.3
Clay products	8.2	14.0	29.1	41.8

6. Per Cent Increases

Industries	1850–60	1860–70	1870–80	1850–80
Pig iron	63.7	166.9	60.3	600.6
Agricultural implements	204.5	99.9	64.8	903.2
Machinery	85.3	113.6	93.5	665.6
Lumber	60.1	73.8	38.7	286.1
Clay products	70.8	108.0	43.8	410.6

tions," [3] vigorous initiative was able and willing to exploit these new technological opportunities. Agriculture, too, was undergoing a process of mechanization and expansion; the increasing emphasis on cash crops helped to provide export balances to pay interest and dividends on the imported capital which was furthering industrial growth.

2. The Corporate Revolution

Beginning in the seventies, these far-reaching changes helped to reshape American economic life. The prevailing individualistic and competitive system began to give way to a corporate system characterized by a high degree of concentration of control. The corporation, originally merely a convenient instrument for the enlargement of the scope of business enterprise, was soon to reveal itself, in Veblen's phrase, as the "master institution of civilized life." [4]

One manifestation of these changes was a vast increase in the size of business units, mainly organized as corporations. Before the Civil War the use of the corporate form in the industrial field was confined almost entirely to the textile industry. With the burst of industrial expansion after the Civil War, the corporation spread rapidly to other sectors as the advantages which it offered in the way of limited liability and pooling investment became apparent. But many manufacturing enterprises, to begin with, continued to be closely held; there was little or no resort to the money markets to obtain funds; expansion was financed, for the most part, by plowing earnings back into the business. The early history of the Carnegie and Rockefeller enterprises illustrates this type of development.

Large-scale economic enterprise offered many advantages. It utilized new technical processes and machinery to attain the economies of specialization and division of labor. It organized quantity production and lowered unit costs. It frequently offered

[3] J. E. Sawyer, "The Entrepreneur and the Social Order," in William Miller (ed.), *Men in Business* (1952), p. 20. Sawyer continues, "By inheritance and diffusion America is, of course, part of a common Western civilization. But the historical timing of the American settlement and the extremely uneven weighting involved in the social and cultural transfer gave the United States a highly selective extraction of the European heritage. Combined with the conditions of the New World, this selective inheritance gave rise to a social structure conspicuously more favorable to the kind of entrepreneurship most conducive to private capitalist development."

[4] T. Veblen, *Absentee Ownership and Business Enterprise* (1923), p. 86.

economies in purchasing and distribution. It made possible greater productivity and opened the way to a higher standard of living and increased leisure for the masses.

Any attempt to generalize about its effects on competition, however, reveals some of the ambiguities of that term. While the growth of corporations typically reduced the number of competitors, thus weakening competitive forces in one sense, it was often associated with changes in transportation which widened markets and with the development of new products or new methods of distribution which broadened the range of competitive alternatives open to buyers or sellers. It must be remembered that in a predominantly rural America, "the most effective monopoly . . . was the small retailer—the general store at the crossroads—whose customers were as dependent on this single source of supply as the desert inhabitant on his oasis." [5]

With increases in size, however, came also increasing concentration of control in many industries. In the first phases of the combination movement, industrialists themselves supplied the driving force. A variety of techniques was employed. Sometimes, competitors merged or were bought out. Sometimes, they were driven out of business by ruthless competition. The more powerful companies expanded their operations. Thus, Carnegie moved in the direction of vertical integration by combining ownership of coal deposits, coke ovens, iron mines, and transportation facilities with manufacture of iron and steel. Standard Oil followed a policy of horizontal integration by combining refineries and controlling pipe lines. Discriminations in railroad rates played a major role in advancing industrial concentration. In some instances, pools were formed to regulate price and output; but since individual members of these pools retained a large degree of independence, conflicting interests usually led to nonobservance and dissolution of the agreements. After 1880, the "trust" method of combination became the fashion, following the lead of the Standard Oil Trust established in 1879. When the "trust" agreement proved vulnerable to legal attack, it was replaced by the holding company. New Jersey modified its general corporation laws in 1889 to permit corporations to hold stock in other corporations. Other states quickly followed suit, and the process of industrial concentration marched onward, though not without resistance. Agrarian and small business discontent expressed itself in a series of state measures directed against the railroads and

---

[5] W. L. Thorp, in U.S. Temporary National Economic Committee, *Problems of Small Business*, Monograph No. 17 (1941), p. 157.

the trusts and in the enactment of the federal Interstate Commerce Act of 1887 and the Sherman Antitrust Act of 1890, but without marked effect in the short run in checking the concentration movement itself.

Beginning in the 1880's and 1890's a new force emerged to give shape and direction to the combination movement. That force was the rising power of the investment banker. Industry needed funds to enlarge its operations. The investment banker supplied these funds by mobilizing accumulated savings through the sale of stocks or bonds and directing them into profitable channels of investment. But the activities of investment bankers soon extended far beyond this middleman function. Operations were expanded to gain and consolidate control over both the supply of, and the demand for, credit. In order to control investment funds and to guarantee credit facilities needed in marketing securities, interlocking relationships were developed with insurance companies, commercial banks, and trust companies. At the same time, the furnishing of funds to industry was used as a strategic lever to enlarge banking influence in this sector, a trend symbolized by the House of Morgan. Between 1898 and 1902, mergers and consolidations followed each other in rapid succession with investment bankers acting as the midwives. After 1902 the pace of consolidation slackened, only to revive again in great bursts of activity in the decades after each of the two World Wars. But there were always areas where investment bankers did not penetrate and their influence has declined in recent decades. Corporations have increasingly been able to expand their enterprises out of their own resources. Many large corporations, with ample internally generated funds and with ready access to capital markets, have asserted their independence from financial control.

Significant shifts in the locus of economic power attended this growth of large-scale corporate enterprise. The typical entrepreneur of the precapitalistic era did his own work, owned his own tools, supplied his own capital, and managed and controlled his own enterprise. There was a concentration of functions. With the development of the industrial and corporate revolution, this concentration began to break up. The first step was the separation of labor from ownership. Workers now hired out for wages; the employer owned the factory and the expensive machinery it contained. This divorce of labor from ownership inspired the Marxian theory of class war, which called for proletarian revolution as the means of collectivizing ownership. Workers, however, turned for the most part to other means of restoring a degree of control, chiefly through trade-unions and collective bargaining.

The next phase involved the separation of management from ownership. Thorstein Veblen was among the first to call attention to this development. In *Absentee Ownership and Business Enterprise* (1923), he pointed to the rise of absentee ownership as a significant aspect of the growth of large corporations. Where formerly owners of enterprises also managed them, Veblen now saw the emergence of a separate managerial group—the administrators—who were hired like workers to perform the function of management.

In the course of the further development of the corporate system, as Berle and Means have pointed out,[6] ownership itself became separated from control. With the dispersion of stock ownership and the perfection of old and new legal devices such as the proxy, the pyramided holding company, the issuance of nonvoting stock, and the vesting of disproportionate power in one class of stock, new concentrations of power emerged in the form of so-called "control groups," who owned only a small percentage of the corporate assets but nonetheless were able to dominate corporate policy and direct the disposition of the corporate income stream. The general body of average stockholders was thus reduced to the status of investors only, disfranchised as far as policy was concerned, no longer working in or managing the enterprises in which their savings were invested, dependent ultimately on the decisions of the control groups for such income as they received. Control over business policy and industrial processes thus came to be centered in the hands of relatively small numbers of men—sometimes a management group, sometimes a combination of management and banking or other investing groups, sometimes primarily a banking or investing group, but in most cases groups operating, in large part, with what Justice Brandeis once called "Other People's Money."

These developments provided an important part of the institutional setting for government activity in the economic realm. As a result of the corporate revolution, traditional notions of private property required modification and rethinking. Property, from something corporeal and tangible, has become incorporeal and intangible, a bundle of expectations, interests, controls, and relationships. With the growth in the size and power of busi-

[6] A. A. Berle, Jr., and G. C. Means, *The Modern Corporation and Private Property* (1933).

ness units, resources and economic relationships are controlled less by the bargaining of the market and more by the administrative decisions of managers. With the separation of ownership from control, as Justice Brandeis once pointed out, "many of the checks which formerly operated to curb the misuse of wealth and power" have been removed. That "control groups" may regard their position as one of trusteeship and impose high standards of responsibility upon themselves there is experience to verify. There is also some evidence that the corporate sector of the economy is becoming more bureaucratized—or, in Schumpeter's phrase, "trustified"—as hierarchical structure solidifies and management becomes more professional in outlook and interest, seeking to promote the long-run welfare of the corporation by striking a balance among the conflicting interests of securityholders, employees, customers, suppliers, and the general public.

Nonetheless, concentration of power in control groups tended to leave consumers, investors, labor, and farmers with minimum influence over industrial activity despite their great and basic interests in it. Out of this situation, as we shall see, arose many of the pressures for government to intervene—pressure to protect investors, pressure to protect labor, pressure to protect farmers, pressure to protect consumers, and pressure to protect a neglected public interest.

3. Impact of Depression and War

In many respects, the boom of the 1920's was the Golden Age of the American businessman, the time when he was the dominant figure of the culture and when his prestige and status were largely unchallenged. This was the period when President Coolidge proclaimed, "The chief business of the American people is business," adding that "the man who builds a factory builds a temple. . . ." [7]

The 1920 census revealed that, for the first time, a majority of the American people lived in urban areas. During the next decade, manufacturing accounted for a larger share of the labor force than did agriculture, forestry, and fishing. Between 1899 and 1929 the value of the goods annually produced by manufacturing industries multiplied 6½ times. And, though hindsight reveals many disquieting elements in the "prosperity" of the twenties, industrial production continued to increase. The automobile industry forged rapidly ahead, bringing along with it

[7] A. M. Schlesinger, Jr., *Crisis of the Old Order* (1957), p. 57.

such related industries as rubber, oil, glass, steel, and road building. By 1929, the physical volume of industrial production was more than 25 per cent above the level of 1922, and the stock market registered wild optimism.

With the collapse of the stock market in October, 1929, however, a spiral of deflation set in. The depression took on catastrophic proportions. National income plummeted from $81 billion to $40 billion, salaries and wages from $49 billion to $30 billion, and gross farm income from $12 billion to $5.3 billion. The industrial production index fell from 125 in June, 1929, to 59 in March, 1933. Businesses and banks went to the wall; thirteen million workers were jobless; and homes, farms, and savings were lost on an unprecedented scale. The few corrective measures that the Hoover administration undertook proved insufficient to check the decline or to alleviate the distress. By the time Franklin Roosevelt took office in March, 1933, the situation was desperate, and the demands for governmental action were overwhelming.

Under the New Deal, the federal government assumed economic responsibilities of a scale and range without precedent in peacetime. Some of its measures were for emergency salvage purposes. Of the more fundamental reforms, a few proved short-lived, but the majority, as will be seen in later chapters, became permanent and accepted aspects of an altered role for government in the American economy. Politically, as the prestige of corporate managers and financiers declined, the New Deal reflected an enhanced sensitivity of government to the claims of labor, farmers, and small businessmen. The programs comprised an extraordinary variety of new regulatory controls, social welfare activities, and public enterprise.

While these programs served many useful purposes and went far to meet the needs of disadvantaged groups, the New Deal met with only limited success in combating depression and unemployment. In March, 1937, the index of industrial production had reached 118 compared with the 1929 high of 125, but it fell again to 76 in May, 1938, before beginning another climb. Some 7½ million were still unemployed in 1937, and their number mounted to almost 12 million in the recession of 1938.

It required the pressure of national defense and wartime spending to reduce unemployment drastically. By 1942, resources were being heavily pressed to meet the requirements of World War II, and new forms of governmental intervention were devised to minimize shortages and keep inflation within bounds. The war's end, contrary to many expectations, ushered in a period of vigorous economic expansion.

4. Basic Characteristics of the American Economy

The American economy has been characterized, over the long run, by constant change, growth, and diversity. Certainly both change and growth were striking features of the period following World War II. Gross national product soared upward, as the following table indicates: [8]

GROSS NATIONAL PRODUCT AT 1954 PRICES

Gross National Product	1929	1933	1940	1946	1950	1955	1957
(in billions of dollars)	181.8	126.6	205.8	282.5	318.1	392.7	407.0

The readjustment from war to peace was cushioned by a backlog of consumer demand which had been dammed up by wartime shortages. Purchasing power was supported by a more even distribution of income. Expansion was stimulated by business investment seeking to profit from technological innovations and from increased levels of consumer spending and accelerated by governmental expenditures to meet the needs of the Cold War and of domestic welfare programs. Since 1941 there has been relatively full employment, only briefly interrupted by the recessions of 1949, 1954, and 1958. Nor did these downturns seriously interfere with the general growth in national income and in capital formation. It has been a dynamic and a buoyant economy.

The American economy is also marked by diversity. Highly industrialized though the United States is, its manufacturing sector employs only about one-fourth of the labor force, and it generates less than a third of the national income. As the table on the following page shows, other sectors of the economy continue to be of great importance.[9]

In the industrial sector, control over resources is highly concentrated. In 1947 there were 113 nonfinancial corporations, each with assets of more than $100 million, which collectively owned 46 per cent of the total net capital assets in manufacturing.[10] In 1948 there were 260 firms with more than 10,000 employees; together

[8] Survey of Current Business, July, 1958, pp. 10–11.
[9] J. F. Dewhurst et al., America's Needs and Resources (1955), p. 732.
[10] Federal Trade Commission, Report on the Concentration of Productive Facilities (1949), p. 14.

PERCENTAGE DISTRIBUTION OF LABOR FORCE, 1870–1950

	1870	1900	1920	1950
Agriculture, forestry, and fishing	50.8	38.0	27.7	12.1
Mining	1.6	2.6	3.0	1.4
Construction	5.9	5.8	5.3	6.2
Manufacturing	17.6	22.1	26.4	25.8
Transportation, communication, and public utilities	4.8	7.1	9.7	8.6
Trade	6.1	8.6	9.9	18.0
Finance, insurance, and real estate	0.3	1.1	1.9	3.2
Professional service	1.6	2.5	3.6	6.3
Personal and domestic service	9.3	9.4	8.1	10.6
Government	2.0	2.8	4.5	7.9

these firms employed 8.2 million workers, or 22.7 per cent of those employed in private, nonagricultural industry.[11] In 1951, of the 114,142 manufacturing firms filing corporate income tax returns, 373 had assets of over $50 million and owned 55 per cent of all of the corporate assets in this sector.[12] Little wonder that ours is commonly called a corporate economy and that there is a frequently expressed fear of monopoly! Yet such figures need to be seen in perspective. Concentration of resources in the hands of a few hundred corporations is by no means a peculiarly American phenomenon. Indeed, a leading authority concludes, "Although many U.S. manufacturing industries are largely concentrated and although the largest firms in the economy account for a significant per cent of economic activity, American industries are less concentrated than similar industries in many other countries, and the general concentration is no higher—it may even be somewhat lower—than in countries showing a comparable degree of industrialization." [13]

For side by side with the giant American corporations are over 9 million other decision-making economic units—700,000 corporations, 3½ million proprietorships engaged in business, and over 5 million separate farm units. And, while the number of farm units is declining, the number of business firms tends to grow at the same rate as does the natural population. In both 1929 and 1952, the number of business enterprises per thousand of population

---

[11] M. A. Adelman, "The Measurement of Industrial Concentration," *Review of Economics and Statistics* (November, 1951), p. 275.

[12] *Statistical Abstract of the U.S.: 1955*, p. 493.

[13] E. S. Mason, *Economic Concentration and the Monopoly Problem* (1957), p. 42.

was the same—25.5. As the following table shows, the degree of concentration also varies in different sectors of the economy: [14]

ROLE OF THE LARGE CORPORATION IN VARIOUS SECTORS
OF THE ECONOMY, 1951

(Corporations with over $50 Million in Assets)
(Percentages)

Sector	Large Corporations' Share of Total Corporation Assets	Share of Total Sector Income Received by All Corporations	Large Corporations' Indicated Share of Total Sector
Agriculture, forestry, and fishing	14.7	0.6	0.1
Mining	30.7	86.6	26.6
Construction	2.8	16.4	0.5
Manufacturing	54.7	94.0	51.4
Transportation, communication, and public utilities	84.2	86.5	72.9
Trade	19.1	31.2	6.0
Finance, insurance, and real estate	64.2	73.3	47.0
Services	16.2	7.8	1.3
Total economy	58.7	50.0	29.4

But is the trend to greater concentration? If the smaller firms are not being eliminated, are they being confined to a shrinking section of the economy? A quarter of a century ago some evidence suggested that they were. In a pioneering study in 1932, Berle and Means concluded that if the growth in concentration continued at the same rate that had held in the period 1909–1929, "then 70 per cent of all corporate activity would be carried on by two hundred corporations by 1950. If the more rapid rates of growth from 1924 to 1929 were maintained for the next twenty years, 85 per cent of the corporate wealth would be held by two hundred large units." [15] This study was only the first in a series which have predicted imminent capture of the whole economy by huge corporations. In 1948, for example, the Federal Trade Commission (FTC) predicted that "if nothing is done to check the growth in concentration, either the giant corporations will ultimately take over the country, or the government will be compelled

[14] Derived from Statistical Abstract of the U.S.: 1955, pp. 493–494.
[15] Op. cit., p. 40.

to step in." [16] Yet the best available evidence simply does not support these gloomy predictions. From 1931 to 1947, the share of manufacturing corporations' total assets held by the 139 largest corporations dropped from 50 per cent to 45 per cent. Over the longer run, while 33 per cent of value added by manufacture around 1901 was produced in industries in which four firms accounted for more than 50 per cent of value added, in 1947 the comparable percentage was 24.[17]

Does corporate concentration of resources mean that the rich are getting richer and the poor poorer? Apparently not. While there is, of course, substantial inequality of individual income, and while the rewards for economic success in this country are high indeed, the trend since the Great Depression, as the following two tables indicate, has been toward greater equality in income even before taxes.[18]

PERCENTAGE OF INDIVIDUALS' INCOME RECEIVED BY:

	1919	1929	1939	1948
Top 1 per cent	12.8	14.5	11.9	8.5
2nd to 5th percentage band	10.1	11.6	11.8	9.4
Lower 95 per cent	77.1	73.9	76.3	82.2

PERCENTAGE OF MONEY INCOME RECEIVED BY EACH FIFTH OF THE NATION'S FAMILIES AND SINGLE PERSONS

	1935–36	1941	1948	1956
Lowest fifth	4.0	3.5	4.2	4.0
Second fifth	8.7	9.1	10.5	11.0
Third fifth	13.6	15.3	16.1	17.0
Fourth fifth	20.5	22.5	22.3	22.0
Highest fifth	53.2	49.6	46.9	46.0

Is corporate concentration to be equated with monopoly? Chapter 18 will deal in more detail with this question and with some of the difficulties inherent in the definition of monopoly and competition. Here it is sufficient to note that corporate concentration does mean that in a substantial proportion of American industries the bulk of the output is controlled by a small handful of firms. In recent years, for example, General Motors, Ford, and Chrysler have produced over 95 per cent of all the cars manufac-

[16] The Merger Movement: A Summary Report, p. 68.
[17] Adelman, op. cit., pp. 289–291; Mason, op. cit., pp. 16–43.
[18] Statistical Abstract of the U.S.: 1955, p. 294; 1958, p. 316.

tured in this country. Even if the industry classification be broadened to include all motor vehicles and equipment, then the four largest firms employ 58 per cent of the industry's employees. Similarly, the four largest aircraft–engine companies account for 55 per cent of the industry labor force. At the same time, on the other hand, many other industries are marked by low concentration ratios. The four largest dress manufacturers, for example, employ only 2 per cent of the industry's workers.[19]

Just as concentration ratios vary widely from industry to industry, so do the forms and degree of competition. There does not, however, appear to be any necessary correlation between concentration and lack of competition. High concentration in the automobile industry is quite compatible with effective and vigorous competition. Yet it also enabled the steel industry for many years both to avoid price competition and to be technologically laggard. The task of evaluating competition in different industries is, as we shall see, one of the most difficult problems confronting public policy.

Although corporate concentration may not eliminate competition, it does endow corporation managers with substantial power over the market. They are in a position to influence prices, if not to control them, to a substantial degree. The existence of a high degree of price control in some sectors of the economy and its absence in others tend to create serious maladjustments. Such disparities accentuate the effective bargaining power of the organized sector of the economy as against the unorganized; they also inspire counterorganization among the unorganized and efforts to utilize the instrumentalities of government to strengthen the bargaining power of weaker economic interests.

In explaining his concept of "countervailing power," Galbraith argues that "power on one side of a market creates both the need for, and the prospect of a reward to, the exercise of countervailing power from the other side." [20] Certainly a notable feature of the past quarter of a century has been the organization of previously unorganized groups for effective economic action. The spread of trade associations, labor organizations, and agricultural producers' co-operatives evidences the strength of this tendency in diverse fields. Particularly significant has been the invocation of governmental authority to buttress the bargaining power of some of these groups. Thus the power exercised by a big manufacturer may be checked by the organization of countervailing

[19] Ibid., 1955, p. 801.
[20] J. K. Galbraith, American Capitalism (1952), p. 120.

power by big labor, by a big buyer, or by big government, the latter acting at the behest, perhaps, of independent distributors or of farmers.

The reliance on government as a balancer or adjuster re-emphasizes another characteristic of the economy—the greatly expanded role played by government. Small independent firms, particularly in distribution, have obtained legislation to compensate for the mass power of large concerns. Labor has strengthened its bargaining power by persuading government to set minimum labor standards and to guarantee and protect the right of collective bargaining. Farmers have organized to obtain large-scale government aid and to impose production, marketing, and price controls on their commodities. The result has been increased economic strength of hitherto weak interests; but it has also involved new rigidities in the economic system, with possible dangers for its adaptive capacity in the face of changing economic conditions.

The obligation of government to provide a measure of economic security is now recognized. The limited, laissez faire view has given way to a new conception of the positive service state, with government assuming major responsibility for maintaining the stability of the national economy and for conserving resources, natural and human. The budget has become a vehicle to redistribute income, to provide social services, and to maintain public enterprise.

The salient aspects of this enormous increase in the economic powers of government will be analyzed in the pages which follow. It is important to remember that this increase is only partly accounted for by the Great Depression, the New Deal, World War II, and their aftermaths. In a larger sense, it represents a response to the new world created by modern technology and industry. The insecurities and the mutual interdependencies which they have generated have led to a growing dependence on government to redress the balance and guarantee well-being. In the old economy of small trade, free competition, and equality of bargaining power, there was relatively little pressure for government to intervene. The new economy of large-scale enterprise, concentration of economic power, and administered prices invites political adjustments. The pressure for intervention comes from business groups as well as from farmers, laborers, investors, and consumers. The new activities of government reflect these demands; they crystallize the adjustments of a democratic community to an altered economic environment.

CHAPTER 2

The Organization of
Economic Interests

THE RELATIVE strength and success of various economic interest groups are deeply affected by public policy. Efforts to influence such policy through appropriate organization have become a cardinal feature of the American economy. In the matrix of thousands of overlapping groupings, three basic interests stand out as of primary importance—business, labor, and agriculture. Each has its own organizational forms and its own tactics and strategy. Each, in turn, is a mosaic of many particular interests, not necessarily harmonious and frequently expressing their aspirations through independent political activity.

The pattern of evolving public policy reflects in part the interplay of these interests, their strength and their weakness, their skill in accommodation, and their ability to capitalize such resources as they have at their disposal. It also reflects the degree to which governmental and party leaders have used this political raw material to muster support for their parties, agencies, or offices. A realistic analysis of the activities of government in the economic system must take these interests into account, must consider their demands and the intensity of the pressure they are able to bring to bear.

1. The Politics of Business

Businessmen's concern with government is not new; wherever business and government have coexisted, the problem of adjusting

19

their relationships has arisen. The adjustment has varied. For centuries the businessman was consigned to an inferior social and political status. In the determination of public policy, he was subordinate to the warrior, the priest, and the landholder. The rise of business influence in the Western World is a relatively recent development. With the industrial and commercial revolution, the modern businessman began to come into his own and assert a new-found independence. He exerted his power to cast off the burdensome restrictions of law and custom evolved to fit the needs of a feudal-aristocratic landholding society. In Europe he met varying degrees of opposition. In England and France he was comparatively successful in overcoming the resistance of agrarian, military, and church groups; in Germany, Italy, and Russia he encountered much more effective resistance from these quarters.

America presented a different picture. There was no feudal heritage to surmount, though the rise of the Southern slaveholding aristocracy presented an American analogue. The slaveholding aristocrats might look upon the businessman with contempt, but while they fought delaying actions, they were unable to check his expanding power. The Civil War brought about their utter rout and ushered in an era of business paramountcy. As the wealth and power of the business community increased, government became increasingly sensitive to its demands and wishes. For three-quarters of a century the influence of the successful businessman permeated the whole life of society. Social values were primarily business values, and politics was geared to the aspirations of the dominant business interests. To be sure, the businessman rarely played a public role in the political process. For the most part, he depended upon professional politicians to effect the necessary adjustments between business activities and public policies. The fact that his influence was exercised indirectly, however, did not make it any less potent.

The post-Civil War consolidation of business influence did not go unchallenged. Beginning at least as far back as the seventies, a ground swell of anti-big-business and antimonopoly sentiment became apparent. But, despite periodic upsurges of popular dissatisfaction, business leadership pursued its course and was able to dissipate dissent with the visible evidence of rising national prosperity. The Golden Age of Coolidge registered this trend at its apogee.

The Great Depression and the New Deal brought about a profound change in this social milieu. Unemployment and other economic distress, together with revelations of abuses of power and trust, undermined public confidence in business leadership. Labor, agrarian, small business, investor, and consumer groups became bolder in demanding the aid of government. The New Deal provided a vehicle for the organization of these groups, thereby institutionalizing counterbalances to the power of large business. Both because of the decline of business leadership and in response to pressures from many sides, government assumed greater responsibility for the over-all functioning of the economy and the co-ordination of economic activity. An expanding network of regulatory statutes bore witness to the new trend. Their own forces divided, businessmen found their calculations hedged about by the decisions of public officials responding to nonbusiness pressures and seeking to protect interests which the businessman could not readily identify as his own. In the face of this apparent threat, business groups re-examined their political strength and resources, and readjusted their political methods in the hope of stabilizing their political relationships on a more satisfactory basis. The American political front, which businessmen first conquered and then largely took for granted, had again become a vital arena and a scene of struggle in which many businessmen felt that the hegemony of business itself was at stake.

The outstanding success of the economy in meeting World War II demands and in providing since the war high employment levels, increasing output, and widely distributed gains in consumption, has gone far to restore the prestige and self-confidence of businessmen. Yet, even though business influence has greatly increased, it has not regained its former pre-eminence. Indeed, a major consequence of the Republican victory in 1952 was an acceptance of many of the reforms of the 1930's, thereby retiring New Deal disputes from politics and converting them into history. Few statutory policies have been revised, although administrative changes have considerably altered the impact of policy. Government continues to exercise a large general responsibility for the functioning of the economy. Both in its attempts to influence government and in its ordinary operations, business has had to allow for the enhanced power and aspirations of other groups.

Consideration of the politics of business suggests a number of questions. Who are the businessmen? Is there a business community in any politically significant sense? To what extent do businessmen share common aims and objectives? To what extent are they organized for effective political action? What are the sources of their power and influence? How do they exercise influence?

Difficulties present themselves at the threshold. How shall the businessman be defined? There are about 4½ million business units—700,000 corporations, 3½ million business proprietorships, and about 250,000 self-employed professionals. Included within this group is every branch of business enterprise from the corner grocery store, whose proprietor employs no labor and perhaps barely makes ends meet, to large-scale industrial, financial, and public utility concerns whose employees number tens of thousands and whose corporate assets run into the billions. Is there any element of community among the various members of this group which justifies treating them as a coherent political unit?

Certainly there are many conflicts of interest and differences of purpose among businessmen. Little business struggles against big business; high-cost producers seek political protection against low-cost producers; independent wholesalers and retailers battle chains; importers oppose those interested in protecting domestic markets; regional economic interests compete politically for freight rate as well as wage differentials; chaotically organized or depressed industries demand government assistance and regulation while more prosperous industries oppose such pleas. The welter of intra- and interindustry competition, and the more than five thousand national and regional trade associations and other business groups which represent individual industries, trades, or areas, serve as a warning against any oversimple characterization of the business community as an organic unit. Indeed, much governmental regulation occurs precisely because of these conflicts of interest, being designed to strike a balance among them.

Business Organization and Influence

The organization of industry trade associations and of local and regional business groups has assisted in, and in part been a response to, efforts to rally and unite business sentiment. In addition to crystallizing and registering the interests of the particular industry or area, these groups are important media for arousing and focusing general business reactions to broader policy issues. They thus provide broader channels for the dissemination of business influence than those directly available to the two more comprehensive business organizations, the National Association of Manufacturers (NAM) and the Chamber of Commerce of the United States.

These organizations attempt to speak for the business community as a whole. They both contain a heterogeneous membership reflecting many of the cleavages within the business world, and some of their policy statements, like party platform planks, are compromises couched in general and ambiguous terms. But on many issues they find it possible to identify and support positions common to most businessmen. The NAM has much the narrower membership base, concentrated in larger manufacturing concerns, and it is consequently more outspoken and aggressive in putting forward its views. For many decades, its main cohesive force was opposition to organized labor, but it has also sought to prevent what it considered undesirable governmental encroachments on managerial freedom and business incentives. The Chamber of Commerce is essentially a federation of state and local chambers, trade associations, and other business organizations; it represents a broader constituency and its policies are correspondingly less sharply defined. By the same token, however, its statements are known to reflect a wider business consensus. It is highly effective in presenting business views to legislative and administrative agencies and in informing the business community of its stake in public policy issues.

But of more fundamental import than these formal organizations in contributing to the consolidation of business influence are the consequences of large-scale corporate enterprise and the concentration movement. The dominance of clusters of large firms in important sectors of the economy fosters homogeneity of outlook in the business community. Also important in promoting homogeneity in the past, although less so now as large corporations have come to finance most of their expansion from retained profits, was the influence of interlocking financial relationships, exercised through the banking and investment houses.

The business community is pyramidal in structure. In its top layers are the managers and directors of large corporations; officers of the major banks, investment houses, insurance and holding companies; corporation lawyers; newspaper publishers; advertising and public relations experts. This group may be described as the "general staff" of "big business." Its members have their internecine battles and rivalries, but on larger issues of public policy they form a fairly solid phalanx of opinion.

Various lines of influence connect this "general staff" with the lower levels of the pyramid. The larger banks and investment houses have their connections with smaller financial institutions; the latter, in turn, serve as a link with small business. The corporate hierarchies, too, have their co-ordinating functions. Closely associated with the top strata of corporation executives is a much wider circle of middle and junior executives and well-paid

technicians who, for the most part, reflect the views of the innei
circle. At a lower level, but yet still within the range of influence
of the top business groups, are the supervisory personnel—the foremen, overseers, and inspectors—and many of the so-called "white-
collar" workers, who, though they receive their income largely as
salaries, frequently adopt the outlook of employers rather than
employees. In addition, the loyalties of those who live largely on
investment income can ordinarily be depended upon to rally
around business leadership. Under favorable conditions, business
influence may even penetrate deeply into the ranks of industrial
workers. An acute observer remarks:

> "Businessmen" maintain a remarkable solidarity on basic political
> issues. A network of common interests pulls the business community
> together on major issues where its security is threatened despite minor
> rifts in its ranks from time to time. . . . Within the business com-
> munity powerful factors operate to discipline the dissident and to bring
> conformity to the predominant views. Unanimity is rare, but a pre-
> dominant business sentiment usually crystallizes and makes itself
> heard on major issues threatening the group as a whole. When most
> segments of business share a common interest, dissenting views are
> neither numerous nor loud. Yet on lesser matters when interests di-
> verge, political differences between types of business may be as bitter
> as a trade-union jurisdictional dispute.[1]

The degree of business solidarity thus depends primarily on a
consciousness of common interest, on an awareness, or belief, that
an issue immediately applicable to one segment of business has
potential significance to all business. When businessmen share
such a belief, their power is great indeed. Typically, major regulations of business are instituted when business interests are divided.
At such times some sections of business support regulation, either
feeling that major issues relating to all of business and the enterprise system are not thereby raised, or that the evils or abuses
being regulated are themselves harming the broad business interest.
The general antimonopoly movement of the late nineteenth century, which led both to the Sherman Antitrust Act and to federal
regulation of railroads, drew some of its firmest and most influential support from among the ranks of businessmen, such as
small competitors squeezed by the growth of large corporations
and trusts or merchants discriminated against by railroad rates
and rebates. Similarly, the New Deal attracted substantial backing

[1] V. O. Key, Jr., *Politics, Parties, and Pressure Groups*, 3d ed. (1952), pp.
86–87.

from some business interests. Many businessmen and their allies supported regulation of stock exchanges and corporate finance by the Securities and Exchange Commission; businesses dependent on sales in rural areas supported Agricultural Adjustment Administration programs; and many small businessmen favored other New Deal objectives of benefit to them.

Business cohesion and unity take different forms. They may produce mutual tolerance of the pursuit of particularistic business goals. For many decades most businessmen, even those with nothing to gain and perhaps something to lose, supported tariffs as a part of the general business interest. Business interests at odds may prefer to settle their own disputes rather than appeal for their resolution to government, since the response of government may introduce a broader framework of considerations which transcend the immediate issues in dispute. The fear of political retaliation may also contribute to cement political unity. Business unity may also express itself in more positive political terms and involve the assumption of direct governing responsibilities. Thus in recent years businessmen have moved into key positions in the Eisenhower administration and called on business to support Republican acceptance of New Deal programs as the price of keeping in power a party friendly to business. At other times, as in the 1920's, business has not felt itself endangered by either party, and has consequently been less impelled to embark on crusading political action.

The extent of business influence is obviously not a fixed quantum. It is capable of expansion and contraction depending on consciousness of common interest, the nature of business leadership, and economic developments. Late in the nineteenth century, discipline and unity disappeared as merchants and other small businessmen joined, or led, the attack on railroads and monopolies. In the face of Bryan and the Populists, Hanna unified business. Early in the twentieth century, this unity was reinforced by corporate growth and consolidation and by the development of further managerial and financial discipline. A breach between the interests of large and small business was reopened in 1912, leading to further regulation. In the 1920's unity was restored, but militancy declined with general acceptance of business leadership and the impotence of any countervailing power—government, union, or farm. The Great Depression shattered this unity, only slowly to be restored during the 1940's.

What are the resources available to the business community for enlisting widespread support? Command of economic wealth is, of course, the keystone of business strength. The prestige of the business community may rise in good times and decline when times are bad, but as long as it retains major control of the economic assets of the nation it possesses a potent weapon. Economic power, moreover, may be transmuted into political power in an even more immediate and direct sense. The cruder varieties of direct purchase of votes, politicians, and officials may no longer be commonly in vogue, but other less direct techniques are available. Campaign contributions to either or both major political parties; the promise of business preferment dangled before the eyes of ambitious public figures; the subsidy of pressure groups; a heavy ownership stake in the press, radio, television, motion-picture, and other industries which mold public sentiment; pressure on economically dependent individuals, firms, or industries to elicit their political support; an intensive cultivation of public relations; the employment of high-priced counsel to erect legal barricades against the expansion of governmental regulation—these and their variants are the levers through which business influence on the political process can be exerted.

The Methods of Business Politics

Practitioners of the politics of business have had various methods at their disposal. They include persuasion, attrition, infiltration, and concession or compromise. Each of these methods may be practiced by the same business groups at different times; sometimes, elements of each may be used at the same time.

The method of persuasion embraces everything from direct economic pressure at one end of the scale to any presentation of business aims and objectives to the general public at the other end. Economic pressure may take the form of threats of injury for undesired conduct or promises of rewards to induce desired conduct. The presentation of business goals may involve the use of mass media or of more selective means to influence public opinion or governmental agencies.

It is the stress on public opinion and on the direct appeal to the electorate which distinguishes the modern application of this strategy. Some old-style, rough-and-tumble businessmen were more defiant of public opinion. W. K. Vanderbilt's "The public be damned," George F. Baker's "It's none of the public's business what I do," and H. O. Havemeyer's "Business is not a philanthropy" were forthright, if incautious, expressions of an indifference to public sentiment characterizing some members of an earlier generation of business leadership. Voters, politicians, and legislators were regarded as commodities to be bought. Nice scruples could not be tolerated in the ruthless pursuit of business objectives. The popular revulsion provoked by such tactics forced a readjustment of business tactics. Businessmen began to think of placating public opinion. A significant reorientation in the character of business politics became evident around the turn of the century. Hanna's management of the McKinley campaign marked the first nationally significant use of the new techniques. To be sure, direct economic pressures were used. But in addition, advertising methods were now imported into politics—the use of slogans and posters, the distribution of "boiler plate" to newspapers, and the marshaling of public opinion on a national scale.

Hanna's methods quickly found imitators among business groups with political problems. The railroad struggle against the Hepburn Act of 1906 reproduced the same pattern of techniques. The campaign of the utility industry during the twenties and its battle against the Utility Holding Company Act in 1935 are more recent instances, though examples could be multiplied. Thus, in 1950, the Buchanan Committee found that in the previous 3½ years 151 large corporations had spent $32,124,835 in attempts to influence congressional and public opinion.[2] Of primary significance is the new disposition of business, particularly big business, to seek safety from political attack through efforts to mold the basic political attitudes of the electorate.

This reliance on persuasion is a by-product of the special relationship between the political and the economic power possessed by business. The very size and concentration of resources which give business economic power make it vulnerable to political attack. Because businessmen are a small minority and are often attractive political targets, they confront a greater need to court public opinion than do more sizable groups. The power of the business community rests ultimately on a general willingness to follow its leadership.

A second method sometimes used by business groups is the method of attrition. This involves attempts to delay, discredit, or prevent the execution of a policy. Litigation to obstruct unpalatable legislation is one example. Nearly every single important expansion of state or national regulatory authority over business was attended at its initiation by an outburst of lawsuits designed to impede the expansion. From the first legal assault on the Inter-

<hr>

[2] Report of House Select Committee on Lobbying Activities, *Expenditures by Corporations to Influence Legislation*, 81st Cong., 1st sess. (1950).

state Commerce Act of 1887, which rendered the ICC almost impotent for nearly twenty years, through the more recent legal barrage against various phases of the New Deal, this technique has been persistently employed. Needless to say, the right to dispute the constitutionality of a legislative act or the legality of administrative action is not in question; it is the abuse of this right as a method of waging guerrilla warfare against undesired regulatory activities which is here identified with the method of attrition.

Such rear-guard action has not been confined to litigation. Unwelcome regulation may be frustrated by withholding business co-operation where it is essential to the effectiveness of the regulation, or business pressure may be exerted to guide the administrative application into more acceptable channels. Indeed, a third method, that of infiltration, involves the placement of sympathetic officials in policy-making administrative posts. Regulatory agencies have shown a tendency to lose their initial zeal for the rigorous administration of statutes regulating business activities as the original personnel are replaced by men less enthusiastic about regulation and more sympathetic to the regulated. Thus, although few New Deal statutes were repealed or amended by the Eisenhower administration, the appointment of new members to such agencies as the National Labor Relations Board, the Federal Power Commission, the Federal Trade Commission, the Bureau of Land Management, and the Tennessee Valley Authority brought about changes in administrative attitudes more agreeable to many business elements.

A fourth method involves concession or compromise. Farsighted and realistic business leadership has recognized the advantages of placating opposition, and, on occasion, has followed the Bismarckian and "Tory Socialist" tactic of controlling or limiting reform by annexing and sponsoring it. Concession or compromise has always loomed large in business politics when the support of other groups is essential. But the price business has been willing to pay for such support has ordinarily depended on the strength of the groups it has had to placate. As both agrarian and labor groups have become more effectively organized, business politicians have found it essential to make greater concessions.

An excellent example of the changing temper of business leadership is provided by the Committee for Economic Development (CED), which, in contrast with more conservative business groups, concedes the premise that large-scale government participation is a permanent part of the economy and attempts to contribute positively to the formulation of public policy rather than merely to oppose the expanding responsibilities of government.

The choice of a method to pursue in the politics of business may be conditioned by various circumstances—the character of the particular business involved, the resources available, the strength of opposition, and the general economic or political setting. Method is subordinate to end; each course of action must ultimately meet the test of proved or probable effectiveness in realizing the goal which businessmen have set.

The general goal of business politics can be minimally and generally stated in survival terms. But the conditions of survival are appraised differently by different sections of the business community. To the small businessman who feels himself threatened by big business, the conditions of survival may be vigorous enforcement of the antitrust laws, enactment of legislation protecting him from big business, or government provision for his credit needs. Big business, on the other hand, is likely to resist every governmental effort to limit bigness. In similar fashion, the peculiarities and special needs of particular businesses dictate very different attitudes toward government. With some, the plea is for direct aid, for tariff protection and subsidies. Infant or ailing industries may seek assistance and regulation. With more prosperous, established, and expanding industries, the goal is nonregulation or a minimum of regulation. With still others, such as the public utilities, the demand is for "reasonable" regulation. The structure of modern business is too complex to expect unanimity of program or strategy over the whole range of its operations.

Nevertheless, efforts to achieve consensus continue to be made. The growth in the strength, organization, and bargaining power of nonbusiness and antibusiness groups has challenged businessmen to unite and rally their efforts. The result has been particularly evident in the growing self-consciousness of big business since 1933. Faced with what it then regarded as a tide of hostile regulation, big business responded with attrition and resistance where possible and with concession or compromise where no alternative was available. But, more significantly, it has recognized that its "old easy-going reliance on the professionals of politics to temper the tides of political unrest has become increasingly untrustworthy." [3] The result has been a vastly increased emphasis on public relations activity in an endeavor to mold the basic political

[3] N. E. Long, "Public Relations of the Bell System," *Public Opinion Quarterly* (October, 1937), pp. 5–6.

attitudes of the electorate.

Yet, over the long run, the effectiveness of public relations campaigns depends on the conduct and performance of those being publicized. The relative success of big business in escaping from the onus of responsibility for the Great Depression, in regaining its stature in the public mind, and in once again exercising great influence in the highest administration circles in Washington has largely been due to its role in the war effort and in the postwar industrial expansion and to its eventual acceptance of, and learning to live with, most of the New Deal reforms. An avoidance of the abuse of its economic power, a continuation of prosperity, and an equitable sharing of the tangible benefits of economic growth—these clearly are the prerequisites for successful public relations and for the maintenance by business of substantial political power.

2. The Politics of Labor

If organization be the *sine qua non* of power, labor has still to realize its full potentialities. About eighteen million workers are members of unions, but this is only one-fourth of the total labor force and about one-half of all "organizable" workers. The merged AFL-CIO musters about fifteen million members—ten million from former American Federation of Labor (AFL) unions, five million from former Congress of Industrial Organizations (CIO) unions—while the remaining three million unionists belong to independent groups.

Organization has been most successful among skilled urban workers, especially in mines, factories, building, and transportation, and has spread only slowly to the unskilled and to clerical and low-income professional groups. Even among the organized, internal cleavages have been widespread and recurrent. Sectional antipathies, opposition of skilled to unskilled workers and of rural to urban workers, craft rivalries, conflicts between craft and industrial lines of organization, ethnic cleavages, opposition between "native" and "alien," violence and racketeering, all have played their part in labor history. Employees in a particular industry often join their employers to urge upon government their common interest in special protection against competitors. Thus, the "labor interest" is far from unified; the labor movement is far from unanimous in agreement on objectives or methods.

The Development of Labor Organization

Before unions could become an effective economic or political force they had to secure a firm organizational base. This task took a century, and it was not until the New Deal that they developed substantial political power. Their delay in reaching political maturity reflected the obstacles confronting any newly emergent group which can win power only by wresting it away from older groups favored by the existing "rules of the game." So it was that labor, although given great numerical strength by the rapid pace of industrialization and placed in a position where the economic benefit or necessity of collective action might seem obvious, was slow in winning common acceptance of unions as such and in generating substantial political power.

Labor's struggle for unions and political power has not been a simple battle with employers; rather it has been, first, a struggle to unify workers. A labor historian once described the history of the AFL as "a perpetual struggle to keep the organization from going to pieces for want of inner cohesion." [4] This striving for unity has clashed head-on with powerful, established ideologies and interests representing many sections of society. The crucial point, in Perlman's words, has been "that under no circumstances can labor here afford to arouse the fears of the great middle class for the safety of private property as a basic institution. Labor needs the support of public opinion, meaning the middle class, both rural and urban, in order to make headway with its program of curtailing, by legislation and by trade unionism, the abuses which attend the employer's unrestricted exercise of his property rights." [5] A brief description of the history of the labor movement illustrates the strength of these barriers to organization.

While rudimentary labor organizations first appeared in this country late in the eighteenth century, it was not until the middle of the nineteenth century that modern trade-unions began to emerge. Two largely parallel but occasionally conflicting trends have characterized the labor movement since the Civil War. The first has been the organization of unions based on craft lines, composed of skilled and better-paid workers. These unions have prospered most in fields least penetrated by mass production, such as the building trades (carpenters, electricians, hod carriers, painters, bricklayers, plasterers, plumbers, structural ironworkers, etc.), printing, metalworking, and railroad transportation. Although

[4] Selig Perlman, A Theory of the Labor Movement (1928), p. 154.
[5] Ibid., pp. 160–161.

representing only a small fraction of American workers, these relatively conservative unions, for the most part enrolled in or allied with the AFL, held unquestioned sway over the labor movement between 1900 and the advent of the New Deal. The second trend, more amorphous and slower to achieve success, consisted of attempts to organize the unskilled and semiskilled workers in factories, mines, and fields. It was manifested sometimes in industrial unionism, sometimes in the demand for "one big union," sometimes in socialist political action, sometimes in syndicalist, antipolitical "direct action."

National craft unions, many of which have maintained their existence unbroken to the present day, first took shape in modern form in the 1850's and 1860's. They concentrated on "business unionism"—the improvement of their own wages, hours, and working conditions—with only incidental interest in wider reform or in general politics. Several short-lived intercraft organizations were formed in the years after the Civil War, but effective and permanent association of craft unions appeared only with the establishment of the AFL in 1886.

A contrary principle of organizing was for some time successfully pursued by the "Noble Order of the Knights of Labor," which sought to unite all labor in "one big union." Originating as a secret society in 1869, it dropped the mantle of secrecy in 1881 and soon became the largest and most significant organization American labor had produced. It suffered, however, from imprecisely defined objectives, conflicts between humanitarian reformers and advocates of revolutionary political and economic action, disputes over politics, and friction with craft unions. Including 700,000 members at its height in 1886, it became the victim of public hysteria after the Haymarket explosion in Chicago, and rapidly lost membership to the more conservative American Federation of Labor.

The American Federation of Labor

From 1890 to 1935, the history of the American labor movement is largely the history of the American Federation of Labor.[6] The only serious challenge to its supremacy came from the Industrial Workers of the World, formed in 1905. The IWW began as a movement for organization of unskilled miners, factory workers, and migratory farm laborers and lumbermen behind a program of militant industrial unionism and socialism. Challenging

[6] The Railroad Brotherhoods, though organized independently, worked closely with the Federation.

the AFL for its acceptance of capitalism and its failure to organize the unskilled, it was assailed, in turn, as an irresponsible mob of "un-American" revolutionaries. Shortly before World War I, a syndicalist faction captured leadership, aiming at seizure of the economic order by "direct action." In the war and immediate postwar years, the organization was widely attacked by federal and state officials under the Espionage Act and the crop of "Criminal Syndicalism" laws which swept the country in an intense wave of antiradical emotion. The IWW declined to a position of slight importance. Yet its rise and prewar strength indicated serious defects in the AFL as a representative labor organization.

AFL policies were stamped with the personality of Samuel Gompers, who was president continuously from 1886 until his death in 1924, except for the year 1895. Formerly a socialist, he had become convinced that under American conditions a stable and effective labor organization must confine itself to business unionism, the "here and now," the search for "a fair day's wage for a fair day's work." While industrial unionism was not forbidden within the ranks of the Federation, and was indeed represented by two of its most powerful constituents, the United Mine Workers and the United Brewery Workmen, craft unions were preferred and craft autonomy jealously guarded. The AFL vigorously condemned as "dual unionism" any effort to organize the unskilled outside the Federation. It set its face against third-party politics, whether independent or in co-operation with farmers. It distrusted reliance upon government but it did adopt the nonpartisan tactics of "rewarding its friends and punishing its enemies" in political life regardless of party affiliation.

The AFL maintained a stable, nationwide labor organization for the first time in American history, but it could organize only a small proportion of the labor force, much smaller than was unionized in other industrialized countries. Its growth was slow, reaching the million mark only by 1902. In its earliest years, a member union lost the spectacular Homestead strike in 1892, and an independent union was smashed in a dramatic strike against the Pullman Company in 1894. Since state militia in the former, and federal injunctions and troops in the latter, had played a decisive role, the demand for independent political action was given new impetus, and quarrels on that issue badly divided the young organization. Its first important successes took place during the prosperous years from 1898 to 1902, a period which saw a great wave of corporate consolidations. These years also witnessed the beginnings of employer organization for militant anti-unionism. The National Association of Manufacturers after 1903, the American Anti-Boycott Association (later the League for Industrial Rights), and certain trade associations made the "open shop," which in practice meant the nonunion shop, the core of their programs. They sought not merely to win over employers, but also to gain sympathy from the general public. Judicial injunctions hampering or crippling union activities first appeared in significant numbers in these years. Thus the Federation had to make its way against employer antipathy, judicial hostility, internal dissension, and leftward challenge from the IWW.

By the beginning of World War I, the AFL was firmly established. It had over two million members; it had won from the Taft administration a Department of Labor and from the Wilson administration the labor sections of the Clayton Act. It had a strong lobby at Washington, paralleled at many state capitals by the lobbies of state federations of labor. While not all reform elements supported the principle of labor organization, the "muckraking" era of the first decade of the century had evoked much public sympathy for exploited workers, and Progressives and Northern Democrats began to espouse protective legislation on behalf of labor. Many went further, and a government Commission on Industrial Relations in 1915 endorsed the principle of unionism.

But the union movement suffered from a basic weakness. AFL craft unions failed to include the mass-production workers whom new technology and large-scale industrial organization were making increasingly numerous and important. It was precisely in those industries that employer organization for collective resistance was strongest; yet, in the face of this united opposition, the craft form of organization divided workers into small separate groups, which often bickered over fine jurisdictional issues. The Federation half-heartedly tried to organize the unskilled and semiskilled into directly affiliated "federal labor locals," but refused to accept industrial unionism as an alternative to craft lines wherever they might conflict. Its encouragement of craft amalgamations was not sufficiently forceful to reduce jurisdictional quarrels appreciably.

The penalties of this structural weakness were temporarily postponed by the war boom and the simultaneous cessation of immigration. The friendly Wilson administration passed the La Follette Seamen's Act to improve the conditions of maritime workers, two federal child labor acts, and the Adamson Act giving railwaymen the basic eight-hour day.[7] Upon our entrance into the war, Federation officials were recognized in a variety of ways as labor's spokesmen. The War Labor Board, established in 1918, gave government sanction for the first time to the right of organization and collective bargaining; it also forbade discrimination in employment because of union membership or activity, although it did not promote the closed shop as such. But in 1919 major strikes by steelworkers and coal miners were beaten, the latter with government aid. The tide had begun to turn against the AFL, which reached its peak in 1920 with over four million members. Enthusiasm for such ideas as "industrial democracy," social reconstruction, and nationalization of railroads was swept away in a wave of reaction. The Federation leadership itself became frightened of labor radicalism and the third-party movement; it set its face against both.

During the 1920's, for the first time in a period of industrial prosperity, labor organization failed to advance. From 1923 to 1931, AFL membership remained almost constant at somewhat under three million. Employer organizations revived militant antiunionism under the name of the "American Plan" open shop. The methods of "scientific personnel management" increasingly adopted by many employers often included employee representation plans or company unions. Labor injunctions were handed down by the courts in unprecedented numbers, together with a series of Supreme Court rulings invalidating labor legislation.[8] Company-operated welfare plans and employee stock-ownership programs often removed the incentive to independent unionism. Meanwhile, technological developments unfavorable to craft unionism proceeded apace. The failure of the Federation to attempt organization of the automobile industry, owing largely to intercraft jealousies and to its reluctance to approve of an industrial union, brought out the weaknesses of the AFL in sharp relief. The general decline in labor cohesion was accentuated by the Great Depression of 1929. By 1933, Federation membership was down to little over two million.

As depression deepened, unemployment widened, and wages diminished, labor leaders were forced to increase their demands for government assistance. In 1932, the AFL reversed its long-

---

[7] Although the leading organizations pressing for the Adamson Act were the four Railway Brotherhoods, the only important craft unions not affiliated with the AFL, the Federation supported them in this move. For further discussion of this and related measures, see Chapter 7.

[8] See Chapter 7.

established stand against unemployment insurance. It also advocated "spreading the work" through the thirty-hour week and a modicum of "economic planning."

The New Deal and the Emergence of the CIO

The New Deal gave a strong impetus, including governmental blessing, to labor organization. Between the summer of 1933 and the winter of 1934–1935, membership in AFL unions increased by more than a million workers. During the next year, however, the pace of growth slackened as employer resistance mounted. Organization in the mass-production industries was seriously hampered by the reluctance of powerful craft unions to surrender jurisdictional claims and permit organization on an industrial basis. Advocates of industrial unionism within the AFL made a determined effort to overcome this reluctance, but met defeat at the 1935 convention. In November, 1935, they organized a new Committee for Industrial Organization (CIO) with John L. Lewis, president of the United Mine Workers, as chairman. Under the auspices of this group a vigorous organizing drive was launched. Striking gains were made in steel, automobile, rubber, radio, electric manufacturing, and other hitherto unorganized fields. By September, 1937, the CIO claimed a membership of over 3½ million. Meanwhile, however, the controversy between the AFL and the CIO unions rapidly came to a head. In 1936 the CIO unions were suspended from the AFL, and in 1938 all of them, with the exception of the International Ladies' Garment Workers' Union, were formally expelled. Later that year, the CIO changed its name to the Congress of Industrial Organizations and established itself on an independent basis.

Among the effects of this split was an accentuation of the contrast between the political tactics and goals of the AFL and CIO, a contrast which persisted in some measure until their reconcilation and merger seventeen years later. From its earliest days, the CIO had taken a far broader interest in public policy and played a more direct role in political campaigns than had the AFL. Since organization of the mass-production industries had required the benevolent assistance of government, the CIO was virtually the child of the New Deal. It consistently supported Democratic presidential candidates (even in 1940, when John L. Lewis declared against Roosevelt) and often took an active part in state or local campaigns. Furthermore, believing that workers have as much at stake in general policies as in direct economic action, the CIO was concerned with all major economic activities of government, from European recovery to the level of the interest rate. Its goals, however, became more conservative over the years. When CIO leaders such as Sidney Hillman and Walter Reuther, who had earlier evidenced socialist skepticism about both the economic order and the two-party system, chose to work within the Democratic Party and to assume a Gomperian acceptance of private enterprise, reconciliation with the AFL became feasible.

The AFL, on the other hand, less in debt to the New Deal, less leavened with intellectuals, and accustomed to bread-and-butter business unionism, was slower to develop deep or broad interests in politics. For many years its principal political concern was only for government to establish labor's right to exercise whatever economic power it could gather. "Over a long period," Key observes, "the policies of the AFL regarding the role of government were astonishingly similar to those of business. Labor insisted as vociferously as business that the true doctrine was that of *laissez-faire:* let the state leave labor alone; it would care for itself through organization, collective bargaining and the strike. Government intervention through social legislation was frowned upon since it might deprive labor of its freedom to employ the economic weapons at its command." [9] Until 1932, as we have seen, the AFL opposed unemployment insurance, and in 1938 it supported the Wage and Hour Act only with great reluctance.

Gradually, however, and partly because of pressure from political leaders and from the CIO, the Federation shifted its political philosophy. In 1939, AFL President William Green stated that "we now seek benefit for the workers and all our fellow men by the use of either direct economic strength or legislation as the situation demands. Neither alone can suffice." [10] And in reaction against the Taft-Hartley Act of 1947, which among other things had attempted to regulate labor's political activities, the AFL organized a permanent agency, Labor's League for Political Education, for continuing political activity. In 1952, the AFL for the first time endorsed a presidential candidate by convention action. With the merger of the AFL and CIO into the AFL-CIO in 1955, a Committee on Political Education was created as the political arm of the united labor movement.

Labor Organization Today

Yet the broad political interest of the newly united labor movement is not easily translated into political effectiveness. The unity of the AFL-CIO is easily strained. It is true that the old craft-

[9] *Op. cit.*, p. 10.
[10] *Labor and Democracy*, p. 67.

industrial union cleavage is much less of a divisive force. During the forties and early fifties, the AFL expanded much more rapidly than the CIO, and came to include a number of industrial unions, so that at the time of the merger thirty-five former AFL unions affiliated 2,629,000 of their members with the former CIO unions in a new combined Industrial Union Department. Nonetheless, jurisdictional conflicts and allegations of "raiding" still plague the new body. The merger took place only after the CIO had purged itself of Communist-controlled unions, the AFL had begun to take action against racketeering, both organizations had new presidents, and imperious John L. Lewis had marched his United Mine Workers out of the CIO, into the AFL, and out again into splendid isolation. Yet the unsuccessful effort during 1957 of the AFL-CIO high command to discipline and to purge the leadership of the powerful Teamsters Union is but one example of the obvious conflicts of interest, philosophy, and personality which still remain. Furthermore, the main business of the new federation is not political; there are many prior claims on its staff and resources.

One major limitation on the political power of labor is the fact that its leaders can seldom deliver the labor vote. While unions may finance campaigns, union staffs may ring doorbells, and union activities undoubtedly create more political homogeneity than exists among nonunion workers and provide some accretion to Democratic strength, nevertheless labor leaders are not in a position to dictate how their rank-and-file membership will vote.

Most unions reflect in their internal operations the "iron law of oligarchy," for, as in most other associations, an organized group of insiders tends to take over effective control of each union. Their leaders are often no more immediately subject to the control of their members than are corporate managers controlled by stockholders, and many union elections resemble in their unreality stockholder elections of directors. Yet there are limits on the ability of union leaders to control the political actions of members, who are often more influenced by their membership in other groups or publics,[11] who are usually supremely un-class-

[11] In 1952, a poll of members of the United Auto Workers, a politically active union, showed that "labor problems" were regarded as among the most important campaign issues by only 13 per cent. Another 23 per cent listed "unemployment, security, and prosperity"; other issues, including Korea, communism, and corruption, were picked by 101 per cent (percentages totaled 137, since some respondents mentioned more than one issue). A. Kornhauser et al., When Labor Votes (1956), p. 55.

conscious,[12] and who are often politically apathetic.[13] John L. Lewis's strong endorsement of Willkie in 1940 had little effect on how the CIO members voted—although it cost Lewis one of his own presidencies, that of the CIO. Even the loyal and disciplined United Mine Workers, who militantly carry out Lewis's orders to strike or to return to work, failed to heed his political command.[14] While the CIO's 1948 campaign against those representatives who had voted for the Taft-Hartley Act was apparently fairly successful,[15] labor's well-publicized campaign against Senator Taft in 1950 boomeranged embarrassingly when Taft won by the greatest plurality ever given an Ohio Senator.

Thus labor's political strength contrasts with that of business. Numerically a small minority, business exercises a major political influence because of its economic resources, its consciousness of common interest, and its ability to capitalize on its economic power, its prestige, and on general acceptance of its economic leadership, especially when its objectives are made to appear harmonious with general middle-class goals and philosophy. Labor, on the other hand, has never exercised the dominance which its numbers might seem to confer upon it. Workers and their families constitute an overwhelming majority of the electorate, and union members and their families comprise one-third of all voters. Yet, as we have seen, union leaders have never been able to harness this political potential. Unions do now participate more actively in politics—with some success—and do promote broad objectives as well as bread-and-butter union issues, but they still operate within the two-party system and compete with other groups and associations to influence their members. For the most part, union members do not regard themselves solely, or even primarily, as union members, but rather as Democrats, Republicans, Catholics, Southerners, Italian-Americans, veterans,

[12] In 1939, when less than one-half of the nation's families had incomes of more than $1,200, seven-eighths of all Americans regarded themselves as members of the middle class. Joel Seidman, "Organized Labor in Political Campaigns," *Public Opinion Quarterly* (October, 1939), p. 647.

[13] In the 1952 poll of United Auto Workers members, 44 per cent were classified as having little political interest. Kornhauser, *op. cit.*, p. 136.

[14] I. Bernstein, "John L. Lewis and the Voting Behavior of the CIO," *Public Opinion Quarterly* (April, 1941), pp. 233–249.

[15] The CIO endorsed 215 candidates, of whom 144 were elected. Of these successful candidates, 74 replaced members of the previous Congress who had voted for the Taft-Hartley Act. In twenty-six of these latter elections, the CIO-endorsed candidates won seats which had been held by another party for the three preceding terms. F. Mosteller *et al.*, *The Pre-Election Polls of 1948* (1949), pp. 227–237.

parents, property-owners, etc. Labor leaders must "sell" their political programs to their followers, and the product sells best when it is compatible with middle-class ideology. The abysmal failure of a 1948 attempt of the Wallace Progressive Party to appeal to the "labor vote" was yet another illustration of how firmly wedded labor is to middle-class politics. Business must adjust to public opinion; labor leaders often find that their members do not differentiate themselves from the general public. As Key concludes, "the socio-political order, by the absorption of talents and the diffusion of benefits has recruited new adherents. A potentially disruptive force has been converted into an essentially conservative or at least antirevolutionary interest." [16]

3. The Politics of Agriculture

Farmers, like businessmen and workers, seek to promote their interests through organization. The business community finds cohesion in financial and corporate interrelationships. The factory provides a natural nucleus around which labor can coalesce. But the task of bringing farmers together presents special difficulties —obstacles of isolation, distance, and inbred individualism which are not easily overcome. (Governmental agencies serving farmers often perform the task of bringing farmers together into significant groupings, which means that the administration of agricultural programs usually is deeply immersed in politics.) Diversities of interests among farmers have accentuated these difficulties. Dairy farmers, grain growers, sheep and cattle raisers, cotton growers, and fruit farmers each have more or less distinct interests which induce commodity consciousness rather than a broader agrarian consciousness. Indeed, the interests of one agricultural group may directly clash with those of another group. Dairy farmers, for example, who must buy feed for their herds, will have their costs raised by price-support measures designed to benefit corn growers. And farm owners do not necessarily share the outlook of farm tenants, farm laborers, or migratory workers.

Despite these differences and difficulties, and despite the dwindling importance of the rural element in the total population, the political strength of agriculture in recent years has been formidable. From the Civil War down to the 1920's, while farmers were frequently rebellious, their revolts were poorly organized and short lived. Bestirring themselves politically only at

[16] *Op. cit.*, p. 85.

times of agricultural distress or over acute economic grievances, farmers would quickly return to a state of disorganization and quiescence. More recently, the increasing commercialization of agriculture, better communication among farmers, and their success in winning government aid and in producing a political economy in which levels of agricultural income are at least in part determined politically, and in which governmental agencies can disburse great benefits, have changed their political role. "These changes have converted agriculture from an amorphous sector of the population . . . into a hard-boiled, crystallized pressure bloc constantly alert to its interests. . . . Instead of a slumbering giant roused only by depression and adversity, farmers have become a well-organized and competently led group, with interest in public policy as keen and continuous as that of any business or labor group." [17]

The ability of farmers to gain political redress of their economic grievances has been greatly enhanced both by the myth of agricultural fundamentalism and by political overrepresentation of agriculture. A nation once predominantly rural and still drawing much of its population from rural areas is bound to be deeply influenced by rural mores and prone to believe "that the essential nature of the American society at its best derives from the rural community of free, independent, landowning, God-fearing farmers." [18] It was to be expected that Thomas Jefferson should assert that farmers are "the chosen people of God, if ever He had a chosen people"; it is a tribute to the continuity of culture and myth that the hardly rustic Bernard Baruch would believe that "cities derive their vitality and are forever renewed from the country . . . to embitter and impoverish the farmer is to dry up and contaminate the vital sources of a nation. . . . Agriculture is the greatest and fundamentally the most important of our American industries, the cities are but the branches of the tree of national life, the roots of which go deeply into the land. We all flourish or decline with the farmer." [19]

This belief in the fundamental position of agriculture is made even more politically potent by the fact that agriculture is overrepresented in Congress. Half the senators come from states in which agriculture is the largest single interest. Rural areas are also overrepresented in the House and in state legislatures. Fur-

[17] *Ibid.*, p. 36.
[18] J. M. Gaus and L. O. Wolcott, *Public Administration and the United States Department of Agriculture* (1940), pp. 17–18.
[19] Quoted by J. S. Davis, *Our Agricultural Policy, 1926–1938* (1939), p. 25.

thermore, since rural districts and states tend to be more dominated by one party than do urban and metropolitan areas, the operations of the seniority system in Congress yield even greater power to farm-bloc congressmen.

In addition, despite recurring agrarian resentment of business, agriculture has frequently benefited from powerful business support. Sometimes in order to still rural criticism of business, sometimes in competing with labor for farm support, business has sought to organize farmers and to promote agricultural goals. Chambers of commerce and other business groups aided substantially in the formation of farm bureaus. When splits occur in the business community, businessmen may seek to recruit agricultural support. Hence the alliance of businessmen and farmers against railroad abuses and monopolies. And firms selling to farmers, ranging from International Harvester and Sears, Roebuck to small-town merchants, have often supported efforts of farmers to invoke the aid of government.

The political posture and power of agriculture have varied greatly throughout our history. Until the post-Civil War era of rapid industrial expansion, the rural population in the United States was a clear majority. The parties of Jefferson and Jackson made their primary appeal to farmers and planters. But the cleavages introduced by the slavery issue and the Civil War accelerated changes already foreshadowed by the gathering force of the New Industrialism. The Republican Party, profiting from the temporary disfranchisement of the South, sought to consolidate the rapidly expanding industrial strength of the East and the agrarian elements of the West in a new political combination. The bid for agrarian support was largely based on the promise of free land contained in the Homestead Act of 1862 and on liberal internal improvements. The appeal to industry centered on a rising protective tariff, although "sound money" policies, banking legislation, railroad land grants, and new opportunities for railroad construction also played major roles.

Agricultural Discontent and Third-Party Movements

As the years passed, it became evident that the Republican Party offered more to industrialists than it did to farmers. Agrarian dissatisfaction began with the decline of agricultural prices in the 1870's, but credit stringency, high railroad rates, alleged gouging by middlemen, and general friction between the agrarian economy and the commercial and industrial world on which it was increasingly dependent played supporting roles.

The first major revolt was the Granger movement. The National Grange of the Patrons of Husbandry started in 1867 as a secret fraternal order, stressing social and educational objectives. During the depression of 1873, it turned to politics, calling for regulation of warehouses and railroads, control of monoplies, creation of a Department of Agriculture, and broader government services for agriculture. In a short time, it built up a membership of a million, captured control of several Midwestern state governments, and passed laws regulating railroads and warehouses. But the triumph was short lived. With the temporary improvement of farm prices and the failure of a number of ambitious co-operative enterprises launched by the Granger movement, its membership and political strength declined, and much of its legislation was repealed. The more radical residue of the Granger movement then found an outlet in the Greenback Party (1876–1884), which called for currency inflation as a cure for agricultural ills.

With the return of agricultural distress in the late 1880's, two separate Farmers' Alliances appeared, one in the North and the other in the South. In 1890 three senators and fifty members of the House of Representatives were elected who were pledged to support the antimonopoly, currency reform, and railroad regulation program of the Alliances. These electoral successes stimulated agitation for organization of a third party on national lines, and in 1892 the Populist Party was born. But again, as with the earlier Granger movement, decay soon set in. Though the Populists polled twenty-two electoral votes and over a million popular votes in 1892, they were then absorbed into the Bryan-led Democracy and went down to defeat in the Free Silver battle of 1896. With returning agricultural prosperity, the Populists dwindled into insignificance.

Since the Populist experiment, no effort has been made to build a national third party on a primarily agricultural base. The Progressive candidacies of Theodore Roosevelt in 1912 and La Follette in 1924 were designed to appeal to farmers, but only as part of a larger combination of interests. Sporadic, and temporarily successful, efforts have been made to build independent farmers' movements in some of the rural states. Perhaps the most notable of these experiments was the Nonpartisan League, organized in 1915, which developed its most effective strength in North Dakota. There it entered the Republican primary, captured control of the party and the state government, and enacted a program providing for state-owned grain warehouses, elevators, and flour mills, a state bank, hail insurance, regulation of railroad freight rates, and a graduated income tax. Internal dissension then set in, and the League declined in influence. Efforts of the Nonpartisan League to invade Republican and Democratic primaries in other states were less successful. In Minnesota the League joined with city workers in establishing an independent Farmer-Labor Party, which for a while played an important role in the politics of the state.

The Farm Bloc

The collapse of the agricultural war boom in 1920, and the prolonged farm depression which ensued, inaugurated a new phase in agrarian politics. This time no effort was made to build a new party; instead, farm strategy was concentrated on electing to Congress sympathetic members of both major parties, welding them into a disciplined farm bloc, and utilizing its balance-of-power position to advance agrarian interests. The American Farm Bureau Federation, established in 1919, provided much of the driving force behind the organization of this bloc. In May, 1921, twelve senators met in the office of the Federation and agreed to work together to relieve agricultural distress. They were subsequently joined by others, and a somewhat less effective agrarian steering committee was established in the House.

The farm bloc showed surprising vigor and political efficiency. Sectional rivalries between South and West sometimes hampered common action but were at least partially reconciled during the twenties. The Packers and Stockyards Act of 1921, the Grain Futures Act of 1922, the Agricultural Credit Act of 1923, and the Co-operative Marketing Act of 1926 may all be credited to the bloc. But more ambitious measures of farm relief encountered difficulty. The McNary-Haugen Bill was twice vetoed by President Coolidge, and the farm bloc was unable to get the vetoes overridden.

The drastic intensification of farm depression after 1929 forced farmers toward greater unity and militancy. At a time when local groups of desperate farmers were taking the law into their own hands, the Farm Bureau Federation in 1932 called a conference of leading farm organizations to agree on a legislative program. President Roosevelt promised in his acceptance speech "to be guided by whatever the responsible farm groups themselves agree on," and farmers in great numbers flocked to his support.

With the New Deal, farm organizations came into their own.

Agricultural politics had completed the shift from apathy, punctuated by sporadic rebellions, to continuous pressure-group activity to influence the definition and execution of policy. Thereafter, farm groups participated energetically in the formulation of legislation affecting agriculture. The Agricultural Adjustment Act of 1933, for example, was drafted in intimate consultation with farm leaders. They became powerful enough to persuade Congress to aid agriculture on a massive scale. Even in the days immediately after Pearl Harbor, farm groups were so strong as virtually to free agricultural commodities from the price controls imposed on other goods by the Emergency Price Control Act of 1942. Furthermore, the sweeping aids and services extended farmers by New Deal, World War II, and Fair Deal legislation further spurred the organization of farm interests. "Nowadays, the chief function of these [farm] organizations is to deal with government agencies which were created by their earlier hell-raising." [20] Just as the American Farm Bureau Federation lives in common-law wedlock with the Extension Service, so later agricultural administrative agencies tended to strengthen other private organizations of farmers. Thus the Farm Security Administration assisted the National Farmers' Union, the Soil Conservation Service created the National Association of Soil Conservation Districts, and the Rural Electrification Administration fostered the National Rural Electric Co-operative Association.

Farm Organizations Today

Three major organizations undertake to represent the general interests of American farmers: the National Grange, the National Farmers' Union, and the American Farm Bureau Federation. The Grange, the oldest and the least aggressive of the trio, traces its origins back to the Granger movement. It claimed 860,000 members in 1955, largely concentrated in the Northeast—New England, New York, Pennsylvania, New Jersey, and Ohio—and in the Pacific Northwest. Its membership includes some non-farmers, residents of small towns attracted by its social activities. Its farmer membership consists mostly of fruit and vegetable growers, dairy and poultry men. On the whole, it has reflected the rural conservatism of the Northeast and the interests of farmers advantageously close to large urban markets. Consequently, during the New Deal it was the most conservative of the trio, supporting the general objective of "equality" for agri-

[20] W. McCune, *Who's Behind Our Farm Policy?* (1956), p. 5.

culture, but critical of production control and for some time opposed to the trade-agreement program. In recent years, however, as the Farm Bureau has more intensively cultivated the interests of the large, commercial farmer, the Grange, deeply committed to the family farm, has shifted to a middle position. In 1956, for example, it urged President Eisenhower not to veto a bill fixing high support prices for farm products.

The mildly radical views of the Farmers' Union, partly a survival from old-fashioned, agrarian populism,[21] sharply contrast with those of the Grange and the Farm Bureau. Claiming a membership of half a million families, its center of gravity now lies in the Great Plains wheat states, and it speaks primarily for wheatgrowers. To a much lesser extent it represents corn, hogs, and cotton. It accepted New Deal programs but deemed them inadequate and demanded guarantees of "costs of production." It vigorously promotes the family farm—"farm families on family farms are a balancing force in the social and political structure that is vital to . . . representative democratic government"— and it lobbies vigorously, its president declaring that the "key to the future of family farming lies in Washington." [22] In recent years it has differed most from the other organizations by leading the battle for high price supports and by endorsing proposals to limit the amount of support any one farm might receive. It alone has been friendly to organized labor.

The American Farm Bureau Federation, with over 1,600,000 members, is the largest and most powerful of the trio. Its constituent units, the county farm bureaus, were called into being originally to provide co-operating local groups to support the work of the county agents. In 1919 these local groups were united into the present national organization. The bulk of its membership lies in the corn-hog-wheat Midwest and the cotton South. It took a leading role in the passage of the Agricultural Adjustment Act of 1933, and for some time it continued to provide the most important reservoir of support for New Deal agrarian controls, pledging itself "to give farmers a national voice that all groups can unite in." But, as agricultural income in the late thirties began a major revival which continued into the postwar

[21] The Union was founded in 1902 by a former organizer of the Southern Farmers' Alliance, and an early statement of its goals echoes the spirit of the nineteenth-century agrarian radicals: "To garner the tears of the distressed, the blood of the martyrs, the laugh of innocent childhood, the sweat of honest labor and the virtue of a happy home as the brightest jewels known." C. S. Barrett, *The Mission, History and Times of the Farmers' Union* (1909), p. 12.
[22] McCune, *op. cit.*, pp. 47–48.

period, and as technological changes enabled the larger farmers profitably to use more capital, the Farm Bureau came increasingly to represent the interests of the more commercialized
farms. It became skeptical of or hostile to programs benefiting
smaller, marginal farmers and farm labor. Southern bureaus
feared that government aid to the Negro sharecropper might
endanger white supremacy. During the war the Federation persuaded Congress to emasculate the Farm Security Administration, which had been serving sharecroppers, farm laborers, tenant
farmers, and marginal farmers. Since the war it has opposed
high support prices and has tended to oppose any administrative
agency which might compete with the Extension Service. It is
usually hostile to organized labor, and now generally pursues
conservative economic policies. For the most part, these views
reflect fairly accurately the innate conservatism of the commercial
farmer, when prosperous. At times, however, Farm Bureau leaders have underestimated the extent to which economic adversity
has changed the views of their constituency and, in the postwar
period, they have been faced with occasional revolts against their
advocacy of flexible support prices.[23]

In addition to these general groups, there is a host of organizations which represent particular commodities or forms of marketing organization. Among these are the National Co-operative
Milk Producers' Association, the National Livestock Producers'
Association, the National Council of Farmer Co-operatives, and
many others. Each commodity has its organizational voice, and
the orchestration of agricultural politics gives most of them full
expression.

The strength of the farmer today is only that of a minority.
In a nation once predominantly agrarian, now less than one-
sixth of the population lives on farms. Yet, paradoxically enough,
in part because of this decline, and because favorable legislation
and administration are often the *sine qua non* of economic survival and welfare, in some senses agriculture is politically stronger
than before. Its role in the political side of our political economy
has changed from that of a majority, sometimes slumbering, sometimes in revolt, but always disorganized and usually inarticulate,
to that of a highly active, crystallized minority, aware of its

[23] It has been claimed that, at other times, Federation leaders have allowed
themselves and their organization to be manipulated by business interests and
have spoken for business, not farm, interests. See G. McConnell, *Decline of
Agrarian Democracy* (1953). For a more extreme and overdrawn, indictment,
see McCune. *op. cit.*

strength, and an effective, experienced bargainer in advancing its welfare.

4. The Problem of Pressure Politics

The organization of economic interests to influence public policy has increased in scope and intensity with the expansion of governmental authority in the economic realm. Pressure politics has become an inextricable part of the American system of representation; the result has been to create what Walter Lippmann has called "a polity of pressure groups."

Many have expressed concern lest the tendency of organized groups to put primary emphasis on their own economic interests lead to a dispersive type of group utilitarianism which completely loses sight of the general welfare and transforms the political arena into a "battle royal of interests." That this danger is real need not be denied. Its very existence emphasizes the need of synthesis and adjustment through the machinery of the democratic process. The ideological environment and political machinery within which this synthesis and adjustment may occur is the subject of the next chapter.

CHAPTER 3

Ideology, Governmental Machinery, and Politics

1. The Ideological Environment

G OVERNMENT'S role in the economy is conditioned by the general ideological environment and by the constitutional framework within which the political processes of policy-making operate. While constitutional restraints have often resulted from interpretations reflecting general ideological positions, policy alternatives have been more limited by the governmental machinery than by ideology. This relative absence of ideological restraints on policy has largely been due to the highly pragmatic tone of American social thought and to the remarkably wide area of common agreement within which the political economy has functioned. Obviously, change there has been. Shifting circumstances have altered men's thoughts, and men's changed ideas have transformed their institutions and their behavior. But these changes have largely been redefinitions of older concepts rather than the substitution of radically different values or beliefs.

Consequently, with the exception of the Civil War, policy clashes have seldom raised questions about the fundamental economic and political order. Both the opportunities offered by an expanding, dynamic economy and the possibility of alleviating economic grievances through political action have prevented any large, articulate group from becoming permanently alienated. Despite the bitter intensity of many disputes, reconciliation and adjustment ultimately occur because the range of alternatives open to the contestants has been contained within a common framework. The battles within our political economy have raged between those with important interests at stake—between agriculture and commerce, between management and a nonrevolutionary labor movement, between large and small business, between old and new industries, between importers and exporters. Property rights as such, however, have seldom been directly challenged.

As Louis Hartz has pointed out, the effects of never having experienced feudalism and, hence, of escaping socialism have contributed to substantial consensus.[1] The existence of atomistic social freedom at the nation's outset transformed property from a barrier to equality or to opportunity into a part of the individual's natural rights. The lack of a rigid class structure made the community into a middle-class society, sharing a respect for property and for law. The comparative absence of classes or estates ("We are all of the same estate—all commoners."[2]) opened wide the door to social mobility and to individual economic enterprise. While American economic life escaped the narrow restrictions of feudalism and has always been characterized by relatively free entrepreneurial activity, it has never, in practice, incorporated the extreme tenets of laissez faire. Rather, the basic attitude toward economic policy was a pragmatic one, easily accommodating itself before the Civil War to a host of public controls and enterprises at the state and local level.[3]

It is true that laissez faire, often stated in highly doctrinaire terms, was the professed faith of many businessmen and their allies in the late nineteenth and early twentieth centuries. But this apparent adherence to laissez faire needs to be read against the fact that its primary standard-bearers, the business interests, had in the first half of the nineteenth century relied on Hamiltonian promotionalism and had supported many public investments. Even in the last half of the century they had demanded and defended land grants, tariffs, subsidies, favorable laws concerning patents, bankruptcy, and incorporation, and other aids

---

[1] *The Liberal Tradition in America* (1955).
[2] General Root, in the debates of the New York Constitutional Convention, quoted in B. F. Wright, *Source Book of American Political Theory* (1929), p. 373.
[3] See footnote 1, Chapter 1.

to business. Pragmatic defense of its own interests rather than doctrinal concern was the prime mover of business statesmanship.

This same pragmatism has continued to characterize American attitudes toward the economy. Even during the New Deal, when the sphere of government was expanded to a major degree, no new philosophy was produced to justify the programs. Pragmatism enabled the New Deal to experiment with new controls and with public enterprise without raising profound ideological issues. It later enabled the Republicans to accept these experiments without affirming any fundamental changes in philosophy.

Side by side with this pragmatism, with its stress on practicality, is a persistent middle-class moral idealism, emphasizing equality of rights and freedom from unfair coercive restraints. Some of the most important public policies affecting the economy have come about because a small group of reformers was finally able to arouse the moral indignation of the middle class against such abuses. For example, it was middle-class reformers, not unions, who initiated and provided most of the impetus for state wage-and-hour and child-labor laws.

Thus the ideological environment exercises its influence on the political economy. Underlying agreement combines with social mobility to minimize class conflict. Most policies are fought out within a framework of middle-class values.

There is a presumption in favor of private enterprise, and, normally, economic leadership by businessmen is accepted. If, however, private enterprise fails the pragmatic test of *results*, then there is no insuperable ideological barrier to regulation or to public enterprise. If substantial groups feel an economic grievance, or if the public feels it is not adequately served, then no cries of "Socialism" will deter the appeal for governmental redress. Similarly, if private enterprise offends middle-class morality—by abuse of power, by financial exploitation, or by coercion —then governmental intervention is readily demanded.

American ideology, then, has been given new application as material conditions have changed and as new moral questions have been raised. It has concerned itself with the changing positions of the major classes or groups in society and with the great shift from an economic life primarily agrarian and individualistic to one heavily industrial or commercial and increasingly organized and interdependent. Traditional ideological presuppositions have tended to erode under the impact of economic change. The

antitrust field furnishes a vivid example. In this area, an individualistic ethic and philosophy first reacted to the industrial forces
of concentration and organization by seeking to eradicate them
as inherently evil. Slowly, as the material benefits and inevitability of consolidation became obvious, the problem was recast
as one of accepting large-scale organization but of checking its
abuses and restraining its power. Ideology has occasionally lagged
in its adjustment to changing material conditions, but, viewed
from a broad historical and cultural perspective, adjustments have
not been long delayed.

2. Governmental Machinery and Economic Policy

Together with the ideological environment of a nation, its
constitutional machinery is of basic importance in determining
the role of government in the economic order. Law is always
the prime instrument of public policy, the medium through
which government makes its impact upon individual and social
life. The mode of legislation, administration, and adjudication
shapes the forms of law and in so doing modifies its substance.
Through the institutions of a written constitution and judicial
review, and because of the preponderance of lawyers in American politics, American governmental activities are colored with
a heavy tint of legalism.

Before the Civil War, government influence on economic
life, especially at the national level, made itself felt largely through
judicial determination of private rights and duties. Common law
and rules of equity were the touchstone of decision more often
than statutes. Through this machinery, supplemented but mea-
gerly by positive administrative action, government provided the
formal context for the old economy. Orderly enforcement of
private contracts was the system's keystone, and, for the most
part, reliance was placed on individual self-interest as the surest
guarantee of common welfare. Where social action was essential
to the release of individual energies, it was provided. Establishment of currency, bankruptcy laws, and the granting of limited
patent and copyright monopolies all helped to provide an institutional framework for economic development.

With the growth of those public economic activities—promotional, regulatory, planning, and operating—which form the
topic of this study, the machinery of government was radically
transformed. Courts were no longer the chief instruments of
policy. Its typical expression was in statute rather than common

law, and it required a huge, complex administrative apparatus. Both the shift of balance between state and federal units and the internal transformations of the federal system occurred wholly within the framework of the Constitution, with its 1787 phraseology but slightly altered by a handful of amendments. The adaptation was achieved in part by informal adjustment through extralegal party organization, in part by expansion of the executive establishment, and in part by judicial reinterpretation. The process on occasion progressed smoothly and rapidly, at other times haltingly and incompletely. At all times it left its characteristic mark on the developing forms and substance of governmental economic activities.

The American Constitution struck a balance between federal and state powers, a balance in part reflecting the interplay between the doctrines of economic liberalism and of mercantilism. While its authors sought above all to give the central government those elements of authoritative strength which experience under the Articles of Confederation had proved essential, in pursuing this objective they were limited by the need to win the consent of the states. The closeness of the ratification battle and the imposition of the first ten amendments as a condition of acceptance indicate that the document as written marked the utmost possible limit of federal centralization at the time. Together with this primary purpose there was the desire to prevent the states from disturbing the economic conditions which, to the fathers, appeared essential to healthy individual enterprise. Central power over currency and prohibitions against state legal-tender laws, against impairment of contracts, and against barriers to interstate trade marked the achievement of this objective. It was implemented by the review of state legislation in the federal courts.

Within the central government, although strength was desired vis-à-vis the states, ingenious efforts were made to provide mechanical checks to the "tyranny of faction" or the "tyranny" of any branch of government or of a popular majority. The intricate apparatus of the separation of powers and the system of checks and balances were consciously intended to make strong government difficult and were defended as protecting both property rights and individual rights. The concept that public action might, by restraining nongovernmental coercions, contribute positively to individual liberty had yet to make its appearance.

Under these circumstances the process of readjustment to meet altered conditions and responsibilities was centered in two areas. The division of power between the states and the Union was shifted to match underlying developments in the economic structure. At the same time, the operating mechanisms of the central government, transformed by group and party, were revised to meet the new responsibilities imposed upon it.

The States and the Union

The formal legal distribution of powers between the states and the Union remains largely what it was in 1789, but the real allocation of powers and functions reflects the change from a loose association of poorly connected settlements and farms scattered along the Eastern seaboard, with a population of but 3½ million, to a well-knit nation-state of more than 175 million, spanning the continent from the Atlantic to the Pacific. In the late eighteenth century, sailing vessels provided the most rapid means of transportation between Eastern cities. The land journey from Boston to New York, over the best road in the country, took a week; that from Philadelphia to Pittsburgh, twenty days. Political attitudes reflected this local isolation:

> Community consciousness showed itself only in the more thickly peopled districts, and even there it was feeble. Generally speaking . . . the idea of a National Government had not penetrated the minds of the people. They managed to tolerate State Governments, because they always had lived under some such thing; but a National Government was too far away and fearsome, too alien and forbidding for them to view it with friendliness or understanding. The common man saw little difference between such an enthroned central power and the Royal British Government which had been driven from American shores.[4]

Rapid and inexpensive transportation, first provided by the railroad and later supplemented by the automobile, the truck, and the airplane, together with almost instantaneous communication, was the basic factor transforming our economy from a congeries of local systems into a single national whole. The entire nation, or regions comprising large blocs of states, became the effective areas of economic and social activity. This change not only produced an enormous expansion in governmental functions; it also altered profoundly the pattern of federalism, shifting power toward the center. For political authority, to be effective, must in the long run be organized over areas as broad as the problems with which it deals.

[4] A. J. Beveridge, *The Life of John Marshall* (1916), Vol. 1, p. 285.

Noticeable even before the Civil War, the growth of federal authority reached a rapid rate of expansion late in the nineteenth century. It took two forms: direct extension of federal power, and employment of the states as instruments of federal policy. Federal intervention in new fields usually occurred only after corresponding state efforts proved inadequate. The state Granger laws of the 1870's failed to regulate railroads effectively; they were supplemented by the Interstate Commerce Act of 1887. State antitrust laws likewise fell short of their objectives; federal legislation began in 1890. Protection against adulterated food and drugs, provided in part by the states throughout the nineteenth century, was assumed as a federal responsibility in 1906. After World War I, increasing interstate transmission of electricity and natural gas, together with the organization of public utility holding companies on a superstate scale, engendered federal participation in these spheres. Only in rare instances, such as the control of radio and television communications, bituminous coal, and atomic energy, has the federal government initiated regulation without prior action by the states.

The supplanting of state by federal action in the most important fields of regulation was not the product of any widespread desire for federal centralization as such. It was adopted by senators and congressmen who were loath, on principle, to diminish the relative influence of the states. Sometimes it followed a Supreme Court decision denying the states constitutional authority over particular objects of regulation. More often, however, federal intervention resulted from the inability of states to deal adequately with activities which extended beyond their boundaries. When markets expand beyond state boundaries, no state can afford to treat its enterprises much more harshly than do its neighbors. To do so presents to its entrepreneurs the alternative of bankruptcy or transfer of their businesses to states exacting less stringent conditions. Interstate competition is a potent pressure toward lower standards. Only a uniform rule can resolve this dilemma. In a few cases such rules have been provided through interstate compacts. But, in the main, federal centralization has appeared to be the only feasible solution.

Extension of federal policy through state instrumentalities has been accomplished chiefly through grants-in-aid. Federal funds, and, in the past, federal lands, have been given to the states for particular purposes under specified conditions of state co-operation. Agricultural and vocational education and road building are the classic examples.

The Social Security Act of 1935 marked a further milestone in the evolution of co-operative federalism. It followed the older model of grants-in-aid for benefits to the aged, the disabled, and the blind, but employed a new technique for unemployment insurance.[5] State-administered and state-financed systems, subject to minimum federal standards, but with a wide degree of local discretion, are virtually required by federal law through the imposition of a substantial tax upon employers in states failing to comply with the Act. Portions of the New Deal agricultural program were also based on this type of federal-state relationship. In addition, during the New Deal, federal funds were given to states and municipalities to enable them to maintain relief programs. First through public works programs and now for slum clearance, housing, and other special purposes, federal funds have been granted to cities and other local units, theoretically creations of the states but frequently having closer ties, or reaching more sympathetic ears, in Washington.

While state functions are drawn increasingly into the federal vortex because so many economic problems extend beyond state boundaries, the appropriate area of jurisdiction is often neither the state nor the nation. The natural geographical influences which promote community of economic interest tend to produce a typically regional pattern. The suitability of particular areas varies for different purposes; over 140 different subdivisions are used today in federal administration. In addition, regional political authorities have been constituted both from the bottom up through interstate compact and from the top down through such federal agencies as the Tennessee Valley Authority. The effort to transform recognition of regional interests and consciousness into responsible regional administration marks a significant phase of the new federal relationship.

The Separation of Powers

Adjustments to evolving needs of public policy within the machinery of central government have been equally far reaching. In a sense, as Arthur Holcombe has pointed out, "The government of the United States is a kind of dual government.

---

[5] A precedent for the tax offset device of the Social Security Act had been established in the federal inheritance tax law of 1926, which allowed taxpayers to credit state inheritance tax payments against the federal tax, up to 80 per cent of the latter. The constitutionality of this measure was unanimously sustained by the Supreme Court in *Florida* v. *Mellon*, 273 U.S. 12 (1927).

There is constitutional government . . . and there is also party government. [Our] government . . . has gradually developed into a combination of the two. . . ." [6] Changes in the governmental process have occurred in both constitutional and party government. The adjustments include the reallocation of functions among the legislative, executive, and judicial powers and the partial bridging over of the separation of powers through party and group.

Adjustments of the governmental machinery center on a major transfer of the policy-making function from the legislative to the executive branch. (The judiciary has sometimes played the leading role and has sometimes been off the stage, but a discussion of its role is deferred until the next chapter.) For a variety of reasons and in a number of ways, Congress has passed on to the President, to administrators, and to the courts a large share of the policy-making power. Faced with an ever increasing number of complex policy problems, Congress has lacked the time, the information, and often the leadership to spell out policy in full detail. In addition, it is generally unable to negotiate a complete agreement among the conflicting interests concerned. Accordingly, it more and more enacts legislation in general terms, leaving to administrators and judges the tasks of giving policy specific application and of striking a precise balance among the interests.

Furthermore, the power of the Presidency has multiplied many times since its low point in the last half of the nineteenth century, when the young Woodrow Wilson described what he saw as "Congressional government." Because of the tremendous growth of the national executive establishment, because of the increased importance of foreign policy and national defense, where he is more influential than Congress, because of his unique ability to focus public opinion, and because he represents the entire nation in a way no congressman can, the President today is Chief Legislator as well as Chief Executive. He now sets the agenda for Congress, and, insofar as he controls the sprawling governmental bureaucracy, he guides both the administrative making of policy and administrative requests to Congress for new legislation.

Congress has shared its power reluctantly and in return has exacted the right of thorough oversight of administration. The development of the independent regulatory commissions, which until World War II were the characteristic, although by no means exclusive, instrument for specialized regulation, testifies

[6] *Our More Perfect Union* (1950), pp. 7–8.

to the unwillingness of Congress to surrender its powers completely to the executive.

Originally developed for railroad regulation in a few states, the commission form was first adopted for federal regulatory purposes with the creation of the Interstate Commerce Commission in 1887. Independent of the executive, endowed with security of tenure for substantial terms, and acting under broad grants of legislative authority, commissions attempt to solve the dilemma of the separation of powers by performing all three functions. They serve as legislators in filling in the terms of general statutory standards, as administrators in actively promoting the policies entrusted to them by Congress, and as judges in applying those policies to particular cases. Congress has tended to prefer the commission to the executive agency because of fear of excessive centralization of power in the executive branch. It views the commission "as a creature of Congress, independent of the president, impartial and objective in the performance of its duties, and expert in the handling of complex, difficult matters beyond the capacity of Congress to handle effectively." [7] The device also produces in limited areas of the American administrative structure a continuity of service and policy comparable to that derived abroad from permanent tenure of high-ranking civil servants.

But the very independence which Congress may prize is attacked by those who believe that all decisions of administrative policy should be made within an all-embracing and unified system of presidential responsibility.[8] In 1937, the President's Committee on Administrative Management, in a classic argument for greater focus of administrative responsibility on the President, assailed the commissions as "a headless 'fourth branch' of the government, a haphazard deposit of irresponsible agencies and unco-ordinated powers. . . . the Congress has found no effective way of supervising them, they cannot be controlled by the President, and they are answerable to the Courts only in respect to the legality of their action." [9]

In the past, the commission form of regulation was supported

[7] M. H. Bernstein, Regulating Business by Independent Commission (1955), p. 67. Bernstein here is summarizing an address of Speaker Rayburn.
[8] To be sure, Presidents have often exercised in fact considerable influence on commission policies through their powers of appointment, budgetary control, and other means. For examples, see E. S. Redford, Administration of National Economic Control (1952), pp. 277–283.
[9] Report of the President's Committee on Administrative Management (1937), p. 36.

on several grounds. Where regulation in a particular field was undertaken as an exception to the general presumption of laissez faire, there was a desire to make the area of regulation narrow and self-contained, separate from more general economic policy. There was perhaps an exaggerated faith in experts, a hope that the regulatory process could be "judicialized" and kept free from politics. But separation from general economic policy is more difficult in an age when government underwrites a minimum standard of living and a commitment to high employment, and when it is deeply involved in the economy for reasons of national security and foreign policy. And commission experience suggests that economic regulation cannot be made wholly nonpolitical. The stakes in economic controls are too large to permit their relegation to specialists entirely outside the general policy guidance of the government; the effort to do so may lead simply to an undue responsiveness of the regulators to the interests they are supposed to regulate.[10]

In recent years, therefore, the device of the independent regulatory commission has fallen into disfavor. With the exception of the Atomic Energy Commission, which has primarily managerial, contracting, and promotional powers, no new commissions have been established since the New Deal. In 1950, the Maritime Commission was reconstituted as the Federal Maritime Board and transferred to the Department of Commerce, where it is subjected to considerable, but not full, department control.[11] Indeed, important and numerous economic policies have long been administered by executive agencies. Even in the area of direct regulation, "the Department of Agriculture is one

[10] Many observers have made this point. ". . . the control of business remains too controversial and too vital a political issue to be entirely relegated to any commission independent of close control by the policy-formulating agencies of the government. Administrators cannot be given the responsibilities of statesmen without incurring likewise the tribulations of politicians." E. P. Herring, Public Administration and the Public Interest (1936), p. 138. "'Independence' . . . facilitates a maximum responsiveness by a commission to the demands and interests of regulated groups." Bernstein, op. cit., p. 101. See also P. H. Appleby, Policy and Administration (1949), p. 149; D. B. Truman, The Governmental Process (1951), p. 420; J. W. Fesler, The Independence of State Regulatory Agencies (1942), p. 65.

[11] The remaining independent regulatory commissions are the Interstate Commerce Commission, the Civil Aeronautics Board, the Federal Power Commission, the Federal Communications Commission, the Federal Trade Commission, the National Labor Relations Board, the Securities and Exchange Commission, and the Board of Governors of the Federal Reserve System. Each will be discussed later in appropriate chapters.

of the largest regulatory agencies in the Federal Government. It administers the greatest number of regulatory acts of any federal agency—acts which vary widely in subject matter and in administrative and enforcement procedures. . . ." [12] Other important economic controls and aids are administered by the Departments of Labor, Commerce, Treasury, Interior, Justice, Post Office, and Health, Education, and Welfare.

Needless to say, departmental administration is not without its problems. Executive agencies, too, confront the danger of losing sight of broad definitions of the public interest through too close an association with, or reliance on, the particular group or interests being controlled or served. The regulatory agency may be a part of a larger clientele-service organization or department. Thus the Food and Drug Administration was moved from the Department of Agriculture to what is now the Department of Health, Education, and Welfare in part out of the fear that Agriculture was too deeply committed to the promotion of agrarian interests to permit one of its units to act vigorously against processors of agricultural products.

Identity of attitude between regulator and regulated may also arise when the agency deals constantly with a particular industry or commodity. This identity is enhanced when agency and industry personnel share the same backgrounds and may shift from industry to agency or vice versa. This problem arose in an acute form in World War II in the War Production Board, in the Office of Price Administration, and in the agencies of the "commodity czars," such as the Rubber Director, the Office of Defense Transportation, and the Petroleum Administration for War. Or the problem may simply take the form of conflict among agencies dealing with interrelated policies. Thus the agencies, both independent and executive, dealing with various forms of transportation have often operated on contradictory assumptions and have worked at cross purposes. And so have some of the subdivisions of the Agriculture Department.

These problems will probably always be with us. While most students of public administration advocate a greater degree of centralized political and administrative responsibility in order to co-ordinate overlapping programs, to mitigate policy conflicts, and to lessen the particularism of too narrowly oriented agencies, there are real limits on the possibility or desirability of

[12] Commission on Organization of the Executive Branch of the Government (Hoover Commission), *Task Force Report on Agricultural Activities* (1949), p. 52.

a substantially increased degree of central responsibility and control. Furthermore, even if the case for greater central responsibility be granted, there remain serious administrative and constitutional barriers to be overcome. The task of central co-ordination is usually assigned to the President by students of public administration, and the Constitution charges him with the duty to "take care that the laws be faithfully executed." But despite extensive reorganization and the institutionalization of the Presidency, the federal government remains an enormously complex and cumbersome machine which presents formidable obstacles to effective co-ordination.

The national budget system, established in 1921, and managed by the Bureau of the Budget, has proved to be an important aid to fiscal policy and administrative planning. The Civil Service Commission and the General Accounting Office also play helpful roles, and the creation of the Council of Economic Advisors in 1946 established a useful staff agency for central information and advice in the field of general economic policy. But the struggle of the President, his Cabinet, and his staff to direct and co-ordinate the executive establishment is a never ending task. Frequent administrative reorganizations are evidence of the struggle, not of its solution. So it is, for example, that in 1942 the Department of Agriculture could say that the "organizational history of the Department for the past twenty years shows that there has never been a year in which major changes have not been made." [13]

The constitutional barriers to greater presidential control over administration derive from congressional authority to control executive agencies. At times the assertion of this claim may produce conflict and deadlock as President and Congress issue contradictory commands to an administrator. More often, however, problems arise from congressional intervention in petty details of organization and operation and from a dispersion of control within the Congress which may give precedence to local interests and promote that narrow group orientation of administration which the broader political responsibility of the Presidency was designed to prevent.

Parties and Groups

Together with governmental machinery, evolving political forces also serve to condition the role of government in economic life. The interrelations between party and group and be-

[13] C. M. Hardin, *The Politics of Agriculture* (1952), p. 167.

tween these informal organs of government and the constitutional machinery are intricate and vary with time, place, and
circumstance. At the time of the writing of the Constitution,
Madison had anticipated that the new government would confront the problem of hammering out sound and broad policies
in an environment of politically active economic interests—what
he called "factions" and defined in these words:

. . . a number of citizens . . . who are united and actuated by some
common impulse of passion, or of interest, adverse to the rights of
other citizens, or to the permanent and aggregate interest of the
community. . . . The most common and durable source of factions
has been the various and unequal distribution of property. Those who
hold and those who are without property have ever formed distinct
interests in society. Those who are creditors, and those who are deb-
tors, fall under a like discrimination. A landed interest, a manufacturing interest, a mercantile interest, a moneyed interest, with
many lesser interests, grow up of necessity in civilized nations and
divide them into different classes, actuated by different sentiments
and views. The regulation of these various and interfering interests
forms the principal task of modern legislation, and involves the spirit
of party and faction in the necessary and ordinary operations of the
government.[14]

The size of the nation, Madison felt, would limit the power
of factions to control the new government. The larger the community, the greater would be the number of factions; and the
greater their number, the less likely it would be that any one
would control the government. Thus the new government would
have enough strength vis-à-vis factions to perform its essential
functions and yet would not be strong enough to abuse its powers.

Madison was not wrong in his belief that "liberty is to faction what air is to fire." [15] The political freedoms granted, or not
denied, by the new instrument of government did encourage
the expression of economic interests, and the very separation of
powers and other limits on the power and unity of government
invited economic groups to participate in the making of policy.
The extreme diffusion of political and governmental power exaggerated the relative power of interest groups, and the geographic
concentration of dominant interests made sectionalism the most
important dimension of national politics. Even as late as 1924,

[14] *The Federalist*, No. 10, Modern Library ed. (1937), pp. 54, 56.
[15] *Ibid.*, p. 55.

Arthur Holcombe could say that from the original business interests of the North Atlantic, the grain interests of the West, the tobacco interests of the Upper South, and the cotton and rice interests of the Lower South "may be traced the economic and social forces which have dominated national politics from the beginning to the present day." [16]

Indeed, so important are interest groups in the political process that some observers equate group activity with politics and government. "All phenomena of government," said Arthur Bentley in 1908, "are phenomena of groups pressing one another. . . . The great task in the study of any form of social life is the analysis of . . . groups. . . . When the groups are adequately stated, everything is stated. . . . Law is a group process, just as government is. It is a forming, a systematization, a struggle, an adaptation of group interests." [17] Without going as far as Bentley, contemporary political scientists argue that "the purpose of the democratic state is the free reconciliation of group interests," that "the public interest can be realized only through promoting certain special interests," and that it "cannot be given concrete expression except through the compromise of special claims. . . ." [18] Thus, "a satisfactory criterion of the public interest is a preponderant acceptance of administrative action by politically influential groups." [19] When "affected private interests are shaping the course of official action . . . Democracy [is] at work." [20]

So starkly primitive an equation of politics with group activity and of the public interest with group interests, however, is too simple as a description of political processes and too narrow as a definition of the public interest. Administrators are not necessarily the helpless pawns of powerful groups; they may be able to point policy in new directions by the character of the leadership they provide. Neither are congressmen and other political leaders inevitably the captives of aggressive, monolithic groups. The history of most legislation is far more complicated than this.

The party may play a crucial role. Clearly a majority party, vigorously led by a strong President, can put pressure groups to rout. A dynamic administration leads more than it is led, putting some interest groups out of business and conjuring up others

---

[16] *The Political Parties of Today*, p. 46.

[17] *The Process of Government*, pp. 208–209, 258–259, 272. For a comprehensive, if somewhat qualified, statement of this group theory of government, see Truman, *op. cit.*

[18] Herring, *op. cit.*, pp. 9, 209, 259.

[19] A. Leiserson, *Administrative Regulation* (1942), p. 16.

[20] W. Gellhorn, *Federal Administrative Proceedings* (1941), p. 130.

where none existed before.[21] Certainly the pressures and desires of interest groups were responsible for much of the New Deal, yet the Roosevelt administration was as much their creator as their instrument. The National Recovery Administration (NRA) doubled the number of trade associations. The New Deal virtually made the CIO and encouraged the growth of farm organizations. Even long-established groups were given new life by the Roosevelt administration. By 1933, the Farm Bureau Federation's membership had fallen to under 200,000—about one-third the size it had achieved in 1931 and would again attain before World War II under the benevolent eyes of the government. The membership of the United Mine Workers fell to 80,000, one-fifth of the total it had achieved in 1917 and would again achieve after its posters had proclaimed to the miners that "PRESIDENT ROOSEVELT WANTS YOU TO JOIN THE UNION."

Thus party and administration can free policy from the cramping confines of narrow group interests. But this is a possibility rather than a certainty. The vigor of presidential leadership may be sapped by an inability to exploit aggressively the majority sentiments to which his office gives such incomparable access, or by deadlock with a Congress controlled by the opposition party or by an opposing wing of his own party. For, while American parties can win elections, they are often unable to govern. A majority party controls the organization of Congress, but it cannot be sure of producing legislative majorities unless it can control the voting of its members. Obviously, the weaker its discipline, the greater the influence enjoyed by pressure groups. More than this, the relative dominance of party or group may mean that different issues are exploited and that different majorities are assembled around them.[22] When party and administration are dominant, they determine which are to be the major political issues, and groups play a secondary role,

[21] . . . not all differences of interest are durable causes of conflict. Nothing is apt to be more perishable than a political issue. In the democratic process, the nation moves from controversy to agreement to forgetfulness; politics is not a futile exercise like football, forever played back and forth over the same ground. The government creates and destroys interests at every turn." E. E. Schattschneider, *Party Government* (1942), p. 32.

[22] "The very fact that people must close ranks in order to engage actively in any conflict compels them to subordinate a great multitude of inconsistent antagonisms, which are then neglected, disapproved of, explained away, and forgotten . . . it is conflict itself which forces people to unite . . . unity is a function of conflicts, and . . . as a consequence the number of conflicts that can be developed in a free society at any one time is limited." E. E. Schattschneider, "Political Parties and the Public Interest," *Annals* (March, 1952), p. 19.

seeking to extract such special benefits as may be open to them. Thus, in connection with the Marshall Plan, shipping companies might seek to protect their special interests, but the initiative in producing the plan lay elsewhere. When party and administration are less vigorous, then groups set the policy agenda and channel the debates. Thus the Smoot-Hawley Tariff Act of 1930, which had such grave consequences in weakening the fabric of international trade during the Great Depression, largely registered the triumph of an intricate network of special interests.

Over the long development of economic public policy, group politics—where factions pursue their own goals as if there were no large questions of public interest—have been more common than what Schattschneider has called "the politics of survival"—where "private and special interest conflicts are strongly subordinated to a dominant concern for the preservation of a common interest of the nation." [23] At times of crisis, however, when strong leadership poses great alternatives, public awareness of policy issues expands, and a broader conception of public interest comes into play. Since crisis has been with us almost constantly during much of the twentieth century, the importance of strong leadership, as indicated, for example, by the spectacular growth in the power and prestige of the Presidency, appears to be waxing. Yet, within this secular trend, we also see short-run cycles when congressional power expands. At times the public seeks relief from strong presidential leadership, and from the air of crisis it creates, and turns to Congress. Since Congress cannot provide effective leadership, the focus of public attention blurs. The policy alternatives seem to multiply, and group politics dominate. New crises then produce a need for leadership which only a President can satisfy.[24]

Thus the political environment in which public policy is forged is in almost constant change. With each shift, different policy alternatives enter the realm of the possible, and different policy considerations come to the fore. Organized interests permeate the

[23] *Ibid.*, p. 22.

[24] ". . . there has been a recurrent cycle of change in the relations between the President and the Congress. Periods of party government under Presidential leadership have alternated with periods of party government under Congressional leadership, separated from each other by periods of government without effective party leadership of any kind. . . . What is normal is the ebb and flow of the leadership from the White House to Capitol Hill and back again. Sometimes one is in the ascendant, sometimes the other, and often neither. Since the beginning of the present century the periods of party government have been longer than before and Presidential leadership has been more impressive than Congressional leadership." Holcombe, *Our More Perfect Union*, p. 202.

processes of policy formation and administration, but their potency varies with time and circumstance. The unending struggle to define the public interest ensures that the role of government in the economic realm will always be subject to re-examination and redefinition.

CHAPTER 4

Constitutional Limitations
on Economic Policy
and Administration

$\mathbf{T}$HE WATCHFUL eye of the Supreme Court
has attended every stage in the transformation of government's role
in economic life from the modest functions of 1789 into today's
pervasive activities. Judicial review, explicitly applied to state action by the Constitution, and to federal action by the doctrine
established in 1803 in *Marbury* v. *Madison*, has often controlled
the courses which policy has taken. The unique power of our
courts casts many of the great issues of American public policy
into the mold of constitutional law. Considerations of intrinsic
desirability have often been subordinated to, or treated in terms
of, the tests of "interstate commerce" or "due process of law."
And the very existence of constitutional limitations has made the
courts more ready to reshape the meaning and application of
statutes, even when constitutional issues are not directly involved.

For the last twenty years, the Supreme Court has restrained its
participation in policy making and has limited its oversight of
administration. Yet so great has been its past role that a full
understanding of present policies requires some historical analysis.
The influence of judicial review on specific phases of policy making and administration will be a recurrent theme of the present
study. Here, however, we only review briefly the historic role of
the Supreme Court in the growth of economic policy and sum-

67

marize analytically the major categories of constitutional limitations.

1. Constitutional Limitations on Economic Policy

Constitutional Law and Economic Development

The nature of the judicial process gives the courts a wide area of discretion within which to guide and confine the evolution of policy. The expansibility of crucial constitutional phrases is amply proven by their adaptation to a wholly altered technological and social environment. Adherence to precedents established in earlier cases where the factual circumstances were of a similar character—the principle of *stare decisis*—does not substantially diminish judicial flexibility. No two cases are identical, and an ample fund of precedents lies on each side of every leading issue. The Supreme Court, moreover, has never held itself rigidly bound by past decisions. Precedents are occasionally explicitly overruled; more often they are simply abandoned.

The Supreme Court is, in a sense, a "third House" of all our legislatures, state and national, but its power is negative, one of veto rather than origination. The great epochs of judicial supremacy have been those in which new restrictions were imposed upon legislators and administrators. Each ruling of unconstitutionality, moreover, may strike down a host of similar measures and smother others in embryo. Thus future policy is diverted into permitted channels and administration confined within the orbit of judicial approval. In periods of liberality the courts may sweep away the earlier bounds; they cannot determine the shape of things to come.

In the historical development of constitutional interpretation affecting public economic policy, five great eras are discernible. From 1801 to 1835, the Supreme Court under Chief Justice Marshall's leadership established a broad scope of national power within which the expanding economy might develop. Only one act of Congress was invalidated, an unimportant section of the Judiciary Act of 1789, but the opportunity was used to affirm the Court's authority over federal legislation.[1] Of greatest importance, Marshall announced in ringing words a sweeping interpretation of the commerce clause, laying a foundation for its use not merely as a major vehicle of later federal regulation, but also as a potent limitation upon the states.[2] State threats to national economic

[1] *Marbury* v. *Madison*, 1 Cranch 137 (1803).
[2] *Gibbons* v. *Ogden*, 9 Wheaton 1 (1824).

expansion were sternly struck down. The constitutional phrase which forbade state laws "impairing the obligation of contracts" became a powerful weapon against legislation considered inimical to individual enterprise.

Under Chief Justice Taney, from 1836 to 1864, the Court maintained the same basic lines of interpretation. Again only a single federal statute fell under the judicial ax.[3] The commerce clause continued to justify broad federal authority, but it was made less of a limitation upon the states in fields where Congress had not taken positive action. State regulatory action was viewed more kindly. The contract clause was less severely applied. The battle between Jackson and the United States Bank, in which Taney, as Secretary of the Treasury in 1833, had played a leading part, left him fearful of the growing power of monopoly, particularly financial monopoly. This experience was reflected in his decisions. But, despite important differences in approach, judicial limitations under his guidance continued to follow the currents set flowing by Marshall.

In the third era, from the Civil War until 1885, the Court supported legislative discretion in the first groping efforts of the states to temper the more flagrant evils of the new industrialism. In the celebrated Granger decisions of 1877, it held that legislative regulation of grain elevators and railroads did not violate the recently adopted Fourteenth Amendment. Utmost leeway was given the states in the exercise of the "police power," their broad authority to protect public morals, public safety, public health, and public welfare. "This is a power," admitted Chief Justice Waite, "which may be abused; but that is no argument against its existence. For protection against abuses by legislatures the people must resort to the polls, not the courts." [4]

In the middle 1880's, however, and for half a century thereafter, the Court so revised its constitutional interpretations as to make itself the chief barrier to governmental economic regulation. As this period coincided with the upsurge of pressures for the limitation of corporations in order to protect disadvantaged groups, constitutional limitations became crucial in the making of policy. The commerce clause was narrowed to prevent federal regulation in certain areas where federal action alone was possible. But the major instruments of restraint were the "due process of

---

[3] The Missouri Compromise of 1820, in *Dred Scott* v. *Sanford*, 19 Howard 393 (1857). While the decision was the most ill fated in American history, it is irrelevant to our concerns here.

[4] *Munn* v. *Illinois*, 94 U.S. 113 (1877).

law" clauses of the Fifth and Fourteenth Amendments.
From a procedural limitation, originally designed to prevent
federal encroachment on individual rights and then extended to
the states to protect the Negroes of the South, the clause was
transformed into a substantive limitation upon any social or
economic legislation which, to the Court, appeared unreasonable,
arbitrary, or capricious. Its protection of "persons" was extended
to corporations. Its prohibition on deprivations of liberty and
property was construed to enact into the Constitution the doctrines of laissez faire and of liberty of contract. So vigorously did
the Court apply this restraint against reform legislation that 228
state laws were held invalid in the period from 1890 to 1937.[5]

Restraints were not always applied. There were always dissenting voices, such as those of the radical Republican Justice Harlan,
who inveighed mightily against "judicial usurpation of legislative
authority," and of Holmes, who pleaded consistently for free legislative experimentation in the states. At intervals their views prevailed. In the decade preceding our entry into World War I, a
new charter of freedom was given to protective labor legislation
and corporate regulation. Accidents of individual appointments
and tenure played no small part in turning the balance of decision
in close cases. During the half-century as a whole, however, the
dominant motif was expressed by Justices Field, Brewer, Mc-
Kenna, and Sutherland, who felt it their duty to protect private
property and corporate freedom against what seemed to them
unwarranted encroachments of radical democracy upon the true
liberalism of unhampered individual enterprise.

The fourth era ended with the constitutional crisis of 1937.
The doctrine of judicial supremacy had reached its apogee in a
three-year period in which the Court all but nullified the New
Deal by striking down twelve acts of Congress [6] and reaffirmed
the unconstitutionality of state minimum-wage legislation. Convinced that existing constitutional interpretations presented insuperable obstacles to his program, President Roosevelt tried to
cut the Gordian knot by enlarging the Court and so reducing the
hostile majority to a minority. He lost the titanic congressional
battle which ensued, but he won the war. With "the switch in

[5] Little wonder that the liberal Justice Holmes should protest, "As the decisions now stand, I see hardly any limit but the sky to the invalidating of
[state laws] if they happen to strike a majority of this Court as for any reason
undesirable." *Baldwin* v. *Missouri*, 281 U.S. 586 (1930).

[6] They included such measures as the National Industrial Recovery Act,
the Agricultural Adjustment Act, the Bituminous Coal Conservation Act, the
Railroad Retirement Act, and the Frazier-Lemke Farm Mortgage Act.

time that saved nine," Justice Roberts and Chief Justice Hughes shifted positions. Beginning in March, 1937, the new majority took the steam out of the drive for Court reform by upholding every New Deal law put before it, including some quite similar to earlier statutes which had been judicially vetoed. This new judicial attitude was crystallized in the next two years as five judges were replaced. The constitutional revolution of 1937 removed barriers to increased federal authority through a liberal reinterpretation of both the commerce and the general welfare clauses. The due process clause was shorn of its restrictive character.

These reinterpretations were part of a general retreat of the Court from a doctrine of judicial supremacy to a policy of self-restraint. It would be a mistake to attribute this change solely to the threat of Roosevelt's "Court-packing" plan, for the anachronism of reading into the Constitution an outmoded conception of the role of government and a discarded economic theory was doomed by the passage of time.[7] "Looking back," said Justice Roberts later, "it is difficult to see how the Court could have resisted the popular urge for uniform standards throughout the country—for what in effect was a unified economy."[8] Judicial self-restraint in the field of public economic policy is the kernel of the new attitude. Since 1937, the Court has voided only three acts of Congress, none of them relating to economic policy. It has also ceased to discourage social and economic experimentation by the states. It has constantly reiterated its new-found conviction that the economic policy-making function belongs with the elected representatives of the people.

In the long course of judicial review, two major categories of substantive limits to economic policy were established. The grant of powers to the federal government was at times so narrowly construed as to forbid congressional action. The due process clause was used to void both federal and state economic regulation.

Limitations on Federal Authority

A basic feature of our constitutional system is that federal authority is limited to the enumerated powers. Some important economic measures have been hung on the constitutional pegs of federal powers over currency, patents and copyrights, and bank-

---

[7] As early as 1905, Holmes protested that a case was being "decided upon an economic theory [laissez faire] which a large part of the country does not entertain." *Lochner* v. *New York*, 198 U.S. 45.

[8] *The Court and the Constitution* (1951), p. 61.

ruptcy, but the vital sources of federal authority are the powers to regulate interstate and foreign commerce and to tax and spend in the general welfare.

The coverage of the commerce clause has by and large been continuously extended, paralleling the transformation in scale of economic activities. "Commerce" was first held to include transportation as well as trading across state lines. New methods of communication were also readily included within its scope. Economic realities and legal adjustments, however, have not always moved in step. In Marshall's hands, the commerce clause released enterprise from state restrictions. But in the late nineteenth century, when federal regulation first began to rival that of the states, the Court became fearful of too wide an extension of its scope. In consequence, interpretation of the commerce clause took two contrasting directions. On the one hand, federal regulation viewed as desirable was permitted to cover even nominally intrastate affairs. Two doctrines were evolved for this purpose. The first extended federal authority to intrastate activities "affecting" interstate commerce. The Shreveport case, decided in 1914, permitted federal control "in all matters having such a close and substantial relation to interstate traffic that the control is essential or appropriate to the security of that traffic, to the efficiency of the interstate service, and to the maintenance of conditions under which interstate commerce may be conducted upon fair terms and without molestation or hindrance." [9] The second doctrine, first introduced in 1922 in a decision sustaining federal regulation of stockyards,[10] viewed certain intrastate operations as elements in a continuous "stream" of interstate commerce. It could be used to bring manufacturing or processing operations within the scope of federal regulation.

On the other hand, regulatory action viewed askance by the Court could be struck down through the doctrine of "dual federalism," which made the "normal" authority of the states over production, as contrasted with commerce proper, an independent limitation on federal authority. Antitrust policy was denied application for a time to the very manufacturing combinations it was designed to combat, on the ground that their operations were matters exclusively of state concern.[11] A federal effort to prohibit the interstate shipment of goods made by child labor was similarly

[9] *Houston, East and West Texas Railway Co.* v. *U.S.*, 234 U.S. 342.
[10] *Stafford* v. *Wallace*, 258 U.S. 495.
[11] *U.S.* v. *E. C. Knight Co.*, 156 U.S. 1 (1895).

frustrated.[12] There was thus created a "twilight zone" in which states were unable to regulate effectively because of either legal restraints or interstate competition, while at the same time federal regulation was forbidden by the Court. Early in the New Deal, this "twilight zone" was extended by narrowing the Shreveport doctrine. It was held that, to bring production or intrastate commerce within federal jurisdiction, a "direct effect" upon interstate commerce must be shown, not merely a "close and substantial effect." This redefinition contributed to invalidation of the National Industrial Recovery Act and was the major ground for disapproval of the Bituminous Coal Conservation Act.[13]

This narrow view of the national power, in striking contrast with more generous interpretations of the past, was overturned by the constitutional revolution of 1937. Indeed, that revolution began with a case, based on the National Labor Relations Act, which involved the power of Congress to regulate manufacturing and production just as did the Schechter and Carter cases, both recently decided against the government. This time, however, the Court turned sharply away from its previous restrictive interpretation, holding now that the test bringing intrastate activities within the scope of the commerce clause was a "close and intimate effect" rather than a "direct effect." [14] Well might the dissenting minority complain that "almost anything—marriage, birth, death—may in some fashion affect commerce," for in succeeding cases the Court held that Congress could regulate building employees who serviced corporations in interstate commerce,[15] oil drillers,[16] a small newspaper which sold forty-five copies outside the state,[17] and a utility whose services were rendered and used within a single state.[18] The furthest authorized penetration of federal power into local affairs occurred when the Court upheld Congress's power to regulate the growing of wheat which was consumed on the same farm. "Even if appellee's activity be local and though it may not be regarded as commerce, it may still, whatever its nature, be reached by Congress if it exerts a substantial effect on interstate commerce, this irrespective of whether such effort is . . . 'direct'

[12] *Hammer* v. *Dagenhart*, 247 U.S. 251 (1918).
[13] *Schechter* v. *U.S.*, 295 U.S. 495 (1935); *Carter* v. *Carter Coal Co.*, 298 U.S. 238 (1936).
[14] *NLRB* v. *Jones & Laughlin Steel Corp.*, 301 U.S. 1.
[15] *Kirschbaum Co.* v. *Walling*, 316 U.S. 517 (1942).
[16] *Warren-Bradshaw Drilling Co.* v. *Hall*, 317 U.S. 88 (1942).
[17] *Mabee* v. *White Plains Publishing Co.*, 327 U.S. 178 (1946).
[18] *Consolidated Edison Co.* v. *NLRB*, 305 U.S. 197 (1938).

or 'indirect.' " [19]

Not merely the extent of federal jurisdiction under the commerce clause, but also its qualitative scope have been given the utmost breadth in recent decisions. Promotion, protection, fostering, and if need be, prohibition of commerce—all are within its terms. With a breadth of interpretation recalling Marshall,[20] these decisions seem to leave the federal government free to deal with any problem of commerce:

In our view, it cannot properly be said that the constitutional power of the United States over its waters is limited to control for navigation. . . . That authority is as broad as the needs of commerce.[21]

This broad commerce clause does not . . . render the nation powerless to defend itself against the economic forces that Congress decrees inimical or destructive of the national economy. Rather it is an affirmative power commensurate with the national needs. . . . And in using this great power, Congress is not bound by technical legal conceptions. Commerce itself is an intensely practical matter . . . once it is established that the evil concerns or affects commerce in more states than one, Congress may act. . . .[22]

At the same time, revived devotion to judicial self-restraint has led the Court to uphold state measures having an impact on interstate commerce, provided there is no discrimination against interstate commerce, and if Congress has not pre-empted the particular field of action.[23]

The second great constitutional vehicle of federal centralization, rivaling the commerce clause in importance, is the power to tax and spend in the general welfare. The debate over the meaning of this clause began early with a sharp clash between Madison and Hamilton in *The Federalist*. Madison contended that the clause —"The Congress shall have Power To lay and collect Taxes,

[19] *Wickard* v. *Filburn*, 317 U.S. 111 (1942).
[20] "Let the end be legitimate, let it be within the scope of the Constitution, and all means which are appropriate, which are plainly adapted to that end, which are not prohibited, but consistent with the letter and spirit of the Constitution, are constitutional." *McCulloch* v. *Maryland*, 4 Wheaton 316 (1819).
[21] *Appalachian Power Co.* v. *U.S.*, 311 U.S. 377 (1940).
[22] *North American Co.* v. *SEC*, 327 U.S. 686 (1946).
[23] *Southern Pacific Co.* v. *Arizona*, 325 U.S. 761 (1945); *Morgan* v. *Virginia*, 328 U.S. 373 (1946); *Cities Service Gas Co.* v. *Peerless Oil & Gas Co.*, 340 U.S. 179 (1950).

Duties, Imports and Excises to pay the Debts and provide for the common Defense and general Welfare of the United States"— was part of the general scheme which allocated to Congress only those powers specifically enumerated elsewhere in the Constitution. Hamilton, on the other hand, argued that the general welfare clause conferred powers distinct from, and not to be limited to, the enumerated powers—a view he forcefully repeated in his famous *Report on . . . Manufactures.*

Clearly, the latter view would produce far more extensive national power over economic and other affairs. And over the years, it is the latter view which has won out. The use of federal funds to promote various national objectives and to induce state participation in federally aided programs and the policy of nationally financed internal improvements have gone far beyond the promotion of interstate commerce. Not only waterways, railroads, and roads, but education, agriculture, maternity welfare, and a host of other services have come within its orbit.

It was difficult to obtain a definitive judicial interpretation of the general welfare clause, since beneficiaries were unlikely to contest the power and individual taxpayers were held to be without sufficient interest to justify restraining suits. Then in 1936 the Court finally accepted Hamilton's broad interpretation in the course of finding the Agricultural Adjustment Act of 1933 invalid for other reasons.[24] A year later, in the Social Security cases, both a direct federal system of old-age benefits and a federally instigated system of state unemployment insurance were sustained as legitimate exercises of the taxing and spending power.[25] The Court took notice of the obstacles to individual state action imposed by interstate competition and explicitly approved co-operative endeavor by the states and the Union to attack a situation injurious to both.

Regulation through taxation, however, has had a checkered judicial career. Although the second act adopted by the first Congress was a tariff measure designed to encourage and protect domestic manufactures, not until 1928 did the Court explicitly sanction the use of tariffs for purposes other than revenue.[26] With a few exceptions, regulation through other types of taxation was permitted only as an alternative means of accomplishing objectives which might have been sought directly under an enumerated

[24] *U.S.* v. *Butler,* 297 U.S. 1.
[25] *Steward Machine Co.* v. *Davis,* 301 U.S. 548; *Helvering* v. *Davis,* 301 U.S. 619.
[26] *Hampton & Co.* v. *U.S.,* 276 U.S. 394.

power.[27] Thus in 1936 the Court invalidated the first Agricultural Adjustment Act, which levied processing taxes upon agricultural commodities and then used the proceeds to compensate farmers who had restricted their production of those commodities. This was held an attempt to regulate production under the mere guise of the taxing power.[28] But in the constitutional revolution of 1937 the Court reversed its position. It upheld the second Agricultural Adjustment Act, which differed from the first only in details.[29] A tax is not void merely because it regulates, discourages, or even deters the activities taxed.[30] It is for Congress, not for the judges, to decide whether a given exercise of the taxing and spending powers will promote the general welfare.[31]

Thus, "what was once . . . a Constitution of Rights, both state and private, has been replaced by a Constitution of Powers." [32] The Court is still the umpire of the system in cases of outright conflict, but it has returned to the legislatures, federal and state, the task of determining the most appropriate distribution of governmental functions.

Due Process of Law

Correlative with the "twilight zone" between effective state and effective federal regulation, judicial interpretation for about a half-century established a "midnight zone" into which the economic policy of neither states nor Union might extend. These restraints arose from a conversion of the procedural limitations of the due process clauses of the Fifth and Fourteenth Amendments, which protect any person against deprivation of life, liberty, or property without due process of law, into substantive limitations.[33]

---

[27] The major exception was approval of a prohibitory tax on oleomargarine when colored to resemble butter, in McCray v. U.S., 195 U.S. 27 (1904). The Court there refused to go behind the fact that the measure on its face was one of taxation rather than regulation. While never explicitly overruled, this doctrine was subsequently abandoned.

[28] U.S. v. Butler, 297 U.S. 1.

[29] Milford v. Smith, 307 U.S. 38 (1939). The Court here only considered the taxing and spending power and did not expressly declare that agriculture came within the definition of commerce. That declaration was not forthcoming until 1955, in Maneja v. Waialua Agricultural Co., 349 U.S. 254.

[30] U.S. v. Sanchez, 340 U.S. 42 (1942).

[31] Helvering v. Davis, 301 U.S. 619 (1937).

[32] E. S. Corwin, "The Passage of Dual Federalism," in R. G. McCloskey (ed.), Essays in Constitutional Law (1957), p. 186.

[33] The associated phrase in the Fourteenth Amendment prohibiting denial of "the equal protection of the laws" is also an important limitation on discriminatory state legislation.

For a century the due process clause of the Fifth Amendment was construed solely as an additional procedural protection for private individuals. Until 1886, moreover, the Court refused to extend the Fourteenth Amendment beyond the purposes for which it had ostensibly been adopted, i.e., the protection of Negroes against discrimination.[34]

Responding in part to a campaign of the American Bar Association to restrict legislative power and to promote laissez faire, a new Court majority in the middle eighties drastically altered this interpretation. Corporations as well as natural persons were brought within the scope of the clause. While the states might still legislate for the public health, morals, safety, and welfare, any exercise of these "police powers" which restricted private or corporate freedom was subjected to judicial censorship. If, in the eyes of the Court, the legislative purposes were unwarranted, the means not appropriate to a justifiable purpose, or the policy discriminatory, arbitrary, unreasonable, or capricious, the statute failed of approval. Congressional action was similarly constrained.

In the first quarter-century of the new interpretation, the Court adopted an extreme stand against interference with private rights and duties for social ends, especially when considering protective labor legislation. The doctrine of freedom of contract, despite radically unequal bargaining power, was mechanically applied in disregard of the theoretical presumption of constitutionality. In a celebrated dissenting opinion, Justice Holmes protested against embodiment in the Constitution of a "particular economic theory." "The Fourteenth Amendment," he said, "does not enact Mr. Herbert Spencer's *Social Statics*." [35]

For a few years after 1910, the Court retreated somewhat. Inroads were made into judicial faith in laissez faire, especially in regard to special protection for women and general limitations on hours of work. Powerful economic and social briefs, detailing the practical effects of lack of regulation, forced actuality upon the Court's attention. In addition, political hostility to the courts, and growing demands for the power to recall judicial decisions,

---

[34] In an oral argument before the Supreme Court in 1882, Roscoe Conkling, a member of the congressional committee which had drafted the Fourteenth Amendment, argued from the contents of the then unpublished Committee Journal that possible application of the amendment to corporate protection had been considered at the time. This interpretation, however, played no part either in congressional adoption of the amendment or in its ratification by the states. It was nevertheless later employed by the Court in justifying its altered construction of the due process clause.

[35] *Lochner v. New York*, 198 U.S. 45 (1905).

doubtless contributed to the result. In the period after World War I, however, a more conservative attitude again dominated due process decisions. Minimum-wage legislation for women and children became the focus of dispute and was repeatedly rejected from 1923 until 1936, although generally by a closely divided Court.[36]

As in other areas, 1937 began a new era for the due process clause. Recognizing the necessity to expand the police power in accordance with changing economic needs, the Court explicitly overruled earlier minimum-wage decisions:

The Constitution does not speak of freedom of contract. It speaks of liberty. . . . The liberty safeguarded is liberty in a social organization which requires the protection of law against the evils which menace the health, safety, morals and welfare of the people.[37]

During the period 1885–1936, the due process clause was also used substantively to restrict the scope of regulation and procedurally to govern the regulatory process. Price control for many decades was limited to businesses "affected with a public interest." This expression, tossed out almost accidentally by the Court to give a common-law precedent for its Granger decisions, for a time created an arbitrary category of industries peculiarly liable to regulation, while all others were free from public control. Although public utilities were, of course, within the concept, this line of interpretation placed regulatory policy in a strait jacket, preventing experimentation in special regulation for other industries which might benefit from, or require, a limited degree of control. Classification of new industries was a difficult task for the Court, and it was hard to find consistent criteria common to the included industries and absent from the excluded ones.[38] One observer concluded that "the only general rule which could be drawn from the decisions was that types of regulation of which

---

[36] The history of protective labor legislation in the Supreme Court is treated in some detail in Chapter 7.

[37] *West Coast Hotel* v. *Parrish*, 300 U.S. 379 (1937).

[38] In 1923 Chief Justice Taft divided the category of "businesses affected with a public interest" into three sections: (1) businesses with a public franchise, (2) businesses traditionally subjected to special regulation at common law, and (3) "businesses which, though not public at their inception, may be fairly said to have arisen to be such and have become subject in consequence to some government regulation." *Wolff Packing Co.* v. *Industrial Court of Kansas*, 262 U.S. 522. This definition proved hard to apply in practice.

the Court sufficiently disapproved were unconstitutional." [39]

The constitutional revolution of 1937 swept this doctrine, too, into discard,[40] leaving it for the legislatures to decide which industries to regulate. "The legislature, acting within its sphere, is presumed to know the needs of the people of the state," said the Court in 1937.[41] "The day is gone when this Court uses the Due Process Clause . . . to strike down state laws . . . because they may be unwise, improvident, or out of harmony with a particular school of thought." [42] "Our recent decisions make it plain that we do not sit as a super-legislature to weigh the wisdom of legislation nor to decide whether the policy which it expresses offends the public welfare." [43] Yet, despite the great deference which the Court now pays to legislatures, it has never yet expressly confined due process to procedural matters. It continues to determine whether questioned legislation has a rational basis or is "substantially related to a legitimate end sought to be attained," [44] although, it admits, "a pronounced shift of emphasis . . . has deprived the words 'reasonable' and 'arbitrary' of the content they once had." [45]

In those areas where extensive regulation had been permitted, the Court retained close supervision over the regulatory process. The Granger doctrine, making reasonableness of regulated prices a matter of legislative discretion, was slowly whittled away over a twenty-year period in favor of thoroughgoing judicial review. In 1898, the Court emerged as the arbiter of public utility regulation by requiring that regulation allow a fair return on the fair value of the property.[46] The obstacles thus placed before utility regulators are treated in Chapter 12. Suffice it to say here that judicial participation in the regulatory process through the rule of *Smyth* v. *Ames* was a major barrier to the effectiveness of public utility regulation and the administrative commission as a device of public control.

[39] R. L. Stern, "The Problems of Yesteryear—Commerce and Due Process," in McCloskey, *op. cit.*, pp. 153–154.

[40] In 1934 the Court had seemed to discard the doctrine in a case upholding a state milk-control law. *Nebbia* v. *New York*, 291 U.S. 502. But the Court then backed away in *Mayflower Farms* v. *Ten Eyck*, 297 U.S. 266 (1936).

[41] *Townsend* v. *Yeomans*, 301 U.S. 441 (1937).

[42] *Williamson* v. *Lee Optical Co.*, 348 U.S. 483 (1955).

[43] *Day-Brite Lighting, Inc.* v. *Missouri*, 342 U.S. 421 (1952).

[44] *Cities Service Gas Co.* v. *Peerless Oil & Gas Co.*, 340 U.S. 179 (1950).

[45] *Daniel* v. *Family Security Life Insurance Co.*, 336 U.S. 220 (1949).

[46] *Smyth* v. *Ames*, 169 U.S. 466 (1898).

2. Constitutional Limitations on the Administration of Policy

Judicial oversight of administration has always been significant and since 1937 has been more important than judicial review of substantive legislative policies. At the same time, the bulk of economic policy making, having first shifted from the common-law courts to the legislatures, has now passed to administrative agencies. Among the many reasons for this shift are the increased technical complexity of specific policies, their vastly greater number as government's economic role has expanded, and the desire to provide official voices for interests unable adequately to represent themselves, whether poorly organized special interests or the broad interest of the whole public.

Judicial concern with administrative forms and processes has developed primarily because administrative agencies seem to violate the constitutional separation of powers in two ways: they make policy, presumably a legislative function; and, in applying rules to cases, they determine private rights and duties, an act of adjudication. And they do this on a heroic scale. The *Federal Register* (containing administrative rules and regulations) dwarfs in size the *Statutes at Large* (laws enacted by Congress). An agency such as the National Labor Relations Board decides more cases each year than do all of the federal courts of appeal combined, and administrative decisions affect greater total dollar values than do the money judgments of federal courts.

To be sure, no subtlety of analysis can classify every governmental action as uniquely legislative, administrative, or judicial. Administrators and judges invariably supplement legislation in applying statutes to particular cases. Adjudication occurs in all administration which touches private interests. Nor does the Constitution enact an absolute separation of powers. Yet the architecture of its first three articles is clearly based upon the triangular pattern, and the Court has viewed the maintenance of intragovernmental equilibrium as one of its duties. Its activities have generally taken the form of limiting the delegation of legislative power and of "judicializing" administrative procedures affecting private rights and duties. In the course of its general abnegation, the post-1937 Court first extended to administration the same deference and presumption of legality which it rendered to legislatures. At congressional insistence, however, it has resumed its scrutiny of administrative procedure.

Administrative Lawmaking

As the abortive experience with direct statutory fixing of rail-road rates amply proved, general legislation cannot provide for the infinite variability of circumstances, and legislatures are not well suited for the enactment of particular policies for each circumstance. The consequent growth of regulatory bodies with substantial discretion in the setting of rates or the making of rules confronted the Court with the question of whether Congress, in apparent violation both of the separation of powers and of the legal maxim that delegated powers cannot be further delegated—*delegata potestas non potest delegari*—might lawfully pass on to administrators the powers given it by the Constitution. The courts resolved the dilemma by permitting extensive delegation of legislative authority, sometimes thinly disguised under the term "quasi-legislative," subject to the requirement that the legislature lay down general standards to guide the exercise of administrative discretion.[47]

For about forty years the Court extended federal executive powers just as resolutely as it restricted legislative powers. Not only did it expand executive discretionary powers; it also granted the President sweeping removal powers over officials in the executive branch, thereby strengthening his control and weakening that of Congress.[48] But in the mid-thirties the Court three times struck down New Deal measures because they involved delegations not circumscribed by any real standards.[49]

Since then, however, the Court has virtually dropped the requirement of a limiting standard. In 1943, it held that the legislative standard of "public interest, convenience, or necessity" given the Federal Communications Commission "is as concrete as the complicated factors for judgment in such a field . . . permit." Setting more detailed standards "would have stereotyped the powers of the Commission to specific details in regulating a field

[47] *Field* v. *Clark*, 143 U.S. 649 (1892); *Hampton & Co.* v. *U.S.*, 276 U.S. 394 (1928).

[48] In 1926 the Court upheld the removal power of the President, granting him a power implicitly denied him by *Marbury* v. *Madison* and explicitly by the Tenure of Office Act of 1867 and by subsequent legislation. *Myers* v. *U.S.*, 277 U.S. 52. A later case permitted Congress to specify the causes for removal of members of independent regulatory commissions. *Humphrey's Executor* v. *U.S.*, 295 U.S. 602 (1935). But the Court refused to intervene when the President removed the chairman of the TVA, an independent, but presumably executive, agency.

[49] *Panama Refining Co.* v. *Ryan*, 293 U.S. 388 (1935); *Schechter* v. *U.S.*, 295 U.S. 495 (1935); *Carter* v. *Carter Coal Co.*, 298 U.S. 238 (1936).

of enterprise the dominant characteristic of which was the rapid pace of its unfolding." [50] In a later case, the Court upheld the granting of regulatory powers, where there were no penal sanctions, even in the absence of an express legislative standard.[51] Thus the Court has now virtually removed judicial limitations on "skeleton" legislation; responsibility for the delegation of power rests with Congress. The need for decentralized policy making has won out over the principle of separated powers.

Procedural Due Process and Judicial Review of Administration

While it has a long-established meaning in criminal procedure, the application of "due process of law" to civil administration is a fairly recent development. Over the past seventy-five years the courts have evolved an elaborate set of procedural rules governing administrative operations which substantially affect private rights and duties. These rules, an important sector of administrative law, are implemented by judicial review.

Delicate and complex issues are at stake in administrative law. They arise out of conflicts between the needs of effective policy enforcement on the one hand and avoidance of arbitrary denial of private rights on the other. Thus, in turn, conflicts are produced between the administrative and judicial arms of government. We adhere to the traditions of a rule of law and of "a government of laws rather than of men," but, since judges and legislators, as well as administrators, are men, in practice the rule of law means that there is a hierarchy of lawmakers. The law made by administrators is on a lower plane than that made by legislators or by constitution writers. Hence administrative actions are valid only if they do not conflict with the Constitution or with congressional statutes, and every administrative act may be challenged by an appeal to law in a court.

In theory, court review is generally confined to questions of law. Administrative findings of fact, on the other hand, must merely be supported by "substantial evidence." Review is limited to ascertaining a reasonable foundation for the findings; it does not extend to the weight of the evidence. Fact finding, indeed, is the very heart of the administrative process. If judicial review reaches here, administrative hearings are only preliminary trials and the

[50] *National Broadcasting Co.* v. *U.S.*, 319 U.S. 190. One observer commented that to tell an administrator to act in the "public interest" is to tell him, "Here is the regulatory problem; deal with it." K. C. Davis, *Administrative Law* (1951), p. 36.
[51] *Fahey* v. *Mallonee*, 322 U.S. 245 (1947).

vital administrative role is transferred to the courts.

In practice, the distinction between law and fact is often a difficult one, and the pre-1937 Court at times seemed to act on the assumption that administrative findings were worthless. Courts sometimes recognized a category of "questions of mixed law and fact." Moreover, over the vigorous dissents of its liberal wing, the Supreme Court repeatedly held that fact findings essential either to the jurisdiction of the administrative agency or to the constitutionality of its action must be reviewed *de novo* by the courts.[52] The post-1937 Court, however, expressing deference for administrative findings, erased both jurisdictional and constitutional fact as a basis for court review.[53] It has also held that the question of whether a particular factual situation fits within statutory terms or concepts is to be regarded as more a question of fact than of law.[54]

In general terms, the procedural requirements imposed upon administration are simple. The agency must give a fair hearing to all affected interests, preceded by adequate notice. Its decisions must be supported by substantial evidence, exhibited in explicit findings. Affected parties must be allowed the right of appeal to the courts to test the validity of administrative action. Substantial flexibility is permitted, on the other hand, in the rules of evidence. Because of their expertise, administrators are presumed to be able to discriminate between the relevant and the irrelevant, and harsh common-law restrictions on hearsay evidence are not enforced.

In applying these principles, reviewing judges have sometimes threatened to convert the requirement of a fair hearing into a rigid procedural framework akin to that imposed upon the lower courts. The Morgan cases [55] illustrate well how the attitude of the Court changed as it came to defer more to administrators. The cases dealt with one of the major problems of the administrative agency, that of the "institutional" decision, in which a case is decided by an administrative entity rather than by an individual. The problem is perhaps as much psychological as it is one of administrative law, for it often arises when the murky anonymity of the decision-

[52] *Crowell* v. *Benson*, 285 U.S. 22 (1932); *St. Joseph Stockyards Co.* v. *U.S.*, 298 U.S. 38 (1936).

[53] *Estep* v. *U.S.*, 327 U.S. 114 (1946); *Railroad Commission of Texas* v. *Rowan & Nichols Oil Co.*, 310 U.S. 573 (1940).

[54] *Gray* v. *Powell*, 314 U.S. 402 (1941).

[55] *Morgan* v. *U.S.*, 298 U.S. 468 (1936); *Morgan* v. *U.S.*, 304 U.S. 1 (1938); *U.S.* v. *Morgan*, 307 U.S. 183 (1939); *U.S.* v. *Morgan*, 313 U.S. 409 (1941).

making process in a large organization denies an individual the assurance that he has talked to the man who is going to decide his case.[56]

The Morgan cases involved the validity of rates the Secretary of Agriculture had set under the Packers and Stockyards Act. In the first case, the Court invalidated the rate order because, while the Secretary technically made the findings and issued the order, another official had examined the evidence. Thus, the Court held, respondents had been denied the "full hearing" required by the statute. In the second Morgan case, the Court struck down the rate order because respondents had not received a trial examiner's intermediate report as a basis for argument before the final decision, and had, therefore, not been afforded a "full hearing." These two decisions seemed to cast into a single rigid mold the internal procedure of every regulatory agency, regardless of the particular administrative problems faced in its activities. They certainly made impossible demands on administrators. The first decision held that the Secretary himself had to "consider" the evidence and argument before making his findings. But the original oral testimony alone filled thirteen thousand pages! The third and fourth Morgan cases, however, marked the turning of the tide. The third directed that greater deference be paid administrators. The fourth in effect nullified the first by holding that interrogation of the Secretary to determine whether his examination of the case had been sufficiently thorough was improper. Thus there would be no way of knowing whether an agency head making a decision had really complied with the Court's doctrine in the first Morgan case.

These four cases, accordingly, first registered the Court's concern over the institutional decision and its fairness to the rights of individuals, then reflected the Court's retreat from its earlier position for fear of crippling administrative processes. In another case, the Court keynoted its new hands-off policy toward administration by pointing out that the vital "differences in origin and

[56] Dean Acheson, a friendly critic of administration, has commented, "The agency is one great obscure organization with which the citizen has to deal. It is absolutely amorphous. He pokes it in one place and it comes out another. No one seems to have specific authority. There is someone called the commission, the authority; a metaphysical omniscient thing which sort of floats around the air and is not a human being. That is what is baffling. . . . Mr. A. heard the case and then it goes into this great building and mills around and comes out with a commissioner's name on it but what happens in between is a mystery. That is what bothers people." Quoted in K. C. Davis, *op. cit.*, p. 357.

function" of courts and administrative tribunals "preclude wholesale transplantation of the rules of procedure, trial and review
which have evolved from the history and experience of the
courts." Unless these differences are respected, "courts will stray
outside their province and read the laws of Congress through the
distorting lenses of inapplicable legal doctrine." [57]

Judicial withdrawal from supervision of administrative procedures was based on the Court's recognition of the need for
substantial administrative autonomy and flexibility. Fearful of
what Justice Frankfurter later termed a "hopeless clogging of the
administrative process by judicial review," [58] the Court gave a
restrictive answer to the question of who had sufficient "standing"
to contest administrative actions in the courts.[59] For the older
requirement that an administrative finding be supported by "substantial" evidence, it substituted that of *some* evidence.[60] The
Court deferred to the expertise of the administrators—"we certainly have neither technical competence nor legal authority to
pronounce upon the wisdom of the course taken by the commission" [61]—and in general enunciated a narrow theory of review.[62]

The Administrative Procedure Act of 1946

Before this new adjustment between the executive and judicial
arms of government could become permanent, however, the third
arm intervened. Congress wished to "judicialize" administration
and to provide for judicial review to a greater extent than did
the post-1937 Court. The Administrative Procedure Act of 1946,
which effectuates this congressional desire, was the culmination of
a long debate. The issue had been precipitated by the American
Bar Association, which in 1933 had begun to express concern over:
(1) the discretionary rule-making authority of administrators; (2)
the mixing of quasi-judicial with quasi-legislative and administrative functions within agencies; and (3) the adequacy of court
review.

The clash between lawyers and administrators was sharp. Administrative agencies, for historical reasons which were defended

[57] FCC v. Pottsville Broadcasting Co., 309 U.S. 134 (1940).
[58] Dissenting, in FCC v. National Broadcasting Co., 319 U.S. 239 (1943).
[59] E.g., City of Atlanta v. Ickes, 308 U.S. 517 (1939).
[60] NLRB v. Nevada Consolidated Copper Co., 316 U.S. 105 (1942).
[61] Board of Trade v. U.S., 314 U.S. 534 (1942).
[62] ". . . the range of issues open to review is narrow. Only questions affecting constitutional power, statutory authority and the basic prerequisites of proof
can be raised. If these legal tests are satisfied, the Commission's order becomes
incontestable." Rochester Telephone Corp. v. U.S., 307 U.S. 125 (1939).

by their officials, functioned in many different ways, through rules and regulations, decisions, proclamations, awards, or decrees, all of them reflecting different objectives pursued by different procedures. But this diversity of procedure was criticized severely by lawyers and laymen. The mixing of functions and the minimizing of court review were defended by administrators as necessary for administrative flexibility and effectiveness. Out of a concern for individual and property rights, many lawyers wished to separate out the quasi-judicial functions, to make administrative procedure more closely resemble the judicial process, and to make administrative action subject to full judicial review of fact as well as law. Accustomed to the advocacy of individual rights, the bar was suspicious of the new agencies, which subordinated individual interests to their interpretation of the public interest. In this view, there was real doubt whether administrators could be "fair." Critics on this ground were joined by those who had opposed the regulatory policies and who now hoped to frustrate their administration by litigation. The enormous expansion of regulatory administration under the New Deal, the need for speed, and the inexperience and zealotry of new administrators had produced some abuses of administrative discretion and contributed to the demand for reform.

In 1940, Congress passed the Walter-Logan Bill, the last of a series of measures sponsored by the American Bar Association during the thirties. It was an extreme bill, prescribing a single, rigid procedure for rule-making and subjecting almost every administrative action to judicial review. That its provisions would have seriously impeded effective administration is indicated by the fact that, while the bill was running the legislative gauntlet, exemptions were provided for those agencies especially popular in Congress at the time—the Interstate Commerce Commission, the Federal Trade Commission, the Federal Reserve Board, federal lending agencies, and those administering laws dealing with taxes, patents, longshoremen and harbor workers, and agricultural marketing. Indignantly protesting that the bill would "turn the clock backward and place the entire functioning of the government at the mercy of never-ending lawsuits and subject all administrative acts and processes to the control of the judiciary," President Roosevelt vetoed it, and the veto was sustained by the House.

Meanwhile, the first two Morgan cases, together with pressure for legislation, led to thoroughgoing re-examination of the problem by the administration on its own initiative. The internal organization and procedure of the Agriculture Department, the

Labor Board, and other agencies were revised. A Committee on Administrative Procedure was appointed by the Attorney General early in 1939 to review existing procedures and to recommend administrative and legislative reforms. The committee made specific reform proposals to the twenty-three agencies studied, and in 1941 a majority of the committee made moderate general recommendations. These included the making public of all policies and procedures, the use of hearing commissioners when agency heads cannot hear all cases, and some formalization of rule-making. The minority recommended wider separation of the quasi-judicial function and a broader scope for judicial review. Bills based on both majority and minority reports were introduced but received little attention in World War II. After the war, the Bar Association again sponsored a congressional campaign which produced the Administrative Procedure Act of 1946.

While the Act is far less demanding of agencies than was the Walter-Logan Bill, critics still describe it as "a lawyer's law, conceived by lawyers and dedicated to the proposition that justice is the exclusive business of lawyers." [63] It classifies all administrative actions as *rules* or *orders*. For rule-making, it requires notice and opportunity for all interested persons "to participate . . . through submission of written data, views, or arguments." When the pertinent law requires a hearing, orders, which are defined most broadly, can be issued only after observing the adjudicatory processes specified by the Act. Separation of the quasi-judicial function is promoted by setting up independent examiners who conduct preliminary hearings and recommend decisions, and who are insulated from other officials of the agency. Judicial review is defined broadly, giving the right of appeal to "any person suffering legal wrong because of any agency action, or adversely affected or aggrieved by such action." And "every final agency action, for which there is no adequate remedy in any court, shall be subject to judicial review."

The Act, as the Supreme Court has said, "contains many compromises and generalities and, no doubt, some ambiguities." [64] This being so, its meaning depends upon how the courts interpret it. In general, while the judges have retreated somewhat from their post-1937 self-denial of control over administration, judicial interferences with administration resulting from this Act have been moderate. The Court has returned to the requirement that there be substantial evidence to support an administrative finding and

[63] R. J. Swenson, *Federal Administrative Law* (1952), p. 121.
[64] *Wong Yang Sung* v. *McGrath*, 339 U.S. 33 (1950).

that in testing its substantiality the courts will consider the whole record. Ordinarily this review is conducted with general respect for the administrative process and deference to the administrators, and a knowledgeable observer can still conclude that "the history of American administrative law has been one of the constant expansion of administrative authority accompanied by a correlative restriction of judicial power." [65] The judges have accepted the administrative state.

Consequently, after the bitterness of the struggle which produced it, the Administrative Procedure Act has been somewhat of an anticlimax. Hailed by its proponents as "the beginning of a new era in administrative law," [66] and damned as "sabotage of the administrative process" by its opponents,[67] it has, in summary, "neither created nor substantially altered a single government agency," and it "neither reduces the number of administrative agencies, nor prevents their growth, nor changes their powers materially. . . ." [68] In short, it seems only to have codified the best prevailing practice after most agencies had already substantially judicialized their administrative procedures.[69]

3. The Future of Constitutional Limitations

The constitutional revolution of 1937 drastically revised constitutional limitations on government's economic activities. A half-century of restrictive interpretation was virtually swept away. Reviving the doctrine of judicial self-restraint as to economic policies, the Court refused any longer to read into the Constitution the prescription of a particular relationship between government and private enterprise. It adhered firmly to constitutional protections for democratic organization, as its civil liberties decisions indicated, but rejected with equal firmness the identification of democracy with laissez faire. Responsibility for policy making was thus placed squarely on the shoulders of elected officials, legislative and executive. Constitutional issues were relegated for the

[65] B. Schwartz, The Supreme Court (1957), p. 136.
[66] A. T. Vanderbilt, in his foreword to G. Warren (ed.), The Federal Administrative Procedure Act and the Administrative Agencies (1947), p. iv.
[67] F. F. Blachly and M. E. Oatman, in Public Administration Review (Summer, 1946), pp. 213–217.
[68] R. Parker, "The Administrative Procedure Act: A Study in Overestimation," Yale Law Journal (1951), Vol. 60, pp. 581, 584.
[69] The provision concerning independent examiners does change the hearing process somewhat at lower levels. It does not affect the procedures by which the commission or agency head reaches decisions.

time being to a minor role.

Less dramatic than the censorship of legislation, the influence of the courts on administration is no less significant in its impact on economic policy. It is a cardinal factor in determining the effectiveness of the administrative processes lying at the heart of the modern service state. Maintaining intact its historic role of protecting the individual from the abuse of administrative discretion, the judiciary must at the same time give sufficient scope to administrators to advance adequately the equally real interests with which they are entrusted. The Supreme Court has now dedicated itself to co-operation between judges and administrators, based on performance by each of the functions to which they are best suited. Yet, now that the Court has revived the doctrine of judicial activism in civil liberties cases, new problems of adjustment may arise. Justice Frankfurter recently suggested some possibilities: "Yesterday the active area in this field was concerned with 'property.' Today it is 'civil liberties.' Tomorrow it may again be 'property.' Who can say that in a society with a mixed economy, like ours, these two areas are sharply separated, and that certain freedoms in relation to property may not again be deemed, as they were in the past, aspects of individual freedom?" [70]

[70] *Of Law and Men* (1956), p. 19.

PART 2

Government as Promoter of Particular Interests

_____

CHAPTER 5

Promotion of Business Enterprise

1. The Concept of Promotion

Promotional activity involves the use of government to encourage, strengthen, protect, or advance the interests of particular groups, industries, or sectors of the economy on the assumption—not always justifiable—that such assistance will contribute to the general welfare. In a larger sense, the protection of property and contract, the law of corporations, the maintenance of a monetary system, the rules for bankruptcy, patent, copyright, and trade-mark privileges, and the establishment of standards may all be viewed as species of business promotionalism. But attention is focused here on the more affirmative assistance rendered through tariffs, subsidies, services, and other direct aids to particular interests.

Promotion may take place for a variety of reasons. It may simply be a bald raid on the public treasury with no conceivable public benefits. Usually, however, it is defended on the ground that, by supporting a given group, government is contributing to the common welfare. Sometimes the reasons adduced may be primarily military or strategic. Thus, George Washington justified the tariff in his first annual address to Congress: "The safety and interests of the people require that they should promote such manufactures as tend to render them independent of others for

93

essential, particularly military supplies." Sometimes the stress is
on economic benefits which will be diffused as a result of aid to a
particular interest. Thus, tariffs on manufactured products have
been defended on the theory that they aid laborers and farmers
as well as manufacturers; bounties to shipowners on the ground
that they foster foreign markets for American products; subsidies
to railroads on the assumption that they bring economic advantages to the regions through which they pass. Sometimes an
economic group or regional interest demands promotional assistance to offset allegedly unfair advantages of competitors; thus
promotion for one group stimulates claims on behalf of others.

The classic statement of the case for business promotionalism
was made by Alexander Hamilton during Washington's first term
in a series of able reports on such subjects as the public credit,
chartering a national bank, instituting a system of currency, and
encouraging manufactures. Hamilton wished to establish a strong
central government drawing its primary support from banking,
commercial, and manufacturing interests and dedicating its energies to promoting the growth of business enterprise. His program, which was in the main enacted, provided for the assumption of the Continental and state debts by the federal government,
the establishment of a national bank, a mint, a system of coinage,
the passage of tariff legislation, and a land policy designed to
bring in revenue to redeem the public debt.

A particularly noteworthy exposition of the Hamiltonian system was the famous *Report on the Subject of Manufactures*
(1791), in which Hamilton argued that the development of
manufacturing would benefit the whole nation. Manufacturing
would increase national wealth, provide employment, stimulate
immigration, multiply the objects of enterprise, encourage the
natural aptitude of the American people for mechanical arts,
and foster the genius for invention. It would directly benefit
farmers by substituting a reliable domestic market for an uncertain foreign market; workers in industry would increase the
home demand for agricultural produce. With little adaptation,
identical arguments are set forth in most "underdeveloped" countries today. To encourage manufacturing, Hamilton advocated
premiums and bounties for new enterprises, but this scheme was
rejected as being too costly. Instead, only his proposals for mild
customs duties were adopted by the early Congresses.

The Hamiltonian program identified the prosperity of the nation with the prosperity of the business classes. It was government's role to dispense privileges to business; the resulting eco-

nomic benefits would percolate through the whole economy. This "trickle-down" theory of economic welfare, which was to become an important strand in the American political tradition, nevertheless rested on a narrow political base. It held out direct and tangible rewards to businessmen; the benefits it promised other groups were frequently remote and indirect. A more inclusive formula had to be evolved if the foundations of business promotionalism were to be secure.

Henry Clay's "American System," which appeared in the first quarter of the nineteenth century, was an effort to satisfy this need. Promising a sound banking system and protective tariffs to businessmen and industrialists of the East, at the same time it offered a program of federally sponsored internal improvements to attract farmers and businessmen in the West. By multiplying the beneficiaries of government largess, it sought to consolidate business and agrarian support. Though the strategy was statesmanlike, the execution proved difficult. The Whig Party, which espoused the "American System," enjoyed only temporary and intermittent success. The fulfillment of the "American System" had to await the emergence of the Republican Party, which succeeded in cementing a more durable alliance between Eastern business and industrial interests and Western agrarian elements.

The early opposition to business promotionalism found its most effective leaders in Jefferson and Jackson. Jefferson's preference for an agricultural society is well known. Yet he was partially converted to a protective tariff on manufactures after interruptions of commerce during the Napoleonic Wars and the War of 1812 had demonstrated the hazards of reliance on foreign supplies.[1] Jackson took a similar view, at least as regards "those leading and important articles so essential to War." [2]

While both Jefferson and Jackson were prepared to make concessions to business promotionalism, they would not tolerate the subordination of agriculture to industry. This is the significance of Jefferson's struggle with Hamilton and of Jackson's fight against Biddle and the Bank of the United States. Jefferson and Jackson, and their followers, were less concerned with utilizing government as a positive instrument to advance agrarian objectives than they were with preventing its exclusive use by business and bank-

---

[1] In 1816 he wrote, "We must now place the manufacturer by the side of the agriculturist. Experience has taught me that manufactures are now as necessary to our independence as to our comfort. . . ." C. A. Beard, *The Idea of National Interest* (1934), p. 317.

[2] *Ibid.*

ing groups to promote commercial interests. The Jeffersonian slogan, "Equal rights for all—special privileges for none," epitomized this attitude. A plank in the Democratic platform of 1840 gave it terse expression: "Justice and sound policy forbid the federal government to foster one branch of industry to the detriment of another, or to cherish the interests of one portion to the injury of another portion of our common country."[3] During the pre-Civil War period, when the Democratic Party and its agrarian followers were in the ascendancy, these views restrained business promotionalism.

The Civil War shifted the balance of political forces. The Republicans achieved the majority status which had eluded the Hamiltonians and the Whigs. They succeeded where the Whigs had failed because of the general economic successes of the new industrialism; because, Hamiltonian aristocratic pretensions having been discarded, the race for the rich material rewards of the new order usually seemed to be open to all comers;[4] and because they joined North and West together in mutual alliance. While the new party depended upon and catered to Western agrarian support, its leadership was closely associated with the rising industrial forces, and its policies were primarily shaped by the needs of business enterprise.

Paradoxically, once business was in the saddle, the friends and foes of business shifted positions on the question of government action. Although policies of business promotionalism were vigorously pursued, business spokesmen, turning a blind eye to the tariff and to manifold public aids to transportation, and perhaps forgetting the promotional effects of the way in which the rules of the business game—incorporation, bankruptcy, banking, patent laws, etc.—were defined and administered, proclaimed a new-found faith in laissez faire and resisted most proposed government efforts to aid other groups. When farm, labor, and other elements felt dissatisfied with their share of the new order's bounty, they pressed for greater government participation in the economic sphere, their reaction taking two somewhat different directions. On the one hand, it involved a demand that business be "regulated," that restraints be imposed to stamp out

[3] *Ibid.*, p. 320.

[4] ". . . the new whiggery was able to attach to the Horatio Alger cosmos the grand and glorious label of 'Americanism' . . . it is the true egalitarian insight of Tocqueville shining through the platitudes of Alger which accounts for the latter's grip on 'Americanism' . . . those platitudes unite Hamilton and Jefferson, making it possible to use a genuinely national label. . . ." L. Hartz, *The Liberal Tradition in America* (1955), pp. 206–207.

alleged abuses. On the other hand, it expressed itself in a plea that disadvantaged groups be given privileges like those enjoyed by more favored groups. If government is to dispense privileges, the argument went, it cannot limit the beneficiaries. The logic of protection for one group led to the call for "protection all around." Thus, business promotionalism inspired movements for agrarian and labor promotionalism, and a competitive race for privileges was set in motion.

2. The Tariff: A Major Instrument for Promotion of Business Enterprise

Historically, the tariff has been perhaps the most effective weapon in the arsenal of business promotionalism. Behind the ramparts of rising tariff walls, one industry after another was guaranteed a domestic market free from foreign competition, and many powerful vested interests were established and consolidated in the defense of the protective tariff system. Although tariffs are, in effect, taxes which tend to raise domestic prices, consumer consciousness of their impact is deadened because their effect is swallowed up in the total price of the protected commodity. At the same time, a persuasive symbolism of national interest has been built up around the protective tariff. The importance of protected industries for national defense, their contribution to national prosperity, the market they provide for agricultural producers, their protection of the standard of living of American workers—these and similar arguments provide a strong compulsion to treat the protective tariff not as an expression of private interest, but as an embodiment of the public interest.

In the history of American tariff policy five distinct periods can be noted:

(1) 1789–1815, when protectionist policy was taking shape, but was not yet applied in full force;

(2) 1816–1832, when there was a considerable rise in tariffs and the system of protection had its first great triumph;

(3) 1833–1860, when, with the exception of a short interruption between 1842 and 1846, protectionist policy was under severe attack and duties were lowered;

(4) 1861–1933, when, with minor interruptions under Cleveland and Wilson, the trend of tariff rates was sharply upward;

(5) 1934 to the present, when, under the influence of the Re-

ciprocal Trade Agreements program, the trend of tariff duties has been downward.

Between 1789 and 1815, the outlines of American protectionist policy first emerged. Although the Tariff Act of 1789 was only mildly protective, Hamilton's *Report on . . . Manufactures* gave the protectionist movement impetus, and later tariff acts cumulatively increased rates. The stimulus to manufacturing was at first slight. With the European wars, much of the carrying trade fell into American hands; international trade was extraordinarily profitable; and capital flowed into commerce rather than manufacturing. After 1807, embargoes and the war with England dealt a severe blow to foreign commerce. The scarcity and high price of imports worked to the advantage of domestic manufactures. Capital which had previously been invested in commercial pursuits was now placed in manufacturing. Manufacturing interests began to flourish, and also to petition for higher duties.

The real victory of the so-called American System of protection came in 1816, when the high seas were once more open to foreign commerce. Industries which had developed in the previous period were apparently threatened with bankruptcy. British goods inundated American markets after the Napoleonic Wars and the War of 1812. The clamor for protection was spurred on by resentment against England. Patriotism dictated emancipation of the country from English influences. The vested interest argument was transformed into national interest; military considerations required that the country nourish industries necessary to its survival. Jeffersonians joined the cry for protection. From the Act of 1816 through the Act of 1828, each tariff revision registered an upward movement of rates.

By 1824, however, high tariffs were encountering increasingly strong agrarian opposition. Farmers who bought manufactured goods in protected markets and sold their crops in world markets were hurt by protective tariffs. Southern cotton planters ceased to regard protection as a phase of national interest and assailed it as a vested sectional interest. The tariff of 1828 became the "tariff of abominations" to its opponents. Though the Act of 1832 reduced duties to about the level of 1824, dissatisfaction continued. "Nullification" sentiment ran strong in the South; in South Carolina it almost flared into open revolt. Only Jackson's firm anti-nullification stand and the further reduction of duties by Clay's Compromise Act of 1833 finally quieted the discontent.

From 1833 until the Civil War, except for a short interlude between 1842 and 1846, tariff duties declined. The politically dominant Democratic Party reflected the tariff views of its predominantly agrarian constituency. The Act of 1842, which raised average rates to the level of 1832, was enacted by the Whigs and repealed in 1846 as soon as the Democrats were returned to power. While industrialists appealed for higher rates in terms of labor and of humanitarian interests, stressing the alleged connection between high tariffs and high wages, they were unable to make headway in an inhospitable political environment.

In 1861, tariff policy was sharply reversed. During the Civil War, rate increases were chiefly inspired by fiscal needs. At the close of the war, however, the high war rates were retained. Protectionists seized the opportunity to consolidate their position, to oppose reductions, and to press for further increases. Reconstruction offered a golden opportunity. The temporary disfranchisement of the South assured Republican ascendancy, and the Republican Party was hospitable to high-tariff advocates. The tariff lobby became an established part of the American scene. Wool, copper, salt, iron, and a host of other commodity interests all set up shop in Washington, and congressmen (like "Pig-iron" Kelley) began to be described by the commodities for which they spoke.

To secure acceptance for high tariffs required considerable political skill. Industrialists rarely opposed each other's appeals for protection, and a solid phalanx of industrial support was thus assured. The farmer was placated with the Homestead Act and free land. When that remedy was exhausted, protection was extended to agricultural commodities. In some instances, as in the case of wool, sugar, and dairy products, real benefits were conferred, and the loyalty of particular agrarian interests to the protective tariff system was thus cemented. In other instances, as in the case of wheat, rye, barley, and other export crops, the benefits were dubious, but the inclusion of these agricultural commodities in the protected list afforded "psychological" satisfaction and helped to disorganize potential agrarian opposition. The appeal to urban workers identified the tariff with high wages —the "full dinner pail." Reduce the tariff, it was said, and unemployment would spread through the land; wages would fall to the "pauper" level of Europe and Asia. Arguments such as these were remarkably effective in winning widespread support for high tariffs. Meanwhile, infant industries grew into giants, and competition began to give way to organization and monopoly.

To be sure, between the Civil War and the New Deal efforts were made to reduce tariffs, but they were, for the most part, ineffective. A slight reduction was made in 1872, only to be restored three years later. The Democratic victory in 1892 produced the lower levels of the Tariff Act of 1894, which provided, however, for some rate increases as well as reductions. President Cleveland refused to sign the Act, and its chief significance was to demonstrate the extent to which local interests of a protectionist nature had honeycombed even the Democratic Party. The 1912 Bull Moose insurgency within the Republican Party originated, in part, in a protest against the high rates of the Payne-Aldrich tariff of 1909. Meanwhile, dissatisfaction with legislative tariff making was mounting. In 1909, President Taft appointed a Tariff Board to help him exercise his discretionary powers under the tariff act of that year, but the board came to an untimely end in 1912 when Congress failed to make appropriations for its continuance.

With a Democratic victory in 1912, a reversal of the traditional high-tariff policy seemed probable. Party leaders had promised "a competitive tariff," which seemed to mean that tariff rates would be designed, not to exclude foreign goods, but to enable American producers to compete with foreign producers on "equal terms." While the formula was evasive, the Underwood Act of 1913, which sought to implement it, marked the first important tariff reduction in over fifty years. The difficulties of deciding what rates made a tariff truly "competitive" led to the creation in 1916 of the Tariff Commission, a bipartisan, fact-finding body to furnish accurate information to guide legislative judgment. Not authorized to recommend policies or to suggest rates, it was only an information-gathering body. Under war conditions it had little influence. In fact, World War I largely nullified tariff reductions. Wartime disturbances in foreign trade, by cutting off or restricting imports from other industrial countries, gave greatly increased protection to many American industries.

After the Armistice, nationalist sentiments and business interests combined to oppose any downward revision of tariffs and, indeed, pressed for new increases. American manufacture of certain products such as dyestuffs and other chemicals had so greatly expanded during the war as to establish practically new industries. These "war babies" stressed their infancy and argued that without protection they would be unable to withstand competition from Germany. Other industries made much of the danger of "dumping" from European countries with depreciated currencies.

Furthermore, farmers, suffering from a severe price collapse in 1920–1921, demanded protection against imports of Canadian, Argentine, and other foodstuffs and raw materials. The Republican victory in 1920 was the signal for upward tariff revision. Insurgent elements in the Republican Party were weak. Farmers were reconciled to high duties on manufactured goods by the promise of protection for agriculture. The Emergency Tariff Act of 1921 and the Fordney-McCumber Act of 1922 inaugurated a new era of protectionism. Tariff levels were higher than ever before.

A feature first found in the Act of 1922 was the so-called flexible provision. Intended to transfer part of the task of tariff revision from Congress to the executive, it gave the President power to raise or lower duties by as much as 50 per cent of the statutory rate. This power was to be exercised only if investigation by the Tariff Commission showed that changes were necessary to equalize differences between foreign and domestic costs of production. The new machinery was cumbersome and impractical. "Costs of production" vary from those of the marginal producer to those of the most efficient. The Act did not make clear which were to be considered, either at home or abroad. Consequently, compilations of cost data and comparisons of costs were hard to make. The hope of some tariff reformers that the new presidential power would be used extensively to lower rates was delusive. In the next eight years, duties were changed on only thirty-nine commodities out of twenty-eight hundred listed in tariff schedules, and only six of these changes were downward. Tariff revision was not a serious political issue during the twenties. Largely financed by loans abroad, exports boomed, but few realized that the shift of the United States from debtor to creditor status required a modification of tariff policy if debts were to be serviced and repaid. Businessmen and the general public were content to let well enough alone. Presidents Coolidge and Hoover exerted their influence to maintain statutory rates, not to tamper with them.

The depression which began in 1929 served to stiffen even more the American protective system. In 1930, the Hawley-Smoot Tariff Act raised import duties well above the already high 1922 levels. Although more than a thousand economists petitioned President Hoover to veto the bill, he approved it somewhat reluctantly and the bill became law. The results were disastrous. The disparity between agricultural and industrial prices was widened. The raising of barriers against foreign goods made debt payments difficult and helped inaugurate a series of debt repudiations abroad. At the same time, the Act provoked retaliatory measures which contributed to the decline of world trade and the ensuing global depression. During 1931 and 1932, a wave of tariff increases and quota restrictions swept across the world, reinforced the tendency toward autarchy, and sharpened political and economic bitterness among nations. American exports declined from $5.2 billion in 1929 to $1.6 billion in 1933, while imports fell from $4.4 billion to $1.5 billion. During Hoover's last year, imports were further restricted by import excise taxes on lumber, coal, copper, crude petroleum, and petroleum products. The Roosevelt administration at first continued this policy by extending import excise taxes to some agricultural products.

On taking power, the Democrats were split on tariff policy. One wing, led by Secretary of State Cordell Hull, wanted to move in the direction of freer trade and to reduce duties sharply. Another wing, particularly strong in the councils of the National Recovery Administration and Agricultural Adjustment Administration, desired a high tariff wall to protect New Deal experiments in price-raising from disturbances abroad.[5] In these circumstances it was uncertain where congressional tariff revision, once initiated, might lead. The dilemma was resolved by making tariff rates a subject for negotiation with other countries and accordingly delegating to the President the power to revise duties. The Trade Agreements Act of 1934, initiating a quarter of a century of tariff revision downward, authorized the President to negotiate executive agreements not requiring Senate ratification. These agreements could lower duties by not more than 50 per cent in exchange for corresponding concessions on American exports. Articles on the free list could not be transferred to the dutiable list, and vice versa. Tariff reductions in a trade agreement are applicable, by the most-favored-nation clause incorporated in the statute, to the goods of all countries, except those which discriminate against American commerce.

The Trade Agreements program proved to be an effective political technique for reducing duties. Transfer of the power of revision from Congress to the executive changed the criteria of policy and the environment of policy making. Congressmen necessarily are more concerned with the particularistic interests

[5] Section 3(e) of the National Industrial Recovery Act gave the President power to exclude, limit, and control imports when it appeared after investigation by the Tariff Commission that the effect of such imports might be "to render ineffective or seriously to endanger the maintenance of any code. . . ."

of their constituencies, while the President, serving the broadest of constituencies, is more concerned with the general impact, at home and abroad, of trade policy. Congress tends to focus on the particular product or industry seeking protection, while the executive must consider the impact of high tariff barriers on our exports and on foreign relations. In contrast with legislative tariff making, where logrolling unites a multitude of local interests behind one omnibus measure, executive tariff bargaining involves piecemeal revision of rates and makes possible the isolation of protected interests. At the same time, by providing for expansion of exports, it induces exporting interests, which expect to benefit by the reciprocal agreements, to rally to the support of the agreements and to counteract the opposition of those who claim to be injured by the concessions the agreement contains.

Between 1934 and 1935, trade agreements were negotiated with twenty-nine countries. The Act was renewed in 1937, 1940, and 1943. In a further extension in 1945, the President's power was increased by authorizing him to lower tariffs by as much as 50 per cent of the rates prevailing on January 1, 1945, thus allowing a total reduction from Smoot-Hawley levels of as much as 75 per cent on rates already reduced to the limit before 1945.

During the postwar period, the Act has been renewed only after bitter legislative battles in which Congress, feeling the strong pressure of industries believing themselves threatened by tariff concessions, has acted only under the spur of urgent presidential appeals. Shifting regional positions have made it more difficult for Congress to make decisions on tariff policy. Some Southern areas, for example, formerly favoring freer trade, have become protectionist as textile mills and chemical plants were established in them, while other interests, such as the Detroit Chamber of Commerce, now desire freer trade in the hope of expanding vehicle and machinery exports. Congressional reluctance to maintain the Trade Agreements program has been evidenced by short renewals and restrictive amendments.

The program was extended again in 1948, but a "peril-point" amendment required that the Tariff Commission investigate the articles on which negotiations are being considered and report to the President what amount of concession, if any, may be granted without causing or threatening serious injury to domestic industries, or whether increases are required. The President may negotiate beyond these peril points only by filing a special report with the relevant congressional committees; in practice they have not been exceeded. Public hearings, moreover, must precede the completion of any agreement. The peril-point amendment was repealed in 1949 after President Truman had made this provision a campaign issue in the 1948 election. It was then restored by the Extension Act of 1951, which granted the program only a two-year additional life and also added an "escape clause." This clause enables any interested party to request the Tariff Commission to investigate and report to the President whether a concession already in effect is causing or threatening serious injury to domestic producers. If the Commission finds injury, it may recommend an adjustment in the tariff level.

All trade agreements must permit the withdrawal of concessions. The President may reject a Tariff Commission recommendation for escape-clause action, but must explain his reasons to the appropriate congressional committees. The tendency of Congress to renew the law for only one to four years at a time makes it difficult for the President to disregard Tariff Commission recommendations regularly, although a substantial number have been rejected. The program was given only a one-year renewal in 1953 at the request of the new Eisenhower administration, pending an examination of American policy by the (Randall) Commission on Foreign Economic Policy. This commission endorsed the reciprocal agreements program, and the President, conscious of a need to reassure other nations of a more permanent American commitment to trade expansion, requested a three-year renewal and broader powers in 1954. The congressional calendar was too crowded to permit adequate consideration in that year; a one-year renewal of the old program was enacted as an interim measure. The President repeated his request for longer-term action in 1955.

Congress then responded with the desired three-year renewal and the grant of broader powers, but only after an intense legislative battle in which the protectionist forces—notably Southern textile interests, independent oil producers, coal operators, wool growers, and chemical and bicycle manufacturers—brought to bear heavy pressure in opposition. The House approved by a margin of only one vote a closed rule on debate necessary to protect the bill from crippling amendments on the floor. To the President's previous powers, the 1955 law added authority to reduce rates by as much as 5 per cent in each of the three following years, or to reduce to 50 per cent rates which exceed that proportion of the value of the import. At the same time, however, the Senate added amendments making it easier for domestic industries to appeal for higher rates when they can show injury. A further amendment authorized special protection through either tariffs or import quotas on a finding that excessive imports of any commodity "threaten to impair the national security." In 1958, after the advocates of liberal trade policies had shown greater political strength than had been expected, Congress enacted a four-year renewal. It granted the President authority to negotiate additional tariff reductions of up to 20 per cent, but the protectionist forces secured a more extensive national-security provision and a clause permitting Congress to override, by a two-thirds vote, a Presidential rejection of a Tariff Commission recommendation for escape-clause action to protect a domestic industry.

Despite the political vicissitudes it has encountered, executive tariff making through international negotiation has thus far stood the test of time and has significantly altered the character of American trade policy. The emphasis on negotiation rather than unilateral protection of individual domestic interests has been especially marked since the adoption in 1947 of the General Agreement on Tariffs and Trade (GATT), which now includes thirty-seven countries.[6] Tariff levels have been greatly reduced, the average rate on dutiable imports during 1956 being 11.3 per cent, compared with 53 per cent in 1930–1933. Protectionist sentiment is still powerful, and more major congressional battles can be expected. Nevertheless, although there are still many cases of highly protected industries, the role of the tariff as an instrument for governmental promotion of American business has been greatly diminished.

3. The Merchant Marine and American Shipping Policy

Government aid to ship ownership and construction provides another case study in business promotionalism. Solicitude for American shipping interests was manifested at the very first session of Congress in 1789. Under legislation enacted in that year, only ships built in the United States and belonging to American citizens could register under the American flag; goods imported in American vessels were granted a 10 per cent reduction in customs duties; and the imposition of a discriminatory tonnage tax had the effect of reserving the coastal trade for American vessels. Under this stimulus, shipyards thrived, and the merchant marine expanded rapidly. The outbreak of war in

[6] See Chapter 28.

Europe created new opportunities for American shipping as the merchant fleets of the belligerents suffered serious losses. Between 1789 and 1810, American tonnage engaged in foreign trade increased from 123,893 tons to 981,000 tons.[7]

The War of 1812 dealt American shipping a heavy blow, but after the war the merchant marine resumed its growth, though at a slower pace than before. By 1855, American tonnage in foreign trade totaled 2,348,000 tons. Until wooden ships were displaced by their iron rivals in the late 1850's and the 1860's, American shipyards and the merchant marine remained prosperous and held their own in competition with the rest of the world. American shipping policy, meanwhile, moved in a liberal direction. The Navigation Act of 1817, to be sure, excluded foreign vessels from the American coastal trade. But in a large number of bilateral treaties of friendship, commerce, and navigation, the United States repealed discriminatory duties and taxes on vessels engaged in foreign trade in exchange for similar concessions by other countries.

Direct subsidies were first used after Britain had provided a mail subsidy to aid Samuel Cunard in establishing passenger steamship service to this country in 1840. In 1845 Congress authorized mail subsidies, with preference to be given to steamships which could be converted into vessels of war. Between 1847 and 1858, over $14 million was spent on subsidies to help establish steamship service to Bremen, Le Havre, Liverpool, Panama, Oregon, and Cuba. The first experience with subsidies was unsatisfactory. Some lines fell into financial difficulties and pressed for increased aid. Subsidies appeared to many as an unnecessary drain on the public treasury. In 1858 they were discontinued.

After the Civil War, the American merchant marine began a decline which continued down to World War I. With the triumph of the iron ship, ship construction became considerably cheaper in Great Britain than in the United States. High tariffs on shipbuilding materials contributed to this disparity. As a result, shipowners pressed for a "free ship" policy, the right to purchase ships abroad and sail them under the American flag. Shipbuilders vigorously contested this policy, suggesting instead that the higher costs of American construction be met by government subsidy. For a short period after the Civil War (1865–1874), mail subsidies were revived. They were granted to steamship lines serving Brazil, Hawaii, and the Far East. The trade expansion expected to result from the Brazil line never developed.

[7] Paul M. Zeis, *American Shipping Policy* (1938), pp. 4–6.

The subsidies to the Pacific Mail Line produced one of the worst scandals of the Grant era, bringing the whole subsidy program into disrepute. In 1874 all subsidy contracts were terminated.

During the next two decades, while our foreign trade fleet shrank, the battle between "free ships" and subsidies continued. A curious realignment of interests developed. Coastal shipowners, then representing the bulk of the American merchant marine, opposed "free ships" lest they be permitted to enter the coastal trade. Some ship operators in foreign trade joined forces with shipbuilders and manufacturers of steel and other shipbuilding materials to call for subsidies. This policy was espoused by the Republican Party. A few adamant shipowners in foreign trade continued to press for "free ships" with the backing of agricultural interests in the Democratic Party, but they failed to enlist sufficient support.[8]

The Ocean Mail Act of 1891 restored mail subsidies, but in much smaller amounts than subsidy advocates had hoped. The Act remained in force until 1928, by which time $29.6 million had been spent. More than half of this total went to the American Line, operating between New York and England. Few new lines were established, and the Act did not appreciably enlarge the merchant marine. After McKinley's election in 1896, the drive for larger subsidies increased in vigor. But despite powerful support from the dominant Republican leadership, new direct subsidies could not be obtained. Indirect aid, however, was made available. In 1898 and 1899 Congress expanded the coastal monopoly by reserving all trade between the United States, Hawaii, and Puerto Rico for American shipping.

Democratic and Progressive strength in Congress after 1909 shifted the emphasis of policy from promotion to regulation and control. The Panama Canal Act of 1912 introduced a limited free ship policy,[9] but its benefits were not sufficient to induce

[8] The "free ship" group won several minor victories. The tariff of 1890 permitted free importation of iron and steel plate for shipbuilding, and the tariff of 1894 extended the free list to include all shipbuilding material. But ships so constructed could engage in the coastal trade only two months a year. This effectively discouraged purchase.

[9] The Act allowed foreign-built vessels not over five years old to operate under American registry in foreign, but not in coastal, trade. Such vessels were eligible for mail contracts. All shipbuilding material was allowed entry duty free, and vessels constructed from such material could engage in the coastal trade without restriction. The policy with regard to shipbuilding material was later reversed by the Tariff Act of 1922, which required payment of regular duty rates.

American shipowners operating under foreign registry to transfer to the American flag. The Seamen's Act of 1915 ameliorated conditions of employment at sea. The Shipping Board Act of 1916 then tried to regulate shipping combinations and to outlaw discriminatory practices by giving the Shipping Board power to "disapprove, cancel, or modify" agreements made by common carriers.

Meanwhile, World War I changed the character of the shipping problem. The United States was faced with a severe shortage of merchant shipping. Ship registry laws were liberalized to admit foreign-built ships owned by American citizens. In 1916 a Shipping Board was established with power to create an Emergency Fleet Corporation, which in turn was authorized to purchase, construct, and operate ships in foreign commerce. The corporation's activities were not to extend more than five years after the end of the war. Total appropriations amounted to approximately $3 billion. This gigantic emergency shipbuilding program was costly, wasteful, inefficient, and slow. Construction was undertaken through private contractors, many of them without any previous shipbuilding experience. Profit levels were extremely high. Of a projected building program of eighteen million tons, less than one-sixth, most of it already under construction when the Fleet Corporation began operations, was delivered before the Armistice. Indeed, the program had just begun to get well under way when the Armistice was signed, and more than one-third of the Shipping Board fleet was begun after the War was over. Meanwhile, surplus construction materials were disposed of at small fractions of their cost.

When the Republicans returned to power, stress was again laid on the promotion of private shipping interests. The Merchant Marine Act of 1920 established a new Shipping Board and directed it to sell the government-owned ships as soon as possible. If unable to sell them, the Board was to charter ships to private companies or to operate them itself. The Act also set up a fund of $25 million for loans to aid private companies to build new ships. The Shipping Board moved rapidly to dismantle the government fleet. Between 1921 and 1928, it sold 1,164 ships for $17 or $18 a ton, a small fraction of the original cost. Ships costing $516 million were disposed of for about $41 million. Many vessels, some still in good condition, were sold for scrap, and much of the remaining fleet was withdrawn from operation in order not to compete with private enterprise. By August 31, 1925, only 228 active cargo and 15 passenger vessels were still under government ownership; most of these were operated by managing agents under contracts guaranteeing the operators against loss. The Mail Subsidy Act of 1928 further assisted the private shipping industry. The construction loan fund was increased to $250 million, and the terms of loans were made easier. Liberalized mail subsidies were gradually increased from $9 million in 1929 to $29 million in 1934. With generous subsidies available, the remaining lines owned or operated by the government became attractive to private interests, and the Shipping Board hastened to offer them for sale. Some sales were made under conditions which laid the Board open to charges of gross favoritism. The subsidy program developed numerous abuses. Subsidies were diverted into high salaries, excessive dividends, and profits for affiliates of the parent shipping company, instead of going into maintenance or new construction. Between 1921 and 1935, American tonnage in foreign trade shrank from eleven to four million tons. Very little new construction was undertaken. By 1935 the American foreign trade fleet was rapidly becoming obsolete.

A new phase in arrangements for shipping was inaugurated by the Merchant Marine Act of 1936, which still provides the legislative framework for current policies. Mail subsidies were abandoned in favor of direct subsidies. The newly established United States Maritime Commission was authorized to grant two types of subsidy: one for construction and the other for operation. Both subsidies were to be determined by the differences between foreign and domestic costs, a somewhat uncertain measuring rod. Additional operating subsidies could be paid to offset foreign subsidies. Safeguards were included to prevent a repetition of the abuses which had discredited the mail-subsidy system. If subsidies failed to stimulate a rebirth of the American merchant marine, the Maritime Commission was empowered to construct ships on its own account, sell or charter them if possible, and operate them itself if necessary.

The Merchant Marine Act of 1936 thus continued the policy of subsidizing private shipping but also authorized government ownership and operation. By 1940 the Maritime Commission had disposed of the last of the World War I vessels, but, spurred by the desire to expand employment, as well as to revive the moribund shipping industry, it also launched a program for the construction of five hundred ships in ten years. It took delivery of a C-2 vessel in 1939, the first cargo ship built in American yards in eighteen years. By mid-1940, contracts had been let for 159 vessels, and 42 had been completed. This program was soon dwarfed by the staggering demands of World War II, when the Commission supervised construction of 4,915 merchant ships with a gross tonnage of 37 million—one of the most remarkable production achievements of the period.[10] By 1945, four-fifths of all the tonnage being built in the world slid down American ways. At first the Commission operated a few of these vessels, but in 1942 the War Shipping Administration was created to purchase or charter all private merchant ships. Thereafter it received all ships built for the Commission, but it then chartered them for operation by private companies.

After the war slightly more than one-half of the world's merchant tonnage flew the American flag. Since then there has been a drastic decline in both American shipping and ship construction. By 1955 the active U.S. fleet was only 14.3 per cent of the world's total, and the annual gross tonnage of ships built had declined from 12.5 million in 1943 to 105,000 in 1955.[11] Indeed, since American costs both for construction and for operation greatly exceed costs in other countries, the industries were able to survive only because of major government aid.

At the end of hostilities about half of the merchant fleet was put in the inactive reserve under the jurisdiction of the National Shipping Authority, an agency of the Maritime Administration. Occasionally, as happened during the Korean conflict, ships are withdrawn from its fleet and put in active service. Most of the remaining fleet was sold at bargain prices, with preferences given to American citizens. In 1950 the Maritime Commission, then under criticism for managerial inefficiencies, was transferred to the Department of Commerce and renamed the Federal Maritime Board. It is under some, but not full, departmental control by the Secretary of Commerce.

Current construction-subsidy programs are still carried out within the general framework of the 1936 Act. The Merchant Ship Sales Act of 1946 contains a stronger declaration of policy on shipbuilding, but the substantive provisions are unchanged. Where the 1936 Act only required that the merchant marine be "constructed in the United States," the later Act declares that the needs of national defense and of commerce require "efficient American-owned facilities for shipbuilding and repair."

[10] W. Gorter, United States Shipping Policy (1956), p. 212. The tonnage built during World War I had been 2.3 million, and an additional 6.5 million had been delivered in the three years after the war.
[11] Ibid., pp. 15, 212–213.

The subsidy basis still used is the construction differential, which permits the Board to pay not more than 50 per cent of the construction costs. Subsidies average about 45 per cent and are in addition to governmental payments for national defense features not essential to commercial operation but desirable for military uses.[12] The program is expensive—from 1936 to 1953, $421 million were spent to subsidize the construction of 247 vessels, and in 1955 the Maritime Administrator forecast ship construction plans over the next fifteen years adding up to $1.2 billion (presumably involving a subsidy of about $540 million).[13] Yet even with such an expenditure, the annual building rate would be only about ten ships, while a year earlier the Undersecretary of Commerce had concluded that sixty ships a year must be built to preserve even the nucleus of a shipbuilding industry.[14]

In addition, construction is encouraged under the 1936 Act by easy payment plans—long-term, low-interest, insured mortgages, and generous trade-in allowances on obsolete vessels. These aids, as well as construction subsidies, are predicated on the assumption that the American shipbuilding industry is essential to national defense and so must be assisted even though it cannot compete in a world market.

Yet policy suffers from a confusion of goals. Maintenance of a merchant marine and of a shipbuilding industry are two distinct objectives. Public policy has attempted to promote building through aids to the shipping lines, using construction subsidies as a means of enabling operators to buy American-built ships at competitive prices rather than as a direct aid to shipbuilders. Thus construction aids accrue in the first instance to the shipowners. Builders benefit only if these inducements—construction subsidies, easy-payment plans, etc.—are sufficient to persuade shipowners to order more vessels. Since shipping lines now possess enough adequate, if middle-aged, vessels, such indirect aids may not produce new orders. Faced with a parallel, although less acute, problem before the war, the Maritime Commission developed new designs, ordered prototypes, and then had

[12] The price of the superliner United States, for example, was about $70 million, of which the government's share was $42 million, $18 million representing the subsidy and $24 million national defense features. In the controversial case of American Export Lines' Constitution and Independence, the company paid $14 million on each, and the government about $9.4 million each.

[13] Gorter, op. cit., p. 48.

[14] Department of Commerce, Office of Undersecretary for Transportation, Maritime Subsidy Policy (1954), p. 29.

vessels built for its own account. The Maritime Administration did the same with the postwar construction of the Mariner class vessels, thereby keeping its shipyards busy. If a shipbuilding industry indeed remains a vital matter for national security, despite the changes in military technology, the question arises whether similar direct stimulation, rather than indirect aid, might not support it more efficiently and at lesser expense.

The operating differential subsidy has been a much more effective device in maintaining the merchant marine. Where aid is required to meet foreign competition and to promote commerce on an essential trade route, the Maritime Administration will pay the difference between foreign and domestic operating costs, provided the American ship is not more than twenty years old. To guard against excess profits, the government can recapture, after a ten-year period, half of a subsidized operator's profits in excess of a 10 per cent return on his capital employed in shipping. Since only costs are subsidized, leaving the operator dependent on his own efforts to secure revenues, the scheme does not guarantee profits. The authors of the 1936 legislation sought to avoid a repetition of the mail-pay scandals under the Act of 1928 by imposing stringent accounting and financial requirements as well as by not guaranteeing a profit. They avoided conflict with the Reciprocal Trade Agreements program by protecting American-flag lines from the lower costs of competitors without directly limiting sales of foreign shipping services. They felt that the public would be better served by a direct, calculable aid than by a hidden subsidy. In recent years, annual subsidy payments, after deducting estimated recaptures, have run to about $60 million. About half of the American-flag ships are subsidized, and their subsidies cover about one-tenth of their cost and amount to about one-third of their pretax profits.[15]

A further aid to shipowners, especially those not receiving operating subsidies, has been the imposition of cargo-preference rules on government-financed shipments abroad. These rules date back to at least 1934, when Congress required that goods exported under Reconstruction Finance Corporation (RFC), Export-Import Bank, or other government loans be carried in American bottoms. But with the enormous expansion of American military and economic activities abroad after World War II, cargo-preference requirements came to be of major importance. Although these rules have aroused vigorous criticism abroad and some opposition at home,[16] Congress has continued to impose

[15] Gorter, op. cit., pp. 95, 98.
[16] For example, both the Gray and the Randall Reports condemned them.

them, listening sympathetically to the pleas of shipping interests and maritime labor unions.[17] Accordingly, all shipments to the Armed Forces overseas must go in American-flag ships, and all cargoes financed by government grants or loans are subject to at least "50–50" division between American and foreign vessels. In the period 1952–1954 about two-fifths of the outbound dry cargoes carried by American ships were traceable to these requirements, which added significantly to the costs of the foreign-aid programs.[18]

This promotional device lacks the clear-cut rationale of the operating subsidy. It is blunt; its hidden costs are unknown; and its promotional results are unfocused. Its main effect is to keep at sea a fleet of middle-aged, slow Liberty ships of only moderate defense value. It arbitrarily restricts the competition of foreign ships, and since the aid recipient designates who is to carry the cargo not carried by American ships, it often bars third nations from performing any of the shipping. It invites foreign criticism and retaliation, and embarrasses American efforts to lower international trade barriers.

Cabotage restrictions, which grant American-flag ships a monopoly on intercoastal and coastwide trades, have been made less significant by economic changes. While in 1924 this monopoly provided employment for over four million gross tons of ships, today only a million tons of shipping find these routes profitable. This change has resulted from altered patterns of production and distribution, technological improvements in trucking and railroads, and increased relative costs of ocean shipping. Government efforts to expand domestic ocean trade could succeed only at the price of injuring land carriers.

The combined effect of all these aids has been to keep an American merchant marine afloat on some scale. Yet the results fall short of some of the stated policy objectives, and the basic objectives themselves remain far from clear. At one time or another, government assistance to shipping has been justified on commercial, employment, and military grounds.[19] The main commercial objective, continuity of service for American shippers on all major routes, has in fact been promoted by the operating

Report to the President on Foreign Economic Policies (1950), p. 89; Commission on Foreign Economic Policy, Report to the President and the Congress (1954), p. 69.

[17] In 1954, by amendment to the 1936 Act, Congress permanently required a 50-50 sharing of all foreign-aid cargo.
[18] Gorter, op. cit., pp. 110–111.
[19] U.S. Maritime Commission, Economic Survey of the American Merchant Marine (1937), p. 5.

subsidies, but not by the building subsidies or the cargo-preference rules. The maintenance of employment, which was a major consideration in the thirties, has seemed less pressing in postwar circumstances.

It is the needs of national defense which, added to the interests of the direct beneficiaries, have engendered consistent congressional support for the subsidy programs. In the eyes of the defense planners, however, the results have been inadequate. In 1955, the American-flag merchant fleet was between two and five million deadweight tons short of estimated defense requirements; it was continuing to decline in numbers, in tonnage, and in share of trade.[20] Despite the subsidies, some American shipowners have found it advantageous to register a large fraction of their fleets under Liberian, Panamanian, and other flags where they could avoid the stringent and expensive requirements of inspection and working conditions imposed on American-flag shipping.

Moreover, the validity of the defense argument, which received strong support from the experiences of both world wars, has now come into question. A nuclear war would hardly permit the slow mobilization of shipbuilding facilities to create an emergency fleet, while in a limited war shipping seems unlikely to be a major bottleneck. Even assuming a large-scale but not unlimited war, involving heavy shipping losses, it is argued by our maritime allies, for some of whom merchant shipping is a major earner of foreign exchange, that their vessels would be equally available with our own in a wartime pool. Flag discrimination and subsidies, in their view, undermine the economic base of the alliance by reducing their ability to earn dollars in one major industry where they possess clear cost advantages.

The conclusion seems inescapable that the goals of policy require more precise definition and the means a more direct relation to the objectives.

4. Public Aids to Domestic Transportation

The transportation industry has also been a major object of government promotion. Railroads, water carriers, motor carriers, and air carriers have all enjoyed public aid in greater or lesser degree and continue to vie with each other for favorable treatment. The character of the aid extended has varied with the particular mode of transportation.

[20] Gorter, *op. cit.*, pp. 84–89, 91, 94.

Public Aids to Railroads

Railroads first benefited from public support, then fell from favor, and finally witnessed new competing modes of transportation claiming an increasing share of public bounty. Before 1850, government aid to the railroads was largely state and local. While Congress regularly defeated bills proposing direct subsidies in the form of land grants—in part because of constitutional scruples, in part because of the local character of the aid sought—it did extend such indirect aids as mail contracts, cuts in the import duties on iron rails, and grants of rights-of-way over public lands.

The great era of federal railway land grants opened in the second half of the nineteenth century. Beginning with the Illinois Central in 1850 and extending through 1871, hardly a session of Congress passed without some grant. This era reached a peak in the years 1862–1866, when over 100 million acres were given to railroads. This was the period of the Pacific railway charters, when the rush to span the continent was in full swing, and a fever of speculative railroad building seized the nation. Then opposition began to mount. Congress had earlier encouraged the railroads as a means of opening up the West to settlement and of binding together the newer and older parts of the nation. Once the railroads were established, the feeling grew that the public lands should be reserved for actual settlement. Railroad scandals and the not-unfounded conviction that some land grants were little more than swindles abetted this reversal of opinion. In 1870 the House of Representatives resolved that land grants cease, and a strong movement was launched for the forfeiture of land by railroads which had been unable to meet the required conditions. Meanwhile, the grand total of federal and state land grants received by the railroads amounted to approximately 183 million acres.[21]

After 1871 public aid to railroads became of relatively minor importance for some time. In the 1920's, when railroad plant and equipment had been worn down during the World War I period of government management, and rates were lagging behind rising costs, the federal government lent more than $350 million to the railroads. During the Great Depression promotional activity took on the character of salvage. Both the Public Works Administration and the Reconstruction Finance Cor-

[21] Federal Co-ordinator of Transportation, *Public Aids to Transportation* (1940), Vol. 1, p. 13.

poration bailed out desperate or bankrupt railroads with loans for maintenance and equipment, for refunding, and even to meet current expenses.

Government promotionalism has not been an undiluted boon to the railroads. For one thing, promotion often leads to regulation. The movement to regulate the railroads, which led to the state Granger Laws and the Interstate Commerce Act of 1887,[22] received much of its impetus from a popular conviction that the roads had improperly profited from land grants and other public aids. Although only a few roads were built with land-grant aid—five companies or their predecessors received more than two-thirds of this aid—all railroads suffered from the reaction against the land-grant abuses. When the RFC made its loans in a later period, it required borrowing roads to change their financial practices.

Furthermore, the government received substantial reductions in rates paid to land-grant railroads for the transportation of official property and military personnel. When this privilege was abandoned on October 1, 1946, total government savings were estimated to have run as high as $1.5 billion.

Estimates of the value of the public aids given railroads vary widely. While it is clear that sales of land granted them yielded the roads about $440 million, the value of other public aids is impossible to determine. One government agency, operating in the early 1930's, estimated the value of all government aid to be $1,503 million. A few years later, another, using different and, on the whole, more reasonable assumptions, put the figure at $624 million.[23]

These past subsidies, finally, are now found by the railroads to be present political liabilities. Enjoying little public aid, they suffer from the competition of means of transportation which are subsidized. When, in the political economy of transportation, the rails assail the public aids extended to their competitors and raise the cry of unfair competition, their arguments are often blunted by opposition references to the aids railroads once received. In the main, the railroads today ask, not for subsidies, but for an end to subsidies to other forms of transportation.[24]

[22] See Chapter 10, below.

[23] Federal Co-ordinator, *op. cit.*, Vol. 2; Board of Investigation and Research, *Public Aids to Transportation* (1945), H. Doc. 159, 79th Cong., 1st sess.

[24] In 1958, however, a number of hard-pressed railroads asked state and local governments to subsidize unprofitable commuter lines, and Congress authorized the Interstate Commerce Commission to guarantee $500 million in loans to railroads for the maintenance or purchase of equipment.

Public Aid to Water Carriers

Inland-waterway transportation is a branch of commerce where private enterprise completely depends for its existence on sizeable government aids. Promotionalism has created the industry. With the exception of the Great Lakes system, where nature has done most of the engineering work and where shipping has flourished since the middle of the nineteenth century, inland waterways have grown and declined in response to a mixture of economic and political factors.

The opening of the Erie Canal in 1825 marked the beginning of an age of great canal and river prosperity and inaugurated an era of canal construction which reached its height between 1830 and 1840. The major vehicle of inland commerce, the canals, were an object of state expenditures from the beginning. And between 1827 and 1866 the federal government granted 6.3 million acres of public lands to aid canal building or river improvements.

Between the Civil War and the turn of the century, inland waterways languished, unable to compete with the growing network of railroads. Expenditures on waterway improvements declined. Toward the end of this period, dissatisfaction with railroad rates and a belief that water transportation could provide cheaper service and operate as an effective regulator of the railroads led to a revival of interest. In 1903 New York decided to rebuild the Erie Canal, and in 1907 President Roosevelt appointed an Inland Waterways Commission to prepare a plan for improving inland waterways. Large expenditures were made after 1910. In the century before 1890, the federal government had spent $214 million for waterway development, but between 1890 and 1931 it spent about $1,370 million.[25] Total state and local expenditures for canals, terminals, and other waterway improvements up to 1936 were $1,250 million.[26] Because of the desire to prime the pump and stimulate employment, federal activities were sharply stepped up in the 1930's, when $1,164 million were appropriated.[27] The political appeal of such "pork-barrel" legislation contributed to a resumption of this faster pace of expenditures after World War II. By the end of 1951, total public aid had mounted to about $4.6 billion, and annual federal expenditures were averaging about a quarter of a billion dollars.[28]

[25] H. G. Moulton, et al., The American Transportation Problem (1933), pp. 434–438.
[26] Federal Co-ordinator, op. cit., Vol. 1, p. 20.
[27] Board of Investigation and Research, op. cit., p. 326.
[28] Domestic Land and Water Transportation (1951), S. Rept. 1039, 82d Cong., 1st sess., pp. 31, 72.

This large annual subsidy is more easily explained in terms of politics than of economics. With the exception of the Great Lakes system, which produces remarkably cheap transportation, most of the inland waterways are expensive when all costs are taken into account. While no recent cost studies are available, research conducted about 1936 showed that total costs of water transportation were seldom lower than rail charges.[29] In this computation, there was added to the cost of performing the actual transportation the annual cost (depreciation, maintenance, imputed interest) of the navigational improvements provided by government, excluding traffic not requiring the improvements. On this basis it found, for example, that the full economic costs per ton on an average haul on the lower Mississippi was $5.97, compared with rail costs of $3.81. On the Black Warrior River in Alabama, it was $2.83, while rail costs were $2.17. On the Ohio River, full water costs were lower than rail on coal, but higher on iron, steel, and petroleum products. The costs of government improvements alone were 5 cents a ton-mile on the upper Mississippi, and 2½ cents on the Illinois waterway, compared with average rail charges of slightly less than 1 cent.[30]

Despite the fact that waterways were toll-free, so that taxpayers, not carriers, paid their cost, private enterprise was slow to use them. Private and contract carriers transporting heavy goods— petroleum products, coal, ore, sand and gravel, etc.—gradually increased their tonnage, but it was difficult to lure common carriers into the field. In an attempt to demonstrate the profitability of common carriage and to encourage the establishment of joint rail-barge rates, Congress in 1924 established the Inland Waterways Corporation to continue the barge-line operations on the Mississippi and the Black Warrior rivers first begun by the Army in World War I. The operation did not prove profitable.[31] In 1950, the corporation showed an accumulated deficit of $7 million, a figure which understated actual losses by several millions. In 1953, the corporation was sold to a private firm.

Thus, despite substantial tonnage increases in recent years, an economic justification for large waterway subsidies is difficult to establish. Even in 1955, inland waterways other than the Great Lakes carried only 7.6 per cent of all intercity freight.[32] Water-

---

[29] To be sure, water traffic has increased greatly since then, and some projects had only partially been completed, but there have also been great additional expenditures.

[30] Federal Co-ordinator, op. cit., Vol. 3, pp. 86, 87, and under Table 37.

[31] Ibid., pp. 792–793; Federal Co-ordinator, op. cit., Vol. 3, pp. 211–298.

[32] In 1940 inland waterways other than the Great Lakes carried 22 billion

ways have had a significant impact on the rates of competing railroads, but with haphazard effects. Rate reductions have accrued to shippers able to avail themselves of water facilities; usually only a few firms, principally those transporting petroleum, coal, and iron ore, find it practicable to do so. At the same time, competitive handicaps have been placed on shippers without access to waterways. They may even suffer a double competitive disadvantage if railroads raise rates elsewhere to make up for rates lowered to meet water competition. Railroad resentment against subsidization of water carriers has produced demands, often seconded by economists and by some governmental reports,[33] that tolls be imposed on the use of water facilities, but so far with no results. Railroad pressure, however, did contribute to the enactment of the Transportation Act of 1940, which provided for more comprehensive regulation of water carriers.[34]

The explanation of these largely uneconomic results of waterway subsidies lies in the political machinery by which policy is made. Inland-waterway projects comprise a major share of "pork-barrel" appropriations, by which congressmen seek to demonstrate their worth to their constituents by maximizing governmental expenditures within their constituencies. Thus, concern with localized benefits, rather than broader economic considerations, tends to control the authorization of waterway projects.

Public Aid to Motor Carriers

One of the most intensively debated issues in transportation has been the question of whether motor carriers receive public aid. Railroad spokesmen have argued that the vast expenditures on public highways since World War I are a direct subsidy to motor carriers; the latter have replied that their industry has, through registration fees, gasoline taxes, and other charges and payments which have gone into the construction of public roads, met all the costs properly attributable to it. In the confusion of charge and countercharge, it has thus far been impossible to achieve any reconciliation.[35]

This issue and the related one of the impact of trucks on high-

---

ton-miles of freight, or 3.7 per cent of all intercity freight traffic. In 1955 they carried 97.7 billion ton-miles or 7.6 per cent. ICC, *Annual Report* (1941, 1956); Chief of Engineers, *Annual Report* (1941, 1956).

[33] For a list, see A. Maass, *Muddy Waters* (1951), p. 161.

[34] See Chapter 11.

[35] For an analysis of some of the problems confronted in attempts to allocate costs among various highway users, see Secretary of Commerce, *First Progress Report of the Highway Cost Allocation Study* (1957), 85th Cong., 1st sess., H. Doc. No. 106.

way safety and maintenance have underlain bitter political and public relations battles between railroads and truckers. In 1957, in a case arising out of the veto of a Pennsylvania law raising truck-load limits, a district judge found twenty-four Eastern railroads guilty of violating the Sherman Act by conspiring to destroy the competition of long-haul trucks.[36] Seeking to cripple interstate trucking in the Northeast by erecting a "Chinese wall" around Pennsylvania, the railroads had subsidized anti-truck articles in national magazines and operated through "front organizations" to give the semblance of grass-roots pressure. Trucker counterattacks have often been conducted on the same level.

While it may be that the motor-carrier industry as a whole does not receive public subsidies, this does not mean, of course, that it does not benefit from highway improvements. Naturally enough, it, together with such allied interests as motor-vehicle and tire manufacturers, oil companies, and the construction industry, were among the leading supporters of the Federal Aid Highway Act of 1956, which committed the government to the spending of $25 billion on the interstate highway system over the next thirteen years.

Public Aid to Air Carriers

The real beginnings of the American air-transport industry date from the Air Mail Act of 1925, and government aid has always played a vital part in its success. Between 1918 and 1926, the air-mail service was operated directly by the Post Office Department. The Act of 1925 provided for the award of mail contracts to private companies by competitive bidding. At first payments were limited to a maximum of four-fifths of air-mail revenue; no subsidy was envisaged. Subsequently, payments were increased and air-mail postage rates reduced. As a result, payments to air-mail carriers exceeded estimated air-mail revenue in 1929 by $9,345,000. Despite these aids, some mail contractors and most other air lines faced serious operating deficits early in 1930, and widespread abandonment of services was threatened.

In 1930 Congress enacted the Watres Act, providing for the issuance of route certificates in place of the air-mail contracts. It also established a more liberal formula for mail payment designed to encourage passenger traffic. The Act created an active demand for new service, and payments to air-mail carriers mounted to $19.5 million in 1933. Charges of collusion between mail carriers

[36] The background of the case is described in R. Bendiner, "The 'Engineering of Consent'—A Case Study," *The Reporter* (August 11, 1955), pp. 14–23.

and Post Office officials of the outgoing administration led to the cancellation of all air-mail contracts in 1934. After a short interval during which the Army flew the mails, experiencing a number of fatal accidents, the Air Mail Act of 1934 restored contract operations under competitive bidding. The level of compensation was lowered and a maximum of 40 cents per plane-mile was imposed. Payments to air-mail carriers exceeded estimated postal revenue for the four years from 1935 through 1938 by only a little more than $4 million; total payments increased from $9 million in 1935 to about $14 million in 1938.

Heavy losses suffered by the air carriers again produced a demand for more favorable legislation, and Congress responded with the Civil Aeronautics Act of 1938. As modified by an executive order in 1940, it established within the Department of Commerce a Civil Aeronautics Administration (CAA), which maintained the national airway system, planned and administered the airport program, and enforced safety, licensing, and traffic-control regulations. A semi-independent Civil Aeronautics Board (CAB) was charged with economic regulation, including the setting of air-mail payments and subsidies.[37] Under legislation enacted in 1958, the functions performed by the CAA were transferred to a newly created Federal Aviation Agency. This new body will develop and co-ordinate air navigation facilities for military as well as civilian aircraft. It will regulate use of air space, establish air traffic rules, and assume the regulatory powers over air safety formerly exercised by the CAB. The Board, however, will continue to investigate accidents.

The promotional activities of the CAA have consumed large federal appropriations and constitute a major, if indirect, subsidy to the scheduled air carriers, as well as to other civilian users of the airways. Through 1951, about $614 million had been spent in establishing, maintaining, and operating over 65,000 miles of federal airways.[38] In 1956, annual appropriations reached $75 million.[39] Although the CAA proposed a tax on aviation gasoline to help meet airway costs, air carriers now pay nothing for these government services. Military craft and private planes also use the airways, but just before World War II scheduled air carriers ac-

[37] For a discussion of its regulatory powers over entry and rates, see Chapter 11.

[38] B. N. Behling, "Subsidies to Transportation," Library of Congress, Legislative Reference Service, *Public Affairs Bulletin* (August, 1950), No. 86, pp. 42–43.

[39] Secretary of Commerce, *Annual Report*, 1956, p. 30.

counted for 24 per cent of their use.[40]

Airports typically have been constructed by state or local governments, but with substantial federal aid. Through 1949 it was estimated that about $1.5 billion had been invested in airports.[41] Under the Federal Airport Act of 1946, as amended in 1950 and 1955, a total of $236 million was appropriated in the fiscal years 1947–1955, and annual appropriations of $63 million were authorized for 1956–1959. These federal funds met half the costs of constructing and improving airports approved by the CAA. While there have been no recent studies of the subsidies involved, in 1940 it was estimated that scheduled air carriers could properly be charged with over one-fifth of the annual airport cost, while their payments for the use of airport facilities covered only about 18 per cent of their share of the cost.[42]

In addition to these indirect aids, the CAB also paid direct mail subsidies to scheduled carriers. The 1938 Act directed the CAB to set mail payments at an amount sufficient, when combined with other items of carrier revenue, to enable the carriers to function profitably. Until 1953, all air-mail payments were made by the Post Office and not separated into payments for service and subsidies, but in 1951, for example, the CAB estimated that about $75 million of the total of $125 million was subsidy.[43] An executive order in 1953 ordered a separation of subsidies from service payments and directed the CAB to pay the subsidies.

In the happy position of confronting steadily mounting passenger traffic, the CAB tried to eliminate subsidies among domestic trunk-line carriers and those flying abroad by allowing competition, through route extensions and new routes, only after carriers already serving a route had begun to make pre-subsidy profits. Similarly, new routes and route extensions expected to be profitable have usually been given to weak carriers to bolster their revenues.[44] Although this policy has delayed the development of competition and has prevented new carriers from entering the field, it has reduced subsidies. By 1956, only one domestic trunk-line carrier and only three of the seven carriers providing foreign service required subsidy.

In 1956, however, the CAB was still subsidizing local-service, or

[40] Civil Aviation, 78th Cong., 2d sess., H. Rept. No. 1893 (1944), p. 5. In 1955, air carriers accounted for over 30 per cent of traffic handled by CAA traffic-control towers. CAA, Statistical Handbook of Civil Aviation, 1956, p. 19.
[41] Behling, op. cit.
[42] Board of Investigation and Research, op. cit., pp. 78–80.
[43] CAB, Annual Report, 1953, p. 14.
[44] See Chapter 11.

feeder, lines, which serve the smaller cities and feed traffic into the points served by trunk-line carriers. These subsidies amounted to about $35 million, or double the sum this kind of service received in 1951. Feeder service was forced on the CAB by popular and congressional pressure on behalf of local business and other interests who argued that in the "air age" all communities had a right to air service. In 1944, despite doubts of its own staff about the profitability of feeder service, the Board declared that it was its duty to promote civil aviation and that it would allow qualified applicants the opportunity to develop such services. Between 1946 and 1949, it certificated feeders on a large scale. Because it did not wish to saddle itself with an unlimited liability for subsidies, it first issued only temporary three-year certificates. But most were subsequently given five-year extensions, and now about two-thirds of the several hundred local-service points have been permanently certificated, thereby committing the government to indefinite subsidization. Feeder lines have expanded greatly, and while the subsidy they require in proportion to their traffic has steadily decreased, the total subsidy obligation has increased.

Promotionalism has been remarkably successful in the achievement of its major objective—the rapid development of civil aviation. Total operating revenues of certificated carriers have grown from $90 million in 1940 to $1.6 billion in 1955. Revenue ton-miles flown grew from 250 million in 1943 to over three billion in 1955. This impressive growth owes much to vigorous promotional policies, yet government assistance in the form of indirect aids and direct subsidies does not disappear as the industry achieves relative maturity. Promotionalism is often hard to stop; it tends to become a permanent part of the economic environment of favored groups, and impressive political power can be summoned to its support. It also raises serious conflicts with regulatory policies designed to enable different modes of transportation to compete with each other on even terms.[45]

The Pattern of Public Policy

The history of public aids to transportation reveals an interesting pattern. In each case, public aid has been highly important in the developmental stages of the industry; in each case, public aid has been followed sooner or later by regulation. In the case of the railroads, aid was withdrawn as the industry expanded and grew prosperous, only to be renewed once again with the onset of a stage of decline and difficulties. The renewal of aid to water

[45] See Chapter 11.

carriers developed as an offset to the power of the railroads, though local vested interests supported its continuation long after the monopoly position of the railroads had been undermined by highway competition. In the case of motor carriers, the tendency has been to increase taxes and payments to the point where it becomes highly questionable whether any form of public subsidy is being received. Air carriers are passing from a developmental and subsidy-receiving stage to one of increasing regulation and restriction of direct subsidies. The competitive relationships among different types of carriers makes public aid to any of them suspect to the others; at the same time, each presses for maximum favorable treatment. In this context, public policy wavers between aid and regulation, though the long-term trend may be toward over-all control and co-ordination.

5. General Services for Business

The aids, services, indirect benefits, and direct subsidies offered business by government are too numerous to be listed. The governmental agencies administering these benefits are many. In addition to the direct subsidies already discussed there is a host of special aids such as the below-cost postal rates which benefit newspapers and periodicals and the preferential tax treatment accorded some firms and industries. Indeed, so great is the impact of taxes, and so great are the benefits of favorable tax treatment, that business interests take great interest in, and exert maximum efforts to influence, the writing of tax legislation. A study of the hearings of the House Ways and Means Committee in 1947 showed that virtually all witnesses represented organized economic groups, with business groups predominant.[46] Examples of special tax treatment include accelerated depreciation allowances for industrial construction essential to national defense during both world wars and the Korean War, and the depletion allowance for oil (and to some extent for other minerals) which permits a flat deduction of 27½ per cent from gross income instead of being limited to actual depletion.

Reconstruction Finance Corporation loans during that agency's

---

[46] Thus, "of approximately 150 organized groups testifying . . . all but twelve clearly represented business, labor, agricultural, or professional interests." There were 94 business organizations, 28 agricultural organizations, 8 professional associations, and 5 labor organizations. R. Blough, *The Federal Taxing Process* (1952), pp. 27–28.

twelve-year life amounted to $50 billion. Other agencies, such as the Small Business Administration, the Export-Import Bank, the Federal National Mortgage Association, and the Public Housing Administration, provide credit which directly or indirectly aids business. And many other agencies offer services profitably used by business.

Most of the aids to business are concentrated in the Department of Commerce, which was established in 1903 "to foster, promote, and develop the foreign and domestic commerce, the mining, manufacturing, shipping, and fishing industries, and the transportation facilities of the United States." In discharging these responsibilities, the Department has become a general service agency for American business, ministering to the needs of its special clientele just as the Departments of Agriculture and Labor do to theirs. Its subordinate units include the Bureau of the Census, the Office of Business Economics, the Business and Defense Services Administration, the Weather Bureau, the National Bureau of Standards, the Patent Office, the Bureau of Foreign Commerce, and the Coast and Geodetic Survey. Each performs a range of promotional, technical, statistical, or advisory services only incompletely suggested by its title.

The position of the Department as a service agency for business, however, reflects the broader political context in which it is compelled to function. Under Secretary Herbert Hoover in the twenties, the Department became a powerful engine of business promotionalism and went through a period of extraordinary expansion. Over fifty foreign offices were established, for example, from which Department agents sought out trade opportunities in the most remote corners of the world. Under the New Deal, the service functions were continued, but on a less ambitious scale and no longer with an eye singly to business needs. Yet, even under the New Deal, the liaison function of the Department as a connecting link between business and government persisted, and the Department made vigorous efforts, through such agencies as the Business Advisory Council,[47] to provide channels by which the businessman's point of view might be presented.

[47] The Business Advisory Council was organized in June, 1933, by Secretary Roper in order "to make available to the Department of Commerce seasoned judgment and experience on matters affecting the relation of the Department and business." It consists of approximately fifty members, most of them leading businessmen, serving without compensation and meeting periodically to study departmental and general business problems.

6. The Importance of Business Promotionalism

The preceding survey has emphasized the importance of special government aid in such areas as tariff policy, shipping, transportation, and the field of general governmental services for business. The assistance rendered in these areas has been highly useful to numerous business enterprises. There remain, however, many businessmen who have benefited little, if at all, by special governmental aid. Even in the areas where aid has been most important, the extent of governmental aid forthcoming has varied with the political strength business groups have been able to muster.

Where business promotionalism has been carried to excess and produced abuses, the result has usually been to inspire counterorganization by farmers, laborers, and other nonbusiness groups. As these groups organized, they became increasingly conscious of their political power. They imposed brakes and restraints on business promotionalism in the form of regulatory controls. They also awakened to a realization that they, too, could use government in positive fashion to promote their own interests.

CHAPTER 6

Promotion of Agriculture

THE PROMOTION of agriculture is a relatively ancient function of American government. Beginning with a land policy designed to open up virgin areas for settlement and cultivation, and expanding to provide farmers with information, education, and a wide variety of services, agricultural policy has gradually evolved a complex pattern of relationships which includes government credit facilities, the stimulation of agricultural co-operatives, promotion of soil conservation, and a linked system of subsidies, crop loans, "soil banks," and production and marketing measures intended to increase the farmer's share of the national income. Behind these expanding controls is a long story of agitation and organization by farm groups operating through both political parties, a gradual turn toward collective action under the pressure of economic maladjustments, and the slow assumption of major responsibilities by government.

Public land policies largely determined the nature of the agricultural system which was to dominate the empty continent. The policy debate was marked by an early clash between Hamilton, who viewed the public lands as a source of public revenue and was indifferent to the social structure which might result from sales to the highest bidders, and Jefferson, who preferred a pattern of settlements based on small farms worked by their owners. The older states, desiring to maximize revenues, to maintain their political power, and to stem the westward flow of their sons and daughters and of newly arrived immigrants, sided with Hamilton. In general, however, under increasing political pressure from poor and land-hungry settlers, the policy of selling to the highest bidder gradually gave way to a more generous system. The Homestead Act of 1862, which opened up the Western public domain for settlement, capped the long struggle of the pioneer farmers for free land. It granted title free of charge for 160 acres to any actual settler after five years of residence. Despite abuses and evasions in the course of which many huge tracts of timberlands were gathered up by individuals and corporations for private exploitation, by 1890, when most of the good land was occupied, it was distributed predominantly among small, owner-operated farms. This pattern of ownership was well designed for the humid, crop-growing areas, but less suitable in the grazing areas and forest lands west of the 100th meridian.

1. The Development of Governmental Services for Agriculture

Governmental interest in the improvement of agriculture was manifested early. "In 1839 Congress took the memorable step of appropriating $1000 to the Patent Office for collecting and distributing seeds, prosecuting agricultural investigations, and procuring agricultural statistics." [1] The year 1862 was particularly important for agricultural legislation, including the Homestead Act; the creation of the Department of Agriculture, with bureau status, as a service agency for farmers; and the Morrill Act, giving land to the states for the establishment of colleges of agricultural and mechanic arts. This statute laid the basis for close co-operation between the federal Department and the state agricultural colleges. The Hatch Act of 1887 provided funds for the creation of state agricultural experiment stations, which also became closely associated with the agricultural colleges. In 1889 the Secretary of Agriculture achieved Cabinet rank.

As scientific research demonstrated the benefits of new farming techniques, attention turned to extension work as a means of carrying the results of this research to the farmers. Soon the agricultural colleges were sponsoring "farmers' institutes," "agricultural trains," and similar devices to disseminate "correct agricultural principles." Beginning in 1902, the Department sent agents to Southern counties to demonstrate methods of combating the ravages of the Mexican boll weevil. This work soon enlisted the enthusiastic support of the agricultural colleges and local farm and business groups, and led in turn to the Smith-Lever Act

[1] A. P. Chew, The United States Department of Agriculture, p. 27.

of 1914, which established county agents to work closely with the Department and the colleges in a federally aided system of extension education. To enlist local financial support and co-operation, county agents were jointly selected by the state extension office and the co-operating county group. Thus the county agent was simultaneously a national, state, and local official. This administrative expedient combined centralized supervision of standards with a form of decentralized administration which ensured personal contacts with farmers in practically every agricultural county.

The governmental machinery thus developed was to prove invaluable much later when the ambitious experiments of the Agricultural Adjustment Acts were initiated. Unlike the National Recovery Administration, the Agriculture Department did not have to improvise. The way had been prepared for years. Competent personnel had been trained; a tradition of close working relationships with states and localities had been built up; and the Department was firmly rooted in the support and understanding of its constituency.[2]

In the late nineteenth century, the Department also began to undertake regulatory duties of incidental benefit to farmers. The Meat Inspection Act of 1890, the Animal Quarantine Act of 1901, the Grain Standards Act of 1901, the Pure Food and Drug Act of 1906, the Plant Quarantine Act of 1912, and the Federal Warehouse Act of 1916 were only the beginning of a wide array of federal standards and inspection services. While most of these activities began largely as marketing aids for farmers, their importance to consumers became increasingly apparent over the years. At the same time, other services were provided. Crop reporting was expanded. In 1916, Congress created the Federal Land Banks. By World War I, the main emphasis of policy was on the improvement of farming methods, on marketing aids, and on meeting the need for improved long-term credit facilities.

2. Emergence of the Agricultural Surplus Problem

The period shortly before and during World War I was American agriculture's golden age. Although its share of national in-

[2] The federal grants-in-aid authorized by the Smith-Hughes Act of 1917 and the George-Reed Act of 1929 for the promotion of vocational education in agriculture and home economics also helped develop working relationships between the federal government and the rural population. The personnel of the Smith-Hughes schools frequently exerted an influence almost as important as that of the county agent.

come had declined as the nation became industrialized, the growth of cities and towns had provided a constantly expanding market for farm commodities. In addition, substantial proportions of many crops found ready sales abroad. While American tariffs made it more difficult for other nations to earn dollars by exporting to us, we were then a debtor nation, and payments for invisible imports, such as interest and dividends on foreign investments here, made it possible for merchandise exports to exceed imports. Accordingly, agricultural output and income mounted. The production of wheat and corn doubled between 1870 and 1900, and that of cotton trebled. From 1900 to 1915, the index of total farm production rose from 87.3 to 107.8, while prices increased 52 per cent in the decade before 1910.

After World War I, American agriculture faced an increasingly difficult economic problem. This problem centered in the inability of farmers to match supply to demand at prices which yielded them incomes comparable to those of nonfarmers. Among agricultural products as a whole, both supply and demand are relatively inelastic, so that major price changes are required to bring about a balance. After World War I, agricultural output, in part because of the very success of governmental research and extension programs, tended to grow faster than the nation's appetite for farm commodities. The rate of population growth (including immigration) slowed. Nonagricultural income increased, but as income rose smaller proportions were spent on farm commodities. Furthermore, the export market dwindled.

Conventional economic analysis would require that farmers respond to this slackening in the growth of demand and to the consequent decline in prices by checking their own production or by shifting to other occupations. But the individual farmer, seeking to maintain his income, ordinarily attempts to increase production when confronted by falling prices. The transfer of farmers to other occupations, though often rational economically, is difficult sociologically and psychologically and occurs only slowly. In a period of heavy urban unemployment it is impossible. And, since one of the most significant farm surpluses is babies, even a substantial annual migration may leave the farm population constant.[3]

This difficulty in matching supply and demand, especially the slowness in adjusting supply to changing conditions of domestic

[3] It should be noted, nonetheless, that the size of the farm labor force, including self-employed farmers, fell from its 1910 peak of 11.6 million to a level in 1950 of only 6.8 million.

and foreign demand, produced extreme fluctuations in farm income. Net annual income realized by farmers rose from $3.5 billion at the outset of World War I to $9.2 billion in 1919, then shrank back to $3.6 billion in 1921. In the twenties it recovered modestly to $6.1 billion, only to fall to a catastrophic $1.9 billion at the beginning of the Great Depression. Under the New Deal it recovered to $4.4 billion by 1939; then, stimulated by war and postwar demands, it shot up to a high of $17.2 billion in 1947. It then dropped to $12.9 billion by 1950, rose to $14.8 billion in 1951, and leveled off to a range of $11 to $12 billion in the mid-1950's.

It is this combination of chronic surpluses and extreme price and income fluctuations which underlies the policy proposals and debates since World War I, which explains the gradual shift of farmers to a demand for vastly increased federal aid, and which has changed an industry historically a bulwark of individualism and a rare example of almost perfect atomistic competition into one subject to complex, direct governmental control and highly organized collective activity.

3. World War I Boom and Postwar Depression

The full dimensions of the agricultural problem were at first concealed by the euphoric boom of World War I, when prices of crops and of farm land went skyrocketing dizzily upward. Wheat, which sold for 93 cents a bushel in 1913, climbed to $2.76 in 1919; corn rose from 70 cents to $1.59; and cotton from 13 cents a pound to 38 cents. Marginal and submarginal land was opened up; American agriculture expanded as never before. Farmers borrowed money, bought land, turned to money crops, purchased machinery, and installed expensive improvements.

In the fall of 1920, the war boom broke as European agriculture made a speedy recovery. Crop prices dropped severely, and land values plunged downward. Deflation left the farmer with overexpanded acreage and a heavy burden of debt. Faced with contracting economic vistas, farmers began to turn to government for relief. The first outlines of a bipartisan farm bloc appeared in Congress. The tariff was tinkered with in 1921 and 1922, but had little effect on farm income. For a while the War Finance Corporation helped dispose of agricultural products in the export market and tried to stabilize the farm credit structure by making loans to livestock loan companies, co-operative marketing associations, and other financial institutions supplying credit to farmers. Efforts were made to extend regulation over processors and distributors of farm products. The Packers and Stockyards Act of 1921 regulated rates and practices in the handling of livestock and live poultry. The Grain Futures Act of 1922 policed trading in futures contracts. The Capper-Volstead Act of 1922 and the Co-operative Marketing Act of 1926 tried to help farmers bargain more effectively with middlemen by facilitating the formation of agricultural co-operatives. The Agricultural Credit Act of 1923 supplied discount facilities in the intermediate credit field. But all of these measures, though useful in their respective ways, did little to ameliorate the consequences of the price collapse of 1920.

Agrarian leaders, striving for "a fair share of the national income," searched for a scheme to raise prices and make government aid more directly available to farmers. The most popular proposal was the equalization fee embodied in the McNary-Haugen Bill.[4] Its aim was to secure the world price plus tariff for the domestically consumed portions of export crops. Under this plan, a federal board would purchase enough agricultural products for sale abroad to raise domestic prices above world prices by the amount of the tariff duties. Losses in marketing surpluses abroad were to be covered by an equalization fee collected from the growers. This proposal, which made no provision for control of production, won great favor among farmers. Twice passed by Congress, in 1927 and in 1928, it was vetoed on both occasions by President Coolidge. It was strongly opposed by the business wing of the Republican Party both because it ran against their view of the proper role of government and because it would raise domestic industrial costs while lowering foreign ones.

Agrarian dissatisfaction continued. President Hoover, backed by the recommendations of the Business Men's Commission on Agriculture,[5] took the line that the primary assistance which government could render was to improve the marketing machinery. The Agricultural Marketing Act of 1929 reflected this recommenda-

[4] The second most popular plan of these years was the export debenture plan. Its essential feature was the paying of a bounty on exports of farm products in the form of "debentures," which could be used by importers to pay customs duties. Growers of staples entering the world market would, in effect, be directly subsidized out of customs receipts. This plan was introduced in Congress in 1926 and in 1928, but without success; efforts to add it as an amendment to the Smoot-Hawley Tariff Act also met defeat.

[5] See Business Men's Commission on Agriculture, *The Condition of Agriculture in the United States and Measures for Its Improvement* (1927). This Commission was established by the National Industrial Conference Board and the Chamber of Commerce of the U.S.

tion. A Federal Farm Board was set up with a revolving fund of $500 million. When price-depressing surpluses appeared, loans were made available through co-operatives and so-called stabilization corporations to enable farmers to hold surpluses off the market. The hope was that the surpluses could be disposed of later as prices improved.

Unfortunately, the experiment was launched at a time of deteriorating general economic conditions and growing world surpluses. The experiments with wheat and cotton were particularly disastrous. Operating through the Wheat Stabilization Corporation, the Board loaned money on some 330 million bushels of wheat. This temporarily pegged the domestic price close to $1.00 a bushel, or 20 to 30 cents above the world price, but the Corporation was finally compelled to withdraw from the market, and the price dropped to a low of 57 cents. The experience with cotton was similar. Loans made at 16 cents a pound could not be continued; ultimately the price declined to less than 7 cents. The huge losses suffered by the Farm Board demonstrated that price-supporting loans could not cope with mounting surpluses as long as production was unchecked. The Board unsuccessfully urged farmers to reduce their acreage, but glut induced more glut, and the more the farmers produced, the lower prices went.

After 1930 the farm decline steepened. As the depression hit industry, domestic demand for agricultural commodities fell off sharply. Foreign buying declined more than ever as purchasing power shrank, import barriers abroad were raised, and other sources of supply were developed. The severe drop in prices made it impossible for many farmers to pay their debts. Wholesale foreclosures were threatened. The failure of farm relief schemes resulted in dramatic incidents—farmers' holiday movements, the dumping of milk, the tarring and feathering of lawyers who sought to foreclose mortgages, and the defiance of courts which ordered foreclosures. The country was faced with a desperate agricultural crisis. After the Farm Board failure, production control programs were winning wider support. The stage was set for government intervention on a grand scale when the Roosevelt administration took office in 1933.

4. New Deal Agricultural Policy

The Agricultural Adjustment Act of 1933

The Agricultural Adjustment Act (AAA) of 1933, hastily framed under Agriculture Secretary Wallace's direction on the basis of recommendations drafted by a conference of farm leaders, opened a new era. It radically altered government's relation to agriculture. For the first time, it committed the nation to the concept of parity, declaring as its goal the re-establishment of "prices to farmers at a level that will give agricultural commodities a purchasing power with respect to articles farmers buy, equivalent to the purchasing power of agricultural commodities in the base period, August, 1909—July, 1914." Full parity was not guaranteed, but this legislation was the first of a series which established the parity standard as a general goal. Although the Act also dealt with the gold content of the dollar and an emergency farm-mortgage refinancing program, its outstanding feature was production control, which was to be exercised through contracts for restriction of acreage or output in exchange for benefit payments, commodity loans, marketing quotas and agreements, export subsidies, and direct purchase of surpluses. At first, production-control provisions applied only to wheat, cotton, corn, hogs, rice, tobacco, and milk.[6] This list was expanded in 1934 to include rye, flax, barley, grain sorghums, cattle, peanuts, sugar beet, and sugar cane.

Contractual regulation of output was especially important in wheat, cotton, hogs, and corn. The farmer who did not want to adjust his production could refuse to co-operate, but benefit payments made "co-operation" quite attractive. Payments were financed from processing taxes on the commodities on which benefit payments were made. Taxes were equal to the difference between actual and parity prices. Contracts were supplemented in a number of ways. The Commodity Credit Corporation (CCC) made nonrecourse loans available to cotton and corn growers, thereby establishing a floor under prices of commodities grown by "co-operating" farmers. To force more growers into the "voluntary" contract system, legislation enacted in 1934 added marketing controls for cotton and tobacco, enforced by taxes on all sales in excess of prescribed quotas. Emergency purchases of pigs and sows in 1933–1934 and cattle and sheep in 1934–1935 helped to reduce supplies and support prices. Subsidies were paid on the export of wheat from Pacific Northwest ports. For milk and dairy products, marketing agreements between producers and distributors introduced greater stability into a number of milk markets.

Thus the first AAA tried to eliminate the disequilibrium between supply and a depressed demand by primary reliance on production and marketing controls. While the slaughter "of every

[6] Control of milk production was never put into effect.

third little pig" evoked some newspaper criticism, production, perhaps checked more by the severe droughts of the period than by
the AAA, did drop considerably. Market-depressing surpluses,
especially in wheat and corn, were dissipated. Indeed, some wheat
was actually imported in the drought years. Prices responded satisfactorily to this change in market conditions. Though parity
prices were not realized, farm prices in 1935 were 66 per cent
higher than in 1932. Farmers' net income rose from $1.9 billion in
1932 to $4.6 billion in 1935; in the latter year, AAA benefit pay-
ments totaled $573 million. The farmers' share of the national in-
come had mounted from 4½ to 9 per cent.

While successful as an emergency salvage operation, the AAA
had some marked deficiencies. In balancing supply and demand,
its efforts were confined to the supply side. Acute disequilibrium
had arisen because of depression-induced underconsumption, but
through the use of processing taxes, the AAA raised prices, thereby
intensifying underconsumption and making consumers pay for
farm relief. The program had an uneven impact. Tenant farmers,
sharecroppers, and small farmers failed to benefit appreciably.
Smaller operators, providing their own labor, could not reduce
their costs as they cut back their acreages. Producers of nonbasic
commodities received fewer benefits, while their own costs were
inflated. While corn and cotton growers, the backbone of the
Farm Bureau Federation, fared well, drought-devastated wheat
and cattle areas of the Great Plains were in dire need. Finally, the
AAA had shown that production curbs alone could not raise prices
and income quickly. It was not until carried-over surpluses had
been substantially reduced by the drought and by subsidiary
features of the AAA program that prices rose appreciably.

On January 6, 1936, the Supreme Court invalidated the
processing-tax provisions of the 1933 Act.[7] While this decision did
not affect the AAA marketing agreements, commodity loans, or
surplus removal through special purchases, it struck at the heart
of the AAA by stopping all adjustment programs dependent upon
contracts with producers. At first stunned, farm leaders soon
sought other ways of continuing benefit payments. A new approach was found in a shift in emphasis from acreage control to
soil conservation.

The Soil Conservation and Domestic Allotment Act of 1936

Even before the Butler decision, drought and dust storms had
dramatized the need for soil conservation, and a number of New

[7] *U.S.* v. *Butler,* 297 U.S. 1 (1936).

Deal agencies had already begun to attack the problem.[8] Soil conservation therefore appeared to offer a legitimate means of furthering the primary goal of agricultural policy—the raising of agricultural income. The Soil Conservation and Domestic Allotment Act of 1936, stating as one of its goals the re-establishment of parity income for farmers, provided for direct payments to farmers following approved conservation practices and abandoning "soil-depleting" crops such as wheat, corn, tobacco, and cotton in favor of grasses and other soil-building crops. It was hoped that some production control in the basic crops could thus be achieved. Despite the general agricultural revival, the pace of spending was only slightly reduced. The AAA spent over $1.8 billion from May, 1933, through 1936, and $470 million were appropriated for the first year of the 1936 Act.

While the conservation aspects of the new program attracted considerable farmer participation, it did not effectively check production. Following the especially severe drought of 1936, the return of normal weather in 1937 made for better than average yields, and a sizable minority of farmers refused to participate. The limitations of the conservation program were fully revealed. The cotton crop increased from 10.5 million bales in 1935 to 19 million bales in 1937. The crop carry-over was almost large enough to meet the next year's domestic demand. This same story of expanded acreage, production increases, and huge carry-overs was repeated in wheat, corn, and other crops, and the same vicious spiral of crop surpluses and sharply declining prices was recurring. Once more farmers were impelled to turn to plans for more rigid control of output.

The Agricultural Adjustment Act of 1938

In 1938 a new Agricultural Adjustment Act became law. This measure, intended to be more permanent than that of 1933 and more comprehensive than that of 1936, saw another shift in emphasis. It stressed price maintenance more than the Act of 1936 and emphasized acreage reduction less than the Act of 1933. Prices were to be maintained primarily by controlling "surpluses," rather than production. The Act provided four ways of eliminating or neutralizing surpluses.

First, it strengthened the soil-conservation and allotment features of the 1936 Act by denying benefit payments, maximum commodity loans, and parity payments to "non-co-operators" who

[8] See Chapter 23 for a more extended discussion of soil conservation and land-use planning.

exceeded acreage allotments. Secondly, should excessive supplies of cotton, wheat, corn, tobacco, or rice develop, the Secretary of Agriculture could, with the approval of a two-thirds vote of the affected producers, impose marketing quotas. Sales in excess of quotas incurred a penalty tax. Thirdly, the Commodity Credit Corporation was authorized to make nonrecourse loans on any agricultural commodity and was directed to make loans on cotton, corn, and wheat when prices fell below, or supplies exceeded, levels specified in the Act. Loans to co-operating farmers ranged from 52 to 75 per cent of parity prices, depending on market price and supply conditions. This provision was described as an "ever-normal granary" program designed to even out production cycles and to protect against the effects of drought and other disasters. As it was administered, and as loan rates were raised by Congress in succeeding years, however, its main effect was to increase prices and it resulted in government-held surpluses of wheat, cotton, and corn larger than those stored by the ill-fated Farm Board. Most of these accumulations were used up during World War II, thereby putting off the need for reconsideration of the basic policy.

Finally, surpluses were also attacked in a number of miscellaneous ways. Attempts were made to find new uses for the surplus commodities. The export of wheat and cotton was subsidized. Consumption was expanded by the provision of free school lunches, by distribution of surplus commodities to needy families through state welfare agencies, and by the Food Stamp Plan. This plan, one of the few attempts to solve the agricultural problem by expanding and upgrading consumption, was begun only in 1939 on an experimental basis and abandoned during the war. It granted families on relief from 50 to 75 cents a week in special stamps which could be used for the purchase of surplus foods from retailers. The stamps were redeemed by the government. The plan was popular with both grocers and relief clients. In effect, it established a domestic two-price system to subsidize the purchase of surplus products by low-income consumers.

All of these efforts to combat surpluses were, of course, intended to raise agricultural prices and income. In addition, annual parity payments, averaging over $200 million a year, were made directly to producers of corn, wheat, tobacco, and rice. The Act also established a Federal Crop Insurance Corporation, but its results were disappointing. Although the Corporation paid out more than it received, many farmers dropped out of the program. It was halted by Congress in 1943 and then revived after the war on an experimental basis with a limited number of commodities.

While the impact of the second AAA was obscured by World War II, some results were clear prior to Pearl Harbor. The greatly expanded use of CCC loans bolstered prices appreciably. Increased prices and generous government payments combined to give farmers a net realized income (from marketings and government subsidies) averaging over $4.8 billion for the years 1938–1941, a figure more than two and one-half times the low of 1932. But the drought had receded, and scientific agriculture enabled farmers to expand steadily their yield per acre. With foreign demand for export crops still drastically reduced, CCC surpluses reached record levels. CCC loans increased prices, but higher prices encouraged greater production, which entailed larger CCC loans. Supply still had not been balanced with demand. The effects of the war only temporarily corrected this disequilibrium. In addition to these fundamental difficulties, the problems of farm credit and of program administration must be examined in order to permit a full understanding of war and postwar production and marketing policies.

5. Farm Credit and Farm Security

Government extension of farm credit began long before the New Deal. After years of complaint from farm groups that interest rates on farm loans were too high, terms too short, and sources of credit undependable, Congress in 1916 enacted the Federal Farm Loan Act, which established a dual system for supplying long-term mortgage loans. One part was composed of twelve federally chartered co-operative land banks organized around associations of borrowing farmers. The second part consisted of joint stock land banks, which were privately owned institutions operating for profit.[9] Both were under the general supervision of the Federal Farm Loan Board.

The farm loan associations which formed the base of the land bank system were made up of farmer-borrowers who had to buy association stock amounting to 5 per cent of their loans. The associations then sold mortgages to the federal land banks and bought stock in these banks to the extent of 5 per cent of the loans sold. The government's investment in the land banks was thus retired as the stock purchased by the associations increased.

---

[9] After a period of rapid expansion, many of the joint stock land banks encountered serious difficulties. In 1933, arrangements were made for their liquidation under the supervision of the Farm Credit Administration.

Since land bank bonds were tax exempt, rates on their mortgages were moderately below prevailing levels. By 1929 the land banks held mortgages amounting to $1.2 billion, about 15 per cent of the total farm-mortgage debt. To improve short-term credit facilities, Congress in 1923 established twelve intermediate credit banks, also under the general supervision of the Farm Loan Board. These banks, wholly government-owned, did not deal directly with individual farmers. They discounted paper for co-operative marketing associations, co-operative livestock companies, and rural banks, and, subsequently, for production credit associations and banks for co-operatives.

Thus a substantial government-sponsored farm credit system already existed before the Great Depression threatened the whole farm-mortgage structure. The precipitous drop in income left farmers helpless to meet even interest payments on their debt. Country banks and joint stock land banks failed; insurance companies and federal land banks found themselves hard pressed. Some one-sixth of all farmers lost their farms in the period 1930–1935 through foreclosures and forced sales.[10] Late in the Hoover administration certain steps were taken to relieve distress. The Farm Board made loans to agricultural co-operatives. In 1932 the land banks were authorized to grant loan extensions to worthy borrowers, and the government bought another $125 million of their stock. The Department of Agriculture made emergency crop, feed, and seed loans. The RFC organized twelve regional agricultural credit corporations to refund short-term indebtedness. But the magnitude of the disaster outstripped these expedients.

The New Deal and Farm Credit

Faced by emergency, the new Roosevelt administration took more drastic action. All existing agricultural credit agencies were quickly consolidated into the Farm Credit Administration (FCA) by executive order. The Emergency Farm Mortgage Act of 1933 provided for large-scale farm debt refinancing. Payments on principal of land bank loans were postponed for five years for borrowers in difficulties, and interest rates were reduced first to 4½ and then to 3½ per cent. With funds provided by the RFC and later by the Federal Farm Mortgage Corporation, "land bank commissioner loans" of up to $7,500 each were made available for first or second mortgages; these might amount to 75 per cent of the "normal" appraised value of farm property.[11] Although gov-

[10] M. R. Benedict, *Can We Solve the Farm Problem?* (1955), p. 138.
[11] The federal land banks were restricted to first mortgage loans and a maxi-

ernmental action had been too long delayed—between 1930 and 1933 about $1 billion in farm mortgages had been liquidated through foreclosures and forced sales—it now proved effective. Between 1933 and 1937, at a time when other credit agencies were reducing their loans by more than $2 billion, the federal government poured about $1 billion into farm bank mortgages and about $800 million into commissioner loans, thereby checking the process of liquidation. By 1939, federal agencies held approximately 40 per cent of the total farm-mortgage debt.

The land banks performed their function well. By 1947, the last of the federal funds had been returned, and the banks and their network of local farm loan associations were firmly established on a self-supporting basis. Long-term, regularly amortized mortgages, both public and private, now prevailed. The total thirty-year cost of this program to the government, aside from interest subsidies, was about $82 million.[12]

Government subsidy of land-bank interest rates, carried on from 1933 to 1945, proved more questionable and reflected some confusion in policy goals. This subsidy, amounting to $277 million,[13] provided a special privilege for farmers with land-bank mortgages and contributed neither to stabilization of the credit system nor to a permanent solution of the farm credit problem. Indeed, during World War II it directly conflicted with efforts of the Agriculture Department to discourage land speculation. When government lending was growing, terms and conditions of loans became, perhaps inevitably, political questions. Congressmen from rural areas tended to make political capital out of low interest rates, and there was danger that the federal system would drive out private credit agencies. With the decline in government loans since World War II, and with the success of the Farm Credit Administration in institutionalizing itself as a bank, run on commercial principles and substantially insulated from political pressures, the problem has disappeared.

In addition to these emergency provisions, the Farm Credit Act of 1933 provided a short-term credit system analogous to the land-bank system in the long-term field. This system consisted of twelve production credit corporations and over five hundred production credit associations. Loans made by the associations were discounted with the federal intermediate credit banks.

mum of 50 per cent of the value of the land and 20 per cent of the value of permanent improvements.

[12] Benedict, *op. cit.*, p. 151.
[13] *Ibid.*

The production credit corporations helped organize the local production credit associations, assisted in capitalizing them by buying their preferred capital stock, and supervised their operations. Their loan volume has constantly grown, reaching $1.4 billion in fiscal 1956, and the government's stock subscription in the production credit corporations was reduced from $120 million to $29 million.[14] The net cost to the government up to that time was $24 million.[15]

The Farm Credit Act of 1933 also established a Central Bank for Co-operatives and twelve district banks to serve the credit needs of co-operatives. They may rediscount paper with the federal intermediate credit banks. Their loan volume, too, has mounted, reaching $567 million in fiscal 1956.[16] Under the provisions of the Farm Credit Act of 1955, the government stock subscription is now slowly being paid back. Because of the large government investment, imputed interest costs to the government total about $80 million.[17]

The Farm Security Program

While the Farm Credit Administration provided improved credit facilities for many farmers, there remained large disadvantaged agricultural groups—tenants and sharecroppers, farm laborers, and owner-operators handicapped by heavy debt burdens, small holdings, or location on submarginal land—who were unable to qualify for assistance under the FCA program. The attempt to use government credit and other assistance to ameliorate their lot embroiled the Farm Security Administration (FSA) in a controversy which cost it its life and which vividly revealed some of the great cleavages within agriculture which have a bearing on public policies.

As the following table shows, American agriculture is characterized by extreme diversity. The situation, and often the problems, of the large commercial operator are entirely different from those of the small family farmer. Excluding the last category—part-time farmers, retired and unemployed people tending a few acres, etc.—the more than 700,000 small farmers make less than one-fortieth of total farm sales, and the smallest 2.5 million less than one-fourth. Since the benefits of the AAA and other action programs previously discussed were usually distributed in proportion

[14] FCA, *Annual Report, 1956*, pp. 26, 36.
[15] Benedict, *op. cit.*, p. 168.
[16] FCA, *op. cit.*, p. 43.
[17] Benedict, *op. cit.*, p. 166.

FARMS, SPECIFIED CHARACTERISTICS (AVERAGE PER FARM), AND SHARE OF TOTAL FARM SALES, BY ECONOMIC CLASS OF FARM: 1950 [18]

Economic Class	Number of Farms (Thousands)	Acres of Land	Investment in Land and Buildings	Value of Farm Produce Sold	Percentage of Total Farm Sales
Commercial farms with sales of					
$25,000 or more	103.2	2,422	$110,008	$56,058	26.0%
$10,000 to $24,999	381.2	567	41,318	14,475	24.8%
$ 5,000 to $ 9,999	721.2	298	22,918	7,017	22.7%
$ 2,500 to $ 4,999	882.3	191	13,162	3,625	14.4%
$ 1,200 to $ 2,499	901.3	123	7,829	1,813	7.3%
$ 250 to $ 1,199	717.2	85	4,648	720	2.3%
Part-time, residential, and other farms	1,672.8	83	5,406	432	2.5%

[18] Bureau of the Census, Census of Agriculture: 1950 (1952), Vol. 2, pp. 1116–1117, 1175.

to output, only a small share of these benefits reached those most in need of assistance on welfare criteria. Almost half of the benefits accrued to the half-million most prosperous farmers.

It was the depressed and submerged bottom half of the nation's farms, often poorly served or never reached by the Extension Service county agents, that the FSA and its predecessor, the Resettlement Administration, sought to serve. The findings of the President's Committee on Farm Tenancy,[19] revealed that 42 per cent of all farmers were tenants in 1935, as compared with only 25 per cent in 1880. In parts of the South, the proportion was over 60 per cent. In the preceding ten years, farm tenancy had grown at the rate of forty thousand per year. In addition, more than a quarter of all persons gainfully employed in agriculture in 1930 were farm laborers. The precarious plight of migratory laborers had been dramatized in John Steinbeck's widely read novel, *The Grapes of Wrath*. Half a million farm families on submarginal land faced impoverishment. Thousands more owned holdings too small to yield a decent living. Other thousands, hopelessly debt-ridden, faced loss of their farms. The President's Committee recommended action along four main lines:

(1) assistance in the form of liberal credit to enable tenants to purchase farms;

(2) modest loans to prevent small owners from slipping into tenancy, and to help tenants and sharecroppers to increase their standard of living and begin the climb toward landownership;

(3) retirement of submarginal land by public agencies, and assistance to enable families living on such land to find homes on good land;

(4) co-operation with state and local agencies to improve the general leasing system regulating relationships between landlords and tenants.

The Bankhead-Jones Farm Tenant Act of 1937, administration of which was vested in the Farm Security Administration of the Department of Agriculture, sought to carry out some of these recommendations. It authorized a long-term tenant purchase program. It also provided for continuation of the relief and rehabilitation program carried on earlier by the Resettlement Administration, and provided for completion of the homestead projects initiated by that agency.

[19] *Farm Tenancy* (1937).

The FSA program embraced a number of activities which contributed greatly to the wave of congressional criticism that later swamped the agency. These included co-operative land-leasing associations, co-operative farm communities, camps for migratory labor, subsistence homesteads, and even three suburban housing developments. Over four thousand small co-operatives of farmers were formed for buying feed, bulls, and machinery. Surrounding farm areas were almost universally suspicious of these collectivist experiments; merchants sometimes lost business as a result of their activity; and landlords and commercial farmers opposed measures to lure away or make more independent their tenants or their hired help. The FSA was also criticized for introducing excessive paternalism; and in the South it appeared to challenge the sharecropping system and perhaps even white supremacy. Some of its programs were poorly administered, and some of its experiments failed. Added to this were the facts that much of the FSA staff was recruited from outside the traditional agricultural-college–Extension-Service system and that the FSA threatened to create a formidable competitor to the Farm Bureau Federation since it served as a potential organizing nucleus for the poorer, marginal farmers who were often looked down upon by the more prosperous members of the Federation.

The legislative campaign against the FSA was spearheaded by the Federation, speaking for the larger, commercial farmers and seeking to capture or destroy any governmental rival to the established Extension Service. In the 1941 appropriations bill, civil service protection was denied FSA personnel. In 1942 and 1943, the FSA was attacked before several congressional committees. In 1943, an unfriendly subcommittee of the House Committee on Agriculture began an investigation of the beleaguered agency. Under attack, and with his appropriations held up, the Administrator resigned in the fall of that year. Most of the staff scattered and much of the program was liquidated. In 1946, Congress established the Farmers' Home Administration (FHA) to succeed the FSA and to continue the tenant-purchase and rehabilitation-loan programs, but forbade it to carry on most of the remaining FSA programs.

The original tenant-purchase program offered extremely liberal loans to tenant farmers for the purchase of farms. The loans could be for as much as the full value of the farm; the interest rate was 3 per cent; and repayments were flexibly amortized over forty years. The demand for these loans was overwhelming, but appropriations were so limited that in some areas there were as many as thirty applicants for every loan that could be granted. The FHA has supplemented this program by insuring private low-interest loans. In its own program, it has shifted emphasis somewhat from farm-ownership loans to farm-enlargement loans, aiding already established farmers now working on uneconomically small farms to purchase additional land. While this policy ensures that the funds available to the Agency can be used to aid more farmers with less risk, it brings fewer benefits to tenants who own no land. Considering the risk involved, the FSA-FHA program has had an impressive record of financial solvency. Through 1953, about $438 million had been loaned to 60,639 farmers; $245 million had already been repaid; only $3.4 million had been, or was expected to be, lost in write-offs; and the net cost, including administrative expense and imputed interest costs to the government, was only $20 million.[20] Despite these loans and expenditures, the program has never been large enough to have a major impact on tenancy. Its loan recipients comprised only 2.6 per cent of farm tenants in 1940 and only 4.2 per cent of the reduced number in 1950. The proportion of tenant-operated to total farms declined sharply from 39.4 per cent in 1940 to 27.2 in 1950, but this drop is primarily due to such general economic factors as changes in the optimum scale and method of farm operation and greater agricultural prosperity. Little of it can be credited to the FSA and FHA.

The rehabilitation lending program had a much wider reach. These loans, begun by the Resettlement Administration, were designed to put destitute farm families, unable to secure credit elsewhere, on a self-supporting basis. Loans were made for the purchase of supplies, equipment, and livestock, for the refinancing of other debts, and for family subsistence. A high degree of supervision, including the drafting of a plan for increasing productivity, accompanied each loan. From 1935 to 1940, loans were made to 856,024 farmers. In 1946, the FHA terminated this program but began a similar one which granted "production and subsistence" loans. Considering that FSA loans were in part the equivalent of relief payments, extended to those farmers poorest in resources or education, and that the necessary supervision entailed high administrative costs, the program achieved considerable success. Of

[20] Benedict, op. cit., p. 204. In addition, $66 million had been lent to 7,982 farmers under FHA-insured loans. The reader is cautioned that these same initials, "FHA," are widely used also for the Federal Housing Administration, whose loan-insurance activities have been confined, however, to nonfarm mortgages.

$1 billion lent, all but $110 million has been, or is expected to be, repaid; the net cost of the program through 1953 was $300 million.

Net costs of the current FHA production and subsistence loans, which totaled $668 million in the period 1947–1953, run to about $30 million a year. They serve about 300,000 low-income farmers. In thus enabling many indigent farm families to become self-supporting, the FHA and its predecessor agencies have provided a measure of previously unavailable security for less-advantaged farmers.

6. The Politics of Agricultural Administration

If it be true that politics is concerned with who gets what, when, and how, then the administration of agricultural policies, involving as it does broad discretion in the disbursement of sizable benefits, is inseparable from the political process. The allocation of benefits tends to reflect the political strength of different segments of the agricultural community. Furthermore, because of the geographical distribution and isolation of farmers, often it is a governmental agency administering a program which ties together a farm group and helps to make it politically effective. One observer has stressed "the tendency for 'private' groups to emerge and grow strong through their association with public agencies." [21] Accordingly, the proliferation of action programs since 1932 has intensified the political organization of agriculture. Program administrators not only take into account existing power configurations but seek to affect their relationships by attempting to confer maximum benefits on their own supporting clienteles.

When the first AAA was launched, direction was vested in the Department of Agriculture (USDA); the alternative of delegating its administration to the decentralized Extension Service, dominated by the agricultural colleges and intimately associated with the Farm Bureau Federation (FBF), would have risked loss of federal control of the program and perhaps failure to reach many farmers. After some experimentation, state and local committees of farmers were employed to administer the program, first under the AAA and later under the Production and Marketing Administration (PMA). These committees determined conservation payments (under the Act of 1936) and acreage allotments. While the Extension Service and the FBF helped mutually to establish the AAA program, friction soon developed between the AAA and the Extension Service. The FBF, realizing that

[21] C. M. Hardin, *The Politics of Agriculture* (1952), p. 259.

the AAA-PMA committee system was part of a rival organization controlling over half of USDA expenditures, came to the support of the Extension Service; the fight broke out into the open in 1942–1943.[22] After the war, the PMA and the FBF differed over the question of flexible versus fixed support prices and over issues of administrative reorganization. At times this struggle involved both groups in party politics.

This campaign was merely one manifestation of the struggle for power and preferential advantage which revolves around the determination of agricultural policy. The different branches of the USDA have found themselves inextricably involved in this struggle. Secretaries of Agriculture have frequently felt their authority threatened by AAA-PMA heads, whose great spending and control powers make them formidable figures in the contest for farmer support. Both Secretaries Wallace and Brannan, for example, had summarily to shift AAA-PMA administrators to other posts. In a reorganization struggle in 1946, the Secretary found the FBF and the Farmers' Union supporting the AAA against him.

The one-sided struggle between the FBF and the FSA, serving marginal and politically ineffective farmers and able to recruit the aid only of the Farmers' Union, resulted in the liquidation of the FSA. Other agencies have been more successful in developing supporting clientele organizations in the contest over agricultural policy, so that the political organization of agriculture is well entrenched.

So high a degree of involvement in politics makes it difficult to develop general policies, leads to frequent conflicts between agencies, and yields much administrative confusion. During the New Deal, while the AAA, bending every effort to restrict production, was limiting acreage, the Extension Service was showing farmers how to increase their yield per acre, and the FSA was helping marginal farmers to expand their production. In 1951, congressional investigators reported that soil-conservation programs were "permeated with duplication, overlap, conflict, and lack of co-ordination . . . a state of 'civil war' exists in many areas between the Extension Service, the Agricultural Conservation Program Branch of the Production and Marketing Administration, Soil Conservation Service, and Farmers Home Administration." [23]

While perhaps more skillful political leadership and better

[22] For a description, see *ibid.*, ch. 9.
[23] House Appropriations Committee, *Hearings on Agricultural Appropriations, Fiscal Year 1952* (1951), Part I, p. 547.

organization within the USDA might lessen such extreme administrative conflict and resulting clientele confusion, they are in large measure inevitable consequences of the politicization of as diverse a sector of the economy as agriculture. They are a perhaps necessary cost of diversity in power structures, diffusion of influence, broad participation in decision-making, and the pluralistic struggle to realize conflicting ends.

7. Wartime and Postwar Agricultural Policies

Agriculture in World War II

World War II offered the American farmer both economic and political opportunities. It greatly improved his economic condition. It also postponed re-examination of prewar policies, which had been piling up CCC surpluses at an alarming rate, and it enabled him to win important political victories. Unfortunately, it did not solve his long-run economic problems; in fact, these were only intensified by his political successes. Current agricultural policies are still importantly shaped by prewar and wartime policies.

The power of the congressional farm bloc was never higher than in World War II, and that power was fully exploited. Although farm prices had risen greatly in the two years before our entry into the war, farm spokesmen refused to approve the Emergency Price Control Bill of 1942 until amendments were adopted forbidding the imposition of price ceilings on certain farm commodities at levels below 110 per cent of parity. Thus, while wheat rose 83 per cent in price from August, 1939, to April, 1942, no ceiling could be imposed until it had risen another 74 per cent.[24] In insisting on these additional gains at the expense of price stabilization, farm congressmen were taking a more extreme position than their constituents, over half of whom appeared satisfied with prices obtained in September, 1941.[25] Later in the same year the ceiling was changed to the higher of (1) the parity price, or (2) the highest price paid between January 1 and September 15, 1942. In 1943, Congress tried to raise the effective ceiling by eliminating parity payments, allotment payments, and conservation payments from the parity computations, but the

---

[24] Comparable percentages for other commodities were: corn, 74 and 34; cotton, 119 and 13; oats, 104 and 28; milk, 43 and 11; eggs, 46 and 33. W. W. Wilcox, *The Farmer in the Second World War* (1947), p. 123.

[25] "Gallup and *Fortune* Polls," *Public Opinion Quarterly* (Winter, 1941), p. 667.

President vetoed the bill.

The height of the price ceilings measured the farm bloc's strength, but it was the accompanying price floors that had more lasting consequences. In 1941, the Steagall Amendment, a rider attached to another bill, provided that when the Secretary of Agriculture asked for increased production of any commodity as a contribution to the war effort, he must support its price through CCC nonrecourse loans, at 85 per cent of parity. The next year, as a condition of supporting the Stabilization Act of 1942, the farm bloc added to the Steagall Amendment postwar price guarantees which set the pattern of subsequent legislation. It was provided that on the so-called "basic" commodities— cotton, corn, wheat, rice, tobacco, and peanuts (the composition of this list reflects the influence of Southern Democrats in the congressional making of farm policy)—CCC loans would be offered at 90 per cent of parity for two years after the first day of January following a declaration that hostilities had ceased. The support level for commodities covered by the earlier amendment was also raised to 90 per cent, and the same two-year guarantee extended.[26]

Although support of forward prices for commodities of special military importance was a sound means of encouraging their production, the pursuit of parity for all commodities not only weakened the price-stabilization effort, but also encouraged the production of some items in greater amounts than were needed while making it harder to persuade farmers to shift to more essential crops. Since those commodities in most abundant supply were also the furthest below parity before the war, the fixing of all farm price ceilings at parity encouraged the production of grains, cotton, and tobacco rather than of more needed meat animals, dairy products, and oilseed crops. Meanwhile, USDA guidance of production was largely confined to exhortation rather than full-scale production planning, which would have required the adjustment of price relationships and the use of incentive payments and penalties to induce the priority production of essential crops.

The index of farm output rose from 106 in 1939 to 129 in 1945, but good weather and the easing of AAA acreage restrictions accounted for much of this increase. Indeed, so fearful of

[26] In 1946, these commodities—the so-called Steagall commodities—were eggs, chickens, dry peas, dry edible beans, soy beans for oil, peanuts for oil, hogs, turkeys, milk and butter fat, flax seeds for oil, American-Egyptian cotton, potatoes, and sweet potatoes.

postwar surpluses was the War Food Administration, that it pursued a "bare-shelf" policy which risked serious dangers had growing conditions been unfavorable.

By the end of the war, American agriculture was healthier than at any time since World War I. There were five million fewer people on the farms than in 1939, and per capita farm income, although still much lower than nonfarm income, had risen 220 per cent in a period when nonfarm income rose only 99 per cent. In contrast with World War I, mortgage debt was steadily reduced; it dropped to only $5.25 billion in 1945, while farm real estate and livestock were valued at $66.1 billion in 1946, and savings in cash totaled $19 billion.[27]

Postwar Policies

Postwar prosperity, together with the two-year guarantee contained in the Steagall Amendment, gave agricultural policy-makers a breathing spell. Instead of the deep recession commonly expected, domestic demand for farm products remained firm; general inflation helped to maintain agricultural prices; and a generous American foreign-aid program financed huge overseas shipments. The price index for farm products, which had stood at 128 in 1945, reached 196 in 1948.

The postwar boom tended to divide agriculture into two camps on the basic question of price-support policy. On the one side, favoring a continuation of fixed, high support prices—even at the cost of acreage allotments, marketing restrictions, and other controls—were the cotton, tobacco, rice, and peanut growers of the South and the wheat farmers of the West. On the other side was a different combination of interests. Many of the corn and hog growers of the Midwest were shifting back to their traditional conservatism. With farm income at comfortably high levels, they were less persuaded of the need for controls and thought they might gain more from unrestricted production even at lower prices. Allied with them were the farmers of the Northeast and the West Coast, who had been least aided by the action programs and some of whose costs, such as feed, were substantially raised by price supports. On this side, too, were many of the land-grant college spokesmen, who doubted the long-run economic viability of high support prices and were hostile to extensive federal controls. This split has continued down to the present, with the Farmers' Union and most Democrats backing

[27] M. R. Benedict, *Farm Policies of the United States, 1790–1950* (1953), pp. 452–453, 459.

the first group while the FBF and most Republicans support the second.

The battle was first joined in 1948, when the Steagall guarantees were scheduled to expire. The House passed the Hope Bill, calling for fixed, high supports, and the Senate approved the Aiken Bill, applying lower, flexible supports and transferring many federal functions to the states. A conference committee remained deadlocked until the closing hours of the session, when, apparently out of desperation, it simply put the two bills together and reported out what became the Hope-Aiken Act of 1948. The Hope part of the Act (Title I) was to apply until June 1, 1950, when the Aiken section (Title II) was to become operative. For the most part, Title I continued the high support prices of World War II. The so-called basic commodities and hogs, chickens, eggs, and milk and its products were to be supported at 90 per cent of parity; the remaining Steagall commodities were to be supported at not less than 60 per cent of parity. Only "co-operators" in the production and marketing controls were eligible for support loans.

Title II attempted to shift farm policy in a new direction. It sought to discourage overproduction by providing flexible price supports which varied with supply. Basic commodities would be supported at 90 per cent of parity only if the supply were not greater than 70 per cent of "normal."[28] With every two percentage-point increase in supply, the support level would drop one point to a minimum of 60 per cent. When acreage allotments or marketing quotas were in effect, support prices would be raised by one-fifth but not above 90 per cent. Provisions regarding nonbasic commodities were less specific but generally similar.

In addition, the parity formula was revised. Existing parity calculations perpetuated intercrop relationships of a third of a century ago. Since 1914, technological changes had greatly lowered the costs of growing field crops, such as wheat and corn, while few economies had been made in the production of cattle, fruits and vegetables, dairy products, and wool. At the same time, demand for the former group had declined, while it had greatly increased for the latter. Accordingly, if the support programs simply increased all farm prices in the same proportion, it would make the growing of field crops quite profitable and encourage

[28] "Normal" supply was defined as domestic consumption for the previous year, plus estimated current exports, plus a carry-over allowance, which ranged from 30 per cent for cotton to 7 per cent for corn.

the production of far greater quantities than would be consumed, while it would discourage the production of commodities in greater demand. The new formula preserved for agricultural income as a whole its 1909–1914 purchasing power but adjusted relationships among different agricultural prices in terms of their average prices in the preceding ten years.

Thus Title II envisaged a more flexible policy designed to reflect technological changes, to adjust supply to demand, and by so doing, to reduce the scale of government subsidies and the scope of federal control. But the unexpected election of President Truman in 1948 was attributed in part to agrarian discontent with the agricultural policies of the Republican Eightieth Congress, and in 1949 the Anderson-Gore Act repealed Title II of the 1948 law. The new legislation was another victory for high, rigid supports, reflecting primarily the influence of Southern Democrats; they rejected both a radically new program proposed by Secretary Brannan and the more moderate bill written by Senator (and former Agriculture Secretary) Anderson. The Act paid lip service to the principle of flexible supports but in actuality called for high support levels. For 1950 and 1951, support of basic crops was maintained at 90 per cent and 80 per cent of parity respectively if acreage allotment or marketing controls were in effect; thereafter a moderate degree of flexibility was envisaged.

In fact, 90 per-cent supports were extended through 1952 by administrative action. Most nonbasic commodities were to be supported at 75 to 90 per cent. The Act retained the new parity formula of the Aiken Bill, but included farm wages, thereby raising parity prices by about five points; until 1954 it permitted the computation of parity prices for each commodity at the higher of the old or new formula.

In 1949, an attempt to eliminate the towering surpluses accumulated under high support prices was proposed by Agriculture Secretary Brannan in what became known as the Brannan Plan. Among farm groups, his program was endorsed only by the Farmers' Union, and it was never put into effect. It did, however, focus discussion on the costs and effects of current programs. Its central objective was to replace price supports by direct income payments as the basic method of sustaining agricultural incomes. Payments would be based on a new "parity income standard," computed on a moving ten-year average. Full parity incomes would be assured to growers of the "basic commodities" plus meat, eggs, chickens, and milk, with discretionary parity

levels for other crops. There would be rigorous production controls to avoid surpluses of storable commodities, and limitations
on the benefits received by any one farm. The plan was defended
as a way of preserving the family farm against the incursions of
large-scale agriculture, of avoiding surpluses, and of lowering
prices on perishables. Cited in its favor was the disastrous potato
program experience, where potatoes were destroyed to increase
prices and the consumer paid both high prices and the taxes
to cover the $600 million cost of the program. The Brannan
Plan was opposed by large farmers, by those who feared its expense, and by most of the farm organizations, who were willing
to receive other direct aid and the indirect guarantees of CCC
price supports, but considered direct income subsidies as both
politically and economically unacceptable.

The Eisenhower administration brought into office Secretary
of Agriculture Ezra Benson, who strongly attacked high, fixed
supports and fervently pleaded for a return to freer agricultural
markets. In the writing of the Agriculture Act of 1954, the battle
between fixed and flexible support prices was again fought, but
the outcome this time was a moderate victory for flexibility. For
the 1955 crop, prices of basic commodities, except tobacco, which
remained at 90 per cent, were to be supported within a range
of 82½ to 90 per cent of parity; thereafter, basic commodities
and such items as dairy products, oats, barley, and wool were to
be supported at between 75 and 90 per cent. A gradual transition to the modernized parity formula was resumed, and up to
$2.5 billion worth of CCC stocks were segregated for disposal
by donation, barter, or bargain sale through noncommercial
channels at home and abroad.

This small degree of flexibility did not discourage production,
and surpluses continued to accumulate relentlessly. Confronted
with falling farm income in the 1956 election year, Congress
tried to restore rigid price supports. To an unusual degree the
struggle had come to be conducted along party lines. In a House
vote in 1955 on a high-support bill, 87 per cent of the Democrats and only 9 per cent of the Republicans voted for the measure. President Eisenhower vetoed the 1956 bill, but under great
political pressure, instructed his unhappy Secretary of Agriculture to use his discretion to raise support levels to a minimum
of 82½ per cent of parity, thereby increasing support expenditures by half a billion dollars.

To restrict production and to funnel more federal funds to
farmers, the President asked Congress for legislation to establish

a so-called "soil bank" somewhat resembling the 1936 Soil Conservation program. The administration strongly supported this measure, on which over $1 billion was spent in the 1957 crop year, as a method of avoiding surpluses through restricting production. Under the soil-bank program, farmers growing specified crops which are in surplus are paid to withdraw land from production. All farmers may be paid under three- to five-year contracts for taking land out of production and devoting it to vegetative cover or trees. Payments are intended to equal the net income a farmer otherwise would receive from the land. This program offers few advantages over crop-storage schemes. Were it to encourage the withdrawal from agriculture of farmers and of whole farms, it would frontally attack the basic farm malady. But by retiring only some of the acreage of farms, it contributes to the already pressing problem of agricultural underemployment. It is expensive, yet payments per acre must be high to entice farmers into withdrawing acreage. Under the good growing conditions of 1958, so many farmers decided not to renew their soil-bank agreements that payments had to be increased from an average of $10 per acre to $13.50. Finally, the gravest indictment of the soil bank is that it failed to reduce output significantly. As had been the case with earlier attempts to restrict acreage, farmers simply concentrated greater effort in fewer acres. Total farm output in 1957 was as high as it had ever been.

In 1958, there were further struggles over the level of support prices, and the farm bloc suffered serious defeats, possibly marking the beginning of a major reversal of farm policy. Early in the session, Congress passed, by small majorities in both chambers, a bill to prevent Secretary Benson from lowering support prices on wheat, rice, and dairy products. The bill was vetoed by the President, and reduced price supports went into effect. Next, the House Agriculture Committee reported out an omnibus measure providing high supports for most major crops. Urban Democrats, apparently out of a concern for consumers, joined with Republicans to reject it. Late in the session, Congress enacted a measure which (1) ended all acreage limitations on corn and lowered support prices to 65 per cent of parity; (2) gave cotton farmers a choice between support at 80 per cent of parity with low acreage or support at 65 per cent with high acreage; and (3) gradually reduced rice supports to 65 per cent of parity. The law did not affect the three other "basic" crops. Wheat and peanuts were then being supported at 75 per cent of parity and tobacco at 90 per cent, but Secretary Benson declared his intention of dealing with them during the next year. While the 1958 law reduced prices, it seemed likely that, because of its easing of acreage restrictions, total costs to the government would remain high.

8. The Problem of Agriculture

Thus, with the exception of the 1958 law, farm policy has been primarily shaped along the lines first established by the Steagall Amendment. But absence of significant change is no proof of its success. Its failure to match supply with demand is most simply and dramatically measured by CCC surpluses. Even with the soil bank, acreage allotments, and marketing quotas, and even though the USDA has speeded up the liquidation of CCC stocks through an aggressive foreign disposal program and by paying the costs of shipping to charitable institutions and processing into edible form for donations to needy persons, the stocks have piled up, and the costs of the CCC program have mounted. From a low of $1.1 billion on June 30, 1952, CCC inventories soared, reaching a high of almost $6 billion in 1956, and declining only to $5.4 billion in 1957. These programs, needless to say, are extremely expensive. Their high costs result primarily from the fixed, high support prices initiated in World War II. From 1932 through 1939, the net realized cost of USDA programs totaled only $3.8 billion. From 1940 through 1956, they totaled $18.7 billion. Of this total, over half was spent on the stabilization of prices and income, and more than another quarter was spent on agricultural conservation and designed for the same primary end. In addition, from 1940 through 1956, the government spent $17 billion on the procurement of agricultural commodities for foreign-aid programs, which had as one of their incidental objectives the bolstering of farm prices.[29] Nor have the best efforts of the Eisenhower administration succeeded in lowering these costs. In fiscal 1957 the CCC's realized costs and losses amounted to $4.2 billion, and it was estimated that they would exceed $3 billion in each of the following two years. The total USDA budget in 1957 slightly exceeded $5 billion, of which $3.5 billion was spent on the stabilization of farm prices and income.

Overproduction is not the only problem. Normally, for example, there are no embarrassingly large surpluses of tobacco in

[29] USDA, *Realized Cost of Agricultural and Related Programs, by Function or Purpose, Fiscal Years 1932–1956* (1957).

CCC storage. The tight tobacco acreage allotment and marketing quota controls are effective. Co-operating tobacco farmers over the years have built up a vested interest in the maintenance of these controls. Thus, land included within acreage allotments has sold for $500 to $1,000 an acre more than similar land without allotments [30]—a measure of the capitalized value of the tobacco program. Such increments, once politically consolidated, are not easily reversed.

Clearly something has gone wrong with our farm policy. Much of farm production is for CCC storage and not for consumption. While some USDA agencies pay farmers not to grow certain crops and impose acreage and marketing controls, others are simultaneously teaching farmers how to grow more. Despite impressive governmental programs of research and demonstration, one observer concludes, "resources—human effort, land, and capital—are poorly utilized in much of agriculture . . . the waste is prodigious, waste chiefly of time and energy of millions of farm people and of a vast amount of natural resources." [31]

Policy has gone wrong primarily because organized farm groups, the policy-making processes in Congress, and executive leadership have all failed to achieve agreement on the character of our basic agricultural problems and on the direction of remedial instead of palliative action. Attempts of the Bureau of Agricultural Economics to do this in the late thirties and early forties were blocked by FBF and congressional opposition.[32] Policy has never yet faced up to the need to accelerate and facilitate the lasting retirement of surplus farm land and the movement of marginal farmers into other occupations, because no means have been found to develop political support for such a program.

"Equality for Agriculture" has long been the banner raised by agrarian leaders and farm congressmen. This vague goal has been given an unfortunately precise application in the parity principle, a statistician's nightmare which seeks to compare incomparables and tends to perpetuate outmoded and economically unsound patterns of agricultural production. Once the idea of "Equality for Agriculture" is disentangled from parity and its complex calculations of price relationships, it becomes apparent that it is concerned with two different policy objectives, one relating to production and the efficient use of resources and the other re-

[30] J. E. Mason, "Acreage Allotments and Land Prices," *Journal of Land and Public Utility Economics* (May, 1946), pp. 176–181.
[31] T. W. Schultz, *Production and Welfare of Agriculture* (1949), pp. 61–62.
[32] C. M. Hardin, *Freedom in Agricultural Education* (1955), chs. 13–15.

lating to the welfare of farm people.[33] It has been assumed that governmental aids to promote production and marketing efficiency—research and demonstration, credit, regulation of middlemen, etc.—would also serve agricultural welfare objectives. Efficient production, on this assumption, would by itself provide farm families with sufficient income to solve their own welfare problems. Admittedly, there is a genuine farm welfare problem. In Professor Schultz's words, "There has been a serious neglect of the welfare of farm people [who] have fallen behind in education, nutrition, housing, modern medical facilities, free time, old age and disability benefits, and other phases of social security." [34] But efforts to attack farm welfare problems in terms of production and marketing have too often brought least benefit to those most needing aid. Raising farm prices is not an effective way of channeling aid to needy farmers.

Agricultural prices do determine what farm incomes will be, and consequently legislative efforts to raise agricultural income to parity with the rest of the economy have focused on price guaranties. A persuasive argument can be made for moderate and flexible price supports as a means of protecting farmers from the excessive instability of unsupported farm prices. But prices perform several other functions, often neglected by policy-makers. They distribute farm income among families and persons. Under existing price guarantees, large commercial farmers receive many times the aid given marginal farmers. The very largest farms may receive in a year government payments of over a quarter of a million dollars. Prices also guide production. High support prices too often encourage farmers to grow commodities already in surplus. Prices also channel trade, both at home and abroad. High support prices for cotton, for example, make it more difficult to sell American cotton abroad, and their effect at home is to accelerate the trend toward synthetic textiles and paper products. Thus high support prices only intensify the basic economic problem of bringing supply into balance with demand. And this basic problem of continuing disequilibrium between supply and demand will not soon disappear. A recent study concluded that "an extension of present trends will give a larger volume of [agricultural] production in 1965 than a 15% larger population with a 20% larger GNP [gross national product] will buy in that year . . . holding price supports at high levels works in exactly the wrong direction from that needed . . . such high

[33] This analysis owes much to Schultz, *op. cit.*, pp. 10–13.
[34] *Ibid.*, p. 11.

fixed price supports are a strong positive subsidy to an over-expansion of production which is already over-expanded." [35]

Concentration on the unsolved policy problems should not obscure the successes which agricultural policy has also achieved. Down to the present, the family farm has, on the whole, been preserved. Action programs since the Great Depression have lifted the farmer out of his desperate plight of 1932. Foreclosures and bankruptcy were staved off, and a sound credit system firmly established. Conservation and soil-building programs have added greatly to a major natural resource. Agricultural prices and income were restored, and surpluses have occasionally been liquidated by sound methods. New farm policies are urgently needed, but the old ones cannot be dismissed as utter failures.

[35] J. D. Black and J. T. Bonnen, *A Balanced United States Agriculture*, National Planning Association Special Report No. 42 (1956), pp. 27–28.

CHAPTER 7

Promotion of the Interests
of Labor

IT IS difficult to distinguish between general
measures designed to help lower-income groups and measures
intended specifically to promote labor interests. Progressive taxation, free public education, recreational facilities, and low-cost
housing were all warmly supported by labor. Compulsory education not only increases the opportunities of a worker's children;
it also reduces the competition of low-paid child labor. To
strengthen its competitive position, labor also supported free
land policies and restrictions on immigration. Social security and
relief legislation decrease some of the risks to the worker in the
modern industrial order. While all these measures bear some
relation to the general topic of this chapter, the discussion here
is focused on (1) protective labor legislation, and (2) government policies toward labor organization and industrial disputes.

Protective legislation aids the economically weakest workers
by setting minimum standards. It has followed a fairly uniform
pattern in most industrial nations. Normally beginning with
work-week limitations for women and children, requirements of
safety precautions in hazardous occupations, factory inspection,
and workmen's accident compensation, it has in most cases
spread to include a limited working week and minimum wages
for all. While pressure from labor has greatly stimulated this
trend, particularly in wage-and-hour legislation, general human-
itarianism prompted a considerable degree of protective action

even before workers had been given the vote. More significant is the attitude of government toward unions and industrial disputes. Organization is not only a prerequisite for successful labor bargaining with employers; it also creates effective political pressure. At the same time, government policies are often crucial in aiding or hindering such organization. Over the decades, American public policy has been transformed slowly, from outright condemnation of unions as criminal conspiracies, to relaxation of restraints, to positive encouragement, and finally to regulation.

1. Protective Labor Legislation

Protective labor legislation assumes that there is unequal bargaining power which, if uncorrected, produces unjust or undesirable results. Although the volume of state and federal legislation of this type is now enormous, its adoption in the United States lagged behind other industrialized nations. Until the 1930's, organized labor for the most part preferred to improve its bargaining position through independent collective action rather than by legislation. There were also high, and at times insurmountable, constitutional hurdles.

Protective statutes modified that "freedom of contract" which the courts formerly read into the due process clauses of the Fifth and Fourteenth Amendments. Accordingly, they were invalid if the judges regarded them as "arbitrary, unreasonable, or capricious"—tests which depended more on social and economic attitudes than on abstract legal principles. Dozens of laws fell before this barrier, and the fate of legislation was often decided by a closely divided Supreme Court. Statutes protecting particular groups of workers were also attacked under the "equal protection" clause of the Fourteenth Amendment. While the law has always recognized children as a class apart which the state might protect as its wards, the reasonableness of laws requiring special treatment of women, miners, seamen, railroad workers, and other groups was established only after a long, uphill battle.

Federalism also seriously hampered the adoption of protective labor legislation. Under pre-1937 interpretations of the commerce clause, federal authority over labor was confined to interstate and foreign transportation, government employees, and the District of Columbia. Indirect control might also be exercised over working conditions on federal contracts. The taxing power, although sustained as a means of outlawing the manufacture of white phosphorus matches, was not permitted to regulate labor conditions through differential levies. The states could regulate labor conditions under their general "police powers." But, with the coming of rapid transportation and large-scale production, economic life became regional and national, and interstate competition set narrow limits on any one state's ability to raise the minimum standards. To secure an effective minimum plane of competition, national action was required, but constitutional interpretation made the federal government impotent until 1937.

Child Labor

Limitations on child labor, the oldest examples of protective legislation, began in Britain with the Health and Morals of Apprentices Act of 1802, which forbade night work and limited the working day to twelve hours for apprentices in textile mills. In this country, the earliest corresponding statute was passed by Massachusetts in 1842. It prescribed a maximum day of ten hours for children under twelve. Shortly after the Civil War, Massachusetts prohibited child labor under the age of ten in manufacturing and extended the ten-hour law to children up to fifteen. Later in the century most states adopted child-labor laws, generally coupled with compulsory education. Except for the very young, child labor was not prohibited outright, even in more hazardous occupations, until the decade before World War I. The proportion of gainfully employed children between ten and fifteen rose steadily until 1910.

In the "progressive era" of the early twentieth century, almost every state adopted or extended child-labor legislation. Gradual extension of state laws continued after World War I and was greatly accelerated in the early years of the New Deal. Half the states now forbid the employment of child labor under sixteen in manufacturing, mining, and mercantile establishments. Most states limit the workday of children to eight hours, bar nightwork, and prohibit their employment in dangerous occupations. Some states extend these restrictions to children up to the age of eighteen. Most states fall far short of the leaders both in age and hour provisions and in enforcement machinery. And most states permit the employment of children, outside of school hours, in agriculture, in street trades, in the home, and in canneries.

Once a few states had imposed serious checks on child labor, the limitations of action by single states became evident. Agitation for supplementary federal legislation led to platform planks by both parties in 1916, but constitutional barriers blocked federal action. The Owen-Keating Act of 1916 forbade the interstate transportation of goods on which child labor had been used. Although the Supreme Court had previously approved similar use of the commerce power to prohibit interstate transportation of lottery tickets, impure and adulterated foods, and prostitutes,[1] this child-labor law was struck down by the Court in a 5 to 4 decision.[2] The majority held that the federal government could regulate commerce in goods which were harmful per se, but could not regulate commerce in order to modify the conditions of production. Congress then attempted to use the taxing power, which had successfully eliminated white phosphorus matches and oleomargarine colored to resemble butter. This attempt, too, the Court vetoed, declaring it to be a penal regulatory measure dealing with production, rather than a real tax.[3]

In 1924, therefore, a constitutional amendment was submitted by Congress to the states, giving the federal government the power to regulate child labor. But Southern textile operators, the Farm Bureau Federation, and the National Association of Manufacturers led such a vigorous campaign against ratification that by 1933 only six states had approved the amendment. In the more favorable atmosphere of the New Deal period, twenty-two more states ratified—still short of the required two-thirds —but the need for the amendment was then removed by federal regulation under a more liberal interpretation of constitutional authority. These federal measures, first on a temporary basis under the National Industrial Recovery Act (NIRA) of 1933, then permanently under the Fair Labor Standards Act of 1938, are discussed below, together with other New Deal protective laws.

Hours of Work

During the past century, the nonagricultural worker's average week has been reduced from seventy to forty hours. The reduction has been gradual and with marked occupational variations. In steel, for example, the twelve-hour day persisted until 1923. Organized labor has demanded shorter hours with a persistence second only to its pressure for increased wages. It has won adherents from other groups through pleas for adequate leisure in which to develop "good citizenship," through evidence of

[1] *Champion* v. *Ames*, 188 U.S. 321 (1903); *Hipolite Egg Co.* v. *U.S.*, 220 U.S. 45 (1911); *Hoke* v. *U.S.*, 227 U.S. 308 (1913).
[2] *Hammer* v. *Dagenhart*, 247 U.S. 251 (1918).
[3] *Bailey* v. *Drexel Furniture Co.*, 259 U.S. 20 (1922).

the deterioration of physical and mental health from excessive hours, and in times of unemployment, by urging programs to "share the work." While in other industrial countries such demands were usually met many decades ago by government action, American hours legislation, until the New Deal, covered only children, women, and special occupations. This contrast is in part attributable to the attitudes of the AFL, which steadfastly refused to endorse general hours laws. Constitutional limitations, only slowly removed, were another obstacle. Comprehensive regulation of working hours began only after 1933.

Limitation of working hours for children dates back to Massachusetts and Connecticut statutes of 1842, and for women to a New Hampshire law of 1847. Early control over women's hours was ineffective, generally allowing employer and employee to "contract out" by mutual agreement.[4] Effective limitation began in the seventies, but its constitutionality was at once questioned. Only in 1908 was the issue finally resolved in its favor.[5] A great number of statutes followed early in the Wilson administration, producing a flood tide of labor legislation unparalleled until the New Deal. By 1939, all but five states limited the work week in one or more industries, although neither domestic servants nor farm labor were protected in most states, and some states had maxima as high as fifty to sixty hours. Here, again, the lack of uniformity hindered legislation on a state basis and produced pressures for federal action.

Hours laws for men began with federal government employees and gradually broadened out into widening circles of public concern. Navy-yard workers were given the ten-hour day in 1840. The eight-hour day was adopted in principle for government employees and workers on public contracts in 1869, although its effectiveness was limited until 1912. Most states have followed the federal example. Hours are usually limited in transportation —in order to protect travelers, freight, and the employees themselves from the unusual risks incident to fatigue—and in other industries regarded as especially hazardous or unhealthful. A federal act of 1907 limited the continuous hours a railroad employee could work to sixteen, to be followed by at least ten hours of rest. Similar standards are set by most states. In 1916, under

---

[4] Thus, the New Hampshire ten-hour law applied only in the absence of "an express contract requiring greater time."

[5] Cf. *Ritchie v. People*, 155 Ill. 98 (1895); *Muller v. Oregon*, 208 U.S. 412 (1908). The latter case was the occasion of Louis D. Brandeis's celebrated brief on the ill effects of long hours for women.

threat of an imminent railroad strike, Congress within four days passed the Adamson Act, giving trainmen the "basic" eight-hour day without wage reduction.[6] Overtime payment at "time and one-half" was required for railroad workers in 1919. Seamen's hours have also been legally limited since 1913, and in 1936 they were lowered to eight a day both at sea and in port.

Hours regulation in other occupations for a long time faced the threat of judicial invalidation. If particular industries were regulated, it had to be shown that they offered unusual hazards to health. Although the Supreme Court had upheld Utah's eight-hour law for miners and Oregon's ten-hour limit for factory employment in general,[7] the constitutionality of such regulation was always in doubt until 1941, when the Court, in dealing with a federal statute, finally removed the judicial barriers to wage-and-hour legislation by either federal or state governments.[8]

Wages

Wages have always been viewed as the heart of the labor contract, and their general regulation has been as foreign to our economic traditions as general price regulation. Even minimum-wage legislation (which was first enacted in New Zealand in 1894, and spread rapidly to the Australian states, to Great Britain in 1909, to France in 1915, and to other industrialized European countries after World War I) was unimportant in America until the New Deal. Minimum wages are usually applied first to women, children, and other "sweatshop" workers, then to the unskilled. At first the insignificant role of these groups in the organized labor movement gave labor leaders little incentive to promote government protection. Not until the CIO industrial unions organized unskilled workers, and the low wage rates of nonunion workers created bargaining difficulties for the new unions, was there a significant shift in union policy. Moreover, the Supreme

[6] Since this law did not forbid overtime work, or even require higher rates of pay for overtime, it was, in effect, a wage-regulating rather than an hours law. On this basis its constitutionality was doubtful, but an argument against it on these lines was rejected by the Supreme Court in *Wilson* v. *New*, 243 U.S. 332 (1917).

[7] *Holden* v. *Hardy*, 169 U.S. 366 (1898); *Bunting* v. *Oregon*, 243 U.S. 426 (1917).

[8] ". . . it is no longer open to question," said Justice Stone for a united Court, "that the fixing of a minimum wage is within the legislative power and that the bare fact of its exercise is not a denial of due process under the Fifth more than under the Fourteenth Amendment. Nor is it any longer open to question that it is within the legislative power to fix maximum hours." *U.S.* v. *Darby Lumber Co.*, 312 U.S. 100.

Court removed the constitutional barriers to minimum-wage laws for women and children only in 1937.

Much state legislation deals with incidental features of wage payments. In most states unpaid wages are given first claim on a firm's assets, and in some states workers are given free legal assistance in collecting them. Other regulations prescribe the place and frequency of payment, forbid the use of "company scrip," and require dismissal payments.

During the late nineteenth and early twentieth centuries, a number of investigations showed that wages paid in certain occupations to unprotected, unorganized, and economically weak workers, particularly women and children, were inadequate to maintain a decent and healthful standard of living, no matter how barely defined. The apparent success of foreign minimum-wage-law experiments and some striking revelations of sweatshop conditions, combined with the powerful humanitarian sentiment of the time, created a movement for legislation which achieved considerable momentum after 1910. Early laws covered only women and children, both because of constitutional doubts about general regulation and because of union fears that a minimum wage for men would tend to become a maximum.

In 1912 Massachusetts enacted a mild measure, whose only sanction was publicity. Other states followed with more effective statutes. In 1917 the Supreme Court divided equally on the constitutionality of Oregon's law, and the statute stood.[9] By 1925, fifteen states and the District of Columbia had enacted such laws. A shift in Court membership suddenly brought the movement to a halt. An unexpected 5 to 4 decision vetoed the District of Columbia statute.[10]

The breakdown of wage standards during the Great Depression, together with an increase in industrial homework and a recrudescence of the worst evils of sweatshops, stimulated renewed efforts to set a "floor" under wages. The most striking results were achieved in 1933–1935 in the National Recovery Administration codes, considered below. In addition, attempts were made to evade the Adkins decision by taking up its apparent suggestion that a law setting the minimum wage at "reasonable value of services rendered," rather than at a minimum living standard, would be upheld. The attempt was unavailing; in

[9] *Stettler* v. *O'Hara*, 243 U.S. 629 (memorandum decision without opinion).
[10] *Adkins* v. *Children's Hospital*, 261 U.S. 525 (1923). Subsequent decisions invalidated the Arizona and Arkansas laws. *Murphy* v. *Sardell*, 269 U.S. 530 (1925); *Donham* v. *West-Nelson Manufacturing Co.*, 273 U.S. 657 (1927).

1936 the Court's majority of five saw no sufficient distinction between the two types of statutes.[11] In 1937, however, the shift of one judge produced a new majority which overruled the Adkins case.[12] By 1941, the constitutionality of minimum-wage legislation was no longer open to question.[13] By 1954, twenty-six states had minimum-wage statutes in force, but twenty-one applied only to minors and women. Meanwhile, the federal law of 1938 inaugurated a permanent, nationwide policy.

Workmen's Compensation

In recent decades, the economic risks of unemployment have come into great prominence. Parallel with them and long antedating them in public attention, although less dramatic, are the risks of illness and accident. The latter grew increasingly severe during the nineteenth century, as powerful and oftentimes dangerous machinery became a regular adjunct of industry. Safety legislation, stimulated by severe accidents, especially in mining and transportation, has become an important body of law, state and federal. No preventive measures could be universally successful, however, and society faced the problem of support for the temporarily or permanently disabled worker and his dependents.

Common-law rules developed in the first half of the nineteenth century made it extremely difficult for an injured employee to recover damages from his employer, even if he could afford to set in motion the machinery of justice. The burden of inherent occupational risk was held to lie with the worker and to be reflected in his wages. Under the doctrine of "assumption of risk," employers escaped responsibility even for abnormal hazards if it could be shown that the worker was aware of them when taking the job. Again, while employers were required to exercise reasonable care in preventing accidents, the doctrine of "contributory negligence" excused them of all liability if the worker were at all responsible for a particular accident, no matter how great the employer's negligence. Nor was an employer responsible for accidents due to the negligence of a fellow worker. During the eighties, various states abrogated these harsh rules, shifting liability to the employer. Even so, the worker often found it difficult to recover damages through the ordinary judicial processes.

Meanwhile, other nations began to experiment with compulsory

[11] *Morehead v. New York ex rel. Tipaldo*, 298 U.S. 587.
[12] *West Coast Hotel Co. v. Parrish*, 300 U.S. 379.
[13] See footnote 8, above.

accident insurance. Germany, in 1884, and Great Britain, in 1897, began the movement which has since spread to all industrialized countries and has become the most highly developed branch of protective labor legislation in the United States. Compulsory workmen's compensation laws substitute payment on a fixed scale for the doubtful chance of large jury damages in a court suit. Procedure is simplified and recovery hastened through the use of administrative commissions for the establishment of valid claims. Insurance funds for payments are built up out of employers' premiums, usually in private insurance companies but in some instances directly operated by the states. Premium reductions are generally given for a good safety record. All of the states now have workmen's compensation laws. In half of them acceptance of the machinery is optional with the employer, but his alternative is the possibility of a large adverse judgment under an employers' liability law depriving him of the common-law defenses.

The principle of workmen's compensation is for the most part now accepted by all interested groups. Since employers must meet the costs of accidents, there is a strong incentive to voluntary preventive measures. Early in this century, however, the idea of workmen's compensation was hotly contested by employers, and the influential railway brotherhoods long preferred the occasional recovery of enormous damages. As successive legislatures adopted compensation, the battle was transferred to the courts. Its constitutionality was for a time successfully challenged in a number of states, chiefly on the ground that it required liability when an employer was not at fault and interfered with freedom of contract, but in a series of Supreme Court decisions in 1915 and 1917, its validity was established beyond doubt.[14] Maryland, in 1902, had been the first state to enact such a law; by 1913 there were twenty state acts; and by 1948 every state had passed one.

In recent years, the greatest legislative advances have been made in compensation for medical expenses. By 1953, thirty-six states and territories were providing full medical benefits. Nevertheless, the aims of the workmen's compensation movement have not been entirely realized. Few states are concerned with rehabilitation of those permanently handicapped or with active programs of accident prevention. Neither death benefits

[14] *Jeffrey Manufacturing Co.* v. *Blagg,* 235 U.S. 571 (1915); *New York Central Railroad Co.* v. *White,* 243 U.S. 188 (1917); *Hawkins* v. *Bleakly,* 243 U.S. 210 (1917); *Mountain Timber Co.* v. *Washington,* 243 U.S. 219 (1917).

nor disability payments are at all adequate in amount. A recent
study concluded that "the evidence is clear that workmen's compensation has left unfulfilled most of its major original objectives." [15] Pressure for expansion of the legislative program has
eased, however, as unions more frequently win comparable benefits through collective bargaining.

Administration of Protective Legislation

The very inequality of bargaining power between employer
and employee, which is the root cause of protective legislation,
also creates a need for special administrative devices to make
that legislation effective. If the enforcement of protective laws
is left to civil court action by employees, or to criminal action
begun on their complaint, experience shows that even the best-
drawn statutes will go unheeded. Successful labor legislation requires sufficient administrative flexibility to apply general standards to the infinite variety of industrial conditions and sufficient
administrative vigor to protect those workers unable to protect
themselves and to promote the interests of those whose interests
would otherwise be neglected. Enforcement of labor legislation
has been most successful when in the hands of administrative
tribunals, with suitable channels of appeal to the courts on questions of law. Hence the development of state corps of factory
inspectors, wage-and-hour commissions, and similar agencies. In
the most advanced states, labor administration is concentrated
in an integrated department. Disparities in administrative standards among the states, however, are even greater than in statutory
requirements. In addition, because of low pay and prestige, lack
of adequate public or group support, antiquated methods and
outlooks, and bureaucratic lethargy, state labor administration
is often of a low order, unaggressive, and routinized.

Apart from the administration of protective legislation, organized labor has long demanded continuing agencies within the
government to represent it in broad policy formation. The United
States Department of Labor and many corresponding state units
were created in response to this demand. The Department is
the second youngest of the Cabinet agencies, reaching that status
only after continuous AFL pressure. Its predecessors, a bureau
within the Department of the Interior (1884), an independent
but noncabinet department (1888), and the Department of Commerce and Labor (1903), were all viewed by the Federation

[15] H. M. and A. R. Somers, "Workmen's Compensation: Unfulfilled Promise," *Industrial and Labor Relations Review* (October, 1953), p. 33.

as incapable of giving labor that independent representation in the highest councils of the nation which it claimed as labor's due. The Department was finally established in 1913 and directed "to foster, promote, and develop the welfare of the wage earners of the United States, to improve their working conditions, and to advance their opportunities for profitable employment."

While the AFL thus won a victory, and Secretaries of Labor were, until 1929, regularly selected from among its nominees, the Department for its first twenty years was a governmental stepchild. Hampered by tiny appropriations and weak personnel, it was but a poor counterpart of its elder brothers in agriculture and commerce. As late as 1932, when Commerce Department expenditures were almost $50 million and those of the Agriculture Department (excluding the Bureau of Public Roads) reached $124 million, the Labor Department spent a mere $14.7 million. Of this figure, immigration and naturalization absorbed $11.6 million, leaving only $3.1 million for promotional and informational service proper. Here, again, the New Deal produced a radical transformation. By 1940, because of additional duties given it, and because of the heightened importance of labor in the national political scene, Labor Department appropriations, exclusive of immigration, naturalization, and emergency expenditures, had risen by almost 500 per cent to $18.2 million. By 1957, with immigration and naturalization having been transferred to the Department of Justice, the Labor Department's expenditures, exclusive of those for veterans' services and benefits, had mounted to $364 million. Of this sum, however, $273 million was granted to the states for the administration of unemployment compensation [16] and employment services, or in payment of unemployment compensation benefits for former federal employees. The creation of the CIO and the great expansion of union membership altered the Department's previous narrow AFL orientation. Its administration of the Fair Labor Standards Act, discussed below, its promotion of, and assistance to, state unemployment compensation and employment services, its co-ordination of state protective standards, and its expanded informational services have now made it especially important to unorganized workers, who are unrepresented by powerful lobbies. In addition, as we shall see in Chapter 25, the various welfare activities—particularly the social security and public assistance programs—now conducted by the Department of Health, Education, and Welfare make a broad contribution to the wel-

[16] Discussed below in Chapter 25.

fare of workers. This aid is usually most needed by the unorganized.

The United States Employment Service (now the Bureau of Employment Security) has filled a need never satisfactorily met before. In a complex economy seeking to maintain full employment and to avoid labor shortages, the matching of men and jobs is best performed on a broad regional or national basis. Except for World War I, prior to the New Deal the task was done poorly. Only 21 states had established public employment offices, and there were only about 250 of them. State regulation had only partially restrained the abuses of some private employment agencies—exorbitant fees, misrepresentation of wages and other conditions of employment, bribing of foremen to fire old workers and hire new, agency-placed recruits. In 1933, the Wagner-Peyser Act offered federal funds to the states for the establishment of state employment offices which conformed to the standards of the federal Employment Service.[17] By 1940, further stimulated by the desirability of using employment offices for the administration of unemployment compensation, all states had established offices, and a total of fifteen hundred were in operation. By 1951, there were eighteen hundred full-time and twenty-seven hundred part-time offices. Aided by federal grants, these state offices, which also administer unemployment compensation benefits, have expanded their services. In fiscal 1957, they received 8.5 million applications for work, conducted 1.5 million counseling interviews, tested 1.4 million individuals, and made 6.2 million nonagricultural placements.

2. Trade-Unions, Industrial Disputes, and the Law

The major instrument of protective labor policy is, of course, the legislature itself, with administrative agencies a close second. By contrast, the reciprocal rights and duties of employers and employees which make up the law of industrial relations were until recent times hammered out almost exclusively by the courts. Where disagreements lead to strikes or lockouts, the attitude of the executive—local, state, or federal—is often decisive. Before 1932, legislative guidance in this area was scanty. Of the few statutes enacted, some were reshaped in the mold of judicial interpretation, and others were invalidated under the due process

[17] At first the national government covered half of their costs. During World War II it operated the offices. In 1946, they were returned to the states, with their expenses thereafter borne fully by the federal government.

clauses. Thus, the framework of law within which labor relations were conducted was to be found primarily in judicial decisions and in the impact of executive action on industrial disputes.

Industrial Relations at Common Law

While the judge-made law of industrial relations is often interspersed with ancient common-law terms, most of its substance dates from the last half of the nineteenth century, when both corporations and unions first appeared in modern form. Following English precedents, American courts originally regarded all labor organizations as unlawful per se, indictable as criminal conspiracies regardless of their objectives or methods. This stern doctrine was, with few exceptions, abandoned with the celebrated Massachusetts decision in *Commonwealth* v. *Hunt* (1842),[18] which sanctioned combined action seeking lawful ends by lawful means. Subsequent case law sought to define legitimate union objectives and legitimate methods for their pursuit. Where ends were forbidden, even otherwise lawful methods could be prevented. Injured employers could get redress through damage suits or injunctions to forestall illegal action. In certain cases the executive could bring criminal charges against union officers and members.

Collective bargaining over wages, hours, and working conditions was universally recognized as legitimate, and resultant agreements were usually treated as legally enforceable, if not precisely contractual, relationships. Courts were more hesitant, however, to approve the closed shop (employment only of union members) or the union-preference shop (hiring of members in preference to nonmembers as long as the former are available).

Reinforced by the Thirteenth Amendment's prohibition of involuntary servitude, the common law gave individual workers an unqualified right to quit work, matched by an employer's right to discharge employees for any or no reason. The strike, however, involving the concerted stoppage of work, stood on a different footing. It might conflict with employers' rights equally sacred to the law—their right to do business free from coercion or intimidation and to receive governmental protection both of their physical property and of their free access to labor, raw materials, and customers. Labor boycotts raised similar issues. Courts conceded the inequality in bargaining power between individual workers and their employer, often a large corporate aggregate treated by the law as a single person. Where to draw

[18] 4 Metcalf 111.

the line between these conflicting rights, however, was a matter of social policy rather than of definitive legal precedent. In formulating this policy, court decisions, as modified by statute, channeled industrial relations and often determined the success or failure of attempts to unionize.

The conduct of strikers has been surrounded by rigid restrictions. In their efforts to persuade "loyal" workers to lay down their tools, and to prevent strikebreakers or "scabs" from entering a plant, they may not use violence or intimidation. Before 1921, even "peaceful picketing" was forbidden by some courts as a contradiction in terms, and others had held picketing of any kind to be unlawful. In that year, the Supreme Court approved the provisions of the Clayton Act of 1914 (see below), which forbade injunctions against peaceful persuasion. A single picket at each gate, limited to "communication or persuasion," was acceptable, but mass picketing, "persistence, importunity, following and dogging" were condemned.[19] For almost another two decades, judicial definitions of peaceful—hence legal—picketing were confused and often contradictory.

Labor's second main weapon in industrial disputes is the boycott. It includes both consumers' boycotts (concerted refusal to purchase boycotted materials) and workers' boycotts (refusal to work on boycotted materials). The latter may take the form of "sympathetic strikes," designed to aid fellow unionists organize the business supplying the products against which the strikes are called. "Secondary boycotts" involve pressure on customers or dealers of the employer concerned in a dispute. Until modified by statute, the trend of the law was strongly against workers' and secondary boycotts, because the interest of boycotters in a dispute elsewhere was held too uncertain and indirect to justify the injury caused. Consumers' boycotts involving action only by workers directly concerned in a dispute are uniformly sustained, but their effects are generally negligible. The most important boycott cases, arising under the antitrust laws, will be treated below.

On the employers' side, also, certain rights and duties have been tested by court action over the last century. Employers are free to combine forces in dealing with labor, either for negotiation or for collective resistance. A number of business associations, including the National Association of Manufacturers during its early years, have devoted themselves largely to work of this na-

[19] *American Steel Foundries* v. *Tri-City Central Trades Council*, 257 U.S. 184.

ture. Individual employers may close their plants in a "lockout" at any time and for any reason. They may demand protection against violence and supply themselves with company police and armed guards. Access to the plant must be maintained by public authority for either "loyal" workers or strikebreakers.

Before the New Deal, the law permitted discrimination against union members at the employer's unlimited discretion. Company unionism, an effective weapon against independent labor organization during the 1920's, might be promoted by any means short of physical violence.

Organized labor regarded as particularly objectionable the use of the so-called "yellow-dog" contract, which bound a worker not to join a union or participate in union activities. Since an employer could discharge men at will in any case, these contracts were at first of little consequence. In 1917, however, a divided Supreme Court sustained an injunction against union officials forbidding them to attempt the organization of workers bound by such contracts.[20] Moreover, the Court had previously invalidated both federal and state statutes forbidding yellow-dog contracts as contrary to the due process clause.[21] Thus, until successfully outlawed by the Norris-La Guardia Act of 1932, this instrument served as a powerful antiunion weapon.

Apart from legal rights, employers had marked advantages accruing from their general social and economic position. Few in number, they could keep secret such illegal activities as concerted blacklisting of union members, while the corresponding workers' boycott was perforce publicly known. Employers involved in disputes usually enjoyed the sympathy of middle-class elements and of the local executive and judiciary. With rare exceptions, the use of state militia and federal troops or a declaration of martial law during strikes presaged union defeat by the combined forces of employers and the "public." A well-disposed police force, or company guards temporarily enlisted as deputy sheriffs, often arrested union leaders on petty charges, holding them for the duration of the strike and releasing them only when their cause was already hopeless. In company towns, private police might deal with union organizers as trespassers. Superior economic resources, coupled with the natural sympathies of newspaper owners and the leverage of advertising control, also helped create a climate of

[20] *Hitchman Coal and Coke Co.* v. *Mitchell*, 245 U.S. 229 (1917).
[21] *Adair* v. *U.S.*, 208 U.S. 161 (1908); *Coppage* v. *Kansas*, 236 U.S. 1 (1915). The former case dealt with portions of the Erdman Act of 1898, applying to railway labor.

public opinion favorable to employers, which might be a decisive factor in closely contested strikes.

In establishing their legal rights against unions, employers have been somewhat hampered by the common-law rule that unions, as unincorporated associations, might not be sued in their own name. Most states retain this rule, although it was reversed for the federal jurisdiction in 1922 in the first Coronado Coal case,[22] which permitted recovery against a union in its quasi-corporate capacity out of union funds, provided that official responsibility could be shown. Elsewhere the action must lie against individual officers and members, whose financial resources are often very limited.

Two factors in the complex of law surrounding industrial relations which played a particularly significant role in hampering trade-union growth deserve special treatment. They are the Sherman Antitrust Law and the use of the injunction in labor disputes.

Labor and the Antitrust Laws

The passage of the Sherman Act of 1890, whose genesis is reviewed at length in Chapter 15, was attributable to fears of large corporate consolidations and price-fixing combinations. Whether its prohibition of "every contract, combination in the form of trust or otherwise, or conspiracy, in restraint of trade or commerce" was meant to include union activities has been hotly disputed,[23] but whatever the congressional intent, judicial decisions for a long time consistently applied it to labor. Not until 1940 and 1941 did the Supreme Court remove this important obstacle to unionization.

Although courts had twice before applied the Act to unions in minor cases, its first such use to attract widespread public attention came during the Pullman strike of 1894. The Cleveland administration felt that all possible legal means must be used to end a railroad strike. For this purpose it secured sweeping injunctions, based partly on the Sherman Act, partly on the power to prevent interference with the mails, and partly on a putative power to forbid hindrances to interstate commerce in general. Eugene V. Debs and other leaders were jailed for contempt. Whereas lower courts stressed the Sherman Act as the basis for the injunctions, the Supreme Court refused to commit itself on this issue, resting

[22] *United Mine Workers* v. *Coronado Coal Co.*, 259 U.S. 344.
[23] For the argument that the Act was intended to apply to labor, see A. T. Mason, *Organized Labor and the Law* (1925); for the opposing view, see E. Berman, *Labor and the Sherman Act* (1930).

its affirmance on broader grounds.[24] The consequent uncertainty was resolved in 1908. An elaborate secondary boycott against Loewe & Co., hat manufacturers of Danbury, Connecticut, had been organized by the United Hatters of America in a campaign for the closed shop. A damage suit against the union's officers and members was appealed to the Supreme Court, which unequivocally declared labor activities to be within the scope of the Sherman Act and held that the boycott was designed to restrain interstate commerce in Loewe's hats.[25] A jury subsequently awarded $74,000 damages, which when trebled, in accordance with the Act's triple-damage provisions, and added to interest and costs totaled $252,000.

The Danbury Hatters' decision, as it was popularly called, was received by labor with dismay. AFL officials not only viewed it as a miscarriage of justice based on an unwarranted reading of the statute, as a serious financial blow, and as an impediment to the use of an important weapon; they saw in it a potential threat to the very existence of unions, which might become the objects of dissolution suits by hostile Attorneys General. These extreme fears proved unfounded. The introduction in 1911 of the "rule of reason" and common-law tests of illegality precluded the outright destruction of organizations almost uniformly sanctioned at common law since 1842. Nevertheless, explicit amendment of the Sherman Act, along with abolition of "government by injunction," became the cardinal legislative objectives of the AFL. It supported Democratic candidates in 1908 and 1912, and claimed its reward from the Wilson administration.

Under Wilson's leadership, Congress responded with several labor provisions in the Clayton Act of 1914. Congress was unwilling to provide exemption for labor, but the possibility of dissolution suits was clearly eliminated by the somewhat grandiose words of Section 6:

That the labor of a human being is not a commodity or an article of commerce. Nothing contained in the antitrust laws shall be construed to forbid the existence and operation of labor, agricultural, or horticultural organizations, instituted for the purposes of mutual help, and not having capital stock or conducted for profit, or to forbid or restrain individual members of such organizations from *lawfully*

---

[24] *U.S.* v. *Debs*, 64 Fed. 724 (1894); *In re Debs*, 158 U.S. 564 (1895).

[25] *Loewe* v. *Lawlor*, 208 U.S. 274 (1908). The applicability of the Sherman Act was re-emphasized three years later in an *obiter dictum* passage in Justice Lamar's opinion in *Gompers* v. *Bucks Stove and Range Co.*, 221 U.S. 418 (1911).

176 PROMOTER OF PARTICULAR INTERESTS

carrying out the *legitimate* objects thereof; nor shall such organizations, or the members thereof, be held or construed to be illegal combinations or conspiracies in restraint of trade under the antitrust laws. [Italics supplied.]

Despite praise heaped on Section 6 by Gompers and other AFL officials, it is evident on its face that the italicized words robbed it of any meaning beyond debarring dissolution suits. Section 20, which somewhat restricted the use of labor injunctions, was of more consequence, especially on the side of procedure, but on balance the Clayton Act took away more than it gave. For, by Section 16, private parties as well as the government could now seek injunctive relief under the antitrust laws. Such private actions soon became more numerous than criminal prosecutions, damage suits, and government applications for labor injunctions combined.

In 1921 the Supreme Court made clear how little the Clayton Act had helped labor, describing it as "merely declaratory of what was the best practice always." Neither intimidation by pickets nor secondary boycotts were freed by its terms from injunctive restraint,[26] and the antitrust laws continued to impede unionization. Sherman Act application to secondary boycotts was reinforced in 1927 by a decision enjoining a relatively weak stonecutters' union from refusing to handle stone taken from a leading nonunion quarry.[27] Justices Brandeis and Holmes, dissenting, argued in vain that the rule of reason should distinguish this nonviolent defensive action of a weak union against a dominant employer from the elaborate coercive tactics, illegal in themselves, condemned in the earlier decisions.

Of even greater potential significance to unions was the second Coronado case,[28] arising from the efforts of the United Mine Workers to unionize the Southern coal mines to prevent competitive undermining of Northern labor standards. In 1925, the Supreme Court held that although coal mining itself was not interstate commerce and therefore not subject to the federal antitrust laws, violence on the part of union members intended to stop the interstate shipment of nonunion coal did fall within the prohibitions of the Sherman Act. Thus, although a strike is primarily a collective withholding of labor, which the Clayton

[26] *American Steel Foundries* v. *Tri-City Central Trades Council*, 257 U.S. 184 (1921); *Duplex Printing Press Co.* v. *Deering*, 254 U.S. 443 (1921).

[27] *Bedford Cut Stone Co.* v. *Journeymen Stone Cutters' Association*, 274 U.S. 37.

[28] *Coronado Coal Co.* v. *United Mine Workers of America*, 268 U.S. 295 (1925).

PROMOTION OF THE INTERESTS OF LABOR

Act declared not to be an article of commerce subject to the antitrust laws, any union action which had the intent (and not merely the incidental result) of interfering with interstate commerce became an illegal restraint of trade.

Beginning in 1937, the concept of interstate commerce was enormously expanded. Had the doctrine of the second Coronado decision been maintained, this expansion might have made the antitrust laws a much more serious obstacle to union activities. In 1940, however, in one of a series of cases which radically altered judicial attitudes toward unionization, the Court majority, although paying lip service to the Coronado case, virtually annulled it. A sitdown strike in a Pennsylvania hosiery plant, although illegal under state law, was held not to be a restraint of trade forbidden by the Sherman Act.[29]

In subsequent decisions, the Court almost completely eliminated the application of the antitrust laws to labor organizations. Ironically enough, this occurred just as the government was seeking to limit unions, not in organizing or collective bargaining, but in undertaking market restraints directly contrary to the competitive goals of the Sherman Act. In the leading case, Carpenters' Union officials had been indicted for violating the Sherman Act because of a strike and secondary boycott arising out of a jurisdictional dispute—acts clearly illegal under the Duplex and other decisions. Holding that the Norris-La Guardia Act had redefined the exemptions conferred by Section 20 of the Clayton Act, the Court dismissed the indictments and practically freed unions from the antitrust laws.[30] Market restraints on the part of unions violate the Sherman Act as now construed only if there is connivance with employers.[31] A union may even drive an employer out of business merely because of an old grudge, and despite his willingness to sign a union contract, without violating the Sherman Act.[32] Regulation of such union activities would require new legislation.

The Labor Injunction

If the Sherman Act was for some decades the chief legislative hindrance to organized labor, the injunction was by far the leading judicial obstacle. Before 1932, the injunction was a major instrument of labor law. Through its terms, the lofty principles of

[29] Apex Hosiery Co. v. Leader, 310 U.S. 469.
[30] U.S. v. Hutcheson, 312 U.S. 219 (1941).
[31] Allen-Bradley Co. v. International Brotherhood of Electrical Workers, 325 U.S. 797 (1945).
[32] Hunt v. Crumboch, 325 U.S. 821 (1945).

reciprocal rights and duties laid down in appellate courts were applied to specific labor disputes. In the hands of unfriendly judges, the injunction was often a more deadly weapon than the common law or the antitrust statutes. Hence the vehemence of labor animus against it, a feeling so intense during the 1920's as to displace almost all other items in the political agenda of the AFL. In those years of organizational weakness and internal strife, the single issue to which all labor would give its unequivocal support was relief from the injunction.

Originally developed by equity courts in contexts wholly differing from modern industrial disputes, injunctions were designed to prevent in advance irreparable damage for which adequate compensation could not be obtained in later legal proceedings. Wide discretion was necessarily placed in the judge, and violation of his writ was punishable as contempt of court. In the federal courts, where controversy over the injunction was sharpest, the instrument was particularly flexible. A temporary restraining order, supported by affidavits describing in the most loose terms the injury to be suffered from a strike, could be issued by the court on the employer's application, without notice to the union. After notice and summary hearing, it was followed by a temporary injunction, and in due course by full hearing and decision to make the injunction permanent. Appeals could be carried to higher courts on questions of law. From the labor viewpoint, the procedural safeguards at the later stages were generally Dead Sea fruit. The strike was often broken by the restraining order alone. Delaying a strike would often defeat unionization, and defiance of the order would cause wholesale arrests of strike leaders, sapping union morale and identifying strikers in the public mind with common criminals. Federal judges frequently directed their writs to "all persons whomsoever." The more far-reaching injunctions prohib*.ed every variety of activity.

Labor regarded imprisonment for contempt of court, without jury trial, as a denial of basic civil liberties. To Gompers the injunction was "personal government foisted upon our people instead of a government by law." [33] Only in a few isolated instances was the writ employed in labor's favor.[34] After repeated interpretations of the Clayton Act as a mere restatement of pre-existing law, pressure intensified for a more effective attack on the labor injunction. One proposal popular in AFL circles would have pre-

[33] F. Frankfurter and N. Greene, *The Labor Injunction* (1930), p. 53.
[34] See particularly *Texas and New Orleans R.R. Co. v. Brotherhood of Railway and Steamship Clerks*, 281 U.S. 548 (1930).

vented its use in protecting the "right to do business" simply by limiting the definition of "property" to things "tangible and transferable." Although both major parties included anti-injunction planks in their 1928 platforms, the Republicans were less condemnatory, noting only that labor injunctions had "in some instances been abused and have given rise to a serious question for legislation." Only with Democratic electoral successes in 1930, and with the imminence of another presidential campaign, did positive action become possible. Under the leadership of Senator Norris and Representative La Guardia, an anti-injunction bill was finally passed in 1932. After lengthy public hearings, the simple AFL proposal was rejected as of doubtful practicability and more doubtful constitutionality. The body of equity rules, procedural and substantive, required surgery rather than butchery, if much of value were not to be lost in the process of eliminating undesirable features. The bill finally enacted, by large majorities in both houses, was substantially as drafted for the Senate Judiciary Committee by a distinguished group of legal specialists, headed by Professor (later Justice) Felix Frankfurter.

A major piece of labor legislation, the Norris-La Guardia Act set about with great care to remedy, one by one, the evils of the labor injunction and the weaknesses of the Clayton Act. In contrast with later, more paternalistic New Deal laws, it was primarily self-help legislation, granting unions as much freedom from injunctive interference when pursuing their normal goals by normal methods as management had possessed for some time. The substantive grounds for the issuance of labor injunctions were circumscribed in three respects. Yellow-dog contracts were made unenforceable in federal courts. Injunctions under the antitrust laws might no longer be more extensive than those based on the common law. And in no case might federal injunctions prohibit the following acts when performed by persons, either singly or in concert, participating or interested in a labor dispute: refusal to work; joining or remaining in a union; giving financial aid to a union or strikers; lawfully aiding anyone in a labor dispute who is also party to a lawsuit; picketing or otherwise publicizing a labor dispute; assembling peaceably to promote their side of a dispute; and "advising, urging, or otherwise causing or inducing without fraud or violence" any of the preceding acts. Thus was sheathed the main judicial weapon against normal union activities, extending even to secondary boycotts.

New procedural limitations were also thrown about the use of the labor injunction. Temporary or permanent injunctions might be issued only after the open hearing of witnesses in support of the complaint, subject to cross-examination, and after formal court findings "that unlawful acts have been threatened and will be committed unless restrained," "that substantial and irreparable injury" will follow, that greater injury would be inflicted on the complainant by denying relief than on defendants by granting relief, that there is no adequate remedy at law, and that the complainant cannot secure adequate police protection. A temporary restraining order, valid for five days, could be issued only after an allegation of unavoidable and irreparable injury had been supported by sworn testimony sufficient to justify a temporary injunction, and after the complainant filed a bond sufficient to recompense defendants for consequent loss or damage. Before obtaining equitable relief, a complainant had to "make every reasonable effort to settle such dispute either by negotiation or with the aid of any available governmental machinery of mediation or voluntary arbitration." Appeals were expedited. Provision for jury trial in contempt cases was strengthened. Union officers or members, and the unions themselves, were liable for unlawful acts of individual members only "upon clear proof of actual participation in, or actual authorization of, such acts, or of ratification of such acts after actual knowledge thereof." By 1947, moreover, sixteen states, covering many of the important industrial areas of the country, followed the federal model with "baby Norris-La Guardia Acts," although in other states courts continued to use labor injunctions against unions and to enjoin even peaceable behavior.[35]

The constitutionality of the Wisconsin act was upheld in 1937.[36] The federal act was affirmed and a broad construction given its scope in 1938.[37] The Norris-La Guardia Act thus has satisfied most of labor's grievances against "government by injunction." One loophole, however, was opened in the Act when, in the dramatic Lewis case of 1947, a divided Court held that it did not forbid labor injunctions when government was the employer.[38]

[35] E.g., see R. E. Mathews, et al., "Survey of Ohio Practice in Issuance of Labor Injunctions," Ohio State University Law Journal (June, 1939), pp. 289–329.

[36] Senn v. Tile Layers' Protective Union, 301 U.S. 468.

[37] Lauf v. E. G. Shinner & Co., 303 U.S. 323; New Negro Alliance v. Sanitary Grocery Co., 303 U.S. 552.

[38] U.S. v. Lewis and United Mine Workers of America, 330 U.S. 258. Because coal operators and the union had been unable to agree on a contract, the government had seized and technically was operating the mines. A district court enjoined Lewis and the union to end the strike and imposed heavy fines

Mediation, Conciliation, and Arbitration

Government agencies at local, state, and federal levels have long used their good offices to obtain adjustment and voluntary settlement of labor disputes. Without special legal authority, city mayors have traditionally intervened in situations threatening stoppage of essential services. Governors and Presidents have played similar roles. Informal mediation or conciliation may avert or shorten a stoppage, eliminating hardship to both sides and to the public. It is ordinarily undertaken on the initiative of the executive or at the request of either party.

Arbitration is a more formalized process, usually eventuating in an award by an impartial board or single arbitrator on disputed claims as to rights and duties. As unionization has grown, this function has become increasingly important, centering on the interpretation of labor-management contracts. Elaborate machinery, both private and public, has been established for arbitration. Awards are frequently made binding in accordance with the prior agreement of both parties.

Specialized agencies for conciliation and arbitration were first set up by Massachusetts and New York in 1886. Most states now provide similar services, varying greatly in adequacy of personnel and in effectiveness. In establishing the Department of Labor in 1913, Congress authorized the Secretary "to act as mediator and to appoint commissioners of conciliation in labor disputes. . . ." In 1917, the United States Conciliation Service was formally organized to carry out this mandate. Its commissioners intervene in strikes or potential strike situations at the request of either party or of local officials and, in rare cases of unusual public importance, on their own initiative. The Service expanded rapidly, commanding a staff of 79 conciliators in 1919; in the trying conditions of 1917–1919, it was able to adjust 2,790 disputes. During this period, as the pressure of rising prices on living standards and the labor shortages in many fields contributed to industrial conflict, mediation boards, with equal representation of employers and employees, were also established for each leading industry, with the machinery capped by the National War Labor Board. This Board for the first time formulated the policy, later adopted by Congress in the

---

when they ignored its injunction. In the Supreme Court, a bare majority held that the Act did not apply and that the injunction was valid. But of the majority of five, only three justices would support a judgment for criminal contempt. Two of the minority of four, although believing the injunction void, argued that Lewis and the UMW were criminally contemptuous of it; they joined forces with the three on this point.

Wagner Act, of affirming the right of workers (as well as employers) to organize and to bargain collectively through representatives of their own choosing. Although it did not completely eliminate strikes, the machinery aided substantially in smoothing industrial relations in a most difficult period of transition.

After World War I, the War Labor Board machinery was swept away, and during the twenties the case load of the Conciliation Service fell off. In the thirties, with the vast expansion of union membership, the number of cases rose rapidly, passing 1,000 in 1934 and reaching an annual rate of 3,700 just before World War II. A good deal of informal conciliation was also done in this period by representatives of the National Labor Relations Board (NLRB). During World War II, the work of the Conciliation Service was further multiplied, over 21,500 disputes requiring its services in fiscal 1944. In 1941, a National Defense Mediation Board, composed of representatives of labor, management, and the public, was established by executive order to deal with cases which the Conciliation Service was unable to settle. When in 1942 a difficult case involving the United Mine Workers and the captive coal mines led to the resignation of the CIO representatives, a similar tripartite National War Labor Board was established, first by executive order and later by law in the War Labor Disputes Act of 1943. This Board and its twelve regional subboards functioned as courts of appeal for cases handled initially by the Conciliation Service. The most important of its policies was a compromise between the open shop advocated by employers and the closed shop demanded by unions. It pursued a "maintenance-of-membership" policy, which provided that all union members who did not resign during a fifteen-day period after the issuance of a Board order had to retain their membership as a condition of employment.

As in World War I, the Board could not forbid strikes. A thirty-day "cooling-off" period, however, was required in disputes involving war contractors, and other sanctions, such as contract cancellation, loss of draft deferments, and plant seizure, were available to the President. Forty-seven plants were seized by the federal government, an action which in wartime conditions resulted virtually in compulsory arbitration of labor disputes. These seizures were made under general war powers, but seizure in peacetime requires legislative authorization. In 1948, the railroads were seized on the basis of a 1916 law, but presidential seizure of the steel mills in 1952 on the basis of his general executive powers was voided by the Supreme Court.[39]

[39] *Youngstown Sheet & Tube Co.* v. *Sawyer,* 343 U.S. 579.

In 1947, the Taft-Hartley Act made the Conciliation Service independent of the Department of Labor, renaming it the Federal Mediation and Conciliation Service. Although the older agency had successfully settled over three-fourths of the cases presented to it, some employers felt that its position within a labor-oriented Department prevented it from being fully impartial. The same Act also provided that in disputes which "imperil the national health and safety," the President may appoint a board of inquiry to ascertain and report the facts. He may then petition a district court to enjoin a strike or lockout for as much as eighty days. During this period the fact-finding board would be reconvened to continue its investigation and to make a second report by the sixtieth day. If the dispute were still not settled, the employer's last offer was to be submitted to a secret ballot of the employees. This procedure was designed to provide a cooling-off period during which a settlement could be negotiated. If the workers voted to strike at the end of the period, however, the strike would not be illegal. The President could only report the facts to Congress "with such recommendations as he may see fit to make for consideration and appropriate action." These emergency provisions have almost completely failed to avert critical strikes. They have been criticized as distorting the bargaining process, for "they neither aid collective bargaining nor create the conditions necessary for amicable agreement between labor and management." [40] In practice, the eighty-day cooling-off period is sometimes a "warming-up period." Nor is last-minute, *ad hoc* legislation, of the sort implied by the Act, likely to make for sound labor law.

Railroad Labor Legislation

Public adjustment machinery has been most highly developed in the railroad field. Because of the utter dependence of the whole community on uninterrupted transportation services, because the railroads formerly had a virtual monopoly of these services, and because most transportation has always been included within the regulatory powers of Congress, the government has experimented for seventy years with attempts to prevent strikes through regularized intervention. Considerable experience with arbitration and mediation and with the balance between voluntary adjustment and public influence has been accumulated, and laws covering railway labor have sometimes served as models for more general legislation.

[40] C. M. Rehmus, "The Operation of the National Emergency Provisions of the Labor Management Relations Act of 1947," *Yale Law Journal* (June, 1953), pp. 1052, 1059.

While an ineffective and unused act providing for voluntary arbitration and for government fact-finding commissions had been enacted in 1888, the seeds of modern law began with the Erdman Act of 1898. It provided for mediation and conciliation by the chairman of the Interstate Commerce Commission and the Commissioner of Labor, on the request of either party to the dispute. If unsuccessful, they were to try to bring about arbitration. Submission of a dispute was voluntary, but awards were binding and enforceable by court order.[41]

In the early years, no use was made of the Erdman Act. Management was not yet generally converted to union recognition. As the unions gained in strength in the years before World War I, however, the Act was invoked in sixty-one cases, all but sixteen of which were settled without arbitration. Success in mediation led to its strengthening by the Newlands Act, passed in 1913 with the support of both railroad management and labor. A permanent Board of Mediation and Conciliation was created and empowered to intervene on its own initiative, as well as on the request of either party. For three years this machinery worked well, but in 1916 the increasingly powerful unions refused to use it in their claim for the eight-hour day. A strike was averted at the eleventh hour only by direct congressional action—passage of the Adamson Act [42] at the urgent behest of President Wilson.

During federal control of the railways from 1917 to 1920, public policy encouraged organization by forbidding antiunion discrimination and by introducing nationwide agreements on hours, wages, and working conditions. Three bipartisan Boards of Adjustment were eminently successful in deciding controversies over the interpretation or application of wage agreements. Like organized labor at large, the railway brotherhoods made great strides during the war years. Seeking the retention of federal control after the war under the "Plumb Plan," they vainly opposed the Transportation Act of 1920, which restored the roads to private ownership.[43]

The labor provisions of this Act ignored most of the lessons of previous decades. Congress created a full-time tripartite Railroad Labor Board, which had been advocated by proponents of compulsory arbitration, but it was unwilling to accept the principle

[41] The Act also sought to outlaw yellow-dog contracts and forbid antiunion discrimination, but this provision was invalidated by the Supreme Court in 1908.

[42] See above, p. 164.

[43] See Chapter 10.

of compulsion itself and gave the Board no sanctions for enforcement of its awards. An abortive effort was made to set out standards for wage decision, but the phraseology was so broad as to create more difficulties than it solved. Mediation machinery was unwisely abandoned. The Act also omitted guarantees of freedom of organization. The new machinery was distrusted by the unions from the start. It failed to prevent the great shopmen's strike of 1922. Public members of the Board were believed to be biased in favor of the carriers, and did approve of company unionism, which now flourished on the railroads for the first time. Nor did the Board gain the full confidence of management. Several roads ignored its awards, and the Supreme Court affirmed their contention that enforcement rested solely on publicity.[44]

In 1926, therefore, Congress passed the Railway Labor Act, which remains the basic law in this field.[45] Amendments in 1934, promoted by the unions together with the Federal Co-ordinator of Transportation,[46] strengthened the Act, elaborating its provisions against company unionism, differentiating the various adjustment stages, and setting up appropriate machinery for each. It places primary emphasis on direct collective bargaining and mediation, but also establishes voluntary arbitration and compulsory investigation. Returning to the model of the Erdman and Newlands Acts, the statute provides for mediation of disputes not settled by conferences through a full-time, three-member National Mediation Board, on request of either party or on its own motion. If mediation fails, the Board tries to persuade both sides to accept arbitration, which is performed by *ad hoc* boards, containing nominees of the parties concerned and neutral members chosen by the other members or, in the event of disagreement, by the Mediation Board. Arbitration awards are binding, are subject to judicial review on limited grounds of law, and are enforceable as court orders. While of substantial importance before 1934, the arbitration machinery has now been supplanted almost completely by the National Railroad Adjustment Board, which is described below.

The National Mediation Board certifies labor representatives for collective bargaining. The 1934 amendments to the Railway Labor Act forbid company unions. The roads must negotiate in good faith with the authorized labor representatives certified by the

---

[44] *Pennsylvania Federation* v. *Pennsylvania R.R. Co.*, 267 U.S. 203 (1925).

[45] In 1936 the Act was amended to cover air transport lines and their employees.

[46] For the creation and duties of this office, see below, pp. 286–287.

Board, although agreement is, of course, not compelled.[47] Carriers may not engage in a number of specified labor practices, such as promotion of company unions, yellow-dog contracts, and other hindrances to independent unions. While these "unfair labor practices" closely approximate those forbidden by the Wagner Act of 1935, railway unions must depend for their enforcement upon ordinary judicial processes,[48] without the aid of a special administrative tribunal.

Mediation procedure relies heavily on delay, looking to a "cooling-off period" to foster voluntary adjustment of disputes. Thirty days' notice is required for changes in agreements on wages, rules, or working conditions, and the status quo must be maintained until final action by the Mediation Board. Moreover, if the adjustment machinery fails to settle a dispute, and the Board deems it to "threaten substantially to interrupt interstate commerce to a degree such as to deprive any section of the country of essential transportation service," the President may create a special emergency board of disinterested persons to investigate and report. Their report is made within thirty days after appointment, and conditions are maintained without change (except by agreement) pending the report and for a further thirty days thereafter.

The 1934 amendments also established a National Railroad Adjustment Board of thirty-six members, operating in four functional divisions and dealing with routine disputes arising out of collective bargaining. Each division represents both parties equally. Deadlocks may be resolved by a neutral "referee" appointed by mutual consent or by the Mediation Board. The Board has jurisdiction, on petition of either party, over disputes "growing out of grievances or out of the interpretation or application of agreements concerning rates of pay, rules, or working conditions," after ordinary negotiations have failed. The Board's operations fall somewhere between arbitration and quasi-judicial decision. Its orders may be enforced only after court review at the instance of the winner, in which the Board's action is to be taken as prima-facie evidence of the facts. All but a handful of its thousands of awards, however, have been obeyed without court action.

Experience under the Act of 1926 has varied considerably.

---

[47] Cf. *Virginian Railway Co.* v. *System Federation No. 40*, 300 U.S. 515 (1937).

[48] The most striking case of the use of an injunction on behalf of organized labor is afforded by *Texas & New Orleans Railroad Co.* v. *Brotherhood of Railway and Steamship Clerks*, 281 U.S. 548 (1930), where the union secured a decree against maintenance of a rival company union under the 1926 Act.

From 1926 to 1941 it worked very well indeed. From 1941 on, it has enjoyed somewhat less success, the number of stoppages and man-days lost rising substantially. Among the causes for this rise have been a drastic decline in railroad employment (causing the railroad brotherhoods to fight hard for the preservation of jobs through restrictive rules—"featherbedding") and limitations on management's ability or willingness to make concessions resulting from the competitive inroads of other forms of transportation and from uncertainty whether regulatory authorities will allow increased rail charges to meet increased wage costs. One consequence of these strains on the bargaining process was a great increase in the number of emergency boards in the 1940's. As these boards became more frequent, their recommendations carried less weight. To make matters worse, twice during World War II emergency board recommendations were disregarded by President Roosevelt under union pressure and new settlements negotiated.

Despite these weaknesses, however, the mediation machinery meets its major objectives. While there are occasional work stoppages, widespread tie-ups of this crucial service are rare, and the proportion of man-days lost from labor disputes is very small.

3. Labor Under the New Deal

The New Deal opened a new era in which the possibility of using government as a positive instrument to realize labor's widening objectives quickly became apparent. Under the stimulus of the National Industrial Recovery Act of 1933, union membership, which had fallen to a little over two million, rebounded. The initial gains made by the mine workers and the needle trades were quickly extended to the hitherto unorganized mass-production industries.

Soon the old issue of craft versus industrial unionism was again rife. "Federal locals" for the newly organized were viewed by craft leaders as temporary devices, to be maintained only until their members could be apportioned among appropriate craft unions. The resultant dissension, coupled with a revival of strong antiunionism among employers, nullified some of the gains of 1933 and 1934. In revolt against the official AFL attitude, leaders of the United Mine Workers, the Amalgamated Clothing Workers, the International Ladies' Garment Workers, and other industrial unions, headed by John L. Lewis of the miners, formed a Committee for Industrial Organization (CIO) in 1935 to organize the unskilled. In 1936 the CIO unions were suspended from the Federation and two years later reorganized their group as the Congress of Industrial Organizations, with a wholly independent constitutional framework. CIO successes in 1936 and 1937 were spectacular. For the first time, the rubber, automobile, and steel industries were organized. Union recognition by the United States Steel Corporation was the most dramatic labor accomplishment in decades. Late in 1937, however, the CIO was defeated in a long-drawn-out strike against four independent steel companies.

Throughout the remainder of the New Deal, the split in the labor movement caused vigorous recriminations, personal and otherwise, between the two organizations. The AFL declared war on the CIO as a revival of radical dual unionism, of the sort which in the past had only disrupted labor. The CIO retorted that AFL leadership ignored the mass of American workmen, that craft domination produced fruitless jurisdictional quarrels and toleration of labor racketeering. The CIO, in its turn, suffered from internal dissension, leading both to a split within the United Automobile Workers and the secession of the International Ladies' Garment Workers and the United Mine Workers. Although, as we have seen,[49] the breach in the labor movement was not healed until 1955, the emergence of the CIO reshaped the structure of organized labor in harmony with the modern pattern of industry. The same period marked a milestone in the evolution of government's attitude toward organized labor. A long tradition of aloofness or hostility, partially modified during World War I, was suddenly transformed into recognition, sympathy, and with some exceptions, open friendliness. Union membership reached a new peak of eight million, almost twice its previous record. Labor legislation, both protective and promotive of organization, was extended to unprecedented lengths.

The National Industrial Recovery Act

The National Industrial Recovery Act (NIRA) of 1933 was the progenitor of New Deal labor policies.[50] Its famous Section 7(a) required all National Recovery Administration (NRA) codes to guarantee labor's right to organize and to bargain collectively, free from the restraint or coercion of employers. Under this impetus, an organizing movement spread through the ranks of

[49] Chapter 2.
[50] The significance of the NIRA as an experiment in industrial control is analyzed below in Chapter 17.

American labor. Between the summer of 1933 and the winter of 1934–1935, AFL membership increased by more than a million. Unions conducting aggressive organizing campaigns made the greatest gains, but it was the collective bargaining provisions of the NIRA which made these gains possible.

The NIRA also provided a new method of enacting protective labor legislation on a nationwide industry basis. The code-making process, in which government, employers, and trade-unions all participated, offered an opportunity to shape labor standards, to outlaw child labor, to fix minimum wages, maximum hours, and other conditions, and to give these standards legal status. Again, it must be noted, labor was most effective in industries where it was strongly organized. Its new-found power was sometimes skillfully used to expand trade-union influence by eliminating or limiting the differential advantage of unorganized regions and employers.

The NIRA experiment, to be sure, was severely criticized by some labor leaders. Those who expected it to usher in a labor millennium were disappointed. Many employers bitterly resisted the spread of unionism, and their influence penetrated into the inner councils of the NRA. Difficulties developed over the application of Section 7(a). Organized labor contended that the law required the NRA to promote unionization, while the agency's high command held that this responsibility rested upon the workers. Disputes developed over the status of company unions and the question of representation of minority worker groups.

Despite these disputes and difficulties, the NRA struck a new balance in employer-employee relationships. It tried both to raise labor standards and to provide a legal environment in which unionism could take root and flourish. It made at least tentative gestures toward giving labor a voice in the determination of industrial and business policies. As labor's economic and political strength increased during the next years, strenuous efforts were made to extend these gains.

The Wagner Act and the Work of the NLRB

The present National Labor Relations Board (NLRB) can be traced back to the NIRA. After an outbreak of strikes during the early summer of 1933, President Roosevelt by executive order established the National Labor Board, composed of industry and labor representatives, with Senator Wagner acting as chairman. Subsequently, special boards for certain industries were created either under their NRA codes or by executive order; the National

Labor Board dealt with alleged violations of Section 7(a) in all other industries. At first, when the prestige of the Board was great and the disposition to obey the Recovery Act strong, the Board and its regional subdivisions were able to settle many labor disputes. After some early successes, the Board's effectiveness was seriously undermined by the informal character of its authority, dissension among Board members, lack of sanctions, certain ambiguities in the terms of Section 7(a), and defiance of the Board's orders by several large companies.

The National Labor Board was succeeded in July, 1934, by the first National Labor Relations Board, established by joint resolution of Congress. Empowered to deal with controversies arising under Section 7(a) and to conduct elections to determine employee representatives for collective bargaining, this Board suffered from many of the same handicaps as the original Wagner Board. It was, if anything, even less successful in obtaining compliance with its decisions. When the NIRA was invalidated by the Supreme Court in 1935,[51] the Board, too, was extinguished. From its experience and opinions, however, were derived many of the principles underlying the unfair labor practices prohibited by the National Labor Relations Act of 1935—the Wagner Act.

This statute, enacted less than a month and a half after the death of the NRA, established a three-man National Labor Relations Board appointed by the President and confirmed by the Senate. Two major tasks were given the NLRB: (1) to protect the right of employees to organize and to bargain collectively through representatives of their own choosing; and (2) to set up machinery to determine bargaining representatives and so reduce strikes for recognition, usually the bitterest of all industrial disputes. While Section 7 of the new Act echoed the language of Section 7(a) of the NIRA, Section 8 in its prohibition and definition of "unfair labor practices" shielded labor's rights by imposing five specific restraints on employers. The first forbade employers "to interfere with, restrain, or coerce employees in the exercise of the rights guaranteed in Section 7." The second, directed against company unions, forbade employers "to dominate or interfere with the formation or administration of any labor organization or contribute financial or other support to it." The third forbade discrimination because of union membership. The fourth outlawed practice was the discharge of, or discrimination against, an employee for having filed charges or testified under the Act. The fifth unfair labor practice, refusal to bargain collectively with employee

[51] *Schechter* v. *U.S.*, 295 U.S. 495.

representatives, placed an affirmative duty on the employer to bargain, although not necessarily to agree.[52]

Section 9 provided that collective-bargaining representatives chosen by a majority of the employees in a unit should be the exclusive representatives of that unit. The NLRB was given full discretion to decide whether the appropriate unit should be "the employer unit, craft unit, plant unit, or subdivisions thereof." Section 9 also authorized the NLRB to determine the bargaining representatives by secret ballot or other suitable methods, and to certify them.

In other sections, the Board was empowered to order employers to cease and desist from specified unfair labor pactices which interfered with the right of employees to organize. Violation of a Board order itself carried no penalty; the Board had to petition a circuit court of appeals for enforcement. Any aggrieved person could try to persuade this court to review the legal issues involved, but the NLRB's findings of facts, if supported by evidence, were conclusive. An NLRB certification of bargaining representatives was reviewable only when it accompanied an order to an employer to bargain with the certified representative.

In examining the administrative record of the NLRB, it is necessary to recall the environment in which it functioned and the nature of the pressures which impinged upon it. At the threshold, it was met by employer hostility and a barrage of lawsuits questioning the Act's constitutionality. Until the Supreme Court spoke in April, 1937,[53] nearly two years after the passage of the Act, the Board's activities were almost paralyzed. After the Act was upheld, an avalanche of business descended upon the Board, straining its resources. Meanwhile, as the battle between the AFL and the CIO became more bitter, employers hostile to unionism were quick to take advantage of the split. Jurisdictional squabbles cast discredit on unionism and forfeited middle-class sympathy. It was in this context that the NLRB was compelled to operate. It could not count on the support of a united labor movement. It

[52] But note the words of Justice Stone in H. J. Heinz Co. v. NLRB, 311 U.S. 514 (1941): ". . . the National Labor Relations Act, while requiring the employer to bargain collectively, does not compel him to enter into an agreement. But it does not follow . . . that, having reached an agreement, he can refuse to sign it, because he has never agreed to sign one."

[53] See Associated Press v. NRLB, 301 U.S. 103; Washington, Virginia and Maryland Coach Co. v. NLRB, 301 U.S. 142; NLRB v. Jones & Laughlin Steel Corp., 301 U.S. 1; NLRB v. Fruehauf Trailer Co., 301 U.S. 49; NLRB v. Friedman-Harry Marks Clothing Co., 301 U.S. 58. With the exception of the second case listed, all of these were 5 to 4 decisions.

could count on the hostility of many employers. And as the feud between the AFL and the CIO developed, the Board was inevitably involved, its decisions attacked by both sides.

The work of the Board fell into two main classes: (1) cases of alleged unfair practices by employers, and (2) cases involving the determination of bargaining agents. The latter category provided the greatest amount of NLRB case work. During the twelve years of the Wagner Act, nearly sixty thousand representation petitions were filed with the Board, together with forty-five thousand charges of unfair labor practices.[54] Elections or cross-checks of union membership cards against payrolls (largely abandoned after 1939) were conducted by the Board prior to certification of bargaining agents. While this part of the NLRB program did much to encourage collective bargaining—unions won better than four out of five elections and cross-checks [55]—the AFL-CIO feud and other inter-union jurisdictional conflicts often aggravated the Board's difficulties in selecting the appropriate bargaining unit. The Board commonly accepted the jurisdictional claims of craft unions when their membership was substantial and there were no conflicting claims. When both craft and industrial unions claimed jurisdiction, the question was decided by the employees in the craft group, under the Globe doctrine.[56]

The NLRB was never able to satisfy fully either the AFL or the CIO. The former contended that the Board was dominated by the CIO, which in turn assailed the Board for bending over backward to be fair to the AFL and for carving up industrial unions into craft groups.[57] Yet NLRB representation cases were clearly of

[54] H. A. Millis and E. C. Brown, *From the Wagner Act to Taft-Hartley* (1950), p. 76.

[55] *Ibid.*, p. 89.

[56] *Globe Machine and Stamping Co.*, 3 NLRB 294 (1937). This doctrine, however, was not applied where an industrial union had already obtained an exclusive bargaining contract and had a record of continuity of bargaining relationships in the plant: *American Can Co.*, 13 NLRB 1252 (1939).

[57] The AFL frequently cited *Shipowners' Association of the Pacific Coast*, 7 NLRB 1002 (1938), in which the CIO Longshoremen's Union was designated as the bargaining representative for all West Coast ports, although an AFL union claimed a majority among particular employees. In fact, statistically at least, the NLRB seemed to steer a course midway between the two organizations. Down to December 1, 1939, the Board had decided 301 cases involving conflicting AFL and CIO arguments over bargaining units. In 187 of these cases, the Board gained complete or substantial AFL and CIO agreement with its decision. In the remaining 114 cases, the Board upheld the contention of the AFL in 51 and that of the CIO in 45. In 14 cases, the contention of each was upheld in part, and no decision was handed down in two cases. *Intermediate Report of the Special Committee to Investigate the NLRB*, H. Rept. No. 1902, 76th Cong., 3d sess. (1940), pt. 2, p. 29.

enormous assistance to unions and helped establish collective bargaining in many industries. Two observers conclude:

. . . the Board built soundly in developing a common law which would protect the right of employees freely to choose their bargaining representatives. Hampered by inadequate staff and by . . . the divided and competing labor movements, and faced by a tremendous volume of cases . . . the Board nevertheless achieved a very large degree of respect and acceptance of its work in this [representation] field. It made an outstanding contribution toward the establishment of collective bargaining on a freely chosen and democratic basis.[58]

About two-thirds of the NLRB's unfair labor practice cases dealt with discrimination against employees for union activity.[59] Almost another third involved allegations of refusal to bargain. In ruling on such cases, the NLRB expected employers to meet with union representatives, to receive their demands, to offer counter proposals, and generally to negotiate in good faith. A major effect of NLRB administration was the virtual elimination of company unionism. Charges of company domination of unions were involved in about one-fifth of the cases filed in the first three years of the Wagner Act but declined substantially thereafter.

The Wagner Act achieved its objectives, permanently altering the course of labor-management relations and the distribution of power in the economy. It was designed to facilitate and encourage, but not to require, collective bargaining and unionization. This it did. Union membership, also stimulated by the concurrent efforts of the CIO, increased fourfold under the Wagner Act, rising from less than 4 million in 1935 to almost 15.5 million in 1947. The percentage of manufacturing employees covered by union contracts increased from 19.5 in 1935 to 69 in 1946.

The economic and political power of unions increased correspondingly. In part because of NLRB sanctions and in part because of union strength, attitudes and practices of employers changed radically, although not without protest. In industry after industry, collective bargaining was substituted for all-out anti-union warfare, which had involved the use of professional strike-breakers, labor espionage, lockouts, and various forms of coercion.

With the spread of collective bargaining and the availability of NLRB elections, strikes to gain union recognition fell off. They accounted for about a third of all strikes in 1934, less than a tenth during World War II, and only a sixth in 1946.

The far-reaching changes in industrial relations occasioned by

[58] Millis and Brown, *op. cit.*, p. 173.
[59] For case statistics, see *ibid.*, pp. 78–79.

the Wagner Act were accompanied by vigorous criticism of the terms of the law and of the manner of its administration. The Act was attacked for onesideness, for imposing restrictions on employers without placing comparable restraints on labor, for requiring employers—but not unions—to bargain in good faith. Freedom of union organizers to try to persuade workers was not matched, it was alleged, by freedom of speech for employers.[60] The Act was also criticized for denying representation to worker minorities. There was some validity to these charges. The law did protect union activities while limiting antiunion activities. This was its declared purpose; it sought to protect the right to organize and to bargain collectively in the belief that the existence of responsible trade-unions would reduce industrial disputes and serve the general welfare.

Apart from the provisions of the Act, the NLRB was strongly criticized for biased administration. The informality of procedures, alleged mixing of prosecuting and adjudicative functions, and overzealousness in fostering unionism were all assailed. While certain of these criticisms really applied to the law itself, in some cases the zeal of NLRB employees had outrun their judgment and they had taken upon themselves direct organizing responsibilities more properly left to the unions. But such activity was not characteristic of the Board's record as a whole. For the most part, it had only obeyed the mandate of the Act to protect the legal right to organize unions.

With the conservative resurgence ushered in by the 1938 elections and the deepening cleavage between the AFL and the CIO, attacks upon the Board intensified and its position weakened. In 1940, by a vote of 258 to 129, the House approved a series of amendments to the Act written by a hostile investigating committee,[61] but friends of the law were still strong enough to prevent action in the Senate. The first chairman of the Board, J. Warren Madden, was not reappointed because it seemed unlikely that he

[60] In fact, after some contrary rulings during the first few years, employers were authorized to express their views on labor problems as long as no coercion was involved and workers were free in their choice of a bargaining representative. See NLRB v. Virginia Electric & Power Co., 314 U.S. 469 (1941).

[61] The majority of the Smith Committee (so called after its chairman, Howard W. Smith) effected a coalition with AFL forces in Congress. The amendments as voted contained protection for AFL craft unions, as well as provisions increasing the privileges of employers and restricting the scope of NLRB activity. The Smith Committee amendments also proposed the separation of administrative and judicial functions by vesting all administrative duties in a Labor Relations Administrator independent of the Board.

would be confirmed by the Senate. World War II delayed further action, but the further revival of conservative strength, the continuing split in organized labor's ranks, and the increase in public concern over the effects of jurisdictional disputes and occasional displays of union irresponsibility all combined to prepare the way for amendment of the Wagner Act after the war.

Wage and Hour Legislation

Meanwhile, New Deal efforts to regulate hours, wages, and working conditions continued after the collapse of the NRA. In 1936, a fresh start was made through the Walsh-Healey Act, which rested the authority to regulate, not on the interstate commerce clause, but on the power of the government as purchaser to insist upon stated contractual conditions.[62] The Act required that all federal contracts involving $10,000 or more must limit working hours to eight per day or forty per week, except as permitted by the Secretary of Labor;[63] that boys under sixteen and girls under eighteen should not be employed; and that rates of pay should not be less than the prevailing minimum wage of the industry as determined by the Secretary. The incidence of this Act has, of course, spread enormously with the expanded volume of government contracts, especially for defense. In addition, since 1931 the Davis-Bacon Act has established minimum-wage standards for mechanics and laborers employed on public works contracts greater than $2,000.

The Fair Labor Standards (or Wage and Hour) Act of 1938, which has much wider coverage than the Walsh-Healey Act, was passed by a somewhat reluctant Congress under heavy administration pressure after the Supreme Court had upheld both the Wagner Act and a State of Washington minimum wage law. Designed to eradicate substandard labor conditions from interstate commerce, the Act prescribed a maximum work week of forty hours [64] and required the payment of time and one-half for overtime work. Minimum wages were first fixed at 25 cents an hour, to be raised to 30 cents in 1939 and 40 cents in 1945. By later amendments, the minimum was raised to 75 cents in 1949 and to $1 in 1956. Child labor under sixteen years of age was prohibited

[62] In *Perkins* v. *Lukens Steel Co.*, 310 U.S. 113 (1940), the Supreme Court held that companies complaining of a wage determination of the Secretary of Labor under the Act lacked standing to sue.

[63] The Secretary has authorized work in excess of the stated minima, if compensated at the rate of time and one-half.

[64] In the third year after its passage. For the first year the maximum was set at forty-four, for the second at forty-two.

except under special conditions laid down by the Children's Bureau (a function subsequently transferred to the Bureau of Labor Standards). The minimum age may be raised to eighteen years in those occupations the Bureau finds to be hazardous or peculiarly detrimental to health and well-being. Enforcement is vested in a single administrator heading a Wage and Hour and Public Contracts Division in the Department of Labor. Criminal as well as injunctive proceedings may be instituted against violators; employees may also bring suit for recovery of double damages.

Coverage of the Act does not extend to the full limits of Congress' power to regulate. As amended in 1949, the Act applies to those workers "engaged in commerce," "engaged in the production of goods for commerce," or performing work "closely related" and "directly essential" to such production. The line is often hard to draw, as the number of cases involving the issue of coverage attests.[65] There are various partial and complete exemptions; those not covered include workers in the retail and service trades, construction, and agriculture.[66] Coverage extends to over twenty mil-

[65] E.g., see *Kirschbaum* v. *Walling*, 316 U.S. 517 (1942); *10 East 40th Street Building* v. *Callus*, 325 U.S. 578 (1945); *Borden Co.* v. *Borella*, 325 U.S. 679 (1945); *Martino* v. *Michigan Window Cleaning Co.*, 327 U.S. 173 (1946); *Mabee* v. *White Plains Publishing Co.*, 327 U.S. 178 (1946); *Boutell* v. *Walling*, 327 U.S. 657 (1946); *Schulte, Inc.* v. *Gangi*, 328 U.S. 108 (1946).

[66] The 1949 amendments added new exemptions and broadened old ones. Wage and hour provisions do not apply to agricultural and nonprofit irrigation company workers; seamen; employees of streetcar, urban railway, or bus systems; taxicab operators; employees of small telephone exchanges or telegraph offices; workers in small forestry and lumbering operations; employees engaged in catching or canning fish; and employees of weekly or semiweekly newspapers with a circulation of less than 4,000. They do not apply to persons employed in a *bona fide* executive, administrative, professional, or local retail capacity, or to outside salesmen. They do not apply to persons employed in any retail or service establishment, the greater part of whose selling and servicing is in intrastate commerce, to laundries or dry cleaners. They do not apply to persons employed to handle or prepare or can agricultural, horticultural, or dairy products or other materials in their raw or natural state.

In addition to these classes which are exempt from both the wage and hour provisions, there are still others—such as employees of railroads, motor carriers, or pipelines regulated by the ICC; air carriers; fish canners; poultry, egg, and dairy buyers; and a number of other specified processors—who are exempt only from the hour provisions. And there are still others—such as employees in seasonal industries and employees who are working under annual or semiannual guaranteed wage plans which have been negotiated through collective bargaining—who are partially exempt from the hour provisions. In addition, there is another whole class of exemptions, which permits the payment of a subminimum wage to learners, apprentices, and individuals whose earning capacity is impaired by age or physical or mental deficiency or injury.

lion employees working in almost three-quarters of a million establishments.

Enforcement is decentralized, with regional and field offices hearing complaints, making investigations, and handing down orders. In the first decade of administration, more than $111 million was ordered paid to three million workers in restitution for employers' failures to meet minimum-wage or overtime-pay standards.[67] The task of enforcement among marginal businesses hiring low-paid and itinerant or seasonal employees, however, is a never ending one. In 1955, over half the firms investigated were violating the law, and $12 million in back wages were ordered to be paid to 130,000 workers.[68]

Federal regulation is now much more important than state law in setting minimum standards. Only in a few respects, such as hours of work for women, are state laws more protective than the federal act. Thus, within the area it covers, the federal law sets standards for the whole economy, minimizing the problems of compliance and interstate competition. Because of the extent and success of collective bargaining, and because of the tight labor market which has usually prevailed in recent years, minimum-wage regulation now has only limited impact, protecting workers where immobility, ignorance, or other factors would otherwise set labor standards well below national averages. When $1 an hour was established as the minimum in March, 1956, it was estimated that only about two million workers were affected.

4. Labor in the Postwar Period

After a period of rapid growth under the New Deal, organized labor entered upon relative maturity during the postwar period. Its substantial power and its new status had been acknowledged in World War II when its leaders were given important posts in administration of the economy and when existing unionization was protected by the National War Labor Board's adoption of the "maintenance of membership" principle.

With labor's greater power and with acceptance of collective bargaining in most manufacturing, mining, and transportation industries, governmental policy, reflecting changes in the political environment, shifted somewhat from promotionalism to regulation. In 1946, the Republicans, who had little following among

[67] W. S. Tyson, "Fair Labor Standards Act of 1938: A Survey and Evaluation of the First Eleven Years," *Labor Law Journal* (January, 1950), p. 282.

[68] *New York Times*, February 27, 1956.

labor organizations, won control of Congress; the curbs on trade unions which they espoused were supported by conservative Southern Democrats who hoped that a nonunionized South could attract new industries. Labor's internal feuds had directly weakened its political power. It also lost public support as a result of jurisdictional disputes and of occasional abuses of power, such as coercion of employers to recognize unions despite the wishes of employees, unreasonable expulsions and denials of membership under closed-shop contracts, unjustifiable boycotts, and failure to bargain in good faith. Communist domination of some unions and control of other unions by racketeers had similar results. Business groups, led by the National Association of Manufacturers and the Chamber of Commerce, had for ten years been advocating amendment of the Wagner Act. Labor's split had prevented it from agreeing on moderate reforms which might have forestalled more far-reaching changes. Circumstances were ripe for a substantial alteration in national labor-relations policy.

The Taft-Hartley Act

The year following the end of the war saw some of the most acute labor-management conflict in recent history. The disintegration of war controls and the termination in August, 1945, of the union pledge against work stoppages were followed by demands for wage increases to cushion the fall in earnings due to reduction of hours, loss of overtime pay, and rising prices. A Labor-Management Conference called by President Truman in November, 1945, to work out a program of postwar labor-management relations was largely unsuccessful. During the fall of 1945 and the first half of 1946, the country was shocked by a wave of strikes, especially those in coal, steel, electrical equipment, meat-packing, automobiles, and railroads. A tie-up of railroad service in May, 1946, occurred despite government seizure and led President Truman to demand emergency legislation empowering him to draft workers striking against the government. A bill to this effect passed the House but failed in the Senate. Instead, Congress passed the Case Labor Disputes Bill, which in important respects foreshadowed the restrictions on unions of the Taft-Hartley Act, but it was vetoed by the President.

Pressure for regulation of labor practices was intensified by the Republican congressional victory in 1946 and by a second wave of wage increases and sharp price rises which followed the breakdown of price control in mid-1946. Then came John L. Lewis's dramatic defiance of the government. In October, 1946, his United

Mine Workers had requested a reopening of its contract with the government. The Secretary of the Interior refused, arguing that the contract could be reopened only by joint consent. When Lewis proceeded to give notice of termination as of November 20, the government, on November 18, obtained a temporary injunction restraining the union. The union defied the injunction, and an almost complete stoppage occurred. Though Lewis and the UMW were fined for contempt of court and the miners were ordered back to work, public sentiment had been outraged by Lewis's high-handed behavior.

In June, 1947, a new Labor-Management Relations Act (generally known as the Taft-Hartley Act) was passed by a coalition of Republicans and conservative Democrats large enough to override a presidential veto. It endeavored to strike a compromise between the objectives of moderate conservatives, who sought primarily to check labor abuses, and the demands of more extreme antilabor forces, who wished to weaken the labor movement itself. Where the Wagner Act emphasized protection of the right to organize unions, the new legislation regulated certain practices and internal arrangements of unions and weakened their position vis-à-vis employers. Where the Wagner Act had promoted collective bargaining, the Taft-Hartley Act gave more scope to individual bargaining. By arming management with new rights, by restricting union practices, and by giving the individual employee opposed to unionism a legal status not enjoyed under previous legislation, the new Act reversed the flow of New Deal pro-labor legislation, which had contributed so powerfully to the growth of the American labor movement.

The character and structure of the NLRB were greatly altered. The Board, increased in membership from three to five, was stripped of authority over the administration of unfair labor practice complaints. Instead, administrative and prosecuting functions were concentrated in a newly created General Counsel, appointed by the President and confirmed by the Senate. He had final authority to issue complaints in unfair labor practice cases and was given direction of all regional employees and all attorneys save trial examiners and the personal legal assistants of Board members.[69] The NLRB itself became essentially a quasi-judicial

[69] A statutory ambiguity as to the power of the Board to hire and fire regional personnel was resolved shortly after the Act's passage when the Board delegated the power to the General Counsel. A similar ambiguity over the initial responsibility in processing representation cases was clarified when this function, too, was delegated to the General Counsel.

board to hear such unfair labor practice cases as were appealed to it. It continues to exercise final responsibility in representation cases.[70]

The Taft-Hartley Act sought a new balance in industrial relations by strengthening the prerogatives of management and restricting those of unions. The five unfair employer practices of the Wagner Act were retained, but the restraints they imposed were lessened. An employee could now be lawfully discharged for engaging in any of the newly defined "unfair union practices," for certain other unlawful practices specified by the Act,[71] or for striking during the sixty-day notice period at the end of a contract. Foremen and other supervisors were denied the protection of the Act. While they could join or organize unions, management was not compelled to bargain with them. Where previously management could petition for representation elections only when it was confronted with the claims of competing unions, it might now request an election whenever a union made a demand for recognition. Petitions of employers or employees asking the NLRB to decertify a union had to be given the same attention as a petition for certification. No representation election could be held within a year after a preceding one. Potentially more important, the Act denied a vote to strikers who were not entitled to reinstatement. The Board has interpreted this provision to mean that strikers who have been replaced by nonstriking workers or strikebreakers, except in a strike caused by unfair employer practices, are ineligible to vote,[72] while their replacements are eligible.[73] The possibilities of using this provision for strikebreaking or "union-busting" are obvious.

The balance between management and union was also shifted by the "free speech" provisions of the law. Designed to protect management's right to express its views on labor relations, so long

[70] The new Act also contained some procedural amendments designed to "judicialize" procedure. Hearings before trial examiners were to be conducted "so far as practicable" in accordance with the rules of evidence of federal district courts. NLRB decisions had to be based on "the preponderance of the testimony." In issuing directive orders, the Board could not award back pay to employees "suspended or discharged for cause." On court review, NLRB findings of fact were to be conclusive, not "if supported by evidence," as the Wagner Act provided, but only "if supported by substantial evidence on the record as a whole."

[71] Thus, an employee may be discharged for making "disloyal" disparaging remarks about his employer. *NLRB* v. *Local Union No. 1229, International Brotherhood of Electrical Workers*, 346 U.S. 464 (1953).

[72] *Pipe Machinery Co.*, 76 NLRB 247; 79 NLRB 1322 (1948).

[73] *Triangle Publications*, 80 NLRB 835 (1948).

as there is no threat or promise of benefits, they introduced new confusion into an area which had been clarified by the Supreme Court in its interpretation of the old law.[74] Although two circuit court decisions have held that these provisions only restate the First Amendment,[75] both the NLRB and other court decisions have interpreted them more broadly. Where formerly an employer's statement was examined in the light of its context to ensure that seemingly innocuous words were not coercive or intimidating in effect, apparently now management's statements may not be used in evidence unless they directly violate express terms of the Act.[76] The Board also interprets this provision as permitting employers to expose employees to antiunion speeches during working hours [77] even if a similar opportunity is not provided for prounion meetings.[78]

The Taft-Hartley Act also established certain unfair union practices as a counterpart to the unfair employer practices of the Wagner Act. It was made an unfair labor practice for unions or their agents "to restrain or coerce" employees in their right to join or not to join labor organizations, except in the case of an authorized union-shop agreement. Other unfair union practices proscribed include attempts to cause an employer to discriminate against a worker except for failure to pay fees or dues; refusal to bargain collectively with an employer; secondary boycotts, jurisdictional strikes in violation of NLRB rulings, or strikes to force an employer to deal with a union other than the one already duly recognized as the bargaining agent; initiation fees found by the NLRB to be excessive or discriminatory; and "featherbedding" rules requiring employers to make payments "in the nature of an extortion, for services which are not performed or not to be performed." [79]

[74] NLRB v. Virginia Electric & Power Co., 314 U.S. 469 (1941); Virginia Electric & Power Co. v. NLRB, 319 U.S. 533 (1943).

[75] NLRB v. LaSalle Steel Co., 178 F. 2d 829 (1944); NLRB v. Bailey & Co., 180 F. 2d 278 (1950).

[76] Pittsburgh Steamship Co. v. NLRB, 180 F. 2d 731 (1950); NLRB v. Ray Smith Transport Co., 193 F. 2d 142 (1951).

[77] Babcock & Wilcox Co., 77 NLRB 577 (1948). For the pre-Taft-Hartley "captive audience" doctrine forbidding this practice, see Clark Brothers Co., 70 NLRB 802 (1946).

[78] Livingston Shirt Corp., 107 NLRB 400 (1953).

[79] But the Supreme Court has interpreted this provision as not forbidding a union to require an employer to accept and pay for unnecessary services. Employers may legally be forced to pay for the setting of "bogus" (unnecessary and unused) type and for the hiring of a local orchestra to sit in the pit while a traveling orchestra plays on stage. American Newspaper Publishers

The above provisions of the 1947 law can be regarded simply as an amendment to the Wagner Act, correcting its alleged one-sidedness and striking a new balance in labor-management relations. But the law also regulates several internal union practices and restricts some types of union activity. In order to enjoy rights under the Act and to use NLRB machinery for representation certification or for investigation of complaints concerning unfair employer practices, unions must file their constitution and by-laws as well as detailed annual reports on finances, compensation of principal officers, internal procedures, and related matters. Union officers have to file affidavits stating that they are not Communists and do not believe in or teach the violent overthrow of the government. Union political contributions and expenditures in connection with federal elections and primaries are illegal, and individual officers as well as unions are liable for violation of this prohibition.

The constitutionality of these provisions was questioned but, for the most part, has been affirmed. The financial and other reports were soon held to be reasonably incident to public policy.[80] The Communist affidavit requirement was vigorously attacked by many unions, including some which were militantly anticommunist, but in 1950 a divided Court upheld its constitutionality.[81] A year later it was held that the requirement applied to the parent AFL and CIO organizations as well as to their constituent unions.[82]

The constitutionality of the ban on political contributions and expenditures has not yet been adjudicated. In 1957, in a case involving an indictment of the United Automobile Workers for sponsoring TV broadcasts which endorsed candidates, the Supreme Court directed a lower court to hear the case but deferred its decision on the constitutional issue.[83]

The provisions of the Act relating to suits against unions contained some of the potentially most important restrictions on union activity. Damage suits for breach of contract could be brought in all cases. Unions were specifically declared to be re-

---

Assn. v. NLRB, 345 U.S. 100 (1953); NLRB v. Gamble Enterprises, Inc., 345 U.S. 117 (1953).
[80] National Maritime Union v. Herzog, 334 U.S. 854 (1948).
[81] American Communications Assn. v. Douds, 339 U.S. 382.
[82] NLRB v. Highland Park Manufacturing Co., 341 U.S. 322 (1951).
[83] U.S. v. International Union UAW-CIO, 352 U.S. 567 (1957). The Court had earlier held that this Taft-Hartley provision, which amends the Corrupt Practices Act of 1907, did not prevent a union from distributing political material to its own members. U.S. v. CIO, 335 U.S. 106 (1948).

sponsible for the acts of their agents. While agents were not specifically defined, the law declared that in cases of "wildcat" or unauthorized strikes, "the question whether the specific acts performed were actually authorized or subsequently ratified shall not be controlling." Damage suits by those injured were also authorized in cases of boycotts, secondary and jurisdictional strikes, and certain kinds of featherbedding. Money judgments were to run only against union funds and not against individual members.

The 1947 Act also regulated some aspects of collective-bargaining procedure. As we have seen, refusal to bargain with an employer is an unfair labor practice. Conferences must be conducted in good faith with the purpose of arriving at a written agreement covering terms and conditions of employment. An existing agreement can be modified or terminated only on sixty days' written notice to the other party. If no agreement is reached after thirty days, both parties must notify appropriate federal and state agencies. For the sixty-day period, both parties are bound by the terms of the existing contract. Workers striking during this period lose their status as employees but can regain it if rehired.

Disputes which threaten to produce work stoppages are divided into three categories. Small disputes, intrastate in character, are no longer considered to be the national government's responsibility where state or local conciliation services exist. At the other extreme, disputes involving national emergencies are singled out for special treatment as already described. Disputes falling between these two categories are to be handled by the Federal Mediation and Conciliation Service.

A jurisdictional strike is an unfair labor practice, and the NLRB accordingly hears all complaints which involve such strikes.[84] The Act also directs the NLRB to "hear and determine" jurisdictional disputes, unless a voluntary settlement is reached within ten days after a case is filed, but the Board has been divided on the question of its powers over these disputes. A majority has ruled that the Board can only facilitate settlements but not decide which union has jurisdiction over the disputed job.[85] Consequently, after a hearing, the Board dismisses the charge, or rules that the accused union has no lawful right to force recognition of its jurisdiction, or assigns the job to a bargaining unit (but not to the union, since this would be equivalent to awarding a closed shop, banned by the Act). The indecisiveness of

[84] *Moore Drydock Co.*, 81 NLRB 1108 (1949).

[85] S. A. Levitan, "Jurisdictional Disputes," *Labor Law Journal* (February 1953), p. 136.

this procedure encourages unions to settle jurisdictional disputes themselves.[86]

Finally, the 1947 legislation also regulates the content of the agreements reached by collective bargaining, thereby injecting government more deeply into labor-management relations than did the Wagner Act. The Taft-Hartley Act strengthens the hand of management by limiting the kind of union-security agreements which can be established. The closed shop, which requires employers to hire only union members, is prohibited as an unfair practice. Union-shop agreements, where workers must join the union after being hired, and maintenance-of-membership agreements, in which workers are free to join or not to join but if joining must retain their membership for the duration of the agreement, are permitted only under certain restrictions. The original Taft-Hartley Act prohibited a union-security agreement unless a majority of employees in the bargaining unit had approved it in an NLRB-conducted election. Such an election could be held only on petition of at least 30 per cent of the employees, and only if the union had complied with other provisions of the Act relating to union registration and reports. In 1951, after 97 per cent of 46,119 polls conducted by the NLRB in slightly more than four years had endorsed union-security agreements,[87] Congress removed the election requirement. Workers may still, however, vote on such agreements if 30 per cent of them so petition.

Union-security agreements can be voided by state action. When state laws are more restrictive of these agreements, the Taft-Hartley Act provides that they take precedence over the national law. By 1957, eighteen states had enacted "right-to-work" laws which guarantee that no employee shall be required to join a union as a condition of employment, thus invalidating union-shop agreements.[88] Bitter legislative battles over right-to-work bills occur each year in other states, but, as yet, only one predominantly industrial state—Indiana—has adopted such a law. One analysis of eight years' experience led to the conclusion that "Virginia's right-to-work law is, for the most part, unenforceable." [89] While

---

[86] *Ibid.*, p. 140. See also, H. H. Reins, "Jurisdictional-Dispute Settlements in the Building Trades," *Labor Law Journal* (June, 1957), p. 385.

[87] NLRB, *Annual Report, 1951*, p. 10.

[88] C. G. Niebank, Jr., "In Defense of Right-to-Work Laws," *Labor Law Journal* (July, 1957), p. 460. A nineteenth state, Louisiana, had enacted such a law but later repealed it.

[89] J. M. Kuhlman, "Right-to-Work Laws: The Virginia Experience," *Labor Law Journal* (July, 1955), p. 453.

the right-to-work principle, sometimes called the "open shop," was enunciated as long ago as 1903 [90] and is still supported by employers' associations seeking to increase their strength vis-à-vis unions, the argument is now couched in terms of voluntarism and individual freedom from coercion. It is pointed out that in Western Europe the decision has gone against compulsory unionism.[91] Union spokesmen, on the other hand, attack such legislation as part of a "union-busting" scheme and argue that it enables "free riders" to avoid paying dues to cover their share of the cost of collective bargaining in their interest. They are supported by some employers who find that union and closed shops make for smoother labor relations. Despite the many barriers to union-security agreements erected by the 1947 law, both the union shop and the forbidden closed shop still flourish where strong unions operate. A third of all workers under union contracts in 1946 were in closed shops,[92] and in 1949 a Senate committee found them still to be prevalent.[93]

Union security was further affected by a Taft-Hartley Act provision that the checkoff, in which the employer deducts union dues from wages and pays them directly to the union, may not be used without receiving from each employee an annual written authorization. Nor may an employer assist union security by discharging a worker for any reason of union discipline except a failure to pay union dues and fees. Even in a union shop, where all employees must be union members, expulsion from the union for any reason except failure to pay dues or fees cannot cause a worker to be discharged. The Act also regulated the content of agreements by requiring equal representation of management in the administration of union health-and-welfare funds established by collective-bargaining agreements.

Thus the Act has expanded management's power and restrained that of unions. While this shift has perhaps hurt weaker unions and hindered the organization of nonunionized firms, it has not seriously affected strong unions. But the Act has been operative only in times of fairly high employment and has been administered first by a prolabor administration and then by one for the

[90] J. L. Toner, "Right-to-Work Laws: Public Frauds," *Labor Law Journal* (March, 1957), p. 191.

[91] A. Lenhoff, "The Problem of Compulsory Unionism in Europe," *American Journal of Comparative Law* (1949), p. 18.

[92] Bureau of Labor Statistics, *Extent of Collective Bargaining and Union Recognition* (1946), p. 3.

[93] Senate Committee on Labor and Public Welfare, *The National Labor Relations Act of 1947*, S. Rept. 99, 81st Cong., 1st sess., p. 20.

most part anxious not to offend union labor. Labor leaders still
fear that in more unsympathetic hands it could be used for
"union-busting." They point out that an employer faced with
a strike, or having instigated one, might petition for union de-
certification, secure an injunction to restrain picketing, have
his striker replacements or strikebreakers vote in a representation election in which the strikers cannot vote, have the NLRB
certify the resultant vote for no union, and be safe from further
representation questions for a full year.

While the Act does not turn its back on collective bargaining, it limits its scope and goes to some length to protect individual bargaining. In this direction are such provisions as de-
certification elections, checkoff rules, limits on union-security
arrangements, and employee votes on the employer's last offer
in national-emergency strikes.

This effect was intended. It is in harmony with the views of
the conservative congressional coalition which passed the law.
But quite unintended was the extent to which the Act has quick-
ened labor's interest in the political process. It was the explicit
purpose of the Act's supporters to restrict union political activities
—hence the ban on political contributions and expenditures. But
the effect of the restrictions contained in the Taft-Hartley Act
as a whole has been to make the AFL more politically active,[94]
and the Act has been a major issue in every presidential election
since its passage.

State Labor-Management Regulation

The scope of state regulation has become less important as
the courts have expanded their definition of activities "affecting
commerce" and so subject to federal regulation. Except for union-
security agreements, mentioned above, the Taft-Hartley Act has
been interpreted as pre-empting for federal regulation the area
of labor-management relations. Under the Eisenhower administration, the NLRB tried to reduce federal jurisdiction by limiting the unfair labor practice cases it would accept. In 1954, it
announced that it would hear cases involving retail stores only
when they had direct out-of-state purchases of $1 million a year
or indirect out-of-state purchases (goods shipped from within the
state but with an out-of-state origin) of $2 million, or out-of-
state sales of $100,000. An interstate retail chain must have
total sales of $10 million. Other business enterprises must have
direct out-of-state purchases of $500,000, or indirect out-of-state

[94] See Chapter 2.

purchases of $1 million, or out-of-state sales of $50,000. Local utility and transit systems must do a business of at least $3 million each year, radio and TV stations a business of $200,000, and newspapers $500,000.[95] A number of states then began to regulate the evacuated areas. In 1957, however, the Supreme Court held that the federal power to regulate was plenary and that, even if federal law was not being applied, state laws were not applicable.[96] This was in harmony with earlier decisions which have consistently barred state action when in conflict with the Wagner or Taft-Hartley Acts,[97] or even when parallel to federal statutes.[98] This doctrine of federal pre-emption applies to representation cases as well as unfair labor practice cases.

Within their jurisdiction, state laws vary greatly in content and administration, generally being most restrictive of unions in Southern and nonindustrial states. There have been three main waves of state legislation, the first two paralleling federal policies. Just as the Norris-La Guardia Act was followed by sixteen state anti-injunction acts, so the Wagner Act was echoed by labor-relations laws in eleven largely industrial states. But, as a reaction began to set in against the Wagner Act in the late 1930's, the states were inundated by a second wave of proposals designed in various ways to limit union power and to protect employers and the public against union abuses. Most of the Taft-Hartley provisions first appeared in one or more state laws. Some states narrowed the scope of their anti-injunction statutes; others broadened their labor-relations laws by proscribing unfair union practices. Among the state measures were limits on strikes and picketing, and prohibitions of closed shops, secondary boycotts, jurisdictional strikes, picketing by nonemployees, and picketing in the absence of a labor dispute. Other states required

[95] Before 1950, the NLRB had on a case-by-case basis rejected enterprises whose effect on commerce was unsubstantial. In 1950, it established certain minimum standards, far below those enunciated in 1954.

[96] *Guss* v. *Utah Labor Relations Board*, 335 U.S. 1 (1957). Sec. 10(a) of the Taft-Hartley Act does permit the NLRB to cede jurisdiction over unfair labor practice cases to the states, but the NLRB has been unable to make any cession agreements with the states primarily because the state law must be consistent with the Taft-Hartley Act. See H. N. Shenkin, "State Power Where NLRB Refuses to Assert Jurisdiction," *Labor Law Journal* (March, 1957), p. 155.

[97] E.g., *Hill* v. *Florida*, 325 U.S. 538 (1945); *International Union, United Automobile Workers* v. *O'Brien*, 339 U.S. 454 (1950); *Amalgamated Assn. of Street, Electric Railway and Motor Coach Employees* v. WERB, 340 U.S. 383 (1951); *Garner* v. *Teamsters*, 347 U.S. 485 (1953).

[98] *LaCrosse Telephone Corp.* v. WERB, 336 U.S. 18 (1948).

unions to register, to file periodic reports, and to charge only reasonable dues. This legislative reaction against unions reached a peak in 1947. By September of that year the closed shop was banned in fifteen states, picketing was restricted in twenty-two, jurisdictional disputes limited in nine, secondary boycotts forbidden in sixteen, and registration and financial reports required in eleven.[99]

After 1947, while there have been crosscurrents, the state antiunion tide ebbed. During the years immediately after 1947, the states generally eased union restrictions. After 1953, there was once again a mildly antiunion trend. Altogether, in the nine years down to 1956, four states repealed closed-shop bans, three states rejected by referenda proposals to bar them, but four states enacted right-to-work laws, and one prohibited the closed shop. A half-dozen states amended existing laws to make them less restrictive of unions, and three states enacted new legislation making union activities easier. Seven states restricted picketing, three limited union political activities, and two limited strikes.[100]

Despite some moderate reversal in sentiment, unions have been unsuccessful in repeated efforts to amend or repeal the Taft-Hartley Act. In 1957, the political strength of union leaders—their ability to influence their members and to gain support from the general public—was seriously, if temporarily, weakened by unsavory evidence recounted before the Senate Select Committee on Improper Activity in the Labor or Management Field. This committee dramatically publicized the corruption and abuses of power of the top officials of certain unions, especially the giant and powerful Teamsters' Union. These leaders had displayed a seeming inability to differentiate between their own and union funds. Some had allied themselves with the underworld. They had at times connived with employers to commit union members to unsatisfactory contracts, and their control over the internal political and administrative machinery of their unions had been firm enough to deny rank-and-file members any real voice in the leadership or policies of their unions.

The AFL-CIO leadership was confronted with the alternatives of "cleaning its own house," so as to head off further regulatory legislation, ejecting corrupt unions at the price of once again splitting the labor movement and centralizing power at the expense of union autonomy, or of losing both public and rank-

[99] Council of State Governments, *The Book of the States, 1948–1949* (1948), p. 454.
[100] *Ibid.*, various years.

and-file support by tolerating corruption and abuse of power. Late in 1957, the AFL-CIO expelled the Teamsters, its largest union, and several small unions, but it appeared likely that Congress would soon turn to the task of devising new regulatory measures of its own.[101]

Emerging Issues of Public Policy

Clearly, this investigation, and its effects on union members and the public, have blasted early union hopes for more favorable legislative action and may well open the door for further restrictive regulation. Although unions have won wide acceptance, are firmly established in many areas of the economy, and throughout the postwar decade have been remarkably successful in winning economic benefits for their members, it can hardly be said that the pattern of industrial relations and the pattern of relationships within unions have achieved mature stability. Accordingly, public policy is still in process of evolution and confronts many knotty issues.

The crucial questions appear to be those of power and responsibility. For a quarter of a century, public policy has been concerned with equalizing the power mobilized on opposite sides of the bargaining table in the belief that a more equitable and sound adjustment of labor disputes will result from reasonably balanced collective bargaining. Obviously, equality of power does not guarantee the elimination of crippling work stoppages and the maintenance of essential services. Yet there does seem to be some evidence for the belief that, as both sides become more adjusted to the bargaining process, their exercise of power be-

[101] In 1958, the Senate passed the Kennedy-Ives Bill, but it failed in the House. A moderate measure designed primarily to deal with the abuses uncovered by the Senate Select Committee, it required disclosure of financial operations by unions and union officials, particularly those affecting welfare funds; periodic elections of officers by secret ballot, with provisions for removal for misconduct; and barred "shakedown" picketing and certain other union abuses. The measure was supported by most AFL-CIO unions. It was opposed by employers' groups, such as the National Association of Manufacturers and the Chamber of Commerce, and by several unions, including the Teamsters, the United Mine Workers, and the United Steel Workers. Employers attacked the measure for not going far enough in curbing certain union activities, for softening the Taft-Hartley Act in several particulars—including that law's denial of voting privileges in representation elections to employees on strike—and for requiring the disclosure of employers' arrangements with "middlemen" to influence employees in the exercise of their lawful rights. Despite the bipartisan origin of this bill, it became a party issue in 1958, Democrats supporting it as wise legislation and Republicans demanding stronger legislation.

comes more responsible and their readiness to compromise increases. Corporation management today more often than not accepts unionism and collective bargaining and is more skilled in human relations. Once the principle of collective bargaining is accepted and the union recognized, its leadership is better able honestly and reasonably to seek a fair settlement.

Yet work stoppages still occur, and some of them seriously affect the community. Governmental policy toward major strikes has changed. During World War II and for some time thereafter, including the period of the Korean War, both President and Congress supported a policy of using the utmost of governmental pressure and even positive action to prevent stoppages in essential industry. This policy is still proclaimed by the Taft-Hartley Act. The Eisenhower administration, however, has tended more to a "hands-off" policy, wishing to discourage reliance on government in industrial disputes in a belief that the parties are more apt to negotiate a settlement if neither side can hope for favorable governmental intervention. In this view, even an occasional strike is justifiable as a means of allowing the parties to learn how to live with each other.

While such a policy probably does facilitate settlements, it does not protect the public from intolerable stoppages. Compulsory arbitration has often been advocated, and a trend in that direction can be discerned in essential industries, but the belief that the rights of unions and managements should be thus circumscribed has not won wide acceptance.

Even when collective bargaining is peaceful, however, problems of public policy are still presented by management-labor power relationships. Not even the apparently optimum situation presented by a relatively equal balance of powers can escape scrutiny, for then the firms are usually large enough in size and few enough in number to command a substantial control over prices. If, in times of labor shortage, firms buy industrial peace with large wage increases, recovered by price increases passed on to their customers—as was commonly alleged to be the case in 1956 and 1957—then dangerous inflationary and distorting forces may be unleashed within the economy.

When power is not so evenly matched and weak employers are confronted with a powerful union, the case for united action among employers is often unanswerable. They pool their strength to avoid being picked off one by one and to muster comparable power. But industry-wide bargaining also presents serious problems. The bringing together of employers to deal with a union may cause or facilitate a unity of action in matters of price and output which shackles competitive forces and is inconsistent with antitrust policy. Perhaps of greater importance, when industry-wide bargaining breaks down, the resulting strike, also industry-wide, is all the more crippling. This is especially true of such industries as transportation, coal, and steel, but the shutdown of almost any large industry is bound to have painful consequences.

When power is unevenly matched, other problems are raised. The weaker the union, the easier it is to destroy its power. The principle of effective collective bargaining then is not effectuated at all. When union power predominates, the temptation to abuse it is sometimes irresistible, and it may fall into wholly irresponsible hands.

Furthermore, the organization of sufficient union power to conduct collective bargaining raises internal political questions. Union leadership must enjoy the support of the rank and file if it is to be responsible in its bargaining and enforce its agreements. Yet strong leadership may easily degenerate into internal union dictatorship indulging in absolutist practices which suppress the rights of union members. On the other hand, when elections of union officers are more democratic, leaders desiring re-election may often be pressed by their rivals to bargain harder; thus they may find themselves in a position where it is difficult to reach compromise settlements with management.

Clearly, the pattern both of labor-management relations and of internal union constitutional arrangements is still in course of evolution. Public policy will continue to confront difficult problems in achieving a healthy equilibrium in these fields.

CHAPTER 8

Government, the Consumer, and the Public Interest

Of ALL basic economic interests, that of the ultimate consumer is the broadest, the most akin to a general interest, and yet the least organized, the least articulate, and therefore the least recognized in the dynamics of policy formation. Organization is a prerequisite for direct participation in political processes, but the consumer's interest is ordinarily too diverse and too widely diffused to be effectively organized. Any individual consumes a wide variety of commodities, and each commodity is consumed by a host of individuals. Large institutional consumers, and producers buying materials for further fabrication, stand on a different footing. They combine a powerful interest in particular commodities with resources adequate to promote and protect that interest. Even in the absence of organization, a developed group consciousness is a political potential which may be competed for by policy-makers, but consumers usually lack this consciousness, identifying themselves more with their producing than with their consuming roles.

Although politically weak, the consumer was sovereign in the theory of classical economics and so might seem to need little governmental aid. Adam Smith succinctly stated the concept in an oft-repeated remark: "Consumption is the sole end and purpose of all production; and the interest of the producer ought to be attended to only so far as it may be necessary for promoting that of the consumer. The maxim is so perfectly self-evident,

212

that it would be absurd to attempt to prove it."[1] As the end result of the economic process, so ran the theory, consumption is the basic motivation of economic activity in an individualistic order. Consumer sovereignty was implemented through the competition of sellers for the consumer's favor. In the real world, however, while the consumer may be sovereign in some senses, he is a part-time and often incompetent sovereign, easily swayed by advertising, increasingly unable to evaluate rationally the array of complex goods and services competing for his purse and attention, and sometimes needing protection from his supposed subjects. Consequently, government has been invoked, not to impose rationality on the consumer, but to protect him from certain of the more extreme consequences of his ignorance.

1. The Nature and Organization of the Consumer Interest

It is sometimes asserted that consumer interest is identical with public interest and therefore requires neither special organization nor special representation in government. It is true, of course, that the consumer interest is broadly based, since consumption is universal. Viewed most widely, the consumer interest does approach the general public interest in a larger and better distributed national income. It may, however, conflict with other functional interests. Consumer interests as such, for example, will presumably always favor low prices, whatever the cost in substandard working conditions or in the destruction of capital. The consumer interest in particular commodities may conflict with other elements of the public interest.

In a narrower sense, consumers share a common interest in the most efficient conversion of their income into goods and services. To this end, they require accurate information about available commodities—their variety, quantity, quality, and prices. They share an interest in defense from misrepresentation and injury. Moreover, although they benefit from any productive improvement which is passed on to them, their immediate relation to retail markets gives them a special interest in distributive efficiency.

The consumer interest in particular commodities is ordinarily too small to serve as a basis for effective organization. Even the slightest increase in income will normally improve an individual's position more than price reduction on any one commodity

[1] Adam Smith, *The Wealth of Nations*, Cannan ed., Vol. 2, p. 159.

he consumes. Only if organization can improve his status with regard to a wide range of goods and services can he afford to contribute to the cost of such organization or protection. Institutional consumers buying in large quantities are an important exception to this generalization. As the area of governmental services broadens, political units—local, state, or federal —perform an increasing share of the purchasing function for their constituents. In recent decades, the military services have been by far the largest consuming group for an important range of goods. Systematic testing and formulation of rigid specifications are highly developed for such consumers. Tests are also employed by educational and charitable institutions and by business concerns purchasing capital equipment, raw or semimanufactured materials, and goods and services for their employees.

Fortunately, consumer interests are often so closely related to those of better organized groups that they may be promoted jointly. Most governmental aids to consumers have resulted from such coincidence of goals. Farmers, for example, share with consumers of farm products an interest in efficient distribution and in reduction of distributive markups. Created primarily to promote producing interests, farm organizations also seek protection for the agricultural community as a leading consumer of manufactured goods. The oldest and best-established federal consumer service agency is the Bureau of Home Economics in the Department of Agriculture, which acquired its present status in 1923. Producers supplied the initial impetus to meat inspection, grain standardization, and compulsory government grading of agricultural commodities; these programs redound to general consumers' advantage as much as to producers'. That the interests of consumers and of farmers as producers often conflict, on the other hand, hardly needs illustration.

Organized labor groups are sometimes active in their capacity as consumers, particularly in connection with large items like housing. In addition, business concerns offering better goods, superior efficiency, or higher standards are often allied with consumer interests, in an effort to capture a larger share of the market. This alliance manifests itself politically, as well as through the "unseen hand" of competition, which classical economists thought would transmute the private self-interest of entrepreneurs into the general interest of consumers. Gathering consumer groups around them, large distributors have led the fight against legislation designed to freeze the channels of distribution. And reputable merchants and manufacturers, often organized in trade associations or Better Business Bureaus, have usually been foremost in battles against fraud, misrepresentation, and deception.

The occasional identification of consumer interests with other and better organized interests, however, does not eliminate the frequent conflicts. The "unseen hand" shows signs of paralysis over wide areas. In response to this situation, only a small movement has arisen to organize the interest of consumers as such.

The Consumer Movement

The oldest type of consumer organization is the co-operative. Originating in Rochdale, England, in 1844, European consumer co-operatives have come to occupy an important position both economically and politically. The Rochdale type, which sets the pattern for the great majority, obtains its capital from members on the basis of a fixed return. Each member is given one vote regardless of the amount of capital contributed. Surplus earnings are returned to purchasers in proportion to the volume of their purchases. Salaried managers are responsible to the consumer-owners. Beginning in the retail field, co-operatives have confederated into large-scale wholesale co-operatives, and for some commodities have even undertaken manufacturing operations.

Consumer co-operatives have flourished in Western Europe, especially in Britain, Scandinavia, and Switzerland. They handle a substantial proportion of retail trade and play a significant political role, usually allying themselves with trade-unions as constituents of labor or social-democratic parties. American co-operative experience has been far more limited. Early efforts to establish the movement were mostly sporadic, utopian ventures in a new way of life rather than soundly organized economic enterprises. In the twentieth century, a more stable co-operative movement developed, centered at first around Finnish or Scandinavian groups. While its growth since 1929 has been substantial, its total economic impact is still very small. In 1953 there were 1,090 retail co-operatives serving 600,000 members, with annual sales of $110 million.[2] Much of the reason for the great difference between Western European and American co-operative development lies in the greater competition and efficiency of American distribution and marketing. While European co-operatives are offered an incentive to expand by the wide distributive margins of their competitors and may even undertake manufactur-

[2] The Co-operative League of the U.S.A., *1954 Co-op Yearbook*, p. vi.

ing to combat a monopoly, in this country the antitrust laws bar most monopolies and enlist much of the popular antimonopoly zeal tapped by European co-operatives. The efficiency and low margins of American grocery chains and supermarkets offer rugged competition to the co-operatives and weaken their appeal to consumers. Groceries, petroleum products, fuel, and electricity are the major commodities handled co-operatively. While the movement is moderately successful economically and some of its ventures are on a large scale, its ability to focus the political activity, even the attention, of its members is usually minimal.

Consumer co-operatives must be distinguished from the firmly established agricultural producer co-operatives, which have been an important part of the American economy for many decades. They provide farmers on a nonprofit basis with common services which are too expensive or elaborate to be undertaken by individuals. They process and market farm products and purchase farm machinery, fertilizer, and other producers' goods. In part, they overlap with consumer co-operatives, since they often buy ultimate consumers' goods as well. Their major interest, however, is in production. When engaged in marketing, their interests may conflict with those of consumers in precisely the same manner as other producers' organizations.

Farm co-operatives have enjoyed a privileged political status through special credit facilities, partial exemption from the antitrust laws, and other aids. Consumer co-operatives have but few similar governmental aids. Some states exempt credit unions from income taxes, and rural electrification co-operatives are assisted by the Rural Electrification Administration; along with public agencies, they are given first call on power generated at public dams. Competing firms often allege that co-operatives are exempt from federal and some state income taxes because they pay no tax on the funds distributed to members as patronage dividends. These are comparable, it is argued, to the profits of private businesses, which are taxed. Co-operatives reply that these are price reductions, not profits, and so are not taxable.

The National Tax Equality Association was founded in 1943 to campaign for the revision of federal and state tax laws so as to tax co-operative patronage refunds. Farm groups have usually been powerful enough to thwart this drive, although in 1951 Congress did require co-operatives to pay corporation income taxes on sums retained for surplus or reserves, but not on patronage dividends. Thus, by and large, consumer co-operatives are given no special advantages and must make their way on their own merits. Although still doing only an insignificant portion of the nation's total retail business, consumer co-operatives do form a small nucleus for potential consumer organization.

Aside from co-operatives, the only organizations performing direct services for the consumer as such are research and testing groups. They seek to afford a rational basis for consumer choice in the jungle of brand names and high-pressure advertising techniques so that the ordinary individual may match the position of the institutional purchaser, who acts on the basis of specifications, quality tests, and careful price comparisons. The pattern for their operations was set by Consumers' Research, Inc., established in 1929 after *Your Money's Worth*, a best-selling book by Stuart Chase and F. J. Schlink, had evoked great public interest in consumer protection. A rival organization, the Consumers' Union of the United States, was founded in 1936 by striking employees of Consumers' Research. The newer group, whose monthly reports have a circulation of 825,000, is now the larger. It takes a broad view of consumer interest and on occasion seeks to mobilize consumer opinion on public issues. It allies itself affirmatively with other consumer elements. The testing groups help to stimulate consumer consciousness by publicizing government protective activities and keeping alive the feeling that further protection may be badly needed.

Both agencies are nonprofit and are supported by membership fees and the sale of publications. They test products purchased on the open market. They are hampered by limited funds and by the intrinsic difficulties of satisfactory testing for certain commodities. They have had to compete, moreover, with various spurious imitations, some of which are pure frauds classifying commodities without any testing, while others accept subsidies for sponsoring the wares of particular manufacturers. The Federal Trade Commission has issued cease and desist orders against a number of these self-styled "testing bureaus."

The consumer movement also manifests itself in groups devoted to general discussion and promotion of consumer welfare, usually as part of a broader program. The medical profession, for example, has supported consumer protection against fraudulent and dangerous proprietary medicines. Home economics teaching provides a focus for organization of the consumer interest in education. Organized women's groups also show a special interest in consumer welfare. The General Federation of Women's Clubs, the American Association of University Women, the League of Women Voters, and similar organizations in lesser degree, give prominent place to this topic among their avowed purposes. While not to be compared in strength with the large agricultural or labor organizations, the "women's lobby" is a not inconsiderable force in the legislative process, most effective when a group with a direct economic interest is allied with it. Thus, chain stores were able to enlist the support of the women's lobby in opposition to special taxes and other antichain measures in the 1930's, and in 1950 margarine, cottonseed, and soybean producers gained the aid of women's groups in their efforts to repeal the margarine tax. The women were not "taken in," for they had real interests at stake themselves; but they were most effective when associated with more sharply defined interest groups. On the whole, however, organization of the consumer interest is weak and seems likely to remain so.

2. Protective Legislation for the Consumer

Almost every governmental action has some effect on consumer welfare, adverse or favorable. Consideration of consumer interests played a leading role in the growth of public utility regulation and a significant part in the development of antitrust policy. Public enterprise is likewise sometimes undertaken in response to particular consumer needs. The traditional identification of consumer interest with the public interest makes the former a touchstone for appraisal of governmental action. In the absence of effective organization, however, it is often disregarded in the formulation of public policy. Its struggle for recognition against well-knit producers' organizations is always a difficult one. But occasional waves of popular indignation, and the more frequent cases of identity of interest between consumers in general and some better organized groups, have brought about several forms of special governmental protection for the consumer. The ancient public regulation of weights and measures in the marketplace set the precedent for such action. The more important modern examples include the pure food and drug laws and legislation against false advertising. With the support of producers, there has also developed regulation of quality standards in certain fields.

Legislation for Pure Food, Drugs, and Cosmetics

General principles of commercial law give the buyer a measure of protection against adulteration or misrepresentation. His legal relations with sellers no longer accord with the rule of *caveat emptor.* The doctrine of "breach of warranty" affords remedies for misrepresentation which can be extended beyond the retailer as far back as the manufacturer. Fraud lays the seller open to criminal as well as civil action. Damages may be collected for injury or death due to a seller's negligence. Except for his rare purchases of expensive, durable consumers' goods, such as houses or automobiles, however, or cases of serious injury with heavy damage claims in the balance, legal protection without administrative enforcement is of little avail to the consumer. A multitude of fraudulent misrepresentations will bilk the public of many fortunes without costing any single individual enough to repay a lawsuit. When adulteration is injurious to health or life, moreover, administrative prevention is preferable to legal remedy.

State and local provisions against the more glaring instances of adulteration or fraud have a long history. Sanitary regulations, inspection of weights and measures, and the like were well-established public functions at the beginning of the nation's history. With relative local self-sufficiency, particularly in foods, municipal regulation protected the public reasonably well. But the development of mass production and the elaboration of processing techniques in the second half of the nineteenth century made the problem of protection more complex. State legislation against adulteration of food and drugs began with Virginia in 1848 and Ohio in 1853. It spread over most of the nation during the remainder of the century. Later, many states offered some protection against false advertising by enactment of the model statute sponsored by the trade journal *Printers' Ink.* As with protective labor legislation, however, interstate competition prevented any single state from raising its standards very far out of line with the others and made federal action essential. The struggle for a federal law began about 1880 but required a full quarter-century to achieve ultimate victory.[3]

The Pure Food and Drug Act of 1906 was adopted only after several decades of accumulating public concern about food adulteration and patent-medicine frauds. Pure-food bills had been introduced as far back as 1890 but were always lost somewhere

[3] Federal legislation in 1872 forbade use of the mails to defraud, and since then Post Office inspectors have investigated allegations of fraud conducted by mail. Hearings are granted those accused, and those found guilty are denied use of the mails, letters addressed to them being returned to the senders, marked *"Fraudulent!"* More serious cases may be criminally prosecuted by the Justice Department. The Post Office acts only on complaint, and even then a swindler need only change his name and address to be back in business.

in the legislative maze. Constitutional scruples, particularly among the Southern Democrats, played some part in the opposition. Its core, however, was the powerfully organized Proprietary Association of America, backed by some of the large business interests which dominated the congressional leadership of that period. Only through a slow process of public education, accelerated early in the twentieth century by a flood of popular writings describing existing evils, did positive action finally become unavoidable.

The educational process was led by Dr. Harvey W. Wiley, chief chemist of the Department of Agriculture from 1883 to 1912, who organized a famous "poison squad" of Department employees for the testing of food preparations. Professor E. F. Ladd, Food Commissioner of North Dakota, made similar but more sensational experiments. Public excitement and irresistible demand for congressional action, however came only with the wide publicity given such investigations by the "muckrakers." Magazine articles by the dozen, together with several popular books, devoted themselves to this topic. Climaxing the entire movement was the publication early in 1906 of Upton Sinclair's *The Jungle*, dealing with the Chicago stockyards. An immediate bestseller, its descriptions of slaughtering practices were so shocking that sales of meat and its by-products were heavily reduced. President Theodore Roosevelt took up the cudgels for Wiley's Food and Drug Bill and was joined by the General Federation of Women's Clubs. Although substantially watered down, it was finally passed with only a few opposing votes. In separate legislation, public meat inspection, applied to the export market since 1890, was extended to the domestic market.

The Act of 1906 sought to protect the consumer's purse as well as his health. It forbade interstate commerce in adulterated or misbranded foods and drugs. Misbranding was defined as: (1) being affirmatively "false or misleading in any particular," (2) failing to state the quantity of ten enumerated habit-forming or dangerous drugs; or (3) imitating another article. Adulteration of food included: (1) substitution of less valuable constituents, (2) abstraction of valuable constituents, (3) hiding of damage or inferiority through artificial coloring or coating, (4) addition of poisonous or other deleterious ingredients possibly injurious to health, and (5) inclusion of decomposed or diseased animal or vegetable substance. Drugs had to conform to the standards of the semiofficial United States Pharmacopoeia and National Formulary, or else to have their standard of quality stated on the label. Detailed regulations were made by the Treasury, Agriculture, and Commerce Departments jointly, but administrative responsibility was placed in the Department of Agriculture because of Dr. Wiley's earlier work.

Criminal prosecution was one sanction, with a fine of up to $200 for a first offense and $300 or a year's imprisonment for subsequent offenses. Forfeiture of adulterated or misbranded articles upon their entry into interstate commerce was a more rapid remedy, essential to prevention of public injury from poisoned substances after they had entered commercial channels. Revision of food and drug laws followed in almost every state, generally bringing definitions into accord with the federal model. In states with effective administration, these laws were an important supplement to federal action, since they could attack directly the manufacture and sale of the forbidden goods within their jurisdictions.

On the whole, the Food and Drug Act was reasonably effective in barring the extremes of dangerous adulteration. Its administration was hampered, however, by inadequate appropriations. In a number of critical instances, heavy pressures to be lenient were brought to bear upon rule-making officials. The popular movement which had brought about enactment of the law left in its wake no organization to keep watch over enforcement. Dr. Wiley himself asserted that administration was so weak as to amount to executive sabotage; after bitter conflict with the Theodore Roosevelt and Taft administrations, he resigned in 1912. The location of the Food and Drug Administration (FDA) within the Department of Agriculture until 1940 sometimes subjected it to pressures from segments of the Department's clientele. Noteworthy examples were the rules on corn sugar in canning and the minimum tolerances of poisonous lead-spray residues on fresh fruit.[4] On the whole, however, given its limited resources, the FDA, in co-operation with the food and drug industry, made great strides in eliminating dangerous products.

Protection against misbranding and misrepresentation was less adequately provided by the 1906 law. Proprietary foods sold under distinctive names and containing no added dangerous ingredients were exempted, as were compounds, imitations, or blends when

---

[4] Transfer of the FDA to the Federal Security Agency and later to the Department of Health, Education, and Welfare did not wholly relieve it from such pressures. Shortly after its transfer out of Agriculture, it allowed a further increase in lead tolerances, thereby aiding the hard-pressed fruit growers of the Pacific Northwest.

plainly so labeled. Moreover, while the courts broadly interpreted the adulteration provisions, in 1911 the Supreme Court defined misrepresentation narrowly, holding that the words "false or misleading in any particular" did not include far-fetched declarations of therapeutic or curative effects.[5] Designed to rectify this decision, the Sherley Amendment of 1912 was gravely weakened by patent-medicine interests, which persuaded Congress to transform its prohibition of "false and misleading representations" into one of "false and fraudulent representations." Since legal definitions of fraud require knowledge and intent on the part of the malefactor, proof of this offense became practically impossible.

In addition, the Act's remedies were seriously weak. Juries were often loath to convict local manufacturers. Fines were small, and some hardened offenders looked upon them as license fees for continuing in business. Imprisonment was practically never imposed. Perhaps the outstanding defect of the law, however, was its failure to include advertising, which influences purchasers more than do labels. The Federal Trade Commission Act offered only modest protection in this field.[6]

Except for the Sherley Amendment and the Gould Amendment of 1913, requiring quantity labels on packaged goods, modifications of the 1906 Act before 1938 were mostly sponsored by agricultural producers. Butter standards were adopted in 1923. The McNary-Mapes Amendment of 1930 required canned products falling below standards of quality, condition, and fill promulgated by the Secretary of Agriculture to be labeled as substandard. No provision was made, however, for grading above the minimum.

With a resurgence of interest in consumer protection during the Great Depression, and with the publication of a number of books exposing advertising abuses, increasing attention was given in the mid-thirties to the defects of the basic Act. The FDA had for some years remonstrated against its limitations, establishing in its Washington office a "Chamber of Horrors" which exhibited some of the filthy, decayed, or insect-infested food it had seized, patent medicines accompanied by users' testimonials and users' death certificates, and cosmetics along with photographs of women disfigured, blinded, or paralyzed by their use. Under its auspices, far-reaching revisions were introduced into Congress in 1933. There followed a five-year battle royal between the proponents of increased consumer protection and affected

[5] U.S. v. Johnson, 221 U.S. 488.
[6] See below, pp. 510–514.

manufacturing and advertising interests. Through advertising channels, heavy pressure was brought to bear on the press, which with few exceptions joined the chorus of opposition. The measure seesawed back and forth between House, Senate, committees, and subcommittees, with weakening amendments being added at almost every stage. In 1936 it appeared unlikely that any bill would pass.

At a crucial stage in the proceedings, however, almost one hundred persons were killed by "Elixir Sulfanilamide"—the new drug sulfanilamide dissolved in a deadly poison—which had been marketed without ever being tested for toxicity. The FDA seized remaining stocks, enough to kill 3,720 people, and prosecuted the manufacturer, but it had not had authority to take preventive action. The situation threatened a repetition of the popular feeling of 1906. Reputable manufacturers hesitated to continue outright resistance to new legislation. The Food, Drug, and Cosmetic Act, finally passed in June, 1938, contained numerous compromises but was a substantial advance over the old law. It expanded consumer protection by enlarging the range of affected commodities, broadening definitions of adulteration and misbranding, increasing penalties, and making special provision for peculiarly dangerous substances. Cosmetics (except for soap) and therapeutic devices were included in its terms. Food adulteration was redefined to cover retention of natural poisons as well as addition of poisonous substances, subject to tolerances set by the Secretary of Agriculture. Substances might not be added to food to increase bulk, reduce quality or strength, or "make it appear better than it is." Coal-tar coloring products might be used only after government certification. Standard drugs had either to conform to the official compendia or be clearly labeled with the precise differences from official standards. The definition of adulterated cosmetics in general followed that for food under the old law, with special provision for coal-tar hair dyes. "Adulteration" of all three classes of goods included their packing, preparation, or holding under unsanitary conditions.

There were substantial modifications in the definition of misbranding, and several loopholes in the old statute were plugged. A food sold under the name of another had to be clearly marked "imitation." Foods bearing proprietary names were to be labeled with the common or usual name of the food and each ingredient. Containers so formed or filled as to be misleading were prohibited. Dietary food had to contain such information about its vitamin, mineral, and other properties as the Secretary determined to be necessary for full consumer protection. Artificial flavoring or coloring and chemical preservatives were to be disclosed on the label. Certain drugs must carry a warning of their habit-forming qualities. Labels had to contain adequate directions for use, warnings against unsafe dosage, and disclosure of ingredients involving special dangers to the user. A general definition of misbranding applying to the entire Act took into account not only misleading representations but also omission of material facts or material consequences. To prevent a repetition of the sulfanilamide experience, full information about new drugs had to be filed and samples submitted for government testing before being introduced into interstate commerce. An emergency permit control system for distribution of foods peculiarly liable to contamination during processing was established.

Penalties were sharply increased, amounting to a year's imprisonment or fine not exceeding $1,000 for a first offense, with subsequent offenses entailing imprisonment up to three years and fine up to $10,000. The old forfeiture provisions remained, although multiple seizures while a forfeiture proceeding was pending were now generally forbidden. Injunctions restraining continuance of prohibited actions were authorized as a new enforcement technique both more rapid and less expensive than criminal procedure in cases not involving moral turpitude.

The 1938 Act closed most of the statutory loopholes.[7] False and misleading advertising, however, remains beyond FDA control and is inadequately controlled. Poultry-processing plants are free from compulsory sanitary inspection and, according to critics, could provide tales of the marketing of diseased birds "to rival the lurid accounts . . . in . . . The Jungle."[8] Control over the use of chemicals with unknown effects in cosmetics and foods is inadequate. And labels of commonly used poisonous products, such as paint, paint remover, polishes, and cleaning fluids, need bear neither a warning nor a list of ingredients.[9]

[7] In 1954 the Miller Amendment empowered the FDA to set tolerances in the final product for poisonous materials used in the growing of fruit and vegetable crops.

[8] "50 Years of the Food and Drug Act," Consumer Reports (July, 1956), pp. 359, 365.

[9] In 1952 a serious statutory breach was opened up by a Supreme Court decision which denied the FDA the power to inspect factories without permission of their owners, holding that the 1938 law had been poorly drafted, not actually conferring the powers it intended, U.S. v. Cardiff, 344 U.S. 174. In 1953 Congress explicitly granted the FDA permission to inspect "at reasonable times" and upon written notice.

The major weakness of current enforcement, however, is budgetary, not statutory. Despite the sweeping scope of its assignment, the FDA is given far less money than agencies with smaller responsibilities but greater political support. In 1955, for example, the FDA had an appropriation of only $5.5 million, while over $14 million was voted for the eradication of farm pests and plant and animal diseases. In 1954, in an attempt to muster support for increased appropriations, the Secretary of Health, Education, and Welfare appointed a Citizens' Advisory Committee to investigate enforcement of the food and drug laws. Stating that "the scope and complexity of the present enforcement and regulatory problems, if dealt with inadequately, constitute a threat to the health and welfare of our citizens," the committee concluded that "the resources of the FDA are woefully inadequate to discharge its present responsibilities." [10] It recommended that the FDA be expanded threefold or fourfold within five to ten years. In his 1955 State of the Union message, President Eisenhower called for "better consumer protection under our existing pure food and drug laws." Congress, however, added only $384,000 to the FDA's appropriation for the next year.

While under the Meat Inspection Act each carcass must be inspected before it can be sold, only in antibiotics and coal-tar dyes can the FDA afford to test a sample from each batch. Only about one-twelfth of all of the establishments processing or storing foods, drugs, and cosmetics can be inspected in any one year, and only one-tenth of 1 per cent of these products can be tested. In fiscal 1954, the FDA seized 32 untested, mislabeled, or low-potency drugs, 150 tons of food tainted with poisonous or harmful materials, and 2,544 tons of filthy or decomposed food. But the FDA itself pointed out how much enforcement was left undone. "Gross adulteration [of food] such as visible filth or decay, has been left largely for detection by the consumer." [11]

Furthermore, the increasing use of chemicals in many foods and cosmetics raises new hazards to health and further strains the capacity of the FDA. Chemicals may be added to foods without prior tests. Only when the FDA has investigated and found the chemical to be unsafe may its use be barred. The FDA may also prescribe food standards which prevent use of a chemical unless its presence is noted on the label. In 1950,

[10] Citizens' Advisory Committee on the FDA, Report, H. Doc. No. 227, 84th Cong., 1st sess., p. 5.

[11] Department of Health, Education, and Welfare, Annual Report, 1954, p. 194.

the FDA and the Public Health Service stated that of 704 chemicals then known to be used in foods, the safety of 276 was unknown.[12] In 1952, the FDA was able to establish standards excluding certain chemicals from bread, unless listed on wrappers, only after ten years of research and hearings which covered 17,000 pages. The need for knowledge and the lack of enforcement are equally serious in the field of cosmetics.[13]

Clearly, budgetary support is as essential as basic legislation to the effectuation of public policy. The lack of organized consumer strength to influence appropriations committees, and the failure of administration leaders to support more effectively the case for the consumer interest, has partially negated policy and leaves this interest inadequately protected.

False Advertising

Opponents of the Food, Drug, and Cosmetic Bill of 1933 succeeded in eliminating its advertising provisions. Consumer groups and the FDA had argued that misleading advertising was so akin to misbranding that it could be defined in almost identical terms and be most effectively prevented by the same agency. Proprietary drug and advertising interests maintained that such control, if imposed at all, should be placed with the agency already active in the advertising field, the Federal Trade Commission. Their view was finally adopted by Congress.

In the mid-thirties, FTC efforts to lessen false advertising in general had been severely curtailed by the Raladam decision of 1931.[14] The Commission's repeated requests for revision of its basic statute, to prohibit "unfair or deceptive acts or practices in commerce" as well as "unfair methods of competition," were not satisfied until the passage in 1938 of the Wheeler-Lea Amendment, which also contained special provisions against false advertising of food, drugs, cosmetics, and therapeutic devices.

While the FTC had long devoted most of its attention to cases of misrepresentation, its main purpose had been the protection of competitors, not of consumers. The new amendment empowered it to protect consumers directly by issuing orders against false advertising of those specified products and against deceptive practices in general. In addition to its usual cease and desist orders, the Commission might also bring suit to enjoin dis-

[12] *Report of the Select Committee to Investigate the Use of Chemicals in Foods and Cosmetics*, H. Rept. 2356, 82nd Cong., 2d sess. (1952), p. 4.
[13] *Ibid.*, H. Rept. 2182 (1952).
[14] See below, p. 511–512.

semination of an allegedly false advertisement pending completion of its ordinary procedure. Where injuries to health might occur from customary or advertised uses of the commodity being falsely advertised, the advertiser was subject to the same criminal penalties as under the Food, Drug, and Cosmetic Act. Falsity in advertising, however, was less rigidly defined than misbranding under the Food, Drug, and Cosmetic Act. A product is misbranded if its label is "false or misleading in any particular," but an advertisement is false only if it is "misleading in a material respect." Although the Wheeler-Lea Amendment also called for advertisements to be judged by what is "suggested" and by the omission of "material" facts, the courts are more lenient in the standards they apply to advertising. In an earlier case of alleged misrepresentation in advertising, a lower court had accepted "pictorial exaggeration" and the "time-honored custom of at least merely slight puffing." [15] Similarly tolerant attitudes have characterized judicial interpretation of false advertising under the 1938 law.[16]

Attempts to eliminate deceptive practices and false advertising in foods, drugs, cosmetics, and therapeutic devices command a large share of the FTC's limited resources. In fiscal 1956, such efforts accounted for over one-fourth of its expenditures and led to 150 of the 192 complaints it issued. In its search for offenses, the Commission's Bureau of Investigation examines, on a sampling basis, newspapers, periodicals, and mail-order catalogs; monitors broadcasts; and checks TV and radio continuities. Most of its cases, however, originate in complaints from those who allege injury. In fiscal 1956, it received 2,221 such complaints. The FTC's first action is usually an inquiry by correspondence. If the case is not disposed of in this manner, it is then referred to a field office for investigation and report. Technical consultation and advice may be sought by the FTC's Division of Scientific Opinions from other governmental agencies, such as the Bureau of Standards, the FDA, and the Public Health Service. In 1956, the Division submitted 1,022 opinions. Most cases are disposed of when the offender agrees, by letter, affidavit, or stipulation, to eliminate the questioned statements or claims. In 1956, the Commission approved 166 stipulations, mostly dealing with deceptive practices and false advertising.[17]

[15] *Ostermoor & Co.* v. *FTC*, 16 F. 2d 962 (1927).
[16] *Carlay Co.* v. *FTC*, 153 F. 2d 493 (1946).
[17] Case statistics in this paragraph from FTC, *Annual Report: 1956*, pp. 21, 22, 28, 65, 69.

Among the stipulations accepted in a typical year [18] were agreements to cease claiming or implying: that Dr. Guild's Green Mountain Asthma Compound is a remedy for asthma; that a Beau-T-Form Maternity Garment will eliminate the discomforts of pregnancy or promote easy or safe delivery; that Dornol Skin Detergent will prevent or cure pimples or acne; that FAB, Tide, Cheer, Surf, or Hum wash clothes as clean without rinsing as with rinsing; that Bulova watches are "Academy Award Watches" unless made clear that the title results from a licensing arrangement with the Academy of Motion Picture Arts and Sciences and not from a meritorious award; that sweaters called Hand Looped Knits are handlooped; that Natcol is an "amazing discovery" or that it is of any value in retarding falling hair; that Con-O-Lite burial vaults are patented; that an Electro-Scope is a cure, treatment, or any aid in relieving arthritis, neuritis, eyeritis, rheumatism, neuralgia, sciatica, lumbago, nasal catarrh, impaired eyesight, intestinal catarrh, kidney inflammation, bladder inflammation, prostate trouble, ovary congestion, female weakness, varicose veins, migraine headaches, high blood pressure, congested circulation, or respiratory ailments; that a Forecaster calendar is an unfailing system of birth spacing; that Snug Denture Cushions will eliminate "denture breath"; that Good Luck Margarine is a dairy product and competing products are not suitable for table use; or that Heart-Shield Bibles afford protection against bullets, shrapnel, or projectiles, or have gold-plated covers.

Cease and desist orders cover a similar range. Firms were ordered to cease and desist from representing that: Bethany College and Divinity School is a college or institution of higher learning; that "Static-Master instantly destroys static-surface attraction with polonium, a harmless by-product of the Uranium-Radium series," when in fact polonium can be highly dangerous; that Parfum de Soir, Danse Apache, or Bois de Rose are imported from France or that they contain gold; that Dolcin is "economical" or "low cost" or that it is effective treatment for rheumatic fever, fibrositis, myositis, neuritis, sciatica, lumbago, bursitis, etc.; or that Thorkon will convert "a nagging, quarrelsome, irritable woman into a good wife and mother . . . unless such . . . conditions are caused by Vitamin B_1, B_2, niacinade, or iron deficiencies," which instances, the FTC assures us, "are quite rare." [19]

[18] FTC, *Decisions* (fiscal 1953), Vol. 49, pp. 1585, 1591, 1597, 1601–1603, 1611–1612, 1616, 1631, 1641.
[19] *Ibid.*, pp. 1ff., 229ff., 466ff., 566ff., 613ff.

While a perusal of FTC dockets offers ample evidence of the continued existence, in modern garb, of the nineteenth-century "medicine man," of the credulity of some of the public, and of the irresponsibility of some advertising, the net result of FTC regulation should not be overrated. Undoubtedly the marketplace is purged of some denizens of the business underworld who positively endanger the health of their customers or push misrepresentation to the point of fraud. But most FTC actions secure only paper victories over advertisers who can invent new deceptive advertising campaigns more rapidly than the Commission can act against old ones. The FTC can act only against the advertiser, not against his advertising agency or his advertising media. It can require no retraction and cannot censor copy in advance. It can eliminate some advertising abuses, but falsity, misrepresentation, and exaggeration in advertising can be expected to continue. A healthy public skepticism may offer more protection than official regulation.

Government Commodity Standards

Another form of governmental defense of the consumer interest is the establishment of commodity standards, which offer an alternative to brand names as a basis for identification and consumer choice. Government action can hardly operate on the exact pattern of private research and testing organizations, but it can help assure to consumers a minimum of objectively established basic quality information. The political impotence of consumers is demonstrated again by the relative lack of such governmental services and by the fact that those which are provided result from the pressure of producers.

The setting of official standards for the use of governmental purchasing units, scientific organizations, and manufacturers dates from the establishment of the National Bureau of Standards in 1901. Growing out of the earlier Office of Standards, Weights, and Measures, the Bureau has developed an elaborate organization for testing qualities of all sorts. Although ultimate consumers may receive substantial indirect benefits from its work, the Bureau's services primarily benefit producers and institutional consumers.

In agriculture, the Agricultural Marketing Service has developed systematic grades which may be used by processors voluntarily. Meat grading has been well established for half a century. The McNary-Mapes Amendment of 1930 to the Food and Drug Act, requiring the labeling of substandard canned goods, was spon-

sored by the National Canners Association in an effort to eliminate the competition of inferior products. Under the leadership
of the NRA Consumers' Advisory Board, vigorous efforts were
made to extend compulsory grading above the minimum standard. While distributors of private brands were not unfriendly,
national-brand manufacturers and allied advertising interests
feared the proposal's effect on existing good will for their products, created at great cost, and were able to have it defeated.
As finally enacted, the Food, Drug, and Cosmetic Act simply
extended the McNary-Mapes Amendment to all foods other than
fresh or dried fruits and vegetables.

Primarily because of the desire of sheep-raisers and woolen
weavers to shield wool from the competition of other fibers, rather
than to protect consumers as such from misrepresentation, Congress in 1940 passed the Wool Products Labeling Act. This measure requires that most products containing wool, with the exception among others of rugs, carpets, and upholstery, must bear
labels showing percentages of virgin wool, reprocessed or reused
wool, and any other fibers or fillers used. Willful violation is a
misdemeanor, punishable by a fine not exceeding $5,000 or im-
prisonment up to one year. Falsification of the label is a violation of Section 5 of the Federal Trade Commission Act, and
the Wool Act is enforced by ordinary FTC cease-and-desist order
procedures.

The Fur Products Labeling Act of 1951 also protects consumers from misrepresentation, but this statute likewise was enacted primarily to protect furriers from unethical competition
and had the firm support of the Master Furriers' Guild. The Act
directed the FTC to determine, after public hearings, the true
English names of furs and to publish them in a Fur Products
Guide. Labels and advertising must disclose the true name of
the fur and whether the fur article is dyed, bleached, damaged,
secondhand, or pieced. Penalties and enforcement procedures
are the same as for the Wool Act.

In 1953, after several serious injuries from the ignition of
clothes made of synthetic fibers, Congress enacted the Flammable
Fabrics Act. This forbids the production or distribution of wear-
ing apparel "so highly flammable as to be dangerous when worn."
The FTC is empowered to issue appropriate rules and regulations,
to conduct tests, and to make investigations and reports. Enforcement measures include cease and desist orders, seizure of offending goods, and criminal penalties of a year's imprisonment or
fines up to $5,000 for willful violations. Tests of flammability

have been established by the Bureau of Standards and testing procedures by the FTC.

Enforcement of these three laws requires the FTC to investigate, police, and counsel actively rather than to wait for complaints. In fiscal 1956, nearly 15 million products were examined for compliance on a sampling basis, and over 5,000 commercial establishments were investigated. There were 7,603 cases of questionable practices disposed of with the acceptance of assurances of their discontinuance; 136 cases were investigated for complaint or stipulation, and 46 complaints were issued. Only one criminal prosecution was undertaken.[20]

The uneven balancing of the political scales against the consumer was also demonstrated during World War II in the work of the Office of Price Administration (OPA). In an attempt to prevent maximum prices from being undercut by quality dilution, the OPA established quality grades for rayon hosiery and for canned fruits and vegetables and required informative labels. Hosiery was to be labeled as to grade, gauge, and price, and canned goods were to be classified A, B, C, or D. The reaction of the affected businesses was violent. Four congressional committees were induced to investigate the OPA. When the dust had settled, the economists responsible for the hosiery and canned-goods regulations had resigned; others had been purged by an appropriations amendment preventing OPA funds from being used to pay the salaries of price administrators who lacked experience in business, commerce, or industry; and a 1943 amendment to the price-control law forbade grade-labeling requirements and prohibited the OPA from using quality standards in fixing maximum prices unless the standards were customarily and generally used, were needed by other agencies, or were necessary to control prices.

This brief but dramatic episode vividly displayed the power configurations arrayed against this part of the consumer interest. Co-operatives and some grocery chains have voluntarily labeled their canned goods with Agriculture Department grades, but consumer response has been disappointing. Unless consumer consciousness is sufficient to promote the cause of greater consumer information through economic support in the market for those who provide informative labels, the odds against political adoption of this form of consumer protection will remain overwhelming.

[20] Statistics in this paragraph are from FTC, *Annual Report: 1956*, pp. 25, 69.

3. Consumer Representation in Government

As other broad functional interests developed powerful organizations, they obtained the creation of executive agencies avowedly devoted to their needs. Departments of Agriculture, Commerce, and Labor were thus established in turn, implementing through functional representation the accepted tradition of special-interest promotion. In their own self-interest, moreover, these three great promotional and clientele Departments cultivate the corresponding outside organizations, and through them the appropriate congressional blocs, as a safeguard for continuance of their funds.

To round out the existing picture, logic might appear to dictate creation of a Department of the Consumer. The form of the executive establishment, however, is not determined by logic. The failure of consumers to secure the services of executive agencies is a direct result of their political weakness. Under the New Deal, several experiments were made in giving consumers governmental spokesmen, in an effort to facilitate the development of consumer consciousness and organization. This was putting the cart before the horse, however, as the failure of these experiments demonstrated.

Consumers were not wholly lacking in executive representation before 1933. Besides the FDA, the Bureau of Home Economics in the Department of Agriculture and the Bureau of Labor Statistics in the Department of Labor were both devoted to consumer welfare along with other objectives. The Home Economics Bureau, in particular, had developed a strong consumer bias. But the weakness of its position was demonstrated in 1933, when a conflict with flour interests over a publication recommending decreased bread consumption for high-income diets led to threats of reduced appropriations. The Bureau took due warning, and the pamphlet, despite a heavy demand, was not reprinted. In addition, in the regulation of public utilities, several states and the District of Columbia have made arrangements to obtain active presentation of the consumer's viewpoint as one element in the conflict of forces out of which the public interest is to be derived. People's Counsels, appointed independently of the regulatory commissions, serve as consumers' attorneys in commission proceedings.

Explicit consumer representation in the federal government, however, was first provided in three emergency New Deal agencies, the National Recovery Administration, the Agricultural Adjustment Administration, and the National Bituminous Coal Commission. The Consumers' Advisory Board of the NRA was created on President Roosevelt's insistence over the strenuous protest of General Johnson, the NRA Administrator. From the outset, the Board was a stepchild. Although it made substantial headway toward a workable and concrete definition of consumers' interest in industrial regulation, its influence on code-making and code administration was almost negligible. The Board's repeated objections to price-fixing and output-limiting provisions were viewed as academic obstructionism, and its first executive director resigned in despair.

Nonetheless, as time wore on, the Board's influence began to make itself felt in NRA attitudes. When complaints of profiteering, price increases, and discriminatory practices multiplied, coming from both intermediate and ultimate consumers, officials gave more heed to the Board's recommendations. The successive policy committees set up within the organization were strongly influenced in their conclusions by its well-reasoned criticisms, which growing factual experience served to confirm. In July, 1934, a rule against price fixing was issued, although it was then too late to modify most of the code structure. To some extent, recommendations of the Consumers' Advisory Board conflicted with the fundamental purposes of the NRA when judged realistically rather than by announced objectives. The Board's basic defect, however, was clearly its lack of an organized constituency. The Board tried to remedy this deficiency by organizing consumers through governmental channels, seeking to establish a consumer council in each of the nation's 3,072 counties. Only 150 county councils were actually established, however, and they did not generate sufficient pressure to balance the organized opposition forces. The NRA experience demonstrated both the need for consumer representation and the formidable obstacles which confront it.

In the AAA, too, consumer representation was instituted at Presidential insistence and over the opposition of its Administrator, George Peek. The position of the AAA Consumers' Counsel was anomalous from the outset. The purpose of the AAA, to raise prices of farm products, had to be accepted as a framework for his operations. He therefore attempted to promote improved distributive efficiency and reduction of price spreads between farmers and the retail market. In practice, however, it proved far easier to align farmers and distributors against consumers than farmers and consumers against the well-entrenched distributors. Two successive Administrators, anxious to obtain quick results, came into insoluble conflict with the Counsel. The conflict was eased in 1935 when a new Counsel decided to concentrate on consumer education. Even then, despite the relative innocuousness of this program, he was occasionally involved in other disputes with the AAA. The office had no real foundation on which to support aggressive promotional activities. In 1941, some of its functions were abandoned and others transferred to the Agricultural Marketing Administration, later the War Food Administration. In 1945, this agency was terminated and its surviving duties shifted to the Secretary of Agriculture. In the process, the functions of the Consumers' Counsel disappeared.

The Bituminous Coal Conservation Act of 1935 and its lineal successor, the Bituminous Coal Act of 1937, called for consumer representation for the first time in specific statutory terms, following the model of state laws creating People's Counsels for public utility commissions. A Consumers' Counsel was set up and directed "to appear in the interests of the consuming public in any proceeding before the Commission and to conduct such independent investigation of matters relative to the coal industry and the administration of this Act as he may deem necessary to enable him properly to represent the consuming public in any proceeding before the Commission."

Under the second Act, forceful steps were taken by the Counsel to obtain a part in the elaborate price-fixing process around which the plan revolved. His early conflicts with the Coal Commission were reminiscent of the NRA and AAA experiences. Anxious to bring immediate relief to the industry by establishing minimum prices as quickly as possible, both producer and labor members resented his intervention. Despite the clear command of the statute, he was at first refused access to data supporting the Commission's decisions. After a reorganization in 1938, the Commission became more responsive to his demands. The Counsel was now given full access to individual cost data. On his initiative, they were also made available to the general public, although only after court action against recalcitrant producers.[21] Testimony was presented on his behalf at several stages in the evolution of price schedules.

Besides legal activities within the immediate framework of the Act, the Counsel took steps to interest domestic consumers in the proceedings and to direct their attention to quality standards and other information essential to intelligent buying. Press releases, a small news bulletin, and a motion picture entitled *Know Your Coal* were all employed to this end. On the whole, the Counsel

[21] *Utah Fuel Co.* v. *National Bituminous Coal Commission*, 306 U.S. 56 (1939).

viewed his position as representing all consumers, large and small. Although conflicts among different consuming groups were potentially serious, issues of this type did not come to the fore.

In July, 1939, when the Coal Commission was transformed into a division of the Interior Department, the functions of the Consumers' Counsel were assumed by the Solicitor's Office in that Department. The independent statutory status of consumer representation in bituminous-coal regulation thereby came to an end, and the entire scheme of regulation expired in 1943.

The Counsel added considerably to the administrative difficulties of the Bituminous Coal Commission. Nevertheless, given a body containing representatives of coal operators and coal unions, this was a small price to pay for whatever broader definitions of policy and wider representation of interests he could inject. The wisdom of having public policy made by such functionally representative bodies, however, is open to serious question. Although it enables face-to-face bargaining among, and adjustment of, those interests immediately concerned, it tends to promote a narrow and particularistic definition of the public interest. The weakness and disorganization of his constituency prevented the Consumers' Counsel from mustering countervailing power at all comparable to that of the operators and miners.

4. Consumer Interest and Public Interest

Pluralistic organization has come to rival individualism in the development of modern democratic societies. The trend is often positively fostered by public policy. Atomization of agricultural, labor, and business organizations is rightly viewed as neither possible nor desirable. In seeking to mediate effectively among such groups, government is compelled to supplement the traditional technique of judicial determination of individual rights and duties with an elaborate administrative organization and a trained civil service directed positively toward eliciting a public interest out of the welter of interacting partial interests. Early recognition of this need in public utility regulation was later followed by its acceptance in antitrust policy and elsewhere.

Meanwhile, a type of unformalized functional representation has been introduced into the executive branch of government. It was carried to an extreme under the NRA, where lawmaking and law enforcement were delegated to private industrial and labor associations. The Bituminous Coal Commission and some of the World War II agencies took lesser steps in the same direction.

The great promotional Departments, particularly Agriculture, which performs among other duties a host of regulatory functions, exemplify the same trend. The ideal of impartial administration, of course, is not wholly abandoned. The unmitigated clash of special interests, without mediation and guidance by active proponents of a public interest, is more likely to produce deadlock than effective governmental action. But direct participation of special-interest representatives in administration is no longer viewed as an unhealthy excrescence on a pure body politic. It is welcomed and encouraged.

Under these conditions, the need for consumer representation is intensified. For their own self-defense, administrators require a constituency of consumers, as well as of more specialized interests, before whom to justify their actions. In a pluralistic world, unorganized consumers are at the mercy of superior forces. But New Deal efforts to substitute active government promotion for organizational initiative failed in the face of superior forces. Consumer strength within and without the government can only develop in step. Until consumers develop consciousness and organization, consumer legislation will continue to be enacted only when producer and consumer interests coincide or when public opinion is aroused by some dramatic incident.

PART 3

Government as
Regulator in the
Public Interest

CHAPTER 9

The Growth of Government Regulation

1. Conditioning Factors

During its first century, the nation underwent many important changes, but none was so pervasive in its influence on government and economic life as the simple physical fact that a vast continent with rich natural resources was being rapidly occupied and exploited. Public policy became inextricably intertwined with exploitation and development. Groups might disagree about terms and conditions, but most of them shared a sense of continental destiny. Seemingly inexhaustible public lands provided material for what Vernon Parrington once called a National Barbecue; one of the main tasks of government was the allocation and distribution of the economic surplus.

The building of roads, the cutting of canals, the construction of railroads, and the invention of the telegraph provided transportation and communications networks which facilitated the march across the continent. Here, too, the resources of government were tapped to promote expansion. At the same time, the United States was evolving from a preindustrial to an industrial economy. The settlement of the West obscured the transformation, but at different rates of speed in different sections, the impact of the industrial revolution was deeply felt.

British colonial policy had retarded American manufacturing, but after the Revolution, and particularly after the War of 1812,

239

numerous manufacturing units were established and the basis was laid for a great era of industrial expansion. Industrialization was accelerated by generous governmental aid. This aid met sporadic resistance from agrarian elements, but the resistance was neither sustained nor effective. Industrialization proceeded with increasing speed. Agrarian groups found their hegemony challenged. Other changes followed. In Massachusetts, in Charles Francis Adams's terms, the Codfish Aristocracy and the Merchant Princes gave way to the Lords of the Loom. The next generations were to witness the rise of the railroad barons, the captains of industry, and the masters of capital as new industrial and financial empires were carved out.

Economic and legal institutions were shaped to facilitate this expansion. The corporate device, although in use in England, had largely lain fallow in this country during the colonial period. The simplicity of economic and social conditions here made widespread resort to it unnecessary. But, as E. M. Dodd has pointed out:

The political and commercial separation from Great Britain led to an immediate demand for American banking and insurance enterprises, and of these the banks from the outset and the insurance companies at an early date generally assumed the corporate form of organization. . . . independence was followed also by an increased interest in such public improvements as canals and toll bridges, and the larger of these enterprises sought and generally obtained incorporation. These early types of corporations were followed during the closing years of the eighteenth century by a substantial number of turnpike and water works corporations and by a few pioneer charters for manufacturing enterprises. . . .[1]

Thus the basis was laid for the expansion which followed. As the century advanced, one sector of economic life after another came under corporate sway.

Resistances to the corporate system were, of course, encountered. As Justice Brandeis described it, "at first the corporate privilege was granted sparingly; and only when the grant seemed necessary in order to procure for the community some specific benefit otherwise unattainable."[2] The relaxation of restrictions on corporate size and activity came gradually. In part, it reflected a general desire for business expansion; more immediately, however, it was caused by the growing political power of corporate promoters

[1] *Harvard Legal Essays* (1934), pp. 66, 67.
[2] *Liggett* v. *Lee*, 288 U.S. 517 (1933).

whose influence in a few strategic states set in motion a "race
. . . not of diligence but of laxity."

The rapid pace of industrialization and the seemingly bound-
less opportunities for development gave direction to the growth
of business enterprise. With improvements in transportation and
with the widening of markets, local businesses became national in
scope. With increases in the size of firms also came increasing
power of businessmen to shape the national economy. The frontier
offered a traditional safety valve for the restless and dissatisfied,
but as the years passed and the frontier reached its Western
limits, the independence of the small farmer and laborer seemed
to become more illusory than real. Agriculture felt the impact of
mechanization and specialization and became closely geared to
the compulsions of a market economy. Becoming conscious of its
decreased bargaining advantages, labor sought through organization and pressure on government to repair its position.

It was against this background that the relations of government
to economic life unfolded. To depict the first century of this history only in terms of the gradual triumph of laissez faire is to miss
much. To be sure, mercantile regulations dating from the colonial
period—such as municipal fixing of the "assize" of bread—were
well on the road to disappearance by the first decade of the nineteenth century. But other trends toward expanded government
activities were already well in evidence.

As population became more closely knit and urbanization proceeded, functions formerly performed by private individuals were
transferred to the domain of public enterprise. Volunteer fire
companies became municipal departments. Education became a
public function. Public hospitals were established. Road building passed from private into public hands. The era of the social
service state was foreshadowed.

At the same time, government vigorously promoted economic
development and laid the foundations for the growth of business
enterprise. The dearth of private capital made public credit essential. Where prospective profits were too small to encourage
private companies to undertake improvements, the state itself took
the lead. Roads were built, bridges constructed, canals cut, and
railroads laid by public authorities in order to advance economic
development. Public resources were made freely available to private individuals. Loans and stock subscriptions were utilized to
promote internal improvements, dams, turnpikes, canals, railroads, and even manufacturing enterprises; such stock ownership
in some instances enabled governmental entities to name directors

and exercise some supervision over internal management. Nor was state aid confined to loans or stock subscriptions. Grants of land, lottery privileges, exemptions from taxation, and other devices were also used to encourage private initiative.

Indeed, a dominating characteristic of early government intervention in the United States is the extent to which public funds and public resources supported, stimulated, and promoted the spread of business enterprise. The exigencies of a young and undeveloped country carried the day for government aid. The demand for internal improvements was a natural outgrowth of the pressing needs of a rapidly expanding country. As the turnpike era gave way to "canal mania" and "railroad mania," construction costs were regularly shouldered or shared, first by state and local governments, and later by the federal government.[3]

2. The Beginnings of the Regulatory Movement

The beginnings of the regulatory movement are often traced to the Granger agitation of the 1870's. In fact, the roots reach deeper. Even as the corporate system was getting under way, alarms and forebodings began to be heard. An aversion to industrialism and a fear that corporate privileges would produce undesirable concentration of power were early expressed by leading agrarian spokesmen such as Jefferson and John Taylor. Jefferson's opinion on the constitutionality of a National Bank (1791) breathes this fear. John Taylor, the philosopher of Jeffersonian Democracy, constantly reiterated the dangers of "condensation" of power. Jackson's attack on the Bank and the "money power" reflected the same underlying concern. Some Jacksonian Democrats labeled the railroads undemocratic because they raised the danger of monopoly; they preferred common roads—"a real people's road." When complaints were made that the government had to pay exorbitant rates for railway mail transportation, Jackson himself cried, "Already does the spirit of monopoly begin to exhibit its natural propensities, in attempts to exact from the public . . . the most extravagant compensation," and asked "whether a combination of citizens, acting under charters of incorporation from the states, can, by a direct refusal, or the demand of an exorbitant price, exclude the United States from the established channels of communication. . . ."[4] In 1838, Congress for the first time regulated

[3] See Chapter 5.

[4] L. H. Haney, *Congressional History of Railways in the United States*, Vol. II, p. 201.

payments for mail transportation.

Regulatory legislation, however, was still extremely rare. Implicit in the concern of Jeffersonian and Jacksonian Democracy were the seeds of later regulation, but they were long in coming to full fruition. The Jeffersonian fears were strong enough to restrain somewhat the distribution of public bounty to private interests; they could not reverse the forces which dictated a policy of government aid in a young and undeveloped country. The dread of private monopoly was mingled with a distrust of centralized political power. Steeped in agrarianism, Jeffersonian political theory had a bias toward local home rule and decentralized political power; it envisaged no large use of central government to direct the nation's economic destinies.

The agrarian inheritors of the Jeffersonian tradition, therefore, focused their early efforts at regulation on local and state action, rather than national. The antimonopolists might try to dislodge privileged groups entrenched in the national government; they would not seek central controls to regulate industries which were rapidly becoming nationwide until the possibilities of local and state control had been thoroughly explored.

The growth of regulation in the United States has not been the product of any farsighted plan or design, inspired by a general philosophy of governmental control. Step by step, whether in state or nation, it has been a series of empirical adjustments to felt abuses, initiated by particular groups to deal with specific problems as they arose.

3. The Massachusetts Experience and the Spread of Regulation

The pragmatic and experimental character of this growth can be illustrated in a variety of fields. The early development of regulatory commissions in Massachusetts furnishes an interesting example of the process.[5] Regulation in Massachusetts was at first primarily legislative. The restrictions on business corporations imposed by some of the early charters, particularly those limiting corporate size and voting rights of large stockholders, seemed to indicate a fear of monopoly; but restrictions did not persist as part of the living law. Among the earliest corporations were the banks. Some public control was provided through a reserved legislative right to examine into the affairs of such banks and

[5] See L. D. White, "Origin of Utility Commissions in Massachusetts," *Journal of Political Economy* (March, 1921), p. 177.

inspect their books, and by a requirement for periodic reports. But the legislative investigating committee, as a device of control, developed serious weaknesses. "Its supervision was necessarily temporary and intermittent; its activities were usually undertaken after the damage had been done; its members, depending on their own genius for discovery, were readily deceived." [6] Accordingly, a Bank Commission was created in 1838 to provide continuous and intimate supervision of banking affairs. Although abolished in 1843, it was restored in 1851, with amplified authority, and became a part of the state's permanent regulatory machinery.

There evolved a similar system of control over insurance companies. Legislative visitation and public reports proved ineffective. Enforcement of rights by private suits was inadequate; it often was difficult to serve writs on out-of-state companies. Frequent frauds and irregular practices culminated in a series of exposures. Again the expedient of a commission was invoked.

Railroad policy also began with special acts of incorporation. The result, according to the first Railroad Commissioners' Report in 1869, was that legislation covering the 550 railroads incorporated was "scattered through 950 special acts: one chapter containing 145 sections of the General Statutes, and 40 general laws passed since those statutes were compiled." This mass of legislation embodied three main regulatory principles, besides the reserved right of the state to alter, amend, or repeal charters: (1) legislative power to reduce rates when the net income of the railroad company exceeded 10 per cent of its actual cost; (2) a reservation of legislative right of purchase after a specified period at a price equal to cost plus 10 per cent interest per annum; and (3) from 1836 on, requirement of annual reports.

These principles, as actually applied, were not particularly restrictive. The first was evaded. The second made the cost of state purchase prohibitive. The third was openly flouted. In the early period of railroad construction, railroad promoters were still treated as public favorites; they were allowed, in Judge Cooley's phrase, "to shape the law to suit themselves." The frenzy of railroad building was attended by the growth of powerful railroad lobbies; in L. D. White's words, they "were able to hoodwink the General Court [legislature], to defy it, and to manipulate it." [7]

Dissatisfaction soon became articulate. High rates and complaints of unfair discrimination against certain firms led to a demand for more effective regulation. In 1869, after five years of

[6] *Ibid.*, p. 180.
[7] *Ibid.*, p. 189.

struggle against bitter railroad opposition, a Railroad Commission was created. Its powers were limited; the "functions assigned to it were wholly advisory in their nature"; enforcement of its recommendations was dependent almost entirely on the force of public opinion. As Charles Francis Adams, Jr., said in 1874, the Commission was "simply a medium, a species of lens by means of which the otherwise scattered and powerless rays of Public Opinion could be concentrated to a focus and brought to bear upon any corporation." [8]

Beginning about 1870, the movement to establish state railroad commissions acquired real momentum. By 1886, thirty states and territories regulated railroads, twenty-five by commission and five by legislation. Although, as the Cullom Committee (a special Senate investigating committee) reported in 1886, there were many regulatory gaps, and some states believed that railroads should not be hampered by regulation, the era of government aid was passing. Restrictive legislation was on the increase. Eastern states tended to follow the Massachusetts pattern of an advisory commission, though the powers of commissions were increased as experience revealed the difficulties of regulation without authority. Entirely different were the Western and Southern commissions which owed their origin to the Granger movement. These agencies were usually vested with rate-fixing power, and frequently maximum rates were set by statute.

4. The Granger Movement

The Granger movement, while now remembered primarily in connection with the growth of effective railroad regulation, also had a wider program. It was anti-money-power, antimonopoly, and antimiddleman. By no means novel in rural America, such sentiments had been foreshadowed in a simpler Jacksonian day when industrial and banking development was far less advanced. In the enthusiasm and buoyant hopefulness of the settlement of the West, the notes of complaint were muffled. But as hope gave way to disappointment and economic depression bred disillusionment, the old war cries were heard again. This time they called for government regulation.

The Granger movement symbolized a remarkable change in attitude toward the railroads, particularly in the West. The frenzied railroad building of previous decades had been welcomed

[8] A. R. Ellingwood and Whitney Coombs, *The Government and Railroad Transportation* (1930), p. 50.

by the farmers. Railroads were blessings; the demand was for more and still more of them; competition would protect the public against unreasonable charges. With the agricultural depression of the late sixties and early seventies, this attitude rapidly changed. Railroads which had been hailed as the "harbingers of dawning civilization" were now condemned as "tools of extortion." Both farmers and merchants complained that rates were extortionate, that gross discrimination was practiced among localities and individuals, that railroads combined to set unfair rates and eliminate competition, that they corrupted state officials, that railroad capital was watered, and that stock which farmers and merchants purchased to aid in railroad building was rendered worthless by the financial manipulation of railroad promoters. While the movement to regulate railroads commanded wide and sometimes fierce agricultural support—hence charges that the West was bound in servitude to "absentee Eastern and European capitalists"—recent research has shown that in both the East and the West merchants strongly supported and perhaps guided the movement.[9] Indeed in New York, for example, merchants and other small businessmen led the crusade for state regulation, upstate merchants charging that lack of railroad competition there made them pay the costs of rate wars elsewhere along the trunk lines, and New York City merchants accusing the railroads of agreeing on rate differentials which penalized the city for the benefit of other ports.

To secure relief, the farmers and merchants turned to politics. Gaining control of a number of Midwestern state governments, they enacted a series of regulatory laws since known as "Granger legislation." In Illinois, a Railroad and Warehouse Commission was created in 1871; the Railroad Law of 1873 vested it with power to prepare a schedule of maximum rates for both freight and passenger transportation; unjust discrimination in railroad rates was outlawed. In 1871, the Minnesota legislature prescribed maximum rates for passengers and freight and created a railroad commissioner to collect statistics and enforce the railroad laws. In 1874, a board of railway commissioners was created with power to fix maximum rates. The Iowa Railroad Act of 1874 followed the earlier Minnesota model of setting maximum rates with provisions for a railroad commission empowered to reduce rates below the maximum when that could be done without injury to the railroad. Similar statutes were enacted in a number of other Western states.

The Granger legislation met intense railroad opposition. Rail-

---

[9] E.g., see L. Benson, *Merchants, Farmers & Railroads* (1955).

roads warned that they would be compelled to abstain from further construction because sufficient capital would not be available for investment in states imposing such restrictions. Some railroads openly defied the laws and refused to obey their provisions. Others appealed to the courts, claiming that the legislation was unconstitutional. Still others applied the statutory provisions in such a fashion as to make their incidence as obnoxious as possible, all inconveniences suffered by shippers and passengers being attributed to the law. Sometimes cries of economy were raised as means of cutting the appropriations and reducing the effectiveness of the regulatory commissions. In almost every instance sustained efforts were made to repeal or modify the law.

Railroad strategy achieved considerable success. In 1874, the Minnesota legislation was modified and made acceptable to the railroads. In 1876, the Wisconsin law was similarly amended. In 1878, the Iowa legislation was practically repealed. The Granger leaders were unable to hold their supporters. By the end of the 1870's, better prices for farm products and lower freight rates, doubtless adopted in part in response to the regulatory measures, robbed the movement of much of its momentum.

The Granger crusade, nevertheless, left its impress on the regulatory movement. "On the whole," comments the historian of the Granger movement, "it is not too much to say that the fundamental principles upon which American regulation of railroads by legislation has developed were first worked out in the Granger states of the Northwest during the decade of the seventies." [10] The establishment of a commission with power to fix maximum rates, the attempt to prevent discrimination by "short-haul" clauses, the effort to preserve competition by outlawing the consolidation of parallel lines, legislation against free passes to public officials—all these were Granger contributions.

Another important result was the opportunity given to the Supreme Court, in the Granger cases, to uphold the constitutional validity of state regulation of railroads and grain elevators. To be sure, Chief Justice Waite's distinction in *Munn* v. *Illinois*,[11] between a business clothed with a public interest and one which is only a matter of private rights (*juris privati*), became in more conservative hands what Justice Frankfurter once called "an imprisoning definition of the allowable scope of legislation." But at the time and in the given instance, the Court sanctioned a major extension of the frontiers of control. The emphasis of the decision

[10] S. J. Buck, *The Granger Movement* (1913).
[11] 94 U.S. 113 (1877).

was on the legislative power to fix rates. In rebuffing the claim that the reasonableness of rates was a matter for the courts to decide, Waite took an advanced position, from which the Court later retreated. But for a number of years, until fears of unrestricted legislative control led to the erection of judicial bulwarks against possible "confiscation" of railroad profits, these decisions gave the stamp of constitutionality to the type of close regulation represented by the Granger laws.

5. National Regulation

The Granger movement greatly strengthened the growing pressure for national regulation of railroad rates. Agitation for federal action affecting railroads, to be sure, antedated the Granger movement. As early as 1846, Congress was memorialized to construct a government railroad to the Pacific. Two years later, Senator Benton of Missouri presented a plan for a similar road to be built by the government and leased in sections to private companies under a stipulation of reasonable rates. Nothing came of these schemes. The Pacific railways constructed in the next two decades received extensive governmental aid, but ownership and control remained private. The Union Pacific charter of 1862 did provide for two government directors out of a total of fifteen, and the amended charter of 1864 provided for five out of twenty, but there is little evidence to indicate that the government's minority representation appreciably affected Union Pacific policy.[12]

Until 1868, relatively little was said in Congress about the regulation of railroad rates. In that year, signs of a policy shift became evident. Three resolutions were introduced which looked toward rate regulation; the House Committee on Roads and Canals submitted a report holding that rate regulation was both constitutional and expedient. Although nothing came of this report immediately, each new session of Congress witnessed continuous and rising interest in railroad regulation.

Agrarian discontent in the seventies intensified this interest. The federal government was urged to construct and operate a railroad from the Mississippi to the seaboard in order to secure cheap transportation to the Eastern markets for Western produce. In December, 1872, President Grant suggested the appointment of a congressional committee to consider "various enterprises for the more certain and cheaper transportation of the constantly increasing Western and Southwestern products to the Atlantic sea-

[12] The provision for government directorships was terminated in the course of the Union Pacific reorganization of 1897.

board." The resultant "Windom Committee" filed its report in 1874. Its key recommendation was more competition to lower railroad rates. To this end, it proposed the improvement of natural waterways. While it did not, in so many words, endorse construction of a government railroad running from the Mississippi to the Atlantic seaboard, it did state that "the only means of securing and maintaining reliable and effective competition between railways is the national or state ownership, or control, of one or more lines, which, being unable to enter into combinations, will serve as regulators of other lines."

By this time, Granger agitation was at its height. In 1873, the Iowa Grange petitioned Congress to "regulate without delay, by a just and equitable law, the freights and fares of all railroads within the United States." Similar petitions poured in from other Granger states. After a stormy debate and a vote in which the sectional alignment of the West against the East was unmistakable, the House in 1874 responded to the clamor by passing the McCrary Bill by a vote of 121 to 116. This bill, introduced by an Iowa Representative, called for the creation of a federal commission with the power to fix maximum rates, summon witnesses, investigate complaints, and prepare charges against the carriers. The Senate took no action on the bill.

Up to this time, the burden of complaints against the railroads had been the high rate level. But as railroad competition became interspersed with monopoly, the regulatory movement focused on efforts to abolish unjust discriminations between persons and places. Railroad rate wars, punctuated by short-lived rate agreements, sometimes produced absurdly low rates for traffic which had a choice of carriers, and railroads granted huge secret rebates to large shippers. The cost of these rate concessions was borne by shippers in monopoly areas—hence the many situations where shippers with a short, monopolized haul were charged more than those with a longer but competitive haul. In 1878, Congressman Reagan of Texas introduced a bill prohibiting discriminatory rates, the granting of rebates and drawbacks, and pools for the distribution of freight earnings. A drastic long-and-short-haul clause was included.[13] Rate schedules were to be posted conspicuously by the railroads, and a five-day notice of rate changes was required. Enforcement was to be through the courts, not by a commission.

---

[13] Long-and-short-haul clauses are intended to prevent railroads from charging more for a short than for a long haul, when the haul is on the same line and in the same direction and the shorter distance is included within the longer distance.

The bill passed the House by a vote of 139 to 104. A comparison of the sectional distribution of the vote with that on the McCrary Bill reveals the impact of the developing concern over discrimination in rates. While New England continued in opposition, the proponents of regulation were now able to muster a majority in the Middle Atlantic and Southern states as well as in the West. The Senate, however, again refused to take any action.

But by this time it was increasingly apparent that federal railroad regulation was only a question of time. Merchants, manufacturers, millers, packers, and boards of trade in increasing numbers were adding their voices and strength to the movement. The railroad question became one of the chief congressional concerns, and bills were introduced and discussed at every session. In 1885, the House passed the Reagan Bill once again. The Senate was finally stirred to action, and in the same year the Cullom Bill, creating a federal commission to regulate railroads, won a favorable vote of 43 to 12. At this juncture, on motion of Senator Cullom of Illinois, a select Senate committee was appointed to investigate and report on the necessity for regulation of railroad and water rates. The investigation was elaborate. Hearings held in all parts of the country showed the demand for federal regulation to be unmistakable. The Cullom Committee report concluded: "It is the deliberate judgment of the committee that upon no public question are the people so nearly unanimous as upon the proposition that Congress should undertake in some way the regulation of interstate commerce."

By 1886, conditions were ripe for federal regulation. The Wabash decision of the Supreme Court made it imperative.[14] In an earlier Granger case, the Court had said: "Until Congress undertakes to legislate for those who are without the state, Wisconsin may provide for those within, even though it may indirectly affect those without." [15] But in the Wabash case, Justice Miller upheld the railroad contention that a state could not regulate that part of an interstate journey which was within its boundaries. Control of interstate shipments was exclusively vested in the federal government, whether or not it chose to exercise its authority. Arguing that to allow each state to establish its own regulatory controls would be "a deleterious influence upon the freedom of commerce among the states," he concluded "that this species of regulation is one which must be . . . of a general and national character, and cannot be safely and wisely remitted to local rules and local

[14] *Wabash, St. Louis and Pacific Ry. Co.* v. *Illinois*, 118 U.S. 557 (1886).
[15] *Peik* v. *Chicago and Northwestern Ry. Co.*, 94 U.S. 164 (1877).

regulations." This decision intensified the pressure for federal regulation, since without federal action a large share of railroad traffic would be outside the reach of any regulatory authority.

The regulatory movement now came to a rapid climax. In February, 1886, Senator Cullom introduced a new bill aimed primarily at outlawing discrimination and establishing a commission. It passed the Senate 47 to 11. The House replied by re-enacting the Reagan Bill by a vote of 192 to 41. The two bills then went to conference committee, which accepted the House demand that pooling be declared illegal and adopted the Senate provision for an administrative commission to regulate rates and limit discrimination. This bill passed the Senate by a vote of 37 to 12 and the House by a vote of 219 to 41.

The creation of the Interstate Commerce Commission laid a foundation for national assumption of economic regulatory responsibilities. If the first steps were feeble and hesitant, the ICC nevertheless had significant and far-reaching effects in the impulse it gave to subsequent expansion of national regulatory authority. The establishment of the ICC was the culmination of a long agitation. That period of preparation, with its shifts in attitude, is a fascinating record of the pragmatic erosion of laissez-faire doctrine. Agrarian forces distrustful of central controls were compelled to invoke national power in order to come to grips with economic organizations that eluded local jurisdictions. Merchants and industrialists, imbued with a profound belief in the virtues of limited government, found it necessary to strengthen government in order to remedy abuses which bore heavily upon them.

The Interstate Commerce Act thus was a dramatic symbol of the ending of one era and the ushering in of another. It marked the end of a century of expansion, in the course of which a continent was occupied, industry became national in scope, and government helped to create new engines of wealth and power that threatened to evade all effective control. It stood at the threshold of a new age when increasingly the consequences of the first period of industrial development and exploitation were critically appraised, and when the resulting uneasiness crystallized in the creation of new instruments of national power to control and direct policy in important sectors of the economy.

CHAPTER 10

Railroad Regulation and the Co-ordination of Transportation

P UBLIC POLICY," an English judge once observed, "—it is a very unruly horse, and when you once get astride it you never know where it will carry you." More than seventy years' experience in federal regulation of railroads has carried us far, but it has yet to vouchsafe an ultimate destination. It has witnessed a transformation in the philosophy of regulation from the negative, restrictive conception which seeks merely to stamp out past abuses to the positive, guiding principle which assumes some affirmative governmental responsibility for planning and directing development. It has been marked by a widening jurisdiction over railroad activities and the penetration of regulatory authority into other fields of transportation, such as air, motor, and water carriers. It has seen a tendency to entrust increasing controls to independent commissions, although in recent years serious questions have been raised both about the scope of existing regulatory powers and about the adequacy of the commission as a device for the effectuation of policies dealing with broad transportation issues. Finally, this experience offers some insight into the long-run consequences of regulation and the ability of regulatory organization and procedure to adjust to basic economic changes in the regulated industry.

1. Public Policy and Parties-in-Interest
in Railroad Regulation

Railroad regulation finds a focal point in the Interstate Commerce Commission (ICC). But other arms of government cannot be disregarded. Congress formulates the policies and controls the budget of the ICC; the President makes appointments subject to Senate approval and may himself initiate important transportation policies; the courts reserve some power to overrule ICC decisions. Public policy is thus a product of the interplay of all these governmental agencies.

The regulatory machinery, moreover, does not operate in a vacuum. Important parties-in-interest have a vital stake in the formulation, execution, and—on occasion—frustration of policy. A realistic examination of the regulatory process must take them into account, consider their claims, their demands, and the intensity of the pressures they bring to bear on the determination of policy. Among the major parties-in-interest the following deserve special notice: (1) consumers of railroad service—shippers and passengers; (2) railroad labor; (3) railroad management; (4) financial control groups; (5) railroad investors; (6) railroad equipment and supply industries; and (7) competing forms of transportation.

Shippers and passengers, whose complaints gave the initial impetus to the regulatory movement, are primarily interested in low rates and adequate service. They will act together to oppose general rate increases, but in the struggle for advantageous rate treatment, cleavages develop between shippers and passengers, between large and small shippers, between commodity groups, and between locality and sectional interests. Consumers vary enormously, moreover, in the degree to which they use railroad service and in the extent of their organized activity. Traffic studies of the Federal Co-ordinator of Transportation estimated that there were 215,000 shippers who annually shipped six or more carloads of freight, and that 100,000 of these shipped more than one hundred cars annually. This latter group has a direct and vital interest in regulation; it is well-informed, organized, and articulate. On the passenger side, there is a somewhat analogous interest on the part of commuters; they are less well organized but are transportation-conscious and capable of being aroused to action. There are, of course, a large number of casual shippers and occasional travelers by rail, whose individual interest is small and indirect, who are unorganized and inarticulate. Accordingly, organized large-scale shippers and functional organizations of shippers on a commodity basis, such as trade associations, claim the center of the stage.

In addition, the national government is itself a shipper, and its agencies may represent specific consumer interests in proceedings before the Interstate Commerce Commission. In their day, the Bituminous Coal Commission and its Consumers' Counsel were authorized to represent the coal industry before the ICC, and the Agricultural Adjustment Act of 1938 permitted the Secretary of Agriculture to appear before the Commission when rates on farm products were at issue. Local government officials frequently testify in the interest of commuters or localities before the ICC or state regulatory bodies.

Railroad labor is a second important party-in-interest. Because of labor-saving technological improvements and because of the in- roads of competing modes of transportation, the number of rail- road workers has been falling ever since World War I. In 1920, there were over two million railroad employees; in 1955, the number had been cut in half. Despite dwindling ranks, however, railroad labor is strongly organized and capable of exerting con- siderable political power to support its demands. An overwhelming majority belongs to unions. While collective bargaining is its first resort, railroad labor often looks to political channels when pri- vate negotiations prove unsatisfactory. A long series of railway- labor acts bears witness to the power it has been able to mobilize.[1] While labor's primary attention is given to bread-and-butter union goals which involve differences with management—wages, work- ing conditions, steady employment, etc.—its aims and those of management converge when the question is one of protecting railroads from the competition of other carriers.

Management constitutes another important party-in-interest. Since this group directs day-to-day railway operations, its at- titude toward regulation is especially important. The group as a whole has long since ceased to oppose the government's right to regulate. It maintains, however, that if railroads are regulated, competing modes of transportation ought also to be subjected to a regulatory regime. Otherwise, railroad management should be left free to meet competition. Painfully aware of the competition railroads now face, it opposes ICC intrusion into the area it feels should be reserved for managerial discretion, and resents its con- sequent inability to adjust rates and services as flexibly as its

[1] See Chapter 7.

competitors. Some managers are part owners and directors of their roads; most of them are responsible to financial groups which dominate the railroad field.

It is these control groups which make the ultimate decisions, subject to such regulatory authority as exists and such independent influence as management may exert. Sometimes they are considerable investors in railroad securities, but in many cases the design of corporate structures and the dependence of the railroads on the capital market have concentrated power over policy in the hands of financial interests whose direct ownership stake is relatively small but whose influence is extensive. Where such financial interests dominate, they oppose regulatory measures which challenge their ascendancy and limit the opportunities for gain inherent in control. The financial history of many railroads demonstrates that interests of the control groups and of small investors are not necessarily the same. While both may unite in pressing for higher rates and lower wages, their interests diverge when control groups divert corporation income and assets to uses which endanger the financial stability of the enterprise. Railroad reorganizations reveal such conflicts of interest in their most acute form; in the past, at least, they frequently provided opportunities for mulcting unorganized investors.

Investors in railroads are today a more organized and coherent interest than in the past. In the early days of railroading, much of the capital came from foreign investors. Such influence on public policy as they enjoyed was largely exerted through the American financial houses which had distributed the securities. With the shift of the United States to a world-creditor position, most railroad stocks have been transferred to domestic ownership, and much of the bonded indebtedness is held by institutional investors, such as insurance companies, banks, pension funds, colleges, and foundations. The interest of the small investor in regulation is reasonably clear. Concerned for the safety of his investment, he is likely to be friendly to regulation of security issues, consolidations, and reorganizations designed to protect him from exploitation by "insiders." At the same time, regulation will not satisfy him unless it affords a reasonable prospect of adequate and stable earnings on his investment. Spokesmen for investors, therefore, urge public policies ensuring continuity in earnings; they favor such increases in rates and such reductions in operating expenses—including the wage bill—as will provide a goodly margin of safety after meeting fixed charges. A wave of railroad bankruptcies and reorganizations in the 1930's gave investors an acute interest in policies governing reorganizations. The declining position of the railroads during the past three decades has made access to the capital market difficult for many of them. During the Great Depression, the national government came to the rescue by investing a half billion dollars in railroad securities through the Reconstruction Finance Corporation and the Public Works Administration. In the 1958 recession, Congress authorized the governmental guarantee of another half billion dollars in private loans to railroads.

Other important but sometimes overlooked parties-in-interest are the railway equipment and supply industries. In prosperous times, railroads are heavy consumers of steel, lumber, oil (formerly coal), and other basic commodities and supplies. Many industrial plants and communities depend upon railroad purchases. Such affiliated interests benefit when railroad plant is maintained and improved. Hence their interest in the profitable operation of railroads and in the flow of capital into the industry. The supply groups, however, also use transportation services, and as consumers, they are as eager as any other shippers to secure low rates. Moreover, some of them, such as the oil industry, are also suppliers for competing forms of transportation.

Other transportation media have always had a stake in railroad regulation. In the early days, the railroads were regarded as invaders, and canal companies sought legal and political protection against this challenge to their hegemony. More recently, railroads have revived the ancient strategy of the canal companies. The extraordinary growth of transportation by highway, water, air, and pipe line has forced railroads to seek defensive political action. The railroad campaign has taken two somewhat different directions: first, a demand for the repeal of regulatory measures which hamper their ability to compete with other transportation agencies, and second, a demand that competitors be regulated in the same manner as railroads. Public policy has incompletely crystallized around the second alternative, but the final outcome is still unclear. Meanwhile, the competition between rival carriers is bitter and intense. This struggle and the agitation it produces in the political arena form an important part of the regulatory process.

This catalog of the more important parties-in-interest does not exhaustively analyze their interrelationships, combinations, and conflicts. At best it simply indicates the intricate web of adjustments which the search for the substance of public interest involves. Out of the complex of these interacting pressures, desires are generated and purposes emerge to which agencies regulating transportation are sensitive in different degrees. The alignment varies with the problem. Yet there are continuities in the dominant purposes of the parties-in-interest which provide a clue to their conduct and set limits of feasibility to public policy.

2. The Pressure for Regulation

Analysis in terms of parties-in-interest illuminates the dynamics of the regulatory process. In the early days of railroading, the dominant government policy was one of aid rather than regulation. Railroad promoters were viewed as public benefactors; there was little disposition or apparent need to erect safeguards to protect other parties-in-interest. New employment opportunities opened up for labor. The prospect of profits attracted investors. Consumers found railroads incomparably superior to roads and waterways. The promise of swift transportation, industrial development, and access to markets dwarfed the problem of costs. Sanguine expectations combined with real benefits to produce a pattern of public policy in which the communal interest was identified with the interests of railroad management and control. The result, as Judge Cooley pointed out in the first annual report of the ICC, was that "the carriers of the country were . . . enabled to determine in great measure what rules should govern the transportation of persons and property; rules which intimately concerned the commercial, industrial, and social life of the people. . . ." [2]

Abuses of the power vested in corporate management produced the demand for regulation. Other parties-in-interest began to assert themselves as independent entities with objectives conflicting with those of management. The community of interest was shattered. The Granger movement of the 1870's symbolized the rupture. Though the Grangers soon lost power and many of their more stringent controls over railroads were abandoned, smoldering resentment persisted, providing support for national regulation in the next decade.

The movement for national regulation began essentially as a shippers' movement. Congressional votes during the seventies and eighties indicate that support for regulation was at first concentrated in Western agrarian regions; however, as small businessmen in the East began to feel the pinch of discrimination, they, too, joined in the demand for regulation. The Cullom Committee hearings, with their long procession of merchants protesting against special arrangements made by the railroads with large manufacturers and distributors, further indicate that it was an

[2] ICC, *Annual Report, 1887*, p. 4.

aroused shippers' interest, consisting mainly of smaller business-men and farmers and protesting primarily against discrimination rather than the general rate level, that provided the driving impetus behind the movement for regulation. "The paramount evil chargeable against the operation of the transportation system of the United States as now conducted," reported the Cullom Committee, "is unjust discrimination between persons, places, commodities, or paticular descriptions of traffic." [3] Other parties-in-interest, although conscious of grievances, were neither suf-ficiently organized nor effective enough to find political expres-sion. Railroad labor was still weak. Investors who had suffered from managerial recklessness were as yet unprepared to press for political remedies. The burden of sponsoring regulation was, therefore, shouldered by shippers; the objectives of the original Act to regulate commerce were shippers' objectives.

3. The Interstate Commerce Commission—Creation and Frustration

The Act of 1887 was a very modest beginning in national regu-lation of railroads. It reaffirmed the common-law principle that rates be "reasonable and just." Carriers were required to publish rate schedules and give ten days' notice of increases. Special rates, rebates, drawbacks, and other forms of unjust discrimination be-tween persons, places, and commodities were declared illegal. The Act sought to enforce competition by forbidding pooling. Its "long-and-short-haul" clause made it unlawful to charge more "for a shorter than for a longer distance over the same line, in the same direction, the shorter being included within the longer distance." The ICC, however, could make exceptions, and the clause applied only if the transportation was "under substantially similar circumstances and conditions."

The Commission's authority was limited. It could gather statis-tical and other information from the railroads and require an-nual reports. It was empowered to receive and investigate com-plaints; it could notify a carrier violating the law "to cease and desist or make reparation," but it could compel obedience only by obtaining an enforcing order in a federal circuit court.

The problem of sanctions did not appear to be crucial during the initial and short-lived honeymoon period of regulation. Car-riers began to put an end to free passes, rebates, drawbacks, and special rates; they announced rate reductions and the disbanding

[3] S. Rept. 46, 49th Cong., 1st sess. (1886), p. 215.

of pools. The ICC concluded that "the operation of the act has in general been beneficial." [4] But the honeymoon was soon over. Rail revenues declined, and railroads blamed the Act. The prohibition of pooling and the long-and-short-haul clause were the subject of particular attack. Within a year after passage of the Act, evasion became commonplace. In 1890, the ICC quoted a railroad manager as saying:

. . . the situation in the West is so bad that it could hardly be worse. Rates are absolutely demoralized . . . certain shippers are allowed heavy rebates, while others are made to pay full rates. . . . The management of rates is dishonest on all sides, and there is not a road in the country that can be accused of living up to the rules of the interstate commerce law. Of course when some poor devil comes along and wants a pass to save him from starvation, he has several clauses from the interstate act read to him. But when a rich shipper wants a pass, why, he gets it at once.[5]

The ICC's efforts to end these discriminations were frustrated from a number of directions. Its staff was much too small to police all railroads. Even when violations were suspected, evidence was extremely difficult to obtain. Witnesses refused to testify, pleading immunity under the Fifth Amendment. After the Supreme Court in 1892 had upheld one such refusal,[6] Congress guaranteed the immunity from future punishment of witnesses before the ICC, in the Compulsory Testimony Act of 1893.[7] The Commission encountered serious obstacles when it sought to enforce orders in the courts. Procedure was unsatisfactory and involved long delays. Cases were tried de novo; railroads were permitted to present new evidence, including evidence held back in the original ICC hearing. Limits on the ICC's discretion and its inability to provide prompt relief to complainants discredited the Commission as an effective enforcement agency.

A series of Supreme Court decisions in 1896–1897 completed the rout of the ICC. While the Act of 1887 gave the Commission no blanket power to set rates, the ICC believed that it was empowered to declare whether particular rates were unreasonable and to prescribe maximum rates in correcting unreasonableness. But in the

---

[4] ICC, Annual Report, 1887, p. 42.
[5] ICC, Annual Report, 1890, p. 25.
[6] Counselman v. Hitchcock, 142 U.S. 547.
[7] Constitutionality of this Act was upheld in Brown v. Walker, 161 U.S. 591 (1896).

Social Circle case (1896),[8] the Court remarked that it could find no such authorization in the Act either "expressly or by necessary implication," and in the Maximum Rate case (1897),[9] it ruled that the ICC "had no power to prescribe a rate for the future, although its right to pass upon the reasonableness or unreasonableness of rates could not be questioned." In other words, the Commission could declare the existence of evils; it could not prescribe remedies. At the same time, a series of decisions virtually emasculated the long-and-short-haul clause, as it had previously been interpreted by the Commission. In the Import Rate case (1896) [10] the Court overruled an ICC prohibition of lower rates for a haul between American points when the traffic originated from a foreign point. Since competition for import traffic was vigorous, circumstances were dissimilar and justified lower rates than prevailed on domestic traffic between the same points. Then, in an 1897 case dealing with domestic rates,[11] the Court again overruled the Commission, holding that competition between railways might be important in determining dissimilarity of circumstances and so justify lower rates for longer hauls. Since this form of discrimination was generally a result of competition, the decision practically nullified the long-and-short-haul clause. Justice Harlan, dissenting, pronounced a requiem over the ICC:

> . . . the present decision . . . goes far to make that Commission a useless body. . . . It has been left, it is true, with power to make reports and to issue protests. But it has been shorn by judicial interpretation of authority to do anything of an effective character.

In its annual report for 1897 the ICC was equally frank about its impotence:

> The Interstate Commerce Commission can conduct investigations and make reports. It can perhaps correct in a halting fashion some forms of discrimination. It collects and publishes statistical information. . . . But by virtue of judical decisions, it has ceased to be a body for the regulation of interstate carriers. . . . The people should no longer look to this commission for a protection which it is powerless to extend.

The ICC met frustration in still another direction. Implicit in the prohibition of pooling was the hope that rates might be kept

---

[8] *Cincinnati, New Orleans and Texas Pacific Ry. Co. v. ICC*, 162 U.S. 104.
[9] *ICC v. Cincinnati, New Orleans and Texas Pacific Ry. Co.*, 167 U.S. 479.
[10] *Texas and Pacific Ry. Co. v. ICC*, 162 U.S. 197.
[11] *ICC v. Alabama Midland Railway Co.*, 168 U.S. 144.

"reasonable" by competition. Prior to the law of 1887, railroads had frequently sought to eliminate rate-cutting through pools to divide traffic or earnings. While these pools usually broke down, efforts to restore them continued to be made. When the Act of 1887 outlawed pools, railroads turned to traffic-association agreements which fixed rates as well as traffic arrangements. Decisions of the Supreme Court in 1897–1898 in the Trans-Missouri Freight Association and Joint Traffic Association cases,[12] holding these agreements illegal under the Sherman Antitrust Act, appeared to indicate that competition would be maintained. Actually, however, these decisions only accelerated railroad consolidation.

"With pooling prohibited," the ICC prophesied, "the tendency among the railroads seems likely to be in the direction of consolidation as the only means of effectual protection against mutual jealousies and destructive rate wars." [13] The panic of 1893 yielded a crop of railroad failures. By June, 1894, a quarter of the total railway capitalization was in receivership. The reorganization period, with its reliance on banking leadership, facilitated consolidation. "During the nineties," as E. G. Campbell has pointed out:

. . . the railroads . . . had gone through a transition which was to be experienced by many of the other great industries. . . . At the beginning of the decade there had been innumerable great independent systems, each with its own group of subsidiaries, but each competing against rival systems in the same regions. At the end of the decade there were practically no independent systems; the various systems had been drawn into a few huge combinations which were dominated by a single man or a small group of men working in harmony with each other. . . . The railroad industry had been transformed from one dominated by hundreds of competing leaders into one controlled by a small group of financiers. . . . Throughout the country competing systems had found it more profitable to form communities of interest and co-operate instead of competing and trying to ruin each other.[14]

The concentration movement aroused considerable alarm. In 1902, Charles A. Prouty, a member of the ICC, declared:

Five years ago the crying evil . . . was discrimination, mainly discrimination between individual shippers. While many rates were too

[12] U.S. v. Trans-Missouri Freight Assn., 166 U.S. 290 (1897); U.S. v. Joint Traffic Assn., 171 U.S. 505 (1898).
[13] Annual Report, 1888, p. 26.
[14] E. G. Campbell, The Reorganization of the American Railroad System, 1893–1900 (1938), pp. 331–332.

high, the general level was low; and in view of competitive conditions
. . . little apprehension was felt of any general unreasonable advance.
Not so today. The vast consolidations of the past few years; the use
of injunctions to prevent departures from the published tariff; the
lesson which railroad operators themselves have learned, that competition in rates is always suicidal, since it does not increase traffic
and does reduce revenues—these have largely eliminated . . . competition. Discrimination is disappearing, but in its place comes the
other danger which always attends monopoly, the exaction of an
unreasonable charge.[15]

4. The Beginnings of Effective Regulation

While the ICC languished and its inability to regulate the railroads effectively became increasingly clear, popular pressure for
more effective control was intensified. The Elkins Act of 1903
made departures from published railroad tariffs a misdemeanor,
subjected to punishment shippers receiving rebates, as well as
railroads granting them, and provided injunctive relief to restrain
deviations from published rates. Enacted primarily at the behest of
the railroads themselves, it received popular support on the theory
that it would check hidden concessions to the so-called trusts.

Rooseveltian trust-busting fervor fanned popular interest in
checking concentration. In 1904, the Supreme Court, in a 5 to 4
decision, ordered the dissolution of the Northern Securities Company, a holding company used by the Hill-Morgan-Harriman
interests to bring two of the largest transcontinental railroad systems under common control.[16] Although James J. Hill was said
to have remarked that the decision made no difference to him
except that he now had to sign two certificates instead of one,
Roosevelt and the public regarded it as a great victory and pressed
on to demand more effective rate regulation. In his annual message in December, 1904, Roosevelt asked Congress to give the
ICC "power to revise rates and regulations, the revised rates to at
once go into effect, and stay in effect unless and until the court
of review reverses it." The House responded by passing the Esch-
Townsend Bill by the overwhelming majority of 326 to 17, but
the railroads succeeded in blocking Senate action. The President's
next annual message again urged Congress to act, and once more
the response of the House was virtually unanimous. Early in 1906,
the House passed the Hepburn Bill, which went even beyond the
President's recommendations by giving the ICC power to initiate

[15] Ibid., pp. 333–334.
[16] Northern Securities Co. v. U.S., 193 U.S. 197.

as well as revise rates. The vote was 346 to 7.

Meanwhile, the railroads were fighting bitterly against the bill. They launched an ambitious publicity campaign designed to persuade Congress that the public was opposed to the legislation.[17] Their opposition reached its climax in the Senate, where conservatives of both parties sought to prevent action. The clamor of the shippers and the widespread public uneasiness aroused by disclosures of corporate abuses and growing concentration of control at last had its effect. The Senate conservatives beat a slow retreat, reluctantly agreeing to grant the Commission rate-making authority but, following familiar strategy, insisting that the courts be given broad powers of review. Jurisdiction of circuit courts "to enjoin, set aside, annul or suspend" ICC orders was recognized; railroads might obtain a temporary injunction to suspend a new rate prescribed by the Commission; new rates were not to become operative during judicial proceedings until the ICC order had been sustained by the courts.

The Hepburn Act of 1906, nevertheless, marks the beginning of effective regulation. ICC jurisdiction was broadened to include

---

[17] The methods used by the railroads in mobilizing opposition to the bill have been succinctly described by Professor Ripley:

"An extensive service, regardless of cost, was set up with headquarters at Washington and with branches in all the leading cities. . . . Bogus conventions, packed for the purpose—such as the 'Alabama Commercial and Industrial Association'—passed resolutions unanimously, to be scattered broadcast by free telegraphic dispatches all over the country. 'Associations for the Maintenance of Property' held conventions, the fact being duly advertised. Palpably garbled news items from Washington were distributed without cost, especially during the hearings of the Senate Committee. . . . An elaborate card catalogue of small newspapers throughout the United States was made, in which was noted all of the hobbies, prejudices, and even the personal weaknesses of the editors. . . . Magazine sections or 'ready to print' insides were also made up, in which appropriate and subtle references to railroad issues were concealed in a mass of general reading matter. Two or three weekly letters were sent gratis to minor newspapers without regular Washington correspondents, containing 'good railroad doctrine,' together with the spicy local news items. Dakota farmers got suggestions as to the danger of the proposed legislation affecting their rates. Kentucky planters were warned of the probable effect upon tobacco prices. As an indication of the formidable proportions of this campaign of education, the Chicago office, alone, employed some forty highly paid experts. Regular reports were rendered by this news service to the railroads' committee, as to the results achieved; setting forth the number of columns of news matter distributed and the changes effected in the proportion of 'pro' and 'con' items published. It was indeed a most astounding demonstration of the lengths to which organized corporate power would go to defeat regulative legislation." W. Z. Ripley, *Railroads: Rates and Regulation* (1912), pp. 496–498.

express companies, sleeping-car companies, pipe lines, railroad facilities, and various other instrumentalities of transportation such as private-car lines and industrial railroads or tap lines. The so-called commodity clause attempted to prevent railroads from engaging in other businesses and to eliminate opportunities for discrimination implict in a dual carrier-shipper status. Subject to exceptions authorized by the Commission, thirty days' notice of all rate changes was required. Sanctions against discrimination were strengthened by subjecting to stiff penalties the givers and recipients of rebates and all those departing from published tariffs. The ICC was also given power to prescribe uniform accounts and to supervise accounting and statistical practices.

The most important change was the explicit grant of rate-making power to the Commission, which now could not only declare existing rates to be unjust and unreasonable, but could also set maximum rates. While these Commission actions could be suspended by a temporary injunction, the courts were directed to compel obedience if, after hearing, the order was found to have been "regularly made and duly served."

Thus, after nearly twenty years of evasion and frustration of regulation, the carriers were at last subjected to a reasonably effective scheme of control by a reinvigorated ICC. From 1906 on, a steady stream of legislation widened Commission powers and jurisdiction. The Mann-Elkins Act, passed in 1910 under pressure from the insurgents in Congress, strengthened the Commission in two important respects: it revitalized the long-and-short-haul clause and it gave the Commission power to suspend proposed changes in rates or classifications, pending an investigation of their reasonableness.[18] The Panama Canal Act (1912) strengthened ICC jurisdiction over joint rail and water traffic, gave the Commission supervisory power over water carriers permitted to remain under railroad control, and sought to stimulate competition between water and rail carriers by making it illegal for railroads to have interests in shipping lines operating through the Panama Canal. The Valuation Act (1913) authorized the ICC to value railroad property as a basis for a more scientific determination of rates. It required a variety of findings as evidence of value but unfortunately failed to indicate the relative weight to be accorded to the various findings, and thus became a fertile

---

[18] It also created a short-lived Commerce Court, sponsored by President Taft as a court of specialized jurisdiction to improve procedure for the enforcement of ICC orders. The tendency of that court to obstruct the Commission led to its abolition after less than three years.

breeding ground of litigation. The Clayton Act (1914), although of primary importance as an antitrust measure, also reiterated the desirability of competition among railroads and provided some control over transactions between railroads and firms with which they had interlocking interests. The latter provisions, which grew out of the New Haven investigation with its revelations of financial buccaneering and wastage of corporate assets,[19] marked the faint beginning of ICC jurisdiction over the financial management of carriers.

Each new legislative accretion increased ICC authority and expanded its power. After the passage of the Hepburn Act, the courts for the first time began to defer to the Commission as "a tribunal appointed by law and informed by experience." The courts gave recognition to the congressional desire to have administrative rather than judicial regulation. Buttressed by congressional support, the ICC carved out a sphere of administrative autonomy relatively free from judicial interference. This administrative discretion meant that the Commission could now generate new principles and give recognition to interests hitherto neglected. Judicial emasculation of the original Act of 1887 had made the regulatory scheme prior to 1906 a harmless concession to public opinion which interfered in no important respect with the objectives and policies of railroad control and management. The reinforcing legislation initiated by the Hepburn Act and the change in court attitude which followed opened the way for other parties-in-interest to make their influence felt. ICC concern for the interests of shippers and passengers was demonstrated in a series of important rate decisions between 1910 and 1917, which in the main denied rate advances proposed by the railroads despite tremendous pressure to grant the increases and in the face of a marked rise in operating expenses, particularly toward the end of the period.

The impact of regulation during these years is difficult to isolate from other factors affecting the railroads. While the Commission undoubtedly restricted profits, it cannot be said that the result was economic disaster for the railroads. In fact, available dividend statistics indicate that investors in railroad securities, as a whole, fared better after 1906 than in the years immediately preceding. While there was also a striking increase in the railroad mileage in receivership, from 4,593 in 1911 to 37,353 in 1916, rate levels and regulation were not the main causes. Ex-

---

[19] 31 ICC 32 (1914).

cessive capitalization and financial manipulation, outside the range of ICC control, were largely responsible for the debacles of the New Haven, the Rock Island, the Frisco, and various other railway systems during these years.

The railroad history of the period, nevertheless, raised crucial questions about the future of regulation. In spite of improved operating records, the financial standing of some carriers weakened. Less prosperous roads found it difficult to sell stock, and the necessity of issuing bonds raised their fixed-income obligations. The shortage of new capital affected maintenance and improvements. Bankers blamed the hesitancies of investors and the deterioration of plant and equipment on the restrictive rate policies of the Commission and on fears of what it might do in the future. Defenders of regulation attributed the decline in investor confidence to financial scandals and asked for ICC supervision of security issues and capitalization to restore confidence. The Commission itself faced a dilemma. If large sums were to be invested in new construction and equipment, rates had to be set high enough to induce investment in weak as well as in strong roads. Yet to sanction rate policies that relieved the financial exigencies of weak railroads was to give strong roads unnecessarily high profits and to place the burden of watered stock, financial manipulation, inefficient management, and unfavorable location on shippers and passengers.

A negative, restrictive policy, confined to protecting shippers against extortion, might restrain avarice; it could not ensure adequate service, progressive management, and a development of transportation facilities to meet national needs. It could deal belatedly with the consequences of abuses; it could not anticipate their occurrence and forestall them. The ICC had power to fix maximum rates, but its criteria were by no means clear. It lacked control over the financial structure of railroads, upon which the rate level was intimately dependent. It had no authority to prevent even flagrant financial abuses. It could not regulate the issuance of securities, although it had asked for this power as early as 1907. Aside from the Safety Appliance Acts, there was no authority to deal with railroad services as such. The ICC had no control over railroad labor-management relations. The conflicting jurisdiction of state and national agencies further complicated the task of the Commission, although the Shreveport case (1914) [20] alleviated the situation somewhat

[20] *Houston, East and West Texas Ry. Co.* v. *U.S.*, 234 U.S. 342.

by upholding the power of the ICC to control intrastate charges for the purpose of preventing discrimination against interstate commerce. Thus regulation created the need for more regulation, but the problem had not yet been visualized as one of developing an integrated national railroad network. Regulation was not yet conceived as implying positive guidance and control as well as negative check and veto.

5. World War I

The weaknesses of railroad organization and control were strikingly revealed under the heavy demands of World War I. To overcome difficulties growing out of conflicts of ownership and competitive aspirations of various railroad systems, federal control and operation were proclaimed by President Wilson on December 26, 1917. The twenty-six months of federal operation provided illuminating commentary on both the potentialities and the limitations of railway nationalization, but this brief experiment was an interregnum outside the main stream of regulatory development. War imposed its own imperatives. The primary need was unity of operation for the most expeditious movement of men and strategic materials regardless of corporate interest or other considerations. All facilities, from terminals to locomotives and freight cars, were pooled and treated as part of one system; nonmilitary passenger service was reduced; priority was accorded to freight needed for defense; and the shortest hauls possible were used.

The war experience significantly influenced the postwar regulatory pattern. Operation of the railroads as a unified, integrated national system directed attention to a new, positive concept of regulation, one not merely of protecting the public against unreasonable exactions but rather of seeking to guide and plan railroad development to meet national needs. If such a conception were to prevail, the regulatory responsibilities of the ICC would have to be increased and its jurisdiction widened.

The war experience also left its impress on the parties-in-interest. Under federal operation, employees were encouraged to join unions, greatly stimulating the organization of railway labor. Working rules as well as wages were determined on a national basis. For the first time, the railway unions were strong enough to be consulted in the formation of important public policies. Investors, too, became articulate. Enjoying a guaranteed standard return under federal operation, they pressed for a continuation of legal safeguards to protect and enlarge their return. For shippers, the war brought rate increases, although the taxpayer bore much of the burden of mounting operating expenses. The strain that extraordinary war demands placed on the transportation system brought home to shippers the importance of adequate service and facilities, and they were prepared to recognize these needs as well as to claim protection against excessive and discriminatory rates. While believing staunchly in the superior virtues of private operation, railway management, having had to assume the duties and responsibilities of public officials during federal operation, now saw the transportation problem in a wider framework than the interests of individual companies. Managers developed a new understanding and appreciation of the problems of regulatory authorities.

6. The Transportation Act of 1920 and the Post-World War I Years

It is against this background that the Transportation Act of 1920 emerged. "Back to normalcy" sentiment was running strong. A vigorous reaction against war controls was under way. Whether justifiably or not, government operation of the roads was criticized as woefully inefficient, and allegedly prolabor wartime policies were castigated by business interests. Proposals to extend federal operation for five years were impatiently brushed aside. The Plumb Plan, sponsored by the railroad brotherhoods and providing for ownership of all railroads by the government and operation by a federal corporation, met with little response outside of labor ranks.

Yet practically every proposal sponsored by groups interested in the restoration of private operation contemplated considerably expanded public control and the further consolidation of existing lines into fewer but stronger systems. Plans put forward by investors, railway executives, and the Chamber of Commerce all called for ICC regulation of security issues, promotion of consolidation, and guarantee of a "fair return" on the value of railroad property. These plans differed in detail but shared a broad view of the transportation problem.

The ICC, agreeing that the railroads should be restored to private ownership and operation, called for a considerable strengthening of its own authority—broad power over the rate structure; power to determine division of rates between carriers; power to regulate water carriers; power to control consolidations, joint use of facilities, and the pooling of freight earnings; power to authorize additions, extensions, and the construction of new lines; power to control security issues and capital expenditures; and power to adjust conflicts between federal and state jurisdiction.

The Scope of the Act of 1920

Out of the maelstrom of these proposals, the Transportation Act of 1920 emerged. Labor's Plumb Plan was rejected, but other parties-in-interest found more comfort in the Act. Earnings were not guaranteed, but the ICC, given the power to determine minimum as well as maximum rates, was directed to set them "so that carriers as a whole (or as a whole in each of such rate groups or territories as the Commission may from time to time designate) will, under honest, efficient and economical management . . . earn . . . a fair return upon the aggregate value of the railway property of such carriers held for and used in the service of transportation. . . ."

The Commission was ordered to determine the aggregate value of railways and what was a fair return; Congress specified, however, that for the first two years the rate of return should be limited to 5½ per cent, to which the Commission might add an additional ½ per cent to provide for improvements. Thus the ICC was given an affirmative duty of providing adequate railroad revenue.

In addition, to meet the special needs of the weak roads, a "recapture" clause required a carrier earning more than a 6 per cent return on the value of its property to divide the excess equally between a "reserve fund" designed to stabilize its own financial position, and a "general railroad contingent fund," to be used by the ICC to make loans or to lease equipment to carriers. The Commission was also given power, in determining the division of joint rates, to take into consideration the revenue requirements necessary to provide a fair return. These provisions, taken in conjunction with the instruction to the Commission to formulate a consolidation plan establishing a limited number of systems, each earning substantially the same rate of return, were designed to provide special protection for investors in weak roads and to ensure adequate revenue for all.

The ICC was given control over railroad security issues and intercorporate assumptions of financial obligations. It was also authorized to supervise the uses to which the capital thus raised was put. At the same time, in furtherance of ICC recommendations for an "emancipation of railway operation from financial dictation," interlocking directorates, except with Commission consent, were prohibited, and it was made unlawful for officers or directors of carriers to profit from dual railroad and banking connections.

Most to the liking of shippers was the grant to the ICC of wide authority over service. Carriers were required to furnish safe and adequate service; the Commission could penalize violations. Extensions, abandonments, and new construction were subject to ICC approval; the Commission might, in addition, order a carrier to acquire facilities or build an extension where the public interest, convenience, or necessity justified such action.

Despite the far-reaching expansion of ICC authority, in some respects opportunities for managerial initiative were widened. Pooling agreements, previously illegal, might now be validated by the ICC. The Commission was authorized to prepare a comprehensive consolidation plan, but it had no statutory power to enforce its scheme. The initiative in consolidation remained with the carriers. Piecemeal consolidation by two or more railroads was dependent upon ICC approval, but control through a non-carrier holding company was not subject to its jurisdiction. The Act's rate-making provisions were viewed as an improvement over previous legislation, although the recapture clause was resented by the executives of strong roads.

The Transportation Act of 1920, taken as a whole, was a striking departure in railroad regulation. Earlier laws had been dominated by concern with railroad abuses; they were designed to prevent extortionate or discriminatory charges. Abandoning this restrictive approach, while continuing the earlier mandate of "reasonable and just" rates, the 1920 legislation explicitly recognized the needs of the carriers for adequate revenue. By protecting the investor, it sought to stabilize railroad credit and stimulate a flow of capital into the industry. The statutory recognition thus given to the long-standing demands of the carriers neutralized the opposition which might otherwise have developed to the ICC's enlarged regulatory jurisdiction.

The authority vested in the ICC by the Act of 1920 appeared impressive. Its power to fix minimum rates extended even to intrastate rates where necessary to remove discrimination resulting from state action. It was given broad authority to supervise railroad financial structures, service, and facilities. The membership of the Commission, increased from seven to nine in 1917, was now further increased to eleven. Armed with its new powers, the Commission seemed able to supervise almost all of the important activities of the industry and to work out "a permanent solution of the railroad problem."

Weaknesses

In fact, these hopes proved illusory. "Permanent solutions" cannot meet the needs of a dynamic society, and regulatory controls, unless they are flexibly adjusted to meet changing needs, run the danger of becoming strait jackets. The Act of 1920 was in many ways ill adapted to cope with the technical and economic changes affecting the railroad industry after 1920. Legislation based on the assumption of a virtual railroad monopoly of transportation was soon outmoded by the rapid growth of alternative transportation agencies—motor carrier, water carrier, and air carrier. Statutory standards that breathed in every pore the hope for industry stability were confronted with a crumbling business fabric, even before the disastrous repercussions of the 1929 panic produced complete demoralization.

In these circumstances, the predicament of the ICC was not a happy one. In the years of relative prosperity from 1920 to 1929, the impact of competitive transportation agencies was somewhat obscured; the Commission could still hope to strike a balance among the parties-in-interest in railroading which would yield general satisfaction. But as the full impact of the depression was felt and the inroads of other types of carriers became more apparent, the ICC found itself in an increasingly unfavorable milieu for a successful composition of interests. The task of a regulatory agency dealing with a declining industry in a period of marked economic instability is far from easy.

Nor was the ICC well equipped to meet the challenge. Its power over water competition was limited. It had no authority over motor and air carriers. The effort made in 1920 to bring water carriers fully under ICC jurisdiction had been defeated. A proposal to authorize ICC regulation of interstate motor carriers in the Transportation Act of 1920 had been rejected because of "a good deal of opposition from motor-truck companies, motor manufacturers, traffic men, and others." [21] Expert witnesses assured Congress that highway carriers would not be seriously competitive with the railroads.

The ICC was thus hampered by inadequate jurisdiction over

[21] Hearings, House Committee on Interstate and Foreign Commerce, *Return of Railroads to Private Ownership* (Transportation Act, 1920), 66th Cong., 1st sess. (1919), Vol. 1, p. 292.

other transportation media. It could control railroad reactions to the incursions of competitors; it had no direct power over the tactics of the competitors themselves. As water and high-way competition became acute, and as the railroads belatedly awakened to the menace, the Commission was faced with pressure for rate adjustments to enable railroads to meet the threat of diversion of traffic to their rivals. If it sanctioned adjustments, it risked disrupting the rate structure and throwing the burden of sustaining railroad earnings on noncompetitive traffic. Whole localities, regions, and industries might thus find themselves disadvantaged. If it resisted adjustments, it accelerated the diversion of traffic from the railroads. The choice of policy was difficult; it was made infinitely more difficult by the ICC's incomplete control of competitive transportation relationships.

The Consolidation Experience

Absence of authority also hampered the Commission in other spheres, consolidation being a notable example. The Act of 1920 envisaged a regrouping of the railroads into "a limited number of systems." The Commission was to draft a comprehensive plan, subject to criteria established by the Act. Competition between systems was to be preserved as fully as possible; existing routes and channels of trade were to be maintained, wherever practicable; systems were to be so arranged as to equalize rates of earnings. The object was to simplify rate making, achieve economies, and support railroad credit generally by combining weak with strong roads. But no compulsory power was given to the Commission. Acceptance by the railroads was to be voluntary. The apparent hope was that the weak would be willing and the strong would be altruistic.

Pending adoption of a "comprehensive plan," railroads seeking to acquire control of other railroads were required to obtain ICC consent, which was conditional on a finding that the acquisition would be in the public interest. The ICC's authority extended to control of one carrier by another but not to cases where noncarrier holding companies were used as instruments for the unification of carriers. This loophole gave actual power over consolidation to the railroad control groups and their affiliated banking connections. As a result, most of the real consolidation during the twenties was immune from Commission control. The ICC went through the motions of formulating a "comprehensive" plan. It held elaborate hearings, accumulated volumes of testimony, and finally, with marked reluctance and only in order to comply with the congressional mandate, announced a plan which could have little practical significance.

Struggle for traffic was the dominating consideration in the consolidations which did take place. Rival systems sought to extend their traffic control by absorbing strategic neutral roads. Other systems, finding their interests endangered by the threatened diversion of traffic, were forced to join in the battle. The struggle frequently involved extravagant expenditures, and it made banking support essential. The boom market of the late twenties provided a ready outlet for railroad holding-company securities, thus replenishing the war chests of the contestants and giving a further impetus to wasteful rivalry while the ICC stood by helplessly. With the Depression came the debacle; securities shrank in value and holding-company empires collapsed. In 1933, the noncarrier holding company was at last brought within ICC jurisdiction, but by that time most of the damage had been done.

Thus the ICC was by no means as well equipped to cope with the realities of business practice and the sweeping changes of the twenties and thirties as a cursory catalog of its extensive powers might have indicated. Operating within legal limits, it had no roving mandate to strike at abuses wherever it found them. It could, and did, recommend that Congress supplement its authority when weaknesses in the law were revealed. But it could not compel action when Congress chose to deny it power.

The climate of opinion in the twenties was unfavorable to aggressive regulatory action. Prevailing sentiment favored private business enterprise; the dominant political forces were solicitous of vested rights. This solicitude was reflected in decisions of the Supreme Court construing the Act of 1920 when occasional ICC forays threatened interference with the prerogatives of management and control. It likewise expressed itself in the Commission's tendency to let well enough alone and in its reluctance to guide railroad destinies actively or to interfere, in any substantial fashion, with managerial discretion.

The Rate Structure

From 1921 to 1929, railroad earnings failed to keep pace with general business conditions, but compared with what was to follow, the period can be described as one of relative prosperity for the railroads. This relative prosperity, in fact, partially concealed the economic inroads of competitive transportation agencies. Passenger revenue shrank during the period as a result of increased use of automobiles; freight revenue, on the other hand, continued to increase.

The 1920 Act had attempted to protect investors and carriers by instructing the ICC to set rates at levels yielding a fair return. In 1920, the Commission granted a 33 per-cent increase in freight rates, followed by a 10 per-cent reduction the next year. This level proved satisfactory for the railroads as a whole, yielding them a return of over 5 per cent from 1923 through 1929. Between 1920 and 1929, investment in plant and facilities increased by $5.5 billion and dividends mounted. Many roads, however, did not share in these benefits. Even in the boom year of 1929, more than 23 per cent of the railroad stock outstanding did not pay dividends, and during the twenties some of the weaker roads were forced into receivership.

The recapture plan, developed to meet the problem of the weak railroads, failed. The constitutionality of the plan itself was upheld,[22] but the valuation criteria used by the ICC in computing rates of return were rejected by the Supreme Court.[23] Accordingly, carriers refused to pay or paid under formal protest. By 1931, less than $11 million had been paid, although the Commission estimated that $359 million was due for the 1920–1930 period.

Apart from enforcement difficulties, the recapture experiment developed unexpected results. The law took excess income in good years but made no allowance for poor returns in bad years. A weak road with a brief period of good business, or with an inflated capital structure but a low physical valuation, might be subject to recapture. A strong railway might choose to increase its operating expenses and so avoid recapture. These anomalies, as well as the endless litigation, discredited the experiment, and the recapture clause was retroactively repealed by the Emergency Transportation Act of 1933. Thus, although investors in general fared well in the twenties, the problem of the investor in weak railroads remained unsolved, and the fair return contemplated by the Act of 1920 was not earned on all roads.

The Commission had to make difficult decisions, and they were as subject to political review as they were to judicial appeal. If it protected carriers and investors with adequate rates, it displeased shippers. Denied relief by the ICC, politically potent shippers turned to the legislative and executive arena for re-

[22] *Dayton-Goose Creek Ry. Co. v. U.S.*, 263 U.S. 456 (1924).
[23] *St. Louis and O'Fallon Ry. Co. v. U.S.*, 279 U.S. 461 (1929).

dress—as illustrated by the tactics of farm groups.

The decline in agricultural prices after 1920 led farmers to seek lower freight rates. The 10 per-cent general reduction of 1922 left them dissatisfied. When their appeals for further relief were rejected by the ICC, they turned to Congress, which in 1925 responded with the Hoch-Smith Resolution. Declaring it "to be the true policy in rate making . . . that the conditions which . . . prevail in our several industries should be considered in so far as it is legally possible to do so, to the end that commodities may freely move," the resolution directed the ICC to investigate existing rates and, "in view of the existing depression in agriculture to effect with the least practicable delay such lawful changes in the rate structure . . . as will promote the freedom of movement . . . of the products of agriculture . . . at the lowest possible lawful rates compatible with the maintenance of adequate transportation service." The Commission accordingly began in 1925 a comprehensive study of rate structures; pending the outcome of this study, it denied a rate increase proposed by Western carriers. But no general reduction of agricultural rates was ordered. In 1927, the Commission did acknowledge the force of the resolution and ordered a reduction in rates.[24] But the carriers appealed, and the Supreme Court upheld the appeal, ruling that the resolution was "more in the nature of a hopeful characterization of an object decreed desirable if, and in so far as, it may be attainable, than of a rule intended to control rate making." [25] Thus, by judicial construction, the resolution was robbed of any controlling effect and dismissed as a meaningless congressional gesture.[26]

While agrarian pressure in this instance failed, in other cases shipper pressure was more potent. Shippers who could turn to other modes of transportation forced the railroads to make con-

[24] 129 ICC 25.

[25] *Ann Arbor Railroad* v. *U.S.*, 281 U.S. 658 (1930).

[26] The investigation growing out of the Hoch-Smith Resolution did lead the ICC in 1930 to order reductions in grain rates to be made effective the following year. The carriers unsuccessfully petitioned for a rehearing. An appeal was then taken to the courts. In January, 1932, the Supreme Court ordered a rehearing. The result has been summarized as follows:
"So by the time the farmers, afflicted by one depression, had raised enough political stir to obtain legislative relief and had pursued their remedy through administrative red tape, a whole economic cycle had swung around and another depression was with us. This time the carriers found public sympathy and took advantage of it to get release in the courts from the small part of the burden that the farmers were about to shift upon their shoulders." H. C. Mansfield, *The Lake Cargo Coal Rate Controversy* (1932), p. 256.

cessions and to plead for ICC recognition of the necessity. Such piecemeal whittling away at the rate structure complicated the Commission's task of arranging satisfactory adjustment of the general level of rates. Existing relationships among industries, localities, and sections were disturbed. Noncompetitive traffic was penalized, since the railroads naturally sought to recoup their losses on that segment of their business. A frequent result was political agitation as groups dissatisfied with the ICC's decisions turned to Congress or the Chief Executive's appointive power to find a remedy for their grievances. Thus the dissatisfaction of the intermountain states with a transcontinental rate structure favoring the Pacific Coast and discriminating against intermountain territory led to demands for representation on the Commission and for legislation to secure a rigid enforcement of the long-and-short-haul clause. The carriers, on the other hand, demanded repeal or such modification of the long-and-short-haul clause as would enable them to meet water competition effectively without disturbing the existing rates at intermediate points.

Even where competitive modes of transportation were not involved, conflicts among rival interests for favorable treatment at times generated political pressures which transformed the Commission into a political football. Of these, perhaps the most famous was the Lake Cargo Coal Rate Controversy.[27] Rivalry between Northern and Southern coal operators to supply lake cargo coal and their pressure for preferential freight rates to Lake Erie ports were so intense as to lead to direct political interference with rate-making. Appointments of ICC members were made and rejected with a view to swaying decision on the issue. The Commission itself was hopelessly divided, finding for the Southern operators in 1925 and for the Northerners in 1927. Appeals were taken to the courts. A compromise was finally worked out among the railroads concerned, more or less independently of both the ICC and the coal operators. The Commission emerged from the battle "somewhat battered and scarred," content to remain a spectator while the rival gladiators arranged a truce.

The controversy illustrated well the operative limits that business and political realities impose on ICC rate-making powers. Intimately involved in the stress of competition among industries and localities, and endowed with powers which make it potentially an arbiter of economic destinies, the ICC cannot intervene too positively without arousing intense political resentment. The safest course is one of relative noninterference. Hence, the

[27] See H. C. Mansfield, *op. cit.*

tendency in crucial cases is often to preserve the status quo or to let the disputants work out a mutually satisfactory compromise. In putting its seal of approval on such solutions, the Commission seeks to ensure itself against attack and to avoid being dragged into the abyss of political controversy.

The Adjustment of Interests (1920–1929)

The adjustment of interests which evolved from the regulatory process in the twenties can now be briefly summarized. The program for the "emancipation of railway operation from financial dictation" turned out, on the whole, a failure. Railway security issues were supervised, but financial control groups discovered legal and other subterfuges which rendered them largely immune from ICC control. Management continued to be dependent on the control groups; consolidations were determined, not by the ICC or by the needs of the weak railroads, but by the stronger roads and their affiliated investment bankers. The effects of extravagant expenditures for stock purchases and wide distribution of dubious holding-company securities were shortly to prove disastrous for many small investors. On the other hand, investors in railroad securities, taken as a whole, fared reasonably well. Railroad earnings were sufficiently attractive to induce $6 billion of new capital to flow into the industry.

The impact of regulation on shippers and other users is more difficult to evaluate. From 1922 on, freight rates were relatively stable; the ICC maintained the status quo. Farmers pressed vainly for rate reductions, but other shippers used the threat of turning to alternative transportation agencies to obtain concessions. Passengers abandoned the railroads in considerable numbers.

Railway labor declined somewhat in influence. Two wage cuts, in 1921 and 1922, reduced wartime wage rates to a lower level, which prevailed until 1929. From 1923 on, traffic increased, but was handled by a steadily declining labor force as output per man grew.

7. The Impact of Depression

With the onset of the Great Depression, railroad earnings took a sharp turn for the worse. Total operating revenue shrank from $6.3 billion in 1929 to $3.1 billion in 1932. In 1929, railroad net income, after provision for fixed charges, totaled $897 million; in 1932, Class I carriers as a whole fell $152 million short of earning their fixed charges. Railroad credit was virtually destroyed. Expenditures for maintenance declined sharply. The number of employees dropped from 1.7 million in 1929 to approximately a million in 1932; the wage bill shrank from $2.9 billion to $1.5 billion.

The regulatory process was thus compelled to operate in an environment of sharp economic contraction. The impact of depression was severely felt by all parties-in-interest, and the more powerful tried to shift the burden of readjustment and sacrifice to the weaker. At first, the financial control groups and management, operating apparently on the assumption that the economic disturbance would pass quickly, maintained dividends so far as possible, although employment and wage bills were cut drastically.

As the gravity of the decline became apparent, the carriers turned to the ICC for relief, applying in June, 1931, for a 15 per-cent increase in freight rates. Railroad security holders supported the application, citing the threat to railroad credit. Shippers protested, pointing out that financial distress was not confined to railroads, that other prices had fallen drastically, that railroad rates had shown no corresponding decline, and that an increase would seriously burden industry and agriculture and accelerate the diversion of traffic to other types of carriers. The ICC denied the 15 per-cent increase but did approve a number of emergency rate advances expected to yield over $100 million a year.[28] These revenues were pooled in a fund administered by the Railroad Credit Corporation (a private corporation controlled by the carriers) and then loaned to carriers failing to earn their interest charges. Because of further traffic shrinkage, the emergency increases yielded only $75 million up to March 31, 1933. Loans made by the Railroad Credit Corporation helped to prevent some defaults, but its resources were inadequate to cope with the desperate situation of the railroads.

The next step in the efforts at railroad rehabilitation was the establishment of the Reconstruction Finance Corporation early in 1932. Among its other functions, the RFC made loans to railroads if funds were not obtainable on reasonable terms through ordinary banking channels, if the ICC approved, and if the loans were adequately secured. By the end of 1932, loans totaling $337 million had been authorized. They were extended to meet maturing funded debt, to repay bank loans, to pay interest on funded debt, and for construction and repairs. The RFC propped up a rapidly crumbling financial structure, mobilizing public

[28] *Fifteen Per Cent Case*, 178 ICC 539 (1931).

credit to salvage the stake of the investor.

A third step in sustaining the railroads financially was a reduction in labor costs. As the depression deepened, railroads cut their labor force drastically. In January, 1932, the railway unions were prevailed upon to accept a 10 per-cent wage reduction for twelve months.

In short, up to 1933, the campaign to save the railroads was essentially an effort to shift much of the burden to labor and shippers. All parties-in-interest lost heavily in the catastrophic decline in earnings. Public policy, however, approached the problem primarily from the point of view of the investor and financial interests concerned. The rate increase and the RFC loans were primarily motivated by the desire to safeguard investors' interests.

8. New Deal Transportation Policy

With the change of administration in 1933 and a shift in the balance of political power, new currents became discernible in the flow of public policy. Labor became more articulate, and shippers, especially farmers, became somewhat more influential. Investors faced sacrifices, but public policy tried to distinguish between financial control groups and small investors. Legislation curbed the power of control groups and protected small investors from exploitation by them. At the same time, the new administration tried to aid railroads generally by bringing competitive modes of transportation under more effective control.

Supervision of financial control groups was furthered by the Emergency Railroad Transportation Act of 1933, which gave the ICC jurisdiction over noncarrier holding companies controlling railroads. With this gap closed, the Commission was at last vested with some power to ensure that future consolidations would further its own goals rather than be determined only by the ambitions of rival railroad financial interests.

A desire to limit financial influence is also discernible in the railroad reorganization legislation of the period. Under the pre-1933 system of equity receiverships, financial abuses were common. Excessive fees to receivers, protective committees, reorganization managers, and legal counsel made deep inroads on the debtor's estate. Financial control groups frequently dominated the reorganization process, and the rights of small investors went unprotected. ICC control over reorganization was, at best, remote, indirect, and exercised at a late stage in the proceeding. After the reorganization plan had been approved by the court, the new corporation formed to take over the railroad had to request the permission of the ICC to issue securities. A Commission refusal would mean that, after months and sometimes years had been spent in developing a plan, the proceeding would have to start all over again. "As a result of this condition the Commission approved many securities issued under plans of reorganization of which it disapproved—solely for the purpose of preventing further delay." [29]

Dissatisfaction with the old system was already widespread when the depression threatened a new deluge of reorganizations. With many railroads unable to meet their fixed charges, the necessity of readjusting capital structures to scale down fixed charges became manifest. In the closing days of the Hoover administration, Section 77 of the Bankruptcy Act of 1933 was enacted to meet the need.

Section 77, somewhat amended in 1935 and 1936, enabled the ICC to participate early in reorganization proceedings and to shape the financial structure of reorganized railroads. The Commission was to ratify the appointment of trustees, fix maximum limits of compensation for them, and pass upon petitions of parties-in-interest to intervene in the proceedings. It was given broad supervisory powers over protective committees and their proxy solicitations and deposit agreements. No reorganization could go into effect without its approval, and it might initiate plans on its own authority. It could thus sponsor interests in reorganization proceedings which in the past had been inadequately represented.

In Section 77 reorganization proceedings, the ICC has sought to protect investors by ruthlessly pruning fees paid to trustees, counsel, and protective committees, and by requiring parties-in-interest to negotiate with each other at arm's length. Yet investors have also lost heavily as the Commission has required reorganization plans to make drastic reductions in railroad overcapitalization. The holders of securities which were thereby written down in value or assigned no value in reorganization have thus borne the cost of earlier mismanagement and financial abuses and the loss in the economic value of railroad properties due to intercarrier competition. The ICC has been guided in reorganizing capital structures by what it believes to be the present

[29] C. S. Rhyne, "Work of the I.C.C. in Railroad Reorganization Proceedings under Section 77 of the Bankruptcy Act," 5 *George Washington Law Review* 754 (1937).

and prospective earning power of the properties.[30] In the first twenty-nine Section 77 plans approved by the end of 1944, funded debt had been reduced by 45 per cent and fixed charges by 78 per cent.[31] Many railroads went under during the 1930's, the low point being reached in 1939 when 108 roads, with 31 per cent of the nation's railroad mileage, were in receivership. As a result of the ICC's Draconian measures, total railroad capitalization was substantially reduced. By 1948, Section 77 reorganizations had eliminated over $2.5 billion of debt.[32] The combined effect of reorganizations and reinvestment of earnings brought the net capitalization of the roads by 1950 down to $15.6 billion, only about 55 per cent of the ICC estimate of the original cost of railway properties plus working capital and present value of land and rights.[33] As a whole, the railroads may now be considered undercapitalized, although their ability to earn an adequate return on even their reduced capital remains questionable.

Such drastic pruning made investors as a group pay the costs of previous overcapitalization and of lower earning power. The impact, however, was uneven. Since most reorganization plans virtually wiped out stockholder equities and gave bondholders capital stock to offset the writing down of funded debt, ownership—and sometimes management as well—has been shifted in many cases to those who before were only creditors.

There has been much criticism of the harshness of ICC reorganization policies, as well as of the inordinate length of Section 77 reorganization proceedings, some of which took more than a decade to complete. World War II and the immediate postwar period brought prosperity to most railroads, which were offered all the traffic they could handle. Temporarily, at least, the earnings of many reorganized railroads handsomely exceeded ICC estimates, which were the basis for reorganized capital structures wiping out stockholder equities.

[30] *Chicago Great Western Co. Reorganization*, 247 ICC 193 (1941). Its position has been blessed by the Supreme Court. "The basic question in a valuation for reorganization purposes is how much the enterprise in all probability can earn." *Group of Investors* v. *Chicago, Milwaukee, St. Paul & Pacific RR. Co.*, 318 U.S. 523 (1943).

[31] Special Subcommittee on Transportation, House Committee on Interstate and Foreign Commerce, H. Rept. 2735, 79th Cong., 2d sess., Part 2, p. 327.

[32] D. P. Locklin, *Economics of Transportation* (4th ed., 1954), p. 584.

[33] ICC, *Statistics of Railways in the United States*, 1950, p. 156; *Increased Freight Rates*, 281 ICC 557 (1951).

In response to complaints of long delays, Congress in 1939 enacted the Chandler Act, which allowed debt readjustment plans to be put into effect without resort to a Section 77 proceeding, if no major reorganization were needed and if holders of two-thirds of the claims involved consented. Originally limited to one year, the Act was extended in 1942 but was allowed to expire in 1945. Criticism of ICC eliminations of stock equities led the House in 1945 to pass the Hobbs Bill, which drastically curtailed Commission powers in reorganizations. This bill died in the Senate, but in 1948 Congress passed the moderate Railroad Modification Act, which permits a railroad, with ICC approval, to modify the terms of any of its debt or securities, except equipment obligations. The ICC must hold hearings on the request for modification, and the holders of three-fourths of the obligations or stock affected must agree to the change.

Thus the ICC was able to bring some order to the financial chaos of the railroads. Assaying the inability of railroads to meet their obligations or to earn a return on their capital, the ICC allocated the cost of readjustments primarily to stockholders. But the losses borne by security holders and the general financial distress of the railroads produced a virtual investor boycott of railroads in the thirties. The government was forced to step into the breach. Through the RFC and the Public Works Administration, the national government became a substantial investor in railroad securities, with a stake in recovering its investment. Even after returning prosperity had rescued most railroads and provided a steady market for equipment obligations, the memory of Section 77 reorganizations and doubts about the long-run financial viability of rail transportation have made it difficult to float new bond issues and all but impossible to sell new capital stock.

Despite its role as an investor in railroad securities, government was sensitive to the claims of other parties-in-interest. The increased influence of labor, evident from the very beginning of the New Deal, offered a formidable obstacle to retrenchment programs designed to safeguard investors' interests. The Emergency Railroad Transportation Act of 1933 was originally conceived by investors who sought to achieve operating economies, chiefly at the expense of labor. Railway labor unions succeeded in adding Section 7(b), which blocked any recommendations of the Federal Co-ordinator of Transportation which would reduce the number of employees or the amount of their compensation below the level prevailing in May, 1933. With this

Act scheduled to expire on June 16, 1936, carriers would once again be free to reduce employment. The Railway Labor Executives Association attempted unsuccessfully for some time to negotiate with management a system of dismissal compensation. When management balked, labor secured administration support for the Wheeler-Crosser Bill, which would have required compensation for anyone discharged as a result of co-ordination projects. Faced with the possible enactment of this drastic bill, management accepted a voluntary dismissal-compensation plan. Thus administration sympathies tilted the scales in the negotiations and facilitated the acceptance of labor's demands.

Other labor gains were also registered in the legislative arena. The Railway Labor Act of 1934, amending the 1926 law, more explicitly recognized the right to organize and bargain collectively; it also strengthened the machinery for adjustment of disputes between employers and employees.[34] In the same year, the first Railroad Retirement Act was passed. When this Act was pronounced unconstitutional,[35] a substitute was promptly enacted in 1935. After the Social Security Act was upheld, a third and broader Railroad Retirement Act was passed in 1937, and in 1938 a further measure provided for railroad unemployment insurance.

Wage adjustments were also favorable to labor. The 10 percent reductions of 1932 were fully restored by April 1, 1935. Two agreements increasing wages were made in 1937. Following the sharp decline in business activity that year and a new period of financial distress for the carriers, management proposed a 15 per-cent wage cut, which was refused by the unions. The President then appointed an Emergency Board under the terms of the Railway Labor Act. The Board recommended that the proposed wage reductions be cancelled, and this course was accepted by management.

The handling of rate questions in the 1930's saw the beginning of a shift in the balance which the ICC struck among the various parties-in-interest and a transformation of its role. In brief, the Commission became more "railroad-minded," increasing the priority assigned to carrier revenue needs, and began to pass judgment on managerial estimates of the rate levels best designed to maximize rail revenues. As the competition offered by other transportation media increased, the problem of preventing exploitation receded and the Commission was faced

[34] See Chapter 7 for further discussion.
[35] *Railroad Retirement Board* v. *Alton R.R. Co.*, 295 U.S. 330 (1935).

with the task of deciding whether rate increases would be likely to increase total rail revenues or to divert traffic. Indeed, the Emergency Railroad Transportation Act of 1933 had introduced a new rate-making formula, instructing the ICC to give due consideration, among other factors, "to the effect of rates on the movement of traffic; to the need . . . of adequate and efficient railway transportation service; and to the need of revenues sufficient to enable the carriers . . . to provide such service." In construing this rule, the Commission gave the revenue needs of carriers controlling weight.[36]

In 1936, following the lead of Southern and Western carriers, the ICC, despite management opposition, ordered marked reductions in Eastern passenger fares in the hope of attracting more traffic and raising total revenues. Passenger receipts did rise, but management attributed this to general economic improvement rather than the lowered fares. In 1938, the ICC, with some misgivings, accepted the carriers' request for a fare increase. When revenues declined, lower rates were again ordered in 1940.

In the setting of freight rates, the ICC charted a somewhat uncertain course, but generally gave more weight to carrier claims than previously. In July, 1933, it rejected the pleas of hard-hit shippers of basic commodities for lower rates, giving priority to the revenue needs of the railroads. Responding to outside criticism and dissents from within the Commission, it next discontinued, from October, 1933, the emergency increases put into effect by the Fifteen Per Cent decision of 1931.[37] In 1935, the ICC rejected a petition for a general rate increase to yield about $170 million but did authorize specified emergency increases.[38] These increases were allowed to expire at the end of 1936, because of rising traffic, but in 1937 the carriers were given a general increase in commodity rates expected to yield about $70 million.[39] No sooner had these increases been announced than the carriers, having had to grant a $130 million wage increase and facing other cost increases of about $120 million while traffic was declining, petitioned for a further blanket increase of 15 per cent in all freight charges.[40] Shippers protested vigorously and in great numbers, arguing "that the proposed increases . . . would simply dry up rail traffic by causing di-

[36] *General Rate Level Investigation,* 195 ICC 5 (1933).
[37] 178 ICC 539.
[38] *Emergency Freight Charges Case,* 208 ICC 4 (1935).
[39] *General Commodity Rate Increases,* 223 ICC 657 (1937).
[40] *Fifteen Per Cent Case,* 226 ICC 41 (1938).

version thereof to competing forms of transport agencies, or a relocation of industry or change of the manner of distribution." [41] The Commission granted a general 10 per-cent rise, but partially or wholly exempted products of agriculture, forests, and mines out of a desire to spare distressed industries. At the same time, the Commission expressed the fear that the decision might only hasten the diversion of other types of traffic to nonrail carriers.

The rate history of the thirties reveals the strains generated by the pressures of rival groups seeking maximum advantages from a declining industry. A shrinking but potent labor force operating in a favorable political milieu gained wage increases and provisions for security. Management acting on behalf of investors tried to shift the burden of increased expenses to shippers. The ICC, seeking to mediate between investors and shippers, temporized. The revenue needs of the carriers made some rate increases imperative; the danger of causing a diversion of traffic led to denials of the full range of rate rises demanded by the railroads. Some shippers faced with rate increases found avenues of escape in relocating their plants or in using other modes of transportation. Others, whose traffic was closely tied to the rails, complained that rate increases had discriminatory effects on their development.

Given this setting, ICC regulation necessarily generated much dissatisfaction. In a period of dynamic industry expansion, a regulatory agency finds its task considerably lightened by the fact that gains may accrue to all the parties-in-interest. The task of regulation in a period of distress and contraction is far more challenging. Parties-in-interest do not contend for the privilege of making the first sacrifice. The regulatory agency is powerless to satisfy the expectations aroused in a more hopeful era. Regulatory principles fashioned to deal with phenomena of expansion reveal themselves as inadequate when contraction comes. Thus, the ICC can neither guarantee the carriers the revenues they demand nor give the shipper the relief he asks. The Commission may adjust railroad rates, but it has little or no control over railroad expenses; and it has only partial control over the competition offered by rival modes of transportation. Labor costs are outside its jurisdiction. Its power to compel capital readjustments and scaling down of fixed charges is limited and subject to court review. It may exercise its persuasive gifts to advance railroad rationalization, but mandatory authority is lacking. These deficiencies in the regulatory instrument led to experimentation

[41] *Ibid.*, p. 75.

with a different device for the promotion of rationalization and for the framing of a constructive national transportation policy.

9. The Problem of Transportation Co-ordination

The appointment of Joseph Eastman as Federal Co-ordinator of Transportation in 1933 involved the first serious effort to address public attention to a revision of national transportation policy as a whole. Unfortunately, the office, created by the Emergency Transportation Act of 1933, went out of existence in 1936 when Congress failed to act on Eastman's recommendation for an extension of its life. Eastman fell victim to pressure politics. Some of his proposals had aroused opposition from both railroad labor and railroad executives, and Congress was content to allow the office to lapse.

The work of the Co-ordinator fell into two general categories: (1) operating and management economies; and (2) the study of public transportation policy. In the first field, Eastman had few successes to report, although valuable studies were published. In the second field, the Co-ordinator had much to do with laying the groundwork for the Motor Carrier Act of 1935 and the Transportation Act of 1940, although his proposal to concentrate all transportation regulation in the ICC was not fully adopted.

The difficulties encountered by the Co-ordinator's "operating economy" program vividly illustrate the obstacles to any thoroughgoing rationalization of railroad operations. The Act of 1933, to be sure, was temporary and did not arm the Co-ordinator with very much power. His staff undertook a number of comprehensive studies, and an imposing list of co-ordination prospects was surveyed. The Co-ordinator made recommendations, but almost nothing came of them. Vested interests in the status quo offered effective resistance. Section 7(b), inserted into the Act of 1933 at the behest of labor, barred economies displacing labor. Carriers possessing strategic advantages were reluctant to share them with other carriers. The Co-ordinator noted that railroad management was "intensely individualistic and suspicious of collective action. . . . Plans for . . . co-ordination in railroad affairs meet resistance because they are foreign to certain habits of thought which are the growth of many years."

Labor [pointed out Eastman] is hostile, fearing loss of employment, and there are railroad officers, both major and minor, who have similar fears. . . . Various supply companies are not friendly to collec-

tive railroad action in such matters as scientific research and purchases. Various large shippers are accustomed to play one railroad
against another to their own advantage and do not like to see such
opportunities reduced. Shippers are particularly antagonistic to increases in the charges for accessorial services.[42]

The Co-ordinator did have some power to issue orders; yet,
with one minor exception, no orders were issued. After first
exhausting the possibilities of voluntary co-operation in a vain
endeavor to win the willing consent of labor and management,
the Co-ordinator announced in February, 1936, his intention to
order the co-ordination of railroad terminal facilities at eleven
specified points. The order was never issued. In response to protests from labor, the President requested the Co-ordinator to
hold up the order until provision had been made for dismissal
compensation. An agreement between labor and management
was not reached until May. In mid-June, the Co-ordinator's
term expired, and in view of the opposition of both railroad
labor and management, Congress refused to extend the life of
the organization. The political context had made the Co-ordinator "a prober of possibilities" rather than "a doer of deeds."
The Federal Co-ordinator enjoyed greater success in the planning of transportation policy. A series of able reports canvassed
the whole transportation situation and explored various policy
alternatives. Three possibilities were envisaged: (1) public ownership and operation; (2) the compulsory consolidation of railroads into a few systems, with possible minority participation
in management by the government; and (3) the extension and
improvement of the present system of federal regulation. The
first and second plans were rejected. "Theoretically and logically
public ownership and operation meets the known ills of the present situation better than any other remedy," Eastman pointed
out, but he argued that it would involve serious financial dangers to the country and that it was "at least questionable whether
the railroads alone could well be nationalized without including
other forms of transport to some considerable extent." The second
plan was also rejected, he reported:

. . . not only because the present uneven distribution of competition
would be accentuated, with enhanced danger that population and
business would tend to concentrate at favored points . . . but also

[42] *Report of the Federal Co-ordinator of Transportation, 1935* (1936), p.
37.

for the practical reason that a consolidation of this character . . . would precipitate a controversy in which many railroads, many communities, and labor would join with equal vigor and from which it would be difficult to emerge.[43]

In advocating the third plan, Eastman recommended that the major transportation media be subjected to co-ordinated federal regulation by the ICC, that the Commission be reorganized in order to perform its new duties more effectively, and that a permanent Co-ordinator of Transportation, selected from the Commission and associated with it, continue to perform functions similar to those exercised by him under the Act of 1933. Two bills, providing for ICC regulation of motor and water carriers, respectively, were recommended for congressional action. The motor carrier recommendations, in amended form, were enacted in 1935 and represented a powerful expansion of ICC jurisdiction. But ICC authority was not extended to water carriers. Instead, Congress in 1936 created the Maritime Commission, and transferred to it the regulatory jurisdiction over water carriers previously possessed by the Department of Commerce. In 1938, the Civil Aeronautics Authority was created and endowed with regulatory jurisdiction over air carriers.

The Co-ordinator's proposals, and Congress's response to them, partially accepting and partially rejecting the logic of unification of regulatory authority in transportation, highlighted the three major problems of public transportation policy, which continued to be of major concern in the next two decades and which are discussed in the next chapter. These problems, then and still unresolved, are: (1) whether competition or monopoly, or which proportion of the two elements, is the goal of policy; (2) how to reconcile the promotion of transportation with its regulation; and (3) how to formulate a broad national transportation policy designed to take maximum advantage of the different available modes of transportation.

[43] *Report of the Federal Co-ordinator of Transportation, 1934* (1935), p. 2.

CHAPTER 11

Transportation Regulation and the Search for National Policy

1. The Regulation of Motor Carriers

THE INCLUSION of motor carriers within the regulatory jurisdiction of the ICC, while a step toward a unified transportation policy, occurred primarily because of the impact of highway competition on the railroads and on their regulation. This experience suggests that further unification of policy depends, not merely on the acceptance of the principle, but on the adjustment of administrative and policy conflicts among existing regulatory and promotional agencies and on the configuration of underlying carrier interests which these conflicts reflect.

State regulation of trucks and buses, which began in the 1920's, was at first concerned with safety, physical characteristics of vehicles, licensing of drivers, and the numbers of hours that a driver might operate. Soon, however, the states began to regulate the rates and services of common carriers. In order to prevent evasion of such regulation, controls were then extended to contract carriers.[1] But the impossibility of regulating interstate motor

[1] At first, the Supreme Court, while permitting economic regulation of common carriers who hold themselves ready to serve anyone, held state statutes

carriers [2] led the National Association of Railroad and Utilities Commissioners to sponsor federal regulation as early as 1925. In the 1930's, the ICC and the Federal Co-ordinator of Transportation joined in this request for federal regulation.

The principal support for the regulatory agencies came from the railroads, who, as they belatedly became aware of the inroads of highway-carrier competition, strongly urged motor-carrier regulation to control the rates of their competitors, to restrict entry, and perhaps generally to check highway competition. Representatives of the Association of Railroad Executives helped draft the motor-carrier legislation.

Shippers and highway carriers were divided in their attitudes. Some shippers hoped that regulation would end unstable rates and unsatisfactory service. Certain small shippers saw in regulation a way of ending the rate concessions extorted from hardpressed motor carriers by large shippers. Bus lines, which operated on a large scale and feared rate wars and duplication of service, generally supported regulation, as did some of the larger trucking firms, who wished to end the chaos of unrestrained competition. Most members of the Chamber of Commerce of the United States supported strong regulation, but the National Industrial Traffic League, representing large shippers, opposed more than a minimum of control. The American Trucking Association approved the bill only in its late stages and after being assured that regulatory authority would be vested in a separate ICC bureau. Thus, supporters of regulation wished to restrict competition, with railroad interests and their governmental allies seeking to limit the inroads of motor-carrier competition, while bus operators and big truckers sought to stabilize conditions within their industries.

With the potential opposition divided, railroad interests and the regulatory agencies were bound to win their fight for at least some regulation. After several years of hearings and debate, Congress enacted the Motor Carrier Act of 1935. The Act was deferential toward state regulatory authority. The ICC cannot interfere with the exclusive right of states to regulate intrastate motor

---

unconstitutional which attempted to regulate contract carriers who serve only shippers whom they have agreed to serve. *Michigan Public Utilities Commission* v. *Duke,* 266 U.S. 570 (1925); *Frost* v. *Railroad Commission of California,* 271 U.S. 583 (1926); *Smith* v. *Cahoon,* 283 U.S. 553 (1931). But it subsequently modified its position so that states could require permits of contract carriers and set their minimum rates. *Stephenson* v. *Binford* 287 U.S. 251 (1932).

[2] See the Duke decision cited in footnote 1.

carriers, and ICC permission to engage in interstate carriage does not thereby convey any right to do intrastate business. Applications or complaints filed with the Commission involving regulated carriers or transportation brokers operating in not more than three states must be referred to a joint board composed of representatives from each of the states concerned. Decisions of the joint boards, however, are subject to Commission review on its own initiative or on the demand of one of the interested parties.

The Act established different degrees of regulation for common carriers, contract carriers, private carriers, and transportation brokers. Common carriers are of course the most completely regulated. A common carrier may operate only under a certificate from the ICC, after a finding that he is able to perform and that the proposed service is required by the public convenience and necessity. A "grandfather clause" entitled carriers in operation on June 1, 1935, to receive a certificate by virtue of that fact. Rates, fares, charges, commodity classifications, and consolidations are subject to ICC control. Rates and fares must be published, and must be reasonable and not unjustly discriminatory. The ICC is also charged with the enforcement of safety standards. Common carriers must provide insurance protection, and those with over $1 million of securities outstanding must obtain ICC approval for any security issues.

Contract carriers, subject to much less supervision, are controlled primarily to make common-carrier regulation effective. Contract carriers need only a "permit" to operate; this is subject to less rigorous conditions than a certificate of public convenience and necessity. While general publication of rates is not required, minimum rates must be made public and filed with the ICC, which can prescribe minimum but not maximum rates.[3] Provisions regarding safety requirements, security issuances, and consolidations are identical with those applying to common carriers.

Private carriers, not available for hire and carrying their own goods, are subject only to controls over hours of service for employees, safety, and equipment. Brokers must be licensed by the Commission and file accounts and reports.

Many vehicles are exempted from all ICC controls except those dealing with hours of work, safety, and equipment. The logic of

[3] Prior to an amendment of the Act in 1940, carriers often violated their filed minimum rates. The ICC has since ruled that carriers cannot charge less than their minimum rates and this ruling has been judicially affirmed. *Auto Transports, Inc., Suspension of Permit*, 51 MCC 600 (1950); *Auto Transports v. U.S.*, 101 F. Supp. 132 (1951).

exemptions such as school buses, taxis, hotel buses, trolley buses, and farm vehicles is obvious. The exemption of vehicles transporting livestock, fish, agricultural commodities, and newspapers, however, is to be explained less by logic than by the political power of the special groups affected. These exemptions, and the private carriage of goods to avoid federal transportation taxes, enable substantial amounts of truck freight to escape ICC economic regulation.

The ICC, operating through its Bureau of Motor Carriers, confronts a regulatory task of staggering proportions. In 1956, there were about 160,000 motor carriers with about 1.4 million vehicles theoretically subject to its jurisdiction. The Commission's economic controls apply to about 19,000 common and contract carriers.[4] As a result of the magnitude of the task and the inadequacy of the Bureau's appropriations, in 1956 about 100,000 carriers had never even been served with copies of the ICC's safety regulations. Substantial but inadequate field inspections are conducted.

The Bureau's early years were largely occupied with the burdens of defining its jurisdiction and classifying carriers. It was often hard to draw a dividing line between contract and private carriers, between contract and common carriers, between exempt agricultural commodities and nonexempt products processed from such commodities. The Bureau also had to deal with almost ninety thousand applications for certificates and permits under the grandfather clause.

In more recent years its attention has focused on questions of entry, combination, and rates. Down through 1956, it had received over fifty thousand applications to institute new operations. Verbally, at least, the Commission has endorsed the principle of competition. It has repeatedly ruled that the existence of adequate rail or water service, or the fact that railroads might be adversely affected, is not sufficient ground for denying a motor carrier permission to operate.[5] A community is entitled to adequate highway as well as rail service.[6] In some cases, the ICC has authorized trucking operations which would compete with existing motor-carrier operations; in its own words: "We believe that when the available traffic permits it, competition should be encouraged."[7]

[4] ICC, *Annual Report, 1956*, pp. 71, 118–119.

[5] *Bowles*, 1 MCC 589 (1937); *Tri-State Transit Co. of Louisiana, Inc.*, 29 MCC 381 (1941); *Clark*, 16 MCC 535 (1939). But see footnote 14, below.

[6] *Petroleum Transit Corp.*, 11 MCC 164 (1939).

[7] *Balch & Martin Motor Express Common Carrier Application*, 47 MCC 75 (1947).

The courts have several times endorsed such decisions, holding that a certificate conveys no necessary immunity from competition.[8] The ICC has gone furthest in promoting competition when considering bus applications.[9]

The preponderance of ICC decisions, however, has substantially limited competition within the motor-carrier industry. In some cases, the Commission has ruled that it will authorize competitive services only when it can be shown that existing carriers cannot or will not provide satisfactory service.[10] It has argued that existing carriers should normally have the right to all the traffic they can handle efficiently;[11] it has rejected applications because they would harm existing carriers without any compensatory public benefit.[12] It has also protected common carriers against the competition of contract carriers, lest the latter skim the cream off traffic, thereby endangering the ability of common carriers to perform their broader functions.[13] Thus, despite some lack of clarity in the decisions, in general the ICC has tended to restrict entry into an industry which in the absence of regulation would be highly competitive. It has seldom, however, restricted entry in order to protect rail carriers.[14]

The issue of competition is also raised in applications for combining motor-carrier operations, through sale or lease of operating rights, consolidations, and acquisitions of control. Through 1956, the ICC had received over forty thousand applications involving intercorporate relationships and had approved the overwhelming majority. In general, the maintenance of competition is not a controlling consideration, for the Commission will weight against

[8] E.g., *St. Johnsbury Trucking Co.* v. *U.S.*, 99 F. Supp. 977 (1951); *Wales* v. *U.S.*, 108 F. Supp. 928 (1952).

[9] E.g., *Pan-American Bus Lines Operation*, 1 MCC 190 (1936); *Mt. Hood Stages, Inc., Extension*, 44 MCC 535 (1945).

[10] E.g., *Omaha & Council Bluffs Ry. & Bridge Co., Common Carrier Application*, 49 MCC 445 (1949); *Gilliland Extension, Storage in Transit, Grand Rapids, Michigan*, 53 MCC 59 (1951).

[11] *Justice*, 2 MCC 699 (1937).

[12] *Public Service Interstate Transportation Co.*, 43 MCC 599 (1944).

[13] *Gollock*, 1 MCC 161 (1936).

[14] There are, of course, exceptions. Sometimes the existence of rail service has been one cause for the denial of motor-carrier operations (*Wilson Extension–Dairy Products*, 61 MCC 51 [1952]), and in one case the existence of rail service seemed to be the only reason for a denial (*Hitchcock Common Carrier Application*, 54 MCC 16 [1952]). The ICC has also blocked the establishment of a coast-to-coast motor-freight system for fear that it would adversely affect the railroads and those dependent on rail transportation (*Pacific Intermountain Express Co.–Control & Purchase*, 57 MCC 341 [1952]).

it the benefits of more efficient operation and better service. In 1942, it concluded that there was little need to fear a monopoly in trucking at that time,[15] and its decisions since then have continued to be favorable toward most proposed mergers. Buses presented a somewhat different picture, but the Commission felt that any threat of monopoly could quickly be checked by the grant of additional certificates.[16] In cases where combination will adversely affect existing weaker carriers, ICC decisions have varied with the particular circumstances.[17] The net effect of ICC policy toward combinations has been to reduce competition within the industry.[18]

ICC rate decisions have had a somewhat similar effect. As with the railroads, the Commission is concerned with carriers as a whole and not with individual firms. It sets rates in terms of average conditions, even though this may yield excessive profits to some carriers and losses to others. Carriers with higher-than-average operating ratios may propose increased rates for themselves, if competition allows them to do so.[19] Since investment is low in proportion to revenues, the Commission does not judge rates in terms of a return on investment but rather on the basis of providing a safe margin of revenues over costs. An operating ratio of 93 (costs being 93 per cent of revenues) is the usual target figure.

When weighing complaints about specific rates, the Commission considers, among other factors, their effect on traffic, the inherent advantages of motor transportation, and the need for adequate revenues. While in railroad rates it emphasizes variable costs, in motor rates it stresses fully allocated costs. It also tends to be more concerned with minimum than with maximum rates, in order to avoid what it believes to be ruinous competition and to protect other carriers. In a number of cases, it has promulgated minimum rates on a territory-wide basis to end rate wars.[20] Re-

---

[15] *Associated Transport, Inc.–Control and Consolidation–Arrow Carrier Corp.*, 38 MCC 137.

[16] *Transport Company–Control–Arrow Carrier Corp.*, 36 MCC 61 (1940).

[17] E.g., *Mason & Dixon Lines, Inc.–Purchase–Coggin & Cox*, 36 MCC 475 (1941); *Nevada Consolidated Fast Freight–Control–Fleetlines, Inc.*, 40 MCC 499 (1946).

[18] For a strong criticism of this policy, see S. Com. on Small Business, *Hearings on Trucking Mergers and Concentration*, and Appendix, "Trucking, Mergers, Concentration, and Small Business," by Walter Adams and J. B. Hendry; 85th Cong., 1st sess. (1957).

[19] E.g., *Increased Common Carrier Rates in the East*, 42 MCC 633 (1943); *Rocky Mountain Increases*, 54 MCC 377 (1952).

[20] E.g., *Middle Atlantic States Motor Carrier Rates*, 4 MCC 68 (1937); *New England Motor Carrier Rates*, 8 MCC 287 (1938); *Trunkline Territory Motor Carrier Rates*, 24 MCC 501 (1940); *Class & Commodity Rates, New York to Philadelphia*, 51 MCC 289 (1950).

gional minima are usually set at or just under railroad rates. Minima for contract carriers are allowed to rest below those for common carriers since to do otherwise would be to deny the former their inherent advantages.

In dealing with intercarrier relationships, the ICC allows both rail and motor carriers considerable leeway in adjusting their rates to meet each other's competition.[21] In general, the Commission has adopted a relatively passive attitude, seeking to "keep everyone in the business." By allowing one mode to lower its rates to match those of the competing mode, but frowning on rate-cutting by the cheaper mode or rate reductions after equality has been achieved, it tends to create and preserve an equality of rates. Although the Transportation Act of 1940, discussed below, directed the ICC to preserve the "inherent advantage" of each mode of transportation, the Commission has never moved directly toward a definition and effectuation of this phrase. Instead it has usually been content to equalize rates.

A carrier may not lower its rates more than is necessary to meet competition,[22] and the reduced rates must be "reasonably compensatory." For a motor carrier, with its low fixed costs, a reasonably compensatory rate tends to approximate fully allocated costs, but a reasonably compensatory rate for a railroad, with its high fixed costs, tends to be defined as one which covers all direct costs and makes some contribution to fixed costs but which is well below fully allocated costs. The ICC also frowns on deep rate slashes on high-value traffic which has been paying high rates, and it blocks competitive rate reductions if they threaten to produce a rate war or to disrupt established rate structures.[23] The effect is to equalize rates, but this often results in serious competitive inequalities, depriving the low-cost carrier of its cost advantage.

One student concludes "that regulation has consistently, over the twenty years since the Motor Carrier Act, deprived the low-cost carrier of its cost advantage, a result often tantamount to depriving it of all opportunity to compete for traffic." [24] This

[21] E.g., *Automobiles & Chassis to Chicago*, 227 ICC 223 (1939); *Petroleum from Los Angeles & El Paso to Arizona & New Mexico*, 287 ICC 731 (1953); *Iron & Steel, Follansbee, W. Va., to McKees Rocks, Pa.*, 52 MCC 589 (1951).

[22] E.g., *Butter from Sully, Iowa, to Chicago*, 53 MCC 448 (1951).

[23] E.g., *Tobacco from North Carolina Points to Southern Points*, 280 ICC 767 (1951). *Alcoholic Liquors from Indiana, Kentucky & Ohio to St. Louis*, 52 MCC 403 (1951). *Paint from Los Angeles to Portland, Tacoma & Seattle*, 52 MCC 337 (1950).

[24] E. W. Williams, Jr., *The Regulation of Rail-Motor Rate Competition* (1957), p. 212.

tendency toward rate equality, of course, deprives the nation of the "inherent advantages" of low-cost transportation. It has also contributed to some unnecessary duplication of facilities, despite the detrimental effect a sharing of the traffic might have on the costs and efficiency of the dominant carrier. On much of their traffic, railroads offer less service than truckers or require ancillary costs to be borne by the shipper. Consequently, railroads seek to maintain a rate differential on such traffic but are often frustrated by the rate equality imposed by the ICC. On traffic with a high value, moreover, which the railroads once charged on a value-of-service principle rather than a cost-of-service basis, rates now are seldom allowed to drop below the average total cost level of the motor carriers.

Although the motor-carrier industry lacks many of the elements usually accounting for detailed economic regulation—such as high fixed costs, undesirability of duplicating services, and invocation of the governmental power of eminent domain—it is today subjected to control resembling that of public utilities. While forces within the industry—notably those who sought stability and relief from unrestrained competition—have supported control, the main imperative for regulation has come from the impact of trucking on the railroads. The major effects of regulation have been to reduce competition within the industry and to lessen and regularize its competitive impact on other transportation media. Even though highway carriers are subject to ICC jurisdiction, the co-ordination of highway and railroad regulation is still incomplete in terms of a national transportation policy dedicated to preserving the "inherent advantages" of each mode of transportation.

2. The Regulation of Water Transportation

Efforts of the ICC to regulate water transportation and of the railroads to minimize the competitive impact of water carriers have been less successful than in the case of motor carriers. Partial and incomplete regulation of water carriers dates from the Interstate Commerce Act of 1887, which gave the ICC jurisdiction over traffic carried jointly by railroads and water carriers under common control or management. The Panama Canal Act of 1912 forbade railroads to operate ship lines using the Canal and allowed them to operate other ship lines only with ICC permission. In such cases, the water carrier was subject to the same ICC regulation as the railroad. The Shipping Act of 1916, amended in 1933 and 1938, gave the United States Shipping

Board and its successor, the Maritime Commission, regulatory authority over common carriers in the coastal trade and on the Great Lakes, and over both common and contract carriers in the intercoastal trade. This legislation was intended to enable the regulatory authority to curb undesirable competitive practices, to protect shippers from monopolistic abuses, and to police conference agreements. Under these agreements, which were legalized and exempted from the Sherman Act by the 1916 law, participating lines agreed on such matters as rates, apportionment of traffic, and pooling of earnings.

Thus, before 1940, the regulatory pattern was both limited and confused. Authority over water carriers was divided between the ICC and the Maritime Commission, each having different powers and procedures. Contract carriers, except in the intercoastal trade, and all carriers on rivers and canals were wholly unregulated. Both in 1934 and in 1936, the Federal Co-ordinator had recommended more effective and unified control,[25] a proposal endorsed by the ICC.[26] Railroads pressed for ICC regulation with an enthusiasm which caused some water carriers and shippers, including farm groups, to oppose such regulation on the ground that it would be "railroad-minded." Congress attempted a compromise in those provisions of the Transportation Act of 1940 dealing with water carriers. The Act did transfer to the ICC jurisdiction over domestic water transportation formerly assigned to the Maritime Commission and made additional water carriers subject to regulation.[27] But what Congress conferred with one hand it took away with the other, for the Act also exempted from ICC regulation about nine-tenths of the tonnage of domestic water carriers. Private carriers; contract carriers whose equipment and cargoes are so specialized that they do not compete with common carriers; common carriers whose cargoes consist of not more than three commodities transported in bulk; carriers of liquid cargoes in bulk in tank vessels; small craft; and ferries and vessels operated incidentally by railroads, motor carriers, or express companies were all free from regulation. These massive exemptions reflected congressional reluctance to force minimum-rate regulation on water carriers generally, and especially on bulk shippers of oil, coal, ore,

[25] *Regulation of Transportation Agencies*, S. Doc. No. 152, 73d Cong., 2d sess., pp. 10–13; *Fourth Report*, H. Doc. No. 394, 74th Cong., 2d sess., pp. 7–22.

[26] *Annual Report, 1937*, p. 105.

[27] The Maritime Commission kept jurisdiction over foreign commerce and over traffic between the continental United States and its territories and possessions.

wheat, and similar commodities.

Where the law does apply, its provisions resemble those applicable to motor carriers. Common carriers must obtain certificates and contract carriers permits. A grandfather clause protects the rights of those carriers operating before the passage of the Act. But where the Commission narrowly interpreted grandfather rights among motor carriers, thereby restricting competitive alternatives, it has broadly interpreted these rights in water transportation. This is due partly to the irregular nature of water transportation, partly to the fact that large water-carrier companies can present stronger cases before the Commission than the typical small trucking firms, and perhaps partly to criticism of the ICC's restrictive policy toward motor carriers.[28] The Commission has also stated that the desirability of using fully improved waterways makes it proper to authorize as broad a range of operation as is consistent with other criteria—a theme which recurs in its joint rail-barge decisions.[29] In cases involving the entry of new firms, the Commission weighs carefully the impact on existing carriers but does not deny applications simply because of the existence of adequate rail and highway service. Instead, arguing that there are inherent advantages in water transportation, it has upheld the right of shippers to be served by water as well as rail.[30]

The Act of 1940 applied the normal pattern of rate regulation to common carriers. Their rates must be reasonable, and the ICC is empowered to fix maxima and minima. Unjust discrimination is forbidden, and there is a long-and-short-haul clause. Only the minimum rates of contract carriers can be regulated by the ICC, and all intrastate rates are beyond its jurisdiction. Through routes and joint rates with other water common carriers and with railroads can be required. The Commission can prescribe methods of accounting and require reports, but it has no power over the issuance of securities.

To meet the fears of many shippers and water carriers that ICC regulation would serve the interests of the railroads, Congress established a general policy of "fair and impartial" regulation, under which the Commission is required "to recognize and preserve the inherent advantages" of each mode of transportation. Furthermore, in an effort to prevent the ICC from setting water

[28] R. E. Westmeyer, *Economics of Transportation* (1952), p. 500.

[29] *Upper Mississippi Towing Corp.*, 260 ICC 85 (1953).

[30] E.g., *Commercial Barge Lines, Inc., Extension*, 260 ICC 701 (1946); *Pan-Atlantic Steamship Corp., Extension*, 265 ICC 169 (1947); *Inland Waterways Corp., Extension*, 265 ICC 207 (1947).

rates to protect rail traffic, the Act makes it a duty of the Commission, in dealing with water rates, to consider their effect on the movement of traffic "by the carrier or carriers for which the rates are prescribed."

These injunctions appear to have had some effect. ICC decisions since the passage of the Act make it difficult to sustain the accusation that the Commission has unduly protected the railroads at the expense of water carriers.[31] In practice, the power to fix maximum rates means little, since the common carrier by water faces so much competition from nonregulated water carriers and from railroads. Nor has the ICC had much occasion to impose minimum rates to stop rate wars. Going rates are usually based on, and are lower than, railroad rates, as they must be to compensate for the slower water service. On the Mississippi River, a differential of 20 per cent under railroad rates has often been the rule. Accordingly, changes in railroad rates are quickly followed by corresponding adjustments of water rates. At the request of the War Shipping Administration (WSA) and the Maritime Commission in March, 1946, the ICC investigated a number of railroad rates on traffic competing with coastwise and intercoastal water carriers. Rail rates had been cut before the war to meet water competition. The WSA realized that water carriers after the war were facing substantially higher operating costs, and could be induced to re-enter the coastal trades only if rail rates were increased.[32] The ICC reopened a number of cases and rescinded or modified the relief granted the railroads earlier,[33] thus raising rail rates so as to facilitate service by water. Before the Transportation Act of 1940, the ICC had rejected the argument that it should raise rail rates to permit motor carriers to compete;[34] but it later declared that the effect of rail rates on the competitive position

---

[31] For a contrary view see S. P. Huntington, "The Marasmus of the ICC," *Yale Law Journal* (April, 1952), especially pp. 499–505. For criticisms of this article, see *Yale Law Journal* (January, 1953), pp. 171–226, and (November, 1953), pp. 44–63.

[32] Before the Act of 1940, at times the ICC and the Maritime Commission had engaged in an administrative rate war, each agency allowing its regulatees successive rate reductions to meet the competition of the other agency's regulatees. See *Citrus Fruit from Florida to North Atlantic Points*, 211 ICC 535 (1935), 218 ICC 637 (1936), 266 ICC 315 (1938); *Citrus Fruit from Florida to Baltimore*, 237 ICC 245 (1940); *Citrus Fruit from Florida to Baltimore*, 2 USMC 210 (1939).

[33] E.g., *All-Rail Commodity Rates between California, Oregon and Wash.*, 268 ICC 515 (1947), 277 ICC 511 (1950).

[34] *Petroleum and Petroleum Products from California to Arizona*, 241 ICC 21 (1942).

of water carriers and other agencies must be considered in setting rail rates.[35]

The problem of joint rail-barge routes and rates illustrates the difficulty which the ICC faces in determining its attitude toward the two modes of transportation. At issue is the general, and still unreconciled, conflict between public promotional and regulatory policies, arising from a somewhat complex interaction of political forces. Governmental promotion of inland waterways is a policy of long standing, commanding the enthusiastic support of shippers and regions which stand to benefit from the construction and operation of waterways.[36] But shippers not directly served by water carriers do not benefit unless joint rail-barge routes are established. The ICC was first authorized to order railroads and water carriers to establish through routes and joint rates in 1906, but opposition of the railroads, understandably not anxious to help their competitors and desirous of maintaining all-rail routings, blocked any significant action for two decades. Demands for rail-barge routes mounted. Shippers not served by water carriers wanted to share in the benefits of cheaper water transportation. Regional groups, such as the Mississippi Valley Association, desirous of promoting the trade of their regions and broadening the support for waterway expenditures, sought rail-barge routes in order to enlist the political co-operation of outside shippers.

In response to these demands, Congress in 1928 passed the Denison Act, which required the ICC to order common carriers by rail and water to establish through routes and joint rates whenever it found them to be in the public interest. The Act also directed the Commission to prescribe reasonable differentials between all-rail rates and joint rates. The Denison Act was repealed by the Transportation Act of 1940, but the new law repeated the same basic policies. Under these two statutes, the ICC has required railroads to make connections with water carriers. It initially established joint rates at levels 10 or 20 per cent below all-rail rates. In 1948, after a long investigation, it prescribed differentials in terms of cents per hundred pounds.[37] These differentials represent a method of passing on the economies of water transportation to interior shippers and of encouraging use of the waterways at the expense of the railroads.

But this same 1948 decision also registered the impact of contradictory congressional policies. The railroads attacked the rate

[35] ICC, *Annual Report, 1948*, pp. 49–52.
[36] See Chapter 5.
[37] *Rail and Barge Joint Rates*, 270 ICC 591.

differentials on the ground that the ICC had failed to prove that they were based on lower costs of service. Indeed, the Commission's experts had concluded "that the cost for the joint rail-barge routing is greater than that for direct all-rail routing." [38] (It should be remembered that these cost estimates take no account of the costs to the government of constructing and maintaining the waterways.) [39] Where before the Act of 1940 the ICC had given important weight to cost considerations, it now held that rate differentials did not have to be supported by cost differences. It argued that Congress's generous financial support to the government-owned Federal Barge Line indicated a legislative desire to promote "the advantages of joint barge-and-rail transportation in the belief that such service eventually will prove to be economical. It is not for us to say that the experiment should now come to an end." [40]

Thus the ICC, under its interpretation of the Act of 1940, undertakes two tasks: (1) the regulatory task of preserving the "inherent advantage" of each mode of transportation and of preventing unjust discrimination and undue preferences; and (2) the promotional task of encouraging water transportation by establishing differentials favoring rail-barge traffic even when not justified by cost differences. Clearly the promotional policy conflicts with the regulatory policy. It discriminates in favor of, and gives undue preference to, shippers able to take advantage of water transportation, and it substitutes high-cost transportation for low-cost transportation. Were the costs of government construction and maintenance of the waterways taken into account, the conflict would be greatly magnified.

On balance, then, the water-carrier provisions of the Act of 1940 contributed little either to the powers of the ICC or to a more rational national transportation policy. The bulk of water traffic is outside ICC jurisdiction, and the conflict between promotion and regulation is exacerbated, not reconciled.

3. The CAB and the Regulation of Air Transportation

At about the same time that the ICC, the Federal Co-ordinator, the railroads, and others were trying to persuade Congress to extend ICC regulatory powers over motor and water carriers, the arrival of the air age introduced still another complication in the

[38] *Ibid.*, at 604.
[39] See Chapter 5.
[40] *Rail and Barge Joint Rates,* 270 ICC 591, at 612.

problem of devising a unified national transportation policy.

Promotion and safety regulation of civil aviation had begun in 1926,[41] but economic regulation dates only from 1934. The Air Mail Act of that year gave regulatory control over service, accounting, and intercorporate relations to the Post Office, and the power to fix rates for the carrying of mail to the ICC, while the Department of Commerce administered safety regulation and promotional activities. This divided authority was ineffectual and confronted air carriers with the trying task of pleasing three masters. There were fears that ineffectively regulated competition would become cutthroat competition to the detriment both of safety and of the development of a commercial fleet which might serve as a national defense transport reserve. In 1937, following a Presidential recommendation, Congress seemed about to enact legislation vesting unified authority in the ICC. But the measure failed because of jealousies among the agencies then concerned with civil aviation and also because the ICC was considered too close to the railroads and too judicial and regulatory in approach to provide forceful leadership in the promotion of a new means of transportation. In 1938, President Roosevelt endorsed the creation of a separate commission, and the Civil Aeronautics Act of that year initiated full and unified regulation.

This Act established the Civil Aeronautics Board and gave it regulatory authority over entry, routes, rates, air-mail payments, and subsidies of common carriers. A certificate of public convenience and necessity is required for entry, with a grandfather clause protecting the rights of carriers operating in 1938. Rates must be just and reasonable, published, and observed. Pooling, combination, intercorporate relations, and abandonments are controlled, but the CAB has no authority over security issues.

The Board has aimed at a mixture of competition and monopoly. Believing that its primary task is to strengthen existing common carriers and to safeguard earnings, thereby lessening the need for subsidies, it has restricted entry. No new trunk lines have been certificated since 1938. As traffic has grown on established routes, however, the CAB has approved applications from existing lines to extend their routes and add new ones, thereby strengthening weaker systems and permitting the duplication of service on major routes. Its aim has been to promote as much competition as is compatible with profitable operations. By the end of fiscal 1956, eighty-four of the one hundred largest markets were served by

[41] See Chapter 5.

more than one line and only one of the twelve domestic trunk line carriers required a subsidy for its trunk-line services.

Protection of the certificated carriers from competition has aroused heated controversy in connection with the CAB's administrative assault on nonscheduled carriers ("non-skeds"), an assault described by Senator John Sparkman as "strangulation by regulation." [42] In 1938, the CAB granted exemptions from its economic regulation to "fixed base operators," who made irregular trips and ran charter flights. After World War II, with air transportation expanding and an abundance of war-surplus transports, the non-skeds multiplied in number and began to provide, illegally, regularly scheduled services. Operating with flexibility and initiative, they met peak demands on routes taxing the capacity of certificated carriers. They made some service innovations, such as air coach and air cargo, which were belatedly copied by the protected lines. They were attacked by their certificated rivals for inferior safety and for skimming the cream off markets. The CAB, under pressure from the certificated carriers, agreeing with their arguments and identifying the public interest in commercial aviation with their financial well-being, began to tighten the regulatory screws. In 1947, blanket exemptions were withdrawn and the non-skeds were compelled to apply for letters of registration. Full reports were required of them and the number of flights they could make was limited. In 1949, they were forbidden to make joint arrangements which had the effect of providing regular service. A number of lines had their letters revoked for providing too-frequent services. In 1951, the CAB limited the number of flights a non-sked could make to three a month on major routes and eight between fixed points.

The non-skeds mobilized considerable political support and obtained sympathetic hearings before House and Senate committees. In 1953, the CAB beat a partial retreat by rescinding its 1951 ruling. The Board then began a full investigation of the problem. Pending completion of its study, in 1956 it established a new category, the "supplemental air carrier." Such carriers are allowed unlimited chartered flights and up to ten flights a month between any two points. Meanwhile, however, the Board had taken action against North American Airlines, the largest of the non-skeds, for violation of its orders. In 1957, the Supreme Court refused an appeal against a CAB order denying North American

[42] For an account, see R. Bendiner, "The Rise and Fall of the Nonskeds," *The Reporter* (May 30, 1957), pp. 29–34.

flight privileges.[43] Thus the amount and nature of competition that the CAB will tolerate are limited.

Until recently, the Board has had to exercise little control over rates. Maximum rates had been effectively limited by the competition of other carriers. Although the Board has generally allowed rate cuts as a means of increasing traffic, in 1947 it fixed minimum cargo rates to protect independent cargo carriers from the subsidized competition of passenger lines. Unlike the ICC, the CAB need not consider the effect of rates on other modes of transportation. Indeed, as long as most carriers were subsidized, the Board justifiably was more concerned with subsidies than with rates. In recent years, however, as subsidies have ceased and as carriers have sought to raise rates in expectation of the higher cost of jet and turbo-jet planes on order, the CAB has had to face the rate problem. In 1958, pending completion of an investigation of the earnings necessary to promote proper development of air services, it granted a 6 per-cent emergency rate increase, an action termed inadequate by the carriers.

Thus the CAB has confronted a somewhat different combination of many of the same regulatory problems encountered in other areas of transportation. Its promotional activities have been impressive. Its regulatory policy has restricted competition substantially, although it has gradually increased the amount of competition among the twelve trunk-line carriers. Its existence as an independent agency regulating one sector of transportation, and the combination of regulatory and promotional responsibilities with which it is charged, contribute to the difficulties of achieving a unified national transportation policy.

4. The Transportation Act of 1940

These various efforts to promote and regulate motor carriers and air carriers, and concurrent demands from the ICC, the Federal Co-ordinator, and the railroads for a unification of transportation policy and regulatory authority, were reflections of what the ICC once described as "a virtual revolution in transportation."

No more extraordinary development of transportation facilities has ever been seen than has taken place in this country in the past 20 years. . . . there is need for readjustments between and within the different branches of the transportation industry. . . . There is a field here both for continuing study and research and for active, aggressive,

[43] *North American Airlines* v. *CAB*, 353 U.S. 941.

and consistent leadership on the part of the Government which has never been occupied. The problem is to fill that void in the best possible way.[44]

Attempts to fill this void, still largely unoccupied nearly two decades later, led to the passage of the Transportation Act of 1940. In 1938, two committees were appointed by President Roosevelt to study and make recommendations for the improvement of transportation. The first, the Committee of Three, was composed of three ICC commissioners, headed by W. M. W. Splawn. It recommended a far-reaching program including immediate financial aid to the railroads, regulation of all forms of transportation by a single agency, presumably the ICC, and the establishment of a Federal Transportation Authority, with most of the powers of the old Federal Co-ordinator. A Committee of Six, with three representatives each from railroad management and railroad labor, also submitted a broad program, looking toward more comprehensive control of the interrelations of the various modes of transportation.

As we have already seen, Congress's hesitation to impose regulation on reluctant water carriers and against the wishes of shippers and its fear that the ICC was too "railroad-minded" led it to confer only limited authority over water transportation on the ICC. The belief that civil aviation needed promotion more than regulation influenced Congress to omit this industry also from the ICC's jurisdiction. The Act of 1940 did confer some minor benefits on the railroads. The discount previously received by the government on shipments over the land-grant roads was repealed, except on military property and personnel —an exception shortly to cover an enormous volume of traffic.[45] RFC lending powers in the railroad field were liberalized, and the time limit on the filing of reparation and undercharge claims against railroads was shortened. Finally, the requirement of the 1920 Act that railroad mergers must follow an ICC "official" plan was eliminated. Instead, the Commission was left free to approve or reject proposals on an *ad hoc* basis.

The Act established a Board of Investigation and Research to study the relative economies of rail, water, and motor-carrier transportation with a view to determining which services should be encouraged or discouraged to avoid wasteful and destructive competition. It was also authorized to inquire into the extent

[44] ICC, *Annual Report, 1938*, pp. 24–25.
[45] All land-grant rate reductions were terminated in 1946.

of government subsidies to various modes of transportation. During the four-year life of the Board, however, its studies were delayed and its reports obscured by World War II, and little resulted from its potentially valuable work.

The most significant contribution of the 1940 Act was its declaration of policy. It read:

It is . . . the national transportation policy of the Congress to provide for fair and impartial regulation of all modes of transportation subject to the provisions of this Act, so administered as to recognize and preserve the inherent advantages of each; to promote safe, adequate, economical, and efficient service and foster sound economic conditions in transportation and among the several carriers; to encourage . . . reasonable charges . . . without unjust discriminations, undue preferences or advantages, or unfair or destructive competitive practices . . . all to the end of developing, coordinating, and preserving a national transportation system by water, highway, and rail as well as other means, adequate to meet the needs of the commerce of the United States, of the Postal Service, and of the national defense.

Unfortunately, as we have seen, the powers conferred by the Act were not sufficient to effectuate these policies. Many carriers and a whole mode of transportation were exempt from its provisions, and the promotional objectives, partly stated in this Act, but mainly established in other legislation and by other agencies, often frustrated the ICC in its efforts to make the Act's regulatory policies effective.

5. A National Transportation Policy

Both the transportation revolution and its disastrous impact on railroad earnings were temporarily held in check during World War II. Freight and passenger traffic strained the railroads to capacity. The rails had to bear a substantial wartime increase in traffic, which was intensified by the sharp curtailment of coastwise shipping, by the rationing of gasoline and tires, and by a shortage of trucks and parts. The railroads met this challenge remarkably well, carrying in 1944 almost twice as many ton-miles of freight as they did in 1918, although their carrying capacity was about the same. This striking improvement in performance was partly attributable to the fact that traffic was moving both east and west, making for fewer empty car movements, and partly to the effective use by the ICC and the Office of Defense Transportation of their powers to order the most efficient and fullest utilization of facilities. But much of the credit for the railroad's performance must be given to management, which not only operated individual railroads much more efficiently than in World War I but also was better organized for co-operative action through such bodies as the car-service division of the American Railway Association (now the Association of American Railroads) and regional shippers' advisory boards.

The Railroads: A Sick Industry

Wartime traffic brought with it high earnings, and the end of the war found the railroads in much improved health with their debt burden substantially reduced. The postwar decade was marked by general prosperity, but it also witnessed a revival and intensification of the competition of other carriers and left the railroads struggling to maintain their financial integrity. The tables on the following pages reveal the steady decline, only briefly interrupted by World War II, in the rail share of traffic. Railroad percentages of total passenger traffic continued to decline, while the roads were burdened with the necessity of maintaining passenger services and facilities. In 1955, total passenger revenues, including passenger-train income from mail, express, baggage, and milk, failed to cover the direct expenses of providing the service by $85 million. If overhead costs were allocated according to ICC formulae, then passenger revenues fell $637 million short of covering costs.[46] Commuter traffic, almost invariably a heavy burden on railroads, often fails to cover even out-of-pocket costs, but state commissions remain extremely loath to allow railroads to abandon commuter runs.

While the railroads have maintained fairly high levels of freight volume, the decline in their share of total freight movements is one indication of their competitive woes. The complex structure of railroad rates was built originally on the basis of a railroad monopoly of transportation. Rates were set according to the value of the goods shipped, costly goods bearing charges far exceeding the cost of the service so that bulky, low-value commodities, which might not otherwise move, could travel at low rates covering variable costs but making little contribution to overhead. Increasingly, however, motor carriers, setting rates based on cost of service, have found it possible, and profitable, to attract high-value traffic away from the rails even over great distances. With the cream thus skimmed off, railroads have had

[46] ICC, *Annual Report*, 1956, pp. 53–55.

INTERCITY FREIGHT AND OTHER GOODS TRAFFIC BY MODES OF TRANSPORTATION [47]

(in millions of ton-miles)

Year	Railroads		Motor Carriers		Inland Waterways [a]		Pipe Lines		Air Lines	
	Volume	% Total Traffic	Volume	% Total Traffic	Volume	% Total Traffic	Volume	% Total Traffic	Volume	% Total Traffic
1937	363,614	61.82	44,000	7.48	110,127	18.73	70,400	11.97	9	b
1940	379,161	61.96	51,003	8.33	118,057	19.29	63,745	10.42	14	b
1943	734,715	71.97	48,199	4.72	141,652	13.87	96,257	9.43	52	.01
1946	602,099	68.19	64,300	7.28	123,973	14.04	92,400	10.48	77	.01
1949	534,694	60.56	93,653	10.61	139,396	15.79	114,916	13.02	235	.02
1952	623,508	54.91	184,106	16.21	170,000	14.97	157,502	13.87	408	.04
1955	631,385	49.41	226,188	17.70	216,508	16.94	203,244	15.91	481	.04

a. Including Great Lakes.
b. Less than .01%.

INTERCITY PASSENGER TRAFFIC BY MODES OF TRANSPORTATION [47]
(in millions of passenger-miles)

Year	Railroads Volume	% Total Traffic	Motor Carriers Volume	% Total Traffic	Private Autos Volume	% Total Traffic	Inland Waterways [a] Volume	% Total Traffic	Air Lines Volume	% Total Traffic
1937	26,652	9.56	12,673	4.72	228,364	85.08	1,309	.49	407	.15
1940	24,766	8.71	b	b	257,346	90.46 [c]	1,317	.46	1,041	.37
1943	89,865	33.53	27,416	10.23	147,131	54.91	1,927	.72	1,632	.61
1946	66,262	18.74	25,576	7.23	253,570	71.70	2,327	.66	5,910	1.67
1949	35,975	9.38	22,411	5.85	316,774	82.63	1,402	.37	6,770	1.77
1952	34,710	7.23	21,118	4.40	410,275	85.46	1,396	.29	12,578	2.62
1955	28,695	4.32	25,117	3.78	585,817	88.21	1,738	.26	22,741	3.42

a. Including Great Lakes.
b. Separate figures for motor carriers and private automobiles not shown.
c. Includes motor-carrier traffic.

[47] ICC, *Annual Report*, various years.

to raise rates on their remaining traffic, often with the result of accelerating its diversion to other modes of transportation.

Furthermore, postwar inflation and the strong bargaining position of labor have confronted railroad management with steadily mounting operating costs and costly operating rules. The rise in labor, supply, and equipment costs has been accompanied by tax increases. Designed to maintain employment, "featherbedding" working rules, such as the one equating a 100-mile trip with a day's work, add substantially to operating costs. In the face of these mounting costs, management has had to appeal to the ICC repeatedly in the postwar years for general rate increases. While the railroads and outside observers have frequently criticized the ICC for the delays involved in its rate procedures,[48] the Commission has granted, if belatedly, increase after increase. By 1957, the railroads had been permitted almost to double rates over World War II levels. But the ICC has hesitated to grant the full amount of each request for fear that traffic diversion would leave the roads worse off than before. Occasionally, as in the 1957 proceedings, some railroads have opposed the increase for the same reason. Indeed, the railroads often have to return to the Commission to ask for exceptions to the increases to prevent traffic diversion. According to some estimates, the railroads have been able to put into effect only half the increases granted.[49]

As a result, even in the generally booming postwar years, the railroads have been able to earn only about 3 or 4 per cent on their net property investment and only 5 or 6 per cent on their capitalization. On the average, only about 70 per cent of the roads have been able to pay dividends.[50] It is little wonder that most railroads have found the security markets somewhat inhospitable and have asked for government loans. It took only the moderate economic decline of 1957–1958 to endanger the financial stability of many rail carriers and the maintenance and improvement of most of the nation's railroad system.

Clearly, technological change has been the prime mover in producing the malady of the railroads. But both management and government must share some of the onus of responsibility for the weakness of what is still, in peace and especially in war,

[48] E.g., see C. L. Dearing and W. Owen, *National Transportation Policy* (1947), pp. 278–288. During the 1950's, several bills were introduced to enable railroads to increase rates more rapidly. Shippers have opposed such legislation and no bill has yet been passed.

[49] "The Railroads: Economics May Be Starting to Work For Them," *Business Week* (July 13, 1957), p. 88.

[50] ICC, *Annual Report, 1956*, pp. 178–179.

the backbone of the nation's transportation system. Railroad management, on the whole, has not been as enterprising as its industrial and commercial counterparts. In the early days, it was unduly preoccupied with financial speculation and the temptation to abuse its monopoly position. In later years, ICC regulation has had a deadening effect, training managers to abide by regulatory rules, curbing initiative, and in general, ill-preparing them for the demands of an increasingly competitive environment. The industry has been slow to the point of lethargy in developing research programs, improvements in equipment and operation, and even adequate tools of management control.

Nor does the organization of the railroads assist their competitive efforts to win traffic from other transportation agencies. Failure to adopt the consolidation envisaged by the Act of 1920 or the co-ordination authorized by the Act of 1933 has burdened the railroads with wasteful duplications of service and facilities and often breaks up what should be a unified traffic flow. An individual railroad is loath to order more costly, but superior, rolling stock when, because of the accidents of car movements, most of its freight cars may be used by other roads, and all cars yield their owners the same flat $2.75 per-diem charge.[51] A railroad competing with other modes of transportation for traffic which, if shipped by rail, must use the tracks of two or more lines, may find that the appeal of its improvements in service is negated by the slowness and inefficiency of its connecting neighbor.

Increased competitive effectiveness of the railroads as a whole vis-à-vis other transportation agencies requires greater unification of, and less competition within, the railroad industry. Yet public policy still stresses the importance of competition within the industry. It is true that in the 1930's considerable support was generated for the Prince Plan, which called for the grouping of all railroads into seven great noncompetitive, regional systems, but the Federal Co-ordinator, after careful study, declined to endorse it.[52] The Reed-Bulwinkle Act of 1948 granted an exemption from the Sherman Act to ICC-approved rate bureaus, in which railroads jointly consider rate changes, but rate-bureau

[51] A recent study of the movements of one freight car showed that it crossed the country five times and spent two years before it happened to be loaded with cargo that brought it home. *Business Week* (July 13, 1957), p. 103.
[52] *Regulation of Railroads*, S. Doc. 119, 73d Cong., 2d sess., pp. 21–29, 106–123.

procedures still preserve the right of the individual carrier to act independently. It is also true that the ICC can approve consolidations and combinations which would otherwise violate the antitrust laws, but the Commission continues to make the maintenance of at least some competition a requirement for its approval of proposed consolidations. In 1947, it approved the merger of the Pere Marquette with the Chesapeake & Ohio only after finding that it "would not lessen competition but would create a strong, well-balanced system that would afford stiffer competition to the New York Central, Pennsylvania, Baltimore & Ohio and other railroads." [53] But later the ICC frowned on efforts to merge the Chesapeake & Ohio and the New York Central. The proposal advanced in 1958 to merge the two largest trunk-line roads, the Pennsylvania and the New York Central, may once again focus attention on this issue.

Whether railroads should be given wider freedom to compete with other carriers is still an unsettled issue of public policy. For some time, students of the problem have argued that ICC regulations should be eased, giving railroads greater rate-making flexibility to meet intercarrier competition.[54] Railroads have supported this view, but it has been opposed by shippers and other transportation media, who fear that railroads would then be free to drive their competitors out of business by unreasonably lowering rates on competitive traffic while recouping their losses by imposing unduly high rates on noncompetitive traffic. In a sense, both views are correct, and it is precisely because both competitive and monopoly elements operate powerfully that a policy solution is so difficult. Rate regulation is partially based on the assumed existence of monopoly power; this assumption is not wholly invalid and there is a need to protect against abuses of this power. But rigid regulation based solely on monopoly premises makes it difficult for the rails to compete effectively with other carriers. Similarly, requiring railroads to maintain unprofitable passenger operations as a public service assumes the existence of a total rate structure permitting a reasonable return on investment, but competition invalidates this assumption.

There are no easy answers to these questions. Probably the gravest indictment of the ICC and the existing system of regulation, however, is that the Commission has not had the time,

---

[53] *Pere Marquette Ry. Co. Merger,* 267 ICC 207.
[54] E.g., J. C. Nelson, "The Role of Regulation Re-examined," in National Resources Planning Board, *Transportation and National Policy* (1942), pp. 197–238; Dearing and Owen, *op. cit.*

the resources, or the drive to explore the broader issues of policy and to propose answers. Preoccupied with the minutiae of specific cases, necessarily concerned with the rights and duties of those who are a party to each proceeding, burdened with administrative functions, and ensnared in a complex web of political pressures and economic interests, the Commission has not been in a position to bring freshness and breadth to the reshaping of basic policy.

Perhaps the best illustration of the ICC's limitations is to be found in its handling of rail-motor competition. Here, as we have seen, the Commission has never actively sought to define and promote the inherent advantages of each mode of transportation. Instead, its passive, case-by-case approach has permitted policy to be shaped by the tactics and objectives of the affected groups. The motor carriers have had a policy—to divert high-value, high-rate cargo from the rails—and have aggressively promoted it. The railroads have simply fought a defensive, delaying action. In such a situation, the fact of motor competition should lead to an examination of the optimum economic division of traffic and a re-examination of the railroad value-of-service rate structure. Instead, the motor-truck operators are invited to bid for high-value freight, since the defensive reactions of railroads are limited by a rate-making standard which prevents them from dropping their rates below the full costs of motor carriage. Thus, in effect, motor carriers set rail rates for whatever traffic they choose to carry. Since both the ICC and the railroads have lacked a policy, the policy of the motor carriers has prevailed.[55]

A National Transportation Policy?

Although many transportation issues have not been dealt with here,[56] at least part of the case for a national transportation policy has been suggested. The pleas for such a policy have been many and persuasive since the need was first clearly articulated in the 1930's.[57] At present there are many different transporta-

---

[55] E. W. Williams, Jr., op. cit., pp. 201–228.

[56] The regulation of pipe lines and of freight forwarders are among the more important topics not discussed here. For an examination of the full range of transportation policies, see R. E. Westmeyer, op. cit., and D. P. Locklin, Economics of Transportation (1954), 4th ed.

[57] In addition to the reports of the Federal Co-ordinator, see Dearing and Owen, op. cit.; National Resources Planning Board, Transportation and National Policy (1942); Locklin, op. cit., ch. 27; Westmeyer, op. cit., chs. 22–23; Secretary of Commerce, Issues Involved in a Unified and Coordinated Federal Program for Transportation (1950); S. Com. on Interstate and For-

tion policies, partially overlapping and highly contradictory. While many carriers are closely regulated, most water carriers escape economic regulation as do private truckers and carriers of agricultural commodities. Thus, regulatory policy is unevenly applied. Regulation also conflicts with promotional policies. While the ICC, at least in theory, tries to regulate so as to protect the inherent advantages of each mode of transportation, Congress and other agencies heavily subsidize some means of transportation, especially water carriers, without regard to the principle of inherent advantage. Nor is there clarity of policy on whether monopoly is to be accepted and regulated, or whether competition is the goal. If monopoly is accepted, then regulation must be extended and the transportation system treated as a unified whole. If competition is to be furthered, there should be a relaxation of rate regulation as well as of limitations on entry.

In 1955, a Cabinet committee designated by President Eisenhower recommended a policy of reduced regulation. Carriers would have been left free to set rates within broad limits determined by the regulatory commissions—mimima based on direct costs and maxima at a just and reasonable level, not below full costs. The regulators would retain the power to investigate rates and to eliminate unfair discrimination.[58] Release of the report, however, was held up for half a year by criticism within

eign Commerce, *Domestic Land and Water Transportation* (1951), S. Rept. 1039, 82d Cong., 1st sess.

[58] The Committee's proposed statement of policy read as follows:

"It is hereby declared to be the national transportation policy of the Congress:

"(1) to provide for and develop under the free enterprise system of dynamic competition a strong, efficient, and financially sound national transportation industry by water, highway and rail, as well as other means, which is and will at all times remain fully adequate for national defense, the Postal Service and commerce;

"(2) to encourage and promote full competition between modes of transportation at charges not less than reasonable minimum charges, or more than reasonable maximum charges, so as to encourage technical innovations, the development of new rate and service techniques, and the increase of operating and managerial efficiency, full use of facilities and equipment and the highest standards of service, economy, efficiency and benefit to the transportation user and the ultimate consumer, but without unjust discrimination, undue preference or advantage, or undue prejudice, and without excessive or unreasonable charges on noncompetitive traffic;

"(3) to cooperate with the several States and the duly authorized officials thereof, and to encourage fair wages and equitable working conditions;

"(4) to reduce economic regulation of the transportation industry to the minimum consistent with the public interest to the end that the inherent economic advantages, including cost and service advantages of each mode

the administration. When published, it was assailed as unduly favorable to the railroads, and its policy was not pressed.

As the financial position of the railroads continued to worsen in 1958, Congress enacted a measure to aid the railroads and revise federal transportation policy. In addition to authorizing governmental guarantee of up to $500 million in private loans to the railroads, it empowered the ICC to permit the discontinuance, curtailment, or consolidation of any unprofitable interstate train or ferry service. States retain original jurisdiction over intrastate services, but the ICC may accept a petition to discontinue or modify services if a state has failed to act within 120 days or if it has refused a proposed discontinuance. The Act also tightened the definition of private motor carriers exempt from regulation and shortened the list of agricultural commodities whose motor carriage is similarly exempt. Finally, in a potentially significant redefinition of transportation policy, the measure provided that rates for any one mode of transportation "shall not be held up to a particular level to protect the tariff of any other mode of transportation." The effect of these provisions clearly depends upon the manner in which they are applied by the ICC, but they may permit a substantial alteration of policy.

If matters are allowed to drift, large-scale governmental financial participation in the railroad industry, and perhaps some outright ownership, may not be too distant. Government support or provision of commuter transportation is already a lively topic of debate among metropolitan planners. A first step in this direction was taken in 1958, when Massachusetts enacted a measure requiring Boston and thirty-seven other communities served by the unprofitable Old Colony line of the New Haven Railroad to pay up to $900,000 in annual subsidies to the railroad.

In the absence of a clear consensus on the nature of the public interest in transportation, the achievement of an efficient, coordinated, and healthy national system remains a distant goal. Its successful accomplishment implies the existence of flexible regulatory instruments, equipped with adequate authority, enjoying widespread public support, and capable of exercising intelligent foresight in shaping transportation developments to meet

of transportation, may be realized in such a manner as to reflect its full competitive capabilities; and

"(5) to require that such minimum economic regulation be fair and impartial without special restrictions, conditions or limitations on individual modes of transport." Presidential Advisory Committee on Transport Policy and Organization, *Revision of Federal Transportation Policy*, p. 8.

national needs. There are many obstacles in the way.

The history of railroad regulation, which still lies at the heart of our transportation policy problems, has been essentially one of pragmatic adjustments to circumstance. The traditional *modus operandi* has been to deal with evils and their effects after they have occurred; rarely has public policy sought to anticipate and forestall them. Consequently, regulators have almost always been confronted with *faits accomplis* in the form of industry situations which have taken shape and crystallized before regulation appears on the scene. Such situations necessarily limit the freedom with which regulators can act. Clusters of interests have grown up; expectations have been aroused; innocent parties have become involved; relationships have been established which the process of regulation must take into account.

Transportation today presents these complications in a particularly acute form. Technical changes have brought other types of carriers into being and imperiled the financial stability of the railroads. The parties-in-interest whose fortune and future are intimately dependent upon the fate of the railroad industry face shrinking rather than expanding vistas. Other transportation media have their own constellations of shippers, suppliers, and workers who are equally involved in their own well-being and vitally concerned with the competitive interrelations of transportation agencies. Thus the transportation revolution has multiplied the numbers of parties-in-interest. The natural tendency is to seek to shift the burden of necessary readjustment to such groups as demonstrate weakness either in private bargaining or in the political arena, and to make public policy itself the vehicle for transferring the costs of technical and economic changes to the general public. The formulation of a national transportation policy will therefore be influenced by the expediencies these conditions generate. How far it can rise above them will depend, in the final analysis, upon whether a political and economic environment can be developed in which the common interest in an adequate transportation system becomes more articulate and influential than the immediate desires for preferential treatment of the special interests concerned.

CHAPTER 12

Electrical Utilities

E LECTRICAL utilities share with the rail-
roads a common legal basis of regulation. Both are recognized
as public utilities and are, therefore, subject to government control
of rates and services. And in both cases there has been a growth in
regulatory powers and a need to relate regulatory activities to
other governmental policies. But there the resemblance begins to
fade. Railroading is a relatively old industry, showing signs of
decline and enfeeblement and increasingly finding itself in a position of competition, not monopoly. Though its owners and management once fought regulation vigorously, they came to accept
it as part of the normal pattern and to ask for its extension to
competing modes of transportation. With electricity, the institutional setting is different. There one encounters a dynamically
expanding industry, whose output increases each year. Regulatory
action is more recent. Industry leaders have vigorously opposed
regulation and aggressively resisted its extension. Public power
projects, which have been promoted in part for their regulatory
impact on private companies, are still violently attacked by the
industry.

1. The Electric Power Industry

The electrical industry is young. Though the first Edison station
was opened three-quarters of a century ago, the real development
of the industry is a twentieth-century phenomenon. Its growth has
been strong and sustained, its output doubling each decade.

Technological advances encompassing the whole gamut of the industry—generation, transmission, distribution, and utilization— have greatly cheapened power and laid the basis for what has come to be called "the power age." The industry's record of accomplishment is remarkable, yet it has been intertwined with abuses of a monopoly position which have contributed to the substantial role which government now plays.

The pressure for extension of regulation has been accentuated by the predominance of large systems within the industry and by the high concentration of control among these systems. At the peak of the concentration movement, before it was reversed by public policy in the 1930's, fifty-seven systems accounted for 90 per cent of the electricity generated by private companies. The twelve largest systems furnished approximately half of the country's total service. Many of these systems, moreover, were subject to further over-all integration and control through investment and financial corporations, banking affiliations, intersystem holdings, and other financial connections.

This high degree of concentration and control emerged from a process of consolidation which started at the beginning of the century, made some headway before World War I, and proceeded at a feverishly accelerated pace during the twenties as machinery for mass distribution of securities was perfected. Originally, electrical companies were local affairs. With advances in technology, larger areas could be served more efficiently by the same operating organization. Enterprising individuals were quick to sense the advantages of consolidation and to capitalize on them. Promoters and banking groups advanced the process for the sake of the possible financial profits involved. Thus consolidation moved forward by successive stages. At first, two or more local properties were brought together. Later other properties were acquired. Purchases were frequently haphazard and uncontrolled. There was little evidence of any public interest in the result or of the exertion of public authority to direct the process toward public ends. The motivation was profit, and the dynamic urge upon which many utility empires were built was supplied by the rivalries of promoters and their affiliated banking groups.

The results became evident in the internal organization of the great utility systems. Some systems confined their operations to single densely populated metropolitan areas or to sizable but contiguous areas. Others operated in noncontiguous territory, but with one or more well-defined main areas of operation. Still others consisted of large miscellanies of scattered noncontiguous properties in many different parts of the country; their only organizing principle was the search for the rewards of financial control and manipulation of operating companies. The results were also evident in the corporate structures of the great systems. A few, very few, had simple corporate structures with only one or two operating subsidiaries. Others had highly complex structures with tier on tier of operating and holding companies and affiliated subsidiaries. The Associated Gas and Electric System had twelve tiers. Ultimate control was exercised by a financial group with a small monetary stake in the underlying physical properties of the empire it dominated. One of the Insull operating companies was controlled by an investment in the top company amounting to but one two-hundredth of one per cent of the value of the operating company.

Consequently, management was usually subordinated to the financial control groups. As utility empires were built up, promoters and financiers frequently had to pay excessive prices for the control of operating companies. Write-ups in book assets concealed inflated purchase prices. Securities based on capitalized expectancies that were wildly optimistic were unloaded on unsuspecting investors. The burden of supporting these expectancies fell on consumers. Financial groups profited not only through security transactions and manipulations but also through control of the operating companies. They forced the operating companies to pay them inflated fees for financial services, for construction and development work, and for management advice. Operating companies could be "milked" through upstream loans on terms advantageous to the holding-company groups. Such profits of the financial control groups were reflected, first, in inflated operating expenses and unnecessary overhead of the operating companies and, ultimately, in excessive rates extracted from the consumers. In so far as rates were regulated, the control groups were necessarily vitally interested in exerting pressure on regulatory agencies to provide rate schedules that would safeguard the financial structures they had erected, as well as swell the stream of income from which their own wealth and power were derived.

But the success of control groups in exploiting profit potentialities depended not only on the tolerance of regulatory agencies, but also on the market for electric power. And this market revealed, and continues to reveal, great variability among different companies and in different regions. In some cases, industrial and commercial demand bulks large; in others, residential or rural consumption is more important. Electric companies, in shaping their rate policies, necessarily take account of the peculiarities of market behavior. Electricity is not always sold under conditions of monopoly. If rates are too high, the large industrial user of power may install his own generating plant. Electric companies must therefore charge rates equal to or less than it would cost large users to provide their own power. Furthermore, comparative power costs are sometimes an important consideration in the location of new industrial plants, and electric companies may compete vigorously to attract new large users.

Competition is not entirely absent in other classes of service. Gas and even fuel oil compete with electricity in some uses. For many purposes, however, residential and small commercial consumers are so tied to electricity that no practical alternative is available. If rates are high, this group may attempt to restrict its consumption, but there remains an irreducible minimum which users cannot forego. In the determination of the price of this minimum, they have no effective bargaining power. They are ultimately dependent on the marketing policies of the utility companies and on public regulation.

The utility management and control groups do have a choice. They may set low rates to promote maximum utilization and so profit from the economies of scale. Or, relying on their monopoly position to guarantee them whatever increase in business develops, they may prefer to concentrate their efforts on maximum immediate profits through high rates. Faced at times with a decline in industrial demand, they may attempt to recoup their losses by raising residential and commercial rates. In such cases, or when utilities compete intensively for industrial users, the interests of unorganized residential consumers and small commercial enterprises are likely to suffer. If dissatisfaction among these groups leads to a demand for governmental action, public policy then confronts the task of attempting to compel utility control groups to redress the balance in favor of hitherto neglected parties-in-interest.

An analysis of the various parties-in-interest is vital to an understanding of the regulatory process in this industry. While enforcement of the Public Utility Holding Company Act of 1935, discussed below, has loosened the grip of the financial control groups, they often are still of great importance and for some time dominated the industry. Closely tied to these control groups, and frequently identical with them, are the financial interests, the banks and investing institutions which mobilize capital, supply funds, and provide financial services for the industry. In fundamental outlook these groups see eye to eye with the utility control groups, as do also, for the most part, the allied industries which draw their sustenance from the electrical utility industry.

Another important party-in-interest is management—the executives, administrators, and supervisory and technical personnel of the industry. Closer to the operating problems than the financial control groups, they are more sensitive to consumer dissatisfaction and more apt to be alive to the industry's technical potentialities for expansion and new services. In recent years, they have achieved greater independence and scope for initiative, though, broadly speaking, they maintain a community of interest with the financial control groups in their appearances before policy-forming tribunals and regulatory authorities.

Another important party-in-interest is the investor. Thorstein Veblen in his *Theory of Business Enterprise* (1904) called attention to the divergence which may develop between the interests of ordinary investors and those of the insiders who dominate the strategic controls of the enterprise. The utility holding companies furnished numerous examples of insiders utilizing their control to exploit small investors. Consequently, it is important to distinguish between the groups who actually control the enterprise and the small investors whose ordinary role is the passive one of receiving or hoping to receive dividends and interest. Even large, institutional investors, such as colleges, foundations, pension funds, mutual funds, and insurance companies normally play a passive role.

Still another party-in-interest is labor. Labor costs do not bulk large in this industry and, because of the skills required, most of its labor force is relatively well paid. Until the thirties, the industry was largely unorganized, and strenuous efforts were made by management to consolidate the loyalty of employees through paternalistic and welfare policies. For these reasons, there have been few efforts by labor in the past to influence public policy. Regulatory statutes focused on the interests of consumers or investors rather than on those of labor. In recent years, however, some electrical unions have on occasion seconded financial control groups and management in their opposition to public power projects.

Still another party-in-interest, and from a regulatory point of view perhaps the most important, is the consumer. As has already been indicated, the consumer interest breaks up into certain well-defined parts. There are the large industrial and commercial consumers; there are the smaller residential and commercial consumers; and there have been at times neglected potential consumers who were denied electricity by virtue of high rates, residence in sparsely populated rural areas, or distance from transmission lines. While consumers, in general, seek low charges, the small commercial, the residential, and the potential consumers do not have the bargaining power enjoyed by large industrial and commercial users, who can construct their own generating units. Consequently, the remedies of the small consumers must be political rather than economic, but they face serious obstacles in making their political influence effective. With numbers on their side, they are always a potential power to be reckoned with, but they are usually scattered and disorganized and cannot readily be consolidated into a coherent political force. Their displeasure may express itself in periodic bursts of indignation to which political leadership responds, but these are soon exhausted. No effective device has yet been found for maintaining articulate consumer interest as a continuous regulatory force.

These groups, then—consumers, investors, management, labor, financial control groups, and allied interests—provide the raw material and the dynamic force from which a pattern of regulation, more or less effective, emerges. Each group puts forth its claims and seeks in varying degree to determine public policy. And when questions of regulatory policy become intertwined with those relating to public power, new political forces come into play, the number of parties-in-interest multiplies, and their interrelations often become very complex indeed.

2. The Development of Regulation of the Electric Power Industry

The development of regulation in electricity offers interesting parallels to the history of railroad regulation. As with railroads, early public policy was largely promotional, primarily concerned with encouraging the development of the industry. The emphasis was on aid rather than control. Later, as abuses developed, particularly in the form of high rates, consumer dissatisfaction laid the groundwork for regulation. As in the railroad industry, regulation came after abuses had been disclosed and vested interests had become entrenched, and not as a process guiding the development of the industry. As with railroads, regulation lagged behind the developing geographical pattern of the industry. State-wide power was not effectively invoked until long after the industry had transcended local boundaries. Similarly, national power was not resorted to until long after industry organization had outgrown the jurisdictional bounds of the states. As in the railroad industry, also, regulation remained for a long time negative in character, concerned with discovering and penalizing abuses and checking excessive rates. As with railroads, too, regulation has tended to become more positive, concerned with reshaping corporate structures, planning the development of new sources of supply, and controlling and directing marketing policies.

At least three well-defined stages marked the development of electric regulation. The first period might be described as promotional, though some local regulation did appear. It lasted from 1882, when the first central electric plant in the United States was established, until 1907, the date of the first effective effort to regulate electrical utilities through commissions. In the second period, from 1907 until 1933, chief reliance for regulation was placed on state commissions. In the third period, which was foreshadowed by the Federal Water Power Act of 1920, but did not gather momentum until the New Deal, national authority was for the first time strenuously invoked. Concomitantly, state regulation became more vigorous and effective.

Of the first period, little needs to be said. The parallel with the early days of railroads is striking. Electrical utility promoters were commonly regarded as community benefactors who should be given incentives to invest in a risky and experimental industry. As a result, franchises of great prospective value were freely disposed of with little attempt to safeguard future community interests. Regulation, such as it was, depended on the terms of the franchise or charter, or it derived from municipal or state legislation providing no instruments of administration. In either case, it was minimal and ineffective. The way was opened to abuse, and consumer complaints began to mount. It was charged that the utilities imposed excessive rates, overcapitalized their properties, and obtained extortionate profits. A demand for more effective regulation culminated in the establishment of state regulatory commissions. The utilities opposed this movement but were finally forced to capitulate as the popular clamor became more insistent.

3. Regulation by State Commissions—Weaknesses

Starting in 1907, commissions were established in New York and Wisconsin and spread rapidly to other jurisdictions. But the movement toward effective state regulation encountered many obstacles. The utilities first fought the establishment of state commissions and then, in the words of one spokesman, tried to "regulate the regulators." In that effort, they very largely succeeded. The history of the electric utilities from 1907 until the 1930's is not only one of remarkable expansion of the industry itself; it is also a record of the rise of financial control groups to a position of ascendancy and concentrated economic power such as has rarely been witnessed.

This ascendancy was inevitably reflected in the regulatory process. Other parties-in-interest were weak and ineffective. The expansion of the industry dissolved such doubts as the cautious investor might have entertained about holding-company structures. While dividend checks poured in and stock-market quotations rose, the investor was only too content to be a passive income-receiver without questioning the financial practices which were so successfully lining his purse. Not until the Great Depression brought many holding-company structures tumbling down did doubts arise. Consumers, meanwhile, were also difficult to stir into action. Relative prosperity made it hard to excite consumers about electric rates. The general downward trend in rates, as costs were reduced through technical advances, mitigated such consumer dissatisfaction as existed. As a result, consumers, despite their large numbers, remained a negligible restraining force. Regulatory commissions found no support for an aggressive regulatory program. Consumer passivity and inertia inspired a similar attitude among commissions. Thus the economic setting created a situation made to order for the control groups. They knew what they wanted—a minimum of regulation—and the vast economic resources they controlled enabled them to attain their objective. By and large, they succeeded in carving out an area of independent sovereignty which left much of the state regulatory machinery an empty facade.

How was this result achieved? First, intensive efforts were made to create opinion favorable to privately owned utilities and unfavorable to state regulation or public ownership. Second, utility interests limited the scope and effectiveness of regulation by direct pressure on legislatures and administrative agencies. Third, appeals were taken to the courts when commission decisions on rates and valuations were unsatisfactory. Fourth, vigorous steps were taken to prevent federal regulation of interstate transmission of electric power. This increasingly important aspect of utility operation remained in the twilight zone where state regulation was unconstitutional and national regulation nonexistent. Fifth, the holding company was used to render state regulation largely in-

effective. Governmental efforts to control holding company transactions were vigorously opposed.

Public Relations Campaigns

Particularly after World War I, utilities embarked upon a vast
"educational" campaign, to "sell" their industry and to convince
the public of the adequacy of existing regulation and the dangers
of further penetration of government into the utility business.
The cost of this campaign ran from 25 to 30 million dollars a year
—all treated as operating expenses and financed out of charges to
the public. Utility executives were advised not to spare their
"educational" budgets. As M. H. Aylesworth, then managing
director of the National Electric Light Association (NELA), the
industry trade association, put it: "All the money being spent is
worth while—don't be afraid of the expense. The public pays the
expense." [1]

Equipped with ample resources, control groups undertook an
intensive organizational drive to win the loyalty of the various
parties-in-interest. Customers, investors, employees, and allied industries were to be persuaded to accept the control groups' interpretation of proper public policy. They were to be welded together
in a united front of opposition to "destructive" governmental
regulation.

Consumers were wooed in many ways. Intensive drives were
undertaken to increase customer stock ownership—much of it in
nonvoting stock—which was saluted at one and the same time as
"the best kind of public ownership" and also as a means of "combating the growing tendency for public ownership." Security
holders were organized for political purposes. As the managing
director of the NELA said: "Information directly submitted to
the congressional representatives of the respective states as to the
number of security holders within their particular state should be
effective in emphasizing in their minds the importance to their
local constituents of any matters which affect these securities." [2]
Banks, insurance companies, chambers of commerce, and other
businesses were mobilized to support the utility program. Utility
employees were widely used to present the utility case to the
public. As one executive put it, "We have in our employees a

[1] From a speech before the 13th Annual Convention of the Southeastern
Division of the NELA, 1925. Quoted in FTC, *Utility Corporations*, S. Doc.
92, 70th Cong., 1st sess., Part 7, p. 129.
[2] From letter of Paul S. Clapp, dated November 4, 1927, quoted in *ibid.*,
Part 71A, p. 12.

great force which, properly informed and properly directed, can be of tremendous assistance in securing and maintaining right public relations." [3] "With the increased activities of some of our advocates of public ownership," stated an article prepared for the NELA, "it is high time we mustered all of our employees, male and female, to demand their right to the rewards of individual initiative and endeavor, which will be theirs only under private operation." [4] Manuals were prepared and study courses and meetings held to equip employees, in the words of Samuel Insull, "to disseminate facts relating to the theories of political ownership and to help the industry from unjust and injurious attack." Utility employees were trained, in effect, to be missionaries for private ownership.

No channel of public opinion was neglected in the effort to mold a public attitude harmonious with the wishes and program of the utilities. Efforts were made to win the good will of the press by advertising, "canned" handouts, and in some instances, outright purchase of organs of public opinion. The importance of the educational system as an opinion-forming agency was recognized. "The aim," according to the Illinois Committee on Public Utility Information, was "to fix the truth about the utilities in the young person's mind before incorrect notions become fixed there." [5] An elaborate program, ranging from special picture books for kindergartens to retainers for college professors, was formulated for this purpose.

This well-organized campaign was designed to convince the public that the utility conception of public policy was the only proper one. Until the economic debacle of 1929, the utilities were for the most part successful. They made state regulation satisfactory to themselves because they largely succeeded in regulating the sources of public opinion from which regulation springs.

Direct Pressure on Legislatures and Commissions

Utility efforts were by no means confined to efforts to influence opinion. Where it promised to be efficacious, direct pressure on legislatures and commissions was frequently exerted.

The effectiveness of a utility commission depends, in large measure, on the powers the legislature gives it. It is the legislature which determines whether the utility commission will be weak or strong; whether it will have sufficient appropriations and an ade-

[3] *Ibid.*, p. 278.
[4] *Ibid.*, pp. 278–279.
[5] *Ibid.*, p. 141.

quate staff of engineers, accountants, and economists; whether they will be well or poorly paid; whether the commission's jurisdiction will be limited or enlarged; whether the commission will have adequate power to control utility accounts and capitalization, scrutinize operating expenses, determine depreciation allowances, and regulate rates and services—in short, whether a commission will be reasonably effective or whether it will be helpless.

Utilities, therefore, found it expedient to maintain lobbies in various capitals to represent their interests and ensure that no "harmful" legislation would be passed. Lobbying techniques were versatile. They ranged from simple presentations of utility views to expensive, elaborate, and assiduous entertainment of legislators, and even to retainers and direct employment of legislators.[6] As a result of the successful use of such tactics, most state utility regulation was notably ineffective in the pre-1933 period. As late as 1934, there were still twelve states in which commissions had no jurisdiction over rates and services.

There were exceptions. Some commissions, such as those in Wisconsin, New York, Massachusetts, and Illinois, did reasonably good jobs under difficult conditions; but by and large, the performance of utility commissions was far from noteworthy. Commissioners, on the whole, were poorly paid. Their average tenure of office was brief, rarely exceeding five years. The problems they faced were often highly technical and complex. Most commissioners were political appointees; they brought to their task little in the way of helpful background and experience. Their staffs were usually inadequate, and financial resources were limited. Their budgets were paltry compared with the resources available to the utilities in opposing regulation. Rate cases were expensive and drained commission resources. As a result, many commissions held

[6] Here, for example, is a letter signed by W. T. Thayer, State Senator in New York and chairman of the committee through which all bills on utilities had to pass. The letter, dated March 28, 1927, was addressed to a vice-president of the Associated Gas and Electric Company:

"In keeping with your instructions of March 22, regarding my expense account . . . I herewith hand you bill as suggested. . . .

"The legislature adjourned last Friday and I have now returned to Chateaugay and will be here most of the coming summer. If at any time I can be of further service to you, please do not hesitate to call on me. I hope my work during the past session was satisfactory to your company; not so much for the new legislation enacted, but from the fact that many detrimental bills which were introduced we were able to kill in my committee."

(*State of New York, Proceedings of the Judiciary Committee of the Senate in the Matter of Investigation Requested by Senator Thayer*, Legislative Document, 1934, No. 102, p. 464.)

that their function was not to initiate crusades against utilities, but to sit as a judicial tribunal to hear such consumer complaints as were brought to them—a view still held in some states. The weakness of the individual consumer under such a procedure can readily be visualized. The timidity of commissions reflected their inability to mobilize public support. Many commissioners and staff aides were subject to temptations difficult to ignore. With salaries small and tenure uncertain, it is easy to understand why some of them eventually found their way into the employ of the utilities they had formerly been charged with regulating.

Such undermining of morale made effective regulation difficult. But organizational weaknesses were by no means the only explanation for the breakdown of regulation. In a more far-reaching sense, the commissions found that the companies they were trying to regulate were escaping from their reach. The rates and valuations they fixed could be appealed to the courts. The transmission of electricity over increasing distances created a growing interstate traffic immune from state surveillance. Furthermore, with the spread of the holding company, itself not subject to direct regulation, utility commissions were increasingly helpless to regulate the operating companies whose costs, and hence rates, were being inflated by many holding companies.

The Role of the Courts

The role of the courts as ultimate arbiters in rate regulation contributed to the regulatory breakdown. This role did not become immediately apparent. In *Munn* v. *Illinois* (1877), the Supreme Court had laid down the fundamental proposition that rate regulation was a legislative matter not reviewable by the courts. "For protection against abuses by legislatures," said Chief Justice Waite, "the people must resort to the polls, not to the courts." [7] This decision was apparently based on the theory that rate regulation, even if it might be deemed confiscatory, did not really involve a "taking" of property. Property was still identified with physical assets.

Gradually the courts shifted their position. In the Railroad Commission cases, it was suggested that "this power to regulate is not the power to destroy." [8] Here was an early intimation that outrageously low statutory rates might be held to violate the Fourteenth Amendment. Soon thereafter, in *Chicago, Milwaukee, and St. Paul R.R. Co.* v. *Minnesota*,[9] the new doctrine began to

[7] 94 U.S. 113.
[8] *Stone* v. *Farmers' Loan and Trust Co.*, 116 U.S. 307 (1886).
[9] 134 U.S. 418 (1890).

flower. "The question of the reasonableness of a rate . . ." said the Court, "is eminently a question for judicial investigation. . . ." The question of what is a reasonable rate necessarily led to the further question of the basis on which reasonableness should be determined. In *Smyth* v. *Ames*,[10] an attempt was made to answer this question. "We hold," said the Court, "that the basis of all calculations as to the reasonableness of rates to be charged . . . must be the fair value of the property being used. . . . What the company is entitled to ask is a fair return upon the value of that which it employs for the public convenience."

Thus the doctrine was developed that rates yielding a material net income might still be enjoined if they were not sufficient to yield a "fair return on a fair value." In other words, the courts redefined property as value rather than mere physical assets, and the due process clause was extended to protect this new concept of property. Not only did the courts forbid the confiscation of values, but they eventually went one step further. They asserted the right to determine value, not only as a matter of law, but also as a matter of fact. As Justice McReynolds said, in *Ohio Valley Water Co.* v. *Ben Avon Borough*,[11] "In all such [rate] cases, if the owner claims confiscation of his property will result, the state must provide a fair opportunity for submitting that issue to a judicial tribunal for determination upon its own independent judgment as to both law and facts; otherwise the order is void because in conflict with the due process clause. . . ." This doctrine did not go unprotested. An eloquent line of dissent pointed out that it made findings of fact by qualified administrative agencies virtually meaningless and tended to transform the Supreme Court into a general appellate body for the revision of utility rates anywhere in the United States.[12]

Meanwhile, however, the courts had taken upon themselves the task of evolving criteria of fair value. But how was fair value to be ascertained? The famous case of *Smyth* v. *Ames* is the starting point for many difficulties.[13] That case arose out of a Nebraska law reducing railroad rates for farm produce. The reduction was challenged in the courts. The period was one of steadily declining prices, and the original cost of the railroads in question was much higher than would have been the reproduction cost at then-current prices. The railroads, in arguing for a fair return on the value of

---

[10] 169 U.S. 466 (1898).

[11] 253 U.S. 287 (1920).

[12] See Justice Brandeis's dissent in the Ben Avon case and his concurring opinion in *St. Joseph Stockyards Co.* v. *U.S.*, 298 U.S. 38 (1936).

[13] 169 U.S. 466 (1898).

the property, offered original cost as a measure of value. Counsel for the state urged the doctrine of reproduction costs and contended that the rates set by the state legislature were reasonable on the basis of present value of the railroad property. Justice Harlan, in deciding against the state, attempted to steer a middle course between these rival theories. The railroad was entitled to a reasonable return on the fair value of its property. But what was fair value?

In order to ascertain that value [said Justice Harlan] the original cost of construction, the amount expended in permanent improvements, the amount and market value of its bonds and stock, the present as compared with the original cost of construction, the probable earning capacity of the property under particular rates prescribed by statute, and the sum required to meet operating expenses, are all matters for consideration, and are to be given such weight as may be just and right in each case.

What weight each of these factors should be accorded, Justice Harlan did not indicate. Legislatures and commissions were left to guess what would meet the favor of the Court in particular cases, and as if to make the problem even more confusing, Justice Harlan added, "We do not say that there may not be other matters to be regarded in estimating the value of the property."

With these highly indefinite and even conflicting criteria, the commissions were embarked on a half-century voyage on uncharted seas. They had no compass, and their destination was subject to change without notice. They had to find out what the fair value of property really was, but specific directions were not vouchsafed them. Indeed, the celebrated formula of *Smyth* v. *Ames* was a challenge to reconcile the irreconcilable. The economic value of productive property depends on the net profit it yields, and profit is the difference between a firm's costs and the income it receives from the prices or rates. Thus the value of its property depends on its prices or rates, but the Court ruled that in a regulated industry the "value" of the property would determine its rates. Since the market value of a utility's securities, one of the criteria listed by Justice Harlan, hinged on the rates set, it could not be used as an independent basis for setting rates. Consequently, legal value depended primarily on the weight given reproduction costs and original costs. (The original-cost formula, when corrected to disallow wasteful investments, later became the "prudent investment" formula.)

In the years following the *Smyth* v. *Ames* decision, the price level began to rise again. As E. C. Goddard put it, "In the nineties, cost of reproduction was far less than actual investment, however prudent; after 1900 it was increasingly greater than investment, however imprudent." [14] This reversal of price movement was matched by a concurrent reversal of positions by regulators and those regulated. The utilities, which in *Smyth* v. *Ames* had advanced original cost as a measure of fair value, now embraced reproduction cost as that theory promised greater advantages. Public representatives, on the other hand, found original cost or prudent investment more attractive, in part because of the greater ease of computation and the greater stability and certainty of the value thereby derived. The Court frequently disallowed rates for failure to accord enough weight to one or the other formula, but never established a clear rule which could guide regulators in future actions.

In the period before World War I, the Court did not make any single factor predominant in the determination of fair value. But its dicta tended to place great emphasis upon reproduction costs.[15] The spread between original and reproduction cost, however, was not so great at this time as to make the problem acute. The rapid rise in prices during and immediately following the war created a very different situation. The utilities were quick to press for valuations which would recognize the greatly enhanced costs of labor, supplies, and construction. Utility commissions offered resistance, but Supreme Court decisions in the 1920's, although occasionally ambiguous, for the most part represented a triumph for the utilities.

In 1923, the Court struck down two valuations for their disregard of reproduction costs,[16] but upheld a third valuation which gave some, but not controlling, weight to reproduction costs.[17] These cases revealed the Court's uncertainty in the face of new conditions. By 1926, when prices were fairly stable, though on a level well above 1914, the Court evidenced a clearer intention to give great weight to reproduction costs. Indeed, in that year the

[14] Association of American Law Schools, *Selected Essays in Constitutional Law* (1938), Vol. 2, p. 561.

[15] *San Diego Land and Town Co.* v. *National City,* 174 U.S. 739 (1899); *San Diego Land and Town Co.* v. *Jasper,* 189 U.S. 439 (1903); *Wilcox* v. *Consolidated Gas Co.,* 212 U.S. 19 (1909); *Simpson* v. *Shepard,* 230 U.S. 352 (1913).

[16] *Southwestern Bell Telephone Co.* v. *Public Service Commission,* 262 U.S. 276; *Bluefield Waterworks and Improvement Co.* v. *Public Service Commission,* 262 U.S. 679.

[17] *Georgia Railway and Power Co.* v. *Railroad Commission,* 262 U.S. 625.

Court seemed fully to embrace reproduction cost, holding that in times of price stability, "the present value of the lands plus the present cost of constructing the plant, less depreciation, if any, is a fair measure of the value of the physical elements of the property." [18] In this case, however, the company had accepted a rate base which did not fully reflect reproduction costs.

In 1929, in the O'Fallon case, a Court majority, while rejecting an ICC valuation based largely on actual legitimate investment because it had not considered reproduction costs, refused to proffer a definite guide for future action or fully to endorse reproduction costs. "The weight to be accorded thereto is not the matter before us." [19]

These pronouncements of the Supreme Court imposed requirements on regulatory agencies which practically ruled out effective regulation. The Court's fair-value doctrine offered no clear guide to action. The weight to be given either original or reproduction costs was never specified, and reproduction costs were almost impossible to determine. Where records were available, finding original cost, adding improvements, and subtracting recorded depreciation was relatively simple. While valuations based on reproduction cost were sometimes necessary because it was impossible to ascertain original cost, the courts went further and required a finding as to reproduction cost even where original cost data were available. To estimate reproduction costs, it was necessary to make a complete inventory of property and to appraise it.

Uncertainties necessarily attended this process. Electric power properties extended over enormous areas and values might run into billions of dollars. The task of merely listing, counting, measuring, or weighing all items was monumental. Moreover, since the physical condition of all properties had to be reported in order to allow for so-called observed depreciation, much depended upon opinion or even guesswork. Such opinions, even when offered by experts, disclosed startling discrepancies. Nor was this the only difficulty. The pricing process revealed even sharper discrepancies. Great strides had been made in devising new electrical equipment. Under the doctrine of reproduction cost old structures and equipment had to be valued "on the basis of what it would cost to reproduce them today even though they are not in fact being produced and would not be reproduced under any imaginable circumstances." Their reproduction costs could be

[18] McCardle v. Indianapolis Water Co., 272 U.S. 400.
[19] St. Louis and O'Fallon Railway v. U.S., 279 U.S. 461 (1929).

computed "only by some sort of legerdemain." [20] The price of virtually every unit was a matter of estimate rather than fact. The result was resort to conjecture and speculation, as the utility valuation experts strove for maximum reproduction costs and the representatives of the public pressed for minimum estimates. Since the valuation required field inventories and the pricing of myriad items, it could not be accomplished in a short period of time, and rate cases frequently stretched over many years.[21] These long-drawn-out proceedings showed the futility of the fair-value method of rate making. With constant price fluctuations, valuations were obsolete almost as soon as determined. With no judicially recognized process to keep valuations current, the regulatory process, for all practical purposes, became unworkable.

Still another factor contributing to the unworkability of the fair-value rule was the enormous expense of making appraisals.[22]

[20] Brief for the U.S., *amicus curiae*, in *Driscoll* v. *Edison Light and Power Co.*, 307 U.S. 104 (1939), pp. 37–38, 41.

[21] Numerous instances are pointed out in *ibid.*, pp. 47ff.:

"The *Ohio Bell Telephone* case, 301 U.S. 292, was in process of adjudication about fourteen years. The Missouri Public Service Commission required over eight years to reach a determination in its proceedings against the Union Electric Light and Power Company, 17 P.U.R. (N.S.) 337; and over seven years in its proceedings against the Ozark Utilities Company, 18 P.U.R. (N.S.) 408. . . . The New York Public Service Commission consumed at least five years in determining reasonable rates for the Long Island Lighting Company, 18 P.U.R. (N.S.) 65. . . .

"The proceedings before the Illinois Commerce Commission to determine rates for the Illinois Bell Telephone Company, initiated in September, 1921, did not reach a final conclusion until twelve and a half years later, in 1934. See *Lindheimer* v. *Illinois Bell Telephone Co.*, 292 U.S. 151. More than ten of these years were consumed in litigation in the federal courts subsequent to the Illinois Commission's findings in the case. The *New York Telephone Company* case was instituted in 1920 and determined by the New York Public Service Commission in 1924; yet it was not until 1934 that the case was finally settled."

[22] These burdens were graphically described by Harry Booth, General Counsel of the Illinois Commerce Commission, as follows:

"In connection with a case recently decided by the Illinois Commerce Commission, the Illinois Bell Telephone Company spent $1,200,000 in preparation of a state-wide appraisal, and this was subsequent to huge expenditures in the *Chicago Telephone* Case. In proceedings . . . involving the Commonwealth Edison Company of Chicago, the company's expenditures totaled approximately $1,000,000, a large part of which was for appraisals; and the People's Gas Light & Coke Company, also of Chicago, spent in excess of $750,000, more than $600,000 of which was for appraisal purposes. By some authorities it is stated that a complete reproduction cost appraisal may be expected to cost from one-half of a per cent to one per cent of the reproduction cost of the property in question. . . ." (Quoted in *ibid.*, pp. 53–54.)

The costly, almost interminable character of valuation proceedings favored utilities in their struggle against effective regulation.[23] As one Pennsylvania utility lobbyist put it, "The public will sooner or later get tired of spending money for costs, and it is to our advantage to increase the costs." [24]

To avoid protracted and expensive litigation, some commissions virtually abandoned formal rate proceedings. Particularly after the onset of the Great Depression in 1929, many turned to negotiation, hoping to secure reductions by mutual agreement. Some concessions were obtained, especially when the utility feared injury to its public relations if rate reductions were not forthcoming, or where it seemed probable that a formal proceeding would cut more deeply into utility profits than would a negotiated reduc-

[23] Testimony before the New York Commission on the Revision of Public Utility Laws in 1930 illustrates a by no means uncommon situation:

"A case is brought before the Commission by complainants who put in such evidence as they can gather. As the public generally has little money available for the hire of experts, the evidence is probably meager. The company replies that it must have time to make a valuation of its plant to determine what it is entitled to earn. They take from two to six months, perhaps more. They present it with experts getting perhaps $200 a day. The public has not the resources to meet such a case but does the best it can. More time elapses while the public representatives attempt to consider and answer the company's evidence. Then the Commission attempts to digest some thousands of pages of evidence and makes its order.

"This does not end the case. If the Commission does not grant eight per cent on what the company claims as its valuation, the company appeals to the Federal Court. Some courts will act like a nickel in the slot machine, the company drops in its nickel and gets its injunction. A Master is to be appointed to take evidence and it may require months to agree on a Master. Then the Master must try the case de novo. The complainants must spend more money to get experts and the company spends more money. The evidence goes to greater length than in the original case. Then the Master must decide the case himself, must review the great volume of evidence without a corps of assistants.

"Masters are generally inclined to the belief that if evidence is not contradicted it must be believed. That favors the utilities because they can put on witnesses to testify on matters concerning which the public representatives may have neither the knowledge nor the facts to refute. Probably another year elapses in this process and the Master makes his report. Then the statutory Court passes on the Master's report and renders its decision. All this takes time. Then there is an appeal to the Supreme Court, where you take your turn. The case is argued before the Supreme Court and decided. Perhaps five years have elapsed, conditions have changed, new values have been created to be adjudicated, and, besides, the Supreme Court cannot make rates. Only the Public Service Commission can make rates. So the whole proceeding may start over again."

See *Report of Commission*, Legislative Document No. 75 (1930), at p. 272.

[24] *Ibid.*, p. 273.

tion. But most negotiations were not especially successful, since utility companies preferred to stand on their legal rights.

In addition to negotiation, state commissions during the depression also turned to various short cuts in valuation methods. In some instances, an effort was made to avoid new appraisals by applying corrective price indexes to prior accepted valuations in order to arrive at present fair value. But this scheme also met legal obstacles. In 1935, the Maryland Commission's use of such a device was rejected by the Supreme Court as inappropriate, although it was unclear whether the Court objected to Maryland's particular price-index plan or to all such devices.[25] In any case, the net effect was to encourage resort once again to the time-honored but burdensome appraisal methods.

Another device utilized in the effort to secure prompt rate readjustments was legislation authorizing utility commissions to issue temporary rate orders pending a final determination of "fair value." These statutes met bitter utility opposition, and their effective application was delayed by litigation. In 1939, however, the Supreme Court upheld the constitutionality of a Pennsylvania statute authorizing temporary orders based on original cost minus depreciation and providing a recoupment procedure to protect utilities against losses from confiscatory temporary rates.[26]

Court decisions during the 1930's were more favorable to the state commissions and more restrictive of utility claims to "fair value," but the Court resisted efforts to commit it to prudent-investment valuation. In 1933, a majority upheld the rate base established by a commission and rejected utility claims for "going value," but it still reverted to the *Smyth* v. *Ames* rule as the test of confiscation.[27] The next year, the Court again upheld a state commission, holding that the rate reduction ordered would not bring about confiscation, but refused to alter the fair-value rule itself,[28] which was again staunchly reaffirmed in 1935 as embracing both historical cost and reproduction cost.[29] Strenuous efforts were made in 1938 and 1939 to persuade the Court to renounce fair value and to endorse prudent investment, but to no avail.[30]

---

[25] *West* v. *Chesapeake and Potomac Telephone Co.*, 295 U.S. 662.

[26] *Driscoll* v. *Edison Light and Power Co.*, 307 U.S. 104.

[27] *Los Angeles Gas and Electric Corp.* v. *Railroad Commission of California*, 289 U.S. 287.

[28] *Lindheimer* v. *Illinois Bell Telephone Co.*, 292 U.S. 151.

[29] *West* v. *Chesapeake and Potomac Telephone Co.*, 295 U.S. 662.

[30] *Railroad Commission of California* v. *Pacific Gas and Electric Co.*, 302 U.S. 388; *Driscoll* v. *Edison Light and Power Co.*, 307 U.S. 104.

Not until 1942 did the Supreme Court bring to a close the unhappy half-century of judicial participation in rate-making. In that year, in *FPC* v. *Natural Gas Pipeline Co.*,[31] the Court finally, although not explicitly, retired the doctrine of *Smyth* v. *Ames* from active service. The majority did not endorse original cost or prudent investment as the proper rate base,[32] but it did clear a path for regulatory commissions to do so. The ambiguity of some of the crucial phrases in the opinion was cleared up two years later, in *FPC* v. *Hope Natural Gas Co.*,[33] when the Court dispelled any doubts that it had interred the fair-value doctrine. It upheld a valuation made substantially on the basis of original cost but stressed that it was not endorsing, or requiring, any particular method. "It is not the theory but the impact of the rate order which counts. If the total effect of the rate order cannot be said to be unjust or unreasonable, judicial inquiry . . . is at an end. The fact that the method employed to reach that result may contain infirmities is not then important."

While the Court does not now require commissions to adopt any particular method of valuation, and in pursuing its general policy of self-restraint, defers to the expertise of commissions and treats the administrative process with respect, it still reserves the right to review rates and to invalidate them if it finds them to be confiscatory. The standard applied in testing whether rates are confiscatory appears to be one of maintaining the utility's credit, "a standard of finance resting on stubborn facts." [34]

. . . it is important that there be enough revenue not only for operating expenses but also for the capital costs of the business. These include service on the debt and dividends on the stock. . . . By that standard the return to the equity owners should be commensurate with returns on investments in other enterprises having corresponding

[31] 315 U.S. 575.

[32] Once the Court had recognized that value for rate-making is not equivalent to economic value, then it became obvious that the end result of the valuation process was not value but a rate base. "The fixing of prices, like other applications of the police power, may reduce the value of the property being regulated. But the fact that the value is reduced does not mean that the regulation is invalid. It does, however, indicate that 'fair value' is the end product of the process of rate making, not the starting point. . . . The heart of the matter is that rates cannot be made to depend upon 'fair value' when the value of the going enterprise depends on whatever rates may be anticipated." *FPC* v. *Hope Natural Gas Co.*, 320 U.S. 591 (1944) at 601.

[33] *Ibid.*

[34] A description of the Hope standard appearing in *Colorado Interstate Gas Co.* v. *FPC*, 324 U.S. 581 (1945).

risks. That return, moreover, should be sufficient to assure confidence in the financial integrity of the enterprise, so as to maintain its credit and to attract capital.[35]

Thus the courts finally restricted their participation in rate-making, leaving the commissions a much freer rein. In the effort to protect investors against "confiscation," the courts had assumed regulatory responsibilities for which they were ill fitted and contributed to the ineffectiveness of utility regulation. Effective regulation implies the ability to adjust rates in accordance with cyclical fluctuations and technical progress. It further implies a close study of operating costs to promote efficient management. It demands an awareness of marketing problems so that new uses can be discovered and consumption encouraged. The courts are not equipped to perform these functions with promptness and dispatch. They do not have the expert technical facilities on which to base an intelligent judgment. Adequately staffed and competently manned commissions may at least make the effort. But they can make the effort successfully only when the courts provide intelligible legal criteria which permit the commissions a sphere of discretion in which experts can operate.

The Hope decision has led to substantial changes in emphasis on the part of the state commissions in the determination of value. A study in 1954 showed that four states used original cost or prudent investment and did so before the Hope decision; nine still followed Smyth v. Ames, in the main because "fair value" is contained in their legislative standards; eight adopted original cost as the measure of fair value; and nineteen explicitly shifted from fair value to original cost or prudent investment.[36]

The Hope decision has also led the commissions to shift emphasis from the assets side of the balance sheet to the liabilities side. Rate proceedings now tend to center more on the adequacy of rates to maintain the credit of the utility, to ensure fair treatment to its security holders, and to enable it to raise new capital. Where before regulators arrived at a fair—usually about 6 per

[35] FPC v. Hope Natural Gas Co., at 603.

[36] J. R. Rose, "The Hope Case and Public Utility Valuation in the States," Columbia Law Review (February, 1954), p. 212. The Wisconsin commission, taking literally the Hope statement that only "the end result" counts, attempted to do away with the rate base entirely. It set rates so as to produce "a reasonable profit" defined in absolute dollar amounts. The Wisconsin Supreme Court rejected this approach. Commonwealth Telephone Co. v. Wisconsin Public Service Commission, 252 Wis. 481, 73 P.U.R. N.S. 97 (1948).

cent—return on a fair value, now they aim primarily at a return which will cover interest and preferred dividend requirements with enough to spare to yield an attractive but not unnecessarily large return on the common stock. This cost-of-capital approach avoids most of the difficulties inherent in the valuation process, and it can be justified now that most of the water has been wrung out of utility balance sheets and book cost approximates original cost. But it still leaves the commissions with difficult tasks of judgment and estimation. Present interest rates must be computed, and future ones estimated. Future capital needs of the utility must be determined, and future conditions of the capital market estimated. Earnings-price and yield-price ratios for the stock of comparable utilities must be computed and compared. But comparison with other utilities is only of limited assistance in determining reasonable returns for any one utility, since the relative proportions of capital represented by bonds, preferred stock, and common stock and the percentage of profits paid out as common dividends also affect the market evaluation of utility stocks.

This kind of proceeding is shorter and requires fewer tedious calculations than did a proceeding under the *Smyth* v. *Ames* rule, but it requires at least as much judgment. It does not lend itself to precision. The range of possible answers is narrower, but it is still sufficient for one observer to remark that "the controversies engendered between utility and commission witnesses fall short by little in violence from those which characterized rate base theory in the past." [37] In the effort to simplify rate proceedings, a few states have experimented with sliding-scale regulatory schemes, in which rates are automatically adjusted in relation to earnings in a manner designed to reward operating efficiency. These plans, however, depend on agreements between commissions and utilities, and such agreements are not easy to reach or to maintain.

There is considerable variation from state to state in the rate of return allowed utilities. In general, utilities in areas with the highest rates of growth in electric consumption, and hence those with the greatest need for new capital, are allowed the highest rates of return. For example, a computation shows that in the period 1951–1955, New England utilities were allowed, on the average, a return of only 5.08 per cent on total capital, making for a return of 8.39 per cent on their equity, while utilities in the South Central states were permitted a return of 6.94 per cent on

[37] E. W. Clemens, "Some Aspects of the Rate-of-Return Problem," *Land Economics* (February, 1954), p. 32.

total capital and 14.42 per cent on their equity.[38]

In the postwar decade, utility witnesses have increasingly protested the cost-of-capital approach on which the commissions have settled. They point to the long-run inflation which has persisted for over twenty years and argue that it is unfair to hold utility common stock to a return based on book value. Such stock, and the return on it, they claim, should be allowed to reflect general inflation.[39] The commissions have thus far rejected this argument. As the Utah commission put it, "Nor do we believe it was the intention of the legislature . . . to empower or require this Commission to take action that would make utility stockholders free from the impact of the economic forces at work in this country." [40] Defenders of the commissions [41] have argued that the cost-of-capital approach has permitted utilities to raise ample capital, that owners of common stock suffer less from inflation than do owners of preferred stock and of bonds, and that any attempt to reintroduce reproduction cost through the back door would seriously unsettle regulation and strengthen inflationary forces.

The Problem of Interstate Transmission of Electric Power

Still another contributing cause of the ineffectiveness of state commissions in the 1920's was the growing importance of interstate transmission of electricity—an excellent example of how technological change can nullify old regulatory devices and make new regulation imperative. At one time, municipal regulation was adequate, since the early lighting companies were almost entirely confined to single communities. Later, as the industry shifted from direct to alternating current and long-distance transmission became possible, large light and power systems extended their field of operations. The economic changes involved in this technological advance necessitated state-wide regulation. But as the industry developed further and spread across state lines, even state regula-

[38] F. P. Morrissey, "Relation of Growth and Rate of Return for Utilities," *Public Utilities Fortnightly* (September 12, 1957), p. 369.

[39] For examples of such arguments, see the articles reprinted by *Public Utilities Fortnightly*, under the title *Should Cost of Capital Limit a Utility's Return?* (1953); W. A. Morton, "Rate of Return and Value of Money on Public Utilities," *Land Economics* (May, 1952), pp. 91–131.

[40] As quoted in L. W. Thatcher, "Cost-of-Capital Techniques Employed in Determining the Rate of Return for Public Utilities," *Land Economics* (May, 1954), p. 104.

[41] *Ibid.*; Clemens, *op. cit.*; "Reports and Comments," *Land Economics* (February, 1955), pp. 75–79.

tion proved increasingly inadequate.

Before the twenties, interstate transmission of electric power was hardly a problem. By 1928, however, 11.7 per cent of all power generated was transferred across state lines. By 1933, the figure had risen to 17.8 per cent. Meanwhile, the Supreme Court, in a pair of important decisions, had decided that neither a receiving nor a forwarding state could regulate the wholesale distribution of power across state lines, since to do so would burden interstate commerce.[42] These decisions created a no man's land where the states could not act and where the federal government had not acted. Efforts to close this gap during the twenties by invoking federal power were strenuously and successfully opposed by the utilities. The gap remained open until the passage of the Federal Power Act of 1935.

The Problem of the Holding Company

Yet another reason for the ineffectiveness of state regulation was the difficulty of regulating the utility holding companies which developed during this period. While, with one hand, states tried to make their control more effective, with the other many seemed to do their best to nullify control. As states engaged in a competitive race to relax corporate restrictions, holding-company organizers were able to create corporate structures so vast and so complex as to pass inevitably beyond effective state control.

Whatever the motive in developing the holding-company systems, whether to achieve operating economies, to obtain easier access to capital markets, to eliminate competition, to increase profits, or to obtain inexpensive control of vast corporate assets, the result was the frustration of state regulation of the underlying operating companies. State agencies encountered great difficulty in controlling operating companies whose policies were determined by corporate officials outside state jurisdiction. The maze of intercorporate transactions enmeshing operating companies was frequently exempt from any scrutiny or control.[43] The holding

[42] Missouri v. Kansas Natural Gas Co., 265 U.S. 298 (1924); Public Utilities Commission of Rhode Island v. Attleboro Steam and Electric Co., 273 U.S. 83 (1927).

[43] As the New York Public Service Commission pointed out in Re New York State Electric and Gas Corporation, II P.U.R. 1932 E-1-45, at pp. 3, 4:

"Twenty-five years ago, the holding company was . . . used principally for the purpose of centralizing control. In recent years . . . the holding company idea has been utilized to siphon funds from operating utilities into holding companies or their subsidiaries and affiliates which are not subject to public regulation; and, in certain instances, funds have been diverted even

companies themselves were largely immune from regulation. The fees they imposed were part of the expenses of the operating companies and reflected in rates. Though fees were frequently set without arm's-length bargaining, state commissions found it difficult to question them, since the commissions ordinarily lacked control over the holding companies and had no access to their records. Nor were the courts particularly helpful. In 1923, the Supreme Court rebuked efforts of a state commission to reduce the fees paid by an operating subsidiary to its holding company, holding that "the state . . . is not clothed with the general power of management incident to ownership." [44] Not until 1930 did the Court allow a regulatory scrutiny of such operating expenses,[45] and really effective regulation of holding-company transactions remained difficult until the enactment of the federal Public Utility Holding Company Act of 1935.

The second period of electrical utility regulation—the period in which chief reliance was placed on state commissions—thus disclosed many weaknesses and difficulties. Holding companies were inadequately supervised, and as a result, operating utilities under

---

from the holding companies to the pockets of individuals. Payments made to unregulated companies . . . have been charged to operating expenses and frequently so submerged that the fact of such payments and the amount thereof do not appear in any report to stockholders or to regulatory bodies. By such means, operating expenses have been inflated, true profits have been hidden, and regulation of rates has been made extremely difficult. . . .

"Management, construction, service, interbuying and selling, auditing, material purchasing, and like services honestly and efficiently performed by one central organization for a group of similarly situated operating utilities might possibly result in lowered costs to operating utilities. When this is not accomplished, however, and when those who own and control the holding company or the operating utilities also own and control various auxiliary and affiliated corporations and companies, it becomes possible to undermine the operating utilities, to dissipate their profits and surplus, and so to impair their financial standing as to destroy their ability to raise funds for their local needs. . . ."

These and other questionable practices indulged in by some holding-company promoters are fully documented in the elaborate investigation of utility holding companies begun by the FTC in 1928. See FTC, *Utility Corporations*, S. Doc. 92, 70th Cong., 1st sess.

[44] *Missouri ex rel. Southwestern Bell Telephone Co.* v. *Missouri Commission*, 262 U.S. 276.

[45] In that year, the Court requested a lower tribunal to make a specific finding as to the reasonableness of intercompany fees. *Smith* v. *Illinois Bell Telephone Co.*, 282 U.S. 133. A general right of commissions to inquire into intercompany transactions among affiliated companies was later stated in *Western Distributing Co.* v. *Public Service Commission of Kansas*, 285 U.S. 119 (1932).

their control escaped effective regulation. Interstate transmission of electric power was immune from state regulation. The role of the courts in the rate-making process impeded effective regulation. Utility control groups succeeded in limiting the scope and incidence of legislative and administrative action and in persuading many people to accept the view that any strengthening of public control was reprehensible. Analyzed in terms of the fortunes of various parties-in-interest, it seems clear, on the whole, that the balance of power in this phase was heavily in favor of the control groups, with whom other financial interests, management, and allied industrial interests maintained a close community of interest. Up to 1929, there was relatively little evidence of consumer or investor dissatisfaction.

4. New Deal Power Policy

After the financial crash of 1929, complaints from both consumers and investors mounted. While businesses collapsed, unemployment increased, purchasing power shrank, and prices in competitive areas declined, electric rates remained practically unchanged. Consumer demands for reductions went largely unheeded. The pressure on state utility commissions to lower rates increased tremendously, but for the most part, these agencies were unable to afford prompt relief. The weaknesses of existing regulatory practices were strikingly revealed, and consumer support grew for more effective public controls. Evidences of investor dissatisfaction were also soon apparent. With the Insull crash, the debacle of other inflated holding-company structures, investor losses running in the billions of dollars,[46] and revelations that investors were often duped and exploited by holding-company "insiders," a cleavage of interest between the "insiders" or control groups, on the one hand, and the small investors, on the other, became manifest. This latter group added its voice to the growing demand for more effective regulation.

This dissatisfaction—as felt and vocalized by large groups of consumers and investors—contributed to the political overturn

[46] It has been estimated that the hundred thousand stockholders who had the misfortune to own Insull stock lost $4 billion. C. D. Thompson, *Confessions of the Power Trust* (1932), p. 248. Stock in the Middle West Utilities Co. plunged from $57 a share in 1929 to 25 cents in 1932. Stockholders who owned Class A stock in Howard C. Hopson's Associated Gas & Electric Co. saw their shares plummet from $72.62 to 62 cents. M. L. Ramsay, *Pyramids of Power* (1937), p. 81.

of 1932 and provided much of the drive behind the vast New Deal expansion of regulatory authority. Declaring that it was shaping its power policy to protect consumers and small investors, the new administration set out to curb the power of the financial control groups who had hitherto dominated the industry. While the Roosevelt administration sought to consolidate the support of consumers and small investors, the financial control groups, extremely hostile to the Roosevelt power policy, tried to drive a wedge between them by assailing the new policy as a threat to all utility investors. Against this background of struggle a new pattern of regulation emerged.

This third period in the history of electric utility regulation is characterized by national government participation on a major scale. To a certain extent foreshadowed by the Water Power Act of 1920 and the creation of the Federal Power Commission (FPC), federal regulation did not really become significant until the 1930's. As New Deal power policy crystallized, certain main directions became apparent. First, the use of water-power resources under federal jurisdiction was more strictly supervised than it had been under the 1920 Act, which was amended to vest greater authority in the FPC. Second, a regulatory gap was closed by endowing the FPC with power to control interstate transmission. Third, efforts were made to plan and co-ordinate, under FPC authority, the development and use of power facilities and resources.

Fourth, the power of control groups was restricted and the interests of consumers and investors protected by the Public Utility Holding Company Act of 1935, which provided for stringent regulation of holding-company activities and simplification of their structures. Fifth, the publicly owned sector of the power industry was expanded, both through large federal projects such as the Tennessee Valley Authority, Bonneville, and Grand Coulee, and through smaller municipal power plants financed by Public Works Administration grants and loans. Public competition was relied upon to reduce rates and stimulate consumption in the private as well as the public sector of the industry. Sixth, the Rural Electrification Administration was created to promote rural electrification projects, and an Electric Home and Farm Authority was established to encourage consumption by financing the sale of electric appliances. Seventh, state regulation was strengthened both by the simplification of holding-company structures and by making the information, facilities, and aid of federal power agencies available to the states.

5. Federal Power Commission—
Background and Development

The movement for the conservation of water-power resources and for their development under federal control and regulation antedates the New Deal. But before that movement became effective, some of the best power sites in the public domain had been practically given away. The national government was slow to assert control over water-power developments on public lands and reservations and on navigable waters. Before 1896, land patents in the public domain were issued without any special recognition of potential hydroelectric uses. Not until 1890 was specific congressional authorization required for dams on navigable streams, and not until 1906 did Congress pass the first General Dam Act, requiring water-power developments on navigable streams to be approved by the Chief of Army Engineers and the Secretary of War, who could make special stipulations in the interest of navigation.

Beginning about 1905, the issue of federal control of future hydroelectric developments became acute. With the growth of the conservation movement, pre-existing congressional policies were severely criticized.[47] During the next decade, the contest over

[47] "We are now," said President Theodore Roosevelt, in vetoing the Rainey River Bill in 1908, "at the beginning of great development in water power. Its use through electrical transmission is entering more and more largely into . . . the daily life of the people. Already the evils of monopoly are becoming manifest; already the experience of the past shows the necessity of caution in making unrestricted grants of this great power. . . . in place of the present haphazard policy of permanently alienating valuable public property we should substitute a definite policy along the following line:

"First, There should be a limited or carefully guarded grant in the nature of an option or opportunity afforded within reasonable time for development of plans and for execution of the project.

"Second, Such a grant of concession should be accompanied . . . by a provision expressly making it the duty of a designated official to annul the grant if the work is not begun or plans are not carried out in accordance with the authority granted.

"Third, It should also be the duty of some designated official to see to it that in approving the plans the maximum development of the navigation and power is assured, or at least that . . . the plans . . . may not be developed as ultimately to interfere with the better utilization of the water or complete development of the power.

"Fourth, There should be a license fee or charge which, though small or nominal at the outset, can in the future be adjusted so as to secure a control in the interest of the public.

"Fifth, Provision should be made for the termination of the grant or

water-power legislation continued. The conservationists demanded strict regulation of water-power grants along the lines marked out by President Roosevelt in his Rainey River veto message, while the power interests sought freedom from control. The latter tried to muster public support by mobilizing states' rights sentiment against federal expansion and by capitalizing the desire of the South and the public-domain states of the West for rapid water-power development.

After a protracted struggle, the Federal Water Power Act of 1920 was enacted. Although ostensibly a victory for the conservationists, it bore many marks of compromise and its administration was to disclose serious weaknesses. The Act established a Federal Power Commission composed of the Secretaries of War, Interior, and Agriculture—all serving ex officio—with the authority to license water-power developments on public lands, on reservations, or on any navigable waters subject to national jurisdiction. Licenses could be granted to either public agencies or private interests, though the Act gave preference to states or municipalities when their plans seemed equally well adapted to conserving and utilizing navigation and water resources. The Act provided for a maximum license period of fifty years, after which the government could recapture the site and property on payment to the licensee of its "net investment" (actual legitimate investment, plus sever-

---

privilege at a definite time, leaving to future generations the power or authority to renew or extend the concession in accordance with the conditions which may prevail at that time." (*Congressional Record*, 60th Cong., 1st sess., pp. 4698–4699.)

This manifesto of the conservation movement was followed by a second Rooseveltian blast in the James River veto message of 1909:

"The great corporations are acting with foresight, singleness of purpose, and vigor to control the water powers of the country. . . . They are demanding legislation for unconditional grants in perpetuity of land for reservoirs, conduits, powerhouses, and transmission lines to replace the existing statute which authorized the administrative officers of the Government to impose conditions to protect the public when any permit is issued. Several bills for that purpose are now pending in both Houses. . . .

"The new legislation sought in their own interest by some companies in the West, and the opposition of other companies in the East to proposed legislation in the public interest, have a common source and a common purpose. Their source is the rapidly growing water-power combination. Their purpose is a centralized monopoly of hydro-electric power development free of all public control. It is obvious that a monopoly of power in any community calls for strict public supervision and regulation.

"I esteem it my duty to use every endeavor to prevent this growing monopoly, the most threatening which has ever appeared, from being fastened upon the people of this nation." (H. Doc. 1330, 60th Cong., 2nd sess.)

ance damages, less depreciation and amortization). The Act also prescribed for licensees a system of accounting designed to facilitate the determination of actual legitimate costs and to ensure against write-ups or other inflation of the capital structure. Provision was also made for reasonable annual charges to cover the cost of administering the Act and for use of government land and property. Where the licensee's rates, services, and securities were not subject to state regulation, these regulatory functions were entrusted to the FPC.

Its pre-New Deal history indicated little disposition by the FPC to use its regulatory authority with vigor. The Commission was subjected to considerable pressure from the power interests, and it was not prepared to resist. The administrations of the twenties did not favor stringent regulation, and the FPC reflected the dominant sentiment of the period. Weakness in interpreting and enforcing the Act was manifest. Faulty organization and administrative difficulties also hampered the FPC. An ex officio Commission, composed of Cabinet officers with many other responsibilities, worked badly. Personnel was inadequate; the Commission had to depend in large part upon employees loaned by the War, Interior, and Agriculture Departments, and these were usually poorly equipped to perform the specialized engineering and accounting work required by the Act. Because of these weaknesses, the FPC was reorganized in 1930 as an independent body of five full-time members, empowered to recruit its own staff. But it continued to be embroiled in difficulties. Its membership was predominantly conservative, and its water-power policies were from the start severely criticized by Senate progressives.

Under the New Deal, changes were made in the Commission's leading personnel, and a new conception of the FPC's powers and responsibilities emerged. This changed spirit was soon evident in a more rigorous supervision of licensees, particularly in controlling accounting practices and in determining actual legitimate costs of licensed projects. The new attitude was also evident in efforts to expand FPC jurisdiction. These efforts were greatly advanced in 1940, when, in U.S. v. Appalachian Electric Power Co.[48] the Supreme Court adopted an extremely broad interpretation of the FPC's powers, holding that a stream is subject to federal authority even if it is not now navigable but can be made so by "reasonable" improvements, or if a substantial part of it is navigable. It further held that this power is not limited to control for navigation but

[48] 311 U.S. 377. Forty-one states entered the case as *amici curiae* to oppose this expansion of federal powers.

may extend to other purposes. The FPC also tried to breathe life into the statutory preference for public rather than private development of water-power resources. The Federal Power Act of 1935, by adding some clarifying amendments to the 1920 law, reinforced FPC control over water-power resources and buttressed its supervision of licensees.

The Act of 1935 also extended the authority of the Commission into new fields. Regulation of interstate transmission of electric energy was established, and the FPC was given certain powers to bring about co-ordination of utility systems through interconnection of facilities and interchange of energy.

FPC powers over utilities engaged in interstate commerce are extensive. It may fix wholesale rates and charges for interstate transmission. It controls security issues and assumptions of corporate liabilities by utilities engaged in interstate commerce and not regulated by state commissions. It also regulates mergers and sales of property, interlocking directorates, services, accounts, records, and depreciation of utilities under its jurisdiction.

These FPC powers, together with its authority over the interstate transportation and sale of natural gas, conferred on it by the Natural Gas Act of 1938,[49] closed an important gap in the regulatory structure. The Commission now can prevent interstate companies from charging exorbitant wholesale rates to intrastate distributing companies. It can also prevent interstate companies from discriminating in favor of consumers in one state at the expense of those in another.

The FPC does not, however, wield any direct control over local rates; that power is reserved to the states. The Act of 1935 supplemented rather than superseded state regulation. It sought to make state regulation more effective, and to facilitate co-operation between the FPC and state commissions. On the request of a state commission, the FPC is authorized to investigate and determine the generating and transmission costs of companies under its jurisdiction and to turn over to a state commission these data, as well as other information and reports helpful to state utility regulation. It may, on the request of a state commission, lend its experts for use in state proceedings. The Act further authorizes the Commission to determine the actual legitimate cost of the property of utilities subject to its jurisdiction. This information may not only promote more efficient state regulation of rates, but may also be of considerable assistance in the regulation of securities issues, mergers, and consolidations. In

[49] See Chapter 21.

an effort to carry out these responsibilities and render aid to state agencies, comprehensive factual data about all aspects of the power industry have been assembled by the FPC staff and made widely available.

The Commission has tried to prevent duplication and conflict with the state agencies. The Act authorizes it to hold joint hearings or conferences with any state commission on matters of common interest. It provides for the establishment of joint boards and agreements to standardize regulations. These co-operative procedures have been widely used in adjusting the regulatory pattern to the demands of the federal system. At one time, the most notable example of conflicting state and federal regulation was found in accounting regulations. Now the FPC, collaborating with the National Association of Railroad and Utilities Commissioners, has worked out a uniform system of accounts widely adopted by the states. Thus there appear to be no insuperable barriers to the adjustment of the respective federal and state jurisdictions, and FPC assistance has made state regulation more effective.

The Federal Power Act also charges the FPC with the positive function of planning the interconnection and co-ordination of power facilities. The Commission is directed to divide the country into regional power districts and to encourage voluntary interconnection within and between these districts. In arranging its regional districts, it is required to consult with the state commissions concerned. Upon application by a state commission or a utility, the FPC may order a company under its jurisdiction to provide additional interconnection for the sale of power in interstate commerce; but it may issue an order only if it finds such action necessary or appropriate in the public interest and if no undue burden is placed upon the utility concerned. The Commission may not compel the enlargement of generating facilities for the purpose of interchanging power nor may it require the utility to sell or exchange energy, if to do so would impair its ability to serve its own customers. The FPC can also prohibit exports of electricity to a foreign country.

To base such a positive and ambitious program largely on voluntary compliance evokes echoes of the unhappy experiences of the ICC in vainly attempting to promote voluntary consolidation of the railroads under the Transportation Act of 1920.[50] And, in fact, intercompany jealousies and rivalries have sometimes presented serious obstacles. Moreover, one unforeseen con-

[50] See Chapter 10.

sequence of the 1935 Act was that some companies tried to end their interstate connections so as to escape FPC control, and other utilities have requested permission to establish interconnections only on a temporary basis for emergency use in order to evade FPC jurisdiction.

However, since interconnections enable utilities to meet peak demands with less generating plant, protect them against the consequences of generating breakdowns, and thus offer obvious economic advantages, the FPC has enjoyed considerable success in promoting voluntary interconnections. In a typical year, the FPC completes several reports showing the economic and technical advantages of proposed interconnections and releases them to utilities, state commissions, federal power agencies, and other interested parties. Most of these reports are eventually accepted and put into effect. In addition, the FPC can use its authority over the transfer of facilities by sale or merger and over the intercompany acquisition of securities to foster some piecemeal co-ordination. Finally, during war or emergency, the FPC has the power to compel emergency interconnections, and a number were ordered during World War II.

6. Regulation of Holding Companies

Federal control of public utility holding companies was preceded by an elaborate process of investigation. In 1928, the Senate ordered the Federal Trade Commission to undertake a comprehensive survey of the public utility industry which accumulated over eighty volumes of testimony and materials.[51] Subsequently, a House committee sponsored a study of holding companies.[52] The 1932 Democratic platform called for full federal regulation of these companies. In 1935, the National Power Policy Committee, headed by Interior Secretary Harold Ickes, recommended regulatory legislation. Its report, and the covering letter which the President sent with it to Congress, reveal four general objectives which the administration had in mind in proposing holding-company legislation:

(1) The proponents of legislation wished to diminish concentration of control in the electric and gas industries. "By 1932," the committee's report pointed out, "thirteen large holding com-

---

[51] S. Doc. 92, 70th Cong., 1st sess.

[52] *Report on the Relation of Holding Companies to Operating Companies in Power and Gas Affecting Control*, H.R. 827, 73d Cong., 2nd sess.

pany groups controlled three-fourths of the entire privately owned electric utility industry, and more than forty per cent was concentrated in the hands of the three largest groups—United Corporation, Electric Bond and Share Company, and Insull." This concentration was regarded by the committee as dangerous to democracy. Pervading the report was the fear of bigness, fear of the "Money Power," a Brandeisian yearning for independent enterprise which was expressed in Roosevelt's statement "that we should take the control and the benefits of the essentially local operating utility industry out of a few financial centers and give back that control and those benefits to the localities which produce the business and create the wealth. We can properly favor economically independent business, which stands on its own feet and diffuses power and responsibility among the many, and frown upon those holding companies which, through interlocking directorates and other devices, have given tyrannical power and exclusive opportunity to a favored few." [53]

(2) The proponents also argued that state and federal regulation could succeed only if the power and the scope of holding-company influence were limited. Again, to quote from Roosevelt: "Regulation has small chance of ultimate success against the kind of concentrated wealth and economic power which holding companies have shown the ability to acquire. . . . No government effort can be expected to carry out effective, continuous, and intricate regulation of the kind of private empires within the Nation which the holding company device has proved capable of creating." [54] Dismemberment of the holding-company structures into smaller units, the President argued, would make them more amenable to regulation.

(3) Nonintegrated holding companies were opposed because they served no demonstrably useful and necessary purpose, such as the achievement of operating economies resulting from economically and geographically integrated public utility systems.

(4) The proponents also wished to raise the standards of corporate finance and management. To this end, holding companies were to be watched over and regulated in all their activities in order to put an end to the predatory practices which had enabled control groups to exploit consumers and small investors.

Few pieces of legislation have been the focus of as intense controversy as the Public Utility Holding Company Act of 1935.

---

[53] *The Public Papers and Addresses of Franklin D. Roosevelt*, Vol. 4 (1938), p. 101.

[54] *Ibid.*, p. 100.

During the debate, Congress was inundated with telegrams and letters from every section of the country intended to demonstrate that investors were solidly opposed to the bill. This tactic boomeranged, however, when investigation showed that much of the supposed investor opposition was synthetic—manufactured by the holding companies themselves.[55] The President entered the fray in a message seeking to arouse investors against what he termed holding-company propaganda. "I have watched the use of the investor's money to make the investor believe that the efforts of the government to protect him are designed to defraud him." [56] After a prolonged struggle, in the course of which some modifications were made in the original bill, the Holding Company Act was finally passed.

It is a reflection both of the intensity of public reaction against previous holding-company abuses and of the vigor with which the administration pressed the bill that the Act was probably the most stringent regulatory statute ever applied to a sector of the American economy. It certainly went farther than any other measure in requiring the wholesale reorganization of corporate structures and the divestiture of property. The Act's powers, conferred on the Securities and Exchange Commission (SEC), were made as sweeping and broad as were the abuses they were to end. The SEC was given far more opportunity for flexible administration than most regulatory agencies. But it of course was not in the position of starting out with a clean slate to design an ideal corporate structure for the utility industry. It inherited an exising structure with all its entrenched arrangements, expectations, and interests. While much of it was a hang-over from past improper financing and needed to be reformed, it could not be fundamentally modified at one fell swoop. The Act itself recognized the necessity that many readjustments would have to be molecular and interstitial rather than grandiose and spectacular. For, in addition to providing for wholesale reorganization of corporate structures and regrouping of physical properties, it also provided for less conspicuous day-to-day improvements in connection with new security issues, accounting practices, service arrangements, and supervision of intercompany transactions.

The Act applied to all electric and gas holding companies and to their subsidiaries, affiliates, and service companies. A holding company was defined as one holding 10 per cent or more of the voting stock of an operating company or another holding com-

[55] See *Hearings*, Senate Special Committee to Investigate Lobbying Activities, S. Res. 165, 74th Cong., 1st sess.

[56] *The Public Papers* . . . Vol. 4 (1938), p. 98.

pany, or which had a "controlling influence over the management or policies" of such companies. Wholly intrastate companies and primarily operating companies with holdings of contiguous properties were exempted.

The first step in the regulatory process was registration. The Act required all holding companies subject to it to register with the SEC before December 1, 1935, on pain of being forbidden to use the mails or engage in interstate commerce if they did not comply. Registration consisted of filing a statement embodying information on corporate organization, structure, securities outstanding, balance sheets, income statements, and other similar data. Having registered, holding companies were then subject to comprehensive regulation, reorganization, and divestment by the SEC. The strongest powers conferred on the SEC were those contained in Section 11, the "death sentence" provisions, which directed the Commission to require the physical integration and corporate simplification of holding-company systems. In addition, the SEC was given control over issuance of securities, acquisition of securities and utility assets, service, sales, and construction contracts and other intercompany transactions, and reports and accounts.

Under Section 11, it was the duty of the SEC, as soon as practicable after January 1, 1938, to require every registered holding company, first, to limit its operation to a single integrated public utility system "and to such other businesses as are reasonably incidental, or economically necessary or appropriate to the operations of such integrated public utility system"; and, second, to "take such steps as the Commission shall find necessary to ensure that the corporate structure or continued existence of any company in the holding company system does not unduly or unnecessarily complicate the structure, or unfairly or inequitably distribute voting power among security holders, of such holding company system." Under the first, or integration, provisions, the Commission might, however, permit a registered holding company to continue to control one or more additional integrated public utility systems if it found that:

(A) Each of such additional systems cannot be operated as an independent system without the loss of substantial economies which can be secured by the retention of control by such holding company of such system;

(B) All of such additional systems are located in one state, or in adjoining states, or in a contiguous foreign country; and

(C) The continued combination of such systems under the control of such holding company is not so large (considering the state of the art and the area or region affected) as to impair the advantages of localized management, efficient operation, or the effectiveness of regulation.

The second, or "anti-pyramiding," provision made it mandatory that there be no holding company beyond the second degree. An operating company thus could have no more than two tiers of holding companies above it, and the SEC might require even further simplification of corporate structures.

These provisions conferred great power on the SEC, but they also bristled with difficulties. What was a "single integrated public utility system"? What businesses were "reasonably incidental, or economically necessary or appropriate to the operation of such integrated public utility systems"? When was a system "so large as to impair the advantages of localized management, efficient operation, or the effectiveness of regulation"? The imprecision of these phrases indicates the range of discretion vested in the SEC in its mandate to reorganize the utility industry.

The SEC began its difficult task in a hostile environment. Judicial vetoes of major New Deal programs in 1935 and 1936 led the holding companies to believe that they could persuade the courts that the Act of 1935 was unconstitutional, and in 1935 a lower court did so find it.[57] Accordingly, most of the companies refused to register. Not until March 28, 1938, did the Supreme Court rule on the issue; it then upheld the registration provisions of the Act but declined to rule on its other provisions.[58] Within a week, virtually all holding companies had registered, but they continued to contest the constitutionality of the remainder of the Act, especially its death-sentence section, thereby further delaying reorganizations. In 1943, a circuit court upheld the Act.[59] The Supreme Court agreed to hear the issue, but lack of a quorum, because several justices disqualified themselves, delayed a hearing for almost three years. Only in 1946 did the Supreme Court finally sustain the Act as a whole. In so doing, it rejected arguments that a holding company was not engaged in interstate commerce and that the requirements of Section 11 amounted to the taking of property without due proc-

---

[57] In Re American States Public Service Co., 12 F. Supp. 667. This decision was later rejected by a circuit court in Burco, Inc. v. Whitworth, 81 F. 2d 721 (1936).

[58] Electric Bond & Share Co. v. SEC, 303 U.S. 419.

[59] North American Co. v. SEC, 133 F. 2d 148.

ess of law.[60]

Most companies, anticipating such a ruling, had begun to comply with SEC requirements before 1946, but it was not until the legal issues had been clarified that the SEC could count on sufficient industry co-operation to begin applying the death sentence provisions. It approached its task with caution. Its conciliatory policy and willingness to recognize that integration and simplification were an essentially evolutionary process assuaged some of the bitterness of the Act's opponents. The case load was heavy. In the nineteen years from 1938 to 1957, a total of 2,335 companies registered with the SEC. They included 219 holding companies, 1,009 electric and gas operating utilities, and 1,110 other subsidiary companies in holding-company systems. Among the latter were brickworks, laundries, orchards, theaters, and even a baseball club.[61]

The Commission invited holding companies to submit voluntary reorganization plans providing for the divestment of non-integrated companies and properties. When these plans were unacceptable, it modified them or issued its own reorganization orders. The 1935 Act did not specify how divestment was to be accomplished, and the SEC permitted many methods. Some holding companies sold on the market the operating company securities they held, or distributed them to their own stockholders. Others sold properties to other holding companies, to independent operators, or to governmental agencies. The SEC carefully scrutinized all disposals. Capital structures were overhauled and reorganized, as the SEC wrung out water, strengthened depreciation reserves, increased the ratio of equity to debt, insisted upon competitive bidding for new securities, and generally buttressed the financial stability of the regulated companies.

In its definition of an integrated system which might be retained by a holding company, some general principles emerged.[62] The primary requisite was that the system be physically interconnected and that substantial interchanges of power actually occur. The size of approved systems varied greatly, ranging from 1 square mile to about 175,000. As technological advances in transmission developed, the SEC expanded its definition of permissible size. It did not go deeply into the question of the effec-

----

[60] *North American Co.* v. *SEC*, 318 U.S. 750 (1943); 327 U.S. 686 (1946).
[61] SEC, *The Work of the Securities and Exchange Commission* (1957), p. 16.
[62] This discussion of SEC interpretations of the Act owes much to R. F. Ritchie, *Integration of Public Utility Holding Companies* (1954).

tiveness of local regulation in approving systems, but it did try to promote local control and management of operating companies.

In dealing with requests of holding companies to retain additional systems, the SEC had to interpret Clauses A, B, and C, quoted above. It read Clause A as requiring a showing that important, not minimal, diseconomies would result from a severance. Clause B, the so-called "Big B," was used to dismember the more sprawling holding-company empires before other sections of the Act were applied. The SEC gave this clause a single-area interpretation, requiring additional, retained properties to be in states adjoining those in which the principal system was located. (Holding companies had urged a two-area interpretation of this somewhat ambiguous clause, unsuccessfully arguing that it permitted retention of additional systems in any one state or adjoining states, no matter how far removed from the principal system.) Clause C was regarded as subordinate to the first two clauses; if an additional system survived the tests imposed by Clause B and then A, it seldom encountered difficulty in passing the requirements of Clause C. This clause was, however, sometimes applied to limit the size of the additional, retained systems, and the issue of local management was given more weight than questions of efficient operation and effective regulation.

Despite fears that sweeping divestments would cost security holders much of the value of their holdings, most of the loss in market value had already occurred by 1935, and property and security divestments in themselves did not generally penalize investors. SEC enforcement of other provisions of the 1935 Act, moreover, considerably enhanced the financial stability of the holding-company systems. Aided by steadily increasing demand for electric power, both holding companies and their operating subsidiaries entered the postwar era in much improved financial condition. Where in 1940, for example, almost $2 billion of their preferred stock was in arrears, all arrears had been eliminated by the mid-1950's and over $1.1 billion in write-ups had been erased, with another $500 million in the process of amortization. In 1935, holding-company systems earned their income deductions plus preferred dividend requirements only 1.23 times. In 1955, the average for registered electric holding companies was 2.73 times.[63]

The Commission's integration and simplification program is

[63] SEC, *Annual Report, 1956*, pp. 158–159.

virtually complete. By June 30, 1957, only 22 holding-company systems, containing 293 companies, were still registered with the SEC, and only 16 systems were expected to remain subject to the Act indefinitely. Thus 2,042 companies, after having been registered, had been released from SEC jurisdiction.[64] The non-utility companies have been cut loose from utility systems; most operating utilities have been freed from holding-company control and returned to independent management and ownership; and a few holding companies have transformed themselves into investment companies.

Thus most of the purposes of the 1935 legislation have been achieved, with the bulk of the task completed between 1940 and 1952. The major portion of the electric and gas utility industry is now free of holding-company control, and the concentration of economic power which once existed has been shattered. Where in 1935 the fifteen largest electric systems controlled 80 per cent of all electric-energy generation and 98.5 per cent of all interstate transmission of electricity, in 1957 it was estimated that the holding-company systems to remain permanently under SEC jurisdiction would control only about one-fifth of the industry.[65] Governmental power, exercised by a vigorous commission brought into being by a political leadership which articulated the strongly felt grievances of investors and consumers, was used to dilute private economic power. But the dramatic success of the SEC in correcting and preventing holding-company abuses and in freeing operating companies from holding-company control, while essential to effective regulation, does not guarantee it. The day-by-day task of seeking this objective remains a responsibility divided among many regulatory agencies and involves the endless task of striking fine political, economic, and legal balances in an environment of rapid technological and social change.

7. Public Ownership and National Power Policy

Another significant aspect of New Deal power policy was the impetus given to public ownership. To a large degree, this extension of government into the ownership and operation of power facilities was unplanned. Of the largest government power agency, the Tennessee Valley Authority, one observer has concluded that "The process by which TVA evolved as a great electric power

[64] SEC, *The Work of the Securities and Exchange Commission*, pp. 16–17.
[65] *Loc. cit.*

utility was a gradual one, with no one step calculated to produce the end result achieved." [66] Furthermore, since most federal power projects have been based on the use of hydroelectric facilities which are part of multipurpose projects also serving such ends as flood control, irrigation, and navigation, the production of electricity has seldom been the exclusive reason for initiating a power project, and often it has only been an auxiliary by-product. Nevertheless, public power projects and their progeny of public power agencies, both federal and local, have had a considerable impact on the private electric companies; this regulatory and competitive impact has often been one of the purposes of such projects. While the TVA has come to symbolize this New Deal policy in the public mind, public power activities have by no means been confined to the Tennessee Valley. Bonneville and Grand Coulee in the Columbia River Valley, the Hoover and lesser dams on the Lower Colorado, the Fort Peck and other dams in the Missouri Basin, the Southwestern Power Administration and the Southeastern Power Administration, the St. Lawrence projects at Niagara Falls and at the International Rapids, and many others bear witness to the rapid spread of large-scale hydroelectric developments.

In addition, the New Deal initiated some programs to expand public or co-operative distribution of power at the local level. To this end, the Public Works Administration (PWA) made loans and grants of over $200 million to local public bodies for the construction of distribution or generating facilities. The Rural Electrification Administration, still in existence, was established to make loans to co-operatives and public bodies for the construction and operation of facilities to serve rural areas, then largely neglected by private companies.

Behind the support thus extended to public ownership lay a mixture of motives. While there was little disposition to press for the socialization of the entire power industry, there was evident in New Deal power policy a well-defined desire to preserve future water-power projects for public exploitation and development and to use public power projects as a device for regulating private power companies. This desire was rooted in dissatisfaction with previous utility regulation—a dissatisfaction which focused on high rates, low utilization, and limited availability of electricity. Through public competition or the threat of competition, the argument went, rates could be reduced and

[66] R. C. Martin, "Retrospect and Prospect," in R. C. Martin (ed.), *TVA: The First Twenty Years* (1956), p. 267.

increased consumption stimulated. Public credit could help make electricity available in rural areas hitherto without this service. New public power projects, moreover, had an added attraction. To an administration intent on combating depression, power projects commended themselves as useful public works which could provide expanded employment. In some cases, as in multi-purpose projects of the TVA variety, where the power aspects were simply one phase of a broader program of regional planning and development, the very nature of the undertaking seemed to make public sponsorship imperative.

The TVA, a major storm center of the New Deal power policy [67] and still a live political issue, well illustrates many of these motivating drives, the way in which the power program grew, and the impact of public power on private companies. The Tennessee Valley Authority Act, as approved in 1933 and amended in 1935, marked an important milestone in the development of national power policy. In terms of the parties-in-interest analysis, the legislative mandate was clear. The TVA was directed to thow its weight on the side of the consumer—the potential as well as the actual consumer. The statement of policy in the Act was explicit:

. . . projects . . . shall be considered primarily as for the benefit of the people of the section as a whole and *particularly the domestic and rural consumers* to whom the power can economically be made available, and accordingly that sale to and use by industry shall be a secondary purpose, to be utilized principally to secure a sufficient high load factor and revenue returns which will permit *domestic and rural use* at the lowest possible rates and in such manner as to encourage increased domestic and rural use of electricity. . . . [italics supplied]

The TVA had even wider implications. Itself a venture in large-scale public ownership and operation, it was directed to encourage the public ownership of distributive facilities. The Act authorized the Authority in selling surplus power, not used in its operations, to "give preference to states, counties, municipalities, and cooperative organizations of citizens or farmers, not organized or doing business for profit, but primarily for the purpose of supplying electricity to its own citizens or members. . . ." Implicit in these statutory directions was the making of a new force in the determination of public policy—the welding together of a public power bloc composed of the TVA, its em-

[67] See Chapter 24 for a further discussion of the TVA.

ployees, and the network of communities which enjoy its benefits and fall within its sphere of influence. The Act thus built up a vested interest in support of public ownership; it laid the basis for a new party-in-interest in electricity, an organized and coherent body of public power exponents capable of mustering considerable political power.

The TVA Act had still another important aspect—its regulatory impact upon privately owned utilities. TVA operations, it was felt, would invite comparisons with privately owned utilities. The very existence of the TVA and the fear that it might be imitated in other parts of the country might stimulate private companies to pursue rate and service policies calculated to dispel dissatisfaction with private ownership. It was this regulatory potentiality that President Roosevelt had in mind in his address at Tupelo, Mississippi, where the first contract for TVA power was signed, when he said: "I can use you as a text—a text that may be useful to many other parts of the nation, because people's eyes are upon you, and because what you are doing here is going to be copied in every state in the union before we get through." TVA rates, added the President, would serve as a "yardstick" to measure the fairness of private utility rates and would help to reduce them where they were unreasonable.

In inaugurating its program, the TVA took over existing power facilities at Muscle Shoals, whose construction was begun to meet World War I needs for explosives. Much of the power generated there had been sold to the Commonwealth and Southern System, which served most of the Valley. With the TVA prepared to build new dams and generate additional power, the problem of the disposition of this power became important. The utilities in the region would, of course, have preferred to have the TVA sell them its power in bulk, leaving distribution and the fixing of retail rates in the hands of the private companies. But this the TVA was not prepared to do, and in fact could not do under the terms of its Act, which directed it to give preference to municipalities and farmers' co-operatives. Rather than duplicate existing private transmission and distribution systems, the TVA tried to buy them out or to encourage municipalities to purchase local distribution systems. At one time early in 1934, it negotiated an agreement with Commonwealth and Southern providing for such purchases within a defined area and establishing a division of territory.

The effectuation of this division of territory agreement, however, met frustrating obstacles. The TVA and the municipalities

attempted to buy utility property at its original cost less depreciation, but the utilities asked for prices representing the capitalized
value of their earning power. Negotiations proved fruitless, and
the utilities, under the leadership of Commonwealth and Southern, struck back against what they felt to be a menace to their
existence. They erected "spite lines" to skim the cream off rural
areas where the TVA was trying to establish rural electrification
co-operatives. They attempted to block TVA expansion with lawsuits. The sale of some Alabama and Tennessee utility properties
to the TVA was held up until early 1936, when the Supreme
Court, in *Ashwander* v. *TVA*,[68] affirmed the validity of the sales
contracts and the constitutionality of the TVA's authority to
dispose of power generated at Muscle Shoals.

After the Ashwander decision, the TVA, with Norris Dam
about to begin generating, again attempted to negotiate an agreement with the utilities in order to distribute its power. Commonwealth and Southern offered to surrender certain areas to the
TVA, including generation, transmission, and distribution facilities, if the Authority would confine its operations to those areas.
As an alternative, the company offered to transfer all its southeastern generating and transmission facilities to the TVA, provided that it received the exclusive right to distribute TVA power.
Neither of these propositions was acceptable to the Authority.
Instead, it suggested a southeastern power pool of both public
and private agencies which would offer a uniform pool gateway
rate to all distributing systems, whether private or public, and
which would permit municipalities to decide whether they preferred to own their own distributing facilities and purchase TVA
power, or be served by privately owned companies. To this scheme,
Commonwealth and Southern objected on the ground that it
gave them no protection against municipal competition. Negotiations continued, including a meeting at the White House. But
the truce came to an abrupt end when Commonwealth and Southern again appealed to the courts, applying for and receiving a
sweeping injunction which, in effect, brought about the virtual
suspension of all TVA power activities.

Charging lack of good faith, the TVA broke off negotiations
with Commonwealth and Southern, and adopted more aggressive marketing policies. Contracts were made with other power
companies and with large industrial users. Applications from municipalities already served by private companies were welcomed,

[68] 297 U.S. 288.

and many applicants, including the cities of Knoxville, Chattanooga, and Memphis, also applied for PWA loans and grants to build competing distribution systems. Actual construction was held up, however, until early in 1938, when the Supreme Court affirmed the validity of PWA loans and grants, ruling that private utility companies were not immune from lawful competition.[69] This decision, together with a district court ruling favorable to the TVA in the Commonwealth and Southern suit, greatly strengthened the bargaining position of the TVA, since municipalities desiring TVA power were now free to construct their own electrical systems. The TVA then resumed efforts to buy up utility properties, and a number of utilities not connected with Commonwealth and Southern were acquired. A Supreme Court decision early in 1939, holding that the power companies had no standing in court to question the validity of the TVA's power program or the constitutionality of the TVA Act, further reinforced the TVA's position.[70] Within a week Commonwealth and Southern capitulated, agreeing to sell its Tennessee properties to the TVA and to local public agencies and beginning negotiations for the sale of some of its properties in Mississippi and Alabama. Negotiators on both sides made concessions. Altogether, the TVA and its distributors paid $125 million for utility properties.

With the completion of these transactions, one of the most controversial aspects of the TVA power program—its relations with privately owned power companies in the region—became of purely historical interest. Competition in the form of duplication of facilities was largely avoided. The TVA was assured of markets for its power, having carved out a service area covering 80,000 square miles and about double the drainage area of the Tennessee River. In this area live about 5 million people and almost 1½ million electric consumers, whom the TVA serves through 98 municipalities, 51 co-operatives, and 2 small private companies.

Significance of the TVA as a Regulatory Device

The marketing of TVA power has also produced controversy, less sharp but longer lasting. The Authority embarked on a low-rate policy in order to develop its markets rapidly and to maximize consumption. The question whether the wholesale rates it charges its distributors cover its full costs for generating and transmitting

[69] *Alabama Power Co.* v. *Ickes,* 302 U.S. 464.
[70] *Tennessee Electric Power Co.* v. *TVA.,* 306 U.S. 118.

power has long been subject to debate. The rates do more than cover the costs of constructing and operating those facilities used exclusively for power generation and transmission. Whether they also cover a fair share of the joint costs of the dams, which provide navigation and flood control as well as power benefits, depends on how the costs of these multipurpose facilities are allocated among the various purposes served.

Allocation of joint costs is a matter of judgment, and a number of markedly different theories have been advocated. They range from the one extreme of charging power with all joint costs to the other of charging power with no joint costs. The TVA allocates the annual costs (depreciation and maintenance) of the common-purpose property 42 per cent to power, 27 per cent to navigation, and 31 per cent to flood control. Other common expenses, largely administrative, are distributed 40 per cent to power, 30 to navigation, and 30 to flood control.[71] These allocations can be defended; so can others; no allocation will satisfy all parties. On the TVA's basis, the total depreciated investment in power facilities, both single and multipurpose, on June 30, 1957, was $1,467 million, compared with about $300 million in navigation and flood-control facilities. On this power investment, TVA rates produced a return of 4 per cent in fiscal 1957 and over the entire twenty-four-year period of operations. The Government Corporations Appropriation Act of 1948 requires the TVA to repay its power investment to the Treasury within forty years. By 1957, the TVA had repaid $240 million, over twice the amount called for by the schedule of this Act. Another $413 million of net income over the years has been reinvested in power facilities.[72]

If it be assumed that TVA wholesale rates are based upon a reasonable allocation of costs, they clearly have yielded a positive return on the government's investment. While the TVA pays no federal taxes, it and its distributors do pay state or local taxes or make payments in lieu of taxes. If federal taxes were paid, they would reduce its net income, not erase it. Even so,

[71] While the TVA, of course, cannot charge for its flood-control benefits and does not for its navigation benefits, it does compute estimated benefits. By mid-1957, $132 million in estimated direct flood damages had been averted by flood-control facilities with an allocated total cost of $184 million and with a useful life of many more decades. Annual transportation savings in 1956 were estimated to be $20 million compared with annual costs (including depreciation) of $3.8 million. TVA, *Annual Report, 1957*, pp. 16–19, 23–24.

[72] Statistics in this paragraph from *ibid.*, pp. 35–36, A8–A10.

the TVA's wholesale rates cannot be taken as a "yardstick" in the sense of an exact measuring rod by which to measure the fairness of private power rates. The TVA is a venture in public ownership and operation under special joint-cost conditions. Costs of generation, transmission, and distribution vary in different parts of the country; multipurpose projects cannot be compared with single-purpose operations; private companies would have difficulty in writing off a share of joint costs against nonpower purposes; any general comparison between TVA rates and private rates must necessarily be crude and subject to many qualifications. Comparing the retail rates of private companies with those of TVA distributors also presents problems. Distributors' rates are controlled by the Authority, which, in effect, serves as a regulatory agency, also supervising their finances and prescribing their accounting methods. The sense in which these retail rates may reasonably be considered a yardstick for private rates is through their demonstration of a market-development policy in striking contrast with those previously followed by many private companies. As the engineering report of a congressional investigation of the TVA pointed out:

The traditional marketing approach of private industry has been to establish rates which will cover as far as it is possible to do so the entire costs of service immediately, and gradually to reduce rates over the long period of time required to develop the market under such rate policies; in other words, to make the rate-payer earn his rate reduction in advance.[73]

The TVA, on the other hand, began with low, promotional rate schedules designed to encourage high utilization of electricity. David E. Lilienthal, the principal architect of these policies as a director of the Authority from 1933 to 1946 and chairman from 1941 to 1946, wrote of yardstick rates in this sense:

[They are not] an absolute standard of precisely what should be charged for electricity anywhere and everywhere in the country, with the implication that any company charging more than the T.V.A. rate was therefore proved an extortionist. [Instead, TVA rates are] a yardstick in a much more important sense. It has been demonstrated here, to the benefit both of consumers and utilities, that drastic reductions in electric rates result in hitherto undreamed-of demands for more and more electricity in homes and on farms. . . . The yardstick in its correct sense has served and continues to serve a public purpose. It

[73] S. Doc. 56, 76th Cong., 1st sess., Pt. 3, p. 201.

has led . . . to a realistic re-examination of the financial feasibility of low rates.[74]

In pursuing this policy, the TVA did two things private enterprise had failed to do. First, it brought electricity to virtually everyone. Where in 1933 only 3 per cent of the farms in the Valley were electrified, by 1956 the proportion had been raised to about 95 per cent.[75] Secondly, its demonstration of the elasticity of demand for power was a striking success. Use by TVA customers doubled in the four years ending on June 30, 1938, compared with a 27 per cent increase elsewhere for almost the same period.[76] Low TVA rates have continued to expand consumption. In fiscal 1956, the average TVA residential consumer, paying 1.16 cents a kilowatt-hour, consumed 5,812 kilowatt-hours a year, compared with a national average of 2,879 kilowatt-hours at an average charge of 2.62 cents.[77] Equally noteworthy were the effects of TVA rates on the policies of private companies in the area. Substantial rate reductions made by neighboring utilities were followed by a striking increase in consumption, as the following table reveals: [78]

| | 1933 | | 1937 | |
	Average rate	Average kwh. per yr.	Average rate	Average kwh. per yr.
Tennessee Electric Power Co.	5.77	612	2.86	1353
Georgia Power Co.	5.16	803	3.04	1313
Alabama Power Co.	4.62	793	2.97	1289
U.S. average	5.49	595	4.39	793

The threat of government competition operated as a gadfly, compelling utilities to strive for efficiency and lower costs, to embark on promotional pricing and aggressive sales campaigns, to stress low rates and high utilization.

The TVA's great expansion over the years has been confined to the geographic area originally marked out for it by its settlement with Commonwealth and Southern in the late thirties. The power needs of the area, enormously expanded by military and

[74] David E. Lilienthal, TVA: Democracy on the March (1944), pp. 26–27.
[75] TVA, Annual Report, 1956, p. 36.
[76] S. Doc. 56, 76th Cong., 1st sess., Pt. 3, p. 208.
[77] TVA, Annual Report, 1956, p. 5.
[78] S. Doc. 56, 76th Cong., 1st sess., Pt. 1, p. 182.

atomic needs, have mushroomed. In 1933, the area now served by the TVA consumed 1.5 billion kilowatt-hours. By 1945, when the Oak Ridge atomic plant alone used 1.6 billion kilowatt-hours, total consumption had risen to 11.5 billion. By fiscal 1956, federal agencies, primarily the Atomic Energy Commission (AEC), used 21.8 billion kilowatt-hours of the 42.5 billion generated by the TVA. Falling water alone could not meet these needs, and the TVA had to construct steam generating plants. By 1956, about two-thirds of its power was steam-generated.

Private utilities have strenuously opposed appropriations for the construction of TVA steam plants, with Republicans generally opposing and Democrats supporting the appropriations. Thus the Republican 80th Congress denied the TVA construction funds later voted by the Democratic 81st Congress. In 1953, the new Republican administration sharply reduced TVA appropriations, canceling new projects and stopping some already under way. At a press conference, President Eisenhower called the TVA an example of "creeping socialism." [79] Then, in 1954, orders were issued in the President's name directing the Atomic Energy Commission to enter into the so-called Dixon-Yates contract. AEC needs for power in the region had further increased, but Congress had denied the TVA the $100 million it had requested to meet these needs. An AEC contract with two utility holding companies, headed by E. H. Dixon and E. A. Yates, called for the AEC to buy 600,000 kilowatts of power from a steam plant constructed and operated by the private companies and to feed this power into the TVA system to replace power taken out of the system elsewhere by the AEC. The contract was defended as a means of saving the government an immediate capital outlay. It was assailed as a plan requiring substantially higher annual and total costs, providing a guarantee of undue profit to private companies on a contract reached by negotiation and not by competitive bidding, and involving the imposition of a White House directive on two supposedly independent agencies, the AEC and the TVA, against their better judgment. Whatever the validity of these criticisms, it was clear that one purpose was to prevent the TVA from expanding its capacity and to reserve a larger scope for the private utilities.

Under heavy criticism, the Dixon-Yates contract was modified to limit the profits of the private companies and to permit the government to acquire the plant during the first three years of its existence. The contract was then approved by a split vote

[79] *New York Times*, June 18, 1953.

of the Joint Congressional Committee on Atomic Energy, which divided on party lines. After the Democrats won control of Congress in the 1954 elections, the issue was reopened by a Senate investigation, which not only revived the previous arguments but disclosed that A. H. Wenzell, a Budget Bureau consultant on leave from the First Boston Corporation, which was to float the Dixon-Yates bond issue, had played a prominent role in the drafting of the contract. The question of conflict of interest was raised. The politically embarrassed administration was quick to drop the proposal when given an opportunity to do so by the decision of the city of Memphis in 1955 to construct its own power plant, thereby reducing its demand on the TVA system.

The TVA continues, however, to confront obstacles in its efforts to expand capacity. Since 1953, it has received virtually no appropriations for the construction of new generating facilities. At the suggestion of Congress, it has been using its power revenues to provide for additional units at existing plants. But, even though its repayments to the Treasury are well ahead of schedule, power revenues can finance barely enough construction to meet its needs until 1960. In 1957, the Senate passed a bill empowering the TVA to issue up to $750 million of power revenue bonds to finance new construction. The legislation failed of passage in the House, leaving the TVA still dependent on annual appropriations to finance its expansion.

Other Public Power Programs

While the TVA was the most dramatic and most publicized of the federal power agencies, many other projects were launched in the 1930's and 1940's. The giant Hoover Dam on the Colorado, generating 1,250,000 kilowatts and authorized in 1928, antedates the New Deal. The Hoover administration, however, was so reluctant to allow the government to enter the power field that no transmission lines were built by the government, and the falling water, not the power thereby generated, was sold to a private power company and to the city of Los Angeles. The price originally set was designed to cover almost all of the cost of the dam, including substantial irrigation and water-supply benefits, and to yield a profit. Accordingly, the power generated at this dam has had little promotional effect or regulatory impact, although its power rates were moderately lowered in 1940.

Under the New Deal, a series of public power projects were initiated, many of which are still being expanded. On the Columbia River and its tributaries, the system includes the 1,944,000-

kilowatt Grand Coulee Dam, the 980,000-kilowatt McNary Dam, the 1,024,000-kilowatt Chief Joseph Dam, and the 518,000-kilowatt Bonneville Dam. The plants already installed have a total capacity of 5,059,000 kilowatts; when all authorized projects are completed, the system capacity will be almost 9 million kilowatts. In 1956, the output from dams of the Bureau of Reclamation and the Bonneville Power Administration totaled 38.4 billion kilowatt-hours, while the Southwestern Power Administration produced 1.6 billion, and the Southeastern Power Administration 2.2 billion.

Like the TVA, these projects are multipurpose, usually providing irrigation, navigation, and flood-control benefits as well as generating electricity. Most of them were begun in the Depression decade, when the pump-priming and employment effects of such large-scale projects were a major reason for their construction. As with the TVA also, the desire to reduce power rates was an important contributing consideration. Where Hoover Dam power was sold at rates intended to subsidize irrigation and flood control and to yield a profit, New Deal power policy sought to ensure that low hydroelectric power costs were passed on to consumers. Accordingly, the government built its own transmission lines and gave priority to the power demands of public bodies and rural co-operatives. It encouraged and financially assisted local governments and rural co-operatives in acquiring or constructing distribution facilities. Low rates were set so as to maximize consumption and promote regional development.

Again as with the TVA, the economic soundness of these rates depends on the allocation of joint costs. The Bonneville Power Administration, which administers the Columbia River system and has sold its power at an average rate of 2.38 mills per kilowatt-hour, bases its rates on an FPC allocation of joint costs. Of its total investment of $1,728 million in 1956, $1,277 million were allocated to power. On this basis, its rates have enabled it to meet current expenses, to pay interest charges of $2\frac{1}{2}$ per cent on the unrepaid federal investment, and to repay $202 million to the Treasury.[80]

Compared with the TVA, a much smaller proportion of Columbia River power is distributed through public or co-operative bodies. Of the total power sales of the Bureau of Reclamation, the Bonneville Power Administration, and the Southwestern Power Administration, about 28 per cent goes to privately owned

[80] Secretary of the Interior, *Annual Report, 1956*, pp. 68–71.

utilities, about 28 per cent to state and local government bodies and other public authorities, 37 per cent to industrial and commercial users and to the federal government, and about 6 per cent to rural co-operatives.[81] The impact of the public power program as a whole is measured by the fact that in 1955 about one-fifth of the kilowatt-hours delivered to ultimate consumers was sold by public bodies or rural co-operatives.[82]

In order to bring electricity to the nation's farms, the New Deal also promoted and assisted the formation of rural electric co-operatives. Private companies had been notably slow in serving rural areas: only 11 per cent of the farms of America were electrified in 1934. In 1936, Congress authorized the Rural Electrification Administration (REA) to make loans for the distribution, transmission, and if need be, generation of electricity, a program initiated in 1935 as a relief activity. The REA aggressively promoted the formation of co-operatives, lending them funds, offering technical and managerial assistance, and establishing construction, operating, and financial standards. The REA was assailed by the utilities and for some years occasional violence flared up as farmers reacted against efforts of private companies to forestall co-operatives by building "spite lines." While utilities still oppose the REA and attempt to limit its appropriations, it has been able to stimulate an impressive expansion in rural service, by both private and public bodies. By 1956, 94.2 per cent of all farms were served by electricity, 54 per cent by the REA and the remainder mostly by private companies. A total of $3.2 billion has been lent out since 1935.[83] Arrears amounted to only $332,000, and no operating co-operatives have failed. While these co-operatives are not directly subsidized, they do receive the benefits of low interest rates and exemption from federal income taxes. Few would have come into existence without the vigorous support of the REA.

The New Deal policy of promoting public power projects and

[81] *Ibid.*, pp. 27, 69, 73, 89–90. The computation is a rough one, for the various agency reports are not completely comparable.

[82] Publicly owned utilities with annual revenues of more than $250,000 sold 79.5 billion kilowatt-hours. Privately owned utilities sold 369 billion. REA co-operatives sold 14.5 billion. FPC, *Statistics of Electrical Utilities in the U.S., 1955, Publicly Owned*, p. v; FPC, *Statistics of Electrical Utilities in the U.S., 1955*, p. xvii; Secretary of Agriculture, *Annual Report, 1956*, p. 51.

[83] Secretary of Agriculture, *Annual Report, 1956*, pp. 50–51. Since 1949, the REA has also had the authority to provide credit for financing of rural telephone services. Telephone loans made through 1956 will provide service for almost 700,000 farms.

public or co-operative ownership of distribution facilities was for a period reversed by the Eisenhower administration. In 1953, Congress sharply reduced appropriations for the REA, the TVA, and other public power projects, delaying or canceling all new projects and stopping some already begun. The Southwestern Power Administration, for example, was forbidden to use its funds for steam plants to "firm up" its hydroelectric power.

In 1953, the new Secretary of the Interior, Douglas McKay, announced a revised power policy. While acknowledging "that many proposed present-day hydroelectric projects are of such large scope and tremendous cost that only the Federal Government is in a position to finance them," he argued that "in engaging in these projects . . . the Federal Government should not assume the primary responsibility for supplying the power needs for an area. This responsibility properly rests with the people locally." For all other projects, the federal government would encourage construction "by local interests—public or private—which are willing and able to undertake them." It would not build transmission lines to load centers if public or private agencies could provide such facilities upon reasonable terms. It would continue to give first preference to public bodies and co-operatives, but would give privately owned utilities preference over industrial users. Control over the resale rates of public bodies and co-operatives would be discontinued. Above all "the trend toward Federal monopoly must be halted." [84]

In pursuance of this policy, the Interior Department dropped its plans to include in the Columbia Valley system a high, multipurpose dam at Hell's Canyon on the Snake River. It withdrew its objection to the private construction of small power dams, which would be completed sooner but add less capacity to the whole river system. These private projects were later approved by the FPC and survived several attempts of congressional Democrats to override the FPC decision. In general, the new administration observed the preferential rights of public agencies in disposing of current power, but negotiated long-term sales of the remaining power to private companies.

The many beneficiaries of New Deal power policies began to mobilize their political strength, merging it with TVA supporters who opposed efforts of the Republican administration to restrict that agency. Power policy became a major issue, especially in the Pacific Northwest, in the congressional election of 1954,

<hr/>

[84] Secretary of the Interior, *Annual Report, 1953*, pp. xvii–xix.

when the Democrats won control of Congress, and again in 1956, when McKay himself was defeated by a public power advocate in the contest for a senatorial seat from Oregon. The outcome of both elections, especially in public power areas, registered dissatisfaction with the new policies. Although the new Secretary of the Interior, Fred A. Seaton, made no formal changes in administration policy, which was still labeled as one of "partnership," the application of policy was somewhat modified. Thus the Southwestern Power Administration was now permitted to help REA co-operatives construct steam plants and was also authorized to erect transmission lines to carry power to the co-operatives.

8. Summary

Taken as a whole, the experience with electrical utilities well illustrates how the effectiveness of various regulatory programs depends on the political support they can muster. Conventional public utility regulation has encountered great difficulty in maintaining a sense of general community awareness and interest. The obstacles formerly erected by the *Smyth* v. *Ames* doctrine, by the problems of interstate jurisdiction, and by the interstate holding company have all been removed. Yet most students are still notably restrained in their enthusiasm for the performance of the regulatory commissions.

The record of the SEC is more impressive. Armed with sweeping powers, and supported by a vigorous administration, capitalizing on the acute disenchantment of investors and consumers with holding-company control groups, it managed, within little more than a decade, to do a thoroughgoing job of industry reorganization. By dispersing ownership and strengthening local management, it modified the power relations within the industry, engendering a more rational organization and perhaps making it more amenable to regulation.

The TVA and the other public power agencies have had lasting effects. Government risk capital has been used to demonstrate the elasticity of demand by promotional rates, the extent to which regional development may be spurred by cheap hydroelectric power from multipurpose projects, and the economic feasibility of bringing electricity to the remote countryside—all areas in which private enterprise had not performed the innovating role usually assigned to it. These agencies have had a major regulatory impact on privately owned electric utilities—in many cases a greater impact than conventional regulation. Their programs have also permanently altered the composition of the industry's parties-in-interest. The many beneficiaries of public power now comprise a substantial political bloc, capable of mustering strong support for maintenance of policies favoring public power.

The electric utility industry, however, remains preponderantly under private control, but it operates within a framework of governmental regulation and competition which strikes a new balance between private and public power and provides substantial protection for hitherto neglected interests.

CHAPTER 13

Communications

THE REGULATION of communications by wire and by radio wave represents an adjustment to many of the same legal, political, economic, and technological factors at work in the transportation and electric utility industries. While radio and television raise some unique problems of civil liberties and of program content, the telephone and telegraph industries fall fairly neatly into the conventional mold of public utility regulation. The interstate character of both modes of wire communication has necessitated federal regulation.

1. Telephone and Telegraph Regulation

Corporate History and Industrial Background

In the telegraph industry, a period of mushroom growth, characterized by the formation of numerous small companies, was followed by an era of consolidation. The Western Union Telegraph Company, organized in 1856, absorbed many of its smaller competitors and soon dominated the industry. The only effective challenge to its hegemony came after 1886, when John W. Mackay formed the Postal Telegraph System in order to provide a land outlet for his cable interests. The System absorbed existing lines, built interconnections and new facilities, and competed with Western Union on a continental scale. Two powerful combinations thus emerged as the dominant factors in wire telegraphy.

The commercial history of the telephone in the United States is almost synonymous with the growth of the American Telephone and Telegraph Company (A. T. & T. or the Bell System) and its steady march toward integrated control of the entire industry. Bell's policies and its techniques of defense and aggression in consolidating its position and extending its sphere of control constitute a unique study in the politics of modern industry.

It is a story of humble beginnings. The telephone was at first dismissed as merely an interesting scientific toy. In 1876, Western Union rejected an opportunity to buy the Bell patents for $100,-000. It speedily recognized its mistake, and armed with its own patents, entered into competition with Bell. Patent litigation followed, but the Bell interests attracted enough capital to protect their patents against legal attack and to embark on a policy of expansion. In 1879, a truce was concluded by which Western Union retired from the telephone field, selling out its telephone ventures to Bell, which, in turn, agreed to keep out of telegraphy.

With valid patents and ample financial support for expansion, Bell's next problem was to ensure that its domination of the telephone industry would outlast the expiration of its patents in 1893 and 1894. In pursuance of this objective, license contracts required local operating companies using Bell patents to turn over part of their stock to the parent Bell Company, which also purchased controlling stock in these companies in the open market. Telephone apparatus was leased but not sold. In order to control the manufacture and sale of telephone equipment, the Western Electric Company was organized as a Bell manufacturing subsidiary and refused to sell apparatus to non-Bell companies until 1907. Rapid construction of a network of long-distance lines offered yet another obstacle to the development of regional or national competition.

Nevertheless, many independent telephone companies were organized soon after the expiration of the patents. The Bell System fought them strenuously with rate wars, refusals to connect with them or to sell them telephone equipment, attempts to block their franchises, purchases of stock control, and other forms of financial pressure. The general success of its efforts left the Bell System in command of the field.

Its entrenchment in the telephone industry was then supplemented by expansion into adjacent communication fields. In 1909, A. T. & T. acquired control of Western Union, but the resulting domination of the entire wire communications field evoked criticism. Postal Telegraph charged that Bell was using its telephone facilities to discriminate against Postal and in favor of Western Union. The surviving independent telephone companies

renewed their complaints that the Bell System was refusing satisfactory long-distance connections. At this point, the government
came into the picture. Its threat to invoke the antitrust laws
produced the so-called Kingsbury commitment (1913), by which
A. T. & T. agreed to sell its Western Union stock, promised not
to acquire control of competing companies (acquisition of noncompeting companies was not mentioned), and agreed to connect
its toll-service system with independent companies which met its
equipment standards. The Kingsbury commitment interposed
obstacles to the acquisition of competing companies, but it did
not put an end to them. When the Willis-Graham Act of 1921
permitted the merger or consolidation of competing telephone
companies subject to the approval of state authorities and the
ICC, the Bell System again embarked upon a policy of active
acquisition of independents.

As a result of these policies, the Bell System achieved a dominating position in the American telephone industry. A. T. & T.
is, indeed, the largest corporation in the nation and probably in
the world. In 1956, the system had almost 800,000 employees
and 1½ million stockholders. Its assets totaled over $16 billion,
and its operating revenues almost $6 billion. It owned over 87
per cent of the nation's telephone plant, and operated almost 50
million telephones. The parent company receives most of its
income from dividends of the subsidiary operating companies,
service charges paid by them, operation of long-distance lines,
and profits from Western Electric, the manufacturing subsidiary.
It provides wire services for Western Union and for radio and
television stations and networks. Its patents have given it important stakes in motion pictures and radio. It has been continually preoccupied with advances in communications, devoting
large resources to research and development. It has been constantly aware of the strategic importance of staking out claims
early when significant advances in technology occur.

Federal Regulation of Wire Communications Prior to 1934

National policy toward wire communications began as one of
aid and encouragement. In 1843, federal funds were appropriated
for an experimental telegraph line between Washington and
Baltimore. The Post Roads Act of 1866 gave construction rights
to telegraph companies over the public domain, post roads, and
navigable streams and waters. This act also authorized the Postmaster General to fix special rates for government telegrams. Legislation in 1888 authorized the ICC to require government-aided

telegraph companies to make connections wherever their lines met and to receive, deliver, and exchange business on equal terms.

General regulatory power over wire-communication carriers was not vested in the ICC until the Mann-Elkins Act of 1910. Even this authority was limited by the fact that most telephone communication and about a fourth of the telegraph traffic was intrastate and not subject to direct federal control. Furthermore, the ICC made little attempt to use its power vigorously. In the twenty-four years that communication companies were subject to its jurisdiction, the Commission dealt with telegraph rates in only eight cases, telephone rates in four cases, and cable rates in two cases. Few of these involved issues of major importance. The Commission undertook no general rate investigations; it acted only on the basis of such complaints as were brought before it. It never established a separate communications division; its primary concern was with railroads. In the absence of serious pressure to exert its power in the communications field, regulation went largely by default. The ICC did establish uniform systems of accounts; it required monthly and annual reports of financial and operating statistics and it made some valuation studies. Under the Willis-Graham Act of 1921, it also exercised some authority over telephone consolidation. But, at best, it did little more than prepare the groundwork for more effective regulation.

State Regulation of Wire Communications

Meanwhile, the main burden of telephone regulation fell upon the states. In most states, the established regulatory commissions were entrusted with the usual public utility controls over intrastate telephone rates and services. But state regulatory efforts proved largely ineffective. Already burdened with many other responsibilities, most state commissions simply were not equipped to cope with the complex problems posed by telephone regulation. The average commission was inadequately staffed and financed. Consumer pressure for vigorous action was at best sporadic. In contrast with railroad rate controversies, where individual shippers may have substantial financial sums at stake, and shipper organizations exist to present the consumer's case, the stake of the individual telephone user is ordinarily small.

Furthermore, Bell public relations policies were carefully developed to hinder any vigorous efforts at regulation. The Bell System enlisted a large army of investors and employees; its influence was wide reaching and pervasive. As bank depositors, as buyers of materials, as purchasers of insurance contracts and other services, the local Bell operating companies became intimately interwoven with the commercial structure of their communities and were able to draw upon powerful reservoirs of support which did much to discourage attacks on their rate structures.

The Bell System's corporate organization also presented state commissions with jurisdictional obstacles which made federal action a prerequisite to effective state regulation. Just as public utility holding companies prevented effective state control of local operating electric utilities, so centralized control of the local telephone companies left the state commissions, in the absence of federal regulation, unable to control or ascertain the true costs of intrastate service.

At the apex of the Bell System is A. T. & T. ("Mother Bell"), which is both an operating and a holding company. It operates directly the Long Lines Department, which provides long-distance service, and controls twenty-two operating companies. It also owns Western Electric, which manufactures telephone equipment and provides much of the plant and supplies for the whole System. A. T. & T. and Western Electric control Bell Telephone Laboratories, which conducts basic and applied research in all aspects of communications.

A state commission, unless aided by federal regulation, cannot effectively regulate an operating company subject to its jurisdiction, for it cannot control payments to other parts of the Bell System. (The fact that many of the operating companies serve more than one state makes the task of regulation even more difficult.) The operating company not only pays dividends and other interest charges to Mother Bell but also pays A. T. & T. a percentage of its principal operating revenues for research, development, patent rights, and managerial assistance. It pays Western Electric for equipment, supplies, and services at prices which the parent company sets. The depreciation it charges against operating income and applies to its rate base is controlled by A. T. & T. Furthermore, it is difficult to separate intrastate from interstate operations. Much of the Bell plant is jointly used for both. A proper allocation of revenues and expenses between intrastate and interstate business is essential to state regulation but requires data and accounting records beyond the control of state commissions.

Moreover, since the telephone industry presents regulatory authorities with problems of greater technological complexity than do other utilities, it becomes understandable why a leading student of utility regulation concluded in 1950 that "state telephone regulation has . . . been far less effective than that of the other local utilities. . . . the state commissions have particularly avoided telephone rate cases." [1] While some of the strong commissions diligently attempted to gather the data necessary for efficient regulation, access to such data was outside their jurisdictional reach. The national character of the Bell System raised problems which could not be solved by state action alone. The resulting demand for an expansion of national regulation was partially answered in the Communications Act of 1934.

The Federal Communications Commission

Soon after President Franklin Roosevelt took office, an Interdepartmental Committee was set up to study communications and to suggest new legislation. Its recommendations led to the Communications Act of 1934, a broad regulatory measure embracing the whole field of communications—by radio as well as by wire. The Act created the seven-member Federal Communications Commission (FCC), to which were transferred all the duties, powers, and functions in communications formerly exercised by the ICC, the Postmaster General, and the Federal Radio Commission. (Title III of the Act contains special provisions dealing with radio and will be discussed separately.)

The Act amplified federal authority over wire communications, vesting the FCC with jurisdiction over interstate telephone and telegraph rates and services. The Commission was empowered to require common carriers to furnish adequate service upon reasonable request, to order physical connections with other carriers, to establish through routes and charges applicable thereto, and to arrange the division of such charges. It could issue or deny certificates of public convenience and necessity for the construction or extension of lines, require filing and observance of rate schedules, and investigate and suspend changes in rates. In general, these provisions were modeled on similar requirements in railroad regulation.

The Commission might make a valuation of the properties of communications companies. It could require carriers to file inventories of their property. The Act laid down no formula for valuation, only stating that the FCC "shall be free to adopt any method of valuation which shall be lawful." The Commission might classify the property of telephone companies according to intrastate or interstate use and at its discretion, value interstate property separately.

[1] J. Bauer, *Transforming Public Utility Regulation* (1950), p. 337.

The Act attempted to maintain some competition in interstate and foreign communications. The Commission was given jurisdiction over telephone consolidations, and it was made unlawful for any person to be an officer or director of more than one carrier subject to the Act without FCC approval. The combination of radio and wire communication companies was forbidden where the purpose or effect may be "substantially to lessen competition." The FCC could also require reports, accounts, and records from the companies subject to its jurisdiction. It might prescribe accounting forms and depreciation charges, inquire into the management of companies, and keep itself abreast of the advance of the arts "to the end that the benefits of new inventions may be made available to the people of the United States."

In several important respects, however, the Act failed to confer regulatory powers adequate to control the complex corporate structure being regulated. The FCC has no authority to pass on intrasystem transactions involving supplies, research services, finances, credit, or personnel. Thus it cannot directly regulate these aspects of the services provided by Western Electric, Bell Laboratories, or A. T. & T.; it cannot set their charges, control their costs, or even prescribe the form of their accounts. It is true that since the Smith case in 1930,[2] state commissions have been empowered to investigate the nature of the services rendered by these companies, to pass on the reasonableness of their charges, and to disallow unreasonable charges. Since that decision, A. T. & T. has presented cost studies in support of its fees, but the state agencies have been unable in practice to obtain adequate information. A. T. & T. accounts do not show the costs properly allocable to each license and service contract, and state commissions do not have full access to Bell records. The FCC can, however, investigate these matters and the information revealed may be used to implement and strengthen both national and state regulation.

Because of the intermixture of intrastate and interstate business, the Act encourages co-operation between federal and state authorities to facilitate the segregation of interstate and intrastate property and to avoid conflict between accounting and other requirements. There is also provision for joint boards on which the FCC and state agencies may be represented, and for joint hearings.

Regulation of the Telegraph Industry

The basic problem of the telegraph industry is one of an industry in decline, and regulatory policy has necessarily had to be con-

---

[2] *Smith* v. *Illinois Bell Telephone Co.*, 282 U.S. 133.

cerned with its consequences. The Act of 1934 sought to encourage competition within the telegraph industry. At that time, Postal Telegraph was still in existence, carrying about a fifth of the traffic. But Western Union, after a long and enviable earning record, began in the late 1930's to show substantial losses, and Postal Telegraph went into receivership. Destructive competition within the telegraph industry itself, the diversion of traffic to other media including long-distance telephone, teletypewriter, air mail, and radio services, and higher costs of operation all contributed to the plight of the industry.

As early as 1935, the FCC developed doubts about the wisdom of intra-industry competition and asked for legislation enabling it to approve and authorize consolidation of telegraph companies. Legislation was finally enacted in 1943, and the two telegraph companies were merged. Western Union continued to suffer from rising costs and the competition of other media, and its prospects were most unpromising throughout the forties. It has several times sought to have shifted to it the teletype business now conducted by A. T. & T., which yields about a third of all domestic record (written) communications revenue. Such a solution, authorized by the 1943 law and endorsed by a Senate committee, would substantially strengthen the competitive position of Western Union.

Though as yet denied this remedy, Western Union's financial health did improve substantially during the 1950's. The FCC assisted it by approving substantial rate increases and widespread reductions in hours of service or closing of public telegraph offices. The company has done much on its own account with a modernization program and by promoting private-wire and facsimile systems. Despite these steps, however, the competition Western Union can offer A. T. & T. remains little more than peripheral.

Telephone Regulation

The FCC had scarcely assumed its regulatory responsibilities over the telephone industry and begun its routine, organizational duties, involving the classification of carriers, the filing of tariffs, the preparation of a system of accounts, etc.,[3] when it became apparent that little information was available on interstate telephone operations, and that one of the Commission's first tasks was to find

[3] The Commission encountered resistance at the outset. The Bell System challenged its proposed uniform system of accounts because of the requirement that the original cost of telephone properties be shown. In 1936, however, the Court upheld the FCC in A. T. & T. v. U.S., 299 U.S. 232.

out about the telephone business. In 1935, Congress authorized the Commission to conduct a comprehensive investigation, for which $1.5 million was ultimately appropriated. The Commission was instructed, among other things, to explore the capital structure of the Bell System, intercompany relationships, license-service contracts, accounting methods, depreciation practices, patent policies, methods of competition, public relations activities, toll operations, Western Electric costs and prices, and other aspects of the business which bear on the problem of regulation. The FCC's elaborate investigation, completed in 1939,[4] was no tale of scandal, corruption, and empire-building for the sake of power, such as that unfolded by its study of electric utility holding companies. But the FCC report did conclude that the Bell System's corporate structure had been manipulated to increase its profits by padding both the operating expenses and the valuations of the operating companies. Thus, as in the case of the electric holding companies, interstate corporate controls had impeded state regulation to the detriment of the consumer.

The study indicated, for example, that A. T. & T. had caused its subsidiaries to handle their depreciation charges so as to have their cake and eat it too. High depreciation allowances, sufficient to accumulate reserves amounting to about 28 per cent of the Bell physical properties, were added to operating expenses, and hence to rates, but only "observable" depreciation, ranging from 5 to 10 per cent, was deducted in determining the rate base. Consequently, the Bell System received a return on property for which the consumer had already paid. And the sum was sizable, since depreciation charges amounted to almost a fifth of operating expenses.

The license contract fees which A. T. & T. collected from its operating companies involved charges not properly allocable to their operating expenses. These payments supported the research and development activities of Bell Laboratories, which produced many patents and processes enabling A. T. & T. to enter other industries or to license firms outside the telephone industry. The resultant profits, patent royalties, and license fees, although largely

---

[4] The record of the investigation is massive. It contains 8,441 printed pages of testimony, 2,140 exhibits, and 77 formal staff reports on various phases of the Bell System. The investigation was criticized by Bell representatives as an unfair *ex parte* proceeding. The only witnesses who testified were those summoned by the Commission. Counsel for the Bell System were not permitted to cross-examine witnesses or present witnesses of their own. A. T. & T. filed approximately fifty volumes of "comment" on the investigation. See FCC, *Investigation of the Telephone Industry in the United States*, H. Doc. 340, 76th Cong., 1st sess. (1939), pp. xviii–xix.

based on activities financed by the operating companies, accrued to A. T. & T. Furthermore, those patents and processes developed by Bell Laboratories which were useful to the telephone industry were available to the operating companies only on payment of additional fees. Thus, in yet another way, operating expenses of the subsidiaries were inflated to benefit A. T. & T.

Mother Bell, moreover, required its brood of operating companies to purchase virtually all their equipment, supplies, and plant materials from Western Electric at prices which were frequently well above those quoted by independent manufacturers. Western Electric prices were subject to no public regulation and yielded extraordinary profits. These excessive charges by Western Electric became a part of the operating expenses and property valuations of the operating companies and were ultimately borne by the consumer.

Finally, the FCC found that A. T. & T. imposed arbitrary financing fees on its subsidiaries and that its long-distance tolls were either excessive or so divided as to favor the parent company at the expense of the operating companies.

Although Congress did not then grant the FCC's request for powers sweeping enough to regulate all parts of the Bell System, the information gathered by the Commission was sufficient to enable both it and the state commissions to negotiate substantial reductions in telephone charges. The Commission estimated that during the course of the investigation interstate rate reductions of more than $30 million were effected, and substantial reductions were also made in intrastate rates.[5] And in the following years the FCC persuaded A. T. & T. to reduce interstate tolls further and to allocate more of the receipts from interstate traffic to the operating companies. In general, however, both because of gaps in the regulatory scheme and because of the magnitude of the accounting and valuation tasks, rate reductions and reallocations have resulted from negotiation and informal pressure rather than from formal actions based on full determinations of costs, valuations, and rates of return. Despite its limited controls, the FCC has managed, in the almost two decades since its report was published, to make good use of its powers to gather facts and prescribe accounting forms so as to influence the Bell companies to lower telephone rates, and help the state commissions to perform their regulatory functions more effectively. By 1949, the FCC had caused the telephone companies to restate their plant accounts on the basis of

[5] *Ibid.*, p. 602.

original cost, thus reducing by $43 million the net book values on which their rate of return was computed.[6] By 1954, the Commission had completed a program of revising depreciation rates for all Bell companies. The net effect of this study was to lower depreciation charges by $29 million annually,[7] although changing conditions have since required some increases.

While the FCC has usually co-operated with state commissions to facilitate their regulatory tasks, there have been occasional clashes between federal and state authorities. The two jurisdictions are largely complementary in dealing with an interstate utility system, but without full co-operation, conflicts may arise from unevenness of regulation. Consumers in an area of weak regulation may have costs shifted to them by more effective regulation elsewhere.

In the early 1930's, Bell interstate tolls were less than those for intrastate calls of the same distance. The success of the FCC in negotiating a $30 million reduction in interstate tolls during the course of its prewar investigation and a further $20 million reduction in 1946 had increased the disparity. In 1950, the National Association of Railroad and Utilities Commissioners (NARUC) asked the FCC not to begin an action to reduce interstate tolls until a joint review could be made of the reasonableness of the separation of Bell expenses and plant between intrastate and interstate business. The NARUC proposed that $200 million in plant and $20 million in annual expenses be shifted from intrastate to interstate operations. The FCC rejected this proposal, and ordered an investigation of interstate rates with a view to lowering them. Further consultation with the NARUC, however, led to a postponement of this investigation and to a joint study of Bell separation procedures. This study resulted in the following year in a shift of $90 million in gross plant and $22 million in annual expenses from intrastate to interstate operations. By 1956, this continuing joint study had reduced Bell's annual revenue requirements for its intrastate operations by more than $35 million.[8]

Similar joint studies have been conducted in other phases of telephone regulation, of which one of the most significant involved Western Electric. Although this Bell manufacturing subsidiary is beyond full regulatory control, the FCC can investigate its operations. After a number of state commissions had questioned the size of Western Electric profits on sales to Bell operating companies and their effect on intrastate rates, in 1948 the FCC joined with

[6] FCC, *Annual Report, 1949*, p. 104.
[7] *Ibid.*, 1954, p. 40.
[8] *Ibid.*, 1951, pp. 46–48; 1952, pp. 44–45; 1956, p. 42.

state commissioners in a study of Western Electric prices, costs, and profits. Within two years of the initiation of this study, Western Electric had reduced its prices, saving the Bell operating companies $77 million annually. In 1952, on the basis of continuing joint studies, the FCC again suggested to Western Electric that, in view of its high profit rate, further price reductions were in order. Two successive price reductions followed rapidly, providing an annual saving to the operating companies of $110 million.[9] Data on Western Electric prices, costs, and earnings are still compiled quarterly and distributed to the state commissions.

The special position of Western Electric presents a continuing problem. Lacking direct regulatory power over it, the FCC has sought to influence it indirectly, by publicity, by persuasion, and by transmission of accounting data to the state commissions. In 1949, the Antitrust Division of the Justice Department offered another solution by beginning a proceeding under the Sherman Act. Charging that A. T. & T. had used its patents to monopolize the telephone industry and then used its control of operating companies to eliminate competing telephone-equipment manufacturers, the government asked the courts to sever the connection between A. T. & T. and Western Electric and to split Western Electric into three parts. One of the purposes of the action was to inject an element of competition into the telephone-equipment business and thus perhaps lower the operating expenses and plant costs of the operating companies. After seven years of legal skirmishes, however, the Justice Department in 1956 negotiated a consent settlement on a much more moderate basis.[10] By the terms of the consent decree, Western Electric retains both its unity and its corporate allegiance to the Bell System, but A. T. & T. must make most of its patents available to other manufacturers without royalties and Western must disclose its manufacturing costs. It is possible, consequently, that new competition may develop in the manufacturing of telephone equipment.

2. Radio and Television Regulation

In the regulation of radio and television broadcasting, the FCC confronts a range of problems quite different from those associated with utility regulation. Utility regulation focuses on the control of

[9] *Ibid.*, 1948, p. 85; 1949, p. 101; 1952, p. 47; 1953, pp. 39–40.
[10] The settlement has aroused some criticism, e.g., W. D. Rogers, "Is It Trust Busting or Window Dressing?", *The Reporter* (November 1, 1956), pp. 21–23; Antitrust Subcommittee of the House Committee on the Judiciary, *Hearings on Consent Decree Program of the Department of Justice,* 85th Cong., 2d sess. (1958), Part II, vols. 1–3.

entry, services, and rates. In broadcasting, entry is tightly controlled, services are casually examined but not regulated, and rates
are not governmentally controlled at all but are limited by competition. Broadcasting regulation also requires the FCC to consider
thorny questions of censorship, program content, and audience
tastes, to anticipate the course of technological development, and
to estimate which new developments can be profitably exploited
by business firms. That there is much criticism of the way in which
the FCC has performed these duties in part reflects their difficulty
and their novelty.

In no field, perhaps, is the technical imperative for government
to regulate more immediate and direct than in broadcasting. The
number of radio channels is limited. More people want to use
the air than can be accommodated. Unless some central authority
allocates channels and confines broadcasters to definite places on
the radio spectrum, broadcasting becomes meaningless chaos. It
must also be borne in mind that commercial broadcasting is only
one of many radio uses. The FCC must not only adjust the claims
of rival broadcasters; it must also mediate between broadcasting
and alternative radio uses, finding room for military communications, ship-to-shore services, aviation and police purposes, commercial radio-telephone communications, press dispatches, ama-
teurs, scientific research, and a variety of other special needs.

Despite the essentiality of central control, the regulation of
broadcasting, like that in many other fields, came after, and not
before, the art was already well advanced and its commercial exploitation was well under way. Prior to the crystallization of regulatory policy, an industry had already grown up, strategic positions
had been occupied, vested interests were established, and the basic
characteristics of American broadcasting had already manifested
themselves.

Patent Control and the Radio Industry

In the initial stages of the radio industry, control of patents was
a strategic factor. The first important patents were controlled by
the Marconi interests. Some American inventors then made important discoveries, and as the commercial possibilities of radio
became clear, a number of American companies, including General
Electric, Westinghouse, and A. T. & T., sponsored research programs in order to gain radio patent rights and to establish priorities. The result was a considerable dispersion of patent control
and widespread threats of infringement litigation.

In the struggle for position, General Electric gained an initial

COMMUNICATIONS

advantage. The Radio Corporation of America (RCA), which was organized by General Electric, acquired the assets and patent rights of the Marconi Company, as well as all rights under radio patents owned by General Electric. RCA's agreement to purchase all of its radio equipment from General Electric aroused immediate reactions from Westinghouse and A. T. & T., both of which threatened patent-infringement suits and other litigation. This conflict was temporarily adjusted in 1920–1921 by a series of cross-licensing agreements which pooled most of the radio patents, gave Westinghouse a stock interest in RCA, and committed RCA to divide its purchases of radio equipment between General Electric and Westinghouse. But disagreement soon developed over the respective rights acquired by A. T. & T. and by the other members of the pool. Meanwhile, A. T. & T., General Electric, and Westinghouse had all established broadcasting stations, while A. T. & T., in particular, aggressively expanded its broadcasting interests, operating several stations itself, and using its control over wire facilities to establish a network and control other stations. In 1926, A. T. & T. and RCA concluded a new peace treaty, under which the Bell System sold its broadcasting interests to RCA, which operated them through the National Broadcasting Company (NBC). In exchange, Bell's firm grip on the wire facilities for broadcasting was reinforced, and its hold on two-way radio-telephone commercial service was strengthened. In 1927, the Columbia Broadcasting System was founded, and network domination of broadcasting was firmly established.

One result of the 1926 agreement was to centralize control of most of the basic radio patents in the hands of RCA and its cross-licensing associates. Other radio manufacturers had to be licensed by RCA and pay royalties to the RCA patent pool. In 1930, an antitrust suit was brought by the Justice Department, charging that the pool restricted competition. The suit was settled by a consent decree in 1932 under which General Electric and Westinghouse divested themselves of their RCA stock, and pooled patents were made available on a royalty basis to all manufacturers on equal terms. RCA, instead of acting simply as a selling agency for Westinghouse and General Electric equipment, began to manufacture its own radios in competition with other manufacturers.

Parties-in-Interest

Although the industry has expanded greatly since then, and the scope of federal regulation has been extended, the basic configuration of parties-in-interest was already well defined by the early 1930's.

Among the parties-in-interest in broadcasting, there are, first, the manufacturers of radios and television sets. In general, they support the expansion of broadcast services, which increases the demand for their products,[11] but any given technological development, normally requiring FCC approval, may greatly affect their profit prospects. Their relations with broadcasters may be used to expand their sales. Thus RCA causes its broadcasting subsidiary, NBC, to promote color telecasts in order to stimulate sales of its color television sets.

Second, there are the broadcasting stations, whose FCC licenses give them exclusive rights to certain portions of the air. These licenses, provided without charge by the government, often make possible a high profit on comparatively little investment. In 1953, independent TV stations showed a pretax profit of 43 per cent on the depreciated cost of their tangible property; independent AM (amplitude modulation) radio and combined AM-FM (frequency modulation) stations made a profit of 33 per cent.[12] Licenses in practice are almost never revoked, but the profitability of a station may be vitally affected by FCC decisions to grant or deny licenses to competing stations. Not all broadcasting stations are profitable, and there are major conflicts of interest between such groups as AM and FM radio stations, or VHF (very high frequency) and UHF (ultra high frequency) television stations, as well as among individual stations and networks.

Third, there are the networks—three in television, and seven in radio, of which four are national and three regional. The networks directly own nineteen TV and sixteen radio stations and buy time from most of the remaining stations. They provide both commercial and sustaining programs, thereby dominating much radio programing and most television programing. Their interests often conflict with those of independent stations and sometimes with those of their affiliates, and they are intimately concerned with FCC licensing and other policies which affect the resolution of these conflicts.

Fourth, there are the advertisers and the advertising agencies, who buy the time sold by networks and stations. They exert con-

---

[11] By mid-1956, it was estimated, about $15 billion had been invested by the public in television receiving equipment. FCC, *Annual Report, 1956*, pp. 93–94.

[12] *Ibid., 1954*, pp. 112–113. The FCC stopped reporting such data on TV stations after that year.

siderable influence on program content. They are not directly affected by most FCC decisions, although issues affecting advertising concern them greatly. So dynamic is technology in the field that many other interests may be involved in FCC policy-making. They include A. T. & T., which owns the inter-station connecting facilities used in network broadcasting, the amusement industry, and such special interests as promoters of toll television. But the fifth main category consists of the listeners and viewers, the consumers of radio and TV. Collectively, the general public has the largest stake in broadcasting, financially and otherwise, but as is true in other industries, consumers tend to be poorly organized and inarticulate. They consequently exercise little direct influence on the FCC. Because of the limited number of broadcasting channels, especially in television, and because of the concern of most advertisers with reaching large audiences, substantial minority groups within the general public may be denied the broadcasting services they would prefer. Thus conflicts of interest among consumers are resolved primarily by a commercial yardstick.

The Beginnings of Public Regulation

Prior to 1927, broadcasting presented the chaos of a new industry, its vitality outrunning the bounds of public control. In the first burst of expansion of radio, between 1920 and 1927, the only important law capable of being applied to broadcasting was an Act of 1912, which was really intended to regulate radiotelephony. This Act forbade operation without a license from the Secretary of Commerce, but an early opinion of the Attorney General held that the Secretary could exercise no discretion and had to grant licenses to all applicants. Since the ether could not accommodate all comers without causing intolerable interference, the Secretary of Commerce sought to assert discretion to refuse a license where technical factors made refusal seem necessary. In 1923, a circuit court, though reiterating that the issuance of a license was a mandatory act, declared that the Secretary might designate the wave length upon which the licensee was to operate. Following this hint, Secretary Hoover called a conference of broadcasters and negotiated an allocation of frequencies in the "broadcast band," 500 to 1500 kilocycles.

But the demand for frequencies far exceeded the supply, and dissatisfaction with allocations developed. In 1926, a Chicago station, compelled to share its assigned frequency with another station and limited to two hours of broadcasting a week, "jumped" to another wave length and extended its hours of broadcasting, thereby testing the Secretary's legal powers. When Hoover's suit to enjoin the station from broadcasting was rejected by a district court, he requested the Attorney General for an opinion. The Attorney General held that the Secretary had no authority under the Act of 1912 to refuse a license, to designate frequencies, to prescribe hours of operation, or to limit station power. Hoover thereupon abandoned his efforts to regulate broadcasting. Stations used whatever frequencies they chose. A mad scramble ensued for favorable wave lengths and greater power, and two hundred new stations went on the air in the next few months. The result was pandemonium. Interference was so general as virtually to destroy the usefulness of broadcasting. The industry joined with the listening public in demands that something be done to "clear the air." The way was at last prepared for more thoroughgoing regulation.

But by the time Congress was prepared to lay down rules for radio regulation, the broadcasting industry had, as we have seen, already largely taken shape. The basic principle was established that broadcasting was available for commercial exploitation by private capital. Advertising was providing the financial means, and the first national network had begun operations. Broadcasting was becoming big business, with substantial investments at stake. Prevailing views of the proper scope of governmental action, moreover, were antagonistic to public occupation of the field. While it was recognized that regulation was necessary to avoid bedlam, the dominant political philosophy dictated that public interference be limited to the necessary minimum.

The Radio Act of 1927 and the Federal Radio Commission

Even that minimum, however, was considerable, and the Radio Act of 1927 appeared to give the newly created five-man Federal Radio Commission (FRC) sweeping powers. In issuing licenses, the Commission could assign wave lengths and fix power output and time of operation. A three-year limit was placed on licenses, and the FRC could, if it wished, reduce this period. The Act specified that licensees were to enjoy no vested rights in the ether. Station construction or additions could not be undertaken without Commission consent. FRC permission was also necessary for transfers of license ownership.

The 1927 Act sought to establish standards for the exercise of the licensing power. The main requirement, that grants, renewals, and modifications of licenses be conditioned on a finding that "public interest, convenience, or necessity" would be served thereby, did little to limit the discretion of the Commission. Other standards were more restrictive. The FRC was directed to allocate broadcasting facilities equitably among states and communities. The Act explicitly forbade the Commission to censor programs. Stations permitting candidates for any public office to use their facilities were required to "afford equal opportunities to all other such candidates for that office." There was no obligation, however, to make facilities available for political purposes in the first instance. If political broadcasts were permitted, the Act forbade censorship by licensees over the material broadcast. The Act also provided that all broadcast material for which payments were made should be so announced. Finally, the Commission was directed to refuse a station license to "any person, firm, company, or corporation, or any subsidiary thereof, which has been finally adjudged guilty by a federal court of unlawfully monopolizing or attempting unlawfully to monopolize . . . radio communication."

The Radio Act of 1927 thus considerably expanded federal regulatory power. It did not make broadcasting a public utility, but it did vest the Commission with discretionary authority which could have been used to determine the future structure of broadcasting and give direction to its development. In practice, however, the Commission was loath to use its authority with vigor; it tended to accept the broadcasting structure as it had already taken shape. While the Commission did not completely freeze the status quo, such piecemeal revision as it did undertake was largely a response to the more powerful pressures which played upon it.

The Commission's lack of initiative was partially explained by the weakness of its position. Because of disagreement between House and Senate as to whether the Secretary of Commerce or a commission should regulate radio, the Commission was created for one year only. Its life was precarious; its authority was renewed only from year to year until 1930, when the agency was placed on a permanent basis. Uncertainty of tenure promoted timidity. The FRC was handicapped by insufficient appropriations, which made it difficult to recruit adequate technical and legal personnel. Appointments to the Commission frequently were made solely on the basis of political patronage. The agency was racked by internal friction.

From the beginning, the FRC was a focal point for pressures of all sorts. Fearful of congressional criticism, it was unduly sensitive to congressional appeals on behalf of local constituents. It found itself embroiled in sectional jealousies. It was reluctant to antagonize powerful commercial-broadcasting interests with their established control of the more desirable facilities; at the same time, it was exposed to demands from spokesmen for other groups who wanted a greater share in the radio spectrum. In this unenviable position, it is perhaps not surprising that the Commission surrendered to the more insistent and powerful interests, and that its course of conduct was largely dictated by the expediencies of the moment.

The power to grant, modify, refuse, or revoke licenses was the heart of the FRC's authority. The Commission never found it possible to set forth a comprehensive definition of its standard of "public interest, convenience, or necessity." Meaning was, however, poured into it by a process of "inclusion and exclusion," as the Commission and the courts decided specific cases which came before them.[13] In a field as overcrowded as radio, where petitioners for channels far exceed the available supply, licensing necessarily involves a constant process of balancing claims, of choosing recipients for public favor, and of justifying the choice in terms of the statutory standard. The record of the FRC reveals that it inaugurated no fundamental changes in the system of broadcasting which had grown up prior to its creation. Commercial broadcasters were encouraged and others discouraged. Nonprofit broadcasters, including educational stations, were relegated to undesirable channels and hours and allowed only low power.

The principles used to justify this policy may be summarized briefly. First, there is the principle of priority. As a circuit court said in 1930: "It is not consistent with true public convenience, interest, or necessity, that meritorious stations . . . should be deprived of broadcasting privileges when once granted to them, which they have at great cost prepared themselves to exercise, unless clear and sound reasons of public policy demand such action." [14] While the court did not go so far as to say that licensees have a vested interest in a license (which the law explicitly forbade), and while it affirmed that broadcasting privileges are sub-

---

[13] The Act of 1927 authorized the Court of Appeals of the District of Columbia in reviewing action of the Commission to "alter or revise the decision appealed from and enter such judgment as to it may seem just." Dissatisfaction with this procedure led in 1930 to termination of "the administrative oversight of the Court of Appeals." The court was then restricted to a purely judicial review: findings of fact of the Commission, if supported by substantial evidence, were to be conclusive. Because much of the work of the Commission was reviewable in the District, the Court of Appeals, in spite of the change in the law, for some time tended to intrude into the administrative process. This intrusion was later rebuked by the Supreme Court. See *FCC* v. *Pottsville Broadcasting Co.*, 309 U.S. 134 (1940); *Fly* v. *Heitmeyer*, 309 U.S. 146 (1940).

[14] *Chicago Federation of Labor* v. *FRC*, 41 F. 2d 422.

ject to the reasonable regulatory authority of the Commission, the principle was clear that the established station had prior rights, other things being equal.[15] Such a principle necessarily favored those who came in on the ground floor. Since licenses are almost automatically renewed, they have become in practice extremely valuable properties.[16]

A second important criterion is that of technical qualification. Here engineering standards, such as adequacy of equipment, tests of interference, and quality of technical personnel, serve as measuring rods. Since these, for the most part, are objectively verifiable and vital to the efficient operation of a radio station, the soundness of such criteria, if fairly applied, is unimpeachable.

A third criterion is the test of economic qualification. Does the applicant have sound financial standing? Is there a showing of adequate commercial support for the station? Will the station which proposes to compete with existing facilities find such support? Will the applicant make the most economic utilization of the license if it be granted to him? These and other economic factors favor those with strong financial backing and resources.

A fourth criterion which is far from clear-cut is serviceability to the listening public. This has been interpreted as implying that the entire listening public within the service area of a station is entitled to service from that station, and that programs must be sufficiently well rounded to be of interest to all substantial groups represented in the listening public. So-called propaganda stations, which are the mouthpieces of particular social or economic groups and designed to appeal to particular groups in the listening public, get short shrift.[17] The application of these principles re-

[15] On the question of whether a licensee should be safeguarded from competition, the Supreme Court ten years later was somewhat less protective of licensees. It held that "economic injury to an existing station is not a separate and independent element to be taken into consideration by the Commission in determining whether it shall grant or withhold a license." This conclusion was qualified, however, as follows: "This is not to say that the question of competition between a proposed station and one operating under an existing license is to be entirely disregarded. . . . It may have a vital and important bearing upon the ability of the applicant adequately to serve his public; it may indicate that both stations—the existing and the proposed—will go under, with the result that a portion of the listening public will be left without adequate service; it may indicate that, by a division of the field, both stations will be compelled to render inadequate service." *FCC* v. *Sanders Brothers Radio Station*, 309 U.S. 470.

[16] WNEW, a radio station in New York City, was recently sold for $3.4 million, and WDTV, a Pittsburgh TV station, changed hands for $9.75 million.

[17] In refusing a request of the Chicago Federation of Labor (WCFL) for

served the more desirable facilities for commercial broadcasters on the ground that their programs were of wide general interest and ministered to popular tastes.

Broadcasting Regulation by the Federal Communications Commission

The abolition of the Federal Radio Commission in 1934 and the transfer of its powers to the newly created Federal Communications Commission (FCC) produced few important changes in radio regulation. Two members of the old Commission were appointed to the new body; the new appointees initiated no fundamental changes in policy. The statutory standards for the FCC were largely taken over from the Radio Act of 1927, and the new Commission showed little disposition to pour new wine into old bottles. The general framework of broadcast allocation and the priorities established earlier were left substantially unmodified. The development of broadcasting on a predominantly commercial basis continued. The FCC, like its predecessor, continued to be a political storm center. Ugly charges of incompetence and corruption produced demands for investigation and reorganization. The appointment in 1937 of Frank McNinch, former Power Commission chairman, as the new chairman of the FCC was hailed as an administration effort to "clean house."

Under McNinch, a number of reforms were initiated. The old organization into Telephone, Telegraph, and Broadcast sections was abolished in order to end divided responsibility. Important changes were made in leading personnel. Efforts were made to bring the docket up to date and to infuse a new spirit into FCC administration. This energizing of the Commission was sufficiently

---

permission to operate during the evening hours, the Commission (Chicago Federation of Labor, No. 4972, June 25, 1929) observed: "There are not enough frequencies within the broadcast band to give to each of the various groups of persons in the United States a channel on which to operate a broadcasting station."

In its Great Lakes Broadcasting Company decision (4900–02, February 1, 1929), denying a license to a religious sect known as the House of David, the Commission wrote: "Propaganda stations (a term which is used here for the sake of convenience and not in the derogatory sense) are not consistent with the most beneficial sort of discussion of public questions. . . . if the question were now raised for the first time, after the commission has given careful study to it, the commission would not license a propaganda station, at least to an exclusive position on a cleared channel. . . . while the commission is of the opinion that a broadcasting station engaged in public service has ordinarily a claim to preference over a propaganda station, it will apply this principle as to existing stations by giving preferential facilities to the former and assigning less desirable positions to the latter to the extent that engineering principles permit."

long lived to permit the issuance of its *Report on Chain Broadcasting*, discussed below, and thereby to offer its first, and only, major challenge to the existing structure of broadcasting. After having secured some reforms in network organization and practices, however, the FCC's new-found energy ebbed. It relapsed into an acceptance of the status quo, and thenceforth almost never used its power to deny a license renewal. Its moderation, however, gained it no respite from heated controversy, nor did it enable the Commission to avoid thorny problems, for acute conflicts of interest are inherent in the structure of commercial broadcasting.

The licensing power conveys such rich rewards and great privileges that the FCC has been inundated with efforts from all sides to influence its awards. Especially in recent years, it has failed to insulate itself adequately from these pressures. Its actions have led to charges that political or personal influence has at times played a determining role in the granting of licenses. A congressional investigation in 1958 dramatically documented the existence of such practices in a number of instances, and led to the resignation of one Commissioner,[18] who was subsequently indicted on charges of conspiracy to defraud the United States.

The major problems currently confronting the FCC can be conveniently considered under the following heads: (1) allocation of air space; (2) competition and concentration of control; (3) regulation and the advance of the art; and (4) censorship and program control.

Allocation of Air Space

The problem of allocating a limited number of broadcasting channels among a far greater number of applicants continually faces the FCC. In 1956, there were only 3,020 authorized AM stations and 650 TV stations. Each license granted gives to one applicant free of charge a potentially profitable privilege and, in effect, denies other applicants the opportunity to enter the field. Each decision also raises questions of the geographic distribution of broadcasting services, of competition and the concentration of control, and of the kind of service offered and the kind of audience served.

Given the Commission's commitment to commercial broadcasting, one of the major problems, first in AM and then in TV allocations, was that of station power. In the standard AM broadcast band, from 535 to 1,605 kilocycles, there is room for only 108

[18] See *Hearings* of the House Committee on Interstate and Foreign Commerce, Subcommittee on Legislative Oversight (1958), 85th Cong., 2d sess.

channels. The number of stations which may use any one channel without interference depends on the hours they broadcast, their locations, and the power of their signals. The FCC could maximize the number of stations by greatly limiting their power, but differences in power have major effects on the quality of broadcasting, its diversity, its geographic coverage, and the degree of competition. In general, low output promotes diversity and competition at the expense of quality and coverage.

The Act of 1927 stressed the goal of coverage, requiring the Commission so to distribute facilities "among the different States and communities as to give fair, efficient, and equitable radio service to each of the same." Dissatisfaction with the Commission's application of this formula led Congress in 1928 to enact the Davis Amendment, which required equal allocation of station facilities to each of five zones and a fair and equitable allocation to states within each zone according to population. The Commission tried to apply this rule by means of a rather rigid quota system, which gave rise to considerable litigation. A greater deficiency of this system was that, with commercial broadcasters naturally anxious to locate their stations in areas of maximum population density, rural listeners in sparsely populated areas found themselves disadvantaged. They received less and poorer broadcast service. The Act of 1934 attempted to correct this disparity by permitting the Commission to license 100-watt stations regardless of quota restrictions, but economic obstacles to the establishment of small stations in rural areas prevented this provision from having much effect.

In 1936, the Davis Amendment was repealed and a new standard substituted which emphasized reception and provided for "a fair, efficient, and equitable distribution of radio service." But economic obstacles continue to hinder adequate rural coverage. As a former Commissioner has pointed out, "One corollary of the American system in which broadcasting is supported by advertising revenue . . . is that . . . stations are located where the advertisers want them, not where they will best serve the country as a whole." [19] At one time, the FCC considered superpower stations as a means of serving isolated rural areas. From 1934 to 1939, it permitted WLW in Cincinnati to broadcast at 500 kilowatts. The experiment was successful but the FCC then ordered WLW back to 50 kilowatts, fearing that superpower stations would have an undue competitive advantage and would concentrate power over

[19] Address by Irvin Stewart, reprinted in R. S. Rankin, *Readings in American Government* (1939), pp. 275–276.

mass communications into too few hands.

Similar issues are confronted in limiting broadcast hours. Because of atmospheric conditions, an AM channel can accommodate fewer stations at night than in the day. Unless some stations are closed down at dusk, rural areas will lack clear reception after dark. The FCC's solution has been to designate some channels as "clear," reserving their use for a single licensee after dark. But closing a station down at sunset imposes severe financial restrictions on it as long as others are allowed to broadcast without limit.

At the present time, stations are classified as local, with up to 250 watts of power; regional, with from one to four kilowatts; and clear-channel, with from 10 to 50 kilowatts. Thus the earning power of stations is radically unequal, and network broadcasting contributes to lessen that regional diversity which low power was intended to provide. Nighttime operation by a second station is prohibited on twenty-five of the clear channels in an attempt to cover the rural areas. But these clear-channel stations are located in major cities, appeal mainly to an urban audience, and lack enough power to ensure maximum coverage. There are some areas where service is inadequate and many areas where local interests are not served. The problem of the remote, sparsely populated sections of the United States has still to be squarely met.[20]

The question of allocating adequate space on the air waves for education has been a continuing problem for several decades. Educational circles have long criticized the FRC and the FCC for sacrificing educational to commercial broadcasting, further charging that most commercia' broadcasters only use educational programs in the absence of sponsored programs. As a result of pressure from educational groups, the Act of 1934 directed the FCC to "study the proposal that Congress by statute allocate fixed percentages of radio broadcasting facilities to particular types or kinds of nonprofit activities." After lengthy hearings, and after assurances by commercial licensees that they would carry educational programs, the FCC concluded that it was inadvisable to make such an allocation. It did, however, aid in the formation of a Federal Radio Education Committee, composed of broadcasters and members of the public, to promote educational programs. Under the Committee's auspices, some experiments in educational broadcasting were launched, but the Committee was not notably

[20] Because of the commercial failure of FM broadcasting, discussed below, this field has presented few allocation problems. TV has presented some of the same allocation problems confronted in AM radio; they are discussed below in connection with regulation and the state of the art.

active or effective. Individual broadcasters have displayed some willingness to co-operate where interesting educational programs were offered, but they demonstrated an understandable reluctance to carry dull programs and a grim determination not to sacrifice lucrative commercial programs in favor of educational programs yielding no tangible income.

The efforts of educational institutions to obtain AM licenses have met frustrating obstacles. With the exception of a few low-power grants, their applications have been rejected. Education has been better served through FM. From the outset, the FCC reserved FM channels for educational broadcasting, in 1945 setting aside twenty of the ninety channels between 88 and 106 megacycles. Even though educational groups were generally slow to muster the resources for station operation and programing and to apply for licenses, the lack of strong pressure from commercial groups for FM licenses has served to protect the educational allocations. In 1956, there were 136 authorizations for noncommercial educational FM stations in thirty-four states and more space is still available. The spread of educational FM stations continues to be limited by inadequate financial backing and the smallness of the audience.

In contrast, TV allocations for education precipitated a major battle. The FCC considered the question at hearings conducted during the "freeze" on TV licenses, discussed below. At these hearings, the supporters of educational broadcasting, headed by the National Association of Educational Broadcasters, attacked the quality of commercial programs, cited the lack of educational programs carried by commercial stations, and asked that one-fourth of the TV channels be set aside for education. This requirement was opposed by the National Association of Radio and Television Broadcasters, which argued that educational groups lacked the funds to establish stations, the competence to produce programs, and the ability to attract large audiences. The compromise solution of the Commission reserved about one-tenth of the channels, enough to accommodate 242 educational stations. This number was later raised to 258, which would cover about three-fourths of the nation's cities.

Educational groups, however, encountered great difficulty in raising the substantial funds necessary for construction and operation of TV stations. By 1956, only twenty stations were in operation, serving areas with less than a third of the population; another twenty-one construction permits had been granted; and eleven applications were under consideration. The slowness of educational groups in securing licenses has caused would-be commercial broadcasters to eye avidly the more than two hundred unoccupied educational channels. While the FCC recognized in 1953 that educational institutions would require more time than commercial interests to prepare for TV operation, it also announced that channels could not be reserved for educational use indefinitely. In 1956, although denying one request for commercial utilization of a VHF channel reserved for education, it granted another such request and substituted a less desirable UHF channel for educational use.

Thus, after failing to do so in AM radio, the FCC has recognized the claim of education to some of the spectrum used for FM and TV. If efforts of educators to gain financial support for broadcasting ventures do not soon bear fruit, however, it is probable that the FCC will be exposed to increasing commercial pressure to obtain some of the TV channels now reserved for education.

Competition and Concentration of Control

Both the 1927 and the 1934 Acts sought to promote competition in broadcasting. Application of this policy has been uneven. While the FCC and its predecessor have been aware of the danger of concentrated control of communications, they have fought it only halfheartedly.

The 1927 Act directed the Radio Commission to refuse licenses to parties guilty of unlawful monopoly in the radio industry. But when RCA in 1931 was adjudged to have violated the antitrust laws, the Commission, by a vote of 3 to 2, decided that the statute did not require revocation of RCA's licenses. The 1934 law gave the courts discretionary power to revoke the licenses of those found guilty of violating the Sherman Act.

Where possible, the FCC has sought to promote competition within a communications medium by granting more than one license in each area.[21] But because of limited revenues available in sparsely populated areas and because of engineering limits on the possible number of channels, this policy has not been applied fully in TV, where the present FCC allocation plan calls for over 1,800 commercial channel assignments in over 1,200 communities. Unless "boosters," community antennae, or other new techniques

[21] In 1940, the Supreme Court held that a license conferred no protection against competition and that the FCC, in considering a license application, did not have to consider the effect of a grant on existing licensees. *FCC v. Sanders Bros. Radio Station*, 309 U.S. 470.

overcome this obstacle, there will continue to be many areas served only by a single TV station.

The Commission has also attempted to limit concentration in station ownership. The possessor of a license cannot receive another license in the same kind of broadcasting service (AM, FM, or TV) in the same service area. Furthermore, no broadcaster may have more than seven licenses in each kind of service.[22] These limitations are fairly generous, however, and have facilitated the development of substantial multiple ownership of radio and TV stations. The trend has been especially strong in TV, where concentration of ownership has developed rapidly. By 1956, half of the stations in the hundred largest markets were controlled by multiple ownership. In the words of a recent FCC interoffice memorandum, "in most large markets the image of a single-station owner with strong local ties giving his individual attention to a particular community is more myth than reality." [23]

Concentration is intensified by the fact that most multi-station TV owners also own AM and FM stations or other communications media, especially newspapers. The Commission has never tried to promote competition among different communications media. A majority of TV licenses and a large share of AM licenses are held by publishers. Expectations that the opening up of FM for licensing would make broadcasting more competitive have not been fulfilled. Confronted by strong pressure from AM licensees, the FCC eventually gave them over nine-tenths of the FM commercial licenses. In considering license applications from newspapers, the FCC has indicated some awareness of the dangers of concentration, and tends to favor other applicants when the newspaper has a local monopoly, but it also sometimes grants licenses to monopoly newspapers and it does not discriminate at all against competitive newspapers. Thus the FCC has neglected an opportunity to promote competition among different media and has tolerated the development of substantial concentration of control.

Concentration of control and standardization of broadcast fare have also been greatly furthered by the development of the broadcasting networks. Not until 1938 did the FCC begin to investigate this problem, and then only because of the complaints of affiliated

[22] FCC authority to limit the number of stations which may be licensed to any one interest was upheld in *U.S.* v. *Storer Broadcasting Co.*, 351 U.S. 192 (1956).

[23] Senate Committee on Interstate and Foreign Commerce, *Hearings: Television Inquiry* (1957), Part V, p. 3381.

independently owned stations who felt themselves disadvantaged in their bargaining with the networks.

The FCC's *Report on Chain Broadcasting*, issued in 1941, documented the stations' grievances. Because of the great audience appeal of network programs, the chains were able to dominate their local radio-station outlets. Contracts with affiliated stations ran for long terms and gave the networks an option on most of the stations' broadcasting hours. Networks usually exercised their options only about one-third of the time, but could, on short notice, do so without regard to the local station's commitments. The local station could seldom reject a network program, could not compete with the network for national advertising, and could not carry programs from other networks. The Commission concluded that network contracts were restraining competition and preventing stations from providing their proper services to the public.

On this occasion, the FCC moved vigorously to eradicate these abuses. Unable directly to regulate the networks, it used its licensing power to assert control over the contracts which its licensees were permitted to sign. Network contracts were limited to two years and the option power over affiliates was restricted. Stations were given greater freedom to reject network programs, allowed to accept programs from other networks, and permitted to compete for advertising.[24] The Justice Department joined in the attack on network power with an antitrust suit to compel NBC to dispose of one of its two networks. NBC sold its Blue network, which became the American Broadcasting Company (ABC). Thus the position of the affiliated stations was strengthened, the powers of NBC and CBS lessened, and the weaker Mutual Broadcasting System and ABC were made better able to compete with the two major networks. The industry became somewhat more competitive, but the dominance of networks and of network broadcasting remained substantially undisturbed.[25] This dominance has been slowly eroded by the greater appeal of TV for audiences who previously listened to network radio broadcasts.

TV stations in the first years of the medium were few enough

[24] These rules were upheld by the Supreme Court in *NBC* v. *U.S.*, 319 U.S. 190 (1943).

[25] Indeed, a minority member of the FCC has argued that FCC network rules had almost no real effect ". . . although the rules prohibited certain types of provisions in affiliation contracts, they left the stations and the networks relatively free to conduct their actual operations in much the same fashion as before, so long as the affiliation contract conformed to the letter of the law." Frieda B. Hennock, in *Television Inquiry*, Part I, p. 303.

in number to have substantial bargaining power in dealing with the three national TV networks. After the FCC freeze on new stations ended in 1952,[26] and the number of stations on the air increased, station complaints about network power and practices mounted. In response to these complaints, as well as out of concern over concentration of control, Congress in 1955 appropriated funds for an FCC investigation of the present operations of television and radio networks. In 1957, committees of both Senate and House explored the subject, evidencing a disposition to restrict network power. In the same year, a special FCC study group concluded that the networks, though "necessary and highly desirable," exercised an unreasonably "high concentration of control" over TV broadcasting. The group recommended to the Commission that it eliminate network option power, that it prohibit network "must-buy" requirements compelling advertisers to buy time on all of a designated group of affiliated network stations, that it further restrict network ownership of TV stations, and that it ask Congress for authority to regulate networks directly. In 1958, the FCC was still conducting hearings on these recommendations, but the Justice Department had added its weight to the pressure for further action by threatening to bring antitrust action against the networks if the FCC did not adopt regulations limiting network option powers and "must-buy" policies.[27] The networks countered with the argument that these practices were necessary to maintain the quality of network broadcasting, but the demand for further controls continued.

Regulation and the Advance of the Arts

Probably the most difficult task confronting the FCC is that of controlling technology and promoting the development of new services. The Act of 1934 directed the Commission to "study new uses for radio, provide for experimental uses of frequencies, and generally encourage the larger and more effective use of radio in the public interest."

The task is a most difficult one. In few fields is the pace of technical change as rapid as in radio and television. The development of each innovation depends on the Commission's willingness to provide channels for experimentation, and ultimately for commercial exploitation. The FCC is exposed to pressure from all sides—from the interests that find their established positions threatened by new discoveries and from the groups which stand

[26] See page 403 below.
[27] New York Times, June 1, 1958.

to benefit. Too speedy approval of innovations may prematurely standardize inferior techniques and equipment; unnecessary delay will deny the public the benefit of new services.

This problem of timing was presented in 1950 when the FCC considered the application of CBS to begin color telecasts. CBS and RCA had been engaged in a scientific and engineering race to develop a system of color television. CBS had won, producing a system based on the use of a spinning disk attached to the receiver. It pressed its application, arguing that the public should be allowed the benefits of this discovery. NBC and most other interests in the industry opposed the application, arguing that the dot-sequential system NBC was still perfecting would produce better pictures and was "compatible" (i.e., its color broadcasts could be received in black-and-white on existing TV receivers). Hasty action, they argued, would establish and perpetuate an inferior method. Important interests were at stake—the question of whose patents would be valuable, which manufacturer would have a headstart, and the possible obsolescence of black-and-white sets then in inventories and in homes.

The FCC decided for CBS after lengthy hearings, but its decision did not become effective until the Supreme Court in May, 1951, upheld its reasonableness, without passing on its wisdom.[28] But in October of that year, the Office of Defense Mobilization requested CBS to postpone its development of color transmitting and receiving equipment because it involved the use of scarce materials needed in the Korean War. RCA and other interests in the industry took advantage of this delay to perfect a compatible system of color telecasting. They requested the Commission to reconsider its decision. In December, 1953, the FCC reversed itself with no objection from CBS, and approved the NBC system. Only the accidental delay imposed by the Korean War had prevented the Commission from committing the industry to a distinctly inferior system.

FM broadcasting also presented the FCC with the difficult problem of defining a role for a new broadcasting medium. FM is superior to AM in major respects. Reception is better, for there is relatively little interference or static. Since FM uses higher frequencies and its signals cover smaller areas, many more stations can be accommodated in the spectrum. Consequently, it was expected that FM would quickly be accepted, would provide greater opportunities for diversity in radio services, and would make the field more competitive.

[28] RCA v. U.S., 341 U.S. 412.

Despite bitter opposition from AM stations, the Commission authorized FM broadcasting in 1940. World War II then caused the Commission to freeze FM licenses until October, 1945. When the FM spectrum finally became available, applications flooded in, and 769 stations were licensed in the next two years. But the FCC grossly underestimated the extent to which existing patterns of operation and reception in AM broadcasting had frozen the mold of radio. FM stations almost immediately found themselves trapped in a vicious circle: there were no FM receivers, because there were no programs, because there was no advertising, because there were no receivers. Listeners were reluctant to buy FM receivers, which were more expensive than AM sets, because of the paucity of FM programs. FM stations had difficulty in providing programs because advertisers would not pay for them until an FM audience existed. The radio networks at first starved FM by denying it permission to carry network programs. After complaints began to descend on the FCC, the networks reversed their position. They then allowed their AM affiliates to carry network programs on their FM stations, provided that the FM stations duplicated all the network programs carried by the parent AM station. This hurt independent FM stations and prevented the affiliated FM stations from offering much independent programing. As a result, the death rate among commercial FM stations was high. There were 1,020 in 1948 but only 546 in 1956. And in 1955 only 38 of the surviving FM stations were independent of AM stations. Thus the FM listener, first denied all network programs, was later offered broadcasting services which differed hardly at all from those on the AM broadcast band.

FM has been a commercial failure, and it has, with one important exception, failed to add to the diversity of broadcasting services. Some of the unprofitable independent FM stations, lacking the financial resources to produce live programs, have begun to broadcast recordings of fine music, thereby serving a small audience largely neglected by AM radio. In other respects FM has not yielded the superior service of which it is capable. The FCC proved unable to overcome the obstacles raised by the prior existence of, and the vested interests in, an inferior service.

Television has presented still other technical and commercial dilemmas. TV broadcasting was inaugurated on the basis of insufficient technical knowledge and inadequate economic foresight. After the war, when the FCC first began to license commercial TV broadcasters, it originally allotted them that portion of the VHF band between 54 and 216 megacycles. When shared with

FM, this provided only twelve channels for TV. The FCC over-estimated the number of stations a channel could carry without interference and grossly underestimated the demand for licenses. Its allocation plan assumed that stations in the same channel could be as close as 150 miles without interfering with each station's service radius of 50 miles. Even with this crowding, how-ever, the FCC allocation plan gave TV service only to the nation's 140 metropolitan districts.

It became apparent by 1948 that 150 miles of co-channel separa-tion was inadequate to protect against serious interference and that a separation of at least 220 miles was necessary. Such a separa-tion would have greatly reduced the number of licenses available at the very time when, with 108 stations already in operation or under construction, there were more applications pending than spaces available. Furthermore, small cities were protesting against the FCC allocation plan, which gave them no TV service. Faced with an impossible situation, the FCC in September, 1948, issued a "freeze" order, which halted the processing of further TV applications. From then until April, 1952, when the "freeze" was lifted, it worked out a new plan, under which allocations were reduced in the VHF band but sixty new channels were opened up for TV in the UHF band between 470 and 880 megacycles. This plan assigned 2,053 licenses, over two-thirds UHF, to 1,291 com-munities. This allocation, the FCC thought, would promote "the full development of a nation-wide competitive system," achieving the basic aims of providing "(a) at least one service to all areas, (b) at least one station in the largest number of communities, and (c) multiple services in as many communities as possible to pro-vide program choice to the public and to facilitate competition among broadcasters, networks and other elements of the in-dustry." [29]

The new allocation plan, however, by failing to anticipate the relations between VHF and UHF, caused the FCC to repeat much the same error it had earlier committed in FM. When the freeze was lifted, applications for UHF and VHF licenses flooded the Commission. In 1952, there were 108 commercial stations authorized to broadcast; by 1956, there were 609. Most of the new licensees were UHF stations handicapped by the fact that virtually all existing receivers were equipped to receive only VHF programs. Furthermore, the Commission had unwisely adopted a policy of "intermixing" UHF and VHF licensees in the same service area. In only three of the one hundred largest markets were there no

[29] FCC, *Annual Report, 1956*, p. 94.

VHF stations. Networks chose to affiliate with VHF stations. As in the case of FM, UHF stations lacked the audience with which to attract advertisers with which to finance programs with which to appeal to audiences. Furthermore, receivers equipped to receive UHF as well as VHF were more expensive. The statistics on TV receivers dramatize the problem. When the freeze was lifted, the public possessed 17 million VHF receivers. In the first two and one-half years which followed, only 3½ million of the 18 million sets sold were UHF-equipped.[30] As a result, it was generally the VHF stations which carried the network programs and were profitable; the UHF stations were denied audiences and network programs and were consequently unprofitable.[31] By June, 1955, thirty-one UHF stations had ceased operation.

Thus television has less competition and less diversity than it might have had with more foresight in FCC policy. Congressional committees have concerned themselves with the plaints of hard-pressed UHF licensees, and in response to pressure from a Senate committee, the FCC in 1956 announced that it was undertaking "a thorough searching analysis of the possibilities for improving and expanding the nationwide television system through the exclusive use of the UHF band throughout or in a major portion of the United States." As an interim measure, it proposed to pursue a policy of "deintermixture," i.e., of changing allocations so as to assign whole service areas exclusively to either UHF or VHF.[32] It has been slow to implement this policy, however, and each passing month increases the public investment in VHF receivers and the size of the vested interest in VHF broadcasting.

Censorship and Program Control

Another difficult assignment given the FCC is that of promoting the freedom of broadcasting, of denying itself and broadcasters the power of censorship, and yet of insuring that programs render a public service. The significance of radio and TV broadcasting in influencing public opinion underlines the importance of the freedom of the air. The relevant sections of law are concise. Section 326 of the Communications Act provides:

[30] *Television Inquiry*, Part I, p. 290.

[31] An FCC survey of the operations for ten months of 1954 of stations licensed after the end of the freeze showed that 71 per cent of the VHF stations and only 27 per cent of the UHF stations had started to earn a monthly profit. Seventy per cent of the VHF stations and only forty-six per cent of the UHF stations carried network programs. *Ibid.*, pp. 159–161.

[32] S. Rept. No. 2769, 84th Cong., 2d sess., pp. 30, 32–33.

Nothing in this Act shall be understood or construed to give the Commission the power of censorship over the radio communications or signals transmitted by any radio station, and no regulation or condition shall be promulgated or fixed by the Commission which shall interfere with the right of free speech by means of radio communication. No person within the jurisdiction of the United States shall utter any obscene, indecent, or profane language by means of radio communication.

Section 315 reads:

If any licensee shall permit any person who is a legally qualified candidate for any public office to use a broadcasting station, he shall afford equal opportunities to all other such candidates for that office in the use of such broadcasting station, and the Commission shall make rules and regulations to carry this provision into effect: *Provided,* That such licensee shall have no power of censorship over the material broadcast under the provisions of this section. No obligation is hereby imposed upon any licensee to allow the use of its station by any such candidate.

In exercising its powers under these provisions, the Commission has taken the position that it cannot regulate the content of programs because of the statutory prohibition against censorship. At the same time, it has made clear that in considering license renewals, it would take into consideration the past conduct of applicants, including the content and character of their programs. Is not this power to scrutinize programs, some critics ask, the virtual equivalent of censorship?

In fact, the power of license revocation is so extreme that the Commission is most reluctant to use it. Licenses are renewed almost automatically. In the very few cases in which the FCC has moved to deny renewals because of program content, the avowed reasons have been objectionable advertising, indecent and defamatory utterances, or in one case, a gross slanting of news commentaries to attack certain groups. On the whole, a good case can be made out for the proposition that the Commission has been more zealous in guarding the freedom of the air, particularly in the case of political broadcasting, than have individual broadcasters. It has on occasion intervened to persuade broadcasters to grant some groups an opportunity to present their views, although it has not insisted that every unpopular minority has a right to broadcast. It has been most vigorous in protecting the right of political candidates to equal broadcasting opportunities, requiring licensees to keep a complete record of requests for time for political broadcasting, the disposition of the requests, and the charges made. It forbids licensees to "editorialize," unless contrary opinions are given equal time.

But there are limits on how much freedom the FCC can guarantee. A licensee necessarily has great discretion over his choice of programs; he can, and sometimes does, refuse to carry programs contrary to his own views and interests. His exercise of "editorial selection" reflects diverse influences—his own economic interest, the pressure of advertisers, and the demands of particularly active pressure groups within his radio audience. News commentaries may be unbalanced, since stations sell time and advertisers are free to fill it with the commentators they select. Yet the air remains relatively free; opposing major groups are usually given some hearing; and while some issues are avoided, many controversial issues are discussed.

Although the FCC is denied censorship powers and generally holds loose reins on broadcasters, it has expressed some interest in program content. It gives substantial consideration to declared program policies in passing upon applications for licenses, although it seldom seriously considers actual programing in approving renewals. In 1946, the Commission issued a report on the *Public Service Responsibility of Broadcast Licensees,* spotlighting the great discrepancy between applicants' stated intentions and their actual performance as licensees. The report documented the excessive commercialization of radio, the failure to develop local programs, and the narrow standardization of broadcast fare to the detriment of balanced offerings. But the FCC proposed no action; instead, it suggested that these abuses and deficiencies be corrected by self-regulation and by public criticism. In 1949, the Commission attempted to prohibit "give-away" programs as lotteries, but in 1954 the Supreme Court held that such shows were not lotteries within the meaning of the law.[33]

Thus the Commission, as in other areas of its jurisdiction, has used its sweeping powers most sparingly. Although broadcasting is a service uniquely dependent on government regulation, program content is virtually unregulated, and licensees, once enabled to operate in this area, are remarkably free from regulation. For the most part, policies of licensees, and ultimately of advertisers, determine what broadcasting services are offered. Public policy, as it is administered, exerts little influence on the quality or the

[33] *FCC* v. *American Broadcasting Co.,* 347 U.S. 284.

content of these services. Current programing for the most part ignores a significant audience, one comparable to that served by the Third Program of the British Broadcasting Company. Policy changes in the interest of this latter group are most unlikely, however, as long as it remains unorganized and politically ineffective and as long as the vast majority of consumers remain well satisfied, as they apparently are, with present broadcasting fare.

CHAPTER 14

Government and the Investor

A CENTURY AGO, wealth took the form largely of physical property such as land, merchandise, ships, and mills. With the growth of corporate enterprise and the consequent spread of investment in corporate securities, ownership of wealth has come to be represented, in large part, by paper claims to property—stocks and bonds which can be bought and sold in small denominations and which are traded on security exchanges. In fiscal 1956, the value of securities traded on stock exchanges was $38 billion, and $13 billion in new security issues were registered for sale.[1]

The security investment system lies at the heart of the private sector of the American economy. Through its mechanism private savings flow into productive enterprise and give direction to the nation's economic development. Proper performance of the investment function is crucial to efficient allocation and utilization of economic resources. Fluctuations in the value and yield of securities have a major impact on levels of national income and on economic welfare. Furthermore, a majority of American families have a direct or indirect stake in security investments. Stock in publicly owned corporations is held by an estimated 8.5 million individuals. And the many millions who have savings accounts or life insurance policies, or who are beneficiaries of endowed institutions, share a stake which is indirect, but nonetheless real.

[1] SEC, *Annual Report, 1956,* p. xi.
408

1. The Rise of Security Investments

The spread of security investments is a relatively recent development. In the first half of the nineteenth century, the few securities issued were sold mainly through private banks to a few wealthy individuals here and abroad. Modern investment banking arose to meet the post-Civil War need to mobilize capital for the expanding programs of corporate enterprise. The investment banker began essentially as a middleman, buying securities from corporations and governmental units and selling them to investors. As investment banking houses gained strength, their aims became more ambitious. Extending their influence into industry, they exercised some control over the sources of the demand for investment funds. At the same time, they expanded their power over the supply of capital through integration with insurance companies, trust companies, and commercial banks. The classic example of successful penetration in both these directions was the House of Morgan; other investment banking firms played lesser roles.

Prior to World War I, fewer than 500,000 Americans invested in securities. The wartime Liberty Loan campaigns popularized the purchase of securities by small investors. During the 1920's, moreover, many large corporations, particularly public utilities, embarked on sales campaigns to promote employee and customer stock ownership and thus added hundreds of thousands of shareholders to their lists. Investment trusts had a mushroom growth and also competed for the savings of small investors. The result was a tremendous increase in the number of direct investors and a revolution in the organization of investment banking. Instead of catering to a market of 500,000, securities sales organizations were developed to tap a potential market of more than 10 million customers.

The distribution of large blocks of securities often involved complex organization. Managing bankers would investigate and sponsor the issue, perhaps inviting other "originating" bankers to join them in assuming initial financial responsibility. The originating group might then organize a larger group of firms to underwrite the securities—i.e., agree to purchase on a fixed day at a fixed price. The underwriting group, in turn, resold the issue to a "selling" group of firms, mostly dealers, who disposed of the securities to the public. This complex organization was necessary to sell large issues to thousands of small investors and to dilute the risks involved.

The spread between the price paid to the issuing firm and the price charged to the investor was divided among the managing bankers, the originating group, the underwriting group, and the dealers. To protect against price weakness in the open market, which would make it impossible for the selling group to dispose of its issues at the agreed retail price, the underwriting group usually maintained what was called a trading account. The manager of this account stood ready to buy the security in the open market at the price fixed. This function was usually called "pegging," "fixing," or "stabilizing" the market. When the security issue had been substantially sold, the manager of the trading account usually pulled the peg, liquidated any remaining holdings, and allowed the issue to find its own price in the market.

2. Abuses in Investment Banking and the Securities Market

This method of disposing of securities sometimes presented serious hazards for the ordinary investor. Unless the originating bankers and underwriters thoroughly investigated the borrower and adequately disclosed all relevant data, unless the investor knew how much of the price he paid went to the borrower and how much to the distributors, unless he could be assured that the investment banker was not abusing his trust by market manipulations in the distributed security or by letting certain favored clients in on the ground floor, the investor would find himself in no position to appraise the value of securities and might lose all confidence in the machinery by which they were distributed.

There was much in the experience of the 1920's to shake the confidence of the small investor in the securities distribution system. The twelve thousand pages of the Senate hearings conducted from 1932 to 1934 are filled with revelations of incompetence and carelessness, of irresponsibility and abuse of trust by prominent investment bankers. In no field were abuses more glaring than in foreign financing. The Senate committee calculated that of $3.2 billion in foreign corporation securities outstanding on March 1, 1934, $1.4 billion were in default. Of $5 billion in foreign government securities, over $1.5 billion were in default. The committee concluded:

The record of the activities of investment bankers in the flotation of foreign securities is one of the most scandalous chapters in the history of American investment banking. The sale of these foreign issues was characterized by practices and abuses which were violative of the most elementary principles of business ethics.[2]

Dubious practices were not confined to the distribution of foreign issues. It was estimated that between 1923 and 1933 investors lost $25 billion through the purchase of worthless securities, the preponderance of which was domestic.[3] One source of abuse since terminated by legislation developed from the interrelationships of commercial and investment banking.[4] Large commercial banks sometimes organized affiliated investment companies and used them to speculate in bank stock, to manipulate the market price of securities, and to conduct other operations legally forbidden to commercial banks. In numerous instances, investment bankers sponsored issues which created unsound and unfair corporate structures. Perpetual option warrants were issued enabling the sponsoring banker to purchase common stock at a fixed price over an unlimited time. In some cases, voting trusts were established which compelled stockholders to surrender their franchise. Stockholders' pre-emptive rights to subscribe to additional stock issues were circumvented. Provisions for substitution of collateral were included in trust indentures without adequate safeguards.

Meanwhile, investment bankers were frequently paid well for their labors. In 1929, for example, J. P. Morgan & Company received, for $1 each, 1,514,200 option warrants on United Corporation stock. Within sixty days the firm was in a position to sell these warrants for at least $40 each, netting a profit of some $60 million.[5] Sometimes investment bankers shared their profits with a selected list of influential individuals by offering them securities at prices well below those charged other investors. J. P. Morgan and Kuhn, Loeb, as well as the National City Company and other prominent investment firms, all had their "preferred lists," and some individuals high in the economic and political world shared in the bounty.

Lax practices in investment banking had their counterpart in serious abuses in the security markets. Corporation directors, of-

---

[2] Senate Committee on Banking and Currency, *Stock Exchange Practices*, 73rd Cong., 2nd sess. (1934), p. 125.

[3] *Ibid., Regulation of Securities*, S. Rept. No. 47, 73rd Cong., 1st sess. (1933), p. 2.

[4] The Banking Act of 1933 completely severed commercial banking from investment banking.

[5] *Stock Exchange Practices*, p. 115.

ficers, and principal shockholders were in some cases able and willing to utilize confidential information, which came to them by virtue of their positions, in their personal market activities. Pools and other varieties of manipulation were common practices. In the late twenties, credit was freely available for speculation, and margin purchasing became a national pastime. While stock quotations soared dizzily upward, the speculative debauch was unrestrained, but with the collapse of the market in 1929 came heavy losses and disillusionment. During the years of depression which followed, attention turned to the reform of investment and financial practices.

A series of laws was enacted to achieve such reforms. The Securities Act of 1933 began a new era of investor protection. This measure, however, focused only on the issuance of new securities. In 1934, the Securities Exchange Act extended regulation to the securities markets and created the Securities and Exchange Commission (SEC), a bipartisan body of five members, to administer the Acts of 1933 and 1934. The next year, the Public Utility Holding Company Act extended SEC regulatory authority into the field of utility holding company organization and finance.[6] Subsequently the Commission was given broadened authority with respect to over-the-counter markets, was enabled to participate in corporate reorganizations, and was authorized to regulate trust indentures, investment trusts, and investment advisers. As a result of this cumulative grant of power, the SEC became the paramount administrative guardian of the interests of investors in the corporate sector of the economy.

3. The Securities Act of 1933

The draftsmen of the Securities Act drew heavily upon British experience in the protection of investors. In Britain, in 1844, a Select Committee on Joint Stock Companies, under the chairmanship of W. E. Gladstone, had issued a notable report embodying what became the two basic principles of our own Securities Act—first, that investors should have adequate means for knowing the real financial state of a concern, and second, that those issuing securities should be legally responsible for supplying full and accurate information to investors. The British Companies Act of 1844, which adopted the recommendations of Gladstone's committee, provided for the registration of company prospectuses. It introduced the principle of compulsory disclosure of relevant in-

[6] The Holding Company Act is discussed at pages 349ff., above.

formation concerning security issues. Subsequent acts widened the area of specific disclosures required. Through this legislation, the principle of full disclosure became established among the accepted and respected conventions of business in Great Britain. The draftsmen of the Securities Act also drew upon earlier American efforts to protect investors. A generation before, there had been much support, including that of President Taft, for a federal incorporation bill. In a volume entitled *Other People's Money*, Louis D. Brandeis had analyzed the traps and pitfalls which beset investors, pointed to the legislative advances made in England, and called for full and complete disclosure of facts in the marketing of securities. In 1920, the ICC was given some control over railroad financing, and some of the stronger public utility commissions had tried to supervise the financial operations of companies subject to their jurisdiction.

Beginning with Kansas in 1911, the states enacted legislation, later called "blue-sky" laws, to regulate the sale of securities.[7] By 1933, every state except Nevada had passed such legislation. The laws varied widely in their scope and character. Some merely provided penalties for fraud. Others required the registration of security salesmen or the licensing of dealers, but not the registration of securities. Still others provided for the registration of securities, but involved no control over dealers. The best type combined both kinds of control. Regulation under these statutes was limited. Some "get-rich" schemes were exposed and other fraudulent promotions discouraged, but inadequate administrative provisions for enforcement, as well as jurisdictional difficulties, condemned the blue-sky laws to but limited effectiveness.

In utilizing this reservoir of experience, the draftsmen of the Securities Act of 1933 made the British Companies Act their primary model. The Securities Act has been aptly called the "truth in securities act." Its declared purpose is "to provide full and fair disclosure of the character of securities sold in interstate and foreign commerce through the mails." The federal government does not guarantee the soundness of securities; it does seek to compel the publication of all relevant information about new issues, so that investors will at least have an opportunity to know and understand what they are buying. The Act applies only to securities publicly offered. Certain transactions and security issues are exempted, such as the issues of government bodies, banks, building-and-loan associations, carriers regulated by the ICC, in-

---

[7] This term apparently was coined by the proposer of the Kansas law, who complained that some companies sought to "capitalize the blue skies."

surance companies and farmers' co-operatives.[8]

To issue securities subject to the Act, a registration statement must be filed with the SEC.[9] The information in this document is publicly available from the date of filing. A prospectus containing a digest of the registration statement must be given to all persons to whom the securities are offered for sale. In order that the Commission and the public may have an opportunity to examine the statement before the securities are put on the market, no public offering can be made until twenty days after filing.[10] This twenty-day "cooling period" was designed to do away with some of the high-pressure methods of the past which frequently forced distributors, dealers, and investors to make commitments blindly.

The information which must be furnished in the registration statement is intended to reveal facts essential to a fair judgment of the security. The statement must truly state each material fact and cannot omit anything necessary to keep a statement from being misleading. In the case of established businesses, the various items required include information about the character and scope of the business; its corporate structure; the specific purposes for which the new money is to be used; balance sheets and statements of earnings and operations for at least the previous three years; compensation of officers, direct and indirect; any arrangements concerning stock options; the nature of the underwriting contract, etc. For new promotions, the information required is even more detailed and is designed to reveal the character of the promoters, the compensation to be received directly or indirectly by them, and other relevant aspects of the promotional process.

The Act provides administrative, criminal, and civil sanctions to ensure full and true disclosure. In exercising its administrative powers, the SEC is authorized to issue a stop order refusing to permit a registration statement to become effective (thus delaying marketing of the securities). It may also issue a stop order revoking a registration statement if further investigation shows the statement to be false or incomplete. In practice this drastic remedy is seldom invoked because the SEC ordinarily gives the registrant

[8] The Act also permits the SEC to exempt offerings not exceeding $300,000. Commission regulations accordingly permit certain companies to make such offerings, after the filing of a simple "Notification" and with the use of an offering circular containing certain basic information.

[9] Until the creation of the SEC in 1934, administration of the Securities Act of 1933 was vested in the Federal Trade Commission.

[10] An amendment in 1940 permitted the SEC to shorten this waiting period if it finds that full disclosure has been made.

advance notice of weaknesses in his statement by a letter of deficiency, perhaps supplemented by conferences, and then delays the effective date of registration until the deficiency is made good. When the Commission has issued a stop order, it becomes illegal to use the mails and other channels of interstate commerce for the sale of the specific securities involved, and the SEC may apply for an injunction to prevent such use. In addition, the Commission may refer cases to the Department of Justice for the institution of criminal proceedings. Willful violation of the law is punishable by a fine of not more than $5,000 or imprisonment for not more than five years, or both.

The Act also imposes civil liabilities on registrants and those participating in the preparation of registration statements. Liability arises if a seller has not filed a registration statement, has not sent a prospectus to a buyer, or makes the sale on the basis of a materially false or misleading oral statement. Persons suffering losses resulting from false registration statements may sue for damages those responsible for the falsehood. The original civil liability provisions were amended in 1934, after charges that their drastic character had deterred new financing. Under the amended Act, a defendant may reduce his liability to the extent that he can prove that any portion or all of the loss suffered was not caused by the mistake in the registration statement. The burden of proof, however, is still on the defendant. The amended Act also requires a purchaser to prove that he relied on a prospectus containing the mistake, if the purchase occurred after the publication of an earning statement covering a twelve-month period after registration. Suits cannot be brought more than three years after the public offering.

When the Act was adopted, it was believed that the investor's principal protection would derive from these civil-liability provisions, which were a focal point of controversy. Opponents feared that impossible burdens and liabilities were being placed on the issuers and sellers of securities. In fact, however, few suits for civil damages have resulted.[11] These provisions have contributed to the main purpose of the Act—to require full disclosure—but they have not established effective machinery to enable investors to recoup losses. Instead, the emphasis in the administration of the Act has been on detecting and exposing false statements before harm can be done.

[11] Between 1933 and 1940, only sixteen civil suits were filed, and only three resulted in the recovery of damages. "Civil Liability under the Federal Securities Act," *Yale Law Journal* (November, 1940), pp. 90–106.

The Act has had a considerable impact on the security distribution system. The power of investment bankers has been lessened. Generally, the distribution "spread"—the difference between the retail offering price and the proceeds reaching the corporation issuing the securities—has tended to narrow.[12] Private placements of corporate securities with such large institutional investors as insurance companies, banks, investment trusts, and pension funds have greatly increased since 1933, averaging well over one-third of all placements in recent years. Since investment bankers play a much smaller role in private placements, this trend has cut off what was once a lucrative source of investment-banking income.

From the point of view of the investor, the Act must be credited with many positive accomplishments. To be sure, it does not guarantee investors against losses. It cannot fully eliminate fraud or gullibility. But it does ensure that investors receive truthful and adequate information and that they have the opportunity to exercise intelligent judgment based on the facts. The affairs of corporate enterprise and the complexities of investment underwriting, previously obscured by scanty balance sheets and income statements, are now fully exposed to the light of day. While it would probably be naive to expect that all, or even most, investors intelligently read prospectuses, and it can be argued that most prospectuses are too bulky and too crammed with bewilderingly detailed information, nevertheless, the data they contain are carefully scanned by professional investment services and publicized in the financial press. The fraudulent promoter hesitates to expose himself to SEC scrutiny and finds large-scale operations difficult. The Commission's careful examination of registration statements has its repercussions in the business world in the form of improved accounting practices and higher standards of corporate administration. In this sense, the Securities Act provides ultimate protection for investors by pointing the way to a healthier corporate economy.

4. Regulation of the Securities Exchanges

The Securities Exchange Act of 1934 was designed to accomplish three major purposes: (1) "to make available currently to the investing public information regarding the affairs of the cor-

---

[12] P. P. Gourrich, "Investment Banking Methods Prior to and Since the Securities Act of 1933," *Law and Contemporary Problems* (January, 1937), p. 69. See also the opinion of Judge Medina in *U.S.* v. *Morgan et al.*, 188 F. Supp. 621 (1953).

porations whose securities are traded in the securities markets"; (2) "to prevent the diversion into security transactions of a disproportionate amount of the nation's credit resources"; and (3) "to eliminate manipulation and other abuses in the security markets." [13]

In promoting the first purpose, the 1934 Act sought to supplement and extend the disclosure requirements of the 1933 law, which applied only to new issues. Accordingly, the 1934 Act required the registration of all securities traded on national exchanges as well as the registration of the exchanges themselves. Registration involves the disclosure of information similar to that required of new issues, including the issuer's business; its capital structure; its officers; their remuneration, options, bonuses, and profit-sharing plans; and annual financial statements certified by independent accountants.

To carry out the second purpose, the Federal Reserve Board was given power to set margin requirements, and the SEC was authorized to restrict borrowing by members of exchanges, brokers, and dealers. Actually, control over margins and loans on securities serves a broader purpose than the Act indicates. Because of the elasticity of the credit base of the American banking system, uncontrolled margin trading, in which a buyer puts up only a small percentage of the cost of securities and has his broker use the purchased securities as collateral for loans to finance the rest of the cost, may serve to accentuate market instability and adversely affect the economy. In a rising market, increased collateral values make possible larger loans to margin traders which may be used to bid up prices and thus to feed an inflationary spiral. When a price decline does begin, there is a deflationary spiral in which falling prices reduce collateral values, causing loan liquidations, which put further downward pressure on prices. Thus control over margins and borrowing on securities is designed to contribute to the stability of the economy as well as to curb unhealthy speculation.

To carry out the third purpose, the Act proscribes a large number of manipulative and unfair practices and vests the Commission with power to check their use. Willful violation is punishable by a fine of not more than $10,000 or imprisonment for not more than two years, or both.[14] Persons engaging in manipulative practices can be sued for damages by injured parties. In order to eliminate the unfair use of corporate information by "insiders," all directors, officers, and owners of 10 per cent or more of a reg-

[13] SEC, *Annual Report, 1939*, p. 35.
[14] If the violator is an exchange, the fine may be $500,000.

istered equity security must file a monthly statement of transactions in the securities of their own company, and any profits
made on such transactions where the securities are held for a period
of six months or less can be recovered by the company or any of
its stockholders. The SEC is empowered to regulate short selling,
in which a seller, anticipating a price drop, sells for later delivery
securities he does not own. While short sales facilitate the normal
functioning of a market, they had often been abused, especially in
"raiding" a falling market. SEC rules are designed to restrain such
abuses. In addition, the Commission is vested with broad power to
suspend or withdraw the registration of a securities exchange or
of particular securities listed on exchanges. It may also suspend or
expel members and may deny or revoke the registration of a broker
or dealer engaged in over-the-counter trading. The SEC may also
impose trading rules on an exchange, if they are deemed necessary
and the exchange refuses to effect the desired changes.

The SEC has used sparingly its broad powers to regulate exchange trading practices, preferring to rely on the self-regulation
of exchanges to control the activities of their members. This SEC
policy is perhaps best exemplified by its relations with the New
York Stock Exchange, which accounts for the preponderance of exchange transactions.[15] The Exchange is a voluntary association
with a constitution and bylaws. Until the passage of the 1934 Act,
it was subject only to internal regulation. Until 1938, its control
was entrusted to a Governing Committee chosen from its members. This Committee and its subordinate committees prescribed
the trading rules; it could fine, suspend, or expel those members
whom it found guilty of violating its rules. Although the largest
group of members were commission brokers, and although commission houses and their allies had a majority of seats on the
Exchange, the Committee was controlled by "inside" elements—
the floor traders, specialists, and odd-lot dealers. The nomination
and election machinery was so arranged as to perpetuate "inside"
control.

The commission brokers and allied groups, having direct relations
with customers, were desirous of restoring public confidence in
the Exchange so as to maximize market activity. Accordingly,
they were more willing to accept SEC regulation. The floor traders and, to a lesser extent, other inside groups were less dependent
on public opinion and were most interested in personal specula-

[15] In 1955, this exchange handled 86.7 per cent of security transactions on
all registered exchanges. SEC, *Annual Report, 1956*, p. 244.

tion and quick, direct trading. They feared that SEC regulation, or even more effective self-regulation, would curtail their activities.

Under its first chairman, Joseph P. Kennedy, the SEC moved slowly. Kennedy had been a successful Wall Street trader and enjoyed the confidence of the trading element in Wall Street. He believed that there were abuses to be remedied, but, as far as possible, he hoped that the Stock Exchange would do its own house cleaning and its own policing. After negotiation and consultation, the SEC persuaded the Exchange to adopt sixteen trading rules designed to check manipulative practices. Some of these rules were so general as to be relatively meaningless. Others merely codified earlier Exchange rules. Still others were aimed at discouraging excessive trading and establishing a parity of advantage between member traders and outside buyers and sellers, but their effectiveness depended on the vigor of Exchange enforcement.

Kennedy then resigned, believing his task to have been accomplished, and was succeeded by James M. Landis. The SEC for a while contented itself with keeping a watch on market manipulations and calling questionable cases to the attention of the Exchange. But as it became apparent that the Exchange was failing to impose adequate punishment on violators of its rules, the SEC's attitude began to stiffen. In 1937, margin requirements were tightened, and more stringent rules governing specialists' transactions were placed in effect. Dissatisfied with the wrist-slapping punishment meted out by the Exchange, the SEC ordered that one of the most prominent Exchange speculators, Mike Meehan, be expelled for stock manipulations. Friction slowly built up as the Commission tried to prod the Exchange into more stringent enforcement.

When William O. Douglas succeeded Landis as SEC Chairman in September, 1937, he signaled an intensification of pressure by a speech warning that "the time is past when the country's exchanges can be operated as private clubs." Still hoping for self-regulation, he expressed doubts that public confidence could be restored, or trading rules effectively policed, so long as the "Old Guard" controlled the Exchange. This speech met a sympathetic response from the underrepresented commission-broker bloc within the Exchange, and pressure for action became intense.

Late in 1937, the president of the Exchange appointed a committee to report on the advisability of Exchange reorganization. This committee, reporting early in 1938, proposed the creation of a new Board of Governors, with increased representation for "members and partners who come into daily contact with the public, plus the addition of public representatives." The Board was to elect a full-time president. Over "Old Guard" opposition, the report was submitted to the Exchange membership in the form of constitutional amendments. Just before the vote, the dramatic arrest for grand larceny of Richard Whitney, former "Old Guard" president of the Exchange, ensured the complete collapse of "Old Guard" opposition. The report was endorsed, and the "reformers" in the Stock Exchange named the new Board of Governors. William McChesney Martin, Jr., a leader in the reform movement, was selected as the first president of the reorganized Exchange.

With the triumph of the "reformers," a new era of co-operation between the SEC and the Exchange began. A series of round-table discussions worked out new trading rules. The Whitney scandal had revealed the inadequacy of existing Exchange provisions for protecting customers' funds and securities, and in 1938 the Board of Governors announced the adoption of a program of safeguards. Member firms were encouraged to organize "affiliated companies" to carry on dealer and underwriting activities separately from their brokerage activities. An annual audit by independent accountants of all member firms doing business with the public was required. Members' periodic financial statements were expanded, as were the Exchange's surprise examinations of its member firms and partners. Members of brokerage firms doing business with the public were not permitted to trade in securities on margin.

The Exchange has since continued to co-operate with the SEC. The Commission has from time to time suggested changes in Exchange rules, and in turn, it has accepted amendments proposed by the New York and other securities exchanges. Since the exchanges have fairly complete control over their own members, the SEC has usually been able to achieve its purposes through exchange self-regulation. Thus the regulation of security trading, a task which is so complex as to strain the administrative resources of a government agency, has been performed with a minimal burden on the SEC. Support from within the financial community, so essential to the initiation of self-regulation, has broadened over time with the general success of SEC-reinforced self-regulation. The dominance of those firms dealing with the public has waxed, and there is general public endorsement of self-regulation and of SEC actions against those traders or companies whose behavior might endanger public confidence in security markets and transactions.

5. Regulation of Over-the-Counter Markets

The same general policy of promoting self-regulation characterizes SEC regulation of over-the-counter markets. These markets embrace all transactions in securities which do not take place on an organized exchange. Many securities can only be bought and sold through dealers and brokers who make a market for such securities. While the dollar volume of securities traded over-the-counter is but a fraction of that of exchange transactions, there are about 20,000 stocks listed by the National Quotation Bureau, and the Bureau's daily quotation sheets carry about 6,000 compared with the 3,686 securities listed on national exchanges. Over five thousand brokers and dealers are registered with the SEC to transact over-the-counter business.[16]

The Act of 1934 empowered the Commission to regulate over-the-counter markets, in order, as the Senate Committee on Banking and Currency put it, "to forestall the widespread evasion of stock exchange regulation by the withdrawal of securities from listing on exchanges, and by transferring trading therein to over-the-counter markets where manipulative evils could continue to flourish, unchecked by any regulatory authority." The Act provided for registration of brokers and dealers in over-the-counter markets and for supervision of their transactions. Because of the complexity and administrative difficulty of regulating these markets, the Act prescribed no specific rules but gave the SEC broad discretionary powers to regulate and to recommend further legislation. The Commission at first moved slowly, but after study and some experience, the Act was amended in 1936 to outlaw manipulation through specific language. In the same year, the SEC adopted rules requiring full disclosure of information on the terms of transactions. In 1937, it issued rules defining manipulative, deceptive, and fraudulent practices. These rules, as amended and interpreted over the years, have gradually applied higher standards of conduct to brokers and dealers by incorporating common-law principles. The law of torts, of equity, and of agency have all been applied to define fraud and misrepresentation and the fiduciary obligations of brokers and dealers.[17]

To avoid the task of directly policing over-the-counter markets, the Commission suggested the expansion of the pattern of self-

[16] *Ibid.*, pp. 90, 94, 105.
[17] W. T. Lesh, "Federal Regulation of Over-the-Counter Brokers and Dealers in Securities," *Harvard Law Review* (October, 1946), pp. 1237–1275.

regulation already applied to the exchanges. Accordingly, in 1938, the Maloney Amendment to the 1934 Act provided for the formation and registration of one or more voluntary associations of investment bankers, brokers, or dealers doing business in over-the-counter markets. These associations were to adopt rules of fair trade practices and to exercise disciplinary powers over their members somewhat comparable to the arrangements of registered exchanges. The SEC was vested with residual power over the associations. Membership in such an association is technically voluntary, but nonmembers may be barred from obtaining brokers' discounts. In 1939, the SEC granted the application of the National Association of Securities Dealers, Inc. (NASD), for registration as a national securities association. This Association, which by 1956 had enrolled 3,634 brokers, dealers, and investment bankers as members, has adopted rules which seek to prevent fraud, manipulation, and unreasonable charges and profits. It takes disciplinary action against its members. Since over-the-counter markets in effect compete with the exchanges for the confidence and trade of the public, there is a strong incentive to make self-regulation effective. The SEC, however, does investigate and inspect on its own initiative and takes appropriate action. In 1956, the SEC inspected 952 brokers and dealers, while the NASD and the registered exchanges inspected 2,228 firms. The NASD took final action in 102 disciplinary proceedings, including 8 expulsions and 6 suspensions, while the SEC instituted 45 proceedings to revoke, deny, or cancel registrations.[18]

6. Other Regulatory Activities of the SEC

Corporate Reorganizations

Chapter 10 of the Bankruptcy Act as amended in 1938 [19] imposed duties on the SEC in connection with corporate reorganizations in federal courts. These provisions resulted from an SEC study of corporate reorganization committees, which revealed serious abuses harmful to investors. The Act provides, first, that the Commission shall participate in corporate reorganizations at the request of the court, or on its own motion, if approved by the

[18] SEC, *Annual Report, 1956*, pp. 106, 113–115.

[19] These amendments, known as the Chandler Act, revise the entire Bankruptcy Act of 1898, as amended, with the exception of those provisions which relate to railroad reorganizations, municipal debt readjustments and extensions, and compositions of agricultural debts. Chapter 10, dealing with corporate reorganization, replaces the former Section 77B of the Bankruptcy Act.

court. Its right to be heard on all matters arising in the proceedings makes independent, expert advice available both to the courts and to investors. Second, the Commission is empowered to prepare advisory reports on tentative reorganization plans. Where the total indebtedness does not exceed $3 million, a federal court *may* and where the indebtedness exceeds $3 million, a federal court *must*, submit reorganization plans to the SEC for examination and report. On the approval of any plan by the judge, the Commission's report must be transmitted to creditors and stockholders who are being asked to vote on the plan.

As this summary indicates, the SEC has no authority to veto or require the adoption of a reorganization plan, or to settle any of the issues which arise in the proceeding. Its functions are purely advisory. Its investigating facilities and expert staff are made available to the courts and investors in an effort to preserve the assets of corporations in reorganization and to ensure that reorganization plans provide sound corporate structures and fair and equitable treatment for different classes of security holders.

The Trust Indenture Act of 1939

The Trust Indenture Act of 1939, which also arose from the SEC investigation of protective and reorganization committees, represents another extension of the frontiers of investor protection. Trust indentures are legal instruments by which an equitable right or interest in property is conveyed to a trustee and in accordance with which the trustee may be required to protect the interests of investors who are beneficiaries of the trust. The SEC investigation [20] had revealed numerous instances where trustees under indenture had failed to protect the interests of security holders. In some cases, trustees had occupied other positions which involved them in conflicts of interest with the security holders to whom they were ostensibly responsible.

The Trust Indenture Act vests the SEC with power to regulate the practices, operations, and security transactions of trustees under indenture. It imposes upon indenture trustees the standards of fiduciary responsibility which have long obtained in the administration of personal trusts. Enforcement of indenture provisions, however, is left to the private actions of investors, and the SEC is primarily concerned with reviewing the qualifications of

[20] SEC, *Report on the Study and Investigation of the Work, Activities, Personnel, and Functions of Protective and Reorganization Committees,* Part VI, *Trustees Under Indentures* (1936). This study was authorized by the Securities Exchange Act of 1934.

trustees and the conformity of indenture provisions with statutory standards.

The Investment Company and Investment Advisers Act of 1940

As a result of catastrophic losses suffered during the Great Depression by many investors in investment-trust securities, Congress in 1935 authorized the SEC to investigate investment trusts and to recommend legislation. The investigation unfolded a sorry chapter in American finance.[21] The attraction of the investment trust was its promise of safety through diversification of risk and expert management in selection of the securities in the trust's portfolio. In numerous cases, these advantages were and continue to be realized. In other instances, also widespread, they were unfortunately not realized. In twenty-two investment companies which had become bankrupt, the SEC estimated that security holders had lost $510 million of their $560 million investment.[22] In some cases, there was outright looting of assets by unscrupulous promoters or groups who had captured control. In others, the companies were operated to benefit sponsors rather than investors. Complicated capital structures were ofttimes devised to give promoters control without any substantial investment of their own funds. Self-dealing was rampant. Boards of directors often consisted of banking, brokerage, or distributor sponsors who used the investment trusts as instruments of speculation, as dumping grounds for dubious securities, or as means of multiplying their brokerage and selling commissions. "Insiders" utilized investment-trust funds to make loans to themselves, to finance companies in which they were personally interested, and to obtain control of other enterprises.

In order to eliminate these and other abuses, Congress enacted the Investment Company and Investment Advisers Act of 1940. Reputable trusts strongly supported the measure, seeing in it a means of ridding themselves of less ethical competitors and of regaining public confidence in this investment device. The Act ensures publicity by requiring investment companies to register with the SEC. Self-dealing is discouraged by requiring at least 40 per cent of a trust's directors to be independent of principal underwriters, regular brokers, managers, or advisers. Transactions with affiliated persons and underwriters are subject to SEC regulation. The Commission is empowered to supervise mergers, consolidations, and reorganizations of investment companies, and

---

[21] SEC, *Investment Trusts and Investment Companies* (1939, 1940).

[22] *Hearings* on S. 3580, Subcommittee of Senate Committee on Banking and Currency, 76th Cong., 3rd sess., Part I, p. 34.

to ensure equitable distribution of voting power among holders of different classes of securities. Management and underwriting contracts and major changes in investment policy must be approved by a majority of voting security holders. Sources of dividends must be revealed. Speculative practices such as buying on margin and short selling are forbidden. Rigid provisions are made for adequate accounting records and an independent audit.

The success of the SEC in preserving the advantages of this type of investment while making its abuse difficult is partly indicated by the great growth of investment trusts since the passage of the Act. In 1956, there were 399 registered investment companies, and the assets of this investment medium had grown from $2.5 billion in 1941 to $14 billion.[23]

The Act also requires that investment advisers register with the SEC. Registered advisers may not make any profit-sharing arrangements with their clients, nor may they assign contracts with clients to others without the consent of the client. They are also prohibited from employing any scheme, device, or artifice to defraud a client. If an investment adviser acts as a principal for his own account in a security transaction with a client, he must disclose to the client the capacity in which he is acting and obtain the client's consent to the transaction. Willful violation of the Act is punishable by a fine of $10,000 or not more than two years' imprisonment, or both.

7. Conclusion

On the whole, the SEC has successfully discharged its responsibility to protect investors and has won widespread acceptance from the interests affected. This acceptance of regulation is all the more remarkable in view of the vehemence with which many elements of the financial community in the 1930's greeted the creation of the SEC. The major reason, as we have seen, is that regulation came to be viewed as in the self-interest of most of those regulated. The revelations of fraud, manipulation, and violation of trust, when added to the shock and disillusionment resulting from the collapse in security prices during the Great Depression, had so thoroughly shaken public faith in the financial community that the reassurance which effective regulation provided was necessary to renew public confidence and participation in the securities markets.

The regulated interests benefit from an investor confidence which can rely upon higher fiduciary standards, a financial struc-

[23] SEC, *Annual Report, 1956,* p. 183.

ture more closely based upon real values, and exchanges in which the informed investor is better protected against extreme and unwarranted fluctuations. To the extent that the SEC exerts its influence to maintain and raise such standards, it will continue to command the support both of responsible elements in the financial community and of investors.

PART 4

The Promotion and Regulation of Competition

_____

CHAPTER 15

Antitrust Legislation and the Attack on Monopoly

S INCE THE late nineteenth century, Ameri-
can public policy in the regulation of business has developed two
well-defined traditions. There has been a basic differentiation in
the treatment accorded public utilities and other industries requiring direct regulation on the one hand and the rest of business
on the other. For the former, a substantial and expanding group,
positive regulation by special public agency has become an almost universally accepted policy, as we have seen above in Part
III. For the latter, competition has generally been viewed as the
most effective regulator in the public interest, although in recent
decades there have also been experiments in special industry regulation, as in the cases of coal and oil.

The rapid industrialization of the country after the Civil
War brought in its train insistent and successful efforts of entrepreneurs toward combination and consolidation, sometimes approaching monopoly. This concentration movement, in turn, occasioned increasingly hostile reactions from farmer and small
business groups, who felt disadvantaged either as suppliers, as consumers, or as competitors. The organized pressures of these groups,
together with the response of unorganized consumers to the antimonopoly campaigns of office-seekers, produced a peculiarly characteristic American policy, unique among the major nations of
the world. Competition was to be maintained and made fair
by law. To this end, the judicial process would be set in motion at

the instance of the public prosecutor. Nationwide acceptance of this policy was signalized by the Sherman Antitrust Act of 1890— a measure destined to be regarded as one of the most significant pieces of legislation in American history.

1. The Combination Movement

The period between the close of the Civil War and the turn of the century witnessed a complete transformation of American economic life. The phenomenal growth of railroads fused a congeries of local markets into a single, nationwide market and made possible the development of mass production and distribution and of large-scale corporations in their modern form. An increasing proportion of a rapidly increasing population was being urbanized, much of it employed in newly erected factories. Meanwhile, the typical scale of business enterprise was being enlarged. As little business became bigger business, it altered its form of organization. Individual enterprise and the partnership gave way to the corporation.

This era of industrial expansion was characterized by two closely related developments of fundamental importance. The first was a natural corollary of the growing scale of enterprise, with its many marked economies; it took the form of increased concentration of production in the hands of a limited number of firms. In many fields competition was virtually unimpaired, but in others a few enterprises came to dominate enough of the market to give them substantial control over their prices. Secondly, and of greater significance for public policy, there was a marked trend toward conscious and positive co-operation among businessmen in order to limit competition and control their markets through consolidation, combination, or agreement. It was this latter movement which constituted the so-called "trust problem"—a problem not yet fully solved.

The combination movement, as distinguished from the movement toward larger-scale enterprise, has developed continually from the close of the Civil War to the present, but with particular intensity in four phases. The first, from 1879 to 1893, saw the formation of the celebrated "trusts proper" and produced the first wave of antimonopoly legislation, state and federal. Giant mergers in the form of holding companies or outright consolidations, initiated by professional promoters, characterized the second phase, lasting from 1897 to 1903. The third intensive phase, from 1922 to 1929, utilized the forms of the second for relatively new industries, such as electrical utilities, motion pictures, radio, and automobiles. It witnessed, in addition, a strong movement for market control through trade associations, a movement which culminated in the National Industrial Recovery Act of 1933. The fourth phase developed shortly after the end of World War II and has continued through the middle 1950's. It has employed the older forms of combination, including vertical as well as horizontal integration, but has been especially noteworthy for its many mergers designed to enable firms to diversify by entering new fields.

A number of impelling causes motivated the first phase. The transportation revolution destroyed a multitude of local semi-monopolies, vastly expanding the geographical extent of the typical market. An entrepreneur could no longer depend upon his own territory for an assured core of demand. The products of a distant rival might now easily be brought to consumers at the very doorstep of his factory.

At the same time, the increasing importance of fixed capital in many industries, a result of technological change, with the concomitant increase in the proportion of overhead to variable costs, made possible "ruinous" or "cutthroat" competition, especially in periods of economic depression, with prices remaining below total costs for long periods. Railway rate wars were only the most outstanding example of this tendency, which was enhanced by a general price decline between 1867 and 1895. It is hardly surprising that businessmen frequently sought to "stabilize" their markets by agreement. Sometimes a single man or group of men, like Rockefeller and his associates in the Standard Oil Company, would see the economic advantages of control over output and price, to say nothing of personal power and social prestige in America's "Gilded Age," and would aggressively promote consolidation by both persuasive and predatory methods. Success in one field stimulated emulation in others. While the movement was in part a by-product of attempts to achieve the economies of large-scale production, for the most part it had its roots in the desire to eliminate competition.

The Forms of Combination

Combination among former competitors took many forms, ranging from the loose "gentlemen's agreement" to the complete merger of assets and corporate identities into a single firm. The most common type of agreement was at first the pool, the lineal predecessor of many modern trade associations and the American counterpart of the European cartel. Strictly used, the term refers only to agreements under which the output or income (or, among railroads, the traffic) of a number of firms is lumped together and redivided in agreed proportions, regardless of what each firm produces or earns. But the expression was commonly applied more broadly, including any agreement on a common price policy, on limitation or sharing of output, on common use of patents, or on allocation of markets. The more effective pools implemented their agreements with institutional machinery, which might enforce fines or other penalties for noncompliance; they also provided common services. Thus, the Michigan Salt Association of 1876 served as a common and exclusive sales agency, in this manner controlling prices and completely eliminating competition for customers.[1]

Pools were particularly popular in the 1880's and 1890's, when they were used in the coal, meat-packing, whiskey, wallpaper, bagging, cordage, and gunpowder industries, and in many branches of the iron-and-steel trade. They suffered, however, both from the adverse attitude of the common (and, later, also statute) law and from certain inherent defects. The very success of a pool in raising prices frequently tempted members secretly to produce in excess of their quotas and sometimes stimulated competition from nonmember producers or from substitute products. Thus, while the pool in one form or another has been used continuously to the present day, many businessmen turned to closer and more effective forms of combination. Among these the most celebrated was the "Trust," devised by Standard Oil attorneys in 1879.

The "trust proper," which gave its popular name to the entire combination movement, was a simple adaptation of an ancient legal device, widely used for other purposes, to unify control over a number of corporations. Owners of a majority of the common stock of each member company transferred their holdings, and therewith the controlling voting power, to a small board of "trustees," receiving in return "trust certificates" entitling them to prorata shares in the distributed profits. In this way, the functions of supplying capital and bearing risk were completely separated from that of control. Once consummated, the trust agreement ensured absolute and unqualified unity of policy, since the trustees were now the legal owners of the entire group of companies. The first Standard Oil Trust, formed in 1879, utilized a "dummy" board of three minor employees; but in 1882 the agreement was rewritten, setting up as the new board the nine

[1] J. W. Jenks, "The Michigan Salt Association," *Political Science Quarterly* (March, 1888), pp. 78–98.

leaders of the Standard group.

Free from the internal defects of pools, although still subject to outside competition, the Trust was widely used during the next few years. The whiskey trade, suffering from chronic overproduction and cutthroat competition, abandoned vain attempts at stabilization through pools in favor of the Distillers' and Cattle Feeders' Trust (1887). The cottonseed oil, linseed oil, white lead, sugar refining, carbon filament, and fruit preserving industries were all similarly organized during the same decade. An official report in 1888 declared that "this form of combination was obviously devised for the purpose of relieving the trusts and trustees from the charge of any breach of the conspiracy laws of the various States, or of being a combination to regulate or control the price or production of any commodity," and that "all trade combinations having similar aims either have adopted this method or speedily will do so." [2] As will be seen below, however, an end was soon put to the use of this device by the common law, supplemented by a host of unfriendly legislative measures.

Having demonstrated the profitability of central control, and having become identified in the public mind and press with every predatory practice indulged in by any type of big business, the trust proper disappeared from the American scene. From 1892 on, the combination movement diverged along two fairly well-defined lines. The first, and relatively less important, continued to employ the informal and necessarily secret pool. The second, which in the years 1898 to 1902 climaxed the entire movement, wore the legal garb either of the holding company or of outright merger.

Outright merger, logically the simplest form of combination, requires little comment. It was utilized extensively during the entire period. The Standard Oil Company bought up many refineries from 1872 on, generally by exchanging Standard stock for the securities of the independents. This device, however, was sometimes impractical as a method of controlling large industries. It required the consent of each class of security holder in the merging companies and involved complex negotiations on terms of exchange. The holding company, a corporation controlling other firms by the ownership of a majority (or less [3]) of their common stock, was equally effective as a means of market control and was much easier to form. Moreover, by pyramiding successive layers of

[2] House Committee on Manufactures, *Report on Investigation of Trusts*, H. Rept. 3112, 50th Cong., 1st sess., p. ii.
[3] Where stock is widely distributed, ownership of as little as 20 or 30 per cent may often ensure effective control.

holding companies one on another, entrepreneurs with a relatively small investment could dominate the operating companies representing a vast investment at the bottom.

Until 1888, no state incorporation laws permitted companies to own stock in other companies, and some common-law decisions had forbidden such acquisitions without express legislative sanction. In that year, the New Jersey law was amended, at the urging of New York lawyers searching for a new device to substitute for the then threatened Trust, to permit unrestricted intercorporate stockholding. Several of the former Trusts, including Standard Oil, as well as a number of new combinations, proceeded to organize holding companies. The income from incorporation fees tempted other states to follow New Jersey's example. So began the competitive race in "charter mongering," which ever since has provided at least one state in which businesses might be incorporated without the restraints thought desirable elsewhere in the nation.

Holding companies appeared in gunpowder, tobacco, and meat. Head and shoulders above all others in size was the United States Steel Corporation, organized in 1901. Large-scale mergers also continued to take place in many industries. Outstanding examples were the Diamond Match Company (1889), the American Tobacco Company (1890), the Distilling and Cattle Feeding Company (1890), the American Sugar Refining Company (1891), the International Paper Company (1898), the National Biscuit Company (1898), the United Shoe Machinery Corporation (1899), the American Can Company (1901), the Amalgamated Copper Company (1901), the International Harvester Company (1902), the E. I. du Pont de Nemours Powder Company (1903), and many others. Most of the new combinations were incorporated in New Jersey.

This intensive second phase of the combination movement was brought to a close by a series of factors. Promoters had run out of attractive industries to combine. The stock market decline of 1903 made it difficult to float new issues on favorable terms. The movement was also discouraged by the failure of the United States Shipbuilding Company and the International Mercantile Marine Company in 1902–1903, and by the dissolution in 1904, under the Sherman Act, of the Northern Securities Company, a railroad holding company. Public policy toward the "trusts," [4] meanwhile, had undergone a marked development.

---

[4] The term "trust" is here used in its common meaning of any large combination, whatever its organizational form, which dominates an industry. The "trust proper" will be referred to by the capitalized form "Trust."

2. The Development of Public Policy

So thoroughgoing a transformation of the economy evoked protective responses from groups adversely affected. Outsiders, deprived of free entry into "trustified" industries, often by methods of dubious commercial morality, envied the profitable business denied them. In so far as loss or the fear of loss was a more powerful stimulant to action than hope of gain, even more potent resentment was kindled in the hearts of former competitors who felt themselves "frozen out" of the market, or forced to sell out at distress prices, by the "unfair" competitive practices of the trusts. Hardly less concerned were the primary producers who no longer enjoyed competition among buyers for such commodities as crude oil, grain (for whiskey), and cottonseed.

These groups were quick to organize and press their interests at the various state capitals and in Washington. Nevertheless, however vociferous, they could not by themselves have created an effective antimonopoly movement. Their cause was favored by a growing popular fear of the inroads of big business industrialism and finance into the simpler patterns of life in an agrarian society. The old freedom of small enterprise seemed threatened with extinction and the lives of ordinary men with domination by corporate octopuses ruled by private and secret oligarchies. Consumers would be at the mercy of the monopolies for the necessaries of life. Like the railroads, trusts were also feared as corrupters of the democratic processes of government. The antimonopolist writers exhibited moral fervor of an intensity rare today. Henry Demarest Lloyd wrote of the destruction of our civilization by barbarian money-makers, "gluttons of luxury and power, rough, unsocialized, believing that mankind must be kept terrorized, [who] claim a power without control, exercised through forms which make it secret, anonymous, and perpetual." [5]

Public sentiment was concentrated with particular severity against the giants of the 1880's, above all the Standard Oil and Sugar Trusts. The Standard Oil Company of Ohio was formed in 1870 by John D. Rockefeller and various associates. In 1874, acting on the conviction that consolidation was essential to stabilize the industry in the depression conditions then prevailing, they began a systematic campaign to gain control over petroleum refining and marketing. First Cleveland, and later Philadelphia, Pittsburgh, New York, and other large refining centers were

[5] *Wealth Against Commonwealth* (1898), p. 510.

brought into the scheme, mainly by amicable negotiation, but sometimes by purchase under threat, or after a period of competition generally disastrous for the independent.[6] In this early period, Standard Oil joined with the leading oil-carrying railroads to organize the ill-famed South Improvement Company. In return for a guaranteed division of its traffic among the Pennsylvania, New York Central, and Erie Railroads, this secret company was not only to receive rebates of 40 to 50 per cent on listed freight rates for its own crude oil, and 25 to 45 per cent on refined, but also similar rebates on oil shipped by its competitors. Detailed reports of competitors' shipments were also to be supplied to the company. However reasonable this extraordinary arrangement may have been for the carriers, who were suffering from chronic rate wars and welcomed any device for stabilizing the division of traffic, it promised to add an invincible competitive weapon to the economic efficiency of Standard Oil.

News of this secret scheme leaked out to the Pennsylvania oil fields and evoked the first organized opposition to Standard Oil. Petitions for relief were addressed to Harrisburg and Washington. A Producers' Protective Association was organized to carry on the fight by boycotting the company. Legislative authorization of independent pipeline construction was prevented through the influence of the Pennsylvania Railroad, but the South Improvement Company's charter was repealed and its contracts automatically dissolved. Nonetheless, the Standard interests continued to receive rebates throughout the seventies, and with their aid the absorption of refineries continued apace. Pipelines, the new means of oil transportation, were also bought up by the Company. By 1879, 95 per cent of the country's refining capacity was either directly controlled by Standard or joined in its policies through voluntary association. Its last severe fight with the organized independents, who constructed the Tidewater pipeline in 1878 to supply their own seaboard refineries, ended in 1883, after a brief but intense rivalry, with an agreement on division of pipeline traffic. By this time, the Standard group had organized itself under the famous Trust Agreement of 1882. It had closely approached monopoly control of oil refining and marketing.

[6] For an analysis of the conditions impelling the oil industry toward efforts to restrain competition, especially during the depression decade of the 1870's, and for general historical background on the early decades of the Standard Oil group of companies, see R. W. and M. E. Hidy, *Pioneering in Big Business 1882–1911*, Vol. 1 of *History of the Standard Oil Company (New Jersey)* (1955).

The Sugar Trust arose with almost equal rapidity. During the early 1880's, technical improvements in sugar refining had increased the most economical size of plant and had led to substantial overcapacity. Cutthroat competition bankrupted a number of refineries. To remedy this situation, H. O. Havemeyer organized in 1887 the Sugar Refineries Company, a Trust owning twenty refineries and producing about 78 per cent of the country's output. Although heavily overcapitalized from the start, the company bought out and shut down competing plants at high prices, recouping its losses by raising refined sugar prices. Transformed in 1891 into the American Sugar Refining Company, a New Jersey corporation, by the next year it controlled 98 per cent of the industry. Its history during the following dozen years was a succession of periods of high prices in the absence of competitors, consequent stimulation of new competition, low prices and a campaign to acquire or destroy the competitors, and a repetition of the entire cycle. Although it never compared with Standard Oil in ability to suppress independents, its profits were enormous over a thirty-year period.

By 1890, these two enterprises were archdemons in the public eye. Standard Oil was criticized, not for its price policy or the quality of its products, but for its apparent goal of monopoly power and for the practices it used in eliminating competitors. While its profits were large, it did tend to reduce the price spread between crude and refined oil, and its kerosene (then the major product) was consistently of the highest grade. Standard's competitive methods, however, constituted a well-nigh exhaustive catalog of measures considered contrary to commercial morality, although they were by no means uncommon in the business practice of the time. In addition to railroad rebates and control of pipelines, it used widespread local price-cutting to eliminate competition, compensating itself by increased prices in noncompetitive markets. Bogus independents, secretly controlled by Standard, were launched in various local areas. Commercial espionage, long practiced by small business locally, was elaborately developed on a national scale. Wholesalers and retailers buying from independent refiners were threatened with destructive competition. Independent pipelines would find their supply of crude oil jeopardized by Standard activities. Crude-oil producers, who felt their prices and sales to be at Standard's mercy, came to be its most relentless enemies.

Besides these practices, the trust indulged in many forms of political pressure. It lobbied in state legislatures against the authorization of new pipelines. It was alleged that members of Congress were on its payroll.[7] Under these conditions, the antagonism which began among producers spread through the remaining independent refiners and distributors and ended by encompassing unorganized consumers. There was a particularly sentimental appeal in the thought that this private "moloch of monopoly" controlled the price of kerosene, the poor man's source of light.

In the case of sugar, price policy and political corruption played a more important role, although here, too, questionable competitive methods were not lacking. A frank policy of increasing prices whenever possible was combined with major influence on sugar tariffs. Elimination of foreign competition was indispensable to the sugar trust's domestic price policy, and it was generally thought to have bought its tariff protection directly. In addition, the Company was later found to have corrupted revenue officers into short-weighing raw sugar, saving itself several million dollars in duties. Havemeyer's blunt "damn the public" attitude also contributed to resentment against this monopoly in an article of universal consumption.

Organization of political action against industrial monopolies went hand in hand with the movement (described in Chapter 9) for railroad regulation. The agricultural depression of the seventies, which produced the Granger movement, was blamed by many farmers on excessive charges for transportation and distribution of their produce. Monopolistic practices, they felt, led not only to low prices for their own products but also to high prices on the things they bought. Railway discrimination was fought partly because it was believed to foster industrial monopoly, a belief borne out by revelations about Standard Oil. While the Grange was chiefly concerned with regulating railroads and promoting farmer co-operatives, it laid the foundations for agrarian political organization. During the seventies, important third parties under the name "Antimonopoly," "Independent," or "Reform," were formed in eleven Midwestern and Northwestern states. In 1874, Iowa's Antimonopoly Party demanded legislation to "secure the industrial and producing interests of the country against all forms of corporate monopoly and extortion."[8] An Antimonopoly presidential candidate campaigned in 1884.

Directed primarily against railroads and grain elevators, the Granger movement obtained no legislation against monopolies in general, but it was the direct ancestor of the various Farmers' Alliances and of the Populist Party of 1892. A vigorous crop of

[7] J. T. Flynn, *God's Gold* (1932), p. 370.
[8] S. J. Buck, *The Granger Movement* (1913), p. 236.

such agrarian organizations arose in both the South and West during the 1880's, some of them reaching out tentatively for an alliance with newly organized labor. Their press thundered against the trusts. Late in the decade, agrarian or farmer-labor parties obtained majorities or balances of power in a number of state legislatures, forcing the older parties into competitive bidding for their support. By 1890, they controlled eight states, forty-four congressmen, and a handful of Senators, and were jockeying for the formation of a national third party. The spirit of the movement, as far as trusts are concerned, is well illustrated by a passage from W. S. Morgan:

> The agricultural masses, the most numerous and important of any class of people forming the great body of the republic . . . are robbed by an infamous system of finance; they are plundered by transportation companies; they are imposed upon by an unjust system of tariff laws; they are deprived of their lands and other property by an iniquitous system of usury; they are fleeced by the exactions of numerous trusts; they are preyed upon by the merchants, imposed upon by the lawyers, misled by the politician and seem to be regarded as the legitimate prey of all other classes. Monopoly names the price of what they have to sell, and charges them what it pleases for what they are compelled to buy. . . . Individual effort is fruitless. The relentless, remorseless, and unyielding grasp of monopoly is upon every avenue of trade and commerce. . . . Monopolies exist by law, are chartered by law, and should be controlled by law. A trust is a conspiracy against legitimate trade. It is against the interests of the people and the welfare of the public. It is demoralizing in its influence, inconsistent with free institutions and dangerous to our liberties. To participate in a trust should be a crime subject to severe punishment. Trust is only another name for monopoly. Monopoly is wielding a greater power in the government than the people.[9]

It was this farmer-labor movement which put the first American antitrust laws on the statute books and injected most of the fire and rhetoric into the campaign for antitrust legislation, although essential support was also forthcoming from disadvantaged small businessmen and from unorganized elements in the general consuming public.

Combinations at Common Law

Even before the enactment of new statutes, the antimonopolists had some legal protection against restraints on competition. The

[9] W. S. Morgan, *History of the Wheel and Alliance, and the Impending Revolution* (1889), pp. 15–17.

tradition of the common law, especially as expounded by American state courts, was in line with their objectives. Two branches of the law, each the product of centuries of exposition and refinement, were in particular conflict with the combination movement. Contracts in restraint of trade were unenforceable in the courts. Monopoly was illegal. Each of these doctrines, however, had a limited and technical meaning, the fruit of experience with an economy strikingly different from that of late-nineteenth-century America.

The doctrine of restraint of trade, going back to the Dyer's case of 1415, originally concerned contracts whereby one party agreed not to compete with the other in a local market—contracts usually made in connection with the sale of a business. As transportation improved and markets expanded, the possibility of outside competition made such agreements less objectionable. The law was then modified to permit restraints when reasonably ancillary to the main purpose of the sale, in order to ensure to the buyer the uncontested use of "good will" built up by the seller, provided that such restraints were not part of a monopolistic scheme injurious to the public.[10] By analogy, however, this branch of the law could be extended to cover restraints upon competition, that is, agreements whereby the parties sought to exclude others from the market.[11] The minds of common-law judges were well prepared for this extension by the second ancient principle, which held monopolies to be unlawful because contrary to public policy.

The term "monopoly" referred originally only to exclusive trading rights granted by the Crown, similar to the modern patent. Such grants were particularly common under the Tudor monarchs, who found it easier to obtain revenue in return for monopolistic concessions than to persuade a recalcitrant Parliament to vote taxes. In *Darcy* v. *Allein* (1602), an English court voided a monopoly in the importation and sale of playing cards, holding that monopoly is accompanied by three inseparable incidents:

1. That the price will be raised. 2. After the monopoly grant, the commodity is not so good as it was before. 3. It tends to the impoverishment of divers artificers and others who before by their

---

[10] A distinction was made at one time between *general* restraints, which were void, and *particular* restraints, limited to one locality, which might be enforceable. See *Mitchel* v. *Reynolds*, I P. Wms. 181 (1711). By the late nineteenth century, however, this distinction was no longer of importance.

[11] See, for example, *Hubbard* v. *Miller*, 27 Mich. 15 (1873); *Diamond Match Co.* v. *Roeber*, 106 N.Y. 473 (1887).

labour had maintained themselves and their families, who now will of necessity be constrained to live in idleness and beggary.[12]

All Crown grants of monopoly were repealed by Parliament in 1624 and 1689.

Subsequently, the word "monopoly" was broadened into its more modern meaning, including substantial or exclusive market control however obtained. Sixteenth-century statutes against "engrossing" (cornering the market), "regrating" (acting by any means to raise the price of victuals), and "forestalling" (buying up commodities on their way to market in order to sell them at higher prices) served as signposts to the courts in extending common-law inhibitions against monopolization. Fearing the same results which had led earlier judges to inveigh against monopoly and restraint of trade in the narrower senses, American state judges in the nineteenth century were ready to apply the common law against pools, trusts, and other devices of the new combination era.

In the narrow and relatively unimportant field of technical *contracts* in restraint of trade, a "rule of reason" had been developed which validated most of them. In the wider field of *combinations* in restraint of trade, or restraints upon competition, the American courts, with few exceptions, recognized no such rule. The cases have been summarized thus: "Wherever any agreement between competitors appears to involve an undue restriction of competition and therefore to be detrimental to the public interest the courts will refuse to aid in its enforcement." [13] Pools of every variety were held illegal in various states during the second half of the nineteenth century. They included agreements to control output, to divide market territory, to pool earnings, and to employ a common sales agency to effectuate price control. The impossibility of holding defaulting members of a pool to their agreement through ordinary legal processes was one important inducement to businessmen to seek tighter and more effective forms of combination. These, too, however, came within the ban.

Two cases of prime importance outlawed the trust. In *People v. North River Sugar Refining Company*, the New York courts vacated the Company's charter on the ground that it had no legal authority to join the Sugar Trust or to place control of its affairs in the hands of another organization.[14] The Court of Appeals re-

---

[12] II Coke 84b.
[13] U.S. Commissioner of Corporations, *Trust Laws and Unfair Competition* (1915), pp. 37–38.
[14] 121 N.Y. 582 (1890).

fused to follow the lower court in declaring the Sugar Trust itself to be against public policy, restricting its decision solely to the question of corporate powers of the North River Company. In *State* v. *Standard Oil Company*, the Ohio Supreme Court went further and held the Oil Trust itself to be an unlawful monopoly.[15] Its words summarize admirably the broad attitude of the common law:

[The object of the agreement] was to establish a virtual monopoly of the business of producing petroleum, and of manufacturing, refining and dealing in it and all its products, throughout the entire country, and by which it might not merely control the production, but the price at its pleasure. All such associations are contrary to the policy of our state and void. . . . Much has been said in favor of the objects of the Standard Oil Trust, and what it has accomplished. It may be true that it has improved the quality and cheapened the costs of petroleum and its products to the consumer. But such is not one of the usual or general results of a monopoly; and it is the policy of the law to regard, not what may, but what usually happens. Experience shows that it is not wise to trust human cupidity where it has the opportunity to aggrandize itself at the expense of others. . . . Monopolies have always been regarded as contrary to the spirit and policy of the common law. . . . A society in which a few men are the employers and the great body are merely employees or servants, is not the most desirable in a republic; and it should be as much the policy of the laws to multiply the numbers engaged in independent pursuits or in the profits of production, as to cheapen the price to the consumer. . . . The effect on industrial liberty and the price of commodities will be the same whether created by patent, or by an extensive combination among those engaged in similar industries, controlled by one management. By the invariable laws of human nature, competition will be excluded and prices controlled in the interest of those connected with the combination or trust.

The Cotton Seed Oil and Whiskey Trusts were likewise attacked successfully in Tennessee and Nebraska.[16] Thenceforth, the trust proper was abandoned, and a few years later some of its successor organizations, including the corporate merger of former competitors and a price-fixing combination of otherwise independent firms, were also defeated in state courts on similar grounds.[17]

[15] 49 Ohio 137 (1892).

[16] *Mallory* v. *Hanaur Oil-Works*, 86 Tenn. 598 (1888); *State* v. *Nebraska Distilling Co.*, 29 Neb. 700 (1890).

[17] The Illinois Supreme Court castigated one corporate monopoly in the following terms: "There is no magic in a corporate organization which can

Thus, American interpretations of the common law were in general harmony with the rising antitrust movement.[18] Judicial declarations of public policy endorsed competition as an automatic regulating device for ensuring the public welfare. No highly refined economic theory went into the decisions, but even professional economists of the day were mostly content with a simple dichotomy between competition and monopoly, the former needing no interference and the latter a potential danger even if it had not in fact unreasonably affected prices. The Ohio decision above shows, too, that some courts, like the Populists, feared monopoly as a serious threat to free enterprise and the "American way of life."

Nonetheless, the growth of the combination movement in the face of these legal obstacles proved the common law to be inadequate. Its defects lay in its method of application. Loose agreements of the pooling variety were generally brought into court only when some disgruntled member began an action or was himself sued for noncompliance. Remedies were difficult to enforce and rarely succeeded in restoring competition. In most cases, the law merely refused to aid the combination, and its only effect was to make combination agreements unenforceable in court. It offered no positive hindrance, and it was silent until spoken to, i.e., until someone brought a case into court. Criminal penalties could be applied only if combinations were adjudged criminal conspiracies, a fate which overtook some early labor organizations but not trusts. Moreover, the common law was state-wide only, and a large combination could operate in other states after being condemned in one. States varied in their interpretation and application of the law, and there was no uniformly applicable federal common law. It became clear that if the trust problem were to be attacked by forbidding and breaking up monopolistic enterprises, statutory enactments and administrative machinery were essential.

---

purge the trust scheme of its illegality, and it remains as essentially opposed to the principles of sound public policy as when the trust was in existence. It was illegal before and is illegal still, and for the same reasons." *Distilling and Cattle Feeding Co.* v. *People*, 156 Ill. 448 (1895). See also *Richardson* v. *Buhl*, 77 Mich. 632 (1889), condemning the Diamond Match Company. And in 1895 the New York Court of Appeals voided the charter of a combination of dealers to control the purchase price of raw milk. *People* v. *Milk Exchange*, 145 N.Y. 267.

[18] In Britain, on the other hand, nineteenth-century interpretations of the doctrine of restraint of trade were making it steadily less effective as a means of limiting anti-competitive combinations. See Thorelli, *op. cit.*, pp. 27–35.

State Antitrust Laws

Although provisions against state-granted monopolies date from the beginning of our national history, state antitrust legislation began only in 1887, as the shortcomings of the common law became apparent and as public support crystallized. Standard Oil's rebates were publicized by the New York Hepburn Committee in 1879 and by various state lawsuits. The role of railroad rate discrimination in fostering industrial monopoly had been described in Henry Demarest Lloyd's *Story of a Great Monopoly* (1881), and was particularly emphasized by the Cullom Committee of the Senate, whose railway investigation immediately preceded the Interstate Commerce Act of 1887.

The rising tide of antitrust agitation in the public press and in petitions to legislatures produced additional official investigations in 1888. A Canadian report on "Alleged Combinations in Manufacture, Trade and Insurance" shed new light on monopolistic practices on both sides of the border. A committee of the New York Senate took testimony on combinations in sugar, milk, rubber, cottonseed oil, petroleum, oilcloth, envelopes, meat, glass, furniture, copper, jute bagging, grain elevators, and groceries, and made public for the first time the text of Standard Oil's Trust Agreement. While most of the members felt that the dangers had been exaggerated and that immediate legislation was undesirable, the evidence produced before this committee served as a basis for action elsewhere. The House Committee on Manufactures also explored the leading trusts in some detail.

Beginning in the Granger states, a wave of antimonopoly statutes swept the country. By the middle of 1890, seventeen states and territories had passed such laws, six of them in the form of constitutional provisions. The marked and significant sectional character of the movement is indicated by the almost solid geographical grouping of the states, beginning with Washington in the Northwest, and running through Idaho, Montana, Wyoming, the Dakotas, Nebraska, Kansas, Texas, Iowa, Missouri, Mississippi, Tennessee, North Carolina, and Kentucky. In addition to this main bloc of agrarian revolt, antitrust laws had been passed by Michigan and Maine. By 1900, thirteen more states had joined the movement: Utah, New Mexico, Oklahoma, Arkansas, Louisiana, Georgia, and South Carolina in the South and West; and Minnesota, Wisconsin, Illinois, Indiana, Ohio, and New York in the North. The laws varied considerably in content, but almost all forbade monopolies and combinations in restraint of trade in

general terms, and provided criminal penalties and administrative
machinery for prosecutions where the common law had merely
made contracts unenforceable. In addition, they attacked particular
forms of agreement and specific practices which were thought
especially likely to bring about market control.

Since the turn of the century, there have been few significant
changes in basic antitrust policy at the state level. Forty-one
states now have antitrust laws. But while state laws are often more
thoroughgoing, both in definition of offenses and in prescription
of remedies, than the federal law, they have had little practical
effect. It has been aptly said that "these laws raise more smoke
than fire." [19] Enforcement has generally been haphazard and ill
financed. Their fundamental difficulty lies in the impossibility
of dealing with national or international economic institutions
through limited political areas. The dominant force in shaping
American public policy toward industry has been, of necessity, the
federal government.

The Sherman Act of 1890

The adoption of the Sherman Act was a curious political phenomenon. Unlike the Interstate Commerce Act, it was not the
fruit of exhaustive investigation and careful debate, a response to
overwhelming demand from directly interested groups. Unlike the
supplementary antitrust legislation of 1914, it was not the product
of a professedly liberal President and party newly installed in
office. While hindsight justly views it as one of the most important measures ever passed by Congress, it is doubtful if any member of the 51st Congress so regarded it. Indeed, so incomplete and
murky is the legislative record and so complex were the political
maneuvers surrounding the enactment that it is impossible to glean
from this history any clear-cut congressional intent.[20] Part of the
problem arises from the fact that, as Hamilton and Till put it,
"the bill which was arduously debated was never passed, and . . .
the bill which was passed was never really discussed." [21] The
further fact that the draftsmanship of the Act, which was long
ascribed to Senator Hoar instead of Senator Sherman, was actually
that of Senator Edmunds is an additional indication of the con-

[19] "Collection and Survey of State Antitrust Laws," *Columbia Law Review,*
Vol. 32 (1932), p. 364.
[20] For a detailed analysis of the legislative history and for a somewhat different interpretation of it, see Thorelli, *op. cit.,* Chapter 4.
[21] W. Hamilton and I. Till, *Antitrust in Action,* TNEC Monograph No. 16
(1940), p. 11.

fused congressional background.[22]

The legislative record itself is short. After its extensive investigation of the trust issue in 1889, the House Manufactures Committee had been unable to agree on any specific legislative recommendation. Sixteen antitrust bills were introduced in the House in that year. Their proposed remedies ranged from a suspension of tariff duties on goods controlled by trusts to the outright prohibition of interstate commerce by trusts, but none of these bills emerged from committee.

In March, 1890, the Senate debated for five days a bill introduced by Senator Sherman, identical with one which had been favorably reported by the Finance Committee in 1888. It declared illegal any arrangements among persons or corporations "made with a view, or which tend, to prevent full and free competition in the production, manufacture, or sale of articles imported into the United States." No hearings had been held on this bill, and the debate dealt primarily with questions of constitutionality and with relations between tariff protection and monopoly. Only Senator Stewart of Nevada opposed the general policy of the bill, arguing that combination was inevitable and that the best remedy against trusts was "counter combinations among the people." By a vote of 31 to 28, the bill was then referred to the Judiciary Committee, a move which the bill's supporters feared was intended to kill it. Surprisingly, only six days later the Judiciary Committee reported out a completely rewritten bill, which speedily passed both houses with almost no debate and little opposition. The vote in the Senate was 52 to 1, and, after two conferences, the House passed it by a vote of 242 to 0. The law was approved on July 2, 1890.

Why were the issues so inadequately debated, and why was so potentially controversial a measure passed with only one dissenting vote? Why was the law couched in such general terms? There are two lines of explanation, not necessarily mutually exclusive. The first stresses interparty competition for support from the vigorously antimonopolist West. Mason of Illinois stated this case succinctly:

You [the Democratic members] use the "trust" as a bugaboo to frighten people away from the Republican party into your ranks. That is the reason you do not want the Republican party to strike a blow at trusts today. The moment that we strike down trusts in this country

[22] Thorelli, *op. cit.*, pp. 210–214.

that moment there is taken away one of the principal elements of your political talk in seeking to drive the farmers away from the Republican party into the Democratic party.[23]

According to this view, the public concern over trusts was too obvious a political issue for wise politicians to ignore. Having lost the Presidency in 1884 for the first time since the Civil War, Republicans were in no mood to risk the defection of substantial geographical sections. (The Sherman Silver Purchase Act of 1890 was another measure designed to strengthen the bonds holding the West within the Republican Party.) Nor could their opponents sensibly refuse an opportunity to pry away the avowedly antimonopolist agrarian Republicans from the increasingly powerful Eastern industrial section of the party.

In 1884, the Democrats had mentioned this issue in their platform; in 1887, President Cleveland suggested a relationship between tariffs and trusts—a favorite Democratic theme—but on neither occasion was legislation suggested. In 1888, the Republicans, hitherto silent, joined the Democrats in writing an antitrust plank into their platform, but its vague terms merely recommended "such legislation as will prevent the execution of all schemes to oppress the people by undue charges on their supplies, or by unjust rates for the transportation of their products to market." In his first message to Congress, President Harrison gave the subject a paragraph, advising "prohibitory legislation" as far as the limited federal jurisdiction might permit.

Thus, antagonism to trusts became an ostensibly bipartisan policy, but it was not in fact believed in strongly by the leaders of either party, least of all the dominant Republican Party, in whose councils big business exercised great influence. Accordingly, it is contended, the congressional leadership only wished to pacify the surging antimonopoly sentiment of the time with a meaningless antitrust law.

This view is supported by the fact that the high-tariff McKinley Bill was the chief business of the 1890 session. Even the ill-reputed Sugar Trust was favored by this law, which preserved a duty on refined sugar while admitting raw sugar free. And an amendment to the Sherman Bill withdrawing tariff protection from monopolistic combinations was beaten in the Senate by a vote of 22 to 16. Finally, the argument concludes, the failure of the trusts and their senatorial allies to oppose the measure proves that it was

[23] 21 *Cong. Rec.* 4098 (1890).

intended to be an empty gesture, so vague, so general, and so impractical as to be innocuous. Indeed, Senator Platt questioned the seriousness of his colleagues:

The conduct of this Senate for the past three days . . . has not been in the line of honest preparation of a bill to prohibit and punish trusts. . . . The question of whether a bill would be operative, of how it would operate, or whether it was within the power of Congress to enact it, have been whistled down wind in this Senate as idle talk, and the whole effort has been to get some bill headed "A bill to punish trusts" with which to go to the country.[24]

The other line of explanation holds that Congress, operating in a new area of legislative policy and armed with only the crudest tools of economic analysis, was simply unable to specify which combinations really restrained competition and promoted monopoly. Neither the legal nor the economic concepts of the time were adequate to deal in explicit terms with the rapidly evolving forms and practices of the new industrial order.

Accordingly, Congress chose simply to apply as federal statute law the old common-law doctrines of monopoly and restraint of trade, leaving it for the courts, applying judicial reasoning and operating case by case, gradually to inject specific meaning into deliberately general and vague prohibitions. Certainly this argument recurs throughout congressional consideration of the measure:

We have affirmed [declared Senator Hoar] the old doctrine of the common law in regard to all interstate and international transactions, and have clothed the United States courts with authority to enforce that doctrine by injunction. We have put in also a grave penalty.[25]

I admit [said Senator Sherman] that it is difficult to define in legal language the precise line between lawful and unlawful combinations. This must be left for the courts to determine in each particular case. All that we, as lawmakers, can do is to declare general principles, and we can be assured that the courts will apply them so as to carry out the meaning of the law. . . .[26]

Whatever the true explanation, the effect of the congressional action was to pass on to the courts the task of defining basic American policy toward competition and monopoly. The Act

[24] 21 Cong. Rec. 2731.
[25] 21 Cong. Rec. 3146.
[26] 21 Cong. Rec. 2460.

would mean nothing until it had been given application in specific cases. Under these conditions, concrete policy would be slow to develop.

3. Early Application of the Sherman Act

The heart of the Act lies in its first two sections, which originally read as follows:

SEC. 1. Every contract, combination in the form of trust or otherwise, or conspiracy, in restraint of trade or commerce among the several States, or with foreign nations, is hereby declared to be illegal. Every person who shall make any such contract or engage in any such combination or conspiracy, shall be deemed guilty of a misdemeanor, and, on conviction thereof, shall be punished by fine not exceeding five thousand dollars, or by imprisonment not exceeding one year, or by both said punishments, in the discretion of the court.[27]

SEC. 2. Every person who shall monopolize, or attempt to monopolize, or combine or conspire with any other person or persons, to monopolize any part of the trade or commerce among the several States, or with foreign nations, shall be deemed guilty of a misdemeanor, and, on conviction thereof, shall be punished by fine not exceeding five thousand dollars, or by imprisonment not exceeding one year, or by both said punishments, in the discretion of the court.

Three methods of court action against violators are provided: (1) criminal prosecutions brought by federal attorneys; (2) equity proceedings instituted by federal attorneys to enjoin and restrain violations; and (3) suits for damages by private parties injured "by reason of anything forbidden or declared to be unlawful by this act"—if successful, the injured parties are to recover thrice the amount of damage sustained.[28]

Couched in these extremely broad terms, the Sherman Act was neither self-explanatory nor self-enforcing. Taken at face value, its words covered, at a minimum, practices heretofore frowned

[27] In 1937, Section 1 was altered by the Miller-Tydings Amendment to legalize resale price maintenance. See below, pp. 562–563.

[28] The Wilson Tariff Act of 1894 imposed similar penalties (but with minima of $100 fine and three months' imprisonment) for combinations, conspiracies, trusts, agreements, or contracts in restraint of trade in the importation of goods from abroad. The Webb-Pomerene Export Trade Act of 1918 exempted from the Sherman Act associations engaged in export trade, provided that they did not restrain trade within the United States or restrain the export trade of any domestic competitor. Export trade associations were subjected to administrative supervision by the Federal Trade Commission.

upon by the common law, and applied that law to interstate commerce. It replaced mere unenforceability of contracts by liability to equitable restraints and criminal penalties. It clearly included the most notorious trusts of the eighties, which were referred to time after time in the congressional debates. At a maximum, a literal reading would proscribe every form of concerted activity—not only by industrial entrepreneurs but also by farmers, laborers, or any other organized group—which in any way adversely affected the flow of interstate commerce.

A more precise definition of the new policy, and its effectiveness, depended upon four factors: (1) the meaning given to it by the courts in specific cases; (2) the sympathy of the Justice Department with its objectives and the vigor with which it attacked violators; (3) congressional support in providing funds for enforcement and in enacting supplementary legislation when necessary; and (4) the adequacy of injunction, dissolution, or criminal penalties in restoring competition in cases where prosecutions were successful. As far as the major trusts whose actions led to the legislation were concerned, the combined working of these factors made it almost a dead letter for its first two decades.

The Harrison, Cleveland, and McKinley administrations displayed little enthusiasm for the Act. Only eighteen actions were brought, many of them by spirited federal attorneys in the field with little or no support from Washington. From 1898 to 1901, when new combinations were being formed at a rate never equaled before or since, the sole suit instituted by the government concerned a relatively minor coal-and-coke pool. Richard Olney, Attorney General from 1893 to 1895, was positively hostile, first vainly attempting to get the Act repealed and later writing: "You will have observed that the government has been defeated in the Supreme Court on the trust question. I always supposed it would be and have taken the responsibility of not prosecuting under a law I believed to be no good—much to the rage of the New York World." [29] There were no special funds for antitrust-law enforcement. The Justice Department was hampered by a lack of investigatory facilities, which made it exceedingly difficult to collect evidence. The first outstandingly successful prosecution, against the Addyston Pipe Pool, was made possible only by the revelations of a disgruntled stenographer.

Two early, halfhearted attempts to reach large trusts both ended in miserable failure. A federal court in Massachusetts quashed a

[29] Quoted in H. S. Cummings and C. McFarland, *Federal Justice* (1937), pp. 322–323.

clumsily drafted indictment against the Whiskey Trust on a narrow technicality.[30] Subsequent decisions in three other districts tended to restrict the Act. The first case to reach the Supreme Court, *U.S.* v. *E. C. Knight Co.*,[31] was a bill in equity against the Sugar Trust, which then controlled 98 per cent of the domestic refining industry. On the ground that control of manufacturing affected commerce "only incidentally and indirectly," and was therefore subject only to state regulation, the Court, with only one dissent, dismissed the bill. Similar rulings disposed of two cases against combinations of livestock dealers in Kansas City.[32] The almost complete reversal of this extraordinary stand within a few years indicates that substantial responsibility for the fiasco rested with government counsel, who failed to stress the effect of the sugar combination on interstate sales of the refined product. The immediate consequence of the Knight decision, however, was a feeling that, without a constitutional amendment, industrial combinations were safe from federal law.[33]

At the same time, the Sherman Act was successfully applied to two fields unrelated to its primary objectives. In 1893 and 1894, lower courts applied the Act to unions, granting injunctions against strikes.[34] In rejecting an appeal from one of these actions, in the famous Debs case, the Supreme Court upheld the use of the injunction on other grounds, declining to rule on the applicability of the antitrust law.[35] But in 1908 the Supreme Court unequivocally placed labor activities under the Act by allowing employers to recover triple damages from their striking employees.[36] These cases lent color to the charges of liberal critics that a reactionary judiciary was abusing the Act by penalizing unions while exempting industrial malefactors.

The government also won two cases against railroad combinations, which many thought to be covered exclusively by the Interstate Commerce Act of 1887. In reversing two lower courts in a 5

[30] *U.S.* v. *Greenhut*, 50 Fed. 469 (1892). On the other hand, the constitutionality of the Act was sustained in *U.S.* v. *Jellico Mountain Coal and Coke Co.*, 46 Fed. 432 (1891).

[31] 156 U.S. 1 (1895).

[32] *U.S.* v. *Hopkins*, 171 U.S. 578 (1898); *U.S.* v. *Anderson*, 171 U.S. 604 (1898).

[33] *Annual Report of the Attorney General*, 1896, H. Doc. 234, 54th Cong., 1st sess., Exh. 1.

[34] *U.S.* v. *Workingmen's Amalgamated Council*, 54 Fed. 994 (1893), 57 Fed. 85 (1893); *U.S.* v. *Debs*, 64 Fed. 724 (1894).

[35] *In re Debs*, 158 U.S. 564 (1895). For a discussion of labor and the antitrust laws, see above, pp. 174–177.

[36] *Loewe* v. *Lawlor*, 208 U.S. 274.

to 4 decision, the Supreme Court in 1897 dissolved the Trans-Missouri Freight Association, a combination of Western railroads which fixed rates by agreement.[37] The majority held the agreement void irrespective of whether the rates actually fixed were reasonable. In the following year, a similar decision outlawed a rate-fixing association of Eastern railroads.[38]

Not until the Addyston Pipe case of 1899 did the Court uphold the Sherman Act's application to manufacturing.[39] Six producers of cast-iron pipe had established an elaborate pooling agreement. Although they controlled only 30 per cent of total national capacity, high transportation costs gave them a limited monopoly power in nearby territory. Orders from designated cities were reserved for each of the member companies. In a further area, known as "pay territory," the pool conducted a secret auction among its members, awarding contracts in return for the highest bonus offered to the pool. Bonuses were later distributed in proportion to members' capacity. In all public auctions, a specious appearance of competition was preserved by prearranged high bids from members other than the one selected. Circuit Court Judge William Howard Taft (later President and Chief Justice) in a lucid opinion held the agreement to be within the prohibitions of the antitrust law. He found the prices to be unreasonable, but argued that even had they been reasonable the scheme would have been invalid at common law and was certainly so under the Sherman Act. The Knight case was distinguished on the ground that the Addyston pool directly concerned itself with sales in interstate commerce, and not merely with manufacturing. The decision was affirmed by a unanimous Supreme Court.[40]

Taken together, the Sugar Trust and Addyston decisions appeared to mean that the federal statute constituted a real danger to loose marketing agreements and pools, but left industrial combinations through holding companies or mergers unaffected. The attitude of the McKinley administration reinforced this conclusion. At the same time, a flood of new combinations aroused public interest and antagonism to a point far beyond the level of the late eighties. From 1899 to 1902, an Industrial Commission of nineteen members, ten from Congress and nine appointed by the

[37] U.S. v. Trans-Missouri Freight Assn., 166 U.S. 290.
[38] U.S. v. Joint Traffic Association, 171 U.S. 505.
[39] U.S. v. Addyston Pipe and Steel Co., 175 U.S. 211.
[40] See also U.S. v. Chesapeake & Ohio Fuel Co., 115 Fed. 610 (1902); Continental Wallpaper Co. v. Voight, 212 U.S. 227 (1909); Montague v. Lowry, 193 U.S. 38 (1904); Shawnee Compress Co. v. Anderson, 209 U.S. 423 (1908).

President, exhaustively investigated combinations in the oil, coal, silver, whiskey, tobacco, salt, wallpaper, thread, baking powder, and other industries. The Commission's factual material proved more fruitful than its recommendations, which proposed increased publicity enforced through federal licensing of corporations and specific prohibitions of price discrimination, together with possible tariff modifications.

In 1899, the Civic Federation of Chicago gathered together an impressive assemblage of legislators, lawyers, governors, and other prominent citizens to discuss means of dealing with trusts. "The Department of Justice was flooded with petitions that trusts be investigated and destroyed." [41] In Congress a new wave of proposed legislation appeared. A constitutional amendment to remedy the Knight decision failed to receive the necessary two-thirds vote because of the Democratic Party's commitment to the principle of states' rights. In 1900, the House passed by 274 to 1 a bill slightly strengthening the Sherman Act and exempting labor organizations, but it was killed in the more conservative Senate. Strong antitrust planks reappeared in the platforms of both major parties. Yet the formation of new combinations proceeded apace.

At this juncture, the assassination of McKinley placed in the White House Theodore Roosevelt, with his belief in a more active role for government in the economy and his concept of expanded Presidential authority. Aggressively opposed to excessive accretion of power in private hands, the new President endorsed thoroughgoing publicity as a remedy against corporate abuses. Under his leadership, Congress created in 1903 a Bureau of Corporations; armed with the power of subpoena, it was to make "diligent investigation into the organization, conduct, and management of the business of any corporation, joint stock company, or corporate combination." In the same year, the House passed a bill to compel general publicity of corporate affairs and to prohibit discrimination in local prices and in railway rates. Administration support was withdrawn in the Senate, however, and the measure was defeated by the Republican majority.

In its ten years of existence, the new Bureau contributed greatly to the fund of economic knowledge about American industry, especially in its studies of meat-packing, oil, tobacco, steel, and lumber. The Roosevelt administration also infused new life into the Justice Department. In 1902, Congress was for the first time asked to grant special appropriations for antitrust enforcement. This was done, and forty-four proceedings were instituted

[41] Cummings and McFarland, *op. cit.*, p. 327.

under Roosevelt, as compared with eighteen under his predecessors. Substantial use was also made of the Act's criminal provisions. The court record was moderately successful, but most of the cases were against minor pools.[42]

Two big cases were brought to a successful conclusion. One enjoined the "Big Four" meat packers from conspiring to depress livestock prices and enhance meat prices.[43] The case on which Roosevelt's reputation as a "trust buster" largely depends was the successful dissolution of the Northern Securities Company, a holding company set up by Hill, Morgan, and Harriman to unite the Northern Pacific and Great Northern Railroads. Outright consolidation had previously been prevented under a Minnesota statute.[44] A divided Supreme Court led by four justices, with one concurring and four dissenting, held the company subject to the Sherman Act despite the existence of substantial outside competition and the alleged reasonableness of the rates fixed by the combination.[45] The chief significance of the case lay in its condemnation of the holding company as a method of control over previously competing companies, and its inclusion of this type of stockholding within the scope of the commerce clause.

Roosevelt left office with no major industrial trust yet dissolved, although suits against Standard Oil and American Tobacco had been initiated. The direct effects of his two major victories were almost nil. Community of interest within the controlling Hill-Morgan group continued to direct the policy of both Northwestern railroads, while the meat packers simply disregarded the Swift case injunction, at least until 1920 and probably until the late 1930's. Despite the lack of solid accomplishment, Roosevelt had furthered the development of antitrust policy. It had been demonstrated to businessmen that henceforth it would be imprudent to disregard the Sherman Act. Some valuable economic data and legal experience necessary to the definition of policy goals had been accumulated. Public attention had been focused on the possibilities and some of the problems of antitrust enforcement.

Late in his term, Roosevelt lost faith in mere publicity as a

---

[42] Eleven pleas of guilty or convictions were obtained in twenty-five criminal cases; fourteen injunctions, dissolutions, or consent decrees were obtained in eighteen equity proceedings; and one suit for forfeiture failed.

[43] *U.S.* v. *Swift & Co.*, 196 U.S. 375 (1905). This success was partly offset when a criminal prosecution failed on the ground that testimony before the Bureau of Corporations gave defendants legal immunity from subsequent criminal proceedings. *U.S.* v. *Armour & Co.*, 145 F. 808 (1906).

[44] *Pearsall* v. *Great Northern Railway*, 161 U.S. 646 (1896).

[45] *Northern Securities Co.* v. *U.S.*, 193 U.S. 197 (1904).

sufficient solution of the trust problem. He popularized a distinction between "good" and "bad" trusts. "Good trusts" gained their position through economies of large-scale operation short of complete monopoly, and took no unfair advantage of competitors or consumers; "bad trusts" competed unfairly and abused their monopoly power. The new attitude emphasized regulation of specific competitive practices and implied a definition of monopoly in terms neither of size nor share of market, but rather of behavior toward competitors and buyers and sellers.

President Taft, generally more conservative than his predecessor, was endowed by his judicial experience with more faith in purely legal remedies for economic problems. He took office with the conviction that the Sherman Act, if properly enforced, would effectively carry out a desirable general economic policy. His sole legislative proposal, which was not pressed, called for federal incorporation as a safeguard against financial mismanagement, and as a means of protecting investors. At the same time, Sherman Act prosecutions were pushed with unprecedented vigor. Seventy-eight suits were instituted during Taft's administration, compared with only sixty-two during the entire previous period since 1890, and in 1911 two major cases, Standard Oil and American Tobacco, were brought to a victorious conclusion in the Supreme Court.

4. The Rule of Reason and Close Consolidations

Roosevelt had recalled the Sherman Act from the limbo of unenforced statutes, but it was the Standard Oil case which marked the first application of the Act to a typical trust. More important, this case provided the first major judicial interpretation of the broadly worded basic provisions of the statute. It laid the foundation for two lines of decision which were to dominate antitrust enforcement for three decades.

After the Ohio decision against Standard Oil in 1892, the nine ex-trustees had maintained their direction of the formerly unified group through a community of controlling interest. Following a trial for contempt of court, the business was reorganized in 1899 under a holding company, the Standard Oil Company of New Jersey, which was given voting control over the other companies of the Standard group. In 1906, the Bureau of Corporations reported that about 91 per cent of the refining industry was directly or indirectly under Standard control, and that the old competitive methods of the group had been continued. In that year, an action in equity was brought for dissolution of the trust. In 1911, the

Supreme Court unanimously affirmed a circuit court decision against Standard Oil.[46]

Chief Justice White's opinion, however, virtually amended the Sherman Act by holding that it condemned only "unreasonable" restraints of trade, despite the text of the statute and clear prior decisions to the contrary, from which he had dissented. Verbose and confusing, the opinion emphasized the intent and methods of the combination rather than its economic results. White claimed to be following the common law, which he believed to prohibit only those:

contracts or acts which were unreasonably restrictive of competitive conditions, whether from the nature or character of the contract or act, or where the surrounding circumstances were such as to justify the conclusion that they had not been entered into or performed with the legitimate purpose of reasonably forwarding personal interest and developing trade, but, on the contrary, were of such a character as to give rise to the inference or presumption that they had been entered into or done with the intent to do wrong to the general public and to limit the right of individuals, thus restraining the free flow of commerce and tending to bring about the evils, such as enhancement of prices, which were considered to be against public policy.

The inarticulate major premise behind the opinion is implicit in phrases expressing a belief in "the inevitable operation of economic forces and the equipoise of balance in favor of the protection of the rights of individuals which resulted," and:

a consciousness that the freedom of the individual right to contract when not unduly or improperly exercised was the most efficient means for the prevention of monopoly, since the operation of the centrifugal and centripetal forces resulting from the right to freely contract was the means by which monopoly would be inevitably prevented if no extraneous or sovereign power imposed it and no rights to make unlawful contracts having a monopolistic tendency were permitted.

Thus the Chief Justice's faith was not so much in competition as in a view of laissez faire which regarded economic maladjustments as almost always automatically self-correcting. This view made it impossible for him to accept a literal interpretation of the statute's condemnation of "*every* combination . . . in restraint of trade."

Against this faith, the forceful and logical concurring opinion of Justice Harlan was unavailing. Harlan termed the majority's insertion of the rule of reason into the Act a piece of "judicial

[46] *U.S.* v. *Standard Oil Co. of N.J.*, 221 U.S. 1.

legislation" and "usurpation." In his mind, it was "a serious departure from the settled usages of this court," which would "entirely emasculate the Antitrust Act" and "throw the business of the country into confusion and invite widely extended and harassing litigation." The entire Court condemned Standard Oil, but the Chief Justice spoke of its size and power as creating only a prima facie presumption of intent to dominate the industry by abnormal methods. The decision really turned upon proof of those methods, including railway rate discrimination, local price-cutting, commercial espionage, use of bogus independents, territorial allocation of markets to member companies, and monopolization of the means of transportation. The implication was inescapable that had the defendants relied only upon "normal methods of industrial development," they would have escaped the condemnation of the Act as now interpreted.

The American Tobacco decision, handed down on the same day, similarly rested on the rule of reason. The Tobacco Trust dated from 1890, when J. B. Duke consolidated five cigarette manufacturers into the first American Tobacco Company. The Company sought to gain exclusive use of the best cigarette-making machinery patents and entered upon a campaign to acquire its leading competitors in all branches of the trade. "Fighting brands" competing with the output of particular competitors and sold below cost were one potent weapon in accomplishing its ends. It also made extensive use of bogus independents, which sought the patronage of groups opposed to the trust on general principles or because of its hostility to organized labor. Large competitors were frequently glad to join the combination at handsome prices, rather than risk the losses of such warfare. Many of the plants thus acquired were then shut down and the ex-competitors were required to agree not to re-enter the business. By 1900, the combination produced from 50 to 90 per cent of every type of tobacco product except cigars, where so little capital was required that independent competition was indestructible. In 1904, a new merger, also called the American Tobacco Company, replaced the former network of interlinked holding and operating companies, although some subsidiaries retained their separate corporate existence. The trust engendered bitter resentment among tobacco growers and surviving independents.

In 1907, dissolution proceedings were brought, and on appeal to the Supreme Court the entire government position was sustained.[47] Chief Justice White, over Justice Harlan's objection, again ex-

[47] *U.S.* v. *American Tobacco Co.*, 221 U.S. 106 (1911).

pounded the rule of reason. Laying great weight on the evidences of "conscious wrongdoing," he found that:

the history of the combination is so replete with the doing of acts which it was the obvious purpose of the statute to forbid, so demonstrative of the existence from the beginning of a purpose to acquire dominion and control of the tobacco trade, not by the mere exertion of the ordinary right to contract and to trade, but by methods devised in order to monopolize the trade by driving competitors out of business, which were ruthlessly carried out upon the assumption that to work upon the fears or play upon the cupidity of competitors would make success possible.

Here again, it was not the monopolistic position actually achieved, but the purposes and methods of the combination, which were held to violate the Act. A month later, similar reasoning was applied by a circuit court in dissolving the Du Pont explosives combination of 1904.[48] Thus the Justice Department had finally won major antitrust victories, but at the cost of a substantial rewriting of the Sherman Act. As far as close consolidations were concerned, the Act was less anti-*trust* than anti-predatory practices.

The enunciation of the rule of reason evoked a storm of controversy. Taking their cue from Justice Harlan, liberals denounced it as judicial legislation, giving to the courts an unwarranted power to exempt "good" trusts. Much of this conflict, as Edward S. Mason has pointed out,[49] was essentially one between law and economics. In the legal discipline, the terms "monopoly" and "restraint of trade" were interpreted in the light of common law. "The antithesis of the legal conception of monopoly is *free* competition . . . a situation in which the freedom of any individual or firm to engage in legitimate economic activity is not restrained by the state, by agreements between competitors or by the predatory practices of a rival." But to an economist, "the antithesis . . . of monopoly is not *free* but *pure* competition . . . a situation in which no seller or buyer has any control over the price of his product."

Consequently, the lawyer (and the judge) tended to view the purpose of the Sherman Act as prohibiting the restriction of competitors, while the economist viewed it as forbidding control of the market. The economic interpretation saw monopoly in the

[48] *U.S.* v. *Du Pont de Nemours & Co.*, 188 Fed. 127 (1911).

[49] E. S. Mason, "Monopoly in Law and Economics," *Yale Law Journal* (November, 1937); reprinted in E. S. Mason, *Economic Concentration and the Monopoly Problem* (1957), pp. 332–350.

position of Standard Oil or American Tobacco because of their overwhelming control of the market; the legal conception required evidence of an intent to restrict competitors or of predatory practices. The legal attitude, derived from common law, was reinforced by the adversary nature of judicial proceedings. It is easier for judges to weigh the evidence of collusion or of predatory practices than to devise and interpret economic tests of such data as prices and outputs. And competitors aggrieved by predatory practices can bring cases into court; abstractions such as competition cannot. The courts, accordingly, tend to focus on private interests injured by unfair practices or exclusion from the market more than on issues such as control of prices.

Thus, critics of the rule of reason, using economic concepts, could for the next three decades complain that the antitrust laws were not being used to prevent monopoly and preserve competition, while its defenders could reply that there was no monopoly because no competitors were being coerced. In 1915, a lower court, while admitting that the Eastman Kodak Company controlled between 70 and 80 per cent of its industry's output "and had accordingly obtained a monopoly theorof," held that this was not enough to indicate a violation of the law:

There is no limit in this country to the extent to which a business may grow, and the acquisition of property in the present case, standing alone, would not be deemed an illegal monopoly; but when such acquisitions are accompanied by an intent to monopolize and restrain interstate trade by an arbitrary use of the power resulting from a large business to eliminate a weaker competitor, then they no doubt come within the meaning of the statute.[50]

Even within the legal approach to antitrust policy, however, White's rule of reason was open to question. Ex-President Taft later defended it on the ground that the common-law standard of reason, which the Court claimed to have adopted, was perfectly precise, that it forbade all monopolization and also all restraints of trade except those ancillary to another dominant, legal objective.[51] The flaw in this argument lay in its premise that the Court would really apply so clear a standard. In fact, the Court read the common law differently, giving itself far more discretion than would Taft's reading. The common law applied reason to ancillary covenants, such as those involving the sale of good will. But the Court applied the rule of reason to all restraints, even when, as in the case

[50] U.S. v. *Eastman Kodak Co.*, 226 Fed. 62.
[51] W. H. Taft, *The Antitrust Act and the Supreme Court* (1914).

of a merger of firms sizable enough to control market prices, trade was being significantly restrained.

One major effect of the rule of reason was considerable uncertainty. While two of the biggest trusts had been humbled, demonstrating that no one was beyond the reach of the law, it was clear that the Court was distinguishing between "good" and "bad" trusts. It was far from clear, however, precisely where the line was between the two, or just which practices were predatory or unfair. Only the Court could answer these questions. As long as Congress remained silent, antitrust policy would be made by the judges. In the antitrust legislation of 1914, discussed in the next chapter, Congress did try to make more explicit the definition of unfair practices and forbidden restraints of trade, but it did not attack the rule of reason. It proceeded to supplement the Sherman Act, rather than to redefine its basic meaning.

The rule of reason caused Sherman Act interpretations to diverge along two fairly distinct paths. In the case of pools, trade associations, and other loose agreements among competitors, the Act continued to be applied with considerable rigor. The rule of reason seldom tolerated these loose combinations because, to the legal mind, they imposed unreasonable restraints on competitors. The doctrine of conspiracy seemed more applicable to loose combinations than to close consolidations. The courts tended to attack any agreement among competitors without asking whether the combination had monopoly power to set prices or to control the market.

At the same time, the close consolidations fared better at the hands of the judges, despite the fact that they were the target at which the Act was originally aimed. Issues of market control were essentially irrelevant so long as no predatory practices or other restrictions on competitors were alleged. As a result, for three decades the Supreme Court condemned no close combinations in manufacturing.[52] In two cases against the United Shoe Machinery Company, which produced about 95 per cent of the shoe machinery made in the United States, the Court found nothing to question in this virtually complete monopoly. In the first, a

---

[52] It applied the law much more severely to railroads. It required a terminal association to admit to membership all railroads it served, and dissolved two railroad combinations. *U.S.* v. *Terminal Railroad Assn. of St. Louis,* 224 U.S. 383 (1912); *U.S.* v. *Union Pacific Co.,* 226 U.S. 61 (1912); *U.S.* v. *Southern Pacific Co.,* 259 U.S. 214 (1922). And it disapproved of two mergers of railroad and anthracite coal companies, even though they controlled only about 33 and 20 per cent, respectively, of the total output. *U.S.* v. *Reading Co.,* 253 U.S. 26 (1920); *U.S.* v. *Lehigh Valley Railroad Co.,* 254 U.S. 255 (1920).

criminal proceeding,[53] the Court found that the original merger had been among noncompeting companies making complementary lines of machinery. In the second, a civil suit for dissolution,[54] the Court repeated this finding, despite evidence of substantial overlap in types of machinery, and held that the fifty-seven subsequent acquisitions "added nothing of obnoxious power . . . nor in any practical or large sense removed competition."

Complaints of rival makers of machinery and of many shoe manufacturers had centered on United Shoe's method of leasing machines. Most of its lines were protected by patents, and it regularly bought up new inventions as soon as they appeared. It made no outright sales of its machinery, and as a condition of leasing certain machines it required the use of its products for other parts of the manufacturing process. These "tying clauses" enabled it to force a complete line upon any manufacturer who found one of its machines indispensable. The legal monopoly attaching to a patent could thus be extended, in effect, to apparatus on which patents had long expired. But the Court approved the tying clauses as legitimate conditions to the use of patented machines. Indicating extreme reluctance to interfere with a long-established combination which had made large investments and which would be difficult to dissolve, the Court concluded:

It is impossible to believe . . . that the great business of the United Shoe Machinery Company has been built up by the coercion of its customers and that its machinery has been installed in most of the large factories of the country by the exercise of power, even that of patents. The installation could have had no other incentive than the excellence of the machines and the advantage of their use, the conditions imposed having adequate compensation and not offensive to the letter or the policy of the law.

The faith in automatically operating natural harmonies and extreme laissez faire, a faith antipathetic in its very nature to a strong antitrust policy, stands out clearly in these words. Three justices dissented, finding that the company dominated the industry and that its leases restrained trade to an extent unwarranted by its patent rights.

The shoe-machinery cases may possibly be explained away because of special rights attaching to patents.[55] But patents were not

[53] *U.S.* v. *Winslow*, 227 U.S. 202 (1913).

[54] *U.S.* v. *United Shoe Machinery Co.*, 247 U.S. 32 (1918).

[55] When suit was later brought against the company under Section 3 of the Clayton Act, which specifically forbade tying contracts on goods whether

involved in the decision of 1920 in favor of the United States Steel Corporation.[56] U.S. Steel, then the nation's largest industrial enterprise, was a holding company formed in 1901 to merge concerns which were themselves amalgamations of smaller companies. It had been set up to forestall a threat of overexpansion and ruinous competition at a time when manufacturers of heavier semifinished products had been about to integrate forward into the finished lines, and manufacturers of finished products had laid plans to integrate backward. The arrangement of the combination also brought large promoters' profits, estimated at over $60 million, to the Morgan firm and others.

Heavily overcapitalized, U.S. Steel evidently expected to gain substantially from the semimonopolistic position thus achieved. It controlled at the time of its establishment over 60 per cent of the country's entire iron and steel capacity, and at first pursued an expansionist policy, absorbing a number of important competitors. Thereafter, possibly because of fear of antitrust prosecution, it became more cautious, and by 1911 its share of the industry had dropped to 50 per cent. It had abstained from predatory practices, its record being almost free from charges of local price-cutting, transportation favors, commercial espionage, or restrictive contracts with customers. It chose rather to tolerate its rivals, sheltering them under the umbrella of its enormous power. Price competition was first limited by agreements and understandings, followed in 1907 by the celebrated Gary dinners. At these "business meetings with a social aspect," [57] Judge Gary exhorted his fellow steelmakers to preserve stability in the industry. Restraint of price competition was assisted by the industry-wide practice of price quotation on a "Pittsburgh-Plus" basing point. How large a role was played in the minds of the independents by fear of a price war against a rival with the size and financial connections of the Corporation, it is impossible to judge. The dinners came to an end in 1911, but price leadership by U.S. Steel remained.

A government suit to dissolve U.S. Steel into its component parts was rejected by a 4 to 3 decision of the Supreme Court. Speaking for the Court, Justice McKenna conceded that the Corporation's promoters had intended to monopolize the industry, but

---

patented or unpatented, if they tended substantially to lessen competition or create a monopoly, a 7 to 1 decision in the Supreme Court condemned its leases. *United Shoe Machinery Corp.* v. *U.S.*, 258 U.S. 451 (1922).

[56] *U.S.* v. *U.S. Steel Corp.*, 251 U.S. 417 (1920).

[57] This phrase was used by the trial judge in the district court's opinion, 223 Fed. 55 (1915).

they had, in his opinion, given up the effort before 1911 when the suit was filed. Despite the statute's condemnation of any "attempt to monopolize," he held that it was directed "against monopoly . . . not against an expectation of it, but against its realization." In its treatment of competition, the majority emphasized the legal, rather than the economic, concept. Competition had not been illegally restrained, the majority concluded, for U.S. Steel had made no efforts to suppress the independents by unfair means. The explicit price-fixing agreements and the Gary dinners had been abandoned before 1911. The economic argument that industry acceptance of price leadership and basing points constituted a tacit agreement to prevent price competition was not strongly presented to the Court. The argument that U.S. Steel had so large a share of the market as to constitute an inherent monopoly or restraint on competition was rejected. "The law does not make mere size an offense or the existence of unexerted power an offense. It . . . requires overt acts and trusts to its prohibition of them and its power to repress or punish them. It does not compel competition nor require all that is possible." The dissenters insisted that the combination had gained its power not through normal growth but in "plain violation and bold defiance" of the Act, and that to let the Corporation remain "would be to practically annul the Sherman Law by judicial decree." Power to dominate the industry, not merely the abuse of such power, was to them the test of illegality.

This narrow construction of the law was confirmed in 1927 in the Harvester case.[58] The International Harvester Company was formed in 1902 by consolidation of the five leading manufacturers of harvesting machines, producing 85 per cent of the American output. An earlier suit for dissolution had led to a consent decree [59] in 1918 which required the sale of three less important brands to independents, and forbade the company to employ more than one agent in any town. (Exclusive agency contracts, limiting each dealer to a single line of the International's products, had given it effective local monopolies in many small communities.) The consent decree reduced its share of the market to about 65 per cent.

[58] U.S. v. International Harvester Co., 274 U.S. 693.

[59] A consent decree is a court decree entered against the respondent in an equity proceeding by his own consent. Obtained by informal negotiation between the government and the respondent, it is enforceable through contempt proceedings in precisely the same manner as a contested decree entered by a court after litigation. Unlike a contested decree, however, a consent decree does not necessarily reflect an authoritative intrepretation of the law. Nor can it be made the basis for triple-damage suits by private parties.

In 1920, the Federal Trade Commission reported that the decree had not been adequate to restore competition and recommended separation of the leading McCormick and Deering brands, as well as separate ownership of a steel-producing subsidiary. The Justice Department thereupon filed a supplemental petition requesting further dissolution. With three of its members not participating, the Supreme Court refused the request. FTC statements were lightly dismissed as "hearsay," not deserving consideration under the legal rules of evidence. The Court re-emphasized its line of argument developed in the Steel decision:

The law . . . does not make the mere size of a corporation, however impressive, or the existence of unexerted power on its part, an offense, when unaccompanied by unlawful conduct in the exercise of its power. . . . And the fact that competitors may see proper, in the exercise of their own judgment, to follow the prices of another manufacturer, does not establish any suppression of competition or show any sinister domination.

The Steel and Shoe Machinery cases, reinforced by the Harvester decision, severely limited the application of the Sherman Act to close consolidations. The government dismissed a number of appeals to the Supreme Court in antitrust cases,[60] and almost no new efforts were made to dissolve combinations until 1937. Where before the Steel decision the government had secured a number of dissolution decrees in the lower courts, including the Du Pont powder trust (1911), the glucose trust (1916), and the Eastman Kodak combination (1915),[61] after that decision the milder remedy of enjoining specific predatory practices was usually used. Consent decrees forbidding particular unfair methods of competition were accepted by a large number of respondents, including the American Sugar Refining Company, the General Electric Company, the American Telephone and Telegraph Company, the Victor Talking Machine Company, the Fox Theatres Corporation, the National Food Products Corporation, and the National Cash Register Company. The most far-reaching consent decree was entered against the leading meat packers in 1920; it forbade them to control public stockyards, wholesale or retail groceries, and

[60] *U.S.* v. *Quaker Oats Co.*, 232 Fed. 499 (1916), 253 U.S. 499 (1920); *U.S.* v. *American Can Co.*, 230 Fed. 859 (1916), 234 Fed. 1019 (1916), 256 U.S. 706 (1921); *U.S.* v. *Keystone Watch Case Co.*, 218 Fed. 502 (1915), 257 U.S. 664 (1921).

[61] *U.S.* v. *Du Pont de Nemours & Co.*, 188 Fed. 127 (1911); *U.S.* v. *Corn Products Co.*, 234 Fed. 964 (1916); *U.S.* v. *Eastman Kodak Co.*, 226 Fed. 62 (1915).

livestock-market newspapers.

In the few cases where dissolution was ordered, the test of legality developed under the rule of reason led to marked caution in the manner and extent of reorganization decreed by the courts. Decrees were intended to shift the position across the border line of legality, but to disturb property rights and the industrial situation as little as possible. Thus, in the Standard Oil case, the holding company's shares in the various operating companies were simply distributed among its own shareholders in proportion to their interest in the holding company. For the time being, accordingly, there remained complete community of ownership in the operating companies. Many observers felt this outcome to be almost farcical. The market value of the securities concerned appreciably increased. For some time, the constituent companies limited their operations to their old market areas.

Nonetheless, the passage of time slowly dispersed ownership of the various companies, through inheritance and sale, until after World War I they began invading each other's territory. New firms grew up as strong as, or stronger than, the old Standard companies. The situation was transformed from one of almost complete monopoly to one of typical "oligopoly," with no single firm dominating the field, with vigorous competition in marketing and service to customers, but with price competition distinctly limited.

The Tobacco Trust was divided into fourteen separate companies, four in general tobacco manufacturing, two in tin foil, two in licorice, three in snuff, one foreign manufacturer, one cigar concern, and one in retail trade. Here, too, no provision was made against community of ownership by individuals. Stock prices again appreciated considerably. The independents, represented by Louis D. (later Justice) Brandeis, strongly criticized this retention of common ownership and the perpetuation of a few large concerns. The judges, however, held that the new situation would not be subject to successful prosecution, that the court was concerned with law and not economics, and that the remedy granted exhausted their power.[62] The long-term result has been an industry dominated by a few leaders, with very heavy advertising rivalry but relatively little price competition.

A somewhat similar dissolution was ordered in the Du Pont case. No attempt was made to produce a more perfectly competitive situation than in these cases, and the difficulties of doing so without sacrificing the economies of large-scale, integrated production may well be insuperable. It has become increasingly

[62] 191 Fed. 371 (1911).

evident that in many if not most industries, while a more vigorous antitrust policy would doubtless have resulted in substantially less concentration of control, the minimum scale of enterprise for efficient production and marketing, and for ensuring technical development, is such that the classical economic model of a perfectly competitive market is simply unattainable.

The net effect of the rule of reason was a substantial abandonment of the frontal attack on close consolidations during the two decades of the 1920's and 1930's. The law had prevented complete monopolization of certain industries and doubtless deterred efforts to monopolize others. Since the Shoe Machinery and Steel cases had both been decided by 4 to 3 votes, and the views of the two abstaining justices were almost certainly on the side of the minority, businessmen would have been poorly advised to assume that these cases reflected a settled interpretation of the law. For the most part, however, the Sherman Act had become a restraint on predatory competitive practices rather than on the accumulation or nonpredatory exercise of market power. In the 1940's, however, as will be shown in Chapter 18, antitrust policy toward close consolidations entered a new phase, both on the side of administrative attack and on the side of judicial interpretation.

5. The Sherman Act and Loose Combinations

Loose combinations, in contrast to close consolidations, were given much less leeway by virtue of the rule of reason, since agreement or collusion among competitors retaining their independence fit clearly into the common-law tradition of conspiracy in restraint of trade. The antitrust legislation was enacted in response to widespread resentment against a number of outstanding, aggressive, monopolistic combinations, but the infinite variety of looser agreements among business firms are equally important in their effects upon the national economy, although less dramatic and less productive of moral indignation. Pools, market-sharing, and price agreements among competitors, and similar methods of limiting competition, are, of course, very old phenomena. Well before the Sherman Act, many such agreements were held to be unenforceable at common law as being in restraint of trade and, therefore, against public policy. The ephemeral character of these agreements, due largely to the impossibility of binding recalcitrant or renegade parties to their terms, had been chiefly responsible for the search for surer means of eliminating competition, through trusts, holding companies, and large-scale mergers.

In Germany, where neither common law nor antimonopoly statutes hindered the development of voluntary associations among competitors, they multiplied apace in the half century before World War II. Called "cartels," their major purpose, frankly proclaimed, was "stabilization" of their markets through the concerted control of prices and output. In Britain, likewise, no positive antitrust policy was initiated until after World War II, and common-law hindrances to business corporations had steadily eroded since 1889. As a result, particularly following Britain's abandonment of free trade after World War I, trade "Institutes" were organized over a wide economic area. Like cartels, they sought to eliminate overproduction, to "rationalize" industrial and commercial practices, to control prices, to allocate output, and so far as possible, to maintain profits.

In this country, the term "cartelization" has always carried an alien and unfavorable connotation. A more rigorous interpretation of the common law, coupled with state and federal antitrust legislation, has outlawed all open price and output agreements among competitors. On the other hand, the same basic trends producing dissatisfaction abroad with unmodified competition have also obtained here. Improved transportation, mass production, increasing proportions of fixed to variable costs, and the business cycle lie at the heart of the movement for business self-regulation. Deflected from cartelization by public policy, American businessmen were not ready to forego all attempts at common action short of merger, particularly when the alternative might be cutthroat competition and bankruptcy. Certain aspects of the business retreat from competition are discussed below in Chapter 17.

Illegal agreements have often been set up secretly, but they must surmount the obstacle of legal nonenforceability as well as the risks of government prosecution or private triple-damage suits under the antitrust laws. Many secret price and output agreements break down of their own accord. There is also, however, a wide area of open co-operative activity, ranging from unqualifiedly beneficial and universally approved operations at one extreme to a zone of doubtful legality at the other. For such purposes, regional or national trade associations, generally incorporated, are set up in particular industries.

The Trade Association Movement

Although a few trade associations flourished at the time of the Civil War, organizations of this sort became common only during the 1870's and 1880's, when they were concerned almost exclu-

sively with efforts at market control. They were generally short-
lived. Later in the century, as state and federal statutes came to
forbid price and output agreements, a gradual transformation set
in. "Constructive co-operation" for promotion of an industry
through product standardization, research, and like activities, as
well as through lobbying for tariff and other favors, were among
their avowed objectives. When the rule of reason was enunciated
in 1911, association promoters saw an opportunity to expand their
functions.

The leader of this new movement was A. J. Eddy, a Chicago
lawyer. His book, *The New Competition* (1912), whose title page
bore the inscription, "Competition is War, and 'War is Hell,' "
set forth a plan for "open competition," designed to meliorate the
consequences of unrestrained competition. Intended to prevent
members of an industry from being played off one against another
and to avoid market surpluses and price "chiseling," the plan called
for systematic interchange and dissemination of statistics on production, sales, prices, costs, and inventories. Trade association
members would thus be enabled to act with greater knowledge,
making their individual policies with due regard to the economic
position of their entire industry. The plan was taken up at once
in many fields, particularly in steel products, lumber, and textiles.

During World War I, the government encouraged formation
of trade associations as instruments for wartime economic planning. By the close of the war there were from fifteen hundred to
two thousand associations. The movement was fostered by the
Commerce Department during the early 1920's, and later by the
Federal Trade Commission as well. Legal difficulties then damp-
ened the enthusiasm of many businessmen until 1933, when, suddenly converted into quasi-public agencies for the administration
of the National Industrial Recovery Act (NIRA), trade associations became almost a *sine qua non* for every industry. Their number shot up into the high thousands. The movement declined
somewhat after the death of the NIRA but once again expanded
during World War II as trade associations again came to play an
important part in the industrial-mobilization program. There are
now about twelve thousand associations, a fourth of them national
in scope.

Many trade association activities have no relation to antitrust
policy. Likewise, of course, numerous anticompetitive agreements
are not institutionalized under trade associations. Nevertheless,
the organization of competitors for legitimate co-operation carries
with it the danger that co-operation may be extended beyond the

border line of illegality. In consequence, antitrust policy toward loose agreements has focused on trade associations.

Association Activities

The major activities of trade associations fall into the following categories:

(1) Government relations, including contacts with administrative agencies and legislative lobbying

(2) Trade promotion, including market research, industry advertising, and development of new uses for industry products

(3) Standardization and simplification of product types and sizes and establishment of quality standards

(4) Annual conventions

(5) Establishment of accepted trade practices, including elimination of supposedly undesirable methods of competition

(6) Collection and dissemination of trade statistics relating to business activity, including production, sales, inventories, shipments, and orders

(7) Employer-employee relations

(8) Special statistical studies and publication of statistics

(9) Technical research and advisory services, including operation of research laboratories

(10) Public relations, designed to promote good will toward the industry as a whole

(11) Cost studies and promotion of uniform accounting

(12) Exchange of credit information concerning customers

(13) Traffic and transportation, including advice on routing, handling of freight claims, and promotion of lowered freight rates

(14) Collection and dissemination of members' prices and bids, including "open price filing"

(15) Commercial arbitration

(16) Bill collection service

(17) Information and assistance with regard to registration of patents, trade-marks, designs, and styles [63]

Obviously many of these activities are directed solely toward cost reduction or market expansion and conflict in no way with antitrust policy. They include research, industry advertising, representation at fairs and expositions, product standardization, simplification of grades and sizes, credit rating of customers, and arbitration machinery for disputes within the industry and between members and outsiders. The Commerce Department positively encourages such activities. Other trade association practices, how-

[63] See TNEC, *Trade Association Survey*, Monograph No. 18 (1941), pp. 22–26.

ever, may involve serious limits on competition, depending on how they are used. This is the case, for example, with the promotion of standard cost accounting and the provision of uniform accounting forms. The object may be merely to supply the services of expensive, skilled accountants on a joint basis. On the other hand, the practice may easily slide over into recommendation of fictitious minima for certain cost elements, arbitrary allocations of overhead costs, or arbitrary profit allowances, thus tending to fix part of the final price regardless of actual cost variations.

Interchange of patent rights can likewise be manipulated for purposes of market control. In highly mechanized industries, the incidental patents on refinements of the basic processes frequently run into the hundreds. Manufacturers may find it convenient to avoid interminable and expensive litigation by pooling their various patents through an association, cross-licensing all the members for their use. Such a pool, far from introducing monopolistic elements into the market, actually reduces them by eliminating the various legally held monopolies on the separate patented processes. On the other hand, a pool may be so administered as to convert separate patent monopolies into a single concerted monopoly over a whole industry. Only a detailed examination of each case can show whether or not such practices conflict with the antitrust laws.

The statistical services of trade associations are particularly likely to run afoul of antitrust policy. These services vary widely. Prices, production, and sales are the most commonly reported items, but some association statistics also cover costs and inventories. It is commonly argued that such information is essential to intelligent competition, reducing, rather than creating, market imperfections. In the early years of Eddy's open-price system, for example, lumber dealers were said to be unwarrantably bid down by unscrupulous large buyers, who made false claims of low-price offers from others. In more general terms, it is asserted that the proper planning of a firm's economic policy must be made in the light of the entire industry's market prospects, and that industry-wide forecasting necessitates the interchange of information.

Yet particular trade association practices may tend to induce price and output policies approximating those of a single monopolist and so may conflict with antitrust policy. Where there are few competitors, full information on each other's output and prices may in itself, without any direct agreement or collusive action, lead them all to restrict output simultaneously. The manner of reporting and the association's analysis or comments on the information may enhance this tendency. If individual transactions are identified in the reports, pressure can be brought against price-cutters. Inventory statistics may induce members to curtail production in order to maintain or raise prices. Cost statistics are the most questionable of all. While circulation of individual costs is rarely permitted by members, figures for average costs are, in fact, often taken as suggestions for minimum prices. Here, again, the precise method of calculation and presentation may be decisive of the practical effects.

Informational activities of trade associations, therefore, may be transformed into efforts to control output, prices, and methods of sale and distribution. These services are most highly developed where the trade is handled by relatively few sellers. Most associations, moreover, disseminate their information only to members, thus depriving outside sellers and all buyers of the advantages of knowledge and "intelligent competition" which the information is supposed to promote. For these reasons, the Federal Trade Commission has at times suggested that statistical reporting be closely supervised by a public agency, and perhaps even removed to a neutral body.

Outright price and production control is potentially implicit in any scheme of institutionalized co-operation among supposed competitors. Adam Smith once propounded the classic remark that "people of the same trade seldom meet together even for merriment and diversion, but the conversation ends in a conspiracy against the public, or in some contrivance to raise prices." [64] Abroad, such market control is usually explicitly sought. Control techniques in this country must be trimmed to meet the limitations of the law; in this respect trade associations are "cartels emasculated by the antitrust laws." [65]

Despite these legal limitations, discussed below, associations have on occasion attempted directly to establish concerted price and output controls. More commonly, "Codes of Ethics" are used to eliminate certain forms of competition, proscribing, for example, "sales below cost," a deceptive phrase which conceals serious ambiguities. Its practical results depend upon the particular cost formula employed—whether the cost of the most efficient producer, that of the least efficient, that of each producer taken separately, or some average—as well as upon the method of allocating overhead and upon the allowance, if any, for profit. The codes also frequently seek to eliminate competition in credit terms and other

---

[64] Adam Smith, *The Wealth of Nations* (Cannan ed., 1904), Vol. 1, p. 130.

[65] A. R. Burns, *The Decline of Competition* (1936), p. 74.

elements going into the composition of actual price. Such provisions arise from co-operative efforts to outlaw "unfair methods of competition," and are often put in final form at FTC Trade Practice Conferences, discussed below in Chapter 16. Associations have also sought legislative action to restrain competition, e.g., legislation against price discrimination, for legalization of resale price maintenance, and for chain-store taxation. These activities are discussed in Chapter 17.

Price and Output Agreements

In striking contrast with their attitude toward mergers, the courts have applied the Sherman Act to loose agreements, apart from a few notable exceptions, with consistent and marked severity. Power to control, or even merely to affect, the market—not abuse of that power—is the criterion of illegality. Nor must an agreement include all or almost all of the firms in a given market to fall within the ban. The rule of reason has some significance in this field, as will be indicated, but its application is very limited, and many activities are held to be illegal per se. As a result, while very few close consolidations were dissolved or prevented between the two World Wars, associations and agreements in restraint of trade were successfully attacked by the dozens. It was frequently claimed at that time, and with some reason, that the combination of lax construction against combinations and strict construction against agreements actually promoted trustification—that the courts had in this way converted the Sherman Act into a positive force for the defeat of its original objectives.

With few exceptions, the antitrust laws have been construed unambiguously to forbid direct price or output agreements. The courts have generally held that any combination to fix prices is illegal per se, refusing to inquire whether the prices set are reasonable or whether business conditions make price control a reasonable activity. This inflexible approach was foreshadowed in the Addyston Pipe case of 1899, discussed above, in which counsel for the pool argued that the prices it fixed were reasonable. The Court rejected this claim as untrue and in any event irrelevant, since the members had power to charge unreasonable prices. This precedent has generally been honored ever since.[66] Price-fixing and pooling of earnings through a common sales agency were also held

[66] Shortly before the Addyston case, the first dealing with industry, both the Trans-Missouri Freight Association (1897) and the Joint Traffic Association (1898) cases had applied the same rule to the fixing of rates by groups of railroads.

illegal in a suit involving a wallpaper association in 1909.[67] The law restrains concerted price-fixing by buyers as well as sellers.[68] An agreement to fix prices need not be explicit to fall within the ban; trade association activities leading indirectly to the same result are equally forbidden. Thus, the FTC was sustained in 1927 in ordering an association of paper dealers to cease distributing price lists actually used by members in their interstate sales, even though association penalties were levied only against price-cutting in intrastate commerce.[69] Similarly condemned were a boycott by retail lumber dealers to prevent wholesalers from selling directly to consumers,[70] and the use of a patent agreement to fix the price of bathtubs.[71]

When he propounded the rule of reason in 1911, Chief Justice White did not distinguish between close combinations and loose agreements. Some trade association lawyers forecast a legalization of agreements to prevent "ruinous competition," as long as they curtailed only "overproduction," or set only "reasonable" prices. These hopes were destined to disappointment. Following the dominant trend of the American common-law cases, the courts almost consistently voided concerted control of output or prices, no matter how good the motives or how allegedly beneficent the results.

The issue was raised in especially clear-cut form in the Trenton Potteries case in 1927.[72] Manufacturers and distributors of 82 per cent of the vitreous-enamel bathroom fixtures produced in this country, associated in the Sanitary Potters' Association, had admittedly fixed prices and sold exclusively through selected jobbers. The Supreme Court, by a vote of 5 to 3, upheld the ruling of the trial court judge that the reasonableness of the prices and good intentions of the members were irrelevant to the question of guilt under the law, and that "an agreement on the part of the members of a combination controlling a substantial part of an industry, upon the prices which the members are to charge for their commodity, is in itself an undue and unreasonable restraint of trade and commerce."

The Court was emphatic in its refusal to apply the rule of reason and in its application of a per se rule:

[67] *Continental Wallpaper Co.* v. *Voight & Sons Co.*, 212 U.S. 227.
[68] *Swift & Co.* v. *U.S.*, 196 U.S. 375 (1905); *Live Poultry Dealers' Protective Assn.* v. *U.S.*, 4 F. 2d 840 (1924).
[69] *FTC* v. *Pacific State Paper Trade Assn.*, 273 U.S. 52.
[70] *Eastern States Retail Lumber Assn.* v. *U.S.*, 234 U.S. 600 (1914).
[71] *Standard Sanitary Mfg. Co.* v. *U.S.*, 226 U.S. 20 (1912).
[72] *U.S.* v. *Trenton Potteries Co.*, 273 U.S. 392.

. . . it does not follow that agreements to fix or maintain prices are reasonable restraints and therefore permitted by the statute, merely because the prices themselves are reasonable. Reasonableness is not a concept of definite and unchanging content. . . .

The aim and result of every price-fixing agreement, if effective, is the elimination of one form of competition. The power to fix prices, whether reasonably exercised or not, involves power to control the market and to fix arbitrary and unreasonable prices. The reasonable price fixed today may through economic and business changes become the unreasonable price of tomorrow. . . . Agreements which create such potential power may well be held to be in themselves unreasonable or unlawful restraint, without the necessity of minute inquiry, whether a particular price is reasonable or unreasonable as fixed, and without placing on the government in enforcing the Sherman law the burden of ascertaining from day to day whether it has become unreasonable. . . . Moreover . . . we should hesitate to adopt a construction making the difference between legal and illegal conduct in the field of business relations depend upon so uncertain a test as whether prices are reasonable—a determination which can be satisfactorily made only after a complete survey of our economic organization and a choice between rival philosophies.

It is to be noted, also, that while the "trust" cases established a test of market dominance approximating complete monopoly, association agreements have been condemned on the basis of "substantial control," which has meant as little as 30 per cent. As one judge put it, the law forbids "all agreements preventing competition in price among a group of buyers, otherwise competitive, if they are numerous enough to affect the market." [73]

There have been exceptions, two minor and one major, to this well-crystallized pattern of decisions condemning all output and price agreements. In 1918, in a case of limited applicability, the Supreme Court upheld a rule of the Chicago Board of Trade, the world's leading grain market, which required the buying and selling of grain outside of trading hours to be done at the closing market price.[74] Applying the rule of reason, the decision held that the Board of Trade rule substituted a public market for private bidding and so promoted and improved competition. Similarly, in 1923 the Court validated an agreement between all the manufacturers in the rapidly dying handblown-glass industry and their skilled workers, which divided the manufacturers into two groups

[73] Learned Hand, *Live Poultry Dealers' Protective Assn.* v. *U.S.*, 4 F. 2d 840, 842 (1924). Cf. also *Indiana Farmers' Guide Publishing Co.* v. *Prairie Farmer Publishing Co.*, 293 U.S. 268 (1934).

[74] *Chicago Board of Trade* v. *U.S.*, 246 U.S. 231.

and allocated the full labor supply to each in turn for half a year. Since prices were set by the competing machine-made product, which supplied 95 per cent of the market, and the number of trained blowers was limited, the Court saw "no combination in unreasonable restraint of trade in the agreements made to meet the short supply of men." [75] These unique circumstances made the case inapplicable as a general precedent.

The Trenton Potteries decision and its per se doctrine, however, were brought into serious question by the Supreme Court's application of the rule of reason to a price-fixing combination in the Appalachian Coals case of 1933.[76] During the Great Depression of the early thirties, many businessmen had vigorously protested the outlawing of all forms of price-fixing under the antitrust laws. Harassed competitors, desperately struggling to keep afloat in the face of declining demand, looked upon "cuttthroat competition" as one potent cause for the fatal spiral of decreasing prices and income. They pled for "reasonable" co-operation, not to exploit the public, but merely to "adjust production to demand" and "keep prices above costs." Arguments heretofore made in the chronically "sick" industries, like bituminous coal and cotton textiles, were now applied more generally, as virtually all industries became "sick." Shortly before Congress responded to this plea with the National Industrial Recovery Act of 1933, the Supreme Court handed down a decision which appeared to reverse much that had seemed firm and unshakable in antitrust law interpretation.

Appalachian Coals, Inc., was an exclusive selling agency set up by 137 soft coal producers. Their output was 12 per cent of the total east of the Mississippi, 54 per cent of the production of the Appalachian fields, and a larger proportion of some Eastern and Southeastern markets. In an industry then suffering acutely from overcapacity, loss of customers to other fuels, and consequent cutthroat competition, this sales agency proposed to eliminate price competition among its members but not to restrict production. Arguing that the scheme would not only benefit mine operators but would also prevent wage cuts and lighten heavy relief burdens on local communities, the scheme's proponents first appealed vainly for Justice Department approval and then for judicial approval. The district court declared its sympathy with the motives behind the program but stated that modification of the Sherman Act was a matter for Congress and not for the courts.[77]

[75] National Assn. of Window Glass Manufacturers v. U.S., 263 U.S. 403.
[76] Appalachian Coals, Inc. v. U.S., 288 U.S. 344.
[77] U.S. v. Appalachian Coals, Inc., 1 F. Supp. 339 (1932).

The Supreme Court displayed no such modesty concerning the judicial function. The Sherman Act was declared to possess a "generality and adaptability comparable to that found to be desirable in constitutional provisions." Emphasizing the industry's distress, its overcapacity, and the existence of sufficient outside competition to prevent undue price increases, the Court decided in favor of the association by an 8 to 1 majority. It had not been shown, they felt, that there would be any effect on prices "which in the circumstances of this industry will be detrimental to fair competition." Chief Justice Hughes continued:

A co-operative enterprise, otherwise free from objection, which carries with it no monopolistic menace, is not to be condemned as an undue restraint merely because it may effect a change in market conditions, where the change would be in mitigation of recognized evils and would not impair, but rather foster, fair competitive opportunities. . . . The fact that the correction of abuses may tend to stabilize a business or to produce fairer price levels does not mean that the abuses should go uncorrected or that co-operative endeavor to correct them necessarily constitutes an unreasonable restraint of trade.

The Appalachian Coals decision, with its generous application of the rule of reason to loose agreements,[78] would have substantially altered the meaning of the Sherman Act, had it served as a precedent for later cases. But in the Madison Oil case of 1940 the Court once again sweepingly reaffirmed the Trenton Potteries precedent, restating the per se rule in circumstances where it would have been easy to invoke the rule of reason. The oil decision was also important as a stage in the shift of the Court's position toward giving more weight to economic criteria of competition and monopoly, a subject discussed below in Chapter 18.

The Madison Oil case involved a criminal prosecution begun in 1936 against the major companies selling gasoline in the Midwest.[79] The companies were charged with conspiracy to raise tank-car gaso-

[78] The Court went out of its way to reject the double standard of differing criteria for close combinations and loose agreements. "We know of no public policy, and none is suggested by the terms of the Sherman Act, that . . . those engaged in industry should be driven to unify their properties and businesses in order to correct abuses which may be corrected by less drastic measures. . . . The question in either case is whether there is an unreasonable restraint of trade or an attempt to monopolize. If there is, the combination cannot escape because it has chosen corporate form, and, if there is not, it is not to be condemned because of the absence of corporate integration."

[79] U.S. v. Socony-Vacuum Oil Co., 310 U.S. 150 (1940). The case is known as "Madison Oil" because the district court trial was held at Madison, Wisconsin.

line prices, and indirectly to raise prices at retail, through a concerted program of buying "surplus" gasoline from independent refiners in order to free the market from the pressure of this "surplus." The defendants admitted the buying program, but claimed that it had had the approval of the National Recovery Administration (NRA) and the acquiescence of government officials after the end of the NRA. Such effect as the program had on prices, they asserted, was a mere incident to the major purpose of eliminating the destructive competition of "distress" gasoline. Under the Appalachian Coals rule, they argued, this was a reasonable and legitimate operation.

The Supreme Court, by a vote of 5 to 2, affirmed a jury conviction of most of the defendants, relying heavily on the Trenton Potteries precedent. Indeed, it broadened that doctrine: any such agreement affecting any portion of a market, and any manipulation of prices, is illegal per se. The Court sharply, if unconvincingly, distinguished the Appalachian Coals case on the ground that neither intention nor power to fix prices had been shown in that case, whereas here the oil companies in their buying program "had as their direct purpose and aim the raising and maintenance of spot market prices and of prices to jobbers and consumers . . . by the elimination of distress gasoline as a market factor." The restatement of the per se rule and the rejection of the suggestion that "reasonable" price fixing might be permissible was so emphatic that the opinion of Justice Douglas warrants quotation at length:

Thus for over forty years this Court has consistently and without deviation adhered to the principle that price-fixing agreements are unlawful *per se* under the Sherman Act and that no showing of so-called competitive abuses or evils which those agreements were designed to eliminate or alleviate may be interposed as a defense. . . .

Ruinous competition, financial disaster, evils of price cutting and the like appear throughout our history as ostensible justifications for price fixing. If the so-called competitive abuses were to be appraised here, the reasonableness of prices would necessarily become an issue in every price-fixing case. In that event the Sherman Act would soon be emasculated; its philosophy would be supplanted by one which is wholly alien to a system of free competition; it would not be the charter of freedom which its framers intended.

The reasonableness of prices has no constancy due to the dynamic quality of business facts underlying price structures. Those who fixed reasonable prices today would perpetuate unreasonable prices tomorrow. . . . Those who controlled the prices would control or effectively dominate the market. And those who were in that strategic position would have it in their power to destroy or drastically impair the competitive system. But the thrust of the rule is deeper and reaches more than monopoly power. Any combination which tampers with price structures is engaged in an unlawful activity. Even though the members of the price-fixing group were in no position to control the market, to the extent that they raised, lowered, or stabilized prices they would be directly interfering with the free play of market forces. The Act places all such schemes beyond the pale. . . . Congress has not left with us the determination of whether or not particular price-fixing schemes are wise or unwise, healthy or destructive. . . . Whatever may be its peculiar problems and characteristics, the Sherman Act, so far as price-fixing agreements are concerned, establishes one uniform rule applicable to all industries alike. . . . Under the Sherman Act, a combination formed for the purpose and with the effect of raising, depressing, fixing, pegging, or stabilizing the price of a commodity in interstate or foreign commerce is illegal *per se*. . . . Whatever economic justification particular price-fixing agreements may be thought to have, the law does not permit an inquiry into their reasonableness. They are all banned because of their actual or potential threat to the central nervous system of the economy.

Moreover, it was held that proof of success in raising prices was not essential to a finding of guilt. The charge of conspiracy to restrain trade could be sustained simply by evidence that the combination had desired and intended to raise prices.

Trade Association Open Price Plans and Statistical Reporting

The Madison Oil decision thus restored the Sherman Act's unequivocal condemnation of loose agreements directed toward market control. Antitrust-law enforcement, however, was still faced with the difficult task of showing in particular cases that the methods employed by an association are, in fact, intended to influence prices or production. This has been no light burden in cases involving the statistical reporting activities of trade associations, and the line drawn by the courts has not always been a clear one.

Of all the trade association activities questioned under antitrust laws, none has received closer attention than the dissemination of statistics in accordance with Eddy's proposals for the "new competition." The popularity of "open competition," and its encouragement by the government during World War I, made it at one time the most characteristic single trade association function. The practice was tested in the Supreme Court between 1921 and 1925 in four major cases, the first two resulting in adverse decisions and the subsequent pair showing a more sympathetic attitude. All four involved trade associations which prepared and disseminated reports on prices, terms of sale, output, inventories, orders, sales, and shipments, which operated delivered-price systems, and which held meetings at which prices and production were discussed. No explicit price and output agreements were proven, but it was alleged that each scheme had the intent and effect of controlling prices and output.

The Hardwood case, decided in 1921, dealt with the most comprehensive of the plans.[80] Producers of one-third of the American hardwood-lumber output organized an association at the close of World War I, focused on the interchange of statistical information. Each member submitted daily reports of shipments, monthly reports of production and inventories, and price lists. These data were collated by the association's manager of statistics, who then sent out to members: (1) monthly reports of production and inventories, indicating separately each member's figures; (2) weekly reports of sales and shipments, including names of purchasers; (3) monthly summaries of price lists; and (4) an interpretative market report letter. The association also held frequent formal meetings, at which market prospects were discussed. During the meetings, a questionnaire was circulated asking for members' estimated future production, expected shutdowns, and observations on the future outlook in general. There was no explicit agreement on either prices or production.

A Supreme Court majority of six looked upon the association's record with the utmost suspicion. To them, the systematic revelation of the most intimate details of day-to-day business transactions to nominal competitors suggested *ipso facto* implied collusion in price and output policy. In addition, the Court found that meetings and market reports were studded with repeated warnings against "overproduction," and with a number of suggestions, scantily veiled, for price maintenance or increase. It found this plan for "open competition" to be in both purpose and effect a scheme to restrict production, and hence illegal. "Genuine competitors do not make daily, weekly, and monthly reports of the minutest details of their business to their rivals. . . . This is not the conduct of competitors but . . . clearly that of men united in an agreement, express or implied, to act together and pursue a common purpose under a common guide."

The Court's minority, led by Justice Brandeis, diverged sharply from the majority. Brandeis could see no coercion in the scheme, no loss of freedom of action on the part of anyone. He thought that it promoted desirable, intelligent competition. The dissenters' argument, however, that "surely Congress did not intend by the

[80] *American Column and Lumber Co.* v. *U.S.,* 257 U.S. 377.

Sherman Act to prohibit self-restraint," failed to recognize that concerted self-restraint is the sum total of any price or output agreement. The real objective of the Court minority, indeed, was not so much to maintain competition as such, as the desire to preserve the open door of opportunity. It appeared to be motivated, above all, by the fear of bigness. It was here that Justice Brandeis made his celebrated comment that so strict an attitude toward loose agreements might well encourage consolidation. In view of the double standard which induced the Court here to strike down a loose agreement covering a smaller proportion of an industry than did either U.S. Steel or United Shoe Machinery, both so recently upheld, Brandeis asked:

May not these hardwood lumber concerns, frustrated in their efforts to rationalize competition, be led to enter the inviting field of consolidation? And, if they do, may not another huge trust, with highly centralized control over vast resources, natural, manufacturing, and financial, become so powerful as to dominate competitors, wholesalers, retailers, consumers, employees and, in large measure, the community?

Two years later, the Court enjoined statistical interchanges among manufacturers of a very large part of the country's linseed oil, cake, and meal.[81] Association members supplied to a central bureau: (1) their regular price lists; (2) telegraphic advice of price concessions from those lists, with names of purchasers and exact terms offered; (3) a daily report of all sales; and (4) a monthly report of inventories. They bonded themselves heavily for observance of the agreement and arranged monthly meetings subject to penalties for nonattendance. Whenever a member bid unsuccessfully for a sale, he could have the entire industry circularized at once through the bureau to learn which member had made the sale. The implied sanctions against price-cutting appeared to the Court an abnormal departure from competitive methods, which "took away [the manufacturers'] freedom of action by requiring each to reveal to all the intimate details of its affairs." The plan was unanimously declared unlawful.

Only two years later, however, the Court seemed to shift its position appreciably in the Maple Flooring and Cement cases.[82] The Maple Flooring Manufacturers' Association, composed of producers of about 70 per cent of the industry's output, had organized the exchange of statistical information among its members. The

---

[81] U.S. v. American Linseed Oil Co., 262 U.S. 371 (1923).
[82] Maple Flooring Manufacturers' Assn. v. U.S., 268 U.S. 563 (1925); Cement Manufacturers' Protective Assn. v. U.S., 268 U.S. 588 (1925).

Court approved this scheme, dividing 6 to 3, with the minority being drawn from the erstwhile majority. Viewing the operation of the plan with a sympathetic attitude in complete contrast with that in the Hardwood case, the Court held "that trade associations . . . which openly and fairly gather and disseminate information . . . without, however, reaching or attempting to reach any agreement or any concerted action with respect to prices or production or restraining competition, do not thereby engage in unlawful restraint of competition." Schemes of this sort are not to be attacked "merely because the ultimate result . . . may be to stabilize prices or limit production through a better understanding of economic laws and a more general ability to conform to them."

There were certain differences between the condemned and the approved plans. In the Hardwood and Linseed cases, future prices were reported, individual firms and their prices were identified, and the statistical information was withheld from customers. These practices were avoided by the Maple Flooring Association. It held regular meetings of members, at which market conditions and similar topics were considered, but on the advice of counsel, future prices were never discussed. Yet its scheme was not as blameless as it might seem. It distributed estimated "average costs" for all grades of flooring and freight-rate books to all members, thereby enabling them to quote identical prices under a delivered pricing system. The government's case was poorly prepared, however, and failed to demonstrate to the Court how the system operated and how it might serve to promote implicit agreement on prices.

Even allowing for these differences, it is apparent that the Court had changed course appreciably. It now emphasized the desirability of the widest dissemination of information, which "tends to stabilize trade and industry, to produce fairer price levels, and to avoid the waste which inevitably attends the unintelligent conduct of economic enterprise." The Cement case was decided on essentially similar grounds, complicated by peculiar industry characteristics which justified co-operative efforts to prevent fraud by consuming contractors. Thus, each of the four decisions depended on the facts of the particular case, and general doctrines are hard to abstract.

The next case in this line to come before the Supreme Court, involving the Sugar Institute,[83] reveals the inordinate complexity of the factual situations often encountered in the application of antitrust policy. During the decade before World War I, the near

[83] *U.S.* v. *Sugar Institute, Inc.*, 15 F. Supp. 817 (1934); *Sugar Institute, Inc.* v. *U.S.*, 297 U.S. 553 (1936).

monopoly of the Sugar Trust had lost its grip on the refining industry as new companies, attracted by the trust's high profits, had entered the industry. By 1927, when the Institute was formed, there were fifteen companies refining imported raw sugar and supplying about four-fifths of total consumption. Overcapacity had led to widespread secret price concessions and rebates, other unfair competitive practices, and severe reduction in profits.

Under the stimulus of these conditions, the refiners met together and evolved a plan for a trade association. Its ostensible purpose was the abolition of price discrimination among customers; its actual purpose was to require adherence to a seller's reported price and to end all indirect methods of competition. Members sold only upon open prices and terms, and price changes were to be announced at least one day in advance. The Institute also compiled and disseminated to members statistics on production, sales, shipments, and inventories. Unlike the Maple Flooring Association, it did not make them available to buyers.

The most striking feature of the Institute was the extraordinary variety of restrictions laid down as to terms of sale and methods of distribution. It was argued in defense of these requirements that they were all essential to the prevention of secret price concessions. Members were forbidden to deal with anyone combining any of the functions of broker, warehouseman, and merchant. Brokers' commissions were fixed. In consequence of Institute discussions, although not through explicit agreement, members developed a basing-point system, concertedly maintained by refusals to sell f.o.b. refinery. Delivered prices were based on all-rail freight rates, buyers thereby becoming unable to benefit from cheaper means of transportation. The Institute reduced the number of consignment points for bulk sugar, to the disadvantage of many communities. The terms of sales contracts were narrowly circumscribed. Quantity discounts were forbidden. Credit terms were rigidly standardized. Guaranties to purchasers against price declines were forbidden. Packing sugar for sale under merchants' private brands was discouraged. Allowances for returned bags were forbidden. Sales of secondhand sugar, damaged stocks, and "frozen" stocks were all limited. In short, every possibility of special concession was eliminated, and every element of the price structure was concertedly regulated and maintained, except for the basis price itself. And the basis price was subject to the requirement of advance announcement.

The government alleged that there was concerted price-fixing by direct agreement as well, but this contention was rejected by the trial court. That court did find, however, that "a direct basis price agreement was not vital to defendants' purpose; in part, at least, they were able to maintain prices through preserving the price structure, withholding statistics from the trade and effectuating the open-price scheme." Under these conditions, the judge felt, the Sherman Act had clearly been violated. Restrictions on the various elements of the price structure had gone far beyond the extent required for the elimination of abuses. The effect of such restrictions was to eliminate competition in terms of sale, transportation, and distribution, and to prevent experimentation in more economical distributive techniques. The withholding of statistics from purchasers was directly condemned. The open-price system itself, when applied to future prices, was judged to "aid both in maintaining price levels without regard to the normal effect of supply and demand and in eliminating, ofttimes, entirely fair competition." The ostensible purpose of preventing discrimination and secret concessions could have been attained through publication of details of past transactions alone. The trial court's decree, while not dissolving the Institute, enjoined the continuation of its central activities, including the open-price system. The court also forbade dissemination of statistics not supplied to purchasers, and all the devices for standardizing terms of sale and methods of transportation and distribution.

The Supreme Court, without dissent, sustained this view of the law and affirmed the decree with only minor modifications. The Sherman Act, it said, does "not prevent the adoption of reasonable means to protect interstate commerce from destructive or injurious practices and to promote competition on a sound basis," but it found the Institute's activities to be beyond the protection afforded by the rule of reason. "As the statute draws the line at unreasonable restraints, a co-operative endeavor which transgresses that line cannot justify itself by pointing to evils afflicting the industry or to a laudable purpose to remove them." Stress was laid on the high proportion of the sugar market supplied by Institute members. Accordingly, "the maintenance of fair competition between the defendants themselves in the sale of domestic refined sugar is manifestly of serious public concern." The Court did make minor modifications in the decree, permitting advance announcement of future price changes so long as they did not have to be observed, and allowing some statistical information to be kept confidential. But these modifications were of little value to the Institute, and it was soon voluntarily dissolved.

While the activities of the Sugar Institute were somewhat more than ordinarily complex, the case is a fair sample of the difficulties of antitrust regulation under the rule of reason. In this instance, the Justice Department, in order to demonstrate how the Institute's restraints operated, and that they were unreasonable, had to build up its record in an investigation lasting several years. The evidence taken in court covered over ten thousand pages, besides nine hundred exhibits; and the trial judge required ninety large, double-column pages to analyze the facts and the applicable law. The cost to the government ran into the hundreds of thousands of dollars.

Since the Sugar Institute decision, most antitrust actions brought against trade associations have been settled by consent decrees. A number of cease and desist orders issued by the FTC, however, have been appealed to the courts.[84] In four cases the Commission was upheld. The compilation and distribution of statistics by the Salt Producers Association were condemned as aiding a system of voluntary production and sales quotas.[85] The Maltsters Association had erred by disseminating statistics among its members but denying them to buyers, by standardizing terms of sale, and by using a system of delivered pricing.[86] The Milk and Ice Cream Can Institute had operated a similar pricing system, had circulated statistics, and had standardized discounts.[87] And an association of crepe-paper manufacturers had administered a system of zone pricing.[88] All of these association activities were held to be illegal.

But in one case the FTC was reversed. The Commission had ordered an end to a plan of the Tag Manufacturers Institute in which prices and terms of sale were circulated and sales below list price had to be reported daily. The Commission had found that the plan limited competition, but the Court of Appeals, honoring the Maple Flooring precedent, disagreed because no future prices had to be reported, statistics were available to buyers, and there was no requirement to adhere to reported prices.[89]

Thus, in this one area of the law regarding loose combinations, the judges have continued to apply a rule of reason. While direct agreements to control price or output are illegal per se, other trade association programs designed to limit certain types of competition or to base it on fuller knowledge are examined in detail to deter-

---

[84] The FTC may act to stop, as unfair methods of competition, trade association practices which the Justice Department might attack as restraints of trade under the Sherman Act. See Chapter 16.

[85] *Salt Producers Assn.* v. *FTC*, 134 F. 2d 354 (1943).

[86] *U.S. Maltsters Assn.* v. *FTC*, 152 F. 2d 161 (1945).

[87] *Milk and Ice Cream Can Institute* v. *FTC*, 152 F. 2d 478 (1946).

[88] *Fort Howard Paper Co.* v. *FTC*, 156 F. 2d 899 (1946).

[89] *Tag Manufacturers Institute* v. *FTC*, 174 F. 2d 452 (1949).

mine whether the program as a whole unreasonably restrains trade. Each decision has depended on the particular set of facts in the case, and the judges have refused to generalize. Accordingly, there remains a considerable area of uncertainty as to the legality of trade association practices and programs. It does appear, however, that among the crucial questions determining legality are whether statistics are available to buyers, whether individual sales can be identified, and whether future prices are reported. Clearly illegal are programs in which terms of sale are standardized in every detail and in which reported prices must be observed.

Supplementing the attack under the Sherman Act on industrial concentration and agreements, the government has sought since 1914 to control directly certain types of trade practices. These efforts are set forth in Chapter 16. In the 1930's, as will be shown in Chapter 17, the Great Depression engendered a substantial retreat from competition, symbolized mainly by the National Industrial Recovery Act but also by other legislation to limit competition in the distributive trades. There followed in the late 1930's a revival of antitrust policy and administration which has maintained its vigor ever since. Chapter 18, in addition to reviewing these recent developments, summarizes the evolution and status of American policy toward monopoly, competition, and economic concentration as a whole.

CHAPTER **16**

The Federal Trade
Commission and the
Regulation of Trade Practices

AMERICAN antitrust policy has been directed primarily toward the maintenance of competition through prohibition of monopoly and restraint of trade. A closely allied development has sought to temper the effects of unbridled competition by confining the competitive struggle within a framework of established rules. Such regulation is, in principle, not strictly within the antitrust concept; it takes for granted the existence of competition and applies alike to small "chiselers" and to dominant enterprises threatening monopolistic control. In the historical unfolding of public policy in this country, however, the two types of regulation stemmed from the same roots and have remained closely intertwined.

The earliest competitive practices attacked by federal statute were considered undesirable first and foremost because of their use by large concerns to eliminate smaller rivals. Except for limited efforts to protect consumers against dangerous fraud, particularly in foods and drugs, it was assumed that maintenance of competition would ensure an economic order in the public interest. Only in later years were legislatures persuaded to strike out into wider territory to fix a basic plane of legitimate action and to forbid practices deemed "cutthroat," "ruinous," or "unfair." At the same time, the familiar regulatory machinery of statutory prohibition, enforced through private lawsuit or through civil or criminal action brought by the public prosecutor, has been supplemented by a newer governmental technique. The Federal Trade Commission, intended to be an impartial, permanent, specialized, semi-independent administrative tribunal, was designed to aid in both the formulation and execution of trade-regulation policy.

1. Competitive Practices at Common Law and Under the Sherman Act

It is of the essence of competition for one competitor to try to obtain the custom of his rivals. If he succeeds by virtue of superior efficiency or other legitimate advantage, they have no legal remedy for the damage suffered. Certain types of practices, however, have long been condemned at common law as violating elementary standards of common morality. The term "unfair competition" was first applied to "passing off," or misrepresenting one's goods as those of another. By adept simulation of a brand name or a packaging style, an unknown firm might trade on the good will built up by an established rival; the courts would give damages and enjoin the deceptive device. Similar relief could be obtained when competitors maliciously disparaged one's business reputation or goods, or when they molested one's employees. Trade secrets were protected to some extent from commercial espionage and from disclosure by once trusted ex-employees.

By gradual extension of the concept of "unfair competition," the law came also to forbid enticement of a competitor's employees with intent to do him injury, or inducing breach of his sales contracts by fraud, intimidation, or coercion. Malicious threats of patent or trade-mark infringement suits against a competitor's customers, with no real intent to carry out the threats, were similarly forbidden. Malice or fraud was at the heart of these offenses. They affected large and small enterprises alike, and an ordinary private civil lawsuit sufficed to deal with them. Some, like "passing off," might defraud the consuming public as well, but the public's interest was considered secondary and adequately protected by a just regard for the rights of those directly concerned.

With the growth of the combination movement, new practices appeared which came to be considered unfair. Not always immoral in themselves, they were felt objectionable because peculiarly suited for the destruction of competitors by large firms seeking to dominate an industry. Commonly known as "predatory practices," the methods included attacks on small rivals through local price-cutting, financed out of high profits elsewhere, or through "fighting brands" sold at a loss in order to destroy the market for a particular competing product. Railroad rebates or other transportation favors, bogus independents (firms ostensibly independent but actually controlled by a combination), exclusive dealing contracts with local distributors, "tying" contracts requiring the use of a full line of goods in connection with a single patented or otherwise monopolized commodity, and measures by a dominant combination to restrict the channels of distribution to certain favored dealers or types of dealer—all such practices were likewise viewed as "predatory."

Against these devices, the common law was poor protection to the small competitor, both procedurally and substantively. In a contest between equals, private litigation might suffice to establish their respective rights, but the small man could not afford a lawsuit against a rival with sufficient economic power to destroy him. Moreover, the substance of the law failed to keep pace with the development of new techniques for eliminating competition. Predatory practices short of fraud upon particular competitors could not be attacked. Moreover, the price policy of any business not "affected with a public interest," however destructive to others, was entirely within its own discretion.

The common law was supplemented to some extent by the Sherman Act of 1890. In its application to mergers, that law focused upon predatory practices as evidences of restraint of trade and intent to monopolize. From 1911 on, decrees under the Act, including consent decrees, frequently outlawed the use of specific competitive devices. This aspect of the statute is illustrated by the opinion of a court in a suit in 1913 against a combination of towing companies:

Even competitive practices, of a nature which as between business rivals standing practically on equal terms may be normal and lawful, yet when employed by a powerful monopolistic combination with the ability to crush, and for the purpose of crushing, a weak rival, may become abnormal and unlawful. It needs no discussion to demonstrate that complete unification of the towing and wrecking facilities at fourteen principal ports, accompanied by restraints with respect to competition imposed upon the sellers of towing properties in excess of the legitimate protection necessary to the preservation of the business purchased, excessive restrictions against competition under joint contracts and on sales of tugs, bitter rate wars, and a system of exclusive contracts with customers such as is found here, all adopted or engaged in for the purpose of effectuating monopolistic control, are abnormal methods of doing business and eliminating competition, and that a restraint of natural competition by such means is undue restraint.[1]

Among the practices sometimes forbidden under the Sherman Act were excessive price-cutting and local price discrimination when clearly intended to eliminate competition, bogus independents, "fighting brands" and the corresponding "fighting ships" (operated by shipping conferences against independents), "tying contracts," and contracts for exclusive dealing. The Act was also applied to concerted efforts of distributors to preserve the traditional channels of distribution from manufacturer to wholesaler to retailer. Conventional distributors might be resisting the advances of manufacturers who were integrating downward, seeking direct contacts with retailers, or those of large retailers, such as department stores, mail-order houses, and chain stores, who were integrating upward, seeking the economies of direct purchases from producers. Efforts of wholesalers to boycott manufacturers who sold direct to retailers, or to circulate black lists and white lists with this object in mind, were enjoined, as were concerted efforts of small retailers to boycott manufacturers giving special concessions to large retailers. These issues, as well as that of resale price maintenance, which also produced considerable Sherman Act litigation, are discussed in Chapter 17.

Application of the Sherman Act to specific competitive practices was unsatisfactory to various groups. Victims of predatory methods felt that the law should intervene before the methods had taken effect. Instead of condemning their future use only after the damage had been done, public policy might thus forestall attempted monopoly before it had taken root. In some instances it was felt that the courts had not gone far enough. Tying contracts and exclusive dealing arrangements, for example, were sometimes upheld as legitimate extensions of patent rights. The permissible limits of price discrimination among localities or among different types of customers were uncertain. Dissatisfaction crystallized into outright criticism and strong pressure for amendment after the Standard Oil and American Tobacco decisions of 1911. Recognizing for the first time that the law unquestionably had teeth, businessmen urged a clearer definition of forbidden acts. The rule of reason seemed to leave to the courts excessive discretion in condemning or approving business practices. Moreover, each antitrust decree covered a number of specific practices, and it was im-

[1] *U.S.* v. *Great Lakes Towing Co.*, 208 F. 733 (1913).

possible to know whether any given practice would be condemned if employed alone. Continuous agitation during the next few years, within and outside of Congress, culminated in 1914 in the passage of the first important supplementary antitrust legislation.

2. The Legislation of 1914

Two streams of thought lay behind the Federal Trade Commission and Clayton Acts of 1914. The first wished to modify the old law by specifying prohibited practices and eliminating the uncertainty introduced by the rule of reason. The second desired new administrative machinery, a specialized body to aid in law enforcement, to supervise and apply guiding rules to the competitive system. If public policy were to distinguish between "good" and "bad" trusts, that judgment, it was felt, could not safely be left to a remote and uncontrolled judiciary, or to a busy Attorney General's office subject to direct political pressures. Distrust of the courts was a potent factor in that day, particularly in the Progressive wing of the Republican Party. These two streams of thought, however, were each the product of widely divergent attitudes.

Among supporters of a broad antitrust policy, the immediate reaction to the Oil and Tobacco decisions, and more particularly to the supposed fiasco of the subsequent dissolutions, was a desire to repeal the rule of reason and to substitute an uncompromising prohibition of all attempted monopolies and restraints of trade. Well represented in Congress, although not coherently organized in the country at large, this group also felt that the experience of two decades warranted extension of the statute to forbid specific practices and methods of organization which had been used time and time again to intimidate or absorb competitors. Its leaders included Louis D. Brandeis, Senator Cummins of Iowa, and Representatives Clayton of Alabama and Stevens of New Hampshire.

Much had been learned since 1890 about America's industrial organization and business practices. The Industrial Commission of 1899–1902, the Bureau of Corporations, the gigantic court records of antitrust prosecutions, and special congressional investigating committees like the Stanley Committee of 1911, which studied the history and operations of the U.S. Steel Corporation, had supplied an enormous mass of data upon which to build new legislative policies. Price discrimination, fighting brands, bogus independents, transportation favors, tying contracts, and exclusive dealer arrangements were the predatory methods most often attacked. The holding company was singled out as a particularly objectionable form of organization. In addition, the Pujo Committee's investigation of the "Money Trust" in 1912 had convinced many observers that bankers' control of industrial firms, implemented through interlocking directorates, was another threat to competition. If these practices and controls could be explicitly prohibited, it was hoped, monopoly might be suppressed in its incipiency and the difficult task of unscrambling trusts largely avoided. Brandeis advanced the thesis that big business was less efficient than enterprise on a moderate scale, that the growth of bigness was due to artificial advantages, and that if government forbade such advantages natural forces would then maintain healthy competition as a regulator of prices and output.

This group advocated a new commission primarily to make antitrust law enforcement more efficient. It would be an enlarged and improved Bureau of Corporations, free from direct political control, and would engage in continuous surveys of business practices and investigations of allegedly monopolistic industries. It would refer apparent violations to the Justice Department for prosecution and aid the courts in working out dissolution plans which would truly restore competition. Only a few members of the group, notably Congressman Stevens, envisaged the commission as a device for building up an administrative law of unfair competition.

Business leaders were, on the whole, more content with the rule of reason. Yet the Sherman Act was now a proven potential danger, and few of them shared President Taft's confidence that the new interpretation could leave no one uncertain as to whether his practices were illegal.[2] While seeking more specific definitions of forbidden acts, businessmen were also anxious to be allowed to eliminate cutthroat or ruinous competition. Judge Gary of U.S. Steel, going further than most, even advocated the creation of a commission to encourage and regulate co-operation among competitors, and authorized in times of depression to restrict production, to allocate it among the members of an industry, and to fix maximum prices.

Some business groups also favored a new commission as a body to review in advance proposed mergers and other potentially illegal acts. Its approval was to immunize the participants against subsequent antitrust prosecutions. Some would have subjected com-

[2] In 1911 the National Civic Federation circulated a questionnaire to leading businessmen containing the following question, among others: "Do you believe that the Sherman Law, as now interpreted, is made clear and workable?" Of 1,033 answers, 841 were in the negative and only 192 in the affirmative. Senate Committee on Interstate Commerce, *Hearings on the Control of Corporations*, 1911–1912, p. 499.

mission decisions to judicial review, thus throwing the ultimate determination of policy back to the courts, but others were willing to leave final discretion with the commission. Surprising numbers of businessmen were also ready to accept federal incorporation, or at least compulsory federal licensing, for interstate corporations, and even a degree of federal price regulation where near monopoly was the only alternative to cutthroat competition.

In addition to these two major competing viewpoints of anti-monopolists and of business leaders, there was a wide range of other opinions more or less vociferously expressed. They spread all the way from satisfaction with the Sherman Act as it stood to suggestions for encouragement of concentration in industries with heavy capital requirements, coupled with stringent regulation on public utiilty lines. President Taft led the defenders of the status quo. A few voices indicated contentment with potential competition as an adequate safeguard against exploitation, without any positive governmental action whatsoever. More important than such proposals were the demands of organized groups interested only in particular phases of antitrust policy. The American Federation of Labor, which played a significant part in the 1912 campaign and was regarded by the resurgent Democratic Party as an essential element of its strength, demanded complete exemption from the Sherman Act as well as restrictions on the use of injunctions in labor disputes. To this proposal the Federation added exemption for agricultural organizations, thus attempting to enlist the support of organized farmers. Legalization of resale price maintenance was advocated by retail druggists and certain manufacturers. Grocery and lumber retailers and wholesalers desired freedom to organize boycotts against manufacturers who sold direct to large retail outlets.

It was in such a climate of opinion that Wilson's administration, backed by solid majorities in both Houses, began its serious efforts at antitrust law revision. Having dealt in 1913 with tariff and currency reform, it turned to trust legislation in the following year. The Democratic platform of 1912 had "regretted" the rule of reason and demanded prohibition of holding companies, interlocking directorates, stock watering, price discrimination, and domination of any industry by a single corporation. Unlike the Republican and Progressive platforms, the Democratic made no reference to a new trade commission, but President Wilson added this item to the program in his special antitrust message of January, 1914. In method of enactment, the resulting legislation contrasted strikingly with the 1890 Act. There had been extended

Senate hearings in 1911 and 1912. Further hearings were held by committees in charge of the detailed proposals in the new Congress. A number of legislators, notably Senator Newlands of Nevada, had been refining the details of a Trade Commission Bill over some years. Instead of a brief and hurried measure pushed through its legislative stages with little attention from Congress and none from the executive, the new statutes were hammered out in months of debate, amendment, and reamendment, always under the careful eye of Wilson and his immediate advisers. Yet the final product was scrappy and incoherent—technically far poorer legislation than the Sherman Act itself.

Without originating any elements of the new policies, President Wilson himself dominated the legislative decisions. His own philosophy, expressed while serving as Governor of New Jersey and in a number of speeches during the presidential campaign, at this time roughly paralleled the Brandeis-Cummins viewpoint described above. To him, the worst vice of the trusts was that they prevented men of enterprise and ingenuity but limited capital from making their independent way to success. He felt that "item by item we can put in *our statutes what constitutes restraint of trade,* not leaving it to courts for generalizations which may fit some cases and not others." [3] Under his guidance, several related bills were submitted, outlawing interlocking directorates, defining a number of acts to be deemed "in restraint of trade," prohibiting explicitly certain predatory methods, and establishing a trade commission. Originally the commission was essentially an enlarged, independent Bureau of Corporations. In the course of the summer, however, the hope of specifying unequivocally all those predatory methods which promoted monopolistic controls proved chimerical and was abandoned.

No statutory definitions could ever be drawn to include the infinite range of industrial and commercial practices. As soon as one set of prohibitions was laid down, new methods, or new variations on old methods, would spring up to circumvent them. If trusts were really to be avoided by nipping monopolistic practices in the bud, government would have to operate through constantly expanding administrative or judicial definition of a comprehensive legislative standard. The fact that some trade practices promoted competition in some circumstances and were anticom-

---

[3] Italics in original. From address on "The Tariff and the Trusts," at Nashville, Tennessee, February 24, 1912, in R. S. Baker and W. E. Dodd (editors), *The Public Papers of Woodrow Wilson—College and State* (1925), Vol. II, p. 414.

petitive in others augmented the argument for administrative or judicial application of general standards to specific cases. Wilson was thus led to endorse Congressman Stevens's proposal to give the new commission authority to enforce a general prohibition of "unfair methods of competition." The various bills were finally fused into two, one dealing with the Federal Trade Commission and the other, named for Chairman Clayton of the House Judiciary Committee, grouping together a host of provisions, including prohibition of two specific types of trade practice. Enactment was favored by most of the Democrats, with the Progressive Republicans voting for them but urging their inadequacy, and the regular Republicans opposing them as dangerous encroachments upon business freedom.

The Federal Trade Commission Act established a commission of five members, holding office for seven years, not more than three of whom may be of the same political party. The FTC was independent of the executive departments, and commissioners might be removed by the President only for "inefficiency, neglect of duty or malfeasance in office." [4] It absorbed the personnel and functions of the Bureau of Corporations and had even wider investigatory powers. It could conduct general economic studies of "the organization, business, conduct, practices, and management" of companies engaged in interstate or foreign commerce. At the request of the Attorney General, or on its own initiative, the FTC might investigate the effectiveness of antitrust decrees, and upon request by a court, act as master in chancery in recommending the form of new decrees.

The FTC's substantive power was derived from Section 5 of the Act, which stated "That unfair methods of competition in commerce are hereby declared unlawful." After formal complaint, notice, and hearing, the Commission might order persons, partnerships, or corporations engaging in such methods to "cease and desist." Until 1938, legal sanction for enforcement depended upon review by a circuit court of appeals, on the initiative either of the defendant or of the FTC, and court affirmation of the order. A violation then was punishable as contempt of court. In 1938, for reasons indicated below, the terms of Section 5 were amplified to include "unfair methods of competition in commerce, and unfair or deceptive acts or practices in commerce." In addition, Commission orders to "cease and desist" were made final sixty days after their issuance, unless the defendant petitioned meanwhile for judicial review. Violators of orders became subject to civil

―――――――――
[4] See *Rathbun* v. *U.S.*, 295 U.S. 602 (1935).

penalties of up to $5,000 for each offense.[5] In 1950, a further amendment provided that each day of continuing violation may be treated as a separate offense.

FTC jurisdiction over enforcement of this general competitive standard was made exclusive, but the Commission shared with the Justice Department responsibility for enforcing the four specific prohibitions of the Clayton Act. Section 2 of the latter statute forbade price discrimination among purchasers where the effect "may be to substantially lessen competition or tend to create a monopoly in any line of commerce," except for discrimination on account of differences in grade, quality, or quantity, or making due allowance for selling or transportation costs, or "in good faith to meet competition." [6] Section 3 outlawed tying contracts and exclusive dealing arrangements, or price concessions to the same effect, likewise where the effect "may be to substantially lessen competition or tend to create a monopoly in any line of commerce." Intercorporate stock acquisitions, except among railroads, were forbidden by Section 7, where the effect "may be to substantially lessen competition" *between the corporations concerned,* or tend to create a monopoly of any line of commerce. Section 8, finally, prohibited interlocking directorates among banks with over $5 million capital or among competing industrial corporations with over $1 million capital. The remainder of the Act dealt with minor procedural reforms, with railroads, and with relief of organized labor from the antitrust laws and from certain types of injunctions in the course of industrial disputes.[7]

The 1914 legislation in fact added little to the substance of the law. The specific practices forbidden by the Clayton Act could already be attacked under the Sherman Act as attempts to monopolize or as conspiracies in restraint of trade. And for the most part, unfair methods of competition now declared illegal by the Federal Trade Commission Act were already condemned by the common law. What was new in the 1914 legislation was the making explicit of what had only been implicit in Sherman Act interpretation, the prohibition of certain practices previously illegal only as part of proven conspiracies or with proven illicit intent, the emphasis on prevention rather than punishment, and the creation

[5] This change in procedure applies to orders only under Section 5 of the FTC Act, but not under Sections 2, 3, 7, or 8 of the Clayton Act.

[6] This section was later greatly expanded by the Robinson-Patman Act of 1936; see Chapter 17 below.

[7] For a discussion of the labor provisions of the Clayton Act, see above, pp. 175–176.

of an administrative tribunal to expand the definition of unfair trade practices and apply it to new situations, rather than leaving this task to the ordinary process of civil litigation.

3. Intercorporate Relationships Under the Clayton Act

Neither Section 7 nor 8 of the Clayton Act made much impact in their first four decades of existence. Like the remainder of the antitrust laws, their meaning is determined by the interplay between judicial interpretation and administrative enforcement. Over the years, the courts first buried Section 7 by means of a highly restricted definition of intercorporate stockholding, only to resurrect it in 1957 in a potentially awesome form.

In 1926, the Supreme Court, in a 5 to 4 decision, distinguished between acquisition of stock and acquisition of assets, holding the latter to be beyond the reach of the FTC even if the merger of physical assets had been based on an illegal acquisition of voting stock.[8] Competitors desiring to merge were free to do so by transferring assets. Even the mild discouragement to holding-company control which remained was later destroyed by judicial interpretation. In 1930, the International Shoe Company, largest manufacturer in the country, was allowed to retain control of the W. H. McElwain Company, ranking fourth or fifth.[9] In 1934, another 5 to 4 decision completed the judicial emasculation of Section 7 by validating a merger of assets executed by a holding company even after a formal complaint had been issued against it under the Act.[10]

Beginning in 1926, the FTC had repeatedly urged Congress to plug this loophole, but not until 1945 was legislation seriously considered. In 1950, Congress passed the Celler Anti-merger Act, which prohibited mergers through acquisition of assets as well as stock. But where the original Section 7 was on its face a per se rule, banning any acquisition which might lessen competition *between* the merged corporations no matter how small they might be, the amended law prohibited mergers only "where in any line of

---

[8] *FTC v. Western Meat Co.*, 272 U.S. 554.

[9] *International Shoe Co. v. FTC*, 280 U.S. 291. The companies were held to be noncompeting because they dealt in different types of shoes generally sold to different classes of consumers, although dress shoes made by both went into the same market areas. Prospective bankruptcy of McElwain also played a part in the decision. Stress was also laid on the continuance of outside competition, although this was irrelevant under Section 7 as it then read.

[10] *Arrow-Hart & Hegeman Electric Co. v. FTC*, 291 U.S. 587.

commerce in any section of the country, the effect of such acquisition may be substantially to lessen competition, or tend to create a monopoly."

In its first proceeding under the 1950 Act, the FTC was urged by its counsel to interpret it as imposing a "substantiality test," barring the merger of firms each of which has a substantial share of the market. The Commission declined to do so, saying that there "must be a case-by-case examination of all relevant factors in order to ascertain the probable economic consequences" of the acquisition. But it did hold that "the Clayton Act requires a lower standard of proof" than the Sherman Act and that "more specifically, the merger in U.S. v. Columbia Steel Co. (1948), which was examined [and approved] under the Sherman Act, would probably not have been approved had the new Section 7 been in existence and invoked against it." [11]

As late as 1958, there had been no judicial interpretation of the Celler Act. But a proposed merger of the Bethlehem Steel Corporation and the Youngstown Sheet and Tube Company, respectively the second and fifth largest steel companies, was being contested in the courts after the companies had announced their intention of proceeding in spite of an unfavorable advisory ruling by the Justice Department.[11a] Meanwhile, in 1957, the Supreme Court, in a surprising 4 to 2 decision involving the Du Pont Company, drastically revised its interpretation of the old Section 7.[12]

In 1949, the Justice Department had brought a civil suit under Sections 1 and 2 of the Sherman Act against Du Pont, charging that its 23 per-cent stock ownership of the General Motors Corporation, acquired in 1917–1919, had given it an illegal preference over competitors in the sale of automotive finishes and fabrics to

[11] *Pillsbury Mills, Inc.*, 50 FTC 555 (1953). For a discussion of *Columbia Steel*, see pp. 608–609 below.

[11a] On November 20, 1958, a decision against the merger was made by Judge Weinfeld of the U.S. District Court for the Southern District of New York. Rejecting arguments of the companies that the merger would facilitate expansion of steel capacity in the Chicago area, would stimulate rather than lessen competition, and would enable Bethlehem to challenge the dominant position of U.S. Steel, the court found that the plan would aggravate the already existing oligopoly situation in the steel industry and would lessen competition substantially, both between the defendants and in the industry generally, in the country as a whole and in a number of specified geographical and product markets. See *U.S. v. Bethlehem Steel Corp.*, Civil No. 115–328, S.D.N.Y. At the beginning of 1959, the companies had not yet decided whether to appeal this ruling.

[12] *U.S. v. E. I. du Pont de Nemours & Co.*, 353 U.S. 586.

General Motors. As somewhat of an afterthought, it was also charged that this stock ownership violated Section 7 of the Clayton Act.[13] In its ruling, the Court found the Du Pont stockholding illegal under Section 7 rather than under the Sherman Act. It held that the Clayton Act was concerned with preventing not only a lessening of competition between two corporations tied together through stock acquisitions—a horizontal acquisition—but also the lessening of competition resulting from a vertical acquisition in which a supplier acquires control of a purchaser, thereby diminishing competition among suppliers for the purchaser's orders. The dissenting judges protested that "over 40 years after the enactment of the Clayton Act, it now becomes apparent for the first time that [Section] 7 has been a sleeping giant all along," but the majority held that "any acquisition by one corporation of all or any part of the stock of another corporation, competitor or not, is within the reach of the section whenever the reasonable likelihood appears that the acquisition will result in a restraint of commerce or in the creation of a monopoly of any line of commerce."

Thus the Court appears to have greatly expanded the scope of Section 7, which may now apply to vertical acquisitions and to intercorporate relationships no matter how old. If the decision stands without modification, it need not be proved that a merger tended to lessen competition or to create a monopoly at the time of acquisition; it has only to be shown that the merger endangers competition at the time the suit is filed. On the other hand, as the Antitrust Division has pointed out, in a complete merger, as opposed to a holding of controlling stock, "the assets of the merged companies may be so scrambled" after some years that any attempt to disentangle the combination would be unworkable.[14]

Section 8, outlawing interlocking directorates, is so loosely drawn and so poorly enforced that it has been of no real consequence. With limited appropriations, the antitrust agencies have concentrated on more serious abuses. The section is open to evasion through the use of dummy directors. It does not bar "indirect" interlocks, in which competitors have directors on the board of a third corporation, or interlocks between potential competitors or between buyers and sellers. In 1951, the FTC issued a report noting the deficiencies of Section 8,[15] but Congress has taken no remedial action.

---

[13] This charge occurred only in the closing pages of the government's brief and occupied but a few minutes of its oral argument.

[14] *New York Times*, January 6, 1958.

[15] FTC, *Report on Interlocking Directorates*.

4. Trade Regulation Under the Clayton Act

Sections 2 and 3 of the Clayton Act, the only remnants of the original 1914 program for prohibiting specific predatory competitive methods, were robbed of much of their vigor by the qualifying clause, "where the effect may be to substantially lessen competition or tend to create a monopoly in any line of commerce." In seeking to interpret and enforce these provisions, the antitrust agencies and the courts were thus confronted with the same task as in Sherman Act enforcement—the definition of "competition" and "monopoly." Developments in the interpretation of these sections, accordingly, have roughly paralleled the judicial and administrative application of the Sherman Act itself.

Tying Contracts

The prohibition of tying contracts in Section 3 has been easier to apply than the ban on exclusive dealing, and it has come closer to producing a per se rule. Tying arrangements, sometimes known as "full-line forcing," make the lease or sale of a particular product conditional on the lessee's or purchaser's use of associated products sold by the same manufacturer. Applying to commodities "whether patented or unpatented," the statute brought about a definite alteration in the law, for previously, in the Mimeograph case, the Supreme Court had allowed the A. B. Dick Company to compel purchasers of its patented mimeographs to use on the machines only ink and paper sold by it.[16]

This prohibition was designed to prevent the extension of a a partial monopoly into a wider field; the classic example had been United Shoe Machinery's use of leasing arrangements, described above in Chapter 15. Since tie-in or package sales are not in themselves objectionable, the antitrust agencies and the courts have generally condemned them only when the seller enjoys substantial monopoly power. When such power has been demonstrated, the courts have almost invariably prohibited the arrangement. Thus United Shoe's tying leases were successfully attacked.[17] The Radio Corporation of America, then doing between 70 and 95 per cent of the business in vacuum tubes, was forbidden to re-

---

[16] *Henry* v. *A. B. Dick Co.*, 224 U.S. 1 (1912). This doctrine was later reversed, without reference to the Clayton Act, but the reversal applied only to cases where the patented article was sold, not when it was leased. *Motion Picture Patents Co.* v. *Universal Film Mfg. Co.*, 243 U.S. 502 (1917).

[17] *United Shoe Machinery Corp.* v. *U.S.*, 258 U.S. 451 (1922).

quire radio manufacturers, licensed to use its patented circuits, to buy from RCA all the tubes needed for initial operation of the sets.[18] Two manufacturers of electric tabulating machines, who supplied the entire market, were enjoined from requiring exclusive use of their own tabulation cards, although they could warn against the use of inferior cards.[19] And in 1947, the Supreme Court declared the prohibition to be a per se rule if a substantial amount of trade is involved. In a case voiding contracts tying the sale of salt to the lease of a patented salt dispenser, the Court ruled:

. . . It is unreasonable, *per se*, to foreclose competitors from any substantial market. . . . Under the law, agreements are forbidden which "tend to create a monopoly," and it is immaterial that the tendency is a creeping one rather than one that proceeds at full gallop; nor does the law wait for arrival at the goal before condemning the direction of the movement.[20]

Thus, these and other cases [21] have made it clear that the courts will condemn any use of tying clauses to broaden the scope of a patent monopoly. They have tended similarly to condemn abuse of any dominant position. The American Can Company, which owned 54 per cent of all can-closing machinery, was forbidden to require lessees of its machinery to use its own cans.[22] In 1953, however, the Supreme Court, in a somewhat confusing decision, declined to prevent a newspaper with a morning monopoly from compelling advertisers buying space in morning editions to purchase equal space in evening editions, which did face competition.[23] The Court reached its conclusion by lumping together the morning and evening markets and thus finding no monopoly. The case probably reflects a failure to analyze adequately the economic facts of the situation rather than an intention to reverse the steady trend toward per se prohibitions of tying contracts.

Exclusive Dealing

Before 1947, the courts generally enforced the rule of Section 3 against exclusive dealing only when the seller dominated a market. Thus, for many years, this provision made no change in policy,

[18] *Lord v. RCA*, 24 F. 2d 565 (1928); affirmed in 28 F. 2d 527 (1928); *cert.* denied, 278 U.S. 648 (1928).

[19] *International Business Machines Corp.* v. *U.S.*, 298 U.S. 131 (1936).

[20] *International Salt Co.* v. *U.S.*, 332 U.S. 392.

[21] See also *Carbice Corp.* v. *American Patents Development Corp.*, 285 U.S. 27 (1931); *Leitch Mfg. Co.* v. *Barber Co.*, 302 U.S. 131 (1938); *Judson Thompson* v. *FTC*, 150 F. 2d 952, *cert.* denied, 326 U.S. 776 (1945).

[22] *U.S.* v. *American Can Co.*, 87 F. Supp. 18 (1949).

[23] *Times-Picayune Publishing Co.* v. *U.S.*, 345 U.S. 594.

since before 1914 exclusive dealing, although not a restraint of trade within the meaning of the Sherman Act,[24] had been outlawed in several cases as part of a monopolistic scheme carried on by a dominant producer or combination.[25]

Accordingly, the courts refused to condemn exclusive contracts of a margarine manufacturer who produced only little more than 1 per cent of the country's output.[26] An attempt of the FTC to stop thirty-five refiners from leasing gasoline pumps and tanks at nominal rentals on condition that only their own brands be sold was rejected by the Supreme Court, which emphasized the large number of refiners seeking to supply retailers and the absence of any indication of lessened competition.[27] The Court also accepted exclusive dealing on other grounds. Schoolboys selling Curtis magazines were held to be agents, not dealers, and Section 3 was interpreted as not barring exclusive agencies.[28] General Motors was permitted to require its dealers to use or sell only its parts for repairs in order to protect its warranty and maintain its good will.[29]

In cases where a dominant seller used exclusive contracts, however, the courts almost invariably condemned them. Concerns making two-fifths of the dress patterns sold to consumers were forbidden to prevent their dealers from carrying competing lines.[30] A firm producing over half of the player-piano rolls made in the country was similarly ordered not to require its dealers to sign exclusive contracts.[31] A number of other exclusive agreements, where the proportion of output controlled ranged from three-fifths to nine-tenths, were also voided.[32]

[24] In re Greene, 52 F. 104 (1892); Whitwell v. Continental Tobacco Co., 125 F. 454 (1903); see also D. R. Wilder Manufacturing Co. v. Corn Products Refining Co., 236 U.S. 165 (1915).

[25] See Commissioner of Corporations, Trust Laws and Unfair Competition (1915), pp. 484–486; Continental Wallpaper Co. v. Voight, 212 U.S. 227 (1909); Standard Sanitary Mfg. Co. v. U.S., 226 U.S. 20 (1912); U.S. v. Great Lakes Towing Co., 208 F. 733 (1913), 217 F. 656 (1914).

[26] B. S. Pearsall Butter Co. v. FTC, 292 F. 720 (1923). Cf. also Excelsior Motor Mfg. & Supply Co. v. Sound Equipment, Inc., 73 F. 2d 725 (1938).

[27] FTC v. Sinclair Refining Co., 261 U.S. 463 (1923).

[28] FTC v. Curtis Publishing Co., 260 U.S. 568 (1923).

[29] Pick Mfg. Co. v. General Motors Corp., 80 F. 2d 641 (1935), affirmed in 299 U.S. 3 (1936).

[30] Standard Fashion Co. v. Magrane-Houston Co., 258 U.S. 346 (1922); Butterick Co. v. FTC, 4 F. 2d 910, cert. denied, 267 U.S. 602 (1925).

[31] FTC v. Q. R. S. Music Co., 12 F. 2d 730 (1926).

[32] FTC v. Eastman Kodak Co., 247 U.S. 619 (1927); FTC v. Carter Carburetor Corp., 121 F. 2d 722 (1940); Fashion Originators' Guild v. FTC, 312 U.S. 457 (1941).

In 1947, in the International Salt decision cited above, the Supreme Court changed its criterion from market dominance to substantial control. The shift in its general views on monopoly and competition, described below in Chapter 18, necessarily had an impact on its interpretation of the Clayton Act. Since 1947, it has made exclusive contracts virtually illegal per se when the seller has any substantial share of the market. In 1949, in a 5 to 4 decision, it condemned the exclusive dealerships of Standard Oil of California, even though that company produced only 23 per cent, and the independent dealers under those contracts sold less than 7 per cent, of the gasoline in the relevant market area.[33] Three years later it followed the same precedent in a case involving an oil company which sold only 3 per cent of the gasoline in its area.[34]

But the FTC has been somewhat more cautious than the Court; in 1953, for example, it remanded a case which involved exclusive dealing contracts, on the ground that no substantial injury to competitors had been proven.[35] Moreover, questions raised by the dissenters in the Standard Oil of California case suggest that there may be still further evolution in the interpretation of Section 3, in line with the Court's recent efforts to reshape the basic notions of competition and monopoly in Sherman Act proceedings. Three judges contended that there had been no evidence that Standard's contracts did in fact lessen competition. And Justice Douglas, in a dissent reminiscent of Brandeis's in the Hardwood case,[36] argued that voiding the contracts would result in their conversion into agency agreements or outright refiner ownership, thereby promoting large-scale organization. These dissents reflect the difficulties of establishing economic policy criteria in areas where elements of monopoly and of competition are intertwined and where it is far from clear how particular practices will affect market structure and behavior.

Price Discrimination

Section 2 of the Clayton Act, forbidding price discrimination, was hedged about with even more exceptions than Section 3. It not only required proof of tendency to lessen competition or create a monopoly, but it also specifically permitted discrimination "on account of differences in the grade, quality, or quantity of the

---

[33] *Standard Oil of California* v. *U.S.*, 337 U.S. 293.

[34] *U.S.* v. *Richfield Oil Corp.*, 99 F. Supp. 280 (1951); sustained *per curiam*, 343 U.S. 922 (1952).

[35] *Maico Co., Inc.*, 50 FTC 485.

[36] See pp. 479–480 above.

commodity sold, or that makes only due allowance for differences in the cost of selling or transportation," or "in good faith to meet competition." Without doubt, the salient practice which Congress sought to outlaw was temporary local price-cutting to eliminate small competitors by a large firm which could recoup its losses elsewhere. Such predatory price-cutting had been condemned by the Supreme Court in the Standard Oil and American Tobacco cases, and on the basis of experience around the turn of the century, was regarded as one of the typical methods of a would-be monopolist.[37]

In practice, the Act has been little used in this connection. Predatory local price-cutting appears to have declined in popularity as a competitive weapon. The decline may be ascribed in part to the Clayton Act, but it is probably more largely due to the development of different methods of competition. The initiator of a price war, moreover, always runs the risk of its extension to his entire market. Consequently, Section 2 has almost never been applied to local price-cutting.[38]

The FTC did, however, try to apply Section 2 to two other kinds of price discrimination, only to be frustrated in both attempts for over two decades. The first was geographical discrimination resulting from the use of basing-point price systems, under which uniform delivered prices are charged.[39] The second involved discriminatory discounts in distribution.

The basing-point system first came into prominence in the steel industry, where a "Pittsburgh Plus" scheme was instituted by U.S. Steel and followed by the other companies. Prices for steel, no matter where produced or how delivered, were fixed as the sum of a Pittsburgh "base price" and the rail freight charge from Pittsburgh to the point of delivery. Price competition was thus eliminated at all points, producers outside Pittsburgh either "picking up" or "absorbing" differences between actual freight charges and charges from Pittsburgh. The system implied willingness of

[37] An earlier version of the Section also referred specifically to the lessening of competition among purchasers of a commodity, as well as in the seller's plane of competition, but this was a secondary consideration.

[38] Of the thirteen cease and desist orders issued by the FTC under this clause before its amendment by the Robinson-Patman Act of 1936, only one dealt with local price discrimination of the traditional sort. *Pittsburgh Coal Co. of Wisconsin*, 8 FTC 480 (1925). Section 2 was also invoked in a private suit involving local price-cutting. *Porto Rican American Tobacco Co.* v. *American Tobacco Co.*, 30 F. 2d 234 (1929).

[39] As shown in Chapter 18, FTC efforts to outlaw the basing-point system finally met with success after World War II. The present discussion is limited to the Commission's earlier unsuccessful efforts.

non-basing-point producers to refrain from price-cutting in their own areas, but fear of retaliation by U.S. Steel and the compensatory opportunity of entering distant markets evoked their support. As important fabricating centers developed outside of Pittsburgh, however, steel consumers in the West and South increasingly resented having to pay "phantom freight" charges. Pressure was consequently brought on producers, on state legislatures, and on the FTC to secure some modification of the practice. Thirty-two state governments banded together in the "Associated States Opposing Pittsburgh-Plus."

While the Justice Department's unsuccessful dissolution suit against U.S. Steel had not seriously raised the issue of uniform delivered prices, the FTC in the early twenties conducted an elaborate investigation of the scheme. In 1924, it issued an order directing U.S. Steel to abandon "Pittsburgh Plus." [40] Instead of contesting the order in court, the Corporation announced its intention of complying "in so far as it is practicable to do so." It substituted a multiple basing-point system, but made base prices at other points higher than those at Pittsburgh. Prices east of Pittsburgh remained Pittsburgh-plus, while those west of Chicago became Chicago-plus. Most of the results of the old system were thus perpetuated. The FTC, nevertheless, made no effort to enforce its order.

From 1933 to 1935, the NRA steel code legalized basing points. In 1938, the Wheeler-Lea Amendment to the Trade Commission Act made all prior FTC orders automatically enforceable unless appealed to the courts within sixty days. U.S. Steel immediately filed an appeal against the 1924 order, but the case was delayed first by agreement and then by World War II. Thus, for its first three decades, Section 2 had little practical meaning for basing-point systems. [41]

The second kind of price discrimination unsuccessfully attacked by the FTC grew out of the struggle for favorable discounts among different types of distributors—wholesalers, chain stores and other mass distributors, and voluntary groups of retailers. Discriminatory discounts can affect competition among distributors as much as among producers. Accordingly, in one early case, the FTC forbade a manufacturer to deny the wholesale discount to a co-operative buying organization of retailers which purchased in

[40] U.S. Steel Corp., 8 FTC 1 (1924).

[41] Efforts of the Justice Department to outlaw a basing-point system in cement were blocked in 1925 by a Supreme Court decision which found nothing illegal in the scheme. See above, pp. 480–481.

as large quantities as did wholesalers. In addition, it condemned a manufacturer who granted discounts to chains on the basis of the combined purchases of their separate stores while refusing to grant a similar privilege to associations of independent stores, even though selling costs did not vary between the two. The Commission was reversed in each instance by a circuit court of appeals, on the ground that the Clayton Act applied only to reduced competition in the *seller's* line of commerce.[42] The Supreme Court refused to review these decisions, and the FTC was thus forced to abandon its efforts.

In 1929, however, the Supreme Court reached a contrary conclusion in a private case, holding that the words "in any line of commerce" meant what they said, including purchasers as well as sellers.[43] The FTC, after some further delay, then renewed its campaign. Early in 1936, after two years of hearings and the assemblage of over 21,000 pages of testimony, it directed the Goodyear Tire and Rubber Company to cease selling tires to Sears, Roebuck & Company, the country's leading mail-order house, at a price differential greater than the savings in costs on Sears orders. Once again, the Commission was overruled in the courts,[44] but meanwhile the terms of Section 2 were substantially altered by the Robinson-Patman Act.[45]

In this area too, then, the FTC was unable to breath life into the Clayton Act, to fulfill that law's purpose of eliminating undesirable trade practices not previously actionable under the Sherman Act. It remains to consider the contribution of the FTC to American trade-practice policy under the broad grant of powers in its own statute, which directed it to prevent "unfair methods of competition."

[42] *Mennen Co.* v. *FTC*, 288 Fed. 774 (1923); *National Biscuit Co.* v. *FTC*, 299 Fed. 733 (1924). In the Mennen case, the court also insisted that wholesalers and retailers were to be defined by their own customers, and gave great weight to the proviso in Section 2 protecting the right of sellers to select their own customers "in bona fide transactions and not in restraint of trade."

[43] *George Van Camp & Sons Co.* v. *American Can Co.*, 278 U.S. 245 (1929).

[44] The final decision in this case held that the word *or* between the phrases *on account of differences in . . . grade, quality, or quantity* and *makes only due allowance for differences in . . . cost* made those phrases independent of each other and so allowed any difference in grade, quality, or quantity to justify any difference in price without regard to the differences in cost to the seller. *Goodyear Tire and Rubber Co.* v. *FTC*, 101 F. 2d 620; *cert.* denied, 308 U.S. 557 (1939).

[45] See Chapter 17.

5. The Federal Trade Commission

Congressional leaders in 1914, as has been shown, added the phrase "unfair methods of competition" to the Trade Commission Act to replace abortive efforts at seriatim definition of predatory competitive methods. No wholly unambiguous "congressional intent" as to its meaning can be drawn from the debates. Various interpretations of the words "unfair methods of competition" were offered. They were substituted for "unfair competition" because that term had taken on a limited meaning at common law, concerned largely with misrepresentation, whereas the new formulation was directed primarily against monopoly-producing tactics. The phrase was generally agreed to cover specific practices already condemned in Sherman Act cases. How much further it might extend was left unsettled. Its very vagueness was considered an asset by many of its proponents, who expected the FTC to build on this foundation a new commercial law—not merely to see that the game of competition was played fairly, but also to ensure that the game continued to be played. The new administrative mechanism was envisaged as a more effective prosecuting agency than the Justice Department and also as a participant with the courts in guiding the flexible development of the legislative standard itself. The Commission, furthermore, was to carry on, presumably on a more independent basis and with more adequate resources, the investigatory activities of the Bureau of Corporations and to develop investigation as a means of regulation.

Success in accomplishing these purposes depended upon three major factors: (1) Commission personnel and policy, (2) congressional support, and (3) judicial co-operation in interpreting the law and in limiting the scope of judicial review so that the Commission retained substantial discretion in applying and developing the new standard. The history of the FTC has, in fact, been characterized by long periods of weakness in policy, internal dissension, congressional hostility, and narrow construction of its legal authority by the courts.

Reluctant in its earliest years to formulate explicit policies for its own guidance and that of businessmen, the Commission soon found its energies diverted by World War I. An effort immediately after the war to protect the small man's "new freedom" and to pursue other Wilsonian goals led only to successive reversals in the courts and to vigorous congressional criticism. Presidents Harding and Coolidge were pledged to "normalcy" and a policy of co-operation and support for business, especially big business, wholly at variance with Wilson's skeptical suspicion. Their appointees to the FTC shared their viewpoints, and by 1925 constituted a majority of the Commission. They saw its proper role as one of aid to business in eliminating those competitive practices which businessmen themselves disfavored.

Tentative gestures were made toward constructing machinery for business "self-regulation," but doubts of judicial approval, conflicts with the Justice Department, and internal uncertainty as to the meaning and desirability of an altered policy prevented the Commission from making much headway on this newer road. The appointment by President Roosevelt of commissioners more in sympathy with the purposes of the 1914 legislation [46] also had little immediate effect, for between 1933 and 1935 antitrust policy was largely suspended by the National Industrial Recovery Act. The FTC, therefore, continued to perform weakly. It was recognized as a useful investigator for specific purposes and as a mild check upon unethical and fraudulent sales tactics, especially in advertising, but it was clearly not an effective instrument for antitrust law enforcement or general trade-practice regulation.

Unfair Methods of Competition

In its first two decades, the FTC was also greatly hampered by the generally hostile or restrictive attitude of the courts. The phrasing of Section 5 of the Trade Commission Act left uncertain not only the content of policy, but also the division of function between the Commission and the courts. The Commission made no attempt to define "unfair methods of competition" by an all-embracing listing. In its first public statement on the subject, in 1916, the FTC emphasized that its administrative authority was meant to supplement the Sherman Act, and that "unfair methods" meant primarily methods lessening competition, restraining trade, or tending toward monopoly. The common-law doctrine of "unfair competition" led the Commission to assume that false and misleading advertising might also fall within its jurisdiction. It envisaged future expansion of the standard as the need might arise. Its expectations seemingly met judicial approval in its first court case, one involving misrepresentation, when a lower court took a broad view of FTC powers:

[46] It was the effort of Roosevelt to remove Commissioner William E. Humphrey, the leading "conservative" of the FTC, which led to the Supreme Court decision in *Rathbun* (*Humphrey's Executor*) v. *U.S.*, 295 U.S. 602 (1935), limiting the removal power of the President over quasi-judicial and quasi-legislative officers.

The commissioners, representing the Government as *parens patriae*, are to exercise their common sense, as informed by their knowledge of the general idea of unfair trade at common law, and stop all those trade practices that have a capacity or a tendency to injure competitors directly or through deception of purchasers, quite irrespective of whether the specific practices in question have yet been denounced in common-law cases.[47]

Taking heart from this decision, the Commission announced in 1919 that it felt itself "empowered to leave the shores defined by the common law and, taking the knowledge of these [common-law] decisions with it, to embark on an uncharted sea, using common sense and common law for its compass." [48] In fact, judicial restraints for some time would be so far-reaching as to push it back, with few exceptions, from uncharted seas to the well-known coastal waters of pre-existing common-law and antitrust-law interpretation.

The courts not only drastically restricted the substantive meaning of the 1914 legislation, as applied to specific cases; they also gave minimal deference to FTC proceedings and findings. Before the Wheeler-Lea Amendment of 1938, an FTC order could not be enforced until the Commission had applied to a circuit court of appeals, where it had to justify its order. Under this procedure, it lay within the court's judgment to give as little or as much weight to FTC discretion as it pleased. The only statutory guide was the provision that "the findings of the commission as to the facts, if supported by testimony, shall be conclusive." Questions of law were subject to final determination by the court.

In practice, however, there was no hard and fast line between matters of fact and matters of law. On questions of law, furthermore, and especially on the all-important issue of the meaning to be given to "unfair methods of competition," the reviewing courts could act within a wide discretionary zone. On the one hand, they might respect the judgment of the presumably expert, quasi-judicial Commission, restraining it from overzealous attacks on legitimate private interests, but permitting it to guide the growth of administrative law in harmony with antitrust policy. On the other hand, they might confine the standard of the law to the minimum, weigh the evidence on the facts for themselves, and reduce the Commission to the role of public prosecutor in a special field. From 1920 to 1933, the latter alternative was adopted. But it must also be noted that from 1925 on the FTC itself took

---

[47] *Sears, Roebuck & Co. v. FTC*, 258 F. 307 (1919).
[48] FTC, *Annual Report, 1919*, p. 45.

few steps to improve its own situation and that the findings of the Commission and its staff were often so presented as to inspire little confidence in the FTC's economic expertise.

The first and most decisive blow from the judiciary fell in 1920, in the initial Supreme Court decision under the Trade Commission Act. The case involved an FTC cease and desist order under Section 5 against a U.S. Steel subsidiary which required purchasers of its steel ties for cotton bagging also to buy from it a proportionate amount of bagging. The Court reversed the FTC on a technical issue of procedure, but speaking through Justice McReynolds, it took the opportunity to announce its conception of the statute in these terms:

The words "unfair methods of competition" are not defined by the statute and their exact meaning is in dispute. It is for the courts, not the commission, ultimately to determine as matter of law what they include. They are clearly inapplicable to practices never heretofore regarded as opposed to good morals because characterized by deception, bad faith, fraud, or oppression, or as against public policy because of their dangerous tendency unduly to hinder competition or create monopoly. The act was certainly not intended to fetter free and fair competition as commonly understood and practiced by honorable opponents in trade.[49]

Taken literally, the Supreme Court's words "never heretofore regarded" would have limited the FTC to administration of pre-existing legal rules, with no authority to define and attack new practices which it found to be unfair. They would have added nothing to the common law and the Sherman Act but a new agency and procedure of enforcement. They were, in fact, largely applied by the lower courts in this discouraging manner, and with few exceptions by the Supreme Court. In consequence, the FTC abandoned any serious effort to strike out into new spheres where pre-existing trade-practice regulation had been inadequate. It concentrated instead upon those few areas where it was able to persuade the courts to open the gates. Through the limitations set by judicial review, the Commission's principal attention was deflected away from preserving competition by attacking competition-destroying practices and into maintaining a minimum plane of honesty and fair dealing for such competition as might persist.

What little headway the FTC did make in outlawing restraints of trade and incipient monopoly went scarcely further than the Sherman Act. The Commission met with outstanding success only

[49] FTC v. Gratz, 253 U.S. 421 (1920).

in its prosecutions of resale price maintenance and of concerted efforts by associations of manufacturers or distributers to restrict the channels of trade, but its substantive addition to antitrust law was almost negligible. Its very success in attacking resale price maintenance led eventually to legislation designed to encourage the practice.[50] Whereas Sherman Act proceedings had only outlawed explicit agreements to maintain prices, the FTC was able to persuade the Supreme Court to adopt the realistic attitude that systematic black-listing of price-cutters and elaborate resale price enforcement machinery were equivalent to an implied agreement.[51]

In attacking co-operative activities of loose associations, the FTC added nothing to the policy content of the antitrust laws, but the fact that, until the late 1930's, it was better financed and staffed than the Antitrust Division enabled it to operate on a wider front. It issued orders against agreements on prices, terms of sale, and division of market territories; against organized boycotts designed to limit business to "legitimate" dealers of the traditional distributive hierarchy; and against trade association activities tending toward establishment of artificial price uniformity. This was a measurable, if modest, contribution to antitrust enforcement.

False Advertising and Misbranding

The more fruitful lines of FTC legal activity sprang from the second branch of its ancestry, the common-law doctrine of "unfair competition." The Supreme Court's dictum in the Gratz case, with its reference to Commission jurisdiction over practices "heretofore regarded as opposed to good morals because characterized by deception, bad faith, fraud or oppression," in effect invited the FTC to supplement private common-law defenses against unethical practices such as systematic disparagement of competitors, commercial bribery, espionage, and passing-off. By a striking Supreme Court victory in 1922, moreover, it was enabled to enter the analogous and far broader field of false advertising and misbranding, a field which has ever since been the subject of most of its cases.

In the 1922 case, FTC v. Winsted Hosiery Co.,[52] a lower court had reversed a Commission order against the common practice of

---

[50] See below, pp. 560–566.

[51] FTC v. Beech-Nut Packing Co., 257 U.S. 441 (1922). But the courts also tried to uphold the contradictory doctrine that a seller could refuse to do business with any purchaser for any reason, leading occasionally to the reversal of FTC orders, e.g., Cream of Wheat Co. v. FTC, 14 F. 2d 40 (1926).

[52] 258 U.S. 483.

labeling clothing knitted of mixed materials as "Natural Wool," "Australian Wool," etc., on the ground that other manufacturers understood the labels and that deception of consumers was irrelevant, since the method was not unfair to *competitors*. The Supreme Court, on the contrary, stressed the deception of consumers, holding that competitors marking their goods truthfully were "necessarily" affected and that the misbranding was consequently an unfair method of competition.

The FTC hailed this decision as "the Magna Carta of truth in interstate trade and of incalculable service to both industry and the public at large." [53] It began to enter large numbers of orders and stipulations dealing with such deceptive practices, and thousands of additional cases were handled through informal negotiation. The practices included misstatements not only of ingredients, but also of quality, origin, and purity of commodities, misleading trade names or slogans suggesting that a dealer saved costs by selling "direct from a manufacturer to consumer," false representations of governmental endorsement, and many other deceptive concomitants of hectic, nonprice competition. A crusade against false advertising and misbranding, conducted frankly in the interest of consumers and the more ethical competitors in any field, thus became the FTC's chief pursuit. There were several setbacks in the courts, but the cases turned largely on the issue of whether there was, in fact, substantial deception of the public or whether exaggerated advertising could be construed merely as legitimate "puffing."

Another turn of Supreme Court interpretation, however, for a time narrowed even this avenue of FTC endeavor. In 1929, the Court dismissed a case involving a controversy between two sellers of lamp shades in the District of Columbia over the use of the firm name "The Shade Shop," holding that no substantial public interest was involved in a simple dispute between private parties.[54] This was followed by the Raladam case of 1931, which sharply restricted the Commission's campaign against false advertising.[55] At the urging of the American Medical Association, the FTC had forbidden the Raladam Company to represent "Marmola," a thyroid extract product, as a "scientific remedy for obesity," and to advertise it without stating that it might be safely administered

[53] R. S. Ely, "The Work of the Federal Trade Commission," *Wisconsin Law Review* (June, 1932), pp. 195, 209–210. The author of this article was then an attorney on the Commission's staff.

[54] *FTC* v. *Klesner*, 280 U.S. 19.

[55] *FTC* v. *Raladam Co.*, 283 U.S. 643.

only under medical advice. The Court's reversal was based on a restatement of the jurisdictional requirements under Section 5, which was now held to demand not only that a practice be unfair, and that its suppression be in the public interest, but also that it be a method of *competition*, and that there be substantial evidence of injury to competitors. In this instance, the FTC had not proven injury to other patent-remedy manufacturers. The suggestion that doctors might suffer was rejected on the ground that they were engaged in a profession, not a trade, The decision led to the paradoxical conclusion that a monopolistic seller, or one in a trade with no honest competitors, could misbrand his product to his heart's content, while the public would be protected against fraud only in a trade where unethical competitors had honest rivals. Aside from this difficulty, the FTC was greatly hampered by having to prove specific injury to competitors in each case.

From 1935 on, the Commission recommended annually that it be relieved of this burden. Its request was finally granted in the Wheeler-Lea Act of 1938, which amended Section 5 to forbid "unfair methods of competition in commerce, and unfair or deceptive acts or practices in commerce." The measure had been opposed by the larger business organizations, and especially by magazine and newspaper publishers, who feared a disturbing effect on advertising revenue. Associations of smaller businessmen, on the other hand, especially independent retailers, had supported it. The Act also gave the Commission special powers to control the false advertising of foods, drugs, cosmetics, and therapeutic devices, paralleling the new powers of the Food and Drug Administration against misbranding and adulteration.[56] This legislation, however, reinforced the earlier tendency of court decisions to concentrate the FTC's activities primarily on attacking deceptive practices, rather than its original purpose of pursuing anticompetitive and monopolistic practices.

Meanwhile, the Supreme Court began to evidence a more kindly attitude toward the FTC, narrowing the scope of judicial review and more broadly defining the Commission's powers. Until 1934, the lower courts had increasingly substituted their own judgments on the facts for those of the FTC. In that year, the Supreme Court suddenly turned against this practice, rebuffing a circuit court for honoring the statutory division of function "with lip service only." [57] And a subsequent Supreme Court opinion declared that "the courts cannot pick and choose bits of evidence to make

[56] Cf. above, Chapter 8.
[57] *FTC v. Algoma Lumber Co.*, 291 U.S. 67 (1934).

findings of fact contrary to the findings of the Commission." [58]

Even more important was a second decision in 1934, which in effect counteracted the Gratz decision. In the course of upholding FTC orders against the widespread practice among candy manufacturers of selling their goods to children by means of lottery devices, the Court stressed the proven injury to competitors who, on moral grounds, refused to follow suit; it also pointed to the long-established policy of many states against lotteries. At the same time, the language of the Court opinion opened for the Commission a road toward expansion of the law of unfair competitive methods which had seemingly long been closed:

But we cannot say that the Commission's jurisdiction extends only to those types of practices which happen to have been litigated before this court. Neither the language nor the history of the act suggests that Congress intended to confine the forbidden methods to fixed and unyielding categories. . . .

While this court has declared that it is for the courts to determine what practices or methods of competition are to be deemed unfair . . . in passing on that question the determination of the Commission is of weight. It was created with the avowed purpose of lodging the administrative functions committed to it in "a body specially competent to deal with them by reason of information, experience, and careful study of the business and economic conditions of the industry affected," and it was organized in such a manner, with respect to the length and expiration of the terms of office of its members, as would "give to them an opportunity to acquire the expertness in dealing with these special questions concerning industry that comes from experience. . . ." If the point were more doubtful than we think it, we should hesitate to reject the conclusion of the Commission, based as it is upon clear, specific, and comprehensive findings supported by evidence.[59]

In this reversal of judicial attitude, the improved form of the Commission's published findings of facts undoubtedly played some part. So also did the generally lessened respect of the courts for the tenets of laissez-faire philosophy. The consequences in the FTC's court record are striking. Whereas from its inception until 1933 the Commission won sixty-nine cases and lost sixty-three, in the following seven years it lost only eleven while winning one hundred. With this encouragement and with increased appropriations, the FTC began to enforce its statutes much more vigor-

[58] FTC v. Standard Education Society, 302 U.S. 112 (1937).
[59] FTC v. R. F. Keppel & Bros., 291 U.S. 304 (1934).

ously.[60] The bulk of its case load, however, continued to be concerned with deceptive and unethical practices rather than with anticompetitive practices. In 1938, for example, of 305 complaints it issued, only 13 were antimonopoly cases. Sixteen involved the Robinson-Patman Act, and the remainder deceptive or unfair practices.[61]

Much the same division of case work continues to characterize the FTC. In fiscal 1956, it filed 15 antimonopoly complaints, 27 Robinson-Patman complaints, and 150 complaints alleging deceptive practices. In the same year, only about 40 per cent of its budget was allocated to antimonopoly investigation and litigation.[62] Thus, even though the courts now allow it greater latitude in its antitrust activities, the Commission's past history, together with the supplementary assignments given it by Congress in the Wheeler-Lea Act and other legislation concerned with false advertising,[63] cause it to devote its energies mainly to restraining commercial deception, fraud, and misbranding.

To be sure, some of the FTC's antimonopoly cases in later years, such as those against basing-point pricing systems,[64] have been more successful, and the Commission has come to share a significant part of the burden of antitrust enforcement with the Antitrust Division. It not only has concurrent jurisdiction with the Justice Department in enforcing the Clayton Act, but also has attacked as unfair methods of competition many agreements which could be regarded as restraints of trade under the Sherman Act. Such agreements, usually involving price-fixing, output limitations, or market allocations, are really agreements not to compete rather than methods of competition, but the FTC's power to forbid them was explicitly stated in 1948.[65]

Orders, Stipulations, and Trade Practice Conferences

In its attempts to eliminate both anticompetitive and deceptive practices, but especially the latter, the Commission has developed techniques supplementing the cease and desist orders provided for by statute. In its legal proceedings, the Commission, after due investigation, issues a formal complaint, which names the respondents accused of violating the law, presents the charges, and

[60] From 1935 through 1941 (fiscal years), the FTC annually docketed an average of 332 cases. Its average from 1921 through 1934 was only 114. FTC, *Annual Report, 1941,* pp. 108–109.

[61] FTC, *Annual Report, 1938,* pp. 42–45.

[62] FTC, *Annual Report, 1956,* pp. 28–32, 69.

[63] See above, Chapter 8.

[64] Discussed below in Chapter 18.

[65] FTC v. *Cement Institute,* 333 U.S. 683.

affords an opportunity for reply. If no reply is made, a formal cease and desist order may then be issued. If the complaint is contested, a hearing is conducted before a trial examiner, who hears the arguments of FTC attorneys and counsel for the respondents. He then issues an initial decision, based upon findings of fact and conclusions of law.[66] Unless appealed to the Commission by either side within thirty days or reviewed by the FTC on its own motion, this decision becomes equivalent to an order. A final hearing before the Commission results either in dismissal of the case or in a cease and desist order. In 1951, respondents were allowed to agree to a consent order after being served with a complaint. By this procedure they do not admit guilt but do promise compliance.

In addition to these legal proceedings, the Commission has also developed two informal techniques. If the Commission regards a violation as relatively unimportant, it will allow respondents to sign a "stipulation" as to the facts and agree to cease and desist from the charged practices, thereby avoiding further action. Of the 22,830 cases from 1915 through 1950 in which applications for complaint had been docketed and final disposition had been made, 31 per cent were settled by stipulations, 23 per cent were closed for such reasons as death or discontinuance of business or of the practices involved; 28 per cent were dismissed, and only 18 per cent led to the issuance of formal cease and desist orders.[67]

The second informal device for eliminating objectionable methods of competition is the trade practice conference. Shortly after World War I, the Commission had discovered that in certain industries fraudulent, deceptive, or oppressive practices were so widespread as to be almost universal. In a highly competitive field, such tactics as misrepresentations as to quality and commercial bribery, once begun by an unethical few, spread perforce to the many, however they might wish to resist them. The FTC therefore began the practice of inviting industry representatives to meet informally with one of the commissioners, and to submit proposed minimum standards together with lists of practices considered unfair by the trade. After the proposed rules had been circulated to the entire industry as "Trade Practice Submittals," the FTC might use them as a guide in its choice of prosecutions.[68] As court decisions in FTC cases multiplied, the Commission became in-

---

[66] Before 1950, his decision was only a recommendation to the Commission, which alone could issue an order.

[67] FTC, *Annual Reports, 1948, 1949, 1950.*

[68] This procedure did not make illegal any practice not construed by the courts as within the Trade Commission or Clayton Acts.

creasingly aware of the limited flexibility of its statute; it therefore began to classify proposed rules into two groups. Group I rules were positively approved. Practices there set forth were construed as legally unfair competitive methods under the 1914 legislation, and the Commission undertook to prosecute violations. Group II rules were merely expressions of industry opinion recognized by the FTC as sound and deserving of general compliance; violation of such rules, however, was not illegal and could not be prosecuted.

From 1919 to 1925, a few Submittals were entertained each year. When the appointment of W. E. Humphrey in 1925 placed the Coolidge appointees in a majority, the Commission elaborated the Trade Practice Submittal procedure as a means of positive co-operation with business. It promoted Submittals, under the new name of "Trade Practice Conference," as a form of "self-government for industry." The content of Conference rules was substantially extended. Group I rules were still for the most part squarely within the bounds of established antitrust law, although one common and doubtful provision forbade sales below cost "for the purpose of injuring a competitor and with the effect of lessening competition." Anti-price-discrimination provisions were also made more far reaching than the terms of the Clayton Act. Group II rules tended to leave the safe and unquestioned domain of quality standards, product standardization, prohibitions of design piracy, arbitration techniques, and other such matters, and to include to an increasing extent uniform terms of sale, agreements to observe basing-point systems, cost accounting methods designed to engender price uniformity, and prohibitions on dealing through "illegitimate" trade channels. In short, from an instrument for preserving fair methods of competition, the FTC was being converted into a device for greatly restricting price competition. Trade associations, some in the mistaken belief that FTC "acceptance" made legal what was otherwise forbidden by the antitrust laws, eagerly took advantage of this opportunity. The number of conferences rose from five in fiscal 1927 to fifty-seven in 1930.

When the Department of Justice became suspicious of certain Conference rules in 1930, the Commission suddenly announced wholesale revisions in order to align them with the judicially declared legal norms. Affected industries were angered by the alterations, particularly since they had been made without prior notice, and business confidence in the Trade Practice Conference was badly shaken. The number of conferences fell to about ten a year. Failure of this procedure to satisfy the demands of trade associations for industrial "self-regulation" was a powerful stimulus in the rapidly growing movement of the late twenties for modification of the antitrust laws, and Trade Practice Conference experience was heavily drawn on in the formulation of "codes of fair competition" under the National Industrial Recovery Act.

After the demise of the NIRA in 1935, the FTC resumed the use of Trade Practice Conferences, but with more modest expectations than in the late twenties and with objectives more in harmony with antitrust policy. Trade practice rules for 160 industries were in force in 1956. These codes do not add to the content of the law, but in the words of the FTC, they "interpret and clarify the requirements of laws administered by the Commission as they apply to a particular industry." [69] They promote voluntary compliance and enlist the co-operation of trade associations in discovering evasions and recommending formal prosecutions, thereby substantially easing the burden of enforcement.

Economic Investigations

The supporters of the 1914 legislation had expected that the FTC's investigatory powers would be an integral part of the process of regulating business conduct. What Woodrow Wilson called "pitiless publicity" would be a major regulatory technique as the FTC explored corporate price and output policies and competitive practices. Market imperfections would be reduced by generalized knowledge, and unfair practices would be exposed at the same time. To this end, Section 6 endowed the Commission with general authority, first, "to gather and compile information concerning, and to investigate from time to time the organization, business, conduct, practices, and management of any corporation engaged in [interstate] commerce, excepting banks and common carriers . . . and its relation to other corporations and to individuals, associations, and partnerships." The FTC may require such corporations to submit special or annual reports, and may publish all the information it gathers, "except trade secrets and names of customers." Second, the Commission is empowered, "upon the direction of the President or either House of Congress, to investigate and report the facts relating to any alleged violation of the antitrust acts by any corporation."

In practice, however, the FTC has not found it possible to use continuous publicity as a regular means of trade practice control. The obstacles have been threefold: in the courts, in Congress, and in the Commission itself. At the start, the Commission undertook to expand and systematize the work of the Bureau of Cor-

[69] FTC, *Annual Report, 1956*, p. 62.

porations by gathering periodical statistical information on market conditions and business organization throughout industry on a voluntary basis. It met with little success. During World War I and the immediate postwar years, the FTC tried to secure such information compulsorily from the food and other essential industries, but its efforts were delayed by court proceedings. Appropriations for this purpose soon expired and Congress no longer approved of the FTC's efforts. In place of the Wilsonian plea for "pitiless publicity," Representative Wood of the House Appropriations Committee declared that "there is too much of sticking your nose into other people's business." [70] A Commission report on the five largest meat packers evoked such congressional hostility that an investigation was threatened, and a number of staff employees participating in the study were discharged, allegedly to placate the Senate Appropriations Committee. Nor did the Commission itself, after the political transformation of 1925 which placed the Wilson appointees in a minority, strongly press for widespread economic investigations. Only in 1939 was general industry reporting reinstituted, "with a view to developing and publishing the significant facts regarding the general trend of, or changes in, the economic situation." [71]

Meanwhile, despite the apparently all-embracing provisions of the statute, the courts seriously limited FTC powers to require the submission of economic information. In 1923, a divided lower court forbade the FTC to demand cost and other data from iron-and-steel companies, on the grounds that the manufacturing activities were intrastate and that the FTC could only investigate alleged violations of Section 5 and of the antitrust laws.[72] The Supreme Court did not pass on these issues, but did rule that the FTC could not itself appeal to the courts to enforce its requests for information. It could only refer cases of refusal to the Attorney General, who could take whatever action he chose.[73] Even the FTC's power to investigate antitrust violations pursuant to congressional resolution was narrowly construed.

In a study of the tobacco industry, conducted in response to a Senate resolution, the Commission tried to examine all correspondence between the leading tobacco companies and their jobber customers. In 1924, the Supreme Court refused to support

[70] Appropriations Committee Subcommittee, Hearings on Independent Offices Appropriations Bill for 1926, 68th Cong., 2nd sess. (1925), p. 117.

[71] FTC, Annual Report, 1940, p. 18.

[72] FTC v. Claire Furnace Co., 285 F. 936.

[73] Ibid., 274 U.S. 160 (1927).

the Commission, holding that the Senate resolution conferred no authority, since it was not based on an alleged violation of the antitrust laws. A construction of the statute permitting the Commission to conduct "fishing expeditions into private papers on the possibility that they may disclose evidence of a crime," the Court held, might violate the Fourth Amendment's guarantee against unreasonable searches and seizures.[74]

In 1950, however, the Court removed this limitation on FTC investigatory powers by a broad new construction of the law. In a case involving an FTC request for a report of compliance with an earlier order against price discrimination, the Court sweepingly reinterpreted the FTC's powers:

An administrative agency charged with seeing that the laws are enforced . . . has a power of inquisition . . . which is not derived from the judicial function. It is more analagous to the grand jury, which does not depend on a case or a controversy for power to get evidence but can investigate merely on suspicion that the law is being violated, or even just because it wants assurance that it is not.[75]

Accordingly, except for the statutory prohibition of the disclosure of "names of customers," judicial restrictions on Commission investigatory powers have now been minimized. Congressional obstacles, however, still remain. Congress has usually been niggardly in its appropriations for investigations. In 1924, the House Appropriations Committee, feeling that many resolutions of the less conservative Senate were "politically inspired," began adding to Appropriations Acts a rider forbidding the use of FTC funds for investigations except when approved by concurrent resolutions of both Houses, unless the investigation involved antitrust violations. Even the latter exception was removed in 1933. The FTC can still investigate on its own motion, but only within the limits of its available funds. In recent years, on the average, less than $300,000 a year has been appropriated for economic investigations.

In view of this partial atrophy of its investigatory power, through voluntary disuse for many years and through outside limitation, it is not surprising that this aspect of FTC activities has not lived up to original expectations. Nevertheless, despite these obstacles, FTC investigations have contributed substantially to the making of public policy. Through fiscal 1956, the Commission had published 127 studies and had conducted another 44 unpublished investigations

[74] FTC v. *American Tobacco Co.*, 264 U.S. 298.
[75] U.S. v. *Morton Salt Co.*, 338 U.S. 632.

at the request of other government agencies.[76] These studies have ranged over the entire industrial and commercial scene. They vary in comprehensiveness from the eleven pages devoted to Southern Livestock Prices in 1920 to the survey in ninety-five volumes of Gas and Electric Utility Corporations in 1928–1935. Of its published studies, sixty have resulted from congressional resolutions, which often carry special appropriations. Another sixteen were made in response to requests of the President or the Attorney General; fifty were initiated on its own motion.[77]

The studies have varied greatly in quality. Some have been shallow and unsound; others have been penetrating and fruitful. They have covered topics of such general importance as mergers, industrial concentration, and international cartels. They have dealt with such trade practices as retail price maintenance, delivered pricing, and open price reporting. There have been reports on many of the most important industries.

The positive results have varied with the immediate political situation and the thoroughness of the investigation. At times, the revelation of unethical or illegal activities in the course of an FTC inquiry has led to discontinuance of these activities by the businesses concerned, without recourse to administrative action. Other investigations have led directly to administrative action by the Justice Department or by the Commission itself. Cases in point are antitrust suits against the meat packers in 1920, the International Harvester Company in 1923, and various lumber trade associations from 1920 to 1923.

FTC studies have also served to lay the groundwork for new legislative departures. The Packers and Stockyards Act of 1921 was a direct consequence of the controversial FTC reports of 1918 and 1919. The Grain Futures Administration (now the Commodity Exchange Administration) was likewise set up in the Department of Agriculture after an FTC investigation. Congress utilized the elaborate Utility Corporation study as the foundation for the Public Utility Holding Company Act of 1935, the Federal Power Act of 1935, and the Natural Gas Act of 1938, and as one of the bases for the Securities Act of 1933. The Robinson-Patman Act of 1936 grew, in part, out of the Chain Store Investigation of 1931–1934. Perhaps equally important is the contribution of these investigations to general understanding of the workings of our economic structure. They have provided many of the concrete data for increasingly sophisticated analyses of competition and monop-

[76] FTC, *Annual Report, 1956*, pp. 104–127.

[77] One was conducted at the request of the Treasury Department.

oly, analyses later reflected in judicial interpretation of the anti-trust laws.

These positive results are no mean return on an expenditure of a few hundred thousand dollars a year. They are far removed, however, from the aspirations of the founders of the FTC. The existence of such an agency, with a corps of trained investigators, has been an important public asset. But the powers of fact-finding and publicity have failed to serve as an integral part of the regulatory process itself. In particular, the process of investigation has seldom been used to indicate solutions to the economic problems raised by antitrust victories in the courts, with the result that remedial decrees have often had little significant economic impact.[78]

The FTC as an Administrative Device

Viewed in its entirety, the record of the Commission is hardly a distinguished one. Many of its basic defects stem from origins beyond the Commission's control. After 1921, the policy which it was founded to administer was no longer accepted by the political arms of the government, executive and legislative. After 1925, that policy was for a while not accepted by a majority of the FTC itself. Until 1934, judicial hostility was a major factor in its successive disappointments. Nor did the legislative standard itself, with its vagueness and ambiguity, provide a basis for forceful administration.

These weaknesses were beyond the Commission's control, but it added others within its own area of responsibility. Its staff has rarely been of outstanding quality. Where it was expected to combine economic expertise with administrative flexibility in a vigorous attack on the problems of monopoly, it has tended to prefer tedious routine to courageous experimentation in administrative techniques. As a quasi-judicial tribunal, the FTC issues public findings of facts and orders which should be akin to the written opinions of appellate courts. In practice, they have often tended to reproduce the legalistic jargon of the formal complaints and statutory standards of illegality, with little economic analysis of the practices condemned or legal analysis of the basis for the orders. Findings of the ICC, NLRB, and SEC contrast markedly with those of the FTC. While not wholly responsible for the early hostile attitude of reviewing courts, the orders too often in the past deserved little better treatment than they received.

Nor have the Commissioners compensated for the unwilling-

---

[78] House Committee on Small Business, *United States versus Economic Concentration and Monopoly*, Staff Report (1946), pp. 22–23.

ness of Congress to define their task more explicitly by themselves undertaking a forthright formulation of policy. Had this been done in the early days, more respect might have been forthcoming from the courts. Had it been done with the Trade Practice Conference procedure, the fiasco of 1930 might have been avoided and the Commission would not have forfeited the growing confidence of the business world. The FTC might then have illuminated in sharper contour the precise defects of its legislative authority and appealed more successfully to Congress for remedial amendments. An independent administrative agency is always ultimately controlled by Presidents, who name its members, and Congresses, which supply its funds. But when an agency is resolved to make full use of its position, it can become a force of no mean significance among the political elements which determine the fabric of public policy.

In its essence, the 1914 legislation was an attempt to take the burden of formulation and administration of antitrust policy out of the hands of the Justice Department and the courts and to set up in their stead an independent regulatory commission. While agencies of this sort are widely used, the scope of the FTC is broader than that of other commissions. The ICC, the FCC, the FPC, the SEC, the CAB, and state public utility commissions all deal with functionally limited portions of the economy. The NLRB covers a somewhat wider field horizontally, but its duties are relatively precise. Concentration upon administration of a policy well outlined by Congress, or upon policy formation in restricted areas in which the commissioners can develop unequaled knowledge and acquaintance with all relevant factors, is largely responsible for such success as these bodies have attained. Federal Trade Commissioners could not possibly acquire as intimate an acquaintance with the whole business world as Interstate Commerce Commissioners can with the railroads, or even with all forms of transportation. Their relatively short terms, which have in practice averaged only six and one-half years, add to the inherent difficulties of their task.

Except for its investigatory activities, the FTC has made little contribution to antitrust policy or enforcement. It is true that after World War II the Commission, taking advantage of new judicial attitudes, was able to win some crucial court cases and thereby to extend the definition and impact of its statutes, but its general attitude has remained passive and its enforcement procedures inordinately slow and cumbersome.

A very heavy share of its efforts continues to be devoted to the

field where policy is relatively simple and least controversial—
that of false advertising and misbranding. It is here that Congress
has been most generous with grants of further legislative authority.

Postwar criticism of the FTC has been extremely harsh. A House
Committee in 1951 pointed to:

. . . the generally low level of morale among its employees . . . The
internal strife and office politics that pervade the agency . . . The
many small cliques and groups whose chief interest is in personal
authority and advancement . . . The pronounced feeling of unrest
and dissatisfaction in many segments of the Commission . . . Among
the older employees an attitude of indifference toward the work of
the agency, a reluctance to face new issues, and a determination that
one's own little domain shall not be disturbed . . .[79]

A Task Force of the first Hoover Commission reported:

[The FTC's] operations, programs, and administrative methods have
often been inadequate. . . . The Commission has become immersed
in a multitude of petty problems; it has not probed into new areas
of anticompetitive practices; it has become increasingly bogged down
with cumbersome procedures and inordinate delays in disposition of
cases. Its economic work—instead of being the backbone of its activities—has been allowed to dwindle almost to none. The Commission has largely become a passive judicial agency, waiting for cases to
come up on the docket, under routinized procedures, without active
responsibility for achieving the statutory objectives. . . . With notable exceptions, appointments to the Federal Trade Commission have
been made with too little interest in the skills and experience pertinent to the problems of competition and monopoly, and too much
attention to service to political party.[80]

And a former Commissioner, James M. Landis, has pronounced
this dismal judgment:

Reference must be made to . . . the utter bankruptcy of the Federal
Trade Commission. As a practical matter, the deterioration of that
Commission has gone beyond the possibility of redemption. If duties
of this kind are to be thrust upon some agency, there is really only one
thing to do, and that is to wipe out the F.T.C. completely and start
afresh.[81]

[79] House Committee on Small Business, *Antitrust Law Enforcement*, H.
Rept. No. 3236, 81st Cong., 2d sess., p. 18.
[80] Commision on Organization of the Executive Branch of the Government,
Task Force Report on Regulatory Commissions (1949), pp. 119–125.
[81] Commenting in G. W. Stocking and M. W. Watkins, *Monopoly and
Free Enterprise* (1951), p. 548.

Under the Eisenhower administration, efforts have been made to accelerate and improve administrative procedure. The Commission's organization was revamped; the backlog of pending cases was reduced; and attempts were launched to check on compliance with outstanding orders. It is not yet clear whether these administrative reforms, together with recent improvements in the quality of formal FTC findings and opinions, have earned it a significantly more generous evaluation.

In the broad task of formulating policies for the maintenance of the competitive structure as a whole, where controversy is all-pervading and vital economic interests are at stake, the Commission has been relatively helpless. In setting the FTC this task, Congress perhaps was demanding the impossible. An administrative agency is no substitute for fundamental definition of policy.

CHAPTER **17**

The NRA, Small Business, and the Retreat from Competition

THE NATIONAL Industrial Recovery Act of 1933 (NIRA) and the National Recovery Administration (NRA) which it spawned are period pieces of the American political economy. Although the Act was described by President Roosevelt, when he signed it, as "the most important and far-reaching legislation ever enacted by the American Congress," it was the child of crisis, of the near-panic conditions in the spring of 1933. Objectives of short-run recovery and long-run reform were blended in its terms, but the emphasis was heavily on the former. The Act was viewed as an emergency measure; it was limited to two years' duration; and its constitutional justification was supposed to rest largely in the state of emergency. Its administration was hampered by haste and confusion. The stress on immediate action, rather than on previsioned choices of policy, contributed to the administrative chaos which hastened the experiment's decay in 1934, months before the Supreme Court declared it unconstitutional.

Yet the NIRA was more significant than its crisis character might suggest. It was the first substantive legislative modification of antitrust policy and it reflected a strong current of views and interests, not limited to periods of crisis, which run counter to general support of competition. It linked together trade association policy and the regulation of competitive methods by turning over to the associations themselves a large share of the responsibility for redefining unfair competition. It permitted them a latitude far beyond any previous conception of "unfair methods of competition." It was, essentially, an experiment in industrial self-government, subject to a mild degree of governmental supervision. Requirements of minimum labor standards and protection for labor organization were exacted in return for the new liberty of association.

In the circumstances of the Great Depression, it is not surprising that business firms were quick to use the NIRA to influence market conditions in ways previously forbidden by the antitrust laws. But the desire, especially on the part of small businessmen, for protection against the rigors of competition was by no means limited to periods of economic crisis; it was also reflected after the NIRA in the pressure for such measures as the Robinson-Patman Act and the "fair-trade" laws.

1. The Background of the NIRA

On May 17, 1933, President Roosevelt requested enactment of a National Industrial Recovery Bill as the basis for a "great cooperative movement throughout all industry in order to obtain wide re-employment, to shorten the working week, to pay a decent wage for the shorter week, and to prevent unfair competition and disastrous overproduction." Vesting the President with sweeping discretionary powers, the measure provided for the establishment of industry "codes of fair competition" by "truly representative" industrial groups or associations. Codes were to be approved by the President through a new agency constituted at his direction. He might modify code provisions in order to protect consumers, competitors, employees, or the public interest. Violations were to to be punishable by fine, and also subject to FTC cease and desist orders, regardless of whether the firm concerned had participated in formulation of the code. If an industry failed to submit a code of its own accord, the President might impose one after notice and hearing. In extreme cases, he might subject an industry to a licensing requirement, no unlicensed firm being permitted to operate. The President might also enter into or approve voluntary agreements among industrialists, or labor organizations, or both.

Codes, licensing requirements, and agreements were all to be exempted from the antitrust laws for the two-year duration of the Act. Every code and agreement was to guarantee employees "the right to organize and bargain collectively through representatives of their own choosing" and to outlaw "yellow dog" contracts. There were also to be provisions concerning wages, hours, and working conditions; maximum hours and minimum wages were to be fixed by collective bargaining wherever possible, but otherwise could be prescribed by the President. All code provisions were to be subject to cancellation or modification at any time, again at the President's discretion.

The bill thus placed in the hopper of the hectically busy "Hundred Days" special session of Congress was compounded of diverse elements, each with its own substantial history and each designed to elicit support from one of the great organized political forces of the nation. The basic elements were three. First came relaxation of the antitrust laws, permitting businesses to modify competitive practices and even to eliminate competition entirely. The new rules would be bulwarked by compulsion on recalcitrant minorities and, in extreme cases, on entire industries. Labor provisions, secondly, were of two kinds: establishment of floors under wage-and-hour standards in each industry, and protection of union organization. The public works program, finally, for which $3.3 billion were provided by Title II of the Bill, was intended to spur immediate re-employment and recovery.

Relaxation of antitrust policy was supported by those businessmen who had for decades urged the recasting of the industrial order into a framework of what they termed "constructive co-operation." But the overwhelming pressure behind it was occasioned directly by the depression. Many small businessmen attributed their troubles primarily to competitors' sales below cost, now to be eliminated by code. Larger business, speaking through the Chamber of Commerce and the National Association of Manufacturers, saw an opportunity for profit "stabilization."

Although "unfair competition" was undefined, and might presumably include any practices disfavored by the majority of an industry, it was generally agreed to include labor "sweating." The precise point at which increased hours, lowered wages, and deteriorated working conditions became "sweating" also went unspecified, but it was understood from the start that each code would contain certain minimum labor standards. Active support from organized labor, however, required more substantial advantages than this. Earlier in the session, the AFL had thrown its full weight behind the Black-Connery bill, which proposed a thirty-hour week in order to reduce unemployment by "sharing the work." This measure, approved by a large majority in the Senate, went well beyond the point accepted by the business community. Its rigid terms were strongly disapproved by the administration as well, but it was prevented from coming to a vote in the House only by a promise to achieve similar results through the forthcoming general industrial-recovery legislation. In the eyes of labor leaders, the prize provision of the NIRA was Section 7, which guaranteed the right of union organization. Once organized, they felt, labor would be assured of sharing in industry's gains from cartelization.

Thus, the measure had the blessing of both business and organized labor. Throughout its texture, moreover, ran evidences of widespread public support for some form of "economic planning," and of a response to the then most popular theory of the depression's causes. If mass purchasing power could only be increased, it was thought, the deflationary spiral would be reversed. With competition relaxed, the pressure of organized labor would force a greater share of the national income into the hands of working-men. Public works were to take up some of the immediate slack and "prime the pump" for a regenerative process which would later become self-operating.

In its rapid passage through the House, the bill clearly demonstrated its character as a compromise between business and labor proposals. Henry I. Harriman, president of the Chamber of Commerce, defended the measure in terms reminiscent of the medieval concept of a "just price." "The time has come," he said, "when we should ease up on these [antitrust] laws, and, under proper governmental supervision, allow manufacturers and people in trade to agree among themselves on these basic conditions of a fair price for the commodity, a fair wage, and a fair dividend." [1] William Green, president of the AFL, welcomed it as "a very definite step forward in industrial stabilization, rationalization, and economic planning . . . the most outstanding, advanced, and forward-looking legislation designed to promote economic recovery that has thus far been proposed." [2] Even the representatives of organized agriculture, who had cause to fear that the measure would increase the prices farmers paid, accepted it in the hope that revived mass purchasing power would stimulate the demand for farm products. A few congressmen were uneasy at its cartel-like implications. A few more disliked the potentially dictatorial licensing powers. But in the House the opposition was able to muster only 76 votes against 325.

In the Senate, the bill had rougher sailing. Business leaders had

---

[1] House Ways and Means Committee, *Hearings on National Industrial Recovery*, 73rd Cong., 1st sess., p. 134.

[2] *Ibid.*, p. 118.

become seriously worried about the labor provisions; they did not succeed, however, in obtaining assurances that the open shop would remain inviolate. On the other hand, industry did gain one further concession in a new clause giving the President power to limit imports when necessary to render code provisions effective. Thus foreign as well as domestic competition could now be prevented. Special regulation for the oil industry was also provided.

The most vigorous Senate opposition arose on three grounds. The licensing provisions, viewed askance from the start by business and accepted only on an administration promise of utmost reliance on voluntary action, were limited to one year and conditioned upon a prior finding of "destructive wage or price cutting." Grave constitutional doubts were expressed concerning the unprecedented delegation of legislative power; federal regulation of intrastate commerce; and wage, hour, and licensing regulation in relation to the due process clause. These objections were swept aside, for they could not be met without destroying the entire bill. The threat of virtual emasculation of the antitrust laws, however, was too much for agrarian senators to accept. Lifelong antimonopolists, like Senator Borah of Idaho, insisted on an amendment forbidding codes to permit "combinations in restraint of trade, price-fixing, or other monopolistic practices." Given the previous Supreme Court interpretation of the phrase "restraint of trade," this amendment would have removed from the Act those cartelization privileges which lay at its very heart. In conference committee, the language was watered down to a prohibition only of "monopolies or monopolistic practices." So heated was the opposition to this change that, despite the most severe pressure from an extraordinarily popular Chief Executive, final Senate approval was granted by a vote of only 46 to 39. Antitrust policy was clearly by no means a dead issue in American politics.

2. The National Recovery Administration

The NIRA became law on June 16, 1933, less than a month after its introduction. In signing it, President Roosevelt laid primary stress on its effects in eliminating competition in substandard labor conditions. He also promised "that the antitrust laws will stand firmly against monopolies that restrain trade and price fixing which allows inordinate profits or unfairly high prices" and expressed the hope that prices would not be increased as rapidly as wages, "lest the whole project . . . be set at naught." But the statute itself contained no such standards. The only guidance it provided for the code makers was contained in the vague generalities of congressional declaration of policy:

A national emergency productive of widespread unemployment and disorganization of industry, which burdens interstate and foreign commerce, affects the public welfare, and undermines the standards of living of the American people, is hereby declared to exist. It is hereby declared to be the policy of Congress to remove obstructions to the free flow of interstate and foreign commerce which tend to diminish the amount thereof; and to provide for the general welfare by promoting the organization of industry for the purpose of co-operative action among trade groups, to induce and maintain united action of labor and management under adequate governmental sanctions and supervision, to eliminate unfair competitive practices, to promote the fullest possible utilization of the present productive capacity of industries, to avoid undue restriction of production (except as may be temporarily required), to increase the consumption of industrial and agricultural products by increasing purchasing power, to reduce and relieve unemployment, to improve standards of labor, and otherwise to rehabilitate industry and to conserve natural resources.

So all embracing were these objectives that, assuming the Act to be constitutional, there were virtually no limits to the legal scope of co-operative action. Congress had given the administration carte blanche. Even the labor provisions of Section 7(a), the least ambiguous of the lot, were to give rise to almost endless disputes over interpretation.

Had the President been able to draw on an experienced civil service, had the administration been able to formulate concrete policies and translate them into action, and had a clear policy of industrial reorganization been grounded on widespread popular support, the NIRA might have formed the basis for a cartelized economy under close government supervision—in effect a planned economy. In the absence of such policies and such administrators, the effects of the Act would depend primarily on the equilibrium of forces in code making and administration, and on the attitudes and methods of those directly charged with its administration.

Except for the public works program of Title II, which was directed by Secretary of the Interior Harold L. Ickes, the Act was administered by a new agency, the National Recovery Administration (NRA), headed by General Hugh S. Johnson. He was subject, in turn, to a Special Industrial Recovery Board, composed of five Cabinet members and three other high officials, and to the President; but the Board members and the President were far too busy with their own problems to be of any real influence in NIRA administration. Immediately under General Johnson were deputy administrators directly charged with code negotiation; at the height of NRA activity they numbered 55, with 151 assistant deputies. Code making and administration were subjected to the criticism and review of three advisory boards. The Industrial Advisory Board, nominated by the Secretary of Commerce, represented the interests of industry as a whole, as contrasted with the interests of a particular industry in any one code. The Secretary of Labor nominated a corresponding Labor Advisory Board, and Johnson himself selected a Consumers' Advisory Board.

The NRA's immediate objective was code negotiation over the widest possible area and in the shortest possible time, so as to make the maximum contribution to re-employment. General Johnson's temperament favored rapid action. He distrusted academic, a priori theorizing and was content to allow policy to develop by precedent. In accordance with the conception of the NRA as a co-operative recovery movement, utmost reliance was placed on voluntary codification. The Act's licensing provisions expired in 1934 without use or even threat of use, and codes were imposed only by the special Federal Alcohol Control Administration set up to supervise the liquor industry. Contingent power to impose codes, however, was undoubtedly a potent force in persuading businessmen to resolve minor differences and organize themselves under the Act. The NRA had hoped to concentrate attention at the start on the ten industries employing the largest number of workers, but its unwillingness to postpone consideration of voluntarily submitted codes made this impossible. By the end of the summer it was literally flooded with code proposals, and the first fifteen completed codes, all in effect by mid-September, included several minor industries.

The President's Re-employment Agreement

Fearing that the speculative boomlet of the early summer of 1933 might soon collapse, and desiring to overcome the reluctance of businessmen to accept increased labor costs until competing industries were also codified, President Roosevelt cast about for a speedier technique of promoting work-sharing and wage increases than the necessarily elaborate formulation of semipermanent codes. A solution was found in the NIRA provision for voluntary agreements. At the end of July, under the impetus of a promotional campaign comparable only to a national election or a war-bond drive, over two million agreements were negotiated directly between the President and the individual employers.

This President's Re-employment Agreement ("PRA" or "blanket code") protected labor standards and collective bargaining. Employers agreed not to use child labor, to reduce the work week to forty hours for white-collar and thirty-five hours for other workers, to maintain specified wage minima ($12 to $15 per week for white-collar workers and 30 to 40 cents per hour for others), to maintain weekly wages despite any reduction in hours, and to respect the guarantees of labor organization in Section 7(a) of the NIRA. Neither acceptance of the agreement nor compliance was required by law. Widespread acceptance, however, was secured by the distribution of "Blue Eagle" signs and labels and by a nationwide campaign for consumer boycotts of nonparticipating firms. Social pressure was backed by the threat of Blue Eagle withdrawal, and in some cases by government's refusal to negotiate public contracts with noncompliers. Although only 184 Blue Eagles were withdrawn, and the effect of withdrawal rapidly waned as the public lost interest in the campaign, the method was successful as a short-run expedient.

The PRA added an incentive to the negotiation of regular NRA codes. Its wage-and-hour conditions were often more severe than those in proposed codes. And code trade practice provisions offered businessmen the prospect of lessened price competition in return for these labor concessions already granted. Hence code applications poured into the NRA office through August and September. By February, 1934, the code-making process was virtually completed. In all, the NRA approved 557 basic codes, 189 supplementary codes, and 19 codes jointly with the Agricultural Adjustment Administration.

The Code-Making Process

Code provisions were of two basic varieties. Those dealing with trade practices were drafted by trade associations or other industry representatives. But as a condition of approval, the NRA required not only the mandatory labor provision of Section 7(a), but also wage, hour, and child-labor regulations on the general lines of the PRA blanket code. Unions, wherever they existed, played a primary part in hammering out details of the labor provisions. Thus code formulation was usually a process of bargaining for reciprocal advantage between organized business and organized labor, with NRA deputy administrators holding the ring and urging the contenders to agree. Labor had no objection to price and production controls if they would assure added wage-and-hour concessions; business had to accept Section 7(a) and was, by and large, quite ready to place a floor under labor standards if given the *quid pro quo* of market controls. In consequence, almost any trade practice provisions upon which most businessmen of an industry could agree were written into their codes and given the force of law, binding upon the entire industry.

NRA machinery provided no adequate protection for the interests of consumers, nor did it consider repercussions of individual codes on the economy as a whole. Proposed codes, drafted by trade associations or industry representatives, were discussed with a deputy administrator. They were then given a formal public hearing at which dissenters of all sorts might be heard, including minority industry groups, distributors, and consumers. But any controversies raised—in practice they centered mainly on labor provisions—were resolved in closed, informal conferences. Under great pressure to get some sort of code completed, deputies exerted themselves to effect compromises between the organized interests. Deadlock was to be avoided at any cost. The deputy's role was that of arbitrator, not of policy-maker in his own right. Throughout the proceedings, he was flanked by advisers from the three advisory boards, but the Industrial Advisory Board's representative generally backed up the demands of the particular industry group, and the Labor Advisory Board was interested almost exclusively in labor provisions. Lacking the support of an organized constituency, the Consumers' Advisory Board's complaints were usually received by NRA officials with a deaf ear. Continuous criticism from this source, among others, led eventually to reconsideration of NRA trade practice policy in the middle of 1934. But code making was by then practically at an end.

While the broad outlines of NRA labor policy were fixed, policy with regard to trade practice provisions was not. But deputies, in their anxiety to get the system operating, avoided broad policy decisions and tended to accept whatever the industry's representatives could agree upon. The deputy's approval was usually followed by speedy acceptance by the Administrator. Presidential signature then converted the code into a legal instrument carrying civil and criminal enforcement provisions.

Businessmen, however, were by no means united on the terms of desired trade practice provisions. The NRA soon learned that great areas of industry were not organized in truly representative trade associations. In some cases, rival groups submitted strikingly diverse code proposals for the same industry. Long-established trade associations often represented predominantly the larger business units, and their suggestions sometimes met with outraged protest from smaller rivals. Geographical cleavages, interests of integrated or full-line firms as against those specializing in single processes or products, cleavages of size, cleavages among different stages of production, and cleavages among different modes of distribution, all served as fruitful sources of dissension. The very definition of an "industry" was a treacherous undertaking. Overlapping of codes became a serious problem. For all the decade of talk about "self-government in industry," business was in no state to govern itself. A slow, organic evolution on a voluntary basis might have prepared the ground for such an experiment, but here business was thrown pell-mell into the process of writing itself supposedly binding law. Internal dissension in code formulation foreshadowed the subsequent breakdown of compliance.

Code Trade Practice Provisions and Administration

Labor provisions have been discussed in Chapter 7, but it should be noted here that they added to the complexities of code administration and compliance. Labor disputes and disagreements over Section 7(a) were major factors in the decline of business confidence in the NRA in 1934–1935. Congressional action to replace this section, although not the wage-and-hour provisions, through the Wagner Act, was well under way before the invalidation of the NIRA.

Although officially denominated "codes of fair competition," NRA codes were, of course, not limited to outlawing trade practices previously considered "unfair" at common law or under the antitrust acts. They included anything an industry desired which it could persuade the NRA to grant. Despite innumerable internecine disputes, most industries found that their lowest common denominator of agreed provisions included substantial breaches of the wall heretofore erected by the antitrust laws against concerted activity. While almost every code forbade false advertising, commercial bribery, harassing litigation, and the like, the basis for business support of the NRA was permission for market controls. Such controls generally took the form of direct or indirect limitations on pricing, with less frequent attempts at production control. As NRA officials slowly became hostile to these provisions, business as a whole lost interest in the Act.

From the start, the NRA disfavored explicit price-fixing. Nevertheless, most of the early codes limited individual firms' discretion in setting prices. In a few cases, machinery was authorized for the direct fixing of price minima. They included bituminous coal, lumber and timber products, and petroleum; in these cases conservation of natural resources was one alleged justification. In cleaning and dyeing, printing, and a few other localized industries with innumerable small units, similar provisions were established in order to outlaw "ruinous" competition. Over two hundred codes also authorized temporary fixing of minimum prices. Although actually applied in only nine industries, such price-fixing was undertaken over an extended period for retail tobacco, ice, waste-paper, and solid fuel. Most codes, however, relied on a clause forbidding "sales below cost," with cost usually defined in accordance with uniform accounting techniques prescribed by the code authority. In retail trades, an effort was made to eliminate "loss leaders" [3] by prescribing a minimum percentage markup on all goods. Well over half the codes called for an open price system, the earlier ones requiring a waiting period between filing price changes and putting them into effect. Adherence to filed prices and minimum-price provisions was promoted by rigidly confining variations in terms of sale, including discounts, credit terms, guarantees against price decline, advertising allowances, returns of unwanted merchandise, combination sales, and premiums.

Complete regulation of output, like direct minimum-price fixing, was sanctioned by the NRA almost exclusively for natural resource industries. Some other codes sought to limit production indirectly by restricting inventories or weekly hours of plant operation. A larger group restricted long-term investment by forbidding acquisition of new machinery or entry of new units into the industry without special authorization. Other more or less common provisions affecting market conditions included basing-point systems, limitations on marketing areas, and attempts to favor one or another distributive channel. In addition, each code outlawed various competitive tactics peculiar to the particular industry.

Just as Congress had rid itself of responsibility for policy decisions by handing to the NRA and to trade associations the duty of crystallizing the vague terms of the Act into code provisions, so the NRA itself often passed on the burden of decision by accepting code provisions so vague that their real effect would depend upon day-to-day administration. The ultimate locus of the legislative powers so grandiosely delegated by Congress to the President was in the code authorities set up to administer the new

[3] This term has no commonly accepted, precise definition. It may mean sales at a price below invoice cost, or at a markup less than the average cost of doing business, or at a markup less than that generally made. Its effect depends on the price being lower than buyers have been led, either by advertising or by experience, to expect.

law for separate industries. In industries with well-established trade associations, the association board often became the code authority. In others, special committees were hastily formed in order to sponsor codes, and subsequently undertook their administration. Industry-wide elections were sometimes conducted. Where intra-industry differences were sharp, and where firms were numerous and widely scattered, recruitment of a code authority was often difficult. Minority groups were generally guaranteed some representation, but complaints of inadequate representation, usually originating with smaller firms, and often justified, troubled the NRA throughout its career. In the iron-and-steel industry, the three largest members had 757 of a total of 1,428 votes, although forty firms were included in all.

In the crucial early days, liaison between code administration and the NRA was maintained only through the deputy administrator who had negotiated the original code. Since the deputies were burdened with the heavy duties of formulating new codes, they at first left code authorities almost wholly to their own devices. Deputies were later replaced with men chosen from outside the NRA and paid for attendance at authority meetings on a per diem basis. This expedient also proved unsatisfactory. At the end of 1934, full-time administration representatives with well-defined liaison duties were employed. By then, however, the NRA was already hopelessly entangled in conflicts over reformulation of policy.

The Development of Policy

The NRA soon had reason to regret its failure to consider general trade practice policy at the start. It had permitted outright cartelization only in a few natural resource industries, but it had handed over to code authorities elsewhere substantial power to control their markets. Despite President Roosevelt's plea for the longest possible postponement of price increases, the NRA had made no effort to set up incentives for voluntary compliance or machinery for compulsory enforcement of such postponement. Many business concerns began to exploit to the full the monopolistic potentialities of their newly enacted codes.

The sudden and widespread reorganization of industrial habits engendered by the NIRA upset the pre-existing balance of commercial advantage and disadvantage in thousands of individual cases. Complaints from the losers, and from those dissatisfied with their gains, flooded the NRA and Congress. The furniture code authority, for example, complained of high prices for lumber and

other timber products. Small businessmen were particularly vociferous. They were less well equipped than their larger competitors
to absorb increased labor costs. When price competition was
eliminated, they were unable to offer as effective nonprice inducements to consumers. They felt discriminated against in the composition of code authorities. Provisions like the elimination of
three-shift operations in cotton textiles, which tended to transfer
business from Southern to Northern mills, evoked complaints on
sectional grounds. Large consumers and farm organizations also
made known their discontents. Senator Nye of North Dakota,
who had helped lead the Senate fight against antitrust law exemption, alone received over fifteen thousand complaints before
the NIRA had been on the books for six months. Public contracts
so regularly evoked identical bids that President Roosevelt issued
an executive order permitting bidders on such contracts to cut their
openly filed prices by 15 per cent.

The swelling volume of complaints, reinforced by attacks in
Congress, led the President in the spring of 1934 to appoint a
National Recovery Review Board, headed by Clarence Darrow, to
investigate the NRA codes. While the Board's inquiry was somewhat unsystematic and reflected the personal bias of its members,
its indictment of the NRA scheme as "monopoly sustained by
government," and "not a planned economy but a regimented organization for exploitation," helped to crystallize the growing opposition to the NIRA as then administered.

Such outside remonstrances gave added vigor to those Cassandras within the NRA, mostly on the staffs of the Consumers' Advisory Board and the Research and Planning Division, who had
always viewed with misgiving the legalization of price and production controls. Throughout 1934, there took place inside the
organization a steady evolution of substantive policy and of administrative machinery. The first real opportunity for considered
policy formation, however, came with the establishment in March,
1934, of an NRA administrative staff, including a full-time administrator for policy. This new group of officials frankly discarded
General Johnson's earlier attitude of developing policy only by
precedent, by trial and error. They set out to formulate standards
against which error could be judged. Their guiding criteria were
short-run recovery, expansion of production, consumption, and
employment, and "the preservation of competitive and prevention
of monopolistic tendencies." This last criterion went directly
counter to the most important trade practice provisions implanted
in the codes, but before it could be applied, four-fifths of the codes

were already in effect.

The NRA reconsidered its attitude toward prohibitions of sales below cost. It became increasingly strict in its supervision of accounting techniques, disallowing a variety of artificial, price-inflating cost elements. Exceptions were made to permit price-cutting in good faith to meet competition, although this rule easily led to nullification of the entire provision. The NRA also experimented for a while with a price floor based on "lowest reasonable cost" of a "representative firm," to be determined by an impartial agency. Meanwhile, constitutional difficulties, hostile courts, and a public opinion averse to condemnation of dealers for selling at low prices soon made the task of enforcement impossible. The policy group recommended that "the inclusion of cost protection provisions in codes . . . is unsound and unwise policy except in cases of declared emergency."

Open-price provisions underwent a similar experience. The policy group favored price filing on principle, but strongly opposed the price-rigidifying requirement of waiting periods before price changes. Yet it was often precisely this feature which endeared the system to businessmen. "Loss leader" prohibitions were also condemned. Recommendations were made against machine-hour limitations and against direct restrictions on output. The new attitude, in short, was a radical retreat from all those cartel-like implications which, at least in the minds of the sponsoring business groups, had been the very core of the NIRA.

The new policy produced a storm of resentment. New codes were required to conform, as were old codes when revised on some other account, but most enacted codes, covering the bulk of industry, were left untouched. Thus, the NRA entered a stage of irresolution and suspended animation, in which it supervised the administration of codes openly in conflict with its newly announced general policy. By the autumn of 1934, the experiment was visibly deteriorating. Compliance difficulties contributed to this decay. Elaborate compliance machinery could not disguise the bare fact that much code verbiage was unenforceable. Increasing uncertainty arose both as to the constitutionality of the Act and as to the likelihood of congressional extension beyond the original two-year limit.

In September, 1934, the NRA was reorganized at the top. Personal attacks on Johnson, coupled with physical exhaustion from his immense burden, led to his resignation. He was replaced by a four-man National Industrial Recovery Board, which later became a seven-man body, two members being identified with labor, two with business, one with consumers, and two without special interest. At the President's direction, the Board began a general appraisal of NRA policy and administration, but with the coming expiration of the Act hanging over it from its inception, it was more interested in laying the groundwork for extension than in attempting a hurried reform of the existing order. Wholesale code revision was postponed.

The End of the NIRA

When Congress convened in 1935, it had to face squarely the question of NIRA extension. Continuation of wage-and-hour protection was generally favored. Organized labor demanded a strengthening of Section 7(a), either as part of a new NIRA or in separate, permanent legislation. Sentiment on the trade practice provisions was more sharply divided. In the Senate, a clear majority, under the leadership of senators from agricultural states, stood for complete restoration of the antitrust laws or, at a minimum, substantial curtailment of code-authority powers. President Roosevelt asked for a two-year extension of the NIRA, but called for elimination of "monopolies and private price fixing . . . We must make certain that the privilege of co-operating to prevent unfair competition will not be transformed into a license to strangle fair competition. . . . Small entrepreneurs especially should be given added protection against discrimination and oppression."

An administration bill was prepared incorporating these proposals, but Senate opponents of the NIRA secured a resolution for general investigation of the Act, with special reference to its effect on small business. After seven weeks of open hearings devoted to charges and countercharges, the Senate Finance Committee reported out a resolution continuing the Act for only ten months and forbidding price-fixing except under government supervision in natural resource industries found by the President to be "affected with a public interest." All existing codes were to expire in thirty days unless revised to conform to the new requirements. This resolution passed the Senate without a record vote on May 14.

The Senate resolution, if made law, would have killed the NIRA. Review of the entire code structure in thirty days was physically impossible. Ten months was too short a time in which to rebuild an effective administrative system. The administration, therefore, put forward in the House a compromise measure, providing for a two-year extension and for elimination of concerted price-fixing except under government control "in order to prohibit discriminatory price cutting, or otherwise to protect small enterprises against discrimination or oppression, or to deter the growth of monopolies, or to prevent the waste of mineral natural resources." At this juncture, however, the legislative process was suddenly cut short by the Supreme Court's sweeping Schechter decision, handed down on May 25, 1935.[4]

A unanimous Court declared the NIRA unconstitutional on two grounds: (1) that it delegated legislative power to the President without adequate standards to guide him in its exercise, and (2) that it invaded the field of intrastate commerce reserved to the states. So broad was the Act's declaration of policy, said Chief Justice Hughes, that "the discretion of the President in approving or prescribing codes, and thus enacting laws for the government of trade and industry throughout the country, is virtually unfettered." The second issue was discussed in connection with the code immediately concerned, a joint NRA-AAA code for live poultry in the New York metropolitan area. Poultry slaughtering was held to be neither "in interstate commerce" nor sufficiently "affecting interstate commerce" to justify federal regulation of wages and hours. Distinguishing between "direct" and "indirect" effects, the Court enunciated an extremely narrow definition of federal regulatory powers.[5]

The first ground raised no insuperable obstacle to NIRA extension. Indeed, the desirability of more concrete congressional definition of code policy had been recognized for some time on all sides. But the Court's narrow construction of the commerce clause seemed to place the nation's entire manufacturing and mining business—everything other than transportation and trade—beyond the power of federal regulation of any sort. Code enforcement came to an end at once. Congress passed a ten-month continuing resolution repealing all compulsory features of the Act, but leaving antitrust law exemption for voluntary agreements which protected labor standards.

Reactions to the Schechter decision were varied. The more conservative sections of the press welcomed it as putting an end to unsound experiments in government regulation of industry. Organized labor condemned it and sought to promote the same labor goals through substitute legislation. The business community was divided. Regret at the loss of opportunities for market control was tempered by satisfaction at the termination of Section 7(a) and by realization that the administration was, in any case, heading

---

[4] *Schechter* v. *U.S.*, 295 U.S. 495.

[5] See above, Chapter 4, for a discussion of judicial interpretations of the interstate commerce clause.

rapidly away from the grant of anything savoring of monopolistic privilege. In September, 1935, the FTC was authorized to approve trade practice provisions in voluntary NIRA agreements, provided that they also contained labor provisions satisfactory to the President. Twenty-two industries submitted agreements, but in no case were their labor provisions approved. Since antitrust law exemptions were no longer granted, businessmen could derive the same benefits from FTC Trade Practice Conferences without labor concessions as from NIRA voluntary agreements with very substantial labor concessions. Thus, the NIRA expired completely in April, 1936. The Blue Eagle had died an ignominious death.

Lessons of the Experiment

The NIRA was a failure, substantively and administratively. It unquestionably contributed to the short-lived boom of the early summer of 1933, and its reduction of the work week doubtless aided in the re-employment of some two million workers. But the larger economic improvement which lasted until the beginning of 1937 was probably hampered by the increased costs and prices attributable to the NIRA. The experiment did succeed in markedly reducing child labor and sweatshop conditions, in encouraging unionization, and in eliminating some undesirable commercial practices, but these results could have been achieved with far less effort and far less elaborate administrative machinery.

As an attempt at basic reorganization of the American economy, the NIRA encountered a fundamental dilemma. The degree of minute governmental control required to prevent abuse of a privately cartelized economic order was found to be immense—far beyond what "economic planners" had envisaged and far beyond what business or the general public would accept. Unsupervised cartelization, on the other hand, at once released a flood of complaints, and engendered a powerful movement for restoration of antitrust policy. NRA officials themselves were unwilling to accept the logical consequences of the codes they had approved. The widespread contention that antitrust policy was an anachronism without real public support, the hobby of a handful of academic economists and misguided senators, proved to be an utter delusion.

The lessons of administration were even clearer than the lessons of policy. The essential defect of the NRA, from this point of view, lay in its attempt to do too much too quickly, without adequate personnel and without guiding lines of policy. The NRA was infected with a feverish desire for action almost regardless of consequences. Trial and error are no substitute for policy-making, for only policy-making can erect criteria for the recognition of error. Congress had not determined policy when it passed the Act; the NRA did not approach this task, as far as trade practice policy was concerned, until codification had been virtually completed. The NRA was most successful in administering its labor policy, which was relatively well defined in advance. The combination of labor and trade practice provisions in single codes under a single administrative body may have been justified for the tactical purpose of evoking business support. Over the long run, however, the purposes and necessary techniques of control in the two areas are so widely separated as to require a special government agency for each. Chronic friction between the NRA and the FTC, moreover, demonstrated the need for co-ordination of various agencies dealing with trade practice regulation.

NRA experience also illumined the boundaries of administratively feasible "self-regulation of industry." To permit associations to make voluntary agreements among themselves, enforced by group sanctions, is clearly possible, whether or not desirable. To let associations make agreements which have the force of law and impose criminal penalties on industry members, whether voluntary parties to the agreement or not, is impracticable save within very narrow limits. Much of the "law" written into NRA codes was literally unenforceable. The difficulty of achieving voluntary agreement over whole industries was also strikingly displayed. Identity of interest and purpose among all businessmen except for the "chiseling 10 per cent," which so many proponents of self-regulation took for granted, proved to be illusory. The complexity of American business physiology was made known for the first time. So, likewise, was the inadequacy of available statistical materials for effective planning and for predicting the results of particular measures.

Finally, and most important, the practical difficulties which beset NRA officials in 1934 and 1935 suggest a basic misconception at the heart of the NIRA. It sought to evoke an industrial order operating in the public interest out of the interaction of organized partial interests in separate industries taken one at a time. It was thought that whatever was mutually agreeable to the industrialists, the workers, and (to a lesser extent) the consumers of separate industries would magically combine into a harmonious pattern for all business. This thought was confused with the older concept that "what is good for business is good for the public." But this older concept assumed that the "invisible hand" of competition would guide entrepreneurs willy-nilly toward public service, whereas under the NIRA competition was largely forsaken. While individual industries, including their workers, might benefit from lessened production and increased prices, provided that they were not followed by others, over-all application of such a principle could lead only to over-all impoverishment.

3. After the NIRA—The Attack on Mass Distribution

With the ending of the NIRA, the pre-1933 legal situation was restored. General economic improvement, coupled with widespread discontent under that Act, had greatly weakened the pressures for antitrust law modification. Now, however, separate groups which had benefited most under various NIRA provisions demanded special legislation to achieve the same results. Organized labor secured passage of the Wagner Act in 1935 and the Fair Labor Standards Act in 1938 to replace Section 7(a) and the wage, hour, and child-labor provisions of NRA codes. The bituminous coal industry likewise received special attention in the Coal Acts of 1935 and 1937, described below in Chapter 19. A third group demanding statutory protection in lieu of the NIRA was composed of wholesalers and independent retailers, who were engaged in a struggle against the newer forms of mass distribution. These smaller merchants failed to generate much public support for a proposal in 1936 for a general statute to outlaw destructive competition, including prohibition of loss leaders, price-cutting, sales below cost, and unfair labor conditions. They did secure, however, three types of new legislation: the Robinson-Patman Anti-price Discrimination Act of 1936 and correlative State Unfair Trade Practices Acts; the legalization of resale price maintenance; and special taxation of chain stores.[6]

These small businessmen had formerly been among the leading supporters of the antitrust laws, and they continued to press strongly for certain kinds of antitrust enforcement. The fact that they also desired to modify the antitrust laws to shield themselves from competition reflects some of the ambiguities of the concepts of competition and monopoly. It further registers the conflict of interest between large corporations and the smaller business firms—a conflict which continues to generate political interest in

[6] Both chain-store taxes and resale price maintenance laws had been enacted by many states before the death of the NRA, although pressure for national legislation did not become intense until the search developed for substitutes for the NIRA.

antitrust legislation and administration.

Large-scale organization had been relatively slow to develop in distribution, but by the decade of the Great Depression it was having a major impact on independent distributors. It took two major forms, each of which displaced or competed with independent merchants. The first was forward integration by manufacturers who wished to sell directly to retailers or even to consumers, the better to promote the sale and servicing of their products. This form is discussed later in this chapter. The second was the development of large retail organizations—department stores, mail-order houses, chain stores, and supermarkets—which competed with independent retailers and tended to bypass wholesalers, brokers, and jobbers by purchasing directly from manufacturers and processors.

The trend toward the newer forms of mass distribution, perceptible ever since 1900, was greatly accelerated by the depression. Chain stores, which had the greatest competitive impact on independent merchants and were the focus of their resentment, had enjoyed a spectacular success in the decade after World War I, increasing their share of total retail sales from 4 per cent in 1919 to 20 per cent in 1929. In the early years of the Great Depression, independents' losses to chains and other mass distributors continued as consumers became more concerned with price savings and more ready to forego the privileges of convenient location, credit, delivery, and return offered by independent retailers. By 1933, chains were making 25 per cent of total sales. The falling volume of business intensified the competitive pressures. The bankruptcy rate shot up among small retail units, and to a lesser extent among wholesalers. With the threat of extinction on the horizon, and with the mass distributors constituting both a real competitive menace and a convenient scapegoat for their economic woes, the independents, over one million in number, became a considerable political force. When organized during the middle and late 1930's, they proved unusually effective in securing protective legislation.

Chain-Store Taxation

The most direct attack on the chain stores was an attempt to tax them out of existence. After retailers and wholesalers had failed in their efforts to prevent chain store growth by boycotting manufacturers who sold directly to chains and gave them special concessions—efforts which had been attacked by the FTC [7]—they

[7] From 1915 to 1933, the FTC brought twenty-one actions against distributor boycotts, black and white lists, etc.

turned to the advocacy of punitive taxes. In 1927, four states adopted special taxes on chain stores. After the Supreme Court in 1931 had upheld the constitutionality of such a tax,[8] and as the depression intensified the need of states for new sources of revenue, the movement to tax chains swelled to a flood tide, reaching its peak in 1933 with the introduction of 225 bills and the passage of 13. "Wherever a little band of lawmakers are gathered together in the sacred name of legislation," commented an observer, "you may be sure that they are . . . thinking up things they can do to the chain stores."[9] By 1939, twenty-seven states had enacted taxes, although some had by then elapsed, been repealed, or been invalidated by the courts.

In the mid-thirties, the chains developed effective public relations and propaganda techniques for eliciting the support of potential allies, such as housewives, employees, farmers, and food processors and manufacturers, and were able to reverse the legislative tide. The reversal was dramatically signaled in late 1936 when California rejected a chain tax by a decisive margin in a popular referendum. Thereafter, few states enacted new laws, and many repealed or lowered existing levies. In 1938, Representative Wright Patman of Texas introduced a bill for a prohibitory federal tax, which would have applied a virtual death sentence to chains extending into more than a few states, but the chains' counter-mobilization had developed sufficiently to prevent the bill from being considered seriously. No hearing was held on it for two years, and it never emerged from committee.

For the most part, these laws provided for graduated license taxes, with the levy on each store in excess of a certain number increasing in proportion to the number of units in the chain within the state. In practice, most of the tax rates were not heavy enough to hamper the chains seriously. They may have caused chains to close some marginal units in certain states, but their effects on national totals were insignificant. At most, they accelerated the trend of chain-store systems to concentrate on high-volume units, notably the supermarkets.

Loss Leaders and Discounts

Of more lasting legislative import in this conflict among the channels of distribution were efforts to deal with "loss leaders" and discounts. Independents had claimed that the lower prices by which mass distributors attracted custom were based, at least

---

[8] *State Board of Commissioners* v. *Jackson*, 283 U.S. 527.
[9] J. T. Flynn, quoted in C. F. Phillips, "State Discriminatory Chain Store Taxation," *Harvard Business Review* (Spring, 1936), p. 354.

in part, on illegitimate competitive methods. Nationally advertised products, or unbranded staples familiar to the buying public, are sometimes sold below cost (or below usual or advertised retail prices) as "loss leaders." The practice was challenged as deceptive on the ground that buyers are led to expect similar savings on everything in the store or that inferior substitutes are "pushed" on them by salespeople. It was particularly damaging to single-line dealers like booksellers or tobacconists, who might lose their entire trade to multiline stores using books or cigarettes as loss leaders. Independent druggists were hurt by loss leaders employed by drug chains and by small, "pine-board" stores, which cut standard markups and often procured their drugs and cosmetics at distress prices from bankrupt producers or wholesalers. The device was defended, on the other hand, as a form of advertising no more deceptive than other forms. Furthermore, prices which seemed to be below cost to independents often were above the costs of the mass distributor, who received larger discounts and often performed the wholesaling function himself. Independents sought to outlaw loss leaders, as well as to decrease or eliminate price competition, through resale price maintenance and through direct statutory prohibitions of sales below cost.

A more significant part of the struggle focused on the mass distributors' advantages in their own buying prices. If part or all of this differential could be outlawed, there would be a substantial benefit to the independent retailers, who suffered not only from loss leaders but from the generally lower selling prices of the mass distributors' whole line. Moreover, in their assault on mass distributors' discounts, the retailers had powerful allies among the wholesalers, who were larger, and in most trades better organized, than retailers. Indeed, wholesalers and other middlemen led the attack, for if mass distributors were denied wholesale or other discounts, then there would be less reason for them to bypass the middlemen.

The issue of discounts was central to the interests of the mass distributors. Their principal sales appeal lay in lower prices; these prices were attributable in part to their retailing economies and in part to their wholesaling economies. The former were made possible by their high volume and limited service, and by the application of uniform principles of management and operation. These economies were reflected in lower markups than those of their independent competitors. But a part of their lower selling prices was also attributable to their lower buying prices. It was natural that both independent retailers and wholesalers would focus on this factor, because it was easier to believe that low chain prices were due to their advantageous discounts than to recognize the relative inefficiency of the conventional distributive channels. Furthermore, chain-store retailing efficiencies could hardly be directly attacked, while secret and allegedly unjustified discounts made a convenient political target. Independents, however, misled themselves by grossly overestimating the importance of discounts as an explanation of lower chain selling prices. In 1929 and 1930, as an FTC study showed, chain-store discounts typically accounted for only about one-fifth of the difference between chain and independent selling prices.[10]

The discounts granted mass distributors fell under three main headings: functional or trade discounts, which are extended in accordance with a functional customer classification (wholesaler, retailer, consumer); quantity discounts; and special discounts and allowances. Independents attacked the discounts received by mass distributors on two grounds. They argued that chain stores, since they sold to consumers, were in fact retailers and should be denied wholesale functional discounts. At the same time, they claimed that all chain-store discounts, and in particular the special discounts and allowances, resulted, at least in part, from the exercise of undue bargaining power rather than from savings to the manufacturers extending the discounts. The first argument could have but little general appeal. Wholesale discounts are granted by manufacturers in return for being relieved of the wholesaling function; if a mass distributor performs this function, or renders it unnecessary, he has earned the discount.

The second argument had more substance. Invoice quantity discounts presumably reflected a manufacturer's cost savings resulting from large sales, and many of the special discounts and allowances granted to mass distributors were payments for specified services, such as brokerage, special sales effort, or featuring a product in advertising and displays. But others of these special price concessions were forced on manufacturers by the sheer bargaining power of the mass distributors and were not in fact payments for services. Here again the independents greatly exaggerated the importance of such power and the size of the concessions gained. They promoted the Robinson-Patman Act in an effort to reduce or eliminate these chain buying advantages.

Rival distributive groups had sought to use NRA code machinery to improve their competitive positions. Mandatory minimum

[10] FTC, *Final Report on the Chain Store Investigation*, S. Doc. 4, 74th Cong., 1st sess. (1934), pp. 53ff.

markups, prohibitions of sales below costs, direct limitations on distributive channels, and mandatory customer classifications, with standard discounts for each class, were all tried in one or another code for the distributive trades. Loss leader sales were effectively discouraged in some fields, although enforcement difficulties led to progressive breakdown. Moreover, in keeping with the general trend of NRA policy against code provisions "freezing" the advantages of vested interests, the administration became increasingly hostile to such codes, especially in regard to mandatory customer classification. While supporting NIRA extension, therefore, the forces opposed to mass distribution had begun to promote special supplementary legislation, state and federal, some time before the Schechter decision.

4. The Robinson-Patman Act

Drafted by counsel for the U.S. Wholesale Grocers' Association, the Robinson-Patman Bill in its original form was frankly announced as an anti-chain-store measure. It was an amendment to Section 2 of the Clayton Act, whose prohibition of price discrimination the FTC had unsuccessfully tried to apply to the struggle over distributive channels.[11] Section 2 did not protect independents from the effects of the use of bargaining power by mass distributors, since it failed to limit quantity discounts to manufacturers' actual cost savings and did not prevent special discounts and allowances. In its final report on chain stores, in 1934, the FTC had recommended a general prohibition of "unfair" or "unjust" price discrimination, direct or indirect, without exceptions or provisos, leaving to the courts authority to determine the extent to which particular concessions might be deemed "fair" or "just" or "nondiscriminatory." Wholesalers and independent retailers, however, demanded more specific protection.

Congressman Patman introduced the measure only a fortnight after the demise of the NIRA. It was patently a "middleman's bill," designed to protect wholesalers' trade discounts but severely to restrict mass distributors' quantity discounts. It flatly banned all discounts, regardless of their effects on competition, except for trade and quantity discounts. The former required no cost justification but had to be based on a classification of customers itself based on the buyer's customers (i.e., classifying chain stores as retailers). Quantity discounts, on the other hand, were illegal unless they made "only due allowance" for differences in manu-

[11] See above, pp. 502–505.

facturing, selling, and delivery costs; the bill's sponsors attempted to define cost savings very narrowly. The bill also forbade broker- age payments by buyers to persons controlled by sellers, and out- lawed special concessions or payments unless offered on "propor- tionally equal terms" to all buyers. The measure was vigorously supported by the well-organized wholesalers, food brokers, and re- tail druggists, and had the approval of the less-organized retail grocers. Opposition came from chain stores, mail-order houses, and department stores. Manufacturers and processors were in an equivocal position, for they desired relief from the bargaining power of large buyers without sacrificing extremely valuable mar- keting channels. They therefore favored the bill, but with substan- tial modifications. In the final result, they probably gained more than any other single group.

The legislative history of the bill was one of initial overwhelm- ing support confronting gradually mounting opposition and criti- cism. Mass distributors, at first not taking the bill seriously, were unable to influence the House's hearings or deliberations. They found that the independents had mustered considerable force against them. An elaborate investigation of the American Retail Federation, a group allegedly dominated by department and chain stores masquerading behind a "front" of independents, had been used to dramatize secret discounts given the chains. Seeking to appeal to popular sentiment of the day, the bill's proponents at- tacked the chains as tools of corporate concentration and Wall Street domination. Equating competition with the continued ex- istence of independent competitors and identifying monopoly with large size, they argued that their measure would promote competition and prevent monopoly. It "will restrict the chain- store and mail-order octopuses which gradually but surely are destroying the small businessman in every section of the coun- try." [12] "There are a great many people who feel that if we are to preserve democracy in government, in America, we have got to preserve a democracy in business operation. . . . we must make some effort to maintain the yeomanry in business." [13]

Only after the House committee had completed its hearings and the Senate committee had reported out the bill without hearings, did the mass distributors fully awake to their danger. They intensi- fied their direct opposition, supported a substitute measure—the Borah-Van Nuys Bill—and persuaded manufacturers and agricul-

[12] Representative Patman, *Cong. Record*, Vol. 80, part 3, p. 3446.
[13] Chairman Sumners, in House Committee on the Judiciary, *Hearings to Amend the Clayton Act*, 74th Cong., 2d sess. (1936), p. 437.

tural producers to support more moderate legislation. Criticism from these groups had its effects. The Senate committee held hearings, ostensibly on the Borah-Van Nuys Bill but actually on the Robinson-Patman Bill. The Senate added a number of moderating amendments, and the House, under pressure from powerful farm organizations, eliminated the classification clause, which would have denied trade discounts to farmer co-operatives as well as to chain stores. A conference committee, confronted with this welter of support, opposition, and criticism, reported out a measure which was less specific than the original bill but was replete with ambiguities and confusions resulting from hasty drafting and inability to compromise serious differences.

This compromise, which became the Robinson-Patman Act of 1936, contained within it, as Section 3, the unaltered version of the Borah-Van Nuys Bill. This section does not amend the Clayton Act. Modeled on a Canadian law, it is a criminal statute which provides penalties for: (1) giving or receiving discriminatory advantages through discounts, rebates, allowances, or advertising service charges, in respect of "goods of like grade, quality, and quantity"; and (2) geographical price discrimination or sales at "unreasonably low prices," with the purpose of "destroying competition or eliminating a competitor." Despite the apparently sweeping character of this section, it has had little effect. The first offense applies only to identical sales, and the second requires proof that a price cut or discrimination was predatory in intent. The Justice Department made no attempt to apply this section until 1948, and the actions it then brought were later dropped for lack of evidence. Moreover, Section 3 may not serve as the basis for private suits.[14]

The remainder of the Robinson-Patman Act was an amendment of Section 2 of the Clayton Act, tightening its prohibitions of price discrimination. The new law forbade price discrimination "where the effect . . . may be substantially to lessen competition or tend to create a monopoly in any line of commerce, or to injure, destroy, or prevent competition with any person who either grants or knowingly receives the benefit of such discrimination, or with customers of either of them." This phraseology made not only restraint of competition but also injury to competitors a test of illegality and erased the limits earlier imposed by the courts on the Clayton Act by specifically requiring consideration of the effects of discrimination on competitors of those receiving discounts as

---

[14] *Nashville Milk Co.* v. *Carnation Co.*, 2 L ed. 2d 340 (1958).

well as on competitors of those granting them.[15] All mention of trade discounts had disappeared from the Act, but quantity discounts now could make "only due allowance" for differences in the cost of manufacture, sale, or delivery resulting from the differing methods or quantities in which such commodities are . . . sold or delivered." The FTC is empowered further to restrict quantity discounts by setting limits beyond which they may not be given, even if justified by cost savings, "where it finds that available purchasers in greater quantities are so few as to render differentials on account thereof unjustly discriminatory or promotive of monopoly." A discrimination, however, may be defended by a showing that it "was made in good faith to meet an equally low price of a competitor."

To prevent evasion of these limits on quantity discounts, the general provisions are reinforced with prohibition of certain specific forms of discrimination. Brokerage payments are forbidden to buyers or to persons controlled by buyers "except for services rendered." Special allowances for services rendered by the buyer, or the furnishing of buyers with facilities or services, are legal only when offered to all buyers "on proportionally equal terms." Finally, the Act covers buyers equally with sellers, making it illegal for buyers "knowingly to induce or receive" a prohibited discrimination.

Thus the Act bristles with ambiguities, with "infelicitous language," with "indeterminate generalities," [16] and with vague principles whose practical effects depend on administrative and judicial interpretation. "I doubt," confessed one court, "if any judge would assert that he knows exactly what does or does not amount to a violation of the Robinson-Patman Act in any and all instances." [17] Consequently, it can be so applied as to promote "soft competition"—by protecting competitors even at the price of diminishing the vigor of competitive forces—or to further "hard competition"—by protecting competition itself whatever the cost to individual competitors. To interpret the Act in a manner placing rigid restraints on pricing policies would go far toward reincarnating "the spirit of the deceased N.R.A. in the corpus of antitrust" and toward codifying "a catalogue of pricing restrictions virtually identical with the Sugar Institute's Code of Ethics which the Supreme Court in the same year condemned as an illegal re-

[15] The courts had at first considered only competition on the seller's level. See above, pp. 502–505.

[16] *Automatic Canteen Co.* v. *FTC*, 346 U.S. 61 (1953).

[17] *U.S.* v. *Great Atlantic & Pacific Tea Co.*, 67 F. Supp. 677 (1946).

straint of trade under the Sherman Act." [18] To make the Act fully consistent with the antitrust laws would be to frustrate the hopes of the Act's backers, who sought an anti-chain-store measure. In general, Robinson-Patman Act application and interpretation have been somewhat promotive of "soft competition," not enough to satisfy the expectations of its backers, but enough to raise questions of the law's compatibility with the Sherman Act. Its implementation, however, has varied considerably from provision to provision and over time, a cautious initial approach by the enforcement agencies being followed in the forties by a more rigorous definition of permissible discrimination and in recent years by a more permissive application which began with the Indiana Standard decision of 1951.[19]

Trade or functional discounts, which favor wholesalers and older types of middlemen, are not limited by the Act. The FTC has explicitly upheld their legality,[20] and they need not be based on cost differences. Thus the older distributors are given an advantage over the mass distributors, if they have the bargaining power to capitalize on it. Since trade discounts based on a special classification of buyers could be used to evade the limits on quantity discounts, the FTC does pass on the methods by which customers are classified and requires that buyers operating on the same level, such as independent retailers and chain stores, be put in the same class.[21] When a buyer operates at more than one level, selling, for example, both at wholesale and retail, the FTC has ruled that the larger trade discounts may be applied only to that portion of the purchases which is resold at wholesale, and this ruling has been upheld by the courts,[22] even though in such cases the buyer is in fact performing the wholesaling function also on that portion which he resells at retail. Thus, in this respect, the Act has been applied to protect a rigid distributive hierarchy. Functional middlemen are eligible for special discount privileges denied to those

---

[18] F. M. Rowe, "The Evolution of the Robinson-Patman Act: A Twenty-Year Perspective," *Columbia Law Review* (December, 1957), p. 1074. For a description of the Institute's price controls, see above, pp. 481–484.

[19] The discussion here is concerned with the application of the Act to discrimination among various buyers regardless of location; its application to *geographical* discrimination, as in basing-point systems, is discussed in Chapter 18.

[20] *Simmons Co.*, 29 FTC 727 (1939).

[21] *Pittsburgh Plate Glass Co.*, 25 FTC 1228 (1937); *American Oil Co.*, 29 FTC 857 (1939); *Sherwin-Williams Co.*, 36 FTC 25 (1943).

[22] *Southgate Brokerage Co. v. FTC*, 150 F. 2d 607 (1945); *Standard Oil Co. (Indiana) v. FTC*, 173 F. 2d 210 (1949). The Indiana decision was reversed on other grounds, 340 U.S. 231 (1951).

who combine marketing functions.

The Act's brokerage provisions have been strictly applied against mass distributors. The majority of FTC orders under the Act have pertained to brokerage payments. Lower courts have held that such payments to a buyer are illegal per se and that it need not be shown that a particular payment actually tends to lessen competition or create a monopoly.[23] In a case brought against A & P, that firm argued that it had advised its suppliers, had helped them dispose of surpluses, and had enabled them to save the cost of using brokers. But a circuit court was unconvinced by this defense and held the Act's prohibition of brokerage payments to be absolute.[24] Thus, in this area, too, the Act has been interpreted to defend the traditional distributive structure, and prices have been prevented from accurately reflecting costs. A number of FTC orders, moreover, have debarred groups of independent retailers from pooling and directly negotiating purchases so as to earn brokerage commissions, thereby preventing independents from matching some of the efficiencies of chains.[25]

The Act's requirement that services and facilities, and allowances for them, be offered to all buyers "on proportionally equal terms" has been less vigorously enforced, and neither FTC nor judicial criteria are yet clear. The courts have upheld FTC orders requiring that services provided to any one buyer be made available to all,[26] but the question of what the terms must be proportionate to is still unclear. In some cases, the FTC has required allowances to be proportionate to the dollar volume of sales. But it has also approved allowances, not proportionate to volume, which differed for newspaper advertising, handbill advertising, and store displays, as long as they were not greater than the cost of the services.[27]

Both Commission and courts have tended, on balance, to apply

[23] *Oliver Bros.* v. *FTC*, 102 F. 2d 763 (1939).

[24] "The phrase 'except for services rendered' is employed by Congress to indicate that if there be compensation to an agent it must be for bona fide brokerage, viz., for actual services rendered to his principal by the agent. . . . In short, a buying and selling service cannot be combined in one person." *Great Atlantic & Pacific Tea Co.* v. *FTC*, 106 F. 2d 667 (1939); *cert.* denied, 308 U.S. 625 (1940).

[25] E.g. *Biddle Purchasing Co.* v. *FTC*, 96 F. 2d 687 (1938); *cert.* denied, 305 U.S. 634 (1938); *Oliver Bros.* v. *FTC*, 102 F. 2d 763 (1939); *Quality Bakers* v. *FTC*. 114 F. 2d 393 (1940); *Modern Marketing Service* v. *FTC*, 149 F. 2d 970 (1945).

[26] *Corn Products Refining Co.* v. *FTC*, 324 U.S. 726 (1945). See also *Elizabeth Arden, Inc.* v. *FTC*, 156 F. 2d 132 (1945); *cert.* denied, 331 U.S. 806 (1947).

[27] *Lever Bros.*, 50 FTC 476 (1954).

quantity discount provisions so as to minimize the advantages of large buyers, although the lines of judicial interpretation have been uneven. Quantity discounts have been held by the Supreme Court not to be illegal per se,[28] but the specific quantity discounts in individual cases have fared poorly indeed. They may be defended by cost estimates which show that the discounts are no greater than the savings to the manufacturer on large sales. But cost accounting is not a precise science; accountants can disagree honestly and strongly on accounting methods. The FTC has endorsed no cost-accounting principles, but it has not been loath to reject cost estimates submitted in defense of discounts. It places the whole burden of proof on the seller, requiring positive proof of any claimed savings. It further requires that the savings apply directly to the questioned discounts. In recent years, the Commission has indicated a willingness to relax the rigidity with which it applies the cost test,[29] but the outcome of this apparent change of course is as yet uncertain.

Furthermore, the FTC has refused to accept savings in manufacturing costs as a justification for quantity discounts. Large orders may enable manufacturers to use otherwise idle capacity, to schedule operations over longer periods, to maintain operations when demand is slack, and to make other economies. But although a manufacturer with idle capacity might be willing to grant such quantity discounts that his prices covered little more than marginal costs, the FTC has set average total cost, not marginal cost, as its standard. Put in another way, overhead costs must be spread evenly over all units produced, even though the mass buyer's large orders have made possible substantial manufacturing economies. The FTC has also held that goods manufactured for a distributor's private brand cannot be subject to larger price concessions than those on like products which carry the manufacturer's brand.[30]

Quantity discounts may reflect differences in selling and delivery costs, although cost allocations are closely scrutinized.[31]

[28] *Bruce's Juices, Inc.* v. *American Can Co.*, 330 U.S. 743 (1947).

[29] In 1953, a committee was appointed to explore the accounting principles involved. A more tolerant attitude was demonstrated in a case in which a manufacturer was permitted to compute his cost savings on all electronic tubes instead of having to compute them individually for each of the six hundred types of tube he sold. *Sylvania Electric Products, Inc.*, 51 FTC 282 (1954).

[30] *U.S. Rubber Co.*, 28 FTC 1489 (1939).

[31] *Kraft-Phenix Cheese Corp.*, 25 FTC 537 (1937); *American Optical Co.*, 28 FTC 169 (1939).

Chain stores and co-operative buying agencies have been denied such discounts when deliveries are made to separate stores.[32] They have also been denied when based on cumulative purchases over a period of time.[33]

In 1948, in the Morton Salt case, the Supreme Court upheld this severe interpretation of the limits on quantity discounts. A circuit court had set aside an FTC order against the Morton Company's quantity discounts. Morton's prices per case were $1.60 for less-than-carload lots and $1.50 for carload lots (1,035 cases). If a buyer purchased as many as 5,000 cases in any consecutive twelve months the price dropped to $1.40, and if the purchases totaled 50,000 cases it fell to $1.35. The circuit court accepted these discounts, finding them open and available to anyone and in conformity with general practice in the trade. It held that the FTC had failed to show that the discounts were not justified by cost savings, and that competition had not been injured.[34] Nevertheless, Justice Black, speaking for the majority of the Supreme Court, held the discounts to be illegal. He argued that the discounts were really not available to all buyers, since no independent retailer and probably no wholesaler would buy as many as 50,000 cases.

The legislative history of the Robinson-Patman Act makes it abundantly clear that Congress considered it to be an evil that a large buyer could receive a competitive advantage over a small buyer solely because of the large buyer's quantity purchasing ability. The Robinson-Patman Act was passed to deprive a large buyer of such advantages except to the extent that a lower price could be justified by reason of a seller's diminished costs due to quantity manufacture, delivery, or sale, or by reason of the seller's good faith effort to meet a competitor's equally low price.[35]

Moreover, he said, the burden of proving the cost justification of the discounts lay with the seller, and he accepted the FTC's finding that Morton had not done so.

The Court further held that the discounts injured competition within the meaning of the Act. This part of the decision involved the provision declaring discounts illegal only where their effect "may be substantially to lessen . . . or to injure, destroy, or pre-

---

[32] *Simmons Co.*, 29 FTC 727 (1939); *Standard Brands*, 30 FTC 1117 (1940); *Sherwin-Williams Co.*, 36 FTC 25 (1943).

[33] *H. C. Brill Co.*, 26 FTC 666 (1938); *American Optical Co.*, 28 FTC 169 (1939); *Simmons Co.*, 29 FTC 727 (1939); *Standard Brands*, 30 FTC 1117 (1940).

[34] *Morton Salt Co. v. FTC*, 162 F. 2d 949 (1947).

[35] *FTC v. Morton Salt Co.*, 334 U.S. 37 (1948).

vent competition. . . ." In interpreting the Clayton Act's similar phrase, the Court had held that the word "may" signified a probability.[36] In the Morton case, however, the Court equated "may" with reasonable possibility, declaring that the phrase "does not require that the discriminations must in fact have harmed competition, but only that there is reasonable possibility that they 'may' have such effect." [37] The Court also defined the competition which was protected by the Act. Morton had argued that its discounts had no substantial effect on competition among its customers because only one-tenth of 1 per cent of its sales were in less-than-carload lots and because salt was but a tiny fraction of the total grocery trade. The Court replied that, since "Congress was especially concerned with protecting small businesses," the Act was violated when "the competitive opportunities of certain merchants were injured." The test of illegality could not be confined to a showing of "general injury to competitive conditions," but now also included (here the Court quoted a congressional committee report on the Robinson-Patman Bill) "a showing of 'injury to the competitor victimized by the discrimination.' "

This decision greatly eased the task of enforcing the Act. Possibility of injury is far easier to prove than probability; it can almost be assumed. And injury to particular competitors can be shown more easily than injury to competition. Thus the Morton decision seemed to favor "soft" rather than "hard" competition. Both the FTC and a lower court have since retreated somewhat from this extreme position,[38] but the Supreme Court has not yet re-examined the issue.

In interpreting the Act's standard of injury to competition, the Supreme Court relied heavily on floor debate and committee re-

---

[36] Congress did not intend, said the Court, "to prohibit the mere possibility of the consequences defined. It was intended to prevent such agreements as would . . . probably lessen competition. . . ." *Standard Fashion Co.* v. *Magrane-Houston Co.*, 258 U.S. 346 (1922).

[37] As a precedent for its definition, the Court cited *Corn Products Co.* v. *FTC*, 324 U.S. 726 (1945). This earlier decision had, apparently inadvertently, used the words "reasonable possibility," but it had also reiterated the Standard Fashion formula, saying that "the use of the word 'may' was not to prohibit discriminations having the mere possibility of these consequences, but to reach those which would probably have the defined effect. . . ."

[38] A circuit court has declared: "We construe the Act to require substantial, not trivial or sporadic, interference with competition to establish the violation of its mandate." *Minneapolis-Honeywell Co.* v. *FTC*, 191 F. 2d 786 (1951); *cert.* denied, 344 U.S. 206 (1952). And the FTC dismissed a complaint on the ground that a "reasonable probability" of injury had not been proved. *General Foods Corp.*, 50 FTC 885 (1954).

ports as an indication of congressional intent. But in interpreting another clause, which permits selling at a low price if done "in good faith to meet competition," the Court appears to have allowed more price flexibility than was intended by the Act's authors. The FTC initially accepted the argument of meeting competition in good faith only as a procedural, not a substantive defense—it shifted the burden of proof to the Commission, which then had to demonstrate that competition had actually been injured. In 1951, in the Indiana Standard case, the Supreme Court reversed both the FTC and a circuit court on this point, holding that "meeting competition in good faith" is a substantive defense.[39] It can be refuted only by proving the absence of good faith—a difficult task.

This decision goes far to nullify the Act's other barriers to price flexibility and integration of distributive functions. Indiana Standard sold gasoline in tank-car lots to jobbers and in tank-wagon lots, with smaller discounts, to retailers. Three jobbers in the Detroit area resold gasoline both at wholesale to retailers and at retail to ultimate consumers. One jobber, "Ned's," sold only at retail and at cut rates. The FTC charged that Indiana's discounts injured competition among retailers and ordered the company to deny jobbers the jobbing discount on gasoline sold at retail and to withhold that discount on all of Ned's purchases. Indiana's successful defense was that it was only matching the offers made by other refiners. The FTC order thus neatly pinpointed the conflict between "hard" and "soft" competition. It was designed to protect small dealers from the competition of those who combined the jobbing and retailing functions. It would have promoted a rigid stratification of the distributive hierarchy and lessened the price flexibility of both refiners and retailers. The effect of the Supreme Court's decision was to protect price flexibility and the vigor of competition at the risk of injuring small dealers.

The significance of this decision extends beyond the "good faith competition" clause, for in it the Court, perhaps influenced by the refusal of the Solicitor General to represent the FTC, also recognized the conflict between an overzealously applied Robinson-Patman Act and the antitrust laws. Holding that "the heart of our national economic policy has been faith in the value of competition," it chose to read the Act in the light of the belief that "Congress did not seek by the Robinson-Patman Act either to abolish competition or so radically to curtail it that a seller would

[39] *Standard Oil Co. (Indiana)* v. *FTC,* 340 U.S. 231.

have no substantial right of self-defense against a raid by a competitor." Two years later, the Court again demonstrated its awareness of this potential conflict, pointing out that rigid enforcement of the Robinson-Patman Act would "help give rise to a price uniformity and rigidity in open conflict with the purposes of other antitrust legislation." It again decided in favor of hard competition and the primacy of the antitrust laws, holding that it had "a duty to reconcile [its Robinson-Patman interpretations] with the broader anti-trust policies that have been laid down by Congress." [40]

A later attempt of the FTC to prove that Indiana's discounts were part of an illegal pricing "system," and hence not made in good faith, was rejected by a circuit court and by a five-man majority of the Supreme Court.[41] The four-man minority vainly argued that Indiana should have been required to prove that the competitive prices which it matched were not in themselves unlawfully discriminatory. The Indiana Standard decisions have been severely criticized by congressional spokesmen for small businessmen, and several bills to restrict the good-faith defense have been introduced.

The Act's attempt to establish the principle of buyers' liability, by forbidding buyers "knowingly to induce or receive an illegal discrimination," has thus far been ineffectual. In 1953, the Supreme Court dismissed an FTC order against a buyer, holding that mere knowledge that he was receiving a lower price did not violate the Act. Rather, the burden of proof lay on the FTC to show that the buyer also knew that the lower price was unjustified.[42] The difficulty of proving such knowledge led the Commission to drop all pending cases.[43]

Neither the results nor the rationale of the Robinson-Patman Act are easy to evaluate. It certainly has protected middlemen and, to a lesser extent, independent retailers by narrowly confining quantity discounts and forbidding or restricting brokerage payments and other special allowances, while imposing no limits on functional discounts. It has erected substantial barriers to price flexibility and to discriminations favoring large buyers. The very complexity and uncertainty of the law, and the difficulty of defending quantity discounts, probably operate to make sellers offer

[40] *Automatic Canteen Co.* v. *FTC,* 346 U.S. 61.
[41] *FTC* v. *Standard Oil Co. (Indiana),* 2 L ed. 2d 359 (1958).
[42] *Automatic Canteen Co.* v. *FTC.,* 346 U.S. 61.
[43] The Commission later initiated action against two grocery chains under Section 5 of the FTC Act. FTC, *Annual Report, 1956,* p. 33.

smaller quantity discounts than might be economically justified. Yet the Act has aided small distributors much less than they had expected. Its emphasis on cost accounting led many manufacturers to re-examine their distribution costs. They often found that cost savings on large sales were greater than they had realized and that their smaller orders were unprofitable. Moreover, since the buying advantages of mass distributors were usually only a small fraction of their total cost advantage over independent competitors, the Act could not be of great value to the independent retailers. Middlemen have been aided more, but the primary beneficiaries have been the manufacturers, who have been helped in resisting the demands of large buyers for special concessions. But the extreme difficulty of enforcing this complex statute, and the limited resources available to the FTC, have made its impact much less than the recital of pertinent court cases and Commission proceedings might suggest, even when the possibility of private suits is taken into account. Certainly the Act has failed to check the growth of the mass distributors or the vigor of the competition which they offer to independent distribution.

State Unfair Trade Practices Acts

Parallel with the pressure for federal legislation, opponents of mass distribution promoted similar state statutes during the 1930's to cover intrastate commerce. The movement began in California in 1931 and spread very rapidly after 1935. The laws were of two general types: anti-price-discrimination acts, similar to the Robinson-Patman Act, and prohibitions of sales below cost, frequently limited to the distributive trades. By the end of the decade, provisions of both types were in force in sixteen states, while eighteen additional states had one or the other. The anti-price-discrimination laws were designed primarily to prevent predatory local price-cutting and arbitrary buying advantages unrelated to differences in cost. They require no further discussion.

Prohibitions of sales below cost have usually served a dual purpose. Aimed directly at loss leaders, they have also been used to promote price-fixing. The blend of these two objectives has varied somewhat from state to state and considerably from trade to trade. The laws generally prohibit sales below cost, or gifts, "for the purpose of injuring competitors or destroying competition." Because of the difficulty of proving intent to injure a competitor, some state acts make a below-cost sale itself, or the proof of actual injury, evidence of intent. In the definitions of "cost," some statutes apply a specific percentage markup over invoice cost, and others place weight on cost surveys of trade associations. These associations also police their trades, since no state enforcement agency is established.

Thus, the laws permit a considerable degree of self-government by distributive trade associations. For enforcement, these groups customarily rely on co-operation rather than coercion, in part because of the expense of legal proceedings, and in part because of the questionable legality of the acts and the way in which they are applied. At least four state laws of this type have been voided by the courts on grounds of price-fixing (violating the due process clause of the Fourteenth Amendment) and vagueness or arbitrariness in cost definitions.[44]

In some areas and some trades, the associations sponsoring the laws were primarily concerned with eliminating loss leaders and preventing price wars. Often chain stores joined with independents in these programs. But in other instances, distributors' associations so inflated and standardized their definitions of cost as to fix prices and eliminate price competition. In 1941, the Antitrust Division brought nine Sherman Act proceedings against such associations. Most of the cases resulted in pleas of *nolo contendere* or in consent decrees, but two were carried to circuit courts. In both cases the associations were found to have used the state laws as means of illegally fixing prices.[45] Despite their limited effectiveness, however, unfair-trade-practice acts still remain on the books in most of the states.[46]

5. Resale Price Maintenance—The Fair-Trade Acts

By far the most notable political victory of the independents in their struggle against mass distributors was the legalization of resale price maintenance by the so-called fair-trade acts. Distributor pressure on manufacturers to control the prices at which their products were resold at wholesale and retail had begun as early as the 1870's. After the formation of the National Association of Retail Druggists (NARD) in 1898, the movement for resale price maintenance became national in scope. In many trades, especially drugs and groceries, distributors were the chief proponents, fre-

[44] E.g., *Great Atlantic & Pacific Tea Co.* v. *Ervin*, 23 F. Supp. 70 (1938); *State* v. *Packard-Bamberger and Co.*, 8 Atl. 2d 293 (1939).
[45] *Food and Grocery Bureau of Southern California* v. *U.S.*, 139 F. 2d 973 (1943); *California Retail Grocers and Merchants Assn.* v. *U.S.*, 139 F. 2d 978 (1943).
[46] V. A. Mund, *Government and Business*, 2d ed. (1955), p. 486.

quently attempting to force price maintenance on manufacturers. Many producers supported the program willingly, finding that consumer acceptance of a branded product and its price, created by extensive advertising, was often depreciated by use of the product as a loss leader. And independent retailers frequently refused to carry or to "push" a product on which the price was severely cut by mass distributors or by independent "price chiselers." The fixing of resale prices was, of course, opposed by mass distributors as an unwarranted interference with their freedom to reduce prices on goods which they owned. They contended that it was both legitimate and desirable to attract custom through price savings for the consumer made possible by superior distributive efficiency. Price maintenance, they claimed, was an attempt to freeze the channels of distribution in the interests of the less efficient. Furthermore, what appeared to the independents to be unjustifiably deep price reductions often actually yielded a profit to the mass distributors, especially in such high-markup trades as drugs and toiletries.

The NARD persuaded leading drug manufacturers to sign uniform resale price maintenance contracts with their distributors and to number their products serially to permit enforcement of the contracts. The Supreme Court found this scheme illegal under the Sherman Act in 1911, holding that the "public is entitled to whatever advantages may be derived from competition." [47] Many manufacturers then made it a practice to announce resale prices and to refuse to sell to wholesalers and retailers who did not honor these prices. In 1919, the Supreme Court appeared to approve this type of resale price maintenance,[48] but it later condemned such refusals to sell if they implied an agreement to suppress competition among retailers.[49] Despite these adverse decisions and vigorous attacks by the FTC,[50] many manufacturers, pressed by distributors to enforce resale prices, continued to pursue refusal-to-sell policies.

Dealers and manufacturers in the liquor, drug, jewelry, confectionery, and book trades, led by the powerful and militant

[47] Dr. Miles Medical Co. v. Park & Sons Co., 220 U.S. 373.

[48] U.S. v. Colgate & Co., 250 U.S. 300.

[49] U.S. v. A. Schrader's Son, 252 U.S. 85 (1920); Frey & Son v. Cudahy Packing Co., 256 U.S. 208 (1921); FTC v. Beech-Nut Packing Co., 257 U.S. 441 (1922). A manufacturer distributing through bona fide agencies and retaining title of the goods until their sale could fix retail prices as he pleased. U.S. v. General Electric Co., 272 U.S. 476 (1926).

[50] In the first five years after the Beech-Nut case, the FTC issued seventy-one complaints against resale price maintenance schemes.

NARD, for many years urged Congress to enact legislation exempting resale price maintenance contracts from the Sherman and FTC Acts. Every session of Congress from 1914 to 1937 saw the introduction of such measures. But after the defeat of one bill in 1930, and adverse FTC reports in 1929 and 1931, the NARD turned to the state legislatures.

In 1931, the organized druggists of California secured enactment of a statute authorizing voluntary price maintenance contracts between manufacturers and dealers. Then in 1933 they hit upon an appealing title and a novel legal technique for applying price maintenance to all dealers. Under the name "Fair Trade Act," a second California law incorporated a "nonsigner clause," which made the prices fixed in a contract signed by any one distributor binding on all other distributors within the state upon the serving of notice. This provision greatly improved the bargaining position of organized retailers in forcing price-maintenance contracts on recalcitrant manufacturers, and made them binding willy-nilly on cut-rate stores and mass distributors. Its clear disharmony with common-law principles of contract raised constitutional questions, but in 1936 the Supreme Court sustained the provision, when limited to branded or trade-marked commodities, as a legitimate means of protecting a manufacturer's good will.[51] So successful were the political techniques of the NARD, and so militant were its members, that a wave of Fair-Trade Acts swept the country. In 1937 alone twenty-eight states passed such laws, and by 1940 they were in force in forty-four states.

Well-nigh nationwide approval of resale price maintenance by the states still left commodities in interstate commerce subject to the limitations of the federal antitrust laws. Even under the NIRA, federal government policy had forbidden the explicit authorization of price maintenance. Its advocates sought to remedy this situation through the Miller-Tydings Amendment to the Sherman Act, authorizing price maintenance for interstate commerce in those states where it was permitted by state law. Politically, this approach had the advantage of appearing to defer to state preferences instead of directly attacking the almost sacred text of the Sherman Act. The bill was temporarily delayed by the objections of President Roosevelt and the FTC, but Congress ultimately enacted it as a "rider" to an appropriations measure in 1937. It was signed by the President with some misgiving, accompanied by caustic criticism of the practice of attaching irrelevant "riders" to urgent

[51] *Old Dearborn Distributing Co.* v. *Seagram-Distillers Corp.*, 299 U.S. 183 (1936).

general legislation. The administration's objections had been met, in part, by a proviso prohibiting price agreements between firms competing with each other at any one distributive level (sometimes known as "horizontal" agreements).

The Miller-Tydings Amendment made resale price maintenance a part of general trade-regulation policy. Legal problems, however, continued to plague the fair-trade movement. In 1951, the Supreme Court, in the Schwegmann case, held that the Amendment did not give antitrust immunity to nonsigner arrangements.[52] Only signed contracts were exempted from the Sherman Act. To rule otherwise, said the Court, would be to permit "a program whereby recalcitrants are dragged in by the heels and compelled to submit to price fixing. . . . That is not price fixing by contract or agreement; that is price fixing by compulsion . . . that is resort to coercion." In addition, a circuit court had held in the Wentling case the year before that state laws approving price-maintenance contracts could not prevent a nonsigning mail-order house from making interstate sales at whatever prices it chose.[53]

The organized drug interests amassed their considerable powers to persuade Congress to reverse these decisions. The opponents of fair-trade, including the Justice Department, labor and farm organizations, department stores, and the American Bar Association, attempted to muster counterforce, but the fair-traders were aided by spectacular price wars which erupted after the Schwegmann decision. In New York City's "battle of Herald Square," Macy's and Gimbel's matched cut with cut until the price of Bayer Aspirin, for example, fell from 59 cents to 4 cents. While customers were benefited, albeit bruised, smaller dealers lost heavily, and many manufacturers believed the worth of their products to have been depreciated. This price war lent drama and impetus to the high-pressure campaign for new legislation.

Deluged with communications and visitations, Congress in 1952 passed the McGuire Fair Trade Enabling Act by large margins. This measure, an amendment to Section 5 of the FTC Act, exempts from the antitrust laws both fair-trade contracts and the use of the nonsigner clause within states which have price maintenance laws. Having thus reversed the Schwegmann decision, Congress also attempted to deal with the Wentling decision by means of a clause declaring that neither contracts nor nonsigner

[52] *Schwegmann Bros.* v. *Calvert Distillers Corp.*, 341 U.S. 384. Schwegmann, a nonsigner, had sold whiskey for $3.25 a fifth, when its fair-trade price was $4.37.
[53] *Sunbeam Corp.* v. *Wentling*, 185 F. 2d 903 (1950); 192 F. 2d 7 (1951).

enforcement "shall constitute an unlawful burden or restraint upon, or interference with, [interstate] commerce."

Congress achieved its first objective but not its second. In another proceeding against Schwegmann, a lower court rejected his argument that the nonsigner provisions in both the federal and the Louisiana laws were unconstitutional, and the Supreme Court refused to review the decision.[54] But in 1957 a lower court decision, which the Supreme Court likewise refused to review, made retail price-fixing impossible when goods are mailed or otherwise shipped into a fair-trade state from an area without fair-trade laws.[55]

Furthermore, legal and enforcement problems continue to create great difficulties for the resale price maintenance movement at the state level. In recent years, as the memory of the price wars of the 1930's receded and as the price-fixing potentialities of fair-trade became more apparent, state judges have become increasingly hostile to this form of legislation. In 1957 alone, the high courts of Indiana, New Mexico, and South Carolina declared the nonsigner clauses of the laws of those states to be unconstitutional. By the end of 1957, fair-trade laws had been held unconstitutional in ten states, the issue was pending before the high courts of five more, and three states—Vermont, Texas, and Missouri—and the District of Columbia had never enacted such measures.[56] In these circumstances, many manufacturers who wished to pursue national marketing policies, including some who had long been outstanding supporters of fair-trade, abandoned the effort to maintain resale prices.

Since no state agency checks on compliance with fair-trade contracts, their enforcement depends primarily on the trade itself. Compliance is policed by manufacturers or by retailer groups and is most effective where the retailers are well organized, where manufacturers are large enough to have a sizable enforcement staff, and where consumers are not very price-conscious. Fair-trade is least successful in seasonal, perishable, or expensive commodities; it is most successful in the sale of advertised, widely distributed, brand-name products.

In the trades where price maintenance has been most effective, it has virtually eliminated price competition among distributors. In

[54] Schwegmann v. Eli Lilly & Co., 205 F. 2d 788 (1953); cert. denied, 346 U.S. 856 (1954).

[55] General Electric Co. v. Masters Mail Order Co., cert. denied, 2 L. ed 2d 39 (1957).

[56] New York Times, January 6, 1958.

theory the contracts set only price minima; in practice almost all dealers quote these prices. Although mass distributors may market more efficiently, their prices on fair-traded goods are not allowed to reflect these efficiencies. Independent retailers are thus partially shielded from the forces of change, and the channels of distribution partially frozen. Moreover, well-organized dealers like the druggists can use fair-trade to increase their margins. Acting together, using or threatening to use black lists or white lists, promising to "push" some products or threatening to put them under the counter, they can persuade manufacturers to set fair-trade prices at levels which will increase the retail markup.[57] The NARD has used fair-trade as a weapon in its long campaign to assure its members a markup of at least 50 per cent.

Price maintenance not only eliminates retail price competition on the sale of the same products; it also tends to promote price uniformity among competing products. It would be suicidal for a manufacturer to set resale prices if the prices of competing products were not maintained or were set at lower levels. Accordingly, whether or not by explicit agreement, fair-trading manufacturers tend to set the same prices for similar products.

While the elimination of competition among retailers and among manufacturers raises prices, fair-trade's impact can easily be exaggerated, for it covers only branded goods. Even in the fields where it has been most successful, such as drugs, the protection it affords small dealers is limited. Mass distributors have been moderately successful in promoting their own private brands, thereby competing in price with independents and making the manufacturers of fair-traded goods reluctant to allow distributive margins and retail prices to be pushed too high. Large margins on fair-traded drugs and toiletries have attracted supermarkets, who now sell the lion's share of many so-called drugstore items. In the same way, high markups on such lines as appliances have brought into existence the "discount houses," who openly flout fair-trade prices. The difficulty of compelling them to comply with maintained prices has brought about the collapse of fair-trade in some areas and has contributed to the trend among leading national manufacturers toward discontinuing efforts at price maintenance.

Thus, despite many legislative victories, final achievement of

---

[57] The Justice Department has successfully prosecuted a number of cases brought against organized retailers for coercing manufacturers into signing fair-trade contracts. House Committee on the Judiciary, *Amending the Sherman Act with Respect to Resale Price Maintenance*, H. Rept. 1516, 82d Cong., 2d sess. (1952), pp. 20–21, 31–39.

their objectives continues to elude the small retailers. In 1958, the supporters of fair-trade, realizing that state legislation and enforcement were inadequate even when aided by the two federal enabling statutes, were seeking a comprehensive federal law which would directly extend to the makers of brand-name products the power to fix resale prices. These manufacturers would thus have the same right to control their ultimate prices as do producers who ship to distributors on consignment or who sell through exclusive franchises. Here again public policy faces the choice between "hard" and "soft" competition.[58]

6. Conflicts Between Dealers and Manufacturers

Examples of conflict between large and small business, and between "hard" and "soft" competition, can also be found in vertical relations within particular trades, where the development of large-scale manufacturing organizations restricts the full independence of distributors. Both gasoline and automobile dealers, for example, complain that the large refiners and manufacturers at times abuse their considerable powers over dealers. There is much justification for these complaints. The large oil companies have sometimes used the threat of lease cancellation or other weapons to force service stations to cut their prices and margins in order to meet competition. These companies have also "persuaded" dealers to carry exclusively, or to give preferential sales effort to, certain brands of tires, batteries, and accessories.

The large automobile manufacturers, for a long time able to cancel franchise agreements on short notice for almost any reason, at times coerced dealers to accept more cars than they could sell profitably, to make excessive trade-in allowances, and to invest more

[58] While fair-trade conflicts with antitrust policy, and so is opposed by the Justice Department and the FTC, it would be possible to outlaw loss leaders, the ostensible target of the fair-trade movement, without creating such a conflict. Sales below cost are not illegal under Section 5 of the FTC Act; they are condemned only when made with the intent to injure competition. *Sears, Roebuck & Co. v. FTC*, 258 F. 307 (1919). (One of the complaints lodged against A & P in its criminal antitrust trial was that it had deliberately taken losses in certain areas in order to drive out competition, but the court did not rule on this issue. *U.S. v. New York Great A & P Tea Co.*, 67 F. Supp. 626, 1946.) It has been suggested, however, that sales below invoice cost might be outlawed "where the effect may be substantially to lessen competition." (Senate Committee on Interstate and Foreign Commerce, *Hearings on Resale Price Fixing*, 82d Cong., 2d sess., 1952, pp. 41–42.) The fact that independent distributors have never backed this proposal suggests that it is competition, not merely loss leaders, from which they seek to be protected.

heavily than they desired in sales, service, and advertising. According to an FTC study, in 1937 the average sale of a new car at a price of $850.19 yielded the dealer a net loss of $4.26 after disposal of the trade-in. Only a profit of $23.35 on related sales of parts, accessories, and service enabled the dealer to show an over-all profit.[59] In 1954, a year in which manufacturers pressed hard for sales, dealers' profits were 0.6 per cent of sales.[60] Until stopped by antitrust action, moreover, manufacturers compelled their dealers to use only specified finance companies.[61]

Thus dealers could justifiably claim that at times their suppliers had abused their great powers. The courts have been of no assistance, for they have held that these powers were based on leases or franchise contracts which the dealers had willingly signed, however one-sided they might be. Dealers have been only slightly helped by state legislation. They have won sympathetic hearings from congressional committees,[62] but in the late thirties, when they sought to initiate a campaign for federal legislation, they were unable to agree on its content.

In 1956, the automobile dealers persuaded Congress to enact the "Day in Court" Act. This measure permits a dealer to sue for damages in a federal court in the event that a manufacturer fails to "act in good faith in performing or complying with any of the terms or provisions of the franchise, or in terminating, canceling or not renewing the franchise with such dealer." While this law is too recent for its impact on manufacturer-dealer relations to be appraised, the hearings and publicity incident to its passage did cause manufacturers to review and modify their dealer policies and contracts. At best, however, dealers have only moderately shifted the uneven balance of power between them and the manufacturers. To protect themselves from "bootleg" dealers and other forms of competition, "legitimate" dealers have frequently sought exclusive territorial franchises. In an indirect effort to obtain the same result, they secured federal legislation in 1958 providing that each new car be posted with its "suggested" retail price and the name of the dealer to whom it was consigned.

Much the same struggle has occurred in other trades. One result

[59] FTC, *Report on Motor Vehicle Industry,* H. Doc. 468, 76th Cong., 1st sess. (1940), p. 481.

[60] *Wall Street Journal,* November 28, 1955.

[61] *General Motors Corp.* v. *U.S.,* 121 F. 2d 376; *cert.* denied, 314 U.S. 618 and 314 U.S. 710 (1941); *Ford Motor Co.* v. *U.S.,* 335 U.S. 303 (1948).

[62] Subcommittee of House Select Committee on Small Business, *Hearings on Distribution Problems,* 84th Cong., 1st and 2d sess. (1955-1956), Parts I, II, VIII.

of the agitation for the Day in Court Act was to encourage independent automotive parts manufacturers and distributors to unite in a campaign against the automobile manufacturers and oil companies, on the ground that their coercion of dealers and allegedly misleading advertising had deprived the independents of their former share of the market.

7. The Problem of Small Business in a Competitive Economy

Thus, in recent decades, the small businessman has raised serious problems for antitrust policy. At one time, monopoly and size were equated, as were competition and large numbers of firms. Small businessmen were among the leading supporters of antitrust policy. They continue to support and benefit from many aspects of this policy, some of them doubtless owing their business life to it and many securing substantial protection against abuses of market power. But as far back as the trade association cases of the twenties, it was becoming clear that the antitrust laws were not an unalloyed boon to small business. The struggles within the field of distribution, where the bulk of small business is to be found, sharpened the issues. In most trades, small business wanted less competition than economic forces and antitrust policy imposed on them.

Viewed in this light, it is remarkable that the general public policies of supporting competition in business were so little modified. For the most part unable through their own resources to achieve the kind of market restraint often gained by larger businesses, small businesses needed governmental assistance if they were to eliminate price competition. But any such program necessarily implied a substantial breach in antitrust policy. This proved possible only during the two-year life of the NIRA, and even then evoked a substantial reaction. Small businessmen themselves seldom advocated an end to competition in general; it was only the competition immediately confronting them that they wished to attack; elsewhere it was to be supported.

The relatively minor modifications of antitrust policy they gained were seldom sufficient to shield them from competitive forces. Proposals like the Robinson-Patman Bill were significantly modified before enactment to provide greater conformity with general policy. Once enacted, the laws were often interpreted and applied in the light of competitive goals. And none of these measures has been able to protect distributors from the forces of change, from the new forms of competition arising in a dynamic economy.

Thus, while the distributive war was waged in part on political battlefields, most of its crucial battles have been economic. While some distributors were winning sympathetic congressional audiences, arguing that the very existence of an economic middle class was at stake, other merchants were sharpening their economic weapons. Many, through such devices as "voluntary chains" or supermarkets, have partly matched the efficiencies of the chains. Others have profited through nonprice appeals. The requiems periodically pronounced over small business in general have continued to prove, at the very least, premature.

Granted that there are compelling reasons, political, social, and economic, for the preservation of small business, it can be argued that the public interest will be better served by affirmative assistance than by legislation which restricts competition and perpetuates inefficiencies and waste.[63] Small businesses typically do not possess the managerial skills, technical information, research facilities, access to highly qualified outside counsel, and financial resources generally available to larger corporations. This lack is now increasingly, but unevenly, met by trade associations, chambers of commerce, state and federal Departments of Commerce, and the Small Business Administration.[64] Assistance of this type could be substantially broadened. Competitive policy, while inhibiting the predatory and the restrictive, might more properly strengthen the weak than hobble the able and strong.

[63] See A. D. H. Kaplan, *Small Business: Its Place and Its Problems* (1948).
[64] The Small Business Administration is discussed at pages 742–743, below.

CHAPTER **18**

The Revival of Antitrust Policy

B EGINNING in the late 1930's, antitrust activity was revived as the cardinal feature of American public policy toward the bulk of industry. Except for the war years, this revival has continued down to the present day. It has been marked by broader judicial interpretation of the Sherman Act, more ample congressional support, and more vigorous executive enforcement by administrations representing both major parties than in any earlier period.

It is somewhat surprising that this revival should have started during the second administration of Franklin D. Roosevelt. The New Deal had begun by suspending the antitrust laws under the NIRA, and thereafter the Roosevelt administration was mainly preoccupied with questions of recovery, reform, and rearmament. Furthermore, many of its economic programs, such as those in agriculture, coal, and oil, were founded on the assumption that certain industries were afflicted with too much competition.

The new vigor of antitrust policy was traceable partly to the sharp economic downturn of 1937 and partly to the aggressive leadership of Thurman Arnold, who in 1938 became Assistant Attorney General in charge of the Antitrust Division. In 1937, the Justice Department had already begun to consider possible means for improving enforcement of the Sherman Act. Public hearings on a bill sponsored by Senators Borah and O'Mahoney had explored the possibility of requiring federal licenses for large corporations, a scheme first seriously considered by the Taft administration. License restrictions were to be used both to safeguard investors and to facilitate regulation. The antitrust laws were to be given new teeth—sharpened beyond recognition—through suspension of the license for serious violations.

These cautious gropings toward a revived antitrust policy were given fresh impetus by the precipitous recession of 1937, which saw industrial production drop by 36 per cent in twelve months. The administration attributed the recession to two major causes: unwillingness of private investors to replace the declining flow of government spending, in the face of labor unrest and a supposedly hostile President and Congress; and monopolistically induced price rigidities and price increases, particularly in heavy industries and in building materials, which were believed to have prevented increased purchasing power from being adequately reflected in increased demand. This second hypothesis, which held that government expenditures, especially on public works, were being dissipated in price increases instead of stimulating employment, seemed to be validated by the recurrent phenomenon of identical bids on government contracts. It led directly to proposals for a new antitrust campaign.

1. Antitrust Policy Revived

The new campaign began on two fronts. One sought both immediate and longer-range objectives through an unprecedented enforcement effort within the framework of existing statutes. The other involved a broad investigation of the whole industrial structure, with an eye toward a renovated long-run trade-regulation policy.

This inquiry, authorized by Congress in 1938 after a special message from the President, was conducted by the Temporary National Economic Committee (TNEC). The Committee was composed of twelve members, six from Congress and six from executive departments and regulatory agencies. It was given a wide investigatory mandate, with particular emphasis on "monopoly and the concentration of power in and financial control over production and distribution." While the TNEC favored antitrust policy as a basically sound attitude of American government toward the industrial order, it carefully eschewed any appearance of a moral trust-busting crusade. It stressed the value of fact-finding as a basis for policy formation. The evidence which it gathered and the material submitted to it by co-operating agencies comprised the most thoroughgoing analysis and description of American industry and trade ever produced.

World War II diverted public attention to other matters. The administration had neither time nor desire to initiate economic reforms after 1941; as a result, none of the TNEC's important legislative recommendations were translated into statute. Nevertheless, the TNEC had a significant impact. It provided a factual and analytical foundation for a more sophisticated understanding of problems of monopoly and competition on the part of economists, Antitrust Division staff, and judges. Its studies suggested many of the targets chosen for antitrust attack.

The strengthening of the Antitrust Division was signaled by the appointment in 1937 of Robert H. Jackson, and in 1938 (after Jackson had been named Solicitor General) of Thurman Arnold, as Assistant Attorney General in charge of the Division. The recently demonstrated willingness of the Supreme Court to review constitutional doctrines in the light of changed conditions inspired hopes of a similar freshness of attitude toward the Sherman Act. Both men were convinced that antitrust policy offered a means of overcoming economic stagnation. While conceding that the Sherman Act had helped to keep the economy from being cartelized, Arnold argued that its beneficial potentialities had been crippled by unfavorable judicial interpretation and lackadaisical and erratic enforcement.[1] The target of enforcement, he contended, should be not bigness per se, but rather those market restraints, whether exercised by large firms or small, which interfered with competitive forces and impeded recovery by raising prices and restricting output. In 1940, he explained the rationale and purpose of the antitrust enforcement campaign in these words:

One restraint leads to another. Every aggressive combination compels others to combine in self-defense. The total effect of all these various restraints is the unbalance of prices which has been the principal cause of the failure of our economy to get on its feet in the last eight years . . . the fundamental objective of the antitrust laws is not to destroy the efficiency of mass production or distribution. . . . It is

[1] Arnold had had the misfortune of earlier committing to print in a popular book so sweeping a denial of the effectiveness of previous antitrust enforcement that Senator Borah, for one, was most hesitant to allow him to assume the task. Senate Committee on the Judiciary, *Hearings on Nomination of Thurman W. Arnold*, 75th Cong., 3d sess. (1938), pp. 3ff. In his book, a coolly anthropological dissection of American economic institutions, Arnold had concluded that "the actual result of the antitrust laws was to promote the growth of great industrial organizations by deflecting the attack on them into purely moral and ceremonial channels. . . . The effect . . . was to convince reformers either that large combinations did not actually exist, or else that if they did exist, they were about to be done away with just as soon as right-thinking men were elected to office." *Folklore of Capitalism* (1937), pp. 208, 212.

not size in itself that we want to destroy, but the use of organized power to restrain trade unreasonably, without justification in terms of greater distribution of goods. . . . Size in itself is not an evil, but it does give power to those who control it. That power must be constantly watched by an adequate enforcement organization to see that it does not destroy a free market.[2]

Arnold's success in expanding the scope of enforcement, in selecting economically significant cases, and in persuading the courts to revise their interpretation of the Sherman Act was so great that thereafter the Act has sometimes been called the "New" Sherman Act (or even the "Thurman Act"!).

Ever since its establishment in 1903, the Antitrust Division has been undernourished. Its appropriations had averaged around $200,000 for many years, first reaching $300,000 in 1935. With full administration backing, Arnold waged a successful campaign for increases. In fiscal 1939, appropriations were raised to $780,000, and in 1940, to $1,325,000. The climb continued in the postwar years, recent appropriations averaging between three and four million dollars. While these funds permit greatly expanded enforcement activity, they are still hardly commensurate with the responsibilities assigned the Division. Since a single important case may cost anywhere between $100,000 and $500,000, the number of suits the Division can launch is still seriously limited.[3]

Nonetheless, increased appropriations afforded the Division an entirely novel breadth of action. From a few dozen lawyers, the staff was enlarged to about 250. The employment of a number of economists enabled the Division to focus more on market data evidence and less on allegations of predatory practices, thereby paving the way for greater judicial acceptance of economic criteria of monopoly or restraint of trade. A team of attorneys and economists could now be detailed to make a comprehensive investigation of an entire industry, or a type of market control wherever found, concentrating on the focal points of price and output determination and laying the groundwork for formal attacks through the courts. Such a study of the housing industry, for example, led to the filing of about a hundred suits against manufacturers and distributors of construction materials and contractors and labor unions in the building trades. Other actions were directed against restraints of trade in the fertilizer, milk-distribution, and food-

---

[2] *The Bottlenecks of Business* (1940), pp. 58, 124–125.

[3] In some years the work of the Division actually shows a profit, in the sense that the fines collected from antitrust violators exceed its appropriations. These fines, however, accrue to the Treasury and not to the Division.

processing industries, and against "management engineering" firms which established restrictive trade association controls.

Antitrust enforcement thus became both more pointed and broader. Before the late thirties, one observer has pointed out, "prosecutions were merely symbolic in character. In any one year, from half a dozen to a dozen instances of law violation were arbitrarily selected for investigation and trial. . . . With all available resources committed . . . the prosecution of a few lawbreakers became in effect a guarantee of immunity to the rest." [4] Now the Division could range far and wide over the economy. In fiscal 1939, it instituted 92 cases and 215 major investigations, as compared with 11 and 59, respectively, in the previous year.

The Division also sought to extend the scope of the Sherman Act by applying it to such areas as medical practice, newspaper associations, insurance, railroads, and labor unions. The Division enjoyed considerable success, although in some instances what the Court gave the Congress took away. The Clayton Act and other laws had exempted farmers' co-operatives from the antitrust laws, but in 1939 the Court applied the Sherman Act to a milk producers' association which had joined with other organizations to fix the price of milk.[5] Similarly, although the Webb-Pomerene Act of 1918 exempted export trade associations from the Sherman Act, the Court now ruled that they could not engage in the restrictive activities of international cartels.[6] The Court also held that the antitrust laws applied to restraints of trade in the medical profession [7] and in the transmission of news.[8] In later years, the Court has continued to expand Sherman Act coverage, applying it to real estate brokerage,[9] newspaper publishing,[10] building construction,[11] the theater,[12] and boxing,[13] although not to organized baseball.[14]

In other areas, the Division was less successful. After the Su-

---

[4] C. D. Edwards, *Maintaining Competition* (1949), p. 293.
[5] *U.S.* v. *Borden Co.*, 308 U.S. 188.
[6] *U.S. Alkali Export Assn.* v. *U.S.*, 325 U.S. 196 (1945).
[7] *U.S.* v. *American Medical Assn.*, 317 U.S. 519 (1943).
[8] *U.S.* v. *Associated Press*, 326 U.S. 1 (1945).
[9] *U.S.* v. *National Assn. of Real Estate Boards*, 339 U.S. 485 (1950).
[10] *Lorain Journal Co.* v. *U.S.*, 342 U.S. 143 (1951).
[11] *U.S.* v. *Employing Plasterers' Assn.*, 347 U.S. 186 (1954).
[12] *U.S.* v. *Shubert*, 348 U.S. 222 (1955).
[13] *U.S.* v. *International Boxing Club of New York*, 348 U.S. 236 (1955).
[14] *Toolson* v. *New York Yankees*, 346 U.S. 356 (1953). In holding that professional baseball was not a trade, the court was following an earlier precedent: *Federal Baseball Club of Baltimore* v. *National League*, 259 U.S. 200 (1922).

preme Court ruled that the Sherman Act applied to agreements among insurance companies,[15] Congress, in the McCarran Act of 1945, suspended application of the Sherman Act for three years to give the states an opportunity to establish or strengthen regulation in this area, and provided that thereafter the federal law would apply only to the extent that regulation was not provided by state law. Similarly, efforts to apply the Act to railroad rate bureaus, which set rates for competing railroads, led Congress to enact, over the veto of President Truman, the Reed-Bulwinkle Act of 1948, which exempted the bureaus. As for labor unions, the Supreme Court held that the Act did not apply "so long as a union acts in its self interest and does not combine with non-labor groups." [16]

Problems of Enforcement

Despite the extension of the Act's scope and impact and the greater emphasis on staff investigation of entire industries or whole ranges of practices, the obstacles to effective enforcement of the Act remain formidable. Because of the limited funds available to the Division, and the volume of complaints received by it, in practice most of its actions are taken not on its own initiative, but in response to complaints of competitors, buyers, or suppliers. Consequently, industries in which aggrieved interests have also been intimidated, or in which all concerned, except the impotent consumer, are satisfied with the operations of an illegal scheme of control, are likely to escape Division scrutiny. Furthermore, since funds and staff are available to bring into court only a few of the complaints received, enforcement still tends to be haphazard rather than uniform and sustained.

In addition, many serious problems are involved in the gathering of evidence and the litigation of cases.[17] For evidence in the field, the Division must rely on agents of the Federal Bureau of Investigation, whose training is not primarily in economics. The evidence found is often fragmentary, and records cannot be subpoenaed or testimony compelled until a suit has been initiated.

The trial of a case presents its own hazards. The numbers and compensation of the government's staff are normally dwarfed by the resources available to the defendants. In a criminal suit, the

[15] U.S. v. South-Eastern Underwriters' Assn., 322 U.S. 533 (1944).

[16] U.S. v. Hutcheson, 312 U.S. 219 (1941). For a discussion of labor and the antitrust laws, see above, pp. 174–177.

[17] For a detailed statement of these enforcement problems, see W. Hamilton and I. Till, Antitrust in Action, TNEC Monograph 16 (1940).

case must be proven beyond a reasonable doubt; in a civil action, it must be supported by a preponderance of the evidence. The practices which have been attacked often seem quite normal, and the facts of the case are usually highly technical and complex. An understanding of the issues customarily requires considerable knowledge of the industry's structure and practices and fairly sophisticated economic analysis. These economic issues are explored within the intricate and confining procedure of courtroom combat, where attorneys and judges alike are more learned in law than in economics.[18] Jury members are usually experienced in neither.

The judicial process and the complexity of most antitrust cases combine to produce long delays between the initiation of a suit and its final determination. A suit was filed against the Aluminum Company of America in 1937, but the first district court injunction, after trial and appeal, was not issued until 1950. Moreover, throughout the antitrust enforcement process, the primary issue for public policy is the future organization and practices of an industry, but the litigation is focused on past wrongdoings.

Many of these problems are the inevitable consequences of attempting to define and enforce a policy through judicial application—the price paid for passing a general statute and leaving it to the courts to define precise meanings in specific cases. While the revived Antitrust Division has improved its presentation of cases and persuaded the judges to give substantial weight to economic factors, most of these defects can never be eradicated completely.

Under Arnold's direction, the Division also strengthened the Act's sanctions. The criminal penalties were too light and too infrequently imposed to deter undesirable activities. From 1890 to 1946, while 108 union members, 75 petty racketeers, and 8 wartime spies were jailed for Sherman Act violations, only 7 businessmen received prison sentences, and those were suspended. Nor were severe fines imposed; in 226 cases involving businesses in the same period, the average fine paid by defendants found guilty was only $2,000.[19] Thus the real punishment imposed by a criminal suit lay in defense costs and unfavorable publicity. Doubtless these are sufficient to act as deterrents in many instances, but where the situation calls for an altered structure of

---

[18] In 1950, for the first time, an economist was employed by a district judge to help him analyze the economic aspects of a case (involving the United Shoe Machinery Corporation).

[19] House Committee on Small Business, *U.S. versus Economic Concentration and Monopoly* (Committee Print, 1946), pp. 257–261.

industry, effective remedies cannot be obtained by means of criminal prosecutions.

The Division attempted to classify illegal situations into those where punitive action might suffice and those where monopolistic conditions so pervaded the industry as to require a substantial modification of existing industry practices. For the former, the criminal provisions of the Sherman Act were to be used almost exclusively, on the ground that the sanctions of the injunctive proceedings were an insufficient stimulus to observance. For the latter, the Division announced a policy of seeking "constructive economic solutions," wherever possible through extended use of consent decrees.[20] This policy was an important departure from tradition. In devising these "constructive economic solutions," the Division aimed not so much at restoration of competition as at business policies of a kind which would be engendered if fuller competition were possible. There developed a notion of "workable competition," based on the analysis of particular industry structures and practices and reflecting the newer economic concepts of imperfect and monopolistic competition, which were replacing the conventional dichotomy of pure competition and monopoly.

The injunctions or decrees previously resulting from successful civil antitrust suits had too often failed to accomplish the purposes of the Sherman Act. An injunction forbids certain behavior, and a decree requires that certain actions be taken. The scope and impact of each are limited. They apply only to the parties named and to the particular actions described. Only those practices found to violate the law may be forbidden. They had been most successful when an otherwise reasonably competitive market had been controlled through agreements or by such market devices as exclusive dealing, tying contracts, or price discrimination. In such instances, civil action could successfully attack market restraints in specific industries.

But in more oligopolistic industries, where markets were dominated by a few large firms, the mere outlawing of specific practices or the requiring of a few actions seldom made the industry significantly more competitive in behavior or market results. Here

---

[20] Needless to say, the Division has not always followed this course. In 1946, it won a sweeping criminal victory over the major cigarette companies (see below, pp. 582–583), but it left the industry and the general nature of its practices unchanged. The market sharing and price leadership of which it complained appeared to continue undiminished. W. H. Nicholls, *Price Policies in the Cigarette Industry* (1951), ch. 28.

rigorous application of antitrust policy would require the dissolution of the dominant firm or firms, or the divestiture by them of some of their corporate assets. In practice, however, dissolution has been ordered in relatively few cases. In the pre-Arnold days it had been used to break up combinations in oil, tobacco, gunpowder, meat-packing, corn products, and photographic equipment, and to free Radio Corporation of America from control by General Electric and Westinghouse. The revival of antitrust policy did not bring about a major increase in the use of dissolution decrees, although the Blue Network (now the American Broadcasting Company) was separated from the National Broadcasting Company, the Pullman manufacturing and operating subsidiaries were divorced, the large motion-picture companies were divided into producing and exhibiting companies, and Du Pont was ordered to relinquish its stockholding in General Motors.

Both the Antitrust Division and the courts have been reluctant to invoke the ultimate sanction of dissolution. The judges have sometimes rejected the Division's pleas for dissolution, as in actions against the Aluminum Company, United Shoe Machinery, and General Electric, but the Division itself has rarely requested dissolution, even in cases where the dominance of the companies concerned made the efficacy of other remedies most doubtful. There is a natural hesitation to upset property rights except in cases of flagrant abuse of the law. Even when radical surgery otherwise might appear necessary, the concentration of productive facilities in one plant, as in the case of United Shoe Machinery, or the concentration of output under one brand name, as with the major cigarette manufacturers, may cast doubt on the economic viability of the fractionated successors which would be produced by dissolution. In the 1950 Aluminum Company decree, the court rejected the plea to split the firm on the ground that dividing its research and managerial staff would be harmful to national defense, as well as making it more difficult for the successor firms to compete effectively with other aluminum companies and with producers of other metals.

Under Arnold, however, the Division greatly increased its resort to the consent decree as an alternative method of settling antitrust cases. While this device is not specifically authorized by the Sherman Act, it has been used since 1906 and was implicitly recognized in the Clayton Act. Since the late thirties, by far the largest share of civil suits has ended in such actions. A consent decree is reached by informal, secret bargaining between the government and the defendants. Once an agreement has been reached, it is usually automatically approved by a district court, and then becomes as binding as any other judicial decree or injunction.

The procedure has many advantages. It is much speedier and less expensive than the full course of litigation. Its flexibility permits a more precise shaping of remedies to the structure and practices of a particular industry. Since a consent decree enables a firm to avoid private triple-damage suits under the Sherman and Clayton Acts,[21] the government can often bargain for more far-reaching remedies than would be imposed by the courts. Sometimes remedies first worked out in consent decrees have later been applied by the courts in contested cases, as with the requirement that patents which had been used to further monopoly be licensed royalty-free to other firms.

While civil remedies have thus been strengthened, the Division still lacks the staff or appropriations for more than spot checks on compliance. Reports of noncompliance usually originate from the complaints of aggrieved firms, rather than on the Division's own initiative.

The Division's increased enforcement activities, its dramatization of cases, and its success in persuading the courts to broaden the meaning of the antitrust laws have had a multiplier effect by inducing a vast increase in private triple-damage suits. Since World War II, private suits have been about five times as numerous as government actions.

2. The "New" Sherman Act

Antitrust policy peculiarly depends on the positive support of all three branches of government. While administration leadership persuaded Congress to increase antitrust appropriations, thereby permitting more vigorous enforcement, the Division's most significant gains were registered in judicial redefinitions of the policy itself. In the main, these gains reflect the Division's success in persuading the courts to apply criteria of market structure as well as criteria of corporate behavior and intent in their interpretations of the Sherman Act. This greater reliance on economic analysis of markets characterizes recent decisions in many aspects of antitrust policy, but it is most sharply seen in cases dealing with monopoly

[21] The Clayton Act states that "a final judgment or decree in any antitrust case," to the effect that a defendant has violated said laws, "is *prima facie* evidence of illegal action" in a private suit. Consent decrees and judgments on a plea of *nolo contendere*, however, have been held not to be "a final judgment or decree."

and oligopoly.

The shift in the criteria for evaluating monopoly and restraint of trade has had major effects on the rule of reason. Where that doctrine had emphasized predatory practices as evidence of an intent to monopolize or unreasonably to restrain trade, the new trend in antitrust interpretation lays stress on such economic data as prices and shares of market. It has tried to eliminate the rule of reason's implied distinction between close consolidations and loose combinations, and has partially avoided the question of reasonableness by outlawing certain practices and arrangements per se.

Monopoly and Oligopoly

While the Madison Oil decision of 1940 [22] was a halfway house between these two stages in antitrust enforcement, it was the Alcoa decision of 1945 which clearly marked the beginning of a new era. The case had been initiated in 1937 by a government suit charging that the Aluminum Company of America had violated Section 2 of the Sherman Act by monopolizing the manufacture of virgin aluminum and the sale of various aluminum products. The government asked that Alcoa be split up. After a trial that lasted more than two years, the company was found by the district court not to have violated the law, but the decision of the circuit court, which in this case had the effect of a Supreme Court ruling, went against Alcoa.[23]

In this decision, Judge Learned Hand, speaking for the court, declared monopolization illegal per se, thus apparently erasing the rule of reason from such cases and removing the distinction between close consolidations and loose combinations. He found that Alcoa controlled over 90 per cent of virgin aluminum production,[24] which "percentage is enough to constitute a monopoly; it is doubtful whether sixty or sixty-four per cent would be enough; and certainly thirty-three per cent is not." The mere

[22] Discussed above, pp. 476–477.

[23] U.S. v. Aluminum Co. of America, 44 F. Supp. 97 (1942); 148 F. 2d 416 (1945). So many justices disqualified themselves because of prior connections with the prosecution of the case that the Supreme Court could not muster a quorum of six with which to hear the appeal. Consequently, Congress amended the judicial code so as to enable a circuit court to function, in such circumstances, as the court of last resort.

[24] This percentage was based on a much-criticized definition of the relevant market. It excluded scrap, which does compete with ingot, and included the ingot which Alcoa itself consumed. Had scrap been included, Alcoa's share would have been 60 to 64 per cent; had consumption of its own ingots been excluded, its share would have been 33 per cent.

existence of such a monopoly, Hand continued, gave the firm as much or more power to fix prices than an illegal combination or contract among several firms, and "it would be absurd to condemn such contracts unconditionally, and not to extend the condemnation to monopolies; for the contracts are only steps toward that entire control which monopoly confers; they are really partial monopolies."

Thus the old double standard was rejected. Furthermore, the ruling of the Steel and Harvester cases that the mere existence of monopoly power, if unexercised, was no offense was explicitly repudiated. The distinction between exercised and unexercised power "is . . . purely formal; it would be valid only so long as the monopoly remained wholly inert; it would disappear as soon as the monopoly began to operate; for, when it did—that is, as soon as it began to sell at all—it must sell at some price and the only price at which it could sell is a price which it itself fixed. Thereafter the power and its exercise must needs coalesce."

It is true that the Act forbids monopolization and attempts to monopolize rather than the fact of monopoly as such, Hand continued, but monopoly was not "thrust upon" Alcoa; the fact that Alcoa expanded with the market and so maintained its position and power is enough to constitute the offense of monopolizing. Alcoa "insists that it has never really excluded competitors; but we can think of no more effective exclusion than progressively to embrace each new opportunity as it opened, and to face each newcomer with new capacity already geared into a great organization, having the advantage of experience, trade connections, and the elite of personnel." Nor is it necessary to prove any specific intent to monopolize, "for no monopolist monopolizes unconscious of what he is doing. So here, 'Alcoa' meant to keep and did keep, that complete and exclusive hold upon the ingot market with which it started. That was to 'monopolize' that market, however innocently it otherwise proceeded."

Thus the fact of monopoly was equated with the offense of monopolization, and it was irrelevant whether the monopoly power had been abused. Congress "did not condone 'good trusts' and condemn 'bad' ones; it forbade all." [25] Nor was economic efficiency a sufficient defense, for it was Congress's "belief that

[25] Alcoa was found to have abused its powers in the past by such tactics as "squeezing" independent fabricators through narrowing the spread between the ingot prices it charged them and the prices it set on fabricated products. These practices had apparently been abandoned, and the court emphasized that Alcoa had violated the Sherman Act "regardless of such practices."

great industrial consolidations are inherently undesirable, regardless of their economic result," and one of Congress's "purposes was to perpetuate and preserve, for its own sake and in spite of possible cost, an organization of industry in small units which can effectively compete with each other." Excessive size itself, then, as measured by share of the market, was illegal.

The Alcoa decision thus sweepingly revised and discarded previous doctrines, but the force and scope of the precedent it established were at first uncertain. While it had been enunciated by the court of last resort in that proceeding, it lacked the authority of a Supreme Court decision. Moreover, it applied directly only to the rare case of a monopoly, and not, on its face, to the far more frequent phenomenon of an oligopolistic industry, where the market is dominated not by one firm but by a "Big Three," "Big Four," or "Big Five."

These two uncertainties were short lived. In the following year, in an equally sweeping decision in the second American Tobacco case, the Supreme Court explicitly endorsed the Alcoa doctrine and applied it to monopolization by three sellers.[26] This was in many respects an extreme decision, which appeared to simplify greatly the task of proving antitrust violations. While the Court has never disclaimed the Tobacco decision, the history of subsequent cases is largely one of qualifying and softening it. The case is probably best explained as an effort of the Court to reverse sharply the trend of previous close-consolidation cases since 1913 and as a reflection of its willingness to accept what it thought were the relevant economic criteria.

The case arose out of a criminal suit against the three leading cigarette producers. A jury had found them guilty on the basis of identical selling prices for cigarettes, identical buying prices for tobacco, and common pricing and purchasing tactics designed to squeeze the so-called 10-cent cigarette producers by raising the prices of tobacco and lowering the prices of the Big Three cigarettes. In sustaining this verdict, the Supreme Court repeated the Alcoa condemnation of monopoly per se and applied it to oligopolists acting in concert. "The material considerations in determining whether a monopoly exists is not that prices are raised and that competition is excluded, but that power exists to raise prices or to exclude competition when it is desired to do so." In fact, the tactics of the Big Three had been unsuccessful, and their share of the market had fallen from over 90 per cent in 1931 to 68 per cent in 1939, but the Court held that "neither proof of

[26] *American Tobacco Co.* v. *U.S.*, 328 U.S. 781 (1946).

exertion of the power to exclude nor proof of actual exclusion of existing or potential competitors is essential to sustain a charge of monopolization under the Sherman Act."

This condemnation of *"the power to abuse* rather than the *abuse of power"* [27] simplified the task of proving an antitrust violation. No specific intent to monopolize had to be shown. More than this, no proof of an explicit agreement among the Big Three was required. Statistics which showed that the companies bought and sold at identical prices and purchased fixed shares of the supply were accepted as sufficient proof of an illegal agreement. "The essential combination or conspiracy in violation of the Sherman Act," said the Court, "may be found in a course of dealings or other circumstances as well as in any exchange of words." Under this doctrine, conscious parallelism of action in an oligopolistic market may be held to be an illegal conspiracy.

From this decision flow three main currents—illegality of monopoly power per se, conscious parallelism of action as an illegal restraint of trade, and judicial reliance on economic data and criteria—each of which passes through and connects later decisions despite their tendency to soften the Tobacco case doctrine. These currents intermingle, and none can be completely isolated. One common factor, however, is the penetration of law by economics. This has led the judges to re-examine previous antitrust precedents and to redefine competition, monopoly, and restraint of trade by laying greater stress on economic results, performance, and market structure in place of the traditional tests of predatory practices or particular forms of anticompetitive agreement.

Basing-Point Pricing

One of the best illustrations of this new judicial respect for economic analysis is to be found in the antitrust cases dealing with basing-point pricing systems. This experience also demonstrates some of the difficulties inherent in interpretation of the "New" Sherman Act.

As shown in Chapter 15, basing-point systems, although operating in steel and cement at the beginning of the century and long the subject of political attack by consumers in the West and the South, enjoyed virtual immunity from the antitrust laws until after World War II. These systems had little to fear from the earlier interpretation of the antitrust laws. Predatory practices

[27] This phrase is that of H. Koontz and R. W. Gable, *Public Control of Economic Enterprise* (1956), p. 340.

584 PROMOTION AND REGULATION OF COMPETITION

were usually avoided; competition was gentlemanly; and individual
competitors were apparently protected rather than abused. Nor
were the economic implications of basing points well understood
for some decades, least of all by the Antitrust Division and the
courts. The Division had failed to attack Pittsburgh-plus pricing in
the Big Steel case of 1920. In the Cement case of 1925, the government did not attack a basing-point system as an agreement to fix
prices; the Supreme Court considered the identical prices actually
charged to be a result of vigorous competition and held the
system not in restraint of trade.[28]

The difficulties of the authorities in deciding how basing-point
systems should stand in relation to antitrust policy was natural
enough, since they involve both competitive and monopolistic
elements. Under the usual arrangement, one or more localities are
designated as basing points. A uniform base price is established
for each such point. A delivered price to any seller is then determined by adding to the base price at the nearest basing point
the cost of transportation, usually by rail, from that point to the
buyer. Since all sellers, wherever located and whatever their actual
transportation costs, use the same base prices and the same freight
charges, they all quote identical delivered prices.

It follows that there is no price competition whatsoever in
delivered prices offered the buyer. Yet when sellers at different
distances from the buyer bid for his order, their net prices (delivered price less actual freight charges) may vary greatly. Thus
sellers compete for orders, but a buyer finds no price competition.
He confronts identical bids, but an individual seller discriminates
in net price among his buyers. The system protects a plant at a
basing point from being undersold by plants not at basing points
and nearer to buyers, but the latter plants are given an advantage
in net price, since their delivered prices include an allowance for
"phantom freight" not actually incurred. The system makes it
easier for a dominant firm to set prices for the industry, but it also
protects smaller firms from predatory pricing practices. A competitive market would also tend toward identity in prices, but the
identical delivered prices of a basing-point system result from an
agreement not to compete in delivered prices.

These systems are usually resorted to by industries whose members believe, with considerable justification, that unrestrained
competition would be ruinous. "The truth is," wrote one frank,
if imprudent, trustee of the Cement Institute to another in 1932,
"that ours is an industry above all others that cannot stand free

[28] *Cement Manufacturers' Protective Assn.* v. *U.S.*, 268 U.S. 588.

competition, that must systematically restrain competition or be ruined." [29] Basing-point systems are used primarily in industries combining standardization of product, heavy investment, and high transportation costs. When products are standardized, competition is mainly a matter of price. When investment is large, and the proportion of fixed to variable costs is high, then under adverse market conditions, especially in depressions, unrestrained competition tends to drive prices down to the level of variable costs, failing to provide a return on investment. The slowness with which large investments can be made, or retired, makes it hard for supply to match changes in demand, and prices fluctuate widely. The necessity of heavy investment also tends to limit the number of firms, making the industry oligopolistic. When transportation charges are a large proportion of delivered prices, effective markets are highly imperfect. Each plant has a natural monopoly in its nearby market area, which other plants can enter only by a substantial lowering of their net price. In such circumstances, unrestrained competition in times of strong demand would give each isolated producer a natural local monopoly, while in bad times competition would become destructive, wiping out capital as prices dropped toward the level of variable costs. Industries reflecting these factors include steel, cement, sugar, lumber, wood pulp, and lead.

In such industries, basing-point systems cannot be evaluated on the assumption that pure competition is a viable alternative form of organization and pattern of operation. The task of public policy, then, is to decide which elements of competition are essential either to prevent abuses of power or to produce the most desirable results.

Abuse of power to injure weaker firms within the industry has seldom been a major issue. Basing-point systems require substantial industrial self-government, for they are not the automatic consequence of the economic factors just discussed. Individual firms must all abide by the rules, and particular care must be taken to ensure that delivered prices are fully identical. The same freight rates must be used in computations; customers must be denied the option of buying at the mill and providing their own transportation; and such matters as credit terms and allowances for the return of containers must be uniform. Usually such restraints are accepted as being in the long-run self-interest of each

[29] *Aetna Portland Cement Co.* v. *FTC*, 157 F. 2d 533 (1946), Respondent's Brief, p. 127, as cited in Clair Wilcox, *Public Policies Toward Business* (1955), p. 214.

producer, the very size of whose investment compels him to forego quick profits for more permanent stability. It is true that industry associations have occasionally punished price-cutters by severe penalties, such as making a maverick's plant a special basing point with a punitively low base price,[30] but the basing-point industries, being comparatively orderly, have usually been able to avoid such naked exercises of power.

The economic results of basing-point systems are more controversial. It is sometimes charged that basing points tend to encourage excessive industry capacity, but neither economic analysis nor an examination of the relevant industries clearly confirms or refutes this charge. This method of pricing discourages the entry or growth of firms in non-basing-point areas, but the related effects of price leadership and protection against severe price declines appear, as in the steel industry, to have encouraged entry in general and diluted industry concentration. The impact on manufacturing costs and efficiency is also unclear.

Effects on transportation costs and industrial location, however, are evident. Since sellers can compete in distant markets and buyers do not pay for actual freight, unnecessary transportation is encouraged and transportation costs have been much higher than necessary. Wasteful cross-hauling may take place in which products made in one plant are shipped to buyers close to another plant while similar products are traversing the same route in reverse. Buyers have no incentive to use cheaper forms of transportation, since they must in any event pay delivered prices based on rail freight. The system also encourages geographical concentration and retards the relocation of industry. Buyers, such as steel fabricators, who convert basing-point priced materials into final products, must compare their freight costs on materials and on products; when the former are higher, these buyers tend to locate around basing points, even though there may be sellers at non-basing points. Despite locational changes in demand, producers at basing points are protected from price competition by closer sellers in servicing distant buyers. While the prospects of collecting for phantom freight may attract a smaller producer to a

[30] The Supreme Court cited an example in its Cement Institute decision: "In one instance, where a producer had made a low public bid, a punitive base point price was put on its plant and cement was reduced 10¢ per barrel; further reductions quickly followed until the base price . . . dropped to 75¢ per barrel. . . . Within six weeks . . . capitulation occurred and the recalcitrant joined a Portland Cement Association. Cement in that locality then bounced back to $1.15, later to $1.35, and finally to $1.75." FTC v. Cement Institute, 333 U.S. 683 (1948).

non-basing point, the fear that his plant might then be made a basing point may deter him.

Antitrust Action Against Basing Points

Clearly, the antitrust laws could not readily be applied to such systems without some sophistication in both economic concepts and goals of competitive policy. Moreover, action on this front involves substantial political repercussions because of the impact of basing-point pricing on industrial location. Existing firms and more developed regions had an enormous stake in the maintenance of the status quo, while other areas, notably the West and South, saw that the system was delaying their industrial development.

A basing-point system could be questioned under the antitrust laws in several ways. The Antitrust Division might attack it as a collusive agreement, a conspiracy in restraint of trade condemned by Section 1 of the Sherman Act. If the system had been imposed on the industry by a dominant firm, then it could be attacked under Section 2 as an attempt to monopolize. In addition, the FTC could attack the practice under Section 5 of its Act as an unfair method of competition. Finally, either agency could charge that the system involved price discrimination which injured competition and so violated Section 2 of the Clayton Act as amended by the Robinson-Patman Act.

Despite the earlier failures, the FTC, encouraged by the success of the antitrust action against the Sugar Institute,[31] began in the late thirties a broad campaign against basing-point pricing in a number of industries. The preparation and prosecution of these cases demonstrated more economic sophistication and more careful delineation of these pricing schemes and their effects than had characterized earlier proceedings. The campaign was initiated in 1937 with a complaint against the Cement Institute and seventy-four cement producers, which led to the issuance of a cease and desist order in 1943. Other orders were directed against producers of corn products, malt, milk cans, crepe paper, rigid steel conduits, and bottle caps. In 1947, the citadel of basing points was attacked with a complaint against the American Iron and Steel Institute and 101 steel producers.

The first case to reach the Supreme Court focused on the price-discrimination aspects of the system. In 1945, the Court held that two glucose producers, by their use of a single basing-point system, had discriminated among their customers, collecting phantom

[31] See above, pp. 481–484.

freight on some sales and absorbing freight on others.[32] This discrimination had injured competition among their customers—candy manufacturers—and so had violated the Clayton and Robinson-Patman Acts. Nor could these prices be defended as having been made "in good faith to meet the equally low prices of a competitor," for they were part of a system and not tailored to meet a specific situation.

The illegality of a single basing-point system having thus been determined, the next issue for judicial decision was collective adherence to multiple basing-point systems. Decisions in the lower courts were mixed. In three cases, common adherence to basing-point systems was held not only to be contrary to the Clayton Act but also to be an agreement to avoid competition and hence an unfair method of competition under the FTC Act.[33] In a fourth case, however, the same behavior was held not in violation of the FTC Act and the price discrimination clause.[34] In 1948, the Supreme Court determined the issue unequivocally, ruling that collective adherence to such a basing-point system constituted a common effort to maintain uniform prices and terms of sale. It thereby violated the FTC Act and was also unlawful under the Robinson-Patman Act, the good-faith proviso not applying since prices were matched "as a practice rather than as a good faith effort to meet individually competitive situations." [35]

In a subsequent series of cases, the FTC charged, and the courts agreed, that "the concurrent use of a formula method of making delivered price quotations with the knowledge that each did likewise" in itself violated the FTC Act, without the necessity of showing that an explicit agreement existed.[36] Thus the doctrine of conscious parallelism of action was applied to condemn common adherence to a basing-point system. While these cases were brought under the FTC Act, the decisions made basing points equally liable to action under the Sherman Act. The basing-point

[32] *Corn Products Refining Co.* v. *FTC*, 324 U.S. 726; *FTC* v. *A. E. Staley Mfg. Co.*, 324 U.S. 746.

[33] *U.S. Maltsters Assn.* v. *FTC*, 152 F. 2d 161 (1945); *Milk and Ice Cream Can Institute* v. *FTC*, 152 F. 2d 478 (1946); *Fort Howard Paper Co.*, v. *FTC*, 156 F. 2d 899 (1946).

[34] *Cement Institute* v. *FTC*, 157 F. 2d 533 (1946).

[35] *FTC* v. *Cement Institute*, 333 U.S. 683.

[36] *Triangle Conduit & Cable Co.* v. *FTC*, 168 F. 2d 157 (1948). This decision was appealed to the Supreme Court but allowed to stand when that body divided 4 to 4 and issued no opinion. *Clayton Mark & Co.* v. *FTC.*, 336 U.S. 956 (1949). For a similar decision, see *Bond Crown & Cork Co.* v. *FTC*, 176 F. 2d 974 (1949).

industries were forced to capitulate. In 1948, U.S. Steel agreed to put into effect the order first issued by the FTC in 1924. Three years later, the other steel companies bowed to an order forbidding joint adherence to a basing-point system.

Having lost their legal battle, the basing-point industries counterattacked on the political front by seeking to persuade Congress to reverse these judicial decisions. In 1948 and 1949, hearings before a friendly Senate subcommittee were used to protest the FTC orders and court rulings. Then, because of the apparent impossibility of winning approval for a bill which would directly legalize basing points, a substitute measure was proposed requiring proof of a probability that such schemes would lessen competition (thereby reversing the Morton Salt decision),[37] permitting individual adherence to basing-point pricing except as part of a "combination, conspiracy, or collusive agreement" (thereby attempting to prevent application of the doctrine of conscious parallelism of action), and expanding the exemption provided by the good-faith competition clause (thereby reversing parts of the basing-point decisions and the lower court's decision in the Standard of Indiana case). The net effect would have been to enable industries to use basing points, provided that their methods of securing agreement and compliance were reasonably discreet. The measure passed the House early in 1949, but its opponents in the Senate fought a strong delaying action. It passed the Senate in 1950 but was vetoed by President Truman.

In 1951, new tactics were adopted. A measure was drafted which on its face seemed only to reaffirm the Supreme Court's ruling in the Standard of Indiana case [38] that the good-faith competition clause provided a substantive defense to a charge of price discrimination. The committee report accompanying this bill, however, stated that identical delivered prices were legal under a system in which each producer was a basing point, and that no conspiracy could be inferred from the price identity. This indirect attempt to legalize one type of basing-point system passed the Senate but was not reported out of the House committee. Similar measures in the following years made no headway.

Some part of what the basing-point industries lost in the courts and failed to regain in Congress, however, has been restored to them by the FTC. In recent years, turning its back on the powers proffered it by the Morton Salt decision, the Commission has limited its intervention to those practices which make it probable,

[37] See above, pp. 555–556.
[38] See above, pp. 557–558.

rather than merely possible, that competition will be injured.[39] The Commission similarly seems to have adopted the view that conscious parallelism of action alone is insufficient evidence of conspiracy.[40] Thus, if recent precedents prevail, the FTC may be less likely to attack some types of basing-point systems in the future, especially if an industry's agreement to employ the method is tacit and if its enforcement machinery is not obtrusive.

While on the whole beneficial in terms of competition and efficiency, the results of the FTC assault on basing-point systems are somewhat ambiguous. This fact is attributable as much to inherent market imperfections and the difficulty of defining clear criteria for competitive policy as to the inadequacy of FTC orders as remedies for noncompetitive market situations. Despite some confusion in statements by Commission members and staff, all that the FTC orders forbade was collective adherence to rigid pricing systems and absorption of freight, or collection of phantom freight, where injury to competition resulted. Otherwise, in the absence of tacit or explicit collusion, firms were free to choose their pricing methods, to absorb freight, and to match prices as they saw fit.

The major industries affected, steel and cement, in 1948 adopted f.o.b. pricing, under which the buyer pays freight charges and chooses his method of transportation. Under the conditions of booming demand then prevailing, the producers lost nothing by this action. Where before they had absorbed freight on a majority of their orders, now their base prices were their net prices. When demand for steel slackened in 1953, U.S. Steel announced that it would again absorb freight, and the other steel companies followed. But absorption was limited to those sales where it was necessary to enable a producer to match prices in distant markets. As demand continued to drop, absorption increased. Thus, the present system is a blend of f.o.b. and delivered pricing. It is

[39] See above, pp. 556–557.

[40] The Supreme Court, too, has weakened this doctrine. While lower courts applied it to basing-point systems, and in 1948 the Supreme Court applied it to the acceptance of identical license provisions by patent licensees (*U.S.* v. *Line Material Co.*, 333 U.S. 287; *U.S.* v. *U.S. Gypsum Co.*, 333 U.S. 364), in 1953 it declared: "This Court has never held that proof of parallel business behavior conclusively established agreement or, phrased differently, that such behavior itself constitutes a Sherman Act offense. Circumstantial evidence of consciously parallel behavior may have made heavy inroads into the traditional judicial attitude toward conspiracy; but conscious parallelism has not yet read conspiracy out of the Sherman Act entirely." *Theater Enterprises, Inc.* v. *Paramount Film Distributing Corp.*, 346 U.S. 537.

unlikely, however, that uniform delivered pricing will ever again be the rule. Most steel is now delivered by trucks, much of it by contract and private carriers, whose rates are not published. Many of the wastes and rigidities of the old system have been erased, as have been some of the barriers to economic relocation of industry.

Despite the ambiguities of the present system, the uncertainties with which it confronts business firms in their price policies, and the problems of determining, not to mention evaluating, present practices, it is probable that there is now about as much competition in pricing as is viable under existing circumstances. This situation appears preferable to either extreme alternative.[41] Even systematic freight equalization, which makes every producer a basing point and so eliminates phantom freight, encourages distributive wastes, maintains rigid price uniformity, and rules out all price competition. Complete f.o.b. pricing, which would eliminate freight wastes and encourage industrial relocation, tends to establish regional monopolies and prevents the use of selective price discrimination to inject a degree of real competition into the market. F.o.b. pricing modified by selective freight absorption appears to offer an optimum combination of these goals, promoting relocation but making best use of existing capacity, preventing market sharing, and working against rigid pricing. In short, in this area the major limits on the ability of antitrust policy to restore competition have been less legal and political than economic; they are inherent in the structure of certain industries.

Patents and Antitrust Policy

A major campaign of the Antitrust Division to apply the Sherman Act to the area of patents was more sure-footed in its approach and more concrete in its results. While there are inescapable difficulties in making the optimum reconciliation between the patent system and a competitive structure of industry, by the late thirties economists were virtually unanimous in the opinion that the American patent system as then operating was unduly fostering monopolistic restraints. Spurred on by TNEC revelations of specific patent abuses, the Antitrust Division succeeded in persuading the courts to make major revisions in their attitude toward patent privileges and to adopt new civil remedies designed to restore competition in patent-ridden industries.

The Constitution specifically empowers Congress "To promote the progress of Science and useful Arts, by securing for limited Times to Authors and Inventors the exclusive Right to their re-

[41] See discussion in Wilcox, *op. cit.*, pp. 221–224.

spective Writings and Discoveries." In 1790, Congress enacted the nation's first patent law, protecting inventors who registered new and useful processes and devices. Beginning in 1793, the State Department issued patents to all who registered, without determining the novelty or usefulness of the inventions. This policy led to a mountain of patents on devices which were anything but useful or novel. The courts were inundated with litigation over the validity of issued patents. Consequently, in a law of 1836 which still serves as the framework for the patent system, Congress established a Commissioner of Patents and a Patent Office. The Commissioner was directed to issue patents only after a determination that the inventions were new and were "sufficiently useful and important."

In its statutory terms, American public policy is more generous in its grant of patent privileges than is that of most other countries. Patents may be taken out on processes of production, devices used in production, and the goods produced, including foods and medicines. The patent grant extends for seventeen years, and during that period the patentee need not use the patent; he may license others to use it on whatever terms he chooses; or he may refuse to license it at all.

This statutory generosity is paralleled by administrative inadequacies. The Patent Office lacks the staff, facilities, and appropriations with which carefully to scrutinize applications. No attempt is made to determine whether the alleged invention really works. It is presumed to be useful unless it appears likely to be positively harmful.[42] The main test of the Patent Office examiner is the novelty of the alleged invention. Accordingly, it is compared with earlier patents, and scientific publications may be searched, but a TNEC monograph pointed out the inadequacy of even this procedure:

. . . a hurried survey, in terms of mechanical likeness to what has gone before, is the most that can be given. . . . The group of examiners has annually to pass upon a minimum of 60,000 applications, a load which runs to 12 per person per week. . . . the usual item involves an extended research into an intricate body of technology, yet only a few hours can be given to it. . . . The examiner can note the claim, glance at the specifications, conduct a casual inquiry, draw

[42] The Office still follows the interpretation of Justice Story in 1817 in which he ruled that the word "useful is incorporated in the Act in contradistinction to mischievous or immoral." *Lowell* v. *Lewis*, 15 Fed. Cases 1018.

upon his experience for anything in point, and allow or reject the application. If he certifies a true invention, the patent issues, without appeal, review, or further ado. . . .[43]

Thus, grants of patents, and of the monopoly privileges inherent in them, are made liberally. In recent years, more than fifty thousand have been issued annually. Furthermore, since the Patent Office usually takes about three years to process an application, the grants really extend for twenty or more years rather than seventeen. To be sure, they confer no absolute privileges; they can be enforced only through the courts; the patentee must himself bring suit to enjoin, and seek damages for, the use of his invention without his permission. In such a suit, the defendant may reply with a patent of his own or the claim that the patent is invalid, and it will be the task of the courts to make a final determination of validity.

It is true that the judges have increasingly voided patents. From 1900 to 1945, the Supreme Court actually held to be invalid a majority of the patents litigated before it—a harsh commentary on the effectiveness of Patent Office procedures.[44] In a case in 1950, Justice Douglas commented on the difference between the judicial and administrative standards of invention: "The fact that a patent as flimsy and as spurious as this one has to be brought all the way to this Court to be declared invalid dramatically illustrates how far our patent system frequently departs from the constitutional standards which are supposed to govern." [45] But litigation is costly; patents are rarely brought into the courts; and the overwhelming proportion are accepted at face value.

Furthermore, a policy designed to encourage individual inventors has had many unanticipated consequences in an age in which the corporate organization of business has profoundly altered the process and significance of invention. An invention today is usually the result of the organized effort of a number of specialists using complex and costly equipment, the product of a corporate research

[43] W. Hamilton, *Patents and Free Enterprise*, TNEC Monograph No. 31 (1941), p. 125.

[44] Of the 109 patent infringement suits considered by the Court in this period, 26 involved patents which were held to be valid and to have been infringed, 23 dealt with patents found to be valid but not infringed, and in 60 cases the patents were found to be invalid. E. B. Inlow, *The Patent Grant* (1950), pp. 142–143.

[45] *Great Atlantic & Pacific Tea Co. v. Supermarket Equipment Corp.*, 340 U.S. 147.

program. Of the patents issued between 1939 and 1955, corporations received 60 per cent, with fifty firms receiving about 20 per cent.[46] An individual may be given the credit, and the patent is issued in his name, but the discovery is in fact a social product and the patent is normally assigned automatically to the corporation employing the researcher.

The patent system still plays a useful role. Patent privileges encourage corporate investment in research and in the development and production of new products. There is much validity to the argument that it is the expectation of exploiting temporary monopoly positions which encourages technological innovation and makes the economy dynamic. But the patent system can also lead to corporate benefits unaccompanied by any social gains. The abuses of the patent system are many, but most of them have in common an effort to extend the monopoly grant.

This grant may be extended in time by withdrawing and amending a patent application while it is pending in the Patent Office. The same end may be served by dividing a basic invention into several parts and applying for several patents over a period of years, or by developing and patenting improvements. Thus, the Hartford-Empire group's patents, which controlled a machine used in the manufacture of glass containers, were held pending for fifteen years and then issued successively over twelve years, thereby converting the statutory seventeen-year grant into one of forty-four years.

Because of the laxity of Patent Office procedure, patent privileges may be taken out on products and processes which are not significantly new discoveries, thereby blocking off competition. As the productivity of patent attorneys exceeds that of inventors, the volume of such pseudo-patents has been great indeed, perhaps comprising a majority of all patents issued.[47] The Johns-Manville Corporation for example, gained a legal monopoly over the insulation of previously constructed buildings by patenting a process for blowing mineral wool between the inner and outer walls—a patent which, in the words of one commentator, "applied, not to the manufacture of the wool itself, nor to the machinery used in

[46] *Business Week* (January 26, 1957), p. 149.

[47] One patent attorney has concluded from his own experience that the overwhelming proportion of patents would not stand up in court. "Out of one hundred patents, ninety can be discarded with little more than a cursory examination. Of the remaining, nine will not withstand a strict examination. This leaves, at the most, one patent that has more than a fighting chance of being declared enforceable." D. G. Cullen, "The General Lawyer and Patent Problems," *Lawyers Guild Review* (September 1946), pp. 585–589.

blowing it, but to . . . the idea of blowing through a hole." [48]

The monopoly privileges conferred by the patent may be extended to other goods or processes. Thus, as we have seen, United Shoe Machinery would lease one of its patented machines to a shoe manufacturer only on condition that he also obtain other machinery and supplies from that firm. American Can, Continental Can, and International Business Machines pursued similar policies. The patent monopoly may also be extended vertically to control other stages of production and distribution. The patents of Hartford-Empire covered only the machinery used in making glass containers, but they enabled that group to control the production and sale of glass containers as well. Similarly, Ethyl Gasoline Corporation's patent on tetraethyl lead was employed in an effort to maintain gasoline prices.

The patents amassed by a single corporation or group of corporations may provide the means of dominating a whole industry, commanding all methods of producing a range of goods. Other firms may then enter the industry only with the permission and on the terms set by the patent holders. Thus, in two suits filed against the Radio Corporation of America in 1954 and 1958, the government charged that that firm's control of more than ten thousand radio, television, and related patents had enabled it to monopolize those industries and to stifle independent research and development. Competitors wanting a license under any one RCA patent had to accept "package licenses" covering all RCA patents. Package licenses restricted the end use of products made under the patents and required that royalties be computed on the basis of the sales price of completed products without regard to the proportion of patented and unpatented components which went into them. A competitor, it was alleged, had the choice of accepting RCA domination and paying full royalties, or undertaking the Herculean task of "inventing around" the roadblock of RCA patents.[49] And in numerous other industries many of the patent

[48] Wilcox, op. cit., p. 144. See also Clair Wilcox, *Competition and Monopoly in American Industry*, TNEC Monograph No. 21 (1940), pp. 161–163.

[49] Late in 1958, these suits were concluded with the imposition of a fine of $100,000 and the acceptance of a consent decree by which RCA was required: (1) to make all of its radio and black-and-white TV patents (numbering some ten thousand) available without charge to the whole industry; (2) to place its color TV patents (about one hundred in number) in an open pool, available on free license to any other firm joining the pool; and (3) to license at reasonable royalties all new patents it received in the next ten years.

applications filed and some of the research performed are in furtherance of patent warfare among corporations:

> The great research laboratories are only incidentally technological centers. From the business standpoint they are patent factories; they manufacture the raw material of monopoly. Their product is often nothing but a "shot-gun," a basis for threatening infringement suits and scaring off competitors; or a "scare-crow," a patent which itself represents little or no contribution but seems . . . to cover an important part of a developing art and hence permits threat of suit.[50]

Litigation is an important weapon in patent warfare. Infringement suits greatly contributed to the market dominance achieved by the Bell System, National Cash Register, United Shoe Machinery, and Eastman Kodak. Since such suits are expensive, the outcome may depend more on the resources, legal and otherwise, of the contestants than on the merits of the case. Thus, in a legal struggle between Eastman Kodak and the Boston Camera Company, begun in 1894, Kodak was finally adjudged to have infringed Boston's patents, but by then the latter company had been economically defeated and absorbed into Kodak.[51] Legal and economic inequality, as well as large research laboratories, may contribute to the concentration of effective patent privileges in the hands of the bigger corporations.

When the contest is among large corporations, however, the outcome is more often cross-licensing or pooling arrangements. These arrangements vary greatly in purpose and effect. An open patent pool, as in the automobile industry, where patents covering all but the newest inventions are open to all without payment or subject to reasonable royalties, encourages entry into the industry and the speedy adoption of technical improvements, while discouraging infringement suits. But pooling arrangements may also be used to restrict entry, divide markets, retard innovations, and fix prices.

Even before the revival of antitrust enforcement in the late thirties, the courts had somewhat limited the extension of patent

---

[50] A. E. Kahn, "Fundamental Deficiencies of the American Patent Law," *American Economic Review* (1940), vol. 30, pp. 475–491. An internal policy memorandum of Hartford-Empire described its policy as one of applying for patents intended "to block the development of machines which might be constructed by others for the same purpose as our machines, using alternative means" and for other patents "on possible improvements of competing machines so as to 'fence in' those and to prevent their reaching an improved stage." Wilcox, *Public Policies Toward Business*, p. 74.

[51] Hamilton, *op. cit.*, p. 47.

privileges designed to cripple competition. Under the Clayton Act, the Supreme Court forbade a firm enjoying market dominance because of a patent monopoly to employ tying contracts so as to force buyers of the patented product also to buy unpatented goods.[52] It had condemned patent pools which enabled members to restrict output, fix prices, and determine the channels of distribution.[53] It had also held that once title to a patented product passed to a buyer the patentee had no further control over it.[54]

Nevertheless, as the TNEC studies showed, American industry was shot through with serious restraints on competition exercised by individual patent-owning corporations or by combinations of firms. The overwhelming majority of these restraints had never been questioned under the antitrust laws. Lack of effective enforcement had been one reason. Another was that the courts had rather consistently upheld the power of a patentee to include restrictive provisions in patent licenses. The Supreme Court so held before the Sherman Act,[55] and in 1902 it ruled that the Act did not impair this power.[56] It permitted patentees to restrict the output [57] and the markets of licensees.[58] The widest patent breach in the antitrust laws, however, was opened by the General Electric decision in 1926.[59]

This case raised two major issues. The first was the power of a

---

[52] E.g., *United Shoe Machinery Corp.* v. *U.S.*, 258 U.S. 451 (1922); *Carbice Corp.* v. *American Patents Development Corp.*, 283 U.S. 27 (1931); *International Business Machines Corp.* v. *U.S.*, 298 U.S. 131 (1936). See above, pp. 499–500.

[53] *Standard Sanitary Mfg. Co.* v. *U.S.*, 226 U.S. 20 (1912). See also *U.S.* v. *Motion Picture Patents Co.*, 247 U.S. 524 (1918). In 1931, the Court tolerated a patent pool covering methods of "cracking" gasoline because the pool's ability to fix prices was limited by competition. It controlled only about one-half of the supply of cracked gasoline and only about one-fourth of all gasoline. *Standard Oil Co. (Indiana)* v. *U.S.*, 283 U.S. 163.

[54] E.g., *Bloomer* v. *Millinger*, 1 Wall 340 (1863); *Bauer* v. *O'Donnell*, 229 U.S. 1 (1913); *Strauss* v. *Victor Talking Machine Co.*, 243 U.S. 490 (1917).

[55] *Mitchell* v. *Hawley*, 16 Wall 544 (1872); *Adams* v. *Burke*, 17 Wall 543 (1873).

[56] "The very object of these [patent] laws is monopoly, and the rule is, with few exceptions, that any conditions which are not in their very nature illegal . . . will be upheld by the courts. The fact that the conditions in the contract keep up the monopoly or fix prices does not render them illegal. . . ." *Bement* v. *National Harvester Co.*, 186 U.S. 70 (1902).

[57] *Rubber Tire Wheel Co.* v. *Milwaukee Rubber Works Co.*, 210 U.S. 439 (1908).

[58] *General Talking Pictures Co.* v. *Western Electric Corp.*, 304 U.S. 175 (1938).

[59] *U.S.* v. *General Electric Co.*, 272 U.S. 476.

patentee to control a licensee's prices. The Court upheld this power, "provided the conditions of sale are normally and reasonably adapted to secure pecuniary reward for the patentee's monopoly." The second issue was the validity of the agency contracts between General Electric and the firms distributing its light bulbs. After the Victor Talking Machine decision had barred patentees from controlling retail prices of their products, General Electric had designated its distributors as agents, shipping them bulbs on consignment and retaining title until they were sold, in order to be able to fix their resale prices. The Court held this to be a bona fide agency system and upheld General Electric's control over resale prices. This decision, which looked at the issues almost entirely in terms of the private interest of the patentee, erected a major barrier against attempts to extend antitrust policies to patents. The task confronting the Antitrust Division was to persuade the judges to consider the public interest in competition as well as the privileges of the patentee.

The offensive launched against patent privileges by the Division in the late thirties was a broad one, but much of it involved the General Electric precedent. In two cases, the Division persuaded the Supreme Court to narrow drastically, if not to deny, the protection of price-fixing offered by agency contracts. In the Univis case,[60] the court struck down an agency system, similar to that of General Electric, which set the prices charged by distributors and finishers of patented eyeglass lenses. And in the Masonite case,[61] it condemned as a conspiracy in restraint of trade an agency system under which Masonite made hardboard for the whole industry, distributed it through competing manufacturers, and fixed the prices at which it was to be sold.

In another series of cases, the Division sought to persuade the Court to reverse its ruling that a patentee could control the prices charged by a licensee. In 1940, efforts of the Ethyl Gasoline Corporation (half owned by Standard Oil of New Jersey) to use its patent privileges to control the price of gasoline were condemned. The company had forbidden its licensee refiners to market their ethyl gasoline through jobbers not licensed by it, and it revoked licenses of jobbers who failed to observe prices posted by the refiners.[62]

In 1948, the Division made a frontal assault on the General Electric decision in two cases, asking the Court to overrule it on

---

[60] U.S. v. Univis Lens Co., 316 U.S. 421 (1942).

[61] U.S. v. Masonite Corp., 316 U.S. 265 (1942).

[62] Ethyl Gasoline Corp. v. U.S., 309 U.S. 436.

the ground that a patent confers only the right to exclude competitors, not to join with them in a price-fixing agreement. In both cases, four justices opposed the 1926 precedent, but a majority, while finding for the government, thought it unnecessary to reverse the General Electric doctrine. The Line Material case involved the two principal producers of fuse cutouts, each of whom possessed an essential patent.[63] Each licensed the other, fixing the licensee's prices, and their cross-licensing agreement also provided that any other licensees maintain the same prices. The Court found this arrangement to be illegal per se: "When patentees join in an agreement as here to maintain prices on their several products, that agreement, however advantageous it may be to stimulate the broader use of patents, is unlawful *per se* under the Sherman Act." In the second case, U.S. Gypsum had modeled its price-fixing activities more precisely on the General Electric precedent, signing separate licensing and price-fixing contracts with each of the major producers of gypsum wallboard.[64] The Court, however, held that the formal separateness of the contracts did not alter the reality of the combination to fix prices. It said:

Lawful acts may become unlawful when taken in concert. . . . The General Electric case affords no cloak . . . for a patentee, acting in concert with all members of an industry, to issue substantially identical licenses to all members of the industry under the terms of which the industry is completely regimented, the production of competitive unpatented products suppressed, a class of distributors squeezed out, and prices on unpatented products stabilized.

In several more recent cases, the restrictive powers given a patentee by the General Electric decision were further narrowed. The New Wrinkle decision condemned a scheme wherein two patent-holding litigants resolved their dispute by forming a separate corporation to hold their patents and to impose price-fixing on all licensees.[65] And in 1949, a district court invalidated General Electric's attempts to update its 1926 arrangements.[66] Its basic patents had expired, and it had sought to continue its control by patenting such improvements as filaments and bulb frosting. It pooled patents with Westinghouse and licensed four other producers. The pool fixed the price and output of all producers. The court held that General Electric had violated both Sections 1 and 2

[63] U.S. v. *Line Material Co.*, 333 U.S. 287.
[64] U.S. v. *U.S. Gypsum Co.*, 333 U.S. 364.
[65] U.S. v. *New Wrinkle, Inc.*, 324 U.S. 371 (1952).
[66] U.S. v. *General Electric Co.*, 82 F. Supp. 753 (1949).

of the Sherman Act by monopolizing the industry and by conspiring with the licensees to restrain trade. Thus any attempt to use patent-licensing provisions as part of an agreement to fix prices and output is clearly illegal. The original General Electric doctrine has never been overruled, but the most that it now permits is the price-fixing involved in an arrangement between one patentee and one licensee covering a single patent.

In its actions against patent pools and cross-licensing arrangements, the concern of the Antitrust Division was not alone with persuading the courts to adopt new doctrines, but also with broadening the coverage of existing rulings and sharpening the civil remedies to be applied in eliminating abuses. As we have seen, the Supreme Court had long held patent pools illegal when used to fix prices or output. In the Line Material and second General Electric cases, the courts extended their condemnation to arrangements apparently protected previously by the General Electric doctrine of 1926. In the National Lead case of 1947,[67] the Court indicated that any cross-licensing arrangement among large corporations is illegal if licenses are not available to other firms on reasonable terms. In 1952, it also condemned joint action by patentees in refusing licenses and conducting patent litigation as a method of limiting competition.[68]

In prosecuting these cases, the Division sought harsher punishments and more positive remedies. In the past, license contracts had frequently been voided and restrictive practices enjoined, but these steps were often insufficient to deter others and inadequate to restore effective competition. From a study of patent-controlled industries, the Division had concluded that the necessity of paying royalties on all existing patents was a formidable barrier to the entry of new firms. In its case against the Hartford-Empire pool, which had enabled its members to allocate production, fix prices, and discourage innovation, the Division persuaded the district court to issue a decree requiring that all abused patents be licensed royalty-free to all applicants and that all future patents be licensed at reasonable royalties.[69] The court also enjoined the defendants from suppressing patents. By a 4 to 3 decision, however, the Supreme Court rejected this latter part of the decree, holding that a patentee, even after abuse of his patent, may still decide whether to use or not to use his invention. While accepting compulsory licensing for the first time, the majority also eliminated the re-

[67] U.S. v. National Lead Co., 332 U.S. 319.
[68] Besser Mfg. Co. v. U.S., 343 U.S. 444.
[69] Hartford-Empire Co. v. U.S., 323 U.S. 386 (1945).

quirement of freedom from royalty payments, holding such harsh treatment to be unnecessary. Two years later, in the National Lead case, the Division again asked for royalty-free licensing.[70] National Lead and Du Pont had joined foreign producers in an international titanium cartel which exchanged patents, allotted market areas, and fixed prices. The government argued that abused patents should be made unenforceable. But, once again by a 4 to 3 vote, the Supreme Court refused to require royalty-free licensing, although it did require compulsory licensing and indicated that it might approve of royalty-free licensing under some circumstances.

Meanwhile, however, the Division had been incorporating both compulsory and royalty-free licensing in a great number of consent decrees.[71] Finally, in 1953, a district court, while rejecting a government plea that General Electric be forced to split off half of its bulb-manufacturing facilities, did require that firm to make its existing patents available royalty-free.[72] And in the following year the Supreme Court affirmed a district court decree requiring United Shoe Machinery to sell its machines as well as lease them and to grant licenses at reasonable royalties.[73] A number of recent decrees, moreover, have required patentees also to provide licensees with the "know-how" necessary to utilize patents.

The final practice involved in the antitrust assault on patent privileges has been the amassing of many patents by a single corporation. In a number of cases, the Antitrust Division has attacked this practice as a means of blocking off actual or potential competitors from a whole industry, but the courts have not yet made direct rulings on this question. Several cases raising the issue, such as those against Western Electric and International Business Machines, have been settled by consent decrees. In the United Shoe Machinery case, this practice, together with others designed to handicap competitors, was not condemned per se, but their combined use, in an industry already dominated by United Shoe, was held to constitute monopolization under Section 2.

Thus the Division was largely successful in persuading the courts to resolve conflicts between patent policy and antitrust policy in favor of the latter. Furthermore, the judges have in other

---

[70] U.S. v. National Lead Co., 332 U.S. 319 (1947).

[71] In the 1940's, more than thirty consent decrees required compulsory licensing, and more than twenty established royalty-free licensing. Wilcox, Public Policies Toward Business, p. 162.

[72] U.S. v. General Electric Co., 115 F. Supp. 835. This civil suit followed the company's criminal conviction in 1949.

[73] U.S. v. United Shoe Machinery Corp., 110 F. Supp. 295 (1953); United Shoe Machinery Corp. v. U.S., 347 U.S. 521 (1954).

areas of patent law narrowed the privileges conferred by these grants. In general, they have come to view patents more in terms of the public interest and less as a species of private property.[74] In 1942, for the first time, the Supreme Court permitted a licensee to attack the validity of a patent.[75] In 1947, it extended the same privilege to a licensee even though his license forbade him to question the patent's validity,[76] and it has refused to enforce patents in infringement cases when the defendants were able to show that the patents had been used in violation of the antitrust laws.[77]

The Court has also raised the standards of patentability. Not only must an invention be new and useful; it must also "reveal the flash of creative genius, not merely the skill of the calling." [78] This "flash of genius" doctrine endangers the validity of patents resulting from the joint efforts of corporate research teams.[79] Congress attempted to reverse the doctrine in the Patent Act of 1952, but that statute's standards for patentability are still so vague as to give the courts virtually as much discretion as they enjoyed before.

While the legal restraints which the patent system can impose on competition have thus been modified in major degree, and while the legal victories won by the Antitrust Division have undoubtedly prevented many monopolistic abuses of patents, the administrative problems which remain are formidable. With a limited budget, the Division cannot begin to check on the use or abuse of the torrent of patents issued by the Patent Office each year. Even when these patents are not abused, the fact that so many of them are held invalid when they are judicially tested indi-

<hr/>

[74] "It is the public interest which is dominant in the patent system." *Mercoid Corp.* v. *Mid-Continent Investment Co.*, 320 U.S. 661 (1944).

[75] *Sola Electric Co.* v. *Jefferson Electric Co.*, 317 U.S. 173.

[76] *Katzinger Co.* v. *Chicago Metallic Mfg. Co.*, 329 U.S. 394.

[77] *Morton Salt Co.* v. *G. S. Supplinger Co.*, 314 U.S. 488 (1942).

[78] *Cuno Engineering Corp.* v. *Automatic Devices Corp.*, 314 U.S. 84 (1941).

[79] In 1944, Thurman Arnold, then attacking patent privileges in his role as a judge of a Circuit Court of Appeals, made this point explicitly: "Each man [in a corporate research group] is given a section of the hay to search. The man who finds the needle shows no more genius and no more ability than the others who are searching different parts of the haystack. . . . The 'inventor' is paid only a salary, he gets no royalties, he has no property rights in the improvements which he helps to create. To give patents for such routine experimentation on a vast scale is to use the patent law to reward capital investment, and create monopolies for corporate organizers instead of men of inventive genius." *Potts* v. *Coe*, 140 F. 2d 470.

cates serious administrative deficiencies in the Patent Office itself. A steady accumulation of unjustified limits on competition can be expected to continue until these deficiencies are remedied.

3. Standards of Competition

A major factor in the revival of antitrust policy during the last two decades has been the willingness of the courts to accept and apply economic concepts of competition. But just as there were ambiguities and uncertainties in the older legal definitions of monopoly and restraint of trade, so are there uncertainties and cleavages of opinion among economists over the question of whether given situations and practices are truly competitive. As has been indicated, a number of developments have combined to confront the Supreme Court, the ultimate maker of antitrust policy, with the necessity of establishing new standards. There has been an evolution of economic concepts of monopolistic competition. There have been the Robinson-Patman Act and the fair-trade acts, which emphasize as a goal of policy the protection of competitors rather than competition, thereby precipitating the issue of "hard" versus "soft" competition.[80] The shift in judicial criteria for resolving these issues is perhaps most strikingly illustrated by the expansion of per se rules and the more stringent attitude toward large firms.

It will be recalled that from 1911 down to the 1940's, the Supreme Court had applied a double standard.[81] To close consolidations, usually attacked under Section 2 of the Sherman Act, it gave the full benefit of the rule of reason, condemning them only when their practices were regarded as predatory. To loose associations, attacked under Section 1 as conspiracies in restraint of trade, the Court applied stiffer standards. With the exception of the Appalachian Coals decision, it adopted a per se rule, condemning outright any price-fixing agreement, and it often found other forms of agreement among competitors to involve unreasonable restraints of trade.

To a considerable extent, the "new" Sherman Act involves a dismantling of this double standard and a substitution of per se rules for the rule of reason. A series of Section 1 cases have considerably expanded the range of business arrangements which are now conclusively presumed to be "unreasonable." Thus market

[80] See above, pp. 550–552, 555–557, 559–560, 566.
[81] See Chapter 15.

sharing [82] and boycotts involving joint action among competitors [83] are now illegal per se. There has also been, as we have seen,
a similar expansion of per se rules in applying the Clayton Act.

Furthermore, it appeared for a time that the Court intended to
remove completely the question of "reasonableness" from its application of Section 1. The Alcoa decision rejected the old distinction
between illegal price-fixing by a group of competitors and legal
price-fixing by a monopolist, and came close to making the existence of a monopoly a per se offense. The second American
Tobacco decision then seemed to extend this condemnation to
oligopoly, holding that the possession of the power to exclude
competitors, when accompanied by a conspiratorial intent to use
it, was illegal. The motion-picture industry cases further extended
this rule. In the Griffith case, a theater chain had used its bargaining power as the owner of the only theater in many towns to obtain major competitive advantages for its other theaters.[84] Here
the Court again virtually condemned monopoly power per se:
"Monopoly power, whether lawfully or unlawfully acquired, may
itself constitute an evil and stand condemned under Section 2 even
though it remains unexercised." In the Paramount case, the five
major producers, who also owned chains of theaters, were found
to have favored their own theaters and to have blocked the distribution of independently produced films.[85] While not condemning
vertical integration per se, the Court did find it illegal when undertaken "to gain control over an appreciable segment of the market
and to restrain or suppress competition."

Similarly, in the Yellow Cab case, the Court condemned vertical
integration by a taxicab manufacturer whose ownership of several
operating companies had prevented competing manufacturers
from selling to those companies.[86] Here the Court held that, given
a demonstrated intent to monopolize, the exclusion of competitors
from any substantial market violates Section 2. In yet another extension of this doctrine, the International Salt decision condemned all patent tie-ins, declaring that "it is unreasonable *per se*
to foreclose competitors from any substantial market." [87] Finally,
the successful action against A & P rested in part on the charge that

[82] U.S. v. *National Lead Co.*, 332 U.S. 319 (1947); U.S. v. *Timken Roller
Bearing Co.*, 341 U.S. 593 (1951).
[83] *Fashion Originators Guild* v. *FTC*, 312 U.S. 457 (1941). This was not a
Section 1 proceeding, but the doctrine of this case applies to Section 1 actions.
[84] U.S. v. *Griffith*, 334 U.S. 100 (1948).
[85] U.S. v. *Paramount Pictures, Inc.*, 334 U.S. 131 (1948).
[86] U.S. v. *Yellow Cab Co.*, 332 U.S. 218 (1947).
[87] *International Salt Co.* v. *U.S.*, 332 U.S. 392 (1947).

that company had used its substantial power in some markets to restrict competition in others.[88]

The Market Structure Test

Thus the Court went far toward condemning monopoly and monopoly power per se. These condemnations were based upon economic analyses which stressed market structure as a criterion of competitiveness. If firms were so few in number or if any one possessed so dominant a share of the market that prices could be fixed or competitors excluded, then the existence of such market power made competition "unworkable." The major test applied to particular industry situations or practices was the measurement of the power possessed.

This approach reflected the efforts of economists who had been searching for criteria of "workable" competition. It can be demonstrated that if technological and institutional conditions were to permit perfect competition, resources would be most efficiently allocated in the short run. But perfect competition is only an abstraction. Actual markets are flawed with many imperfections. Almost no market can meet the requirement that buyers and sellers be so numerous and they all be so small as to deny to any one the power to influence prices. Yet few markets, on the other hand, are so inherently monopolistic as to warrant public utility regulation. Accordingly, economists searched for means of defining market structures which, although only imperfectly competitive, would be sufficiently so to produce results and performance approximating the competitive ideal. Most definitions of such "workable competition" center on market structure as a restraint on the power of buyers and sellers. Edward S. Mason summarizes the literature by saying that "workable competition is considered to require, principally, a fairly large number of sellers and buyers, no one of whom occupies a large share of the market, the absence of collusion among either group, and the possibility of market entry by new firms." [89] In essence, the structural test of workable competition

[88] U.S. v. New York Great A & P Tea Co., 67 F. Supp. 626 (1946); 173 F. 2d 79 (1949).

[89] Economic Concentration and the Monopoly Problem (1957), p. 354. J. M. Clark, who was the first to use the term, defined "workable competition" as "rivalry in selling goods . . . under conditions such that the price or prices each seller can charge are effectively limited by the free option of the buyer to buy from a rival seller or sellers . . . necessitating an effort by each seller to equal or exceed the attractiveness of the other's offerings to a sufficient number of buyers to accomplish the end in view." American Economic Review (1940), vol. 30, p. 243. Clair Wilcox defines it as "the avail-

involves a measurement of the market power wielded by an individual firm or by a group of firms acting together.[90]

This was the economic basis for the judicial assault on market power. It attacked the power resulting from collusion or tacit agreement among firms when that power was used to fix prices, set output, and exclude competitors. It also attacked the market power of a single firm when it was of such a degree as to constitute "monopoly power." Monopoly power, too, was defined primarily in terms of the power to fix prices and exclude competition:

. . . the material consideration in determining whether a monopoly exists is not that prices are raised and that competition actually is excluded but that power exists to raise prices or to exclude competition when it is desired to do so.[91]

In considering the matter of monopoly power, two ingredients are of outstanding significance: viz., the power to fix prices and the power to exclude competitors.[92]

The Business Performance Test

In its condemnation of certain forms of market power, the Court went far in accepting economic criteria, but it soon became apparent that economists themselves were far from agreed that the essence of competition was the existence of effective structural restraints on market power. Equating the antitrust attack on market power with an attack on bigness, critics of this policy stressed the innovating role of the large corporation. Joseph A. Schumpeter, for example, argued that the most effective kind of competition was the "creative destruction" by which new products, processes, and organizational forms, usually introduced by a large firm seeking temporary monopoly profits, displaced older products,

---

ability to buyers of genuine alternatives in policy among their sources of supply." *Competition and Monopoly in American Industry*, p. 9. Corwin Edwards goes into greater detail, but stresses the requirements of an appreciable number of buyers and sellers, with no one dominant, and an absence of collusion. *Maintaining Competition* (1949), pp. 9–10.

[90] "Given the available information on market structure and the behavior of firms, the primary focus of an evaluation of the effectiveness of competition is presumably on the extent or degree of market power possessed by individual firms or a number of firms acting in concert. Competition becomes unworkable if a firm or firms possess an 'unreasonable' degree of market power. A major tenet of antitrust philosophy is that a policy of enforced competition is possible, only if the rivalry of all firms in a market is such as to limit sharply the ability of each to earn more than competitive profit." Mason, *op. cit.*, p. 328.

[91] *American Tobacco Co.* v. *U.S.*, 328 U.S. 781 (1946).

[92] *U.S.* v. *Aluminum Co. of America*, 91 F. Supp. 333 (1950).

processes, and forms. The kind of competition which really limits market power is:

the competition from the new commodity, the new technology, the new source of supply, the new type of organization . . . competition which commands a decisive cost or quality advantage and which strikes not at the margins of the profits and the outputs of existing firms but at their foundations and their very lives. This kind of competition is as much more effective than the other as a bombardment is in comparison with forcing a door. . . . competition of the kind we now have in mind acts not only when in being but also when it is merely an ever-present threat. It disciplines before it attacks. The businessman feels himself to be in a competitive situation even if he is alone in his field. . . . In many cases, though not in all, this will in the long run enforce behavior very similar to the perfectly competitive pattern.[93]

This argument held that only the large corporation, often wielding substantial market power because of its size, could engage in the research and development necessary to introduce new products and processes. And it was the technological dynamism of the large corporation which contributed most to the economy, making it more competitive by injecting the new product or process and adding significantly to the choices offered the consumer. Most often, it was argued, these beneficial results could be obtained only at the cost of accepting substantial power. Thus the fiber-and-fabric industry was made structurally less competitive by the entrance of the large producers, initially monopolists, of such new synthetics as rayon, nylon, orlon, and dacron. These producers possessed substantial market power and enjoyed monopoly profits. But they made the industry more competitive in terms of performance, results, and consumer choice.

To this argument, J. K. Galbraith added the supplementary theory of "countervailing power," which held that market power could best be checked, not by antitrust action, but by the organization of countervailing power by those who confront dominant power in the market.[94] Thus the power of a large buyer, such as A & P, may be the most effective check on the power of large manufacturers.

Perhaps because of similar misgivings about the wisdom of an unqualified condemnation of market power, Supreme Court decisions, especially in the framing of civil remedies, began to

[93] *Capitalism, Socialism, and Democracy*, 2d ed. (1947), pp. 84–85.
[94] *American Capitalism: The Concept of Countervailing Power* (1952).

take into account other criteria of competition. To some extent, as Mason has pointed out, this shift can be viewed as a concurrent use of business performance and market structure tests.[95] Where in the cases cited above the Court had seemed to condemn per se the mere existence of substantial market power, in a number of others it gave weight to the performance of the firms possessing this power. In the National Lead case, the titanium industry was vulnerable on the basis of the market structure test; there were only four producers, two of whom made 90 per cent of the sales, and there had been collusive agreements.[96] Yet the Court rejected the government's plea that the two dominant producers be split up, apparently because it thought that the industry had been sufficiently competitive in performance:

From 1933 on there was active competition . . . for customers. There has been a vast increase in sales; and repeated reductions in the price of titanium pigments have taken place and a very few increases. . . . The findings show vigorous and apparently profitable competition on the part of each of the four producers, including an intimation that the smaller companies are gaining ground rather than losing. Keen competition has existed both before and after the elimination . . . of certain patent advantages from among the weapons of competition.

Then in 1948, a 5-to-4 Court decision held that the acquisition of the largest independent steel fabricator on the Pacific Coast by the Columbia Steel Company, a subsidiary of U.S. Steel, did not violate the Sherman Act. Although the majority gave close attention to the industry's market structure, and found that Columbia's share of the regional market would be increased to 24 per cent, it refused to be bound by any single statistical measure of market power as a criterion of illegality. Instead, it re-emphasized the concept of reasonableness, and laid stress on intent in determining whether the acquisition was an unreasonable restraint.

Nor can we find a specific intent . . . to accomplish an unreasonable restraint . . . Granting that the sale will to some extent affect competition, the acquisition . . . seems to reflect a normal business purpose rather than a scheme to circumvent the law. . . . In determining what constitutes uneasonable restraint, we . . . look . . . to the percentage of business controlled, the strength of the remaining

---

[95] *Op. cit.*, pp. 351–371. These pages reprint his article, "The Current Status of the Monopoly Problem in the United States," *Harvard Law Review* (June, 1949).

[96] *U.S. v. National Lead Co.*, 332 U.S. 319 (1947).

competition, whether the action springs from business requirements or purpose to monopolize, the probable development of the industry, consumer demands, and other characteristics of the market. We do not undertake to prescribe any set of percentage figures by which to measure the reasonableness of a corporation's enlargement of its activities by the purchase of the assets of a competitor. The relative effect of a percentage command of a market varies with the setting in which that factor is placed.[97]

The minority, speaking through Justice Douglas, strongly assailed this apparent retreat from a market test to the rule of reason in a dissent which evoked the memory of Brandeis.[98] The extent of the retreat should not be exaggerated, however, for the margin of decision was slim, and the majority was influenced by the fact that the Attorney General in 1946 had found no objection to the sale to U.S. Steel of the government's Geneva, Utah, plant, built during World War II, giving that firm half of the Pacific ingot capacity. The government now appeared to be "straining at the gnat of Columbia after swallowing the Geneva camel." [99]

The courts have seemed also to adopt a form of business performance test in connection with the definition of the relevant market. Obviously the broader the market, the smaller is any one

[97] U.S. v. Columbia Steel Co.. 334 U.S. 495 (1948).

[98] "This is the most important antitrust case . . . in years . . . because it reveals the way of growth of monopoly power—the precise phenomenon at which the Sherman Act was aimed.

"We have here the problem of bigness. Its lesson should by now have been burned into our memory by Brandeis. [Size] can be an industrial menace because it creates gross inequalities against existing or putative competitors. It can be a social menace—because of its control of prices. Control of prices in the steel industry is powerful leverage on our economy. . . . In final analysis, size in steel is the measure of the power of a handful of men over our economy. That power can be utilized with lightning speed. It can be benign or it can be dangerous. The philosophy of the Sherman Act is that it should not exist. For all power tends to develop into a government in itself. Power that controls the economy should be in the hands of elected representatives of the people, not in the hands of an industrial oligarchy. Industrial power should be . . . scattered into many hands so that the fortune of the people will not be dependent on the whim or caprice, the political prejudices, the emotional stability of a few self-appointed men. The fact that they are not vicious men but are respectable and social-minded is irrelevant. That is the philosophy and the command of the Sherman Act. It is founded on a theory of hostility to the concentration in private hands of power so great that only a government of the people should have it.

"The Court forgot this lesson in [the Steel and Harvester cases]. The Court today forgets it when it allows United States Steel to wrap its tentacles tighter around the steel industry of the West."

[99] Mason, op. cit., p. 361.

firm's share of it. The determination of whether trade is being monopolized, whether a firm or combination has a substantial amount of market power, often depends on whether the competition of close substitutes is assumed to be significant. Those who, with Schumpeter, stress interproduct competition, argue that market power is limited by the actual or potential development of new products.[100] They further argue that the possession or expectation of substantial power is necessary to encourage and protect the innovator, the agent of dynamic competition. Those who stress market structure, and urge a narrow definition of the relevant market, are skeptical of the restraints actually imposed by interproduct competition. They argue that "inter-industry competition as an economic force is more apparent than real" and point out that it is "perfectly compatible with a fully monopolized industry." [101] Economists cannot offer any reliable measure of when the substitutability of one product for another is sufficient to warrant inclusion of the substitute in the relevant market.[102]

In the Alcoa case, Judge Hand refused to consider the competition of other materials or even of scrap aluminum. But in the preparation of a district court decree, after the return of the case from Judge Hand, Judge Knox stressed the performance criterion and gave weight to the competition between aluminum and other materials. While requiring Alcoa to sever its ties with Aluminium, Ltd., of Canada, and to license its American competitors, he refused to order it split up into two parts. Interproduct rivalry is so significant a market factor, he argued, that competitive success "can be achieved only by companies that are rich in resources, and which are capable of undertaking extensive scientific and market

[100] Thus the Business Advisory Council of the Department of Commerce pointed out in a report to the Secretary of Commerce that aluminum "must compete with steel, copper, zinc, lead, tin, wood, textiles, plastics, paper, clay, glass, leather and cork. . . . Timber, the ancient material, has been rejuvenated through modern chemistry and by technical machinery. The former transport dominance of the railroad industry has long been lost to highway and air competition." *Effective Competition* (1952), p. 70.

[101] Walter Adams, "The Rule of Reason: Workable Competition or Workable Monopoly?" *Yale Law Journal* (January, 1954), pp. 363–364.

[102] Economists have developed a theoretical measure of substitutability— the cross-elasticity of demand—but even if this device could give precise results, it would not determine when two or more markets become one market. "Economists have long been puzzled to find a satisfactory definition of a 'market.' In final analysis, it may be ventured, without attempting to solve this riddle, that no transaction or series of transactions in any area, or in any trade, is uninfluenced by transactions, present and prospective, in other areas and other trades." M. W. Watkins, *Public Regulation of Competitive Practices in Business Enterprise* (1940), p. 237.

experimentations. At the present juncture, the weakening of any aluminum producer would lessen the buoyancy of the industry as a whole." [103]

Similarly, in the Cellophane case, the choice of the relevant market was the crux of the decision. Here, by a 6 to 3 vote, the Supreme Court defined the relevant market as including all flexible wrapping materials, and thus exonerated Du Pont from the charge of monopolization. The precise basis for the majority's definition is unclear,[104] but the district court's similar ruling was apparently influenced by Du Pont's business performance and its abstinence from predatory practices.[105] Protesting that "the majority virtually emasculates [Section] 2 of the Sherman Act," the dissenting Supreme Court justices preferred the narrower definition on the basis of market structure criteria:

Du Pont's independent pricing policy and the great profits consistently yielded by that policy leave no room for doubt that it had power to control the price of cellophane. . . . The public should not be left to rely upon the dispensations of management in order to obtain the benefits which normally accompany competition. Such beneficence is of uncertain tenure. Only actual competition can assume long-run enjoyment of the goals of a free economy.

On the other hand, in the Du Pont-General Motors case the next year, the Supreme Court, in a 4 to 2 decision, reversed course sharply and adopted a narrow definition of the relevant market.[106] Although Du Pont's sales of finishes to General Motors were only 3.5 per cent of all such sales to industrial users and its fabric sales to General Motors were only 1.6 per cent of the total, the Court held that the revelant market was the fabric and finish purchases of automobile manufacturers. Monopolization of this market was threatened by Du Pont's controlling stock ownership in General

[103] U.S. v. Aluminum Co. of America, 91 F. Supp. 333 (1950).

[104] "In considering what is the relevant market for determining the control of price and competition, no more definite rule can be declared than that commodities reasonably interchangeable by consumers for the same purposes make up that 'part of the trade or commerce,' monopolization of which may be illegal." U.S. v. E.I. du Pont de Nemours & Co., 351 U.S. 377 (1956).

[105] "There has been no monopolization or conspiracy or attempt to monopolize shown. The record reflects not the dead hand of monopoly but rapidly declining prices, expanding production, intense competition stimulated by creative research, the development of new products and uses and other benefits of free economy. Du Pont nor any other American company similarly situated should be punished for its success." U.S. v. E.I. du Pont de Nemours & Co., 118 F. Supp. 41 (1953).

[106] U.S. v. E.I. du Pont de Nemours & Co., 353 U.S. 586 (1957).

Motors, with its consequent power to bar sales of competing fabric and finish producers. Thus, here the Court once again placed primary emphasis on the market structure test.

In the United Shoe Machinery case of 1953, the district court's decision similarly stressed market structure.[107] To the company's performance argument that its monopoly position was necessary to permit efficiency and research, Judge Wyzanski replied that "the law does not allow an enterprise that maintains control of a market through practices not economically inevitable, to justify that control because of its supposed advantage." While avoiding a per se condemnation of monopoly power, he called for a much stricter standard of conduct for monopolists than for members of a competitive industry. United Shoe's business practices, such as its refusal to sell its machines and its insistence on long-term exclusive contracts, were not in themselves illegal, but they had enabled a dominant firm to establish and maintain an illegal monopoly. That monopolization was not illegal per se; it was illegal because it resulted, not solely from United Shoe's "ability, economies of scale, research, and adaptation to inevitable economic laws," but rather from practices which, given United Shoe's dominance, "are unnatural barriers; they unnecessarily exclude actual and potential competition; they restrict a free market." The doctrine that the possessor of monopoly power may be prevented from following practices which are legal when engaged in by competitive firms was upheld by the Supreme Court in 1954.[108]

4. Current Policy: The Doctrine of Permissible Power

Edward S. Mason has observed:

What the courts appear to be reaching for, above and beyond the range of traditional Sherman Act violations, is a doctrine of permissible power. Some power there has to be, both because of inescapable limitations to the process of atomization and because power is needed to do the job the American public expects of its industrial machine. There is no reason, however, to tolerate positions of market power that can be lessened by appropriate antitrust action unless it can be shown that this lessening substantially interferes with the job to be done.[109]

Despite some backing and filling, the courts have greatly extended their condemnation of market power of all kinds. The out-

---

[107] U.S. v. United Shoe Machinery Corp., 110 F. Supp. 295.
[108] United Shoe Machinery Corp. v. U.S., 347 U.S. 521.
[109] Mason, op. cit., p. 387.

lawing of price-fixing agreements per se has been broadened by an expanded definition of what constitutes such an agreement. Tying contracts are now condemned per se, but the courts retreated from their apparent per se condemnation of exclusive-dealing arrangements and integration when it became clear that this doctrine was based on questionable criteria of competition. Similarly, the courts for a while tended to condemn monopoly power per se on structural criteria. They paused in response to the criticism of those who emphasized business performance. While the Court considers illegal monopoly power simply as "power to control prices or exclude competitors," [110] this test cannot be applied until the relevant market is defined, thereby accepting or rejecting interproduct competition as an effective force. Even then, there may remain the problem of an industry where efficiency seems to require greater power than is tolerable under structural standards. Nor can intent be entirely forgotten in evaluating concentrations of market power.[111]

Market power, consequently, is viewed by the courts with suspicion but is not necessarily condemned. Some of its forms and exercises are presumed to be so unfair or to have such undesirable results as to be outlawed per se. Others are questioned but may be accepted as permissible if they are regarded as inescapable, fair, competitive in performance, or beneficial in result. Mr. Dooley's analysis of many decades ago still applies: "Th' thrusts are heejous monsthers built up be th' inlightened intherprise iv th' men that have done so much to advance pro-gress in our beloved country. On wan hand I wud stamp thim undher fut; on th' other hand not so fast." [112]

Obviously, such a policy of accepting "permissible" market power and rooting out the impermissible vests the judges with great discretion. Yet the much-criticized uncertainty of the antitrust laws can be exaggerated. A very substantial proportion of

[110] U.S. v. E.I. du Pont de Nemours & Co., 351 U.S. 377 (1956).

[111] Two economists have argued fairly persuasively that the rule of reason has continued to be of greater influence than is generally recognized in interpretations of the "new" Sherman Act, and that the courts have rightly weighed intent heavily in passing on the legality of questioned practices or structures. See J. B. Dirlam and A. E. Kahn, Fair Competition: The Law and Economics of Antitrust Policy (1954); also A. E. Kahn, "Standards for Antitrust Policy," Harvard Law Review (November, 1954), p. 29; ibid., "A Legal and Economic Appraisal of the 'New' Sherman and Clayton Acts," Yale Law Journal (January, 1954), p. 293.

[112] Finley Peter Dunne, Mr. Dooley at His Best, ed. Elmer Ellis (1938), pp. 104–105.

business practices falls squarely inside or outside the law. While much uncertainty remains, it is doubtful whether the existing state of economic analysis or the blend of economic, political, social, and ethical values furthered by antitrust policy will allow for a more precise policy statement than that enunciated by Judge Knox in 1950:

In determining the extent of permissible power that is consistent with the antitrust laws in a particular industry, the following factors are relevant: the number of the firms in the market; their effective size from the standpoint of technological development, and from the standpoint of competition with substitute materials and foreign trade; national security interests in the maintenance of strong productive facilities, and maximum scientific research and development; together with the public interest in lowered costs and uninterrupted production.[113]

5. Judicial Administration of Policy

Thus, many of the same factors which led the framers of the 1890 legislation to vest the courts with broad discretionary power still apply. The impossibility of agreeing at that time on more than the broadest statements of policy led to the decision to give the judges the task of slowly injecting specific meaning, case by case, into the statute. Nearly seventy years of interpretation have added much concreteness to the broad terms of the Sherman Act, which, as the Court once observed, have a "generality and adaptability comparable to that found to be desirable in constitutional provisions." [114] But given the problem of reconciling such goals as limitation of market power and efficiency, given the innate deficiencies of economic analysis, and given the perennial task of applying old standards to the new forms and practices of a dynamic economy, much generality must continue to characterize antitrust policy.

There is also a strong political case for extensive judicial participation in policy-making in this field. While antitrust policy in the abstract tends to be an accepted, almost revered, part of the basic rules of the game—in this respect, too, resembling a constitutional provision—and while particular interests may strongly urge and support antitrust attacks on certain firms or practices, there is no stable pattern of organized groups which will consistently support antitrust administration. Groups which favor the

[113] U.S. v. Aluminum Co. of America, 91 F. Supp. 333.
[114] Applachian Coals, Inc. v. U.S., 288 U.S. 344 (1933).

application of the antitrust laws to others may themselves be subject to antitrust prosecution. The only group which fairly consistently benefits is the notoriously unorganized body of consumers. These factors are the primary reasons for the inability of
the FTC to develop vigor and effectiveness; indeed, what little
success it has finally enjoyed has been largely attributable to its
ability partially to "judicialize" itself.

In such circumstances, there is much to be said for vesting
primary responsibility in the courts. The judges can secure greater
acceptance for their policy decisions than could a more obviously
political agency. Judicial decisions in particular cases are in reality
policy decisions—e.g., that it is unsound to allow a firm as large
as Du Pont to control a firm as large as General Motors, when the
latter makes substantial purchases from the former—but they are
the more acceptable for being regarded as a declaration of legal
rules. Furthermore, while an individual case is costly and time-
consuming, and while important policy questions may lie un-
answered for many years until an appropriate case is completed, in
some senses judicial administration is remarkably economical. The
decision enunciated in a major case will often have direct repercussions on the practices of thousands of business firms. Businesses
can ignore these precedents only at the risk of incurring prosecution or private suits.

Yet, since the courts can make policy decisions only when cases
are brought before them, the Antitrust Division has the power to
determine which questions will be posed and thus to exert considerable influence over the answers given. These powers, and the
great discretion the Division enjoys in the negotiation of consent
decrees, give it, too, a crucial role in the making of policy. Such
discretionary powers can, of course, be abused. Yet the Division's
decisions have been remarkably well immunized from the pressures of businesses with immediate and often great interests at
stake.[115] Its record of impartiality and of insulation from affected
businesses and their congressional supporters compares favorably
indeed with that of the independent regulatory commissions.

The Division naturally is influenced by the general policy posi-

[115] Absolute immunity, of course, is too much to hope for. The Radio Corporation of America (RCA) was accused of bribery in connection with its
1932 consent decree. And in 1952, H. Graham Morrison, then head of the
Division, was dismissed by Attorney General James P. McGranery, apparently
at the urging of Senator McCarran and allegedly because of his refusal to call
off action against RCA. After his dismissal, the suit was dropped, although new
ones were filled in 1954 and 1958. *New York Times*, February 22, 1958. These
later suits culminated in the consent decree of 1958. See above, p. 595.

tion of presidential administrations. Thurman Arnold was promoted to the bench during World War II, when it was feared that too vigorous antitrust enforcement would endanger the cooperation of business leaders in the war effort. But his revival of the Division was maintained after the war under both Democratic and Republican administrations. Its support by the Eisenhower administration meant that this revival, initiated under the New Deal, had been accepted by a political leadership strongly oriented toward business. Vigorous antitrust enforcement has become a bipartisan policy.

6. Trade Regulation in Review

American trade-regulation policy has undergone striking changes in its seven decades of development. Its course is marked by four distinct phases. The Sherman Act of 1890 was a vaguely conceived direct attack on large, dominant firms. As such it was ineffective. The 1914 legislation sought to maintain an open door of opportunity for the little businessman by outlawing unfair methods of competition, which were thought to be his main obstacle. It was likewise ineffective, not merely because of unsympathetic judicial construction, but also because its assumptions were fundamentally erroneous. The concentration of economic power was not caused solely by immoral, predatory tactics. In 1933, the NRA relaxed the antitrust laws in favor of industrial "self-government." While administrative haste, undigested policies, and the complexity of the economy doomed this experiment, its general emphasis on the preservation of competitors at the expense of competition was repeated in such later legislation as the bituminous coal acts, the fair-trade laws, and the Robinson-Patman Act. Since 1937, finally, there has been a revival of antitrust policy on a new basis, unprecedented both in methods and objectives.

That policy is no longer envisaged solely as a means of protecting competitors and consumers from the exploitation of predatory monopolists. Since a substantial degree of market power is now recognized as the inevitable consequence of large-scale organization, the problem has become one of determining what is "permissible power." Concentration of market power is viewed with suspicion, but its possible contribution to efficiency, to innovation, and to the effective operation of the economic order is now taken into account. The "trust problem" is no longer a peripheral pathological phenomenon on the fringes of a seemingly healthy organism; it has become a problem of the capacity of an industrial system to make full use of its human and material resources.

With this stress on the inevitability of much market power and on the results of industrial behavior has come an increasing dissatisfaction with the old dichotomy between the "natural monopoly" industries and the rest of the economy. In the first area it was believed that public utility regulation was necessary to limit power and to ensure operation in the public interest. In the second, it was assumed that something resembling pure competition would reign, automatically limiting power and serving the public interest, requiring government only to prevent predatory and unfair practices and occasionally to dissolve a trust. The unreality of so simple a classification is now obvious. Just as competitive factors play an important role in the closely regulated industries, so also does the degree to which competition is a viable goal vary greatly in the remainder of the economy.

In addition to the now less distinct public utility sector, at least four broad categories stand out, with innumerable gradations. First, in a large portion of commerce and industry where capital needs are slight, entrance to and exit from the field are easy, and firms are numerous, competition may be enforced through a vigorous application of the traditional methods. The basic objective there need simply be that of free opportunity to compete and protection from unfair methods of competition.

Second, there are industries where capital requirements are high, entry is limited, and product standardized. In this area, where competition has proved most evanescent and basing points and price leadership have tended to prevail, many elements of sound public policy remain uncertain. The risks of cutthroat competition are so enormous, and the gains from restrictions on competition are so palpable, that elimination of one restraining device can hardly be accomplished before another has arisen to replace it. While unlimited competition may have undesirable results, the public interest would be served by greater price flexibility and locational mobility. Less reliance on defensive restrictions might lead these industries toward more vigorous technological development.

A closely related third area includes many industries producing consumer goods on a very large scale. Here the economies of mass production, together with the large volume of resources necessary to utilize new processes and to discover, develop, and market new products, make for concentration in a few large units. Price competition is often somewhat attenuated, but there is keen competition in other respects, including product development. While the economic results of this type of industrial structure are generally welcomed, the concentration of market power can be abused, and it is here that the doctrine of permissible power is most directly relevant. The exercise of market power must be held within bounds, and public policy should seek to ensure that no greater concentrations are permitted than are clearly justified by criteria of economic performance.

Finally, there is a fourth area where some of the hazards of unrestricted competition have led to explicit legislative modification of the basic public policy of supporting competition. These industries, usually exploiting natural resources, have pressed for special protection on the ground that the wastes of excessive competition injure not only entrepreneurs, workers, and local communities but also an underlying public interest in conservation. Examples of such special industry regulation are discussed in the following chapters.

Thus, the very complexity of our economy has contributed to a considerable broadening of trade-regulation policy. From a simple espousal of competition and an almost instinctive abhorrence of predatory power, it has expanded to include a recognition of the inevitable limitations on pure competition, a reconciliation of structural and performance standards, and an evaluation of competition in terms of the over-all functioning of the economy. It has further modified general competitive policies by special industry regulation. These changes constitute a significant departure from the earlier antitrust concepts. Experimentation along these lines, rather than either the atomization of industry, so as to give the market the entire task of regulation, or the adoption of inclusive economic planning, denying the market any regulatory function, appears to offer substantial promise of success coupled with the least dislocation of our economic and political traditions.

PART 5

Special Industry Regulation

_____

CHAPTER 19

Bituminous Coal: Regulation of a Sick Industry

THE INCREASING complexity of regulatory action in the industrial sector of the American economy is demonstrated by the emergence of special industry regulation in the basic fuel industries—coal, oil, and natural gas. Lying midway between the categories of public utility and antitrust regulation, this area displays a diversity of pattern resulting from varying combinations of competitive and monopolistic elements. It confronts public policy with special problems because of the unique market factors, political forces, and social goals characterizing each industry. In a sense, special industry regulation is a bridge between the other two great types of regulation and combines elements of each, but the problems of these industries, and the policies they have evoked, have few elements in common.

1. The Malady: Too Much Competition?

Public policy toward the bituminous (soft) coal industry [1] has been directed primarily toward eliminating what were felt to be

[1] The anthracite (hard) coal industry, with about a tenth the annual tonnage of the bituminous industry, presents entirely different problems. Although competition of other fuels, notably heating oil, has made serious inroads into its demand, the industry's reaction to the change is conditioned by highly concentrated control in the hands of a small group of producers. Since production is almost wholly within the single state of Pennsylvania, public policy in this field remains a matter primarily of state concern. The present discussion is restricted to the bituminous industry.

the excesses of competition. Similar purposes have motivated public policy in other areas, such as oil and agriculture; what was unique in the soft coal industry was the dominant role of organized labor in bringing about regulation. The effects of destructive competition within the industry were greatly intensified by the competition of other energy sources and by the technological backwardness which until recently has handicapped industry efforts to meet the challenge of other fuels. These effects were also magnified by the chronic depression of the industry during the entire period between the two World Wars. Already a "sick industry" in the 1920's, its troubles were accentuated beyond endurance by the Great Depression.

The regulatory schemes erected during the 1930's were allowed to expire, largely unmourned, during World War II. Nonetheless, these efforts to bring stability to an economically unstable industry, and to make an intensely competitive industry less competitive, are of considerable interest. Like the NIRA experience, they offer an insight into the administrative and political problems of substituting regulation for the market. Whenever bituminous coal has suffered serious relapses since World War II, there have been pleas for a restoration of government regulation. And since the industry is now in effect substantially regulated by the United Mine Workers, a study of the prewar experience permits a comparison between public and private regulation.

The Background of Federal Regulation

Although the relative importance of coal has been declining throughout most of this century, it is still a major source of the nation's energy supply, meeting most of the fuel needs of the electric power, steel, cement, and other manufacturing industries. Coal and its by-products are also important raw materials for a wide range of chemical processes. Although the work force has declined from over two-thirds to less than one-third of a million, the industry is still the backbone of the economy of West Virginia and occupies a prominent position in Pennsylvania, Illinois, Ohio, Kentucky, and significant areas of other states.

If competition were the sole goal of policy, coal would require little attention. It offers one of the rare examples of an industrial structure approximating the standards of pure competition. There are many producers. From World War I down to the present, five to six thousand firms have operated between six and nine thousand mines with an annual output exceeding a thousand tons each, and there are many thousands of smaller mines. No one company is big enough to influence prices subtantially. The product is standardized. Grades, qualities, and sizes of coal vary considerably, as does its utility for specific uses; but these differences can be measured fairly precisely, and its heating value is accurately calculated in British thermal units (BTU). Since new mines can be opened readily and cheaply, entry into the industry is easy and production can be expanded rapidly. In the absence of public or private regulation, competition would reign unchecked.

In practice, however, these competitive forces operate most vigorously in one direction, that of depressing prices and promoting overcapacity. Ease of entry and the substitution of other fuels tend to limit price increases, except over the very short run, for supply can quickly be expanded to match increases in demand. But there are few influences which can check downward pressure on prices. Once demand eases, hard bargaining by the large buyers of coal drives prices down. Exit from the industry is difficult, and falling prices fail to reduce supply except over the long run. Neither do price declines increase demand appreciably, for, below a certain price level, consumption of coal is more sensitive to the general level of business activity than it is to further price reductions.

In consequence, overcapacity tends to characterize the industry. Production expanded rapidly throughout the nineteenth century, but after 1890 the rate of expansion declined sharply and actual contraction set in shortly after World War I. Yet overcapacity persisted as a result of declining demand. The fall in demand was attributable chiefly to increased efficiency in consumption and to the substitution of other energy sources. In a variety of uses, coal was being increasingly displaced by fuel oil, diesel oil, natural gas, and hydroelectric power. The proportion of total energy supplied by bituminous coal has fallen from almost 90 per cent in 1900 to 64 per cent in 1930 and less than 40 per cent in recent years.

The disproportion between capacity and demand was magnified by the sudden increase in consumption during World War I, when many new mines were opened and abandoned workings were brought back into operation. There was, to be sure, a marked postwar contraction; between 1923 and 1932, the number of mines and miners both fell by about 42 per cent. For both technical and economic reasons, however, the reduction of capacity did not nearly keep pace with the shrinkage in demand. Once opened, mines often could not be shut down without permanent damage and abandonment. Local taxes on coal in the ground stimulated owners to resume operations whenever the slightest margin over direct costs was in prospect. Since the industry was the only source of livelihood for the inhabitants of most coal-mining communities, labor transfer was difficult. By means of wage reductions, even below normal subsistence standards, it was sometimes feasible to maintain unremunerative production for long periods. At the same time, unusually wide dispersion of ownership and control prevented output restriction by voluntary co-operative action.

The peculiar labor conditions of the twenties also contributed to the maintenance of overcapacity. Wages then approximated three-fifths of the total cost of coal at the mine, a larger proportion than in almost any other industry. Pressure on wage rates and disputes over union organization were consequently common. The coal industry's labor history is replete with episodes of bitter and violent conflict. Like many other unions, the United Mine Workers of America had expanded greatly during World War I. Organization was most effective in the northern Appalachian fields and in Ohio and Illinois. In the immediate postwar years, organization and wages were maintained in the North but the union was broken in the South. In consequence, there was a marked southward shift of production and an over-all increase in capacity. Many Northern mines which closed temporarily were later reopened with nonunion labor and lowered wage rates.

Overcapacity imposed steady downward pressure on prices and, in turn, on wages. The average price at the mine fell by more than half between 1923 and 1932, from $2.68 per ton to $1.31, while total annual wage payments dropped from $851 to $235 million. Although the most precipitous decline occurred after the onset of the Great Depression in 1929, the problem of falling prices had been serious throughout the late twenties. Despite the reduction in labor costs, producers as a whole were losing heavily. Bankruptcy and reorganization were common.

The troubles of the coal industry were accentuated by competitive practices growing out of a market structure where the buying side was dominated by large consumers. Coal cannot be stored economically above ground for any length of time because of deterioration, fire hazard, and the large amount of space required. Various sizes and qualities produced jointly are marketable at differing prices; the less desirable types must often be sold immediately at any price obtainable. By strategic use of their heavy buying power, large industrial, utility, and rail consumers could lower prices by playing off one producer against another.

Under these conditions, impoverishment of worker and entrepreneur alike was reflected in demoralized communities and growing demands for remedial action. In the formulation of public policy, conservation played a negligible part. It is nonetheless a factor of considerable objective significance. Although total bituminous reserves are adequate at present consumption rates for many centuries, they are concentrated, for the most part, in relatively inaccessible areas of the Rocky Mountains. The better seams in the easterly regions, especially of coals used for steelmaking, are being exhausted fairly rapidly. Their useful life must be reckoned only in decades. Extreme competitive pressures force operators to extract only the most easily workable material, at the cost of permanent abandonment of only slightly inferior coals. Economic stability encourages practices which avoid a considerable degree of physical waste, and provides a framework within which minimum conservational requirements can be imposed.

2. Federal Regulation

Active federal intervention in the bituminous coal industry was first undertaken in World War I when the problem was one of shortage, intensified by severe bottlenecks in railroad transportation.[2] Under the Lever Act of 1917, the United States Fuel Administration fixed maximum coal prices, allocated shipments, and aided in the adjustment of labor disputes. Price control was terminated early in 1919, but during the next three years, repeated labor disturbances prolonged the threat of coal shortage and on two occasions brought about partial restoration of wartime controls. A strike in April, 1922, the worst in the industry's history, led to the creation of an investigatory commission, which recommended increased government control, implemented through supervision of distributive channels by the Interstate Commerce Commission. The end of the strike, however, brought the industry out of the era of temporary shortage and high prices into a long downward swing into chronic depression and cutthroat competition. With this change, beginning in 1923, the movement for public control shifted its focus away from consumer protection and toward the welfare of operators and miners.

For a time the well-organized United Mine Workers (UMW) succeeded in maintaining labor standards. The 1922 strike, how-

---

[2] The unusually hazardous nature of this industry led many decades ago to state legislation promoting mine safety. The Bureau of Mines was established in the Department of the Interior in 1910 to supplement these provisions. The Bureau also engages in general promotional and research activities in connection with coal and other mineral resources.

ever, weakened the union's influence in the South. Although the "Jacksonville Agreement" maintained wage rates in the Northern fields between 1924 and 1927, the industry's movement southward was accelerated by the wage differential, and in the latter year union organization was largely broken down in the North. The union was further weakened by a series of antitrust prosecutions and the enforcement against it of "yellow-dog" contracts. At the pit of the depression, it reached its weakest point since the end of the nineteenth century.

Efforts at voluntary control by operators were equally unsuccessful. The antitrust laws ruled out binding arrangements, while looser agreements were unable to withstand competitive pressures. In 1932, producers in the Appalachian territory established a joint sales agency, Appalachian Coals, Inc. Its operation was suspended pending a determination of its legality. By the time it had received judicial approval,[3] more effective organization was in operation under the National Industrial Recovery Act.

The failure of voluntary controls, whether initiated by labor or by management, to remedy the industry's woes led to increasing pressure for government intervention. In the late twenties and early thirties, a number of measures were introduced into Congress. All called for antitrust exemption, and some sought to bolster coal prices through such devices as joint marketing agencies, federal licensing of interstate producers, and direct minimum-price fixing. Producers were sharply divided in their attitude toward government control. At first a majority preferred some form of industry "self-government," but as conditions became desperate, increasing numbers came to favor protective legislation. The UMW, more anxious for government action, was then too weak to attract serious legislative attention. With the passage of the National Industrial Recovery Act of 1933, the demand for special bituminous coal regulation was temporarily dropped.

The NRA Period

Although the Bituminous Coal Code was approved only three months after passage of the NIRA, its negotiation was as complex and difficult as any in NRA history. The savage interregional competition characterizing the industry was transferred to the code-drafting offices. Nonunion operators were hostile to guarantees of collective bargaining. Southern producers, favored by recent industry trends, were loath to permit any reduction in wage differentials

[3] See pp. 475–476, above.

or other action which might prevent further gains for them by freezing the existing regional pattern of production. Operators as a whole were suspicious of the intrusion of government representatives into code administration. A vital part in the entire proceeding was played by the UMW, which had begun an extremely effective organizing drive immediately after passage of the Act.

The code followed the general NRA pattern in exchanging labor concessions for restrictions on competition. Because of the industry's extreme distress, outright minimum-price fixing was adopted as the basic instrument of producer protection. Agreement on a code, however, was achieved only at the cost of studied vagueness in many provisions. Administration, moreover, including control of prices, had to be geographically decentralized among five divisional code authorities, which included union representation at a later stage. During the code's brief existence, a series of eight amendments substantially clarified its terms. The evolution followed two paths. Increased labor protection developed in step with growing UMW strength. At the same time, standards and techniques for minimum-price fixing were restated with greater precision, although they still left vast discretion with the divisional code authorities.

The position of both workers and operators was clearly improved under the NRA. Union organization was extended to over 90 per cent of the industry. Child labor was eliminated. The thirty-five-hour week became standard. Annual earnings rose by 35 to 50 per cent, and the number of mineworkers increased moderately. Price increases were sufficient not only to absorb increased labor costs but also to eliminate most of the operating deficits of previous years and, in many cases, even to provide a moderate profit. From the low point of $1.31 per ton in 1932, average mine realizations rose to $1.75 in 1934 and $1.77 in 1935. In the major producing areas, they were as high as $1.86, providing a 3-cent margin over total costs.

Individual dissatisfaction with the regulatory system, however, was rife. Small producers charged that their larger competitors dominated the code authorities. Particular regions alleged unjust discrimination in the setting of wage or price differentials. Enforcement proved impossible and, as noncompliance mounted, the price structure broke down in ever-widening areas. By the time of the Schechter decision in May, 1935, the coal code had virtually disintegrated. Steps were taken in the winter of 1935, therefore, to replace it with a "little NRA," based upon special legislation with more adequate standards and administrative procedure. The movement culminated in passage of the Bituminous Coal Conservation Act in August, 1935.

Special Bituminous Coal Legislation

As originally introduced, the 1935 bill provided not only for labor protection and price control, but also for production quotas and the retirement of marginal coal lands by government purchase financed out of a tax on the industry. It was announced as seeking to regulate bituminous coal "as a public utility." Guided through Congress by Senator Guffey of Pennsylvania, its leading sponsor was the UMW. The operators were as divided as they had been in the formulation and administration of the NRA code. While there was general agreement on the desirability of production control, each proposed formula for the allocation of quotas was warmly opposed by some of the important producing groups. Large buyers opposed any regulatory plan. Spokesmen for smaller consumers were also troubled by the proposals; their representations resulted in the establishment of the consumers' counsel device previously discussed.[4] Since acceptance of any legislation necessitated the support of a substantial proportion of the operators, positive action was obtained only by eliminating production controls and the national coal reserve. Southern Appalachian operators opposed the bill to the very end. Its final passage was achieved only by close votes in both houses.

Establishing a five-member National Bituminous Coal Commission as the administrative agency, the Bituminous Coal Conservation Act built upon the NRA experience by limiting itself to minimum-price fixing and regulation of labor conditions. Producers were induced to submit themselves to regulation by a 15 per-cent tax on the sale of coal at the mine, 90 per cent of which was remitted upon acceptance of the new "Bituminous Coal Code." Minimum prices were to be determined by twenty-three district boards of producers, each board including a labor representative. The entire process was subject to Commission scrutiny and modification. The Act's labor sections guaranteed the rights of free organization and collective bargaining, provided for union checkweighmen, and forbade employers to require workmen to live in company houses or trade at company stores. As its ultimate sanction in enforcing compliance, the Commission could revoke code membership, thereby reimposing the prohibitory tax upon an offending producer.

The Act of 1935 was never put fully in effect, for only ten

[4] See p. 233, above.

months after passage it was invalidated by the Supreme Court.[5] Its labor provisions were declared beyond the scope of federal authority under the commerce clause, since they regulated production rather than commerce. And that portion of the Act which made maximum hours binding on all members, after their approval by operators accounting for two-thirds of the nation's tonnage and half of the workers, was held to be an unconstitutional delegation of legislative power to private persons. The labor and price-fixing provisions were found to be so closely related that with invalidation of the one the other had necessarily to fall as well, but four of the justices expressed the conviction that the price-fixing provisions alone would have been constitutional.

Proponents of regulation wasted no time in taking this cue. Within three weeks of the decision, a new measure was introduced into Congress to re-enact the price-fixing provisions with only minor alterations, but omitting the labor sections. Collective bargaining was now protected by the Wagner Act of 1935, and as to wages and hours, the UMW felt that "we could deal with the industry and rely on our own power if the industry was not chronically insolvent." [6] Deletion of the labor provisions and a slight broadening of the standards guiding the price-fixing process eliminated much of the producer opposition. Although a few producing groups, notably those of Alabama, together with many large consumers, remained hostile to the bill, general sentiment was more favorable than in 1935. Actual passage was delayed until the 1937 session of Congress, but the bill then passed both houses easily.

Price-Fixing Under the Bituminous Coal Act of 1937

In a sense, the Act of 1937, also known as the Guffey Act, was an exercise in futility. Despite all the effort which went into its administration, the first complete schedule of minimum prices was issued only in 1940, when the effects of national defense expenditures were already eliminating the need for such protection. The schedule's major use was to serve as a basis for maximum prices set by the Office of Price Administration during World War II. Yet experience under the Act did demonstrate forcefully the magnitude and complexity of the problems inherent in the process of substituting administrative decisions for those of the market.

The task of administering the Act was given to the National Bituminous Coal Commission, now expanded to seven members,

---

[5] *Carter* v. *Carter Coal Co.*, 298 U.S. 238.

[6] Senate Interstate Committee, *Hearings on S. 4668, to Regulate Interstate Commerce in Bituminous Coal* (1936), 74th Cong., 2d sess., p. 36.

two of whom were to have had previous experience as operators and two as mineworkers. This provision for industry representation thus carried over the motif of industrial self-government from the NIRA. It was balanced only inadequately by the independent consumers' counsel. The Commission was placed within the Interior Department for housekeeping purposes, but was otherwise independent.

While a vestigial trace of the 1935 Act's labor provisions could be found in a grant to the Commission of authority to protect collective bargaining from company domination, and while the Commission had broad authority to conduct research on production, distribution, utilization, and conservation, the heart of the statute lay in its price-fixing provisions. Once again, the taxing power was used to compel compliance. Failure to accept the Commission's Bituminous Coal Code entailed a 19½ per-cent tax on the market value of all coal subject to the jurisdiction of the Act.

The price-fixing process prescribed by the Act was long and complex, as it had to be to replace the fixing of prices through the many and vigorously competitive markets in which coal was sold. Coal-producing regions were divided into ten minimum-price areas, subdivided in turn into twenty-three districts. In each district there was established a board composed of producer representatives and one labor representative. Price-fixing involved six distinct steps:

(1) On the basis of statistical reports from code members, each district board determined the weighted average cost per ton for coal produced in its district. Costs included all ordinary operating expenses, royalties, depreciation and depletion, selling and administrative costs, but excluded interest on bonded debt, income taxes, and allowance for profit.

(2) These cost determinations were reviewed by the Commission and combined into weighted average costs for each minimum price area.

(3) Each district board proposed minimum prices at the mines "for kinds, qualities, and sizes of coal produced in said district"— together with "classification of coal and price variations as to mines, consuming market areas, values as to uses and seasonal demand." Proposed prices were to be so calculated as to return for the district as a whole a yield per ton equal to the weighted average per ton costs for the minimum-price area in which the district was included.

(4) The proposed prices were submitted to the Commission

for review and modification.

(5) Where coal from several districts entered common market areas, the district boards (or, in cases of their failure to act, the Commission) were to co-ordinate district prices. Co-ordinated prices had to "be just and equitable . . . between and among districts"; they had to "reflect . . . relative market values, at points of delivery in each common consuming market area, of the various kinds, qualities, and sizes of coal . . . taking into account values as to uses, seasonal demand, transportation methods and charges and their effect upon a reasonable opportunity to compete on a fair basis, and the competitive relationships between coal and other forms of fuel and energy"; and they had to yield a return per ton in every minimum-price area as close as possible to the area's weighted average total cost per ton.

(6) The co-ordinated prices, together with appropriate rules and regulations, were then submitted to the Commission for further review and final promulgation.

Such a procedure obviously presented major problems of economic analysis and administration. Before the economic data necessary for pricing decisions could be compiled in a meaningful manner, many assumptions had to be made regarding the definition of costs, the value of various coals in different markets, and the impact of competition. Cost statistics had to be gathered from twelve thousand code members, shipping annually from 350 to 400 million tons of coal from more than thirty states to ninety thousand carload-lot buyers. The prices to be set would apply to coals moving by every conceivable manner of transportation and for any widespread use.

The National Bituminous Coal Commission thus faced perhaps the most complex administrative undertaking ever assigned a peacetime regulatory agency. Some 400,000 separate prices were to be established. Since the task had to be performed in accordance with the intricate criteria and procedural limitations of the 1937 law, and in the environment of a chaotic industry rent by savage interregional and intercompany rivalries, any group of administrators might well boggle at the assignment.

A possible legal barrier to this form of regulation had been removed by the altered trend of Supreme Court decisions after 1937. Challenges to the constitutionality of the Act were instituted immediately, but were rejected in 1940 by an 8 to 1 decision. The regulatory scheme was held to be within the commerce clause and not violative of the due process clause. "If we undertook," said the

Court, "to narrow the scope of federal intervention in this field . . . we would be blind to at least thirty years of history. . . . If the strategic character of this industry in our economy and the chaotic conditions which have prevailed in it do not justify legislation, it is difficult to imagine what would." [7]

Despite its many economic and administrative problems, the Commission, under heightened pressure to protect coal prices because of the sharp industrial recession of 1937, set about its task with celerity. The Act had become law on April 26. On June 21, the Commission promulgated the Bituminous Coal Code, which was accepted by 96 per cent of the industry within nine days. The Commission immediately took up the task of setting prices; it made its own tentative determination of costs, and the district boards were ordered to propose minimum prices on this basis. Since the boards proved unable to agree on interdistrict coordination, this function was likewise assumed by the Commission. Final price schedules were promulgated early in December, 1937, without prior public hearings. This hurried procedure, however, clearly conflicted with statutory requirements. The Commission was immediately faced with a flood of temporary injunctions secured primarily by large coal buyers. Although price levels improved for a month or two, the price structure again collapsed as injunctions freed increasing numbers of buyers from the necessity of observing the established minima. The price schedules were revoked in February, 1938.

In its next phase, the Commission leaned over backward to observe statutory procedural requirements to the full. Every effort was made to forestall complaint through informal co-operation. Since it was feared that the entire earlier proceeding had been tainted, even the old cost determinations were discarded. The first chairman, a producer representative who had been severely criticised for the initial fiasco, resigned in April, 1938; he was replaced by a more conciliatory member from the labor side. After a series of conferences with the district boards and the consumers' counsel, a new and highly formalized procedural schedule was arranged. It provided for public hearings at each of the three major stages: cost determination, price proposals, and price coordination.

The first stage occupied two months in the summer of 1938. It was followed by three months of minimum-price hearings in the autumn. Considerable delay was occasioned by litigation over the

---

[7] *Sunshine Anthracite Coal Co.* v. *Adkins*, 310 U.S. 381.

right of the Commission to open individual cost data to public inspection and cross-examination.[8] Minimum-price hearings were completed only at the end of March, 1939. The district boards were once again unable to co-ordinate prices, and the Commission itself undertook this final task in mid-May.

At this point, the form of the agency was radically altered by abolition of the Commission and transfer of its functions to a Bituminous Coal Division directly under the Secretary of the Interior. In explaining the transfer, carried out under the Reorganization Act of 1939, President Roosevelt declared that "experience has shown that direct administration will be cheaper, better, and more effective than through the cumbersome medium of an unnecessary Commission." The Commission had, in fact, been widely charged with incompetence, wastefulness, and favoritism toward particular producers and large consumers. In an industry as battle-scarred as bituminous coal, such criticism of regulators drawn from within was almost inevitable. The new Division's relations with the industry were far smoother. It is noteworthy that this shift from an effort at industrial self-government to outside governmental supervision occasioned little or no opposition.

While substantially modifying internal organization and personnel, the Division maintained the price-fixing procedure intact. Hearings on co-ordinated prices were continued throughout the summer and autumn of 1939; they were finally closed early in 1940. Opportunity was afforded for the filing of briefs and oral argument, first before trial examiners and later before the Division Director. Further briefs were submitted for consideration by the Secretary of the Interior. The final schedules were promulgated during the summer of 1940 and came into effect on October 1.

The process was so cumbersome and time-consuming, and various determinations were so hotly contested, that it is a tribute to the patience and determination of the Division's personnel that the task was ever completed. The record of hearings on co-ordinated prices included 26,000 pages of testimony and argument, two thousand exhibits, seven hundred written protests, and 112 briefs. After it had been summarized in the 2,800-page proposed report of the trial examiners, the Division Director heard nearly three hundred oral arguments. After receiving his report, the Secretary of the Interior had to hear some one hundred protests before issuing the final report.

This enormous investment of time and effort proved largely

[8] The issue was resolved in the Commission's favor in January, 1939. *Utah Fuel Co.* v. *National Bituminous Coal Commission*, 306 U.S. 56.

wasted. The minimum prices did operate as an effective floor under actual prices,[9] but this was primarily due to the fact that defense expenditures greatly strengthened demand. In 1941, the Guffey Act of 1937 was extended for two years, but in 1943, after a further extension of thirty days and another of ninety, it was allowed to die. Congress believed that industry conditions had so improved as no longer to justify a regulatory scheme so sharply at odds with free market practices. The decision was also influenced by resentment at some of the UMW's vigorous wartime bargaining methods.

While experience under the Act was too brief and too much affected by the industrial revival of the forties to permit a full and definitive appraisal, certain conclusions can be drawn from it.[10] The Act's price-fixing criteria displayed unmistakable signs of the effort to achieve compromise among a welter of conflicting interests. The very complexity and multiplicity of standards, which sought to combine criteria both of cost and of market value, necessarily left to the Division a wide area of administrative discretion. Yet, given the disorganization of the industry and the diversity of its interests, it is doubtful if much greater precision in legislative draftsmanship would have been possible.

The Act's general intent was clear: it sought to raise the *level* of prices while leaving pre-existing competitive *relationships* untouched. It seems equally clear that achievement of this purpose under normal or depressed conditions would have strained the administrative resources of the Division and the enforcement devices of the Act. Any price-fixing system tends to allocate production, to determine which mines will operate, what share of various markets they may claim, and what their level of profits will be. Accordingly, the Division would have had to withstand the inevitable discontent of thousands of individual producers desiring betterment of their relative positions. Moreover, the Act contemplated the freezing of a price structure and the competitive relationships it reflected. But coal prices are dynamic and their relationships highly fluid. As the Division Director pointed out, it "is a relatively chaotic, fluctuating industry, which is characterized not by settled, standard conditions, but at most by general trends, including

---

[9] Enforcement, even in this chaotic industry, was a relatively minor problem, perhaps because of the favorable turn in general economic conditions. The Division issued only 198 cease and desist orders and revoked only 139 code memberships (of which 69 were later restored) because of violations by producers.

[10] For a thorough appraisal, see W. E. Fisher and C. M. James, *Minimum Price Fixing in the Bituminous Coal Industry* (1955), ch. 10.

diverse and even contradictory specific trends." [11]

The Act sought to remedy an immediate situation, and this objective it bid fair to accomplish. Even in its brief period of operation, it largely succeeded in removing labor standards from competition. Effective minimum-price regulation was able to protect conditions of employment and to strengthen the bargaining power of the union. It was also of obvious short-run benefit to producers and the coal communities.

Minimum-price maintenance, however, has longer-run implications which might have aggravated the industry's malady. Most important, it tends to widen the gap between capacity and demand by enabling high-cost producers to remain in operation and by accelerating the shift of consumers to competing energy sources. It hampers technological innovation and industry efficiency by its tendency to freeze existing competitive relationships. Thus it deals with the symptoms of a sick industry but makes a basic cure more difficult.

It is probable that price control as a permanent policy under less buoyant conditions would have entailed so many enforcement problems as to lead almost inevitably to the imposition of production controls. Indeed, this prospect was envisaged by the 1937 Act in a provision directing the Commission to investigate the subject. British and German experience shows that production controls are feasible and administratively far simpler than minimum-price maintenance. It is essentially through production control that the UMW has sought to deal with the industry's ills since World War II. Such a program, however, involves many of the same harmful long-run effects as direct minimum-price regulation.

3. Union Regulation and Corporate Concentration

As a result of New Deal labor and coal policies and the enhanced wartime demand for coal, conditions became favorable during the 1940's for a great increase in the power of the United Mine Workers. Since the war the union has become the main instrument for stabilization of the industry. By the end of World War II, the UMW had organized all but 10 or 15 per cent of the mines.

The union's strength is not based on numbers alone; it has long been one of the nation's most militant and cohesive unions, its

[11] *Findings of Fact, Conclusions of Law, and Order of the Director of the Bituminous Coal Division Establishing Effective Minimum Prices and Marketing Rules and Regulations under the Bituminous Coal Act of 1937* (1940), p. 11.

members responding to President John L. Lewis's strike calls with discipline and unity. The militancy of its members derives from the peculiar unattractiveness of coal mining as an occupation and from the bloodiness of the industry's past labor relations. In past decades, living in company towns, the miners' whole lives seemed to be controlled by the producers. They were economically, geographically, and socially isolated. Their work was unusually demanding and hazardous; their employment was highly insecure. Accordingly, to them

the union is more than a collective bargaining association, it is the pillar of their hopes. As long as the union is preserved they are not serfs, they retain a glimpse of freedom and an awareness of potential power. The fortunes of the union are completely entwined with their own personal histories.[12]

During the thirties, while industry stabilization was being attempted by legislation, the UMW concentrated its growing bargaining power on wages. Its main efforts were to increase wage levels, to stabilize and standardize payments for skill and shift differentials, and to eliminate regional differentials. It enjoyed great success. Average weekly earnings have risen from less than $20 in 1935 to as much as $85 in some recent years, a rate of growth substantially higher than that of wages in general. Skill differentials have been made uniform, and the North-South wage differential, on which unionization had foundered in the twenties, was eliminated after a long struggle.

These wage concessions, often secured by the UMW by playing off one region against another, or "captive mines" (owned by steel companies) against commercial mines, have had important consequences on industry organization and practices. Miners no longer compete with each other in wages, and operators no longer compete on the basis of wage rates. Since wages still comprise more than half the total cost of coal, the floor under wage rates

[12] J. A. Wechsler, *Labor Baron: A Portrait of John L. Lewis* (1944), pp. 8–9. In the words of another observer: "Miners are haunted men. Their minds are vexed with the memories of bloody struggles for higher pay and for the preservation and growth of their labor union. Their thoughts are constantly troubled by insecurity of work, for they know that, although the calendar year contains 365 days, they have worked as little as 142, and only nine times out of the last 25 years have they averaged more than 200 days a year. Their hearts grow weary repressing the importunate warnings of the dangers that lurk underground, which may at any time cut them off from their livelihood. Their families silently share their burdens." C. A. Madison, *American Labor Leaders* (1950), p. 157.

places narrow limitations on the range of competitive price reductions. The union has provided that stability hitherto precluded by the extremely competitive structure of the industry.

High wage rates have had other effects. They have slowly forced some of the less efficient mines to close. The UMW does not object to this, since it believes that excess capacity is an important factor in the industry's ills. Viewing the problem as one of too many miners as well as too many mines, the union has also sought to reduce employment by forbidding child labor, by strictly enforcing seniority provisions (thereby discouraging the entry of younger men), and by encouraging mechanization.

Since World War II, the UMW has used its power directly to stabilize the industry and maintain prices. In 1947, it incorporated in its collective bargaining contracts a "ready and willing" clause which, in effect, gave the union the power legally to call work stoppages whenever it chose. On June 13, 1949, when mounting stockpiles of coal threatened existing price levels, the UMW began what Lewis called "a brief stabilizing period of inaction." After the work stoppage, the union, following a "divide-the-orders, share-the-work" program, then ordered its members to work only three days a week. This program had the enthusiastic support of hard-pressed producers, although it was opposed by the captive mines and certain other producers who would have been able to dispose of a full week's production. These tactics have been repeated on several occasions. Thus, a form of private regulation by the UMW has been substituted for the prewar government regulation.

Union stabilization of the industry raises important policy questions. "The unhappy truth," concludes one comment, "is that the UMW is attempting to apply the 'remedies' of monopoly (in the broad sense) to what it envisions are the central problems of the coal industry." [13] Many of the criticisms which were leveled against the Guffey Acts can also be applied to UMW controls. Its share-the-work programs protect the inefficient and penalize the more efficient mines. Its very success in maintaining and raising coal prices has accelerated the shift to other energy sources—a shift given further impetus in the 1940's by the frequency with which work stoppages interrupted the flow of coal to markets. The UMW campaigns vigorously in the political arena against competing energy sources—hydroelectric power projects, extensions of natural-gas pipelines, and imports of oil—but it is a losing battle.

Yet the great market power wielded by the UMW has had fewer questionable consequences than might be expected. The share-the-

[13] M. A. Baratz, *The Union and the Coal Industry* (1955), p. 141.

work program is pursued only in times of depressed demand; at other times, UMW policies tend to weed out the less efficient mines, and union leaders have consistently promoted mechanization. Restriction of employment in an occupation as hazardous and unattractive as coal mining is not entirely blameworthy. Reduction of the number of mines, promotion of mechanization, and the counter-organization of employers have all tended toward greater corporate concentration among coal producers. Such a development, while anticompetitive in the structural sense, may promote more dynamic technological improvements in methods of extracting and transporting the energy that coal contains.[14] Only the resources of large corporations or of government are sufficient, it can be argued, to discover and develop economic means of improving the industry's technology by increasing the yield of chemicals, and by liquefaction, gasification, or conversion into electricity at the mine. Some progress along these lines has taken place in recent years, primarily through research conducted by the Bureau of Mines, the Battelle Institute, and the Pittsburgh Consolidation Coal Company, the largest producer. In this industry, the excessively competitive structure of the past has militated against technological or economic dynamism.

Thus, it is not interference with competition as such that calls UMW controls into question. Indeed, were an economic downturn or other circumstance to weaken UMW strength and were conditions like those of the 1920's to recur, there would probably be renewed pressure for legislation resembling the Guffey Acts. Such a program would have more undesirable economic consequences than the present UMW controls and would be administratively cumbersome, if not unworkable.

Instead, UMW controls may be challenged under the general philosophy which holds it undesirable for any private group to possess so much market power. This danger is reinforced by the crucial importance of energy to the whole economy and the interrelations of coal and other energy sources. The economy's appetite for energy has grown rapidly and will continue to do so, but known oil and natural-gas reserves and undeveloped hydroelectric sites are more limited than coal reserves. If oil availabilities in fact become inadequate before atomic power is sufficiently developed, it is possible that coal's many decades of stagnation and decline may come to an end. In those circumstances, UMW restrictive controls which were acceptable in a declining industry may well be challenged in an expanding industry of vital national importance.

[14] This is the argument of a series of articles in *Fortune*, March, April, and July, 1947.

CHAPTER 20

Oil and the Mixed Economy

REGULATION of the oil industry, like that
of coal, falls outside the broad patterns of public utility and
antitrust policies. Here, too, regulation arose out of the problems
of excessive competition and received the enthusiastic support of
most producers. And here, also, the forms of regulation were peculiarly conditioned by the technology of production. But the
differences between these two great energy industries are more
significant than the similarities. The oil industry has enjoyed almost constant dynamic expansion. While oil production and retailing have been keenly, sometimes excessively, competitive,
refining, transportation, and wholesale marketing have been concentrated in huge corporations. The role of labor unions is relatively unimportant.

1. Regulation of Oil Production

In one phase or another, the oil industry has occupied the attention of government for about eighty years. Concentrated control
of refineries and pipelines played a leading part in producing the
antimonopoly movement of the late nineteenth century. Pipelines
were given public utility status and placed under the control of the
ICC in 1906. After the dissolution of the Standard Oil trust in
1911, a single near-monopoly in refining and distribution was replaced by a somewhat oligopolistic situation, in which about
twenty major integrated companies control the great bulk of refining capacity and crude oil and product pipelines. Allegations of

concerted price-making among these "majors," and of undue control by them over the business practices of their distributors, have made the industry the object of an almost continuous stream of antitrust prosecutions.[1]

Our primary concern here, however, is with a different sector of the industry—the production of crude oil. In this sector, concentration is far less marked. In the early phase, Standard Oil, sure of its control of transportation and refining, was quite willing to let others bear the risks of exploration and production, but over the years, as the majors grew in number, they increasingly undertook production.[2] As intricate geophysical and geological exploration techniques have come to the fore and as oil deposits become harder to find, capital requirements have mounted and the role of the large corporation has expanded. Offshore and foreign production are almost completely controlled by the large companies. In domestic onshore production, however, the independent remains a significant factor, still accounting for a large share of production. The rewards for discovery are so rich that independents still "wildcat" in great numbers in the hope of striking bonanzas. The independents, moreover, are a powerful force in the politics of the oil states, one of the fundamental determinants of the modern regulatory system.

The pattern of oil regulation is a blend of three elements: (1) direct production control is imposed by most oil states through proration laws; (2) interstate collaboration is provided by an interstate oil compact; (3) state regulation is supplemented by federal assistance, (a) in determining production quotas, and (b) in forbidding interstate shipments of oil or petroleum products pro-

---

[1] For an analysis of the oil industry leading to a strong plea for the vigorous application of the antitrust laws, see E. D. Rostow, *A National Policy for the Oil Industry* (1948). For the contrary viewpoint, stressing the competitiveness of the industry, see Ralph Cassady, Jr., *Price Making and Price Behavior in the Petroleum Industry* (1954).

[2] The discovery of rich pools in the Southwest shortly after the turn of the century enabled some independent producers, notably the Texas Company and the Gulf Oil Corporation, to integrate toward the consumer and ultimately to become major companies. The splitting of the Standard Oil combination into thirty-four parts by the antitrust decree of 1911 left most of the resultant companies with gross imbalances among their production, refining, transportation, and marketing facilities. As the community of interest and control among these Standard Oil companies gradually eroded, many integrated backward or forward in order to assure themselves of ample supplies of crude oil and of markets for their refined products. Subsequently, other refiners increased their exploration and production activities because of the special tax advantages offered to producers by the allowance for depletion.

duced in violation of state law. In recent years, moreover, the viability of state production controls has come to depend on the federal restriction of oil imports. Before discussing these developments, it is essential to consider the technological, legal, and economic factors motivating the imposition of public controls.

The Basis for Government Intervention

Common-law rules governing the rights of surface owners and leaseholders, as they developed in this country after the discovery of oil in 1859, were singularly inappropriate to the oil industry. Their effect was actively to promote waste. Ownership of land overlying an oil pool is ordinarily divided into numerous holdings unrelated to the subsurface petroliferous structure. The oil is trapped in porous sands or limestone strata surrounded by impervious rock. Since oil usually occurs together with water and is lighter than water, it is found in the highest points of the porous stratum, usually where there is a bending or break or where the stratum "pinches out" in a stratigraphic trap. Natural gas is usually present in addition, and the oil is in a complex physical equilibrium of overlying gas pressure, dissolved gas pressure, underlying hydrostatic pressure, and peripheral rock pressure. By far the most economical means of recovering oil is to make optimum utilization of natural reservoir pressures to drive the oil to the surface once the reservoir is punctured by drilling. Both gas and water assist production in other ways. As long as pressure is maintained, dissolved gas reduces the viscosity of the oil and permits it to move readily. And an even water drive, with the water following the oil, tends to flush the oil out from the rock and sand and to push it up the well. Exploitation designed to maximize the long-run yield of oil demands careful spacing of wells, drilling to carefully selected depths, and limitation of the relative rates of flow of gas and oil in order to maintain the maximum natural pressure as long as possible. In areas where entire pools are managed under unified auspices, such as the Middle East, these practices are readily followed. Diversity of ownership under American conditions, however, produces far different results.

As a general common-law principle, a landowner holds title to all minerals directly underlying his property. This doctrine is fairly easily applied to metals and coal, but the physical facts of oil and its production fit poorly into this framework. Release of reservoir pressure through tapping the system at one point induces migration of oil toward that well from the rest of the reservoir. In determining the ownership of oil raised to the surface by one landowner but drawn out from under the property of his neighbors, the courts had at least three different strands of precedent to draw from. The first, the doctrine of riparian right, gave owners of lands bordering on running streams equal interest in the preservation of their flow. The second granted owners of water wells the right freely to withdraw percolating waters beneath the surface. The third, the rule of capture, gave ownership of wildlife to whoever captures it on his own land.

Unfortunately,[3] the courts rejected the first rule and accepted the analogies of percolating waters and wildlife in proclaiming the applicability of the rule of capture. ". . . There can be no definite sale and delivery of oil and gas in place," said a Texas court in 1921, "since they are supposed to percolate restlessly about under the surface of the earth, even as birds fly from field to field and the beasts roam from forest to forest. . . ." [4] Under this rule of capture, as a Pennsylvania court admitted in 1907,

. . . every landowner or his lessee may locate his wells wherever he pleases, regardless of the interests of others. He may distribute them over the whole farm or locate them on only one part of it. He may crowd the adjoining farms so as to enable him to draw oil and gas from them. What then can his neighbor do? Nothing; only go and do likewise. He must protect his own oil and gas. He knows it is wild and will run away if it finds an opening and it is his business to keep it at home. This may not be the best rule but neither the legislature nor our highest court has given us any better.[5]

In consequence, no sooner is a pool discovered than every nearby property owner begins drillings in order to obtain as large a share as possible from the pool. The owner of a large tract will place "offset wells" at frequent points around his boundaries in order to balance the withdrawals of his neighbors. The rate of recovery will be as high as reservoir pressure permits, since restriction by any single producer will merely redound to the benefit of others. Such "flush production" exhausts the natural reservoir energy with great rapidity. Depending on the particular geological formation, as little as 10 per cent of the oil may be recovered without pumping,

[3] That is, in the light of hindsight. At the time that the rule of capture was accepted, the judges were impressed by the technical difficulties of attempting to measure the quantity of oil under particular tracts of land and by the fact that they were deciding a conflict between one landowner who wished to produce and one who wished not to. The public interest in such disputes appeared to lie on the side of production.

[4] *Medina Oil Development Co. v. Murphy,* 233 S.W. 333.

[5] *Bernard v. Monongahela Natural Gas Co.,* 216 Pa. 362.

contrasted with up to 50 or 60 per cent under the best engineering practice. Not only does this condition waste capital through excessive drilling and acceleration of the substitution of "stripper well" (i.e., pumping) operations; it may also make much of the oil permanently nonrecoverable. The unduly rapid escape of gas from solution increases the oil's viscosity and sometimes makes it impossible to pump. In addition, encroaching water may cut off sections of the pool. Thus, the combination of a unique technological situation with diffused surface ownership, together with the rule of capture, necessitates public intervention in order to achieve the objectives of conservation.

While the need for conservation is invariably placed at the forefront of arguments for regulation of oil production, no precise meaning can be given to the term. The wastes of competitive drilling cover a wide range. Direct overground wastes are caused by the venting and flaring of gas, which could have been used both for reservoir pressure and as a fuel; by the loss of the natural gasoline mixed with the gas; and by the escape through seepage, evaporation, or fire of oil stored above ground. Then, too, there are the underground wastes involved in the loss of pressure, increased viscosity, and flooding. In the earliest fields, as much as 75 to 90 per cent of the oil remained underground after production had been terminated, and as recently as 1938 it was estimated that "perhaps as much as 65 per cent" of the oil discovered was not being recovered.[6]

In addition to these physical wastes, there are the economic wastes resulting from the unnecessary expenditure of capital and labor in offsetting and other superfluous wells, the use of pumps because of the squandering of reservoir pressure, and the storage above ground of oil better left underground. It has been estimated that waste of materials and labor in drilling and operating unnecessary wells in the East Texas field alone may have exceeded $1 billion.[7] Finally, there may be a question of the desirability of using scarce, exhaustible energy sources for "lower uses," e.g., natural gas to make carbon black or as a boiler fuel.

Omitting consideration of natural gas, which is discussed in Chapter 21, the major public interest in oil conservation is a function of the relatively low ratio of known reserves to present

[6] National Resources Committee, *Energy Resources and National Policy* (1938), p. 138.
[7] Subcommittee of the House Committee on Interstate and Foreign Commerce, *Hearings on Petroleum Investigation*, 76th Cong., 1st sess. (1939); Pt. 1, p. 503.

production. The most recent estimates of proven reserves in the United States total 30.6 billion barrels, compared with an annual production rate of about 2.6 billion barrels. The reserve-production ratio is therefore about 11½ years. This figure should not be construed as implying imminent depletion of our domestic reserves, since proven reserves are continually being increased by the extension of already discovered fields, the improvement of extraction techniques to make more of the oil recoverable,[8] and the discovery of new deposits. Despite a tremendous expansion of production, additions to reserves over the decades have more than kept pace with withdrawals. The reserve-production ratio has therefore remained almost constant since World War I. On the other hand, new discoveries and other additions to proven reserves become harder to make each year. Higher proportions of dry holes are drilled, discoveries occur at greater depths, and the new pools are smaller. In 1957, for the first time in many years, more oil was produced than was added to reserves. The conclusion of the National Resources Committee in 1939 is even more applicable today: "We have produced a larger proportion of our reserves; we are now using our reserves at a faster rate than the rest of the world; and probably we have discovered a much larger percentage of our total possible reserves because of the more intensive search for oil in this country."[9] The United States now consumes about 55 per cent of the free world's annual oil production but has only 15 per cent of the free world's known reserves.

The vital role of petroleum products in our present economy and their essentiality to national defense need no emphasis. Synthetic liquid fuels could be made from oil shale and coal, but in the present state of technology the costs would create serious dislocations in an economic structure geared to abundant use. Oil imports could meet our needs at reasonable costs, but to rely fully upon them would raise serious questions of national security. Consequently, since the recovery of a higher proportion of known deposits through improved production techniques appears to offer

[8] Improved methods of secondary recovery have been growing in importance. In 1958, a study by the Oil Compact Commission indicated that in addition to present proven reserves, another 13.1 billion barrels could be recovered from existing fields by fluid injection. *Oil and Gas Journal* (June 30, 1958), pp. 46–47. Of the 309.8 billion barrels of oil-in-place discovered in the United States, 57.8 billion had been produced by 1958 and 30.6 billion more—the proven reserves—could be recovered through existing techniques. This amounts to a recovery rate of only 28.5 per cent. Obviously any significant increase in this rate would add enormously to reserves.

[9] *Energy Resources and National Policy*, p. 143.

as great an augmentation of supplies as probable future discoveries, the public interest in extending conservation can hardly be questioned.

Despite this clear-cut general interest, the needs of conservation alone would almost certainly not have engendered the present regulatory machinery. Active state intervention was induced rather by pressures for economic stabilization and for the protection of correlative individual interests. Like "conservation," the term "stabilization" has no universally accepted meaning. In this context, it may be taken as the maintenance of crude-oil prices above the total production costs of relatively inefficient producers. Under the conditions peculiar to the oil industry, this objective is partially conducive to conservation. For restrictions on production not only maintain prices; they may also, if properly administered, bring production techniques into conformity with high engineering standards and thereby increase the total ultimate recovery. Indeed, any restriction of production normally increases ultimate recovery. And while state-wide production quotas or "allowables" are set with only the price level in mind, engineering factors serve increasingly as the basis for fixing allowables for fields within states. In addition, the state agencies regulating production also prevent direct waste by such measures as fixing maximum gas-oil ratios, prohibiting earthen storage, enforcing precautions against pressure blowouts and fire, and requiring proper well casings to seal the oil-bearing strata. In addition, price levels higher than would otherwise prevail encourage exploration and development and prevent the abandonment of "stripper wells" during temporary periods of "flush" production from newly discovered fields.

Yet the objectives of conservation and stabilization, while overlapping, are not identical. Their harmony in practice depends in large measure upon the particular restrictive measures imposed. Allowables for fields are determined by demand, not by optimum rate of flow, and the quotas allotted some fields have been set so low as to use reservoir pressure inefficiently. Allocation of quotas on the basis of numbers of wells has encouraged excessive well drilling—a waste only inadequately restrained by spacing regulations. And the granting of at least one well to each tract of land, combined with equal well allowables, permits such close drilling in settled areas as to enable "fingers" of water to cut off oil in some fields.

The immediate impetus to present control mechanisms came from the desire for stabilization. It arose from the conjunction early in the 1930's of new discoveries on an unprecedented scale, above all in the extraordinary East Texas field, with an absolute falling off in demand for the first time in the industry's history. Crude oil prices fell in 1931 from nearly one dollar to less than 10 cents a barrel. The situation threatened total demoralization of the industry, and led the producing states to undertake comprehensive restrictions.

The Pattern of State Regulation

Regulation of oil production began in Pennsylvania and New York in 1878 and 1879, and soon spread to other states. The early statutes provided minimum safety standards, discouraged the more dramatic forms of overground waste, and protected fields against malpractices by individual well owners.

Production control, associated with the concept of "economic waste" (i.e., production beyond market requirements at remunerative prices), was considered by Oklahoma in 1915 as a result of temporary oversupply, but was not put into effect because a war-induced increase in demand resolved the problem. Until the late twenties, in fact, more anxiety was expressed over prospective shortages than over excessive production. Only with the sudden spate of new discoveries between 1926 and 1931, coinciding with a sharp reduction in demand, was outright restriction undertaken. The producing states had good reason to be concerned. Their tax revenues depended in large measure on the prosperity of the oil industry, and the depression was placing new burdens on hard-pressed state treasuries. Producers clamored for public aid. The Oklahoma law of 1915 was therefore revived; Texas followed with similar action. At the height of flush production from newly discovered pools, however, ordinary regulatory mechanisms did not suffice to stem the tide.

Litigation was one obstacle. Although the principle of statutory restriction had been sustained by the courts for many years, both as a legitimate conservational measure and because it tended to protect correlative rights in particular fields, the methods of restriction adopted in the emergency were struck down under the Fourteenth Amendment. While producers as a group favored state control, as individuals they maintained a hectic race for recovery under the rule of capture. A flood of "hot" oil, produced in disregard of restriction laws, flowed from the Texas and Oklahoma fields. The governors of these states even resorted to martial law, policing production controls with the aid of the militia, but this extreme measure was invalidated by the Supreme Court. Stability was finally achieved only in 1933, with the aid of federal intervention under the National Industrial Recovery Act.

Despite the temporary failure of state restriction at the pit of the depression, legislative and administrative techniques devised at that time remain at the heart of the control machinery. All the important producing states, except Illinois and California, follow a similar regulatory pattern, although with significant differences of detail. In California, where the restriction statute of 1931 was repealed in the following year, like results are achieved through voluntary curtailment under a producers' association. The core of the production controls is the system of prorationing, which allocates to each producer a maximum production quota. Determination of total national production and allocations among the states are made through federal machinery described below. The state problem is one of allocation to individual producers within its boundaries.

In seeking a workable proration plan, administrators face a tangle of technical, economic, and political considerations. At first, allowables were set on a flat per-well basis, but this encouraged wasteful drilling and was inequitable unless wells were evenly spaced and reservoir pressure was uniform throughout the field. Principles of equity, implemented to some extent by judicial application of the Fourteenth Amendment, required that allowables be distributed as nearly as possible in proportion to the oil in place under each tract. A second method allocated quotas in proportion to potential output, but this involved the wasteful measurement process of running each well for a time at full capacity. Moreover, it, too, encouraged the duplication of wells. A third method set quotas in proportion to the area drained by each well. This discouraged excessive drilling on individual tracts but failed to reflect differences in reservoir conditions. In recent years, formulas have been devised combining such elements as well depth, tract acreage, thickness of strata, viscosity, and differences between static and flowing bottom-hole pressures. But if a field's quota is only a small fraction of its potential, a strict prorata distribution will make many of the smaller properties unremunerative. A minimum per-well allowance is therefore usually set for such "marginal wells."

While proration formulas are expressed in engineering terms, the weighting of the different elements is heavily conditioned by the political influence of various producing groups. Since small producers, and the small tract owners who receive production royalties, are numerous and politically active, in some fields the bulk of output is produced under flat per-well allowances, while the potentially more productive wells have on occasion been cut back to as little as 2 per cent of capacity. For some years, such issues were fought out in the federal courts and administrative action frequently fell by the wayside, but in 1940 the Supreme Court, recognizing that proration presents "as thorny a problem as has challenged the wisdom and ingenuity of legislatures," decided that its solution should be left to state administrators.[10]

Whatever the formula applied, proration almost inevitably leads the state into more intensified regulation of productive methods. As long as the single well unit or the open-flow rate plays any part in the determination of allowables, an incentive is provided to multiplication of wells. To an increasing extent, therefore, particularly since 1935, states have undertaken drilling restrictions. Most producing states now have well-spacing laws which limit or discourage drilling. Texas provides a general minimum acreage per well but gives to its regulatory agency, the Railroad Commission, administrative discretion to grant exceptions so as to avoid individual hardship. The pressure of small tract owners has been so great that in some fields more drilling occurs under the exception than under the rule. Each tract owner is granted one well as a matter of right. Owners of larger tracts may then be permitted to increase their well density up to the average on neighboring tracts. Thus, although a ten-acre spacing pattern was prescribed for the East Texas field, in fact the average density was one well to less than five acres.[11]

Over the years, engineering standards promoting underground conservation have been given increasing weight in the administration of prorationing.[12] Price stabilization undoubtedly remains the governing motive. This objective, however, is satisfied merely by the restriction of production to given figures. Ample scope remains for the application of conservational criteria, both in the distribution of allowables and through the requirement of improved production practices as an incident to state protection of the market.

---

[10] *Railroad Commission of Texas* v. *Rowan & Nichols Oil Co.*, 310 U.S. 573.

[11] Seventeen states, not including Texas, now have compulsory pooling laws, however, requiring the owners of small lots to integrate them so as to form a drilling unit whose average complies with drilling regulations.

[12] For analyses which argue that prorationing makes little or no contribution to conservation, see Rostow, *op. cit.*, and M. W. Watkins, *Oil: Stabilization or Conservation?* (1937). For more recent analyses which show how the conservational effects of prorationing have grown, see Y. Y. Willburn, "Administrative Control of Petroleum in Texas," in E. S. Redford (ed.), *Public Administration and Policy Formation* (1956); E. W. Zimmerman, *Conservation in the Production of Petroleum* (1957).

Unnecessary loss of reservoir pressure is now limited in several ways, and a number of wasteful and inefficient operating practices are prohibited.

It is clear that unitization—operation of a field as a single unit —alone provides the conditions for optimum exploitation. Voluntary unitization has been slow to develop. It requires agreement of all owners or their lessees, and small owners have usually felt that they stood to gain more under the rule of capture or under a proration formula, receiving a larger slice of a smaller pie. Compulsory unitization has long been urged [13] and now is supported by the major oil companies. Because of the opposition of small operators, however, the states have been reluctant to adopt it, although the federal government has strongly encouraged unitization of pools which underlie national lands. In the postwar years, there have been important technological advances in the extraction of oil through reinjection of gas and water and in methods of secondary recovery. These measures normally require unit operation and have augmented the demand for unitization. A few states now authorize compulsory unitization under certain conditions, and since 1947 Texas has twice amended its laws to encourage voluntary unitization.

Interstate Co-operation and Federal Assistance

The whole fabric of state regulation depends upon interstate co-operation. Unrestrained output in a single major producing state would endanger the entire carefully built market structure. Restriction elsewhere would then simply benefit the nonco-operator. The mutuality of interest among producing states has not proved sufficient to hold them all in line without federal action.

Federal interest in oil production is more generalized than that of the producing states. As trustees for the nation's defense, federal officials have long been concerned with the possibility of shortage in time of war. The Interior Department, through its control of oil leases on public lands, has experimented with conservational techniques, including compulsory unitization, and played a part in claiming offshore oil reserves for the federal government. Active participation in the general regulatory machinery, however, largely takes the form of supplementing state prorationing. It provides that minimum degree of outside aid without which state controls would be impotent.

A Federal Oil Conservation Board, first appointed in 1924 to promote conservation, later turned its attention to promoting in-

[13] E.g., see National Resources Committee, *op. cit.*, pp. 24–25, 216–223.

terstate co-operation for production restriction. Brief success was achieved in 1931–1932, but it was followed by an even greater demoralization of the industry than before. A number of proposals were then made for direct federal controls, but they were displaced by action under the National Industrial Recovery Act.

The NIRA affected the industry in two ways. Section 9 authorized the President to prohibit interstate and foreign transportation of petroleum and petroleum products produced or withdrawn from storage in conflict with state law. This power was applied almost immediately and succeeded, by the end of 1934, in stemming the flood of "hot" oil from East Texas. The industry's NRA code, adopted in the summer of 1933, transferred the state regulatory systems to federal hands. Imports were limited; production was restricted to estimated consumer demand at remunerative prices and allocated among states, pools, and individual wells; prices were controlled; and refining and marketing were surrounded with a network of limitations designed to maintain the price structure. Unlike that of many other NRA codes, petroleum code administration was not delegated exclusively to industry representatives. It was withdrawn from NRA supervision and placed under Interior Secretary Ickes. There followed a period of sharp conflict between the federal administrators and industry representatives. On the whole, the industry welcomed the end of the NIRA.

A few months before its decision condemning the NIRA as a whole, the Supreme Court invalidated Section 9 as an improper delegation of legislative authority.[14] It was replaced almost immediately by the Connally "Hot Oil" Act, which forbade interstate commerce in contraband oil and provided appropriate sanctions for enforcement.

Meanwhile, earlier proposals for interstate co-operation bore fruit in 1935 in a compact among the producing states. Administrative machinery was established in the form of an Interstate Oil Compact Commission, including a representative from each member state. The compact proclaims conservation to be its goal and specifically renounces the objective of limiting production "for the purpose of stabilizing or fixing prices . . . or to create or perpetuate monopoly or to promote regimentation." In practice, however, the Commission has been laggard in dealing with the problems of conservation, while in August, 1939, it moved quickly to secure agreement on a temporary complete shutdown of production in the face of a price cut by a major refiner. Its

[14] *Panama Refining Co.* v. *Ryan*, 293 U.S. 388 (1935).

main function has been to bring together representatives of the industry and of the state regulatory commissions.

The federal government also provides the basis for establishing national and state production quotas. The Bureau of Mines makes monthly forecasts of demand for petroleum products at existing prices, computes the equivalent crude oil demand, and divides this total among the producing states. Its allocations are based on past output, present capacity, and established channels of supply to refineries. These state "estimates" are in reality production quotas, which are then subdivided by state authorities for prorationing among its fields and wells. While state acceptance is wholly voluntary, the Bureau of Mines estimates are generally closely followed, although independent action by Illinois in 1939 for a while threatened the entire apparatus of control. State prorationing controls, in turn, are supported by the Connally Act.

Conflict Between Federal and State Authority

One of the most striking aspects of this entire regulatory system is the limited character of the federal government's policy-making role. Through the Bureau of Mines, it provides the necessary statistical foundation, and under the Connally Act, it helps to police the controls. As described below, it also limits imports in order to protect prorationing. Nevertheless, although the problems of oil production are national, if not international, policy is made by agencies of the producing states, led by the Texas Railroad Commission.

This federal self-restraint is especially surprising in view of the importance of oil policies to national defense and economic welfare, and the fact that prorationing, which in a sense cartelizes domestic oil production, runs contrary to the general tenor of antitrust policy. The explanation lies in the relative strength of the oil industry in a number of states with far-reaching influence in the political system as a whole. The welfare of the oil-producing states is inextricably intertwined with the economic condition of the industry. They share an understandable fear of control by a political unit potentially more responsive to consumer than to producer interest.

The concern of the national government, on the other hand, derives from the need for conservation and the possibility of abuses of regulatory power by the producing states. Since no crisis of shortage is obviously imminent, the consumer, always hard to arouse, has remained quiescent. The price-raising impact of prorationing has been largely offset by impressive technological economies in refining crude oil and in utilizing its products. Accordingly, recommendations for federal regulation to promote conservation, such as those made by the National Resources Committee in 1939, have won little support.

2. The Offshore Oil Controversy

Occasionally federal and state authority have come into direct conflict. A leading example is the controversy over control of off-shore oil deposits.

As the search for oil broadened and as drilling techniques were improved, rich fields were discovered on the continental shelf between the low-water mark and the three-mile limit, primarily off the coasts of Texas, Louisiana, and California. Although owner-ship and governmental jurisdiction over these lands had not been definitively settled at law, the federal government had never exer-cised any control over them, except in connection with navigation, and the states had assumed authority, licensing oil operations and collecting royalties. But beginning in 1937, the Interior and Navy Departments initiated a vigorous campaign to claim federal juris-diction. The reasons were summarized by the National Resources Committee in 1939, in advocating:

. . . a bold assertion of the national interest in any petroleum or natural-gas reserves that may be found in those [offshore] areas. It is . . . unfortunate . . . that early in our history the public ownership of all subsurface mineral wealth was not declared; such a step would have been so simple at an early stage and would have meant so much in terms of conservation, and it would be so complex and costly at this stage—not to speak of the wastes of irreplaceable resources that have already taken place. But here and now in 1939 we have one last opportunity to take steps which will reserve to the nation petroleum deposits that may be of considerable extent. . . . At this stage in our history it is sheer folly to overlook any opportunity for safeguarding the national interest in petroleum reserves.[15]

At the administration's request, a number of congressional reso-lutions were introduced to establish federal control over the off-shore areas. The first two proposals asserted federal title, but most of the later ones omitted mention of title and instead declared that conservation of the offshore deposits was essential for national defense and the protection of interstate commerce and that rights of the federal government in these areas were an "attribute of its

[15] *Op. cit.*, p. 29.

sovereignty, paramount and exclusive." The Attorney General was directed to protect these rights by appropriate judicial proceeding.

Measures of this type were given fairly extensive consideration by Congress in the period 1937–1939. They were supported almost exclusively by the executive departments, who urged the cause of conservation and stressed the need of the navy for oil reserves. They were opposed by state and local governments, who feared the loss of actual or potential royalties, and by the oil producers, who feared the loss of existing licenses and preferred state to federal regulation. In 1937, before the groups favoring state control had been able to mobilize their forces in strength, the Senate passed one of the resolutions, but no action was taken in the House.

Meanwhile, the Interior Department had been pursuing its objective on other fronts. Until 1937, the Department had always denied applications for prospecting permits on the offshore lands on the ground that they were state property. In that year, however, Secretary Ickes began to hold such applications in abeyance, thereby clouding the titles of state-licensed oil producers and also many titles not involving oil production. Having failed to persuade Congress to declare federal jurisdiction, Ickes sought to have the Attorney General bring suit to secure a judicial determination of the ownership and control of the contested lands. This precipitated a behind-the-scenes struggle of several years' duration within the administration whose details are still unclear and disputed.[16] Although it led ultimately to Ickes's resignation, it also persuaded President Truman in 1946 to order the filing of a federal court action against California. Moreover, while disclaiming any intention of prejudicing judicial or legislative determination of the issue, Truman issued a Continental Shelf Proclamation, which claimed the offshore areas under the high seas "as appertaining to the United States, subject to its jurisdiction and control."[17]

Meanwhile, the opponents of federal control had seized the offensive in Congress, introducing a number of bills and resolutions which would quitclaim any federal "right, title, interest, claim, or demand." Hearings on these measures were dominated by the well-organized forces supporting quitclaim. Forty-six state attorneys-general endorsed it, while Ickes was almost alone in his

---

[16] For an account of this episode, as well as of the whole offshore controversy, see E. R. Bartley, *The Tidelands Oil Controversy* (1953).

[17] The proclamation was deliberately ambiguous as to the federal-state controversy concerning the immediate offshore area then being litigated, but clearly asserted federal jurisdiction beyond the historic limits of state control.

opposition. A quitclaim resolution passed the House easily in 1945 and passed the Senate by a fairly close vote in 1946, but President Truman vetoed it on the ground that the issue was then before the Supreme Court.

In 1947, the Supreme Court ruled against California in a 6 to 2 decision.[18] Disregarding the question of title, the majority held the issue to be "whether the state or the Federal Government has the paramount right and power to determine in the first instance when, how, and by what agencies, foreign and domestic, the oil and other resources of the soils of the marginal sea, known or hereafter discovered, may be exploited." It found that "not only has the acquisition, as it were, of the three-mile belt been accomplished by the National Government, but protection and control of it has been and is a function of national external sovereignty. . . ."

In 1950, similar decisions were made against the claims of Louisiana and Texas.[19] The Louisiana decision followed the California precedent, but the Texas case raised new issues, since that state had enjoyed independent sovereignty for a decade before admission to the Union. In a 4 to 3 decision, the Court nonetheless upheld national authority, arguing that Texas had been admitted on an "equal footing" with the other states.

There is much truth to de Tocqueville's observation that "scarcely any political question arises in the United States that is not resolved, sooner or later, into a judicial question." But this does not mean that the judges are always allowed the last word. No sooner had the Supreme Court spoken than congressmen set about to reverse its ruling. From 1948 to 1952, literally scores of quitclaim bills were introduced in every session of Congress. Many hearings were held, and many parliamentary maneuvers attempted, but the policy struggle remained at an impasse. Supporters of quitclaim legislation always commanded a majority in both houses, but their margin in the Senate was not large enough to override the presidential veto which awaited any full quitclaim bill. Thus, neither a return of control to the states nor an exercise of the federal controls authorized by the decisions of the Supreme Court was possible. Compromise measures to split the majorities supporting state control were introduced, but none mustered sufficient support for passage. One such bill, introduced by Senator O'Mahoney, would have legalized prior state licenses but vested future licensing power in the Interior Department, giving the

---

[18] U.S. v. *California*, 332 U.S. 19.
[19] U.S. v. *Louisiana*, 339 U.S. 699; U.S. v. *Texas*, 339 U.S. 707.

affected states three-eighths of the royalties collected and placing the remaining royalties in escrow until Congress took further action. In 1952, Senator Hill offered yet another alternative, providing for the federal collection of all royalties but earmarking them for aid to education. The strength and cohesion of the state supporters, however, were sufficient to prevent compromise during four inconclusive years.

"States' rights" was the battle cry of the congressional majority. While the material interest of the oil industry and the three states primarily affected obviously transcended any abstract considerations of the proper allocation of governmental powers, most other states, apparently genuinely alarmed about the possible implications of the paramount rights doctrine, also supported the states' rights argument. Congressional supporters of national control, on the other hand, now placed less stress on conservation and focused on other types of potential benefit from federal jurisdiction. They alleged that great sums were being spent on lobbying for state control, and argued that royalties then accruing to only a few states should be shared, through the federal government, by all states. The Hill proposal was designed to dramatize this argument.

Attempts at compromise having failed, in 1951 the House passed a quitclaim measure by a vote of 270 to 92. In 1952, the Senate approved a similar bill by a 50 to 35 vote, and a conference bill was accepted by both houses a few months later. On May 29, President Truman vetoed it, arguing that it transferred a "precious national heritage" to a few states. Since supporters of the bill were unable to muster the necessary two-thirds majority in the Senate, no effort was made to override the veto. Truman's veto message was moderate, emphasizing his willingness to compromise and his support of a number of the earlier compromise proposals. But twelve days earlier, in a public speech, he had been much less restrained. Laying the groundwork for a major campaign issue and using such terms as "corruption" and "robbery in broad daylight —and on a colossal scale," he assailed the oil industry for seeking "to turn that vast treasure over to a handful of states, where the powerful private oil interests hope to exploit it to suit themselves."

The issue was settled by the presidential election of 1952. Early in the campaign, General Eisenhower pledged himself to quitclaim. The Texas Democratic organization, then controlled by Governor Shivers, declined to endorse either candidate until Adlai Stevenson committed himself on the question. After Stevenson announced that he would maintain the position adopted by Truman, the Shivers organization cast its lot with Eisenhower and

656 SPECIAL INDUSTRY REGULATION

probably carried Texas for him. The Submerged Lands Bill of 1953 was almost the first order of business for the new Congress. It quitclaimed to the states the offshore areas within their "historical limits," a phrase designed to give California and Louisiana control for three miles seaward and Texas for three leagues, although Texas' special claims have not been judicially determined and are now being opposed by the Justice Department.

An unusually complicated episode of political pulling and hauling had thus finally come to an end. Federal control of the immediate offshore area had been rejected. Further exploration, however, indicates that by far the greater share of continental shelf deposits lies outside the states' historical limits, thus remaining under federal control.

3. Restriction of Oil Imports

There are no national boundaries to the oil industry, and public policy has been significantly affected by the overseas activities of American oil companies. Long before the offshore controversy, a number of major companies had begun oil exploration, production, and marketing abroad. These activities have not only impinged upon foreign policy; they have also had repercussions on domestic oil policies, especially in the past decade, when the United States has become a net importer of oil.

In recent years, oil has met about one-third of our total energy needs. But, as we have seen, domestic reserves are limited, while our appetite for oil continues to grow. It is true that the continuing discovery of new deposits has thus far delayed the era of domestic shortage first forecast by conservation-minded pessimists as long ago as the early 1920's. But the stubborn fact remains that the United States accounts for more than half of free-world oil consumption while it has only one-seventh of free-world reserves. Indeed, the postwar years have seen consumption finally overtaking discovery. From 1946 to 1955, proven reserves of oil and natural-gas liquids grew at an annual average rate of 4.4 per cent while demand increased at a rate of 6.0 per cent, and in 1957 production actually exceeded additions to reserves. Furthermore, demand is expected to continue its growth. Projecting its estimates from 1950, when domestic consumption was 6.5 million barrels a day, the President's Materials Policy Commission predicted that demand would reach 13.7 million barrels by 1975.[20] It had almost reached 8.5 million by 1957.

[20] *Op cit.*, Vol. 3, p. 4.

Consequently, it is fortunate for our energy supply prospects that there are ample oil reserves elsewhere in the world and that American oil companies still have access to a large share of them. In fact, by far the major share of the free world's oil reserves outside the United States is controlled by five giant American firms —the so-called "international companies"—and by the British Petroleum Company and the Royal Dutch Shell group. Since the early 1950's, imports have accounted for an increasingly important share of American oil consumption, the proportion in 1957 exceeding one-fifth. Moreover, total production outside the United States is expanding much more rapidly than domestic output.

This swelling tide of foreign production has had a serious impact on domestic oil policies, threatening to engulf the prorationing system. Involved are serious problems concerning both the long-run reliability of overseas oil supplies and the short-run effects of imports on the domestic industry. By far the richest overseas reserves are in the Middle East; others are in Indonesia and northern South America; and prospecting appears promising in North Africa. These regions of the world need only be named to indicate the grave political and military uncertainties involved in foreign oil. Yet in the Middle East, costs of production are so low that oil can be shipped all the way to the American East Coast at a profit of more than a dollar a barrel. Closer at hand and much more reliable are the Canadian oil deposits which have been discovered since World War II. While these reserves are being expanded at a rapid pace and will undoubtedly total several times the three billion barrels now proven, Canadian consumption, too, is increasing rapidly. Canadian supply, consequently, is regarded as a helpful supplement to dwindling American reserves, but not as an adequate replacement.

The issues involved in maintaining the availability of oil on reasonable terms from the Middle East, Southeast Asia, North Africa, and Latin America reach into aspects of foreign relations and national defense policy far beyond the compass of this book. Immediately relevant to the domestic system of oil regulation, however, is the impact of oil imports. Here public policy must attempt to balance short- and long-run considerations, to give proper weight to broad national objectives, and to reconcile fuel policy with foreign policy.

In a sense, oil imports present a problem because of the very success of the major companies in developing the huge overseas fields and because of the effectiveness of the American prorationing scheme in raising prices. While, as we have seen, the long-run trends almost surely will increase our relative dependence on imports or synthetics, at the present time domestic wells, if not subjected to production limitations, could meet our current requirements in full. In order to maintain crude prices, however, prorationing controls are limiting production severely, so that output is well below the levels that would be set if the objective were only to maximize ultimate recovery. Prorationing designed to stabilize the market must obviously reduce domestic production to offset any increase in imported supplies. At the same time, the economic incentives operating on the major oil companies favor an expansion of imports. Once having made their discoveries abroad, they must find markets for their foreign production or risk cancellation of their concessions. Moreover, since American prorationing maintains high prices to protect domestic high-cost producers and since foreign production costs are far lower than domestic, it is usually much more remunerative, even after an equal division of profits with the concession-granting governments, to import oil than to buy or produce domestic crude.

In this situation, the proper course for public policy is hard to chart. On the one hand, it can be argued that the greater the proportion of current needs met with imports, the longer will domestic supplies be available for use in possible national emergencies. In addition, a high import rate safeguards American overseas concessions and encourages the search for other foreign reserves. A liberal import policy may also be essential to friendly international relations with the producing countries. On the other hand, by lowering the "allowables" allotted by prorationing authorities, imports endanger the marginal domestic producer and risk the shutdown of stripper wells, making some of our reserves nonrecoverable. They also retard the search for new domestic oil resources.

These conflicting factors must be resolved in a political environment of unusual complexity. Domestic producers have long been politically active and strongly organized in such groups as the Independent Petroleum Association of America. Knowing that imports have necessitated lower allowables, they have for the last decade mobilized steadily mounting pressure for governmental restriction of imports. Allied with them are those integrated oil companies without foreign holdings.[21] Another powerful ally is the

---

[21] For an interesting example of the debate between large, integrated companies with and without foreign holdings, compare Standard Oil Co. (New Jersey), *Facts about Oil Imports* (1953), with a statement of R. E. Wilson, chairman of the board, Standard Oil Co. (Indiana), in *Interstate Oil Compact Quarterly Bulletin* (April, 1953), p. 28.

coal industry, which in the postwar years has continued to lose domestic markets to other fuels. Unable to protect itself by political means from the competitive incursions of natural gas in the home-heating and fuel oil in the locomotive markets, this industry has fought hard to protect its sales to Eastern seaboard electric utilities and industrial consumers from the competition of imported residual fuel oil.

Throughout most of the first postwar decade, the main importers were the giant international companies—Jersey Standard, Socony, Texas, Gulf, and California Standard. Although not without political influence of their own, these firms found it necessary to adjust their policies in the light of the mounting political pressure for import restrictions. In this period, imports were regulated, not by government, but by the international companies' own estimates of how far they could go without inviting the imposition of outside control.

Import policy was thus being determined by the international companies but influenced by their appraisal of political forces. Imports of crude and residual oil tended to steady at about 15 per cent of domestic production. The uneasy balance between the desire to import and the fear of political reaction could be maintained only so long as imports were handled by a small number of firms. By the mid-1950's however, other American oil companies, sometimes at the invitation of producing countries desiring greater competition for concessions, had undertaken foreign production and were beginning to import in substantial quantities. In 1957, for example, the Tidewater Oil Company, controlled by the Getty interests, completed a giant refinery in Delaware designed to use the Middle Eastern oil produced by another Getty company, thereby freeing Tidewater from its dependence on purchased domestic crude.

Fearing that the dikes were about to crumble, the independent oil producers and the coal industry intensified their pressure for legislative restraints on imports. Congress was disposed to be sympathetic, but the executive branch, more concerned with the foreign policy implications, was at first strongly opposed. In 1955, however, Congress was dissuaded from enacting mandatory import curbs only by an administration assurance that effective steps would be taken to secure a "voluntary" restriction program. This was accompanied by administration acceptance of an amendment to the Reciprocal Trade Agreements Act of that year, empowering the President to impose mandatory controls whenever imports of any commodity endangered national security. Earlier that year, a Cabinet committee, the President's Advisory Committee on Energy Supplies and Resources Policy, in a report clearly designed to forestall more drastic congressional action, had urged oil importers voluntarily to restrict their imports to the same proportion of domestic production as had obtained in 1954. In its view, if imports significantly exceeded the 1954 ratio, "the domestic fuel situation could be so impaired as to endanger the orderly industrial growth which affects the military and civilian supplies that are necessary to the national defense." It also noted that the coal industry was even then suffering "serious unemployment and business distress," and urged a further study of that industry.

The government has experienced considerable difficulty, however, in securing voluntary compliance. In efforts to forestall rigid congressional limitations, it has had to rely on increasing degrees of compulsion. In 1954, 656,000 barrels a day of crude oil were imported, or about 10.3 per cent of domestic production. Another 396,000 barrels a day of residual oil were shipped from foreign refineries, raising total imports to 16.6 per cent. During the next two years, the Office of Defense Mobilization, charged with supervision of the voluntary restriction program, sought to cajole, persuade, or bully oil importers to stay within the limits of the 1954 ratios. Despite these appeals, backed by warnings that the failure of self-restraint would lead to compulsory restrictions, imports rose steadily. By mid-1957, domestic production was about 7 million barrels a day, but crude imports had soared to about 1¼ million barrels a day, half a million barrels in excess of the permissible amount under the 1954 ratio. Most of this increase resulted from the activities of smaller companies seeking cheaper sources of oil. A temporary world surplus led to the offering of some oil for importation at price concessions as great as 70 cents a barrel. As imports increased, prorationing allowables were lowered, thereby raising domestic costs of production and further encouraging imports.

During 1957 and 1958, therefore, although the term "voluntary" continued to be applied to the program, import restrictions were shifted to a more mandatory basis. First, individual quotas were assigned to each company, in place of the general exhortation to stay within 1954 ratios. No penalties were prescribed, however, and quotas were exceeded by a number of importers. Pressures for restriction became more intense as the 1958 recession curtailed demand and prorationing in Texas lowered permissible production to the equivalent of eight days per month. At this point, federal buying agencies, including the defense services, were instructed by the President not to buy from companies exceeding their import quotas. This sanction brought most recalcitrants into line, but in mid-1958 a few small oil companies, not interested in sales to the federal government, were still exceeding their quotas, and other importers were partially evading them by bringing in refined oil products.

In the 1958 Trade Agreements Extension Act, the national security clause was strengthened, partly at the behest of opponents of oil imports, through a provision that the President must take into account any "substantial" unemployment resulting from imports. It also permitted him to restrict imports of derivatives of a commodity as well as the commodity itself. There was mounting pressure on the President to do so in the case of oil.

The present uneasy equilibrium leaves serious doubts as to the viability of both the domestic production control system and the method of import restriction. Prorationing is bound to become a steadily less effective means of market stabilization if the share of consumption provided by imports increases. Yet import restriction is at best an indirect and inefficient means of promoting domestic exploration or maintaining a reserve for war emergencies. Curtailment of imports has had serious international repercussions in areas of great importance to the foreign policy interests of the United States. It also entails great difficulties in equitable administration and engenders serious intraindustry and interregional frictions. With anything like the present disparity in costs of expanding reserves and production overseas and at home—and the comparison bids fair to become still less favorable to domestic producers—import restriction can hardly be more than a delaying action. The basic facts of world geology appear to dictate an increasing dependence of the United States on imported oil unless an efficient and large-scale synthetic liquid-fuel industry can be established in the fairly near future.

4. Synthetic Liquid Fuels

Liquid fuels—gasoline and various fuel oils—can be made from natural gas, oil shale, and coal; but with present methods they cannot compete with lower cost fuels derived from natural petroleum. The most advanced technology involves synthetic production from natural gas, but gas is also the least desirable source, since its reserves are about as limited as those of oil. After World War II, full-scale facilities were built for this purpose, partially financed by government loans, but they were abandoned in 1958 as technical problems and rising natural-gas prices rendered them uneconomic. Other private concerns undertook pilot operations to produce liquid fuel from coal shortly after the war, but these efforts were also abortive.

Under the strong urging of Western interests desirous of promoting exploitation of that area's mineral resources, Congress in 1944 enacted the Synthetic Liquid Fuels Act. This measure authorized the Bureau of Mines to construct and operate pilot plants for the production of liquid fuels from coal, oil shale, and agricultural and forestry products. In the eleven-year life of this somewhat novel venture, about $88 million were spent in governmental research and development.

Under this program, the Bureau made substantial progress. It built pilot plants for producing liquid fuels by both the Fischer-Tropsch process, which employs gases derived from coal, and the hydrogenation process, which directly converts solid coal into liquid fuels. In recent years, the Bureau has directed much of its attention to a search for cheaper methods of coal gasification, including underground burning. Neither of these processes can yet yield liquid fuels at competitive prices, but further research and development may uncover new techniques and lower costs.

The extraction of liquid fuels from oil shale represents another promising line of development. Vast quantities of oil are contained in the shale strata of the West, especially in Colorado, which has potential reserves of several hundred billion barrels. There are technical problems both in mining the shale and in processing it to obtain the oil, which is roughly comparable to low-grade crude petroleum. The Bureau has progressed to the point of lowering total production costs to about $2 a barrel, which is in a range comparable with the highest domestic petroleum costs. One oil company has become sufficiently interested to undertake its own developmental work, but no immediate commercial production is in sight. Many problems remain, moreover, before this source can be exploited on a significant scale.

The Bureau of Mines' activity in this area has been opposed by most of the oil industry, perhaps out of fear of eventual large-scale governmental production and competition. In 1953, the Interior Department, on the ground that the government was performing functions best left to private enterprise, ordered the major oil-from-coal pilot plant at Louisiana, Missouri, shut down, and announced its intention to close the oil shale plant at Rifle, Colorado. It also declined to ask for a renewal of the Synthetic Liquid Fuels Act, which expired in 1955. The Missouri plant remained closed, but substantial support for continued government activity persuaded the Interior Department to reconsider its decision on the Rifle plant. The states containing potential fuel sources wished to speed their exploitation, and a number of oil companies with leases on major blocks of oil-shale land favored further experimentation with shale. As a result, the Bureau of Mines continued its operations, although on a more modest scale.

5. Government and the Oil Industry

The case of oil demonstrates the difficulty of fitting special-industry regulation within any pattern of neat categories. Concern for conservation of a scarce and essential raw material was made a justification for regulation, but the real stimulus to regulatory action was the desire of oil producers and allied interests to promote their own economic welfare. The techniques of control which emerged represent a blend of production and import restrictions largely reflecting the intricate interplay of interests within the industry. The resultant compound of policies can hardly remain settled, for they involve continuing tensions between the goals of conservation and of price maintenance and conflicts between the interests of domestic independents and integrated overseas producers, as well as vital considerations of foreign policy.

CHAPTER 21

The Law and Politics of Natural Gas

NATURAL gas offers yet another example of special industry regulation in which factors of competition, monopoly, and conservation come into intricate interplay. The natural-gas and oil industries share many common problems of discovery, production, and conservation, and are often bound together, at the producing level at least, by overlapping economic and political interests. The natural-gas industry, however, differs from oil in that it also displays many of the characteristics of a public utility. Local distribution is a typical natural monopoly conducted under public franchise, and facilities for gathering and transportation of natural gas also tend to be monopolistic. At the same time, natural gas must compete with alternative energy sources. The very mixture of competitive and monopolistic elements within the industry makes for major difficulties in defining a sound public policy. The industry has been the center of a hotly contested political struggle in which producing interests have pressed for a relaxation of price controls over their sector while consumers have demanded a tightening of such controls.

1. State Regulation: Rates and Conservation

The beginnings of state and local regulation paralleled that of electric utilities, discussed in Chapter 12. Its purpose was to ensure that the gas rates charged consumers be no higher than necessary to cover operating costs and yield a fair return on the fair value of the utility plant. In this first phase, little gas flowed across state lines; the problem of jurisdiction was therefore not a barrier to state control. Originally most gas used by utilities was locally manufactured from coal or oil. Where natural gas was employed, it usually came from wells within the same state, since facilities for long-distance transportation were then unavailable.

While urban consumers were burning an expensive, manufactured gas, immense quantities of natural gas were going to waste. Natural gas is found either in so-called dry pools, containing almost no petroleum, or in some form of combination with petroleum. Since, to begin with, natural gas had little or no commercial value and the primary interest was in obtaining oil, gas produced along with oil—so-called "casing head gas"—was regarded as a nuisance and a hazard, and was usually vented (released into the air) or flared (burned off) to get it out of the way.[1] Wells which tapped dry gas were at first regarded as useless unless they were close enough to a city for the gas to be piped there. Before long, new industrial uses for natural gas began to be developed. The carbon-black industry, for example, became a large-scale consumer. Beginning in 1930, facilities were built to extract or "strip" natural gasoline and others of the valuable heavier hydrocarbons from dry gas. The residue, however, about 95 per cent of the gas, was still vented or flared.

As long as there was no immediate market for natural gas, the states took no action to check its waste. But in the late 1920's the development of strong, seamless pipe made it possible to transport gas over great distances. By 1931, it was being sent from the Texas Panhandle field as far as Indianapolis. As soon as gas began to have some value in the field, the twin issues of conservation and of correlative property rights came to the fore. Pipeline companies who owned wells often refused to buy from others in the same field, since by producing from their own wells they could draw gas from under their neighbors' property. Many well owners produced gas only to strip it of its heavier hydrocarbons and then vented the remainder. In Texas alone, more than a billion cubic feet of gas were wasted each day in this manner. During the thirties, the producing states enacted legislation to limit gas withdrawals. The purpose was to conserve the gas and to protect the property rights of all owners in the field. After a great deal of litigation, the

---

[1] In more recent years, especially where unitized operations are possible, the gas has often been reinjected underground to maintain pressure and to keep the oil viscous.

Supreme Court held in 1937 that a state could validly regulate the production and use of natural gas.[2] In 1947, the Texas Railroad Commission finally began to prohibit the flaring of gas produced along with oil. This wasteful practice has now largely disappeared. A majority of the producing states have given further impetus to conservation through laws encouraging unitized operation of gas fields.[3]

A number of states have also used their authority to prevent waste to set minimum prices for gas sold at the wellhead; this practice has been upheld by the Supreme Court.[4] Such price floors are designed to increase available supplies by encouraging wild-catting and greater activity in the gathering of natural gas. By raising prices, however, they also precipitate a conflict of interest between producing and consuming states.

2. The Natural Gas Act of 1938

As natural gas began to move across state lines in substantial quantities, the problem of regulating this flow became increasingly crucial. It had long been held that a state lacked the jurisdiction to regulate the rates charged an intrastate utility by an interstate pipeline company.[5] In the absence of federal authority, no regulation was possible. It was to fill this gap that Congress enacted the Natural Gas Act of 1938.

The Act vests the Federal Power Commission with important powers. Pipeline companies are required to file rate schedules with the Commission and may not change such schedules without its approval. The FPC is authorized to set "just and reasonable" rates, and to eliminate any "undue" preferences. To assist it in determining rates, the Commission is empowered to prescribe accounting methods and to ascertain the "actual legitimate cost" of the pipelines.

The Commission may order pipeline companies to extend their facilities and to make physical connections with local distributors if it finds that no undue burden is placed on the natural-gas company ordered to make the extension or interconnection. Commission approval is required both for abandonment of interstate facilities and for voluntary extension of facilities. Under an amend-

---

[2] *Henderson Co.* v. *Thompson*, 300 U.S. 258.

[3] Unitized operations are similar to those in oil production, briefly described above, p. 649.

[4] *Cities Service Co.* v. *Peerless Oil & Gas Co.*, 340 U.S. 179 (1950).

[5] *Missouri* v. *Kansas Natural Gas Co.*, 265 U.S. 298 (1924).

ment enacted in 1942, companies which were not in operation prior to that date are required to obtain certificates of public convenience and necessity from the Commission as a condition precedent to the construction, extension, acquisition, or operation of any facility. The Commission may determine the service area to which each authorization is limited. Within that area, the pipeline company is free to enlarge or extend its facilities without further authorization. The company is not, however, protected from an invasion of its service area by another pipeline company if the Commission finds that additional service is in the public interest. While the FPC enjoys only limited authority to control the financial aspects of pipeline companies, the security transactions of officers of these companies are subject to regulation. The Commission is also authorized to control exports and imports of natural gas and to co-operate with state regulatory agencies through the establishment of joint boards.

Unfortunately, the Act contained serious ambiguities as to the precise jurisdiction of the FPC. The Commission was empowered to regulate the transmission of natural gas in interstate commerce and the sale in interstate commerce of natural gas for resale. The Act specifically exempted direct industrial interstate sales, control over "the local distribution of natural gas," and "the production or gathering of natural gas." [6] The first two exemptions raised few problems, but the legislative history surrounding the third exemption is obscure. It had long been accepted constitutional doctrine that any sale to an interstate pipeline was a sale in interstate commerce, whether it took place at the wellhead, at the tail gate of a processing plant, or after gathering.[7] But since Congress did not define "production" or "gathering" and failed to mention processing, it is uncertain whether it intended to exempt from regulation the field prices at which gas was sold to the pipelines.[8] This uncertainty, as we shall see shortly, has been the focus of an intense legal and political struggle.

[6] Natural gas destined to enter interstate commerce is usually "gathered" from various wellheads by a network of lines, "processed" to extract valuable by-products and to remove such impurities as water and sulfur compounds, and then delivered to the interstate pipeline. Many pipeline companies own gas reserves of their own, producing and gathering much of the gas they transport. About nine-tenths of the nation's gas reserves, however, are owned by "independent" producers, who sell gas to the pipelines at the wellhead, after processing, or at the terminus of a gathering system.

[7] *Dahnke-Walker Milling Co. v. Bondurant*, 257 U.S. 282 (1921).

[8] See R. W. Gable, "The Jurisdiction of the Federal Power Commission over the Field Prices of Natural Gas," *Land Economics* (February, 1956), p. 44.

3. The FPC and Fuel Policy

Although the 1938 Act appeared to give the FPC fewer regulatory powers over gas-pipeline companies than it had earlier been granted over interstate electric utilities, it shortly became apparent that, in fact, the Commission had been entrusted with broader responsibilities in the natural-gas industry. This was due to two factors: first, that the industry underwent its major growth not before, but after, the initiation of federal regulation; and second, that many aspects of the industry poorly fit the usual public utility mold and require the FPC to go beyond the customary criteria of utility regulation.

While there was substantial interstate transmission of natural gas before World War II, the postwar years saw an enormous expansion. Pipes and pumps were developed capable of transporting gas over vast distances. Postwar prosperity provided a congenial atmosphere for the investment of billions of dollars. By 1956, the total plant investment of FPC-regulated companies was $8.2 billion. Natural gas was being brought to all of the states; pipeline mileage exceeded railroad mileage by 1953; between 1938 and 1956, consumption had increased almost sevenfold; and over 25 million customers were being served. This explosion of the industry across the whole nation confronted the FPC, in its exercise of the certificating power, with a unique opportunity to shape the development of a regulated industry. In so doing, it also raised issues transcending the usual tests of public convenience and necessity; it involved "no less than an attempt to redefine in the broadest terms the public interest in respect to natural gas." [9]

In calmer days, the Commission had developed more conventional criteria for certification. These had included the adequacy of gas reserves, physical facilities, financial resources, and market demand.[10] When the industry began its rapid expansion, and when gas came to rival oil and coal as a major source of energy, these criteria were inadequate either to define the public interest or to reflect the political forces concerned. The policy problem was more than one of utility regulation because gas is a scarce resource, because its interstate transmission can raise conflicts of interest between producing and consuming states, and because the impact of gas on other fuels presents questions of national energy resource policy.

[9] R. K. Huitt, "Federal Regulation of the Uses of Natural Gas," *Amer. Polit. Sci. Rev.* (June, 1952), p. 455.
[10] *Kansas Pipe Line and Gas Co.*, 21 FPC 29 (1939).

These broader questions were forced upon the FPC's attention when it allowed the various parties-in-interest to intervene extensively in cases involving the establishment or expansion of gas service, making them a political battleground for the rivalry between coal and gas. Gas producers (who are often primarily oil producers) and pipeline companies desired full freedom for the transportation of gas anywhere, for any use, and in any quantities. Railroad and coal companies and labor unions in these industries fought all extensions of gas lines, wishing to preserve markets for coal, which is a major user of the rails. Communities and industries desiring gas service, or lower gas rates, argued for certification. State governments frequently participated. Consuming states favored pipeline extension, while producing states were uncertain of their interest. The latter welcomed increased gas revenues but feared that substantial gas exports might limit their economic role to mere resource extraction, exhaust their reserves, and delay their industrialization.

Recognizing that these conflicts raised broad policy questions unlikely to be fully examined or satisfactorily answered through case-by-case decisions, in 1945 and 1946 the FPC conducted a broad, "stocktaking" investigation, inviting the participation of all parties-in-interest. This study began with the fact that gas is an exhaustible resource; its reserves are adequate to meet present consumption needs about twice as long as petroleum, but its life expectancy is computed in decades whereas coal reserves appear sufficient for centuries.[11] Given this fact, those who wished to restrict the expansion of natural gas contended: first, that gas should be barred from markets now adequately served by coal, so as to prevent the displacement of coal miners and railroad workers whose valuable skills would once again be needed when the gas was gone; second, that restraints on pipelines would attract industries desiring gas as a fuel to the underindustrialized producing states, promoting regional development and strengthening the economies of the South and Southwest; and third, that natural gas, being an ideal household fuel and a valuable chemical raw material, should not be wasted on such low-quality end uses as boiler-firing.[12]

The FPC was divided in its conclusions, issuing two reports.[13]

[11] At the end of 1957, gas reserves totaled 247 trillion cubic feet, enough to last 21.4 years at the current production rate of 11.5 trillion cubic feet.

[12] This analysis is derived from Huitt, *op. cit.*

[13] FPC, *Natural Gas Investigation: Smith-Wimberly Report*; and *ibid.*, *Draper-Olds Report* (both 1948).

Commissioners Olds and Draper accepted, at least in part, the case for restriction and recommended that the FPC give "increased consideration to the conservation aspects in the delivery of natural gas" from gas-producing states to coal-producing regions. They asked the Commission to consider the end uses to which the gas would be put and to give weight to the needs of the producing states for greater industrialization. Commissioners Smith and Wimberly were less persuaded by these arguments, contenting themselves with a recommendation that producing states and the industry increase their conservation efforts and that gas suppliers take steps to develop long-run alternative resources, such as the gasification of coal.

In effect, the divided Commission was inviting a reconsideration of the industry's problems and a clarification of its policy directives.[14] Neither Congress nor the administration accepted the invitation, and the 1938 Act, with its implicit assumption that the industry requires only traditional utility regulation, remains the basic statute.

In subsequent years, the FPC majority has come to support the views expressed by Smith and Wimberly. In considering certification applications, the Commission largely restricts itself to exploring the adequacy of supplies, markets, and financial resources,[15] although it may frown upon deliveries to large industrial users if they jeopardize the needs of residential and commercial consumers.

Even this avoidance of the conservation issue, however, has not gained the FPC relief from controversy, for, beginning in 1949, it began to receive increasing numbers of competitive applications for certificates to serve substantially the same market areas. These applications are usually filed by established pipelines which wish to extend into adjacent areas. Since the FPC requires a showing of adequate supplies and markets, competing pipelines attempt to negotiate understandings with producers and local gas utilities. Consequently, the Commission is confronted with the necessity of choosing between two or more broad combinations of associated interests. Many of these competitive applications have precipitated bitter legal and political struggles. One such dispute, involving

---

[14] Four years earlier, Justice Jackson, dissenting, had raised much the same question, asking the Commission to use its powers over rates to encourage conservation and domestic household use. *FPC v. Hope Natural Gas Co.*, 320 U.S. 608 (1944).

[15] For a list of typical applications denied for such inadequacies, see FPC, *Annual Report, 1951*, pp. 83–84.

applications to serve Chicago and nearby Midwestern markets, led in April, 1958, to the issuance of a grand jury criminal indictment under the Sherman Act charging that three large natural-gas companies had conspired to monopolize those markets. They were accused of seeking to exclude a fourth company from that area and of boycotting its sales. The suit was supported by the governors of five Midwestern states, who favored entrance of the fourth company "because it would give our states a new source of natural gas at competitive prices to the consumers." [16] Thus, the Antitrust Division sought to maintain competition in a field which the FPC regulates as a public utility. In 1958, the Supreme Court supported the competitive approach to pipelines by permitting the Division to take action under the Clayton Act to block the merger of two pipeline companies.[17]

4. Public Utility Regulation and Field Prices

Although disregarded by Congress, the stubborn fact that the natural-gas industry differs from the traditional utilities has also plagued the FPC in its efforts to regulate rates. In setting the rates charged by a pipeline company to local distributors, the FPC can satisfactorily handle most of the relevant cost elements—operating costs, depreciation charges, and a return on the depreciated original cost of the pipeline property. But what value is to be assigned to the gas received by a pipeline company—either by purchase or by means of its own production?

For the gas produced by a pipeline company itself, the Commission first chose to value on the basis of cost, taking the operating expenses of production and gathering, and adding a 6 per-cent return on the depreciated original cost of the producing property and the dry-hole costs on nonproductive lands. Thus, the FPC assumed that the value and nature of gas-producing properties were essentially similar to those of a utility. It implicitly argued that utilities should not be allowed to benefit from the increases in value due to gas discoveries and to higher field prices of gas, especially when the pipelines themselves may have been instrumental in raising those prices.[18] This valuation method led also to the regulation

[16] *New York Times,* May 1, 1958.

[17] *El Paso Natural Gas Co.* v. *U.S.,* 2 L ed 2d 528.

[18] *Billings Gas Co.,* 2 FPC 288 (1940). In 1945, the Supreme Court, in a 5 to 4 decision, accepted this procedure, permitting the FPC to include the producing and gathering facilities of an affiliated company within the rate base of the regulated parent company. *Colorado Interstate Gas Co.* v. *FPC,* 324 U.S. 581.

of stripping profits, for in one case the Commission ordered, with judicial approval, that what it regarded as excessive profits from the extraction of liquid products from natural gas be credited to the pipeline's gas operations.[19]

The companies objected vehemently. Many of their leases had been acquired for prices which were only a tiny fraction of their value once gas had been discovered. They argued that wildcatting was a risky enterprise, requiring and justifying greater profits than those attainable by the relatively riskless utilities. They also found ways of circumventing FPC regulation. Some companies sold their producing properties in order to obtain their real value, and the FPC was denied the power to restrain such sales.[20] Others greatly reduced production from their own properties. Pipeline companies produced 35 per cent of their needs in 1945, but only 15 per cent in 1952. The Commission recently attempted to abandon the original cost of reserves in favor of a new standard of "fair field value," computed on the basis of the weighted average of prices of identical gas in the same field sold at arm's-length bargaining. A circuit court, however, rejected this standard in the absence of any showing by the FPC "that the ultimate public interest will be better served thereby." [21]

A somewhat analogous problem, with acute political implications, concerned the field prices paid by pipeline companies to independent gas producers or gatherers. As we have seen, the 1938 Act did not make clear whether Congress intended field sales to interstate pipeline companies to be regulated as sales in interstate commerce or to be exempt from regulation as pertaining to production and gathering. In 1940, the Commission first denied itself this power, both because of its interpretation of congressional intent and because of insufficient administrative resources to undertake the task.[22] But in 1943, the FPC asserted jurisdiction over the sales to interstate pipeline companies of a firm which, in a complex series of operations, delivered gas gathered and produced both by other firms and from its own properties.[23] In 1947, the Supreme Court approved this assertion of authority and extended the FPC's jurisdiction even further. It held that all sales in interstate commerce are subject to federal regulation and that the 1938 Act's

---

[19] Cities Service Natural Gas Co. v. FPC, 155 F. 2d 694 (1946); cert. denied, 329 U.S. 773 (1947); rehearing denied, 329 U.S. 832 (1947).
[20] FPC v. Panhandle Eastern Pipe Line Co., 337 U.S. 498 (1949).
[21] City of Detroit v. FPC, 230 F. 2d 810 (1955).
[22] Columbian Fuel Corp., 2 FPC 200.
[23] Interstate Natural Gas Co., 3 FPC 416.

"exceptions to the primary grant of jurisdiction . . . are to be strictly construed." [24]

The FPC's action and lower court approval of it were sufficient to stimulate a congressional campaign to amend the 1938 Act, even before the Supreme Court made its ruling. Congressmen from the gas-producing states of the South and Southwest led the movement, but oil and gas interests were also able to muster considerable support from other sections. In 1947, bills were introduced to deny the FPC any control over sales to interstate pipelines, either by independent producers or gatherers or by integrated companies. The Commission opposed the legislation, arguing that Congress should defer action until after the completion of the broad investigation then under way. It did, however, endorse a bill, introduced by Representative Priest, which specifically exempted sales by independents to the pipelines from FPC jurisdiction, and in 1947 it issued Order No. 139, which interpreted the 1938 Act as denying it this power.

Meanwhile, the battle to limit FPC jurisdiction was being fought on many fronts. The Commission itself was divided and slowly shifted its position. Although the FPC had originally unanimously endorsed the Priest bill, Commissioner Draper dissented from Order No. 139. At the conclusion of its natural-gas investigation in 1948, the Commission, with one vacancy, split evenly on the subject. The Smith-Wimberly Report asked Congress to exempt the field sales of independents; [25] the Draper-Olds Report opposed any amendment.[26] In 1949, however, the Commission vacancy was filled by Thomas Buchanan, who sided with Draper and Olds in opposing the exemption. Chairman Olds was particularly outspoken in his opposition.

Now the controversy shifted to the Congress. In 1949, Senator Kerr of Oklahoma had introduced a bill to exempt sales by independent producers, and the House had passed a similar measure by a vote of 183 to 131. In part because of the strong opposition mobilized by Olds, the Senate Committee on Interstate and Foreign Commerce refused to report out the Kerr Bill. Accordingly, the proponents of legislation centered their fire on Olds, whose renomination came before the Senate in the same year.[27]

[24] *Interstate Natural Gas Co. v. FPC*, 331 U.S. 682.
[25] FPC, *Natural Gas Investigation: Smith-Wimberly Report* (1948), pp. 40–41.
[26] FPC, *Natural Gas Investigation: Draper-Olds Report* (1948), p. 12.
[27] For a discussion of this episode, see J. P. Harris, "The Senatorial Rejection of Leland Olds: A Case Study," *Amer. Polit. Sci. Rev.* (September, 1951), pp. 674–692.

In 1944, the electric utilities had strongly opposed his nomination for a second term, but he had been easily confirmed. Now the electric groups remained in the background, while oil and gas interests joined the Senate proponents of new legislation in attacking Olds's character and beliefs. Many witnesses attested to his ability and integrity, and some senators, largely from gas-consuming areas, pointed to his opposition to the Kerr Bill as the real reason for the attacks on him. President Truman first vainly tried to persuade the Senate Committee to confirm the nomination. He then took the unusual step of attempting to make the reappointment a party issue. The Democratic National Chairman requested all state chairmen to urge their senators to vote for confirmation. This appeal for party unity had no effect on the Democrats and may have contributed to the virtually unanimous Republican opposition. The final vote against Olds was overwhelming, 53 to 15. The only sizable group in favor comprised Democrats from the gas-consuming areas. For a while, however, it appeared that Truman had retained control of the FPC by those favoring field-price regulation through the appointment of former Senator Mon C. Wallgren to replace Olds.

Having disposed of Olds, the Senate joined the House in approving the Kerr Bill. Passage was by a vote of only 44 to 38, as the gas-consuming states of the North and the East stiffened in their opposition. A majority of the FPC—Draper, Buchanan, and Wallgren—recommended to the President that he veto the bill, while Smith and Wimberly though it should be approved. Truman exercised his veto, and the FPC rescinded Order No. 139.

With legislative action thus checked, the struggle shifted back to the FPC. In 1951, the Commission's Phillips decision marked another stage in the conflict.[28] The Phillips Petroleum Company was one of the largest of the independent producers of gas, its sales comprising about 8 per cent of total marketed production. To gather gas from the many wells it owned or controlled and to deliver this gas to its processing plants and then to interstate pipelines, it had constructed a pipeline network of 4,380 miles in five states, and some of its lines crossed state borders. It raised its prices, and the state of Wisconsin and several cities, in the interest of consumers, requested the FPC to determine whether these prices were reasonable and just. The Commission, by a divided vote, ruled that it had no power to fix field prices of independents. This decision in effect enacted the Kerr Bill and reversed Truman's veto. Buchanan dissented, and Draper concurred separately, while

[28] *Phillips Petroleum Co.*, 10 FPC 246.

Wallgren voted with Smith and Wimberly.

The plaintiffs then appealed to the courts, and in 1954 the Supreme Court, in a 5 to 3 decision, held that Phillips' sales fell within the jurisdiction of the 1938 Act and directed the FPC to regulate them.[29] The Court was thus in the unusual position of ordering a regulatory agency to assume more authority than it desired to exercise.[30]

Oil and gas interests now exerted the most extreme pressure on Congress in an effort to induce that body to reverse the Phillips decision. They were encouraged by President Eisenhower's announcement that he favored such legislation as a means of countering excessive centralization of government. In 1955 and 1956, Congress hotly debated the Harris-Fulbright Bill, which would have denied the FPC any control over field prices. The oil and gas interests were able to mobilize great resources. The many thousands of gas producers placed the weight of numbers behind the bill. Virtually all of the oil-producing industry was in the fight because most producers, through sales of casing-head gas or ownership of gas wells discovered while drilling for oil, had major interests in gas, and because all of them feared the possible extension of government regulation. The stakes were high: an increase of only 5 cents per 1,000 cubic feet in the field price of natural gas would amount to $116 million a year at current sales for the seven Southwestern states, and would add $3.5 billion to the value of their present reserves. Producers argued that price regulation of a risky, dynamic industry based on limited natural resources would discourage exploration, production, and conservation. They pointed out that gas prices to the consumer had risen far less than had the prices of coal and oil. And they contended that the effective regulation of retail gas prices did not require field-price regulation, for prices at the wellhead were but a small fraction of the final cost to the consumer. In 1952, when the household consumer paid about 83 cents per 1,000 cubic feet, wholesale rates were about 30 cents, and Texas field prices averaged only 7 cents.

[29] *Phillips Petroleum Co.* v. *State of Wisconsin*, 346 U.S. 934.

[30] Once before, the Court had taken an expansive view of the FPC's jurisdiction only to have Congress contract it. In 1950, it had permitted the FPC, upon the request of the city of Cleveland, to ascertain the operating costs and property valuation of a large gas distributor and pipeline company which operated only within Ohio but also carried gas which had crossed state lines. The Court held that the company was engaged in interstate commerce even though it sold directly to consumers. (*FPC* v. *East Ohio Gas Co.*, 338 U.S. 464.) In 1954, however, Congress reversed this decision by a law denying the FPC any jurisdiction over wholly intrastate pipelines.

The opponents of such legislation, however, had recruited new allies. Northern and Eastern cities, labor groups, and gas consumers generally testified in opposition. Many local gas utilities were against the bill, fearing that it would raise the prices they paid. Their major argument was that successful regulation required control over all major cost elements, and that exemption of field prices would impose a squeeze on distributors.

Despite the support of the administration and of the Southern wing of the Democratic Party, in 1955 the bill squeaked through the House by the narrow margin of 209 to 203. In 1956, the proponents seemed to have final victory in their grasp when the Senate passed the measure by a vote of 53 to 38. At this point, however, it was vetoed by President Eisenhower, who charged its supporters with "arrogant tactics" after Senator Case's indignant disclosure that a clumsy oil-company lawyer lobbying for the bill had given $2,500 to his campaign fund.

In 1957, it was reported that oil and gas interests had succeeded in moderating utility opposition. The Eisenhower administration still endorsed the principle of exemption, but did not press for immediate action. Fourteen bills dealing with the regulation of independent producers were introduced in that year, but none was acted upon by either house. The FPC, still seeking to avoid utility regulation of producers, endorsed the Harris bill. This measure would eliminate the necessity for certification of producers. It would regulate field prices on sales by either independents or pipeline subsidiaries on the basis of a "reasonable market price," taking into account both the interests of consumers and the need to assure future supplies.

Unless Congress amends the 1938 Act, however, the FPC will remain charged with the task of regulating field prices on sales to interstate pipelines. This is no small task. Where the FPC had previously to regulate only a few hundred pipelines, now it must control thousands of producers.[31] With limited appropriations, the FPC has been unable to keep up with this vast expansion of its regulatory responsibility, and its backlog of pipeline as well as producer rate cases has mounted.[32]

The long policy struggle is now being fought out on the ad-

[31] From the Phillips decision through the 1957 fiscal year, 8,496 independent producers applied for certificates. And in fiscal 1957 alone, 6,947 independent rate schedules were filed. FPC, *Annual Report, 1957*, pp. 79, 85.

[32] In the 3½ years between the Phillips decision and the end of 1957, the FPC suspended 1,144 proposed rate increases, but was able to complete action on only 140 of these rate changes. R. S. Knappen, "Give FPC Credit for Trying," *Oil and Gas Journal* (July 28, 1958), p. 162.

ministrative and judicial fronts. In fiscal 1957, the Commission had 409 rate proceedings concerning independents pending before it, and many more of its rulings were being appealed to the courts than before the Phillips decision.[33] As yet, however, case law has been insufficient to make clear the principles governing the regulation of producers' prices. The Commission has accepted field prices in force at the time of the Phillips decision and has concerned itself only with proposed increases. In July, 1954, it ordered that all field prices on gas sold for interstate transmission be frozen. It directed that producers apply for certificates and file their prices. It has not reduced prices below their levels in June, 1954, but has attempted to control all subsequent increases as well as the prices charged on new sources of supply. In 1957, the Commission ruled that evidence of arm's-length bargaining, comparable prices elsewhere in the field, and market value of the gas was not sufficient to justify proposed increases. There must also be a showing that the increases are no higher than necessary to encourage exploration and production.[34] But in a split decision in 1958, the Commission majority took quite a different line. It now held that in the absence of protests from distributors and consumers, a producer could justify his proposed prices by showing that there is a market for the gas at those prices, even though they may substantially exceed the prices of other nearby producers.[35]

The task of regulating field prices requires the FPC to mediate between producers and pipelines on the one hand and distributors and consumers on the other. The enormous postwar expansion in consumption has radically altered the economic balance of power within the industry. Unregulated field prices have increased severalfold. A high proportion of the presently uncommitted gas reserves is held by large oil companies able to bargain vigorously for high prices and to withhold their gas in the absence of satisfactory offers. Increased competition among pipeline companies for service extensions leads to competitive bidding for these uncommitted reserves. Since the pipeline companies must show about twenty years' reserves under contract in order to secure FPC approval of extensions, and since they have hitherto been able to cover rising costs by higher charges to distributors, they have made little objection to increases in field prices. The distributors, however, have objected strongly, because at the retail level natural gas must

[33] FPC, *Annual Report, 1957*, pp. 1, 87.
[34] *Union Oil of California*, Docket No. G-4331.
[35] *Hope Natural Gas Co.*, issued March 31, 1958, and reported in *Public Utilities Fortnightly* (July 31, 1958), p. 195.

compete in price with other energy sources. Field-price increases have also been opposed by large consumers and by state agencies representing small consumers.[36]

This interindustry struggle promises to continue. It has already led to numerous judicial challenges to FPC decisions. Before 1957, the process of passing on rate increases to consumers had been facilitated by Commission procedures. The FPC had permitted regulated companies to impose increased charges after the new tariffs had been filed with it but before it had completed the lengthy process of determining the reasonableness of the new rates. If it later disallowed part or all of the increases, the difference would be refunded. But the Memphis decision, handed down by a circuit court late in 1957, held that such increases could be imposed only after full FPC hearings, or after the negotiation of agreements with the purchasers.[37] Although the Supreme Court subsequently overruled the circuit court and upheld FPC procedures, gas consumers can be expected to continue to use every channel open to them to block pipeline rate increases.[38]

While consuming states have been supporting regulation of field prices, producing states have attempted to raise field prices. Several states have enacted laws permitting the establishment of minimum prices on gas in the name of conservation. Consequently, jurisdictional clashes seem likely between state minimum-price orders and federal maximum-price orders. The Supreme Court has already held that states may set minimum prices,[39] but a circuit court has ruled that the FPC may require an integrated company to account in its rate calculations for gas it produces from a regulated field on the basis of cost rather than the state-fixed minimum price.[40]

The struggle thus bids fair to be a hardy perennial, but the way in which the issues are framed unfortunately omits some major dimensions of the public interest. The mere conflict between those who favor and those who oppose higher field prices slights the

[36] Regulatory commissions and attorneys-general of consuming states have frequently participated in FPC and judicial proceedings to protest producer and pipeline rates. In 1958, for example, the New York Public Service Commission and several distributors persuaded a court to set aside FPC approval of a pipeline contract for offshore gas supplies. *Oil and Gas Journal* (July 7, 1958), p. 182.
[37] *Memphis Light, Gas & Water Division v. FPC*, 250 F. 2d 402.
[38] *United Gas Pipe Line Co. v. Memphis Light, Gas & Water Division*, no. 23, U.S. Sup. Ct., December 8, 1958.
[39] *Cities Service Gas Co. v. Peerless Oil & Gas Co.*, 340 U.S. 179 (1950).
[40] *State Corporation Commission of Kansas v. FPC*, 206 F. 2d 690 (1953); cert. denied, 346 U.S. 922 (1954).

question of conservation, which is perhaps the salient component of the public interest in this industry. It is true that producers justify their plea for nonregulation and higher prices on grounds of conservation and encouragement of exploration, but there are more effective ways of conserving gas for future generations and for high priority uses than by liberating producers from price regulation. The FPC might possibly use its control over price and certification to prevent an ideal household fuel from being used in large quantities as a boiler fuel and for other inferior uses where coal would suffice. Direct promotion of conservation, however, would require further action by Congress. But an adequate program for gas conservation cannot be developed in isolation from the whole complex of related energy sources. It requires a consideration of the relations among gas, oil, coal, atomic energy, and hydroelectric power, and a definition of their respective contributions to the totality of national energy requirements.

CHAPTER 22

The Challenge of
Atomic Energy

THE IMPACT of technological change on government's relations with the economy is nowhere more striking than in the field of atomic energy. A new industrial revolution was foreshadowed on August 2, 1939, when Albert Einstein wrote to President Roosevelt that "it may become possible to set up a nuclear chain reaction in a large mass of uranium by which vast amounts of power . . . would be generated." The harnessing of atomic energy was first made public on August 6, 1945, when the bomber *Enola Gay* exploded a single bomb over Hiroshima, virtually destroying the city and killing seventy thousand people. Within four days, Japan surrendered, ending World War II. Since then, nuclear fission and fusion have revolutionized the relations among nations, have become dominating elements in foreign and military policy, and have raised the threat of mankind's extinction unless effective controls can be devised.

Against this dramatic backdrop, our concern here with atomic energy may seem rather pedestrian. Yet its impact on the relations between government and the American economy has already become substantial and promises even more far-reaching consequences. Since atomic energy, in its various forms, is potentially almost unlimited in quantity, public policies toward it will become increasingly important as it is substituted for other forms of energy whose sources are limited and being rapidly depleted. At the same time, it is easy to overestimate the speed with which atomic energy will be substituted for other fuels. This new form of energy has already evoked a unique relationship between government and private enterprise, and much of atomic energy's political environment is inherited from the long struggle over the merits of public versus private power, discussed in Chapter 12.

1. The Pattern of Control: The Atomic Energy Act of 1946

For obvious reasons, atomic energy, unlike any other energy source in this country, began as a tight government monopoly. In 1940, the government initiated a program of research. After the first primitive nuclear reactor at the University of Chicago had demonstrated that a chain reaction was possible, a "crash" program was launched to make atomic bombs. Direction of this vast effort, which cost almost $2 billion, was entrusted to a branch of the Army Corps of Engineers, concealed during the war behind the enigmatic title "Manhattan Engineer District." Most of the work was performed by civilian contractors, primarily industrial concerns but also including universities and research institutes. With the successful manufacture of bombs and the end of the war, Congress, only now apprised of the existence of the Manhattan Project, was confronted with the task of determining general atomic policy and devising an administrative organization to implement it.

The first legislation in the new field, the Atomic Energy Act of 1946, emerged out of a full year of broad study and debate. Once the primary policy had been laid down—that the security of the United States required the rapid development and manufacture of more atomic weapons—congressional discussion and the resultant Act centered on organizational issues. So little was known about this revolutionary new force, its impact on existing institutions and programs, and the policy issues it was likely to raise, that legislative emphasis was on the administrative pattern within which policy would grow, rather than on the substance of policy. Congressmen, executive agencies, and interested individuals and groups participating in the legislative process nevertheless were acutely aware that organizational choices would have policy implications. Thus, the debate over the degree of military and civilian control of the atomic program reflected a struggle over the relative emphasis to be given military utilization on the one hand and scientific and commercial uses on the other.

There was virtually no debate over continuation of governmental ownership and operation. It was felt that the international position and national security of the United States depended upon the maintenance of our monopoly of atomic weapons.[1] The case for direct governmental control was enhanced by the desire for absolute secrecy and the special need for rigid safety precautions. Furthermore, too little was known about existing applications and future developments to permit the disentangling of the enterprise's military and civil aspects, so that governmental control of its military applications appeared to require control of the whole venture. Finally, in an argument which later merged with the endemic debate over public versus private power, it was urged that the atomic energy program, which had been paid for by public funds, was a public trust and should therefore be kept in governmental hands to prevent private exploitation of a public investment.

Given the initial general agreement on a continuation of the government monopoly, there remained many important questions of organization and control. The first issue was that of military versus civilian control. The May-Johnson Bill, strongly supported by the armed forces, would have perpetuated military control. It was vigorously opposed by those who feared that military control would hamper the promotion of peaceful uses. Prominent in the opposition were many scientific groups and individual scientists, who felt the future course of research and development to be at stake. A special Senate committee, chaired by Senator McMahon of Connecticut, was appointed to study the problem. In addition to the question of military or civilian control, the McMahon Committee also had to consider the crucial questions of where and how to insert the new agency into the existing structure of government. How much control should President and Congress have, and how was this power to be exercised? What should be the structure of the agency? What role should scientists, as opposed to laymen, be assigned in this program so dependent upon and important to science?

The Committee's answer to these questions was the McMahon Bill, which, after passing both chambers by large margins, became the Atomic Energy Act of 1946. The Act opted for civilian rather than military control by vesting responsibility in a five-man Atomic Energy Commission. Commissioners were to be appointed

[1] In 1946, however, the United States recommended to the United Nations that full control over atomic energy be vested in an international body and offered to give up to that agency, over a period of time, access to and control over its technology and facilities. The proposal was unacceptable to the Soviet Union and became an early casualty of the Cold War.

by the President and confirmed by the Senate, with the Chairman designated by the President. Their terms were so staggered that one expired each year. A Military Liaison Committee, appointed by the defense departments, was established to advise the AEC on military aspects of the program and to facilitate the flow of information and plans. If the Committee disagreed with Commission policy, it was empowered to appeal to the War and Navy Departments and ultimately to the President. The military was given additional representation by a requirement that the Director of the Division of Military Applications, one of the AEC's four operating units, be a member of the armed forces.

Similarly, scientists were given explicit organizational channels through which to influence atomic policy. While the AEC would always have available to it the technical advice of the many scientists on its own staff, Congress wished to ensure that the Commission also have frequent access to the judgment of eminent and disinterested outside scientists. Accordingly, the Act created a part-time, nine-man General Advisory Board, whose members were to be appointed by the President from among the nation's leading scientists.

The new agency was headed by a commission rather than a single administrator because of the complexity of the policy problems it would face. Speed of decision was sacrificed for some assurance that policy alternatives would be fully explored and not confined to the limited perspective of any one person. Yet the program also envisaged a vast industrial organization. To meet the need for managerial direction, Congress delegated administrative authority to a General Manager, first appointed by the President, later, under the terms of a 1950 amendment, by the Commission. Under his supervision, operations are conducted by four divisions: Research, Engineering, Production, and Military Applications.

The AEC's relations with the President were also specified by statute. In addition to his appointive powers, the President was assigned certain specific authority over the AEC in connection with high policy problems. He was to determine at least once each year the amount of fissionable material and of atomic weapons to be produced. He was to direct the AEC to deliver to the armed forces such materials or weapons for such uses as he deemed necessary. No administrative instrumentalities were established for the discharge of these responsibilities, however, and not until the National Security Council was created did an institutional framework for systematic and sustained presidential review of AEC policies emerge.

The problem of congressional control over the atomic program presented special difficulties. Because the program was shrouded in secrecy, Congress could not rely on the usual processes of public discussion and political debate to acquaint it with the important issues. Consequently, the Act established a permanent Joint Committee on Atomic Energy, composed of nine members from each house, and charged with unusual responsibilities for overseeing the work of the AEC. It was directed to "make continuing studies of the activities of the Atomic Energy Commission and of problems relating to the development, use and control of atomic energy." Furthermore, making it plain that the AEC was to share its secrets with the Committee, the Act required the Commission to "keep the Joint Committee fully and currently informed with respect to the Commission's activities."

In the field of industrial development and production, virtually exclusive control was vested in the AEC by the 1946 Act. These provisions were somewhat modified in 1954. Private enterprise was permitted in mining the ores from which fissionable materials are refined, but all subsequent processing or producing stages were reserved for government monopoly. Private ownership of fissionable materials, productive facilities, and patents was forbidden, as was the private production, importation, or exportation of fissionables. The AEC might, however, lend or lease fissionables for research and therapy, and it could, after a ninety-day notification to Congress, license them for industrial use. It was authorized to construct its own facilities or enter into contracts for research and production. Contracts could be let without competitive bidding. All information about the manufacture or use of atomic weapons, the production of fissionable materials, and the use of such materials in the generation of power was classified, but the AEC could declassify data whose disclosure would not endanger national security. This sweeping grant of power reflected the unique importance of atomic energy and its essentiality to national defense.

2. The AEC Program in Action

The AEC inherited a vast enterprise, which was soon to be expanded to a scale comparable with the nation's largest industrial corporations. The task was not easy. The Commission's jurisdiction embraced 5,000 federal employees and 50,000 employees of contractors engaged in AEC activities, facilities representing a capital investment of $1.4 billion, and the management of three towns—Los Alamos, New Mexico; Oak Ridge, Tennessee; and Hanford, Washington—with a combined population of 62,000. It was entrusted with the knowledge and technology to carry forward the manufacture of atomic bombs. But with the ending of the war, the emergency program had been halted and many of the key scientific and engineering personnel had returned to civilian life. The weapons stockpile was small; there was little diversification in weapons; raw materials were scanty; many of the installations were experiencing unanticipated operating difficulties; and peaceful applications had been neglected.[2]

In its first decade, the AEC created a whole new industry, investing more than $12 billion in additional facilities. They included great new plants for the production of fissionables at Portsmouth, Ohio; at Paducah, Kentucky; and on the Savannah River in South Carolina. The Commission now has installations in half the states, including plants for the extraction of uranium from ore, for processing feed materials, and for the manufacture of weapons, a commercial power plant and several power prototypes, testing ranges, and laboratories and other research facilities. The AEC is now a substantial force within the economy, whose expenditures and policies are of major consequence to certain industries and to whole communities.

While this great new industry is government-controlled, and tightly so, virtually all of its work is done by private contractors. They build plants, process ores, produce fissionable materials, manufacture weapon components, conduct research, and provide public services. A small portion of the contracts, about 15 per cent, is let after competitive bidding. They usually cover the purchase of equipment and materials or the construction of routine facilities. Other contracts cover the research being performed by universities and research institutes. But the great bulk of the contracts are negotiated with a few large, research-oriented corporations. The AEC's major plants, for example, are operated by General Electric, Du Pont, Union Carbide, and Goodyear Tire and Rubber.

This system, inherited from the Manhattan District, has many advantages for the AEC. These large corporations offer the services of great numbers of managerial and technical personnel already organized into an operating unit. They can handle the large-scale atomic projects, which would severely tax the resources

[2] Joint Committee on Atomic Energy, *Hearings on Investigation into the United States Atomic Energy Project*, 81st Cong., 1st sess. (1949), Pt. 19, pp. 770–777.

and abilities of any smaller organization. Their profits from AEC work are apparently modest, but enough firms are desirous of accumulating experience and expertise in a growing industry to give the Commission some choice. Being private bodies, they can be more flexible in their methods than the AEC, and they relieve the Commission of much of the burden of administrative detail attendant on the management of a vast atomic program. Finally, by diffusing experience and knowledge, the contract system hastens the day when the government monopoly can be ended.

Despite these advantages, the system also has its drawbacks. Many are inherent in the cost-plus contract, which requires the government to pay all actual costs. This device is perhaps necessary in an experimental program with emphasis on speed of accomplishment, where final costs can only be guessed and construction and operating problems are often wholly unanticipated. The cost-plus-fixed-fee contracts typically used by the AEC place no premium on wastefulness, but they also lack any positive incentive to efficiency. The Commission attempts to promote efficiency through supervision of contractors, but the line between excessive supervision, which jeopardizes managerial flexibility, and inadequate supervision, which risks possible losses in economy and safety, is a hard one to draw.

The system also creates a somewhat hazardous relationship between government and private enterprise. While the contract device had been widely used previously, especially in wartime, never before has 95 per cent of a public agency's expenditures and personnel been under private management. This marriage of public ownership with private operation has been described as "a 'missing link' between capitalism and socialism," [3] but the character of its offspring is still uncertain. There is always the possibility of favoritism, whether innocent or corrupt, in the award of contracts and the potentially profitable experience they confer. That possibility is enhanced when, as in the atomic program, the requirements of competitive bidding and publicity are lacking. The nature of its program requires the AEC to negotiate most of its contracts. But the fact that security considerations shroud the whole proceeding means that there can be little check on the performance and judgment of the Commission. Much more reliance thus must be placed on the good faith and judgment of the AEC than in the case of ordinary governmental agencies.

Moreover, once a contract has been let, an unusual relationship between Commission and contractor is established, blurring the

[3] R. A. Tybout, *Government Contracting in Atomic Energy* (1956), p. vii.

ordinary distinctions between government and private enterprise. The AEC exercises a high degree of control and offers a great deal of counsel, much as a parent company does with its subsidiaries. It sets the contractors' goals and standards, suggests techniques, advances money, and requires reports. It checks for fraud, inspects for safety, and enforces security requirements. One can only speculate on the long-run consequences of such a relationship for both government and the affected businesses. Among the results which have been suggested are: greater government involvement in labor relations, since it is the real employer; a tendency toward runaway labor costs, since the government foots the bill; and a further impetus to the substitution of administered prices for free market prices.[4]

Yet another consequence of the contracting system is its effect on the future structure of the industry. For the reasons already indicated, the AEC found it desirable at the start to give its most important contracts to a few large corporations. Once this pattern had been established, the Commission then found it easier to continue to deal with these concerns, with their previous experience, technical ability, and other resources, than to interest, train, and finance less experienced smaller firms. It was also administratively convenient for the AEC to deal with and supervise a handful of large firms, rather than an army of smaller ones. There are fewer than a half-dozen companies deeply involved in power reactors.[5] Consequently, when private enterprise is permitted to enter the field, it seems reasonably certain that this new industry will be launched from the beginning on an oligopolistic course. The contracting corporations, already large firms, will command a long head start in knowledge and in operating experience over any smaller would-be entrants.

The problem of entry into the new industry is also presented in connection with patents. The 1946 Act made government property of all patentable processes and products discovered and developed on AEC projects, and it narrowly restricted private rights in any other inventions pertaining to atomic energy. No patent privileges could extend to the production and military use of fissionable materials. Patents covering peaceful applications were to be made available for licensing at reasonable royalties determined by the Commission.

When the Act was amended in 1954 in an effort to encourage

[4] Ibid., ch. 8 and p. 140.
[5] Oliver Townsend, "The Atomic Power Program in the United States," American Assembly, Atoms for Power (1957), p. 78.

limited private entry into the field (a development discussed more fully below), it was argued that private enterprise would not come in unless the inventions it developed were protected from competition. Many business groups accordingly asked for normal patent protection for improvements in atomic technology. Congress split on this issue, approximately on party lines, with most Democrats wishing to limit patent protection, while the Republican leadership sought to expand it. After a long struggle over this and many other features of the 1954 Act, a compromise was finally achieved. It permits patents on nonmilitary applications, but requires compulsory licensing of all comers for the first five years at royalties set by the AEC. It also affirms the government's rights in inventions resulting from operations under an AEC contract. It further extends these rights to include any invention made or conceived under any "other relationship" with the Commission, whether or not involving the expenditure of public funds, although the AEC may waive the government's claim.

While these issues were being vigorously debated and partially resolved, the AEC bore the major responsibility for extending the frontiers of nuclear technology. Its progress in developing and producing instruments of destruction, if this be progress, was impressive. The atomic bomb exploded over Hiroshima unleashed a force equal to that of twenty thousand tons of TNT. In recent years, a single hydrogen bomb explosion has reached the equivalent of twenty million tons of TNT, while at the other end of the scale a whole family of low-yield "tactical" atomic weapons has been developed. The stockpile, has mounted steadily, reaching an explosive potential estimated to equal that of a billion tons of TNT by the end of 1954.[6] Atomic energy has also been adapted to other military uses, notably submarine propulsion.

With respect to the peaceful application of atomic energy and its products, the AEC has also made striking contributions. Even before passage of the McMahon Act, the Manhattan District had begun a wide and generous distribution of isotopes for research in the sciences, medicine, and agriculture. The AEC continued and expanded this program. Many fruitful uses have already been uncovered. Reactors can be employed to make radioactive isotopes,

[6] Ralph E. Lapp, "Does the Superbomb Add to Our Security?" *The Reporter* (May 11, 1954), p. 10. This is an informed guess; disclosure of the exact size is punishable by death. In 1957, it was estimated by a member of the Joint Committee that the American material stockpile was sufficient to make 35,000 atomic weapons, while the Soviet Union was believed to be able to muster 10,000. *New York Times* (April 17, 1957).

which can then trace the progress of an element through biological, industrial, or agricultural processes. They may be used to understand the bodily functioning of humans and animals, and to study how plants absorb fertilizers and other nutrients from the soil. They can register the flow of liquids through pipelines, indicate engine wear, measure the thickness of materials, and detect flaws in metals. Atomic emissions may also be used to combat disease.

These new tools may have advanced medical science by more than twenty-five years.[7] In 1958, it was estimated that American industry was already saving about $500 million a year through the use of isotopes.[8] J. Robert Oppenheimer has argued that the potentially most significant effect of the whole program has been its function as "the taking-off place for a new attitude toward the cultivation of science and the training of scientists. . . . These men who are being trained, these specialists in biophysics, medicine, the chemistry of fertilizers, genetics, and nuclear particles, stellar constitution . . . become a part of the many networks of specialists. They find themselves at some point on the incredibly steep curve of growing learning" and so contribute to a virtual revolution in basic and applied science.[9]

In the third area of its responsibility, the development of atomic power for nonmilitary purposes, the Commission has been much less vigorous. Indeed, it has been strongly criticized for failure to promote this program sufficiently and for neglect of some promising methods of generating electricity from atomic energy. This program is an integral part of the political life of the AEC.

3. The Politics of Atomic Energy

Congressional consideration of atomic legislation in 1945 and 1946 was largely nonpartisan and, aside from the struggle over military versus civilian control, essentially nonpolitical. The program was so new and so secret, and its nonmilitary applications so unknown, that the McMahon Act could hardly do more than establish the formal framework within which future policies would be made. As awareness spread of the significance of AEC decisions, various agencies, groups, and individuals began to fill the political vacuum surrounding the Commission, seeking to influence its de-

[7] Statement by Dr. J. C. Bugher, Director of the AEC's Division of Biology and Medicine, Subcommittee on Research and Development of the Joint Committee on Atomic Energy, *Hearings*, 83d Cong., 2d sess. (1954), p. 4.

[8] AEC, *Twenty-Third Semiannual Report* (1954), p. 25.

[9] "The Environs of Atomic Power," American Assembly, *op. cit.*, pp. 23–24.

cisions. For the most part, this interest centered on the question of the AEC's power programs. Some of the Commission's military decisions, such as those involving the development of the hydrogen bomb, had profound political implications, but decision-making in this area, being surrounded by secrecy requirements, was confined to the highest levels of government. The domestic distribution of radioactive by-products raised no political questions. Patent and contract policies have on occasion aroused Congress, but the discussion of issues in this sphere has usually been assimilated into the debate over power policy, which has evoked the most political attention. An explanation of the political environment in which the AEC functioned throws light on the way in which these issues have been handled.

Just as outside forces seek to influence an agency making decisions of potential importance to them, so an agency which wishes to develop its own positive program must seek to mobilize political support if it is to be effective. In embarking upon its voyage on a new and uncharted sea, the AEC cast about for advice and support. For the first two years, its relations with the Joint Congressional Committee, charged with the task of holding unusually close reins on the Commission, were unhappy.[10] The normal friction between a Congress and an administration controlled by opposing parties was exacerbated by the fact that the first AEC Chairman, David E. Lilienthal, was regarded by many Republicans as a particularly provocative symbol of the New Deal. The friction finally culminated in a full-scale attack, led by Senator Hickenlooper, chairman of the Joint Committee for its first two years, who charged Lilienthal with "incredible mismanagement." A six-week investigation of these charges in 1949 dealt only with peripheral matters but led the new Democratic majority to congratulate the AEC for its management and accomplishments; the Republican minority condemned it, largely on the basis of evidence which it said could not be disclosed, for a "leisurely" approach, insufficient attention to secrecy, and inadequate supervision of its delegations of authority.[11]

To counter this opposition and to secure the counsel not proffered it by the Joint Committee, the AEC looked elsewhere.[12] The executive provided little real assistance. The Military Liaison

[10] For a discussion of the AEC's relations with Congress, see Morgan Thomas, *Atomic Energy and Congress* (1956).

[11] Joint Committee on Atomic Energy, *Investigation into the United States Atomic Energy Commission*, S. Rept. 1169, 81st Cong., 1st sess. (1949).

[12] This analysis owes much to Thomas, *op. cit.*, especially ch. 11.

Committee was the battleground for a struggle among the three armed services and seldom exerted a unified influence on AEC decisions. In part because the National Security Council was not yet fully operative, the President did little more than discharge his prescribed statutory duties and did not concern himself overmuch with atomic policies. In these circumstances, the AEC turned for its main support to the General Advisory Committee (GAC), which proved a rich source of counsel and advice, and wielded much influence over the fledgling Commission during the Lilienthal period.

The GAC could exercise this influence, however, only so long as it monopolized access to the AEC. After the Soviet Union had shattered the assumptions of our defense and foreign policies by exploding an atomic bomb in September, 1949, years before we had expected it, other forces began to intrude themselves. Although the possibility of using fusion rather than fission to produce the explosive release of vast quantities of energy had been discussed within the Manhattan project as early as 1942, the AEC had decided not to support a full-scale effort to develop a hydrogen bomb—a decision which apparently was not communicated to the Joint Committee at the time.[13] Immediately after the President's disclosure of the Soviet explosion, the Joint Committee pressed the AEC to regain American supremacy. The GAC, headed by J. Robert Oppenheimer, who had contributed as much as anyone to the development of the atomic bomb, unanimously opposed any "crash" thermonuclear program, on moral and political as well as on technical grounds. The Commission, by a divided vote, recommended against a crash program, but passed the problem on to the President, feeling that so important a decision should be made at the highest level. On January 31, 1950, after some administrative lobbying for the program by the Joint Committee, and after hearing his Secretaries of State and Defense urge the program and Lilienthal oppose it, President Truman ordered the thermonuclear program begun. Lilienthal left the AEC shortly thereafter, and Commissioner Gordon Dean soon became Chairman.

The collaboration of Dean with Senator McMahon, now Chairman of the Joint Committee, instituted a period of harmonious relationships between the two bodies. "Without other fields to deal with, and for some time without burdensome legislation to consider, the Joint Committee concentrated on atomic policy and administration with enthusiasm and determination and assumed

[13] *Ibid.*, p. 87.

the uniquely influential and responsible role which has made it one of the most potent committees on Capitol Hill." [14] The support of the Joint Committee was all the more valuable because the appropriations committees found themselves hampered by secrecy in their efforts to control the AEC budget.

The honeymoon with Congress came to an end in 1953 with the installation of the Eisenhower administration. Two factors operated to disturb the pre-existing relationships. First, the executive began to exercise much of the control and influence formerly concentrated in the Joint Committee. Second, as commercial generation of electricity from atomic energy began to appear feasible, the stage was set for a struggle between the advocates of public and private power.

The new administration pressed for closer co-ordination between atomic policies and other national policies. This desire was intensified by the growing importance of the atom in international affairs. Accordingly, the new Chairman of the AEC, Lewis L. Strauss, was also appointed atomic advisor to the President. Strauss regularly attended meetings of the National Security Council and participated in many other policy consultations with the President and his close advisers. Certain important atomic policy decisions began to originate in the National Security Council, somewhat to the discomfiture of the other Commissioners and of the Joint Committee. When the McMahon Act was amended in 1954, it was proposed that this situation be recognized by a provision making the Chairman the "principal officer" of the Commission. Three Commissioners objected, complaining that Strauss had failed to consult with them and had not kept them informed of major policy decisions.[15] The provision was defeated, but Strauss continued to participate in policy planning at the presidential level. To the extent that the Commission no longer made atomic policy, the Joint Committee, too, was reduced in influence. There followed a period of strong Committee resentment against Strauss, especially on the part of Senator Clinton Anderson, who became Committee Chairman in 1955. In 1958, Strauss declined renomination to the Commission, although he continued to serve for a few months as presidential adviser on atomic energy.

Increased executive control over the AEC, and the consequent diminution of the role of the Joint Committee, contributed greatly

---

[14] *Ibid.*, p. 233.

[15] Joint Committee on Atomic Energy, *Hearings, To Amend the Atomic Energy Act of 1946,* 83d Cong., 2d sess. (1954), Pt. 2, pp. 781, 793, 805, 809, 831.

to the "politicization" of the Commission. Now that the administration had assumed the direction of many atomic policies, those policies became the subject of partisan defense and attack. Added to this were the bitter political recriminations inspired by the President's directive to the AEC to enter into the controversial Dixon-Yates contract as a means of limiting the growth of the TVA.[16] In addition, one of Strauss's first acts as Chairman led to the dismissal of J. Robert Oppenheimer from his position as a consultant to the Commission on the grounds that his access to atomic information endangered national security. This withdrawal of security clearance from the man who had directed the research leading to the atomic bomb and who was one of the nation's most distinguished scientists plunged the AEC into violent controversy. The Commission's doctrine of personnel security was defended by some as absolutely necessary and attacked by others as abhorrent.[17]

Especially important in the politicization of the AEC was the imminence of commercial generation of atomic power. As this prospect approached, the interest of private power groups, public power groups, and potential manufacturers of reactors and generating equipment led them to concern themselves more and more with AEC policies. Even had there been no Dixon-Yates contract, the AEC would necessarily have been involved in the struggle between the advocates of public power and the defenders of private power. That contract only hastened the process.

AEC development of civilian power reactors was slow in getting under way. Despite our head start in experience, technology, and equipment, both the Soviet Union and Great Britain reached certain important milestones before we did. A Russian 5,000-kilowatt power reactor, larger than any of the American experimental reactors, became operational in June, 1954, and the British 70,000-kilowatt Calder Hall power plant, the first full-scale reactor, began service late in 1956. The early American nuclear program was preoccupied with military applications. Because of cheap fuel and advanced technology, American costs of generating electricity conventionally have been lower than those in most of the world, and our short-run supply of energy resources is ample. There was thus no pressing domestic need for the speedy development of atomic power, and the possible political importance of being able to ex-

[16] This episode is described above, pp. 365–366.
[17] See AEC, *In the Matter of J. Robert Oppenheimer; Transcript of Hearing* (1954); and *Texts of Principal Documents and Letters* (1954). See also C. P. Curtis, *The Oppenheimer Case* (1955); Joseph and Stewart Alsop, *We Accuse* (1954).

port power reactors and technology to less fortunate areas was not immediately grasped. Before April, 1950, there had been only one major AEC project unrelated to military purposes, and that project, a power-breeder reactor at Knolls Laboratory, was never completed.

In the fall of 1948, the AEC decided upon its first reactor-development program.[18] As supplemented in 1950–1952, it included the construction of five reactors and the undertaking of three developmental projects. While construction and operation of the reactors accumulated much knowledge valuable for any civilian power project, this was not their central purpose. Two, for example, involved the construction of prototype nuclear engines for submarines. One of the developmental projects, however, was concerned directly with civilian power.

In January, 1951, the AEC invited industry to conduct studies of dual-purpose reactors, which would produce both plutonium for weapons and power for civilian use. Four groups of companies responded. As industry interest mounted, the Commission issued a second general invitation in April, 1952, which evoked a response from six new combinations of firms. The number of teams studying atomic power soon reached twenty-five.

Encouraged by this show of interest, and now for the first time subject to strong pressure from the Joint Committee to begin a nonmilitary power program, in late 1952 the AEC drew up plans for what would have been the nation's first, albeit pilot, atomic power plant. This project, however, together with several others of military importance, was eliminated in the first Eisenhower budget, submitted to Congress in May, 1953. Both the Joint Committee and the AEC strongly protested this cut before the House Appropriations Committee. They persuaded it to amend the budget to permit the AEC to begin work on a civilian power plant out of funds appropriated for other purposes. Accordingly, in October it was announced that the Commission had embarked upon the construction of a full-scale power plant, which involved the use of a reactor originally intended for an aircraft carrier. This reactor was installed in a plant built by the Duquesne Light Company near Pittsburgh and "went critical" on December 2, 1957.

Meanwhile, the Joint Committee, after conducting hearings which revealed many criticisms of the existing program, pressed the AEC for greater speed, breadth, and clarity in its civilian

[18] For analyses of AEC reactor programs, see Townsend, *op. cit.*; and W. H. Zinn's article, "An Appraisal of the United States Nuclear Power Program," in the same work, pp. 80–99.

power program. Complaining of "the indefiniteness of Commission plans for research and development in the field of atomic power components, pilot plants, and prototypes," the Committee asked the AEC to prepare and announce a long-range program "in a concise manner so that all interested companies, groups, organizations, or individuals can henceforth have no doubt about the Federal program." [19] The Commission responded to this request in February, 1954, with a so-called five-year program which included four reactors in addition to the full-scale Duquesne project. Two were pilot models of a type not built before; two were enlarged and improved versions of reactors already successfully built on a smaller scale.

4. Nuclear Power and the Atomic Energy Act of 1954

Announcement of this program and the findings of the various study groups had persuaded industry that developmental work had now progressed to the point where it would be possible for private enterprise to perform a greater share of the work, if the restrictions of the McMahon Act were lifted. The Joint Committee had begun in 1953 hearings on revisions of the 1946 Act. Members of Congress and of the executive branch wished to encourage private entry in the hope of accelerating economic development of atomic power. The most decisive impetus for new legislation, however, arose from considerations of military and foreign policy. Greater co-operation with our allies required that the McMahon Act be amended to enable us to share some of our atomic information and weapons. And it had become apparent that we were on the brink of international competition for the good will of smaller nations through the export of civilian atomic devices and technology. This required both an amendment to permit the flow of information and of devices and an acceleration of the power program, to which it was hoped that private enterprise could make an important contribution.

The legislative machinery was put in motion in February, 1954, by President Eisenhower's proposals for three major changes: (1) that the government be permitted to share with its allies information about atomic weapons used for mutual defense; (2) that it be permitted to exchange information about peaceful applications of atomic energy with friendly nations; and (3) that the government monopoly of fissionable materials, atomic facilities, and patents

---

[19] Joint Committee on Atomic Energy, *Hearings on Atomic Power Development and Private Enterprise*, 83d Cong., 1st sess. (1953), p. 571.

concerning atomic processes be sufficiently relaxed to enable private enterprise to generate atomic power. While the Joint Committee chose to write its own bill, the President's three proposals formed its core. His first two recommendations occasioned little controversy and, in a more limited form, easily became part of the 1954 law. The proposals relating to the role of private enterprise in the future development of atomic power, however, raised crucial questions of public policy, touched upon many important interests, and engendered a long and heated congressional debate.

In this most unusual of industries, where government regulation and ownership preceded private activity, the common denominator of the many issues raised in the course of the legislative process was how much private enterprise was to be permitted and encouraged. As already noted, the issue of patents provided one focus for the struggle. A second major issue was that of private versus public power. This was bound to be a major concern in the consideration of a great new source of power, but the intensity of the debate which it precipitated was greatly increased by the Dixon-Yates episode already described. Proponents of public power, largely Democrats, wished to authorize the AEC to generate and sell electricity, and to give public and co-operative bodies the same preference in its distribution that they enjoyed with respect to other federal power. They further desired that public agencies, as well as private companies, be eligible to produce atomic power. They argued that purely private exploitation of the new resource would lead to monopolization in the manufacture of reactors and of related generating equipment and to greater concentration among electric utilities. They also suggested that private enterprise lacked the incentive and the capital to develop atomic power rapidly enough to maintain American superiority in international competition.

The opponents of public power, largely Republicans, wished to bar or narrowly restrict the development of atomic power by public agencies. Relying on the ability of private enterprise to develop atomic power, they sought to confine the AEC to experimental and military work. The final measure, which became law in August, attempted to compromise the immediate issue of public power. More importantly, despite some confusion in its draftsmanship, the 1954 Act charts a unique and complex relationship between government and industry.

It forbids the AEC to engage in the commercial production and sale of atomic power, although it may sell the power generated from experimental reactors and produced as a by-product from reactors producing plutonium. Public agencies, however, have an equal right with private utilities to apply for licenses to produce atomic power, and in granting commercial licenses the AEC is directed to give preference to public agencies and co-operatives, and to areas with high power costs. The effect of these provisions is more to defer the public power issue than to resolve it, for, in the absence of later amendments, future public atomic power activities will depend on legislative authorizations and appropriations for particular public agencies, rather than on the terms of the 1954 Act.

On the broader question of governmental and private roles in the new industry, the clear intent of the Act is to open up the field for private activity. It permits the private construction, ownership, and operation of power reactors, the private use of nuclear fuel, and the private sale of by-products. It permits private patents, under the conditions mentioned earlier. And it provides for the declassification of information needed for industrial progress, substituting for the old declassification criterion of "not endangering security" the easier requirement of "no undue risk" to security. The progress of declassification, however, depends as much on AEC interpretation and administration as it does on these necessarily vague statutory provisions. Finally, the AEC is empowered to subsidize private ventures. While some of the Act's subsidy provisions are ambiguous, if not contradictory,[20] they clearly allow the AEC to subsidize private activity directly by research and development contracts, and to do so indirectly by performing research itself on behalf of private firms and by adjusting its charges for nuclear fuel and its payments for the plutonium "ash" produced by private reactors.

While thus promoting private entry, the AEC must also regulate. This regulation, largely exercised through its licensing power, is primarily oriented toward security and safety. Indeed, Congress felt so strongly on these scores that it refused to allow private ownership of the nuclear material itself. The reason for its concern is obvious. A reactor capable of generating power can also produce substantial quantities of plutonium, which can be used in weapons. And the use of reactors presents many grave hazards to health and safety, not the least of which is the danger that a "runaway" reactor might produce an explosive chain reaction like that of an atomic bomb.

The AEC is also directed to regulate entrance into the industry

[20] J. G. Palfrey, "Atomic Energy: A New Experiment in Government-Industry Relations," Columbia Law Review (March, 1956), pp. 388–390.

with a view to establishing and strengthening competition. Violation of the antitrust laws in the atomic field entails revocation or suspension of the AEC license, whether commercial or experimental. The AEC is directed to report any apparent antitrust violation to the Attorney General and to consult with him on the antitrust implications of any commercial licenses it intends to issue.

This is a unique combination of different governmental roles. They require of the AEC difficult judgments and a deft hand on the controls. The Commission must encourage private enterprise, but not at the risk of endangering secrecy and safety. Presumably those firms with a head start in the new industry will have an advantageous position, but the AEC must also restrain such firms in the interest of facilitating competition by late-comers. The AEC thus finds itself with the responsibility of attempting to promote, to guide, and to shape activities usually left to the initiative of the private sector of the economy. As one commentator has put it:

> The atomic statute appears to represent the culmination of the blurring process that has been taking place in recent years between private and public sectors of our economy . . . but as similarities increase, basic distinctions remain, and the new atomic statute sharply exposes the resulting conundrum. Under this statute, the Government is undertaking to release the automatic processes of our private economy through affirmative measures of government intervention. It is undertaking to create, regulate, and assist processes of private enterprise which have flourished in the past because they were self-created, self-regulated, and unassisted. Acting as partner, employer, promoter, rival, and policeman, the Government is endeavoring to create a new relationship with industry.[21]

5. The Partnership of Government and Industry

While the 1954 Act attempted to compromise opposing views on the proper role of government in atomic power, it did not close the debate. Later years have been marked by increasingly acrimonious conflict, with the Democratic majority on the congressional Joint Committee spearheading one camp and AEC Chairman Strauss, until his retirement in June, 1958, leading the other. This debate has centered on the question of whether private enterprise, as assisted by the AEC under the terms of the 1954 law, can develop an atomic power industry rapidly enough, or whether direct government construction of atomic power plants is necessary.

The AEC's efforts to promote private development and con-

---

[21] *Ibid.*, p. 391.

struction of power reactors got off to a promising start. In January, 1955, it issued its first call for proposals for power reactor construction. Under this program, the Commission arranged to assist construction and operation by waiving fuel-use charges in the early stages of operation, by performing research, and by paying for the technical and economic information derived from reactor projects. Three proposals for large-scale reactors were made in response to this invitation, two for private utilities, and one for a public power district in Nebraska. In addition, somewhat to the Commission's surprise, two utilities asked for permission to construct large-scale plants without any assistance from the AEC. All five of these proposals were ultimately accepted, as well as one for a small prototype reactor.

Encouraged by this response, the AEC in October, 1955, issued a second invitation, this time for smaller plants of from 5,000 to 40,000 kilowatts, with the provision that the Commission would finance and keep title to the reactors themselves, but not the power plants. There were seven responses to this call, of which six came from rural co-operatives or from small, municipally-owned utilities. It was a hopeful sign that most of the manufacturers associated with these applications were new to the field. Unfortunately, this group encountered serious difficulty as estimates of costs soared, and up to mid-1958 only one AEC contract was actually negotiated.

Early in 1957, the AEC issued a third invitation for proposals, again for large-scale plants. By the end of 1957, four applications had been made, and one had been granted.

Thus, in addition to the operational Duquesne plant, by the end of 1957 six large-scale reactors had been authorized. One private and seven AEC small, experimental reactors had been completed.[22] It is notable, however, that the numbers of applications and licenses slowed down after the first expressions of interest. Both private enterprise and public power agencies confronted many difficulties. Early cost estimates were often woefully inadequate as unanticipated construction and operating problems arose. The Duquesne plant started out as a $47-million project, but its costs finally exceeded $110 million.[23] A small reactor proposed by a rural co-operative was originally estimated to cost $3.6 million. The AEC canceled negotiations when the estimate rose to $14.4 million.[24] The sharp rises in construction costs have not only in-

[22] AEC, 23rd Semiannual Report (1958), pp. 77–136.
[23] Business Week (December 7, 1957), p. 33.
[24] Business Week (October 12, 1957), p. 48.

creased the size of the necessary investments; they also raise the cost of the power to be generated. While conventionally generated power costs on the average about 7 mills a kilowatt-hour, early costs at the Duquesne plant have averaged about 63 mills. In the face of such sobering statistics, both manufacturers and utilities have lost much of their initial enthusiasm for early entry into the new industry.

There also have been other, less formidable handicaps. One, the high cost of insuring against damages from reactor accidents, was dealt with by federal legislation in 1957. This law provides for low-cost coverage over and above that granted by private insurance companies. Secrecy also apparently still hinders private development. Both the Joint Committee and industry representatives have complained that the AEC has proceeded with excessive caution in declassifying information.

As private entry slowed down, Democratic criticism of the AEC mounted. The administration position, generally supported by congressional Republicans, was one of firm and confident insistence that private enterprise would develop, and was developing, atomic power as rapidly as the need justified and that the American rate of development was unmatched elsewhere in the world. This position commanded the enthusiastic support of private utilities and, for a time, of electrical manufacturers.

Congressional Democrats, with the support of public power groups, alleged that the existing program was insufficient. They argued that, with consumption of electricity doubling every decade, and with reserves of oil and natural gas limited, atomic sources of power had to be developed without delay as a supplement to conventional fuels. They further argued that our international position demanded that we not lag behind the Soviet Union and Great Britain in the development of atomic power.

In addition, the Joint Committee criticized the AEC for not adequately exploring the various means of producing atomic power. Different combinations of fuels and moderators may be employed to produce controlled chain reactions. Uranium, enriched uranium (containing more than the normal amount of U-235), and plutonium may be used as fuels. Ordinary water, heavy water, and graphite have been successfully used to moderate the reaction. AEC programs have tended to concentrate on the use of enriched uranium and water. The Joint Committee argued that if future development were left entirely to private enterprise, only the tested methods would be used, thus neglecting the other, more risky but possibly more productive, methods. They also urged the AEC to develop natural uranium reactors, since other nations would be most apt to desire this type so as to avoid dependence on the United States for enriched uranium fuel.

Congressional Democrats waged a vigorous battle to achieve their objectives. They forced the AEC to broaden its reactor program. In 1957, over the Commission's opposition, they persuaded Congress to direct the AEC to design a natural uranium and graphite reactor. They also elicited from the Commission an agreement to construct a natural uranium and heavy-water reactor, if no outside group submitted an acceptable proposal for one of this type. Similarly, in 1958, legislation was passed authorizing almost $250 million in appropriations to which both the AEC and the President objected. Congress authorized a $145-million plutonium-producer which, if additional expenditures were made, could be converted to generate about 300,000 kilowatts of electricity. It also provided that the AEC design four more power reactors which Congress might later order constructed. Finally, it required that the AEC itself begin construction of a $51-million gas-cooled power reactor if no private proposal for one had been negotiated within six months.[25]

Thus, no federal power reactors have yet been constructed, and in the period 1956–1958 numerous bills calling for the appropriation of as much as $400 million for power reactors were rejected. But the AEC has been forced to design plants and to take steps leading to possible power generation. The issue still hangs in balance. The array of interests supporting and opposing these measures was virtually identical with that prevailing in other public power debates, and the administration took a strong position of opposition. Undoubtedly, future sessions of Congress will continue to wrestle with the problem. And late in 1957 there were signs of an important shift in the pattern of interests. Manufacturers, anxious to begin the development and production of reactors and related generating equipment, and impatient with the delays of private utilities, were reported to have decided to support federal construction of reactors in the belief that government expenditures were necessary to speed the growth of the new industry.[26]

Whatever the outcome, it is clear that the atomic power indus-

[25] On November 21, 1958, just within the deadline imposed by Congress, a consortium of more than fifty private power companies offered to construct a gas-cooled type of reactor, which would be installed within the utility system of the Philadelphia Electric Company. If approved, the plant would produce 30,000 kilowatts of electricity and would ultimately be expanded to turn out 40,000 kilowatts. New York Times (November 22, 1958).

[26] Business Week (October 12, 1957), pp. 48–50.

try will for many years present a unique combination of private and governmental activity. Government is assigned the difficult task of nurturing and directing the growth of an infant industry. For a period at least, government has also been given the task of supplying much of the initiative and innovating drive usually reserved for private enterprise.

Finally, future developments in atomic power promise to have important economic and political consequences over the whole range of energy industries. Atomic fuels will probably be substituted rather gradually for other energy sources, for the fuel costs of generating electricity by conventional means are low. But the availability of atomic power will become increasingly important as reserves of other fuels are exhausted. Moreover, the fact that present fuel costs vary greatly from one geographical area to another means that future atomic policies will have a most uneven regional impact. In all probability, atomic power will first be used on a large scale in areas of high fuel costs. It may, for example, become as much in the interest of New England, now a high-fuel-cost area, to press for government construction of atomic power plants, as it was in the interest of the Pacific Northwest and the Tennessee Valley in the past to urge expanded federal expenditures on hydroelectric facilities. Thus, the shaping of public policy in this field is inextricably involved with broader issues of regional and industrial development.

PART 6

Government as Manager and Trustee

CHAPTER 23

Conservation of Natural Resources

CONSERVATION is an evolving term. In its early development, it was focused on the maintenance of renewable resources and the avoidance of waste of nonrenewable resources. It has also come to include preservation of natural beauties and curiosities and recreational areas. In recent years, especially in the key fields of soil, forest, mineral, and water conservation, a distinction has been drawn between physical and economic waste, the latter occurring when resources are lost whose value exceeds the cost of saving them.[1] Conservation also involves

[1] "Conservation," the Interior Department once declared, "is the management and wise use of natural assets to prevent their depletion and at the same time produce wealth." S. Doc. 142, 75th Cong., 3d sess. (1938), p. 3. And the President's Materials Policy Commission in 1952 similarly defined conservation as the avoidance of *economic* waste: "Most thoughtful persons agree that conservation is a good idea, but there are wide differences as to how best—and how much—to protect the future claimants against the nation's treasure of resources. . . . One popular fallacy is to regard our resource base as a fixed inventory which, when used up, will leave society with no means of survival. A related fallacy is that physical waste equals economic waste: the feeling that it is wasteful to use materials in ways that make them disappear . . . these fallacies together lead to a hairshirt concept of conservation which makes it synonymous with hoarding. A sound view of conservation . . . is one which equates it with efficient management—efficient use of resources and of manpower and materials: a positive concept compatible with growth and high consumption in place of abstinence and retrenchment. . . .

"Conservation is something very different from simply leaving oil in the ground or trees in the forests on the theory that by sacrificing lower value

a systematic effort to balance the present and future needs of society.

Taken in this sense, conservation is a peculiarly appropriate subject of governmental action. Save in the narrow domain of immediate family interest, concern for the distant future will rarely be translated into effective action except by public agencies. Some large corporations, notably in forestry and mining, are exceptions; they take a long-run view of corporate interest and are prepared to sacrifice immediate gains for future benefits. But in most cases, unmodified competitive forces do not provide adequate safeguards against wasteful depletion of natural resources. In resource exploitation, moreover, individual interest rarely takes account of full social costs and benefits. Careless stripping of upland forests, for example, may destroy adjacent farm land by soil erosion, pollute the valley waters with the resultant silt, and shorten the useful life of a downstream dam by siltation of its reservoir. The ultimate costs and damages imposed upon others may far exceed the lumberman's profits. Yet, without public intervention, such costs and damages will play no part in shaping his course of action. American land-tenure conditions and traditions have been unusually conducive to rapid exploitation and "mining" of renewable as well as exhaustible resources.

Both the abuses of the natural environment and the development of a conservation movement have been conditioned by the manner in which the United States was settled. Most of the nation's land was once owned by the government. A policy of unrestricted immigration and rapid settlement, applied to unrivaled natural conditions, produced the unique phenomenon of the American frontier, with its legend of inexhaustible resources and its intransigent individualistic philosophy. For a century, the federal government was first and foremost a giver of gifts, and the largest element of its bounty was the public domain. The lands were distributed without any attempt to control their future use.

---

uses today we will leave something for higher value uses of tomorrow when supplies will be scarcer. Using resources today is an essential part of making our economy grow; materials which become embodied in today's capital goods, for example, are put to work and help make tomorrow's production higher. Hoarding resources in the expectation of more important uses later involves a sacrifice that may never be recouped; technological changes and new resource discoveries may alter a situation completely. It may not be wise to refrain from using zinc today if our grandchildren will not know what to do with it tomorrow. But following a course of conservation which . . . weighs economic factors carefully, is very different from the eat, drink, and be merry philosophy which sees no point in judicious self-restraint and no cause for worry over posterity's welfare." *Resources for Freedom*, Vol. I, p. 21.

The policy developed the continent at a rate attained nowhere else in the world, but it also brought in its train unparalleled physical wastage and a good deal of political corruption.

As the best lands ran out at the close of the nineteenth century, and as shortages in specific resources began to threaten, a reaction in public sentiment set in. Governmental restraints upon the exploitation of natural resources, however, ran counter to a century-old tradition, as well as to organized particular interests with a heavy stake in the old order. Forging of the conservation movement into a political cause sufficiently powerful to achieve significant results was accomplished only at the beginning of the twentieth century. The movement has always suffered from the inherent difficulties of mobilizing public concern for broad goals. Its strength has been intermittent, highly dependent on vigorous leadership to arouse and direct it.

1. The Conservation Movement

Concern over the rapid exploitation of our natural resources was first expressed by geographers, geologists, foresters, and other scientific observers in the decades after the Civil War. Eastern experience with forest destruction, water pollution, and wildlife extinction suggested to these specialists the danger of parallel abuses and ultimate shortages in the West. During the 1870's, the American Association for the Advancement of Science and the newly organized American Forestry Association pointed out these dangers in statements to Congress. The celebrated report of Major J. W. Powell of the Geological Survey on *Lands of the Arid Regions of the United States* (1878) stimulated interest in systematic land classification and in irrigation.

These forebodings, however, coincided with the most hectic land boom of American history. Land was liberally granted to states, to railroads, and to individuals. The General Land Office viewed its function as one of promoting the most rapid possible transfer of the public domain to private hands. While preference was nominally given to family farms, actual administrative practice also relinquished every type of resource—land, forest, mineral, and, later, water power—to corporate interests as well. Permanent public retention of natural resources was hardly seriously considered, for it ran counter to the dominant philosophy of the period.

Against the momentum of feverish exploitation, the warnings of scattered scientific Cassandras made little headway. A policy of reserving public lands, which had been applied until 1845 in connection with mineral properties, was reinstituted for limited purposes. Thus, Yellowstone National Park was created in 1872. The President was authorized to reserve irrigation reservoir sites in 1888, and forest lands in 1891. Under the latter authority, Presidents Harrison, Cleveland, and McKinley created forest reservations totaling 45 million acres. During the same period, most states undertook scattered action to protect wildlife, to prevent the more obviously destructive forest malpractices, and to reduce oil, gas, and other mineral wastage.

The sum effect of such measures, while not inconsiderable, was far from constituting an effective or comprehensive program. With the frontier at an end and the consequences of unrestrained exploitation obtruding themselves increasingly upon public consciousness, an eventual trend toward conservation was probably inevitable. But it was greatly accelerated by the enlistment of Theodore Roosevelt's crusading zeal. Roosevelt, in turn, was inspired mainly by Gifford Pinchot, who had become chief of the Agriculture Department's Forestry Bureau in 1898 and was probably more responsible than any other single individual for the widespread public interest in conservation early in this century. Conservation became a watchword of the Theodore Roosevelt administration.

The new development took three forms: (1) popularization, which welded scattered enthusiasts into a national movement; (2) systematic surveying of natural resources and planning for their interrelated development; and (3) reservation of great areas of the remaining public domain and assumption of federal responsibility on an unprecedented scale for natural resource preservation and development.

In his first annual message to Congress, Roosevelt declared that "the forest and water problems are perhaps the most vital internal problems of the United States." Under the Reclamation Act of 1902, the federal government undertook development of irrigation projects in the West. The forest reserves were increased to 150 million acres, including practically all important forest lands still within the public domain. Coal, oil, and phosphate lands were likewise withdrawn from entry, together with a number of water-power sites. The Inland Waterways Commission, appointed in 1907, laid down for the first time the principles of interrelated, multipurpose water-resource development. Enormous impetus was given to state conservation activities by such devices as the first White House Conference of Governors in 1908. A National Conservation Commission was established to inventory the nation's natural resources as a basis for future policy. And the Geological Survey began systematic classification of the remaining public lands.

Politically, Roosevelt's enthusiasm for conservation was closely associated with his campaign against monopolistic corporations. Wholesale withdrawals of public lands engendered fierce hostility from well-entrenched lumbering, mining, and power interests. They received substantial support from wider groups in the Western states who were alarmed by the threat of permanent loss of tax jurisdiction over large areas. Before the close of Roosevelt's term, a congressional reaction severely curtailed the work of the Conservation Commission and forbade further forestry withdrawals without specific legislative consent.

President Taft, while sympathetic to conservation, did not approach the subject with his predecessor's vigorous enthusiasm. Important mineral lands and water reserves were withdrawn during his administration, but the tempo of the movement was sharply decreased. In the public mind, the reaction was emphasized by the dramatic quarrel between Pinchot, who had been placed in charge of the national forests upon their transfer from the Interior to the Agriculture Department in 1905, and Secretary of the Interior Ballinger. Pinchot charged the Interior Department with serious corruption in connection with Alaskan coal lands; President Taft, concluding upon investigation that the charges were unwarranted, removed Pinchot from office. Ballinger, although exonerated by an official inquiry, resigned under a cloud shortly thereafter.

Conservation thus became a political football in the widening Republican schism. In the struggle between the Departments of Agriculture and Interior for control over the national forests—a controversy which recurs to this day—the momentum of the movement was seriously slackened. Like many policies initiated in the flush of temporary excitement, conservation suffered from the absence of a solid core of continuing interests devoted to its maintenance. Nonetheless, by the close of the Taft administration, natural resource conservation had become an accepted and permanent function of American government.

During World War I and the 1920's, substantial, although undramatic, advances were made in the clarification of conservation policy. The Federal Water Power Act of 1920 established federal supervision of water-power development. Other measures provided for control of coal and oil recovery from public lands under a leasing system. Further substantial areas of the public domain were withdrawn from entry by every President. Increasing attention was given to demonstration, research, and assistance to the states in promoting conservational practices on private lands. For a time, during the Harding regime, doubt was cast upon the integrity of the administration of reserved public lands by the Teapot Dome oil-lease scandal.[2] On the whole, however, the period was one of slow but steady development toward effective conservational techniques.

With the deepening of the Great Depression and the election of Franklin Roosevelt, conservation policy was restored to a position of prominence reminiscent of the new President's namesake. In this revival, a leading part was played by the desire for useful public works, noncompetitive with private enterprise, as a means of providing employment. Conservational activities of one form or another became a primary objective for the Public Works Administration, the Works Projects Administration, and the Civilian Conservation Corps. Interest was further intensified by the critical needs of the marginal farm population, which was no longer able to find urban employment. In 1934, dramatic emphasis was given to the disastrous results of soil erosion by the dust storms which arose from the northern Great Plains.

Under these conditions, the conservation movement reached a new peak. Large-scale measures to combat soil erosion were undertaken. Under the Taylor Grazing Act of 1934, most of the remaining unreserved public domain not suited to crop production was withdrawn from entry and incorporated within grazing districts. This Act established, for the first time, general land classification authority and marked a virtual end to the disposal of the public domain. Through tax revisions and purchases, the extent of the public lands was even somewhat increased, and the conservation and planned development of natural resources were extended to many new fields.

During the decade after World War II, the conservation movement once again lost momentum. There was little need for the government to provide employment; there was a reaction against planning; and there was a resurgent emphasis on economic individualism. Few new conservation measures were launched. The

[2] This scandal arose from the granting of leases in the Wyoming Naval Oil Reserve to private interests on unduly generous terms. A number of high government officers, including Cabinet members, were accused of flagrant corruption in connection with the transactions, and the leases were later canceled by the Supreme Court.

potentially significant conservation issues raised in the offshore-oil controversy [3] and in natural gas policies [4] failed to arouse popular concern. The President's Materials Policy Commission of 1950–1952 failed in its efforts to extend conservation policy to the broad range of industrial raw materials. Under Eisenhower, the administration of some conservational policies appreciably slackened, and the conservation movement slipped back, but not to the level prevailing before 1933.

2. Major Spheres of Conservation Policy

Public Lands

Historically, the major emphasis of the American conservation movement has been on the public domain. Of the total United States land area (excluding Alaska) of about 1,900 million acres, 1,462 million acres were once public domain and some 411 million remain in federal hands. In addition, nearly all of Alaska's 375 million acres are under federal ownership.

About 97 per cent of the non-Alaskan federal land lies within eleven Western states, comprising more than half of their total area. Their complaint that federal ownership deprives them of an adequate tax base has been met by a sharing with the states of federal receipts from licensees operating on the federal lands.[5] But the major local opposition to federal reservation of land arises from lumbering, mining, and grazing interests, who would prefer the opportunity to purchase the lands or to exploit them under the laxer controls which might prevail under state ownership and management.

It is in the operation of these lands that most of the important conservational practices were first developed. Several federal agencies are involved. Excluding Alaskan and federally administered but not owned (mainly Indian) lands, in 1955 about 44 per cent of the public lands were managed by the Bureau of Land Management, 41 per cent by the Forest Service, 6 per cent by the Department of Defense, 4 per cent by the National Park Service, and 2 per cent each by the Fish and Wildlife Service and the Bureau of

[3] See above, pp. 652–656.
[4] See above, pp. 668–671, 678–679.
[5] A recent study shows that federal contributions to state and local governments in lieu of taxes on the national forests exceed the payments which would be entailed were these forests taxed. These contributions include 25 per cent of gross receipts from the forests, plus federal expenditures for roads and fire control. E. T. Williams, "National Forest Contributions to Local Governments," *Land Economics* (August, 1955), pp. 204–214.

Reclamation.[6] (All these agencies except the Forest Service and the armed forces are within the Interior Department.) The operations have gradually passed from a custodial phase to one of intensive management. An important milestone in this process was reached in fiscal 1951 when, for the first time, gross cash revenues from these lands exceeded total direct appropriations.

Governmental management usually involves the supervision of private firms and individuals permitted to use the public lands upon payment of fees or royalties. In some cases the level of payments is determined by auction. Land use includes lumbering, grazing, mineral production, and occupancy for business purposes, as well as recreation, hunting, and fishing. Occasionally, as in the case of watershed protection, public land management may yield substantial benefits off the site.

Management of these lands affords many opportunities for the development of conservational practices which are often applicable to private properties as well. Education, demonstration, pecuniary inducements, and legal regulation have all been marshaled to promote the adoption of such practices on private lands. In some areas, notably forestry, conservationists have expressed serious doubts as to the possibility of effective action without a substantial increase in public ownership. In others, among which soil and mineral conservation are outstanding, large-scale public ownership is regarded as neither feasible nor desirable.

Forests

Forest resources were the primary concern of the early conservation movement and retain a central position in conservation policy. They are closely related to a wide range of other natural resources. Watershed protection and soil-erosion control both depend in large measure upon related forest activities. Forests contribute to wildlife preservation and to recreation. But the principal source of conservational interest in forests arises from their intrinsic importance as the raw material for a number of major industries. In 1950, the value of timber cut was only about $1 billion, but the total output of timber-based industries was about $15 billion. Although timber is a renewable resource, the necessary time span for full renewal is long, fifteen to forty years for pulpwood varieties and fifty to eighty years for lumber.

American forests were long treated as obstacles to farming or as mines to be exhausted, rather than as lands capable of producing

[6] General Services Administration, *Inventory Report on Federal Real Property in the United States as of June 30, 1955*, S. Doc. 100, 84th Cong., 2d sess.

annual wood crops. Only in recent decades have any private lumbering operations been conducted on a permanent sustained-yield basis. The old rule was logging of particular areas and subsequent abandonment, often followed by complete destruction through fire and insects. Yet, during the period of large-scale lumbering, local communities become directly or indirectly dependent upon these operations. Forest depletion brings in its train unemployment, the drying up of tax revenues, and community impoverishment. Although other materials are increasingly substituted for wood, moreover, traditional cutting practices threaten grave shortages in the near future. In 1950, for example, the drain on saw timber, including the effects of fire and insects as well as cutting, was about 56 billion board feet, but the growth was only about 36 billion. Under the pressure of diminishing supplies, wood prices have increased greatly in the last two decades.

The problem of managing our forests to meet future needs involves an unusual combination of public and private controls. Excluding Alaska, where economic accessibility to timber tracts raises special problems, there are about 460 million acres of land suitable and available for the commercial production of timber crops. About one-fourth of this land is government-owned, most of it by the federal government. Of the privately-owned land, about 12 per cent is in large tracts owned by pulp and lumber companies. The rest is in scattered patches, 40 per cent in woodlots on several million farms and 48 per cent in a million nonfarm holdings.

The task of improving yields thus calls for both public and private action. It is generally on the federal lands that sound conservational practices are most consistently observed. The national forests comprise 167 million acres, 139 million reserved from the public domain and 28 million acquired through purchase, donation, or exchange.[7] Additional timber is grown on some of the land supervised by other agencies, primarily the Bureau of Land Management. Since its creation in 1905, the Forest Service has devoted itself to the maintenance of existing stands and restoration of growth on cutover or otherwise depleted areas. Carefully organized fire protection results in a substantially smaller pro-

---

[7] The Weeks Act of 1911 permitted the Forest Service to acquire "such forested, cutover, or dead wood lands within the watersheds of navigable streams as . . . may be necessary to the regulation of the flow of navigable streams," and the McNary-Clarke Amendment of 1924 authorized further purchases of such lands for the production of timber. The General Exchange Act of 1922 permitted the exchange of federal tracts for private land of at least equal value, thereby permitting the simplification of complex land-ownership patterns.

portion of loss than on private lands. The program includes large-scale planting, nursery operations, and efforts to restrict the ravages of insects and disease.

On these lands, the primary problem has been insufficient cutting rather than too much. Commercial timbering is permitted under close Forest Service supervision by private operators who bid for tracts designated by the Service. Because these lands were often in remote sections and because there were few access roads, as recently as 1940 only 2 billion board feet a year were being taken from the national forests out of the 9 billion available on the basis of modern management practices and sustained yield. Overripe trees were thus hindering younger growth. In later years, however, with increased prices for timber products and the building of more access roads, annual harvests from the national forests have sharply increased, reaching 7 billion feet in 1956. Timber sales now exceed $100 million, well over the Forest Service's total expenditures. Similarly, the forests on the public domain, which are managed by the Bureau of Land Management, have yet to be fully utilized.

The private forest lands present the gravest problems of policy and administration, imposing upon government the tasks of regulation, promotion, and education. Together with the public forests, they are more than sufficient, under adequate management, to meet national needs. But private forestry practices, while much improved in recent years, are still grossly inadequate. An investigation by the Forest Service in 1945 showed that two-thirds of the private commercial forests lacked adequate fire protection and were being poorly cut. The management of less than one-tenth met good forestry standards.

Most of the better managed private forests are held by the larger companies. Able to plan in long-range terms, they have steadily improved their practices in recent decades. Beginning with an NRA code which banned destructive cutting, they have progressed to the point where many of their holdings are now operated on a sustained-yield basis. But the concept of timber as an annual crop has been slow in winning adherents among the millions of farmers and others who own most of the nation's private forests in small woodlots. Not being full-time lumbermen, lacking the knowledge and skills necessary for proper management, and often without the funds to finance long-term development, they tend to regard a woodlot as a source of incidental income and think in terms of selling off all of the timber at once. Fearing that such small tracts could never be well managed, the Forest

Service and the National Resources Board recommended in the thirties that 200 million acres be added to the national forests.[8]

This recommendation, however, went unheeded, and other efforts have been made to bring about better practices under private ownership. Most of the timber states have forestry departments which seek to improve practices through demonstration and education. New Hampshire has enacted special tax laws encouraging woodlot owners to adopt better practices. Many states attempt in other ways to promote conservation. A number of state laws authorize control of cutting practices, but enforcement is sought mainly through persuasion rather than compulsion. Only in a few states, notably Oregon and Washington, is cutting stringently regulated.[9]

While there is no direct federal regulation of private forests, the federal government has adopted various means to protect these forests and to promote conservation practices in them. It aids the states in research in insect and disease control, and in the provision of planting stock. It helps forty-four states to provide fire protection on about 90 per cent of the private holdings. The Norris-Doxey Act of 1937 authorizes the Forest Service to assist the states in the support of resident foresters, somewhat akin to county agents in agriculture, who counsel woodlot owners on forest management. Under this Act, 285 co-operative projects have been established in 1,376 counties.[10]

These federal and state programs have contributed greatly to forestry conservation, especially in fire prevention and in the encouragement of new plantings. But the improvement of management practices in the nation's woodlots, involving as it does the education of millions of small owners, has been painfully slow. Each of the 285 Norris-Doxey foresters, for example, can give tech-

[8] U.S. Forest Service, A National Plan for American Forestry, S. Doc. 12, 73rd Cong., 1st sess. (1933).

[9] The constitutionality of such controls was affirmed in Dexter v. Washington, 338 U.S. 863 (1949).

[10] In addition, the Sustained Yield Act of 1944 unsuccessfully sought to encourage better management practices in private forests by permitting the combination of private and public forest lands into "sustained-yield units." In return for managing his own land on a sustained-yield basis, the private owner is privileged to buy all the timber cut from the federal tract on the basis of appraised prices rather than by competitive bidding. Only one such agreement has been concluded. Another section of the Act permits the creation of entirely federal units which are to be managed for the benefit of adjacent communities primarily dependent upon timber. Sales are competitive, but the timber must be processed within the area. Five such units have been established by the Forest Service.

nical assistance to only about a hundred people per year, and most small woodlots require such services at least once a decade. In 1952, the President's Materials Policy Commission recommended increased federal technical assistance and financial and other aids to help the states in controlling destructive cutting. It further recommended that if a five-year trial of such a program still left important gaps in the state system, federal cutting-practice regulations be enacted. Congress took no action, and reliance continues to be placed on the slower methods of education, assistance, and persuasion.

Wildlife and Fish

Conservation of fish and wildlife is an important program in itself and also a goal which often merges with other conservation programs. Thus, the maintenance of the national forests and the revegetation of the plains contribute to the preservation of fish and wildlife. Through such measures, the support of both private and commercial hunters and fishermen can often be enlisted for broad conservation campaigns. Fish and wildlife provide a broad base for recreation and for commerce. Almost twice as many people each year receive hunting and fishing licenses as buy tickets to baseball games. And commercial fishing, hunting, and trapping are sizable industries.

The states have long regulated hunting and fishing in a variety of ways. They have established wildlife refuges, hunting preserves, and fish hatcheries, and have stocked lakes and streams with fish. The federal government has contributed to these efforts. In 1900, it became a federal offense to transport across state lines animals killed in violation of state laws. The federal government has regulated the taking of sponges from extraterritorial waters since 1906 and salmon fishing since 1924. In a number of cases, it has also entered into treaties governing fishing in international waters. Under the terms of a 1913 treaty with Canada, it protects migratory birds.

In 1903, the federal government established the first national wildlife refuge. In 1957, the Fish and Wildlife Service administered 270 refuges containing about 18 million acres. It also conducts research and demonstration work, and the Fish and Wildlife Act of 1946 directs the Service to co-operate with state and private agencies in the conservation and rehabilitation of fish and wildlife.

Soils

It is ironic that the largest and most basic conservation problem, that of maintaining soil fertility, has so long been obscured by the embarrassing overproduction of our farms. Indeed, the destruction of soils has often been hastened by price-support measures which stimulate the unnecessary production of highly erosive crops. "We have ruined more good land in less time than any other nation in recorded history," declares a leading apostle of soil conservation.[11] And in the words of the Department of Agriculture: "It is doubtful whether any other long-time social loss is so great as the loss caused by destructive exploitation of soil, the result of unlimited competition for short-time individual advantage in the 'mining of the land.' " [12]

Abusive exploitation of the soil characterized American agriculture in the early years, when it was often easier to stake out a new farm than to maintain a depleted one. Only in this century have scientists become aware that soil is an impermanent and complex resource. Remedial action has been hampered by the fact that soil conservation requires a degree of skill in diagnosis and treatment comparable to that needed for the ailments of the human body.

The primary cause of permanent soil destruction is erosion. By the time the federal government undertook to combat this threat, erosion had already progressed far. A survey in 1934 indicated that 57 million acres had been essentially destroyed for tillage, another 225 million acres were severely eroded, and 775 million acres had suffered moderate damage. Remedial programs since that time have only slowed the process, rather than reversed it. About a half-million acres of cropland are lost to erosion each year, and the total annual economic loss approximates $4 billion. The problem varies in intensity and form in different regions. Water-induced sheet and gully erosion is most severe in the South, while wind erosion is extremely serious in the Great Plains. The consequences for individual farmers range from moderately reduced crop yields and increased fertilizer requirements to total abandonment and migration away from affected areas. Soil erosion also creates water-resource problems, since it intensifies the severity of floods and silts up navigable streams and river-control reservoirs.

The types of action required to reverse the processes of soil depletion and erosion are by now well known in their broad outlines. In general, they involve the shift of many millions of acres from crops to grazing, substitution of soil-building for soil-depleting crops, systematic crop rotation, prevention of overgrazing

[11] Hugh H. Bennett, former chief of the Soil Conservation Service, in "The Coming Technological Revolution on the Soil," *Science* (January 3, 1947).
[12] Department of Agriculture, *Agricultural Adjustment, 1937–1938* (1939), p. 36.

on range lands, supply of more water in semiarid areas, afforestation to check water runoff, mechanical checks to rapid runoff, construction of windbreaks, cultivation of sloping land along the contours, and a host of similar practices.

Before the 1930's, the various agricultural agencies had undertaken much research, and through demonstrations and educational efforts the Department of Agriculture and the Extension Service had promoted soil conservation activities by individual farmers. But the individualism of American farmers has handicapped corrective action. The problems are often social; gullies, for example, are no respecters of property lines. The failure of any one farmer to observe proper practices may endanger his neighbors' lands. Farm tenancy, rapid turnover in ownership, and general agricultural distress have discouraged individual adoption of conservation practices.

Effective governmental action began with the New Deal. An emergency erosion-control program was authorized by the National Industrial Recovery Act, and the Civilian Conservation Corps and Works Progress Administration undertook many conservation projects. Permanent and broader programs were initiated under the Soil Conservation Act of 1935 and the Soil Conservation and Domestic Allotment Act of 1936.

The 1935 Act created the Soil Conservation Service (SCS) to establish demonstration projects and to offer farmers technical assistance in combating erosion. Under state enabling legislation, soil conservation districts are organized by farmers or ranchers and administered by them as units of local government. Upon the request of a district, the SCS will draft a plan, classifying the land on the basis of its suitability for particular uses. Individual farmers within the district may then voluntarily agree with the SCS and the district to carry out long-range conservation plans for their farms. Each plan is worked out by the farmer and an SCS representative. The SCS and the district provide the farm with many services, including free technical advice and supervision and help in procuring equipment, fertilizer, seed, and planting stock. The farmer commits himself to carry out certain portions of his plan each year. The district may also, by a majority vote of its members, establish mandatory regulations governing land use, but voluntary co-operation is the normal practice.

Since only advice and supervision are provided without charge, the cost of the program is modest, amounting in 1957 to $67 million out of total Agriculture Department expenditures of $5 billion. By 1957, there were 2,770 soil conservation districts containing most of the nation's farm land; 1,160,000 individual farm and ranch plans had been agreed upon; and in that year the Service assisted 732,000 farmers and ranchers in applying their SCS plans.

Despite its substantial success and the continuing need for its programs, the SCS soon became involved in political controversy. Friction built up in the field between SCS representatives and county agents, who enjoyed the support of the land-grant colleges, state departments of agriculture, and experiment stations. The Farm Bureau Federation, closely associated with the Extension Service's county agents, joined the attack, wishing to absorb the SCS program within the Extension Service. In 1948, a bill to transfer the SCS to the Extension Service was defeated because of protests from the districts, organized into a national association. The issue was rejoined in the first year of the Eisenhower administration when Agriculture Secretary Benson proposed a transfer of the SCS program to the states, abolishing its regional offices, and cutting loose its technicians to seek employment with the states. This reorganization plan evoked so much protest that it had to be substantially modified. Most of the dismissals were canceled, and Congress used its appropriating power to shift the bulk of the program back to the SCS from the Extension Service. While staff morale was badly shaken, the SCS managed to ride out the political storm.[13]

The Soil Conservation and Domestic Allotment Act of 1936 established an Agricultural Conservation Program only a year after the creation of the SCS. But its main purpose, initially at least, was the raising of agricultural income, rather than conservation. The Agricultural Adjustment Act of 1933, which paid farmers for restricting their acreage of certain "basic" crops, had been invalidated in 1936. The 1936 law paid farmers for restricting their acreage of "soil-depleting" crops. The crops in both cases were the same, but the explicit purpose of the first Act was to raise prices and the ostensible purpose of the second was conservation. Local committees of farmers were organized to administer this program. The emphasis at the start was primarily on curtailment of output, but during World War II it was shifted to conservation. The 1936 program is concerned with the restoration and preservation of fertility, while the SCS concentrates on

[13] In 1955, the President's Commission on Intergovernmental Relations recommended keeping the SCS "as presently organized." A majority would permit any state submitting a satisfactory plan for taking over the program to do so, assisted by federal grants in aid. A minority opposed any change.

longer-run plans for the prevention of erosion. Materials and advice are given to farmers and ranchers free of charge, and the government assumes about half the cost of performing the conservation practices. Most of these practices are a normal part of sound farming; the program therefore probably still contributes as much to farm income as it does to conservation. In 1956 about $215 million were spent on this program, contributing to the observance of conservation practices on 1.2 million farms and ranches containing 36 per cent of all farm land.

Another phase of soil conservation arises from the overgrazing of public lands. During the nineteenth century, ranchers freely grazed their livestock on the public domain. No permission was required, and no rules were imposed. In the national forests, regulation of grazing was begun in 1900, although it was not brought under satisfactory control until after World War I. The Forest Service still allows grazing, but only under permit, and the length of the grazing season and numbers of livestock are controlled to protect the forest floor. It has been a different story on the public domain. There grazing was entirely unregulated until 1934. The consequences were summarized in 1931 by President Hoover's Committee on Conservation in the Public Domain:

> Today overgrazing has taken its toll in the form of large areas unfit for grazing, or greatly reduced carrying capacity for livestock generally. Erosion has been increased by the destruction of forage cover, and the silting of stream and river flow as an aftermath has added to the problems of ranch and farm reclamation. The damage done may never be wholly repaired, nor yet its progress wholly arrested, but as a continuing evil it may be diminished, and by proper scientific treatment and regulation many ranges may be steadily improved and carrying capacity increased.[14]

The Taylor Grazing Act of 1934 boldly attacked this problem by authorizing withdrawal from entry of 80 million acres for the creation of grazing districts. The area was extended in 1936 to 142 million acres. The Interior Department was given full authority to control grazing in such districts, "to regulate their occupancy and use, preserve the land and its resources from destruction or unnecessary injury and to provide for the orderly use, improvement and development of the range." Administration of the Act was vested in a Grazing Service. Advisory boards of local stockmen were established in each district to assist in the making of grazing

[14] *Report of the Committee on Conservation and Administration of the Public Domain* (1931), p. 13.

rules. Grazing permits specified the number of livestock and the months in which grazing was allowed.

Despite the comprehensive language of the Taylor Act, there have been serious political obstacles to the effective administration of grazing controls. Stockmen, with considerable influence over Western senators and congressmen, have pressed for low fees and liberal rules. In 1946, after a hostile seven-year investigation of the Grazing Service by Senator McCarran of Nevada, appropriations were so curtailed that only fifty men were left in the field to supervise 142 million acres. This placed actual control in the hands of local boards of stockmen. Similar efforts to weaken grazing regulation in the national forests were defeated by the more alert and numerous defenders of forest conservation. In the last decade, the Grazing Service, now merged with the General Land Office into the Bureau of Land Management, has been able to muster congressional support for the imposition of higher fees and for larger appropriations. Since 1955, fees have been related to livestock prices, and they now suffice to finance a reasonably effective program of grazing control and range improvement.

Over the entire scope of soil conservation activities, water conservation plays an important role. Optimum distribution of the limited water supply in the arid and semiarid areas of the West is an essential prerequisite to proper land use. In the easterly regions with more rainfall, soil erosion, flood control, and afforestation are mutually interrelated. Land and water conservation policies, in consequence, necessarily overlap over a wide zone.

Water Resources

Water conservation embraces control, development, and utilization of water for a wide variety of objectives. It includes promotion of navigation, flood control, irrigation, power development, drainage, control of soil erosion and siltation, pollution abatement, maintenance of domestic and industrial water supplies, recreation, and fish and game protection. Federal, state, and local governments have always been concerned with one or another phase of water conservation. Canals were a leading element in the various internal improvement programs of the early nineteenth century. The New England states took measures shortly after the Civil War to protect fish in their streams from industrial pollution. As urban centers grew in size, water supply became a leading function of local government. In the arid areas of the West, state courts and legislatures developed elaborate rules of law governing individual rights to the appropriation of water.

Since the turn of the century, irrigation, power, flood control, and pollution abatement have come within the range of federal policy. But it has not yet proved possible to bring about a unified policy, taking into account all the interrelated purposes of water control, in keeping with the physical unity of the national river systems. One major obstacle to the unification of water policy has been the disagreement among various federal, as well as state and local, agencies, each with its own partial outlook and task, its different constituency and purpose.

From the very start, a prominent role was played in water conservation by the federal government. The interstate character of almost all the great drainage basin systems, and the importance of rivers as channels of inland transportation, made their control a matter of more than state concern. Constitutional authority for federal programs is derived from the interstate commerce clause, here usually given a broad reading by the courts, from the power to spend in the general welfare, and from control over the public lands. River development for navigation has been broadly sketched in Chapter 5. It is important to note, however, that navigation may be a significant element in the multipurpose type of water development which has become characteristic of twentieth-century water policy.

For exposed communities, protection against floods has always been a principal concern of local government. Construction of levees and flood walls was until recent decades almost the sole means of protection. When floods brought disaster to particular areas, the federal government intervened to provide temporary relief, but then withdrew as the water subsided. Minor assistance in flood control, particularly in the form of plans and surveys, was provided by the Mississippi Valley Commission, established by Congress in 1879. Moderate financial support was also given to Mississippi flood control in 1917 and 1923. After the catastrophic lower Mississippi flood of 1925, however, the balance of governmental responsibility for flood control was radically altered. While affirming the desirability in principle of a division of costs between local and national governments, Congress in 1928 authorized appropriations of $325 million for flood control in the Mississippi Valley. It held that these floods were on such a scale as to be of national concern and pointed to the $292 million spent in the past on flood control by state and local governments in the Valley.

The comprehensive Flood Control Act of 1936 extended throughout the nation the principle of federal support for flood control. Local authorities were still to provide the cost of land, easements, and rights of way, but the bulk of the financial burden was now assumed by the federal treasury. Two years later, the requirement for local contributions was even further reduced. Thus flood protection became a matter predominantly of national concern. The federal flood-control program, planned and constructed by the Army Corps of Engineers, has grown greatly in the past two decades. Between 1936 and 1949, $1,750 million was spent on it, and in 1948 the Corps estimated that the total cost would run to $12.3 billion. In 1958, an appropriation of $181 million was requested, not including multipurpose projects which contribute to flood control.

As this program progressed, it became increasingly evident that flood control could not be dealt with as an isolated objective. Initially, flood-control projects involved clearing and maintaining river channels and building protective devices such as levees, flood walls, and floodways. It soon became apparent that dams and reservoirs on tributary streams were essential to effective flood control. These dams and reservoirs could also serve other purposes, such as navigation, irrigation, and power generation. Such joint benefits could lower the costs of achieving flood control and make economical some projects not justifiable solely as flood-control measures. Moreover, a failure to develop other phases of water control can defeat the flood-control objective itself. Soil erosion in the watershed can speedily fill reservoirs and river channels with silt. Nevertheless, although the Boulder Canyon Act of 1929 and the Tennessee Valley Act of 1933 both recognized the use of multipurpose reservoirs for flood control, the 1936 Flood Control Act adopted this principle for only a portion of the country. Later measures have paid greater attention to power development, but in general the program still fails to give sufficient recognition to other aspects of water conservation.

The third major aspect of water-resource conservation is irrigation. In large parts of the seventeen states lying west of the 100th meridian, successful farming is virtually impossible without an artificial water supply to supplement the limited rainfall. Even grazing often requires supplemental water. Beginning with the Mormon Project near Great Salt Lake in 1848, co-operative, privately-financed irrigation developed quite rapidly. But private capital was unavailable to finance the more costly, large-scale prospects. In 1894, the Carey Act authorized the granting to any state of up to a million acres of federal lands within its borders if it would agree to reclaim them. Because of insufficient funds and inadequate technical knowledge, few Carey Act projects succeeded.

The pressure for federal assistance mounted. Under the leadership of Theodore Roosevelt, promotion of irrigation became a national policy in the Reclamation Act of 1902.

The Act of 1902 established a reclamation fund, into which proceeds of public land sales in the West were to be deposited. The fund was to be employed for irrigation projects, the cost of which would gradually be repaid, without interest, by the water users. At first, settlers were required to complete their repayments in ten years. This period was later increased to twenty, and then to forty years. Repayments would flow into the fund and be available for further projects. A share of the oil and mineral royalties from the public lands and of license fees for water-power sites was subsequently added to the fund. After 1906, power development was carried on in conjunction with reclamation projects wherever possible, in order to cover part of the cost. Since the late twenties, power revenues have accounted for a large portion of the repayments made into the reclamation fund. Repayments on irrigation contracts have for the most part been maintained, although moratoria and extensions of payment periods have sometimes been necessary.

So rapid, however, has been the pace of investment in reclamation projects that the rotating funds have been insufficient to provide the capital required. Through fiscal 1957, a total of $3.7 billion had been appropriated, only $1.2 billion of which had come from rotating funds. Of the total investment of $2.7 billion in completed plant, property, and equipment, 39 per cent was invested in multipurpose facilities, 35 per cent in irrigation facilities, and 24 per cent in power facilities.[15]

Operations under this program vary in size from garden patches on Indian reservations to the spectacular Boulder, Grand Coulee, and Colorado-Big Thompson dams. Constructed and operated by the Bureau of Reclamation, these projects have transformed large sections of the semiarid areas of the West into thriving farm land. Of the more than 25 million acres of irrigated land in the seventeen Western states, the Bureau serves about 7 million acres, on which about 125,000 family farms and an equal number of suburban homes have been developed.

This achievement, however, has entailed heated political struggles, and irrigation development now faces considerable criticism. Many of the challenges to irrigation policy have come from

[15] Secretary of the Interior, *Annual Report, 1957*, pp. 72, 74. The remaining 2 per cent of the investment was in flood-control works, municipal projects, and other physical properties.

Easterners who look upon it as an unwarranted sectional subsidy. While direct irrigation costs are repaid, on long-term projects imputed interest charges, which are not repaid, can amount to more than half of the construction costs. And unrepaid secondary benefits, such as those accruing to businesses serving the irrigated farms, may exceed the repaid direct benefits. It is also argued that it makes little sense to open up more farm land at a time when general agricultural policy favors land retirement—an argument seconded in recent years by influential voices in the Agriculture Department.

In the West, however, reclamation is regarded as a prerequisite of economic development and of community stability. Without it, large areas would remain barren and empty. Its beneficiaries emphasize the contrast between the repayment features of irrigation policy and the wholly unreimbursed federal contributions to river and harbor development and flood control. In addition, the beneficiaries of other aspects of the Bureau's multipurpose programs rally to their defense. Flood-control and recreational benefits and the provision of domestic water supply, as well as over 25 billion kilowatt-hours per year of low-cost power, have won many adherents and contributed to the development of the West.

Yet the Bureau's success in harnessing falling waters and thereby enlisting the support of the beneficiaries of cheap public power has made enemies as well as won allies. Its new projects are now sometimes debated as much in terms of the conflict between public and private power, discussed above in Chapter 12, as in terms of reclamation. The Bureau has also had to survive other attacks, some arising from its vigorous espousal of acreage limitations. The Act of 1902 limited the holdings to be furnished with water from a reclamation project to 160 acres for any landowner. This was construed to permit joint holdings of 320 acres by man and wife.[16] This provision has been fairly easy to enforce in regions not tilled before irrigation, but the Bureau's large Central Valley project in California served an area where large-scale patterns of land ownership and management had already been established. The large landowners vigorously contested the Bureau's homestead limitations. Legislation exempting the Central Valley was introduced in 1944 and 1947 by California congressmen, but the Bureau was able to muster countersupport from small landowners, and the proposals were not enacted. The conflict in this Central Valley

[16] The Columbia Basin Act of 1943 established "farm units" of no more than 160 acres and prohibited the delivery of water to more than one unit for each family.

also involved rivalry between the Bureau and the Army Corps of Engineers, each competing for authorization to construct part of the project. At stake were not only bureaucratic interests but also the weights to be accorded alternative water uses and the allocation of costs, since the Engineer Corps normally does not charge water users for irrigation benefits.

As supplies of uncommitted water in the West grow slimmer, the Bureau increasingly finds that its new proposals for reclamation and power projects conflict with other possible uses. Thus its plan for a series of irrigation, power, and storage dams on the Upper Colorado was attacked by California, with its interest in securing the largest possible share of Colorado River water for its own use. An even stronger attack came from conservationists, who pointed out that the projected Echo Park Dam would flood out part of the Dinosaur National Monument. The conservationists won, and the Echo Park Dam was dropped from the project as finally authorized in 1956.

At the same time, projects recommended by the Bureau show an alarming tendency to mount in cost. Thus, while the cost of existing irrigation projects in the Columbia Basin in 1950 was on the average only $65 per acre of land provided with water; projects then under construction averaged almost $350; and those in the Upper Colorado about $952. Similarly, the power investment at Grand Coulee amounted to $90 per kilowatt of capacity, but in the Upper Colorado it would range from $463 at the most efficient dam to $640 at Echo Park. With costs at this level, it is essential that Bureau of Reclamation projects be reconciled with general agricultural and power policies. The Bureau estimates that there is sufficient unused water available to irrigate 16.7 million acres of Western land and to provide 8.7 million acres of presently irrigated land with additional water. Our present cropland acreage is less than 400 million, and additional acreage may be required at some time in the future, perhaps to replace marginal farm land. But any such additions should be in keeping with a general agricultural resources policy, which estimates national requirements and considers the possibility and comparative costs of cropland additions through other means. Over twice as much land can be added from flood-protection drainage and land clearance as from irrigation.[17] Considerations such as these point to the need for

[17] The President's Water Resources Policy Commission estimated that the equivalent of 9 million acres of cropland could be added through irrigation by 1975, and 20.5 million acres through flood protection, drainage, and land clearing. It estimated ultimate possible additions through irrigation at 25

careful planning of resource allocations and more unified treatment of river-basin developments.[18]

Water Pollution

Water problems are not confined to the West. Shortages of clean water are now beginning to plague areas throughout the nation. Industry requires enormous amounts of water, by weight about fifty times as much as of all other materials combined. In 1950, industrial use was about 80 billion gallons a day, while irrigation and municipal and rural water systems accounted for 105 billion gallons. By 1975, these figures are expected to mount to 215 billion and 135 billion gallons respectively.[19] But available supplies are already under strain. In more arid areas, competitive pumping has gravely lowered water tables and along the coasts has sometimes permitted invasion by salt water. Even in the more humid areas, running streams, which supply about five-sixths of national needs, no longer yield sufficient supplies of clean water.

Many of the abuses mentioned earlier, such as stripping watersheds of their forest and vegetative cover, contribute to this problem, but the major villain appears to be pollution. Sediment, industrial wastes, and raw sewage are all too freely dumped into streams. Over half of the cities in the East, for example, thus dispose of their sewage. The President's Materials Policy Commission concluded that:

The United States has reached the point where the costs imposed upon its economy by using streams and rivers as open sewers may exceed the apparent savings. Many downstream communities are forced to pay large sums to purify water or to develop alternative supplies, sometimes from distant sources. Valuable wildlife and recreational assets are destroyed, public health is menaced. Industries that require relatively clean water are discouraged from locating along heavily polluted rivers even though good plant sites, labor supply and other attractions exist. Some plants whose water supplies have deteriorated have moved to other localities rather than incur the high cost of purification.[20]

million acres, and additions through other means at 43 million. A *Water Policy for the American People* (1950), Vol. I, p. 165.

[18] Two recent studies concur that present methods of benefit-cost analysis in federal water-resource development seriously overstate benefits and understate costs. See Otto Eckstein, *Water Resources Development: The Economics of Project Evaluation* (1958); and Edward F. Renshaw, *Toward Responsible Government: An Economic Appraisal of Federal Investment in Water Resource Programs* (1957).

[19] President's Materials Policy Commission, *op. cit.*, Vol. I, p. 51.

[20] *Ibid.*, p. 53.

The solution might seem deceptively simple: each industrial plant and municipality should treat its waste or sewage before dumping it into a river. But the costs involved are great. In 1951, the Public Health Service estimated that a moderate ten-year pollution-abatement program, designed mainly to keep the situation from becoming worse, would cost between $9 billion and $12 billion. Individual municipalities and companies are especially reluctant to incur heavy expenditures when effective results can come only from simultaneous action by all concerned with a given stream. Since all will benefit if all abstain from pollution, but few will act unless all act, there is presented a classic case for public regulation.

A good deal can be done through state action. Most states have pollution laws, and some have made substantial progress, but they are reluctant to subject their industries to higher costs than apply in other states. Moreover, most important watersheds cross state lines. The interstate compact is a weak device to overcome these limitations. The Water Pollution Act of 1948 marked the beginning of federal action in this field. In this measure, Congress recognized the primary responsibility of the states in pollution control, but provided federal assistance through the Public Health Service in preparing pollution-abatement plans for interstate streams, encouraging the states to enact uniform laws, helping municipalities in pollution investigations, and promoting the formation of interstate authorities. The Act also authorized federal loans of not more than $250,000 to finance up to one-third of the cost of sewage-treatment plants. Mandatory controls were limited to cases where pollution originating in one state endangers health in another; if no remedial action was taken, a federal suit might be filed against the offender, but only with the concurrence of the state authorities in his state.

When the 1948 Act was being considered by Congress, the Senate Public Works Committee warned that "unless the very reasonable enforcement procedures provided for in the bill bring about the needed results, it is reasonable to anticipate that a later Congress will enact very much more stringent enforcement legislation." In 1950, the President's Water Resources Policy Commission recommended larger appropriations and more vigorous enforcement. In 1952, the President's Materials Policy Commission advocated a further five-year testing of the 1948 Act, then to be followed, if necessary, by a federal tax on industrial operations which pollute navigable waters and interstate streams.

In 1956, Congress moved in the direction of firmer controls by adopting the Water Pollution Control Act. This law permits the federal government to bring action to abate pollution on request of an affected downstream state and without concurrence of the upstream state. The Act also authorizes annual grants of $50 million to municipalities, states, and interstate agencies to stimulate the construction of sewage-treatment works. Individual grants, not to exceed $250,000, may cover up to 30 per cent of the project costs. In 1957, 446 projects were approved, involving a total cost of $167 million.

3. Co-ordination and Planning for Conservation

Modern conservation policy is a compound of many measures stemming from a great variety of needs, interests, and pressures. Some were a direct response to concern over resource wastage, but others were by-products of promotional programs, reactions to dramatic catastrophes, or simply pretexts for the widespread local distribution of federal funds. Whatever the origin of particular measures, the interlocking relationships among various natural resources tend to produce a pattern of general conservation policy, and to create a need for more effective co-ordination of conservation activities.

The broad area of water resources offers an excellent example. Proper water control can serve many interrelated purposes, including agriculture, flood protection, navigation, power generation, industrial and household use, and recreation. The single-minded pursuit of one or some of these purposes may frustrate the achievement of others. In order to ensure the optimum multipurpose combination of uses, watershed developments must be carefully planned in advance. As the President's Water Resources Policy Commission of 1950 put it:

Once they are completed, major water control structures can be altered only with difficulty, or not at all. There are only a relatively few possible dam sites, and once they are appropriated, the possibilities for economic multiple-purpose development are very limited. Once an irrigation project is developed, it cannot be moved because unfavorable soil or climate factors are discovered. There is a sobering finality in the construction of a river basin development; and it behooves us to be sure that we are right before we go ahead.[21]

It was for this reason that the Commission strongly urged a policy of river-basin planning directed toward broad national and

[21] *Op. cit.*, Vol. I, p. 18.

regional goals. With the striking exception of the TVA, however, unity in river-basin programs has seldom been attained. The mere fact of federal participation by no means ensures unity, for some of the most serious conflicts in conservation policy have occurred between federal agencies. Notable examples are the recurring disputes between the Forest Service and the Bureau of Land Management over logging and grazing, and between the Army Corps of Engineers and the Bureau of Reclamation (occasionally allied with the Department of Agriculture) over dams and the uses of the impounded waters.

These are far from being merely bureaucratic conflicts arising out of faulty organization. They also reflect struggles between opposing interests over the distribution of benefits and costs. This is well illustrated by the issue of water control in the Missouri Valley, an area containing one-sixth of the land in the United States and including all or a part of ten states. Its waters could be controlled to provide irrigation in the upper Basin, to generate power, to serve recreational uses, and to promote flood control and navigation on the lower Missouri and the Mississippi. These various purposes are competitive as well as complementary, for there is not enough water to permit the full accomplishment of all of them. In the 1940's, several bills to establish a Missouri Valley Authority on TVA lines were introduced, but they mustered little organized support. The plan lacked strong administration backing, since Roosevelt was preoccupied with World War II, and Interior Secretary Ickes opposed an independent agency, preferring a river-basin authority within his own department. After the 1943 floods, Congress requested the Army Engineers to draft a control plan. The resulting "Pick Plan" concentrated on downstream flood control and navigation through big upstream dams and downstream levees; it took virtually no account of irrigation or power. It called for hydroelectric capacity of only 35,000 kilowatts, and would have flooded out 21,000 acres recently irrigated by the Bureau of Reclamation. Shortly afterward, the Bureau produced its "Sloan Plan" for the upper Missouri; this called for ninety dams to store two years' flow of water, irrigation of nearly 5 million acres, and 758,000 kilowatts of power capacity. It also provided for municipal water supplies, recreation, and upstream flood control. The Sloan Plan, however, largely neglected downstream navigation and flood control, and some of its irrigation aspects were questionable.

The ensuing struggle between the Corps and the Bureau centered on the differing distributions of costs and benefits. Supporting the Pick Plan were the various interests which hoped to benefit from downstream flood control and irrigation and the private electric utilities opposed to public power. The Sloan Plan was defended by farm organizations, upstream communities, public power agencies, and hunting, fishing, and camping organizations. Under presidential direction to agree on a single plan, the Corps and the Bureau adopted the shotgun wedding device of the Pick-Sloan Plan, for the most part a simple addition of the two original plans. The Bureau dropped its objections to most of the big upstream dams, and the Corps accepted the Bureau as a partner in the development. The first projects were authorized in the Flood Control Act of 1944; when completed, the program will contain five big dams, over a hundred smaller ones, 1,500 miles of levees, and many associated activities. But since the Pick-Sloan Plan resulted from mere addition, rather than co-ordination, of the two original plans, it is marred by many inconsistencies and poses serious problems for future decision. In dry periods, for example, there will not be enough water to meet the requirements of both irrigation and navigation.[22] Nor have administrative means yet been devised for co-ordinating these decisions or resolving the inherent local and regional conflicts of interest.

While the obstacles to effective river-basin planning are formidable, the need remains great, and gradual progress has been registered. Theodore Roosevelt's Inland Waterways Commission laid a foundation in 1907 for this type of comprehensive approach to water conservation. Partial co-ordination has been provided by subsequent water legislation in a number of respects. Thus the Army Engineers are required to obtain the advice of the Federal Power Commission on power potentialities in the design of flood-control projects. They are supposed to co-operate with the Department of Agriculture in devising measures for runoff retardation and soil-erosion prevention on watersheds above navigation or flood-control works. And in the Columbia and Missouri valleys some degree of voluntary co-ordination is achieved by interagency committees, although they lack either statutory authority or administrative power.

[22] In dry cycles, which can last twelve years, the river above Sioux City produces only 16 million acre-feet of water per year. Irrigation plans call for the use of 9.2 million acre-feet per year, and the need might increase in dry years. The Corps' 9-foot-deep navigation channel from Sioux City to the Mississippi will require 14.5 million acre-feet per year. Storage capacity of the dams is insufficient to provide the more than 7 million acre-feet needed each year during a twelve-year dry cycle. D. C. Coyle, *Conservation* (1957), pp. 161–162.

Over the years, state governments have grown accustomed to co-ordinating their water policies in a number of ways, although many conflicts, disagreements, and legal disputes over division of water still occur. Adjacent states have agreed on common policies and enacted identical legislation. They have adopted reciprocal laws, such as those enabling Delaware, New Jersey, New York, and Pennsylvania—through an Interstate Commission on the Delaware River (INCODEL)—to plan and co-ordinate the activities of state and federal agencies in flood control, pollution abatement, and supply of water. Interstate compacts, approved by Congress, have established commissions which apportion water on the Rio Grande and Upper Colorado and which abate pollution on the Ohio. Too often, however, such interstate agreements operate only at the lowest common denominator of agreement and exclude controversial issues. Thus the INCODEL plan seeks to avoid the power question, developing only 65,000 kilowatts out of a potential estimated by the Federal Power Commission at 1 million kilowatts. Planning for unified control in most watersheds remains for the future.

The planning concept as applied to natural-resource conservation should not be confused with general economic planning as practiced by totalitarian regimes. It is concerned with the physical framework within which the economy operates rather than with day-to-day economic operations. Its emphasis is on the co-ordination of policies and administration and the harmonizing of immediate objectives with longer-run considerations. Planning of this type, in greater or less degree, has always accompanied conservational activities. An identifiable planning movement, however, is a product of the twentieth century. It first arose in the realm of urban local government, where the socially undesirable consequences of uncontrolled land use were particularly evident. The planning profession is still concerned mainly with metropolitan-area problems. On a larger scale, New York, New Jersey, and Wisconsin established state planning agencies during the 1920's, while the desirability of national planning for natural-resource conservation was expressed by the short-lived National Conservation Commission of 1908.

The vast New Deal public-works program brought the public planning movement to an unprecedented level of activity. A National Planning Board (later succeeded by the National Resources Planning Board) was established in 1933 in the Federal Emergency Administration of Public Works, to assist the Administrator through (1) preparation of comprehensive regional public-works plans, (2) surveys of population distribution and trends; land use; industrial, housing, and natural resources; and general social and economic trends; and (3) project analysis to ensure co-ordination in location and sequence. Planning at the state level was also greatly stimulated; by 1937, all the states but two had established one or another form of official planning agency.

By the end of the New Deal, however, a reaction against the planning movement had set in. The very word "planning," which ranked high in popular esteem in the early thirties, often became a red flag to those who opposed the broad expansion of governmental controls and activities. And Congress, fearful of excessive centralization in the executive and hostile to interference with its traditional prerogatives of distributing federal "pork-barrel" largesse through river and harbor appropriations, terminated the National Resources Planning Board in 1943. A number of states also abolished their planning boards. Yet planning, in the sense of marshaling relevant facts, applying available techniques in order to secure wiser decisions, and attempting to co-ordinate, schedule, and assign priorities to a set of interrelated objectives, necessarily remains vital to effective action in many aspects of governmental activity, especially in the field of conservation.

The conservation of natural resources is significant only in relation to human needs. The tendency of some enthusiasts, in the first flush of the conservation movement, to view the preservation of natural resources as an end in itself, has given way to a more sober appraisal which seeks to balance the claims of present and of future generations on the efficient use of the nation's natural assets.

CHAPTER 24

Public Enterprise and the
Public Corporation

IN CONTRAST with experience elsewhere in the world, direct government ownership and operation of business-type activities have not played a major role in the American economy. While there has been a vast expansion of regulatory and service activities in the twentieth century, especially by the federal government, only a small part of this expansion has taken the form of public enterprise. In 1953, for example, public enterprise accounted for only 10 per cent of total government employment and only 1½ per cent of total national employment.[1]

While the expression "public enterprise" might be broadly interpreted to include the entire range of governmental activities, it is usually limited to economic activities, businesslike in character, for which some direct payment is made. Taken in this narrower sense, the expression is analogous to "private enterprise," and distinguishes the operation of postal services, transportation, electric utilities, and the like, from activities financed out of general taxation such as education, police, and national defense.

[1] These ratios are based on statistics of employee compensation, which weight the compensation per job as well as the numbers employed. National income in 1953 amounted to $305 billion; total compensation of all employees was $209 billion; the total for federal, state, and local government employees was $35 billion; for employees of federal enterprises $2.3 billion; and for employees of state and local enterprises $1.1 billion. Department of Commerce, *National Income* (1954), pp. 178–179.

1. The Motivation for Public Enterprise

Public enterprise has never developed in the American economy as much as elsewhere for a number of reasons. One lies in our ideology. Classical economic liberalism, which dominated nineteenth-century American views about the appropriate functions of government, was particularly hostile to such activity. When there did come to be a demand for, and acceptance of, an expanded economic role for government, public regulation and the governmental provision of services without charge were the major avenues chosen. Socialism as a creed has never enjoyed much appeal here. On the European continent, on the other hand, extreme laissez-faire liberalism never completely overpowered the firmly established and toughly resistant etatist tradition. Preliberal mercantilism, with its emphasis on positive governmental promotion of national economic welfare, and the neoliberal service state (or sometimes the modern garrison state) merged into one another without any sharply defined intervening period. In Britain and the Commonwealth nations (except for Canada, whose position closely resembles our own), humanitarian neoliberalism and the mild socialism of labor parties have carved out for the state a sizable share of direct economic activity. Among the newly independent underdeveloped nations seeking to force the pace of industrialization and economic development, shortages of private risk capital and entrepreneurship and the necessity for radical changes in traditional social and economic patterns, coupled in most cases with a socialist ideological orientation, have led to heavy reliance on government enterprises.

Public enterprise may also be adopted for pragmatic reasons having nothing to do with ideology; it is such reasons that account for most of the American examples. One important group of public enterprises has been established to meet the needs of war or preparation for war; they include the atomic energy facilities, the military arsenals, the naval shipyards, the synthetic rubber plants of World War II, and the Panama Canal. Another group, including the Reconstruction Finance Corporation and the Home Owners' Loan Corporation, was created in response to the Great Depression. In these cases, the required resources were too large, the risks too great, or the likelihood of profit too small to attract private enterprise, and government was compelled to perform the tasks. Similar factors have led to government operations in rural electrification, farm credit, river development, the Alaska Railroad, and the Mississippi River barge line.

Some public enterprises are incidental to the accomplishment of other purposes. Thus the Atomic Energy Commission has found itself operating whole municipalities and their associated services; prison industries have arisen; and dams constructed primarily for irrigation have produced power. The Government Printing Office is a service agency for other governmental operations. Governments have also taken over enterprises when private operations providing essential services have broken down or become unremunerative; this was the case with the railroads in World War I and with many urban transportation systems.

Many other factors have also contributed to the creation of public enterprises. As shown in earlier chapters, government ownership has been developed as a technique of electric utility regulation; it has been an instrument for the conservation of natural resources; and it has been involved in certain welfare programs. Such activities as postal communications and municipal water supply have long been regarded as basic services of universal use which are appropriately provided by governmental agencies.

Unlike the development of public regulation, the growth of public enterprise has never been seriously hampered by judicial restraint. Of course, where private property is taken by eminent domain, just compensation must be paid and the property must be put to a public use. Governmental expenditures on business-type ventures must be for a public purpose or to promote the general welfare. But the courts have accepted legislative judgments on what constitutes a public purpose. As Chief Justice Taft put it in a leading case, a state may engage in "almost any private business if the legislature thinks the state's engagement in it will help the general public and is willing to pay the cost of the plant and incur the expense of operation." [2] The Supreme Court has permitted cities to establish municipal fuel yards and to open a wholesale and retail gasoline business.[3] And it permitted North Dakota to socialize banking, grain storage, milling, and other enterprises.[4]

Judicial tests of the legality of federal enterprises have revolved around public power operations. While the Court has never ex-

---

[2] *Wolff Packing Co.* v. *Court of Industrial Relations of the State of Kansas*, 262 U.S. 522 (1923).

[3] *Jones* v. *Portland*, 245 U.S. 217 (1917); *Standard Oil Co.* v. *Lincoln*, 275 U.S. 502 (1927).

[4] *Green* v. *Frazier*, 253 U.S. 233 (1920).

plicitly upheld federal authority to generate, transmit, and distribute electricity, it has rejected three attempts to void such activity. In one such case, the Court held that the water falling over TVA dams was government property and that the government was entitled both to sell its property and to acquire transmission lines and other facilities useful in making its sales.[5] It has also ruled that utility companies have no standing in court to question the legality of the TVA power program.[6] And it has held that the addition of power facilities does not derogate from Congress's undoubted authority to build a dam for navigation and flood control.[7]

2. The Extent of Public Enterprise

While the impelling motives behind the development of public enterprise in the United States have been pragmatic and its growth has been rather haphazard, its scope somewhat resembles the pattern of development in other industrial nations. This pattern is focused around basic services and industries, many of them natural monopolies. They include postal service, water supply, transportation, power, credit, insurance, and natural resources. In 1949, the first Hoover Commission found that on the federal level there were approximately one hundred important public enterprises, which it classified under five headings: (1) public lands; (2) public power; (3) transportation; (4) lending and insurance agencies; and (5) manufacturing. Federal activities under the first two headings have been discussed in Chapters 12 and 23, and will not be dealt with here. In addition to the remaining three categories, the Post Office deserves special mention.

The Post Office

Postal service has universally been a public function for two centuries. The Constitution authorized the establishment of a postal system. The Postmaster General was admitted to the Cabinet in 1829, and the Post Office, originally responsible to the President but submitting reports to the Treasury Department, was made a separate executive department in 1872. Today it is the largest government enterprise in the free world, employing more than 500,000 workers, operating over 37,000 post offices, handling about 60 billion pieces of mail a year, and taking in

[5] *Ashwander* v. *TVA*, 297 U.S. 288 (1936).
[6] *Tennessee Electric Power Co.* v. *TVA*, 306 U.S. 118 (1939).
[7] *Oklahoma* v. *Atkinson Co.*, 313 U.S. 508 (1941).

gross receipts (1956) of over $2.5 billion.

The Post Office Department well illustrates two common features of public enterprise: the subordination of economic to social and political objectives and the degree to which management, especially when organized within executive departments, lacks the initiative and freedom enjoyed by its private counterpart. Economic return is considered secondary to the basic desirability of an inexpensive and widespread system of communication. The Post Office has always extended service to the most remote areas, despite the inability of many of them to repay the cost on the basis of uniform postal charges. A substantial subsidy is also involved in the low-rate carriage of newspapers, periodicals, and books. Postal charges for third-class matter, consisting largely of advertising, fail by a wide margin to cover costs. The establishment of parcel post service and the postal savings system occasioned serious controversy, since they involved clear incursions into the domains of express companies and banks. However, considerations of convenience and the desirability of an easy savings medium for low-income groups were sufficient to overcome the objections. In addition, the Post Office offers many free services. Government mail is carried free, as are reading matter for the blind, and bulletins and reports from agricultural colleges and experiment stations. Free delivery is also provided for newspapers within the county in which they are published when mailed at or to post offices with only rural delivery service.

These subsidies are established through congressional determination of rates and directives to undertake certain services. Only parcel post rates may be set by the Department, and even they, together with weight and size restrictions, must be approved by the Interstate Commerce Commission. Thus this public enterprise has little power to select or price its services. Furthermore, it has little control over its costs. Salaries are fixed by Congress. The annual public-works appropriation measure, with its "pork-barrel" characteristics, determines which new post offices will be built. The mail-transportation charges paid to the railroads are set by the Interstate Commerce Commission, and those to the air lines by the Civil Aeronautics Board. The Post Office cannot use its receipts directly to defray costs, for they must be paid into the Treasury. All of its expenditures go through the regular appropriation procedure, being broken down in considerable detail, and its books are audited by the General Accounting Office. Nor can it select its own personnel. Its twenty thousand top positions, including first-, second-, and third-class postmasterships, are patronage appointments, normally turning over as a new party enters office. And recruitment and promotion for its other positions are controlled by the rules of the Civil Service Commission.

When to this long list of inhibitions on management it is added that in most administrations the Postmaster General has been patronage chief and principal professional politician of his party, it is hardly surprising that postal management has been poor. Recognizing the deadening effects of these arrangements, the Hoover Commission Task Force concluded that "circumstances beyond [the Department's] control have created a philosophy of management which is sluggish, irresolute and wasteful rather than imaginative and cost conscious. . . ." [8] The Hoover Commission itself attributed the deficiencies of the Post Office to the facts that "(a) The administrative structure is obsolete and overcentralized, (b) a maze of outmoded laws, regulations, and traditions freezes progress and stifles proper administration, (c) . . . it lacks the freedom and flexibility essential to good business operation." [9]

The Eisenhower administration has inaugurated a major reform of the postal administration, revising organization, introducing operating efficiencies, establishing fifteen regional offices, and budgeting funds for research and engineering. The large increases in postal rates put into effect in 1958 should also contribute to reducing the postal deficit. But it remains to be seen how effective the reform program will be in view of the rigid limitations imposed on the postal administration by legislative restrictions and political patronage.

Transportation

There have been significant examples of public enterprise in water transportation. Primarily to meet defense needs, the various maritime agencies have constructed and operated merchant vessels. In an effort to demonstrate the profitability of river barges, the Inland Waterways Corporation for several decades maintained barge service on the Mississippi and Black Warrior rivers. These cases have been briefly discussed in Chapter 5, as a part of policies promoting business.[10]

The federal government also owns and operates two railroads. One, the Panama Railroad Company, was purchased in 1904 to aid in the construction of the Canal. Thereafter its activities were

---

[8] Commission on Organization of the Executive Branch of the Government, *Task Force Report on the Post Office* (1949), p. 33.

[9] *Ibid.*, *The Post Office* (1939), p. 3.

[10] See p. 118.

rapidly expanded, coming to include a shipping line and most of the business activities in the Canal Zone, where private persons are not allowed to own land. In 1948, the Railroad Company was absorbed into the Panama Canal Company, which operates the Canal and now is responsible for all businesses in the Zone. Its stock is held by the Secretary of the Army, who appoints its directors. The Governor of the Canal Zone serves as its president. The business ventures, including the railroad, have been operated with efficiency; prices have been reasonable and labor relations peaceful. The operations have also been profitable. The Railroad Company paid about $25 million in dividends to the Treasury, and the successor Canal Company now usually shows a profit, after paying the Treasury interest on the government investment. The business success of the enterprise may be attributed to its monopoly position, the substantial freedom given its management, and the fact that defense considerations do not add appreciably to its costs.

The federal government also owns and operates the Alaska Railroad Company. After several private railroads had gone bankrupt or had failed to run lines into the interior, this government venture was undertaken in 1914 to promote the territory's development. For administrative purposes, it is located in the Interior Department. Its main line extends 470 miles from Seward to Fairbanks. It also owns and operates a number of other minor businesses. Because of its low, promotional rates and its sparsely populated service area, it has never been profitable. It failed even to earn its operating expenses until 1940. In more recent years, it has shown small net earnings, but these take no account of depreciation and no interest is paid on the government investment of $125 million.

Credit and Insurance

The federal government supplies a broad range of services in credit and insurance.[11] In 1949, the Hoover Commission reported that forty federal agencies, with three hundred offices and thirty-five thousand employees, were making loans or providing insurance. Many motives contributed to the establishment of these programs. Public banking and insurance have attained some of

[11] We omit consideration here of the Federal Reserve System, which might be considered a form of quasi-public enterprise. Each of the twelve Federal Reserve Banks is owned by its member banks, who elect six of its nine directors. The other three are named by the Federal Reserve System's Board of Governors, who, in turn, are nominated by the President and confirmed by the Senate. The Board, however, exercises substantial control over the Reserve Banks. For a discussion of the system, see pp. 798–800, 807–808. below.

their most far-reaching development in sectors of the economy which appear unattractive to private capital but which occupy a strategic position in the political framework. In the forefront of these sectors stands agriculture, whose public credit institutions are described in Chapter 6. Postal savings once played an important role in affording a safe outlet for the savings of low-income groups. Small business and housing loans, both discussed below, also fall into the same general category.

But the largest loan programs had their origins in depression and war, when credit was used on a large scale for salvage operations or to facilitate defense production. The largest credit agency of them all, the late Reconstruction Finance Corporation (RFC), served both purposes. Modeled in organization and general powers after the War Finance Corporation, which had used government credit to support the rural banking structure in the first shock of the agricultural depression after World War I, the RFC was established in 1932 on President Hoover's recommendation and with the support of banking and financial interests. Management was vested in the Corporation's Board of Directors, and its capital funds provided from the Treasury. RFC lending powers were originally confined to banks, insurance companies, other financial institutions, industrial corporations, and railroads. The aim was to avert the spread of bankruptcy by making available funds which private lending agencies were then unable or unwilling to supply. The Corporation was viewed as an emergency agency; its lending authority was at first limited to one year, renewable for another two by the President.

The need for public credit during the New Deal was so great, and the RFC proved such an effective instrument, that its powers were expanded and its life extended. It was authorized to lend to state and local governments as well as to such federal institutions as the Export-Import Bank, home loan banks, and farm credit agencies. Congress invoked its assistance whenever the existing debt structure in an important sector of the economy threatened to collapse. During its New Deal phase, the RFC loaned about $12 billion. Since its loans required collateral and were offered only when repayment appeared likely, the RFC was self-supporting, although its profits represented a low rate of return on the government investment.

In the succeeding phase of rearmament and World War II, the RFC was given a new range of functions. It was empowered to finance government or private plants manufacturing arms or strategic materials, and many of the wartime plants were built with RFC funds. Much of this program was conducted by subsidiaries such as the Defense Plant Corporation, the Defense Supplies Corporation, the Metal Reserves Company, and the Rubber Reserve Company. In 1947, the RFC's authority to finance other government agencies was terminated, but it was authorized to make loans to small businesses unable to obtain private credit. After the outbreak of the Korean War, the Defense Production Act of 1950 enabled the RFC to make loans to private businesses similar to those of World War II. RFC loans financed new plants and additions to old ones, the production of strategic materials, and the development of new processes.

After a record of successful performance in depression and war—one which received the praise of the Hoover Commission's Task Force on Lending Agencies—the RFC fell into bad repute under the Truman administration. A Senate investigation suggested that the quality of RFC management had deteriorated and that political influence had played a part in the making of some questionable loans. Consequently, in 1953, Congress directed the Corporation to liquidate itself and to complete its operations on June 30, 1954.

Despite its dubious reputation in its last years, the twenty-two-year RFC record as a whole was impressive. It had loaned about $50 billion and shown a modest profit on its operations. While the primary goals were economic, the RFC also successfully furthered other objectives. Through its lending power, it brought about a number of changes in the financial practices of railroads, banks, and insurance companies who wished to borrow from it. RFC competition with private capital also induced a liberalization of private business-loan policies.

The Act which terminated the RFC created a Small Business Administration (SBA) to assume some of its functions. By 1958, some $430 million had been authorized to provide this agency with funds for loans to small businessmen and to victims of disasters, and to wind up a few remaining RFC activities. The SBA may make loans up to $350,000 to small businesses unable to secure funds on a reasonable basis from private sources. It makes direct loans and also participates in other loans with private institutions. Through fiscal 1957, it had made 7,096 loans of both types, whose average amount was $45,770. Despite interest charges of 6 per cent (lowered to $5\frac{1}{2}$ per cent in 1958), the high administrative costs involved in such small loans caused its operations to show a cumulative deficit of $14 million by mid-1957. In 1958, in response to continuing complaints of small businessmen about the inadequacy of private credit sources, the SBA was made a permanent agency, and it was empowered to lend up to $250 million to investment companies formed to provide venture capital, rather than short-term loans, to small businesses. These investment companies must be formed by at least ten people and have at least $300,000 in capital, half of which they may obtain from the SBA. They are also given a number of special tax advantages.

Another product of the Great Depression was the Federal Deposit Insurance Corporation (FDIC), which in 1935 was established to take over the Temporary Deposit Insurance Fund, created in 1933. With the paralyzing wave of bank failures fresh in mind, Congress intended the FDIC to protect bank depositors from losses and to restore and maintain confidence in the stability of the private banking system. It insures deposits up to $10,000 in all banks belonging to the Federal Reserve System and in all other mutual savings or commercial banks which so desire. It finances itself with assessments, originally set at $\frac{1}{12}$ of 1 per cent of deposits, levied on insured banks. These assessments, now cut by more than half, have been sufficient to retire the $289 million originally invested by the Treasury and the Federal Reserve Banks and to accumulate an insurance fund of $1.8 billion, or 1.5 per cent of insured deposits. The Corporation is also authorized to borrow up to $3 billion from the Treasury.

In foreign trade, the Export-Import Bank has been a major source of public credit since its establishment in 1934. Originally created by Executive Order to finance trade with the Soviet Union, it was continued by Congress in 1935 and its functions have been expanded greatly to include the financing of general foreign trade through loans to American exporters and their foreign customers, where private funds are not available on reasonable terms. During World War II and thereafter, it came to serve as an instrument for intergovernmental loans. Extensively used now to promote foreign economic development and to enable foreign nations or banks to meet foreign-trade requirements, it has come to be more an instrument of foreign policy than a business enterprise. At the same time, such programs do assist in financing American exports; moreover, the Export-Import Bank has rigorously adhered to "bankers' standards," assuring repayment of loans and a strong profit record. The more uncertain areas of foreign financing are handled by other agencies.

Governed by a board of directors, which includes the Secretary of State ex-officio, the Bank has $1 billion in capital stock, owned by the government, and may borrow interest-bearing funds from the Treasury. It has a lending authority (most recently increased in 1958) of $7 billion. In 1957, it had $2.6 billion in loans outstanding, of which $1 billion had been devoted to foreign development projects, $1.4 billion in emergency foreign-trade loans, and only $100 million in loans to exporters or on commodities. It pays dividends on its stock and has accumulated retained earnings of $465 million.

Housing

A great complex of federal agencies provides credit and insurance in the area of housing, achieving a breadth of scope paralleled only in the field of agricultural assistance. The immediate impetus to federal assumption of responsibility was the disastrous deterioration of the home-financing system, approaching total collapse, during the Great Depression of 1929–1933. Difficulties affecting every aspect of the nation's debt structure were peculiarly aggravated by special features of the mortgage market. They included the inflation of real estate values during the boom of the late twenties; loss of income by houseowners; unsatisfactory short-term, unamortized mortgages; and the inability of local sources of credit to meet the needs of the mortgage market. In 1933, a thousand foreclosures were being ordered daily.

Congress's response to the housing problems of the Great Depression was the creation, beginning in 1932, of a series of interrelated corporate agencies designed to achieve four objectives:

(1) Long-run reform of the mortgage system to provide adequate credit facilities was promoted through the Federal Home Loan Bank system, including the federal savings-and-home-loan associations, the Federal Savings and Loan Insurance Corporation, the Federal National Mortgage Association, and the RFC Mortgage Company.

(2) A large-scale salvage operation for distressed homeowners was carried out through the Home Owners' Loan Corporation.

(3) The Federal Housing Administration sought to stimulate the private construction and modernization of homes.

(4) The United States Housing Authority was created to subsidize slum clearance and low-rent housing.

In 1942 and 1947, these and other housing agencies were combined into a new Housing and Home Finance Agency, which operates through five divisions: The Home Loan Bank Board, the Federal Housing Administration, the Federal National Mortgage Association, the Public Housing Administration, and the Division of Slum Clearance and Urban Redevelopment.

The Federal Home Loan Bank Act of 1932 sought to improve the mortgage system and to provide home-financing institutions better able to serve borrowers. It created a structure modeled after the Federal Reserve System and consisting of a central Federal Home Loan Bank Board, appointed by the President, twelve (now eleven) Federal Home Loan Banks, and numerous member institutions. The banks are authorized to borrow funds by issuing debentures or bonds guaranteed by the United States and to make loans to their member institutions on the security of mortgages. The member institutions in turn make loans to home-owners. The banks were originally financed in part through stock subscription by member institutions and in part by federal funds, but by 1951 the federal investment had been fully repaid. All federal savings-and-loan associations must become members of the system, and other financial institutions may join upon purchase of bank stock and by conforming to the system's regulations. In 1957, there were 4,469 members, with total assets of $44.6 billion and total mortgage loans of $37 billion.

The Federal Savings and Loan Insurance Corporation, operating under the supervision of the Federal Home Loan Bank Board, insures savings accounts up to $10,000 in federal savings-and-loan associations and in such similar state-chartered associations as apply and are admitted. It is financed by assessments on its members and has retired three-quarters of the original federal investment of $100 million. The 3,723 institutions it insures have assets of $42 billion.

Salvage operations were conducted by the Home Owners' Loan Corporation, established under authority of the Home Owners' Loan Act of 1933. This Corporation refinanced home mortgages at low interest rates for owners threatened with foreclosure and unable to refinance on reasonable terms elsewhere. It also made mortgage loans to finance home repairs. Its lending authority was ended in 1936, but by that time it had advanced nearly $3.5 billion to over a million homeowners. When its last mortgages were repaid in 1951, it showed a small surplus of almost $14 million. Not only had it thus saved homes from foreclosure; its program also had a major impact on mortgages granted by others, leading to a lowering of interest rates, a lengthening of maturity dates, and regularized amortization.

In the third phase of this program—the encouragement of home building and modernization—the National Housing Act of 1934 established the Federal Housing Administration (FHA) and provided for a Federal National Mortgage Association ("Fanny May"). The FHA's primary task is to insure mortgages, thereby stabilizing the mortgage market and encouraging private sources to provide the necessary credit. It also seeks to improve home-financing practices. It insures mortgages on one- to four-family houses in amounts and at interest rates which Congress has changed from time to time in response to changing economic conditions. It also makes loan insurance available for co-operative, rental, and defense housing. Under the Housing Act of 1957, the FHA may issue mortgages amounting to as much as 97 per cent of the first $10,000 of appraised value, 85 per cent of the next $6,000, and 70 per cent of value in excess of $16,000. Insured mortgages may not run for more than thirty years or three-fourths of the remaining useful life of the house. Interest rates may not exceed $5\frac{1}{4}$ per cent. The FHA charges an insurance premium of $\frac{1}{2}$ of 1 per cent of the unpaid principal, a rate which has been sufficient to permit the accrual of half a billion dollars in retained earnings. The FHA is free to reject mortgages on its appraisal of value or its judgment of the soundness of the loan. By 1957, it had written $45 billion of insurance, of which $21 billion was outstanding.

As a further means of stabilizing the mortgage market and to provide some liquidity for government-insured mortgages, the Federal National Mortgage Association is empowered to make a "secondary market" for FHA or so-called "GI" mortgages.[12] It buys, sells, and services these mortgages, thereby helping to maintain their prices.

Finally, two agencies now carry on the program of subsidizing low-rent housing and slum clearance. An Act of 1937 created the United States Housing Authority and empowered it to assist, with loans and subsidies, local housing agencies which build and operate low-rent housing for families unable to afford adequate private housing. The Authority, permitted to raise money by the issuance of up to $500 million in government-guaranteed notes or bonds (raised to $800 million in 1938), could then lend

---

[12] The Veterans Administration also insures mortgages. Under the Servicemen's Readjustment Act of 1944, home, business, and farm loans to veterans are guaranteed up to 60 per cent of the principal amount, or $7,500, whichever is less. By mid-1957, almost five million GI home mortgages had been insured.

funds at low rates of interest to local agencies for construction. It was also empowered to pay up to $28 million in annual subsidies, one-fifth matched by local governments, thereby lowering the rents charged in housing projects. The Housing Act of 1949, which replaced the Authority with the Public Housing Administration, extended the program. Contemplating the eventual construction of an additional 810,000 low-rent units, it increased the Administration's borrowing power to $1.5 billion, and lifted the annual subsidy authorization to $336 million. In succeeding years, however, Congress has imposed low ceilings on the construction permitted in specified periods, so that the actual pace of the program has been much slower than expected in 1949. By mid-1957, a total of 430,000 dwelling units had been completed under these programs and were receiving an annual subsidy of $90 million. The Public Housing Administration is also engaged in the sale to private interests of a number of emergency war, defense, and veterans' housing projects.

Supplementing the program of the Public Housing Administration, the Housing Act of 1949 empowered the Public Housing Administrator, operating through the Division of Slum Clearance and Urban Redevelopment, to assist local governments to clear slums and make the underlying land available for private or public redevelopment. This assistance takes the form of both loans and grants. The Administrator may lend funds to finance the necessary planning, which includes studies of the blighted areas and preparation of detailed plans for the acquisition and clearance of slums, rehabilitation of less acutely affected areas, improvement of public facilities, relocation of displaced occupants, and disposition of cleared land at its fair value for its best new uses. He may also advance temporary loans to cover execution of the plans. He is authorized to borrow up to $1 billion from the Treasury for these purposes. In 1957, there were $135 million in outstanding loans and planning advances. In addition, the Administrator may make outright capital grants covering two-thirds of net project costs, i.e., the difference between the cost of acquiring and preparing the land and the amount realized by selling or leasing the land for its new uses. Grants are also available to pay for certain limited costs of relocating displaced residents and small businesses. The 1949 legislation authorized $500 million for capital grants, later increased to $1.25 billion. By mid-1957, there were 264 cities engaged in redevelopment projects, and it was estimated that $297 million in grants would be disbursed by the end of fiscal 1957.

A new housing program was initiated by the Housing Act of 1950, which provided for low-interest loans to colleges, universities, and nursing schools to finance construction of housing and related facilities. The Public Housing Administrator is authorized to lend up to $925 million at a rate ¼ of 1 per cent above the average rate on the outstanding public debt. In fiscal 1957, he received 318 applications and authorized 270. Outstanding loans totaled $209 million.

Expanded use of government credit, first undertaken to prevent total collapse of the national-debt structure at the pit of the Great Depression, has now become a permanent field of public activity. Many of these lending operations involve no direct loss to the government. Public enterprise of this type, particularly in agriculture and housing, fulfills a need left unsatisfied by the private credit structure. It carries with it two significant implications for the role of government in the economy. Participation in capital supply gives public agencies a direct influence upon economic policies of the businesses concerned, and may provide an important means for their regulation. At the same time, choice of objectives for the application of public credit invests government with a large and sometimes decisive role in guiding the flow of investment funds. It thereby influences at a strategic point the dynamics of the economy for the future. And by braking or accelerating the flow of credit and the rate of investment, it can greatly assist pursuance of a countercyclical policy with regard to general levels of employment and income.

State and Municipal Enterprise

State governments operated many businesses early in the nineteenth century, including turnpikes and canals, and even a few railroads. The depression of 1837–1842, the development of the privately-owned railroad network, and a lack of sound business practices and standards doomed most of these ventures.

Today most state enterprises are clustered under the headings of transportation, power, insurance, and liquor. A number of states operate canals, toll bridges, and ferries, and provide harbor facilities. In recent years, the role of state enterprise in transportation—through the operation of toll roads, for example—has been greatly expanded to meet the needs of the automotive age.

A notable instance, and one of the largest public enterprises in the nation, is the Port of New York Authority. This agency was established in 1921 under an interstate compact between

New York and New Jersey. It is directed by a board of twelve commissioners, six appointed by the governor of each state. After capital funds of $17.5 million, to be repaid with interest, were contributed by the two states, the Port Authority raised further sums by bonds, secured by a first lien on net revenues. Its initial purpose was to construct and operate toll bridges and tunnels leading into New York City and to plan for development of the port. It is authorized, however, to build, buy, lease, and operate all kinds of transportation and terminal facilities. Its growth has been spectacular. Enjoying substantial toll revenues from its bridges and terminals, and paying low interest rates on its bonds, it has commanded the credit with which steadily to build or acquire new facilities. Its primary emphasis has been on interurban transportation, and it owns and operates bridges, tunnels, truck terminals, a railroad freight terminal, a bus terminal, and an airport. It also operates the New York International (Idlewild), La Guardia, and Newark airports. And it owns a number of industrial and marine properties. Its total investment had reached $625 million by the end of 1956. Its gross revenue in that year was $77 million, and its net operating income almost $40 million. Over the years, its net income has been sufficient to retire $290 million in debt and to set aside $33 million in reserves.[13]

The Port Authority is thus a remarkably successful public enterprise. Yet the reasons for its financial well-being also raise questions of policy direction.[14] Its financial success and reputation for competent management are partly attributable to the Authority's independence, but its virtual political irresponsibility may mean that financial considerations receive undue weight in its fixing of tolls and its decisions on new facilities. Its financial health is also attributable to its monopoly power, which enables it to charge what the traffic can bear. By pooling its revenues, it uses high toll charges from bridges and tunnels to cover its losses on terminals and other projects. Thus high tolls may continue to be imposed on a particular facility long after its costs have been repaid.

State governments operate many insurance programs. Since 1936, all states have administered compulsory unemployment-

[13] Port of New York Authority, *Annual Report*, 1956, p. 71.

[14] See A. J. Tobin, "The Port of New York Authority," *State Government* (September, 1947), pp. 233–239; W. S. Fairfield, "The New York Port Authority, Guardian of the Toll Gates," *The Reporter* (September 23, 1953), pp. 21–27.

compensation systems (see Chapter 25). The oldest form of state insurance is workmen's compensation for industrial accidents (see Chapter 7). Eighteen states operate workmen's compensation funds, seven of which allow for no participation by private insurance companies. There have been a few other scattered state ventures in insurance. Wisconsin operates a life-insurance system; Massachusetts, New York, and Connecticut assist savings banks in offering life insurance.

The repeal of the Eighteenth (Prohibition) Amendment in 1933 returned to the states control over commerce in alcoholic beverages. Many states thereupon established their own agencies for liquor distribution, in part to secure revenue and in part to prevent socially undesirable stimulation of demand and assure close regulation of retail sales. Of the forty-seven states which permit the sale of intoxicating beverages, sixteen monopolize the retail sale of packaged liquor, and a seventeenth has a wholesale monopoly. Because of the relative inelasticity of demand, the fewness of outlets, the absence of a need to advertise or promote sales, and the simplicity of the distribution and merchandising task, state liquor stores have been highly profitable. Profits have averaged between 12 and 21 per cent of sales, although retail prices have usually been lower than those in nonmonopoly states.[15]

Local governments conduct an extremely wide array of enterprises, including such ventures as slaughterhouses, zoos, golf courses, cemeteries, coal yards, ice plants, laundries, liquor stores, and radio stations. The main fields of municipal enterprise, however, are in water supply, local passenger transportation, electricity, and housing. Although early in the nineteenth century most waterworks were privately owned, now three-fourths of American cities own and operate their own systems. This has come to be generally accepted as a public function and gives rise to few important policy questions.

The scope of municipal power and housing activities reflects federal programs described elsewhere in this book. In 1957, there were about 425,000 federally-assisted, low-rent public housing dwelling units being operated by local authorities. And largely as a result of federal power policies giving preference to public agencies in the distribution of cheap power generated at federal dams, there is substantial municipal ownership of electric-dis-

[15] B. Y. Landes, "Economic Aspects of State Alcoholic Beverage Monopoly Enterprises," *Quarterly Journal of Studies on Alcohol* (September, 1946), pp. 258–269.

tribution plants.[16] Today about one-fifth of all cities with a population of more than 5,000 have municipal systems, less than half of which generate their own power. Among the largest cities, however, only Los Angeles owns its own system.[17]

Thirty-eight urban transit systems are now municipally owned. Some have been so for many years; others have had to be taken over when private operation became unprofitable. In the nation's twelve largest cities, six systems are publicly owned and operated, one is publicly owned but privately operated, and five are in private hands. The entire industry has suffered from a steady decline in traffic, confronting cities owning transit systems with difficult policy decisions. If rates are raised, more traffic is diverted, some of it adding to the congestion strangulating the streets of most large cities, and some of it shifting to suburban shopping centers. Maintaining low rates wins the support of the transit user, but requires a subsidy from the taxpayer; this raises property taxes, which are often close to their economic or statutory limits. Most of the larger municipal systems do not pay their own way. New York reluctantly raised its subway fare from 5 to 10 cents in 1948 and to 15 cents in 1953. Even at 15 cents, however, the fare does not meet the full costs of the subway system. The problem is beyond the control of many large cities, requiring for its solution transportation plans devised to meet the needs of entire metropolitan areas. Establishment of a tri-state commission, for example, has been under consideration in an effort to seek integration of commuter and local transportation in the New York City area.

3. Attitudes Toward Public Enterprise

Early in 1933, a special House committee, the Shannon Committee, reviewed the then existing range of federal public enterprises. It recommended, with only one dissent, the abandonment of government competition with private enterprise and the appointment of a standing committee to guard against "unwise and unprofitable encroachments of government activity." It stated as a "fundamental consideration" that:

[16] In addition, five states generate hydroelectricity, and all of the power sold in Nebraska is distributed by Public Power Districts.
[17] For some statistical indications of comparative efficiency, see FPC, *Rates, Taxes, and Consumer Savings in Publicly and Privately Owned Electrical Utilities, 1935–1937* (1939); Twentieth Century Fund, *Electric Power and Government Policy* (1948), pp. 405–409.

. . . the entrance of the government into commercial and industrial undertakings, backed by public credit and resources and its military and civilian personnel, for the purpose of competing with the business establishments and the opportunities for livelihood of its citizens is . . . in general, repugnant to our fundamental democratic institutions and aspirations.[18]

During the following two decades, however, the New Deal and World War II resulted in a vast expansion of government enterprise in a variety of areas on both federal and local levels. The 1952 election brought into office the Eisenhower administration, which, pledged to "getting the government out of business," attempted to reverse this tide. Former President Herbert Hoover was asked to head a second investigation of the federal executive. Where the first Hoover Commission, whose reports had been published in 1949, had examined internal organization and management, the second Hoover Commission, a more partisan body, sought to limit government to its "proper" functions. The second Commission recommended a curtailment of public power programs; indeed, at the outset Hoover had declared that the aim of policy "should be to get the federal government out of generating and distributing power as soon as possible." [19]

As in the case of the Shannon Committee, the Hoover Commission's criticisms of federal business activities were based on the assumption of the undesirability of governmental competition with private enterprise. Except for public power, however, most public enterprises provide services which are supplementary or complementary to, rather than directly competitive with, the operations of private business. These services were also opposed by the second Hoover Commission. It was especially critical of many federal lending and loan-guaranteeing programs. Its Task Force on Lending Agencies accepted the use of public credit for defense and war procurement and for the promotion of private credit facilities, but it strongly condemned programs designed to help particular groups or businesses and so discriminating against those not qualifying for special assistance. Believing that these programs also saddle government with business risks and discourage private risk-taking, it concluded that "the Federal Government should contract its lending and that it should encourage the direct investment of savings in property ownership

[18] *Report of the Special Committee Appointed to Study Government Competition with Private Enterprise* (1933), H. Rept. 1985, 72d Cong., 2d sess., p. 18.
[19] *New York Times*, April 2, 1953.

and in the equity shares of business enterprises." [20] Accordingly, it recommended the abolition or curtailment of the lending programs of the Commodity Credit Corporation, Farmers' Home Administration, Export-Import Bank, Rural Electrification Administration, RFC, and Small Business Administration, the loan guaranties of the Veterans Administration, and the lending and subsidy programs of the Public Housing Administration.

These proposals were not adopted. Against the argument that such aids were discriminatory could be summoned the argument that appropriate kinds of aid to selected groups may actually contribute to the common welfare. Perhaps more to the point was the fact that these programs had met genuine needs and were firmly entrenched in the strong support of their many beneficiaries. Consequently, while the Eisenhower administration reversed the trend toward expansion of public enterprise, relatively little divestment occurred. The growth of public power was checked or slowed. The RFC was liquidated, but a part of its program was resurrected in the Small Business Administration. The federal barge line was sold, as were the synthetic rubber plants. And several hundred small activities in the Department of Defense, ranging from landscape nurseries to bakeries, were eliminated. The great bulk of federal enterprises, however, remain essentially undiminished.

4. Organizational Forms of Public Enterprise

Public enterprises not only confront the immediate policy issues inherent in their fields of endeavor; they also face broader problems of both public and business administration. Involved are questions of the relation between policy and administration, efficient operation, and the need of an enterprise to cover its costs, to meet its capital requirements, and to be flexible in the face of changing conditions. The executive department is the conventional unit for public administration, and the corporation the most successful form of organization for large businesses. Consequently, it is hardly surprising that public enterprise has sought to combine features of both departmental and corporate organizational forms.

Departmental Management

The government department or ministry of state has developed in various countries with remarkable parallelism as the normal

[20] Commission on Organization of the Executive Branch of the Government, *Task Force Report on Lending Agencies* (1955), p. 5.

instrument for performing governmental functions. The various department heads compose together a collegial co-ordinating cabinet, supervised by the chief executive. Departments are functionally subdivided under assistant ministers and secretaries, each with a staff and line organization.

Such administrative machinery is often applied to the operation of public enterprise as well as to other governmental activities. Before World War I, the preponderance of government-owned businesses was controlled in this manner. The advantages of departmental organization are by no means inconsiderable. Cabinet meetings and a uniform relationship to the chief executive provide for unification and consistent application of over-all policy. Responsibility is focused on the single department head. Channels of authority and responsibility are well defined; assisted by such staff aids as the Bureau of the Budget, they flow up to the chief executive and down to every echelon of the departmental organization. Through appropriate hierarchical arrangements, decisions may be graded by importance and systematically distributed among the suitable levels of administration. In the American system, a direct and routine channel for legislative control is afforded by the annual review of appropriation requests by subcommittees of the House Appropriations Committee. Financial requirements are co-ordinated and controlled through both executive and legislative budget procedures, and detailed expenditures are scrutinized by the General Accounting Office.

In large measure, the advantages of departmental management in general administration apply equally to the administration of public enterprise. Even when complete fiscal independence is desired, with neither subsidy nor profit, the operation of a public business cannot be wholly divorced from wider considerations of public policy. The very prevalence of noneconomic objectives in dictating the establishment of public enterprise suggests the necessity for some control by general policy-determining agencies to ensure the satisfaction of these objectives. Where special subsidies or public guarantees are involved, there is additional need for a degree of central control.

Yet departmental control also displays many disadvantages for public enterprise. These disadvantages lie in the realms of organization, personnel, finance, and psychology. An agency selling goods or services bears a relation to the public quite different from one administering traditional governmental functions. It must adapt itself readily to unpredictable fluctuations in market conditions. Rapidity of decision and ability to take advantage of favorable short-run opportunities may often be more vital to efficient enterprise than the rigid devotion to strict legality, or even legalism, which necessarily characterizes the ordinary bureau. A degree of secrecy is often warranted in commercial operations; while obtainable in some circumstances through departmental management, it is achieved more readily with an autonomous form of organization. The very responsibility of the department head in the public eye will often militate against the devolution essential to administrative flexibility. Another barrier to flexibility in a department lies in the complex controls exercised by the Bureau of the Budget, the Department of Justice, the Comptroller General, and the Civil Service Commission.

The personnel system developed for recruitment and promotion of civil servants is frequently ill devised to fit the needs of commercial administration. In general, public service offers relatively high salaries in the bottom ranges, but low salaries in the upper ranges, depending upon security and noneconomic satisfactions for added compensation. Rapid promotion is rarely the reward for special merit, since a minimum level of morale is most easily maintained through promotions based on seniority. The faithful completion of set tasks is often valued in civil service organizations more highly than imagination or initiative in experimenting with new methods.

Ordinary governmental financial arrangements are based on considerations utterly different from those applying to public enterprises. Primary and often exclusive emphasis is laid by government accounting upon the cash account. A well-organized system provides a detailed check upon each penny received and each penny spent. Public financial controls are directed toward two central objectives: avoidance of corruption, and insurance that no expenditure is made without appropriate legislative authority. Accounting methods rarely distinguish between capital expenditures and expenditures on revenue account. The audits conducted by the General Accounting Office have traditionally been concerned with legality of expenditure rather than with efficiency of operation.[21]

Under departmental management, revenues from an enterprise flow into the Treasury. An increase in business may lift an enterprise's revenues more than its expenses and yet leave it short

---

[21] It should be noted, however, that in recent years major reforms have been introduced into the governmental accounting system to make it serve as an instrument for promoting functional efficiency instead of merely ensuring legality in expenditures.

of funds since it can pay its expenses only out of appropriations. The real financial position, as opposed to the merely superficial cash balance, is often impossible to determine. Variation of capital expenditures from year to year may be entirely justified by particular needs, yet in years of heavy expenditures the financial record will appear poor despite the usefulness of the resulting equipment over a considerable future period. Adequate financial appraisal of public enterprises, no less than of their private counterparts, requires accounting on a commercial basis. Flexibility in general administration, moreover, demands in the financial field a degree of freedom from the rigidity of ordinary budgeting and accounting controls.

The psychological connotations of departmental organization, finally, are not conducive to enthusiastic and imaginative administration of an economic enterprise. The very word "bureau" suggests a "bureaucratic" attitude, one of slow and methodical routine, replete with checks and counterchecks, hampered by red tape, and delayed by interminable reviews. The spirit which favors innovation, promotion, and salesmanship may be developed in an ordinary civil service agency, but the process is a struggle against ponderous tradition. The very creation of special administrative forms for public enterprise puts the managers on their mettle, at least during the initial stages, in order to prove the worth of the new agencies.

To these typical weaknesses of departmental management when applied to public enterprise there must be added a type of positive danger suggested by the expression "political influence." In the sense of policy formation in accordance with broader considerations, noneconomic and economic, political influence is, of course, highly desirable. But depending on the nature of the political structure, these is also the danger that special group and sectional interests quite unrelated to broad policy considerations may find channels for influencing administrative decisions in undesirable ways. Despite the undeniable connection between the management of public enterprises and considerations of broader policy, their primary concern is the efficient supply of goods and services. In most respects, this function bears little or no relation to the issues dividing political parties. Frequent turnover in top managerial positions in accordance with party fluctuations, therefore, is likely to be a serious impediment to effective management. Perhaps the best examples of the undesirable restraints which politically inspired legislative control can impose upon the management and operation of a departmentally organized

public enterprise are offered by the Post Office, whose difficulties
have been described above.

The Public Corporation

Because of these many weaknesses of departmental organization, there has been a world-wide trend toward autonomy in the
operation of public enterprises. The public or government corporation is the fullest embodiment of this trend. American experience with public corporations, barring some notable early
experiments like the First and Second Banks of the United States,
is primarily a product of the three periods when government
felt impelled to experiment with vast new programs of public
enterprise—the two World Wars and the Great Depression.
World War I saw the creation of a fairly small number of corporations to perform business functions.[22] Then, in dealing with
the pressing problems of the Great Depression, the federal government created new public corporations almost indiscriminately.
The largest of them all, the RFC, was established in 1932. It
was followed under the New Deal by a host of others.[23]

In a few instances in the late thirties, the corporate form
proved to have no substantial advantages; the activities were
soon absorbed into larger agencies and the corporations lapsed.
World War II, however, with its need for vast programs of
government procurement, construction, and production, saw another expansion in the number of corporations. A high point
was reached in 1946, when there were over 110, with an investment of more than $20 billion. Peace and the postwar years
brought about a contraction. The first Hoover Commission in

[22] They included the Emergency Fleet Corporation of the United States
Shipping Board, the United States Grain Corporation and the Sugar Equalization Board of the Food Administration, the War Finance Corporation, the
United States Spruce Production Corporation, and the Russian Bureau, Inc.
[23] In order of their creation, they were the Tennessee Valley Authority; the
Home Owners' Loan Corporation; the Production Credit Corporation, the
system of Banks for Co-operatives, and the Federal Farm Mortgage Corporation of the Farm Credit Administration; the Federal Deposit Insurance Corporation; the Federal Surplus Relief Corporation; the Commodity Credit
Corporation; the Public Works Emergency Housing Corporation; the Federal
Subsistence Homesteads Corporation; the Electric Home and Farm Authority,
Inc.; the Tennessee Valley Associated Co-operatives; the Public Works Emer-
gency Leasing Corporation; the Export-Import Bank; the Federal Savings
and Loan Insurance Corporation; Federal Prison Industries, Inc.; the RFC
Mortgage Company; the Disaster Loan Corporation; the Farmers' Home
Corporation; the United States Housing Authority; the Federal National
Mortgage Association; and the Federal Crop Insurance Corporation.

1949 counted 75 active corporations and 12 which were being liquidated.[24] This count can give a false impression, for 51 active corporations were associated with the Farm Credit Administration and 13 (now 14) were in the Housing and Home Finance group. Since 1949, the RFC has been dissolved and the Inland Waterways Corporation sold, but the Federal Facilities Corporation has been established to operate the synthetic rubber plants and to administer the contracts for their disposal, and the Saint Lawrence Seaway Development Corporation was created to construct, operate, and maintain the American part of the Seaway.

In the states and municipalities, the trend toward incorporation for public enterprises has been less marked, although a number of notable examples are at hand. The device has proved useful for regional administration in areas not covered by pre-existing political units. The widespread development of public utility districts, irrigation districts, and other special authorities, encouraged under the New Deal by the Public Works Administration loan and grant policy, is a similar phenomenon, although such units share in part the character both of traditional local governmental authorities and of public corporations proper. In a few instances, like the Port of New York Authority, the corporate form has been used under interstate compact to construct and operate public projects affecting two or more states.

In the first phase of enthusiasm for this new device of public administration, it appeared that the corporation might provide all the desired autonomy and flexibility which was denied under departmental organization. Use of the public corporation seemed to permit an almost infinite degree of flexibility in internal organization and in relationship to the central organs of government. It might carry devolution to the extent of acting merely as a holding company for subordinate operations. It made possible varying degrees of autonomy in four major respects: political (freedom from legislative controls); administrative (freedom from ordinary executive controls); personnel (freedom from ordinary civil service requirements); and financial (freedom from dependence on the legislature for funds and from ordinary budgetary and auditing controls).

The autonomy provided by use of the corporate form is of greatest importance in the realm of finance. Through separation

[24] Commission on Organization of the Executive Branch of the Government, *Task Force Report on Revolving Funds and Business Enterprises of the Government* (1949), pp. 172–173.

from the general treasury and the requirement that the enterprise be economically self-supporting, corporate managers may be stimulated to high standards of commercial efficiency. Realization that losses will not automatically be made up from the public purse and that profits may be employed for improvement of the service directly under their control both play important roles in this connection.

At the same time, the divorce from central direction has never been complete. Various corporations were given different degrees of freedom in each of the four major categories.

The Tennessee Valley Authority

The outstanding example of far-reaching autonomy is the Tennessee Valley Authority. When the TVA was established in 1933, it was charged with a variety of different functions. It was to develop and control the waters of the Tennessee River and its tributaries for the combined purposes of hydroelectric power, navigation, flood control, and recreation. It was also to produce fertilizer at the World War I nitrate plants at Muscle Shoals. It was to develop the local production of fertilizer, to improve land use in the Tennessee Basin through soil-erosion control, reforestation, and allied operations, and to promote the national defense through the manufacture of artificial nitrates.

In view of the many different programs, some of business type and some not, and in view of its unique responsibility for the co-ordinated planning and management of the region's water and land use as a whole, President Roosevelt recommended the creation of "a corporation clothed with the power of Government, but possessed of the flexibility and initiative of a private enterprise." Accordingly, the 1933 Act vested the TVA with unique autonomy and power. As a body corporate under the direction of a three-man Board, appointed by the President and confirmed by the Senate, it may enter into contracts, purchase and lease real and personal property, sue and be sued; it can exercise the governmental power of eminent domain. It is given a remarkable degree of freedom in its internal organization. The TVA is exempted from civil service requirements, but the law forbids consideration of political tests in appointments and promotions and requires that they be made solely on the basis of merit and efficiency.

The general economic situation when the TVA began operations made available an unusual field of professional and administrative ability and induced a flood of applications for employment. The Authority developed its own merit system, based on examination of qualifications, recommendations, and personal interview. The remarkable *esprit de corps* and staff enthusiasm for the Authority's welfare have been noted almost unanimously by observers of its operations, although some have argued that the general civil service system should have been applied once its basic staff was assembled.

TVA construction has been carried on under direct supervision (so-called "force account") rather than by contract. Laborers are selected from applicants, preferably living in the region, by an examination following the model developed by the Civil Service Commission for workers in the navy yards. Turnover has been low, and labor relations good.

In its early years, the TVA's highly satisfactory personnel policy was not paralleled by equal wisdom in internal organization. Instead of concentrating executive functions either in a general manager immediately under the Board, or in a single member of the Board as a managing director, the Authority divided operations into three broad fields, with a director assigned to each for executive supervision. While the Board nominally acted as a corporate body for determining general policy, the directors inevitably became primarily interested in their separate sectors and acted as their partisans in cases of competing interests. Such severe frictions built up that the Board was unable to work as an effective unit, and in 1938 President Roosevelt was forced to remove its chairman. While these frictions were engendered primarily by clashes of personality and divergence in fundamental attitudes toward the Authority's operations, they were intensified by this division of executive responsibility. The error was remedied in 1937 by the appointment of a general manager, and the internal lines of organization were subsequently improved.

The TVA's financial arrangements are less conducive to autonomy. The Authority combines commercial functions in the generation and distribution of power and in part of its fertilizer operations with noncommercial functions in flood control, navigation, agricultural demonstration, and general planning and development of the Valley. Unless its great variety of operations were all financed out of power revenues and fertilizer sales, it could not in its nature be financially self-supporting. Because of its noncommercial functions, it necessarily depends in part upon congressional appropriations. This fact conditions the entire status of the TVA as a public corporation and imposes upon it important congressional restraints.

Not only are funds for noncommercial operations supplied by annual appropriation; this method has also been used in preference to the issuance of TVA bonds for the bulk of the Authority's capital investments. And the government investment in power facilities must be paid back over forty-year periods, thereby limiting the Authority's ability to finance new power construction from depreciation or amortization charges. As of mid-1957, the total TVA power investment had been financed by $1,357 million in appropriations, $413 million from retained earnings, and only $65 million from bonds (largely issued for the purchase of private utility properties).

The practice of financing most of its construction program by congressional appropriation has forced the TVA to fight a continuing political battle for the development of its power program. Again and again, opponents of public power have used the control of appropriations to restrict or delay the construction of power dams and steam generating plants, while the beneficiaries of TVA programs and other supporters of public power have rallied to defend TVA construction appropriations.

The TVA's accounting methods have involved it in a number of clashes with the General Accounting Office. In the Authority's first year of operation, the Comptroller General severely criticized departures from general government accounting practices and took exception to $2 million of expenditures. But upon further investigation all but $81,000 of the exceptions were recommended for release by the General Accounting Office field auditors. The conflict appeared to arise from the TVA's emphasis on flexibility and the Comptroller General's strict interpretation of the Authority's statutory powers. In the words of a congressional investigating committee, "The objections made illustrate clearly the difference between the freedom of a corporation and the strait jacket of red tape which the General Accounting Office sought to impose on the Authority." [25] The Comptroller General has always made postaudits of the TVA, and the Government Corporation Control Act of 1945 directed him to make an annual commercial audit.

Viewed in its entirety, the TVA is a unique experiment in planned regional development under semiautonomous public enterprise. The unusual devotion of its staff members to their tasks has doubtless in large measure been actuated by a vivid con-

[25] Report of the Joint Committee on the Investigation of the Tennessee Valley Authority, S. Doc. 56, 76th Cong., 1st sess. (1939), p. 125.

sciousness of the pioneering character of the Authority's efforts. While the Authority has always been a storm center in the protracted struggle between public and private power, and while there can be legitimate disagreement over the extent to which its low power rates are a legitimate "yardstick" with which to measure the efficiency of private power companies, it has an impressive record of accomplishment in promoting the social and economic rehabilitation and development of the Valley.

The corporate autonomy enjoyed by the Authority seems to have contributed to these results, enabling it directly to co-ordinate many different aspects of water use which elsewhere have to be co-ordinated, usually less successfully, through interagency agreements. The TVA's flexibility has enabled it to handle novel problems in new and fruitful ways. Its relative autonomy from Washington has helped it to serve the peculiar needs of the Valley. As is usually the case with problems of administrative organization, each of these virtues bears with it potential liabilities. Thus autonomy may entail irresponsibility; flexibility may produce corruption and maladministration; and regional decentralization may entail neglect of broad, national considerations.[26] The TVA has succeeded in avoiding most of these pitfalls, in part because it has always been a center of interest and controversy.

The Reaction Against Corporate Autonomy

Nevertheless, the autonomy enjoyed by the TVA has seldom been granted any other agency, just as its unified control of water resources has not been vested in any other authority. As pointed out in Chapter 23, much of the opposition to the creation of similar river authorities stems from other government agencies with a stake in water control. And only a few years after the creation of the TVA, a general reaction developed against the granting of far-reaching autonomy to public corporations. A series of measures, beginning in 1935, tended to erase those features which differentiated the corporation from other forms of public enterprise.[27] One observer remarked that these

[26] It can be argued, for example, that the TVA's regional focus has led it to commit itself too closely to the Extension Service and the Farm Bureau Federation, thereby causing it to keep the Farm Security Administration and the Soil Conservation Service out of the Valley, and so bringing it into conflict with national policies being pursued by the Department of Agriculture. See Philip Selznick, *TVA and the Grass Roots* (1949).

[27] For a discussion of this post-1935 trend, see V. O. Key, "Government

features "have been disappearing before our eyes, like the Cheshire cat. Soon there may be nothing left but the smile to mark the spot where the government corporation once stood." [28]

In the first two years of the New Deal, a veritable spate of government corporations had flowed out of emergency needs, without adequate attention to details of form, maintenance of lines of authority, financial accountability, or means of co-ordination. Thereafter, both the executive and the legislative branches began gradually to exercise more control to assimilate the new agencies into more routine organizational patterns, and to limit their flexibility in procedure. In 1935, the President directed a number of corporations to submit their budgets for "administrative expenses" to the Bureau of the Budget for review and approval. This rule was soon extended to the RFC and the TVA. In 1942, all corporations were made subject to it. In 1936, Congress began in its appropriations acts to limit the amount which individual corporations might spend on administrative expenses. By executive order in 1938 and by the Ramspeck Act of 1940, the civil service laws were applied to every corporation except the TVA. Under the Reorganization Act of 1939, all existing corporations, except the TVA and the Federal Deposit Insurance Corporation, were brought under executive departments or agencies.

In 1945, the framework for public corporation activity was further standardized by the Government Corporation Control Act. This measure had three main provisions:

(1) All corporations were required to re-incorporate under federal law; incorporation of new federal government units under state laws was prohibited; and the power of the President and of cabinet officers to create subsidiary corporations was limited.

(2) Each corporation must submit a "business-type budget" for inclusion in the annual budget and for the scrutiny of the Bureau of the Budget and of Congress.

(3) Corporate accounts were to be audited by the General Accounting Office, but in accordance with customary commercial auditing procedures.

Corporations," in F. M. Marx (ed.), *Elements of Public Administration* (1946), pp. 236–263; C. H. Pritchett, "The Government Corporation Control Act of 1945," *American Political Science Review* (June, 1946), pp. 495–509.

[28] C. H. Pritchett, "The Paradox of the Government Corporation," *Public Administration Review* (Summer, 1941), p. 389.

One observer concluded that the 1945 Act:

. . . goes far toward completing the task of eliminating the features which have made government corporations useful instruments for enterprise purposes. . . . The pattern of control imposed means that, for good or ill, American experience with autonomous public corporation is substantially at an end.[29]

While this is perhaps an overstatement, the distinction between the corporation and other types of agencies which conduct public enterprises has certainly been sharply reduced. The considerations favoring flexibility, autonomy, and financial self-sufficiency have largely been subordinated to the desire for central policy guidance and co-ordination, and to congressional demands for continuing legislative control. At the same time, some of the business-type practices first introduced into public administration through the use of the corporation have now been taken over by nonincorporated agencies.[30] And while incorporation as such is acknowledged to be of only nominal significance, there is continuing recognition that public enterprise requires substantial departures from the conventional administrative arrangements of government.[31]

5. Public Enterprise and General Economic Policy

As the scope of public enterprise broadens, it impinges with increasing force upon the economy as a whole and demands correlation with other elements of public policy. Municipal water supply could be undertaken as an isolated function of government without significantly affecting the remainder of the eco-

[29] Pritchett, "The Government Corporation Control Act of 1945," p. 509.

[30] For example, the operation of all public enterprises, whether or not in the corporate form, are now better reflected in the Budget. In addition to the usual budgetary analysis of program and financing and of expenditures classified by object, the Budget now shows for each enterprise the source and application of its total funds; its revenue, expense, and retained earnings; its financial condition; and the status of its fund balances. Thus, while the enterprise is still subject to full budgetary review, reviewing officials are now in a better position to pass upon the agency as a business enterprise.

[31] In 1958, for example, the Development Loan Fund, established by the Mutual Security Act of 1957 to aid underdeveloped countries, was shifted by Congress to a corporate form of organization. It is also noteworthy that in countries where important sectors of manufacturing and service industry are wholly or partly owned by the government, the public corporation or the "mixed corporation" (combining governmental and private stockholders) remains the favored instrument of administration.

nomic order. But when transportation, power, housing, and large-scale credit operations come within the public sphere, the governmental sector comes to have considerable influence in the total economy. Policy pursued in one field ramifies everywhere and reacts back upon the government itself in its other capacities. Hence the pressure for reintegration of public corporations into the general administrative framework, in an effort to ensure consistency in over-all policy, perhaps even at the cost of the demonstrated advantages of administrative flexibility and autonomy derived from the corporate form.

Beyond the requirements of internal harmony among the administrators of public policy, whether in promotional, regulatory, or operating agencies, lies the significance of the increased scope of all three types of activity taken in conjunction. The growth of public enterprise has been only one reflection of a shift in motivation from mere elimination of abuses to satisfaction of positive demands. The changing pattern of promotion and regulation follows the same trend. Particular policies arise one by one out of special demands and pressures of the moment; their sum effect is to transform the role of government from partial rule-maker and haphazard intervener in the economic process into continuous participant and guide. The trend of recent decades has given to governments throughout the world increased responsibility for shaping the broad pattern of the national economies.

CHAPTER 25

The Welfare State

1. The Rise of the Welfare State

IN 1850, when Herbert Spencer's *Social Statics* proclaimed that "the poverty of the incapable, the distresses that come upon the imprudent, the starvation of the idle, and those shoulderings aside of the weak by the strong, which leave so many 'in shallows and in miseries,' are the decrees of a large far-seeing benevolence," many worthy people of the day were prepared to applaud. Though they might seek to alleviate misery by private charity, they shared Spencer's aversion to any assumption by government "of the office of Reliever-general to the poor." The dominant laissez-faire philosophy consigned government to a limited role—that of maintaining order, enforcing contracts, and protecting property. As for the rest, each individual was expected to make his most effective contribution to the common interest by pursuing his own self-interest.

Even at the height of its popularity, this theory was not altogether successful in impressing its stamp on public policy. The English Industrial Revolution was accompanied by a gradual, if haphazard and intermittent, growth of public services to alleviate misery and raise national well-being. Government was invoked to protect the worker in mines, factories, and workshops—to establish minimum standards of sanitation and hygiene, to provide community services such as public education and housing, and to give some measure of social security to the sick, the elderly, the widowed, the orphaned, and the unemployed. A similar course of development was recorded in the history of most other industrial countries. In the United States, this pattern was slower to unfold. Education was early recognized as a state responsibility, and progress there was rapid. While other welfare activities expanded much less quickly, the long-term trend was always toward a broadening of public obligations. Many public hospitals were constructed, and public institutions were established to care for the aged, the insane, and other special groups of needy persons. Local and state governments assumed an increasing share of the burden of providing relief to the poor.

Prior to the Great Depression, however, these developments were gradual and intermittent. Whether justified or not, the assumption was widespread that the wealth and unique economic opportunities of the United States could provide security for all without the necessity for large-scale government intervention. This assumption was rudely jolted by the prolonged depression which began in 1929. The insecurities generated in that period produced widespread demands that government provide the security which the private sector of the economy was apparently unable to make available.

During the thirties, first local and state governments, and then the federal government, assumed an unparalleled burden of new welfare responsibilities. Government entered the field of slum-clearance housing.[1] Expenditures on relief, work relief, and public works soared. Steps were taken to build a permanent social security program around unemployment compensation and old age insurance as a central core. The night-watchman state began to give way to the service or welfare state, and government was faced with the challenge of making systematic efforts to provide social security for large numbers of insistent citizens. A review of relief and social security developments will give some measure of the dimensions of this transformation.

2. Public Relief Before the New Deal

Prior to the 1930's, relief of the poor and the needy was primarily a local responsibility, borne by private philanthropy or the local community. The Elizabethan system of local poor relief which had been transplanted from England to the Colonies provided the organizational framework for public relief until well into the twentieth century. Poverty was regarded as a sign of

[1] See above, pp. 746–747.

shiftlessness; in order to discourage pauperism, relief grants were meager, and every effort was made to render their reception as unattractive as possible. Before the nineteenth century, paupers were dealt with through various methods. These included "outdoor" relief, that is, relief to the needy in their own homes; "farming out" or "contracting," by which the lowest bidder undertook to care for a single pauper or all the paupers in a given locality; care in an almshouse; and indenture, or "binding out," a form of apprenticeship particularly applicable to children.

During the nineteenth century, "outdoor" relief was granted more sparingly; it was regarded as too costly and as encouraging idleness. The tendency was to turn more and more toward the almshouse or "poor farm," which became a dumping ground for persons of every age and with every kind of handicap or disability. Frequently the almshouse was turned into a workhouse on the theory that compulsory labor would improve the character of the poor and also make them less costly to the community. Each community sought to limit its load of poor relief by "settlement" laws which confined relief to local residents; the "unsettled poor" could receive no relief and were frequently expedited on their way to neighboring jurisdictions.

State responsibility for poor relief was slow to develop. A few states made provision for the so-called "unsettled poor" early in their history. Emergency appropriations for droughts, floods, and other disasters were occasionally made to meet specific needs, but these were sporadically assumed responsibilities. After the Civil War, various states provided relief for needy veterans. During the nineteenth century, there also developed considerable "categorical relief," that is, aid to special classes or categories of needy persons. State institutions were established for the insane, the deaf and dumb, the blind, the feebleminded, the crippled, and juvenile delinquents. The merely poor were left to subsist on local relief. Beginning with Massachusetts in 1863, State Boards of Charities were created to supervise these institutions. But state supervision of local relief developed haltingly; in 1913, twenty-seven states supervised almshouses only; the rest supervised no form of local relief.

State assistance to persons outside of institutions was a twentieth-century development. Again, it took the form of categorical assistance—aid to the blind, mothers' aid, and old age pensions. In 1907, Wisconsin passed the first state law for aid to the blind in their own homes; in 1911, Illinois and Missouri pioneered with a mothers' aid law; in 1923, Montana enacted an old age pension law.[2] Other states followed. By 1930, twenty states aided the blind; forty-five gave aid to mothers with dependent children. But available funds were small; many local units were not rendering the aid authorized by state law; and only a fraction of those in need of assistance was reached. The expansion of these types of categorical assistance had to await the enactment of the Social Security Act of 1935.

Meanwhile, federal welfare activity developed even more slowly. Aside from emergency appropriations to meet catastrophes and the provision of pensions and care for veterans, perhaps the first important step was the establishment of the Children's Bureau in 1912 "to investigate and report . . . upon all matters pertaining to the welfare of children and child life among all classes of our people." The Bureau from the beginning devoted its efforts to assisting in the enactment and administration of state legislation for child care and protection. It also administered federal grants-in-aid for maternity and infant hygiene under the Sheppard-Towner Act of 1921. This activity, however, lapsed in 1929 when Congress failed to continue necessary appropriations.

Prevailing doctrine was hostile to public relief, which was denounced as lending itself to political corruption and as creating an undesirable obligation of state support. It was widely felt that it was preferable to rely on the established private charity societies, and many leaders in social work joined in the protest against "socializing" relief. Yet despite these protests, the trend toward public relief was already clearly apparent in the two decades before 1929.[3] In 1928, 71.6 per cent of all relief granted in fifteen important cities came from public funds.[4]

The Effect of the Great Depression

The 1929 depression induced a remarkable change of attitude toward public relief. As unemployment soared from four million in January, 1930, to eight million in the spring of 1931, and then to thirteen million in the winter of 1932–1933, the very magnitude of the catastrophe dispelled the notion that the victims were in any personal sense responsible for their plight. Mounting need

[2] The Arizona old age assistance law of 1915 was declared unconstitutional. *Board of Control of the State of Arizona* v. *Buckstegge*, 18 Ariz. 277, 158 Pac. 837 (1916).
[3] See Anne E. Geddes, *Trend in Relief Expenditures, 1910–1935*, Division of Social Research, Works Progress Administration.
[4] Josephine C. Brown, *Public Relief 1929–1939* (1940), p. 55.

forced increasing resort to government to provide relief.

At first, private charities tried to carry the increased load. But they were swamped by applications for aid, and their funds did not begin to meet the demands made upon them. By the summer of 1931, they were calling for public relief. But President Hoover's Emergency Committee for Employment, appointed in October, 1930, had taken the position that relief needs should be met locally, as far as possible through private agencies. While it called upon industry to "spread the work" and "give a job," unemployment continued to mount, and many local governments were hard pressed to bear the relief burdens thrust upon them. They called increasingly for state aid. As local funds became exhausted, the pressure to invoke the broader borrowing and taxing powers of the states became difficult to resist. In 1931, state governments began to act, and by May, 1933, twenty-two states had appropriated funds for unemployment relief.

The demand for federal relief, meanwhile, became more insistent. Hoover continued to assert that relief was primarily a local responsibility, but largely as a result of congressional initiative, some federal assistance was forthcoming. During the winter of 1930–1931 federal emergency relief was made available in drought-stricken areas, and an effort was made to accelerate federal public works. In February, 1932, as the crisis worsened, Congress authorized Red Cross distribution of government-owned wheat and cotton to the needy. In July, 1932, the Emergency Relief and Construction Act was passed. This was a major, but still inadequate, effort to provide for the unemployed. A total of $300 million was appropriated for federal public works, and the Reconstruction Finance Corporation was authorized to lend up to $1.5 billion to states, local governments, and in some instances, private corporations, for revenue-producing or self-liquidating projects. As a result of the self-liquidating requirements and the high interest rates charged, relatively few loans were made. The Act also authorized the RFC to make $300 million available to state and local governments for relief, but required that the grants be in the form of loans to cities and counties, or advances to the states to be deducted from future grants-in-aid for highway construction. Because of these conditions, state and local governments were slow to act. Hoover was still reluctant to recognize any federal responsibility to provide subsidies for the relief of unemployment. The hopes of the administration fastened on a "natural" business recovery which failed to develop.

3. New Deal Relief and Public Works Programs

Under the New Deal, a different conception of the role of government emerged. Federal leadership was given to a many-sided effort to develop a new welfare program. Until 1935, emergency conditions prevailed. Chief reliance was on direct relief, supplemented by a public works program. After 1935, the federal government attempted to stabilize its responsibilities on a different basis. It undertook to provide work for a large portion of the able-bodied unemployed, to supply grants-in-aid to the states to assist them in caring for the aged, the blind, and dependent children, but otherwise to limit its activities in the field of direct relief as far as possible. The residual groups in need of relief, particularly the so-called "unemployables," were to become the primary responsibility of local and state governments. At the same time, through the Social Security Act of 1935 and related legislation, measures were taken to provide old age insurance and unemployment compensation and to deal with the problem of security on a more permanent basis.

One of the first acts of the New Deal was the establishment in April, 1933, of the Civilian Conservation Corps (CCC). An initial allotment of $300 million was made to provide work camps for several hundred thousand youths from families on relief. Work consisted largely of forest protection, park developments, and soil conservation projects. The federal government undertook to provide each enrollee with subsistence and a monthly wage of $30, of which $25 had to be remitted to his family. The program won widespread approval and was later expanded.

In May, 1933, the Federal Emergency Relief Act (FERA) made $500 million available for direct relief. Half of this sum was distributed to the states on a matching basis of $1 in federal funds for each $3 of public relief expended in the states. The other half went in outright grants to those states whose needs were so great and whose funds were so exhausted that the matching provisions could not be met.[5]

In June, 1933, the Public Works Administration (PWA) was established, with appropriations of $3.3 billion. Through a rapid expansion of "pump-priming" public works expenditures, the administration hoped to stimulate a great increase in direct and

---

[5] While the main emphasis was on federal-state co-operation, in six states, where efforts to agree on reasonable relief standards failed, the President authorized the federal administrative agency to expend the federal funds directly.

indirect employment. The PWA program included three types of projects: (1) those undertaken directly by federal agencies; (2) those undertaken by state or local bodies, which were to be financed in part by grants and in part by loans; and (3) those undertaken by railroads and financed by loans. The program, however, moved with unexpected slowness. Absence of advance planning and legal and economic barriers encountered by state and local governments in working out their projects delayed action, and by the fall of the year the program was still largely in its preparatory stages.

As a result, the Civil Works Administration (CWA) was hurriedly improvised in November to provide quick employment in the form of work relief. It was a wholly federal enterprise. Work projects were chosen primarily with a view to speedy increases in employment, and wages were paid at "standard rates" for a 30-hour work week. Initially, $400 million was allotted from the PWA fund; in February, 1934, an additional appropriation of $550 million was made to carry the program through the winter. At the height of the program, over four million workers were employed, but available funds were soon exhausted, and criticism of CWA projects mounted. By April, 1934, the program was practically terminated.

After the liquidation of the CWA, readjustments became necessary. Since PWA employment at its peak, reached in mid-1934, amounted only to about 600,000, further measures were necessary. The FERA relief program took up much of the slack. In addition, some of the abandoned CWA programs were resumed through an Emergency Works Program, which employed about two million men from the relief rolls, paying them on the basis of their families' relief needs.

On January 4, 1935, President Roosevelt's annual message to Congress outlined a new relief program. There were then about five million families and single people on emergency relief rolls. Of these, one and a half million were deemed "unemployables," people who for one reason or another would be dependent on outside assistance even in normal times. Roosevelt suggested that this group become the primary responsibility of local communities, with special assistance for certain categories to be made available through federal grants-in-aid to the states. He then proposed that the federal government assume responsibility for giving useful work to the three and a half million "employables." The Emergency Relief Appropriation Act of 1935 incorporated the President's suggestions. The $4.8 billion it appropriated were used to liquidate the FERA program, to provide further funds for the PWA, and to finance a newly created Works Progress Administration (WPA) to provide work for "employables."

For the remainder of the depression period, the WPA assumed the major burden of providing work relief. It hired unemployed workers certified as in need of relief, but in contrast to the FERA work-relief program, it paid them a fixed "security wage" instead of sums adjusted to family needs. This "security wage" varied with skill and locality and ranged from $19 to $94 a month. In 1939, sectional wage differences were reduced, and the minimum monthly wage was raised to $31.20. At first, hourly wages were below locally prevailing wages, but in 1935, after vigorous protests from organized labor, hours of work were reduced to bring the hourly wage up to the prevailing rate. In 1939, however, a work month of 130 hours was prescribed, thereby lowering hourly wages. WPA projects varied with the skills available and were chosen with an eye to minimum expenditures on materials.[6]

Employment on WPA projects reached an initial peak of slightly over three million in February, 1936, and then began to taper off. As a result of the 1937 recession, WPA employment mounted to a new peak of 3,346,000 in October, 1938, but with business improvement the next year, WPA appropriations were sharply curtailed, and the program was terminated early in World War II. Because of inadequate appropriations the WPA program never fully achieved its goal of relieving state and local agencies of all responsibility for employables. Discontinuance of FERA support for direct relief at the end of 1935 imposed a heavy burden on local authorities. A period of confusion, inadequate funds, and considerable suffering ensued. Although general relief appropriations by states and localities later increased, running at some $450 million a year for the period 1936–1939, average monthly benefits showed wide variations in different states and localities. In December, 1939, for example, the average amount distributed monthly per relief case varied from $2.91 in Mississippi to $36.43 in New York.[7]

Meanwhile, however, the federal government still bore some of the load of direct relief. Emergency relief to farmers, begun under

[6] In order of decreasing expenditures, the major types of WPA projects were: highways, roads, and streets; professional and service projects; public buildings; sewer systems and other utilities; parks and other recreational facilities; sewing projects; conservation; and sanitation. A. W. Macmahon, John Millett, and Gladys Ogburn, *The Administration of Federal Work Relief* (1941), p. 6.
[7] *Social Security Bulletin*, February, 1940.

the FERA, was continued by the Resettlement Administration and its successor organization, the Farm Security Administration. At the peak of the program early in 1937, about 300,000 farmers were receiving relief payments in addition to other aid.[8] Surplus farm commodities were also distributed to relief clients through state and local welfare agencies and, beginning in 1939, by means of the Food Stamp Plan.[9] In fiscal 1939, two billion pounds of surplus farm commodities were distributed to some three million families.

4. The Social Security System

While the New Deal was thus responding to the emergency demands of the Great Depression, it was also seeking through the Social Security Act of 1935 to provide a more balanced, long-term welfare program. One part of this legislation, providing for various public-assistance programs, involved no new principle; it simply expanded federal aid to the states for the benefit of particular categories of the needy. The novel contribution of the 1935 Act was its initiation of *insurance* programs, with the hope that they would eliminate much of the need for *assistance* programs. Insurance, unlike assistance, does not connote charity and so involves a quite different welfare policy.

Public-Assistance Programs

The Social Security Act of 1935 greatly broadened the federal obligation to provide public assistance to defined categories of needy persons. It provided for federal co-operation in state plans for public assistance to the needy aged, the needy blind, and dependent children, to be administered by the Social Security Board (now Social Security Administration). The Act also extended federal aid to the states for various health and welfare services and for vocational rehabilitation.[10]

---

[8] See above, pp. 138–146.

[9] See above, p. 137.

[10] These aids have been further extended by other legislation and are administered by various agencies of the Department of Health, Education, and Welfare. The Office of Vocational Rehabilitation makes grants to the states on a matching basis for programs designed to make physically disabled and handicapped people self-supporting. The Public Health Service makes grants in-aid for a variety of state public health programs and facilities, including programs to combat particular diseases. The Children's Bureau, now under the Social Security Administration, administers grants to the states for three programs: maternal and child health, services for crippled children, and child-

Of the programs administered by the Social Security Administration's Bureau of Public Assistance, aid to the blind has been the least important in terms of cost. At the end of fiscal 1957, there were 108,400 people receiving total government aid of $87 million, of which the federal share was $41 million. The federal government contributes four-fifths of the first $30 paid to each recipient and at least half (65 per cent for those states whose per capita incomes are below the national average) of any additional payments up to a maximum of $65 per month. In addition, as is the case in all such assistance programs, the federal government pays one-half of the costs of state and local administration. In 1957, the national average monthly payment under this program was $63.87. Payments, however, varied greatly from state to state, ranging from $37.77 in West Virginia to $116.78 in Washington.[11]

Another relatively small assistance program initiated in 1950 authorizes the Social Security Administration to make matching grants to the states to provide help for permanently and totally disabled needy adults. In 1957, there were 283,900 recipients of such aid. Total governmental expenditures were $211 million, of which the federal share, computed on the same basis as for the blind, was $109 million. The national average monthly payment was $59.10, covering a state range from $24.60 in Mississippi to $116.91 in Connecticut.[12]

Aid to dependent children is given on a more extensive scale. Here the federal contribution is $14 of the first $17 payment per child per month, plus half of any additional payments up to $32 for the first child and $21 for each additional child in the same family. At the end of 1957, there were 647,200 families receiving aid for 1,831,900 children. Total governmental expenditures were $776 million, of which the federal contribution was $443 million. The national average monthly assistance payment was $96.52 per family. Family payments in the states ranged from an average of

welfare services. Some indication of the scope of these programs and of their growth over the years is afforded by a comparison of their 1935 authorizations and their 1957 expenditures:

Program	1935	1957
Vocational Rehabilitation	$1,938,000	$ 36,053,000
Public Health	8,000,000	131,091,000
Maternal and Child Health	3,800,000	14,913,000
Services for Crippled Children	2,850,000	14,845,000
Child Welfare Services	1,500,000	7,920,000

[11] Secretary of Health, Education, and Welfare, *Annual Report, 1957*, pp. 40–41, 79.

[12] *Ibid.*

$28.18 in Mississippi to $150.12 in Wisconsin.[13]

In terms of expenditures and in numbers of recipients, old age assistance is still the most important form of public assistance, although it is slowly being replaced by old age insurance. At the end of 1934, just before passage of the Social Security Act, twenty-eight states had statutes providing for old age assistance. "In only 10 states, however, was this program state-wide in operation, and in three states the old-age assistance law was entirely inoperative because of lack of funds." [14] Pensions actually paid were grossly inadequate. The average monthly pension in North Dakota was 69 cents, in Nebraska, $1.22, and in Indiana, $4.50. More than half the states paid pensions of less than $10 a month.[15] Meanwhile, organized pressure for special provisions for the aged was intensifying. Led by its founder, Dr. Francis Townsend, the Townsend Movement, with its promise of $200 a month for all persons over 60, attracted extraordinary support among the old and "near-old," and petitions and letters poured in by the thousands calling upon Congress to adopt the Townsend Plan.

While this plan was not adopted, the Social Security Act as finally enacted provided two types of support for the aged—one, a national scheme for compulsory old age insurance, which, however, was not to begin to provide annuities until 1942; and the other, a system of matched grants to finance state plans for old age assistance, which could go into effect immediately. Under the latter, the federal contribution was originally limited to $15 a month per individual. State plans for old age assistance had to provide aid to persons 65 years of age or older and meet other conditions prescribed by the Act. The states were quick to qualify under the law, and by September, 1938, every state and territory eligible for grants was administering old age assistance under plans approved by the Social Security Board. In 1957, two and a half million people received $1.8 billion in old age assistance payments, of which the federal share was $1 billion.[16]

Over the years there has been substantial political support for an expansion of these benefits. In 1939, for example, there was a strong revival of support for the Townsend Plan. Although it was voted down in the House by a 3 to 1 majority, the movement had

[13] Ibid.

[14] Social Security Bulletin (November, 1940), p. 67.

[15] H. A. Millis and R. E. Montgomery, Labor's Risks and Social Insurance, Vol. II of The Economics of Labor (1938), p. 381.

[16] Secretary of Health, Education, and Welfare, Annual Report, 1957, pp. 77–79.

some effect in stimulating a liberalization of benefits in that year. When increases in the federal contribution for old age assistance have been under consideration, the richer states have regularly pressed for increasing federal grants on a matched basis. The poorer states, unable to scrape together the funds with which to match and take full advantage of available federal grants, have asked the federal government to pay a higher proportion of the total.

The present formula for federal contributions represents a compromise between these two opposing views. Identical with that for assistance to the blind, it provides for federal payment of four-fifths of monthly benefits up to $30 plus half of any additional benefits up to a maximum of $65. Beginning in 1958, the federal share of these additional benefits was increased to 65 per cent for those states with per capita incomes below the national average. As a result, disparities in old age assistance payments among the states are smaller than they were in the early years of the program, but they are still striking. At the end of fiscal 1957, the national average monthly payment was $58.66, but the average in Mississippi was only $28.67, while Washington paid $94.15.[17] Moreover, while federal law establishes residence and age requirements for state programs, states are free to employ their own tests of need. Some apply means tests rigidly and require relatives to bear much of the burden; others are more liberal in dispensing benefits. Within states where local governments share the costs and help administer the program there often is considerable variation in standards from one locality to another.

The role of the federal government in financing public-assistance programs has become increasingly important. In June, 1957, there were 5.9 million people, or 3.4 per cent of the total civilian population, receiving public assistance. Total governmental expenditures for assistance payments in 1957 were just under $3 billion, of which the federal government provided slightly over $1.5 billion. These welfare payments would be much more sizable were it not for the expanding social insurance programs. Both the young and the old, who account for most of the assistance needs, represent a much larger proportion of the total population than they did two decades ago. While insurance can be expected to meet many needs formerly covered by assistance, it can never fully displace assistance programs. The need for aid to the young arises from situations which for the most part are not covered by the old age and survivors insurance program or the provisions for unemploy-

[17] *Ibid.*, p. 40.

ment compensation. And some of the old will continue to depend on public assistance either because they are ineligible for the insurance program or because the benefits to which they are entitled fall short of meeting their needs. At present, about one-fourth of all old age assistance recipients obtain such aid to supplement inadequate old age insurance benefits.

Old Age and Survivors Insurance

Until the mid-thirties, American legislation to provide security for old age lagged behind that of most other industrial nations, despite a steady growth in the number and proportion of aged people. In 1900, the 3,080,000 people aged 65 and over constituted 4.1 per cent of the population. In 1930 the 6,634,000 people in this age group made up 5.4 per cent of the population. In 1956, people 65 or older numbered 14,700,000, or 8.5 per cent of the population. Before old age insurance, the great majority were dependent for their support on others. In 1939, it was estimated that "approximately 65 per cent of all persons aged sixty-five and over are wholly or partially dependent on public or private social agencies and two-thirds on friends and relatives." [18]

The Social Security Act of 1935 attempted to deal with the problem by establishing a national system of old age insurance. Through a contributory scheme which related benefits to contributions, protection was made available as a matter of right, without the use of a means test.[19] The objective was to prevent future old age dependency on the part of persons covered by the program, while old age assistance protected needy persons who were already old or who would become old without the opportunity to benefit from the insurance program.

The 1935 Act covered about two-thirds of the privately employed population. Since then, coverage has been extended until it now includes, or is available to, about nine-tenths of all persons in paid employment in the continental United States. In 1957, about 75 million workers were covered.[20] Protection now extends

[18] Statement of A. J. Altmeyer, Chairman of the Social Security Board, Senate Committee on Finance, *Hearings on Social Security Amendments*, 76th Cong., 1st sess. (1939), p. 35.

[19] In order to ensure constitutionality, receipts for taxes levied under the Act were to go into general funds and benefits to be paid by appropriation. But a 1939 amendment provided for automatic appropriations into the trust fund of an amount equaling the tax receipts. The Act's constitutionality was upheld in *Helvering v. Davis*, 301 U.S. 619 (1937).

[20] An additional 1.5 million people are protected by the Railroad Retirement Acts.

to members of the armed forces and is available on a group-election basis to employees of state and local governments and of nonprofit organizations. It is also available to the self-employed. Of the workers not covered, about one-third are included in various federal, state, or local programs for government employees. The remaining two-thirds, or about 6 per cent of all employees, are ineligible. They consist principally of self-employed persons with annual net earnings of less than $400, doctors, farm workers who earn less than $100 a year from any one employer, and domestic workers who earn less than $50 a quarter from any one employer.

To finance the system, the 1935 Act imposed taxes on all covered employees and their employers. Initially, employers and employees each paid taxes of 1 per cent on all wages and salaries under $3,000 a year. The tax rate was scheduled to be increased over the years, reaching a maximum of 3 per cent in 1949. In fact, Congress raised the rates more slowly than was originally contemplated. Arguments that these taxes were regressive and deflationary in their effects played some part in early decisions to delay tax increases, but the main reason then and later seems to have been a natural reluctance to increase the tax burden of a vast majority of the public. In 1958, the tax rate for the next year on employer and employee was raised to $2\frac{1}{2}$ per cent on earnings up to $4,800 a year. The self-employed, for whom there are no matching payments by employers, pay a tax of $3\frac{3}{4}$ per cent.[21] Under the 1958 law, the tax on employers and employees is scheduled to reach $4\frac{1}{2}$ per cent in 1969, and that on the self-employed, $6\frac{3}{4}$ per cent.

The structure of benefits provided by the amended act represents a compromise between the private insurance principle of adjusting benefit payments to individual contributions and the broader social principle of determining benefit payments on the basis of need. Benefits are paid to retired workers, and to their wives, dependent children, and survivors. Retired workers become eligible at the age of 65.[22] They may then continue to earn up to $1,200 a year without losing their old age benefits. For each $80 earned in excess of $1,200, they lose one month's benefits. No earnings test is applied after they reach the age of 72. To be fully insured, a worker must have been engaged in employment covered by the system for at least: (a) forty quarters; or (b) one-half of

---

[21] Of these tax rates, $\frac{1}{4}$ of 1 per cent on employees and employers, and $\frac{3}{8}$ of 1 per cent on the self-employed, are imposed to establish a reserve for the disability payments discussed below.

[22] Women have the option of retiring at the age of 62, but any such retirement before the age of 65 involves actuarially-reduced benefit payments.

the quarters between 1950 and his retirement or death, subject to a minimum requirement of six quarters of coverage; or (c) all of the quarters between 1954 and his retirement or death, again subject to a minimum requirement of six quarters of coverage.

The retirement benefits to which a worker is entitled, his "primary insurance amount," is equal to 66 per cent of the first $50 of his average monthly earnings, plus declining percentages of the next $350.[23] Under this formula, monthly retirement benefits range from $33 to $127. Substantial benefits also accrue to the worker's family. When his wife reaches the age of 65, she receives benefit payments equal to one-half of her husband's primary insurance amount.[24] Dependent children under 18 receive the same benefit subject to a general limitation of $254.10 on the total benefits received by any one family.[25] The widow of an insured worker receives benefits equal to three-fourths of her husband's benefit upon reaching the age of 62. A widow with dependent children immediately receives payments equal to three-fourths of her husband's primary insurance amount, and the first dependent child receives a like amount. If there is more than one child, each receives half of the primary insurance amount plus one-fourth of this amount divided by the number of children. If a worker does not leave a widow or dependent children, each parent dependent upon him at the time of his death is entitled to three-fourths of his primary insurance amount. Finally, a lump sum payment, equal to three times a worker's primary insurance amount, but not exceeding $255, may be made to relatives or friends for payment of his burial expenses.

These provisions reflect a series of amendments which have liberalized the benefits conferred by the 1935 Act. The changes introduced have been designed to protect the whole family, rather than just the individual worker, from economic dependence in old age or from the loss of the family provider. Within a framework of basic rules of eligibility, amendments also have eliminated length of covered employment as a determinant of benefits, thereby penalizing workers who are covered for all of their working lives in order to provide full benefits to late-comers. Moreover, minima have been increased by a greater relative amount than have

[23] A "dropout" rule permits the omission from this computation of five years of low earnings, unemployment, or employment not covered by old age insurance.

[24] She has the same option of early retirement as the woman worker.

[25] Beginning in 1957, disabled children who are unable to work because of some permanent physical or mental impairment may continue to receive social security benefits after reaching the age of 18.

maxima.[26] Consequently, the lower-paid worker receives a greater return from the taxes paid on his income than does the higher-paid worker.

In 1956, disability insurance benefits were incorporated within the social security system, taking effect in July, 1957. Totally disabled workers between the ages of 50 and 65 who meet specified work and disability standards can receive monthly benefits under the old age and survivors insurance program. Workers must be fully insured and must also have had twenty quarters of coverage in the ten years immediately before the beginning of disability. An additional tax of ¼ of 1 per cent each on employer and employee, and of ⅜ of 1 per cent on the self-employed, maintains a special trust fund for this program. It is administered in close relationship with the vocational rehabilitation program. By mid-1957, some 273,000 workers had been awarded disability benefits, and 234,000 had been denied them.

The old age insurance program inaugurated by the 1935 Act greatly expanded the welfare role of the federal government. It involved a broad assault on the general problem of old age security, and it sought to substitute insurance for charity. Its coverage now extends to nine-tenths of all workers. Of the 14.7 million people aged 65 or over at the end of 1956, 62 per cent were eligible for old age benefits; 47 per cent were actually receiving them, and 15 per cent were not because they or their husbands were still earning substantial income. The percentage of those eligible will rise, exceeding 70 per cent by 1970, as recent extensions of coverage take full effect. Liberalizing and broadening amendments have been sponsored by both Democratic and Republican administrations. This once-controversial New Deal program has now been retired from partisan politics. Nonetheless, important policy issues remain, and the problem of old-age insecurity cannot yet be regarded as fully solved.

The most immediate problem involves the size of the benefits. Despite the fact that the system favors those with low incomes and with brief coverage, in 1957 average benefits for a retired worker with no dependents were only $59.90 a month. For a retired worker and his wife, the average was $107.80; for a widow and two dependent children, it was $144.60.[27] Even the maximum pay-

---

[26] This trend was reversed by the 1958 amendments, which raised minimum monthly benefits for an individual worker from $30 to $33, but maximum benefits from $108.50 to $127. The combined effect of changes since 1935, however, has been to increase minima by greater percentages.

[27] Secretary of Health, Education, and Welfare, *Annual Report, 1957*, p. 25.

ments, which are $127 for a single individual, $190.50 for a retired couple, and $254.10 for a widow with two or more dependent children, do not suffice to purchase more than the barest necessities. Since the minimum payments are still very small, it is not surprising that 555,000 beneficiaries also required old age assistance in 1957. Even then, their average monthly benefits from both sources averaged only $48.[28]

To some extent, the social security program has been supplemented in recent years by the spread of private pension schemes. Insurance companies have enjoyed great success since World War II in selling pension programs to individuals and to companies. And the concentration of many labor unions on bargaining for "fringe benefits" in the 1950's has brought about the adoption and expansion of many corporation and industry pension plans. As a result, an individual worker may have, in addition to his social security privileges, corporation, individual, union, military, or government employee pension rights. The sum of these various programs provides an adequate retirement income for many. To increase social security benefits, and presumably taxes, would in these cases mean an unnecessary and costly displacement of apparently satisfactory, and for the most part private, schemes. But the beneficiaries of private programs are largely concentrated in the better-paying occupations and professions and in union-organized industries. Consequently, a failure to increase social security benefits may mean that a high proportion of workers in low-paying occupations, such as farming and domestic labor, will still be dependent upon private or public assistance. In this respect, even an insurance program with broad coverage will not eliminate the need for a substantial assistance program.

Another major problem centers on the future cost of the system. The 1935 Act contemplated the establishment of reserves comparable to those of private insurance companies. But in later amendments, Congress held taxes below the levels required to create a reserve which would provide full coverage for risks. Accordingly, present arrangements represent a compromise between a reserve-backed insurance scheme and a "pay-as-you go" program.[29] At mid-1957, the reserve fund totaled $23 billion, invested

[28] *Ibid.*, p. 41.

[29] The difference is partly semantic. The Trust Fund is not fully comparable to that of a private insurance company. Tax receipts in excess of benefit payments and of administrative costs are invested in interest-bearing government bonds. When benefits and costs exceed tax receipts, then the Fund must be drawn upon by withdrawing the interest receipts or by cashing in the bonds. In either case, the government must then obtain the funds to be paid

in government securities bearing an average interest rate of 2½ per cent.[30] Because of recent increases in the size of benefits and more generous eligibility arrangements, expenditures almost equaled receipts in fiscal 1957, and the Old Age and Survivors Trust Fund enjoyed only a modest growth. Expenditures totaled $6,723 million, and tax receipts were $6,540 million. An interest credit of $561 million on the bonds in the Trust Fund accounted for the surplus. It was anticipated that the Trust Fund would shrink from mid-1957 to 1959, whereupon new tax increases going into effect were expected to replenish the Fund.[31]

Despite some tardiness in raising tax rates, Congress has repeatedly expressed its desire that the insurance program be self-supporting. The current reserve falls far short of what a private insurance company following normal actuarial practices would have to maintain, but government insurance programs are usually less conservative than private ones. The actuarial soundness of the reserve and of current and scheduled tax rates is difficult to determine. It involves many uncertainties, including the proportion of people who will choose to remain at work rather than retire, future mortality rates, the interest rate, and future levels of earnings. Prior to the passage of the 1958 amendments, which raised both taxes and benefits, actuarial cost estimates, assuming an interest rate of 2.6 per cent and earnings at the levels prevailing in 1955, indicated the level-premium cost of old age and survivors benefits to be 7.43 per cent of covered payroll. The level contribution rate, based on the pre-1958 schedule of tax increases, was 7.23 per cent of covered payroll, leaving a small actuarial deficiency.[32]

The closeness of this actuarial balance and the uncertainty of its many assumptions mean that future policy-makers will face difficult problems. Current tax schedules call for an ultimate combined employee's and employer's tax of 9 per cent (including disability insurance) on payrolls. As the proportion of aged in the population continues to mount, both the total size of benefits and the political pressure for further increases will grow. Workers with many years of coverage may well press for greater benefits to differ-

out by selling other bonds elsewhere or out of general tax revenues. Thus, in this case, as well as in a pay-as-you-go system, the ability of the government to pay the benefits to which it is committed rests upon its tax revenues and credit.

[30] The newly established Disability Trust Fund totaled $337 million.

[31] Secretary of Health, Education, and Welfare, *op. cit.*, p. 73; Bureau of the Budget, *Budget of the U.S., 1959*, pp. 827–828.

[32] Secretary of Health, Education, and Welfare, *op. cit.*, pp. 37–38. The disability insurance program showed a small actuarial surplus.

entiate them from those whose contributions have extended over only a few years. But if benefits are substantially raised, then retirement will be encouraged, further increasing total costs and necessitating additional tax increases. The demand for a sharp increase in taxes is likely to precipitate a serious conflict of interest between the actively employed and the retired. The adjustment of these divergent interests does not promise to be easy and will find its inevitable reflection in the politics of tomorrow.

Unemployment Compensation

Just as the Social Security Act of 1935 attempted to replace assistance with insurance in providing security for the aged, so it sought to substitute insurance for some of the relief and public works programs used to combat unemployment.

Unemployment compensation seeks to provide a measure of security by building up reserve funds through taxes during periods of high employment and by drawing on those funds to pay out benefits to workers in periods of unemployment. These payments must be distinguished from relief. Benefits are paid as a matter of right rather than as charity and without resort to a means test. Benefits, however, are available to eligible individuals only for a limited period of time. If a protected worker exhausts the benefits to which he is entitled without finding a job, he may be forced to go on relief. Unemployment compensation systems thus deal with problems of short-run rather than long-run unemployment. They may help to tide workers over temporary periods of unemployment and moderate recession. They also may help to even out cyclical fluctuations by adding to purchasing power in depressed periods and serving as a restraint in periods of expansion and boom.[33] Given a prolonged crisis of mass unemployment, however, these systems would have to be supplemented by relief and public works.

Although Britain adopted a system of unemployment compensation in 1912, and other industrial nations soon followed her example, serious American interest did not develop until the Great Depression. Prior to that time, there had been some local experimentation with voluntary plans by particular firms, unions, and industries. But workers covered by them were probably not more than 1 per cent of all wage earners.

With the prolonged depression of the 1930's, pressure for government action grew rapidly. In 1932, Wisconsin enacted the first state unemployment compensation law. Other states began to study proposals. In 1932, the AFL abandoned its traditional opposi-

---

[33] But see p. 810, below.

tion to government unemployment insurance, and now approved it. The movement came to a head with the appointment of the President's Committee on Economic Security, charged with formulating a plan for submittal to Congress. Fears of unconstitutionality and a desire to permit states to experiment with different schemes led the Committee to reject a national plan. But it was also unwilling to leave unemployment compensation exclusively to the states. It felt that progress would be slow and uncertain because of the likelihood that some states would fail to take action and others would hold back out of a desire to avoid the assumption of heavy competitive burdens. Accordingly, the Committee decided in favor of a system of federal-state co-operation.

As finally enacted by Congress, the Social Security Act of 1935 provided a tax-offset plan designed to promote action by the states in accordance with certain minimum standards rather than to prescribe the provisions of state plans in detail.[34] A federal tax was levied on the payrolls of all covered employers with eight or more employees.[35] The tax was fixed at the rate of 1 per cent in 1936, 2 per cent in 1937, and 3 per cent thereafter. A credit of up to 90 per cent of this tax was allowed to employers who pay taxes into state unemployment funds under state laws which meet the standards prescribed by the federal act.[36] State funds are deposited in the Unemployment Trust Fund in the federal Treasury, where they are invested in government bonds. A separate account is maintained for each state, from which it may draw to make benefit payments. Benefits must be paid through public employment offices or some other federally-approved agency.

Out of the 10 per cent of the tax retained by the federal government, grants are made to support the administration of state unemployment compensation laws. To qualify for these grants, states must meet certain administrative requirements, since 1939 including a merit system for their administrative personnel, the opportunity of a fair hearing before an impartial tribunal for anyone

[34] The plan was held constitutional by the Supreme Court, in a 5 to 4 decision, in *Steward Machine Co.* v. *Davis*, 301 U.S. 548 (1937). On the same day the constitutionality of state unemployment compensation laws was also upheld in *Carmichael* v. *Southern Coal and Coke Co.*, 301 U.S. 495.

[35] In 1939, the Act was amended to exempt all wages over $3,000 a year from payment of the payroll tax.

[36] States cannot deny unemployment benefits to eligible unemployed workers who refused to fill vacancies due to a labor dispute. Nor can such workers be required to accept wages, hours, or other conditions of work substantially less favorable than those prevailing for similar work in the community, or employment conditioned on joining a company union or resigning or refraining from joining a bona fide labor organization.

whose claim for compensation is denied, and various prescriptions as to administrative expenses. Thus, while the states actually administer the program, the federal government sets the standards, brings about the levying of the taxes, and handles the reserve funds.

Since taxes paid by employers in states failing to enact laws would have gone into the federal Treasury, the tax-offset device proved extraordinarily effective in stimulating state action. Within two years of the passage of the Social Security Act, all the states had enacted legislation. As with the old-age insurance program, one mark of the popularity of unemployment compensation is that its coverage has been repeatedly extended. The federal law now covers all firms with four or more employees for twenty weeks in the year and almost half the states have extended coverage to smaller firms. It also includes civilian employees of the federal government and veterans who served in the armed forces between June 27, 1950, and January 31, 1955; annual federal appropriations are made for these groups. A separate federal program covers railroad workers. The principal exceptions, in addition to firms hiring fewer than four workers, are farm laborers, employees of state and local governments, domestic servants, employees of nonprofit organizations, and the self-employed.[37] In 1957, over two-thirds of the civilian labor force was protected by unemployment insurance, 40.3 million workers being covered by state laws and 2.4 million federal civilian employees being insured by federal provisions.[38]

States were permitted considerable leeway in working out the details of their programs. One of the first and most controversial issues involved the type of state fund to be established. Under the law, states might adopt pooled funds, under which all taxes were paid into a single reserve from which all benefits were also paid, or they might establish a separate reserve account for each employer, available only for the payment of benefits to his employees. Most employers, particularly those with good employment records, preferred the latter scheme, while organized labor, apparently with some unofficial backing from the Social Security Board, insisted upon pooled funds. Even though employer-reserve plans require that the tax rate on an employer be raised when his reserve falls below a certain point, there is the danger that his reserve will be depleted, leaving his employees with no benefits. Accordingly, all

---

[37] These are the exceptions under federal law. Many states, however, include workers in some of these categories.

[38] Department of Labor, *Annual Report, 1957*, p. 117.

but two of the states finally adopted pooled funds, thus spreading the risk and assuring all eligible unemployed workers of benefits as long as any funds remain in the state's pool.

Employers, however, continued their criticism. Simple pooled funds, they argued, impose the same taxes on all employers, regardless of whether they have good or bad employment records. Nor do they provide any incentive for an employer to prevent unemployment. To meet these objections, most states now follow merit-rating systems by which tax rates on individual employers are adjusted according to their unemployment experience. If the system meets federal standards, tax rates may be set below the 2.7 per cent level. Indeed, since World War II they have averaged well under 1.5 per cent. In rare cases, employers with poor records may have to pay higher than standard rates, usually not exceeding 4 per cent. To the extent that merit rating is applied, a pooled fund comes to resemble an employer-reserve plan. Labor has usually opposed merit rating both because of the lower average tax rates, and hence smaller reserve funds, and because it believes that unemployment ought to be treated as a social risk and that any attempt to allocate responsibility for unemployment to individual employers is likely to be futile and harmful to labor's interests.

While states vary greatly in their methods of computing benefits, especially maxima and minima, average benefits fall into a fairly well defined range. Eligibility is dependent on a short waiting period (one week in most states), earnings of a specified amount in the previous year, and legitimate reasons for unemployment. To encourage the unemployed to take part-time employment, most states pay benefits for partial unemployment. Maximum weekly benefits range from $24 to $45 for a maximum period of from 16 to 30 weeks. The populous, industrial states have the most liberal benefits. Seventy per cent of the workers live in thirty-two states which pay a maximum of $30 or more. Seventy-five per cent live in twenty-seven states with benefit periods extending for 26 or more weeks. Benefits have been considerably liberalized over the years. In 1955 alone, for example, twenty-one states increased maximum benefits. In 1939, the average weekly benefit was $10.66; by 1957, it had increased to $27.53, or about one-third of average weekly wages in covered employment. The average potential duration of benefits was raised from 17.8 weeks in 1946 to 22.5 weeks in 1955.[39]

The Unemployment Trust Fund totaled $9 billion at mid-1957,

[39] Department of Labor, *op. cit.*, pp. 117–122; *The American Worker's Fact Book* (1956), pp. 282, 287.

and state reserves have thus far been sufficient to meet all of the demands made upon them. They have tided substantial numbers of unemployed over short periods of unemployment. Thus, in fiscal 1946, benefits totaling $1,091 million, covering 59 million weeks of unemployment, helped to soften the impact of the shift from a war economy. At various times, however, the reserves of particular states suffering from prolonged unemployment have been drawn down substantially. At the close of 1951, Rhode Island had reserves amounting to only 3.7 per cent of payrolls, enough to finance only a little more than a year's benefits at prevailing rates. Only the imposition of a tax rate of 2.7 per cent enabled it to build up its reserves by 1957 to 4.3 per cent of payrolls, while several states had reserves sufficient to finance benefits at current rates for more than ten years and were taxing at rates of less than 1 per cent.[40]

Nationalization of the program has been urged by some as a method of spreading the risk and preventing the unemployed of any one state from losing protection because that state has been especially hard hit by unemployment. Union leaders argue the case for nationalization by criticizing the considerable variation in amount and duration of benefits which exists among the states. They fear that states may engage in a competitive race to reduce tax rates. They may also believe that Congress would fix benefits at higher levels than those set by state legislatures. Defenders of the present system argue that diversity in terms and administrative arrangements rightly reflects regional differences in employment standards, and that experimentation is thereby encouraged. Meanwhile, the prospects for nationalization appear dim, since the states have acquired a vested interest in the present system. Accordingly, the struggle over benefit levels occurs primarily within the states, although Congress has often been asked to raise the federal minimum standards to which the states must conform.

Labor also strongly questions the adequacy of the whole system of benefits in the face of a major depression. Benefit periods are so short that the program could in fact bear only a small share of the direct cost of widespread sustained unemployment.[41] The insur-

[40] I. C. Merriam, *Social Security Financing*, Federal Security Agency, Bureau Report No. 17 (1952), p. 61; Department of Labor, *Annual Report, 1957*, pp. 146–147.

[41] Even in the moderate recession of 1958, unemployment benefits expired for so many workers before they could resume their old jobs or find new ones that Congress authorized advances to the states to permit them to extend benefit periods. By July of that year, twenty states had accepted federal advances, and over half a million workers were receiving extended benefits. *New York Times*, August 2, 1958.

ance it offers is not sufficient to do away with the need for relief and public works in periods of prolonged economic crisis; hence the importance of other methods of combating unemployment through monetary and fiscal policy, discussed in the next chapter.

5. Frontiers of Welfare: Health and Education

Public Health

Government has long been concerned with various aspects of health. Local boards of health or health departments were common by the beginning of the nineteenth century. After the Civil War, state health departments were established. Late in the century, medical science began to make spectacular advances in understanding the causes of communicable diseases and the health hazards created by the growth of industries and cities. Under the leadership of the American Public Health Association, campaigns were conducted to professionalize and expand public health services. Today state and local public health agencies perform a wide array of functions, including regulation, information, and the provision of a variety of sanitary and health services.

The states, moreover, have always assumed a primary responsibility to care for the mentally ill. The task was first undertaken when it was believed to be as much government's function to protect society by confining the mentally ill as by incarcerating criminals. The high cost of medical and hospital care for these unfortunates ordinarily was beyond the means of most families, so that public institutions became the general rule. The mentally ill occupy over half of all hospital beds in the nation, and the bulk of them are in state or county institutions. States also operate hospitals for certain physical illnesses, such as tuberculosis, where treatment is prolonged and too costly for most families.

The central, and oldest, federal agency in this area is the Public Health Service, headed by the Surgeon General and now a part of the Department of Health, Education, and Welfare. It was established in 1798, as the Marine Hospital Service, to provide medical and hospital facilities for merchant seamen. Today it still provides these services, not only for merchant mariners, but also for Coast Guard personnel, Indians, federal prisoners, lepers, and drug addicts. It conducts medical examinations of immigrants and enforces quarantine regulations on travel into the country. It licenses the manufacture and interstate sale of such biological products as vaccines, serums, and toxins, seeking to guarantee their potency and freedom from contamination. Through the National Institute of Health, it engages in and sponsors research on a number of major diseases, including cancer, heart disease, and mental illness. Finally, it administers grants-in-aid to assist the states in improving their general public health programs. One of its largest grant programs is designed to promote the construction of hospitals, nursing homes, and associated diagnostic, treatment, and rehabilitation facilities. Under this program, one federal dollar is contributed for every two dollars appropriated from state and local funds. Between 1948 and mid-1957, there were authorized 3,514 hospitals and other facilities containing 153,000 beds and 824 projects for outpatient care, involving federal expenditures of $903 million.

The Veterans Administration conducts a vast program of medical care and hospitalization as part of its general responsibility for the welfare of veterans.[42] Hospitalization and inpatient care are provided to veterans with service-connected disabilities, and to the extent that facilities are available, to other veterans willing to swear that they cannot afford private facilities.[43] Outpatient medical and dental care is provided veterans with service-connected disabilities and those receiving vocational rehabilitation benefits. In fiscal 1957, $671 million was spent on the hospitalization and inpatient or domiciliary care of a daily average of 140,000 veterans, and over $81 million on outpatient treatments or examinations for 1.2 million veterans.[44]

[42] In fiscal 1957, the agency paid $1,440 million in disability benefits to slightly more than two million veterans with service-connected disabilities. It paid $435 million in death or dependency compensation benefits to 385,-000 dependents of veterans who died in service or as a result of a service-connected disability or disease. It also paid $657 million in pensions to 688,000 veterans unable to secure gainful employment as a result of a permanent, non-service-connected disability. Some 464,000 dependents of deceased veterans whose death was not due to service-connected causes, but who had had service-connected disabilities (this requirement is waived for World War I veterans), received $294 million in pensions. *Budget of the U.S., 1959*, pp. 200–202. This agency also administers various insurance programs, which cover over six million veterans. In addition, substantial benefits have been extended for education and training and for loan guaranties.

[43] The Veterans Administration is prohibited from challenging such a statement. As a result, in recent years almost twice as many beds in veterans hospitals have been occupied by those suffering from non-service-connected disabilities as from service-connected disabilities. Commission on Organization of the Executive Branch of the Government, *Federal Medical Services* (1955), p. 32. A presidential proclamation, however, denied the privilege of hospitalization for non-service-connected disabilities for veterans entering service after January 31, 1955.

[44] *Budget of the U.S., 1959*, pp. 197–200.

Federal, state, and local assistance programs also involve provisions for medical care. Those receiving categorical and general assistance include a high proportion of people suffering from physical and mental ills. Under the Social Security Act of 1935, federal assistance payments could be used to meet some costs of medical care, but only within the limits of the federal maximum monthly assistance payment. The amount of medical care was therefore limited, and it varied greatly among states and often between localities within a state. In 1950, the Act was amended to broaden authorized payments for medical care, but these still had to come within the individual assistance-payment maximum. In fiscal 1957 (before a 1956 amendment described below had taken effect), $288 million, or about 10 per cent of total governmental expenditures on categorical and general assistance, were spent for medical care. Only about a fifth of this amount came from federal funds, and only the richer states made substantial payments. Over half of the medical expenditures for the aged, for example, were made by three states—New York, Illinois, and Massachusetts.[45]

In order to increase the availability of medical care for the needy, Congress in 1956 amended the Social Security Act to permit federal sharing in medical payments outside the monthly assistance maxima. When this amendment became operative in July, 1957, thirty-five states took advantage of it, eleven providing for medical costs for the first time, and eleven expanding their existing medical care programs.

Health Insurance

Thus federal welfare activities extend deeply and broadly into the field of health. In 1955, a task force of the second Hoover Commission reported that "federal medical service is big business." In all of its aspects, including the medical branches of the armed forces, it provides thirty million people with some or all of their medical care. It involves the expenditure of over $2 billion a year, employs about 10 per cent of the nation's physicians, 9 per cent of its dentists, and 6 per cent of the graduate nurses, and it uses 13 per cent of all hospital beds.[46]

Despite this very substantial activity, all proposals for government health-insurance schemes have met with strong opposition. The case for health insurance rests on the fact that the one major threat to continuity of income for which there is now no public insurance protection is that of nonoccupational illness and acci-

[45] Secretary of Health, Education, and Welfare, *op. cit.*, pp. 43–44.
[46] *Task Force Report on Medical Services*, p. 1.

dent. Costs of illness in a worker's family are another unprotected hazard. The impact of medical costs, moreover, is highly uneven. In the average year, 92 per cent of all families require some medical care, but 11 per cent face medical bills of $500 or more, and 4 per cent have to pay hospital charges of more than $500.[47] Although private health-insurance programs, such as Blue Cross and Blue Shield, have expanded greatly, they are apt to be too expensive for those with the lowest incomes, and they usually do not cover all costs. One study, for example, found that insured patients had themselves to pay, on the average, 21 per cent of their hospital bills and 55 per cent of surgical bills.[48] Nor does the coverage of most private plans extend to extraordinary medical expenses.

In Europe, health insurance was one of the first types of social insurance to be adopted. After the passage of the British legislation of 1911, a lively movement seeking parallel action began in the United States. Bills were introduced in a number of state legislatures and commissions appointed to investigate health insurance, but powerful opposition prevented action from being taken, and attention died down. During the thirties, interest revived, and a number of expert committees supported health insurance.[49] But strong opposition from the American Medical Association (AMA) prevented its inclusion in the Social Security Act of 1935.

After World War II, President Truman championed the cause of health insurance, and the Federal Security Administrator in 1948 proposed a national program of compulsory prepaid health insurance.[50] While his proposal received support from labor organizations and liberal groups, it encountered strong opposition from private insurance companies, drug manufacturers, and a substantial part of the medical profession. The vigorous campaign waged against it by the AMA was largely instrumental in its defeat.

The issue, nevertheless, remained alive. After rejection of his plan for compulsory insurance, Truman urged that government assist in broadening the coverage of private hospital- or medical-insurance plans, which at that time extended only to about thirty million people. This proposal also made no headway. Through vigorous promotion during the next several years, the coverage of

[47] U.S. News and World Report (July 5, 1957), p. 36.

[48] Ibid.

[49] The Committee on the Costs of Medical Care, Medical Care for the American People (1932); Report to the President of the Committee on Economic Security (1935); Technical Committee on Medical Care of the Interdepartmental Committee to Co-ordinate Health and Welfare Activities, The Need for a National Health Program (1938).

[50] The Nation's Health, A Report to the President (1948).

the private plans was greatly extended, applying by 1955 to some one hundred million people, but this still left a large part of the population unprotected. In 1954, President Eisenhower in turn advanced a plan for expanded private health insurance. He recommended a federal insurance fund of $25 million to underwrite voluntary programs designed to aid low-income families and poor health risks. This plan was assailed from both sides. Supporters of public health insurance regarded it as inadequate on the ground that it would not greatly lower the cost of medical insurance to those with low incomes. Opponents of public insurance condemned it as an opening wedge. In 1955, Eisenhower offered a revised proposal calling for federal aid to provide incentives for private insurance groups to extend coverage to chronic invalids. This plan, too, was rejected.

While these insurance proposals, never very strongly backed by the administration, were all rebuffed, the President was more successful in promoting expanded federal medical services. In 1956, as we have seen, Congress approved grants-in-aid to the states to provide better medical care to persons receiving public assistance. In the same year, there was enacted a three-year, $90-million program of matching payments to finance the construction of research facilities by medical schools and other health organizations. In addition, training and advanced study programs have been initiated for nurses and for various types of professional personnel needed in state and local health agencies.

Thus, although public health insurance has not been adopted, the steady expansion of federal medical services on all other fronts continues. Private health insurance now provides much of the protection for which public insurance schemes were designed. But as medical costs rise, it remains to be seen whether private programs can provide adequate coverage for low-income families and others faced with extraordinary medical expenses. If private programs fail to do this, pressure for governmental action will mount. Because of the strong opposition to a direct general insurance program, even one supplementing private plans, it is not unlikely that such action will take the form of expanded medical payments to recipients of public assistance, a further relaxing of the means tests and other restrictions on medical aid to veterans, and other similar benefits to special groups.

Federal Aid to Education

Public education represents another area where there is strong pressure for greatly enhanced federal support. Local governments originally assumed virtually the entire financial responsibility for public education. But this burden has been growing heavier. In 1870, for example, 57 per cent of the children in the five to seventeen age group were enrolled in the public schools, with an average attendance of less than 80 days in the year. In 1952, 85 per cent were in school for an average of 178 days.[51] For the school year 1956–1957, the total costs of public elementary and secondary schools, including capital outlay, reached $12 billion. The ability of the local property tax to pay for the steadily expanding costs of education as well as most other functions of local government has been severely strained. As a result, pressure for state aid to education has built up over many decades.

By 1957, states were paying about 40 per cent of the cost of public education. But the tax resources of the states are far from unlimited, and the public school system as a whole lacks adequate funds. In 1956–1957, public school enrollment exceeded capacity by about 2.3 million children, of whom about 840,000 were on half-day schedules and the others in overcrowded classrooms or makeshift facilities. There was a shortage of 120,700 teachers, and of the 1.2 million teachers, 89,400 did not meet state standards for the lowest teaching certificate.[52] Moreover, regional variations in average income produce striking differences in the amount of education various states can provide. Thus residents of the relatively poor Southern states spend a much larger share of their income for education than do the residents of the more prosperous Northern states, yet they spend far less per child.

Accordingly, there has been mounting pressure for federal assistance. The federal government has long played a minor role in public education. The Northwest Ordinance of 1787 reserved the sixteenth section of land in every township in the Northwest Territory for education. The two Morrill Acts (1862 and 1890) assisted the states in the establishment and maintenance of colleges offering instruction in agriculture and the mechanic arts. In 1867, the Office of Education was established. It gathers facts and statistics on educational conditions, conducts research, disseminates information, and administers grant-in-aid programs. The Smith-Hughes Act of 1917 and later legislation authorized federal matching payments to the states in support of vocational education.

More recently, the Veterans Administration has operated a generous program of educational benefits. Many federal departments and agencies, including the Defense Department, the Atomic Energy Commission, and the Public Health Service, make

[51] Secretary of Health, Education, and Welfare, *Annual Report, 1954*, p. 9.
[52] *Ibid.*, 1957, pp. 160–161.

grants or contractual arrangements for scientific research in the universities. In addition, the federal government assumes responsibility for the education of children living on federal property, including Indians on public reservations.

These programs, however, do not contribute substantially to a solution of the central problem of financing locally controlled education. Accordingly, throughout the postwar period, pressure for federal aid has built up as financial need has intensified. Numerous bills have been introduced, but they have encountered frustrating obstacles. It is difficult to achieve agreement on an allocation formula. The poorer states argue that the main federal concern should be with raising standards by channeling maximum aid to those most needing it, while the richer states object to paying federal taxes in order to benefit education in other states. School bills have sometimes foundered on the segregation issue. Advocates of Negro civil rights tend to oppose any bill which would benefit segregated schools, and Southerners are rigidly opposed to any bill requiring desegregation as a condition of aid. Whether to extend federal aid to parochial schools has been another divisive issue. And the tradition of local responsibility for public education is so well established that many oppose any federal aid for fear that it will necessarily lead to some degree of federal control.

Some proposals have centered on aid to school construction, on the theory that this would be less apt to involve federal control than would aid to school operation and maintenance. President Eisenhower several times asked Congress to authorize such aid. In 1955, the administration focused public attention on the issue by holding a White House Conference on Education, which capped a series of four thousand local, regional, and state conferences, involving more than half a million people. The participants approved federal construction aid by a ratio of more than 2 to 1. They divided almost evenly on the issue of federal aid to school operation. In response to the President's urging, the House considered construction-aid bills in 1956 and 1957, but they failed of passage because of disagreement on the kinds of issues described above.

Meanwhile, considerable federal aid, authorized by legislation in 1950, was being extended to local public schools in so-called "federally-affected" areas. Through fiscal 1957, some $712 million had been provided to assist 3,705 school construction projects to accommodate 950,000 pupils. These projects, whose total cost exceeds $1 billion, were made necessary by nearby federal activities, such as military installations or Atomic Energy Commission contracts.

In addition, substantial contributions for operating costs were made in school districts deemed federally affected because of: (1) the loss of revenue through the tax-exempt status of federal properties; (2) the attendance of children who live, or whose parents are employed, on federal property; or (3) an increase in enrollment growing out of federal contract activities. In 1957, $113 million were paid on this basis to help meet the operating expenses of 3,400 school districts with a total enrollment of over 7.6 million pupils.[53]

Finally, in large part as a response to the demonstration of Soviet scientific achievements symbolized by the sputniks, Congress enacted in 1958 a measure primarily designed to improve the teaching of science. Authorizing the total expenditure of $900 million over four years, the law provided $300 million in matching grants for the purchase of scientific equipment for public and private schools, $295 million for loans to students in institutions of higher learning (with half of any loan to be forgiven for a student who teaches for five years after graduation), and the remainder for such purposes as teacher-training institutes, fellowships for teachers, and vocational education for skilled trades necessary for defense.

With these programs paving the way, it appears not unlikely that general federal aid to public education will be the next major extension of federal welfare activity.

6. The Welfare State

As the developments reviewed here indicate, the quest for security in recent years has taken the form of increased dependence on government to provide at least the minimum conditions of well-being. In 1930, total welfare expenditures (excluding public health and medical services) amounted to $2.6 billion, of which veterans' assistance accounted for $700 million. Of the remainder, the private share was 76 per cent and government's share 24 per cent. By 1950, total expenditures had risen to $16.9 billion, and expenditures, excluding veterans' assistance, amounted to $12.4 billion; of this the private share had now decreased to 37 per cent and government's share increased to 63 per cent.[54]

The quest for security has not been a peculiarly American phenomenon. It has served as a test of the adequacy of govern-

[53] *Ibid.*, p. 186.
[54] Calculated from J. F. Dewhurst, *et al.*, *America's Needs and Resources, A New Survey* (1955), p. 432.

ment in most industrial nations. Governments unable or unwilling to satisfy this demand have lost popular support and fallen prey to the exponents of dictatorial regimes. Constitutional democracies which took vigorous measures to deal with problems of mass unemployment and economic disintegration have consolidated the loyalties of their citizens.

Once highly controversial, existing welfare services are now almost universally accepted and enjoy widespread favor. Bitter political struggles still occur on the forefront of advancing federal welfare activities, as in health insurance. Even in the accepted areas, there is division of view on such issues as the allocation of costs and benefits and the patterns of administrative implementation. But the underlying purposes of the new security measures enlist broad community support, and they have emerged as a response to felt needs.

CHAPTER 26

Monetary and Fiscal Policies for Economic Growth and Stability

O NE of the most significant developments in the role of government in the American economy since World War II has been the explicit assumption of governmental responsibility for maintaining high employment levels and promoting continuous economic growth without undue inflation. This is not a uniquely American experience; it has occurred in one form or another in all democratic nations with advanced economies. Full employment is also an explicit objective of international cooperation under the Charter of the United Nations (Article 55).

The almost universal acceptance of so far-reaching an expansion of government functions results from the combined influences of the Great Depression of 1929–1933, the persistence of massive unemployment in the thirties, the consequent development of new tools of economic measurement and analysis, and the economic impact of the second Great War. The business cycle had been a well-recognized phenomenon long before the Great Depression. Many of the earlier economic downswings had led to emergency governmental action, mainly in the field of banking and currency, to halt deflation and bankruptcy and to stimulate economic revival. But the Great Depression was unprecedented in both size and duration, and it followed a near-decade of continuous expansion which had led to hopes for "permanent prosperity." Almost one-fourth of the work force was unemployed in 1932, and throughout the thirties unemployment remained higher than ever before in this century.

The immediate impact was softened by the vast expansion of government welfare activities described in the previous chapter, but as unemployment persisted the fear arose that something was amiss with the basic economic mechanism, that the nation might be facing chronic stagnation instead of permanent prosperity. This fear was fortified in the minds of some by the brilliant theoretical work of the British economist John Maynard Keynes, and his proposed remedies seemed validated by the experience of World War II. It was then only a short step to formal acceptance of government's responsibility for over-all economic growth and stability, a step symbolized by the Employment Act of 1946.

1. The Development of Policies for Economic Stabilization

The Federal Reserve System and Monetary Controls

To provide the ready supply of money and credit necessary for the proper functioning of the economy, but notably lacking during previous financial panics, Congress in 1913 established the Federal Reserve System. Although it performs the functions of a central bank, Congress was fearful of excessive centralization of financial power; the System therefore comprises twelve Federal Reserve Banks, which hold the deposits of, and extend credit to, the commercial banks which are members of the System. As the System now operates, the Reserve Banks make loans to member banks on the security of bonds and commercial paper, rediscounting the paper which member banks have received as security for their loans to business and other borrowers. The Reserve Banks also issue Federal Reserve notes, now the principal form of currency.

Their capital stock is owned by member banks. All national banks are required to become members of the System, and state-chartered banks which meet certain requirements may do so. Member banks comprise fewer than half of all commercial banks, but they account for over 85 per cent of all commercial banking assets.

Control of the System is vested in its seven-man Board of Governors, appointed for fourteen-year terms by the President and confirmed by the Senate. The Board possesses broad authority over the Reserve Banks and their member banks, enjoying considerable discretion in the formulation and application of banking regulations.[1] It commands sweeping monetary powers, enabling it to

[1] For a detailed account, see E. W. Kemmerer and D. L. Kemmerer, *The ABC of the Federal Reserve System* (1950).

control or influence the supply of money, the availability of credit, and prevailing interest rates.

While the 1913 legislation only directed the Board to take action to "accommodate commerce and industry," economists in the twenties widely believed that its powers, which permitted counter-cyclical action on interest rates and credit supplies, would suffice to avert both inflation and depression. Faith in the efficacy of the Board's monetary policies and powers was shattered by the events of 1929 and thereafter. It prevented neither the excessive credit boom of the late twenties nor the calamitous monetary deflation which followed. Economists today disagree on whether the primary reason was the inadequacies of the monetary control instruments themselves or the failure to make proper use of them. There is fairly general agreement, however, that the tight money policy adopted in 1931 was grossly inappropriate, accentuating deflationary forces by encouraging the hoarding of gold and money and leading ultimately to a disastrous tidal wave of bank failures. Thus faith in monetary policy was rudely shaken at a time when the federal government faced unprecedented problems of depression and unemployment.

The Great Depression, "Pump-Priming," and the New Economics

The prevailing economic theory of the period offered little help to policy-makers who were struggling with their new responsibility to combat unemployment. Classical economics tended to assume a stable economy with full employment of labor and capital. One of its primary tenets, Say's law, held that supply created its own demand. (The money spent in a given period of time to produce the supply of goods available, whether paid to the factors of production or invested, creates the funds to purchase that supply and to provide the savings to finance the investments. The interest rate equates savings and investment; therefore effective demand equals supply.) Hence prolonged unemployment or underconsumption was impossible. Unemployment could only be temporary, for falling labor costs would lower prices; this, in turn, would stimulate a revival of demand.

Confronted with general economic distress and mass unemployment, government could not afford to wait for the economists to agree on new explanations and prescriptions. Both Hoover and, to begin with, Roosevelt believed that an unbalanced budget impaired the national credit and worsened business conditions, and they vainly attempted to bring the budget into balance.[2] But both

[2] In 1932, individual and corporate income taxes were raised substantially, and a sales tax was nearly enacted. One of the first measures of the New Deal

administrations were forced by the emergency into increasing deficits. Hoover initiated the process by expanding public works and establishing the Reconstruction Finance Corporation, but the floodgates were opened under the New Deal. The economic justification of most New Deal antidepression measures tended to come after their enactment rather than before. There was at first little coherent understanding of the full dimensions of the problem, and in the light of hindsight, certain of the policies pursued were mutually contradictory. But the total effect of the many *ad hoc* programs, each designed to meet a particular need or to assist a particular group, was greatly to expand government expenditures.

Probably no aspect of the New Deal engendered greater controversy than its liberal attitude toward government spending. Assailed by many as destructive of business confidence, it came to be defended by the "purchasing power" theory. This analysis held that revival of the economy required an expansion of consumer spending. If government could "prime the pump" by placing more purchasing power in the hands of consumers, then increased consumption expenditures would raise employment, profits, and prices, ultimately requiring consumers' goods industries to install more capital equipment. Thus the way would be prepared for a full-scale, cumulative business revival. Later, the argument became somewhat more sophisticated. It was maintained that an increase in government spending would constitute a net addition to total spending if it were deficit-financed or financed from taxes on funds which otherwise would have been saved. Furthermore, it would have a "multiplier effect" on national income since most of the funds spent by government would be respent by its initial recipients. Secondary recipients in turn would spend most of what they received, and so on. Because of this "multiplier," it was felt that the total regenerative effect would be two or three times the original expenditure.[3]

One of the pioneers in achieving a better understanding of how government might seek to maintain national income and employment was John Maynard Keynes (later Lord Keynes). His *General Theory of Employment, Interest, and Money* was published in 1936, but it was some years before economists and policy-makers became familiar with his analysis and able to clarify its possible applications to current problems. It would be a mistake, moreover, to label as simply "Keynesian" the economics upon which con-

---

was the Economy Act of 1933, which reduced salaries of federal employees and the appropriations of many departments.

[3] J. M. Keynes, *The Means to Prosperity* (1933), p. 12. See also J. M. Clark, *The Economics of Planning Public Works* (1935).

temporary countercyclical policies rest. The income-expenditure approach to problems of employment and inflation has been greatly expanded and refined since Keynes, and it also draws heavily on three lines of study which preceded Keynes: analysis of money supply and price levels, business cycles, and national-income accounting.

The earlier economic theories had held that the normal or equilibrium state of a free economy was always at full-employment levels, and that temporary departures from full employment were inherently self-correcting. Developing a new concept of the factors determining levels of desired investment and voluntary saving, and using the steady improvements in measurement of aggregate components of national production and income, Keynes now hypothesized that depression and unemployment could result from a continuing insufficiency of aggregate demand, something denied by Say's law, and that an economy might come to rest in equilibrium at low levels of employment. If investment levels were inadequate, the mere fall in interest rates might not suffice to expand them to a point matching voluntary savings. In these circumstances, the solution to unemployment would require deliberate policies to augment the total flow of national income.

As subsequently further developed and refined, modern income analysis seeks to understand fluctuations in national income, production, and employment by studying the relation between the incomes received by the units which make up the economy and their ensuing expenditures. It is the failure of these expenditures to equal incomes which causes levels of national income and employment to fluctuate. In the three major sectors of the economy —consumers, businesses, and government—the great bulk of expenditures is determined by incomes. Consumer spending is closely related to income levels; both current production expenses and investment are largely shaped by business receipts; and legislatures are reluctant to allow expenditures to diverge too greatly from tax receipts. Consequently, most changes in expenditures are induced by changes in income. There are, however, certain autonomous changes in spending, and it is these which make for changes in levels of income and employment. These changes can take three primary forms: [4]

(1) Consumers may alter the proportion of their disposable income which they wish to spend (or save). The relation of con-

_____
[4] To simplify matters somewhat, we here omit consideration of the effect of import-export balances.

sumption to income is relatively stable, so that autonomous changes here are least likely, although once a depression has begun workers fearing unemployment may save more and spend less, thus aggravating the depression.

(2) Businesses may vary the amount they invest (on plant, capital equipment, and inventories) or the proportion of net income they save (retained earnings). This is regarded as the most volatile relationship, primarily responsible for the major fluctuations.

(3) Governments may spend more or less than they receive. The possible effects of fiscal policy, i.e., the deliberate use of budgetary deficits or surpluses to counterbalance cyclical fluctuations elsewhere in the economy, had not been fully appreciated before Keynes, and it is one of the main elements of the new economics.

New Deal experience with unbalanced budgets only partially validated the earlier pump-priming theory and the later income-expenditure analysis. The cash deficit in the 1933–1939 period amounted to $21 billion, a fairly modest sum today but regarded as an astronomically high figure in the thirties. This was sufficient to assist in bringing about a substantial increase in national product, which rose from $55.8 billion in 1933 to $91.3 billion in 1939. (After correcting for price changes, the increase amounted to 50 per cent.) But the recovery was not steady and the pump did not remain primed. When federal deficit spending was cut back in 1937, a precipitous decline in business activity followed. And in 1939, there were still nine million unemployed. The failure of these budgetary deficits to produce full and lasting recovery was probably attributable to three causes:

(1) The deficits were not large enough, and government's role in the economy was insufficient to enable government alone to perform the task. Even in 1940, when national defense expenditures had achieved some importance, federal expenditures on goods and services accounted for only 6.4 per cent of gross national product. Moreover, a series of tax-rate increases during the thirties had a retarding effect partially offsetting the expansionary tendency of the deficits.

(2) Much of the effect of government spending was diverted into upward price and wage adjustments rather than the stimulation of additional employment. Many New Deal programs, notably the NRA and the legislation favoring labor organization and wage

increases, contributed to this result.

(3) Adverse psychological factors, although difficult to measure, undoubtedly played some role in dampening the enthusiasm of businessmen for new investments, although they did expand substantially. In addition to the many New Deal reforms which typically sought to satisfy the needs or complaints of other groups at the expense of the interests, power, or prestige of businessmen, the very deficits prescribed by the new economics served to confirm the gloom of business leaders who, reared in an earlier school of economics, could regard mounting deficits only as harbingers of disaster for both the government and the economy.

What the moderate deficit financing of the thirties failed to do, for whatever reason, the enormous deficits of World War II accomplished. To meet the unprecedented needs of the war effort, government spending mounted rapidly, reaching almost half of the gross national product. Tax increases covered only a small portion of these vast added expenditures; the deficit in fiscal 1943 was $56 billion, or over 30 per cent of gross national product. Under this powerful impetus, the economy expanded with remarkable speed. Even after correcting for price changes, gross national product rose by more than 70 per cent from 1939 to 1944. Unemployment fell to less than a million, despite a large increase in the work force (including the armed services), and manpower shortages were the main limitation on the war effort from 1943 on. By taking up the prewar slack and stimulating maximum expansion, the economy was able to provide the goods and services necessary to win the war, producing almost $200 billion of major munitions from mid-1940 to mid-1945, without any severe sacrifices on the part of the civilian population.

This experience provided support for the claims of the new economics. While there remained a wide area of disagreement over which measures to apply and in what proportions, most economists and policy-makers had come to share a common belief in the ability of monetary and fiscal policies in combination to go far in stabilizing income and employment. Among the public, there was a general feeling that if large-scale government activity could so increase national production and maintain employment in time of war, it could do likewise in time of peace.

The Employment Act of 1946

Out of these experiences there emerged the Employment Act of 1946. This measure, passed by overwhelming majorities, gave formal congressional endorsement to the concept of federal responsibility to maintain income and employment. It also reflected the hope, derived from the war experience, that the proper use of monetary and fiscal instruments could operate to stabilize the economy. Its immediate impetus was the widespread concern that the initial postwar years would be marked, at best, by an economic readjustment like that of 1920–1921, or at worst, by a drastic decline comparable to the 1929 depression.

The legislative history of the Act was marked by sharp conflict over its wording.[5] Administration leaders and labor and liberal groups, such as the AFL, the CIO, and the Farmers' Union, with high confidence in the new economics, wished to commit the federal government to the full use of fiscal policy to ensure full employment. Their opponents, who included business and conservative groups such as the National Association of Manufacturers, the Chamber of Commerce, and the Farm Bureau Federation, had greater faith in the ability of the private sector of the economy to provide jobs. Although they believed that monetary policy still had a useful function to perform, they were reluctant to rely fully on fiscal measures, and they feared that undue concentration on full employment as the sole policy objective would lead to high labor costs, mounting deficits, rising prices, and expanded government activity. The Act's final wording was a considerably altered version of the original bill as proposed by Senator Murray. The Murray Bill's goal of "full employment" became "maximum employment"; its specific commitment to use public works and federal loans to maintain employment was dropped in favor of a policy of using "all practicable means"; and the purpose became to "promote," not to "assure," employment. But the significance of the Act lies less in the precise wording of its stated objectives, which are somewhat ambiguous, than in the general direction it gives to policy, the amount of agreement which it did register, and the machinery it established to enable both the executive branch and the legislative branch to assume their new responsibilities for the over-all functioning of the economy.

The Act's declaration of policy, in Section 2, stated that:

The Congress declares that it is the continuing policy and responsibility of the Federal Government to use all practicable means consistent with its needs and obligations and other essential considerations of national policy, with the assistance and cooperation of industry, agriculture, labor, and State and local governments, to coordinate and

5 For a detailed account, see S. K. Bailey, Congress Makes a Law (1950).

utilize all of its plans, functions, and resources for the purpose of creating and maintaining, in a manner calculated to foster and promote free competitive enterprise and the general welfare, conditions under which there will be afforded useful employment opportunities, including self-employment, for those able, willing, and seeking to work, and to promote maximum employment, production, and purchasing power.

Thus the Act places primary reliance on private enterprise to discharge the responsibility of maintaining employment. It also makes maximum employment only one of three objectives of public policy. The other two are maximum production and maximum purchasing power (which was probably intended to mean partly price stability and partly high incomes for nonlabor as well as labor groups). It is recognized, therefore, that full employment is not the sole goal of over-all economic policy. Full employment might well be achieved in a highly inflationary or an inefficient economy, but the Act rejects such solutions. Employment, price stability, and economic growth are related goals of public policy, which are to be advanced conjointly.

To facilitate the pursuit of this policy, the Act established a Council of Economic Advisers (CEA), charged with the duties of gathering and analyzing information on current and prospective economic trends and developments, preparing such data for presentation to the President, and making recommendations on how existing programs may contribute to the goals of the law and on new programs in need of development. In particular, the Council is directed "to develop and recommend to the President national economic policies to foster and promote free competitive enterprise, to avoid economic fluctuations or to diminish the effects thereof, and to maintain employment, production, and purchasing power."

The Act further provides that the President shall transmit to Congress at the beginning of each regular session an "Economic Report," which analyzes current economic conditions and presents "a program for carrying out the policy declared in Section 2, together with such recommendations for legislation as he may deem necessary or advisable." At the legislative level, the Act provides for a Joint Committee on the Economic Report. Composed of seven members each from the House and the Senate, its task is to advise Congress on the President's recommendations. Both the Council and the Joint Committee are intended to focus attention on the over-all functioning of the economy.

2. Instruments of Control for Stabilization and Growth

There is available to policy-makers in pursuance of the goals of the 1946 Act a considerable array of monetary and fiscal instruments. While their use for controlling or influencing economic activity raises many problems, they are here considered primarily as instruments of countercyclical policy. In addition to promoting the long-run development of the economy, such a policy seeks to give an extra impetus to expansion at times when economic downturn is threatened and to apply brakes in periods of full employment and inflationary pressure.

Monetary Policy

The most pervasive instruments are those of monetary policy. Largely under the direction of the Board of Governors of the Federal Reserve System, they are concerned with the volume of money, the availability of credit, and the rate of interest. While monetary policy fell into disrepute as a consequence of the Great Depression, and there remains considerable controversy as to the precise extent of its effectiveness, it is clear that measures in this field can have a powerful and far-reaching impact on the economy.

The Federal Reserve Board exercises major influence over the supply and cost of loanable funds. Most of the contraction or expansion in the nation's supply of money (including bank deposits) occurs as the result of changes in the volume of commercial bank credit. Commercial banks expand the money supply by making loans and creating new deposits. They must, however, maintain minimum legal reserves expressed as a percentage of their total deposits. The Federal Reserve Board may raise or lower legal reserve requirements against demand deposits for member banks in the Federal Reserve System within a range from 13 to 26 per cent for central reserve city banks, 10 to 20 per cent for reserve city banks, and 7 to 14 per cent for country banks. (The range is 3 to 6 per cent for time deposits in all member banks.) Alterations in reserve requirements, accordingly, raise or lower the total volume of permissible bank loans. (It will be seen, however, that in a depression period, when there is inadequate demand for bank credit, lowered reserve requirements may merely create excess reserves.)

Secondly, the Board may accomplish the same objective through open-market operations of Federal Reserve Banks in the purchase or sale of government securities.[6] When the Banks buy securities, the payments for them are ultimately deposited in member banks, constituting an addition to those banks' reserves and hence to their lending power. Thus, if the reserve requirement is set at 20 per cent, the purchase of $1 in bonds by the Reserve System enables the member banks to lend an additional $5. If the Federal Reserve sells government securities, deposits and reserves are reduced, forcing a contraction in outstanding loans (again unless there are excess reserves).

In the third place, Federal Reserve Board actions influence the level of interest rates. Since the interest rate is the price for borrowed capital, its level in turn affects the volume of business investment. Variations in reserve requirements and open-market operations not only control the supply of loanable funds held by the banks; they also indirectly influence the whole interest-rate structure. Thus an increase in the supply of loanable funds held by commercial banks tends to lower the interest rate on all loans, whether by the commercial banks themselves or by other lenders. The reverse also holds true. In addition, in boom conditions when bank loans are at the legal limit and banks are seeking to increase reserves by borrowing from the Federal Reserve System, the Reserve Board may affect the interest rate directly by changing the rate which it sets for the rediscounting of commercial paper accepted from member banks.[7]

Finally, the Federal Reserve Board in conjunction with certain other federal agencies may influence the availability of credit through selective direct controls. Since 1934, for example, the Board has had the power to set margin requirements for the purchase of securities on credit and frequently uses this power to encourage or discourage such purchases. During World War II and the Korean War period, it also had the power to regulate the

[6] These operations are controlled by the Federal Open Market Committee, rather than directly by the Board. But a unanimous Board can dominate the Committee, since it is composed of the seven Federal Reserve Governors plus five representatives of the Reserve Banks.

[7] Being "bankers' banks," or wholesalers of credit, the Federal Reserve Banks may rediscount commercial paper (loans made by the member banks) and so provide the member banks with additional funds to add to their reserves, enabling them to make more loans. Usually, however, commercial banks have preferred to expand their reserves in other ways, normally through the sale of government securities. The rediscount rate, accordingly, has a direct impact on going interest rates only when member banks are "fully loaned up," cannot readily sell government securities, and must turn to the Reserve Banks to replenish their own reserves. In any case, however, the rediscount rate has considerable significance as a barometer of Federal Reserve monetary policy.

terms on which banking institutions could make loans to consumers for the purchase of such items as cars and large appliances.[8] Furthermore, other federal agencies make loans or influence credit terms in special areas, notably housing and agriculture, and thus help to determine the extent of credit available to particular sectors of the economy.

Thus, monetary controls provide the government with substantial power to expand available credit and lower the interest rate at times when the economy lags, and to contract credit and raise interest charges at times when inflation threatens.

Fiscal Policy

Fiscal policy is concerned with the management of government expenditures and receipts as they flow into and out of the national-income stream. Put simply, the contribution of fiscal measures to countercyclical policy is so to vary governmental income and outgo as to compensate for the deficiencies or excesses of demand in the nation's current income-expenditure balance. Thus, when the economy is underemployed, the government can exert an expansionary influence by spending more than it receives. The opposite course of action should tend to relieve inflationary pressures in times of full employment. The countercyclical impact of government can be measured very roughly by the size of the deficit or surplus in the cash budget (including operations of trust funds).

While the effects of fiscal policy are not always easily or precisely determinable,[9] its countercyclical potentialities led many economists and policy-makers at the time of the passage of the Employment Act to hope that fiscal and monetary measures together would suffice to guarantee full employment without inflation. This hope was not without some basis. The very size of the postwar budget meant that government could hardly avoid exercising a major influence on the economy. While the federal government had entered the depression decade with a budget of

---

[8] This authority was repealed in 1952.

[9] For example, the way in which revenues are collected and the way in which they are spent can determine their countercyclical impact. Estimation of the precise impact is difficult. Thus, if the goal is to increase spending in times of underemployment, it is argued that even a balanced budget may make a contribution to the extent that taxes are collected from those with high incomes who otherwise would have saved (not spent) a high proportion of the taxes they paid, and expenditures are paid to those with lower incomes who spend a high proportion of what they receive. Against this, it can be argued that such taxes may discourage risk-taking, thereby lowering private investment and to that extent depressing the economy.

but $3.3 billion and its purchases of goods and services accounted for only 1½ per cent of the gross national product, in the postwar period federal expenditures constituted a much larger share of the national product. Even before the Korean War, with its intensified defense spending, annual federal expenditures in the period 1946–1950 ranged from $36 billion to $41 billion, and federal purchases of goods and services amounted to $16 to $22 billion, or about 8½ per cent of gross national product.[10] Since the Korean War, they have averaged over 13 per cent.

Moreover, in the postwar period, fiscal policy has been greatly facilitated by a number of "built-in stabilizers"—devices which tend automatically to counteract fluctuations in the business cycle. The most powerful of these involves the relationship of taxes to expenditures. Most federal revenues are derived from personal and corporate income taxes. Since personal taxes are quite progressive (the higher the income, the higher the tax rate) and since the corporate tax is levied on profits, tax revenues change more than proportionately with changes in national income. As incomes fall, taxes fall at a more rapid rate, thereby easing some of the impact of the decline on individuals and corporations. Following the wartime reform which placed most personal income-tax collections on a "pay-as-you-go" basis, a part of this effect has been manifested immediately.

The reverse process characterizes rises in national income. At the same time, government spending programs are not automatically curtailed with a fall in tax receipts. Some of them, indeed, tend to rise, thereby providing additional "built-in stabilizers." This is notably true of unemployment insurance payments.[11] It is partly true of old-age payments (which increase as more older people withdraw from the labor market), and if the depression affects agricultural markets, as is likely, it is also true of farm price-support expenditures.

In addition to these built-in stabilizers, a number of other, supplementary devices are available or might be provided. Thus, for example, it has frequently been proposed that countercyclical

---

[10] The difference between federal expenditures on goods and services and total federal expenditures is accounted for by transfer expenditures, which are not part of the gross national product.

[11] While unemployment compensation *benefits* certainly vary countercyclically, unemployment compensation *taxes* may not. Indeed, total tax receipts may rise in periods of substantial unemployment, since merit rating of employers has lowered average tax rates from 2.7 per cent to about 1.3 per cent, and because heavy claims on the state accounts would necessitate an increase in tax rates. See J. D. Maxwell, *Fiscal Policy* (1955), pp. 142–147.

state and local public works programs be encouraged through federal grants-in-aid which would increase the federal share of total costs in proportion to increases in unemployment. Measures to influence business investment and private housing construction may also be utilized. Corporate income taxes may be adjusted to exercise a stabilizing effect on investment, although this has been very little done in the past. Indeed, the various forms of accelerated depreciation to assist defense industry expansion during and since World War II worked in the opposite direction, since they encouraged investment in periods already marked by inflationary pressures. Allowable depreciation rates could be varied counter-cyclically, however, and an extension of the present privilege for tax purposes of carrying back current losses to cancel out profits of the two preceding years would make for refunds in depressed years, although only after a time lag. The various credit and insurance aids to housing, discussed in Chapter 24, offer the federal government a powerful tool with which to influence residential construction. Available credit and subsidies can be contracted or expanded; interest rates on mortgages and the size of required down payments can be lowered or raised to stimulate or discourage new building.

Another instrument with both monetary and fiscal aspects which is used to promote economic stability is management of the public debt. In boom times, a shift to long-term securities will reduce the liquidity of bondholders. During economic downturns, a shortening of maturities will add to liquidity. The budgetary deficit can greatly enlarge the available supply of credit if the funds are borrowed through the sale of short-term securities to commercial banks.

Public works were once considered a particularly desirable means of helping to stabilize the economy. Their construction adds government funds directly to the income stream in the form of wages and payments for materials, while providing useful structures and perhaps stimulating some private investment. Since the construction industry is notably cyclical, public construction in depressed periods employs the labor and the materials most in need of employment. In practice, however, it is extremely difficult to vary the volume of public works flexibly as general economic conditions change.

Finally, it should be noted that fiscal and monetary measures are to some degree complementary. Monetary controls are potentially strongest in inflationary periods, when they may impose restraints on credit expansion and business investment. In depressed periods, they can do little by themselves, since they can make credit available and cheap but offer no positive inducement to investment and spending. (This point is graphically expressed in the phrase: "You can't push with a string.") In such periods, they are mainly a supplement to the prime instrument of fiscal policy, which can inject massive amounts into the national-income stream. In periods of expansion, on the other hand, even large budgetary surpluses, which in any event are difficult to achieve, may prove inadequate to check inflationary pressures which are taking the form of a price-wage spiral, and a combination of vigorous monetary and fiscal measures is then indicated.

Policy Inadequacies

Unfortunately, neither fiscal nor monetary policies have yet proved as efficacious as their more ardent supporters once expected. Their deficiencies consist less in their weakness than in their bluntness and unintended side effects.

As already indicated, fiscal measures are most effective in combating a decline. But much of the hoped-for impact of New Deal deficits in stimulating employment was cancelled by other policies working in the reverse direction and was diverted into price increases rather than additional employment. Income-expenditure analysis with its rationale of stabilization policies has now become fairly well understood and more widely accepted, and actively destabilizing policies are much less likely to be adopted. But in an economy where many prices and wages are, at least in the short run, administered by corporations and labor unions rather than established in a competitive market, there is continuing reason to fear that the import of government deficit spending will be dissipated in price rather than employment effects.

Deficits, moreover, are blunt instruments, good for meeting broad deflationary trends resulting from an imbalance in the income-expenditure relationship, but far less effective when unemployment is uneven and concentrated in regional or industry "pockets." In such cases, a broad fiscal program will spread its influence over the whole economy, and as successive areas and industries come to operate at or near capacity, inflationary effects will appear even though other sectors have as yet received relatively little stimulus. Proper selection of public works may prove of some assistance, but only if the construction industry is itself suffering from deflation or can be readily expanded and if satisfactory and desirable projects can be found in the depressed areas. This difficulty is heightened by the fact that the impact of the postwar recessions has been concentrated on particular industries and areas. Moreover, deflation, as well as inflation, may result from maladjustments in price-wage-profit relationships, rather than investment-consumption relationships. In such cases, while broad fiscal and monetary measures may counteract the deflation itself, they will not remove the underlying maladjustments.

In periods of inflation, fiscal measures alone are still less effective. In 1947–1948, for example, a large surplus in the cash budget, reaching an annual rate of $12.5 billion early in 1948, did not prevent substantial inflationary price rises. Among the reasons were the inflationary monetary policy being conducted at the same time and the fact that the surplus could not check the wage-price spiral then under way.[12] A deflationary fiscal policy clearly cannot work if it is being counteracted by a policy of loose money. Moreover, fiscal policy cannot deal with a wage-price spiral, in which price increases lead to wage increases, which cause further price increases, etc. It is this phenomenon which suggests that the "inflationary bias which may be characteristic of a high employment economy of the future is likely to operate largely from the cost and price rather than from the demand side. This possibility certainly limits the effectiveness of fiscal policy as a stabilization device and requires the use of other supplementary policies." [13]

Monetary policy must be invoked to supplement a fiscal attack on inflation. Since the 1951 accord between the Federal Reserve Board and the Treasury, discussed below, it has been so used. But monetary instruments, too, have difficulty in controlling inflation based on a price-wage spiral. Moreover, the use of credit restraints may have some undesirable side effects, for example, tending to restrict small businesses more than it does large. When the Reserve Board raises interest rates and reduces the supply of loanable bank funds, small businesses ordinarily are most affected. Commercial banks are likely to restrict first the credit lines of small businesses, where the risk factor is greatest. In addition, the larger corporations usually have access to other suppliers of credit, such as insurance companies or the security markets, and in recent years they have increasingly relied on internal sources, such as depreciation allowances and retained earnings, to finance their needs.

[12] See Gerhard Colm, "Fiscal Policy and the Federal Budget," in M. F. Millikan (ed.), *Income Stabilization for a Developing Democracy* (1953), pp. 221–223.

[13] Joint Committee on the Economic Report, *Hearings on the Economic Report of the President* (1950), p. 72.

814 MANAGER AND TRUSTEE

Finally, one of the gravest problems in managing a stabilization policy lies in the difficulties which attend accurate forecasting of trends in the economy. Time is of the essence in dealing with forces of recession, which, unless checked, can gather cumulative weight with great rapidity. Thus a former Chairman of the CEA stated that:

the supreme lesson of the last great depression [is] that it is easier to retain prosperity with mild measures than to regain a lost prosperity with heroic measures. Those in the area of economic policy who do not acknowledge this are as far behind the times as those physicians who remain unaware that the early detection and prevention of disease now weighs more heavily in the scales of the nation's health than surgery or the treatment of epidemics.[14]

At the same time, there is a tendency to hold off deflationary measures on the upswing for fear of setting off a recessionary spiral; yet if corrective measures are too long delayed, creeping inflation may be the result.

Unfortunately, accurate forecasting is far from easy.[15] At any given moment, many forces are at work in the economy. Some industries may be booming, others declining. Some factors cannot be quantified; many data are not immediately available; there may be errors in the information from which quantitative relationships have been derived; and causal relationships within the economy undergo change. The striking inaccuracy of many forecasts is understandable in the light of these difficulties.[16] One observer, accordingly, concludes that the "minimum probable margin of error in present forecasting methods is much greater than the permissible margin. . . . In its present stage of development economic forecasting is much too inaccurate to be used as the basis for changes in stabilization measures." [17] Hence, once again, the importance of the built-in stabilizers.

Political and Administrative Obstacles

Effective execution of a countercyclical policy requires prompt and well-designed government action. The organization of American government and the nature of our political processes, how-

[14] Leon Keyserling, "The Economic Test: Will We Act in Time?" *New York Times Magazine* (June 13, 1948), p. 7.
[15] For an analysis, see E. E. Hagen, "The Role of Economic Forecasting in Income Stabilization," in Millikan, *op. cit.*
[16] Thus the downturns of 1937 and 1948 were unpredicted, and recessions were falsely predicted in 1945 and 1947.
[17] Hagen, *op. cit.*, p. 200.

ever, do not always facilitate such action. The autonomy of state and local governments means that attempts by the federal government to pursue a countercyclical policy may be partially cancelled by contrary actions at lower levels of government. The fact that state and local revenues tend to vary with the business cycle means that these governments will normally expand their spending in good times and contract it in bad times. Thus, in the years 1933–1936, the federal government increased its construction of public works to an annual rate of $1.1 billion, compared with only $200 million in 1929. But this increase was more than negated by a drop in the rate of state and local public works spending from $2.3 billion to $900 million. Thus, except to the degree that federal grants-in-aid may induce countercyclical spending by state and local governments, the federal budget must compensate for variations not only in the private sector of the economy but also in the remainder of the public sector.

The separation of powers also presents serious hurdles. Authority is divided between the President and Congress, and Congress guards nothing more jealously than its taxing and spending powers, which are at the heart of fiscal policy. It is true that the evolution of federal budget procedures has involved greater executive influence on the expenditure side, and over the past two decades increasing use has been made of the budget as a tool of fiscal policy. There has been close co-operation between the CEA and the Budget Bureau. The placing of the Bureau in the Executive Office of the President in 1939 led to a broader concept of the budget as a monetary statement of the President's program as a whole and as a powerful lever in the national economy. But a full countercyclical use of the budget would require substantial discretionary flexibility in both spending and revenues, an objective which both congressional control and the mechanism of executive budget-making render extremely difficult to achieve.

Executive and legislative budget-makers, naturally enough, tend to concentrate on particular agencies and programs, rather than on the general fiscal impact on the economy. Budget procedures were originally devised to enable Congress to control government operations. They are now designed to facilitate: (1) program formulation, through providing cost estimates for programs as a whole; (2) program control, through relating expenditures, obligations, and appropriations to legislative authorizations; and (3) financial planning, through estimating cash flows which will have an impact on Treasury cash balances and the public debt. Accounting statements designed for the first two purposes are of little assistance to fiscal policy. Only the third of these purposes is directly relevant to fiscal policy, and it is likely to be of subordinate interest to both congressional and executive participants in the budgetary process.

Since most efforts to institute stabilizing action must survive congressional scrutiny, one consequence is frequently delay. Another is that the influence of particular groups and sections will be fully felt. Group pressures are more likely to prevent or delay countercyclical reductions in spending and increases in taxes than the reverse, but they may also make it difficult to utilize fiscal policy to meet specialized needs. It might be desirable, for example, to concentrate public works in depressed areas, but public works are the mainstay of the congressional "pork-barrel," of which each congressman in good standing feels entitled to his fair share.

There is, of course, a broad, overriding public interest in providing some degree of economic stability, and the 1932 election drove home the lesson that the electorate will deal harshly with any President and party who fail to prevent a major depression. As economic analysis has improved, Presidents and congressional party leaders alike have come to lay greater stress on policies directed toward general economic stability and growth. But this corrective to the group and sectional bias of the legislative process has been only partially effective. It is especially ineffective in combating inflation, where the temporary gains are many and the losses are only slowly appreciated.

Every fiscal policy measure has other policy implications and any public policy which involves the spending or receiving of money has a fiscal impact. Public works offer a good illustration. Those who are primarily mindful of countercyclical considerations have always argued that public works offer a unique opportunity for varying public spending to achieve economic stabilization. But public works serve functions which are needed or desired in good times as well as bad. Throughout most of the postwar period, for example, a stabilization policy would have delayed the vast construction programs carried on by all levels of government. But their supporters argued, with much force, that we had an immediate need for schools, highways, dams, irrigation projects, and housing developments. Similarly, the opponents of the St. Lawrence Seaway or public power projects would continue to oppose them in depressed periods. Action on such projects, except perhaps at times of acute depression, is likely to be determined by nonfiscal considerations. Indeed, fiscal policy is always subject to modification by the need for compromise with other objectives. Even in the monetary field, where the Federal Reserve System occupies a central position, its actions are often ill co-ordinated with agricultural, housing, and veterans' benefit programs which greatly affect the total credit position, and it must sometimes compromise its stabilization objectives to facilitate the Treasury's task of public debt management.

Because of these limits on the ability of government to act, the first line of defense against economic fluctuations will probably remain the built-in stabilizers, which operate automatically and often before there is general awareness that the economy is veering onto another course. Strengthening of such automatic devices is one of the most promising avenues for improving the effectiveness of stabilization policy. The next range of stabilizing actions is likely to be in the monetary field, where the Federal Reserve Board has very wide discretion and can act promptly and flexibly. Beyond these steps government can, and in serious circumstances will, almost certainly adopt further stabilizing measures which require legislation, but only after an inflationary or deflationary trend has been well established.

3. Exercise of Fiscal and Monetary Controls in the Postwar Period

As pointed out above, the Employment Act of 1946 created two staff agencies, the CEA and the Joint Committee, to focus attention on the broad economic implications of existing programs. These agencies have come to exercise considerable influence.

The Council of Economic Advisers

The major function of the Council is to study current trends in the economy and advise the President in the light of its conclusions. It has little authority of its own but attempts to guide the President, and through him the whole executive branch, on the broad economic implications of their actions. This is a difficult role to play. The CEA must be independent enough to bring the President the benefits of expert economic analysis and judgment, yet it must be sufficiently close to him in economic philosophy and broad political outlook to win his confidence. In its early years, CEA members disagreed publicly with one another on a number of policy questions, leading to some loss of confidence in the Council's judgment. Its second chairman often testified before congressional committees in support of particular measures, leading some to the conclusion that the President regarded the CEA as an instrument for winning legislative support rather than as a professional staff advisory agency.[18]

The Eisenhower administration, when it took office in 1953, had some hesitation about preserving the Council, and for a few months the President had only a single economic adviser. When a full Council was appointed, it spoke mainly through its chairman, Arthur F. Burns, who transmitted its recommendations and advice to the President. The Council's published reports confined themselves largely to problems bearing directly on economic stability. During the 1954 recession, the Council played a substantial part in guiding the application of corrective action, although it was by no means the sole source of economic advice tendered the President.

The scope of the Council's influence within the executive branch was also widened through the creation in 1953 of an Advisory Board on Economic Growth and Stability. This Board is headed by the chairman of the CEA and includes representatives (usually undersecretaries, assistant secretaries, or office directors) from the Departments of the Treasury, Commerce, Labor, Agriculture, and State, the Bureau of the Budget, the Federal Reserve Board, and the White House Office. Meeting regularly, this body has proved a valuable instrument for the exchange of views and informal co-ordination of many different programs.

The Joint Committee on the Economic Report

The other creation of the 1946 Act, the Joint Congressional Committee on the Economic Report, has also enjoyed growing respect. In developing its recommendations for Congress, the Committee functions like other legislative committees, hearing witnesses, publishing staff studies, and making reports. It has no authority, however, to recommend or report on specific legislation. It has provided a convenient forum for the testimony of those interested in broad economic questions. It welcomes the views of industry, labor, and farm groups, and has actively solicited the contributions of economists and government officials. Its studies and reports have earned increasing acclaim, and its members, assisted by an able staff, have achieved a high level of economic understanding. The Committee has had an impact on several important policies, both legislative and executive, but it encounters

[18] For a criticism of the CEA on this and other counts, see P. J. Strayer, "The Council of Economic Advisers: Political Economy on Trial," *Amer. Econ. Rev.* (May, 1950), pp. 144–154.

considerable resistance to its efforts to cause other congressional committees to give substantial weight to the general economic implications of their legislative and budgetary decisions. Being a new force, at variance with established patterns of organization and procedure, the Committee could not be expected to have a major impact on congressional action in the short run, but its growing stature suggests a steadily increasing, if undramatic, gain in influence.

Development of Stabilization Policy

During the postwar period, the economy has presented somewhat different problems from those generally expected when the Employment Act was passed. While there have been three moderate recessions (in 1949, 1954, and 1958), inflation has been more of a continuing problem than unemployment. Thus far, relatively mild monetary and fiscal measures have sufficed to reverse whatever broad downtrends have occurred. The fact that, primarily because of defense spending, the federal budget has been larger than was expected has augmented the power of the built-in stabilizers. Thus, in the recession of 1954, the deflationary impact of a decline of $4.4 billion in personal incomes was largely offset by a consequent drop of $1 billion in personal income taxes and an increase of $2.2 billion in social security payments. And the effect of a drop in corporate income of $7.4 billion was more than halved by a decline of $4.5 billion in corporate income and excess-profits taxes. In this case, the automatic countercyclical developments were helped by the fortuitous timing of the expiration of certain Korean War taxes. A considerable number of other actions were taken, at least in part for purposes of economic stabilization. The Federal Reserve Board made more credit available; social security benefits were increased (although social security taxes were simultaneously raised); the terms for home mortgages were liberalized; and defense spending was accelerated.

Much the same pattern seems to have sufficed to reverse the recession of 1958, when unemployment came to exceed five million. Automatic declines in tax receipts and accelerated defense spending combined to produce an estimated budgetary deficit of $12 billion for fiscal 1959, the largest since World War II. In addition, housing credit was again liberalized; highway construction was speeded up; and unemployment benefits were extended. And the Federal Reserve Board, by pursuing an easy-money policy between November, 1957, and August, 1958, assisted in bringing about an expansion of $4.7 billion in bank loans and investments (other than government securities) in the first half of 1958.

Policy has been less successful on the high side of the cycle. Persistent inflation, although proceeding at variable rates, has characterized almost the whole postwar period. The Truman administration tried to deal with the problem through fiscal policy, but substantial cash surpluses in the calendar years 1947 to 1948 (totaling $14.5 billion for the two years) failed to reverse inflationary forces, mainly because no simultaneous monetary restraint was applied. Thereafter, partly as a result of the 1949 recession and partly because of Korean War expenditures, the budget again shifted into a deficit position, the five-year negative balance for 1949–1953 totaling $9.5 billion. The Eisenhower administration made strenuous efforts to eliminate the deficit, and did succeed in achieving a $4.1 billion cash surplus in 1956. As in 1947 and 1948, however, this was too small to bring about price stability. Given congressional unwillingness to raise taxes, the demands, military and other, made upon government to spend money have been too great to permit government the full use of fiscal policy to counter inflation. The built-in stabilizers continue to operate, but they are partially offset by new spending programs or by reductions in taxes.

While the Truman administration made use of selective credit controls, such as restrictions on consumer credit, it did not employ monetary policy vigorously as a means of combating inflation. In part, this neglect arose from the disrepute into which monetary policy had fallen at the outset of the Great Depression. It also resulted from the subordination of monetary policy to the immediate requirements of Treasury borrowing and public debt management.

During World War II, the Federal Reserve Board had agreed to maintain the existing level and pattern of interest rates on federal securities. By mid-1947, it had allowed some market freedom in the prices (hence yields) of short-term and intermediate Treasury issues, but through open-market operations it supported the prices of long-term bonds so as to maintain a yield of 2½ per cent. Thus two of the Board's monetary instruments—open-market operations and the rediscount rate—were sheathed, for it was obligated to purchase at a fixed price whatever long-term federal securities the commercial banks cared to offer. Since the Board's power to increase the reserve requirements of member banks was soon exhausted, it was left helpless to control the supply of loanable funds and it was committed to a low interest rate. Monetary policy was denied the opportunity to restrain inflation.

The Treasury insisted that the Board continue to support federal securities. Its main reason was that these operations held down interest charges on the federal debt (which had mushroomed under the impact of World War II from $51 billion in 1940 to $260 billion in 1946) and greatly eased the Treasury's task of refunding and conversion. It was also argued that low interest rates stimulated private borrowing and so contributed to economic progress. This second argument tended to minimize or disregard the danger of inflation and the necessity for countercyclical operations on upturns as well as downturns.

Under the pressure of powerful inflationary forces unleashed in the last half of 1950 by the Korean War, the Board struggled to assert its independence from the Treasury in order to pursue a deflationary monetary policy. In this effort, the Board had strong support from the Joint Committee. In 1950, its subcommittee, headed by Senator Douglas of Illinois, urged that monetary as well as fiscal restraints be invoked. It declared "that the freedom of the Federal Reserve to restrict credit and raise interest rates for general stabilization purposes should be restored even if the cost should prove to be a significant increase in service charges on the Federal debt and a greater inconvenience to the Treasury in the sale of its securities for new financing and refunding purposes." [19] In 1952, a second subcommittee came to the same conclusion, arguing that the independence of the Federal Reserve Board "within and not from the Government" would contribute to this end.[20]

After a period of controversy in which the Board enjoyed substantial congressional support and the Treasury had the backing of President Truman, an "accord" was negotiated between the Board and the Treasury in March, 1951. Under its terms, the Board was committed to maintain an "orderly" market for government bonds but otherwise was left free to use its powers to control credit and the interest rate, even if this meant allowing government bonds to fall well below par. Since this accord, the Board has used its monetary tools energetically. In pursuing this policy, it has had the support of the Eisenhower administration, which has relied much more on monetary policy than did its predecessor. While the actions of the Federal Reserve Board have imposed sharp brakes on inflation, they have not stopped it. After two

[19] Senate Document 129, 81st Cong., 2d sess., p. 2.
[20] Subcommittee on General Credit Control and Debt Management of the Joint Committee on the Economic Report, *Monetary Policy and the Management of the Public Debt*, 82d Cong., 2d sess., p. 4.

years of stable prices in 1953–55, uneven but continuous inflation has marked most of the later years of the Eisenhower administration. Price levels did not fall even in the 1958 recession.

Nevertheless, stabilization policy has some achievements to its
credit. The evidence thus far suggests that large-scale unemployment can be avoided. Currently available techniques and policies
have served to check with reasonable speed the recessions which
have developed since World War II, although persistent unemployment in certain depressed areas and industries continues to
present difficulties. On the other hand, the problem of inflation
is far from solved. Our relatively high-employment postwar economy appears to have a marked inflationary bias. The same forces
which support employment, especially the vast spending programs
of government, stoke the fires of inflation. For the most part, we
have been unable to use fiscal measures vigorously to combat it,
and while monetary restraints have helped to reduce its pace, it is
felt by some observers that more effective control would require
much broader use of selective limitations on credit.

One major element of the problem seems to lie within the
private sector of the economy in a price-wage spiral which is not
easily amenable to government control. While sustained inflation
ultimately hurts the whole economy, its immediate impact is hard-
est on those with relatively fixed incomes and with little bargaining
power. Groups with strong bargaining power are able to maintain
or even improve their relative positions in times of inflation. They
include businesses at least partially able to "administer" their
prices (i.e., the prices are not fully controlled by the market),
labor unions able to raise wages, and those agricultural and other
producers who can command governmental support in raising their
prices. These groups, of course, strongly oppose any proposals for
government control over their prices or wages, preferring to rely
on their own bargaining power to protect themselves from inflation.
Yet the very success of their efforts to obtain differential advantages makes for further inflation.

Until means are found for restraining the power of such groups,
stabilization policy will be incomplete, and the price of high employment will continue to be slow but persistent inflation. Indeed,
there are some who contend that this is a price which must be paid
to achieve satisfactory rates of growth, and that government policy
should be directed toward alleviating the impact of inflation on
fixed-income groups in the community, rather than seeking absolute stability in price levels.

Moreover, despite the remarkable progress over the last generation in measurement and analysis of the facts of the economy and in understanding of economic forces and relationships, economic science is still a long way short of precision in either diagnosis or prescription for the problems of stability and growth.[21] The broad goals of sustained development command wide support, but much remains to be done in refining and perfecting the tools to achieve these goals.

[21] In the spring of 1958, a major effort to advance both technical understanding and public consensus on these issues was set in motion by the Committee for Economic Development, supported by a large grant from the Ford Foundation, through the formation of a National Commission on Money and Credit. The Commission was composed of twenty-five prominent citizens representing a variety of backgrounds and interests, and was to make "studies and recommendations concerning monetary and financial institutions, and their powers and policies, with a view to promoting more effectively the major objectives of national economic policy [including] balanced economic growth, sustained high employment and production, and the prevention of cumulative general price movements or the avoidance of their undesirable effects."

CHAPTER 27

Mobilization of the Economy
for War

U NTIL World War I, American public policy
was virtually unaffected by considerations of economic mobilization
for a possible war. Behind ocean barriers, the Constitution's injunction "to provide for the common defense" seemed amply satisfied by a modest navy and minute regular army. Even when the
United States emerged as a world power after 1898, with commitments extending to the Philippines, a sizable navy in being was
thought sufficient to meet the needs of national defense.

Out of the experience of 1917–1918 arose a new concept of total
national mobilization, in which war industry played a role comparable to the military front. The economic mobilization of
World War I, however, was short and incomplete. Only in the
Second World War did the United States begin to approach an
all-out war effort, with its far-reaching implications for government's economic role. Thereafter the Cold War, highlighted by
the hostilities in Korea, made it necessary to maintain defense and
foreign military-aid programs on a scale without peacetime precedent, driving home the lesson that considerations of national security must be given due weight in almost every realm of public
policy.

As experienced in the pre-nuclear age, full-scale war implied a
gigantic diversion of energies and resources from peaceful pursuits
to supply of the armed forces. By taking up slack in existing capacity, enlarging capacity, and shifting capacity from civilian to

war uses, resources of every variety were channeled directly or indirectly toward the overriding objective of military victory. Such a transformation could not be achieved by peacetime methods.

The simple process of bidding for supplies in the open market would give no assurance of producing war material either soon enough or in the necessary quantities. Ordinary economic incentives would not induce the enormous new investments needed in plant and capital goods, since the demand was of uncertain duration and offered no peacetime future. Without impossibly drastic fiscal measures, military procurement would be in direct competition for resources with expanding consumers' purchasing power, which would seek to bid supplies away into increased, rather than curtailed, civilian use. Nor could the distribution of residual civilian supplies be left wholly to the workings of the market mechanism. In place of the market as a governor, a war economy demanded positive direction and co-ordination on a national scale.

This direction and co-ordination were achieved through government controls which reached into every segment of economic life. Production controls were designed to direct facilities, materials, and manpower into their proper slots in the total war economy. They were complemented by comprehensive measures of economic stabilization, including heavy taxation, price control, wage stabilization, and consumer rationing. Yet despite this great overlayering of compulsory controls, the mainspring of a war economy in a free society remained voluntary. To be effective, the system of governmental direction had to be willingly accepted as a necessary means to the common national end. Thus a war economy required full co-operation between government and public, sustained by public participation in devising and executing control policies and by active promotion of continuing public support and understanding.

With the advent of nuclear weapons and long-range missiles, it is doubtful whether protracted economic mobilization, approaching an all-out war economy, will ever happen again in anything like the form experienced in 1940–1945. A global war would involve the United States at the outset and would be fought mainly with material already in being. Limited hostilities, in which both sides refrained from use of weapons of mass destruction, would scarcely require total economic mobilization, although partial mobilization on the lines of the Korean experience remains a clear possibility. Nevertheless, the war mobilization experience, with its demonstration of both capabilities and limitations of governmental action in a period of national crisis, provides significant lessons for peacetime relations between government and the economy. It is also an essential background for understanding the national security factor in the economy in an era of protracted cold war.

1. World War I and the Era of Mobilization Planning

The Experience of World War I

World War I gave Americans their first real insight into the problems of economic mobilization. Despite some earlier production for the allies, the United States entered the war in 1917 almost completely unprepared. Through a faltering process of trial and error, a war economy was gradually created, and by the fall of 1918 was producing in large volume. It was far from an all-out effort; the peak munitions output was less than 30 per cent of the total national product as compared with almost 50 per cent in the Second World War, and it was only briefly sustained. Nevertheless, sufficient experience was accumulated to indicate the pattern and many of the problems of a war economy.

The most clearly demonstrated lessons of 1917–1918 were in organization for economic mobilization. It required months to rectify the confusion in military procurement occasioned by fierce competition between the Army and Navy and among the independent purchasing branches within the Army. Industry and the public were also slow to recognize the needs of a mobilized economy. But the most striking development was that of the central civilian control agencies. The need for such agencies had not been foreseen, and their final form emerged only after a succession of ineffectual experiments. They began with the creation at the end of 1916 of a seven-man Advisory Commission to assist the Council of National Defense (a Cabinet committee). The Commission was weak and never regarded itself as a working part of the government. In July, 1917, it was supplemented by the first War Industries Board, also a weak body with no legislative authority and unclear executive authority. This Board broke down during the winter of 1918, when the whole war effort was threatened by coal and power shortages and a failure of rail transportation.

The crisis of disorganization was resolved in March, 1918, by the reconstitution of the War Industries Board with clear authority over the military services and the other civilian agencies and with power concentrated in its chairman, Bernard M. Baruch. The

Board rapidly established a sound working organization covering military requirements and clearance of orders, priorities, facilities, conservation, prices, labor, and planning and statistics, with fifty-seven commodity sections embracing the entire field of war industry. Priorities authority and the right to commandeer plants and supplies were placed under the Board's control. In a few months, it brought order into the war economy and laid the foundation for a major expansion in military output.

By standards of total mobilization, the World War I control system was rudimentary. Certain major elements were developed: co-ordinated military requirements, a crude but reasonably effective system of priorities, far-reaching measures of materials conservation and substitution, the beginnings of a system for curtailing nonwar construction and less essential civilian production, and substantial expansion of facilities for some munitions. On the other hand, manpower was not systematically controlled. Economic stabilization measures were only piecemeal, and inflation got seriously out of hand. The problem of allocating the nation's entire resources scarcely arose, for war output was too small to stretch the economy to its limits. Indeed, few military end products had been supplied to our own forces by the time of the Armistice. Our major productive contribution was in raw materials and partly fabricated supplies for finishing in France and Britain. A large stream of munitions, ships, and the like was only beginning to flow when the war ended.

Planning for Industrial Mobilization—The Interwar Period

When World War I ended, Baruch was convinced that the nation could not again afford such total industrial unpreparedness, and he earnestly recommended the creation of a top-level civilian agency to plan for future mobilization. This advice was not heeded. In the tide of postwar reaction, the public lost interest. The notion of preparedness and mobilization planning was kept alive only within military circles and among a few who had been most active in the war.

Under the authority of the National Defense Act of 1920, however, some modest planning for economic mobilization was conducted. A small Planning Branch of the War Department, assisted by the Army Industrial College and the Army and Navy Munitions Board, sought to anticipate the needs for wartime military procurement and general economic mobilization. Army procurement planning was the most highly developed. Based on the assumption of an army of four million (its size at the time of the 1918 Armistice), requirements were subdivided into individual items and assigned to specific plants. The Army developed with manufacturers "accepted schedules of production" to which they would shift on the declaration of "M-Day"—the first day of general mobilization. Potential war plants were "allocated" between the Army and the Navy and to the individual branches of the services. Efforts were made to develop stockpiles of the most critical imported materials. Detailed conversion plans were worked out for some plants. Authorization was sought for "educational orders" to give manufacturers experience. Considering the lack of congressional support and the inadequate staffing, the work was surprisingly thorough. The Navy, supposedly always in readiness as the nation's "first line of defense," was less interested in special planning for wartime procurement. And the immense air force requirements of World War II simply were not foreseen.

On the side of general economic mobilization, plans were developed first in the War Department and later in the Army and Navy Munitions Board. A formal Industrial Mobilization Plan was first made public in 1930; revisions were published in 1933, 1936, and 1939. The Plan envisaged a War Resources Administration as the key control agency covering raw materials, facilities, fuel, transportation, and power. In addition, the planners dealt in some measure with the whole spectrum of wartime controls and organization, including foreign trade, price control, and manpower.

On the whole, this work was little noticed by the public. Such attention as it did receive was largely hostile. In the twenties, there was little concern with the possibility of war. In the thirties, there set in a wave of isolationist sentiment. The investigations of the Munitions Committee under Senator Nye and the teachings of a new school of historians evoked widespread disillusionment with American participation in World War I and a frantic search for legislative neutrality to avoid another like occurrence. This movement culminated in the neutrality laws of 1935 to 1939, just as the international situation was deteriorating and new aggressions were occurring year by year in Europe and the Far East. The "peace movement" systematically attacked the mobilization plans, castigating them as a big-business–military conspiracy to impose dictatorship.

As the European crisis came to a head in the summer of 1939, a War Resources Board was appointed, under Edward Stettinius, Jr., to review the industrial mobilization plans and presumably to serve as the War Resources Administration in the event of war.

The Board's predominantly conservative make-up, coupled with the peak of isolationist and neutrality sentiment, led to a strong reaction against it. Its report was withheld from publication until 1946.

In the event, the United States moved into its defense program and finally into the war without substantial benefit from the prewar plans. Inadequacies in the plans themselves were partly responsible; more important was the absence of any clear-cut "M-Day." But beyond that, the need for mobilization planning had not been adequately conveyed to the public at large. And the administration, seeking in an antiwar climate to obtain approval for large-scale armament and aid to our allies, felt unable to take any overt action which seemed to imply eventual American participation. On the sides of both military procurement and civilian organization for economic mobilization, therefore, the years 1940–1943 were, like 1917–1918, an era of trial and error and gradual evolution under the pressure of day-to-day events. Fortunately, the United States was again given time to mobilize gradually, and the delays in developing a large-scale war effort did not prove disastrous.

2. Mobilization for Production in World War II

The whole pattern of American production mobilization for World War II was conditioned by the long period of uncertainty between the launching of the major "defense program" in May, 1940, and the formal entry of the United States into the war in December, 1941. During these months, the foundations were laid for full-scale production. But the pace of mobilization, the methods of control, the organization of emergency agencies, and the responsiveness of the public were limited by the deep cleavages of opinion as to American participation and by the absence of clear targets to guide the production program.

In the face of this climate of opinion, the administration moved gradually in asking for mobilization powers and in developing an organization for production mobilization. Major legislative campaigns were required to obtain defense appropriations, the enactment of Selective Service in August, 1940, and the passage of the Lend-Lease law in March, 1941. The defense period was also marked by internal political divisions and conflicting pressures. The business world was suspicious of the Roosevelt administration and feared the imposition of controls by an unsympathetic government. Organized labor feared the loss of its newly won gains and resisted direction of the defense production program by industrialists.

By the fall of 1941, these obstacles were rapidly giving way. Public opinion had come to favor full-scale American armament and the greatest possible assistance to Britain and Russia. Defense production was beginning to flow. Large-scale orders were being placed under Lend-Lease appropriations. Legislative authority and the defense control organization were rapidly being perfected. The nation had accepted the convoying of goods across the Atlantic, and something close to a shooting war between American warships and German submarines had broken out on the high seas. But all-out mobilization became possible only after the Japanese attack on Pearl Harbor on December 7.

As late as November, 1941, about $28 billion of munitions were programed for production in 1942; the potential munitions production, given complete industrial mobilization, was then estimated at $40 billion. No time was lost after Pearl Harbor in raising the sights. The President's message to Congress of January 6, 1942, charted a massive effort, calling for the production in 1942 of 60,000 aircraft and 45,000 tanks, in 1943 of 125,000 aircraft and 75,000 tanks, and in the two years together of 55,000 antiaircraft guns and 18 million dead-weight tons of merchant shipping. The services' estimates of a complete program matching these targets amounted to $60 billion in 1942 and over $100 billion for 1943—quantities clearly beyond the nation's then capacity. Thenceforth, there was no further question as to the need for production mobilization on a scale never previously conceived.

Organization and Authority for Production Mobilization

Faced with sharp divisions of opinion on both international and domestic affairs, the administration was unwilling in 1940 to adopt the one-man type of control established in 1918 and proposed under the Industrial Mobilization Plan. Instead, in May, 1940, the Advisory Commission to the Council of National Defense was re-created under a 1916 statute. Special areas of responsibility were assigned to each of its seven members, as follows: Industrial Materials, Industrial Production, Employment, Farm Products, Transportation, Prices, and Consumer Protection.[1]

The Defense Commission had no legal authority. There was no

---

[1] Shortly thereafter, Donald M. Nelson was appointed Co-ordinator of National Defense Purchases and for all practical purposes became an eighth member of the Advisory Commission.

chairman; each member reported directly to the President. Only two or three members were expected to serve full time. The Commission was to function as a clearing house between the military procurement services and the national economy, guiding the placement and pricing of contracts, enlisting the voluntary support of industry, arranging labor-training programs, investigating delays, and recommending action to the operating agencies. In practice, however, as the program rapidly expanded in magnitude and as British war orders mounted, the Commission took on the character of a collective policy-making agency and acquired a number of important operating jobs. By the end of 1940, it was evident that a more closely knit and more authoritative production-control organization was essential.

Still fearing adverse political reactions from one-man control, the administration then adopted the somewhat bizarre expedient of a two-headed organization. This was the Office of Production Management (OPM), jointly directed by William S. Knudsen (formerly president of the General Motors Corporation) as Director-General and Sidney Hillman (president of the Amalgamated Clothing Workers of America) as Associate Director-General. Both men had been members of the Defense Commission. The Secretaries of War and Navy were also members of the OPM Council.

Unlike the Defense Commission, the OPM had operating responsibilities from the start. During the one year of its life, it expanded rapidly toward more complete production mobilization. It undertook the planning of raw materials expansions, conservation measures, the first curtailments of civilian production, more systematic steps toward industrial conversion and subcontracting, and a substantial development of the system of priorities.

As 1941 progressed, the civilian sector of the economy became increasingly affected by the defense program. In April, 1941, the former Price and Consumer Protection Divisions of the Defense Commission were reconstituted in a new Office of Price Administration and Civilian Supply (OPACS), under the direction of Leon Henderson, charged with combating price inflation and providing for the equitable distribution of residual civilian supplies after the satisfaction of military needs. The distinction between the OPM's authority over direct defense requirements and the concern of the OPACS with the remainder of the economy proved untenable, and in August, 1941, civilian supply responsibility was transferred to the OPM. At the same time, a Supply, Priorities, and Allocations Board (SPAB) was created, to determine total requirements of materials and commodities for all purposes, and to establish policies on the expansion of output, the allocation of available supplies, and the application of priorities. The administration of priorities was delegated to the OPM.[2] This arrangement was a substantial improvement, since related operating functions were now centralized under the OPM. But responsibility was still not clearly focused. In addition to the two-headed direction of the OPM, there were now uncertain lines of authority between the OPM and the SPAB. The attempt to divide policy and operations and the failure to give any one individual a determining voice in SPAB decisions left civilian direction of the production effort far from satisfactory.

With American entry into open hostilities, production mobilization was strengthened by the swift passage of two major statutes. The First War Powers Act, approved in December, 1941, granted the President complete discretion in redistributing executive functions and suspended all restrictions on government procurement. The Second War Powers Act, approved in March, 1942, consolidated and broadened the priorities powers and restated the authority for allocation in the following terms:

Whenever the President is satisfied that the fulfillment of requirements for the defense of the United States will result in a shortage in the supply of any material or of any facilities for defense or for private account or for export, the President may allocate such material or facilities in such manner, upon such conditions, and to such extent as he shall deem necessary or appropriate in the public interest, or to promote the national defense.

On the foundation of these few but comprehensive words, the entire elaborate wartime system of production control and consumer rationing was erected.

On the administrative side, little time was lost after Pearl Harbor in moving to a straightforward production-control organization under one-man control. In January, 1942, Donald M. Nelson was appointed chairman of a newly established War Production Board (WPB). The Board took over the functions of both the OPM and the SPAB and was authorized to "exercise general direction over the war procurement and production program" and to "determine policies, plans, procedures, and methods of the several federal departments, establishments, and agencies in respect to war procurement and production including purchas-

[2] Executive Order 8875, August 28, 1941.

ing, contracting, specifications, and construction; and including conversion, requisitioning, plant expansion, and the financing thereof. . . ." [3]

Throughout the war, the WPB remained the principal operating and policy-determining agency for production mobilization. Despite the sweeping terms of its initial executive orders, however, the WPB did not retain unchallenged responsibility. Partly because of political pressures, partly because of a deliberate policy of its chairman to delegate authority as far as possible, and partly because of unsatisfactory relations between the WPB and the armed services, a series of independent agencies was established in closely related production-control fields. Their relations with the WPB were often ill defined. As a result, the initial hopes for effective over-all co-ordination of production mobilization by the WPB proved vain. It became necessary in 1943 to create the Office of War Mobilization, a "superagency" at White House level, for supervision of the entire home-front effort.

Parallel with the development of the civilian agencies, there took place major reorganizations of the military services for their colossal job of munitions procurement. Prior to Pearl Harbor, this process also had proceeded in halting fashion. Instead of following the major changes called for by the Industrial Mobilization Plan, peacetime procurement methods were expanded and adjusted only under the pressure of immediate needs. On the Army side, co-ordination of procurement was at first entrusted to the Undersecretary of War, but in March, 1942, a major reorganization created the Army Service Forces to handle all ground-force procurement. Aircraft procurement was placed under a special Army Air Forces Materiel Command. The traditionally powerful Navy bureaus retained greater independence, but here, too, the enormously expanded program required special provision for co-ordination. An Office of Procurement and Material, reporting to the Undersecretary, was created for this purpose. In merchant shipbuilding, a large emergency organization for procurement and production supervision was developed by the U.S. Maritime Commission.

The role of these military organizations went far beyond mere procurement. It included production scheduling and expediting; control of the flow of material to contractors; mediation of labor disputes; and transportation, storage, and distribution operations of unprecedented magnitude and complexity.

[3] Executive Order 9024, January 16, 1942, Section 2. See also Executive Order 9040, January 24, 1942.

Procurement

Procurement is the mainspring of production mobilization, for it is the placing of war orders which sets in motion the forces drawing economic resources into munitions. Peacetime procurement procedures, based on competitive bidding to preclude corruption and reduce costs, are wholly inapplicable to wartime conditions. They must be replaced by the more flexible procedures of negotiation, which permit the geographical dispersion of war production, the use of relatively high-cost facilities in addition to the more efficient ones, and the systematic relating of available plants to needed products. Limited authority to negotiate contracts was granted in mid-1940, but the shift was made only gradually until after Pearl Harbor, when all war contracts were negotiated.

The armed services retained responsibility for military procurement. The civilian control agencies gave some guidance, first through clearance of major contracts and from 1942 on through the establishment of basic procurement policies covering such matters as distribution of contracts to areas with available manpower, maximum use of subcontractors, and favoring of contractors requiring the least additional new equipment. From time to time, civilian control of munitions procurement was proposed, following the British and Canadian patterns, but the issue was seriously raised only in 1942, after military procurement was on a going basis and transfer would have been scarcely practicable. There are clear merits, as well as disadvantages, in both methods—procurement by the armed services combining the functions of buying and using, while procurement by civilian agencies combines the functions of buying and production control.

Facilities

The mobilization of war production required the organized contribution of three basic factors: industrial facilities, materials, and manpower. The problem of mobilizing facilities arose first, since the nation entered the defense program without a munitions industry. The specialized World War I plants had been largely dismantled, and government arsenals, while vital as pilot plants, could handle only a tiny fraction of the defense program. Thus virtually whole new industries for aircraft, shipbuilding, tanks, explosives, guns, and ammunition had to be provided, partly through conversion of existing facilities, but mainly through new construction. In total, war construction increased the nation's prewar industrial plant and facilities by over 50 per cent.

The early launching of the facilities program, despite uncertain estimates of needs and other obstacles, was the most signal contribution of the defense period to ultimate war production. To encourage private plant expansion for products expected to have no peacetime market, the corporate tax laws were revised to permit the amortization of defense plants over five years instead of the usual twenty or thirty years. Even with this aid, however, private financing could not meet the need. Some two-thirds of the total war-plant expansion was directly government-financed, the plants being operated under management contracts by private concerns.

Raw material requirements were peculiarly difficult to project under the limited defense-period program, and expansion projects in this field were a source of chronic dispute. But with the coming of full-scale war, the expansion of raw material supplies became a major part of the production effort. Capacity was increased manyfold for synthetic rubber, aviation gasoline, aluminum, and magnesium, and was raised by one-third in steel. The output of machine tools and industrial equipment was also greatly enlarged.

The enormous industrial-plant program, coupled with direct military construction of cantonments, supply bases, training fields, and other installations, severely burdened the construction industry, which had shrunk during the Great Depression. Early in 1942, all construction not contributing to the war effort was rigidly limited. Even so, total construction reached a peak in 1942 almost a third above the previous record levels of 1927.

The systematic programing of war construction became one of the most perplexing tasks in the mobilization of production. With military requirements fluctuating, and with serious uncertainty as to the potential output from certain types of new plants, some facilities were overbuilt, while in other cases capacity was still inadequate in 1944. Even at the close of the war, when the flow of materials and components was well in hand, and the process of forecasting requirements was running smoothly, the forward planning of construction remained far from satisfactory.

Materials

The supply of materials is the second major factor in production mobilization. In World War II, materials were mobilized far more effectively than either facilities or manpower. Indeed, materials became in many respects the governor or balance wheel of the wartime economy, partly because they were the limiting factor on war production during the crucial years 1941 to 1943, but also because materials lend themselves more readily to flexible control than do the other productive resources.

In the early defense and war years, raw material supplies were greatly enlarged by the facilities expansions noted above and to some extent by public purchase and stockpiling, primarily of imported materials. But supplies could not keep pace with the insatiable demands of expanding military production. Beginning with the light metals in the spring of 1941, materials were diverted to the war industries by a series of conservation orders directly forbidding or limiting their use in less essential applications. By late 1942, virtually every type of material was under such control. This diversion was further advanced by limitation orders prohibiting or limiting the output of automobiles; consumers' durable goods, such as refrigerators and washing machines; and many other end products not required for the war effort. Inventories were also restricted.

Overlaying the elaborate system of individual supply actions and orders controlling usage, there was established a more generalized system of priority and allocation controls. At first voluntary and limited in scope, priorities were made mandatory as the volume of defense orders expanded. They were then gradually expanded to include almost all materials, components, and end products. Shortly after Pearl Harbor, the issuance of priorities without quantitative limits had created an inflationary condition, in which manufacturers required ever higher preference ratings to obtain their supplies. It became necessary in mid-1942 to revalue the entire priorities currency on a simpler basis.

The survival of qualitative priorities, which remained throughout the war the most comprehensive device of materials control, was made possible only by quantitative systems of allocation bringing supply and demand into balance for the most important materials. Broad quantitative control was first attempted in the summer of 1942 under the Production Requirements Plan, but this method proved defective and was replaced in the spring of 1943 by the Controlled Materials Plan. This plan became the outstanding single control instrument for production mobilization. Its core was the allocation of steel, copper, and aluminum to manufacturers of end products, covering their entire production schedules; they, in turn, passed allocation certificates down through their chains of subcontractors to cover requirements for components. Allocations were based on the relative essentiality of end-product programs, which were reviewed in detail each quarter. The vertical flow of allocation certificates directly balanced end-product and component schedules. In practice, major exceptions to the vertical principle were necessary for components such as nuts and bolts, electric motors, and others common to a great variety of end products; their flow was determined by priority ratings associated with Controlled Materials Plan allocations. In principle, production schedules and materials allocations were directly integrated, although here, too, numerous exceptions were necessary in practice. In subsequent war years, other comprehensive allocation systems were devised for textiles, lumber, rubber tires, chemicals, and other materials not adequately controlled through the distribution of the basic metals.

In 1943, certain critical common components threatened the success of the most urgent war programs, notably the construction of destroyer escorts and of plants for synthetic rubber and aviation gasoline. For these components, even the revalued priority system was an inadequate control. A series of component scheduling devices was therefore instituted, assuring the production and delivery in proper sequence of the most urgent orders through a case-by-case evaluation at the component manufacturing plants.

Thus the flow of materials came to be governed by a series of interrelated and interlocking instruments—conservation and limitation orders, priorities, scheduling, allocations, and the Controlled Materials Plan. These controls had to operate within a framework of more fundamental decisions on the scale and balance of the war programs. But within such a framework, they proved a flexible and efficient means of adjusting resources to changing requirements and of obtaining important margins of production from a seriously stretched economy.

Manpower

Manpower is the third basic factor in war production, and the one which sets the ultimate limits on war potential. It is the most difficult to mobilize effectively. Human and political considerations must be given their full weight, over and beyond technical obstacles even more complex than those confronting the control of facilities and materials.

Despite the withdrawal of twelve million of the most able-bodied workers into the armed forces, war industry was successfully manned through the re-employment of some eight million unemployed; the drawing into the labor force of another eight million women, youths, and older persons not normally seeking work; a major transfer of workers into munitions and other war industries; an increase of the standard work week from forty to forty-eight hours; and large increases in productivity flowing from the application of mass-production techniques to the munitions industries. Manpower mobilization was at first voluntary, induced by favorable wage differentials, recruitment drives, and patriotic stimuli. Until 1943, facilities and materials were narrower bottlenecks than labor supply. Thereafter, the economy began to bump the ceiling of available manpower, first in particular areas and skills and later more generally.

Government organization for labor mobilization was comparatively slow to develop. The Defense Commission's Labor Division was primarily concerned with special training programs, settlement of disputes in defense industries, and maintenance of labor standards. After Pearl Harbor, the state-controlled U.S. Employment Service (USES) was federalized, and a War Manpower Commission was established to co-ordinate the government's manpower activities. Voluntary measures were supplemented in 1942 by local employment-stabilization agreements, under which employers in essential industries undertook to recruit only through the USES and to refuse employment to workers not possessing "certificates of availability"; the Employment Service in turn referred job-hunters to the more important war-production plants. These measures were assisted by Selective Service deferment policies, which provided a powerful incentive for younger men to shift to war work. But this contribution to industrial manpower recruitment was limited by poor administrative co-ordination; by an emphasis on dependency rather than occupation as the basis for draft deferment; by public hostility to the designation of specific occupations as "nonessential"; and by its inapplicability to those unfit for military service, to women, and to the exempt age groups.

In 1943, when general labor stringency on the West Coast seriously threatened the aircraft and shipbuilding programs, it became evident that more intensive measures were required to channel manpower supplies into war production. Under the West Coast War Manpower Program, made nationwide in 1944, local interagency Production Urgency and Manpower Priority Committees in each major center were to review new war contracts in the area, to recommend curtailments of less essential production, to establish employment ceilings for major plants, and to channel job-seekers to the plants of highest priority. In practice, little was done to control the placement of war contracts or to reduce less essential employment, but the controlled referral system and the mere fact of concentrated local interagency attention on the labor-supply problem brought useful results. A subsequent attempt to introduce a so-called "forced release" program, lowering employment ceilings in certain plants and directing the workers thus released to critical plants on a man-by-man basis, was opposed by organized labor and industry and ended in failure.

As manpower supply increasingly emerged as a limit on war production, attention was directed toward the possibility of statutory authority to compel labor to move into essential work. Authority for industrial conscription had been granted in Britain and other major belligerent countries. Consideration in 1942 of a possible National Service Act was dropped after strong opposition by both management and labor, but the proposal was revived in 1944 and given Presidential endorsement. Early in 1945, the House of Representatives passed a bill imposing compulsory control on all draft registrants. The Senate passed a substitute bill providing penalties for employers' violations of the then voluntary hiring regulations of the War Manpower Commission. The bill was still in conference when victory was achieved in Europe. Despite general dissatisfaction with existing measures, there was little agreement on appropriate remedies.

Apart from the problem of matching labor supply with production requirements, effective manpower mobilization required the minimization of strikes and alternate means for the speedy settlement of industrial disputes. At a conference shortly after Pearl Harbor, labor and management pledged themselves against strikes or lockouts for the duration and agreed to the establishment of a National War Labor Board (NWLB), representing industry, labor, and the general public. The Board's mediation activities have been briefly described in Chapter 7, and its problems in dealing with wage levels are reviewed later in this chapter. The NWLB received substantial co-operation and support. While strikes were by no means eliminated, the time lost on their account was kept to about 0.2 per cent of available working time.

On the whole, manpower mobilization left much to be desired. It suffered from lack of advance planning, poor co-ordination between Selective Service and civilian labor policies, and the absence of adequate statutory authority. Labor turnover in many war industries was exceedingly high, and absenteeism was a chronic cause of concern. War industry was not well located in relation to labor supply, and housing and community facilities were often inadequate. Fortunately, the production program was not unduly hampered by these defects, primarily because the American economy was not stretched to the utmost.

Food and Agriculture

Wartime mobilization of food and agriculture posed problems similar in some respects to those encountered in war industry: determination of military, export, and civilian requirements; expansion of production of war-essential items; and control of distribution. The central need was to increase total production and to induce many farmers to shift to essential crops. With its thousands of small producing units, however, agriculture was far harder to control effectively than manufacturing, and its mobilization affected strong political interests with unusual power in Congress.[4]

Government organization to deal with these problems emerged only gradually. The Food Section of the Defense Commission was relatively inactive. As shortages developed in 1942, successive reorganizations occurred, authority first being concentrated in the Department of Agriculture and in April, 1943, transferred to the semi-independent War Food Administration.

Through these agencies, the government undertook to expand and plan production, establishing production and acreage planting goals and seeking to meet them through a complex system of incentives, including price supports, commodity loans, government purchases, and subsidies. Military and export needs were assured through a system of "set-asides" at the wholesale level. For the major items, despite a level of civilian supply greater than prewar, it became necessary to institute consumer rationing. The program was on the whole successful, although marked by a series of political compromises which worked counter to the economic stabilization program and which hindered the transfer of agricultural resources from less essential to more essential crops.

Transportation, Fuel, and Power

In World War I, failures in the supply of three essential ancillary production resources—domestic transportation, fuel, and power—nearly strangulated the productive effort during the severe winter of 1917–1918. In World War II, no such failures occurred, although overseas shipping was a most serious bottleneck. These areas were all handled through special civilian control agencies— the Office of Defense Transportation, the Petroleum Administration for War, and the Solid Fuels Administration for War (these latter two being loosely connected with the Interior Department), and the Office of War Utilities (nominally a part of the WPB but

[4] See above, pp. 44–45.

in practice a semi-independent unit). Relatively simple control devices were employed, and heavy reliance was placed on the co-operation of the respective industries through representative industry associations.

At the wartime peak, domestic transportation carriers handled twice the prewar quantity of freight and almost three times the prewar passenger traffic. The process was fostered by regulations stimulating full utilization of capacity and rationalization of freight movements, but general transportation priorities did not become necessary and temporary embargoes were used only briefly to relieve local congestion. The rail regulations were largely administered through the Association of American Railroads. When submarine attacks required suspension of the normal flow of tankers from Gulf Coast to East Coast ports, a catastrophic reduction in Eastern petroleum supplies was averted through government construction of two large and four smaller pipelines and heavy expansion of rail tank-car movement.

Petroleum was, of course, a major factor in the wartime economy. Crude-oil production was expanded by more than 30 per cent in this country and by an even higher proportion in allied countries; aviation gasoline production was increased twelvefold. The mobilization of petroleum resources required drastic shifts from civilian to military use, construction of new refineries, and integrated controls over production, allocation, transportation, and distribution, including consumer rationing. Under the supervision of the Petroleum Administration for War, acting in close co-operation with a special representative industry association, operations of the American industry were in effect placed on a unified basis and co-ordinated into a worldwide international plan. Analogous but simpler problems of coal transportation and distribution were managed by the Solid Fuels Administration for War.

In a similar manner, the Office of War Utilities supervised electric power and other public utility operations. Breakdown or crisis was avoided by radical readjustment of peacetime patterns. Shortages were forestalled by advance planning started in 1939 and by a large construction program in the three following years, which was substantially terminated late in 1942 to prevent interference with other war requirements. Regional interconnections and operating pools permitted greatly increased utilization of capacity.

Overseas shipping posed a wholly different type of problem. In 1942, German submarines threatened the allies with military defeat, and shipping continued to limit the military effort until 1944. This problem was met through the development of technical antisubmarine devices, the use of destroyer escorts and escort aircraft carriers, a huge merchant shipbuilding program, and rigorous control of all shipping operations. The building program, under supervision of the Maritime Commission, produced some 52 million dead-weight tons of new merchant shipping, equal to about three-fourths of the entire world merchant fleet in 1939. Control of shipping developed hesitantly during the defense period, but from April, 1942, on, government control was absolute. Through the War Shipping Administration, cargoes were governed by priorities on both exports and imports; the routing of all ships was closely scheduled; and port operations were likewise controlled. Shipping operators became in effect simply agents for the federal government. American shipping was loosely co-ordinated with British operations through the Combined Shipping Adjustment Board.

Each of these specialized agencies performed with considerable effectiveness. But the creation of control units on commodity or relatively narrow functional lines involved difficult problems of relationship with the broader control agencies such as the War Production Board, the War Manpower Commission, and the Office of Price Administration, as well as with the military services. The very freedom of the so-called "commodity czars" from concern with the over-all balance of total resources, together with their relatively strong bargaining positions, tended to encourage a disproportionate favoring of their needs at the expense of other sectors of the war economy.

Wartime Foreign Economic Relations

While more economically self-sufficient than any of the other belligerents, except possibly the Soviet Union, the United States was vitally dependent on certain imports. Moreover, American supplies not only supported our fighting allies through the operations of Lend Lease, but were also important in preserving friendly attitudes in neutral countries. Large-scale development and production programs were required in areas supplying raw materials, especially in Latin America and Africa, and certain materials were bought to preclude enemy purchases. Export controls were required to prevent enemy acquisition of supplies, to conserve materials by eliminating nonessential exports, to relate exports to public purchase and import programs, to maintain the basic civilian economies of friendly countries, and to make the best use of available shipping. The physical controls of economic warfare were supplemented by control of foreign funds. Toward the end of the war, export controls were modified to meet the expanding requirements of the liberated areas, a prelude to the postwar programs of international relief, rehabilitation, and reconstruction.

The administration of wartime foreign economic relations was built up outside the Department of State, which was considered unsuited to technical operations carried on under the pressures of defense and war needs. After much administrative experimentation during the defense period, the major agencies created were the Office of Lend-Lease Administration and the Board of Economic Warfare, which were consolidated late in 1942 into the Foreign Economic Administration. The program was marked by considerable administrative conflict, both among the various new agencies and between them and the Reconstruction Finance Corporation subsidiaries which served in the earlier years as fiscal and purchasing agents for the import programs.

A decision of President Roosevelt and Prime Minister Churchill to embark on a novel experiment in co-ordinating the war-production efforts of the United States and Great Britain, later joined by Canada, led to the creation in 1942 of the Combined Raw Materials and Combined Production and Resources Boards. The American members of these Boards were top officials of the WPB. In principle, the combined boards were to arrange for the administration of the allied wartime economies as one. The practice was not nearly so far-reaching. Rationalization of production between the allies was limited to a few military items. The Raw Materials Board did not seek to assert jurisdiction over those materials, such as steel and aluminum, of which the United States and Canada were the only important surplus producers. The balance of authority always remained heavily on the side of the national production authorities. Nevertheless, the combined boards developed joint standards for the wartime economies and allocated materials from sources outside the United States and Britain to the best advantage of the United Nations as a whole. They also provided effective means for direct dealing between the parallel production-control agencies of the two governments, similar to the direct co-ordination of military operations.

The Problem of Civilian Supply

In theory, a truly all-out war mobilization would deny to the underlying civilian economy all resources except those necessary to enable that economy to support the war effort. The United

844   MANAGER AND TRUSTEE

States never came close to this extreme position in World War II. It started with an accumulation of economic "fat"—inventories of consumers' durable goods, clothing, and other civilian-supply items. Moreover, aggregate production of civilian goods and services was higher during the war than in 1939. In certain sectors of the economy, however, civilian supplies were greatly reduced or eliminated. Acute civilian supply problems were also created by heavy population shifts to war-production centers. As a result, the direct competition of munitions with war-supporting industries and with the needs of civilian workers raised sharp issues in the allocation of many materials.

The basic problems of civilian supply were twofold: (1) to ensure the equitable distribution, among areas, groups of consumers, or individuals, of residual supplies after military requirements were met; and (2) to define and protect, even against competing military needs, those minimum civilian requirements a shortage in which would directly hamper the war effort. To accomplish these purposes, a wide variety of control devices was developed, including special priorities for replenishing distributors' stocks in shortage areas, wholesale and retail inventory controls, and several types of individual consumer rationing. But with only moderate pressure on general civilian standards, and in view of the complexity and unpopularity of controls applying to individuals, as well as resistance to drastic alterations in the economic structure not clearly necessitated by the war, control measures were generally much milder than would be warranted under maximum mobilization. As textiles became scarce, for example, looms were assigned to more essential fabrics, and production of staple, low-cost garments was encouraged. But clothing was not rationed nor production of nonessential textiles prohibited. Similarly, a program to concentrate civilian output of certain items in a few plants, releasing the remainder for war use, was abandoned after a brief and inconclusive trial. Standardized utility items were not developed. And such nonessentials as jewelry and toys continued to be produced.

Nor did the effort to define minimum civilian standards achieve genuine success. It was confused by widespread political pressures and by mutual suspicion between the military services and the civilian war agencies. The military felt that claims of civilian essentiality were often a pretext for "business as usual," while some civilian officials doubted the full validity of the military-supply programs and felt that the services desired to curtail civilian standards simply to create wider appreciation of the seriousness of the war, and thus improve home-front morale. Such issues of civilian-supply policy were a principal source of friction between the WPB and the military.

Late in the war, as manpower shortages increasingly limited production and prewar inventories dwindled, problems of civilian supply became increasingly acute. Victory was won, however, before adequate solutions were devised, either in the definition of civilian minima or in the optimum distribution of available supplies.

The War-Production Accomplishment

The result of America's wartime mobilization was a volume of production far surpassing anything previously experienced and even the most optimistic prewar surmises. Gross national product, without correcting for price changes, rose from $90 billion in 1939 to over $200 billion in the last year of the war; even at constant prices the increase was over 60 per cent. The production of munitions reached a rate of $65 billion per year and amounted in total to $182 billion. It included some 300,000 aircraft, 1,200 warships, 52 million dead-weight tons of merchant shipping, 87,000 tanks, and comparable volumes of other war items. At its peak, American war production was almost equivalent to the combined military output of the United Kingdom, the Soviet Union, Germany, and Japan. At the same time, the aggregate output of civilian supplies was also slightly increased.

These results were accomplished through a remarkable, integrated, threefold organization of industry, the military-procurement services, and the civilian-control agencies. Into its achievement went the powerful unifying drive of war, channeled by a whole armory of control techniques, most of them developed without precedent and under the stress of acute time urgency.

By 1944, the economy as then organized was beginning to brush the ceiling of its production potential. Manpower shortages became ubiquitous and in turn created new material shortages. By that time, the armed services were fully equipped, and through concentration on programs of immediate urgency the military effort was adequately sustained by war production. It was clear, however, that in an even more severe and prolonged war, the American economy could have been geared to still higher levels of war production. Such a genuinely total war economy would have called for more thoroughgoing controls, especially in the field of manpower, together with a far closer integration of strategy, logistics, procurement, production control, and measures of economic stabilization.

3. Wartime Economic Stabilization

Total national mobilization requires that physical controls be complemented by measures of economic stabilization, comprising war finance; the direct control of prices, wages, and consumer credit; and the rationing of scarce essentials to individual consumers. Without such stabilization measures, the injection of massive defense expenditures into the national income stream would produce rapid and potentially explosive inflation. Spiraling costs would disrupt the war effort, cause great individual suffering, and create overwhelming problems of postwar readjustment. But the relation of these stabilization measures to the prosecution of the war is less immediate and less obvious than production measures, and the indirectness of this relation creates obstacles to public co-operation in carrying out the stabilization measures. For example, the diversion of steel from the manufacture of refrigerators to the production of artillery presents a simple, clear-cut issue which in wartime can hardly be contested, but the validity of a price ceiling for a particular article of clothing or a decision against wage increases in a particular industry bears no such incontestable relation to war needs. The technical complexities are extreme, and stabilization measures are peculiarly susceptible to direct evasion and to resistance through organized political pressure. The wartime efforts to control prices and wages were subjected to a constant and intensive barrage of such pressure from producer, distributor, and labor organizations. The most successful resistance was offered by agricultural producers and processors, operating through the powerful congressional farm bloc, and to a lesser extent by organized labor in delaying wage controls. Effective action was further hampered by the general unpopularity of consumer rationing. No aspect of wartime administration was more difficult or more thankless.

Economic stabilization was also adversely affected by the protracted uncertainties of the defense period. Statutory authority for price and wage control was wholly lacking until 1942, and when granted it was qualified by major political concessions, especially to farm interests. The sheer magnitude of the task posed administrative problems of the most difficult order. In consequence, effective economic stabilization was not accomplished until well into 1943, when war production was already virtually at its peak. Yet despite this slow start, the over-all record was creditable. In the face of far greater inflationary pressures, the cost of living was maintained much closer to prewar levels than in World War I, without visiting undue economic hardship on any significant group.

Organization and Authority for Economic Stabilization

Wartime organization and authority for economic stabilization evolved through a series of halting steps following a succession of crises in which inflation threatened to get out of hand in one or another sector of the economy. Even after the pattern was completely developed in mid-1943, the stabilization agencies had to struggle repeatedly for renewal of their legislative authority, on which narrow time limits were placed. These struggles, together with annual battles over appropriations, kept them constantly in the center of the political arena. The closeness of congressional supervision, the complexity of the stabilization statutes, and the frequent direct imposition by Congress of specific standards or limits was in marked contrast to the almost unqualified delegation of authority for production control in the Second War Powers Act.

The severe inflation of World War I had made economic stabilization a matter of grave concern in mobilization plans for another war. Especially noteworthy was Bernard M. Baruch's plan for an immediate freeze of all prices on the opening of hostilities. Others advocated selective price controls as pressure developed on particular commodities. But economic conditions in 1940 made adoption of the Baruch plan out of the question. The nation was still suffering from large-scale unemployment, and prices were generally regarded as too low, particularly in agriculture. Although the Defense Commission did include a member, Leon Henderson, charged with promoting price stabilization, the President stressed that little was to be done in this field at the start.

By the fall of 1940, those raw materials most in demand for defense production began to experience sharp price rises. The wholesale price index started a steady upward climb in August, 1940, and a rise in the cost of living began in February, 1941. Henderson responded with a series of informal efforts at voluntary industry co-operation in maintaining "reasonable" wholesale prices. Industry meetings were called; oral and written warnings were issued; and five so-called "price schedules" were published. There were no means of enforcement; the process was limited to exhortation and admonition, commonly termed "jaw-bone" price control. By the spring of 1941, price rises were becoming general and a more effective organization for price stabilization was clearly indicated.

In April, the President created by executive order the Office of

Price Administration and Civilian Supply (OPACS), directing it to fight inflation with "all lawful steps necessary or appropriate." With the transfer of the civilian-supply functions to the Office of Production Management in August, 1941, the OPACS became the Office of Price Administration (OPA), the principal economic stabilization agency for the remainder of the war. Its staff was expanded and the broad pattern of organization became set. In the prestatutory period, some seventy-three price schedules had been issued, over a hundred voluntary agreements had been negotiated, and several hundred warning letters had been sent out; these devices in aggregate affected about 50 per cent of all wholesale prices. But price trends continued sharply upward. By the end of 1941, wholesale prices had risen 21 per cent from August, 1940, and the cost of living 10 per cent. The defense program was becoming larger and the country was faced with the threat of general inflation.

In these circumstances, the administration had submitted to Congress in July a bill authorizing general price control. After long debate, this measure passed the House a few days before Pearl Harbor. After Pearl Harbor, the Senate treated it as an urgent war measure. The Emergency Price Control Act of 1942 became law on January 30.

This Act gave the OPA a statutory foundation. It confirmed the organization of price control as a separate function under a single administrator, the post continuing to be filled by Leon Henderson. It authorized establishment of "generally fair and equitable" maximum prices over any commodity when prices were rising or threatening to rise in a manner inconsistent with the Act's general goals of price stabilization. Actual prices during the first half of October, 1941, were to be employed as a standard, with appropriate adjustments for costs, profits, and other relevant factors. The Act also permitted the freezing of rents in so-called "defense rental areas." It provided adequate sanctions and a novel scheme of specialized judicial review through an Emergency Court of Appeals with exclusive jurisdiction over appeals from OPA regulations. On the other hand, the Act did not authorize wage stabilization. And under pressure from the well-organized farm associations, the prices of farm products were virtually excluded from control.[5] Furthermore, the plans for agricultural production were based largely on incentive pricing. Throughout the war, the stabilization program was hampered by the basic conflict of purpose between the OPA, with its general mandate for securing economic stabilization, and

[5] See above p. 148.

the war food agencies, which were supported by the powerful congressional farm bloc.

Under the new law, the OPA undertook a broad expansion of selective price control at the wholesale level, but general price levels continued to rise, stimulated by the absence of effective control over wages and farm prices and by the enormous expansion of government war expenditures, which far outran increases in tax revenues. In April, 1942, the President announced a seven-point stabilization program. The OPA responded promptly by issuing its General Maximum Price Regulation, setting March, 1942, prices as a ceiling over most consumer commodities, and by a broad extension of rent control. Exempted from the General Maximum Price Regulation, however, were many important food items, which aggregated about 40 per cent of all food expenditures. In July, 1942, the National War Labor Board issued its "Little Steel" decision, fixing the 15 per cent cost-of-living increase between January, 1941, and May, 1942, as a general standard for permissible wage-rate increases, subject to exception only to remove inequities or substandard conditions. But the statutory limitations on farm-price control and the enormous administrative burden of the OPA —a burden which the agency was not yet effectively organized to handle—combined with the continuing stream of additional purchasing power to limit the effectiveness of these measures. The cost of living continued to rise, notably in foods, and strikes for higher wages were threatened. By the end of the summer, the entire fabric of anti-inflation measures was in danger of dissolution.

In September, therefore, the President called for new legislation to stabilize all prices, wages, and salaries, imposing a price ceiling on farm products at 100 per cent of parity. In effect, the program sought to achieve stabilization by balancing the powerful political forces of agriculture and labor, offering wage control to the one and food-price stabilization to the other. The President asked for congressional action by October 1, stating that, in its absence, he would take the necessary action on his own initiative. Despite warm congressional resentment over executive pressure, the Stabilization Act of 1942 was approved one day after the President's deadline.

This law directed the President "to issue a general order stabilizing prices, wages, and salaries affecting the cost of living . . . so far as practicable . . . [at] the levels which existed on September 15, 1942." The farm-price standard was reduced to parity or the maximum price between January 1 and September 15, 1942, the same base period being applied to wage stabilization.

Under the executive order accompanying the Stabilization Act, the President rounded out the wartime pattern of stabilization agencies by establishing the Office of Economic Stabilization (OES) to exercise general policy direction and co-ordination. Justice James F. Byrnes resigned from the Supreme Court to accept this post. His office was placed in the White House, and he soon came to be regarded as an "assistant President." He chose to limit the OES primarily to the settlement of disputes arising among the stabilization agencies or between them and the production agencies, although in rare instances broad lines of policy were initiated in his office.

The Stabilization Act laid the foundation for effective control of all the major factors tending toward inflation. It took some months, however, for the process of administration to catch up with the new legal authority. The OPA was under severe attack both outside and within Congress. Henderson resigned in December and was succeeded by Senator Prentiss Brown of Michigan. It was charged that the agency was being mismanaged by economists and college professors not familiar with business practices; Congress responded in the summer of 1943 by requiring that policy-determining officials have at least five years' business experience. Meanwhile, the cost of living continued to rise by about 1 per cent a month, bringing new demands for wage increases and once more threatening collapse of the stabilization effort. Pressure within Congress for new agricultural concessions continued, and a bill to exclude subsidies from parity-price computations was stopped only by a Presidential veto.

By April, 1943, the stabilization program was again in critical condition. The challenge was met by a vigorous executive order to "hold the line." [6] Price ceilings were to be made general, reductions instituted where warranted, and increases kept to the minimum required by law. Wages were to be controlled by the "Little Steel" formula, and concessions on the ground of inequity or inequality were to be halted. Rationing was to be expanded. Subsidies were to be used where necessary, particularly to prevent food-price increases.

The hold-the-line order was the climactic point in the battle for economic stabilization. From then on, the cost of living was largely kept in check. In the twenty-eight months between the order and the end of the war in August, 1945, wholesale prices rose only 2 per cent and the cost of living only 4 per cent; in the previous twenty-eight months the respective increases had been

[6] Executive Order 9328, April 8, 1943.

29 and 23 per cent.

The decisive turning point of April, 1943, did not mean a relaxation of inflationary pressures. It meant only that the government finally had devised and consolidated the interrelated series of measures required to cope with those pressures. Effective administration of these measures required constant modification and improvement. So far as possible, the OPA issued specific dollars-and-cents ceilings to replace the General Maximum Price Regulation, which involved inordinate difficulties in enforcement. The price agency, after a period of internal demoralization, was reconstructed by Chester Bowles, who was appointed General Manager in July, 1943, and Administrator in November. Clearer price standards were developed and methods of accounting and control improved. Many specific price and wage concessions were made, but the broad line was held.

Both in 1944 and 1945, when the Stabilization Act had to be renewed, the operating agencies were put under severe cross-examination, and new restrictions were imposed by statute to forbid specific control measures objectionable to politically powerful groups. In the 1944 Extension Act, for example, the duration of food subsidies was restricted; the government was enjoined against changing business practices or accounting methods; grade labeling and other devices for quality standardization were forbidden; and certain features of distributors' price control were eliminated.

Thus throughout the war, despite the general popular interest in holding down the cost of living and the patriotic incentive for conformity with wartime regulations, the stabilization agencies had to fight a constant series of rear-guard actions to maintain adequate legislative authority and to preserve the foundation of effective administration.

War Finance

In the armory of measures for wartime economic stabilization, the most powerful single weapon is taxation. Although less selective in their impact than direct controls, taxes check inflation at its source by drying up the excess of purchasing power over current supplies of goods and services and thus reducing the so-called "inflationary gap." Government borrowing from sources other than banks has a similar effect. These instruments were an important part of the anti-inflationary campaign of World War II. They were used less extensively in the United States than in other belligerent countries, however, and the failure to make greater use of them contributed to the severe pressures of suppressed inflation which were centered on the OPA and the War Labor Board and which, when unleashed after the war, substantially raised price levels.

No government has been able to devise or collect taxes which would cover the entire cost of a major war out of current revenue. During World War II, the United States financed 43 per cent of its total expenses through current taxes, and 46 per cent in the peak year. This compares favorably with less than 30 per cent of a far smaller expenditure in World War I. On the other hand, the United Kingdom met out of taxes 49 per cent of its total wartime government expenditures and 55 per cent in the peak year; Canada was only slightly behind in this regard.

Wartime tax revenues increased from $5.4 billion to $46.5 billion as the result of a series of new revenue laws in each year from 1940 through 1944. A corporate excess-profits tax was introduced in 1940; individual income tax rates were sharply raised; and in 1943, a system of current tax payments and tax withholding from payrolls was introduced. The tax base was, of course, constantly increasing, national income about doubling during the course of the war.

From 1942 on, increasing disagreement developed, both within the administration and, more significantly, between the administration and Congress, on the extent of possible or desirable further tax increases. In 1942, the Treasury rejected proposals of an administration anti-inflation committee for compulsory savings, for sales taxes, and for extremely heavy income tax increases. Congress was unwilling to accept even the less drastic Treasury program; it rejected a proposed tax on spending and reduced the additional tax yield of the 1942 law from the recommended figure of $7.6 billion to about $3.6 billion. Late in 1943, even sharper conflict developed. A Presidential budget recommendation for a $16 billion tax increase was whittled down before Treasury presentation to $10.5 billion and cut by Congress to a mere $2.2 billion. For the first time in American history, the President vetoed an internal revenue measure; it was passed over his veto and was an important step in the deepening hostility between the two branches of government.

Technical studies and the experience of other belligerents leave little doubt that the economy could have borne higher taxes. The administration itself was unwilling to risk the political consequences of further taxation in the $2,000-to-$5,000 income group, where the largest inflationary potential was concentrated. Congress was unwilling to increase upper-bracket or business surtaxes beyond their already very high rates. In effect, the American system of government, with its responsiveness to organized pressure, was politically unable to tax to the degree considered technically feasible, even in the face of wartime needs.

War taxation was supplemented by legal restrictions on consumer credit and by an elaborate system of encouragement for voluntary savings and purchase of government bonds. The Treasury endeavored to borrow primarily from individuals and other nonbanking sources, in order to remove excess purchasing power. Every device of propaganda and public opinion stimulation was employed in the voluntary savings campaigns. They met with a fair degree of success: out of the total wartime public debt increase of $232 billion, somewhat over half was obtained from nonbank lenders. But the financing of the remainder through bank borrowing injected a large inflationary pressure into the economy as a whole.

Direct Controls

Direct price control was the most complex of all wartime control measures. It affected innumerable transactions and millions of prices. The OPA developed a broad variety of pricing methods, attempting to fit them to the diversity of business conditions and procedures. Special techniques were applied to various kinds of manufacturing, wholesale and retail distribution, service trades, exports, and imports. While the technical adequacy of controls was greatly improved over the war years, in some fields, notably clothing, satisfactory answers had not been found when the war ended.

The basic method of control was the freeze, either selective or general, at the base-period level, with subsequent adjustment. In allowing such adjustments, the OPA required the absorption of cost increases so long as industry-wide profits remained above the 1936–1939 level and no individual item was being produced at a direct loss. These standards were upheld by the courts; and despite widespread complaints of undue stringency by those subject to control, profits in virtually every field, even after high wartime taxes, were well above prewar levels. Special formula-pricing methods were devised for new products. In the clothing field, new products and quality deterioration were major devices of price-control evasion; there was also a tendency to concentrate on high-price lines, denuding the market of staple low-cost goods. In the late war years, the WPB and the OPA sought jointly to remedy this situation, but the measures proved unenforceable and subject to effective resistance both directly and through political channels. Similar resistance greatly limited OPA efforts to standardize quality to provide a firm basis for pricing.

One major device of price control used extensively in other war-time economies was the subsidy, by which supplies could be obtained from high-cost producers without raising price levels as a whole. In the United States, food subsidies were of considerable importance, but they were limited by opposition from farm groups, who preferred over-all price increases. On the other hand, the "Premium Price Plan" for subsidizing marginal increases in production of copper, lead, and zinc was an outstandingly successful stabilization and production measure.

Rent control was in many ways the most effective of the OPA's operations. Here, too, the basic technique was a freeze at prewar levels, supplemented by locally enforced control over evictions and sales of dwellings. While there was some evasion through reduced services, forced sales, and overcharges for furnishings, the broad results were a more complete stabilization than in any other single area. This relative success can be attributed partly to vigorous administration, but it was also made possible by the political popularity of rent control and the inability of landlords to develop organized opposition comparable to that of farmers or manufacturers.

The control of wages was a matter of particular delicacy involving grave political implications, especially for an administration strongly supported by organized labor. During the defense period, no effort was made to control wages. The wage differential between defense and civilian industries provided the greatest single incentive for the necessary shift of manpower into war work. By 1942, however, war plants were competing with one another for labor, and the pressure for further wage increases was a constant threat both to production and to economic stabilization.

After the no-strike pledge of January, 1942, and the establishment of the National War Labor Board, with virtual powers of compulsory arbitration, some months were required to develop standards for wage stabilization. The "Little Steel" decision of July, 1942, the Stabilization Act of October, 1942, and the "hold-the-line" executive order of April, 1943, were the major steps in this development. From April, 1943, on, an effective strategic front was maintained, but the Labor Board had to make numerous tactical concessions. Like price control, wage control remained a matter of flexible day-to-day adaptation to particular pressures within a broad stabilization framework.

Another essential instrument of direct control was individual consumer rationing of essential commodities. The generally ample supplies of consumers' goods made it unnecessary to extend rationing to the scope adopted by other belligerents, but at the height of the war, tires, gasoline, fuel oil, fats and oils, meats, certain canned foods, and shoes were controlled in this manner. Consumer rationing involved peculiarly difficult problems of administration, which were solved in part through decentralization to voluntary local War Price and Rationing Boards. While the program was generally successful, enforcement methods never completely checked the various devices of evasion and black-market dealings.

Stabilization and Production

From the viewpoint of the war economy as a whole, production mobilization and economic stabilization reinforce one another and are both essential to the total result. In particular instances, however, the two purposes may come into apparent or real conflict. Such conflicts were intensified by a wartime government organization which placed responsibility for the respective functions in different sets of war agencies.

Prices and wages are the principal governors of the normal economy; in wartime they are not suspended, but merely channeled within the framework established by the system of controls. When a production increase for a particular item was clearly necessary for military or essential civilian use, and adequate capacity existed, the supply agencies tended to favor the granting of price or wage increases. To the price and wage controllers, however, such action threatened to break the stabilization front and make it more difficult to hold the line elsewhere. Agreeing on a common objective, each set of agencies sought to place the burden of action on the other. This inherent conflict created chronic friction between the WPB, the War Food Administration, the Petroleum Administration for War, and the other supply agencies, on the one hand, and the OPA and War Labor Board on the other.

4. Co-ordination of the War Agencies

The emergency organization of government to provide detailed direction of the wartime economy created many novel problems of administration. The scale and scope of government activities and the great variety of attempted solutions make the war period a mine of valuable case material for administrative study. Areas of significant new experience included delegated legislation, decentralized administration, and civil-military relations. But of all the problems of wartime administration, none appeared so consistently and urgently as the need for co-ordination among the agencies responsible for related programs. Manpower and production, production and stabilization, prices and wages, procurement and priorities, agriculture and industry, foreign economic warfare and domestic controls—these were but the clearest among innumerable examples of the need for co-ordination.

The difficulties were intensified by the peculiar development of emergency governmental organization before Pearl Harbor. The seven Defense Commissioners were wholly unco-ordinated. This weakness was only partially and gradually rectified during the era of the Office of Production Management and the Office of Price Administration and Civilian Supply, and to a somewhat greater extent under the Supply, Priorities, and Allocations Board. The WPB, with its broad charter of authority concentrated in the chairman, appeared for a brief time to meet the need. Even within the production area, however, important functions were soon divorced from effective WPB control; they included food, manpower, transportation, housing, fuel, and synthetic rubber. At the same time, the WPB's authority over the armed services was weakened. On the economic-stabilization side, it became increasingly evident that farm and nonfarm prices, wages, and related stabilization measures must be placed within a general pattern under common direction. And at an even higher level, co-ordination was essential among the three broad areas of procurement, production, and economic stabilization.

In response to these needs, the Office of Economic Stabilization (OES) was established by executive order in October, 1942, with general responsibility to "formulate and develop a comprehensive national economic policy relating to the control of civilian purchasing power, prices, rents, wages, salaries, profits, rationing, subsidies, and all related matters." [7] The OES was authorized to issue directives on policy to the relevant operating agencies. In May, 1943, taking into account increasing congressional sentiment for even broader co-ordinating machinery, the President established the Office of War Mobilization (OWM). Its director was "to develop unified programs and to establish policies for the maximum use of the nation's natural and industrial resources for military and civilian needs, for the effective use of the national manpower not in the armed forces, for maintenance and stabilization of the civilian economy, and for the adjustment of such economy to war needs and conditions." He was also to unify the activities of the services and the various war agencies and to issue any

[7] Executive Order 9250, October 3, 1942.

necessary directives on policy or operations.[8] In October, 1944, this agency was renamed the Office of War Mobilization and Reconversion (OWMR) and was given additional statutory responsibility to draft reconversion plans.

These offices played a vital role in resolving disputes among the operating agencies and in providing top direction for the war economy.[9] They received a virtually total delegation of home-front authority from the President, who was already overburdened by the problems of high military strategy, interallied negotiation, and preparation for the peace settlement and postwar international organization. Justice James F. Byrnes, the first director of both offices, and his successor, Judge Fred M. Vinson (subsequently Chief Justice of the United States), chose to keep their staffs small and their functions concentrated on the arbitration of disputes rather than initiative in policy formulation. Entering the scene after the operating agencies were well established, they recognized the difficulties of initiating sound policy without the understanding derived from intimate contact with day-to-day operations, and felt it unwise to interfere unduly in operating policies.

After the establishment of the OES and OWM, public interagency disputes were sharply reduced in number and the various phases of war administration were kept in reasonable balance. Nonetheless, the attitude of umpire rather than director assumed by these agencies often promoted an unfortunate crystallization of conflicting viewpoints, an undue prolongation of differences, and a tendency toward compromise for its own sake. The top coordinating agencies, as they functioned in practice, were not an effective substitute for sustained co-operation at working levels, and they not infrequently failed to take enough initiative on major mobilization issues.

5. Demobilization and Reconversion

Military victory brought with it the task of economic demobilization, comparable in magnitude, if not in difficulty, with that of mobilization. Eleven million men and women being discharged from the armed forces had to find their places in civilian life, and twenty million were to shift from war production to normal civilian pursuits. The reconversion of industry from the manufacture of war goods to civilian products involved the settlement of tens of thou-

[8] Executive Order 9347, May 27, 1943.
[9] For a history and analysis of the OWMR, see H. M. Somers, *Presidential Agency* (1950).

sands of contracts, retooling, the removal from plants of partly finished military products, the refilling of production pipelines with materials for civilian output, the re-establishment of distribution channels, the creation of smooth industrial relations for the postwar period, and the determination of price and production policies. Demobilization also required the unwinding of the great complex of wartime government controls.

Contrary to many expectations, the process of physical demobilization and reconversion took place remarkably swiftly and smoothly. Economic stability, on the other hand, was not maintained, and the problem of inflation remained acute long after physical reconversion was completed.

The Development of Demobilization Policy

Reconversion planning was begun in a sporadic fashion as early as 1942, but systematic attention could not be shifted from the immediate and urgent problems of war until 1944, when the military balance had clearly turned in our favor. Even then, and until the German surrender, reconversion planning was hampered by concern over its possible adverse effect on war output. There was particular fear of a premature flight of manpower from war plants, a fear magnified by the absence of direct manpower controls and the expectation of a postwar depression with sharp job competition.

Leadership in reconversion planning fell to the Office of War Mobilization and its successor Office of War Mobilization and Reconversion. At the end of 1943, the OWM created a special advisory unit for war and postwar adjustment policies under the direction of Bernard M. Baruch. This unit reported in February, 1944, a series of specific recommendations on major problems of demobilization. Congress responded with the passage of four statutes: the Servicemen's Readjustment Act of 1944 (the so-called "G.I. Bill of Rights"), the Contract Settlement Act, the War Mobilization and Reconversion Act, and the Surplus War Property Act. At the same time, the war agencies began systematic planning of their own demobilization programs.

Reconversion plans were founded on the expectation of a substantial lapse of time between the German and Japanese surrenders. The WPB assumed that at V-E Day, the day of German surrender, there would be heavy military cutbacks and a consequent release of materials and manpower more rapidly than plant reconversion could absorb them. The plans, therefcre, called for the rapid elimination of almost all civilian production controls not directly essential to continuing military production and a "free" rather than a government "programmed" reconversion. In fact, the demands of the one-front war, during its brief existence, proved much more onerous and scarcities more persistent than anticipated. Had the Japanese conflict continued into 1946, there would have been serious difficulties in maintaining the required munitions output. Since hostilities with Japan fortunately ceased on August 15, 1945, only three months after the German surrender, this brief interim proved helpful in launching the processes of physical reconversion.

The stabilization agencies were more cautious than the WPB. The OPA planned for the selective decontrol of prices for goods in ample supply and establishment of more favorable pricing standards for reconversion products. But it emphasized the dangers of postwar inflation and envisaged the prolongation of general price control for a considerable period.

Economic policy for V-J Day was based on a recognition of three possibilities: general inflation, sharp general deflation, or a mixture. The emphasis, however, was on anticipated heavy transitional unemployment, which was expected to reach five to eight millions a few months after the Japanese surrender. Support was therefore given to the maintenance of purchasing power through wage increases and broadened unemployment compensation, the speedy restoration of all forms of civilian construction, including public works, and price-sustaining policies in agriculture and in the liquidation of war surpluses. The forecasts proved grossly in error. The resulting policies magnified the difficulties of maintaining transitional stability, already serious enough with the loss of wartime incentives for the subordination of individual and narrow group interests. Nonetheless, advance planning for demobilization and reconversion put the nation in a far better position than at Armistice Day in 1918, even in relation to its greater task.

Industrial Reconversion and the Demobilization of Production Controls

When the test came, the transfer of manpower out of the armed forces and from war to civilian work, and the reconversion of industry to high-level civilian output, took place with unexpected rapidity. Industrial reconversion was carried out primarily on the initiative of individual firms, facilitated here and there by government action, but not closely guided. By mid-1946, ten million men and women had been discharged from the services, a number far greater than scheduled at V-J Day. Yet unemployment never exceeded 2.7 million and by the fall of 1946 was down to about two million.

The smooth demobilization of military manpower was greatly facilitated by the "G.I. Bill of Rights," which extended comprehensive assistance for the readjustment of veterans to civilian life. In addition to special benefits for disabled veterans, it provided employment-placement services, guaranteed loans for the purchase of homes or farms or for entry into business, allowances for unemployed veterans, and generous financial assistance for education and vocational training.

Contract termination and the physical clearance of plants also proceeded very smoothly. The disposal of war surpluses was slower, and was complicated by an elaborate statutory system of priorities for various classes of consumers and by other difficult administrative problems. However, with civilian demand rising to extraordinarily high levels, surplus disposal offered no serious interference with reconversion, and the gradual liquidation helped to some extent to check inflationary pressures.

Production controls were dismantled with great rapidity, but scarcities were persistent, not only in the consumers' durable goods which had been cut off during the war, but also in basic materials of all kinds, notably steel, the heavy nonferrous metals, lumber, and other building materials. The forecasts had underestimated the speed of reconversion and had not appreciated the magnitude of requirements for a postwar civilian economy operating at almost double prewar levels.

In November, 1945, therefore, when the WPB was terminated, it was replaced by a Civilian Production Administration, charged with expanding the production of materials in short supply, continued limitation of end-product manufacture where materials or facilities were insufficient, inventory control to prevent speculative hoarding, granting of priorities to break bottlenecks impeding reconversion, facilitation of foreign relief and other essential export programs, and allocation of scarce materials and facilities to promote the continuing program of economic stabilization.[10] The agency operated for about a year, focusing its attention on the expansion of supplies of building materials and on a vain endeavor, in conjunction with the OPA, to continue the programs for low-cost clothing initiated toward the end of the war.

The greatest continuing scarcity of the immediate postwar period was in housing. Building had been at very low levels during the depression, and except for war housing was virtually suspended during the war years. At the close of 1945, the President created the Office of Housing Expediter to apply to the housing shortage the

[10] See Executive Order 9638, October 4, 1945.

combined techniques of incentives and controls successfully employed in expanding war production. While housing construction was in fact greatly expanded, the effort to apply wartime control techniques broke down in the face of concerted industry opposition and increasing public reaction and antagonism to all forms of direct control. Little rental housing was built, and construction costs soared. At the end of 1946, the program was virtually abandoned.

Despite the many continuing scarcities, the country was in no mood to maintain wartime production controls. The Second War Powers Act was finally permitted to lapse in the spring of 1947, when the First and Second Decontrol Acts were passed, leaving only a minor residue of temporary production-control powers.

Economic Stabilization in the Postwar Transition

Demobilization of wartime stabilization measures followed a more uneven course than the removal of production controls. The objective was sufficiently clear: to minimize unemployment, to avoid an inflationary hump and subsequent collapse like those of 1919–1921, and to emerge at a plateau of high-level economic activity. The methods chosen, however, were not always consistently designed to achieve these ends, and in large measure they proved unacceptable to a public increasingly restive at the continuance of direct price and wage controls.

The problem of wage control and its relation to price policy was particularly baffling. With the war over, the no-strike pledge could no longer be relied on, and it was desired to return as quickly as possible to free collective bargaining. Wholly unregulated wages, however, were incompatible with regulated prices. The administration, moreover, wished to promote wage increases in order to maintain "take-home" pay despite loss of overtime earnings and downgrading of jobs, with the double purpose of countering the expected deflation and retaining the political support of organized labor.

In these circumstances, the government endeavored to restore partially free collective bargaining and to promote wage increases which would not be reflected in price increases.[11] The policy proved unworkable. Many businessmen felt that the OPA's administration of the price standards was too rigid, and organized increasingly effective resistance to continued price control. Attempts to persuade labor and management to reach a broad wage-price agree-

[11] See Executive Order 9599, August 18, 1945, and Executive Order 9651, October 30, 1945.

ment failed, and the wage-control structure was speedily liquidated. In the winter of 1945–1946, a series of protracted strikes occurred in automobile, steel, and other heavy industries, and their settlement required abandonment of the earlier policy.

The OPA consequently adopted looser pricing standards in February, 1946, but with its price-control authority due to expire at midyear, a bitter political battle ensued over the terms of its continuance. Late in June, Congress authorized its extension, but required the translation of all cost increases into price increases. Condemned by President Truman as "a sure formula for inflation," the measure was vetoed. There followed a month of total absence of legal price control, during which prices rose rapidly. On July 25, a bill extending greatly modified price control for one year was enacted. By this time, however, matters were out of hand. The position was most difficult in the related fields of grain, meat, and dairy products, where the termination of price control had brought forth a temporary flood of supplies which at once dried up with the attempt at recontrol. Shortly before the November election, virtually all food controls were abandoned. Although the cost of living had risen 14 per cent between June and November, 1946, and the cost of food had increased no less than 29 per cent in the same five months, the sweeping Republican congressional victory under the slogan "Had Enough?" appeared to confirm the loss of popular support for the government's stabilization efforts. A week after the election, all price controls were removed, although rent control was extended in modified form. Continuing inflationary pressures were to remain a major problem of public policy for the postwar period, but direct controls were ruled out as a method for dealing with them in peacetime.

6. The National Security Factor
in the Peacetime Economy

World War II and the ensuing "Cold War" between the free nations and the forces of Soviet Communism created in the American public a new consciousness of the position of the United States in world affairs. In contrast with the isolationist reaction of the 1920's and the obsession with neutrality of the 1930's, this country was now participating fully in the United Nations and was the principal partner in a series of regional collective-security alliances ranging from Europe to Southeast Asia. After the beginning of hostilities in Korea in 1950, the arms race with the Soviet Union dominated federal budget-making. Since any global conflict and many possible limited wars would involve the United States immediately, defense policy was concentrated on continuous readiness rather than planning for gradual war mobilization. A large part of the armed forces was stationed in foreign countries or in distant seas. For the first time, the continental United States was directly exposed to the menace of large-scale attack. In these conditions, national security considerations not only played a major part in foreign policy, including foreign economic policy; [12] they also impinged on many governmental relations to the domestic economy.

A simple measure of the impact of national defense lies in the annual budgets. In fiscal 1957, for example, federal expenditures exceeded $69 billion. Almost two-thirds of this total, or over $44 billion, was spent on major security programs (military functions of the Defense Department, atomic energy, and foreign military aid under the mutual-security program). This was more than 10 per cent of the gross national product. Even this figure somewhat understates the resources devoted to national security, for many other programs are partly justified by defense considerations.

Nor is any decline in military expenditures in sight. National security costs have been magnified by the simultaneous need for conventional weapons necessary for "brush-fire" hostilities and for research, development, and production of complex new weapons required to deter massive aggression—weapons such as atomic and hydrogen explosives, supersonic aircraft, intercontinental ballistic missiles, radar warning systems, and possibly anti-missile missiles. Requirements for passive defense were only beginning to receive serious consideration in the late 1950's, and it appeared that even a shelter program limited to protection against radioactive fallout would cost some tens of billions of dollars.

While the scale of the Cold War and the pace of weapons technology were not fully anticipated at the close of World War II, they were sufficiently foreshadowed for defense mobilization to be given new recognition as a major peacetime function of government. After two years of debate, Congress adopted the National Security Act of 1947, creating the National Military Establishment under a Secretary of Defense to co-ordinate the Army, the Navy, and the Air Force. This statute also established other new security agencies, notably a National Security Council to integrate domestic, foreign, and military policies relating to national secu-

[12] See Chapter 28, below.

rity; a Central Intelligence Agency; and a National Security Resources Board, charged with responsibility for the broad planning of industrial mobilization.[13]

The Korean War: Limited Mobilization

This organization for the planning and administration of defense mobilization was tested, and considerably amplified, by the Korean War of 1950–1953. That experience entailed a partial economic mobilization to support the fighting in Korea; at the same time, it was decided to increase substantially our armed forces elsewhere and to encourage and assist a large rearmament effort by our allies, especially in Europe. Steps were also taken to establish an industrial-mobilization base which would permit a very rapid expansion of defense production if the hostilities should spread.[14]

The United States entered upon this limited mobilization with better organizational machinery than had existed in the two World Wars. While the 1947 Act had not had time to become fully operational, it did provide a central control mechanism which could be readily developed as the needs grew. After the Chinese intervention in November, 1950, the Office of Defense Mobilization (ODM) was established and charged with full control over "all mobilization activities of the federal government, including but not limited to production, procurement, manpower, stabilization, and transport activities." Thus machinery for co-ordination, evolved only toward the end of World War II, was functioning from an early stage of the Korean mobilization effort.

The Director of the ODM divided his over-all responsibility into six areas, each to be handled by a subordinate agency. Four of these areas—Foreign Supplies and Requirements, Manpower, Transportation, and Scientific Research—were directed by temporary committees chosen from interested departments and agencies. The other two areas—Stabilization and Production—presented larger problems and required greater organization. The first was assigned, subject to broad policy direction by the ODM, to an Economic Stabilization Agency. It handled direct stabilization controls through three subordinate bodies, the Office of Price Stabilization, the Wage Stabilization Board, and the Salary Sta-

[13] As a result of developments during and after the Korean War, the latter Board was subsequently absorbed into the Office of Defense Mobilization; in 1958, it was also charged with civil-defense responsibilities and became the Office of Civil and Defense Mobilization.

[14] For a discussion of this limited mobilization effort, see G. A. Lincoln et al., Economics of National Security (1954), pp. 86–98.

bilization Board. Indirect stabilization measures, such as taxation and credit controls, were administered by the Treasury and the Federal Reserve System, subject to co-ordination by the Economic Stabilization Agency. Production control was assigned to a Defense Production Administration, closely integrated with the Commerce Department, but also subject to the ODM's general policy direction.

Thus policy was generally set by the temporary mobilization agencies, but, except for direct stabilization controls, it was implemented by permanent departments and agencies. The latter usually functioned through special defense offices. This system involved a degree of friction between the permanent departments and the mobilization agencies, but it had the advantage of providing administrative manpower promptly. It served in effect as a halfway house between normal arrangements and the full consolidation of emergency controls under temporary agencies—a halfway house appropriate to the task of partial mobilization.

Requirements for industrial mobilization and economic stabilization were quite different from those of World War II. Only about 15 per cent of total national output was devoted to defense at the peak of the Korean War. Substantial, although unbalanced, supplies of military equipment were on hand. The shipping built in World War II was readily available, and many war plants had been maintained on a stand-by basis, especially those for producing explosives, aircraft, and synthetic rubber. On the other hand, real difficulties were involved in diverting even a moderate proportion of civilian plant, materials, and labor to war production, for the 1950 economy was already functioning at record levels. There were few idle resources, and military output could be increased only at the cost of cutbacks in civilian production.

An important aspect of the Korean War program was the development of an industrial mobilization base which would be only partly used in limited hostilities but could be adapted without delay to the larger needs of a global war. The goal was to induce existing plants to convert some of their facilities to munitions production, or to be immediately ready to do so. Full-scale and "educational" orders were placed for this purpose. The government procured specialized equipment, especially machine tools, for use or storage in such plants. Industry was also induced, through accelerated depreciation tax allowances and through commitments to future orders, to expand facilities beyond the levels which ordinary commercial demand would dictate. The stockpiling of strategic and critical materials, which had been begun under the

Strategic and Critical Materials Act of 1946, was greatly enlarged, in order to secure a ready store of those materials essential to war production which are scarce or largely imported or whose production or processing is slow. Thus, the emphasis was more on an organized reserve of industrial productivity than on the accumulation of stocks of munitions.

To deal with the immediate need to divert resources to war production, conservation orders were issued restricting the non-defense use of a number of materials, especially the nonferrous metals. Priorities were also used, but sparingly and with only a single preference rating. Contractors could extend their priorities to their suppliers. In mid-1951, the Controlled Materials Plan was re-instituted to allocate steel, aluminum, copper, and a number of other materials.

The main emphasis of manpower policy was on adding workers to the labor force and upgrading their skills—an extension of the policy of broadening the mobilization base. Since the need for additional manpower was relatively small, it was generally met by lengthening the average work week and by the attraction of high wages. The problem of securing skilled workers was more difficult; it required special training programs, some of which were sponsored by the government.

The Economic Stabilization Agency (ESA) confronted a more difficult task, and its actions reflected the one clear failure of the Korean mobilization program. With the economy already operating close to capacity, even the limited diversion of resources to defense was bound to unleash inflationary forces. The imposition of higher taxes on personal and corporate incomes, the levying of an excess-profits tax on corporations, and the natural increase in tax receipts due to higher levels of national income only slowed these forces. Taxes were not raised sufficiently to counteract inflation. While a cash surplus of $7.6 billion was realized in fiscal 1951, and the 1952 cash budget was nearly in balance, this was followed in 1953 by a deficit of $5.3 billion. Monetary controls were wholly in suspense until the Treasury-Federal Reserve accord of 1951.

Consequently, nearly the entire burden of checking the inflationary pressures was left to direct controls, but under limited war conditions there was too little sense of urgency for them to be effective. The result was substantial inflation. The wholesale price index rose from 99.2 in 1949 to 110.1 in 1953, and the consumer price index from 101.8 to 114.4.

Three months after the start of the Korean War, and after substantial price increases had already occurred, Congress passed the Defense Production Act of 1950, authorizing either selective or comprehensive control of prices. Remembering the difficulties of attempting to extend price control after World War II, President Truman wanted to impose controls gradually and flexibly. Congress, at the urging of Bernard Baruch, authorized somewhat more extensive controls than the President requested, although far less than Baruch had recommended. Neither the terms of the Act nor the manner of its administration, however, permitted effective stabilization.

The Act required that prices be controlled only if wages were also controlled. Once again, farm products were given special consideration. Their prices could not be fixed below parity or the levels prevailing in May, 1950, whichever was higher. The ESA first attempted to hold prices down by persuasion, but without much success. It then attempted to apply selective controls, e.g., on automobiles. But the Agency could not fix prices without fixing wages, and it was politically impossible to freeze wages in some industries and not in others. Accordingly, selective controls also failed. Finally, in January, 1951, the ESA issued a general wage-price freeze, assigning its administration to the Office of Price Stabilization (OPS) and the Wage Stabilization Board. But by freezing prices as of that time, the order incorporated the already substantial inflation which had taken place since the outbreak of hostilities. And the terms of the law ensured at least some degree of continuing inflation. Farm prices could rise to parity, and parity itself rose automatically as its computation reflected higher prices elsewhere in the economy. Wages were allowed to rise in proportion to increases in the cost of living, and in conformity with escalator clauses in union contracts. The OPS attempted to "roll back" some prices, but Congress in mid-1951 required that producers' ceiling prices be raised to allow for past increases in production costs. These increases were passed on to final consumers, pyramided in size by the further requirement that distributors be permitted their pre-Korea percentage markups. Thus inflation was made virtually compulsory. The OPS began dismantling its regulatory arrangements in the spring of 1952, and the program was liquidated a year later.

A similar effort to control wages also met difficulties and ultimate frustration. The Wage Stabilization Board followed a liberal policy, allowing all wage rates to rise 10 per cent above the levels of January, 1950, as a rough equivalent to the increase in the cost of living. It also permitted increases in particular occupational rates believed to be unduly depressed, increases reflecting average improvements in productivity for the whole economy, and increases to ease manpower shortages in particular defense plants. So loose a policy greatly hampered the OPS in its efforts to hold down or roll back prices. The costly steel strike of 1952, which caused the loss of about twenty million tons of steel, was partly the result of the OPS view that the steel companies should absorb wage increases without an increase in prices. Even the powers so gently used by the WSB, however, were restricted in 1952, when Congress drastically curtailed the Board's jurisdiction over industrial disputes. Without the power to rule on labor-management disputes, it was foreclosed from maintaining a consistent wage policy.

Congress also reacted adversely to the imposition of credit controls. The Defense Production Act authorized the Federal Reserve Board to regulate consumer credit. Since installment buying had doubled after the beginning of the Korean War, adding significantly to the upward pressure on prices, the Board adopted a rigorous policy, requiring down payments of 25 per cent and full payments within fifteen months. Credit expansion was thereby swiftly checked, but under pressure from manufacturers, distributors, and credit companies, Congress restricted the Board's powers in July, 1951. Maximum payment periods could not be set at less than eighteen months, and down payments on furniture and household appliances could not be required to exceed 15 per cent. Even this diminished authority, which might have been a useful instrument of general countercyclical policy, was terminated by Congress in June, 1952; there ensued a rapid expansion of installment credit.

National Defense and the Mixed Economy

The Korean Armistice did not bring with it any promise that defense expenditures could safely be lowered. The Eisenhower administration made vigorous efforts to reduce them, curtailing the size of the Army and limiting conventional weapons to a scale felt by many observers to be dangerously low. In fiscal 1956, defense spending was 20 per cent below the Korean War peak, but still more than three times the pre-Korean level. The almost fantastic pace of developments in military technology was requiring steadily increased expenditures on newer weapons, and the Soviet launching of the first earth satellite in October, 1957, showed dramatically that a grim race was under way for superiority in long-range missile development. Nor was there any significant slackening in atomic energy development or in military assistance to our allies. As a result, total security expenditures again began to creep upward from $41.8 billion in fiscal 1956 to $45.8 billion budgeted for fiscal 1959, and no prospect of reduction was in sight.

So high a level of defense expenditure has substantial implications for government's role in the economy. It is a determining factor in the magnitude of the total budget and in the necessary levels of taxation. It makes government the sole or largest customer for a number of major industries, such as aircraft, electronics, atomic energy, and missiles, and a significant buyer for many others. The labor force is directly affected by the manpower needs of the military services, and there is sharp competition between industry and the armed forces for many special skills. Applied research, both in industry and in the universities, is heavily weighted toward security projects. Stockpiling has a major impact on markets for certain commodities. The regional distribution of defense installations deeply affects the local communities concerned and their needs for community facilities. If a shelter program were set in motion, it would place a wholly new type and scale of demand on the construction industry. As is shown in Chapter 28, defense considerations are also a paramount factor in foreign economic policy.

Pessimistic observers have speculated on whether a projection of the arms race will not lead inevitably to a "garrison state," a society in perpetual full mobilization where all freedoms are jeopardized by the overriding needs of national survival. Such fears would appear grossly to underrate the capacity of a growing American economy to generate surplus resources for defense without serious impairment of its basic structure. Yet the fact remains that large security programs inescapably add to the economic responsibilities of government and greatly increase the public component of the mixed economy. Until or unless some adequate basis is found for effectively controlled limitation of arms on a global scale, it is difficult to see how this trend can be reversed.

CHAPTER **28**

The United States and the World Economy

IN THE brief period since World War II, the new dimension of foreign economic policy has been added to government's role in the economy. This does not imply that foreign trade and international investment have only recently become important to the United States. In the early nineteenth century, foreign trade accounted for a much larger proportion of our national income than it does today, and throughout that century foreign investment played a major part in the nation's westward expansion and industrialization. Moreover, certain of our domestic economic policies have had an important bearing on international economic relations. The outstanding example is the tariff, which was for many decades the principal governmental instrument for the promotion of business enterprise.[1] Other cases in point include shipping policy,[2] agricultural price supports,[3] and stabilization of oil production.[4]

For the first century and a half of our national existence, however, the central focus of public economic policy was on the peopling and development of our own nation, the resolution of our interregional conflicts, and the regulation of various sectors of the economy according to the interplay of domestic political forces.

[1] See Chapter 5.
[2] See pages 105–114.
[3] See Chapter 6.
[4] See Chapter 20.

The very notion of a consciously designed American foreign economic policy scarcely existed before World War I and was developed in only rudimentary form in connection with the Reciprocal Trade Agreements Program of the mid-thirties. In recent years, by contrast, foreign economic policy has become a central focus of governmental and public attention, a major instrument of American leadership in world affairs.

In bringing about this transformation, economic factors have exercised a significant but only secondary influence. For certain critical materials, the American economy is becoming increasingly dependent on imports. A widening range of agricultural and industrial producers look to exports and to overseas investment for an important share of their income. Expanding world trade based on orderly commercial and financial arrangements is recognized as making an important contribution to economic growth and stability in the United States. The main impetus to the postwar development of American foreign economic policy, however, has come from broader considerations of foreign policy and national security. The key objectives have been twofold: (1) added strength and cohesion in the alliances for collective security against Communist aggression, and (2) the promotion of economic development as a basis for stable and mutually beneficial long-range relationships with the less-developed nations of the world, many of whom achieved political independence only recently.

Thus foreign economic policy has been shaped mainly by the same forces that have projected the United States suddenly and with little preparation into the unaccustomed role of free-world leadership. In contrast with the political and military aspects of foreign relations, however, the implementation of foreign economic policy often bears directly on the interests of organized and politically influential segments of the domestic economy. The effort to avoid or to reconcile conflicts between those interests and broader international political and security objectives is one major strand in the formation of policy in this field.

1. America's Stake in the World Economy

Except for the Soviet Union and Communist China, the United States approaches economic self-sufficiency more closely than any other nation in the world. In 1957, when our international transactions reached an all-time high, exports of goods and services (excluding military assistance) amounted to $26.3 billion, less than 6 per cent of gross national product; the proportion of imports was less than 5 per cent. Corresponding proportions for such countries as Brazil, Mexico, Japan, and Indonesia ranged from 10 to 15 per cent; for Canada, Germany, and Britain, from 20 to 25 per cent; and for the smaller nations of Western Europe and Australasia, from 25 to 40 per cent. The United States is a net exporter of basic foodstuffs and meets from its own resources most of its needs for energy supplies and agricultural and mineral raw materials. These basic facts explain the relatively small role of foreign economic considerations in determining American domestic economic policies. Elsewhere in the free world, the balance of international payments is in all cases a leading, if not the dominant, factor in the formulation of economic policies.

The Direct Impact of Foreign Trade

To look alone at these general averages, however, is seriously to underrate the direct importance of foreign trade to the American economy. On the import side, apart from tropical foodstuffs and beverages not produced at all in the United States, we are heavily and increasingly dependent on imports for substantial proportions of many raw material supplies. In recent years, for example, foreign sources have supplied one-sixth to one-third of our consumption of petroleum, iron ore, copper, and rubber; about one-half of our wool; and the major part, if not all, of our tin, nickel, bauxite, lead, zinc, newsprint, ferro-alloying materials, industrial diamonds, mica, asbestos, and other products. Some of these imports could be replaced fairly easily, although at higher cost, from domestic sources; others are almost indispensable for both strategic and industrial reasons.[5]

The likelihood, moreover, is for increasing dependence on imported raw materials. The President's Materials Policy Commission (Paley Commission) pointed in 1952 to the fact that:

By the midpoint of the twentieth century we had entered an era of new relationships between our needs and resources; our national economy had not merely grown up to its resource base, but in many important respects had outgrown it. We had completed our slow transition from a raw materials surplus Nation to a raw materials deficit Nation.[6]

[5] See Department of Commerce, "The Role of Foreign Trade in the United States Economy," House Ways and Means Committee, Subcommittee on Foreign Trade Policy, *Compendium of Papers on U.S. Foreign Trade Policy*, 85th Cong., 1st sess. (1957), pp. 15–22. See also Department of Commerce, *Contribution of Imports to U.S. Raw Material Supplies, 1955*, World Trade Information Service, Part 3, No. 57-1 (1957).

[6] *Resources for Freedom*, Vol. I (1952), p. 6.

It is only to be expected that a country, even richly endowed with natural resources, which accounts for almost 40 per cent of the world's total production while occupying only 6 per cent of the earth's land surface, would use up its materials more rapidly than the rest of the world and would become increasingly reliant on imports to support continued economic growth. The trend would already have gone much further had it not been for important technological developments, such as production of synthetic rubber, nylon and other artificial fibers, chemical fertilizers, and plastics. On balance, however, the outlook appears to be for gradually increasing dependence on imported raw material supplies, and in consequence an enhanced importance of access to such supplies with assurance and on reasonable terms.

On the export side, American agriculture is traditionally the economic sector most interested in foreign markets. In recent years, between 25 and 40 per cent of the output of cotton, wheat, rice, fats and oils, and tobacco has been sold abroad. In addition, as the pace of American industrialization has outstripped that of Europe during the last several decades, increasing numbers of industrial producers have come to depend on export markets for a substantial share of their business. This is especially true for tractors, trucks, and other vehicles; construction, mining, and industrial equipment; and certain chemicals and pharmaceuticals. A growing number of service industries in the fields of shipping and aviation, banking and insurance, tourism and communications, also derive much of their revenue from foreign business. Altogether, some 7 per cent of the total labor force gains its livelihood from foreign trade.[7]

Moreover, despite its superficially marginal character, foreign trade, together with international capital movements, has had at times a marked effect on the general level of American economic activity. The collapse of international financial arrangements in 1931 and the acute contraction in international trade which ensued were important factors in deepening and prolonging the Great Depression. The maintenance of foreign trade is given some credit, on the other hand, for moderating and shortening the recession of 1953–1954.

The Indirect Stake

The indirect stake of the United States in the world economy is still larger. It derives from the enormous importance of American

[7] See Department of Commerce, *Exports in Relation to U.S. Production, 1955*, World Trade Information Service, Part 3, No. 56-31 (1956).

trade and investment to the rest of the world. The sheer weight of the American economy is so great that what is relatively small for us is of vital concern to others. American imports are more than one-eighth, and exports more than one-fifth, of the free world's totals. The United States accounts for well over half of Canada's foreign transactions and about half of those of Latin America. The United States is by a wide margin the leading market for almost all the world's production of primary products. Exports to the United States of foodstuffs and raw materials represent the bulk of the foreign-exchange earnings, and in some cases the bulk of the national income, of many underdeveloped countries in Asia, Africa, and Latin America. The dollar has come to rival sterling as an international trading currency, and since World War II it has outranked sterling as a form of foreign exchange reserve and international liquidity. For almost ten years after the war, the problem of "dollar shortage" was the central concern of public economic policy in Western Europe and many other parts of the world. Changes in American business conditions can induce serious inflation or grave deflation and unemployment in other countries by altering their market prospects, terms of international trade, or availabilities of foreign exchange for essential imports of raw materials and capital equipment.

In addition to its leading position in current trade, the United States has become by far the most important supplier, actual and potential, of international capital. In the nineteenth century, American development had been substantially assisted by foreign investment. Although Americans began increasingly to invest abroad around the turn of the century, in 1914 the net long-term investment position of the United States was still more than $3 billion on the debit side. The shift to a creditor position was vastly accelerated by the two world wars. In the 1920's, the United States for the first time entered the foreign investment field on a large scale, building up by 1930 a long-term net credit position of almost $10 billion; but the Great Depression caused a reduction of this figure to less than $5 billion on the eve of World War II. During the war, the remaining foreign investments in the United States were largely liquidated. While they have been somewhat rebuilt in recent years, the expansion of American foreign investment, both private and public, has been so large that by the end of 1957 the net long-term credit position of this country in relation to the rest of the world had been increased to almost $37 billion ($51 billion gross, less $14 billion foreign long-term investment in the United States). Of the gross total of $51 billion, about two-thirds was on private account, and one-third public.[8]

This profound shift in the international economic position of the United States has had three important effects. First, other nations are no longer able to rely on net income from investments as a means of financing an excess of American exports over our imports. That excess has been very considerable in recent years, but it has been offset by foreign-aid programs, the disposal at governmental expense of agricultural surpluses, and American overseas military expenditures. The only other means of maintaining a high export volume would be expanded imports; hence the increased pressure, sometimes under the slogan "trade not aid," for a more liberal American import policy.

Secondly, the United States has become the main reliance for outside capital to accelerate development in other sectors of the free world, not only in the underdeveloped countries but also in advanced areas such as Canada and Western Europe. This is true of both private and governmental capital. If foreign investment on the part of free-world nations is to play an important role in accelerating development, most of the capital under present circumstances must come from this country.

Thirdly, the growth in private investment has given American business an increasingly important stake in foreign branches, subsidiaries, licensees, and joint ventures. In contrast with the prewar period, postwar private investment has been mainly "direct," i.e., involving the establishment of wholly or partly controlled concerns in other countries. Most such investment has been in the fields of petroleum and minerals extraction, and is related to the increasing dependence of the American economy on foreign materials sources. In the last few years, however, foreign direct investment has become increasingly diversified, including a wide variety of manufacturing industries and services for local markets, especially in Canada, Latin America, and Western Europe. In 1957 alone, direct new dollar investment was about $2.1 billion; reinvestment of profits of subsidiaries amounted to a further $1 billion. Thus, American business has come to have an increasing interest in political and economic conditions abroad.

In summary, then, the United States has a substantial and growing direct stake in the world economy, and a still larger indirect stake because of the importance of our economic actions to other nations. American foreign economic policy is now a major force in influencing the strength and cohesion of the free world; it has be-

[8] See Department of Commerce, *Survey of Current Business* (September, 1958), pp. 15–23.

come a leading instrument of foreign and national security policy. At the same time, the predominant position of the United States in the world economy has made our actions decisive in almost any efforts to provide an orderly framework for expanded international trade, finance, and investment.

The resulting opportunity for leadership has been affirmatively seized. In the wartime and immediate postwar years, much effort was devoted to the design of international economic arrangements to replace the prewar chaos; this was an economic counterpart to the political and security system which the United Nations was intended to provide. Parts of this system in fact came into being and have survived; others were cut short or modified by unanticipated developments, including the Cold War. A second stream of postwar policy was a response to *ad hoc* emergencies and to forces which had been underestimated: the dollar shortage and the threatened economic collapse of Europe, the direct and indirect military imperatives of the Cold War, the vigor of the drive for economic advance in the poorer countries, and the development of economic regionalism in some areas of the world. The rest of this chapter outlines the principal elements of these two streams of policy, now partially merged and still in the course of rapid evolution.

2. The Bretton Woods System—Design and Reality

The array of international economic arrangements planned for the postwar period may be called the Bretton Woods system, named for the United Nations Monetary and Financial Conference held at that New Hampshire resort in the early summer of 1944. The Bretton Woods conference itself was focused mainly on international finance and public investment, the results comprising the Articles of Agreement of the International Monetary Fund and the International Bank for Reconstruction and Development. Parallel negotiations on commercial policy, private investment, and international commodity arrangements took place in 1947 and 1948 at Geneva and Havana, but the broad design for a postwar system was fully sketched out and widely agreed on at Bretton Woods.

The idea of new forms of postwar international economic cooperation had been touched on in the original Atlantic Charter signed by President Roosevelt and Prime Minister Churchill in the summer of 1941, and was given further elaboration in the various Lend-Lease agreements, especially that with the United Kingdom. It was the subject of intensive expert discussion within the United States government during the war years and of negotiation between America and Britain in the latter stages of the war as victory came in sight. The Bretton Woods conference was attended by representatives of forty-four nations, including the Soviet Union, but the Communist countries later withdrew from international collaboration in the economic field and did not participate in the trade negotiations at Geneva or Havana.

The broad design covered the fields of international trade, finance, investment, and development. The general inspiration was liberal in the nineteenth-century sense of that term. It sought the maximum possible freedom in the international movement of goods and capital without discrimination among nations, a gradual lowering of trade barriers, the elimination of private cartel restrictions, stable exchange rates with monetary reserves large enough to permit free multilateral financial settlements and to avoid competitive depreciation, and codes of conduct to ensure the good behavior of both governments and private parties in international economic dealings.

The design, however, was not one of doctrinaire laissez faire. It did not call for universal free trade or re-establishment of the gold standard, or otherwise seek to recreate the vanished nineteenth-century world economic order. The liberal objectives were rather to be achieved through intergovernmental co-operation, buttressed by international institutions in each major field. Thus, there was to be an International Trade Organization (ITO) to establish and supervise the ground rules for trade, commodity markets, and private investment; an International Monetary Fund (IMF) for financial co-operation, exchange-rate adjustment, and the supplementation of national gold and foreign exchange reserves; and an International Bank for Reconstruction and Development (IBRD) for public investment in basic fields such as transportation, communications, energy supplies, and water-resource control, fields where private capital would not flow in adequate amounts.

For the United States to lead in developing and implementing such a broad design, and to support it with large financial resources and important new commitments for international commercial and financial co-operation, implied a revolutionary change in national attitudes. On the trade side, to be sure, it involved a logical progression from the Reciprocal Trade Agreements policy initiated in 1934 and outlined in Chapter 5, but even in this respect it was a radical forward step. In the other areas it was wholly novel. The proposed scheme of financial co-operation was in dramatic contrast with the unilateral action of the United States in 1933, which devalued the dollar and broke up the London Economic Conference.

The Bretton Woods agreements required congressional endorsement and large-scale appropriations, but they were accepted in 1945 with surprisingly little dissent. So rapid and far-reaching a transformation in the nation's approach to foreign economic affairs was possible only in the same flush of war-born idealism and aspiration for a new start in international co-operation which also gave birth to the United Nations. Within a few years, this mood had given way to concentration on new forms of international action to deal with the Cold War between the free world and the forces of Soviet Communism. As a result, the Havana Charter for an International Trade Organization failed of ratification.[9] The central features of the ITO trade rules, however, survived in the General Agreement on Tariffs and Trade (GATT), which had been negotiated at Geneva in 1947 as an interim arrangement pending completion of the ITO charter.

The architects of the Bretton Woods system were, of course, aware that the ultimate world order for which they were planning could not be brought into being overnight. Their plans were shaped at the end of the most destructive war in history. It was apparent that there would be immediate need for relief on a massive scale to avoid starvation, disease, and civil unrest, and that this would have to be followed by a phase of physical reconstruction. The concept of a transition period was therefore built into the plans, with an expected duration of about five years—perhaps longer for a few countries. In reality, the world has never fully emerged from this transition period.

Hindsight now permits us to recognize that a number of the basic assumptions of the planners were in error. First, they grossly underestimated the extent of the war-induced dislocations in Europe, Japan, Southeast Asia, and the Middle East. Secondly, they were overly concerned with the dangers of a new world-wide depression, especially one initiated by a postwar slump in the United States, and insufficiently concerned with inflation and its international economic consequences. Thirdly, they did not sufficiently foresee the intensity of the desire in underdeveloped countries for accelerated economic development, the scale of necessary international technical assistance and capital flows required

---

[9] For an analysis of the various factors which led to the failure of the ITO, see William Diebold, Jr., *The End of the ITO*, Princeton Essays in International Finance, No. 16 (October, 1952).

to satisfy even a reasonable fraction of this desire, and the difficulties of restoring a large-scale international flow of private capital. Fourthly, and perhaps most important, they did not foresee the Cold War, including its "hot" phase of Korean hostilities, or the profound effects which this basic division of the world would have for the whole range of international action in the political, military, and economic spheres.

Despite these errors, some portions of the Bretton Woods design have been brought into being and the pattern as a whole remains as a kind of ideal against which other measures are tested, a pointer to desirable directions of foreign economic policy even if sober realities require interim measures outside the Bretton Woods framework or in conflict with it. For this reason, it is useful to set forth a brief comparison of the design and the reality in each of the three main fields of finance, trade, and investment and development, before describing the various programs specifically addressed to the unforeseen requirements of the postwar era.

Finance

During the 1920's, strenuous efforts had been made to re-create the pre-1914 pattern of international finance based on the gold standard. This system had made all major currencies automatically convertible with gold and therefore with one another at fixed exchange rates. It depended on gold flows and related Central Bank adjustments of internal interest rates to ensure equilibrium in each country's international payments with the rest of the world. In fact, the dislocations created by World War I, including large residual claims for reparations and inter-allied war debts, were too far-reaching to permit a full restoration of the gold standard. Under the impact of the Great Depression, the system collapsed completely and the gold standard was abandoned formally by the United Kingdom in 1931, the United States in 1933, and other leading countries in the subsequent few years. During the rest of the thirties, international finance degenerated into sheer chaos. Many countries sought to "export unemployment" by using competitive exchange depreciation to foster exports and restrict imports. German National Socialist Finance Minister Hjalmar Schacht introduced bizarre techniques of bilateral barter and multiple exchange rates, in which objectives of political infiltration were mixed with economic motives. "Beggar-my-neighbor" became the guiding principle of foreign economic policy in most of the world.

The Bretton Woods system was intended to avoid a repetition

of these evils. Large-scale inter-allied war debts to the United States were forestalled by Lend-Lease, since the settlements forgave the "loans" insofar as Lend-Lease supplies had been used in fighting the common enemies. Reparations were to be taken in kind rather than in financial obligations.[10] For the longer run, it was recognized that the gold standard could not be re-established, partly because the United States held too large a share of the world's monetary gold stocks, but mainly because high employment levels had become a major objective in almost all leading countries and governments were no longer prepared to see their domestic economic policies determined by external gold flows.

The International Monetary Fund

In effect, the financial side of the Bretton Woods system, as embodied in the Articles of Agreement of the International Monetary Fund, sought to secure the international advantages of the gold standard without its rigidities and without its limitations on domestic policies of economic stabilization. To this end, the member nations undertook to maintain stable exchange rates, to abstain from exchange controls affecting current account transactions (i.e., purchase or sale of goods and services, as distinct from movements of capital), and to avoid discriminatory currency arrangements or multiple currency practices. All member currencies were thus to be freely convertible, except for the possibility of restrictions on capital movements. Competitive currency depreciation was to be avoided, but exchange rates might be altered to correct a "fundamental disequilibrium" in a nation's international payments position, subject to the concurrence of the IMF Executive Board for changes beyond 10 per cent.

Since the gold reserves of most countries outside the United States were too small to offset even moderate short-term fluctuations in foreign exchange earnings, the IMF provided a supple-

[10] There were some important exceptions to both these principles. For example, the wartime credits to Britain from India, Egypt, and certain other sterling-area countries were not forgiven or scaled down, but remained as sterling balances in London which could be drawn upon after the war. From the Indian viewpoint, these were forced loans from a poor to a rich country; from the British viewpoint, they were contributions to a common cause. Whatever the merits of the moral arguments, the sterling balances created during the war were a major factor in the United Kingdom's postwar international financial difficulties. With respect to reparations, likewise, some of the Japanese settlements provided for long-term financial obligations. Nonetheless, the decision of the United States and Canada to forego war debt or reparations claims prevented this type of obligation from becoming an unmanageable obstacle to the restoration of a workable postwar world economy.

mentary source of reserves in the form of an international currency pool. Total quotas of some $8 billion were established,[11] based on the volume of international transactions of the members (with a larger proportional contribution of $2.75 billion by the United States); each nation paid one-quarter of its quota (but not over 10 per cent of its 1946 level of gold and dollar holdings) in gold and the rest in its own currency. When a country's foreign exchange reserves were depleted as a result of short-term fluctuations, it might buy foreign currencies from the Fund up to a total of twice its quota, but at an annual rate not exceeding one-quarter of its quota, subject to extensive discretionary powers of the IMF's executive directors, whose voting power was weighted substantially in proportion to the quotas. In practice, drawings up to one-half of quotas have in recent years been authorized almost automatically, but additional drawings are permitted only after negotiations between the Fund and the applicant government concerning adjustments in economic policies designed to correct the foreign exchange shortage. Drawings must be repaid under a complex formula designed to limit them to covering short- or medium-term needs.

The Bretton Woods agreement contemplated a transitional period of three to five years, during which interim postwar exchange controls would be rapidly dismantled. Thereafter, currency convertibility and nondiscrimination in payments were to be the rule. The major potential exception permitted discrimination against a creditor country whose currency was formally declared "scarce"; this was intended to allow for discrimination against the dollar in the event of a large-scale and prolonged American economic depression.

The IMF agreement thus combined a code of governmental behavior in international finance with a pool of supplementary resources to make that behavior possible, administered through a new international institution with considerable authority to influence the economic policies of member countries when they sought to use the Fund's resources. But those resources, which included only about $4 billion in gold and dollars, were obviously much too small to cover anything more than short-term fluctuations once a reasonably stable order had been established. In addition to postwar relief, which was separately provided, the planners

[11] The original agreement covered forty-four nations, including the USSR, Czechoslovakia, and Poland. The Communist countries soon dropped out, but additional members have joined over the years, so that by 1958 the IMF had sixty-eight members, with quotas totaling about $9.1 billion.

recognized that at least one major financial blood transfusion was indispensable if the Bretton Woods system were to have the slightest chance of being realized in practice.

Since sterling was the main international currency apart from the dollar, it was hoped that a sufficiently large-scale and long-term credit to the United Kingdom to permit the re-establishment of sterling-dollar convertibility might constitute an adequate transfusion. To this end, in connection with the Lend-Lease settlement with the United Kingdom negotiated late in 1945, a long-term American loan at low interest rates was provided in the amount of $3,750 million; this was paralleled by Canada to the extent of $750 million. The British negotiators were reluctantly persuaded to agree in return that sterling would be made freely convertible on current account during the summer of 1947. Smaller stabilization loans to France, the Netherlands, and other European countries were made through the Export-Import Bank.

The Marshall Plan and the European Payments Union

By the early summer of 1947, however, it had become evident that the Anglo-American loan was a pittance compared with Europe's needs. Not only was there no prospect of achieving the Bretton Woods ideal in the foreseeable future; there was imminent danger that without a much larger American aid program, the European economy would collapse. There simply had not been enough time to overcome the wartime destruction of productive capacity, to offset the loss of European overseas empires and foreign investments, or to adjust to the political splitting of the Continent by the Iron Curtain. A severe winter and drought-stricken summer compounded the difficulties. Europe was incapable of earning enough foreign exchange to cover even current needs of imported food, fuel, and raw materials, to say nothing of capital goods for reconstruction. The Western Hemisphere, especially the United States, was the only possible source of supply. At the same time, political relations between the Soviet Union and her former Western allies were steadily deteriorating, and the formidable Communist parties of France and Italy were making it clear that the Soviets stood ready to expand the Communist system to the whole of Western Europe if economic chaos should provide them an opportunity.

The American response to this dramatic crisis was the Marshall Plan, a four-year program for massive assistance to European recovery. All thoughts of early achievement of currency convertibility were laid aside. The terms of the Anglo-American loan were duly implemented by the United Kingdom in July, 1947, but the British financial position was wholly incapable of sustaining convertibility; the loan was largely drawn in a few weeks; and the convertibility experiment was called off by mutual agreement.

For most of the following ten years, the IMF was relegated to a minor role while other agencies and measures not dreamed of at Bretton Woods held the center of the stage. Since the Marshall Plan was providing Europe, and indirectly many other areas, with additional dollar exchange on a scale and on terms far beyond IMF capabilities, it was decided to suspend the availability of IMF resources for European members. With respect to exchange-rate adjustment, there did take place in September, 1949, a major realignment of rates to correct "fundamental disequilibria"; but the adjustment was initiated by Britain under the immediate pressure of a massive run on her dollar reserves—a run which occurred despite strenuous efforts at control. The devaluation of the pound from $4.03 to $2.80 was followed by most other nondollar free nations, but in this whole process IMF consultation played a negligible role.

On the institutional side, since general convertibility was now obviously well beyond the horizon, in 1950 the Western European countries, with vigorous American encouragement and financial support through the Marshall Plan, established a European Payments Union (EPU). The EPU provided mutual currency convertibility among the seventeen member countries, and through Britain and France with the rest of the sterling and franc areas. Fluctuations in individual payments positions within the Union were partly financed by a system of automatic credits. Through the EPU Managing Board and other organs of the Organization for European Economic Co-operation, additional intra-European financial assistance might be negotiated for members in special difficulties. The EPU was in effect a supplementary IMF for its members, geographically restricted but functionally more flexible in a number of respects.

A corollary of the creation of the EPU was acceptance by the United States of discrimination against the dollar for a far longer period than the Bretton Woods transition. Individual European countries enjoying a relatively favorable dollar position were delayed in lessening their restrictions on dollar transactions. In the early 1950's, some specialists, including officers of the IMF itself, criticized these arrangements as doing violence to the Bretton Woods ideal and threatening to perpetuate the division of the free world into hard- and soft-currency blocs. The EPU advocates, on the other hand, argued that limited convertibility was better than the probable alternative of bilateral financial settlements, that the resultant strengthening of the European economy would permit the progressive reduction of dollar discrimination, and that ultimate general convertibility would be better facilitated by this route. In practice, the EPU worked with great effectiveness, making possible a very large expansion of intra-European trade and payments without sharpening appreciably the division between the dollar and nondollar worlds. With the help of the Marshall Plan and vigorous national and co-operative efforts, European economic recovery proceeded more rapidly than anyone had dared hope. American aid for European recovery as such came to an end in 1951; it was followed by a period of economic aid to support expanded defense efforts by Atlantic Treaty members; but by the mid-fifties, the European economy was fully self-supporting.

The Movement Toward Convertibility

With the improved economic position, restrictions against dollar transactions were gradually dismantled. By early 1955, sterling had approached a position of *de facto* convertibility, but the important step to formal convertibility, although actively discussed on several occasions, was put off. Both British and American authorities were determined not to repeat the fiasco of 1947, and were content to rest on a pragmatic system in which effective exchange discrimination was being steadily reduced. Some other European currencies, notably the West German Deutschemark, achieved in the late 1950's a position of strength superior to sterling, but the unique role of sterling in international finance was such that other countries continued to await a British lead before taking further action toward implementation of the Bretton Woods ideal.

Meanwhile, other factors came to dominate the financial policies of the less-developed free countries. For them, especially in Latin America, the IMF played a significant role during the entire period, providing supplementary resources to help them over short-term emergencies and also offering important technical assistance in the design and operation of their foreign exchange control systems. As accelerated economic development came to occupy an ever more prominent position in their policies, however, they turned to exchange control as an important instrument for promoting development. It was used in varying degrees for such purposes as fostering "infant industries," taxing exports of staple primary commodities to provide governments with larger developmental resources, and restricting the consumption of imported luxuries. In most of Latin America, these control systems involved multiple currency practices directly contrary to the terms of the Bretton Woods agreement. Nonetheless, the IMF adopted a tolerant attitude toward such practices, seeking to work for their simplification and smooth operation rather than condemning them outright.

In 1956–1957, the broad movement toward progressive world financial stability was seriously threatened by the Suez Canal crisis. Sterling was again endangered by a run on reserves, and France was experiencing serious difficulties as a result of domestic inflation and the pressures of the fighting with Algerian Arab nationalists. In combatting this new world financial crisis, the resources of the IMF, which had largely been husbanded over the previous decade, now played a leading part. Combined with special credits from the Export-Import Bank and arrangements for financial assistance from West Germany, they were used on a large scale to offset speculative financial drains, to assist an orderly devaluation of the French franc, and to avoid the reimposition of severe exchange controls and other import restrictions by the leading trading nations. Similar co-operative arrangements on a smaller scale were devised to assist Chile, Colombia, Turkey, and several other countries. In the 1958 recession, which seriously lowered the foreign exchange incomes of a number of underdeveloped countries dependent on raw material exports, the ability to draw on IMF resources also served to reduce the severity of the impact.

Thus, after ten years of comparative inactivity, the IMF emerged in the later 1950's as a major instrument to support international financial stability. To do so, however, it was forced to draw heavily on its reserves. In the two years ending in mid-1958, IMF drawings amounted to almost $2 billion, twice as much as in the entire previous decade, and supplementary stand-by credits were arranged of about $1 billion. The Fund's remaining gold and convertible currencies were reduced to $2.4 billion, of which one-third was committed under the stand-by arrangements. Moreover, since world trade had greatly expanded, and world prices had substantially increased, IMF quotas were seriously reduced in proportion to possible needs. At the same time, gold and foreign exchange reserves in the hands of national governments were still not well distributed; for all countries outside the United States they averaged only about 40 per cent of annual imports, and in the important case of the United Kingdom, with its responsibilities for the whole sterling area, only 25 per cent. There was increasing concern as to the adequacy of international financial liquidity, i.e., whether national reserves and international funds together were sufficient to cover even modern swings in payments positions without necessitating a potentially disastrous spiral of import restrictions. For many countries, reserves were so close to the margin that rates of domestic growth and foreign investment had to be held below otherwise desirable levels. In response to this concern, the United States took the lead in October, 1958, at the New Delhi meetings of the Fund Governors, in sponsoring a general increase in IMF quotas; the expectation was for an increase of some 50 per cent.

In summary, fourteen years after Bretton Woods, the international financial scene as a whole was still short of the ideal contemplated by the postwar planners. Apart from the Canadian dollar and the Swiss franc, no major currency was completely convertible with the American dollar. Exchange controls over capital transactions were almost universal, and there were also substantial restraints on current payments. In Europe, there was still significant discrimination against dollar imports, especially of consumer goods. In Latin America and Asia, there were still widespread multiple-currency practices and a degree of domestic inflationary pressure which ruled out foreign exchange stability.

Yet compared with the 1930's, or with the first few years after World War II, the degree of progress toward a workable financial order had been remarkable, and actual practice was far closer to the Bretton Woods ideal than the formal restrictions would suggest. The European Payments Union and the sterling area together provided for currency transferability over almost the entire non-dollar free world, permitting payments on a multilateral basis for perhaps three-quarters of world transactions. Parts of South America had been linked with this system, and most of Central America, as well as Canada, was in the dollar area. Despite the absence of formal convertibility, most European currencies could be traded for dollars on free markets at only nominal discounts from their official values. The restoration of earning power in Europe and Japan, together with American aid programs, overseas dollar expenditures on military account, and the growth of foreign private investment, had almost eliminated the specter of chronic worldwide dollar shortage which had haunted the world's finance ministries for many years after the war.[12] Three moderate American

---

[12] From the end of 1950 to the end of 1957, total gold and dollar reserve holdings outside the United States increased by over $7 billion. The increase, however, was very unevenly distributed, no less than $5.5 billion accruing to West Germany alone. In 1958, a fall in American exports, accompanied by

business recessions had been weathered without plunging the world into financial chaos; indeed, two of them had scarcely caused a ripple. Technical assistance from the IMF, combined with skillful negotiation on the extension of credits, was helping to simplify exchange control systems and to assist underdeveloped countries in reducing the pressures of inflation. For the most part, remaining exchange controls existed to promote other objectives, such as protection of agriculture or promotion of industrialization, rather than being forced on governments by the pressures of unmanageable balance-of-payments deficits.

In short, there was a kind of working financial order underpinned by an increasingly active world-wide international institution and by powerful regional institutions, and backed by continuing American leadership and resources. It was by no means an automatically self-sustaining order, and its evolution had been punctuated by periodic crises and salvage operations. But it did suffice to free a growing volume of international business from the threat of financial chaos. As the largest world trader, the United States had a major stake in its further healthy evolution.[12a]

Trade

The principal purpose of an orderly world financial structure was to make possible an expansion of trade and private investment. Restrictions on trade can take the form either of exchange

---

surprising buoyancy in imports despite the business recession, led to a gold outflow from the United States of some $2 billion. This heavy outflow was a cause for concern in some American financial circles, being attributed in part to domestic inflation and a consequent weakening of the competitive position of certain American exports. On balance, however, it seemed to reflect the growing health of other free world nations more than any basic unsoundness in the American economy, and its causes included significant short-term factors which were unlikely to persist.

[12a] In the closing days of 1958, a further dramatic step in this direction was taken by the major European nations, including Britain, West Germany, France, Italy, Belgium, the Netherlands, and the Scandinavian countries, all of whom made their currencies formally convertible at the official exchange parities for all external earnings on current account. In the French case, the step was accompanied by a further 17 per-cent devaluation of the franc. The residents of the currency areas concerned were still subject to various restrictions on purchases of foreign exchange, and capital transactions were still limited for both residents and foreigners. Under the terms of a European Monetary Agreement negotiated in 1955 in anticipation of an ultimate move to external convertibility, the EPU was liquidated as of January 1, 1959. In its place, there was established a mechanism for multilateral clearing of intra-European transactions and a pool of funds for discretionary assistance to European member countries in temporary financial difficulties.

controls or of direct commercial policy measures such as tariffs or import quotas. Moderate tariffs had been widely used in the nineteenth century to protect both agriculture and industry; the British policy of free trade between 1846 and World War I was the outstanding exception.[13] During the 1920's, despite a general upward drift in tariff levels, world trade expanded rapidly, reaching a 1929 peak one-third above 1913, but it then declined disastrously in the depression years of 1929–1933 and did not fully recover until well after World War II. During the 1930's, moreover, in addition to the spiral of upward tariff changes initiated by the Smoot-Hawley Tariff, many countries turned to quantitative import restrictions as a major instrument of commercial policy. As part of the "beggar-my-neighbor" actions in the financial field referred to above, export subsidies, bilateral barter arrangements, and other governmental trade restrictions became common. Depression conditions also fostered the growth of organized private cartels in many industries designed to maintain prices by restricting production and dividing markets. A major breach was opened in the hitherto generally accepted principle of nondiscrimination in the form of the British Commonwealth system of imperial tariff preference negotiated at Ottawa in 1932.

The ITO Charter

For the postwar planners, therefore, a fresh start on world trade arrangements was at least as important as the new financial order. In their eyes, the capstone of the new system was to be the charter for an International Trade Organization (ITO). An international agreement for "expansion of world trade and employment" was formally proposed by the United States in 1945, but the charter was so elaborate a document, covering so wide a range of issues, that it took three years of intensive negotiation to produce an accord. As it finally emerged in Havana in 1948, the ITO charter contained 106 Articles and sixteen Annexes, with separate chapters covering co-operation in the promotion of high employment levels, economic development and reconstruction, commercial policy, restrictive business practices, intergovernmental commodity agreements, and the constitution of a new international agency to supervise the charter's operation. It was signed by representatives of fifty-three countries, virtually the whole world outside of the Communist bloc.[14] At the next stage, however, it met with heavy

[13] For a survey of American tariff history, see pages 97–105.

[14] The authoritative exposition of the charter by the head of the American delegation at Havana is Clair Wilcox, A *Charter for World Trade* (1949).

opposition from interested elements of the American public. The hostility of protectionist groups was reinforced by others who mistrusted the emphasis on planning for full employment or who felt dissatisfied with the investment provisions. By 1950, it seemed clear that ratification by Congress would be impossible, and the administration ceased to press it. Without American participation, the ITO was of little interest to the rest of the world, and the project quietly died.

No effort was made to revive the sections of the Havana charter concerning employment or investment, which had been opposed with special vigor by American business and other groups. In 1952, the United States promoted the negotiation of a separate agreement on restrictive business practices, but it reconsidered its position in 1955 after an agreement had been drafted and this project was likewise abandoned. The commodity agreement chapter was accepted as a guide by the United Nations Economic and Social Council for its work in this field.

The General Agreement on Tariffs and Trade

The central core of the Havana Charter, the rules on commercial policy embodied in Chapter IV, did survive the demise of the ITO almost inadvertently. At Geneva in 1947, parallel with negotiations in preparation for the Havana Conference, twenty-three countries participated in the world's first simultaneous tariff negotiation; among these countries, 123 bilateral negotiations were conducted in a multilateral framework. To safeguard the resulting agreements, which covered more than half of the world's total trade, general provisions were adopted, based on the draft of the ITO charter and comprising international rules for commercial policy. The tariff agreements and general provisions together were incorporated in the General Agreement on Tariffs and Trade (GATT). When the Havana charter died, the GATT remained.

Successive administrations in this country have taken the position that this was essentially a trade agreement within the scope of the Reciprocal Trade legislation, and therefore did not require formal congressional ratification. Congress has never endorsed the GATT, and in postwar extensions of the Trade Agreements legislation has explicitly avoided either endorsement or condemnation. Through subsequent accessions, thirty-seven countries, which account for the overwhelming bulk of free world trade, have now become parties to the GATT, and in 1955 its general provisions were renegotiated and simplified. Despite its somewhat tenuous legal status, and its almost complete lack of formal organization, the GATT serves as a *de facto* charter of commercial policy, and the United States plays a leading role in its operation.

Following the general Bretton Woods pattern, the basic objectives of the GATT are the progressive reduction of trade barriers and the elimination of discrimination in commercial policy. Its philosophy is in keeping with the Reciprocal Trade Agreements program developed for the United States by Secretary of State Cordell Hull before the war. The experience of the later 1930's, however, had shown that tariffs could not be handled in isolation from other types of import restrictions and that an effective commercial-policy agreement must contain specific and detailed rules of considerable complexity. It also required careful drafting of exceptions and escape clauses to take account of special interests of the various member countries.

With respect to tariffs, the GATT is a forum for the sponsorship of multilateral negotiations, or, more precisely, simultaneous bilateral negotiations among all major trading countries. In this bargaining process, benefits of bilateral concessions are extended automatically to all other member countries through the most-favored-nation principle. In addition to the original Geneva session of 1947, multilateral tariff negotiations were conducted at Annecy, France, in 1949; Torquay, England, in 1950–1951; and Geneva in 1955–1956. Another was scheduled for 1959 or 1960. Detailed rules are prescribed by the GATT to prevent the frustration of tariff concessions through discriminatory internal taxes, customs-valuation practices, or other trade regulations and administrative procedures sometimes described as the "invisible tariff." The escape clause written into the American legislation after the war is an integral part of the General Agreement and is available to all member countries; if a nation withdraws agreed concessions, it must make compensatory concessions or permit withdrawal of corresponding concessions by the other interested parties. Judgments on the fairness of reciprocal concessions are made, in the absence of direct agreement between the parties concerned, by committees of the members acting as a group.

Perhaps the most important provisions of the GATT concern import quotas and other quantitative restrictions on trade. Here the basic rule is to forbid quantitative restrictions, but there are many exceptions. A country in balance-of-payments difficulties may impose quotas to protect its general balance of payments; this exception is linked with the exchange-control provisions of the IMF. Quotas on agricultural products may be used to prevent imports which would disrupt a domestic agricultural price-support program; this exception was required by United States policy. Quotas may also be imposed to prevent imports injurious to national defense. Underdeveloped countries may also employ quotas, within elaborately defined limitations, to promote the establishment and development of new industries, but the rules seek to prevent such quotas from negating tariff concessions. Periodic consultations are required in which a nation imposing quota restrictions must justify them specifically as falling within the agreed exceptions.

The third basic area of agreement concerns nondiscrimination in the application of both tariffs and other import restrictions. Here again, exceptions are made for pre-existing systems of discrimination, such as British Commonwealth preference, the French Union system, and American preferential arrangements with Cuba and the Philippines. Rules are also established for the creation of customs unions or free-trade areas among two or more member countries; such unions may be formed if they embrace substantially all the trade of the participants and if the common external tariffs are no higher than the average of the previous individual tariffs.

As a framework for international economic behavior, the trade rules of the GATT are less clear-cut than the financial rules of the IMF. There are, for example, so many exceptions to the rules against quantitative import restrictions—exceptions for balance-of-payments reasons, for developing countries, for agriculture, and for national security—that in the eyes of many critics they outweigh the principle itself. The GATT also suffers from the ambiguous legal status of American membership and from the absence of a formal administrative structure. In 1955, the member governments sought to rectify this latter weakness by an agreement to create an Organization for Trade Co-operation (OTC) to administer the GATT, to sponsor trade negotiations, and to make studies and facilitate intergovernmental consultation on problems of international trade and commercial policy. Although its powers were carefully limited, American participation in the OTC, along with continued support of the GATT, was vigorously opposed by protectionist groups. The arguments were couched largely in constitutional terms, involving an alleged surrender of tariff policy-making to an international body. Despite a large favorable majority for ratification in 1956 in the Ways and Means Committee, the issue was not pressed to a vote in the House, and the President's request for ratification in 1957 and 1958 went unheeded by Congress.

Apart from rather dubious constitutional arguments, opposition to the GATT reflects in part protectionist dislike of the whole Reciprocal Trade Agreements program and in part a conviction that the agreement is one-sided, permitting widespread exceptions for the whole soft-currency world and all underdeveloped countries, but only few exceptions for the United States, which cannot claim balance-of-payments difficulties. The record does not justify this view. While progress has been slow, pressure over the years through the GATT for removal of quantitative restrictions on American exports, as other countries' balance-of-payments positions have improved, has played an important part in reducing discrimination against the United States.

On balance, however, the *de facto* situation in the field of trade is much further from the Bretton Woods ideal than in the field of finance. In all countries, commercial policy impinges much more directly than financial policy on specific domestic economic interests, often with disproportionate political influence. Given the prominent position of the United States in world trade, a very firm lead from this country would have been required to secure greater results. Through the entire ten-year life of the GATT, however, neither the Truman nor the Eisenhower administration, despite their own inclinations, was in a position to offer such leadership. There were simply too many difficulties in securing congressional support for successive extensions to the Reciprocal Trade Agreements legislation, and the extensions were accompanied by increasingly broad escape clauses which seemed to show a revival of protectionist sentiment. Whether the four-year extension of the Trade Agreements Program enacted in 1958 may change this situation it is still too soon to judge.

Regional Economic Integration

The Bretton Woods ideal had emphasized the reduction of trade barriers on a world-wide and nondiscriminatory basis. In face of the apparently persistent dollar shortage of the early postwar years, however, and in view of the halting nature of global progress, a number of countries turned to regional arrangements as a more promising avenue for expanding their trade and broadening their opportunities for economic growth. This viewpoint was especially strong in Western Europe, where economic integration was supported by the United States with great vigor on political and military, as well as economic, grounds.

Before the war had ended, the governments-in-exile of Belgium, the Netherlands, and Luxembourg had agreed on the goal of economic union, and during the ten years after the war this "Benelux" Union was pushed through many difficulties to a generally successful implementation. Beginning in 1949, as a by-product of the Marshall Plan, the Organization for European Economic Co-operation (OEEC) developed a program of intra-European trade liberalization, focused on the progressive elimination of quantitative import restrictions among the seventeen member countries; this program also made great progress, with the indispensable help of the European Payments Union. In 1950, French Foreign Minister Robert Schuman proposed the establishment of a European Coal and Steel Community. The purpose of the Schuman Plan was primarily political, to bring West Germany more firmly within a Western European framework and to serve as a symbol of Franco-German reconciliation, but its substance was economic—in effect a common market for coal and steel. The plan was accepted by six countries, the three in Benelux together with France, Germany, and Italy, and became operative in 1952. An effort at military integration of the same six countries through a European Defense Community came to naught in 1954, when its ratification was defeated in the French National Assembly, but the proponents of European integration pushed ahead in other fields. In 1957, the six Schuman Plan countries agreed on two major treaties, one for collaboration in the development of atomic power, known as "EURATOM," and the other for a European Economic Community or Common Market. All six parliaments ratified the treaties promptly, and they became effective at the beginning of 1958.

The Common Market Treaty, which promises consequences of far-reaching significance for world trade and the world economy at large, calls for a full customs union to be achieved by progressive stages in a period of twelve to fifteen years, together with the elimination of quantitative trade restrictions within the group and close co-operation in financial and other economic matters. Its sponsors made no secret of their hope that this major step might lead ultimately to political federation.

Regional arrangements of this type necessarily imply discrimination against nonmembers. Western European countries outside the Common Market group—notably Britain, Switzerland, Sweden, Norway, Denmark, and Austria, who for various reasons were unwilling to join the Customs Union as full members—were deeply concerned as to the possible impact on them of the Common Market. In 1957–1958, they sought to negotiate a free-trade area covering the whole of Western Europe (a free-trade area implies the absence of internal trade restrictions, but leaves each member free to determine its own external tariff levels). The European example also stimulated thinking on regional trade arrangements in other areas; serious studies were undertaken in Latin America and in the Middle East. The United States generally supported these movements, but always on condition that the elimination of intraregional restrictions was not accompanied by increased restrictions of the regional grouping as a whole against the outside world, including the United States.

In this objective, American policy was aided by the rules and commitments undertaken in the GATT. At the end of 1958, the outcome of the European Free Trade Area negotiations was in considerable doubt, and it seemed clear that outside of Europe the regional movement would develop only slowly. Nevertheless, these developments posed important new challenges to American trade-policy leadership and confronted American business concerns, as well as the government, with the prospect of far-reaching adjustments in their export-market opportunities and their policies on foreign investment.

Intergovernmental Commodity Agreements

One major aspect of international commercial policy not covered by the GATT concerns intergovernmental commodity agreements. The attitude of the Bretton Woods planners toward such agreements was ambiguous. The basic philosophy of minimizing trade restraints was naturally hostile to any such far-reaching interference with free-market forces, and American policy was generally opposed to them. On the other hand, the same types of political pressures which had led to agricultural price support and production control in domestic American policy operated with even greater force in countries where primary products are a major part of the total output. In many less-developed nations, agricultural staples or minerals account for almost all their foreign exchange earnings and much of their public revenue. Prices for such commodities tend to fluctuate far more widely than for manufactured goods, and this market instability in turn may induce serious inflation or severe depression in the producing areas. Such fluctuations have a major bearing on national incomes, the ability to import manufactured goods, and the prospects for orderly economic development. Any international agreement which was to win the assent of the nations of Latin America, Africa, and Asia had to give some recognition to the desire for stabilization of primary-product markets.

Most of the prewar efforts on this line were agreements among producers seeking to raise prices by limiting production or exports. In the prevailing conditions, especially during the depression years, these agreements generally broke down through nonco-operation of certain producers. The chapter of the ITO charter concerning intergovernmental commodity agreements, which was bitterly disputed in the course of negotiation, attempted to compromise producer and consumer interests. It recognized the possible need for stabilization in some circumstances, but sought to confine the range and duration of agreements as narrowly as possible and to prescribe procedures which would ensure equitable treatment of producer and consumer interests alike. Despite the nonratification of the Havana charter, these principles have been accepted as a guide to the postwar work of the United Nations in this field.

Although it is sometimes argued that an effective primary-product market stabilization system should cover a large number of commodities simultaneously, thus balancing off the differing interests of participating countries, serious discussion in the postwar period has been limited to *ad hoc* schemes for individual products. Pressure for stabilization has varied with market conditions, being slight in the immediate postwar years and during the Korean War boom, and heavy in the post-Korean commodity slump and the recession of 1957–1958; it should be noted, however, that not all commodities follow an identical time pattern of fluctuations. International commodity studies are guided by an Interim Co-ordinating Committee for International Commodity Agreements, composed of four experts and reporting to the United Nations Economic and Social Council; in 1955, this body was supplemented by an eighteen-member advisory Commission on International Commodity Trade, established to conduct analytical studies and make recommendations on measures to reduce excessive market fluctuations or price inequities.

Behind the facade of United Nations debate and documentation, the major importing countries, led by the United States and Great Britain, have fought a delaying action against constant pressure for stabilization agreements from raw-material producing nations, especially those of Latin America and Southeast Asia. Prior to 1958, only three major agreements had been adopted: the Wheat Agreement beginning in 1949, the Sugar Agreement beginning in 1953, and the Tin Agreement, negotiated in 1953 but entering into force only in 1956. It is significant that the United States itself is the largest surplus producer of wheat, and has special interests in sugar because of commitments to Cuba and the Philippines, while the United Kingdom was concerned with tin-producing interests in Malaya. The general American attitude was summarized by the Randall Commission on foreign economic policy in 1954 in the following terms: "The Commission does not believe that extensive resort to commodity agreements will solve the problem of price instability; and it believes that such agreements introduce rigidities and restraints that impair the elasticity of economic adjustment and the freedom of individual initiative, which are fundamental to economic progress." [15]

During 1958, however, the authorities in Washington became increasingly concerned at political antagonism being generated in Latin America and elsewhere by the traditionally negative American attitude, and indicated, if not a change of conviction, at least a readiness to discuss commodity stabilization with the affected producing countries. This shift of attitude at once gave new life to efforts at coffee stabilization, on which active discussions were proceeding toward the end of 1958. There are formidable technical, as well as political, difficulties in devising ways and means of limiting market fluctuations without undesirable consequences in freezing production and market patterns. There are serious administrative complexities in enforcing quota-control systems, and there are serious risks of accumulating burdensome surpluses which must somehow be financed. Yet the consequences of unrestrained fluctuations on the less-developed countries are so severe, and the political interest of the United States in the welfare of these nations has been growing so rapidly, that renewed efforts to resolve these dilemmas for an important segment of international trade appear more likely than not.

East-West Trade

One other significant aspect of postwar trade policy which could not be fitted into the Bretton Woods framework arose from economic relations between the Sino-Soviet bloc and the free world. All the arrangements described so far were limited to the free nations, who account for the great bulk—perhaps 90 per cent— of world trade. Throughout its history, the USSR has followed a policy of maximum self-sufficiency, and when Eastern Europe and mainland China came within the Communist orbit after the war, their trade relations were sharply diverted toward a largely self-contained Communist economic system. East-West trade was reduced to almost insignificant dimensions.

[15] Commission on Foreign Economic Policy, *Report to the President and the Congress*, (January, 1954).

As the tensions of the Cold War increased, especially after the attack on South Korea, the Western nations, led by the United States, took steps to limit such trade even more narrowly. They arranged a concerted embargo or limitation on exports of military goods and of industrial goods which might strengthen the Communist military effort. Trade with Communist China was completely forbidden by the United States and severely limited by the Western European nations and Japan. As the years passed, however, increasing doubts arose as to the efficacy of this program in retarding Communist military strength, and business interests, especially in Europe and Japan, pressed for a relaxation in categories not immediately or exclusively of military value. In 1954 and 1958, the control lists on items other than weapons and atomic-energy supplies were greatly reduced.

Meanwhile, the Communist bloc was making use of its steadily increasing economic strength to initiate new trade and economic-aid programs, especially in the underdeveloped nations which were politically uncommitted. Barter arrangements were made to relieve such countries of burdensome surpluses, of which Icelandic fish, Egyptian cotton, and Burmese rice were among the outstanding examples. In exchange, supplies of badly needed items, for which foreign exchange resources were scarce, were offered on apparently favorable terms. By 1958, increasing attention was being given to this problem by the United States and its allies, and means were being sought to avoid the excessive dependence of friendly countries on Soviet trade, for fear of possible political abuse of such dependence.[16] Whatever Western response might ultimately be developed, it was plain that it would involve governmental restraints and intervention sharply in contrast with the general objectives of the Bretton Woods system.

In trade as in finance, the over-all free-world position in the late 1950's was far healthier than might be assumed from a review of the many divergences from the Bretton Woods ideal. Despite the continuing prevalence of quantitative import restrictions, the slowing down of the movement for tariff reduction, the new emphasis on regional groupings rather than world-wide nondiscrimination, and the uncertainties injected by the policies of the Soviet bloc, the volume of trade was mounting steadily and free-world exports in 1957 reached a peak of over $100 billion. After correction for price changes, world trade in 1950 had passed the

[16] See U.S. Department of State, *The Sino-Soviet Economic Offensive in the Less Developed Countries* (May, 1958).

previous peak levels of 1929, and by 1957 its volume was almost 60 per cent above 1950 and about double the level of the late thirties. The recession of 1958 interrupted this expanding trend, but even in that year the trade volume was second only to that of 1957. The most important single factor contributing to these results has been the avoidance of serious domestic economic depressions in the industrialized countries. The programs of foreign aid described in the next section have also helped to sustain world trade, although they account directly for only a very small share. A vital contributory part has been played by the new arrangements for international co-operation, both financial and commercial.

Despite the expanding trade statistics, however, the picture contained a number of disquieting factors. The increasing Soviet economic potential has already been mentioned. Fears of insufficient international liquidity, which were strong in 1957, seemed likely to be set at rest by the proposed expansion of the IMF. But there were also major new uncertainties in the relations between the advanced and the underdeveloped countries, uncertainties which might jeopardize the flow of fuel and raw materials to the former and thus limit their continued growth. There were political dangers arising from aggressively anti-Western nationalism in Asia, Africa, and the Middle East; there was also concern at the small extent to which the poorer countries were participating in world economic expansion. Their terms of trade in the postwar period were generally much better than in the depression years, but in the latter fifties, especially, neither their internal growth rates nor their economic relations with the industrialized world were showing satisfactory progress.[17] The problem of accelerating their development and finding ways and means to integrate them effectively into the free-world economy was emerging insistently as the most challenging aspect of international economic policy, and the one least adequately treated by the plans of Bretton Woods.

Investment and Development

The third leg of the triangular Bretton Woods design, dealing with international investment and development, was least clearly worked out by the postwar planners. The main emphasis was on re-establishing the channels of private international capital flow which had been almost completely blocked since 1931. Given sound financial conditions and progressively freer trade, it was hoped that foreign private investment, especially in mining and

[17] See GATT, *Trends in International Trade: A Report by a Panel of Experts* (1958).

manufacturing, would rapidly reappear on something like the nineteenth-century scale. For the basic utility services, on the other hand, now in government hands in almost all countries, it was recognized that new means would be needed to promote international public investment; for this purpose, the Bretton Woods conference established the International Bank for Reconstruction and Development, which is described below.

The Promotion of Private International Investment

With respect to private investment, rules and institutions played a less prominent part than with finance or trade. The draftsmen of the Havana charter were somewhat reluctantly persuaded to include provisions designed to protect private investors from unreasonable harassment by host governments. During the negotiations, these had to be counterbalanced by phrases to protect underdeveloped countries from private economic exploitation. The resulting compromise satisfied almost no one; it played an important part in the ultimate nonratification of the ITO; and its loss was not widely lamented.

As the postwar pattern of international relations gradually developed, it soon became clear that the restoration of large-scale private capital flows would be much more difficult than had been hoped. Defaults on foreign bonds during the 1930's had almost wholly dried up this type of foreign investment, except for very safe areas such as Canada. In many parts of the world, there were grave risks of international or civil war, political upheaval, aggressive nationalism hostile to Western enterprise, and close governmental control of foreign business—all discouraging to companies or individuals choosing between investment abroad or at home. There had also been a shift in the sources of investment funds. Little surplus capital was available in Europe, and in the United States the sustained postwar boom afforded attractive domestic opportunities. Foreign investments were too risky for large institutional savers such as insurance companies and pension funds. On both the demand and the supply side, therefore, the situation differed radically from nineteenth-century conditions.

Nevertheless, against the background of steadily improving international financial order and growing world trade, a gradual increase in private capital flows did take place, especially in the extractive industries. An important share was provided by the vast expansion of the international oil industry, which put petroleum in the leading place among commodities in world trade. Other minerals and a widening array of manufacturing industries also played an important part. The total of American direct investment, including reinvested profits of subsidiaries, built up to a rate of over a billion dollars a year by the late 1940's and reached three billion in both 1956 and 1957.

In the absence of an international code of rules, the United States government took many actions bilaterally and unilaterally to stimulate private foreign investment. Diplomatic negotiations were undertaken to promote a favorable investment climate abroad. In renegotiating the traditional treaties of friendship, commerce, and navigation, provisions were often included for nondiscriminatory treatment of American investors, freedom from harassing limitations on operations, assurances against expropriation or for adequate compensation in the event of expropriation, avoidance of double taxation, etc. Government agencies assisted in finding and evaluating foreign investment opportunities. In 1954, the administration recommended to Congress a general 14 percentage-point reduction in taxes on income from foreign investment, but the proposal was not adopted. As part of the foreign-assistance programs described below, governmental guarantees were made available for certain types of American investment approved by the host country; for a small fee, guarantees could cover the risks of nonconvertibility of earnings or repatriated capital, risks of expropriation without adequate compensation, and (since 1956) war risks. Through the Export-Import Bank, the government has also become an important source of loan funds for private investments abroad.

Despite the growing volume of investment, and the many types of governmental assistance already provided, there remained in the late 1950's a general conviction that much more was needed. The ordinary channels of private capital flow were clearly working well for Canada, Western Europe, and some countries of Latin America. The needs were greatest, however, in the poorer underdeveloped countries and especially in the nonextractive industries. Here the private capital flow was very small indeed. In 1957, for example, almost half the new American direct investment went to economically advanced countries, and only one-seventh went to nonextractive industries in underdeveloped countries. From the viewpoint of foreign and security policy, with its increasing interest in the aspirations and attitudes of the uncommitted nations of Asia, Africa, and the Middle East, and even in relation to Latin America, additional action on both the private and the public investment fronts seemed essential.

The International Bank for Reconstruction and Development

It is to the credit of the Bretton Woods planners that they did identify economic development in the poorer nations as one of the major areas for postwar economic policy, even though they did not fully foresee the intensity of the demand or the difficulties of satisfying it. They also recognized that a major element of balanced growth, and a prerequisite to any sustained growth, was the construction of so-called "economic overhead" projects— transportation and communication systems, power and water supply, and river-control works. Since there was no realistic prospect of attracting private capital directly into such ventures, they devised an ingenious intergovernmental institution to accomplish this purpose indirectly. This was the International Bank for Reconstruction and Development, commonly known as the World Bank.

The World Bank, like the IMF, now represents almost all the non-Communist countries of the world (in mid-1958, there were sixty-eight members). Its Board of Governors meets annually, the member countries normally being represented by their finance ministers. Between annual meetings, control is delegated to a group of seventeen executive directors, whose voting power is weighted by the capital subscriptions of the member countries they represent. The staff of the Bank, which actively guides its policies, is headed by a president, elected by the Governors, and three vice-presidents. The three first presidents have all been Americans, and the United States is heavily represented in the staff as a whole, although the Bank maintains its character as an international institution.

The Bank is financed through subscriptions from member governments related to the size of their economies; subscriptions originally totaled about $8.3 billion and have been raised through additional memberships to over $9.3 billion. The United States subscription was $3,175 million, or 34 per cent of the total. Of each member's subscription, 2 per cent must be paid in gold or dollars, and 18 per cent in its own currency; the remaining 80 per cent is a contingent liability which in effect guarantees the servicing of the Bank's borrowings on private capital markets. By the end of 1957, such borrowings, together with repayments of loans and operating profits, somewhat exceeded the total of paid-in subscriptions. Most of the borrowing had been on the New York market, but substantial issues had also been floated in Britain, Canada, Switzerland, and the Netherlands.

Except for an early period of reconstruction loans to European nations, the Bank's operations have been concentrated on lending to underdeveloped countries for economic overhead projects. The Bank has established rigorous standards for scrutinizing the engineering quality and the financial and management arrangements for each project, and it has provided technical assistance to improve project designs. In many countries, before making any loans, it has undertaken elaborate development surveys, covering physical and human resources, investment priorities, financial institutions, availability of managerial talent, and other elements bearing on the over-all credit-worthiness of the borrowing nation and the soundness of individual projects. The Bank has also sponsored an Economic Development Institute in Washington to assist in the training of senior officials from underdeveloped nations who are responsible for developmental planning and operations. World Bank loans are made either directly to governments or government-owned agencies, or to private borrowers with servicing guaranteed by the host government. The Bank set about its task cautiously, so that up to 1956 the rate of loan disbursement was less than $300 million a year, but in fiscal 1958 the volume of loans rose to $700 million.

As a means both of channeling investment funds and of improving the standards of developmental activities, the World Bank quickly established a high reputation. A decade of experience, however, suggested some limitations on its usefulness as the only intergovernmental instrument for promoting accelerated development. Its strict banking standards and legal requirement for government-guaranteed projects foreclosed it from financing more risky ventures. For this purpose, there was established in 1957 an affiliated International Finance Corporation, which could assist nongovernmental ventures with loans or nonvoting participation in equity financing. This was a much smaller organization, and its financing in the first year was limited to a few million dollars.

At the end of 1958, the World Bank had sufficiently proved itself so that its Governors agreed to a large increase in member-nations' subscriptions, thereby providing guarantees for the servicing of several more billions of dollars worth of World Bank bonds. At the same time, urgent consideration was being given to ways and means of providing additional capital for economic development on easier terms, possibly through the establishment of an "International Development Association" to make loans repayable in local currencies. This project, a conception far removed from the Bretton Woods design, was a product of experience under the series of emergency foreign-assistance programs now to be described.

3. The Foreign-Assistance Programs

The second broad element of postwar foreign economic policy involved a series of measures to deal with the consequences of the Cold War, the urgent pressures for economic assistance to the poorer nations, and other unanticipated developments. Some of these measures, such as the limitation on strategic exports to the Sino-Soviet bloc, have already been described as modifications in the Bretton Woods design. Most of them have involved one or another form of foreign aid.

At the start, each of the aid programs (except for technical assistance) was undertaken as a temporary measure to achieve a limited objective. As the years passed, however, other requirements replaced those which had been fulfilled, and in recent years foreign assistance has come to be accepted as a major long-term instrument of American foreign policy.

Rehabilitation and Recovery—The Marshall Plan

The initial foreign-aid programs were clearly short-term measures to avoid starvation, disease, and unrest in the wake of World War II and to begin the process of economic rehabilitation in the devastated areas. Initial responsibility for this task, except in areas under military occupation, was given to the United Nations Reconstruction and Rehabilitation Agency (UNRRA), to which the United States was by far the largest contributor. When the new Communist regimes in Eastern Europe imposed serious restrictions on the impartial administration of UNRRA supplies, Congress became dissatisfied with the agency and withdrew American support, substituting a bilateral program of "post-UNRRA relief." These measures succeeded in their immediate task and were wound up a few years after the war's end.

Economic recovery, however, was to prove more difficult, more time-consuming, and more costly. By early 1947, with production still far below prewar levels and trade badly disorganized, the gold and foreign-exchange reserves of the Western European nations were rapidly running out and no means were in sight for financing their minimum import requirements of food, fuel, and raw materials. At this juncture, American policymakers concluded that further short-run palliatives were inadequate to the needs.

They felt that the problem must be attacked through a co-operative endeavor of several years' duration, designed to cure the dollar shortage at its roots by restoring Europe's productive capacity and the channels of both intra-European and world-wide trade. This concept, broadly outlined by Secretary of State Marshall at a Harvard Commencement address in June, 1947, was eagerly taken up by British and French Foreign Ministers Ernest Bevin and Georges Bidault, and became the genesis of the European Recovery Program or Marshall Plan.

The Marshall Plan had many unique features. Its essence was the annual provision of several billion dollars worth of American and other dollar-area goods and services to European participating nations, three-quarters as free grants and one-quarter as long-term loans. While of limited duration, it involved a four-year commitment of large-scale support for a program not clearly to the interest of any organized domestic constituency. Its enactment was the result of exceptional co-operation between the Truman administration and a Republican Congress, and owed much to the leadership in the Senate of Arthur Vandenberg of Michigan. Public support was developed and maintained by an interlocking series of executive, legislative, public, and unofficial studies and reports.

The detailed program content was worked out through highly organized collaboration between the European governments and the United States. To this end, new forms of administrative organization were developed. In Washington, a special agency of Cabinet rank, the Economic Co-operation Administration, was created to administer the program. It was represented in each participating European country by a special mission organized separately from the embassies although under ambassadorial guidance. The regional character of the program was emphasized by creation of a high-level Office of Special Representative in Europe, which co-ordinated the work of the individual country missions and dealt directly with the newly formed Organization for European Economic Co-operation (OEEC), a European intergovernmental institution established to help effectuate the Marshall Plan but subsequently continued as a permanent organization. The OEEC's first major function was to recommend the intercountry division of aid to the American authorities; this was followed by a European trade-liberalization program and the formation of the European Payments Union, and later by long-run co-operative ventures including the enhancement of European productivity, development of peaceful uses of atomic energy, assistance in training of scientific and technical manpower, and other activities of broad interest to the whole of Western Europe.

As presented to Congress in 1948, the Marshall Plan contemplated a four-year expenditure of almost $17 billion, about 20 per cent less than the Europeans' estimates of their own needs. In fact, the program did not last in its original form into 1952, since the outbreak of the Korean War and the decision to build enlarged military forces in Europe diverted it during 1951 largely into defense purposes. Actual expenditures on account of the original objectives have been estimated at some $12 billion. The results exceeded the most optimistic hopes of 1947. Western European production was restored to prewar levels by 1950, and a foundation had been laid for large continuing gains in European output and trade levels. Intra-European trade and payments were placed on an orderly basis, a necessary precondition to the more ambitious later plans of European economic integration. By the mid-1950's, not only was Europe completely self-supporting, but it was financing a military effort which would have been unthinkable in the forties.

The success of the program can be attributed to a combination of several factors: sound diagnosis of the essential problem, close working relations between European and American officials, effective recovery policies on the part of European governments, and provision by the United States of critical resources in sufficient volume and at the needed time. Although the European Recovery Program has often been regarded as a model of foreign-aid program design and administration, it has not proved possible to duplicate these factors fully in other areas or for other purposes.

Military Assistance and Mutual Security

In the development and achievement of public support for the Marshall Plan, Cold War considerations played some part, although there was strong sentiment for action to avoid economic collapse in Europe entirely apart from the danger of Soviet encroachment. This danger was becoming clearer year by year, however, as Communist control was clamped solidly on the Eastern European nations. It was emphasized by such major episodes as the Soviet fomenting of civil war in Greece, the Communist *coup d'état* in Czechoslovakia, the Berlin blockade, and the attack on South Korea. The maintenance of huge Soviet armed forces, the failure of efforts at international atomic energy control, and the explosion of a Soviet nuclear weapon in late 1949 all made clear that economic recovery alone was no guarantee of Western security.

Beginning with the Truman Doctrine of 1947 and the provision of military assistance to Greece and Turkey, American policy therefore rapidly developed a system of collective military security. The most far-reaching commitments were made under the North Atlantic Treaty of 1949 (NATO), which obligates each member to treat an attack on one as an attack on all. It was followed in the mid-1950's by the Anzus (Australia, New Zealand, and United States) and Southeast Asia Treaties, strengthening of collective security arrangements in the Western Hemisphere under the Organization of American States, support (although not formal membership) for the Middle Eastern Baghdad Pact, and bilateral security treaties with several countries in the Western Pacific. In the first instance, these were mainly political commitments, but it soon became clear that they had to be implemented by some degree of ready military forces. To this end, a substantial fraction of the American armed forces was stationed abroad, and programs were developed to provide direct and indirect military assistance for allied countries. Since the European allies had not yet completed their postwar recovery, they were in no position to finance large additional defense burdens unaided, while the poorer allies had neither the internal financial strength nor the foreign-exchange earning power to secure costly modern military equipment.

Apart from Greece and Turkey, military assistance began with the Mutual Defense Assistance Act of 1949. It was greatly expanded after the outbreak of the Korean War, and the decision was made to transform NATO into an armed peacetime alliance with active defense forces in being. Along with residual economic assistance to Europe, and the small beginnings of technical and developmental assistance then under way, military assistance was fused into the Mutual Security Act of 1951; this law, as amended, remains the legislative framework for most American foreign-assistance activities. Military assistance has been provided to some forty-one countries, the annual expenditures for this purpose reaching a peak of $4 billion in 1953 and leveling off in recent years to somewhat over $2 billion. While the expansion of allied forces was substantially complete by 1954, the evolution of weapons technology was so rapid that continued American military assistance seemed likely for a long period, although it was becoming a smaller share of total allied military expenditures.

Apart from weapons and military training in their use, the programs have also had a large component of so-called "defense support," i.e., economic assistance required to permit the recipient nations to support the added burdens of greatly enlarged defense forces. In the early 1950's, these funds went mainly to Europe, but with the completion of economic recovery on that continent the emphasis was shifted to the Western Pacific, Southeast Asia, and the Middle East. Apart from these forms of direct assistance, the collective military effort has also assisted allied countries in meeting their dollar requirements through American expenditures on foreign air-base and other military construction, procurement abroad of certain types of military materiel (usually called "off-shore procurement"), and expenditures of forces stationed abroad. Taken together, these expenditures have played a large role in relieving the dollar shortage of the immediate postwar years and in adding to the gold and foreign-exchange reserves of other nations.

Technical and Economic Assistance for Underdeveloped Areas

Assistance for economic development was the last major element to be incorporated into the foreign-aid program. Questions as to its proper scope, magnitude, duration, and methods are still hotly debated.

The self-conscious and vigorous drive for economic development in the poorer nations of the world was one of the major forces affecting postwar American foreign policy. Many reasons have been adduced for this drive. Among them are improved communications and the consequent spreading of awareness that advanced countries enjoy higher living standards and less burdensome ways of life; expectations in the former colonial nations that national independence would automatically entail material well-being; broadening of the social and political power base in many countries; and the example of Russian development under Communist leadership. Whatever the reasons, the effort to accelerate development has become a central focus of domestic political concern in long-independent areas of Latin America and the Middle East as well as in the newer nations of Asia and Africa. In most instances, the professed goal is not only to advance from relative stagnation but to close the gap with the West. Since the West is very far ahead, is generally under less population pressure, and is continuing its own growth, this implies for the underdeveloped world a very rapid pace of development under forced draft.

Despite the intense concentration of policy-makers and social scientists on these issues in recent years, the processes of economic development, historical or contemporary, are by no means fully understood. Capital investment and industrialization are clearly necessary, but not sufficient, conditions. Development also involves changes in cultural attitudes and social institutions, altered individual incentives and interests, provision of basic education and training, stimulation of savings and entrepreneurship, enhancement of agricultural as well as industrial productivity, monetization of the economy and the creation of financial institutions, and many other ancillary changes.

The great variety in developmental conditions is matched by variety in national approaches to the problem. Most underdeveloped countries have prepared four-, five-, or six-year plans for development, but they range from mere descriptions of planned public-investment projects at the one extreme to purported blueprints of all economic activity, public and private, at the other. In some cases, detailed means of implementation are employed in the effort to see that plans are carried out; in others, the plans are simply statements of broad aspirations. There is also diversity in the degree of governmental direction or participation in development, although in all cases the governmental role is substantially greater than in nineteenth-century England or America.

Almost all of the developing countries have looked to the more advanced nations for assistance in speeding the developmental process. It is generally recognized that the primary effort must be domestic. This is true both of the cultural and institutional foundations of development and of the bulk of capital formation. But outside capital to supplement domestic efforts may make a critical difference in the pace of development and the degree of pressure on current consumption standards. Perhaps of greater importance, outside help may be essential to the application of advanced techniques. In some areas, a special effort is made to attract private foreign investment, but there is also a universal desire for foreign public capital and technical assistance. Sometimes such assistance is claimed almost as a right—a moral duty from the rich to the poor; more often, it is urged as being in the mutual interests of advanced and underdeveloped countries alike.

The wealthier nations, notably the United States, have responded affirmatively to these desires. Technical assistance for economic development accounts for most of the work of the United Nations in the economic and social fields, including the central Secretariat, the regional economic commissions, and the main specialized agencies. The World Bank, as already described, was established to supply capital for basic economic overhead projects in less-developed areas. But here again, as in the case of European recovery, the magnitude and intensity of demand have been far too great to be accommodated by the international agencies alone.

A new phase in American attention to this problem was opened by "Point Four" of President Truman's Inaugural Address of 1949, in which he called for "a bold new program for making the benefits of our scientific advances and industrial progress available for the improvement and growth of underdeveloped areas." This program was not intended to involve multibillion-dollar grants on the model of the Marshall Plan. Its major emphasis was on expanded technical assistance, partly through the United Nations and partly bilateral, as a basis for a greatly enlarged flow of private developmental capital. The Act for International Development of 1950 reflected this limited concept, expenditures under it being reckoned in the tens of millions rather than the billions of dollars. A parallel effort was organized under British Commonwealth sponsorship in the form of the Colombo Plan for South and Southeast Asia; this was later extended to include non-Commonwealth countries.

The original Point Four administrators were mainly concerned with "grass roots" technical assistance for improving agricultural productivity, technical and vocational training, and small-scale industrialization. Other American policy-makers, however, were impatient with this approach. They felt that existing sources of public and private capital must be supplemented by a large-scale injection of government funds as grants or "soft loans" (i.e., loans on very easy repayment terms), especially for the politically uncommitted nations on the periphery of the Soviet bloc. Some believed that rapid development in Communist China unmatched in the free Asian countries would attract vast new regions to the Communist cause. Others argued that only substantial outside capital supplies could permit the realization of aspirations for growth in a manner compatible with the survival of free institutions. These considerations were fortified in the mid-fifties by a new Soviet strategy of offering substantial economic aid to countries whose political orientation was especially important in the Cold War.

In 1953, an explicit category of "development assistance" was included in the Mutual Security Program for the first time. In 1956–1957, a series of official reviews, legislative, executive, and public, concluded that assistance for economic development must be accepted as an important instrument of American foreign policy for the indefinite future and recommended that it be established on a more systematic basis. In the Mutual Security Act of 1957, therefore, Congress created a new Development Loan Fund, designed to supplement private capital, the World Bank, and the Export-Import Bank by providing additional resources for promoting sound development projects which could not meet normal banking standards. It was expected to offer unusually generous repayment terms, both as to duration and interest rates, and in many cases to accept repayment in local currencies. Although the administration had originally requested a $2 billion authorization for three years, Congress appropriated only $300 million for the first year and $400 million for the second. By mid-1958, over $2 billion worth of proposals had been received, against which some $100 million of loan agreements had been signed. The administration had indicated that it hoped for a very large expansion of the Development Loan Fund during the next several years.

Meanwhile, the United States was also assisting economic development through other programs. The Export-Import Bank, originally created in 1934 to stimulate a revival of American export trade, was converted after World War II into the major foreign lending instrumentality of the government, and used for economic stabilization loans and development assistance along with its trade-promoting functions. By mid-1958, its total outstanding loans amounted to almost $3 billion and its loans to underdeveloped areas in fiscal 1958 alone totaled over $700 million. The projects thus financed were in many cases similar to those supported by the World Bank, but they also included many industrial projects and there was a heavy regional emphasis on Latin America.

Another major contribution to development financing was made under the Agricultural Trade Development and Assistance Act of 1954, generally known as Public Law 480. The main impetus to this statute was the desire to reduce the increasingly burdensome surpluses accumulated by the government under the agricultural price-support programs described above in Chapter 6. The method employed, however, was to permit the sale of such surpluses against payment in foreign currencies, and then to make a portion of those currencies available to the recipient countries as loan funds for promoting their own economic development. Sales under Public Law 480 were to be in addition to normal purchases and were to be so administered as to avoid disrupting the markets of friendly foreign countries. By mid-1958, almost $4 billion worth of farm products had been sold under these programs, roughly one-quarter of all American agricultural exports during the four years in question. These supplies have made an important contribution to economic development by freeing foreign exchange resources for other needs and relieving the inflationary impact of development programs.

Thus, through a series of laws and agencies, bilateral and multilateral, aid for economic development has become an increasingly important element of American foreign policy. In the late 1950's, however, there was still no universal consensus on the adequacy of this effort or the soundness of the methods employed. Many observers felt that a larger share of public investment should be managed by international agencies, notably a new affiliate of the World Bank. It was also widely believed that more effective means could be found for bringing the managerial techniques and productive skills of private enterprise to bear in pursuit of the national objectives. Policy toward development assistance, therefore, was still evolving within a framework of debate and reappraisal.

Foreign Assistance and Long-Range Foreign Economic Policy

Taken as a whole, postwar governmental grants and credits (net of repayments) to foreign countries amounted by the end of 1957 to over $63 billion, including some $37 billion since the start of the Korean emergency. Of this latter amount, direct military assistance accounted for over one-half and indirect military support for another large component. The magnitude and direction of these expenditures have been shaped predominantly by Cold War considerations. While geographical patterns and functional composition were constantly shifting, there was no discernible downward trend in the annual level of expenditure of about $5 billion.

With no end in sight of the basic international tension between the Soviet bloc and the allied free nations, foreign aid has become an important and apparently durable element of the world economic scene. It has helped to underpin the growing volume of international trade and the increasing freedom of international finance. It has also become a major element in the calculations of underdeveloped countries concerning their prospects and possibilities for economic growth.

Since most of the individual aid programs were instituted on a temporary basis, their administration has been marked by improvisation and experimentation in governmental organization and in co-ordinating machinery. Only in recent years has either the executive or the legislative branch come slowly to the conviction that these programs must either be merged with established departments of government or entrusted to new agencies with sufficient assurance of continuity to attract and train qualified manpower. There is still much to be done before foreign assistance is effectively integrated into the body of broader international economic policies.

4. The Interweaving of Foreign and Domestic Economic Policies

The description of postwar foreign economic policy presented above, like much of the public debate on these issues, is stated largely in terms of broad international political or security interests. In its application, however, foreign economic policy necessarily impinges on the same types of economic interests and groupings which are affected by domestic economic policies, and it is subject to the same types of political pressures that have been discussed in other chapters of this book.

The individual measures which in aggregate comprise foreign economic policy cover a spectrum from those which are incidental by-products of domestic policies to those where the motivation is almost wholly international. Over this whole spectrum there is some degree of tension between considerations of general foreign policy and domestic policy considerations, including the pressures of organized interest groups. These tensions play an important role at both the legislative and the executive levels in the working out of foreign economic policies.

An example at one extreme is antitrust policy, which is overwhelmingly domestic in origin and application, but also limits certain types of business activities abroad. In the eyes of some critics, its foreign application creates unnecessary difficulties in relations with countries not sharing American antitrust philosophy and even frustrates certain types of constructive foreign business activity which would promote our general national objectives.[18] In other cases, the primary motivation is a response to domestic pressure, but the specific action may be directed mainly at changes in international trade. Examples in point are quota restrictions on agricultural and petroleum imports and the disposal of agricultural surpluses abroad. In the latter case, however, special efforts have been made to employ the resources arising from this program in a manner contributing to the general foreign-policy objective of promoting economic development.

The tensions are most evident in the field of trade policy. There the shift to executive negotiation of tariffs within the framework of the GATT has placed the main weight of policy on the progressive liberalization of trade and the reduction of import barriers, but with many exceptions and qualifications which give play to

[18] For an exhaustive and balanced treatment of this subject, see Kingman Brewster, Jr., *Antitrust and American Business Abroad* (1958).

the interests of affected domestic competitors. The interweaving of these factors was well exemplified in 1958 by the cases of lead and zinc. Domestic mining of these metals had been contracting for many years as the better ore reserves were worked out, and imports were constituting an increasingly large share of total supplies. When the 1958 recession sharply reduced demand and prices, many domestic producers were in critical straits. The Tariff Commission unanimously recommended an increase in duties, some members supporting import quotas as well. But the imposition of quotas was at variance with the administration's general policy of avoiding such restrictions on nonagricultural products. The foreign suppliers, notably Peru, Mexico, Australia, and Canada, were all allied nations whose economic welfare was considered important to the American national interest. The administration sought to resolve the dilemma through a production-subsidy program, but when this was rejected by Congress, import quotas were reluctantly imposed. At the same time, international discussions were initiated to explore the possibility of a more equitable international sharing of the burden of any future fluctuations in lead and zinc markets.

Even the foreign economic policy measures most clearly based on broad considerations of national interest are often modified by special provisions required by organized domestic interests. Foreign procurement of military supplies has been restricted where potential American suppliers, even at higher cost, are located in areas of substantial unemployment. In promoting expanded production in underdeveloped areas, assistance is usually withheld from the agricultural commodities which the United States produces in surplus, even though the country concerned may have natural advantages in that field. Loans for foreign industrialization made to American firms from proceeds of agricultural surplus sales may not be used for the manufacture of products to be exported to the United States in competition with American domestic producers. Many other examples could be cited. The legislative history of almost every important foreign economic policy statute has involved conflict between efforts to maintain the integrity of the broad policy and pressures for response to affected domestic economic interests.

On the executive side, it has been found necessary to create special machinery as a bridge between agencies mainly concerned with foreign and security policy and those oriented toward the large domestic interest groups. The Department of State has the leading voice in setting the broad lines of foreign economic policy, but this area is also of great concern to the Treasury, the Departments of Agriculture, Commerce, Labor, and Interior, the Atomic Energy Commission, the Federal Communications Commission, the Civil Aeronautics Board, and many other agencies. A host of interdepartmental committees has been established to assure consideration of all affected interests and to reconcile views on particular programs.

In 1954, a Foreign Economic Policy Council was created at White House level, chaired by a Special Presidential Assistant. This group endeavors to determine administration policy on foreign economic matters within the framework of broad national strategy as determined in the National Security Council, but also taking account of domestic economic interests. Its task is not easy. There are, indeed, few areas in which the resources of governmental leadership are so severely challenged as in devising and winning congressional and public support for foreign economic policies conducive to the nation's widest interests.

CHAPTER 29

Conclusion—Public Policy and the American Economy

1. The Evolution of Public Policy

PUBLIC policy over the years has come to play an increasingly significant role in giving shape and content to the American economy. This role, however, is neither novel nor recent in origin. In every generation, diverse economic groups have sought, in greater or less degree, to utilize the instrumentalities of government to guide and direct the course of economic development. Even before the Constitution was ratified, an acute statesman like Madison recognized that "the regulation of these various and interfering interests forms the principal task of modern legislation. . . ."

Public policy, as embodied in fundamental constitutional provisions for the maintenance of order, the protection of property rights, and the enforcement of contracts, contributed to the establishment of the legal framework for the expansion of business enterprise. In the first decade of our national history, the economic program sponsored by the dominant Federalist Party furnished an important impetus to the growth of banking, mercantile, and manufacturing interests. Such Hamiltonian policies as the establishment of a national bank, the funding of the publc debt, and the enactment of a protective tariff were consciously designed to achieve this end.

915

In the period from Jefferson's inauguration in 1801 until the outbreak of the Civil War, agrarian interests were in the ascendancy. The extension of the frontier and the widening of the suffrage favored the growth of agrarian influence. Agrarian statecraft in its initial phase, however, did not operate to impede the growth of manufactures or the spread of business influence. Indeed, in the desire to liberate the United States from dependence on foreign- and particularly English-fabricated goods (a motive which became particularly strong during and after the War of 1812), every encouragement was held out to the proprietors of manufacturing enterprises. Until 1832, the tariff rose steadily and proved a potent influence in accelerating the early stages of the American industrial revolution. The subsequent lowering of the tariff was largely a response to the pressure of Southern plantation owners, who became increasingly aware that they stood to gain by a low tariff policy which would facilitate the sale of cotton in foreign markets and at the same time reduce the price of manufactured articles in the domestic market.

The content of public policy in the pre-Civil War period had to be fitted to an agrarian mold. Public aids to promote the building of roads, canals, and, later, railroads found their strongest political support in the demand of farmers for improved transportation facilities. While business interests might also benefit from such improvements, agrarian well-being furnished the immediate justification. At the same time, the agrarian leadership of the day was prepared to rebuff the efforts of banking and business groups to use the instruments of central government to advance their interests unduly. The Jacksonian war on Biddle and the Second Bank of the United States was such a rebuff. It arose, not only out of agrarian demands for easier credit which the Bank was unwilling to meet, but also out of a deep-seated fear of the Bank as an engine of undesirable concentration of power. But while agrarian spokesmen were prepared to struggle to dislodge opposing economic interests from positions of economic and political influence in the central government, they envisaged government in less positive terms than the followers of Hamilton. In so far as they depended on government, they preferred to utilize it at the local and state level, rather than at the national center.

Over much of the pre-Civil War period, Western and Southern agrarian interests maintained an effective working political liaison which ensured their dominance. As the slavery issue came into prominence, however, and as the conflict over the disposition of the Western lands intensified, agrarian interests began to divide along sectional lines. The inability of the Democratic Party to find a formula that would keep its Southern and Western wings together prepared the way for a political realignment. Under the aegis of the Republican Party, a new political alliance was achieved between the agrarian interests of the West and the business, banking, and industrial interests of the East.

With the triumph of the Republican Party in 1860, public policy began to reflect the aspirations of the new patterns of leadership. Two major forces were combined in this movement. Western agrarian interests received recognition in the enactment of the Homestead Act of 1862, the Land Grant College Act of the same year, and also in 1862, the establishment of the Department of Agriculture as a service agency for farmers. Policies of liberal internal improvements and extensive government aid to advance railroad construction in the West were also calculated to appeal to Western agrarian interests. Concern with the promotion of business interests was even more immediate and direct. The steady elevation of the tariff became a powerful instrument for safeguarding many business enterprises against foreign competition. Monetary and banking policies contributed to the strengthening of the position of business and financial groups. Land grants and other public aids fostered the growth of railroad corporations. Business promotionalism bulked large.

During the 1870's, signs of a shift in public policy became apparent. Promotionalism began to give way to regulation. Agricultural depression accentuated cleavages of interest between railroads, processors, and other business interests on the one hand, and farmers on the other. The appearance of pools, combinations, and monopolies in important sectors of the economy drove nonparticipating small businessmen to turn to government to restore a competitive order. Increasingly farmers and independent small businessmen sought to find common cause. The first important manifestation of the growing regulatory movement, the Granger agitation, was primarily agrarian in origin. Its most significant contribution was in the field of state railroad regulation, where it elaborated a pattern of control of rates and practices which was later to be widely applied to other public utilities in more comprehensive and positive terms

Difficulties encountered in applying state regulation to businesses which transcended the jurisdiction of the states forced the advocates of regulation to invoke federal power. Thus, in the eighties, independent businessmen joined with farmers in pressing for federal regulation of the railroads. The establishment of the Interstate Commerce Commission in 1887 marked a response to these demands. The enactment of the Sherman Antitrust Act of 1890 registered the influence of the same combination of farmers and small businessmen. However, the first great thrust of national regulatory power—symbolized by the passage of these acts—soon exhausted itself. During the nineties, both the Interstate Commerce Commission and the Sherman Act met frustration in the courts. While agrarian discontent found a sounding board in Populist rumblings and the Bryan-led Democracy, the dominant political leadership of the day was content to let well enough alone.

The second major expansion of national power had to wait for the leadership of Theodore Roosevelt. In his administration, a number of new regulatory responsibilities were assumed by the federal government. An effort was made to inject life into the Sherman Act. The passage of the Hepburn Act marked the beginning of effective railroad regulation by the ICC. For the first time, the problem of conservation of natural resources was seriously attacked. Labor received recognition in the passage of the Employers' Liability Act. Consumer interests found expression in the enactment of the Meat Inspection and Pure Food and Drug laws. At the same time, a number of states enacted laws providing for the establishment of commissions to regulate the rates and services of utility companies, and state legislation designed to improve the conditions of labor began to appear on a significant scale.

After a period of slackened tempo under Taft, the expansion of federal economic power was resumed with Wilson. This time the New Freedom served as the rallying cry for agrarian, small business, and labor forces. Again instrumentalities of national power were invoked. The Federal Reserve Board, the Federal Trade Commission, the Federal Farm Loan Board, the Tariff Commission, and the Federal Power Commission were among the important new additions to the structure of controls. The Clayton Act was designed to increase the effectiveness of antitrust policy and at the same time to liberate labor from some of the restrictions of the injunction and of antitrust legislation. The increased strength of labor was also reflected in the enactment of two federal child-labor laws, which were later declared unconstitutional by the Supreme Court. The war emergency of 1917–1918 concentrated a hitherto unparalleled accretion of economic power in the federal government; although many of the specially created war agencies were subsequently demobilized, a residue remained. Wartime experience influenced the strengthening of the powers of the ICC under the Transportation Act of 1920. The activities

CONCLUSION 919

of the Shipping Board persisted into the postwar period.

The decade of the twenties was ushered in with the slogans of "Back to Normalcy" and "Less Government in Business," but the more conservative political leadership was only partially successful in arresting the trend toward increasing the responsibilities of the federal government in the economic realm. Thus, in 1924, the Inland Waterways Corporation, the residuary legatee of a public enterprise undertaken to relieve transportation shortages during the war, was established on a long-run basis. The postwar agricultural readjustment and depression produced insistent demands from farm leaders for federal assistance. Although the more ambitious of these proposals failed to become law, there was a partial response in the enactment of the Packers' and Stockyards Act of 1921, the Capper-Volstead Act of 1922, the Agricultural Credit Act of 1923, the Co-operative Marketing Act of 1926, and the Agricultural Marketing Act which established the Farm Board in 1929. Technological necessities reinforced the clamor of the radio industry and the listening public to produce the Federal Radio Commission of 1926. In 1930, the Federal Power Commission, originally a cabinet committee, was reorganized and made independent. These and other analogous developments of the twenties were neither large nor peculiarly significant in terms of their impact upon the total economy; what gives them particular interest is that they reveal the continuing strength of the forces making for expanded government action even in a political environment which was ostensibly hostile to such expansion.

With the depression of 1929, forces were set in motion which produced a surge of federal economic power unparalleled in scope and purpose. As the depression deepened, public policy was pushed far beyond the traditional regulatory techniques which had been elaborated in the fields of public utility regulation and antitrust policy. The principal concern became the stability of the whole economy; the problems which called for action transcended the boundaries of any single industry. Public policy was increasingly forced to address itself to broader issues of large-scale unemployment and problems of conservation of natural and human resources, to ways of stimulating production and new investment, to wide-ranging problems of the interrelations of fiscal and monetary policies, wage policies, price policies, trade practices, and foreign economic policies in fostering a return of prosperity and an increase in national income.

The initial response to the depression was couched in purely emergency terms. Under Hoover, the Reconstruction Finance

Corporation was organized to give assistance to banks, railroads, insurance companies, and other enterprises which were threatened with insolvency. Vain efforts were made to stabilize the price of some agricultural commodities through purchasing programs sponsored by the Federal Farm Board. An ambitious public works program was inaugurated. As local and state resources were exhausted, federal funds were made available for unemployment relief.

The New Deal's response to the depression was on a broader scale. The RFC widened its activities, though emergency salvaging operations continued to be stressed. Public credit was extensively used to prevent farm and home foreclosures, to finance public works, and to provide relief for the unemployed. Promotional activity was markedly expanded in the agricultural and labor fields. Agricultural control legislation was focused on improvement in farm income, and government-sponsored farm-credit facilities were considerably extended. In the labor field, Section 7(a) of the National Industrial Recovery Act and the activities of the National Labor Relations Board furnished a powerful stimulus to union organization, and the Walsh-Healey and Fair Labor Standards Acts were adopted to improve wages and working conditions. Additional consumer protective legislation was provided, of which the most important was the Food, Drug, and Cosmetic Act of 1938.

Many new regulatory controls appeared on the scene. In transportation, the jurisdiction of the ICC was broadened to embrace motor and domestic water carriers as well as railroads. Air carriers and the merchant marine were subject to additional controls, though legislation in this field was primarily promotional in nature. In communications, a new agency, the Federal Communications Commission (FCC), was created to replace the old Radio Commission, and it was vested with considerable power to regulate interstate telecommunications. Changes in the public utility field were even more significant. The jurisdiction of the Federal Power Commission was expanded to embrace interstate activities of electric and natural-gas companies. The Securities and Exchange Commission was vested with power to regulate utility holding companies and to secure simplification in their corporate structures and geographical integration in their operations. There was a marked expansion of public enterprise in the electrical utility field, and public ownership became a significant regulatory device in the drive to reduce electric rates.

Developments in the area of trade regulation followed a more erratic course. After the mammoth National Recovery Administration experiment in government-sponsored cartelization was dealt its deathblow by the Supreme Court, public policy at first wavered and then, after the recession of 1937, found new direction in a vigorous revival of the antitrust laws. At the same time, independent retailers and wholesalers joined with sympathetic manufacturers to secure legislation to remove some of the competitive advantages of large-scale distributors. The struggle to control the channels of distribution was waged in both federal and state jurisdictions. A number of states enacted laws providing discriminatory chain-store taxation, and many more adopted fair-trade acts which were designed to legalize resale-price maintenance and to outlaw price discrimination. The same impulse to remove the differential advantages of the mass distributor led to the enactment of the federal Robinson-Patman Act and the Miller-Tydings Resale Price Maintenance Law.

During this same period, the range of regulatory authority was being expanded into new fields. Protection was provided for investors through the Securities and Exchange Commission and other agencies. Bituminous coal was subjected to a special regulatory regime which embraced perhaps the most complex venture in price-fixing ever undertaken by any single peacetime agency in the United States. In the case of oil, production restraints in the form of state proration laws, which had begun to be enacted earlier, were extended and supplemented by a federal prohibition of interstate shipment of oil produced in violation of state proration laws.

Novel and far-reaching changes were also evident in the form of an expansion of public enterprise and increased concern with the conservation of natural and human resources. Public enterprise became particularly important in the banking and credit field, in electricity, and in the provision of low-cost housing. The device of the public corporation, which had been widely used abroad and which had been resorted to for emergency purposes during World War I, was increasingly employed in the organization of public enterprise. Conservation of natural resources bulked more important, and a powerful impulse was given to the development of machinery to secure the planned utilization of land, water, and mineral resources. Concern with social security and the conservation of human resources was even more strongly evident. From haphazard and makeshift measures, public policy gradually moved to the stage of making systematic provision for old age, unemployment, and other risks through such measures as old-age insurance, unemployment compensation, regularized public assistance, work relief, and long-range programs of public works.

During World War II, the imperatives of national mobilization further expanded the role of government into an all-pervading direction and control of the entire economy. Through a combination of incentive and regulatory measures of great complexity, administered by a host of specialized emergency agencies and backed by the powerful drive of a united national will for military victory, production was raised to new heights; manpower, materials, facilities, and other resources were channeled into the output of munitions; and prices were held on a relatively even keel. With the ending of the war, emergency controls were for the most part promptly demobilized.

But new problems were quick to emerge in the postwar world. The United States had to assume the onerous burden of providing security in the face of revolutionary developments in military technology and a formidable challenge from the Soviet Union and its allies. The unexplored applications of nuclear energy called for imaginative action by both government and business to take advantage of the novel opportunities which this development foreshadowed. New vistas appeared of the productive potentialities of a high-level, full-employment economy. The United States found itself inextricably committed to a new array of international responsibilities which were entailed by its leadership position in the free world.

The response of the nation to these challenges and opportunities took various forms. Military expenditures mounted and accounted for an increasingly important segment of the national budget. The Atomic Energy Commission was created to deal with the wide array of problems in its field. The Employment Act of 1946 affirmed the government's responsibility to promote high employment, economic stability, and maximum growth. The new ventures in the international area included the reduction of trade barriers, economic and military aid to our allies, economic assistance to underdeveloped areas, and generous support to a variety of international institutions which were established to stimulate world trade and foster economic reconstruction and development.

2. Problems of a "Mixed Economy"

The increased economic responsibilities of government, both national and international, involved significant modifications in the structure of controls in the American economy. Government had come to play a far more important role than it did a half-century ago. While the extent of governmental intervention varied considerably in different sectors of the economy, the impact of public action was widely felt, and in some areas it was of crucial significance. The structure of controls had come to embrace such diverse methods and objectives as enforcement of competition through the antitrust laws; direct price-fixing (all-encompassing in time of war and specifically directed in time of peace to utilities, transportation, and such special commodities as milk); influencing production, price, and supply as in agriculture and oil; providing information as under the Securities Act; a species of cartelization as under the now defunct NRA and the bituminous-coal legislation; licensing as in radio broadcasting and the security markets; subsidies as in agriculture, ocean shipping, and air transport; the utilization of governmental purchasing to set labor standards as under the Walsh-Healey Act; public enterprise as in power, atomic energy, banking and credit, and housing; conservation of natural resources; the development of social security programs; the increasingly significant impact of national defense expenditures; large-scale foreign-aid and loan programs; the use of monetary and fiscal policies as instruments of countercyclical control; and promotion and regulation of the activities of labor, business, and agriculture in a variety of ways. The result of these developments was to produce a "mixed economy" in which relatively uncontrolled private enterprise, governmentally-regulated private enterprise, and public enterprise all existed side by side.

The phrase "mixed economy" may cover a considerable variety of possible permutations and combinations of private enterprise with public guidance, control, or ownership. The American mixed economy, despite the marked expansion in government's role in recent years, remains one in which private enterprise predominates. A mixed economy of this kind means that responsibility for the economic welfare of the nation is decentralized. Over much of the economy, businessmen make the important decisions determining output, prices, and profits. Their decisions are in turn affected by the demands and bargaining strength of labor, by the power exerted by agricultural and other raw materials producers, by the reactions of competitors, consumers, and other market forces, and by the public policies which governments at various levels pursue. The policies of government are particularly important in the area of fiscal and monetary policy and over the whole range of publicly owned or regulated industries. But the American "mixed economy" does not operate under a rigidly determined central plan. Business, labor, agriculture, and government all divide and share responsibility for making the important economic choices which, taken together, spell depression and stagnation or prosperity and growth.

An economy so constituted presents both dangers and opportunities. The principal danger consists in the possibility that particular economic interests may make their decisions with an eye only on what they conceive to be their own short-run interests. But the opportunities for constructive statesmanship are no less apparent. The basic problem is to achieve fruitful working relationships among the various economic interests so that each can make a maximum contribution to the common well-being.

In a constitutional democracy such as ours in which organized interests find free expression, no single pattern of relations between government and the economy can be ordained as fixed and unalterable. The development of public policy reflects the changing aspirations of the dominant political groups as well as underlying technical, social, and economic developments. The vast expansion of the economic powers of government during the thirties represented an adjustment to the demands of political forces and disadvantaged groups which had been stirred to activity by a severe depression and a slow economic recovery. The altered framework of relations between government and business in that decade produced serious tensions which expressed themselves in the existence of widespread mutual distrust between government and business leaders.

Such tensions were perhaps the inevitable accompaniment of a period of rapid change. The increased responsibilities which had been assumed by government ran counter to previously accepted tenets of business leadership concerning the appropriate functions of government. The resultant frictions and cleavages had destructive potentialities in terms of community well-being. The full possibilities of synchronizing governmental and business efforts to overcome economic maladjustments were not adequately realized.

It became fashionable in some circles to insist that efforts to mingle public control and public enterprise with private enterprise were doomed to futility. Some proponents of the Either-Or method of analysis argued that the only ultimate choice was between complete government regimentation on the one hand, or wholly unrestricted and uncontrolled capitalism on the other. Although this posing of alternatives had a certain polemic value in controversy over public policy, it became increasingly clear, as the American political mood became more conservative in the postwar decade, that the new leadership was quite unprepared to conduct a great crusade to sweep away the whole structure of inherited government controls. Indeed, in the interim, the Social Security Act and much of the social legislation of the thirties had passed from an area of sharp controversy into one of widespread public acceptance. While legislation such as the Taft-Hartley Act marked a considerable reversal of the labor policy of the thirties, it in no sense presaged an attempt to repeal all that the New Deal stood for. The bulk of the American electorate appeared committed to an intermediate position which sought to preserve the advantages of private enterprise and which at the same time looked to government to provide basic securities and to guide entrepreneurial dynamics in the direction of economic expansion and community welfare.

Stress on such values excluded both the possibility of totalitarian economic planning and reliance on an unlimited laissez-faire view of governmental functions. Despite profound differences at the polar extremes of American opinion, there remained a hard core of agreement which a substantial proportion of the electorate was apparently prepared to endorse. This area of agreement may be briefly summarized:

(1) Government should exert its efforts to promote economic stability and growth, seeking the maintenance of high employment levels and the avoidance of undue inflation or deflation. While disagreement persists on how these objectives may best be achieved, a general recognition of the broad responsibility is embodied in the Employment Act of 1946.

(2) Public policy should be directed toward the maintenance of competition over as wide an area as possible, on a plane of minimum fairness and commercial decency. Where competition is ineffective, it should be replaced by positive regulation of price policies, by public enterprise, or by other special treatment.

(3) Government should fix reasonable minimum wages and maximum hours, eliminate child labor, and provide adequate care for the aged and the helpless.

(4) Government should accept an obligation to sustain and improve the position of agriculture in the national economy.

(5) Government should guarantee the provision of adequate basic services, preferably through private enterprise, but if necessary by providing them itself.

(6) Government should be charged with the responsibility of conserving natural and human resources.

(7) Government should be viewed not as a substitute for private enterprise, but rather as a positive guiding force, helping to adjust the economy to the needs of the basic economic groups —consumers, agriculture, labor, and business—to whom it is ultimately responsible.

The effective discharge of these functions poses the problem of instruments, of the establishment of adequate administrative machinery capable of coping with America's increasingly complex domestic economy and new international responsibilities. The expansion of governmental activities creates two types of administrative needs: (1) the need for specialization and differentiation of machinery to fit the diverse requirements of government intervention in different areas of the economy; (2) the need for co-ordination to ensure that the policies which are developed in different areas of the economy follow a common stream of tendency and avoid needless conflict. The basic challenge of government remains that of facilitating accommodations, building community of purpose among conflicting groups, and shaping public policies which both reflect common purpose and provide a creative response to the urgent problems of the contemporary world.

The agenda of unfinished business promise no easy solutions. Despite the powerful upward surge of the American economy since World War II, serious social deficits persist in the area of public services. The need for enhanced support for education and scientific research, for schools, hospitals, slum clearance and urban redevelopment, sanitation, parks, playgrounds, roads, and other community needs is urgent. The problem of maintaining economic growth without inflation and without periodic recessions is far from resolved. With a national budget in the neighborhood of eighty billion dollars, the wise management of fiscal policy looms more important than ever before. New technological developments such as atomic energy open up vistas that are awesome in their potentialities both for good and evil. Large-scale expenditures on national defense arising out of conflicting Soviet-American aspirations in the world give new shape to the economy, while escape from an increasingly burdensome arms race waits on the uncertain prospect of a stabilization of relations between the Soviet Union and the Western world. Meanwhile, America's global responsibilities show no signs of lessening; indeed the position of leadership which it has attained imposes a continuing obligation to help the nations of the free world maintain the dynamic momentum of growth and development. The problem of using government creatively and effectively to balance freedom and security and to reconcile economic progress and economic stability offers an unceasing challenge to free societies and democratic governments from which there is no turning back.

Selected Readings

Publishers' addresses are New York City unless otherwise indicated. The initials "GPO" indicate that the publication is obtainable from Government Printing Office, Washington 25, D.C.

CHAPTER 1—*The Economic Background*

Berle, A. A., Jr.: *The 20th Century Capitalist Revolution*, Harcourt, Brace, 1954.

—— and G. C. Means: *The Modern Corporation and Private Property*, Macmillan, 1933.

Dewhurst, J. F., *et al.*: *America's Needs and Resources: A New Survey*, Twentieth Century Fund, 1955.

Drucker, P. F.: *The New Society*, Harper, 1950.

Galbraith, J. K.: *American Capitalism: The Concept of Countervailing Power*, Houghton Mifflin, Boston, 1952.

Hacker, L. M.: *American Capitalism*, Van Nostrand, Princeton, 1957.

————: *The Triumph of American Capitalism*, Simon & Schuster, 1940.

Kaplan, A. D. H.: *Big Business in a Competitive System*, Brookings Institution, Washington, 1954.

National Resources Committee: *The Structure of the American Economy, Part I, Basic Characteristics*, GPO, 1939.

National Resources Planning Board: *The Structure of the American Economy, Part II, Toward Full Use of Resources*, GPO, 1940.

CHAPTER 2—*The Organization of Economic Interests*

Beard, M.: *A History of the Business Man*, Macmillan, 1938.

Blaisdell, D. C.: *American Democracy Under Pressure*, Ronald Press, 1957.

Brady, R. A.: *Business As A System of Power*, Columbia, 1943.

Buck, S. J.: *The Agrarian Crusade*, Yale, New Haven, 1920.

Commons, J. R.: *Legal Foundations of Capitalism*, Macmillan, 1924.

929

Dulles, F. R.: *Labor in America*, Crowell, 1955.

Hardin, C. M.: *The Politics of Agriculture; Soil Conservation and the Struggle for Power in Rural America*, Free Press, Glencoe, Ill., 1952.

Key, V. O., Jr.: *Politics, Parties, and Pressure Groups*, 4th ed. (Chapter 2, "Agrarianism"; Chapter 3, "Workers"; Chapter 4, "Business"), Crowell, 1958.

Kornhauser, A., H. L. Sheppard, and A. J. Mayer: *When Labor Votes*, University Books, 1956.

Kyle, O. M.: *The Farm Bureau Federation through Three Decades*, Waverly Press, Baltimore, 1948.

Lane, R. E.: *The Regulation of Business Men*, Yale, New Haven, 1954.

McConnell, G.: *The Decline of Agrarian Democracy*, University of California Press, Berkeley, 1953.

McCune, W.: *Who's Behind Our Farm Policy?*, Praeger, 1956.

Truman, D. B.: *The Governmental Process*, Knopf, 1951.

Temporary National Economic Committee: *Economic Power and Political Pressures*, Monograph No. 26, GPO, 1941.

CHAPTER 3—*Ideology, Governmental Machinery, and Politics*

Appleby, P. H.: *Policy and Administration*, University of Alabama Press, University, Ala., 1949.

Bernstein, M. H.: *Regulating Business by Independent Commission*, Princeton University Press, Princeton, 1955.

Clark, J. P.: *The Rise of a New Federalism*, Columbia, 1938.

Cushman, R. E.: *The Independent Regulatory Commissions*, Oxford, 1941.

Hartz, L.: *The Liberal Tradition in America*, Harcourt, Brace, 1955.

Herring, E. P.: *Public Administration and the Public Interest*, McGraw-Hill, 1936.

Holcombe, A. N.: *Our More Perfect Union*, Harvard University Press, Cambridge, 1950.

Latham, E.: *The Group Basis of Politics*, Cornell University Press, Ithaca, 1952.

Leiserson, A.: *Administrative Regulation: A Study in Representation of Interests*, University of Chicago Press, Chicago, 1942.

Lerner, M.: *America as a Civilization*, Simon & Schuster, 1957.

Redford, E. S.: *Administration of National Economic Control*, Macmillan, 1952.

Schattschneider, E. E.: *Party Government*, Rinehart, 1942.

Sutton, F. X., et al.: *The American Business Creed*, Harvard University Press, Cambridge, 1956.

Veblen, T.: *The Theory of Business Enterprise*, Scribner, 1904.

CHAPTER 4—*Constitutional Limitations on Economic Policy
and Administration*

Attorney-General's Committee on Administrative Procedure: *Final Report*, GPO, 1941.

Blachly, F. F., and M. E. Oatman: *Federal Regulatory Action and Control*, Brookings Institution, Washington, 1940.

Corwin, E. S., and J. W. Peltason: *Understudy the Constitution*, rev. ed., Holt, 1958.

Davis, K. C.: *Handbook on Administrative Law*, West Publishing Co., St. Paul, 1951.

Gellhorn, W., and C. Byse: *Administrative Law*, Foundation Press, Brooklyn, 1954.

Haines. C. G.: *The American Doctrine of Judicial Supremacy*, rev. ed., University of California Press, Berkeley, 1932.

Hale, R. L.: *Freedom Through Law*, Columbia, 1952.

Jackson, R. H.: *The Struggle for Judicial Supremacy*, Knopf, 1941.

Jaffe, L. L.: *Administrative Law*, Little, Brown, Boston, 1954.

Kelley, A. H., and W. A. Harbison: *The American Constitution: Its Origins and Development*, Norton, 1948.

Landis, J. M.: *The Administrative Process*, Yale University Press, New Haven, 1938.

McCloskey, R. G. (ed.): *Essays in Constitutional Law*, Knopf, 1957.

Schwartz, B.: *An Introduction to Administrative Law*, Oceana Publications, 1958.

Swisher, C. B.: *American Constitutional Development*, 2d ed., Houghton Mifflin, Boston, 1954.

Warren, C.: *The Supreme Court in United States History*, 2 vols., Little Brown, Boston, 1937.

Warren, G. (ed.): *The Federal Administrative Procedure Act and the Administrative Agencies*, New York University School of Law, 1947.

Wright, B. F.: *The Growth of American Constitutional Law*, Reynal & Hitchcock, 1942.

CHAPTER 5—*Promotion of Business Enterprise*

Beard, C. A.: *The Idea of National Interest*, Macmillan, 1934.

Beckett, G.: *The Reciprocal Trade Agreements Program*, Columbia, 1941.

Bidwell, P. W.: *What the Tariff Means to American Industries*, Harper, 1956.

Board of Investigation and Research: *Public Aids to Transportation*, H. Doc. 159, 79th Cong., 1st. sess., GPO, 1945.

Dearing, C. L., and W. Owen: *National Transportation Policy*, Part I—"Promotion of Transportation Facilities and Services," Brookings Institution, Washington, 1949.

Federal Co-ordinator of Transportation: *Public Aids to Transportation,* 4 vols., GPO, 1938–1940.

Gorter, W.: *United States Shipping Policy,* Harper, 1956.

Humphrey, D. D.: *American Imports,* Twentieth Century Fund, 1955.

Locklin, D. P.: *Economics of Transportation,* 4th ed., Richard D. Irwin, Inc., Homewood, Ill., 1954.

Maass, A.: *Muddy Waters,* Harvard University Press, Cambridge, 1951.

Taussig, F. W.: *State Papers and Speeches on the Tariff* (Chapter 1, "Alexander Hamilton's Report on the Subject of Manufactures"), Harvard University Press, Cambridge, 1893.

——: *The Tariff History of the United States,* 8th ed., Putnam, 1938.

Westmeyer, R. E.: *Economics of Transportation,* Prentice-Hall, 1952.

Zeis, Paul M.: *American Shipping Policy,* Princeton University Press, Princeton, 1938.

CHAPTER 6—*Promotion of Agriculture*

American Farm Economic Association: *Readings on Agricultural Policy,* McGraw-Hill, 1949.

Baker, G.: *The County Agent,* University of Chicago Press, Chicago, 1939.

Benedict, M. R.: *Can We Solve the Farm Problem?* Twentieth Century Fund, 1955.

——: *Farm Policies of the United States, 1790–1950,* Twentieth Century Fund, 1953.

Black, J. D.: *Agrarian Reform in the United States,* McGraw-Hill, 1929.

——, and M. E. Kiefer: *Future Food and Agriculture Policy,* McGraw-Hill, 1948.

Blaisdell, D. C.: *Government and Agriculture,* Farrar and Rinehart, 1940.

Gaus, J. M., and L. O. Wolcott: *Public Administration and the United States Department of Agriculture,* Public Administration Service, Chicago, 1940.

Halcrow, H. G.: *Agricultural Policy in the United States,* Prentice-Hall, 1953.

Wilcox, W. W.: *The Farmer in the Second World War,* Iowa State College Press, Ames, 1947.

CHAPTER 7—*Promotion of the Interests of Labor*

Bernstein, I.: *The New Deal Collective Bargaining Policy,* University of California Press, Berkeley, 1950.

Bowman, D. O.: *Public Control of Labor Relations: A Study of the National Labor Relations Board,* Macmillan, 1942.

Commons, J. R., and J. B. Andrews: *Principles of Labor Legislation,* 4th ed., Harper, 1936.

Daugherty, C. R.: *The Labor Problems of American Society,* Houghton Mifflin, Boston, 1952.

Derber, M., and E. Young (eds.): *Labor and the New Deal*, University of Wisconsin, Madison, 1957.

Fitch, J. A.: *Social Responsibilities of Organized Labor*, Harper, 1957.

Frankfurter, F., and N. Greene.: *The Labor Injunction*, Macmillan, 1930.

Gregory, C. O.: *Labor and the Law*, rev. ed., Norton, 1949.

Kaltenborn, H. S.: *Governmental Adjustment of Labor Disputes*, The Foundation Press, Brooklyn, 1941.

Killingsworth, C. G.: *State Labor Relations Acts*, University of Chicago Press, Chicago, 1948.

Lecht, L. A.: *Experience Under Railway Labor Legislation*, Columbia, 1955.

Leek, J. H.: *Government and Labor in the United States*, Rinehart, 1952.

Lester, R. A.: *Labor and Industrial Relations*, Macmillan, 1953.

Lindblom, C.: *Unions and Capitalism*, Yale University Press, New Haven, 1949.

Mathews, R. E.: *Labor Relations and the Law*, 2 vols., Little, Brown, Boston, 1953.

Miller, G. W.: *American Labor and Government*, Prentice-Hall, 1948.

Millis, H. A., and E. Brown: *From the Wagner Act to Taft-Hartley: A Study of National Labor Policy and Labor Relations*, University of Chicago Press, Chicago, 1950.

————, and R. E. Montgomery: *Organized Labor* (Vol. III of *The Economics of Labor*) McGraw-Hill, 1945.

Reede, A. H.: *Adequacy of Workmen's Compensation*, Harvard University Press, Cambridge, 1947.

Seidman, J.: *The Yellow-dog Contract*, Johns Hopkins Press, Baltimore, 1932.

Slichter, S. H.: *The Challenge of Industrial Relations*, Cornell University Press, Ithaca, 1947.

————: *Union Policies and Industrial Management*, Brookings Institution, Washington, 1941.

Somers, H. M., and A. R. Somers: *Trends and Current Issues in Social Insurance*, University of California Press, Berkeley, 1957.

Taft, P.: *The Structure and Government of Labor Unions*, Harvard University Press, Cambridge, 1954.

Werne, B.: *The Law of Labor Relations*, Macmillan, 1951.

Witney, F.: *Government and Collective Bargaining*, Lippincott, Philadelphia, 1951.

Witte, E. E.: *The Government in Labor Disputes*, McGraw-Hill, 1932.

CHAPTER 8—*Government, the Consumer, and the Public Interest*

Bowen, E. R.: *The Cooperative Road to Abundance; the Alternative to Monopolism and Communism*, Henry Schuman, 1953.

Campbell, P.: *Consumer Representation in the New Deal*, Columbia, 1940.

Casselman, P. H.: *The Cooperative Movement and Some of Its Problems*, Philosophical Library, 1952.

Chase, S., and F. J. Schlink: *Your Money's Worth*, Macmillan, 1927.

Citizen's Advisory Committee on the FDA: *Report*, H. Doc. No. 227, 84th Cong., 1st sess., GPO, 1955.

Coles, J. V.: *Standards and Labels for Consumer Goods*, Ronald Press, 1949.

Committee on Public Administration Cases: *The Consumers' Counsel and the National Bituminous Coal Commission, 1937–1938*, rev. ed., Washington, 1950.

Fowler, B. B.: *The Cooperative Challenge*, Little, Brown, Boston, 1947.

Kallen, H. N.: *Decline and Rise of the Consumer*, Appleton-Century, 1936.

"The New Food, Drug, and Cosmetic Legislation," *Law and Contemporary Problems*, Durham, Winter, 1939.

Select Committee to Investigate the Use of Chemicals in Foods and Cosmetics: *Reports*, H. Reports 2182 and 2356, 82d Cong., 2d sess., GPO, 1952.

Sinclair, U. B.: *The Jungle*, Doubleday, Page, 1906.

Sorenson, H.: *The Consumer Movement*, Harper, 1941.

Wilson, S.: *Food and Drug Regulation*, American Council on Public Affairs, Washington, 1942.

CHAPTER 9—*The Growth of Government Regulation*

Benson, L.: *Merchants, Farmers & Railroads*, Harvard University Press, Cambridge, 1955.

Buck, S. J.: *The Granger Movement*, Harvard University Press, Cambridge, 1913.

Davis, J. S.: *Essays in the Earlier History of American Corporations*, 2 vols., Harvard University Press, Cambridge, 1917.

Dodd, E. M.: "The First Half Century of Statutory Regulation of Business Corporations in Massachusetts," *Harvard Legal Essays*, Harvard University Press, Cambridge, 1934.

Handlin, O., and M. F. Handlin: *Commonwealth: A Study of the Role of Government in the American Economy: Massachusetts, 1774–1861*, New York University Press, 1947.

Haney, L. H.: *Congressional History of Railways in the United States*, 2 vols., Democrat Printing Co., Madison, 1910.

Hartz, L.: *Economic Policy and Democratic Thought*, Harvard University Press, Cambridge, 1948.

White, L. D.: "Origin of Utility Commissions in Massachusetts," *Journal of Political Economy*, Chicago, March, 1921, pp. 177–197.

CHAPTER 10—*Railroad Regulation and the Co-ordination of Transportation*

Adams, C. F., and H. Adams: *Chapters of Erie*, Cornell University Press, Ithaca, 1956.

Campbell, E. G.: *The Reorganization of the American Railroad System, 1893–1900*, Columbia, 1938.

Cherington, C. R.: *The Regulation of Railroad Abandonments*, Harvard University Press, Cambridge, 1948.

Federal Co-ordinator of Transportation: *Public Aids to Transportation*, 4 vols., GPO, 1938–1940.

———: *Reports*, GPO, 1934–1936.

Leonard, W. N.: *Railroad Consolidation under the Transportation Act of 1920*, Columbia, 1946.

Locklin, D. P.: *Economics of Transportation*, 4th ed. (Chapters 1–27), Richard D. Irwin, Inc., Homewood, Ill., 1954.

Lowenthal, M.: *The Investor Pays*, Knopf, 1936.

Mansfield, H. C.: *The Lake Cargo Coal Rate Controversy*, Columbia, 1932.

Sharfman, I. L.: *The Interstate Commerce Commission*, 5 vols., Commonwealth Fund, 1936.

Troxel, E.: *Economics of Transport*, Rinehart, 1955.

Van Metre, T. W.: *Transportation in the United States*, 2d ed., Foundation Press, Brooklyn, 1950.

Westmeyer, R. E.: *Economics of Transportation* (Parts I and II), Prentice-Hall, 1952.

CHAPTER 11—*Transportation Regulation and the Search for a National Policy*

Board of Investigation and Research: *Public Aids to Domestic Transportation*, H. Doc. No. 159, 79th Cong., 1st sess., GPO, 1944.

Dearing, C. L., and W. Owen: *National Transportation Policy*, Brookings Institution, Washington, 1949.

Federal Co-ordinator of Transportation: *Regulation of Transportation Agencies*, S. Doc. No. 152, 73d Cong., 2d sess., GPO, 1934.

———: *Fourth Report*, H. Doc. No. 394, 74th Cong., 2d sess., GPO, 1936.

Keyes, L. S.: *Federal Control of Entry into Air Transportation*, Harvard University Press, Cambridge, 1951.

Locklin, D. P.: *Economics of Transportation*, 4th ed. (Chapters 28–38), Richard D. Irwin, Inc., Homewood, Ill., 1954.

National Resources Planning Board: *Transportation and Public Policy*, GPO, 1942.

Presidential Advisory Committee on Transport Policy and Organization: *Revision of Federal Transportation Policy*, GPO, 1955.

President's Air Co-ordinating Committee: *Civil Air Policy*, GPO, 1954.

Secretary of Commerce: *Issues Involved in a Unified and Co-ordinated Federal Program for Transportation*, GPO, 1950.

Senate Committee on Interstate and Foreign Commerce: *Domestic Land and Water Transportation*, S. Rept. 1039, 82d Cong., 1st sess., GPO, 1951.

Senate Committee on Small Business: *Hearings on Trucking Mergers and Concentration* (and Appendix, "Trucking, Mergers, Concentration, and Small Business," by W. Adams and J. B. Hendry), 85th Cong., 1st sess., GPO, 1957.

Transportation Association of America: *Sound Transportation for the National Welfare*, Chicago, 1953.

Westmeyer, R. E.: *Economics of Transportation* (Parts 3–7), Prentice-Hall, 1952.

Williams, E. W.: *The Regulation of Rail-Motor Rate Competition*, Harper, 1957.

Hardin, C. M.: *The Politics of Agriculture: Soil Conservation and the Struggle for Power in Rural America*, Free Press, Glencoe, Ill., 1952.

Hickman, C. A.: *Our Farm Program and Foreign Trade: A Conflict of National Policies*, Council on Foreign Relations, 1949.

Johnson, D. G.: *Forward Prices for Agriculture*, University of Chicago Press, Chicago, 1947.

Nourse, E. G., J. S. Davis, and J. D. Black: *Three Years of the Agricultural Adjustment Act*, Brookings Institution, Washington, 1937.

President's Committee on Farm Tenancy: *Report*, GPO, 1937.

Schickele, R.: *Agricultural Policy*, McGraw-Hill, 1954.

Schultz, T. W.: *Agriculture in an Unstable Economy*, McGraw-Hill, 1945.

————: *Production and Welfare of Agriculture*, Macmillan, 1949.

————: *The Economic Organization of Agriculture*, McGraw-Hill, 1953.

CHAPTER 13—*Communications*

Archer, G.: *Big Business and Radio*, American Historical Society, 1939.

————: *History of Radio to 1926*, American Historical Society, 1938.

Danielian, N. R.: *American Telephone and Telegraph*, Vanguard, 1939.

Edelman, J. M.: *The Licensing of Radio Services in the United States, 1927 to 1947; A Study in Administrative Formulation of Policy*, University of Illinois Press, Urbana, 1950.

Federal Communications Commission: *Investigation of the Telephone Industry of the United States*, H. Doc. 340, 76th Cong., 1st sess., GPO, 1939.

Friedrich, C. J., and E. Sternberg: "Congress and the Control of Radio-Broadcasting," *American Political Science Review*, October and December, 1941, pp. 797–818, 1014–1026.

————, and J. Sayre: *The Development of the Control of Advertising on the Air*, Radiobroadcasting Research Project at Littauer Center, Harvard University, Cambridge, 1940.

Frost, S. E.: *Is American Radio Democratic?* University of Chicago Press, Chicago, 1937.

Mosher, J. G., and R. A. Lavine: *Radio and the Law*, Parke & Co., Los Angeles, 1947.

President's Communications Policy Board: *Telecommunications: A Program for Progress*, GPO, 1951.

"Radio and Television—Part I," *Law and Contemporary Problems*, Durham, Fall, 1957.

Robinson, T. P.: *Radio Networks and the Federal Government*, Columbia, 1943.

Seager, H. R., and C. A. Gulick, Jr.: *Trust and Corporation Problems*, Harper, 1929.

Taft, W. H.: *The Anti-Trust Act and the Supreme Court*, Harper, 1914.

Thorelli, H. B.: *The Federal Antitrust Policy*, Johns Hopkins Press, Baltimore, 1955.

CHAPTER 16—*The Federal Trade Commission and the Regulation of Trade Practices*

Blaisdell, T. C., Jr.: *The Federal Trade Commission*, Columbia, 1932.

Commission on Organization of the Executive Branch of the Government: *Task Force Report on Regulatory Commission* (Appendix N), GPO, 1949.

Commissioner of Corporations: *Trust Laws and Unfair Competition*, GPO, 1915.

Federal Trade Commission: *Control of Unfair Competitive Practices through Trade Practice Procedure of the Federal Trade Commission*, TNEC Monograph 34, GPO, 1941.

Gaskill, N. B.: *The Regulation of Competition*, Harper, 1936.

George Washington Law Review: Federal Trade Commission Silver Anniversary Commemorative Issue, Washington, January–February, 1940.

Hall, H. M., Jr.: "The Investigatory Function of the Federal Trade Commission, 1933–1953," in E. S. Redford (ed.), *Public Administration and Policy Formation*, University of Texas Press, Austin, 1956.

Henderson, G. C.: *The Federal Trade Commission*, Yale University Press, New Haven, 1925.

House Select Committee on Small Business: *Antitrust Law Enforcement by the Federal Trade Commission and the Antitrust Division, Department of Justice*, H. Report No. 3236, 81st Cong., 2d sess., GPO, 1951.

————: *Hearings on Functional Operation of the Federal Trade Commission*, 81st Cong., 2d sess., GPO, 1950.

McFarland, C.: *Judicial Control of the Federal Trade Commission and the Interstate Commerce Commission*, Harvard University Press, Cambridge, 1933.

Miller, J. P.: *Unfair Competition*, Harvard University Press, Cambridge, 1941.

Papandreou, A. G., and J. T. Wheeler: *Competition and Its Regulation*, Prentice-Hall, 1954.

Temporary National Economic Committee: *Hearings*, Part 5-A, "Federal Trade Commission Report on Monopolistic Practices in Industry," GPO, 1939.

Wallace, R. A., and P. H. Douglas: "Antitrust Policies and the New Attack on the Federal Trade Commission," *University of Chicago Law Review*, Summer, 1952, pp. 1–40.

Watkins, M. W.: *Public Regulation of Competitive Practices in Business Enterprise*, 3d ed., National Industrial Conference Board, 1940.

Rose, C. B., Jr.: *National Policy for Radio Broadcasting*, Harper, .

Siepman, C. A.: *Radio's Second Chance*, Little, Brown, Boston, 19

White, L.: *The American Radio*, University of Chicago Press, Chic

CHAPTER 14—*Government and the Investor*

Atkins, W. E., G. W. Edwards, and H. G. Moulton: *The Regulatio Security Markets*, Brookings Institution, Washington, 1946.

Brandeis, L. D.: *Other People's Money*, Stokes, 1914.

Cherrington, H. V.: *The Investor and the Securities Act*, Public Affairs Washington, 1942.

Dice, C. A., and W. J. Eiteman: *The Stock Market*, 3d ed., McGraw 1952.

Edelman, J. M.: *Securities Regulation in the 48 States*, Council of State ernments, Chicago, 1942.

Flynn, J. T.: *Security Speculation*, Harcourt, Brace, 1934.

Haven, T. K.: *Investment Banking under the Securities and Exchange Cc mission*, University of Michigan Press, Ann Arbor, 1940.

Lesh, W. T.: "Federal Regulation of Over-the-counter Brokers and Deale in Securities," *Harvard Law Review*, October, 1946, pp. 1237–1275.

Loss, L.: *Securities Regulation*, Little, Brown, Boston, 1951.

McCormick, E. T.: *Understanding the Securities Act and the S.E.C.*, American Book Co., 1948.

Senate Committee on Banking and Currency: *Stock Exchange Practices*, S. Rept. No. 1455, 73d Cong., 2d sess., GPO, 1934.

Stein, E.: *Government and the Investor*, Farrar & Rinehart, 1941.

Twentieth Century Fund: *The Security Markets*, 1935.

CHAPTER 15—*Antitrust Legislation and the Attack on Monopoly*

Brandeis, L. D.: *The Curse of Bigness; Miscellaneous Papers* (Part II, "Industrial Democracy and Efficiency"; Part III, "The Curse of Bigness"), Viking, 1935.

Burns, A. R.: *The Decline of Competition*, McGraw-Hill, 1936.

Clark, J. D.: *The Federal Trust Policy*, Johns Hopkins Press, Baltimore, 1931.

Commerce Clearing House, Inc.: *The Federal Antitrust Laws with Summary of Cases Instituted by the United States, 1890–1951*, 1952.

Handler, M.: *A Study of the Construction and Enforcement of the Federal Antitrust Laws*, TNEC Monograph 38, GPO, 1941.

Hidy, R. W., and M. E. Hidy: *Pioneering in Big Business, 1892–1911*, [Vol. I of *History of Standard Oil Company (New Jersey)*], Harper, 1955.

Jones, E.: *The Trust Problem in the United States*, Macmillan, 1921.

Oppenheim, S. C.: *Cases on Federal Antitrust Laws*, West Publishing Co., St. Paul, 1948.

Rozwenc, E. C. (ed.): *Roosevelt, Wilson, and the Trusts*, Heath, Boston, 1950.

CHAPTER 17—*The NRA, Small Business, and the Retreat from Competition*

Austin, C.: *Price Discrimination and Related Problems Under the Robinson-Patman Act*, American Law Institute, Philadelphia, 1950.

Commerce Clearing House, Inc.: *Robinson-Patman Act Symposium*, New York, 1946, 1948.

Committee on Industrial Analysis: *The National Recovery Administration*, H. Doc. 158, 75th Cong., 1st sess., GPO, 1937.

Cover, J. H., et al.: *Problems of Small Business*, TNEC Monograph 17, GPO, 1941.

Dirlam, J. B., and A. E. Kahn: *Fair Competition: The Law and the Economics of Antitrust Policy* (Chapters 4, 7, 8), Cornell University Press, Ithaca, 1954.

Federal Trade Commission: *Final Report on the Chain Store Investigation*, S. Doc. 4, 74th Cong., 1st sess., GPO, 1935.

———: *Resale Price Maintenance*, GPO, 1945.

———: *The Bearing of the Robinson-Patman Act upon the Policy of the Sherman Act*, GPO, 1952.

Grether, E. T.: *Price Control under Fair Trade Legislation*, Oxford, 1939.

House Committee on the Judiciary: *Amending the Sherman Act with Respect to Resale Price Maintenance*, H. Report No. 1516, 82d Cong., 2d sess., GPO, 1952.

House Select Committee on Small Business: *Fair Trade: The Problem and the Issues*, H. Report No. 1292, 82d Cong., 2d sess., GPO, 1952.

Johnson, H. S.: *The Blue Eagle: From Egg to Earth*, Doubleday, Doran, 1935.

Kaplan, A. D. H.: *Small Business: Its Place and Problems*, McGraw-Hill, 1948.

Lyon, L. S., et al.: *The National Recovery Administration*, Brookings Institution, Washington, 1935.

Palamountain, J. C., Jr.: *The Politics of Distribution*, Harvard University Press, Cambridge, 1955.

Pearce, C. A.: *Trade Association Survey*, TNEC Monograph 18, GPO, 1941.

Rowe, F. M.: "The Evolution of the Robinson-Patman Act: A Twenty-Year Perspective," *Columbia Law Review*, December, 1957, pp. 1059–1088.

CHAPTER 18—*The Revival of Antitrust Policy*

Adams, W., and H. M. Gray: *Monopoly in America*, Macmillan, 1955.

———: *The Structure of American Industry: Some Case Studies*, rev. ed., Macmillan, 1954.

Arnold, T. W.: *The Bottlenecks of Business*, Reynal & Hitchcock, 1940.

Attorney General's Committee to Study the Antitrust Laws: *Report*, GPO, 1955.

Berle, A. A., Jr.: *The 20th Century Capitalist Revolution*, Harcourt, Brace, 1954.

Bowie, R. R.: *Government Regulation of Business: Cases from the National Reporter System*, Foundation Press, Brooklyn, 1952.

Clark, J. M.: "Toward a Concept of Workable Competition," *American Economic Review*, Evanston, June, 1940, pp. 241–256.

Commerce Clearing House, Inc.: *The Federal Antitrust Laws with Summary of Cases Instituted by the United States, 1890–1951*, 1952.

"Delivered Pricing," *Law and Contemporary Problems*, Durham, Spring, 1950.

Dirlam, J. B., and A. E. Kahn: *Fair Competition: The Law and the Economics of Antitrust Policy*, Cornell University Press, Ithaca, 1954.

Edwards, C. D.: *Maintaining Competition: Requisites of a Governmental Policy*, McGraw-Hill, 1949.

Hamilton, W. H., and I. Till: *Antitrust in Action*, TNEC Monograph 16, GPO, 1940.

————: *Patents and Free Enterprise*, TNEC Monograph 31, GPO, 1941.

Handler, M.: *Antitrust in Perspective: The Complementary Roles of Rule and Discretion*, Columbia, 1957.

House Select Committee on Small Business: *Antitrust Law Enforcement by the Federal Trade Commission and the Antitrust Division*, H. Report No. 3236, 81st Cong., 2d sess., GPO, 1951.

Kaplan, A. D. H.: *Big Enterprise in a Competitive Economy*, Brookings Institution, Washington, 1954.

Kaysen, C.: *United States v. United Shoe Machinery Corporation: An Economic Analysis of an Antitrust Case*, Harvard University Press, Cambridge, 1956.

Machlup, F.: *The Basing Point System*, Blakiston, Philadelphia, 1949.

————: *The Political Economy of Monopoly*, Johns Hopkins Press, Baltimore, 1952.

Mason, E. S.: *Economic Concentration and the Monopoly Problem*, Harvard University Press, Cambridge, 1957.

Oppenheim, S. C.: *Recent Cases on Federal Antitrust Laws*, West Publishing Co., St. Paul, 1951.

"The Patent Problem," *Law and Contemporary Problems*, Durham, Autumn, 1947, and Spring, 1948.

Quinn, T. K.: *Giant Business: Threat to Democracy*, Exposition Press, 1953.

Rahl, J. A., and E. W. Zaidins (eds.): *Conference on the Antitrust Laws and the Attorney General's National Committee Report*, Federal Legal Publications, Inc., 1955.

Schumpeter, J. A.: *Capitalism, Socialism, and Democracy*, 2d ed. (Part II, "Can Capitalism Survive?") Harper, 1947.

Stocking, G. W., and M. W. Watkins: *Monopoly and Free Enterprise*, Twentieth Century Fund, 1951.

Subcommittee on Antitrust and Monopoly of the Senate Committee on the Judiciary: *Concentration in American Industry*, committee print, 85th Cong., 1st sess., 1957.

Whitney, S. N.: *Antitrust Policies*, 2 vols., Twentieth Century Fund, 1958.

Wilcox, C.: *Public Policies Toward Business* (Part II, "Maintaining Competition"), Richard D. Irwin, Inc., Homewood, Ill., 1955.

CHAPTER 19—*Bituminous Coal: Regulation of a Sick Industry*

Baratz, M. S.: *The Union and the Coal Industry*, Yale University Press, New Haven, 1955.

Bituminous Coal Institute: *Bituminous Coal Annual*, Washington.

"Coal," *Fortune*, March, April, July, 1947.

Fisher, W. E.: *Collective Bargaining in the Bituminous Coal Industry: An Appraisal*, University of Pennsylvania, Philadelphia, 1948.

———, and C. M. James: *Minimum Price Fixing in the Bituminous Coal Industry*, Princeton University Press, Princeton, 1955.

National Resources Committee: *Energy Resources and National Policy*, GPO, 1939.

Parker, G. L.: *The Coal Industry*, American Council on Public Affairs, Washington, 1940.

Schmookler, J.: "The Bituminous Coal Industry," in W. Adams, *The Structure of American Industry; Some Case Studies*, rev. ed., Macmillan, 1954.

Whitney, S. N.: *Antitrust Policies* (Vol. I, Chapter 7, "Bituminous Coal"), Twentieth Century Fund, 1958.

CHAPTER 20—*Oil and the Mixed Economy*

American Petroleum Institute: *Petroleum Facts and Figures*, 12th ed., 1956.

Bain, J. S.: *The Pacific Coast Petroleum Industry*, 3 vols., University of California Press, Berkeley, 1944–1947.

Bartley, E. R.: *The Tidelands Oil Controversy*, University of Texas Press, Austin, 1953.

Cassady, R., Jr.: *Price Making and Price Behavior in the Petroleum Industry*, Yale University Press, New Haven, 1954.

Cook, R. C.: *Control of the Petroleum Industry by Major Oil Companies*, TNEC Monograph 39, GPO, 1941.

Dirlam, J. B.: "The Petroleum Industry," in W. Adams, *The Structure of American Industry: Some Case Studies*, rev. ed., Macmillan, 1954.

Fanning, L. M.: *Foreign Oil and the Free World*, McGraw-Hill, 1954.

Federal Trade Commission: *International Petroleum Cartel* (staff report), GPO, 1952.

McLean, J. G., and R. W. Haigh: *The Growth of Integrated Oil Companies*, Harvard Graduate School of Business Administration, Boston, 1954.

O'Connor, H.: *The Empire of Oil*, Monthly Review Press, 1955.

Rostow, E. V.: *A National Policy for the Oil Industry*, Yale University Press, New Haven, 1948.

Watkins, M. W.: *Oil: Stabilization or Conservation?* Harper, 1937.

Whitney, S. N.: *Antitrust Policies* (Vol. I, Chapter 3, "Petroleum"), Twentieth Century Fund, 1958.

Willbern, Y. Y.: "Administrative Control of Petroleum Production in Texas," in E. S. Redford (ed.), *Public Administration and Policy Formation*, University of Texas Press, Austin, 1956.

Williamson, R. deV.: *The Politics of Planning in the Oil Industry Under the Code*, Harper, 1936.

Zimmerman, E. W.: *Conservation in the Production of Petroleum*, Yale University Press, New Haven, 1957.

CHAPTER 21—*The Law and Politics of Natural Gas*

Blachly, F. M., and M. E. Oatman: *Natural Gas and the Public Interest*, Granite Press, Washington, 1947.

Federal Power Commission: *Natural Gas Investigation: Smith-Wimberly Report; Olds-Draper Report*, 2 vols., GPO, 1948.

Gable, R. W.: "The Jurisdiction of the Federal Power Commission over the Field Price of Natural Gas," *Land Economics*, Madison, February, 1956, pp. 39–56.

Huitt, R. K.: "Federal Regulation of the Uses of Natural Gas," *American Political Science Review*, Washington, June, 1952, pp. 455–469.

————: "National Regulation of the Natural-Gas Industry," in E. S. Redford (ed.), *Public Administration and Policy Formation*, University of Texas Press, Austin, 1956.

"Regulation of Natural Gas," *Law and Contemporary Problems*, Durham, Summer, 1954.

Zimmerman, E. W.: *Conservation in the Production of Petroleum* (Chapter 8, "Conservation of Natural Gas"; Chapter 9, "Evaluation of Oil and Gas Conservation"), Yale University Press, New Haven, 1957.

CHAPTER 22—*The Challenge of Atomic Energy*

American Assembly: *Atoms for Power: United States Policy in Atomic Energy Development*, 1957.

Atomic Energy Commission: *AEC Contract Policy and Operations*, Government Printing Office, Washington, 1951.

"Atomic Power Development," *Law and Contemporary Problems*, Durham, Winter, 1956.

Dahl, R. A., and R. S. Brown, Jr.: *Domestic Control of Atomic Energy*, Social Science Research Council, 1951.

Dean, G.: *Report on the Atom*, Knopf, 1953.

"The Impact of Atomic Energy," *Annals of the American Academy of Political and Social Science*, Philadelphia, November, 1953.

Isard, I., and V. Whitney: *Atomic Power: An Economic and Social Analysis*, Blakiston, Philadelphia, 1952.

Joint Committee on Atomic Energy: *Atomic Power and Private Enterprise*, committee print, 82d Cong., 2d sess., 1952.

———: *Investigation into the U.S. Atomic Energy Commission*. S. Report No. 1169, 81st Cong., 1st sess., GPO, 1949.

Lapp, R. E.: *Atoms and People*, Harper, 1956.

Newman, J. R., and B. S. Miller: *The Control of Atomic Energy*, McGraw-Hill, 1949.

Report of the Panel on the Impact of the Peaceful Uses of Atomic Energy to the Joint Committee on Atomic Energy, committee print, 84th Cong., 2d sess., 1956.

Schurr, S. H., and J. Marschak: *Economic Aspects of Atomic Power*, Princeton University Press, Princeton, 1950.

Thomas, M.: *Atomic Energy and Congress*, University of Michigan Press, Ann Arbor, 1956.

Tybout, R. A.: *Government Contracting in Atomic Energy*, University of Michigan Press, Ann Arbor, 1956.

CHAPTER 23—*Conservation of Natural Resources*

Bennett, H. H.: *Soil Conservation*, McGraw-Hill, 1939.

Clawson, M., and B. Held: *The Federal Lands: Their Use and Management*, Johns Hopkins Press, Baltimore, 1957.

Coyle, D. C.: *Conservation: An American Story of Conflict and Accomplishment*, Rutgers University Press, New Brunswick, 1957.

Eckstein, O.: *Water Resources Development: The Economics of Project Evaluation*, Harvard University Press, Cambridge, 1958.

"The Future of Our Natural Resources," *Annals of the American Academy of Political and Social Science*, Philadelphia, May, 1952.

Gulick, L. H.: *American Forest Policy*, Duell, Sloan, 1951.

Hardin, C. M.: *The Politics of Agriculture: Soil Conservation and the Struggle for Power in Rural America*, Free Press, Glencoe, Ill., 1952.

Hart, H. C.: *The Dark Missouri*, University of Wisconsin Press, Madison, 1957.

Huffman, R. E.: *Irrigation Development and Public Water Policy*, Ronald Press, 1953.

Leuchtenberg, W. E.: *Flood Control Politics: The Connecticut River Valley Problem*, Harvard University Press, Cambridge, 1953.

Lyons, B.: *Tomorrow's Birthright: A Political and Economic Interpretation of Our Natural Resources*, Funk & Wagnalls, 1955.

McKinley, C.: *Uncle Sam in the Pacific Northwest*, University of California Press, Berkeley, 1952.

Maass, A.: *Muddy Waters*, Harvard University Press, Cambridge, 1951.

Marshall, R.: *The People's Forests*, Smith & Haas, 1933.

National Resources Board: *Report on National Planning and Public Works in Relation to Natural Resources and Including Land Use and Water Resources*, GPO, 1934.

Parks, W. R.: *Soil Conservation Districts in Action*, Iowa State College Press, Ames, 1952.

944 SELECTED READINGS

Peffer, E. L.: *The Closing of the Public Domain*, Stanford University Press, Stanford, 1951.

Pinchot, G.: *Breaking New Ground*, Harcourt, Brace, 1947.

President's Materials Policy Commission: *Resources for Freedom*, 5 vols., GPO, 1952.

President's Water Resources Policy Commission: *A Water Policy for the American People*, 3 vols., GPO, 1950.

Renshaw, E. F.: *Toward Responsible Government: An Economic Appraisal of Federal Investment in Water Resource Programs*, Idyia Press, Chicago, 1957.

"River Basin Development," *Law and Contemporary Problems*, Durham, Spring, 1957.

Robbins, R. M.: *Our Landed Heritage: The Public Domain, 1776–1936*, Princeton University Press, Princeton, 1942.

Van Hise, C. R.: *Conservation of Natural Resources in the United States*, Macmillan, 1910.

"Water Resources," *Law and Contemporary Problems*, Durham, Summer, 1957.

Wengert, N.: *Natural Resources and the Political Struggle*, Doubleday, 1955.

CHAPTER 24—*Public Enterprise and the Public Corporation*

Commission on Organization of the Executive Branch of the Government: *Federal Business Enterprises; Task Force Report on Revolving Funds and Business Enterprises of the Government;* and *Task Force Report on the Post Office*, GPO, 1949.

————: *Business Enterprises;* and *Task Force Report on Business Enterprises*, GPO, 1955.

Dimock, M. E.: *Developing American Waterways*, University of Chicago Press, Chicago, 1935.

————: *Government-Operated Enterprises in the Panama Canal Zone*, University of Chicago Press, Chicago, 1934.

Gordon, L.: *The Public Corporation in Great Britain*, Oxford, 1938.

Joint Committee Investigating the Tennessee Valley Authority: *Report*, S. Doc. 56, 76th Cong., 1st sess., GPO, 1939.

Key, V. O., Jr.: "Government Corporations," in F. M. Marx (ed.), *Elements of Public Administration*, Prentice-Hall, 1946.

Lilienthal, D. E. and R. H. Marquis: "The Conduct of Business Enterprises by the Federal Government," *Harvard Law Review*, Cambridge, February, 1941, pp. 545–601.

McDiarmid, J.: *Government Corporations and Federal Funds*, University of Chicago Press, Chicago, 1938.

Pritchett, C. H.: "The Government Corporation Control Act of 1945," *American Political Science Review*, Washington, June, 1946, pp. 495–509.

————: *The Tennessee Valley Authority*, University of North Carolina Press, Chapel Hill, 1943.

Robson, W. A. (ed.): *Problems of Nationalized Industry*, 2d ed., Oxford, 1952.

Seidman, H.: "The Theory of the Autonomous Corporation," *Public Administration Review*, Chicago, Spring, 1952, pp. 89–96.

Selznick, P.: *TVA and the Grass Roots*, University of California Press, Berkeley, 1949.

Splawn, W. M. W.: *Government Ownership and Operation of Railroads*, Macmillan, 1928.

CHAPTER 25—*The Welfare State*

Becker, J. M.: *Problems of Abuse in Employment Benefits*, Columbia, 1953.

Brown, J. C.: *Public Relief: 1929–1939*, Holt, 1940.

Burns, E. M.: *The American Social Security System*, Houghton Mifflin, Boston, 1949.

Commission on Intergovernmental Relations: *Federal Aid to Public Health*; and *Federal Aid to Welfare*, GPO, 1955.

Commission on Organization of the Executive Branch of the Government: *Federal Medical Services*; and *Task Force Report on Medical Services*, GPO, 1955.

————: *Social Security, Education, Indian Affairs*; and *Task Force Report on Public Welfare*, GPO, 1949.

Corson, J. J., and J. W. McConnell: *Economic Needs of Older People*, Twentieth Century Fund, 1956.

Ewing, O. R.: *The Nation's Health: A Ten Year Program*, GPO, 1948.

Gagliardo, D.: *American Social Insurance*, Harper, 1949.

Haber, W.: *Unemployment and Relief*, Public Administration Service, Chicago, 1956.

————, and W. J. Cohen (eds.): *Readings in Social Insurance*, Prentice-Hall, 1948.

Harris, E. E.: *Economics of Social Security*, McGraw-Hill, 1941.

Macmahon, A. W., J. Millett, and G. Ogden: *The Administration of Federal Work Relief*, Public Administration Service, Chicago, 1941.

Means, J. H.: *Doctors, People, and Government*, Little, Brown, Boston, 1953.

Meriam, L.: *Relief and Social Security*, Brookings Institution, Washington, 1946.

Millis, H. A., and R. E. Montgomery: *Labor's Risks and Social Insurance* [Vol. II of *The Economics of Labor*], McGraw-Hill, 1938.

Mustard, H. S.: *Government in Public Health*, Commonwealth Fund, 1945.

President's Commission on the Health Needs of the Nation: *Building America's Health*, GPO, 1951.

Riesenfeld, S. A., and R. C. Maxwell: *Modern Social Legislation*, Foundation Press, Brooklyn, 1950.

Sinai, N., O. Anderson, and M. Dollar: *Health Insurance in the United States*, Commonwealth Fund, 1946.

CHAPTER 26—*Monetary and Fiscal Policies
for Economic Growth and Stability*

Abbott, C. C.: *The Federal Debt,* Twentieth Century Fund, 1953.

Bach, G. L.: *Federal Reserve Policy-Making,* Knopf, 1950.

Bailey, S. K.: *Congress Makes a Law: The Story Behind the Employment Act of 1946,* Columbia, 1950.

Duesenberry, J. S.: *Business Cycles and Economic Growth,* McGraw-Hill, 1958.

Economic Reports of the President, GPO.

Gordon, R. A.: *Business Fluctuations,* Harper, 1952.

Hansen, A. H.: *Business Cycles and National Income,* Norton, 1951.

Harris, S. E.: *Twenty Years of Federal Reserve Policy,* Harvard University Press, Cambridge, 1933.

Hart, A. G.: *Money, Debt, and Economic Activity,* rev. ed., Prentice-Hall, 1953.

Joint Congressional Committee on the Economic Report, Subcommittee on Fiscal Policy: *Federal Expenditure Policy for Economic Growth and Development,* GPO, 1957.

Joint Congressional Committee on the Economic Report, Subcommittee on Tax Policy: *Federal Tax Policy for Economic Growth and Stability,* GPO, 1955.

Kemmerer, E. W., and D. L. Kemmerer: *The ABC of the Federal Reserve System,* Harper, 1950.

Keynes, J. M.: *The General Theory of Employment, Interest and Money,* Harcourt, Brace, 1936.

Maxwell, J. A.: *Fiscal Policy: Its Techniques and Institutional Setting,* Holt, 1955.

Millikan, M. F. (ed.): *Income Stabilization for a Developing Democracy,* Yale University Press, New Haven, 1953.

National Bureau of Economic Research: *Policies to Combat Depression,* Princeton University Press, Princeton, 1956.

Ruggles, R., and N. D. Ruggles: *National Income Accounts and Income Analysis,* 2d ed., McGraw-Hill, 1956.

Samuelson, P. A.: *Economics,* 3d ed. (Part II), McGraw-Hill, 1955.

Senate Committee on Banking and Currency: *Federal Reserve Policy and Economic Stability, 1951–1957,* S. Report No. 2500, 85th Cong., 2d sess., GPO, 1958.

Smithies, A.: *The Budgetary Process in the United States,* McGraw-Hill, 1955.

Strayer, P. J.: *Fiscal Policy and Politics,* Harper, 1958.

CHAPTER 27—*Mobilization of the Economy for War*

Backman, J., et al.: *War and Defense Economics*, Rinehart, 1952.

Baldwin, H. W.: *The Price of Power*, Harper, 1948.

Baruch, B. M.: *American Industry in the War: A Report of the War Industries Board*, GPO, 1921 (supplemented ed. published by Prentice-Hall, 1941).

Bureau of the Budget: *The United States at War: Development and Administration of the War Program by the Federal Government*, GPO, 1947.

Chandler, L. V., and D. H. Wallace: *Economic Mobilization and Stabilization*, Holt, 1951.

Civilian Production Administration: *Industrial Mobilization for War: History of the War Production Board and Predecessor Agencies*, GPO, 1947.

Connery, R. H.: *The Navy and the Industrial Mobilization in World War II*, Princeton University Press, Princeton, 1947.

Elliott, W. Y.: *Mobilization Planning and the National Security*, Public Affairs Bulletin No. 81, Legislative Reference Service, Library of Congress, GPO, 1950.

Gordon, D. L., and R. J. Dangerfield: *Hidden Weapon: The Story of Economic Warfare*, Harper, 1947.

Harris, S. E.: *Price and Related Controls in the United States*, McGraw-Hill, 1945.

———: *The Economics of Mobilization and Inflation*, Norton, 1951.

Janeway, E.: *The Struggle for Survival*, Yale University Press, New Haven, 1951.

Lincoln, G. A., and associates: *Economics of National Security*, 2d ed., Prentice-Hall, 1954.

Mansfield, H. C.: *A Short History of O.P.A.*, Office of Price Administration, GPO, 1947.

Nelson, D. B.: *Arsenal of Democracy: The Story of American War Production*, Harcourt, Brace, 1946.

Novick, D., et al.: *Wartime Production Controls*, Columbia, 1949.

Scitovsky, T., et al.: *Mobilizing Resources for War—The Economic Alternatives*, McGraw-Hill, 1951.

Somers, H. M.: *Presidential Agency: OWMR, the Office of War Mobilization and Reconversion*, Harvard University Press, Cambridge, 1950.

Thompson, V. A.: *The Regulatory Process in O.P.A. Rationing*, Columbia, 1950.

Wallace, D. H.: *Economic Controls and Defense*, Twentieth Century Fund, 1953.

War Production Board: *Wartime Production Achievements and the Reconversion Outlook*, GPO, 1945.

Witney, F.: *Wartime Experiences of the National Labor Relations Board*, University of Illinois Press, Urbana, 1949.

CHAPTER 28—*The United States and the World Economy*

American Assembly: *International Stability and Progress*, 1957.

Berliner, J. S.: *Soviet Economic Aid*, Frederick A. Praeger, Inc., 1958.

Brewster, K.: *Antitrust and American Business Abroad*, McGraw-Hill, 1958.

Brown, W. A., and R. Opie: *American Foreign Assistance*, Brookings Institution, Washington, 1953.

Buchanan, N. S., and H. S. Ellis: *Approaches to Economic Development*, Twentieth Century Fund, 1955.

——, and F. A. Lutz: *Rebuilding the World Economy*, Twentieth Century Fund, 1947.

Commission on Foreign Economic Policy (Randall Commission): *Report* and *Staff Papers*, GPO, 1954.

Condliffe, J. B.: *The Commerce of Nations*, Norton, 1950.

Elliott, W. Y., et al.: *The Political Economy of American Foreign Policy*, Holt, 1955.

Harris, S. E.: *International and Interregional Economics*, McGraw-Hill, 1957.

Hirschman, A. O.: *The Strategy of Economic Development*, Yale University Press, New Haven, 1958.

House Ways and Means Committee, Subcommittee on Foreign Trade Policy: *Compendium of Papers on United States Foreign Trade Policy*, GPO, 1957.

Kindleberger, C. P.: *Economic Development*, McGraw-Hill, 1958.

Lewis, C.: *America's Stake in International Investments*, Brookings Institution, Washington, 1948.

MacDougall, D.: *The World Dollar Problem*, St. Martin's Press, 1957.

Mikesell, R. F.: *Foreign Exchange in the Postwar World*, Twentieth Century Fund, 1954.

——: *United States Economic Policy and International Relations*, McGraw-Hill, 1952.

Myrdal, G.: *An International Economy*, Harper, 1956.

Piquet, H. S.: *Aid, Trade and the Tariff*, Crowell, 1953.

Price, H. B.: *The Marshall Plan and its Meaning*, Cornell University Press, Ithaca, 1955.

Schelling, T. C.: *International Economics*, Allyn & Bacon, Boston, 1958.

Senate Special Committee to Study the Foreign Aid Program: *Reports, Studies*, and *Hearings*, 85th Cong., 1st sess., GPO, 1957.

Thorp, W. L.: *Trade, Aid, or What?*, Johns Hopkins Press, Baltimore, 1954.

Triffin, R.: *Europe and the Money Muddle*, Yale University Press, New Haven, 1957.

Vernon, R.: *Organizing for World Trade*, in *International Conciliation*, No. 505, Carnegie Endowment for International Peace, November 1955.

Wilcox, C.: *A Charter for World Trade*, Macmillan, 1949.

Woytinsky, W. S., and E. S. Woytinsky: *World Commerce and Governments*, Twentieth Century Fund, 1955.

CHAPTER 29—*Conclusion—Public Policy and the American Economy*

Clark, J. M.: *Alternative to Serfdom*, Knopf, 1948.

———: *Economic Institutions and Human Welfare*, Knopf, 1957.

Finer, H.: *The Road to Reaction*, Little, Brown, Boston, 1945.

Galbraith, J. K.: *The Affluent Society*, Houghton Mifflin, Boston, 1958.

Hamilton, W. H.: *The Politics of Industry*, Knopf, 1957.

Hayek, F. A. von: *The Road to Serfdom*, University of Chicago Press, Chicago, 1944.

MacIver, R. M.: *Democracy and the Economic Challenge*, Knopf, 1952.

Schumpeter, J. A.: *Capitalism, Socialism, and Democracy*, 2d ed., Harper, 1947.

Steiner, G. A.: *Government's Role in Economic Life*, McGraw-Hill, 1953.

Table of Cases

958 TABLE OF CASES

Glossary of Alphabetical Abbreviations

AAA	Agricultural Adjustment Act (*or* Administration)
ABC	American Broadcasting Company
AEC	Atomic Energy Commission
AFL	American Federation of Labor
AFL–CIO	American Federation of Labor and Congress of Industrial Organizations
AMA	American Medical Association
A. T. & T.	American Telephone and Telegraph Company
CAA	Civil Aeronautics Administration
CAB	Civil Aeronautics Board
CBS	Columbia Broadcasting System
CCC	Commodity Credit Corporation
CEA	Council of Economic Advisers
CED	Committee for Economic Development
CIO	Committee for Industrial Organization; *later,* Congress of Industrial Organizations
CWA	Civil Works Administration
EPU	European Payments Union
ESA	Economic Stabilization Agency
FBF	Farm Bureau Federation
FCA	Farm Credit Administration
FCC	Federal Communications Commission
FDA	Food and Drug Administration
FDIC	Federal Deposit Insurance Corporation
FERA	Federal Emergency Relief Act
FHA	Federal Housing Administration; *also,* Farmers' Home Administration
FPC	Federal Power Commission
FRC	Federal Radio Commission
FSA	Farm Security Administration
FTC	Federal Trade Commission
GAC	General Advisory Committee
GATT	General Agreement on Tariffs and Trade
GPO	Government Printing Office

IBRD	International Bank for Reconstruction and Development
ICC	Interstate Commerce Commission
IMF	International Monetary Fund
INCODEL	Interstate Commission on the Delaware River
ITO	International Trade Organization
IWW	Industrial Workers of the World
NAM	National Association of Manufacturers
NARD	National Association of Retail Druggists
NARUC	National Association of Railroad and Utilities Commissioners
NASD	National Association of Securities Dealers
NATO	North Atlantic Treaty Organization
NBC	National Broadcasting Company
NELA	National Electric Light Association
NIRA	National Industrial Recovery Act
NLRB	National Labor Relations Board
NRA	National Recovery Administration
NRPB	National Resources Planning Board
NWLB	National War Labor Board
ODM	Office of Defense Mobilization
OEEC	Organization for European Economic Co-operation
OES	Office of Economic Stabilization
OPA	Office of Price Administration
OPACS	Office of Price Administration and Civilian Supply
OPM	Office of Production Management
OPS	Office of Price Stabilization
OTC	Organization for Trade Co-operation
OWM	Office of War Mobilization
PMA	Production and Marketing Administration
PRA	President's Re-employment Agreement
PWA	Public Works Administration
RCA	Radio Corporation of America
REA	Rural Electrification Administration
RFC	Reconstruction Finance Corporation
SBA	Small Business Administration
SCS	Soil Conservation Service
SEC	Securities and Exchange Commission
SPAB	Supply, Priorities, and Allocations Board
TNEC	Temporary National Economic Committee
TVA	Tennessee Valley Authority
UMW	United Mine Workers of America
UNRRA	United Nations Reconstruction and Rehabilitation Agency
USDA	United States Department of Agriculture
USES	United States Employment Service
WPA	Works Progress Administration
WPB	War Production Board
WSA	War Shipping Administration

Index

James River Bill of *1909*, 345n
Japan, 680, 858–859, 872, 878, 880n, 886, 897
Jefferson, Thomas, 41, 95–96, 127, 242, 243, 916
Jenks, J. W., 432n
Johns-Manville Corp., 594
Johnson, Hugh, 233, 530, 531, 537, 538
Joint Committee on the Economic Report, 806, 817, 818–819, 821
Joint Congressional Committee on Atomic Energy, 366, 684, 690–692, 694–701
Joint Traffic Assn. of *1898*, 261, 472n
Judicial review, 52, 82–85; *see also* Supreme Court *and* Constitutional limitations
Judiciary, 57; *see also* Courts *and* Supreme Court
Judiciary Act of *1789*, 68
Jungle, The, Sinclair, 220, 224
Jurisdictional disputes, 208
Justice, Department of, 60, 169, 563, 755
antitrust actions, 383, 385, 450, 453–454, 484, 570–571
broadcasting actions, 399
fair-trade actions, 565n
Robinson-Patman Bill actions, 550
trade practices actions, 495, 497, 504–510, 514

Kahn, A. E., 596n, 613n
Kansas, "blue-sky laws," 413
Kansas City, 451
Kaplan, A. D. H., 569n
Kelley, "Pig-iron," 99
Kemmerer, E. W., and D. L., 799n
Kennedy, Joseph P., 419
Kennedy-Ives Bill of *1958*, 209n
Kerr Bill of *1949*, 673–674
Key, V. O., Jr., 24n, 37, 40, 762n
Keynes, John Maynard, 799, 801–803
Keyserling, Leon, 814n
Kingsbury commitment, 374
Knappen, R. S., 676n
Knight case, 451, 452
Knolls Laboratory, 694
Know Your Coal, film, 234
Knox, Judge, 610, 614
Knoxville, Tenn., 361
Knudsen, William S., 831
Koontz, H., 583n
Korean War, 110, 210, 401, 742, 808, 810, 819, 820, 821, 824, 825, 862, 864–868, 879, 905, 906
economic mobilization for, 862, 864–868
Kornhauser, A., 38n, 39n
Kuhlman, J. M., 204n
Kuhn, Loeb, 411

Labor, 17–18, 918
antitrust movement, 439, 451
in coal mining industry, 624, 625, 626, 629
conservation and, 710
in early industrial history, 9–10
in economic mobilization, *see* Mobilization, economic
fair-trade and, 563
jurisdictional disputes, 198, 203–204
migratory farm, 143

New Deal era, 187–197
NIRA and, 526–534, 539, 540–542
oil industry, 639
percentage distribution, *1870–1950*, table, 14
post-World War II period, 197–211
Social Security System and, 782
unemployment insurance attitude, 786–788
utilities, 321
Labor, Department of, 34, 60, 168, 169, 181, 183, 196, 232
Labor Advisory Board, 531, 533
Labor legislation, 35, 70, 920
administration of, 168–170
on children, 161–162
court handling of industrial relations, 170–187
federal-state aspects, 160–162, 166, 168, 170, 197
on hours of work, 162–164, 195–197
New Deal, 188, 189
plant seizure by government, 182
protective, 159–170, 189
railroad, 183–187, 254
state laws, 206–209
on wages, 164–166, 195–197
workmen's compensation, 166–168
Labor-Management Conference of *1945*, 198
Labor-Management Relations Act of *1947* (Taft-Hartley), 199–206
Labor organizations:
development of, 31–32
government attitude toward, 160
legal aspects, 170–187
workers' right to, 188–191
Labor politics, 30–40, 193
influence on policy, 168–170
New Deal and, 36–40
post-World War II, 197–211
tariff and, 99
Labor promotionalism, 97, 159–211
New Deal, 188–197
principles and policies evolving in, 209–211
protective legislation, 159–170
regulation by federal contract, 195–197
state regulation, 206–209
Taft-Hartley effect on, 206
Labor, railroad, 254, 266, 277, 286–287, 310
in the Great Depression, 279
under the New Deal, 279, 282, 283
Labor's League for Political Education, 37
Labor unions, *see* Unions
Ladd, E. F., 220
La Follette, Robert M., 43
La Follette Seamen's Act, 34
La Guardia, Fiorello, 179
La Guardia Airport, 749
Laissez faire, 18, 50, 52, 70, 77, 96, 241, 456, 735, 766
Lake Cargo Coal Rate Controversy, 276
Lamar, Justice, 175n
Land bank system, 138, 139, 140
Land classification, 710